3e

COMMERCIAL REAL ESTATE

Analysis and Investments

DAVID M. GELTNER
Massachusetts Institute of Technology

JIM CLAYTON
Cornerstone Real Estate Advisers
University of Connecticut

NORMAN G. MILLER
University of San Diego

PIET EICHHOLTZ
Maastricht University

OnCourse Learning

Commercial Real Estate Analysis and Investments, Third Edition
David M. Geltner, Norman G. Miller, Jim Clayton and Piet Eichholtz

Executive Editor: Sara Glassmeyer

Developmental Editor: Hyde Park Publishing Services

Rights Acquisition Director: Audrey Pettengill

Rights Acquisition Specialist, Text and Image: Amber Hosea

Senior Manufacturing Planner: Charlene Taylor

Art and Cover Direction, Production Management, and Composition: PreMediaGlobal

Cover & Internal Images:

Top Right: © Jupiterimages/Photos.com/Thinkstock

Top Middle: © iStockphoto/Thinkstock

Top Left: © iStockphoto/Thinkstock

Bottom Right: © iStockphoto/Thinkstock

Bottom Left: © iStockphoto/Thinkstock

© 2014, 2007 OnCourse Learning

ALL RIGHTS RESERVED. No part of this work covered by the copyright herein may be reproduced, transmitted, stored or used in any form or by any means graphic, electronic, or mechanical, including but not limited to photocopying, recording, scanning, digitizing, taping, Web distribution, information networks, or information storage and retrieval systems, except as permitted under Section 107 or 108 of the 1976 United States Copyright Act, without the prior written permission of the publisher.

For product information and technology assistance, contact us at **www.oncourselearning.com**

Library of Congress Control Number: 2013932026

Package Edition:

ISBN-13: 978-1-133-10882-5

ISBN-10: 1-133-10882-2

Student Edition:

ISBN-13: 978-1-133-10883-2

ISBN-10: 1-133-10883-0

OnCourse Learning
7577 Central Parke Blvd. Suite 100
Mason, OH 45040
USA

Visit our corporate website at **www.oncourselearning.com**

Printed in the United States of America
1 2 3 4 5 6 7 17 16 15 14 13

This book is dedicated to our parents,
our wives, and our children,
and to all the students we have known who
wanted to know not just what, but why.

BRIEF CONTENTS

CD-ROM

Answers to Odd-numbered Study Questions

Appendices and Resources for Selected Chapters

ARGUS® Software (student version for completing selected exercises)

CONTENTS

CD-ROM

PREFACE

What This Book Is About

What is real estate? You could say that it is land. In that sense, real estate is the quarter of the earth's surface on which all 7 billion human beings live. Or you could say it is built space, the structures in which we live, work, and play, that shape and define our cities, and shelter our dreams. Or you could say that real estate is one-third of the value of all capital assets in the world, over $30 trillion worth of assets in the United States alone. No matter how you define real estate, you can't ignore it. Real estate is important, regardless of what line of work you are in.

But think a bit more about what real estate is. Perhaps most obviously, it is not called "real" for nothing. Real estate is real. It is dirt and bricks and concrete and steel. Like any major aspect of the real world, real estate can be studied academically from several different perspectives, bringing to bear several different academic and professional disciplines. So if you ask someone, *What is real estate?* the answer you get will likely depend on the profession of the person you are asking. While an architect will describe real estate from an aesthetic and functional perspective, an engineer will describe it from a physical structural perspective. An environmental scientist will describe it from an ecological perspective, and a lawyer will describe it as a bundle of rights and duties associated with "real property," that is, land and the permanent structures on it. All of these answers would be correct, and a complete study of real estate requires a very comprehensive *multidisciplinary* approach.

Yet this book, while not ignoring these various perspectives, is not intended to be a complete multidisciplinary text. In order to provide sufficient depth and rigor to our study, this book will have to concentrate on one of the major disciplines for studying real estate. The discipline we will be using is that of economics. Indeed, we need to be more precise even than that. Within the economic study of real estate, there are two major branches: urban economics and financial economics. The former is the branch of economics that studies cities, including the spatial and social phenomena relevant to understanding real estate. The latter is the branch that studies capital markets and the financial services industry. These are the two major branches of economics we will be using in this text because they are the most relevant for understanding commercial property from an investment perspective. Our major emphasis, however, will be on the second of these two branches, the financial economic aspects of real estate.

Why is the financial economic study of real estate so important? To answer this question, let's go back to our original question, *What is real estate?* Just as the architect's or engineer's answer to this question emphasizes the physical (bricks and mortar), and the lawyer's answer emphasizes the legal (bundle of rights), the successful real estate business professional's answer is likely to emphasize the financial economic aspects. The investor's fundamental answer to the question is, *Real estate is potential future cash flows.* The nature of these cash flows, their magnitude, timing, and risk, will fundamentally be determined in the rental market, which is where urban economics comes in. But whatever is the specific nature of the potential stream of future cash flows generated by real estate, any such stream is, more generally, nothing more and nothing less than what is called a capital asset. And capital assets trade in capital markets. So that is where financial economics takes over.

Capital markets determine the opportunity costs and values of investments and capital assets, and allocate the flow of financial capital (aka "money") to and among the underlying physical assets, which in turn produce the future real benefit flows that are the defining characteristic of capital assets. But perhaps more to the point for those with a more public policy or urban planning perspective, financial capital ultimately determines what real estate assets will be built, where, and when, in an entrepreneurial capitalist society such as that of the

United States and many other countries. The physical structures and aesthetic characteristics studied by the engineer or architect would not and cannot exist in reality without the financial capital to command the resources to produce them. Therefore, the academic discipline that studies financial capital is of vital importance to any real estate professional. As noted, this discipline is financial economics.

Once again, we should be more precise. Within the discipline of financial economics, two major fields are typically covered in the core curriculum in graduate-level business schools: corporate finance and investments. Corporate finance concentrates on applications relevant to the financial and strategic management of large corporations whose equity is usually traded on the stock exchange. The investments field studies applications relevant to individuals and institutions making investment decisions about the wealth they own or manage. Both of these fields are relevant to analyzing commercial property from an investment perspective. Indeed, more so than in the classical (or "mainstream") presentations of these two fields, in real estate, the topics and applications addressed in corporate finance and investments are more closely interwoven. In real estate, we need to integrate these two fields that have grown apart in the mainstream literature and pedagogy.

To do this, we must address a number of features that make real estate unique—different from both the typical corporate finance and the securities investment contexts. For example, most commercial property is not held by publicly traded, taxed corporations. It may be held directly by taxed individuals or tax-exempt institutions, or it may be held by real estate investment trusts (REITs), which are publicly traded corporations that are not taxed at the corporate level. But only relatively rarely is commercial property actually owned (as opposed to rented or used) by the taxed corporations that dominate the stock market. Commercial property assets themselves also differ from the underlying assets held by the typical publicly traded, taxed corporation in that there is almost always a well-functioning market for commercial property. The productive physical assets of most corporations (machines, laboratories, factories) are not usually traded in so well-established and liquid a market as the commercial property market. In this respect, real estate assets are more like the assets studied in the mainstream investments field, primarily stocks and bonds. But the commercial property market is not as liquid or efficient in its operation as the securities markets dealt with in mainstream investments. (When was the last time you went online and ordered the sale of half of your ownership of 1000 North Main Street "at market" before close of business that day?) Another fascinating difference between real estate and the mainstream corporate and securities environment is the simultaneous existence of two parallel asset markets in which real estate trades. Commercial properties are traded directly in the private property market, and they are traded indirectly in the stock market through the equity shares of REITs and other real estate firms. (The analogy would be if you could buy pharmaceutical laboratories both directly and indirectly through the purchase of drug company stocks.)

These and other differences require a specific, real-estate-oriented treatment and synthesis of the topics covered in mainstream corporate finance and investments. This treatment can be, and needs to be, consistent with, integrated with, and built on the mainstream financial economic fields. A seamless intellectual continuum should exist from the typical finance course taught in the MBA core to the typical graduate course in Real Estate Finance or Real Estate Investments, an intellectual continuum from "Wall Street" to "Main Street." After all, since capital and information flow freely between these loci in the real world, real estate investment knowledge and practice should be built on the same principles that underlie the corporate and securities world.

The real estate treatment we need must also present an intellectually coherent framework, rigorous from an academic perspective, built on a few solid underlying concepts and principles, not a hodgepodge of vaguely connected, *ad hoc* methodologies and rules of thumb. Modern real estate is crying out for a framework of fundamental principles, rigorously grounded analytical tools. The student needs a solid foundation in order to develop fundamental understanding. Yet such an elegant framework should include practical procedures and methodologies that can be applied directly to help answer typical real estate investment decision-making questions in the real world. Built on fundamental economic principles, such methods will allow the student to apply creatively the real estate investment analysis framework she learns in academia to the infinite variety of situations she will no doubt encounter in the real world.

The purpose of this book is to present such a framework, a corpus of principles, methods, and knowledge, at a level that the typical graduate student can readily understand (with a little time, effort, and study, of course). Our intention and hope is that, whether you are pursuing an MBA, MRE, or MCP, whether or not you already have some background in mainstream finance or in real estate or in urban economics, you will find this book useful.

One final point: We know that some people claim that real estate is too complex, or lacking in hard data, to study "scientifically"—that it is an art, not a science. The implication is that we can do no better than to support real estate decision making with purely ad hoc analytical techniques. In effect, the implication of this claim is that real estate decision making should be "shot from the hip," or based on vaguely articulated intuition, even though this decision making governs one-third of the world's assets.

But by now, in the twenty-first century, such an attitude truly is ignorance. We can do much better than "seat-of-the-pants" decision making. Yes, real estate is complex, data are less than perfect, and decision making will always be somewhat of an art and require good judgment. Real estate is neither rocket science nor heart surgery, and we will never outgrow our need to always apply common sense. But both financial and urban economics are highly developed, sophisticated fields of study. They contain a very impressive corpus of knowledge and toolkit of methodology, as rigorous as any branch of the social sciences. They encompass a long history and a vast body of scientific literature, both at the theoretical and empirical levels, and have several Nobel laureates to their credit. Quantitative data in real estate data are getting better and more widespread all the time. Financial and urban economics are out there waiting to be applied to real estate investment decision making. Read this book and *do it*!

Organization of the Book

This book is designed to be useful for several types of students, in several types of graduate courses. The most typical users will be business students who already have some basic finance background, or urban studies or real estate students who already have (or will elsewhere receive) a background in urban economics. With this in mind, students should be able to use this book somewhat flexibly.

In general, as is typical of textbooks, this book progresses from basic underlying concepts and principles to more specific and specialized considerations and applications. However, we would characterize the structure of this book as being more akin to a spiral than a straight line. This is because everything is related to everything else. So we start at an introductory level touching several aspects then circle back around again as we progress deeper into the subject matter. The result is some degree of repetition, but in different contexts or different levels of depth. This keeps the treatment always more practical and broad-minded, and also facilitates use of the book by specific chapters or parts without necessarily having to use the entire book in chapter order, thereby giving the book flexibility to be relevant to a broad range of students.

With this in mind, the book is organized into eight parts.

Part I. This is a brief two-chapter introductory overview designed to be especially useful to students who have little or no previous experience or exposure to the commercial real estate industry. A number of terms and basic practices that are widely used in real world practice are described here, as well as the fundamental real estate markets, and the parts and articulation of the overall "real estate system."

Part II. This is the urban economics part of the book: four chapters introducing the fundamental concepts and principles of that branch of economics as they relate to commercial property investment analysis. This is the part of the book that deals directly and in some depth with the "space market," as opposed to the asset market, including rental market analysis. This topic is fundamental, underlying the cash flow generation potential of all commercial property assets. Because this is not an urban economics textbook, however, we confine our coverage to a practical level, focused sharply on issues directly relevant to investment analysis. Students in urban studies programs may skim or even skip Part II and still be able to follow the remainder of the text, but we highly recommend it to business students who will not get this material elsewhere.

Part III. This part begins the in-depth presentation of financial economics for the study of real estate from an investment perspective. It contains three introductory chapters presenting a brief overview and history of real estate in the capital markets; the fundamental mathematical tools and formulas of present value analysis; and the basic definitions and measures of investment performance, periodic, and multi-period return measures. These are the fundamental building blocks of the rigorous study of real estate as an application of the financial economics discipline. Most of the material in Part III (along with Chapter 10, the first chapter in Part IV) should already be familiar to graduate business students who have passed through the core finance courses in their curriculums. Such students can skip or skim Chapters 7 through 10 and still be able to follow the rest of the book. However, concepts and applications particularly relevant to real estate are emphasized in these chapters, and some real estate-specific terminology is introduced, so students without prior real estate exposure should at least skim these chapters.

Part IV. This part presents the fundamental principles, concepts, and methods of micro-level real estate valuation and investment analysis, that is, the analysis of individual properties and transactions. The three chapters in Part IV present the core and basic foundation of the entire book. Recognizing that real estate assets trade in generally well-functioning markets, we present a framework that applies the fundamental economic principles of market equilibrium and opportunity cost to real estate investment analysis. Including the wealth-maximization principle, the DCF and NPV methodologies, and the concept of investment value and its relation to market value, this core framework is entirely consistent with and based on classical financial economics as taught in mainstream graduate-level corporate finance and securities investments courses. However, the implications of real estate's unique features and context are explicitly addressed and incorporated into the framework.

Part V. The three chapters in this part complete the coverage of basic investment analysis concepts and procedures begun in the previous part, extending them from the property level to the owner level. Thus, Part V treats the role of debt and income taxes in real estate investment, including the effect of leverage and the capital structure question. In a nutshell, while Part IV addresses the question of how to analyze the decision of *which* micro-level properties or projects to invest in, Part V addresses the question of *how to finance* those investments.

Part VI. This is the part of the book where we focus on the debt side of real estate investment (mortgages), in which we examine real estate debt primarily from the perspective of the lender (debt investor). The focus is primarily on commercial mortgages, including mortgage analysis fundamentals, commercial loan underwriting, and some basic mortgage economics and investment considerations. Part VI concludes with an introduction to commercial mortgage-backed securities (CMBS). Our treatment in Part VI remains at the introductory level, however, because the primary focus of this book is on equity investment.

Part VII. This part presents the basic macro-level concepts and methods for dealing with real estate from a "top-down" perspective, that is, from a perspective encompassing aggregates of many individual properties, such as portfolios, funds, and REITs. Part VII thus complements Parts IV and V (which present a more "bottom-up" view). The six chapters in Part VII deal with many of the more recent developments in the real estate investment industry. They cover topics such as modern portfolio theory and capital markets equilibrium pricing theory as these relate to real estate, international investments and REIT analysis, unique characteristics of real estate investment performance data (such as the "smoothing" and lagging problem in appraisal-based return indices and the recent advent of transaction price-based and stock market based commercial property indices), and issues related to real estate investment management (including an updated section on real estate equity derivatives).

Part VIII. The four chapters in this last part of the book treat in greater depth than was possible earlier some of the most fundamental topics relevant to property investment: land valuation, real estate development, and leasing. Both land valuation and the economic analysis of investment in real estate development projects are treated as applications of a relatively new academic field that is beginning to make its way into real world practice: *real options*. While option theory is also introduced briefly where it is relevant elsewhere in the book (most notably in Part II's treatment of land value and property life cycle, and Part VI's treatment of mortgage default and refinancing), it is in Part VIII that a complete and practical model is presented.

A final word on how this book "reads" is in order. Economics is a very technical subject with heavy emphasis on analysis and quantitative techniques (i.e., *lots of math and formulas*). Because this is an economics text, we can't get around this, even though we know it makes this subject tough for many students. We do sympathize, however, and we have tried to address the problem in several ways.

First, we have tried to clarify concepts intuitively whenever possible, and we have tried to present lots of simple numerical examples. Second, we have tried to identify sections of the text that are particularly advanced or difficult from an analytical or technical perspective and to set these aside to some extent. They are indicated by a preceding asterisk (*) in their section numbers. Less advanced or more "analytically challenged" students may want to skim these sections and not worry too much about the analytical details. While the points covered in these sections are important (or we would have left them out altogether), the overall implication of the point is more important than the technical details.

Finally, we have tried to systematize the presentation of all the material in this book, so as to clarify the underlying structure of the knowledge presented here. The concepts and tools presented in this book are essentially all based on a few simple foundational economic principles, including market equilibrium, opportunity cost, and wealth-maximization. This gives this material an underlying unity. If you look carefully, we hope you will see not only utility, but also some beauty and elegance in the material presented in this book.

Features in the Third Edition

We continue to be very gratified by the reception of this book since its first edition was published in 2000. Its increasing use by leading graduate programs, both in the United States and other countries, has confirmed our original belief that the real estate industry and its Academy are ready for the more advanced and economically rigorous treatment that is the hallmark of this text. With over 350 Google Scholar citations as of late 2012, this book has become the most such cited text in the field of real estate finance and investments.

The Third Edition features a complete review and updating of all 30 chapters, with a view particularly toward reflecting lessons from the Global Financial Crisis of 2008. These include a greater sensitivity to cyclicality in commercial property asset markets and to the tendency of property investors to rely on debt financing (sometimes to excess). Historical narrative and perspective has been enhanced or introduced in several chapters. Chapters and sections on REITs, CMBS, price indices, and derivatives have been substantially updated. This edition also features attention to sustainability in commercial property development and investment. Increased attention is paid to international considerations, including an updated Chapter 24 on International Real Estate Investment by Professor Eichholtz of Maastricht University. Throughout the text, authors have used updated and expanded quantitative data from leading data purveyors who have generously contributed to the book. The Third Edition continues to include:

- **Accompanying CD:** The book is accompanied by a CD that includes additional and supplementary materials, including appendices, more depth on certain topics, spreadsheet examples of methodologies, data used in exhibits, answers to odd-numbered study questions, and more.
- **Accompanying Specialized Software:** The book's CD includes a special student edition of **ARGUS®**, a software package widely used in commercial real estate analysis for cash flow projection. An introductory tutorial for using ARGUS software is also included on the CD.

New to This Edition

Overall, this edition has been updated and streamlined for better comprehension. The use of a second color makes the exhibits easier to understand and key terms more visible within the text. Most of the exhibits have been revised to include more recent data. Answers to all of the study questions are available to instructors; answers to odd-numbered questions are available on the student CD.

Chapter-specific updates include:

Chapter 2 now includes historical lessons from the recent financial crisis.

Chapter 4 has been revised to include international examples and information about recent developments and projections for the twenty-first century.

Chapter 5 now includes a new boxed feature entitled "Tools to Measure Building Sustainability" and a new reference list "References on Sustainability in Real Estate Investment Considerations."

Chapter 6 includes new content related to office space demand.

Chapter 7 now includes a new section 7.3 which provides a brief history of commercial investment during recent decades and addresses sources of debt and equity capital.

Chapter 9 includes a feature about real estate volatility, which has been revised extensively.

Chapter 10 has been updated to include lessons from the recent financial crisis.

Chapter 11 has been updated throughout and two subsections have been added.

Chapter 13 includes new content about the temptation of leverage in section 13.1, and section 13.2.3 has been renamed and contains additional content.

Chapter 14 has been streamlined and clarified while continuing the previous edition's rigorous treatment of the use of debt in real estate investment.

Chapter 15 includes a revised and expanded section 15.3 on project level finance and deal structuring including elaboration of joint venture waterfalls.

Chapter 16 has been expanded with new exhibits as well as discussion about the financial crisis and the evolution of the residential mortgage landscape.

Chapter 20 has been completely revised including reflection of the Great Financial Crisis.

Chapter 22 opens with a new section, 22.1, and section 22.4 has been completely revised.

Chapter 23 has been reorganized and streamlined.

Chapter 24 has been completely revised.

Chapter 25 now includes a section about innovations in commercial property returns indices—section 25.4.

Chapter 26 has been revised and restructured. Learning objectives have been revised and new sections have been added.

Chapter 28 includes a new feature about the trend toward greener development.

Chapter 29 now includes an exhibit that illustrates the "canonical" formula and a new subsection focused on the development risk ratio and implications for characteristic development regions—section 29.1.3.

Chapter 30 includes an expanded introduction, two new features, and a new list of sustainability references.

With all these improvements, we are very excited about this new edition. It is our hope that it will be used even more widely around the world, and that through its wise use by our very intelligent and thoughtful readers, the efficiency and quality of real estate investment and development around the world will be improved as a result, for the betterment of humankind.

Cambridge, Massachusetts
San Diego, California
Hartford, Connecticut
Maastricht, Netherlands

March 2013

ACKNOWLEDGMENTS

This book would not have been possible without the contributions of a number of individuals who helped in a variety of ways. The original germ of the idea for this project goes back to Christopher Will at South-Western College Publishing in Cincinnati in 1994. But this project would have died without fruition if it were not for the enthusiasm of Elizabeth Sugg, the acquisitions editor for the first edition at Prentice Hall, combined with the opportunity provided by Tim Riddiough at that time at MIT for Professor Geltner to teach the Real Estate Finance & Investments course at MIT in the fall of 1998. The first edition of this book is a direct outgrowth of that teaching project, just as the more recent editions have been particularly inspired and driven by the students of MIT's MSRED Program since Professor Geltner moved back to MIT full-time in 2002. We have also had high-quality assistance from a number of reviewers and class-testers of the working drafts of this book. Most notable in this regard are David Ling and Wayne Archer at the University of Florida, who class-tested most of the first edition of this book and provided us with detailed and in-depth feedback. Excellent review and class-testing feedback of the first edition was also provided by Brent Ambrose, Tony Ciochetti, Terrence Clauretie, Jim Clayton, Ron Donohue, Richard Knitter, Michael Young, Jianping Mei, Tim Riddiough, and Tony Sanders. For new material in more recent editions, the class-testing role has been borne primarily by the students in MIT's real estate finance and investment courses. A particular contribution was made by Konstantinos Kalligeros in the real options material. We would also like to acknowledge the contribution of the real estate investment professional staff at the State Teachers Retirement System of Ohio, the members of the research committee of the National Council of Real Estate Investment Fiduciaries (NCREIF), and the Pension Real Estate Association (PREA). These leading professional practitioners continue to provide us with an invaluable real-world perspective for the micro-level and macro-level portions of this book, respectively. For this third edition we are also particularly indebted to data providers in CoStar Group and Real Capital Analytics, Inc., as well as PricewaterhouseCoopers and Green Street Advisors, among others. The patience and wise guidance of our editor for both the second and third editions, Sara Glassmeyer, has made the development of this new edition not just feasible but actually enjoyable. And, of course, our thanks go to colleagues and assistants at MIT, San Diego, and Maastricht, including with particular note to Sheharyar Bokhari at MIT. Finally, much of the underlying inspiration and character of this book is owed to Stewart Myers, the lead author's Ph.D. dissertation supervisor at MIT back in the 1980s, and a mentor to more people than he probably realizes. Stew's contributions to finance's corpus and toolkit of theory and methods are so fundamental and widespread as to now be taken for granted, and they are ubiquitous in this text.

Courtesy of David Geltner

David Geltner has been at Massachusetts Institute of Technology since 2002 where he has held the George Macomber Chair and currently is Professor of Real Estate Finance in the Department of Urban Studies & Planning with a joint appointment in Engineering Systems in MIT's School of Engineering. Geltner served as Academic Director of the MIT Center for Real Estate from 2003 to 2008. Currently, he is the faculty chair of MIT's Master of Science in Real Estate Development (MSRED) program. Recipient of the U.S. Pension Real Estate Association's Graaskamp Award in 2011 for excellence and influence in real estate investment research, Geltner has served as Academic Advisor to the National Council of Real Estate Investment Fiduciaries (NCREIF), and as Director of MIT's Commercial Real Estate Data Laboratory which has developed pioneering commercial property price and investment performance indices based on transactions prices. Geltner is an editorial board member and frequent contributor to top academic real estate journals and is a past editor of *Real Estate Economics*. Geltner served from 1999–2012 as the External Academic Member of the Real Estate Investment Committee of the State Teachers Retirement System of Ohio. Prior to MIT, Geltner was the REEAC Professor of Real Estate in the Finance Department of the College of Business Administration at the University of Cincinnati. He has been teaching graduate level real estate investments and finance since 1989. Geltner received his Ph.D. in 1989 from MIT's Civil Engineering Department in the field of infrastructure finance and economics. He also has degrees in urban studies from Carnegie-Mellon University and the University of Michigan. A 2006 study published in Real Estate Economics found Geltner to be the most influential academic real estate writer, based on number of citations during 2000–2004 in top academic real estate journals. Geltner is a recipient of the American Real Estate Society David Ricardo Medal. He is also a Fellow of the Homer Hoyt Institute, the Real Estate Research Institute, and the Royal Institution of Chartered Surveyors.

Courtesy of Norm Miller

Norm Miller is a professor at the University of San Diego, Burnham-Moores Center for Real Estate He was at the University of Cincinnati from 1980 to 2007. He received his Ph.D. from the Ohio State University in 1977. He is active on the Editorial Board of several national and international journals and a past president of the American Real Estate Society (ARES).

Dr. Miller has authored numerous academic articles, books and articles in trade market publications on housing, brokerage, mortgage risk, valuation, sustainable real estate, and many other topics. His research on housing market analysis and forecasting spans three decades. In 2009, he founded the *Journal of Sustainable Real Estate* (www.josre.org). He is part of the Collateral Analytics research team, a premier valuation and forecasting firm (www.collateralanalytics.com).

Dr. Miller is currently a Homer Hoyt Land Use Institute Faculty and Board member, based in North Palm Beach, Florida, where he is involved with some premier thought leaders among academics and industry professionals in a think-tank setting for annual conferences on real estate issues and trends. The Hoyt Land Use Institute promotes commercial real estate research, education, and career path awareness (www.hoyt.org).

Courtesy of Jim Clayton

Jim Clayton is Vice-President of Research at Cornerstone Real Estate Advisers LLC, a global real estate investment adviser with subsidiary and affiliate offices in the United States, the United Kingdom, Europe, and Asia. Cornerstone provides core and value-added investment and advisory services, including a comprehensive suite of real estate debt, equity and securities expertise, to institutional and other qualified investors around the globe. Cornerstone is a member of the MassMutual Financial Group. At Cornerstone, Dr. Clayton is responsible for monitoring and forecasting real estate and capital market trends and delivering applied research and strategic thought pieces to the firm's leadership and investor clients. Prior to joining Cornerstone in December 2008, he was the Director of Research at the Pension Real Estate Association (PREA). Before joining PREA in 2006, Dr. Clayton held faculty positions at the University of Cincinnati and at Saint Mary's University in Halifax, Nova Scotia, and was an instructor at the University of British Columbia. He is currently an Adjunct Professor in the Real Estate Program in the School of Business at the University of Connecticut, where he teaches the MBA Real Estate Investment and Portfolio Management course. He also teaches in executive education programs at the Real Property Association of Canada (REALpac).

Dr. Clayton's research has been, and continues to be, published in the major academic and practitioner real estate journals. He is a co-editor of the bi-annual special issue of the *Journal of Portfolio Management* devoted to real estate, and he has been named a Fellow of both the Real Estate Research Institute (RERI) and the Weimer School of Advanced Studies in Real Estate and Land Economics. Dr. Clayton is a member of the PREA Research Committee and co-chairs the PREA Research Affinity Group. He is active in a number of industry groups and is a frequent presenter at both industry and academic events in North America and abroad. Recent speaking engagements include events organized by the Urban Land Institute (ULI), RERI, American Real Estate Society (ARES), REALpac, University of Cincinnati, University of North Carolina Charlotte, Ernst and Young, Altus Group, Investment Property Databank (IPD), Global Property Forum, Florida Public Pension Trustees Association (FPPTA), and MIT Center for Real Estate.

Dr. Clayton received his Ph.D. degree in Real Estate Finance and Urban Economics from the University of British Columbia, an undergraduate degree in Economics from Queen's University, and an M.A. degree in Economics from the University of Western Ontario.

Courtesy of Piet Eichholtz

Piet Eichholtz is Professor of Real Estate and Finance and chair of the Finance Department at Maastricht University in the Netherlands. He teaches courses in Finance and in Real Estate Finance and Investments. His practical experience includes positions at the ABP and at NIB Capital, and nonexecutive board memberships with IPD, Oppenheim Immobilien, NSI, and Redevco.

Prof. Eichholtz has also earned a solid reputation as an entrepreneur. In 1996, he started GPR, a firm that specialized in international property company indices. (GPR was sold in 2001.) In 2004, he became co-founder of Finance Ideas, a financial consultancy company. In 2011, he was one of the founders of GRESB, the Global Real Estate Sustainability Benchmark. He is currently a member of the Investment Committee of Loyalis and of the Housing Scenario Group of Bouwfonds Development.

Prof. Eichholtz has provided extensive services to public society, mainly through board memberships of industry organizations in the property sector but also as an advisor to various government agencies. In early 2004, for example, he was a special property advisor to the UN Good Offices Mission in Cyprus.

Prof. Eichholtz's academic work has been widely published in the Netherlands and internationally. He is a frequent speaker at industry and academic conferences. Most of his work regards real estate markets, with a focus on international investment and portfolio management, performance measurement, housing markets, and sustainability.

PART

I

INTRODUCTION TO REAL ESTATE ECONOMICS

Let's begin with the big picture, with an overview of the commercial real estate system from an economic perspective. The main purpose of Part I is to provide this overview. But we will also present here some of the fundamental nuts and bolts and tools useful in the economic study of real estate. These will help to bring the big picture down to everyday business practice, and be useful in subsequent chapters. As noted in the preface, two major branches of economics bear on the analysis of commercial property from an investment perspective. The first is what is usually referred to in the United States as *urban economics*, and the second

is *financial economics*. In later parts of this book, we will explore real estate from one or the other of these two perspectives, separately. In this first part, by contrast, we will attempt to provide some integration and overview, bringing both of these perspectives together. The first chapter introduces the two major types or levels of markets relevant to commercial property analysis. The second chapter then discusses the development industry that links these two markets in a dynamic system and presents some tools for understanding and analyzing this system. As in other parts of this book, we will also endeavor to bring in some historical perspective on the topics introduced here.

REAL ESTATE SPACE AND ASSET MARKETS

LEARNING OBJECTIVES

After reading this chapter, you should understand:

⊃ How to apply the basic economic concepts of supply and demand to commercial real estate markets.

⊃ The difference between the real estate space and asset markets.

⊃ The concept of market segmentation within the space market.

⊃ Why the long-run supply function in the space market is "kinked" and what that means to future rents.

⊃ The difference between, and relative magnitudes of, the public versus private asset markets, and the difference between equity and debt capital.

⊃ What a cap rate is and what determines cap rate prevailing in real estate markets.

Markets are perhaps the most basic of all economic social phenomena. In essence, a **market** is a mechanism through which goods and services are voluntarily exchanged among different owners. Prior to, or apart from, market exchange, the transfer of real property possession was (and in some cases remains) effected by traditionalistic or ritualistic mechanisms, or by marriage or inheritance, or even by war. The development of well-functioning real property markets during and subsequent to the Renaissance has been an important part of the development of the modern economy and, indeed, modern civilization itself. In this chapter, we will present a basic introduction to the two major markets that are relevant for analyzing commercial real estate: the space market and the asset market.

1.1 Space Market

The **space market** is the market for the usage of (or right to use) real property (land and built space). This type of market is also often referred to as the real estate **usage market** or the **rental market**. On the **demand** side of this market are individuals, households, and firms or institutions that want to use space for either consumption or production purposes. For example, a student renting an apartment is using space for housing consumption. A law firm renting an office is using space for production. Both these types of users are on the demand side of the space market. On the **supply** side of the space market are real estate owners who rent space to tenants.

The price of the right to possess and use space for a specified temporary period of time is commonly called the **rent**. It is usually quoted in annual terms, per square foot (SF), though other methods are also used (such as monthly per apartment). The rental price (determined by supply and demand in the space market) thus gives a signal about the current value of built space, reflecting the current balance of supply and demand for that space. If usage demand grows and space supply remains constant, rents will tend to rise; if supply grows while demand stays constant, rents will fall.

1.1.1 Segmentation of Space Markets: The Immobility of Real Estate

Users in the market for built space generally need a rather specific type of space in a rather specific location. A law firm needs an office building, not a restaurant or retail shop or warehouse, and it may need the building to be in downtown Cleveland, for example. If so, office space in downtown Detroit, or even office space in suburban Cleveland, will probably not satisfy the firm's needs.

The supply side of the space market is also location and type specific. Buildings cannot be moved. A vacant office building in downtown Detroit may be architecturally perfect for the Cleveland law firm, but it is not in the relevant location. Similarly, buildings generally cannot change their type, for example, from shop to office, or office to apartment. While some buildings have been converted from one usage type to another (for example, the warehouses that have been turned into "loft" apartments in New York and other large cities), such conversions are relatively rare and often require considerable construction expenditure.[1]

Because both supply and demand are location and type specific, real estate space markets are highly **segmented**. That is, space markets tend to be local rather than national, and specialized around building usage categories. The market for warehouse space in Dallas exists as a functioning market. A market for warehouse space in the United States as a whole does not really exist as a single space market. This is in contrast to nationally "integrated" markets, such as that for gasoline, for example, or cars, or financial capital. These latter are homogeneous commodities that can be moved easily from place to place.

Because of space market segmentation, rental prices for physically similar space can differ widely from one location to another, or from one type of building to another, in virtually the same location. For example, office rents on new leases in Chicago's Loop can be $23 per square foot (SF) while space in similar office buildings in Midtown Manhattan is not available for less than $33/SF. Similarly, apartment buildings can provide their owners with annual rents of $7/SF in suburban Dallas when retail buildings there are yielding $13/SF on new leases.[2] The office buildings in Chicago cannot be picked up and moved to Manhattan to earn a higher rent, nor can the apartments in suburban Dallas readily be converted into shopping centers.

The economic "Law of One Price" states that, at a given point in time, the same thing cannot trade at different prices. Otherwise no one would pay the more expensive price, and/or no one would sell at the lower price. But this law only applies *within a single well-integrated market*. If there are barriers between market segments, effectively creating separate markets, so

---

[1]An exception that proves the rule: conversion of rental apartments into owner-occupied condominiums. There was a boom in such conversions in the United States between 2003 and 2005 as the demand for, and therefore the value of, condominiums surged far above that of rental apartments, and the two types of real estate are very similar physically. However, even in this case there were substantial barriers and expenses to conversion, and the collapse in the condominium market that spearheaded the subsequent collapse in the owner-occupied housing market in the United States after 2005 led to many failed condominium development or conversion projects which subsequently faced difficulties converting back to rental properties (e.g., with some of their units by then owned and occupied as condominiums including the associated governing rights of the condominium owners over the entire property).

[2]These were the actual average rents reported in late 1992 by the National Real Estate Index.

that buyers cannot go to where the price is cheaper and sellers cannot go to where the price is higher, then different prices can prevail across the segments. This is the case across the real estate space markets.

The primary geographic units of space market segmentation are **metropolitan areas** (also known as "metros," or MSAs, short for "metropolitan statistical areas"). An MSA, encompassing a central city and its surrounding suburbs, tends to be relatively integrated economically, culturally, and socially. By definition, most points within a metropolitan area are more or less within automobile commuting distance of most other points in the area. The entire metropolitan area is largely built on the same economic base, although that base may be diverse in some areas. However, even within the metropolitan area important geographic submarkets exist. For example, the **downtown** (or **central business district—CBD**) is a different submarket from the suburbs, and individual suburbs will differ from one another. So even within a single metropolitan area considerable geographic segmentation of space markets exists.

In addition to geographical segmentation, real estate space markets are segmented by **property usage type**. The major types of space markets for rental property include office, retail, industrial, and multifamily residential. Other smaller and more specialized markets also exist, such as hotels, health facilities, self-storage facilities, and a wide variety of others. Because each of these markets has different types of firms or individuals on the demand side wanting to use the space, and different physical, locational, and architectural requirements on the supply side, the real estate industry serving these various space markets also tends to be segmented. Individual real estate professionals tend to specialize in serving one market segment or another. Real estate firms, such as national brokerage businesses, that do encompass more than one market segment tend to be organized in divisions that focus on the various segments.

1.1.2 Supply, Demand, and Rent in the Space Market

Let us "zoom in" on a specific, historic real estate space market and see how the economist's basic concepts of supply and demand and market equilibrium can help us to understand what goes on in a typical functioning space market. We will consider (a somewhat stylized

Cincinnati skyline circa 1990.

Cincinnati Museum Center-Cincinnati Historical Society Library

version of) the market for class A office space in downtown Cincinnati, Ohio, during the late 1980s and early 1990s.[3]

From the 1970s to the 1980s, office employment grew substantially in downtown Cincinnati. From roughly 24,000 office workers in class A buildings in the 1970s, by the mid-1980s there were 30,000 such workers. This growth in office usage demand was due partly to national factors, such as a structural shift in the U.S. economy (out of manufacturing and into services) that increased the number of office jobs. The growth was also due to local factors, as several national firms relocated their headquarters from other cities to Cincinnati. The 30,000 workers in the mid-1980s were occupying some 5 million square feet (SF) of space in about a dozen office towers typically 20 to 40 stories tall that defined the skyline of the city. The average rent being charged in these buildings was about $16/SF (per year).

This growth in demand is pictured in Exhibit 1-1. The underlying source of the space demand was the need of office workers for space in which to work. As the number of office workers increased, this need grew. The need for office space also grew because technological change, such as the rise in the office use of personal computers and fax machines, made more space necessary per worker. The growth in class A office demand is represented in Exhibit 1-1 by the movement up and out to the right of the demand function line, for example, from a previous time when there were 24,000 workers to the time (by the mid-1980s) when there were 30,000 workers. Notice that if the underlying need for office workers in downtown Cincinnati increased further, to 36,000 workers, for example, then demand in the market would support an additional 1 million SF of space (a total of 6 million SF would be needed) at the same $16 rent. Increase in demand thus refers to potential tenants being willing and able to pay higher rent on average for the same total amount of space leased in the market, or equivalently, to more total space leased at the same rent. (A reduction in demand would imply just the opposite.)

The demand functions pictured in Exhibit 1-1 look essentially like the classical demand functions of economic theory—downward-sloping continuous lines that move up and to the right as demand grows. This is typical of demand functions in the space market. The supply side is a different story, however. The supply function in the real estate space market does

EXHIBIT 1-1 Office Demand as a Function of Employment

© OnCourse Learning

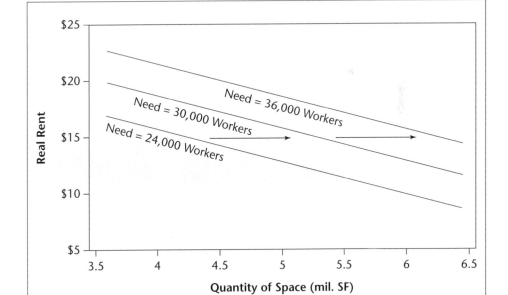

[3]Real estate markets are often divided into classes, A, B, and C, to distinguish the physical and locational quality of the buildings, and therefore the levels of rent and types of tenants that are in the market on the demand side. Class A refers to the upper end of the market, where in the case of office buildings typical tenants would include prestigious law firms, corporate headquarters, and financial service firms. The particular historical period in this example is selected because of its educational value in illustrating a classic boom and bust cycle in the space market.

EXHIBIT 1-2 Real Estate
Space Market Supply
Function

© OnCourse Learning

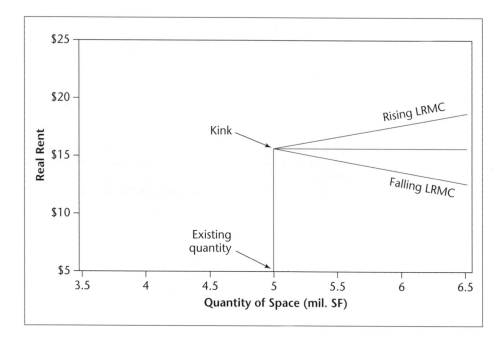

not look like the upward-sloping continuous line depicted in the classical supply/demand diagrams. Instead, the possible supply function shapes shown in Exhibit 1-2 give a better representation of the supply side of most real estate space markets. This uniquely shaped supply function has important implications for understanding the functioning of the space market.

1.1.3 Supply Is "Kinked"

Economists often depict the typical real estate supply function as being "**kinked**"—that is, it is not continuous, but has a "corner" or break in it. The supply function starts out as a nearly vertical line at the current quantity of space supply in the market (in this case 5 million SF). This reflects the fact that the supply of office space is almost completely inelastic: if demand falls, office space cannot be reduced (at least in the short to medium term). This is a consequence of the extreme longevity of built space. Indeed, compared to most other products, buildings last much longer. Rarely is a building torn down within less than 20 or 30 years from the time it is built, and it is much more common for buildings to endure 50 years or more (especially large-scale structures such as class A downtown office buildings). While some buildings can be converted to different uses, such conversions are expensive, time-consuming, and would often be substantially encumbered or constrained by existing long-term leases and zoning regulations. So at least for several years the market will maintain pretty much the quantity of supply it already has, in the case of a fall in demand.

The kink in the supply function represents the fact that this situation is not symmetrical with respect to an *increase* in space demand. The kink (or corner) in the supply function occurs at the current quantity of built space at a rent level that equates (on a capitalized present value basis) to the long-run marginal cost of supplying additional space to the market. At this rent the addition of new supply into the market can be quite elastic even over a relatively short to medium term. Recall that the supply function for any competitively supplied product is simply the marginal cost function for producing additional increments of the product. In the case of built space, the marginal cost is the cost of developing new buildings, including the site acquisition cost as well as the construction cost and necessary profit for developers.

The level of rent that is just sufficient to stimulate profitable new development in the market is called the **replacement cost** level of rent, and this tends to be the long-run **equilibrium rent** in the market. If rents are said to be "below replacement cost" in a market, it means that developers cannot profitably undertake new development in that market. If rents rise above the replacement cost level, new development will be very profitable and will normally occur quickly in most U.S. cities, forcing rents back down to the long-run equilibrium level within a few years at the most.

1.1.4 Relation among Supply, Development Cost, and Rent

To understand the preceding point more clearly, let us return to our numerical example of the Cincinnati class A office market. Suppose that in the mid-1980s it would have cost $200/SF to develop a typical new class A office building in downtown Cincinnati, counting site acquisition cost as well as construction and other development costs, and including sufficient profit for the endeavor to be worthwhile to the developer. Thus, $200/SF was the marginal cost of adding additional class A office supply into the downtown market.

If we could sell new buildings for $200/SF, then additional development would be feasible. But the price at which one can sell buildings depends on what investors are willing to pay for them. This in turn depends on how much income the investors can expect to obtain from the buildings in the future, and how much investors will pay for that income. It is helpful in this context to quote property prices in terms of how much investors are willing to pay per dollar of annual net rent they would initially receive from their investment. Suppose, for example, that in the mid-1980s investors were willing to pay $12.50 to purchase a class A Cincinnati office property for each dollar of current annual net rent the property could produce. Then if a building could charge $16/SF annual net rent for office space, and expect to keep that space rented, the building would be worth $200/SF (as $16 \times 12.5 = 200$). Using typical real estate terminology, we would say office buildings were selling at an 8 percent **cap rate**, as the annual net income, $16/SF, divided by the building value of $200/SF, equals 8 percent. In these circumstances, the net rent that equates (after dividing by the cap rate prevailing in the asset market) to the marginal cost of adding office supply into the Cincinnati market is $16/SF. So $16 would be the replacement cost rent level. According to Exhibit 1-2, this was indeed the case, as indicated by the kink point at the $16 rent level.

The rest of the supply function in Exhibit 1-2 consists of a line moving out to the right away from the kink point. This part of the supply function represents how new additional supply will respond to rents. This part of the line will exhibit one of three possibilities—rising, level, or falling. A rising supply function results when the development cost of new buildings is greater as more total stock of rental space is added into the market. Roughly speaking, if it would cost more to develop the next office building than it did to develop the last one (in real terms, after subtracting general inflation, and including the cost of site acquisition and any necessary demolition), then the supply function is rising beyond the kink point.[4] If it would cost less, then the supply function is falling. If it would cost the same, then the function is level beyond the kink point.

1.1.5 Forecasting the Future Direction of Rents

One of the most basic and important things you must have in the real estate business is an intelligent idea about the future direction of rents in the space market. The shape of the supply function is important, for it fundamentally determines the level of real rents as demand changes over time. In general, the kink means that if a space market is currently in equilibrium, future growth in demand will result in very little (if any) real increase in rent levels in most markets in the long run.

On the other hand, the kink implies that declines in demand will cause relatively rapid and severe reductions in market rents for new leases due to the inelasticity of supply reduction. Such reductions may be expressed, particularly at first, not so much in a reduction in the rents landlords *ask for*, but in an increase in vacancies and in landlords' offering of "concessions" to potential tenants, such as months of free rent up front, as an inducement to sign a long-term lease.

The kink in the supply curve is one reason real estate space markets have often tended to be cyclical, with periods of excess supply followed by periods of tight markets. A modest

---

[4]In general, the term *real prices* refers to prices quoted in constant purchasing power dollars, after removing general inflation (or deflation).

EXHIBIT 1-3 Change in
Supply and Demand and
Rent over Time

© OnCourse Learning

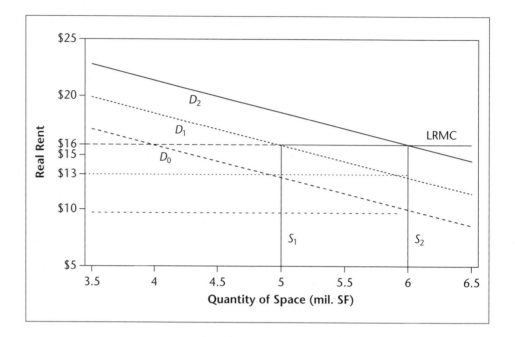

example of this occurred in the Cincinnati office market of the 1980s–1990s. In the late 1980s, developers in that market, apparently anticipating further growth in office demand, built an additional 1 million SF of new office space, expanding the supply from 5 million to 6 million SF. This change in supply is indicated in Exhibit 1-3 by the movement of the supply function to the right, from S_1 to S_2, assuming a flat long-run supply function. Had the demand continued to grow, from D_1 to D_2 for example, this expansion of supply would have been justified, and rent levels in the market would have remained at the long-run equilibrium level of $16/SF. However, as happened in many real estate markets in the late 1980s and early 1990s, the supply overshot the demand. The demand growth did not materialize. The market remained stuck essentially with the same demand function, D_1. Combined with the new supply function of S_2, this caused market rents to plummet to levels around $13/SF. Indeed, during the general economic recession of 1990–1991 and the subsequent corporate downsizing, demand for class A office space in downtown Cincinnati probably actually fell, at least temporarily, from its previous level, perhaps to the level indicated by D_0, resulting in market rents temporarily in the $10/SF range.

With demand at a level such as D_0 or D_1 and supply at a level such as S_2 in Exhibit 1-3, the market rents are below their long-run equilibrium level. That is, rents are below the level that can support new development, below replacement cost. At such a point, the space market is poised for a substantial surge in real rents if demand begins to grow again. Until rents rise back up to the long-run equilibrium level, the inelasticity of supply works in favor of landlords when demand is growing, enabling substantial hikes in real rents. (These may manifest at first as the filling up of vacancy and disappearance of widespread rent concessions in the market.) By the late 1990s, the class A office market in downtown Cincinnati was back up to long-run equilibrium rents.

1.1.6 Is the Supply Function Rising, Level, or Falling?

The principal cause of a rising supply function is the cost of land. In the space market this is caused by land scarcity in the presence of growing usage demand. This results in increasing **location rent**, as space users are willing to pay more real dollars per year for use of the same location.[5]

---

[5]The term *location rent* will be discussed in more depth in Chapter 4. It should also be noted that it is possible for land costs to rise as a result of effects within the other major relevant market, the real estate asset market. This latter possibility will be addressed in Chapters 2 and 27.

The real cost of building construction (apart from land cost) does not usually increase over time or from one site to another. However, if demand keeps growing in the face of fixed land supply, the real price of site acquisition will rise, and this will add to the cost of development.

One way that this occurs is that as more space is built in the market, the remaining supply of good buildable sites becomes scarcer. Construction will be more expensive on remaining unbuilt land sites that are hilly or swampy or less desirable for other reasons. Also, when new construction is undertaken on a site that already has a major existing structure on it, this greatly adds to the site acquisition cost. Not only must the existing structure be demolished, but the opportunity cost represented by the present value of the potential future income that the existing structure could otherwise generate is a major component of the site acquisition cost. For these reasons, it is possible for the supply curve to rise to the right of the kink point, as indicated by the upper line in Exhibit 1-2.

It is also possible, however, for the supply curve to decline to the right of the kink point. This can occur in areas where the location rent is declining over time in real terms, such as when a location is losing its relative **centrality**. For example, during the last half of the twentieth century, the traditional CBDs of many metropolitan areas in the United States lost value relative to suburban locations. Recall the earlier illustration about downtown office rents in Chicago and New York. We noted that in 1992 these averaged $23/SF and $33/SF respectively. Nearly two decades later, in 2010, class A office rents in downtown Chicago and New York averaged $26/SF and $38/SF. At first this might seem like growth, and in nominal terms it is. But if we remove the effect of general inflation, the 2010 rents expressed in constant-purchasing-power 1992 dollars was $17/SF and $25/SF respectively in Chicago and New York, a decline in real terms.[6] In general, the development of the automobile and transport infrastructure, telecommunications, the personal computer, Internet, and smartphones, have all reduced the relative value of central locations compared to peripheral ones. This has caused a reduction in the real level of long-run equilibrium rents for some types of commercial property in the United States.

Evidence suggests that in typical or average space markets in the United States the long-run supply function has tended to be nearly level beyond the kink point, perhaps slightly rising or slightly falling. How do we know this? We can observe that rent levels in the economy have not generally tended to rise faster than inflation even as the total supply of built space has greatly expanded. For example, Exhibit 1-4 depicts a famous index of U.S. home prices produced by economist Robert Shiller. The chart traces home prices adjusted for inflation over 120 years from 1890 to 2010. Note that despite ups and downs (most notably the down period of the 1920s–1930s and the bubble of the 2000s), the overall net direction of the index is essentially flat. This means that real house prices have not been increasing on average over more than a century, in spite of the fact that the demand for housing over this period has grown (as population has grown five-fold and household formation and real incomes many times that) and supply has been greatly added. The chart suggests that building costs have increased in real terms only very modestly (less than half a percent per year) and not at all since the early 1970s.

In judging the likely shape or change in level of the long-run supply curve in U.S. real estate markets, several general historical and geographical factors must be kept in mind. A fundamental consideration is that the United States is, relative to many other nations, a "land rich" country, or anyway perceives itself as such as part of our social and political culture. As a result, in the United States urban land use expansion is relatively lightly controlled. A fundamental historical factor that must also be kept in mind is that during recent history, massive transportation and telecommunications infrastructure investments

---

[6]The source for the 2010 rents is CBRE Econometrics. Note that both 1992 and 2010 were near the bottoms of rental market cycles in both locations, thus providing a "fair" (trough-to-trough full-cycle) comparison across time. It should also be noted that declines in rent/SF refers to rent per square foot of rentable space. If the average density of built space (that is, rentable SF per acre of land) is increasing over time (as was in fact the case in downtown Chicago and Manhattan between 1992 and 2010), then the change in rent/SF will track below that of location rent or land value (See Section 5.3.4 for more discussion.)

EXHIBIT 1-4 Long-Run History of Real Home Prices, Building Costs, Population, and Interest Rates in the United States

Source: Shiller, Robert J.; Irrational Exuberance, Second Edition. 2005 © Princeton University Press. Reprinted by permission of Princeton University Press.

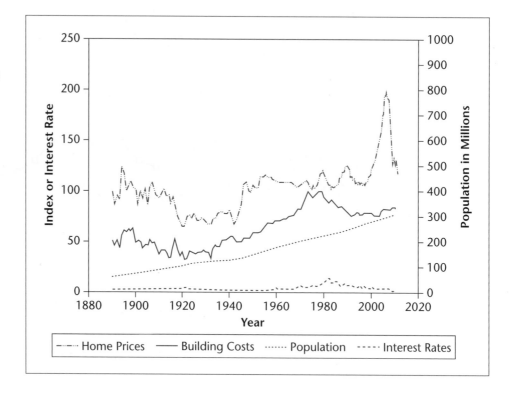

occurred, including the development of the urban expressways that serve virtually all U.S. cities, as well as more recent developments in information and communication technology that tend to reduce the need for physical transportation and commuting. The result has opened up vast tracts of land for urbanization and exurban development by making all points readily accessible or serviceable for living or working. As a result, the supply of land has not been at all fixed in most metropolitan areas, but able to grow and expand with the demand. Large quantities of lightly used land still remain in and around many U.S. cities.

As noted, the effect of this physical expansion of urban land has been pronounced in the traditional CBDs. For example, in the downtowns of most U.S. cities, surface parking lots are not uncommon. These represent a ready supply of unbuilt, lightly used land available for development. The historical evidence is that real rents in U.S. downtowns have not generally risen over the past half century, and indeed they have fallen in many cities. Exceptions to this rule are generally found only in severely space-constrained areas such as islands or peninsulas like Manhattan, Honolulu, and San Francisco. Even in such places, increasing real rents are not guaranteed, as seen in Exhibit 1-5 depicting class A office rents in Manhattan from 1988 to 2010.[7]

In general, unless you have a good and specific reason to believe otherwise, it is probably safest to assume that the shape of the supply function is similar to the middle line portrayed in Exhibit 1-2 in most of the space markets you will probably be dealing in, at least in the United States. This may not be true in some other countries, however.

---

[7]Note that the rents in Exhibit 1-5 are not same-property or constant-quality rents, but reflect the average asking rents within the changing stock of class A office properties in Manhattan which evolves by including new buildings added by construction and by removing older buildings that drop from class A status. As will be discussed in Chapters 5 and 11, same-property rents would tend to track below the market average represented in Exhibit 1-5. (See Chapters 5 and 11 for more discussion.)

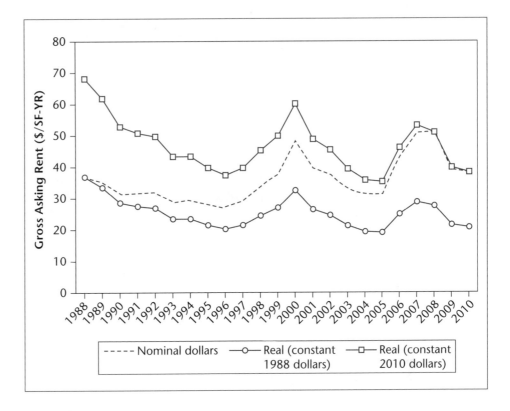

EXHIBIT 1-5 Manhattan Class A Office Market Rents, 1988–2010 Nominal and Real

Source: Data from CBRE Econometrics.

1.2 Asset Market

While the space market is the most fundamental type of market relevant to the real estate business, the **asset market** is of equal importance. The real estate asset market is the market for the ownership of real estate assets. Real estate assets consist of real property, that is, land parcels and the buildings on them. Therefore, this market is often referred to as the **property market**.

From an economic perspective such assets consist essentially of claims to future cash flows, namely, the rents the buildings can generate for their owners. As such, these real estate assets can be compared to, and indeed compete in the capital market with, other forms of capital assets, such as stocks and bonds. The net rents generated by a building are analogous in this respect to the dividends paid out by stocks or the interest paid out by bonds, and property competes for investors' capital against these other forms of investments. The real estate asset market must be viewed as part of the larger **capital market**, the market for capital assets of all types.

1.2.1 Capital Markets

Broadly speaking, the capital markets can be divided into four categories according to whether they are public or private markets, and according to whether the assets traded are equity or debt. (See Exhibit 1-6.) **Public markets** are those in which small homogeneous units (or "shares") of ownership in assets trade in public exchanges in which many buyers and sellers are generally simultaneously participating in the market with price quotes available for all to observe. The stock market is the classic example of a public capital market. In such markets, transaction prices at which the units of the assets trade are typically reported publicly on a daily or more frequent basis. Public markets are characterized by a relatively high degree of **liquidity** in that it is generally possible to quickly sell units of the assets at or

EXHIBIT 1-6

Major Types of Capital Asset
Markets and Investment
Products

© OnCourse Learning

	Public Markets	**Private Markets**
Equity Assets	Stocks REITs Mutual funds	Real property Private equity Hedge funds
Debt Assets	Bonds MBS Money instruments	Bank loans Whole mortgages Venture debt and LBOs

near the last quoted price. This liquidity is both a cause and effect of the fact that in public markets asset share prices can adjust rapidly to relevant news about their value. This ability of asset prices to respond quickly to relevant news is known as asset market **informational efficiency**.

In contrast, **private markets** are those in which the assets are traded in private transactions arranged between individual buyers and sellers who have found each other through some sort of search process, often through the aid of brokers. (Private markets are also sometimes called "search markets.") In private markets, it is common (though not necessary) for **whole assets** (e.g., an entire company or property or oil well or mortgage) to be traded in a single transaction. This can mean that the governance or control of the operation of the underlying physical asset is traded along with the ownership and resulting financial claims. The average size of the individual transactions tends to be larger in the private markets than in public capital markets.

Private markets generally are less liquid than public markets, in the sense that it takes time for sellers to find buyers and it is more difficult to ascertain a fair price for a given whole asset. Transaction costs (the cost of buying and selling) are typically higher in private asset markets, as a fraction of the value of the asset being traded in any one transaction. As a result of transaction and search costs, privately traded assets are generally traded less frequently than publicly traded assets. The fact that whole assets are traded in private deals between (typically) one buyer and one seller (rather than many buyers and sellers simultaneously trading identical shares) also has consequences for the nature of the asset price information that is available to the public.

In private asset markets, it will generally be more difficult (or expensive) to observe the prices at which assets are trading, and the public observability of the price may be delayed until after the transaction closes (perhaps sometime afterwards). Furthermore, as whole assets are generally unique (such as a piece of art or a parcel of land), it is difficult to know how relevant an observed transaction price is for judging the value of any other asset. This problem is compounded by the fact that the parties to each trade are also typically unique, so the observed price represents only the agreement of two individual parties, not a broad market consensus. The same assets are not usually sold repeatedly very frequently, which makes even the trend in prices over time difficult to observe. For all these reasons, asset values in private markets tend not to incorporate or reflect news and information as quickly as do prices in public asset markets. In other words, *private asset markets tend not to be as informationally efficient as public markets*; the "price discovery" process is slower.

Perhaps a quick example will be useful to make this point more concrete. Suppose you own an apartment complex near Los Angeles International Airport. You think the property is worth about $10 million, but of course you are not sure. Now you hear news that should affect the value of your property in a negative way. The Federal Aviation Administration has announced new regulations that control the flight patterns approaching the airport, causing more noise and safety problems for your neighborhood. Logically, this reduces the value of your property, other things being equal, below the $10 million you previously thought it was worth. But by how much does it reduce the value? Is it now $9 million, or $9.9 million?

If another similar property near yours would sell, and you could observe that transaction price, this might give you some idea about how the value of your property has changed, but even this would not give a very clear or definitive picture. The other property is not just like yours, and the buyer or seller in that deal may be unique in some way, or may not have negotiated the way you would. And anyway, there may be no other similar property nearby that sells anytime soon. In short, you don't know how much to mark down your appraisal of your property's value as a result of the FAA news.

Contrast this situation with that of publicly traded assets. Suppose, for example, ownership of your apartment complex was divided into thousands of small homogeneous shares that were constantly being traded by numerous buyers and sellers at publicly quoted prices on the stock exchange, effectively as in a public auction. In that case, you would know very quickly and certainly the effect of the FAA news on the value of your shares, simply by observing the change in the share price.

On the other hand, it may be easier for public market asset prices to *overreact* to news, resulting in a subsequent "correction" to the price. This can cause "excess volatility." Some analysts believe that the stock market can be subject to fads or herd behavior that can move the market broadly for a time in a direction that may not be related much at all to any real news or true information. The public markets' faster response to news than the private markets' does not necessarily guarantee that asset prices will generally be "better" or more "sensible" in one market form or another at any given time, in terms of being able to protect investors against making buy or sell decisions that, at least in retrospect, can look, well, pretty stupid.

Now let's move from a comparison of the columns in Exhibit 1-6 to a comparison of the rows, to consider debt versus equity. Debt and equity are two different types of capital assets, both of which can be traded in either public or private types of asset markets.

Debt assets are essentially the rights to the future cash flow to be paid out by borrowers on loans they have taken out (e.g., interest payments and retirement of principal). The characteristic feature of debt assets is that they give their owners (e.g., the lenders or bondholders) a relatively "senior" or "preferred" claim for obtaining the cash that the **underlying asset** (the source of the cash flow) can generate. Also, debt cash flows are contractually specified, so the recipients know more precisely with relative certainty how much future cash flow they will be receiving, and when. Debt assets are therefore typically less risky than equity assets. Debt assets also typically have specified "maturity," that is, finite lifetimes after which there will be no further cash flow. For example, a bond might pay 8 percent of its stated (par) value in interest each year for 20 years, and then be retired by payment of the par value.

By contrast, **equity** assets are those that give their owners the "residual" claim on the cash flows generated by the underlying asset (e.g., a company or a property). Such a residual claim is "subordinated" to any debt owed by (or on) the underlying asset, meaning it lacks seniority or claim priority. Because equity claims are what are left over after senior claims, equity tends to be more risky than debt. But the equity owners also typically have more control over managing the underlying assets and are better able to benefit from growth or "upside" potential in the cash flows generated by the underlying assets. Equity assets, such as stocks and real property, are typically infinite-lived. Infinite life means that owners of an equity asset must sell the asset in order to "cash out" or liquidate their holding. It also means that more of the present value of the asset derives from the expectation of cash flows in the distant future, where there is the most uncertainty. This is another reason that the value of equity assets tends to be more volatile than the value of debt assets.

Capital asset products based on real estate have been developed for, and are traded in, all four of these branches of the capital markets. For example, REITs (Real Estate Investment Trusts) offer publicly traded common stock shares in companies that essentially do nothing but own (and manage, and buy and sell) income-producing properties and mortgages.[8]

---

[8]In fact, most REITs primarily own equity interests in real property, as opposed to mortgages. To be more specific, a REIT is a corporation or trust that has elected REIT tax status. As long as the REIT conforms to certain government requirements, the REIT is exempt from corporate income tax. These requirements essentially limit the REIT to real estate investment and development type activity and require that the REIT pay out 90 percent of its earnings each year as dividends to its stockholders. For the most part, REITs must hold for at least four years properties that they develop or purchase, which prevents merchant builders, such as home developers, from electing REIT status. The original idea behind the law that established REITs in 1960 was that REITs would be a vehicle through which small investors could invest in commercial real estate through the stock market, much the same way mutual funds allow small investors to hold diversified portfolios of individual stocks.

Mortgage-backed securities (MBS) include publicly traded bondlike products that are based on underlying pools of mortgages, which are real-estate-based debt products. There are both residential MBSs and commercial MBSs (the latter known as CMBS). On the other hand, many mortgages, especially large commercial mortgages, are held privately as "whole loans," and these would be traded privately (if at all).

But the most fundamental form of real estate asset, the direct ownership of whole properties, is traded in a private market known as the property market (or real estate asset market), in which individual real properties (ranging from single-family homes to income-producing commercial and residential or institutional buildings, to land parcels or other such assets) are bought and sold among parties who have often found each other through the services of real estate brokers. Ultimately, all the other forms of real-estate-based capital asset products are based on privately traded property as the underlying assets. That is to say, property assets produce the cash flow that is the ultimate source of any income or value for any real estate investment products or vehicles, including REITs and mortgages.

The demand side of the property market is made up of investors wanting to buy property. The supply side consists of other investors (or developers or owner users) who want to sell some or all of the property they currently own. Investors in the property market fall generally into two main types: individuals or smaller entrepreneurial firms, and larger financial institutions. The major types of institutions include REITs, pension funds, life insurance companies, and various types of funds, as well as banks and other financial institutions. Private individuals invest in the property market both directly (typically via partnerships or corporations) and through funds or syndications. In addition to U.S. institutions, many investors in the U.S. real estate asset market today are foreign individuals and institutions.

In a modern highly developed economy such as that of the United States, the capital markets are highly integrated and sophisticated, well-functioning arenas in which vast quantities of money and information are managed and exchanged. The capital markets determine how the wealth and capital resources of the society are allocated, which in turn determines the future growth rate and economic production patterns in the economy. For example, if investors decide that the future earnings potential of, say, airplane manufacturers looks relatively good, while that of office buildings looks relatively bad, then airplane company stocks will rise and capital will flow to that industry, while office building prices will fall and developers will find it hard to obtain the funds necessary to build new office buildings. In this way, the capital markets govern the real physical allocation of the productive resources of the economy.

Because real estate makes up a large and important part of the overall capital market and of the physical capital formation of the economy, the real estate components of the capital markets are quite important in this overall allocation process. In fact, the value of all real estate assets is comparable to (or often greater than) that of the stock market in the United States.

1.2.2 Magnitude of Real Estate Assets in the Overall Capital Market

Exhibits 1-7 and 1-8 give some idea of the absolute and relative magnitude of real estate assets in the capital markets in the United States as of the early 2000s. Exhibit 1-7 shows the approximate proportion of the total market value of all U.S. assets found in each of the four sectors of the capital markets—public and private, debt and equity. Exhibit 1-7 also indicates the percentage of each of these sectors represented by real estate assets.[9] Altogether, real estate represents over one-third of the value of the investable capital assets in the United States. Real estate is particularly dominant in the private capital markets. Evidence suggests that these proportions are typical of most other advanced economies, with the real estate and private market shares being larger in less developed countries.

Exhibit 1-8 presents a more detailed breakdown of the capital asset "pie" by category of assets. The categories roughly between three o'clock and eight o'clock on the pie chart are

---

[9]The figures in Exhibits 1-7 and 1-8 have been adjusted as far as possible to eliminate overlap. For example, a $100,000 house with an $80,000 mortgage would be counted as $20,000 of housing equity in the private equity segment and $80,000 of residential mortgages (public debt if the mortgage was part of an MBS pool, or private debt if the mortgage was still held by the bank).

EXHIBIT 1-7 U.S. Capital Market Sectors, a $70 Trillion Pie

Source: Authors' estimates based on Miles and Tolleson (1997), updated with FRB statistics.

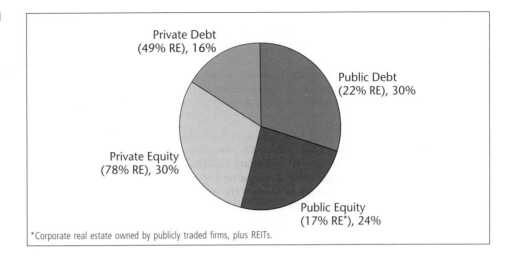

Private Debt (49% RE), 16%

Public Debt (22% RE), 30%

Private Equity (78% RE), 30%

Public Equity (17% RE*), 24%

*Corporate real estate owned by publicly traded firms, plus REITs.

EXHIBIT 1-8 U.S. Investable Capital Market with Real Estate Components Broken Out

Source: Based on Miles and Tolleson (1997), updated with FRB statistics.

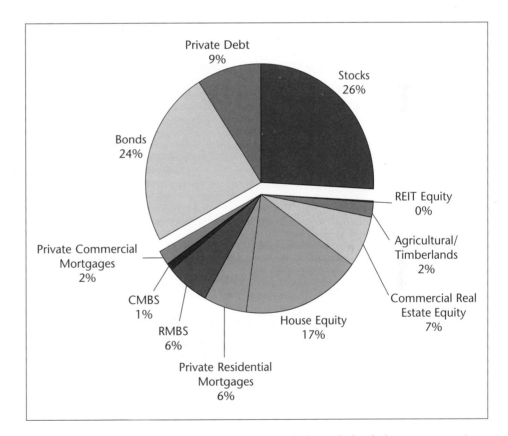

Private Debt 9%

Stocks 26%

Bonds 24%

REIT Equity 0%

Agricultural/ Timberlands 2%

Commercial Real Estate Equity 7%

Private Commercial Mortgages 2%

CMBS 1%

RMBS 6%

House Equity 17%

Private Residential Mortgages 6%

real estate categories. The largest value categories include single-family housing equity (over $10 trillion in value), commercial real estate equity (over $5 trillion including over $300 billion held by REITs and another $2–$3 trillion of corporate real estate held by publicly traded non-real-estate firms, which is categorized as part of the value of the stock market), residential mortgages (over $10 trillion, about half of which is included in publicly traded MBS products), and commercial mortgages (almost $3 trillion of whole loans plus over $600 billion in CMBS). Agricultural and timberlands represent over $1 trillion in assets. Altogether, real estate and real-estate-backed assets represented over $30 trillion in the United States in the early 2000s, about two-thirds of that value in the form of single-family homes and the remainder mostly commercial or income-generating and institutional property. This compared to an approximate stock market valuation at that time of only about $17 trillion.

Exhibits 1-9A and 1-9B present an additional perspective on the magnitude of commercial property in the United States. Commercial property is the main subject of this text, and represents income-generating properties (including residential multi-family or apartment buildings) that underlie the major real estate investment equity asset class. Exhibits 1-9A and 1-9B depict the major categories of such property as enumerated in a 2010 study by analysts at CoStar Group, a commercial real estate information firm. Exhibit 1-9A depicts the breakout on the basis of the physical magnitude of property, as measured by the total rentable square footage.

EXHIBIT 1-9A U.S. Commercial Property by Physical Stock (billions of square feet) Total = 84 BSF (excluding Specialty/ Entertainment)

Source: Based on Florance et al. (2010).

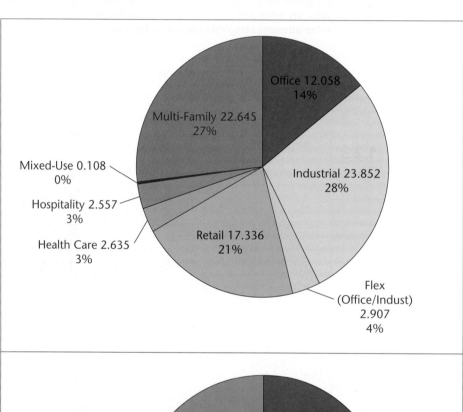

EXHIBIT 1-9B U.S. Commercial Property by Valuation ($ billions) Total = $9,173 billion

Source: Based on Florance et al. (2010).

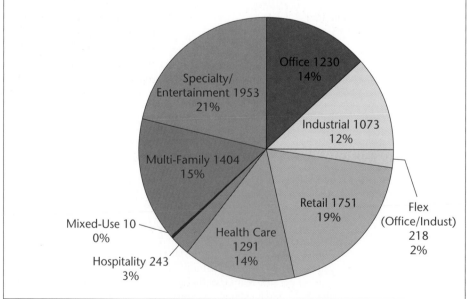

Exhibit 1-9B depicts the same property categories by total dollar value of market capitalization. The exhibit enumerates some 84 billion square feet of commercial property with total market valuation over $9 trillion.[10]

The property inventory in Exhibits 1-9A and 1-9B include essentially all income-producing properties in the United States, large and small, old and new. In particular, the pie charts include the larger and more expensive properties in major metropolitan areas that are actively traded by national and international institutional investors (so-called "institutional" or "investment-grade" commercial property), as well as smaller and generally less expensive properties that are largely traded by private investors and user/owner-occupiers (sometimes referred to as "general" or "mom-&-pop" commercial property).[11] In this overall population, the largest categories by physical size are industrial and multi-family properties, while the greatest by value are retail and multi-family. The overall average value per square foot is $109. The most value-intensive categories include health care facilities (such as hospitals, clinics, and nursing homes) at $490/SF, and office and retail properties at just over $100/SF. The least value-intensive categories include industrial (largely consisting of warehouses and rental industrial spaces) at $45/SF, and multi-family residential (rental apartment buildings) at $62/SF. Accordingly, it is important to note that hospitals, office, and retail properties tend to be found in more central and valuable locations in terms of value per acre of land, while industrial and apartment properties are often not as centrally located.[12]

1.2.3 Pricing of Real Estate Assets

Now that you have some introduction to the magnitude and nature of the property market, you are ready to consider, at an introductory level, *how* it is that real estate assets get their values in this market.[13] As noted, the supply side of the property market consists of property owners wanting to sell or reduce their holdings of real estate assets, while the demand side of the market consists of other investors wanting to buy or increase their holdings of real estate assets. The balance between supply and demand determines the overall level of real estate asset values relative to other forms of physical and financial capital in the country. Within this overall general valuation context, the specific values of individual properties or buildings is determined by the perceptions of potential investors regarding the level and riskiness of the cash flows that each individual property can generate in the future.

As individual properties and buildings differ greatly in size and magnitude, when speaking of property prices and values in general it is common to think in terms of property value *per dollar of current net rent or income*. This way, one can more easily compare prices across properties of different sizes or values. In fact, in real estate, especially in commercial property markets, a measure that is the *inverse* of this price/earnings multiple is most widely used to describe property prices and values. We introduced this measure back in section 1.1.4, as the **capitalization rate (cap rate** for short, also known as an **overall rate**— or **OAR)**, or sometimes as the "return on assets"—ROA). The cap rate is simply the property operating earnings divided by the property asset price or value.[14] The cap rate is similar to a **current yield** (the amount of current income the investor receives per dollar of current value of the investment). So while the cap rate is an inverse measure of asset value (per dollar of

---

[10]Note that the square footage in one of the categories is not enumerated and therefore excluded from Exhibit 1-9A, that of specialty and entertainment properties (which includes sports facilities), though this category is included in the dollar valuation in Exhibit 1-9B. The multi-family category in Exhibits 1-9A and 1-9B is defined as properties having at least five rental units.

[11]See Chapter 11 for evidence on the difference in price performance between the smaller "non-institutional" properties and the institutional properties, based on CoStar data.

[12]The relationship between property value and location will be discussed in depth in Part II, especially in Chapters 4 and 5.

[13]This subject will be treated in much more depth later in this book, especially in Part IV (Chapters 10, 11, and 12).

[14]By convention, cap rates apply to property operating income and property value (i.e., as if there were no mortgage), not the equity investor's income or equity value if there is a mortgage. We will have more to say about the cap rate particularly in Chapter 10.

earnings), it may be thought of as a direct measure of the current component of the return on the investment.

Thus, *property values can be represented as earnings (i.e., essentially, net rents) divided by the cap rate.*[15] The cap rate is determined by capital investment supply and demand in the asset market, based on three major factors.

1. *Opportunity Cost of Capital.* The prevailing interest rates and opportunities for earning returns in other forms of investments in the capital markets (e.g., stocks, bonds, money market instruments) are a major determinant of how much investors are willing to pay for any property per dollar of its current income. As noted, real estate assets are in competition for the investor's dollar in the capital market, competing not only with other properties but also with other forms of assets. When interest rates and yields on bonds and stocks are low, for example, investors cannot earn as much return from those alternative investments. At such times, investors will tend to be more eager to put their money into property, and they will not expect to earn as high a return from property as they otherwise would. This will raise the price they are willing to pay for the property per dollar of its current income, and reduce the cap rate.

2. *Growth Expectations.* Potential investors will be "forward-looking," considering the likely amount of growth (or decline) in the net rent they can expect the property to generate in the future. Of course, the net rent the property will be able to produce in the future depends on what the balance between supply and demand will be in the *space* market in the future. So to consider the growth question, investors must, in effect, try to forecast the future of the space market in which the property is situated. The greater the expected growth in future net rent, the more investors will be willing to pay for the property today per dollar of current net rent, and hence, the smaller the cap rate. (For example, if investors were willing to pay $15.00 instead of $12.50 per dollar of current net income, then the cap rate would be 6.67 percent instead of 8.00 percent, as $1/15 = 6.67\%$.)[16]

   As described previously, growth prospects for rents in a market depend on the current state of the market (e.g., are rents currently below the long-run equilibrium level?), how usage demand will change in the future (will it grow or stagnate?), and the shape of the long-run supply function in the market (is it flat or rising or declining?). In addition to marketwide considerations, each individual property may have unique attributes that affect its own growth prospects, such as existing leases, need for capital improvements, and so forth.

3. *Risk.* If investors regard the future potential net income from the property as less risky and more certain (perhaps because they view the space market as relatively stable and easy to forecast), then they will be willing to pay more per dollar of current income for the property, also reducing the cap rate. Other things being equal, investors do not like risk and will pay more for less risky assets. Of course, investors' aversion to risk and their preferences for certain types of investments may change over time. For example, some investors may want certain types of assets or properties in order to diversify or balance their overall investment portfolios. The more investors prefer the type of asset that a given property is, the more they will pay for it and the lower will be its cap rate. Holding interest rates and growth expectations constant, such preference based pricing differences might be broadly assumed to be related to perceived risk.[17]

---

[15]This is merely a conventional way to quote asset prices. It is not a statement of causality. That is, it would be too simplistic to suggest that property values are *caused by* the current income generated by the property and the current cap rate prevailing in the asset market for similar properties. As will be discussed in more depth in Chapters 9 and 10, property investors are more interested in total return (income and capital appreciation) than in current income alone, and such investors take a multiyear long-run view of the potential and risks in the property's future income and value, not just current income.

[16]Note that this does not imply that investors are willing to settle for a lower *total* return, only that more of that return is expected to come in the form of future increases in earnings or in appreciation or capital growth in the future value of the property, and less in the form of initial income.

[17]The nature and role of risk in real estate asset pricing will be a major subject in Chapters 7, 11, and more fundamentally in Part VII (especially Chapters 21 and 22).

1.2.4 Is the Asset Market Segmented Like the Space Market?

Now that you are familiar with both the real estate space market and asset market and the role of the capital market in the latter, we may draw an important distinction between the real estate asset and space markets. While the building users who make up the demand side of the space market require the *physical* characteristics of real estate assets (i.e., they are looking for built space of a particular type in a particular location), this is not generally or fundamentally the case with the investors who make up the demand side of the real estate asset market. Asset market investors are seeking future cash flows—*financial* rather than *physical* assets. Fundamentally, they do not care how or from where the cash is generated. "Money is fungible," is how this point is often expressed. Cash generated from rents in Chicago warehouses is the same as cash generated from rents in Los Angeles shopping centers and as cash generated from Procter & Gamble or any corporation's stock dividends or bond coupons. This means that real estate asset markets are much more integrated than real estate space markets.

Recall that an important consequence of the lack of integration in the real estate space markets is that prices (in the form of rents) can differ greatly among cities or among types of property, even for properties that are physically similar. In the same way, the much greater degree of integration in the real estate asset markets has the opposite effect. Two properties with cash flows perceived as having similar risk and growth potential will sell at very similar cap rates, even if the properties are physically very different and they are in different locations and their space rents at very different rental prices.

To demonstrate this point more concretely, Exhibit 1-10 shows typical cap rates for a range of different types and locations of commercial property in 1994.[18] This is an interesting year to examine because at that time there were wide disparities in the level of risk perceived by investors in different space markets. Notice that the cap rates for office, retail, warehouse,

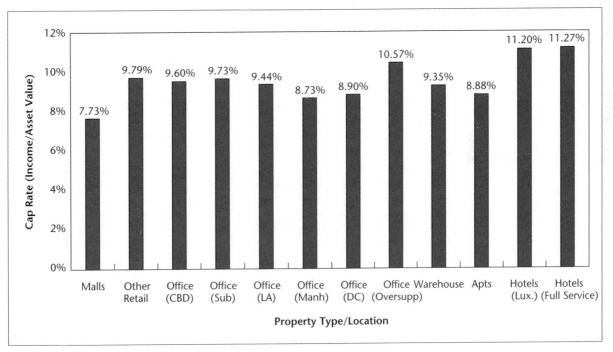

EXHIBIT 1-10 Cap Rates (OARs) for Commercial Property as of Third Quarter, 1994

© OnCourse Learning

---

[18]Exhibit 1-10 is based on the *Korpacz Real Estate Investor Survey*, a widely used survey of professional investors and brokers published by the Korpacz Company, Frederick, Maryland. Other such data sources include Real Capital Analytics, CoStar Group, and NCREIF, among others.

and apartment properties were very similar (roughly around 9 or 10 percent per year), and this was true even across different cities. Where cap rates differed, it was not necessarily because rent levels differed or buildings were physically different, but rather because risks or growth prospects were perceived as being different.

This is seen in the cap rates reported for several types or locations of property in particular. For example, the "oversupplied office market" refers to office buildings in markets experiencing particularly high vacancy. Investors perceived such markets as being more risky than markets that were more in balance. So they required a higher expected return for investing in overbuilt markets, which equates to their being unwilling to pay as much per dollar of current income for such properties. In this case, we can see that the 10.57 percent cap rate indicates investors were generally not willing to pay more than about $9.46 per dollar of current income for office buildings in overbuilt markets, whereas in more typical CBD and suburban office markets they would pay over $10 per dollar of current income.

Hotel properties were perceived as being even more risky due to the lack of long-term leases from tenants and the volatile and highly competitive nature of the hotel business. In 1994, hotels were selling at cap rates in excess of 11 percent (price/earnings multiples less than 9). At the other extreme, regional shopping malls were perceived in 1994 as being relatively low risk, with relatively good growth prospects. Malls had average cap rates of only 7.73 percent in 1994, indicating property values of $12.94 per dollar of net income.

Exhibit 1-11 shows that prevailing cap rates tend to change over time. Note that while apartments had similar cap rates on average to the other major types of income property in the early 1990s, as revealed in Exhibit 1-10, by the beginning of the 2000s apartments tended to sell at lower cap rates (higher prices per dollar of current income) than the other types of property. Apparently investors began to perceive less risk, or more growth prospects, in apartments. Moreover, Exhibit 1-11 highlights a substantial decline in cap rates across the board during the decade of the 2000s. This reflected a general decline in dollar-denominated real interest rates (risk free interest rates net of inflation) as globalization and evolution in the financial markets increased dollar liquidity (that is, investors had more money, especially dollars, to invest, which tended to drive up asset prices).

The boom (or *bubble*) of 2004–2007 appears vividly in Exhibit 1-11 as the decline in cap rates during that period. (Other things equal, falling cap rates imply rising asset prices and vice versa, as prices equal incomes divided by the cap rates.) The 2004–2007 decline in cap rates largely reflected a decline in risk premia; that is, during the boom, investors did not

EXHIBIT 1-11 Average Commercial Property Transaction Cap Rates, 2001–2010

Source: Data from Real Capital Analytics Inc. used with permission.

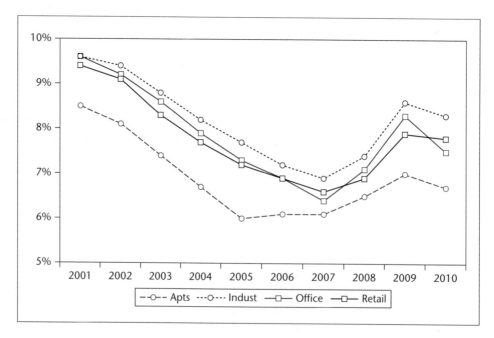

require as much extra expected return premium to invest in risky assets (whether they would have admitted that at the time or not!).[19] From 2008 to 2009 cap rates shot up across the board (though less so for apartments), reflecting the associated collapse in property values. This period saw a dramatic loss in liquidity in real estate markets, and investors suddenly demanding sharply higher risk premia associated with the financial crisis. The rise in cap rates also reflected reduced rental growth expectations due to the deep and prolonged economic recession that grew out of the financial crisis. A sharp recovery in the market in 2010 is reflected by a drop in cap rates.

1.3 Chapter Summary

This chapter has described the two major types of markets relevant to the analysis of commercial property: the space market and the asset market. The space market is the more fundamental of the two in the sense that it determines the cash flows property can generate, and these cash flows underlie any value the property asset can have. However, the asset market is of equal importance because it determines the valuation of property assets, and this in turn both causes and affects the flow of financial capital to and from real estate. Also, the asset market is most directly relevant to the analysis of investment in commercial property, which is the main subject of this book. In introducing these two real estate markets, this chapter has also presented a few of the most basic analytical tools and measures that are widely used in real estate investment practice, including such concepts as the kinked space market supply curve and the cap rate shortcut measure of real estate pricing in the asset market. And we have provided a brief historical perspective and empirical overview of the field. Chapter 2 will continue this introduction.

KEY TERMS

market	kinked supply function	informational efficiency
space market	replacement cost	private markets
usage market	equilibrium rent	whole assets
rental market	cap rate	debt
demand	location rent	underlying assets
supply	centrality	equity
rent	asset market	capitalization (cap) rate
segmented markets	property market	overall rate (OAR)
metropolitan areas (MSAs)	capital market	current yield
downtowns, CBDs	public markets	
property usage type	liquidity	

STUDY QUESTIONS

Conceptual Questions

1.1. What is the real estate *space* market? What is the real estate *asset* market?

1.2. Draw and label a supply curve for real estate (income-property) space, and explain why it is "kinked."

1.3. What are typical causes of a rising long-run marginal cost function in the market for built space?

---

[19]Note that cap rates fell first and farthest in apartments, but then stopped falling earlier in that sector (in 2005 instead of 2007). This reflected the condo-conversion boom and subsequent bust, which we noted earlier in section 1.1.1. The boom in condos drove up the prices of apartments because investors could convert the apartments into condos, until the housing market weakened famously after the middle of the decade.

1.4. Why, or along what dimensions, are real estate space markets *segmented*? What is an important implication of space market segmentation?

1.5. Suppose that demand for built space in a local market is growing. Does this imply that rents will rise? Why or why not? Differentiate between rent changes in the short run and the long run. [Hint: For the long run, explain the conditions necessary for real rents to rise in a market.]

1.6. If demand for built space is declining, does this imply that real rents (that is, rents measured net of inflation) will fall in the market? Why or why not? As in the previous question, differentiate between short-run and long-run rent adjustments.

1.7. What is the difference between a *private* and a *public* asset market? Why do public asset markets tend to be more *informationally efficient* than private asset markets?

1.8. Create a four-quadrant table showing on one dimension the two major types of capital asset products and on the other dimension the two major types of capital markets in which these assets are traded. [Hint: See Exhibit 1-6.] In which panel of this table would an individual commercial mortgage that is held by an insurance company fall? In which panel would ownership of a commercial building fall? In which panel would real estate investment trust stock (REIT) shares fall? In which panel would mortgage-backed securities (MBS) traded on the bond market fall?

1.9. What are the three major factors influencing property prices or cap rates (OARs) in the real estate asset market? How (i.e., in which direction) does each of these influence the rate?

1.10. Exhibit 1-12 shows cap rates for office, industrial, retail, and apartment properties as well as the 10-year Treasury yields over the years 2001 to 2006.

a. Based on what you know about the three major factors upon which cap rates are based, what might explain why suburban office and industrial property have the highest cap rates, apartments the lowest cap rates, and CBD-office in the middle?

b. Cap rates fell quite dramatically over this period for all property types. How much of this decrease can be attributed to a decreasing opportunity cost of capital, as reflected in long-term (and risk-free) interest rates? Do cap rates appear to move one-to-one with Treasury yields? What else might be going on?

EXHIBIT 1-12 Average Cap Rates for Major Property Types, Monthly, 2001–early 2006

Sources: Treasury yield data from the Federal Reserve Board. Property data from Real Capital Analytics Inc. used with permission.

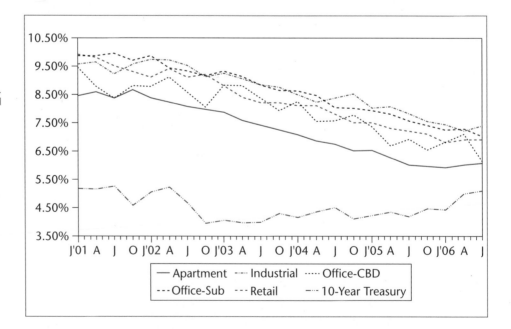

1.11. Approximately what percentage of the total market value of investable assets in the United States is made up of real estate or real-estate-based assets? [Hint: See Exhibit 1-8.]

Quantitative Problems

1.12. A property has a net rent (cash flow or net income) of $1.5m per year and is selling at a cap rate of 8.5%. What is the price of the property? Recalculate the price assuming a 9.75% cap rate and a 7.25% cap rate. [Note: This method of valuing income property, dividing the current net income by the cap rate, is known as direct capitalization, a widely used shortcut valuation method, which is discussed in greater depth in Chapter 10.]

1.13. Use the definition of the cap rate, equal to property income divided by property value, and the data on prevailing market cap rates for early 1994 presented in Exhibit 1-10 to estimate the value of (a) a typical high-quality downtown office building with a net operating income of $10 million per year and (b) a large apartment complex with a net operating income of $3.5 million.

1.14. Total development costs are $250/SF. Investors are willing to pay property prices of $11.76 per dollar of current rental income.
    a. What is the implied cap rate?
    b. What is the "replacement cost rent" in this market?

1.15. Recall that we said in section 1.1.2 that the average rent in downtown Cincinnati for class A office buildings in the mid-1980s was around $16/SF, being charged in about a dozen skyscrapers totaling about 5 million SF. By 2010 the class A office stock in downtown Cincinnati had expanded to some 18 buildings totaling over 8 million SF, and the average asking rent was $19.50/SF (according to CoStar Group). If the Consumer Price Index grew from about 110 in the mid/late 1980s to about 218 in 2010, then what does this history suggest about the shape of the long-run supply function in downtown Cincinnati office space, as depicted in Exhibit 1-2 and discussed in section 1.1.6? What would the $19.50/SF rent of 2010 be expressed in mid-1980s dollars (when rents were around $16/SF in those dollars)?

REAL ESTATE SYSTEM

LEARNING OBJECTIVES

After reading this chapter, you should understand:

⊃ The real estate system and how it relates to investment analysis of commercial property.

⊃ The short- and long-run linkages among the real estate space market, asset market, and the development industry that convert financial capital to new physical supply in the space market.

⊃ How negative feedback loops keep the system in balance in the long run, and positive feedback can lead to destructive spirals.

⊃ The role of forward-looking behavior, as well as forms of behavioral "discipline," on the part of participants in various aspects of the real estate system in keeping the system in balance.

⊃ How cycles or periods of imbalance between supply and demand can occur in the absence of perfect foresight or result from systematic behavioral errors or positive feedback loops.

T   he previous chapter introduced the two basic markets relevant to commercial property investment analysis: the space market and the asset market. These two markets are linked and related in ways that are vital for real estate professionals to understand. In addition to the direct short-run relationship that translates current property cash flow to current property asset value, the two markets are structurally linked over the medium to long run by the commercial property development industry. This industry converts financial capital into physical capital, thereby governing the stock of supply in the space market. This overall system, consisting of these two markets and the development industry linking them, is the subject of this chapter.

2.1 Commercial Property Development Industry

The real estate development industry is the engine of entrepreneurial activity that assembles and applies the financial and physical resources to construct new built space (including the major rehabilitation or conversion of existing buildings). Development is a complex and creative function that, at its best, displays great vision and, at its worst, enormous greed but, in almost all cases, considerable risk-taking on the part of developers and/or their financial backers. Development often requires intense interaction and cooperation between government officials in the public sector and developers in the private sector.

While literally thousands of firms are involved in the real estate development industry, large-scale commercial development in the United States is dominated by a few dozen firms of national scope and a number of regional firms. Beginning in the 1990s, a number of publicly-traded REITs became highly active in commercial development, generally specializing in one or two property types. Traditionally, and even still, however, most development firms are privately held, often dominated by one or a few partners typically consisting of the first or second generation of the firm's founders. Private entrepreneurial development firms typically have specialized expertise in the local space markets, but may lack the connections to "deep pocket" sources of capital held by larger developers or investment funds such as real estate "opportunity funds" (private equity funds that target high-return/high-risk real estate investments). Joint ventures are common in the development industry, especially for large projects, combining the strengths of entrepreneurial firms with those of financial institutions or the abilities of specialized local experts with those of large national firms.

Even an economy in recession needs large quantities of existing built space just to continue to function. But the addition of new increments to the stock of built space is primarily required only by economic growth or by structural changes in the economy and activity patterns, such as those brought about by technological change as well as migration and other demographic shifts. As noted in Chapter 1, built space is an extremely long-lived commodity. Buildings do not wear out fast. It is only the demand for additional and new built space that supports the development industry. For this reason, development is the most cyclical of all branches of the real estate industry. This is seen graphically in Exhibit 2-1, which traces the level of development activity by square footage of projects completed for three major commercial property types (office, industrial, and retail) from 1959 to 2011. (The shaded vertical bands indicate periods of GDP contraction in the national economy.)

Exhibit 2-1 graphically reveals the extent of cyclicality in the development industry. In an extreme example, office building development peaked at more than 300 million square feet (MSF) completed per year in the mid-1980s to a trough of barely 50 MSF per year in the early 1990s, a collapse of more than 80 percent in less than a decade. We also see that, while all types of commercial development often rise and fall more or less together, this is not always true. For example, office development kept growing in the early 1980s when industrial

EXHIBIT 2-1 U.S. Commercial Property Construction Completions by Property Type (MSF): 1959–2011

Sources: Construction start data from Property and Portfolio Research (CoStar Group Inc.) used with permission. Recession data from National Bureau of Economic Research.

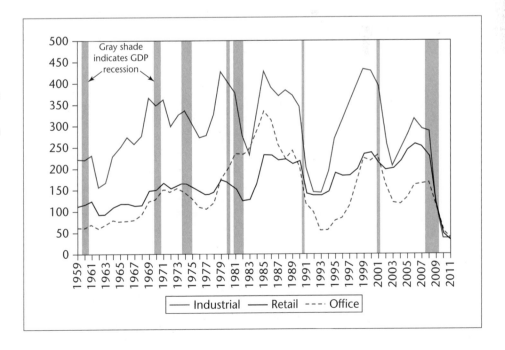

and retail development hit a major downcycle. In general over the 50-year span in the exhibit, the trough construction rates per annum were only half or less than the peaks, and we see that the commercial property development cycle is strongly linked to the general macroeconomic business cycle (with a bit of a lag, as GDP recessions are difficult to predict in advance and commercial property construction can take a long time to permit and finance and complete). The collapse in development was particularly severe during and subsequent to the 2007–2009 recession associated with the financial crisis of 2008, bringing new construction almost to a standstill for the first time since the 1930s, and taking new space delivery well below replacement rates nationwide (implying shrinking absolute levels of the stock of space, as demolitions and retirements exceeded new deliveries). Since the 1990s, the cutback in construction in response to negative demand shocks has tended to be quicker and deeper than had been the case in the preceding three decades, perhaps reflecting a quicker and sharper cutoff in the supply of financial capital from the capital market.

From the perspective of commercial property investment analysis, the development industry is best viewed in its role as a converter of financial capital into physical capital as a feedback link from the asset market to the space market, adding to the supply side of the space market, as described in the next section.

2.2 Overview of the Real Estate System

You have now been introduced to the three major components of what may be called the **real estate system**: the space market, the asset market, and the development industry. Exhibit 2-2 presents a visual overview of this system, including the major elements in and linkages among these three major components. The exhibit allows one to model how the system and its components evolve over time, dynamically, and hence this exhibit is a type of representation referred to as a "**systems dynamics model**."

Exhibit 2-2 also shows how the real estate system is linked to other, exogenous systems, including the national and local macroeconomies, and the national and international capital markets. Let's briefly "walk through" the real estate system depicted in Exhibit 2-2.[1]

The three large (enveloping) boxes in the exhibit represent the three main elements of the real estate system: the space market, the asset market, and the development industry. Within the space market, we see the interaction of usage demand with the current stock of physical space supply, which determines current rents and occupancy levels in the space market. Underlying the demand side of the space market are the national and local economies, which determine the need for certain quantities of physical space of various types as a function of the cost (rent) for such space (i.e., the space demand function as described in Chapter 1). Governing the amount of physical space on the supply side are the past and current activities of the development industry (the result of the long-run supply function described in Chapter 1).

Moving down to the asset market, we see that the space market determines the current operating cash flows produced by the real estate assets that are the fundamental subjects of the asset market. This operating cash flow interacts with the cap rates required by investors to determine current property market values in the asset market. Both the supply and demand sides of the real estate asset market consist of investors, those currently on the "buy" side and those currently on the "sell" side, either in general or for specific assets. All of these real estate investors are operating within the broader capital markets, which encompass other forms of asset and money markets. Investors' desires and perceptions about the investment risks and returns of real estate assets, as compared to other types of investment opportunities available elsewhere in the capital markets, determine the current market cap rates investors require in real estate deals. A key determinant of cap rates is also investors'

---

[1] Exhibit 2-2 has two types of elements: boxes and arrows. The solid boxes represent decision-making agents and empirically observable phenomena. The dashed boxes represent key decisions or actions that drive the system. The solid arrows represent causal linkages and the direction of causality. The dashed arrows represent information flow or information gathering and usage activity.

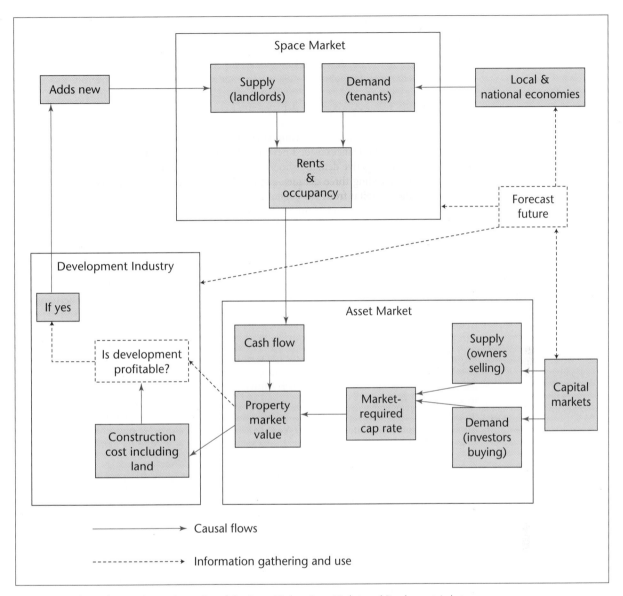

EXHIBIT 2-2 The Real Estate System: Interaction of the Space Market, Asset Market, and Development Industry
© OnCourse Learning

forecasts about the future of the relevant space market, on both the demand and supply sides, so as to predict the likely future course of rents (as we introduced in Chapter 1).

Thus, we see how the space and asset markets, reflecting the underlying economic base and the capital markets, interact to produce current real estate asset market values. These values represent the key signal, or output, from the asset market: input into the development industry, the third major box in the exhibit.

Within the development-industry component of the system, a crucial comparison is made. Current development costs, including construction and land costs (incorporating necessary profit for the developer), are compared against current asset values. If asset values equal or exceed development costs, then development will proceed, thereby adding to the physical stock on the supply side of the space market. As noted in Chapter 1, a key component of development costs is the opportunity value of the land (including all site acquisition costs). This opportunity value is determined in the real estate asset market, as land is a type of real estate asset. Of course, the asset market values land as potentially developable sites, therefore related fundamentally to the space market that each site could serve once developed (or redeveloped). And development takes time, which requires that the development industry be forward-looking. The developer succeeds only if the newly completed built property's value exceeds its total development cost at the time of completion of the project, which may take several years.

Indeed, the real estate system depicted in Exhibit 2-2 is, in principle, forward-looking to varying degrees in several aspects of the system. Not only must developers be forward-looking to account for construction time, but the space market is also forward-looking in that many users of space require long-term planning for their space needs and much space is rented out under long-term leases lasting typically from two to ten years. But the greatest incentives for peering into the long-run future probably reside in the asset market part of the system.

Asset market participants are inherently forward-looking. Investors make or lose money depending on how their investments do subsequent to their purchase. Even when an investor sells relatively quickly to another investor, the price the second investor is willing to pay depends on her perception about the future. Fundamentally, when you "unfold" each subsequent sale transaction of a given asset, you realize that the present value of the asset depends ultimately on the entire future stream of cash flow the asset can generate into the infinite future. To forecast future income streams from the real estate assets they are holding or considering buying, investors must forecast both the local economic base underlying the demand side of the relevant space market and the activity of the development industry on the supply side of that space market. They must also attempt to forecast capital-market and national macroeconomic factors, such as interest rates, inflation, and investor preferences, all of which affect the opportunity cost of capital and therefore the future values of assets.

It is important to note that within the real estate system depicted in Exhibit 2-2 there exist what are called **negative feedback loops**. These are dampening mechanisms that tend to make a system self-regulating, preventing it from spiraling out of control. The principal negative feedback loop in the real estate system is the ability of the asset market to regulate the flow of financial capital to the development industry. If either supply or demand threatens to get out of balance in the space market, the resulting expected effect on assets' operating cash flows will trigger a pricing response in the asset market.

For example, if new development threatens excess supply in the space market, investors will expect lower future rents, which will cause a reduction in property market asset values today. If this reduction is sufficient, it will make additional development unprofitable. The development industry will cut back and/or the capital market will reduce the flow of money to it. This may happen by investors demanding higher returns (such as higher interest on mortgages), reflecting a greater concern about the risk of such real estate investments. On the other hand, if usage demand for space grows without addition of supply, occupancy and rents will be pushed up in the space market, increasing current and expected future cash flow to investors in the asset market and pushing up prices in that market until new development is triggered, just the reverse of the case with excess supply. Such new development will then service the growth in demand and eventually bring rents down to their long-run equilibrium level.

If the participants in the system are sufficiently forward-looking and quick in their reactions, the negative feedback loop in the real estate system can keep built space supply and demand in pretty good balance most of the time, in principle. Of course, the real estate system has not always operated exactly like a well-oiled machine in this regard. Commercial property markets have been subject to pronounced boom and bust cycles. In part this results from the asymmetry caused by the long physical lifetime of buildings, as represented by the kinked supply function described in Chapter 1, which makes it easier or quicker to add new supply than to reduce the existing stock of built space. And in general, even on the up-side, demand can move quicker than supply, as it takes time to build. But there may be other problems as well, besides those centered on the physical development process.

During and after the 1990s, improvements in asset market efficiency related to the increased role of the more informationally efficient public capital markets and the securitization of real estate assets gave hope that the system as described above would work better. Indeed, in the U.S. commercial property market (in contrast to the housing market), there appeared to be greater discipline and less tendency to overbuild on the part of the development industry. There were quick cut-offs in the money spigot from the capital market in the late 1990s after the Asian financial crisis and again after the global financial crisis of 2008, particularly for the financing of new construction. However, a belief in the efficiency of this system may have partly contributed to a mentality that became associated with asset price bubbles, including in commercial real estate, that formed during the 2005–2007 period.

As financial capital flowed into real estate assets, it drove up their prices (perhaps in part because the physical supply of assets did not expand commensurately, and/or because the capital targeted a too narrow segment of the asset base). As commercial property prices rose, investors effectively began to lose sight of the risk and the fundamental basis of asset values, as rising asset prices tempted yet more money into the market. In effect, asset prices were rising simply because they had been rising. This is a type of **positive feedback loop**, which is the opposite of the dampener provided by the negative feedback loop noted above. Positive feedback loops are "explosive" elements in a system, tending to cause spirals in one direction or another.[2] It seems that both public and private capital markets can be susceptible to positive feedback, as was painfully illustrated by the great financial crisis of 2008 and its immediate aftermath. Nevertheless, the lack of overbuilding (relatively speaking) in commercial space markets prior to the 2007-09 recession helped put a floor on how far rents fell and enabled more recovery in asset pricing than would otherwise have been possible.[3]

2.3 Four-Quadrant Model

A graphic representation of the real estate system we just described, which is useful for performing some basic analyses of the system, has been developed by DiPasquale and Wheaton.[4] This model consists of a **four-quadrant (4Q)** graph, as shown in Exhibit 2-3. The four quadrants depict four binary relationships that together complete the linkages between the space market, the asset market, and the development industry.

The 4Q graph is most useful for examining simultaneously the effect on the **long-run equilibrium** both within and between the space and asset markets. The concept of long-run equilibrium in real estate involves allowing the markets sufficient time for the supply of built space to adjust to the demand. Equilibrium in the 4Q graph is represented by a rectangle whose sides are vertical and horizontal connections between four points, one lying on each of the four binary-relationship lines in each of the four quadrants. Where the sides of this rectangle cross the four axes represents the equilibrium stock of built space, rent, asset prices, and rate of new construction in the market. In Exhibit 2-3, the rectangle is indicated by dashed lines and the equilibrium prices and quantities by the points Q^*, R^*, P^*, and C^*. The northeast quadrant depicts the determination of rent in the space market. The horizontal axis in this quadrant is the physical stock of space in the market (e.g., in square feet), and the vertical axis is the rent (e.g., in $/SF per year). Thus, the axes of this quadrant are those of

---

[2]Positive feedback loops are not generally an example of lack of forward-looking behavior on the part of market participants, but rather they may reflect, at least in part, a systematic *mistake* in judgment about what the future is likely to bring, a type of bias that may be based in human psychological behavior that somehow is not checked (and may even be exacerbated) by the relevant market institutions. In real estate one hallmark can be "flipping," the purchase of properties (typically using large amounts of debt) only with the intention of selling them again soon thereafter in anticipation of higher prices. (See further discussion in Chapters 7 and 12.)

[3]The implication of a large run-up in commercial property prices not stimulating a commensurately large building boom would suggest that development costs must also have been increasing in real terms. In contrast to the 1980s, there may have been more brakes on new construction during the 2000s, such as regulatory constraints and pressure on costs of building materials, as well as sharply rising land values in some locations. There may also still have been some institutional memory of the experience of the 1980s/90s cycle, both within the development industry and in the capital markets.

[4]See DiPasquale and Wheaton (1992). A similar four-quadrant depiction of the link between the space and asset markets was presented by Fisher (1992).

EXHIBIT 2-3 The DiPasquale-Wheaton Four-Quadrant Diagram
© OnCourse Learning

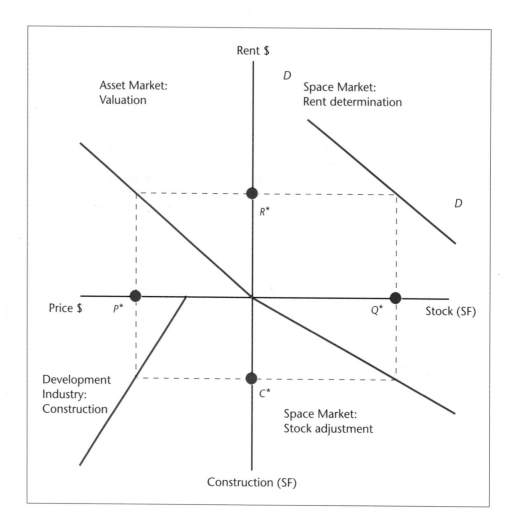

the classic price/quantity diagram in the space market, and the space usage demand function is represented in the northeast quadrant by the downward-sloping *DD* line. If we draw a vertical line from the point on the horizontal axis representing the existing supply of space in the market (Q^*), the point at which that line intersects the demand function will tell us the current equilibrium rent, given that amount of space in the market. The equilibrium rent with Q^* amount of space in the market is R^*.

The northwest quadrant depicts the asset market valuation process, relating the equilibrium property prices (on the horizontal axis, in $/SF) to the level of current rent (on the vertical axis shared with the northeast quadrant, also in $/SF). (Note that in the 4Q diagram the point in the center where the axes cross is the "origin" of all four graphs, so that in the northwest and southwest quadrants the horizontal-axis values increase as one moves from right to left.) The line in the northwest quadrant represents the cap rate or OAR (or its inverse, the price/earnings multiple), which we described in Chapter 1. The steeper the line, the higher the cap rate (lower property price per dollar of current rent). By continuing a horizontal line from the current rent point R^* on the vertical axis to the cap rate line in the northwest quadrant, and then drawing a vertical line down from that point to the price axis, we determine the property price (per SF) implied by the current rent. The point P^* represents the property price. Thus, the two top (or "northern") quadrants depict the short-run or immediate price link between the asset and space markets.

The two bottom (or "southern") quadrants depict the long-run effect of the real estate development industry by showing the impact of construction on the total stock of built space in the market. The southwest quadrant depicts the operation of the development industry—the physical asset production process. The relationship in the southwest quadrant is between property prices and the annual amount of construction activity (including rehabilitation and redevelopment as well as new development). The line in this quadrant relates a given level of property prices to a given rate of construction. The vertical (upside-down) axis represents the physical rate of construction in SF/year produced by the development industry. The farther down the vertical axis you go, the greater the level of the construction activity.

The construction function line in the southwest quadrant is outward-sloping in Exhibit 2-3 (i.e., down and to the left), indicating that in the space market modeled by the diagram, higher property prices will stimulate a greater rate of new construction, as higher prices enable more costly sites to be developed, possibly at higher densities and/or development to proceed at a faster pace due to greater availability of capital. The outward slope of this line therefore represents rising long-run marginal costs in the supply of built space. Greater long-run supply elasticity (i.e., a flatter long-run marginal cost curve for real estate development) would be represented by a more steeply falling line in the southwest quadrant.[5] The construction function line intersects the property price axis at a positive value rather than at the origin, because when property price is below some threshold level, no construction will occur, as it would be unprofitable. A vertical line dropped down from the horizontal (asset price) axis at the current asset price P^* will intersect the construction function line at a point that corresponds on the downward vertical axis (drawing a horizontal line over to it) to the amount of new construction in the market per year (point C^*).

Finally, the southeast quadrant completes the long-run integration of the space and asset markets by linking the rate of construction to the total stock of built space available in the usage market.[6] The line in the southeast quadrant relates the average rate of space construction per year to the total stock of space that can be indefinitely maintained in the market. The concept behind the southeast quadrant is that, in the long run, in the absence of new construction, older space will be removed from the stock as it "wears out" and old buildings are either abandoned and demolished or converted to other uses. Thus, on average over the long run, a certain amount of new construction per year is necessary just to maintain a given stock of space available in the market. The greater the total stock, the greater the annual new-construction rate necessary just to maintain that stock in the long run (hence, the outward-sloping line from the origin). The line in the southeast quadrant thus links the C^* level of construction activity to the Q^* level of total supply of built space. The 4Q picture thus depicts a long-run steady-state equilibrium.[7]

---

[5]The line in the southwest quadrant is not exactly the same as the long-run-supply curve presented in Chapter 1, because the southwest quadrant determines the rate of construction per year, rather than the accumulated total stock of built space supplied in the market. The interaction of the two bottom quadrants fully depicts the long-run-supply function in the space market. The long-run-supply function "kink" described in Chapter 1 does not appear in the 4Q diagram because this diagram shows purely long-run-steady-state relationships. However, the equivalent of Chapter 1's kink could be represented in the 4Q diagram by placing a kink in the stock adjustment line in the southeast quadrant at its corner of the initial rectangle, so that the line bends vertically up to the horizontal axis at Q^*.

[6]The line in the southeast quadrant is not a continuation of, or related in any way to, the line in the northwest quadrant.

[7]For example, in a market where there are 100,000 apartment units, 1,000 to 2,000 units per year will likely be lost (generally older units) due to conversion into other uses, demolition to make way for other projects, or simple abandonment. So, to maintain 100,000 apartments in the market, 1,000 to 2,000 new units must be built per year. Similarly, an average construction rate of 2,000 to 4,000 new units per year will eventually support a steady-state stock of 200,000 units. This reveals how the 4Q diagram depicts long-run average relationships. In particular, the construction function in the southwest quadrant does not represent the amount of construction in any single year, but rather an average rate of construction maintained across a long span of time.

2.4 Using the 4Q Diagram to Help Understand Boom and Bust in Real Estate Markets

Historically, real estate markets have often experienced boom and bust periods. The space markets have exhibited extended periods of rise in building occupancy and rents followed by extended periods of falling or low occupancy and rents.

In addition, property prices in the real estate asset market, along with liquidity and volume of sales transactions in that market, often appear to go through extended periods of rise and fall, usually related to the ups and downs in the space market, but not necessarily identical in terms of period or phase of the cycle.[8]

In this section we will apply the 4Q diagram presented in the previous section to gain some understanding of the famous commercial property cycles that climaxed in the United States in the late 1980s through early 1990s, and again nearly 20 years later in the 2000s.

Turning first to the 1980s–1990s cycle, we begin by noting that the early 1980s were characterized by two economic phenomena in the United States: a sharp increase in user demand for new commercial space and an increase in investor demand for real estate assets. While it is not surprising that such phenomena would stimulate new construction of commercial space, our question is whether these phenomena caused not only the rise but also the subsequent fall in the real estate markets. In other words, how inevitable was the over-shoot? Did the boom contain the seeds of the subsequent bust? If so, why and how was this so, and would such behavior tend to repeat in real estate in other times and places?

To explore this question, we will use the 4Q diagram in a slightly extended way. In the previous section, we noted that the rectangle in the 4Q diagram depicts a long-run steady state. In the present exercise, we will use the diagram to examine both the long run, the short run, and the relation between the two. In this way, the 4Q perspective can show us one way in which the boom could indeed have contained the seeds of the subsequent bust. We will first consider the effect of growth in space usage demand, holding the capital market constant. Then we will consider the effect of a growth in investor demand for real estate, holding space usage demand constant. Finally, we will put these two phenomena together, since in fact they both occurred simultaneously in the United States during the latter half of the 1970s and first half of the 1980s, and again in the decade of the 2000s.

First, consider the effect of an increase in demand for space usage, holding the real estate asset market constant. This is depicted in Exhibit 2-4A, where we see the demand function in the northeast quadrant moving out to the right, from D_0 to D_1. In the 1980s, a booming economy, an aging population, and a pronounced structural shift in the economy away from traditional manufacturing and toward high-technology and service jobs, all fueled growth in demand for several types of commercial property. This growth was especially pronounced on the East and West Coasts and in some southern states. Some of this growth was certainly anticipated in advance by some in the real estate and capital markets, but the exact magnitude and specific nature and location of the space demand growth was, no doubt, to some extent unanticipated, and indeed unanticipatable, as no one can have a true crystal ball.

In the short run (say, a year or two) there is not time for new space to be built in response to an unanticipated surge in usage demand, so unless developers and the capital markets have adequately anticipated the demand growth, rents might initially rise to levels that cannot be supported in the long-run equilibrium. This is indicated in Exhibit 2-4A by the movement of rent on the vertical axis from the original level of R^* to a temporary high level of R_1, found by relating the original stock of space (Q^* on the horizontal axis) to the new demand function D_1. The long-run equilibrium effect of the growth in demand, however, results in rents that are not as high as the R_1 level. This suggests a run-up followed by a

---

[8]For example, the early 2000s were generally a sharp downcycle in many space markets after the dot.com bust and 2001 recession, but most asset markets experienced little or no decline in prices at that time (i.e., an actual increase in price/earnings multiple or drop in cap rates). A similar phenomenon occurred in the early 1980s, with sharp declines in the space market associated with a double-dip recession, but relatively little trouble in the asset market.

EXHIBIT 2-4A Effect
of Demand Growth in
Space Market
© OnCourse Learning

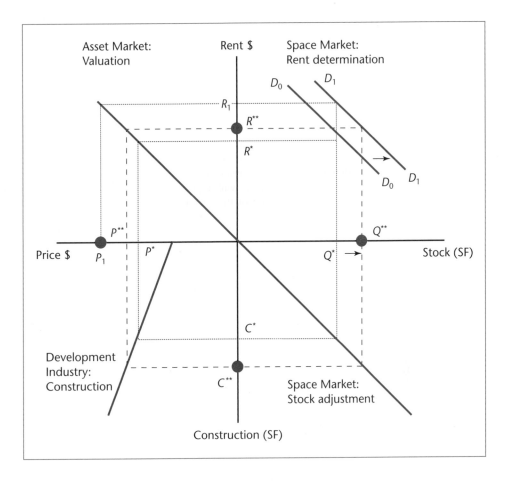

fall-back in rents. The severity of this reversal, and the extent to which it is anticipated by decision makers in the system, can determine the significance of any resulting "boom and bust cycle."

The new long-run equilibrium based on the new D_1 demand function is indicated by the rectangle traced in the dashed lines. The new equilibrium is represented by the points with the double asterisks, where the new rectangle crosses the axes. Note that while the new equilibrium rent (R^{**}) is above the old equilibrium rent (R^*), it is below the temporary R_1 rent level. The fact that R^{**} is above R^* indicates that this space market is characterized by at least a slightly upward-sloping long-run-marginal-cost function, i.e., increasing real development costs (presumably reflecting land or location values increasing over time in real terms). Also, note that while the long-run equilibrium quantity of built space is higher than it was at the old demand level ($Q^{**} > Q^*$), the "absorption" (increased occupancy) of space is not so great as would have occurred if rents had been maintained at the old R^* level. This is due to the effect of usage demand sensitivity to rent (i.e., price elasticity of demand), indicated by the slope of the demand function in the northeast quadrant.

A little experimentation with the 4Q graph will demonstrate an important point. The condition for the new equilibrium rectangle lying outside the old one as a result of growth in underlying usage demand (holding the capital market in the northwest quadrant constant) is that the asset construction function in the southwest quadrant must be outward-sloping (rising marginal costs). Rents, property prices, and stock of space must all increase under these circumstances in response to rising usage demand in the northeast quadrant. But the increase need not be proportionately the same across all of these variables. The amount of the increase will depend on the relative elasticities of supply and demand and the capital market's appetite for more investment in real estate, that is, on the shapes of the lines (or they could be curves) in the two upper quadrants.

EXHIBIT 2-4B Effect of Demand Growth in Asset Market

© OnCourse Learning

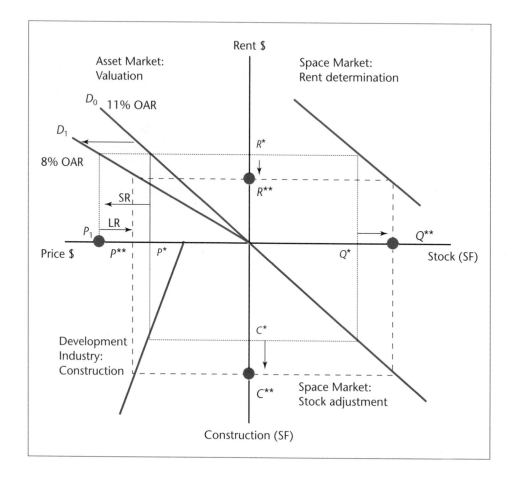

The fundamental key to whether rents must rise with a growth in demand lies in the shape of the construction function in the southwest quadrant. As we noted in Chapter 1, if development costs are constant (completely vertical construction function in the southwest quadrant), then rents will remain constant in the long run even with growth in space usage demand. In that case, the long-run equilibrium rectangle will expand only to the right in its width dimension, and only downward in its height dimension, that is, greater steady-state construction and stock of space but no greater rents or asset prices. Indeed, if the long-run marginal cost of development is declining in real terms (inward-sloping construction function in the southwest quadrant, bending down toward the vertical axis), then the long-run result of an increase in usage demand will actually be lower rents and lower asset prices than before the usage demand grew. Because this result is somewhat counter-intuitive, and also seemingly belied by the initial short-run (but unsustainable) run-up in rent (to level R_1), it may not be properly anticipated by decision makers in the real estate system, perhaps especially in the asset market and development industry, leading to initial gains followed by losses—a "boom and bust" result.

Next, consider the effect of an increase in demand for real estate investment assets among investors in the capital markets. By this, we mean a relative shift in preferences among investors, so that they are willing to pay higher price/earnings multiples for real estate assets than they previously were. Such a shift might occur because investors now perceive real estate to be less risky relative to other investment asset classes (such as stocks and bonds). Or perhaps investors for some reason don't mind or care about real estate's risk as much as they did previously (maybe because their investment holdings are more diversified). Or perhaps investors now tend to expect more future growth in real estate rents than they previously had been expecting, so they don't require as much current return. Or perhaps there is just a general increase in global liquidity (the amount of money available to invest, including some earmarked for U.S. commercial property). The point is that for some reason investors are now willing to pay more for real estate assets, per dollar of current real estate rental income, than they were willing to pay before.

Evidence suggests that something like this did in fact happen in the period from the late 1970s to the mid-1980s in the United States, and again less than 30 years later.[9]

This type of capital market shift is indicated in Exhibit 2-4B by the movement down (to a shallower slope) of the valuation line in the northwest quadrant. For example, suppose that prevailing cap rates had been 11 percent (on average, for typical properties in a given real estate market), and now they have moved down three points to 8 percent, as indicated in Exhibit 2-4B. This represents a substantial upward revaluation of property. Indeed, property values would rise some 37.5 percent if rents remained constant (from 1/0.11 to 1/0.08 per dollar of rent). And, of course, at first rents would remain constant, holding supply and usage demand constant in the space market in the northeast quadrant. Thus, if investors are somewhat **myopic** and cannot foresee what the surge of financial capital into the real estate asset market will do to stimulate new construction, then property prices could rise temporarily to a level above what is sustainable in the long run. This is indicated in Exhibit 2-4B by the short-run rise in asset prices to the P_1 level from the original P^* level.

The new long-run equilibrium is found, as always in a 4Q diagram, by the new rectangle connecting the four quadrants based on the new 8 percent OAR line in the northwest quadrant. This equilibrium is shown in Exhibit 2-4B by the dashed lines, which intersect the axes at the new equilibrium prices and quantities indicated by the double asterisks. Note that this new equilibrium involves a substantial increase in the amount of built space, which reflects the effect of a real estate development boom that brings the stock of space up to the new Q^{**} level. This is the **physical capital** result of the flow of **financial capital** into the real estate asset market (and development industry) caused by the shift in investor preferences toward real estate assets.

The new equilibrium involves lower rents ($R^{**} < R^*$) and therefore more use of space ($Q^{**} > Q^*$) than the original equilibrium holding usage demand constant in the space market. The lower rents mean that the lower cap rates in the asset market do not result in as high a long-run rise in property prices as you might have thought at first, even with rising marginal development costs (outward-sloping construction function in the southwest quadrant). The new equilibrium property market prices of P^{**}, although possibly higher than the old P^* prices, may not be much higher, though the short-lived jump to P_1 may have been much higher. Again, we have the potential ingredients of a "boom and bust," but this time only in the asset market (as the effect on rents in the space market is purely downward pressure).

If development marginal costs are declining (construction function bending down inward toward the vertical axis in the southwest quadrant), then this result is only more extreme. Asset prices end up lower than they started out, even though cap rates are lower (higher asset price/earnings multiples), because the supply of space ultimately increases so much as to bring rents down so far (holding usage demand constant) that asset prices fall in spite of the lower cap rates. And all of this occurs in a sustainable steady state (i.e., with sufficient profit for all "players"). But again, the long-run result is somewhat counter-intuitive and opposite to the initial short-run result, ingredients for potential overshooting and a "boom-and-bust" result that could expose some investors or developers to losses.

Now you can see how these examples using the 4Q graph shed light on the question of what could explain booms and busts in the real estate system. From 1975 to 1985, and again from 2002 to 2007, both usage demand growth and investor demand growth occurred in the United States. If both of these phenomena can individually cause a temporary overshooting of real estate asset re-pricing in the absence of perfect foresight by market participants, imagine that the simultaneous occurrence of demand growth in both of the top two quadrants would exacerbate this danger of asset price overshooting. This would cause real estate prices to rise at first and then fall back, even without a subsequent reduction in underlying demand for either space usage or for real estate investment. The fallback in prices would of course only be deepened as a result of a subsequent reduction in demand (particularly given a kinked supply function, which is not pictured in Exhibits 2-4A and 2-4B). Such a reduction in demand

---

[9]See section 7.3.1 for a more detailed account of the historical cycles.

did in fact happen in the early 1990s and again from 2008 to 2010. In both cases, economic recession and cutbacks in employment occurred in the national economy, undercutting space usage demand growth, and financial shifts (including temporarily decreased liquidity and increased risk aversion among investors) undercut investment demand in the asset market.

Viewing these two historical cycles, separated by some 20 years, from the perspective of the 4Q model, we see some interesting commonalities. In both cases cap rates compressed even as rents soared, exaggerating the asset price run-up. That is a powerful and heady combination, with both the asset and space markets moving upward together. The danger of the system tipping into a positive feedback loop, as described previously, may be particularly acute during such coincidences.

Exhibit 2-5 suggests that there were also differences between these two cycles. In the 2000s the asset market price cycle was less tied to the space market rent cycle, and in the commercial property market there was less overbuilding in the 2000s boom than in the 1980s. The 2000s cycle was more strongly driven by events purely in the capital markets (including extensive securitization and use of derivatives during 2005–2007). This appears to have led to a greater price bubble to burst in the asset market, but less of a rent bust in the space market, compared to the earlier cycle, especially given the relative severities of the two subsequent macroeconomic recessions (the 2007–2009 recession being much more severe than that of 1991). Clearly Exhibit 2-5 reveals how the cycles in the two markets are not exactly the same, as the 25-year period depicted covers two full space market cycles but only one full asset market cycle.

So, where does this leave us? Do booms in general contain the seeds of a subsequent bust? Clearly, there is no iron-clad law. No two cycles are identical. History does not exactly repeat, though it does "rhyme," as Mark Twain noted. We see how in principle cycles can be dampened by the ability of the asset market and development industry to react quickly with foresight to relevant new information and perhaps by the application of supply inelasticity in the development industry (what may be referred to in the industry as "discipline") and by conservative use of debt (limited leverage) in the asset market (another point of "discipline").

EXHIBIT 2-5 Example Space Market Rents and Asset Market Prices (adjusted for inflation): 1986–2011*

Sources: Based on data from CoStar Group Inc., NCREIF, MIT/CRE.

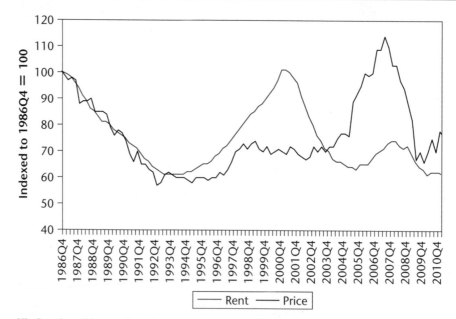

*The lines depicted here are illustrative examples typical of the US commercial real estate markets, but not exact correlates of the same markets. The rent line is based on asking rents for office space in seven major metro areas (source: CoStar); the asset price line is the NCREIF-based TBI (source: MIT) transaction price index for institutional investment property. Both the rent line and the asset price line are net of CPI inflation.

Such discipline may be most needed when it is most difficult to apply: when demand is growing in both the space usage and asset investment markets (both top two quadrants). In any case, the 4Q model helps to elucidate how cycles can happen.[10]

2.5 Chapter Summary

This chapter has completed our overview of the big picture of the commercial real estate industry as it relates to investment decisions. In Chapter 1, we presented the two major markets, the space market and the asset market. In this chapter, we introduced the development industry as the third major component in the overall system, and we sketched the dynamic linkages among these three components in what can be called the "real estate system." We introduced the four-quadrant (4Q) model as a simple visual tool for analyzing this system. We showed how the 4Q model can shed light on the traditional concept of the real estate cycle and suggested something about how such a cycle may be caused by differences between short-run and long-run perturbations of equilibrium in the absence of perfect foresight by market participants, as well as by behavioral phenomena that may in some circumstances trigger positive feedback loops in any of the three major elements in the system.

KEY TERMS

real estate system	four-quadrant model	myopic price forecasts
systems dynamics model	long-run equilibrium	physical capital/assets
negative feedback loop	real estate market cycle	financial capital/assets
positive feedback loop		

STUDY QUESTIONS

2.1. What are the three major components of the real estate system? Describe how the asset and space markets are linked.

2.2. Describe three ways in which participants in the real estate system must be forward-looking, that is, anticipating future responses to current changes in the system, in order for the system to maintain the balance between supply and demand in the space market.

2.3. What is a negative feedback loop? Give an example of a negative feedback loop within the real estate system shown in Exhibit 2-2.

2.4. Describe each of the quadrants in the four-quadrant diagram. Set up the four-quadrant diagram, carefully labeling each quadrant.

2.5. Long-run equilibrium in the four-quadrant diagram is characterized by a fixed stock of space (in the northeast quadrant), yet the southeast quadrant shows that new construction is taking place. What is going on?

2.6. Suppose user demand for space in a certain market grows from 4 to 5 million square feet (MSF) at $10/SF net rent. Assuming property market cap rates remain constant at 10%, show on a four-quadrant diagram similar to Exhibit 2-4A the short- and long-run effects of this change in user demand. [Hint: You can answer qualitatively or recognize that specific quantitative answers will depend on the shapes and slopes of the curves (i.e., the elasticities) in each quadrant.]

---

[10]For additional discussion of real estate cycles and theories to explain them, see section 6.2 in Chapter 6 and section 27.6 in Chapter 27. There is also relevant discussion in Chapters 12 and 22.

2.7. In Question 2.6, in what sense do rents "overshoot" the new long-run equilibrium level? What about for the short run? Why does this happen? What role does forward-looking behavior play in terms of the extent of overshooting?

2.8. Suppose investor demand for real estate assets grows in the sense that prevailing cap rates (OARs) in the property asset market fall from 10% to 8%. Assuming usage demand remains constant in the space market, show on a four-quadrant diagram, similar to Exhibit 2-4B, the short- and long-run effects of this change in investor demand. [Hint: You can answer qualitatively or recognize that specific quantitative answers will depend on the shapes and slopes of the curves (i.e., the elasticities) in each quadrant.]

2.9. Explain what factors might have caused investor asset demand for real estate to grow in Question 2.8.

2.10. Is there a "disconnect" between space and asset markets? The 2002–2005 period was another interesting one for U.S. income-property markets. Capitalization rates declined significantly for all property types (see Exhibit 1-12 within Question 1.11) at the same time that growth in property income was flat or even negative. Property prices generally rose or held firm, and there was relatively little new development (beyond that required in the long run). The phenomenon of rising prices (falling cap rates) at a time of weak space market performance led many market observers to question the rationality of real estate investors and to suggest that property was overvalued because space and asset markets had become "disconnected." Try to explain what took place during this period using the four-quadrant diagram. Do we need to appeal to investor irrationality? [Hint: You may have to shift/change more than one curve at a time.]

Archer, W., and D. Ling. 1997. The three dimensions of real estate market: Linking space, capital, and property markets. *Real Estate Finance* 14(3): 7–14.

Case, K., and R. Shiller. 1988. The efficiency of the market for single-family homes. *American Economic Review* 79(1): 125–37.

Davis, E. P., and H. Zhu. 2011. Bank lending and commercial property cycles: Some cross-country evidence. *Journal of International Money and Finance* 30(1): 1–21.

DiPasquale, D., and W. Wheaton. 1992. The markets for real estate assets and space: A conceptual framework. *Real Estate Economics* (formerly *AREUEA Journal*) 20(2): 181–98.

DiPasquale, D., and W. Wheaton. 1994. Housing market dynamics and the future of housing prices. *Journal of Urban Economics* 35(1): 1–27.

DiPasquale, D., and W. Wheaton. 1996. *Urban Economics and Real Estate Markets*. Englewood Cliffs, NJ: Prentice Hall.

Fischer, D. 1999. An integrated property market model. *Journal of Real Estate Practice & Education* 2(1): 33–43.

Fisher, J. 1992. Integrating research on markets for space and capital. *Real Estate Economics* (formerly *AREUEA Journal*) 20(2): 161–80.

Fisher, J., D. Geltner, and R. B. Webb. 1994. Value indices of commercial real estate: A comparison of index construction methods. *Journal of Real Estate Finance & Economics* 9(2): 137–64.

Florance, A., N. Miller, R. Peng, and J. Spivey. 2010. Slicing, Dicing, and Scoping the Size of the U.S. Commercial Real Estate Market. *Journal of Real Estate Portfolio Management* 16(2): 101–118.

Grenadier, S. 1995. The persistence of real estate cycles. *Journal of Real Estate Finance & Economics* 10: 95–119.

Gyourko, J., and D. Keim. 1992. What does the stock market tell us about real estate returns? *Real Estate Economics* 20(3): 457–486.

Kaiser, R. 1997. The long cycle in real estate. *Journal of Real Estate Research* 14(3): 233–256.

Khandani, A., A. Lo, and R. Merton. 2009. Systemic risk and the refinancing ratchet effect. MIT Sloan Research Paper No. 4750-09, Harvard Business School Finance Working Paper No. 1472892.

Korpacz Real Estate Investor Survey, The Korpacz Company, Frederick, MD (various issues).

Malpezzi, S., and S. Wachter. 2005. The role of speculation in real estate cycles. *Journal of Real Estate Literature* 13(2): 141–64.

Miles, M., and N. Tolleson. 1997. A revised look at how real estate compares with other major components of the domestic investment universe. *Real Estate Finance* 14(1).

Mueller, G. 1995. Understanding real estate's physical and financial market cycles. *Real Estate Finance* 12(3): 47–52.

Pyhrr, S., W. Born, and J. Webb. 1990. Development of a dynamic investment strategy under alternative inflation cycle scenarios. *Journal of Real Estate Research* 5(2): 177–94.

Shiller, R. 2009. *Irrational Exuberance*, 2nd ed., Princeton University Press.

Wheaton, W., M. Baranski and C. Templeton. 2009. 100 years of commercial real estate prices in Manhattan. *Real Estate Economics* 37(1): 69–83.

URBAN ECONOMICS AND REAL ESTATE MARKET ANALYSIS

Just as financial economics is the primary branch of economics useful for studying the real estate asset market, so urban economics is the primary academic discipline for studying the space market. We saw in Part I the fundamental importance of the space market in the overall real estate system, both to the asset market and to the development industry. The focus of Part II, therefore, is to introduce some topics of urban economics that are most relevant to commercial property investment analysis. We will include some topics in related fields as well, such as urban geography and real-estate space-market analysis. The objective is to gain a depth of understanding of the spatial and temporal patterns of urban development that underlie the functioning of real estate space markets.

The first three chapters in Part II present the principles and tools of urban economics and other related academic disciplines that are useful for understanding cities and making informed real estate decisions. A particular focus of these three chapters that is important in real estate investment analysis is the fundamental determinants of land value within a metropolitan area, how land value changes over time in different parts of the city. Recall that land values are the key determinant of the shape of the long-run supply function in the space market, which in turn governs the long-run trend in rents. The last chapter in Part II focuses on the practical application of urban economics in the analysis of specific real estate space markets.

CENTRAL PLACE THEORY AND THE SYSTEM OF CITIES

LEARNING OBJECTIVES

After reading this chapter, you should understand:

➲ Why cities form, grow, and decline.

➲ The centralizing and decentralizing forces that explain the number and sizes of cities.

➲ What constitutes a "system" of cities and the essential characteristics of the U.S. system of cities.

➲ The key practical insights and principles of central place theory and urban hierarchy theory and how real estate decision makers can use these.

➲ What is meant by the economic base and export base of a city.

➲ Employment and population multipliers.

It would not be a great oversimplification to say that in a modern society real estate is an urban phenomenon. While most of the value of real property throughout most of history was based on agricultural production, in the United States today over 90 percent of the value of all real estate is found in urban areas, even though these comprise only a small percent of the total land area of the country. An understanding of cities is therefore basic to an educated perspective on commercial property investment analysis. In this chapter, we will begin with an overview of the big picture, the "system of cities." In the process of doing this, we will introduce one of the most fundamental concepts of urban geography and spatial economics, central place theory, together with related concepts, including urban hierarchy and regional economic base. The basic objective is to understand the forces that underlie the rise and fall of cities and, related to that, some basic determinants of successful locations for various types of activities.

3.1 Pattern of City Size

Cities do not exist as isolated or purely random phenomena. Rather, each city has a place and a role as an element in a **system of cities**, which serves a functioning economy and geographic region. The nature of the system of cities has implications for the nature of the space markets underlying the real estate assets in those cities. Let's begin by considering the patterns in city size (in terms of population) and location.

Of these two, city size is perhaps the simplest characteristic to describe and measure. Yet the population of a city, and how that population changes over time, has important impacts on its space markets. For example, larger, more rapidly growing cities will generally be able to sustain higher real rents, other things being equal. In fact, the sizes of cities tend to follow a rather striking pattern. This pattern is known as the **rank/size rule** (also referred to as Zipf's Law). The rank/size rule can be expressed as follows:

$$City\ population = \frac{Largest\ city's\ population}{Rank\ of\ city}$$

In other words, if you rank all the cities in a system of cities (that is, all the cities in a coherent geographical region corresponding to an integrated economy), such that the most populous city has a rank of 1, then the population of each city will approximately equal the largest city's population divided by the rank of the city.

If you plot Zipf's Law on a bar graph, it results in the theoretical pattern of population and rank shown in Exhibit 3-1A. Note the exponentially declining pattern in the length of the bars representing population as we go down the rankings of the cities. Now examine the population/rank bar chart for the United Nations' projected 2015 populations of the largest metropolitan areas in the world's three largest countries, shown in Exhibit 3-1B. Notice the similarity between the actual empirical patterns in 3-1B and the theoretical pattern in 3-1A. The rank/size rule describes the distribution of U.S. city sizes remarkably well. This phenomenon is found to hold across a wide variety of countries and regions. To be more precise, the pattern tends to slightly deviate from the pure rank/size rule, with major cities (such as those depicted in Exhibit 3-1B) tending to be a bit larger than the pure application of the rule would predict. While the exact cause of this pattern is not fully resolved among geographers, it seems to evolve organically from

EXHIBIT 3-1A Theoretical
Rank/Size Rule
© OnCourse Learning

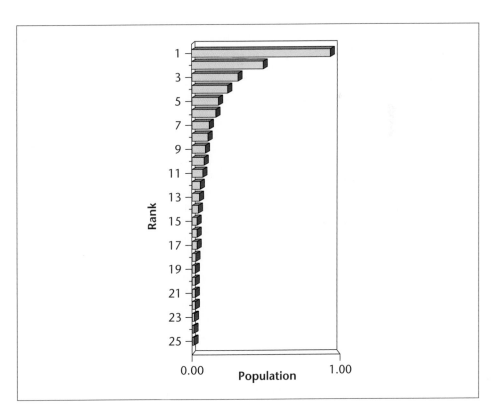

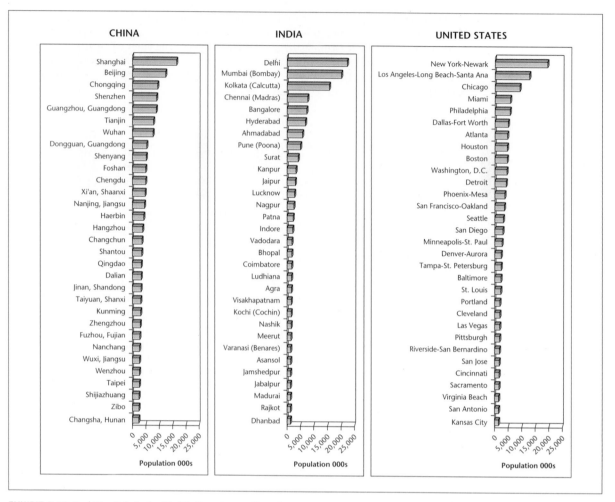

EXHIBIT 3-1B Rank/Size Rule in the World's Three Largest Countries
Source: U.N. Urban Agglomeration Population, 2009.

the way cities grow over time, and it may also be related to location. (See the feature "What Causes the Rank/Size Rule?" on page 46.)

3.2 Pattern of City Location

Let's bring location into the picture. Look again at the rank/size chart of U.S. cities in Exhibit 3-1B. Notice that the three largest cities are far apart, each in a different region of the country: New York in the East, Chicago in the Midwest, and Los Angeles in the West. Similarly in China, Shanghai is in the East, Beijing the North, and Chongqing the Southwest; in India, Delhi is in the North, Mumbai the West, and Kolkata the East. With some exceptions, *cities of similar size are not located near each other geographically.*[1] This is seen graphically in the map in Exhibit 3-2 showing the 20 largest metropolitan areas in the United States.

---

[1]The major exceptions to this rule is the formation of conurbation clusters of cities, such as the East Coast "megalopolis" in the United States or the Pearl River Delta cluster in South China (including Guanzhou, Shenzhen, Hong Kong, and others).

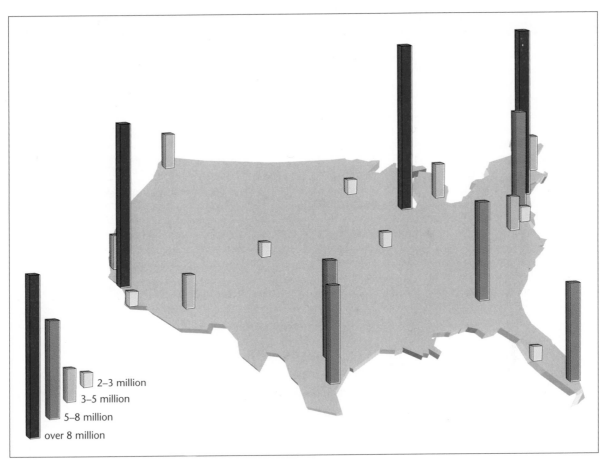

EXHIBIT 3-2 The 20 Largest U.S. Metropolitan Areas
Source: U.N. Urban Agglomeration Population, 2009.

3.3 Factors Underlying the Pattern: Centripetal and Centrifugal Forces

The rank/size rule and the geographical regional dispersion noted earlier together suggest a hierarchical structure of cities and a division of territory into zones of influence.[2] This, in turn, suggests two points:

1. **Centralizing** city-causation (**centripetal**) **forces** are counterbalanced by opposing **decentralizing** (**centrifugal**) **forces**.
2. The relative strength of the centralizing and decentralizing forces differs for different functions and activities.

The centralizing forces cause cities to form in the first place and to tend to agglomerate into fewer and larger cities over time. The decentralizing forces tend to limit the growth of city size and tend to make more, smaller cities dispersed throughout the territory.

---

[2]The major exceptions to this rule are the clusters of cities in the Northeast along the Boston-Washington corridor, the Great Lakes Milwaukee-Pittsburgh corridor, and the relative proximity of Los Angeles and San Francisco.

WHAT CAUSES THE RANK/SIZE RULE?

What causes the rank/size rule? Geographers and economists have long puzzled about the answer to this question, and proposed various theories. Perhaps the simplest explanation has been offered by Xavier Gabaix.

Suppose we begin with any arbitrary distribution of city sizes. Now suppose each city grows randomly over time, but with all cities tending to grow at the same common mean annual percentage rate over the long run, and with the same "volatility," that is, the same relative randomness of actual annual growth around the long-run average. Over time, the distribution of city sizes will converge toward Zipf's Law, and the convergence will be pretty rapid. This is simply a consequence of mathematics. But why would cities all tend to grow at the same rate on average over the long run? Perhaps because the number of new jobs is proportional to the number of existing jobs. Why would all cities tend to have the same volatility in their annual percentage growth? Perhaps because once a city is large enough, it will have a relatively diversified economic base, and this diver-

sification will reduce volatility to a common level. Smaller cities may lack sufficient diversification in their economic bases, and may therefore have greater volatility in their growth. If there is a minimum "critical mass" for city size, below which a city will tend to wither and die away, then the volatility in smaller cities' growth will cause many of them to sink below the critical size at some point. This will result in fewer "small cities" than there should be according to Zipf's Law. This is what we observe in the real world. There are fewer small towns than would be predicted by the theoretical rank/size rule. What this mathematical model cannot explain is why the ranking is relatively stable over time. Rarely do cities significantly change rank, and most such changes are systematic (such as the rise of western and southern cities at the expense of eastern cities). Thus, to understand the size pattern of cities, we must also consider location.

Source: See Gabaix, X. 1999. Zipf's Law for Cities: An explanation. *Quarterly Journal of Economics* 114(3): 707–738.

3.3.1 Centripetal Forces

Three primary centralizing forces cause cities to coalesce:

1. Economies of scale
2. Economies of agglomeration
3. Positive locational externalities

Operating together, these three forces underlie an important characteristic of urban growth dynamics known as cumulative causation.

Economies of scale refers to the phenomenon whereby it is cheaper and more efficient to produce more of a good or service in larger volume at fewer sites. Fundamentally, economies of scale are caused by fixed production costs at a given site. The fixed costs are independent of the quantity produced at that site. The physical plant and equipment in an automobile factory are examples. As a result of scale economies it is typically more efficient to produce 200,000 automobiles per year in one factory than to produce 50,000 automobiles per year in each of four factories at different locations.

Economies of agglomeration are cost or productivity advantages to the clustering of firms or work sites physically near each other. Unlike scale economies, which require increasing quantity of production to obtain greater efficiency, agglomeration economies do not require increased quantity of production per se, but merely the clustering of production work sites. Agglomeration economies result from the ability of different types of workers and production processes to help each other if they are physically near each other. This may result from "vertical linkages" ("upstream" and "downstream" linkages in production processes) or from "horizontal linkages" ("synergy" across firms or work sites, such as the sharing of a common pool of skilled workers or the existence of a critical mass of experts in a given field, resulting in a creative cross-fertilization and stimulation of income-generating ideas).

A closely related economic concept is that of **positive locational externalities**. This occurs when one firm benefits from the nearby location of another firm without the first firm being able to capture all of these benefits for itself. This concept is similar to agglomeration economies. The difference is that locational externalities may occur between as few as two firms or plants, not necessarily requiring a critical mass of firms or workers. An example of a positive locational externality would be the benefit obtained by a trucking firm whose operations are centered, say, in Nashville, Tennessee, when a major airline establishes an air-freight hub in that city. The airfreight operations will increase demand for the trucking company's services.

A more subtle example of external economies occurs in the interaction of scale economies and agglomeration economies and the interaction of supply and demand. As more firms cluster together, the local population and production swells, providing a larger local market for all manner of goods and services. This allows larger-scale production, which, in the presence of scale economies, allows lower cost and more efficient production. This, in turn, stimulates further demand for additional production. Thus, in the presence of scale economies, firms can experience external benefits merely from their proximity to each other, even if they are not directly technologically and physically related to one another. In other words, scale economies can integrate the notions of agglomeration economies and positive locational externalities, at least for goods and services that are locally produced and distributed.

The sort of growth spiral just described has been referred to as **cumulative causation**. It suggests that there can be *momentum* in the growth (or decline) of cities and regions. Growth breeds growth (and decline breeds decline). If we look at the overall system of cities in the United States and define *growth* and *decline*, relatively speaking, by the rank of a city's population, we see that when a city commences growing, it tends to continue growing for at least a few decades; and vice versa: when a city begins to decline, the decline tends to persist for at least a few decades.

3.3.2 Centrifugal Forces

The decentralizing forces that put a brake on urban agglomeration and result in a larger number of smaller cities include factors that make it less efficient or more costly to produce goods and services in large cities, or that reduce the quality of life of the inhabitants. For example, congestion, pollution, crime, high intra-urban transportation costs, as well as high rents and urban-land costs, are some of the negative features of large cities that tend to get worse as cities increase in size (at least beyond some critical limit).

Also, a larger average size of cities relative to the total population of a country implies that the number of cities in the population must be fewer. For example, a country with 100 million city dwellers can have at most only 10 cities with 10 million inhabitants, but it could have as many as 100 cities with 1 million inhabitants. Spread out over the same geographical territory, the 10 "super-cities" would be on average much farther apart from each other and from the average rural point in the territory than would 100 cities of 1 million inhabitants each similarly spaced throughout the same territory. Thus, larger (and therefore fewer) cities will tend to increase rural-to-urban transport costs, due to greater average transport distances (possibly offset by reduced city-to-city transport requirements).

3.3.3 Balance of Forces

When centralizing forces become more powerful or more important in a society, one or a few large cities tend to siphon population and grow faster than smaller cities. For example, reductions in transport and communication costs and the rise of highly centralized governmental and administrative institutions resulted in the development of dominant capital cities in imperial nations, such as London, Paris, and Moscow during the nineteenth century and the first half of the twentieth. These cities often had larger populations than the rank/size rule would predict. When decentralizing forces become more powerful or important, small- or medium-size cities will capture most of the population growth in a society. For example, in the United States in the late twentieth century, medium-size cities generally grew faster than the largest cities.

A fundamental key point about the role of centralizing and decentralizing forces in shaping the system of cities is that centralizing forces are relatively stronger than decentralizing forces for some types of activities. For example, upper-level national governmental functions and international financial services are highly concentrated in only a few of the largest and most expensive cities. For these functions, the centralizing forces must be relatively strong, or they would not concentrate in such high-cost locations. In contrast, light manufacturing, distribution, corporate and governmental research, and lower-level governmental and corporate-managerial functions are widely spread out among cities, including many small- to medium-size cities. For these activities, the centralizing forces must be relatively weak, and/or the decentralizing forces relatively strong.

3.3.4 Central Place Theory and the Urban Hierarchy

The empirical geographic observations and economic intuition described earlier have been developed into a body of geographic theory known broadly as **central place theory** (CPT), including an extension known as the **theory of urban hierarchy**. Perhaps the most famous names associated with the development of CPT are the German geographers August Losch and Walter Christaller.

Losch developed CPT by examining the problem of location on a homogeneous "featureless plain." In such a land, homogeneous agricultural products are produced everywhere but must be marketed at a number of identical dimensionless points (i.e., the "cities") where, incidentally, the industrial population lives and needs to use the agricultural products while producing the homogeneous industrial goods that the farmers need. The greater the economies of scale in industrial production are, the fewer and farther apart will be the cities, other things being equal, for this will allow the factories to be larger in scale. The greater the transportation costs are, the more numerous and closer together will be the cities in the optimal configuration, for this will allow minimization of transportation distances (since any farmer can be served by any city, and any city by any farmer).

Losch's key geometric insight was that city "service areas," or **hinterlands**, would assume a hexagonal shape (like a honeycomb) on such a homogeneous plane, because this is the shape that minimizes the average distance from each city to all points in its service area and still covers all the territory. But while the hexagonally shaped service areas are visually striking in the abstract, the key practical insight of central place theory is the resulting *even spacing* of cities. *Even spacing is what minimizes total transportation costs,* given the total number of cities in the region (e.g., given the scale of industrial production).

Christaller enriched the picture presented by Losch by considering different economic functions or types of production, each of which might be characterized by different degrees of scale economies in production and by different transportation costs in distribution. The optimal configuration of cities on the featureless plain now includes a geographical *urban hierarchy*, in which *higher-order* cities (those containing functions that require more centralization) are fewer and farther apart than *lower-order* cities. But the tendency toward even spacing between cities suggested by Losch's basic CPT still comes through, only now the even spacing applies within each rank or "order."

PROVE CENTRAL PLACE THEORY TO YOURSELF

This even-spacing rule is very fundamental to urban geography. To prove it to yourself, look at a 12-inch ruler and imagine that it is the space or territory that must be served. Suppose there are 13 "inhabitants" (i.e., the people or sites needing to be served by transportation to and from a single point) spaced evenly across the ruler, located one on each inch mark (including the 0-inch point at the end of the ruler). Suppose the "city" to and from which the inhabitants must travel or be served is located in the exact center, at the 6-inch mark. The person living right on the 6-inch mark has no transport costs; the people living at the 5- and 7-inch marks have costs of one inch each, because they are located one inch from the city, and so on. The total transport costs of the society is the sum across all 13 inhabitants, which equals 42 "person-inches." Now imagine locating the city one inch mark away from the center, moving it, say, to the 7-inch mark. This will increase the transport costs of some people and decrease those of others, but the number of people whose costs increase exceeds that of the people for whom the costs decrease. In particular, all seven people living below the 7-inch mark (those at 0, 1, 2, ..., 6) suffer an increase in costs of one person-inch each. Only six people (those on marks 7, 8, ..., 12) see a cost decrease, also of one person-inch each, as their distance to the city is reduced by one inch. So, the total transport costs of the society is now 43. By induction, you can see that if we move the city to any other point farther away from the center, we will only further add to the total costs, in the same manner as has been described here. So the cost-minimizing location for the city is in the center. This is the essence of central place theory.

The larger the population is that is needed to support an efficient production process, the larger we would say is the minimum or **threshold market** for that product or activity. The larger the threshold market population, the fewer the number of suppliers.

Cities with more specialized and larger-scale producers that require a larger threshold market, such as steel and aerospace manufacturers, national government, international financial services, are the higher-order cities, supplying such unique and specialized goods and services to the more numerous and ubiquitous lower-order cities. Lower-order cities contain less specialized and more ubiquitous producers of goods and services that are characterized by either denser markets, lower-scale economies, or higher transportation costs relative to the value of the product. A city's hinterland now includes the territories served by all the lower-order cities that depend on the higher-order city for the higher-level functions and goods or services. Higher-order hinterlands are thus superimposed over the smaller lower-order hinterlands. (See Exhibit 3-3.) Higher-order cities tend to be, but are not necessarily, larger in population than lower-order cities. In the modern economy, higher-order cities are characterized not so much by large-scale manufacturing production, but by major *control* functions, such as corporate headquarters, government capitals, and major financial markets or service centers. Large-scale manufacturing and physical distribution services are more characteristic of mid-level cities.

In a nutshell, let us summarize CPT and hierarchy theory with the following statement:

> *In order to reduce "spatial friction," places of similar size, rank, or function will tend to be* evenly spaced *across geographical space and/ or population.*

EXHIBIT 3-3 Central Place Theory and Urban Hierarchy

The diagram shows the theoretical configuration of 34 lower-order cities (single dots) and 5 higher-order cities (circled dots), with their "hinterland" territories indicated as on a "featureless plain." The hexagonal shapes minimize aggregate transportation costs. The even spacing of the central points is the key point.

© OnCourse Learning

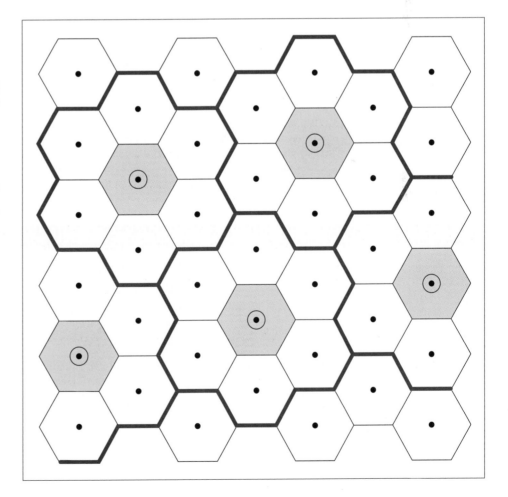

3.3.5 Why Does CPT Matter?

Geographical theories such as CPT may seem rather academic and removed from the real world. But in fact this stuff is very practical and underlies the most basic decision making in real estate development and the operation of the space market. Ignorance of these fundamental geographical principles can spell disaster in the real estate business. Insightful application of these principles is the hallmark of the successful real estate entrepreneur. In this regard, it is important to note that while we have introduced CPT and hierarchy theory to explain the location patterns of cities, these theories also apply to the spatial dimension of any economic activity.

In practical real estate terms, the implication of CPT is, therefore, that every territory must be covered (or served) by at least one central service point. Just as every hinterland needs a city, every market area needs a store or franchise, and every production region needs a branch office to manage it. This gives you the broad outlines of the nature of where it is reasonable to locate certain sites, that is, where sufficient demand for real estate of various types may exist. The emphasis is on the word *where*, for CPT is fundamentally *location theory*, and the oldest cliché in the real estate business is that what matters is: *location, location, location*.

From a practical perspective, central place theory suggests two important principles, each of which is really the opposite side of the same coin, so to speak. The two principles are:

1. If a territory is underserved, there is room for a new central site.
2. If a central site is already effectively located to serve a territory, it is going to be very hard to develop a new such site nearby.

Combined with the hierarchy theory, these principles apply at various levels, ranging from location of retail sites within a metropolitan area to predicting which cities in a country have better potential to grow and develop faster over the long run. The second principle can be thought of as implying that existing central places cast **agglomeration shadows** around themselves, making it difficult for other places of similar size or rank to develop within that shadow. For example, it would be difficult for another city the size of Atlanta to develop anywhere near Atlanta. Based on the same principle, it would be difficult to develop successfully a second regional shopping mall near an already successfully functioning mall (unless the market has grown sufficiently to support a second mall, and/or the second mall differentiates itself sufficiently from the first). Locational patterns are "fractal" in nature, which means they repeat at different scales.

3.4 Economic Base and the Growth of Cities and Regions

While the broad perspective on the overall system of cities examined in the previous section offers important insights, it still paints a very broad-brush-stroke picture, without paying much attention to the specific details that characterize individual cities. CPT cannot explain why two cities equally ranked and equally well-located may fare differently over time as some industries rise and others fall in the economy. To explain this, we need to know more about the specific differences in the local economies of the two cities.

By looking more specifically at the micro-level of individual cities, urban economists have developed perspectives and tools that can increase greatly our understanding of individual cities and how they function economically. The theory that explains what industries are important to a city's growth starts with a deeper investigation of the economic base, the engine that drives a city's sources of income. Understanding which businesses or industries are important to an area has obvious and direct implications for the economic growth prospects for the area.

3.4.1 Definition of Economic Base

The **economic base** of a city or region can be thought of as the source of its income. As such, this is the engine that drives and underlies all real estate activity and values in the region. Economic base analysis is thus a tool to help

- identify which cities or regions will grow,
- characterize what kind of growth (e.g., blue collar versus white collar) will take place, and
- quantify how much growth will occur.

Conceptually, the economic base of a region has three major potential components: (1) the local production of goods and services both for local needs and for export beyond the local urban area; (2) the investment returns to or of capital owned in the local area, such as investment returns on the stored financial wealth of retirees; and (3) government transfers, such as Social Security payments. Of these, the production of goods and services is by far the most important in most urban areas.

3.4.2 Export Base

When we examine the local production of goods and services, we can make an important distinction between goods and services produced in excess of the needs of the local area and those produced only in quantities equal to or less than local usage. Excess production is exported outside of the local regional market, and this brings income that can be used by the local population to buy goods and services either locally or from other areas. Such production is referred to as export production. It seems reasonable that this type of production would be most important in determining the growth or decline of the local area.

Recognition of the importance of export production provides the rationale for the most widely used urban economic theory of local economic growth, **export base theory**. The key principle of export base theory states that

> *Economic growth of the city or region is dependent entirely on growth in the* export *(so-called "basic") sector of the local economy.*

All employment is classified as being part of either the **export (basic) sector** or the **service (nonbasic) sector**. Industries that produce more goods and services than are likely to be consumed locally are presumed to be part of the export sector. Thus, according to export base theory, forecasting the growth of a metropolitan area consists of two steps:

1. Identifying the export base industries in the local region
2. Forecasting employment growth in those industries

This process is facilitated by the fact that there are not many major export industries in most local areas.[3]

3.4.3 Location Quotients and SICs

While the export base theory is intuitively reasonable, to apply it in practice we need a way to identify which industries and businesses are part of the export sector for a given

---

[3]A general trend in economic development has been for production and trade to become more geographically integrated, taking advantage of technological advance and economies of scale. This results in industries that were once purely local and very common becoming part of the export sector in some cities and disappearing in others. For example, breweries traditionally provide beer for a specific city. As the industry developed and storage and transportation technology improved, the concentration of activity greatly increased, with the brewery industry becoming a part of the export base of some regions, while retaining its traditional service-sector character in others. But while increasing integration has been the general trend, there can be counter-examples. More recently in the United States there has been a revival of "micro-breweries," as people discovered that large-scale industrial brewing and transportation of beer lost some of the flavor and variety in the product.

region. The most widely used tool for doing this is a quantitative measure known as the **location quotient** (often referred to as the **LQ** for short). The LQ is defined as the proportion of total local employment in a given industry divided by the proportion of total national employment in that same industry. City m's LQ for industry i is given by the following formula:

$$LQ_{mi} = \frac{N_{mi}/N_m}{N_i/N}$$

where N_{mi} = Employment in city m in industry i

N_m = Total employment in city m in all industries

N_i = National employment in industry i

N = Total national employment in all industries

A location quotient of 1.0 indicates that the same proportion of local workers work in a particular industry as work in that industry in the nation as a whole. A location quotient greater than 1.0 indicates that the local area is more heavily concentrated in that industry than is the average city or region across the country. In practice, it is usually considered that a location quotient must be significantly greater than 1.0 in order to indicate that the industry is part of the export sector of the local economic base.

As an example, the figures in the following table represent the employment statistics for New York City and the nation as a whole regarding total employment and employment in the securities trading industry.

Total U.S. employment	115,000,000
U.S. securities trading industry employment	870,000
Total New York City employment	3,260,000
New York City securities trading employment	190,000

We would compute the location quotient for the securities trading industry in New York City as follows:

$$NYC\ Securities\ Industry\ LQ = \frac{190/3,260}{870/115,000} = \frac{5.8\%}{0.8\%} = 7.3$$

This means that there are over seven times the typical proportion of securities industry workers in New York as in the nation as a whole. As the New York securities industry LQ of 7.3 is considerably greater than 1.0, we clearly confirm that the securities trading industry is indeed part of New York City's export base. Growth in the securities trading industry in New York will increase the total number of jobs in the New York region, implying growth in the region.

When combined with an analysis of large employers in a region, location quotients are an excellent way of determining the importance of a particular industry or firm to an area. Location quotients are readily calculable using employment data from the Bureau of Labor Statistics available from the federal government, as well as most state governments.[4] Industries are classified in hierarchical layers of aggregation known as the **standard industrial classification** system, or **SIC** code. SIC codes are available in many areas to a five-digit depth of disaggregation, as illustrated in the following table in increasing subcategorization for Cleveland, Ohio, as an illustrative city.

---

[4]Reports are available monthly on the Internet or through the mail. Note that in 2002 the U.S. Census Bureau replaced the previous SIC codes with a new industrial classification system designed to be integrated with those used in Canada and Mexico. The new system is called the NAICS and is described on the Census Bureau Web site at http://www.census.gov/eos/www/naics/.

SIC #	Descriptions	Number of Employed Persons
20000	Professional, paraprofessional & technical occupations	200,000
21000	Management support professionals	28,000
21100	Accountants & financial specialists	13,000
21111	Accountants specializing in tax preparation	480

The table gives an example of the branching indicated by one-digit, two-digit, three-digit, and five-digit levels of disaggregation within the SIC code scheme. (The four-digit level was left out of this example.) You can see how the definition of the employment sectors or industries becomes narrower as the SIC code number increases.[5]

3.4.4 Service Sector and Export Multiplier

Workers that are not part of the export sector (nonbasic jobs) serve the local population, as grocery clerks, divorce attorneys, child care workers, utility line repair-people, and so on. All of these jobs depend ultimately, directly or indirectly, on the export base of the region. The location quotient for nonbasic occupations will tend to be near 1.0 in most cities. The nonbasic sector is also known as the service sector of the region. If the export sector declined, there would be less need for the service sector. Since the service sector depends on the export sector, the change in the demand for service-sector jobs is a function of the change in the number of export-sector jobs.

An important feature of regional economies is that the *number of jobs in the nonbasic or service sector generally greatly exceeds the number of jobs directly in the export sector.* As a result:

> *Expansion in the export sector creates an **employment multiplier effect** on total local employment.*

As an example, suppose that in the town of Metropolis a new biotech research center needs 1,000 scientists, lab workers, administrators and facility managers, and maintenance workers. Most of the scientists, lab workers, and managers are brought in from around the country, while a few people are simply hired away from other local firms, who must then replace these workers with new workers, most of whom come from outside the region. First, the new research facility has to be built. This will create some temporary jobs. Then the research center must be maintained, which creates permanent new jobs. Most of the 1,000 new workers have families, which means a population increase of at least 2,000 in the metropolitan area, directly related to the new lab. These 1,000 new households (2,000 people) spend much of their paychecks on local goods and services, such as housing, food, entertainment, and so forth. This expands the demand for local goods and services. Local business retailers expand or new retailers move into the area and add employees as a result of this new business, resulting in more employees, more paychecks, and more people moving into the area. After the market has worked through the entire chain of effects, the net population increase due directly and indirectly to the original 1,000 research-facility workers might be 5,000 people, a **population multiplier** ratio of 5.0.

---

[5]It should be recognized that some industries do not classify well under the SIC system. For example, we might suspect that tourism would be important to economic growth in Hawaii, but there is no tourism grouping in the SIC codes. Rather, workers within the industry of tourism are classified as aircraft pilots, retail suppliers, food servers, housekeepers, bartenders, travel agents, taxi drivers, and so on, which do not group together easily. For this reason, location quotients based simply on SIC codes alone will not always suffice for a thorough analysis of the economic base of an area. But LQs do serve well to indicate which jobs are more or less important in predicting economic growth.

Every net new job in an area within the export sector creates a multiplier effect on the total employment including the export and service sectors. Two types of multipliers are often considered in forecasting the growth effects of changes in the export base:

1. Employment multiplier:

$$\frac{Net\ total\ employment\ increase}{Export\ employment\ increase}$$

2. Population multiplier:

$$\frac{Net\ total\ population\ increase}{Export\ employment\ increase}$$

Typical employment multiplier ratios are in the range of 2.0 to 4.0. Population multipliers are, of course, higher than employment multipliers. Typical population multiplier ratios range from 2.5 to 9.0, depending on the pay rate or income level of the net new jobs and the business income of the newly expanding export-sector firms. Higher-paying export-sector jobs have larger population multipliers.

It is important to note that the multiplier effect goes both ways. If jobs within the export sector are lost, the effect is the eventual loss of many indirect service-sector jobs and eventually population as well. Since people do not immediately move into or out of an area when jobs increase or decrease, the population effects lag behind the employment changes by several months to a few years.

Several steps are involved in using the export base approach to economic base analysis for the purposes of forecasting future city growth or decline. One first performs an analysis of location quotients on SIC classified workers in an area, relative to the United States, focusing on those high location quotient groupings that also have a significant number of local employees. The next step is to forecast the future employment prospects in each of these groups, both positive and negative, and to use these to suggest a population or total employment-growth impact (after considering the multiplier, depending on the income levels of the key industry workers). Such forecasts should take into consideration broad national and international trends, as well as possible unique local firms and situations. Employment forecasts by occupation and SIC or NAIC group are available from many state government economic agencies, such as state-level employment or economic-planning agencies, as well as from professional economic consulting firms.

3.4.5 Classification of Cities by Economic Base

The concept of the economic base, and especially the notion of the export base, suggests a useful way to classify and group individual cities within the overall system of cities in the United States. Such analyses can be used to identify **economic clusters**—cities that are similar in the nature of their economic bases, and which might, therefore, be expected to have similar growth patterns over time.

The most straightforward way to identify economic clusters is to compare the industrial concentrations of the economic bases, particularly the export sectors, across the cities. In this approach, industries are grouped into similar or related categories, such as heavy industry, high technology, government, and so forth. Using location quotients, one then groups cities into those whose export bases appear to be relatively dominated by one industry group or another. Typically, some cities' export bases will be highly diversified across the industry groups. Thus, one ends up with groups such as heavy-industry-dominated

Economic Base Classifications*

Diversified	Farm	F.I.R.E.	Government	Manufacturing
Albuquerque	Bellingham	Anaheim	Albany	Akron
Alton & Granite	Chico	Bloomington, IL	Ann Arbor	Allentown
Baton Rouge	Dubuque	Des Moines	Austin	Aurora & Elgin
Beaver County	Eau Claire	Hartford	Baltimore	Bridgeport
Birmingham	Johnson City	New York	Columbia, SC	Charlotte
Boulder	Joplin	Phoenix	Columbus	Cincinnati
Buffalo	Lexington	San Francisco	Dayton	Cleveland
Du Page	McAllen		Galveston	Detroit
Fort Lauderdale	Merced		Raleigh & Durham	Gary & Hammond
Fort Worth	Modesto		Richmond	Grand Rapids
Hamilton	Ocala		Sacramento	Greensboro
Harrisburg	Oxnard		Salt Lake City	Greenville
Indianapolis	Richland		Trenton	Milwaukee
Joliet	Santa Rosa		Washington	Minneapolis
Kansas City, KS	Stockton			New Bedford
Little Rock	St. Cloud			Providence
Los Angeles	Yakima			Rochester
Louisville	Yuba City			San Jose
Manchester				Scranton
Middletown				Seattle
Mobile				St. Louis
New Haven				Wilmington
Oakland				Worcester
Orlando				Youngstown
Portland				
Riverside				
Springfield				
Syracuse				
Tampa				
Toledo				
Tucson				
Vancouver				

Military	Mining	Service	Transportation
Charleston	Bakersfield	Atlantic City	Atlanta
El Paso	Dallas	Boston	Bergen & Passaic
Honolulu	Denver	Las Vegas	Chicago
Jacksonville	Houston	Philadelphia	Essex & Union
Lake County	New Orleans	Pittsburgh	Jersey City
New London	Oklahoma City	Reno	Kansas City, MO
Norfolk	Tulsa		Memphis
Omaha	Wichita		Miami
Orange County			Middlesex
San Antonio			Nashville
San Diego			Nassau
Tacoma			

EXHIBIT 3-4 Example of U.S. City Classification by Dominant Economic Base

*Location quotients do change over time causing cities to move from one EBC to another—however, this is infrequent.

Source: G. Mueller, "Refining Economic Diversification Strategies for Real Estate Portfolios," *Journal of Real Estate Research* 8(1), winter 1993. © American Real Estate Society. Reproduced by permission. All rights reserved.

cities, high-technology-dominated cities, government-dominated cities, diversified cities, and so on.

An example of this approach is shown in Exhibit 3-4. This study's author, Glenn Mueller (1993), classified cities into nine groups:

1. Farm
2. F.I.R.E.[6]
3. Government
4. Manufacturing
5. Military
6. Mining (including oil & gas)
7. Service
8. Transportation
9. Diversified

Mueller examined employment data for each city and calculated location quotients for each of the nine industrial classifications based on SIC codes. The highest location quotient in each city determined its classification. If no industry group had an LQ much greater than 1.0, then the city was classified in the diversified group. Notice that the economic clusters identified in Mueller's study do not particularly correspond to geographic regions. For example, manufacturing-based cities are not all in the Northeast or Midwest, but include at least some cities in the South and West, such as Charlotte, San Jose, and Seattle. Mueller's analysis indicated that a real estate investment strategy using economic-based categories such as those listed would provide better diversification than a purely physical geographic diversification strategy, such as putting investments in each major geographic region of the country (like Northeast, Southeast, Southwest, and so on).

Of course, real estate investment performance depends not only on patterns in the space market which reflects the city economic bases described in this section, but also on behavior in the asset market. And even performance just within the space market, rents and occupancy, depends not only on the demand for space, which is the focus of economic base analysis, but also on the response on the supply side of the space market.

A city may have strong growth in demand for real estate usage based on its economic growth and still not produce good real estate investment performance (in the sense of growth in rents or property values). If the city's real estate demand growth is eagerly matched by equal or even greater supply growth from new construction and development, rents will not increase in the long run. (See Part I.)

3.5 Chapter Summary

This chapter presented a brief introduction and overview of the major theories and principles that have come from geography and spatial economics to explain the rise and fall of cities. This is obviously knowledge fundamental to making rational and informed real estate investment decisions. Some of the concepts covered in this chapter, such as central place theory and economic base theory, are relevant not only at the big-picture level of understanding the overall system of cities, but also at the more applied level at which real estate professionals make specific location analyses and decisions.

---

[6]Stands for "Finance, Insurance, and Real Estate," a category of professional business occupations characteristic of office employment.

KEY TERMS

system of cities
rank/size rule (Zipf's Law)
centralizing (centripetal) forces
decentralizing (centrifugal) forces
economies of scale
economies of agglomeration
positive locational externalities
cumulative causation

central place theory (CPT)
theory of urban hierarchy
hinterlands
threshold market
agglomeration shadows
economic base
export base theory
export (basic) sector

service (nonbasic) sector
location quotient (LQ)
standard industrial classification (SIC)
employment multiplier effect
population multiplier
classification of cities
economic cluster of cities

STUDY QUESTIONS

3.1. What is the "rank/size rule" (or Zipf's Law)? What is the implication of this rule for patterns of city size in an economy?

3.2. In 2000, the Census Bureau's estimate of the population of the New York City Consolidated Metropolitan Statistical Area (CMSA) was 21,199,865. For Boston, it was 5,819,100. According to the rank/size rule and the rank of Boston as indicated in Exhibit 3-1B, what should the population of Boston have been?

3.3. While the rank/size rule generally describes the distribution of city sizes remarkably well, it does tend to overpredict the number of small cities in an economy; there are fewer small towns than predicted by the theoretical rank/size rule. What explanation, based on volatility of growth, has been proposed to explain the discrepancy? [Hint: See the text box "What Causes the Rank/Size Rule?"]

3.4. Look at the rank/size chart of cities in the European Union (EU) shown in Exhibit 3-5. Do European cities' rank/sizes appear to conform to the exponential shape predicted by Zipf's Law as well as U.S. cities seem to do? Why do you suppose the rank/size

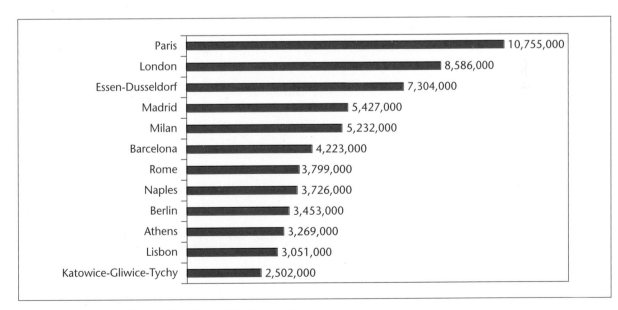

EXHIBIT 3-5 Population of Largest Urban Areas of the European Union

Source: "Demographia World Urban Areas." *Demographia.* July 2012. http://www.demographia.com/db-worldua.pdf

rule might not apply as well for Europe? [Hint: Has Europe historically been a single system of cities like the United States, based on a geographically integrated economy?] Suppose that the EU is far along the way to becoming a geographically integrated economy. What implications does this hold for the system of cities in Europe, the rank/size rule, and the likely growth pattern of European cities in the twenty-first century?

3.5. Carefully explain the difference between *economies of scale* and *economies of agglomeration*.

3.6. Explain how the three major centripetal, or centralizing, economic forces can interact to create the phenomenon known as cumulative causation.

3.7. Use the concepts of agglomeration economies and positive locational externalities to explain why automobile dealerships tend to cluster (e.g., in auto malls). From an economic perspective, does it make sense that competitors locate close to each other? Can you use the same logic to justify the existence and layout of shopping malls?

3.8. Draw a diagram of the essential implication of central place and urban hierarchy theories. [Hint: Can you draw hexagons?]

3.9. What would you say are the implications of central place theory and hierarchy theory for a developer contemplating building a new shopping center at a site in a metropolitan area where there is already a similar size shopping center nearby?

3.10. What is *economic base analysis* (EBA)? According to EBA, what is the main factor underlying growth in city employment and population?

3.11. Which of the following are examples of a basic industry in a city?

a. Grocery store
b. Motel serving primarily traveling salespeople
c. Aircraft engine factory
d. Large hotel serving primarily out-of-town convention business

Explain your answer.

3.12. Explain why an increase in employment in the export (or basic) sectors leads to an even larger increase in total employment in a local area (i.e., explain the employment multiplier effect).

3.13. Consider the following simple model of employment growth due to growth in export sector employment: Total employment, N, is divided into export (basic) and service (nonbasic). Service employment is assumed to be a constant proportion, k, of total employment. Algebraically this implies $N = N_E + N_S$ and $N_S = kN$, where the subscripts "E" and "S" denote export and service, respectively, and k is a constant with $0 < k < 1$. Combine these two equations and simplify to derive an equation that relates total employment to export employment and an employment multiplier. [Hint: Start by substituting out N_S with kN in the total employment identity.]

3.14. The following are local and national employment figures for three industrial sectors. Calculate the location quotients for each industry, and state which industries are part of the export base of the local economy.

Industry	Local Employment	National Employment
Automobile assembly	10,000	1,500,000
Legal services	3,500	2,000,000
Alcoholic spirits production and distribution	2,500	400,000
Total all employment	300,000	120,000,000

3.15. One mayor candidate wants to support expansion of the convention center, another Mayor candidate wants to spend the same amount on a sports stadium, while the third candidate wants to spend this money on supporting a high tech research center and enterprise zone with lower property and business taxes. Compare these three alternatives in terms of which is more likely to create more jobs in the region and be explicit about the theory behind your answer.

INSIDE THE CITY I: SOME BASIC URBAN ECONOMICS

LEARNING OBJECTIVES

After reading this chapter, you should understand:

➲ What determines land rents in a city.

➲ Why and how a freely functioning, competitive land market will lead to land being used at its "highest and best use" (i.e., most productive use).

➲ What determines the relative land values at different locations within a city and the relative growth rate of these values at different locations.

We return to the cliché about the only three things that matter in real estate: location, location, and location. Chapter 3 dealt with the first level of location in this cliché, the big picture: why cities or other "central places" (such as shopping centers within cities) locate where they do, and why some such places grow more than others. The "places" treated in Chapter 3, however, were essentially dimensionless points on the plane, just dots. In this chapter and the next, we will address the second level of location in the cliché as we consider the nature of land use spatial patterns *within* cities.

Land use spatial patterns and dynamics exert tremendous influence on neighborhood property values and on what types of buildings and land uses are feasible and most productive at a given location at a given time. The study of location value we will embark on in this chapter (and continue in the next) is also of crucial importance in linking the space market to the asset market through the development industry, a link that is of vital importance in real estate investment performance. Keep in mind that location value is the major component in land value, and recall from Chapter 1 that land value plays the key role in determining the shape of the long-run supply function, which, in turn, governs the trend in rents.

A Threshold Concept: Urban Form

The general subject of both this chapter and the next is what is often called **urban form**. This term refers to the physical spatial characteristics of a city.[1] How big is the city spatially? What are its overall density and geographical dimensions? How does this density vary across different parts of the city? What are the patterns of the locations of different land uses, such as residential, commercial, and industrial, within the city? Where do high-income and low-income neighborhoods tend to locate? Obviously, urban form and how it changes over time vitally affect land values and rents and, therefore, a whole range of real estate business decisions within any city.

4.1 Some Basic Economic Principles of Urban Land Value and Use

Land is the most fundamental defining characteristic of real estate. If you want to deepen your understanding of real estate, a good place to start is by considering what determines the value of land.

4.1.1 Location and the Residual Nature of Land Value

Land derives its value from the fact that it is a necessary input, or **factor of production**. The real estate value of land therefore comes from what is known as derived demand: people are willing to pay for land not because of the value land has in and of itself, but because land is necessary to obtain other things that have consumption or production value. Urban land value derives from the fact that land is necessary to construct buildings, and buildings are necessary or useful for most types of production of goods or services and for some types of consumption, such as housing, shopping, and many forms of entertainment and learning. What makes one urban land parcel worth more than another is primarily location. Indeed, when you are buying a piece of urban land, what you are usually buying primarily is a particular location relative to access to other points of attraction. In this section, we will introduce an important, though simplified, perspective on land value known as the **residual theory of land value**.

Let's begin with a specific example. A factory produces clothing from bolts of cloth by combining inputs from labor, machines, energy, and land. The machines actually produce the articles of clothing from the raw cloth, but labor and energy are needed to operate the machines and move the output. Land is necessary because the machines and people and inventory take up space and need somewhere to locate. Indeed, where the factory is located will affect how profitable the manufacturing operation is because it will determine the costs of getting the raw material (bolts of cloth) to the factory and the finished products (articles of clothing) from the factory to the ultimate points of retail sale. The cost of the labor and energy to operate the machines will also likely be affected by the location.

Now consider all of these four basic types of inputs in the production process, known as production factors: land, labor, capital (i.e., physical capital, such as machines), and raw materials (including energy). All of these factors of production must be paid for by, and will therefore derive their value from, the value of the finished product. In dividing up the value of the finished product among the four factors of production, we can see that the defining characteristic of land that differentiates it from the other three factors is that land is fixed in location, even in the long run. If you own a parcel of land, you can never move it. You can never take it away to some other site where it might be able to earn more rent. The perspective of the residual theory of land value is that the three more **mobile factors** have to get paid first, in order to keep them from "running away" if they don't get paid an amount equal to what they could earn elsewhere, something the land cannot do. The gross value of the production on the site, measured by the total revenue earned by the clothing factory, will therefore go first to the mobile inputs. Only what is left over after the mobile factors have been

---

[1]The terms *urban spatial structure* and *urban morphology* are also used to describe this topic.

paid the necessary prevailing market costs will be available to the landowner. This is the residual theory of land value.

Let's consider this theory in our clothing-factory example. Suppose the factory earns gross sales revenues of $10 million per year. We can see that the raw materials must be paid for first based on their market values, or else the sellers of those materials simply would not sell to this factory, but rather take their goods elsewhere in the market. Let's suppose these raw materials cost $4 million, leaving $6 million of value to be added by the factory. Next, the factory labor has to get paid the prevailing market wage, or else the workers will quit and take jobs elsewhere. Let's suppose the workers (including the factory management team) earn $5 million. This leaves $1 million per year in profit after subtracting the $9 million cost of goods sold and management overhead from the gross revenues.

But, in the long run, this profit must provide a return on investment to the financial capital that was contributed to establish the factory. In particular, the physical capital—the machines, plant, and equipment (including the building)—must be paid for in the forms of return on and return of the financial capital that was invested. Otherwise, the financiers and investors who provided this capital will take it back (or in the long run they will not replace it when it wears out). Suppose this cost of built physical capital is $900,000 per year. (You can think of this $900,000 per year as rent for machines that are leased or as an annual mortgage payment to pay off a loan of the financial capital invested in the plant and equipment.) In the long run, all of this total $9,900,000 cost per year must be paid first to these more mobile factors, before the landowner can get her share: only $100,000 per year, the "residual" that is left over after the other factors have been paid. This $100,000 is the amount potentially available from the factory operation to pay rent for the land itself, for the location and space that it provides to the production process.[2]

While we have used the example of a clothing factory, it should be easy to see that we could have picked any other type of factory. Indeed, any type of urban land use can be seen as producing some output of goods or services of value, by combining some more mobile inputs with that of land (space and location). For example, a corporate headquarters office provides executive and control services for the rest of the corporation; a law office provides legal services for its clients; a shopping mall provides a convenient or stimulating environment for people to buy goods they need; and a house or apartment provides shelter and a conducive environment for the abode of a household.

The land is last in line to get paid among the inputs because it is "trapped"; it cannot go elsewhere. Of course, the residual theory of land value is a simplified model. The real world is a bit more complicated. But this model captures much of the essence of reality, at least in the long run, in a world where exchange of ownership is governed by free markets.

There is a flip side of the coin from the perspective of the residual theory of land value. Land may get only, but it also gets *all of*, the residual after the mobile factors have been paid their market values. In a well-functioning market system, competition among providers of the mobile factors of production ensures that no such factor need be paid more than its market value. This means that, at least in the long run, land can receive as rents all of any increase in profit that would occur either from an increase in the market value of production (holding the market values of the mobile input factors constant) or from a decrease in the cost of the mobile factors (holding the value of the output constant).

For example, if the factory in our previous example could sell its clothing output for $11 million instead of $10 million and the mobile factor costs remained the same, then the land could claim $1,100,000 per year. The same would occur if the costs of the mobile factors could be reduced to $8,900,000 instead of $9,900,000, holding the output value at $10,000,000.

---

[2]How do the owners of the factory get their profits? They have not really been left out of the model. The factory owners would typically either be owners of the machines and/or the land, or they can be viewed as providing some of the labor, in the form of the managerial and entrepreneurship services necessary to run the business. Apart from their possible role as landowners, the factory owners are therefore part of the mobile factors of production that must be paid prior to the landowner, in the long run, or they will take their contributions elsewhere.

How would the landlord "capture" the extra profit from the tenant? In the long run (which is what we are talking about here), the tenant's lease would expire, and the present tenant would then be in competition with other potential tenants for the land. That competition would lead the potential tenants to bid up their offered land rent to a level at which the tenants will just be making sufficient profit for themselves, that is, just covering their own costs including normal profits. All other remaining revenues from production on the site would be included in the land rent offer.[3]

4.1.2 Competition, Equilibrium, and Highest and Best Use

While the residual theory of land value offers some important insight, economists note that it is a somewhat simplified perspective. In a well-functioning land market, competition exists both among providers of the mobile factors of production and among landowners. The residual theory considers the competition among the providers of the mobile factors, but it seems to ignore or discount the effect of competition among landowners. While each parcel of land is unique to some extent, a number of parcels are usually similar enough that they could substitute well for one another for the purposes of most potential users. So, there is competition in the land market among alternative sites. Similarly, while each potential land user may be unique in some respects, a number of potential users usually provide competition on the other side of the market as well. Of course, the long-lived nature of buildings means that land uses have limited flexibility to change quickly, but in the long run, land use can and does change, so that the urban form we observe does tend to reflect basic economic forces and values.

Among the most powerful of economic forces is the tendency of markets to move toward equilibrium between supply and demand. Equilibrium is defined as the condition in which the market does not need to adjust the level of output any further, because all consumers and producers are satisfied with the current level of consumption and production, given the current prices prevailing in the market (the equilibrium prices). A condition of market equilibrium that is relevant to the consideration of land value is reflected in a famous economic principle known as "Euler's Theorem." According to this theorem, each factor of production will be paid an equilibrium price (or wage) equal to its marginal product, that is, equal to the marginal value of what it contributes to the production process. This applies to land as well as to the mobile inputs to production. From the perspective of Euler's Theorem, land is not necessarily any more "residual" than are the other factors of production. In a sufficiently well-functioning land market, competition among landowners will drive the price of each land parcel to equal the value of its marginal contribution to the production process. But this raises the question: *Which production process?*—that is, to produce which good?

To begin to answer this question, first consider another important characteristic condition of equilibrium in a well-functioning competitive market. In such a market, no participant on either side of the market can be made better off by a change away from the equilibrium without making someone else worse off. Indeed, with perfect markets, any benefits to gainers from a change away from the equilibrium could not offset the losses to the losers from that change.[4] This condition is known as Pareto optimality.[5] In the case of the land market, such equilibrium will be reflected in the fact that each landowner will rent to the user who is willing to pay the highest rent for the land. Otherwise, at least in the long

---

[3]The picture presented here is simplified by the assumption of "perfect competition." That is, we are assuming that there are sufficient numbers of potential tenants for the land competing with each other so that they bid away any excess profit. A more realistic rule of thumb that is often applied in the practice of valuing specific land parcels is to say that the land value is determined by the "second best" developer of the land. The very best developer (or tenant in the present model) for the land may have unique abilities to make profitable use of the site. This uniqueness could allow the very best user to capture and retain for themselves much or all of the value they add above the "second best" use for the site.

[4]Suppose not. If one or more parties can be made better off without making anyone else worse off, then why would the market outcome not adjust to enable such "free" benefits to be captured? Until such adjustment is complete, the market is not in equilibrium.

[5]See more on Pareto optimality, in the context of negotiation procedures, in the CD Appendix to Chapter 12.

EXHIBIT 4-1
Highest and Best Use
Example
© OnCourse Learning

	Site 1		Site 2	
	Clothing Factory	**Grocery Store**	**Clothing Factory**	**Grocery Store**
Revenues	$10,000,000	$4,600,000	$10,000,000	$5,000,000
Mobile Factor Costs	9,900,000	4,550,000	9,990,000	4,625,000
Residual (Land Rent)	100,000	50,000	10,000	375,000

run, the dissatisfied landowners would kick out their current users and rent or sell to those who are willing and able to pay more. This maximizes the total rent earned by all the land (thereby maximizing the productivity of the society). Equivalently, from the perspective of the other side of the market, equilibrium is characterized by the condition that no land user would rather be located at a different place, given the cost or rent they would have to pay for another location. Otherwise, they would simply move to that other place and pay the rent charged there.[6]

Because of its importance, let us consider a bit more concretely what the concept of equilibrium in the land market means by extending our previous example of the clothing factory. Suppose there are two alternative potential uses for the site in question, either the clothing factory or a grocery store. Let us further suppose that there are two possible locations, the one previously described and an alternative site located a bit closer to most residences in the neighborhood but a bit farther from the main interstate highways. Exhibit 4-1 summarizes the revenues and mobile factor costs for each use at each site.

As described previously, the clothing factory at site 1 can earn revenues of $10 million per year, with mobile factor costs of $9.9 million, implying that the clothing factory could pay $100,000 per year in rent to the landowner at site 1. The same factory at site 2 could still earn $10 million in revenue, but would face $90,000 in additional transport costs getting the raw material to the factory and shipping out the finished product, due to the greater distance from interstate-highway access. The result is that, located at site 2, the clothing factory would have only $10,000 residual left over with which to pay land rent.

The grocery store faces a somewhat different situation. While it too would experience lower transport costs by locating at site 1, it would be less conveniently located to serve its retail customers in the residential neighborhood. Consequently, it would have to discount its prices and, therefore, would earn less revenue at site 1. Indeed, the loss in revenue more than offsets the delivery cost reduction for the grocery store. At site 1, the grocery store would earn revenues of $4.6 million with mobile factor costs (including delivery costs for receiving its merchandise) of $4.55 million, leaving only $50,000 residual available to pay rent. At site 2, the grocery store would earn $5 million in revenues, with $4.625 million mobile factor costs, leaving $375,000 to pay land rent.

The grocery store can pay more than the clothing factory for site 2 ($375,000 vs. $10,000 annual rent), while the clothing factory can pay more for site 1 ($100,000 vs. $50,000 annual rent). In the long run, both the factory and the store could move, and both the site 1 owner and the site 2 owner could remove any tenant (and redevelop the site). Therefore, only one result can be consistent with long-run equilibrium in the land market: the factory must locate at site 1 and the store at site 2.

---

[6]Once again, we are simplifying by describing "perfect markets." Pareto optimality in land markets requires not only perfect competition on both sides, but also a lack of locational externalities, also known as spillover effects. Recall from Chapter 3 that externalities occur when what is done on one land parcel affects the value of adjacent or nearby land parcels. Such spillover effects can be either positive or negative. The existence of spillover effects in the real world is the major reason for land use control and regulation by communal authorities, such as zoning ordinances enacted by local governments.

The equilibrium described in this example results in each location being used at its **highest and best use (HBU)**. This means that each site is used in the way that is most productive for that location. Note that productivity in this sense is represented by the *net* difference between the value of what is produced on the site and the costs of the mobile factors of production, that is, the land residual as we have defined it. Thus, equilibrium in the land market tends to result in land parcels being used at their highest and best use in the long run.[7]

4.1.3 Role of Transport Costs: The Bid-Rent Curve

From the preceding section, you can see that land rent (and hence land value) differs from one place to another because the HBU residual value differs from one place to another. And the HBU residual value differs from one place to another primarily as a result of differences in transportation costs. When the transportation costs faced by the users of the site are lower, the residual value is higher, other things being equal. For example, the clothing factory could make more profit located nearer to the highway where the delivery costs of both its inputs and outputs were lower. The grocery store could make more profit located nearer its customers, who then would not incur as much transportation costs getting to and from the store.

To understand the importance of transport costs, you must conceptualize these costs broadly. Transport costs include the costs of moving both inputs and outputs, costs borne both directly by the sellers and indirectly by the buyers. Of particular importance for the value of nonindustrial land, transport cost is not limited to the direct monetary outlay for transportation, such as gasoline cost. For passenger transportation, travel *time* is usually the most important component of transport cost. In our grocery store example, it is likely not gasoline cost, but the value of the time wasted in travel to and from the store, the inconvenience of shoppers having to travel farther, that would force the store to discount its prices at site 1. The implication is that land market equilibrium, the highest and best use of land, will be characterized by the *minimization of aggregate transportation costs* for the society as a whole (for the given allocation of production and consumption).

The role of transport costs in determining HBU and land value leads to a key concept in classical urban economics, the **bid-rent curve** (or **bid-rent function**). The bid-rent is the maximum rent that a potential user would "bid," or be willing to pay, for a site or location. This bid-rent is essentially the same thing as the residual value discussed previously. Each potential user of land has a bid-rent curve (or function), which relates the user's bid-rent to the location of the land site, showing in particular how the bid-rent changes as a function of the user's distance from some **central point**. The central point is the point at which the transportation costs are minimized for that use, the point at which the bid-rent or residual value is maximized.

Each potential land use has its own bid-rent function. We might imagine the entrance to a nearby interstate highway as being the central point for the clothing factory, because the highway reduces travel time and cost for its inputs and outputs. If site 1 is one mile from this highway entrance and site 2 is four miles from it, then the value of the bid-rent function for the clothing factory is $100,000 at one mile, and $10,000 at four miles from this central point. The relevant central point for the grocery store would be different, perhaps the intersection of two arterial streets at the center of the residential neighborhood it serves. Suppose site 2 is at this intersection and site 1 is three miles from it. The grocery store's bid-rent function would be valued at $375,000 at site 2 and $50,000 at site 1.

Graphically, a bid-rent function is depicted on a chart with the vertical axis located at a central point and the horizontal axis representing distance from that point. At the central point, transportation costs are minimized, and the bid-rent is therefore maximized. The amount of the bid-rent at the central point (the height of the intercept on the vertical axis in the graph) depends on the inherent productivity or value of the land use when

---

[7]The social desirability of preserving undeveloped some land parcels can be represented in this model by recognizing that some parcels may have, due to their aesthetic or environmental qualities, a *direct* demand value (i.e., value in "consumption" as undeveloped land) exceeding any *derived* demand value in production, which they would have under development.

EXHIBIT 4-2 Bid-Rent
Functions of Three Land
Uses with Differing
Productivity and Sensitivity
to Transport Cost
© OnCourse Learning

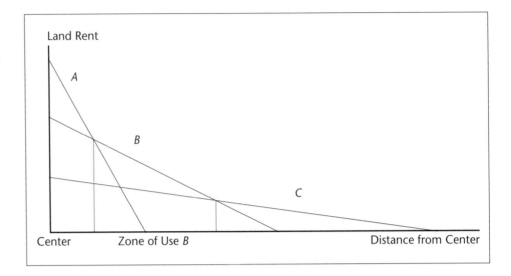

transportation costs are minimized. Land uses that are more productive (when transport costs are minimized) will have higher bid-rents at the central point. As you move away from the central point, the bid-rent falls as the transportation costs rise due to the less-central location. The rate at which the bid-rent falls, the slope of the bid-rent function, depends on the magnitude of transportation costs in the production process of the given land use and on how sensitive these transportation costs are to distance from the central point. Land uses that are more sensitive to transport costs will have bid-rent curves with steeper downward slopes, bid-rents falling more quickly with distance from the central point.

This is depicted in Exhibit 4-2, which shows the bid-rent function for three different land uses, labeled *A*, *B*, and *C*. Use *A* has the greatest productivity when transportation costs are minimized, and so has a higher bid-rent at the central point. Use *A* also is more sensitive to transport costs, perhaps, for example, because use *A* requires a lot of people with a high value of time to commute to it every day. If they have to travel even just a little farther, on average, then use *A* will suffer a lot of loss in productivity or value generation. Use *C* has the lowest productivity in general, but also the least sensitivity to transport costs, and so has the "shallowest" bid-rent function. Use *B* is between the other two in both respects. The result is that, *in equilibrium* in the land market, assuming all three uses have the same central point, use *A* will prevail closest to that center, being able to outbid the other uses, followed by use *B* a bit farther out from the center, followed by use *C* farthest out.

4.1.4 Summary of Basic Urban Land Value and Land Use Principles

The preceding section presented several of the basic economic principles of land value and use determination. Because the underlying demand for land is a derived demand, and other more mobile factors are required to produce value from land, land value is based on the residual available after the other factors (labor, capital, energy, etc.) have been paid their going market rates. This residual is strongly influenced by transportation costs, which, in turn, are strongly influenced by location, making land value largely a function of location. Different types of land uses have different productivities, different sensitivities to transportation costs, and different relevant geographical central points, that is, locations where their relevant transportation costs would be minimized. Therefore, different land uses have different residual values, or bid-rents, they would be willing and able to pay for any given site. In long-run equilibrium in a well-functioning, competitive land market (when, in principle, even built structures can be changed through the development or redevelopment process), each land site will be used for its highest and best use, the use that can pay the highest bid-rent. This will tend to maximize the aggregate land value (residual value) and minimize the aggregate transportation costs of the society.

Finally, let's consider a stylized, extreme case for twenty-first century pedagogical purposes. Suppose all transportation was costless (or, equivalently, no transportation was necessary for physical production). Bid-rent functions would flatten out, and centrality would lose value. However, recall our point in section 3.3.1 of the previous chapter about centripetal forces, including the value of agglomeration. Some of this value derives from, or may simply reflect the fact that, people like to get together. Humans are social creatures. Even in a world with completely flat bid-rent functions, there would still be "central places," locations of agglomeration where people would want to be and would congregate, even if fundamentally only because others *are there*. But such places would be more free to locate or spring up anywhere, irrespective of (nonexistent) transport costs. They would be fixed in location only because of the longevity of structures and the inertia of pre-existent patterns or else because of natural amenities or attractions. Within such centers land value would be high. This is why "virtual real estate" has real value even in virtual worlds such as Second Life® where avatars can move freely and instantaneously through virtual space.[8]

4.2 Classic Monocentric City Model

The basic economic principles and concepts regarding land value and use described in the previous section have been combined in a very simple and elegant model of urban form known as the **monocentric city**. While this model greatly simplifies and abstracts from the complicated reality of modern cities, it captures enough of the essence to offer useful insights. Indeed, the monocentric model is a classic example of how theory, by simplifying reality, reveals important insights into the nature of that reality.[9]

In the monocentric city model, only one central point exists in the whole city, and this central point applies to all potential uses of the land. Indeed, in the simplest version of the model, which we will consider here, there is only one type of land use in the city, housing. The simple monocentric city is a circle of a certain radius extending out from the central point. The central point might be thought of as representing the downtown or central business district (CBD), to which all the households must commute every day to produce some good that enables them to earn the income they must use to meet their housing costs, as well as all their other consumption needs. From this income, they also must pay the transportation costs for their daily commute. These transportation costs are, of course, a function of the distance of their houses from the CBD.

4.2.1 Circlopolis, the Quintessential Monocentric City

To make this model a bit more concrete, let us quantify a stylized example city we will call Circlopolis, which exists in the land of Agricolia. Outside the city, the land is farmed; inside the city, all land is residential, built to a density of two persons per acre, or 1,280 per square mile. The metropolitan population of Circlopolis is 1 million, which gives Circlopolis an area of 1,000,000/ 1,280, or 781 square miles. This determines the **radius to the urban boundary**, recalling that the formula for the area of a circle is π times the radius squared, so the radius is the square root of the area divided by π, which in this case is about 16 miles.

---

[8]Another way rent gradients flatten out in the twenty-first century: polycentrism in metropolitan development. (But that is a topic for the next chapter.).

[9]The following discussion draws heavily from DiPasquale and Wheaton (1996), to which the reader is recommended for a more detailed and in-depth treatment of this topic. In general, the monocentric city model, as well as much of the location theory described in the previous section, has its origins in the theories developed by German economist Johann von Thunen early in the nineteenth century. While von Thunen focused on an agricultural state, much more recent extensions of the city model (of which the monocentric model described here is only a very simple version) have been attributed to such American economists as William Alonso, Edwin Mills, Richard Muth, and Dennis Capozza. (See the references and additional reading for Part II for some specific references.)

Now consider the annual rent for housing at the edge of the city, 16 miles from the center at the boundary between the urban and agricultural land use. In order to induce a farmer to sell his land to enable it to be converted from agricultural production to urban housing, you must pay the farmer the opportunity value of the land in its agricultural use. This would be the agricultural use residual (bid-rent) for the land, equal to the net profit per acre from agricultural production after all the mobile factors have been paid. Suppose this **agricultural rent** is $500 per acre per year. In addition, you must pay the annualized cost of building a house. Suppose there is one resident per house, and houses cost $50,000 to build, which can be paid for by a permanent mortgage at 10 percent per year, giving an annual **construction cost rent** of $5,000 per house. With two houses per acre, that makes the total annual housing rent per acre at the city edge $10,500, consisting of $10,000 to pay for the construction and $500 to pay for lost agricultural rent.

How does this real property rent change as we move in from the urban boundary toward the city center? The residents of houses at more central locations will not have to pay as much in commuting costs, so they will be able to pay more rent for housing and still maintain the same overall level of welfare. In fact, the *real property rent must rise as we approach the center at exactly the rate that the transportation costs fall.* This condition is required by equilibrium.

To see this, suppose this condition did not hold. Suppose, for example, that the real property rent rose by less than the decrease in transportation cost as you moved toward the center. Then residents living closer to the center would be better off than those living farther out. This would cause everybody to want to move closer to the center. Demand would then outstrip supply for more central locations, while houses near the periphery would go searching for residents. Competition among residents bidding for centrally located lots, and among landlords owning peripheral lots trying to find tenants, would force the rent for the more centrally located lots up and the rents for the peripheral lots down until the relative levels were such that everybody was equally well off, considering both their housing rents and their commuting costs. A symmetrical argument would apply if housing rents rose more than the decrease in transportation costs as one moved closer to the center. In that case, everyone would want to live farther out, bidding up the rents there until the incentive for peripheral houses was eliminated. In equilibrium, therefore, the rents must be such that the total of housing and commuting costs is the same across all distances from the center.

This tells us that the bid-rent curve for housing in Circlopolis must have a slope equal to the transportation cost per mile per acre. This slope is known as the **rent gradient**. It tells you how much the equilibrium real property rent per acre declines per mile of additional distance from the center of the city. *The rent gradient equals the transportation cost per mile per person times the number of people per acre.*

Suppose that in Circlopolis the transportation cost per person is $250 per year per mile of distance from the CBD (round-trip commuting cost). Then, with two inhabitants per acre, the rent gradient must be $500 per mile. Housing located one mile from the urban boundary will rent for $250 more per year than housing on the boundary, or $500 more per acre of land. By the time we get to the center of the city (16 miles from the edge) where there is no transportation cost, the housing rent will be $4,000 more per house (or per person), or $8,000 more per acre, than it is at the periphery. So, the total real property rent per year at the center will be some $18,500 per year, including $500 in agricultural opportunity cost rent, $10,000 in construction cost rent, and $8,000 in **location rent** (reflecting the **location premium** in the site). Note that the location rent per acre at the center exactly equals the transportation cost per acre at the periphery.

Now that we know the housing and transport costs for the inhabitants of Circlopolis, we can see how they are using their income. Suppose they have annual incomes of $50,000 each. They are spending per year $9,250 each on the combination of housing and transportation. (Recall that there are two persons in the form of two single-individual households per acre.) So they must each be spending $40,750 per year on "other consumption" besides housing and transportation.[10] We have "backed into" this observation about other consumption

---

[10]In the magical city of Circlopolis, there are no taxes!

EXHIBIT 4-3 Cross-Section of Real Property Rents in Circlopolis and Agricolia

© OnCourse Learning

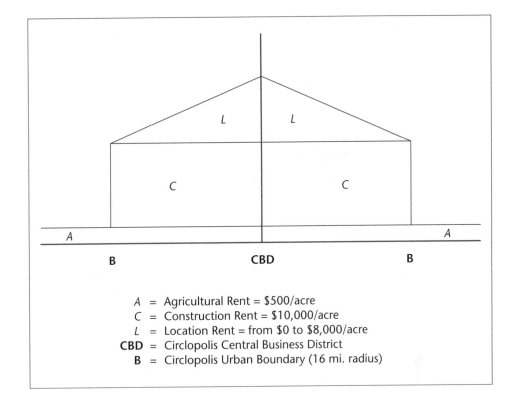

A   = Agricultural Rent = $500/acre
C   = Construction Rent = $10,000/acre
L   = Location Rent = from $0 to $8,000/acre
CBD = Circlopolis Central Business District
B   = Circlopolis Urban Boundary (16 mi. radius)

expenditure, but in reality the direction of causality may go both ways in the long run. How much the Circlopolites want to spend on other consumption (given their income level) also determines how much they have available to spend on housing and transportation, and this, in turn, will in the long run determine the size and density of Circlopolis. This can explain why we see such different densities in cities in different countries, since income levels and culturally based preferences for different types of housing and lifestyles differ widely across countries.

The simple monocentric city model represented by Circlopolis in the land of Agricolia is depicted graphically in Exhibit 4-3. The exhibit depicts a cross-section of real property rents from the agricultural hinterland just beyond the urban boundary through the center of the city.

4.2.2 Using the Model: Some Principles about How Rents and City Size Change

The usefulness of the monocentric city model is that it reduces a very complex phenomenon, a city, down to a simple interaction among a few basic economic forces. This allows us to see easily what causes some of the essential features of the urban form. This, in turn, enables us to examine how rents and urban form may be affected by changes that can happen over time in an economy or society, such as growth in population or income, or changes in transport costs. These changes can have very important effects on real estate opportunities. So let us now use the monocentric city model to examine these effects in our Circlopolis example by changing one variable at a time and seeing how this affects the land rents and urban form variables within the model.

Population   We begin by examining the effect of an increase in the population of Circlopolis, holding density and transportation cost per mile constant. With density constant, the area of the city, and hence the radius, must expand. In particular, for every percent increase

EXHIBIT 4-4 Effect of Population Growth with Density and Transport Cost Constant

© OnCourse Learning

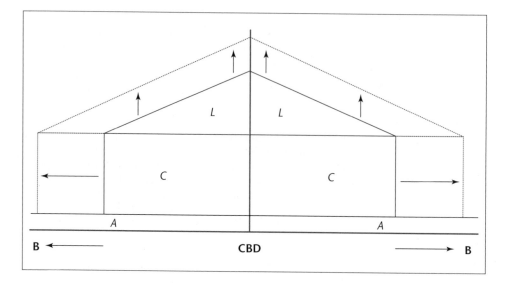

in population, the area must increase by an equal percent (for constant density), and the radius must increase by about half that percent.[11] The housing rent at the new periphery must equal the construction cost rent plus the agricultural rent, based on the same arguments as before, which have not changed. Likewise, the rent gradient as we move in from the new periphery must still be the same $500 per mile (because transport cost and density are the same as before), again based on the same equilibrium argument. So this means that population increase, holding density and other prices constant, must increase rents all over Circlopolis. This is depicted in Exhibit 4-4.

We can summarize the analysis up to now in an important principle:

Principle 1:
Other things being equal, larger cities will have higher average location rents.

This basic principle, derived from such a simple model of urban form and land values, is no doubt a major reason that land prices, rents, and housing costs are so much higher in the nation's largest cities, such as New York, Chicago, Los Angeles, and San Francisco. (For example, in 2010 the median house price in San Francisco was $549,000, while in Cincinnati it was $129,000.)

Perhaps this size principle seems intuitively obvious. But the monocentric city model allows you to deepen your understanding of why larger cities have higher rents. In particular, notice what caused the higher rents when we considered the growth in population in Circlopolis. In our simple model, we were holding density constant. Therefore, land rents (per acre of land) would tend to be higher in larger cities, even if such cities were no denser than smaller cities. This suggests that if larger cities are to keep rents per housing unit at the same level as those in smaller cities, then some combination of higher density and/or lower construction cost must prevail in larger cities. This, in turn, means that, if we hold rent per household constant across cities of different sizes, larger cities must be characterized by some combination of greater density and/or smaller housing units. The 500-square-foot efficiency apartment in Manhattan, stacked 40 on top of each other, might rent for the same as a 1,000-square-foot garden apartment in central Atlanta.

---

[11]If the area of the circle increases by p percent (that is, $AREA_{NEW}/AREA_{OLD} = 1 + p$), then

$$\frac{RADIUS_{NEW}}{RADIUS_{OLD}} = \frac{\sqrt{AREA_{NEW}/\pi}}{\sqrt{AREA_{OLD}/\pi}} = \sqrt{1+p} \approx 1 + p/2$$

for relatively small values of p. For example, if $p = 10\%$, then the more exact value of $\sqrt{1.1} - 1$ is 4.9%.

In fact, we can say more than this. We can see that what caused the higher rents in the population example was *not* the population per se, or even the area of the city, but the *length of the radius,* the distance of the urban boundary from the CBD. The rent gradient is fixed, based on transportation costs and density. The rent at the urban boundary is fixed, based on the agricultural opportunity cost and the building construction cost. Therefore, what governs the change in the average rent is the change in the distance each point finds itself from the urban boundary.

This is important because, for a given population and density, the radius of the city (i.e., the distance from the CBD to the urban edge) must be greater if the city cannot avail itself of an entire 360-degree arc. In reality, geographic constraints on the urban arc are quite common as, for example, with a city on a coastline or peninsula.[12] Most of the largest U.S. cities are on coasts or are cut by waterways or mountain ranges that effectively prevent the use of a large proportion of the arc around the CBD. This no doubt extends the radius of cities such as New York, Chicago, Los Angeles, and San Francisco, further adding to their tendency to support high rents.[13]

It is also interesting to note that if incomes were constant across cities of different sizes, then inhabitants of larger cities would either have to consume less housing (i.e., live in smaller houses and/or have less land per house) or spend more on transport costs, compared to residents of smaller cities. Either way, inhabitants of larger cities would have less economic welfare than inhabitants of smaller cities. Over time, such an imbalance in economic welfare between citizens of smaller and larger cities would not be tenable in an integrated economy. People would migrate from larger to smaller cities, *unless the larger cities offered higher incomes,* on average. But this is exactly what happens in the real world. Larger cities do tend to have higher average per capita incomes than smaller cities. Put the other way around, cities that are able to offer higher incomes tend to attract migration and over time grow larger in population relative to other cities, until an equilibrium across cities is reached. The reality is that the average resident of New York or Los Angeles is, in fact, more productive than the average resident of Cincinnati or Cleveland, for example.

If we consider population changes within one city over time, then the monocentric city model can give some insight into how much, or how fast, rents may change over time, and how such changes may differ in different parts of the city. For example, it is not uncommon for a metropolitan area to increase 10 percent in population over a 10-year period, or indeed over a 5-year period in many Sunbelt cities. Holding density constant as before, such a population increase will result in approximately a 5 percent increase in the urban radius, from 16 miles to 16.8 miles in our Circlopolis example. All locations now have 0.8 mile additional location rent, or an increase in rent of $400 per acre per year.[14] Notice that the increase in rent is constant across all the preexisting points in the city, but the previous rent was higher for more centrally located points. This implies that the *percentage* increase in rent due to urban growth will be greater closer to the periphery of the metropolitan area. For example, at the old boundary, the rent grows from $10,500 per acre to $10,900 per acre, a 3.8 percent increase. At the center, the increase from $18,500 to $18,900 is only 2.2 percent.

---

[12]The existence of lakes or unbuildable wetlands, slopes, or preserved open spaces or conservation land has the same effect of reducing the effective arc, even if the effect may occur at all points of the compass.

[13]When the arc around which a city can expand is limited by, say, bodies of water or mountain ranges, the same total area must fit into a fraction of a circle. The radius equals $\sqrt{A/(\pi F)}$, where A is the area and F is the fraction (less than or equal to 1) of the full 360-degree arc around the CBD that can be used for growth. This is consistent with our point in Chapter 1 that a rising long-run marginal cost curve (increasing development costs including land cost), implying increasing real rents in equilibrium in the space market, would tend to occur in areas where land supply is constrained in the face of growing demand. Growing demand may be thought of as population growth in the present example. Keep in mind that the radius is the distance from the CBD to the edge of the developed urban area, for example, from Manhattan north up the Hudson Valley.

[14]Recall that the additional rent occurs because there are more total people now in the city competing for (i.e., bidding for) the locations within the city, including some people who are farther from the center than anybody used to be when the periphery was not as far out. In order for all these competing citizens to be indifferent about their present location versus any other location (the characteristic of equilibrium), rents must settle at a level so that the people at the periphery are satisfied to live that far out considering the amount of location rent they are saving by doing so.

EXHIBIT 4-5 Effect of Population Growth with Area Constant

© OnCourse Learning

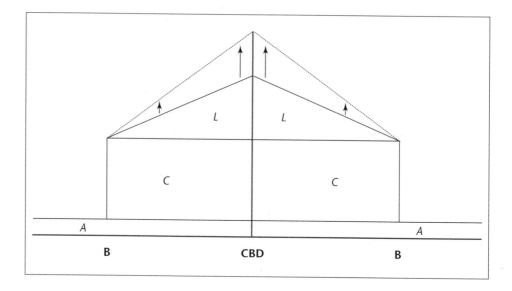

This difference is much more pronounced for the location rent component of the total real property rent.

Now suppose that instead of holding density constant we held the area of the city constant, as might occur through regulatory or geographic constraints on land use (zoning, "green belts," islands, or mountains, for example). Not surprisingly, the model reveals that population growth would still result in higher land rents. But in this case the reason is different. The radius is fixed, so the reason for the higher location rents cannot be greater distance from the urban edge. However, with the radius fixed and the population growing, the density must increase. Now recall that the land rent gradient in equilibrium must equal the difference in transportation cost per mile *per acre*. We are holding the transportation cost *per person* constant, but with more persons living per acre, the transportation costs per acre must increase. So the rent gradient would increase. For example, if Circlopolis's population increased by 50 percent to 1,500,000, there would be three inhabitants per acre instead of two, and this would increase the rent gradient from $500 per mile to $750 per mile. The rent at the urban boundary would still be the same, but land rent everywhere else would increase due to the increased location premium. The new peak rent at the center would be $22,500 (including $12,000 per year of location rent) instead of the old center rent of $18,500 (a 22 percent increase). This is depicted in Exhibit 4-5.[15]

Thus, while population growth will always tend to increase land rents in a city, *how* the city grows will affect the nature and geographic distribution of those increases. This can be expressed in a second basic principle derived from the monocentric city model:

> Principle 2:
> *If a city grows by increasing area rather than density, property rent growth will be relatively greater closer to the periphery; but if a city grows by increasing density instead of area, property rent growth will be relatively greater the closer to the center of the city.*

It is likely that these two principles will continue to be important in the twenty-first century, but may play out differently in different regions. Metropolitan population growth in many cities in mature regions such as the United States and (even more in) Europe will likely

---

[15]Note, however, that in this example the rent *per person* would actually decline in the center, from $18,500/2 = $9,250/year, to $22,500/3 = $7,500/year. This is because in our simple model we kept construction cost the same per acre (increasing from 1.0 to 1.5 persons per room).

be much slower in the twenty-first century than in the twentieth century, but such growth will likely be a major factor in many emerging regions that are still undergoing substantial urbanization. For example, for the leading metro areas listed in Exhibit 3-1B of the previous chapter, the U.N.-projected population growth from 2015 to 2030 is only 9 percent in the United States, but 24 percent in China and 32 percent in India. The tendency or ability to expand effective metropolitan geographic boundaries (commuting radius) may also vary. Rapidly developing countries such as China and India may rapidly expand urbanized spatial areas. In contrast, mature U.S. cities with extensive exurban commuter-sheds may already be near their effective limits (unless technological developments further reduce transport frictions, as discussed below).

Transport Costs   Population growth is not the only basic phenomenon that typically affects the modern city. A second important point to consider is what would happen as a result of a reduction in transport costs per person per mile, holding population and income constant. This could occur, for example, through improvements in transportation technology or infrastructure. In fact, the twentieth century witnessed almost continual improvements in these areas. It is likely that such improvements will continue well into the twenty-first century, especially if one considers the partial substitutability between telecommunications and transportation.[16] The advent of cell phones, laptop computers, the Internet, and other telecommunications developments will allow more flexible location and timing of work and shopping activity, which effectively reduces transport costs. Technological improvements in the automobile and mass transit, including greater fuel efficiency, greater safety and reliability, more efficient traffic control, and a more pleasant or productive travel environment (such as is provided by vehicle air-conditioning, stereo sound systems, cell phones, etc.), all act effectively to reduce transport costs.[17]

We know that a reduction in transport costs per person per mile per year will reduce the rent gradient.[18] This can have various effects on land values and urban form. The two extreme alternatives are depicted in Exhibits 4-6 and 4-7. In the first case (4-6), the residents of Circlopolis have elected to spend at least some of the transport cost savings on purchasing more urban land. Such urban-density-reducing behavior might be reflected in the purchase of, for example, houses with larger lots farther out in the countryside, or neighborhoods with more parkland and golf courses, or even shopping centers with more parking spaces. Such a density-reducing result of transport improvements would have the effect of increasing land rents near the periphery and reducing land rents at the center.

Indeed, the pure effect of a density reduction of the city, even without a reduction in transport costs, is to reduce the *absolute* land rents in the center of the city.[19] Transport cost reduction will only magnify this reduction.

---

[16]Even in the absence of any reduction in transport cost per person-mile of movement, telecommunications and computing developments may allow a reduction in the number of commuting or shopping trips per capita per year, for example, by enabling people to work at home or shop on the Internet. This reduces transport costs per acre (per unit of time), at a given density and given distance from the central node. Transport cost per acre (per unit of time) is what affects the land rent gradient.

[17]As noted previously, we need to think of transport costs as not merely the monetary outlay for travel, but also all forms of "disutility" and inconvenience associated with travel. Even if average speeds do not increase (and travel time therefore does not decrease per mile), transport cost may fall if the disutility of the travel time decreases as a result of added comfort, productivity, or utility during the time traveling.

[18]Recall that the rent gradient is determined as the transport cost per mile per person times the density, and it would not make sense for transport cost reductions to increase the urban density. Therefore, transport cost reductions must reduce the rent gradient.

[19]This is because the location rent at the center of the city equals the rent gradient times the radius, and the rent gradient equals the transport cost per capita times the density. Thus, the rent gradient is directly proportional to the density, which is, in turn, inversely proportional to the area of the city. But the area of the city is not directly proportional to the radius, but rather to the *square* of the radius. Therefore, a decrease in density holding all else constant will result in a less-than-proportional increase in city radius, but a fully proportional reduction in rent gradient. For example, if density (and therefore rent gradient) were reduced by half, the radius would only increase by a factor proportional to the square root of two. Location rent at the center would be $\sqrt{2}/2$ times the previous location rent.

EXHIBIT 4-6 Effect of
Transport Cost Reduction
Savings Applied to Greater
Purchase of Land
© OnCourse Learning

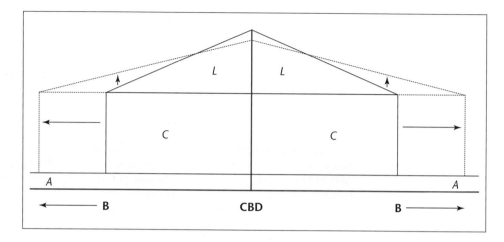

The second alternative possible effect of transport improvements occurs if the inhabitants of Circlopolis elect to keep their same level of residential density, that is, not to expand the spatial area of the city in spite of the transportation improvements. This would tend to happen only in cities that face severe physical or governmental constraints on spatial expansion (or perhaps in cultures where there is a positive preference for urban residential density, as might be the case, for example, in some Mediterranean countries). Then the transport cost reduction causes land rents to decline everywhere in the city (except on the very periphery). But even in this case, rents decline more for locations closer to the center of the city, as depicted in Exhibit 4-7.

It may seem counterintuitive that a technological improvement that increases the overall welfare and productivity of society, namely, transport cost reduction, would result in an absolute *decrease* in total aggregate land value in the city, which is what is implied by the real rent reduction possibility in the spatially constrained case depicted in Exhibit 4-7. To understand this, keep in mind that the value of urban land inside the urban boundary is due essentially to its location premium. This premium only exists because of each location's ability to save transport costs. As improved transport technology or infrastructure reduces those costs, the value of this savings is reduced.

More broadly, transport cost reductions reduce the value of geographic centrality of location, making all locations more equal. Even if this results in an expansion of the urban area, this greater equality across locations must reduce the value of more central locations, at least relatively speaking.

EXHIBIT 4-7 Effect of
Transport Cost Reduction
Savings Not Applied to
Purchase of Land
© OnCourse Learning

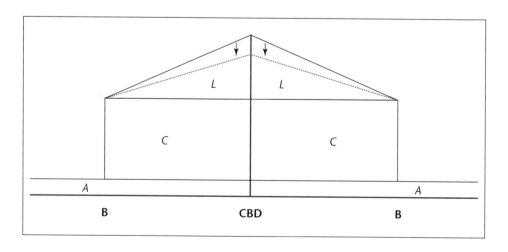

This leads to a third important principle derived from the monocentric city model:

Principle 3:
Declining transport costs (per person, per mile, or per year) holding population and income constant, will always reduce the value of location rent in the center of the city; the effect on the location rent near the periphery is generally ambiguous, depending on changes in density, but the overall result is certainly a flattening of rent gradients.

This third principle can probably go a long way to explaining why we have not seen much increase in real rents over time in most U.S. cities during the twentieth century, in spite of tremendous population and income growth. It may clarify especially how rents have typically declined in real (inflation-adjusted) terms in the central parts of many cities, including in the traditional CBDs, throughout the last half of the twentieth century.[20]

Once again, it is interesting to consider how Principle 3 may play out differently in different regions in the twenty-first century. While technological progress (especially in the areas of telecommunications, computing, and the Internet) may affect all regions, rapidly developing countries such as China and India have much more potential for transport cost reductions than more mature regions, due to infrastructure improvements (including mass transit) and rising automobile ownership, but only if these are not offset by greater densities and the resulting congestion, or perhaps more importantly, by the effect of more rapidly rising real incomes, as discussed below.

Income   The third and final phenomenon to examine is income growth, holding population constant. Income growth is more pervasive than population growth, as some cities are not growing in population, but per capita incomes have increased virtually everywhere and are likely to continue to do so, especially in rapidly developing regions such as Asia and Latin America. The effect of income growth is more complicated to examine because people can elect to spend their additional income in various ways, and income growth can have secondary effects on transport costs.

Normally, we would expect that people would elect to spend at least some of any additional income on purchasing more urban land (such as houses on larger lots, neighborhoods with more parkland and golf courses, more houses per capita—that is, smaller households due to people living on their own more, etc.). Thus, a rise in incomes would spread the city out spatially, reducing its density. While density reduction in general reduces the rent gradient, increasing the amount of unbuildable open space (parks, golf courses, etc.) reduces the "effective arc" of urban development, extending the urban radius without reducing the rent gradient, thereby increasing the central rent.[21] In any case, the effect will be to increase location rents near the periphery, similar to the case of transport improvements shown, for example, in Exhibit 4-6.

This city-expanding, potentially gradient-decreasing, result of income growth would be further complicated (at least to some extent), however, by the indirect effect that higher incomes have on per capita transport costs. Recall that a major component of urban transport cost is the value of people's time wasted in traveling or commuting. This value per hour or per mile of travel is normally a positive function of per capita income. (Higher-income individuals are able and willing to pay more to save travel time, because their opportunity cost of wasted time, in terms of forgone income, is greater, as is their ability to pay for leisure time.) So, this indirect effect of income growth will act (if density were held constant) to steepen the rent gradient, thereby offsetting, at least to some extent, the previously noted potentially gradient-decreasing effect of a rise in incomes.

---

[20]We noted in Chapter 1 that the LRMC (development cost, including land cost) curve in most U.S. cities appears to be only slightly upward-sloping, if at all, as evidenced by a lack of significant increase in real rents over time. Of course, many other factors are involved in real cities, including social and political considerations not contemplated in the monocentric city model.

[21]The key issue is whether the growth in real income changes the *percentage* of unbuildable land.

Normally we would expect at least some expansion in city area (hence, reduction in density) to result from income growth. However, if there are severe constraints on the ability of the city area to expand, then the transport cost effect of income growth would dominate. This would result in a steeper rent gradient and greater percentage increases in land rent nearer to the center of the city. This has probably not occurred in most U.S. cities, but may have been a noticeable phenomenon in some other countries.

We can summarize this income effect in a fourth principle:

> Principle 4:
> *Increasing real income per capita (holding population constant) will tend to decrease rent gradients, with a possible result of absolute reductions in land rent at the center of the city, although a secondary transport cost increase effect (and/or increased open space reservation) due to higher incomes may mitigate this result or even reverse it, especially if the spatial expansion of the city is constrained.*

4.2.3 Summarizing the Monocentric Model

Although greatly simplified, the monocentric model of urban form we have examined here has clarified some basic and very important points about location rents in cities. Other things being equal, larger populations, or geographic constraints on the arc of growth which add to the radius of the city, will be associated with higher land rents. This, in turn, will require the city's inhabitants to spend larger amounts on the combination of transportation and housing costs, or else accept smaller houses in denser neighborhoods. In general, equilibrium among cities (reflecting the results of people's free ability to move among cities) means that larger cities in a country must be characterized by higher average per capita income levels for their citizens. Transportation improvements will tend to reduce the value of geographic centrality of location, tending to equalize land values throughout the city. Income increases have a more ambiguous effect, depending on how spatially constrained the city is and on the degree to which income increases result indirectly in an increase in transport cost.

Circlopolis may seem unrealistically simple. Yet the principles of location value it demonstrates are realistic and all pervading. Students often criticize academic theories as being excessively simplified, too abstractly removed from the real world. But the beauty of a good academic theory lies precisely in its simplicity, in its ability to eliminate aspects of reality that are less important to the subject at hand, so that the aspects of reality that are more important can be clearly seen, and thereby understood. This is why the monocentric model—indeed, the monocentric model in its simplest form as presented here—holds such enduring value.

everywhere in real estate there are "centers" and "peripheries." For a given real estate decision, the center that matters (and the associated periphery) may not be the downtown of a metropolis. The relevant center for an apartment development expected to house university students may be the location of the university campus. The relevant center for the clothing factory in our previous example might be a highway node. The point is, you can apply the monocentric model in a variety of ways to obtain useful insights.

As an example, consider the very practical question of whether real rents for commercial properties will tend to increase over time in a growing city (or the related question of whether commercial property values will tend to grow faster or slower in the long run than single-family home values). At first glance, many people would say, yes, commercial rents should grow in a growing city. But the monocentric city model should give you pause before answering so quickly. Commercial property tends to be located at or near central locations. We have seen in the monocentric city model two major conditions that can cause absolute real location rent levels to decline in central areas: transport improvements or (possibly) growth in real per capita income. If these phenomena dominate over the pure population growth effect, location rents in central areas, such as where most commercial buildings are built, could decline in absolute terms over the long run (after adjusting for inflation), even in a growing city. On the other hand, the monocentric model suggests that low-density housing values might tend to grow over time, at least the land value component of their values, even in cities that are not growing in population. This is because low-density housing tends to locate near the periphery, where the monocentric model suggests location values tend to rise over time in a spatially expanding city.

4.3 Chapter Summary

This chapter presented the basic determinants of urban form, how cities are shaped and configured. Urban form is intimately linked to land values and to basic real estate business activities such as building construction location and investment decisions. In this chapter, we described the fundamental economic principles and concepts that underlie the joint determination of land value and urban form. Concepts such as the residual value of land, bid-rent functions, land market equilibrium, the highest and best use principle, and rent gradients are basic to understanding how cities grow and develop and change over time. These economic fundamentals therefore can be used to inform real estate business decisions. We also introduced a classic model of urban form that teaches through its elegance: the monocentric model. But in fact a major feature of much late-twentieth-century urban form that is likely to be even more prominent in the twenty-first is polycentric and mixed-use development, a topic we'll take up in the next chapter.

KEY TERMS

urban form
factor of production
residual theory of land value
mobile factors
highest and best use (HBU)

bid-rent curve (function)
central point
transportation cost minimized
monocentric city
radius to the urban boundary

agricultural rent
construction cost rent
rent gradient
location rent (location premium)

STUDY QUESTIONS

Conceptual Questions

4.1. What is meant by a *factor of production*? Name four categories or types of production factors. How does land differ from the other factors?

4.2. Explain the residual theory of land value. Why is land value only the residual after other factors have been paid?

4.3. What is bid-rent, and what is the relationship between the bid-rent and the residual value of land?

4.4. Explain the following statement: Bid-rents enforce a "spatial equilibrium" (i.e., meaning that firms do not have an incentive to move if they are paying their bid-rents for land).

4.5. If we were all able to transport ourselves, and all goods and services, anywhere in the world in a few seconds with very little cost, what would the bid rent curves look like? What would determine site value in such a world?

4.6. Consider two uses of a site. Use A is more sensitive to transportation costs, while use B is less profitable apart from transportation costs. Which use is likely to prevail near a transportation node such as a highway intersection?

4.7. How does the highest and best use principle result from long-run equilibrium in the land market?

4.8. What does the following statement mean? Land value determines use, and at the same time, use determines value. Explain your answer.

4.9. Why are denser or more intensive land uses typically found closer to central locations?

4.10. What is meant by a rent gradient? What is the relationship between the rent gradient and transportation costs in a homogeneous monocentric city?

4.11. Why is the classic monocentric city model a long-run equilibrium model?

4.12. Describe the two possible effects of population growth on both relative and absolute land values within a monocentric homogeneous city.

4.13. Describe the two possible effects of transportation cost reduction (per mile, per person) on both relative and absolute land values within a monocentric homogeneous city. Which one do you think dominates in the real world? Explain.

4.14. Describe the two possible effects of income growth on both relative and absolute land values within a monocentric homogeneous city, considering both direct and indirect effects. Which one do you think dominates in the real world? Explain.

4.15. If there are no constraints on the area of a city, what does the monocentric city model say about the relative growth of land rents in the center versus the edge of a city that is growing either in population or in income?

4.16. The classic monocentric city model assumes that all commuting is into the city center. Consider a two-person household in which one person commutes to the city center while the other commutes in the reverse direction to the edge of the city.

   a. Draw the household's bid-rent function assuming round-trip commuting costs are the same in either direction.

   b. Now assume that round-trip commuting costs are higher commuting in to work in the CBD.

4.17. What does the monocentric city model say about the relative level of rents in two cities that are otherwise identical except that one city is located on a coastline and so cannot expand around all points of the compass?

4.18. Holding density constant, for every 1 percent growth in population, approximately what will be the percent growth in city radius?

Quantitative Problems

4.19. Suppose the most productive use of a particular site is as a high-volume, upscale restaurant that can generate revenues of $600,000 per year. The operating expenses, including labor, food, and utilities (everything except rent) are $450,000 per year. The building can be built and equipped for $1 million, which can be paid for by a perpetual loan with interest of $100,000 per year. According to the residual theory, how much is the land parcel worth in terms of annual land rent?

4.20. A firm in industry A is making a location decision, and has narrowed the choice to two different locations, which we will call site 1 and site 2. The firm's revenue is independent of location and equals $5 million per year on each site. The firm's nonland production costs, however, differ at the two sites, being $4 million at site 1 and $4.5 million at site 2.

   a. Assuming the land (rental) market is competitive, what is the firm's bid rent for each site?

   b. Now suppose a firm in industry B is competing for sites with the industry A firm. The industry B firm would have profits before land rent of $750,000 at site 1 and $650,000 at site 2. How is the land allocated, and what is the equilibrium land rent we would observe at each site?

4.21. Consider a simple, homogeneous monocentric city with a circular shape. If the location rent premium at the center is $6,000 per year per acre and the density is three persons per acre, what is the annual transportation commuting cost per capita for residents at the outer edge of the city? Supposing that the annual transportation cost per person per mile of distance from the CBD is $200 (round-trip), how big is the radius of the city?

INSIDE THE CITY II: A CLOSER LOOK

LEARNING OBJECTIVES

After reading this chapter, you should understand:

⊃ The difference between land value and land rent and the key determinants of land values in and around a city.

⊃ Why uncertainty can result in higher land values but less land development in a city.

⊃ Why different land uses and densities occur at different locations within a city.

⊃ How neighborhoods or urban districts grow and mature and sometimes decline and rise again.

⊃ The concept of property life cycle and its implications for real estate investors.

⊃ The nature and cause of the major characteristics of urban form and how this can evolve.

The previous chapter presented just the basics, the bare bones of economic theory for understanding what shapes urban form and the pattern of land value changes over time and space within a city. The simple monocentric city model we explored in Chapter 4 was not only very simple spatially, but it was essentially only a long-run or static model with little consideration of the dynamics of growth. This chapter presents some more advanced concepts and introduces some broader considerations that are important in real world cities. The first two parts of this chapter deal with real property asset value, as distinguished from the annual rents that were the focus of the previous chapter. This will clarify two very important concerns of real estate investors: growth expectations and uncertainty. The remainder of this chapter will then enrich the simple monocentric model of the previous chapter by introducing some important features of real world cities, neighborhoods, and property investments.

5.1 From Property Rent to Property Value: The Effect of Rent Growth Expectations

Real property value is not the same thing as real property rent, although the two are closely related. Property value is the present value of the expected future rents the property could receive. Therefore, other things being equal, property value will be greater where rents are greater. But two other factors also affect property value in addition to the current level of rent the property can earn. The first factor is the expected future *growth rate* of the rents. The second is *uncertainty,* or risk, in the future level of those rents. In this section we consider the effect of the first of these two factors.

A higher growth rate in future rents will increase the present value of those rents, thereby increasing property value, other things being equal. As we saw in Chapter 4, the location premium component of the equilibrium rents within a city can grow over time in real terms, and even more so in nominal terms given inflation. The potential for city expansion will cause the value of nonurban land just beyond the current boundary of the city to exceed the mere present value of future agricultural rents. This is because the present value of the expected future urban location rent premium is incorporated in the current undeveloped land value. The closer an external location is to the boundary of the city and the more rapidly that boundary is expanding toward that location, the greater will be this **growth premium** in the value of the nonurban land.

Indeed, even developed property within the urban boundary will be more expensive per dollar of current annual rent to the extent that the location rent premium is expected to grow. As a result of this growth premium, property will be more expensive (that is, it will sell at higher multiples of the current rent, or lower "cap rates" as we defined that term in Chapter 1) in cities that are expecting greater future growth in rents. But should such growth expectations result in a delay of urban development? That is, will land be held undeveloped in anticipation of such future growth, even after it is profitable to develop the land?

Consider the simple numerical example as depicted in the table below. Suppose that growth in demand for a location suggests that by next year it will be possible to build a structure that will be 30 percent larger than the structure that would be optimal today. If building the smaller structure that is optimally sized for today's demand precludes building the larger structure that is expected to be optimal for next year's demand (i.e., no "expansion or conversion option"), and if investors require, say, a 20-percent expected return for land speculation, then the economics are as depicted in the table. Building today and building next year are mutually exclusive, and the present value today of waiting to build next year is $217 ($260/1.2), whereas the present value of building today is only $200. The land would sell for $217 today, and the rational landowner would choose to wait rather than develop immediately.[1]

	HBU	
	Today (Known)	Next Year (Expected)
Value of Completed Built Property	$1,000	$1,300
Construction & Development Cost (Excluding Land)	$800	$1,040
Profit from Immediate Construction (Excluding Land)	$200	$260
NPV @ 20% Discount Rate (Expected Return)	$200	$217

But note that such optimal delay circumstances depend not just on expectation of future growth in rent location premium, but that the evolution of the location premium will also imply a different optimal structure, in effect, an evolution of the highest and best use (HBU) of the location. It is only such expectation of HBU evolution (in the absence of flexible structure expansion or conversion) that could make delay of initial development a reasonable option. This is because, in the absence of such HBU evolution, building today does not forego the opportunity to take advantage of future rental growth applying to the same fixed use (the same structure). Building today is not mutually exclusive with building next year from the perspective of taking advantage of the rental growth, because the structure you

---

[1]Implicit in this problem setup is the assumption that if the large structure costing $1,040 were built today, it would not be able to rent out sufficiently for a year, such that its value today would be less than $1,240.

build today will serve to provide that same rental growth as the (identical) one you would build next year.[2]

As a result, same use growth expectations alone provide neither an option premium in land value nor a reason to delay construction. This is the situation we face in the simple monocentric city model that we introduced in the previous chapter, where there is only one use in the urban development, namely, housing of a fixed density. But this situation is in contrast to the effect of volatility or uncertainty in growth expectations, the subject to which we turn in the next section.[3]

5.2 Effect of Uncertainty on Speculative Land Value

Unlike the *expected* future location rent growth, the risk or uncertainty surrounding such growth does have implications for possible land speculation and delay of development, and hence can be a determinant of land value and city size. In recent years, mathematical techniques first applied by financial economists to valuing stock options have been used to analyze the effect of uncertainty on land values and urban form.[4] Professor Sheridan Titman was the first to point out that in the presence of uncertainty, it is rational for developers to wait longer than they otherwise would before starting construction, but that such uncertainty actually tends to increase land value.[5] This is because land provides its owner/developers with a "call option." The owner of a land parcel has the *right without obligation* to develop the land at any time. When development is undertaken, this option is surrendered, the cost of construction is incurred, and in return the value of the developed property is obtained.[6]

This option-like characteristic allows the owner/developer to profit from uncertainty in the following way. Uncertainty in the real estate market can be thought of as the possibility of the occurrence of unexpected upswings and downswings in building values.[7] The option characteristic of land ownership allows the owner/developer to take advantage of the "upside" of uncertainty while avoiding full exposure to the "downside." If and when an upswing occurs in the property market, the owner can choose to develop the property and make particularly large profits. If a downswing in the market occurs, the owner can simply choose not to develop for the time being, thereby avoiding potential losses. But once a structure is built, this optionality is lost; the property is now fully exposed to the downside (as well as the upside).

Capozza and Helsley (1990) integrated this options-analysis approach into the classical monocentric city model and showed that uncertainty results in a smaller, denser city with higher rents than would prevail in the absence of uncertainty (other things being equal). The key reason for this is the irreversibility of construction. Once a structure is built on a land parcel, it is normally very difficult and expensive to remove or significantly alter it. In the analogy with stock options, once the option is exercised, you no longer have the option. The loss of the option is part of the cost of development (inherent in the land value).

Logically, if uncertainty gives value to options, then the optionality inherent in undeveloped (but developable) land will be more valuable the more uncertainty (or "volatility") there

---

[2]Here, for simplicity we are ignoring the effect of long-term lease commitments. See Chapters 27 and 30 for discussion of the option value of leasing and other issues of long-term leases.

[3]We will discuss the evolution of the HBU of a location further in section 5.3.4, regarding neighborhood succession and life cycle. Part VIII will carry the discussion of optimal development investment analysis to greater depth.

[4]In fact, the option model has a number of applications in real estate that are of interest to commercial property investment analysts. Some of these applications will be described later in this book, primarily in Parts VI and VIII.

[5]See Titman (1985). The implication of option value theory for optimal development timing will be discussed in more depth in Part VIII of this book, where we will discuss the relationship of the "real options" literature to development decision making. A widely used summary is contained in Dixit and Pindyck (1994).

[6]The analogy with stock options is that upon surrendering the option and paying the "exercise price," you receive the underlying stock shares.

[7]The upswings and downswings are unexpected, not in the sense that people don't expect there to be upswings and downswings, but rather in the sense that these changes in the market cannot be perfectly forecast.

is in the underlying real estate market. This is why, in the presence of uncertainty, it makes sense to wait longer than one otherwise would (that is, to wait for higher rents) to develop a parcel of land. Like surfers waiting for that perfect wave, developers will wait for some sign of an upswing in the market, or at least wait out any likely downswings.[8]

This is reflected in the fact that landowners demand a premium in the rent the developed property must be able to charge (over and above the construction cost rent and the agricultural opportunity cost rent) before they are willing to develop raw land and thereby convert it to urban use at the boundary of the city. Capozza and Helsley labeled this extra rent the **irreversibility premium**. This premium is necessary because the present value of the urban rents must compensate not only for the construction cost and for the forgone agricultural rents, but also for the value of the call option that is being surrendered, the value of the fact that the landowner could wait and possibly develop the property even more profitably at a later date.

The implications of growth and uncertainty on property rent and value within the city and in the as yet unurbanized region just beyond the city boundary are shown in Exhibits 5-1 and 5-2. Exhibit 5-1 shows the property rents, and Exhibit 5-2 shows the property values. The property values depicted in Exhibit 5-2 are, as we have noted, based on investor projections regarding the future levels of (and uncertainty surrounding) the property rent components shown in Exhibit 5-1, in particular regarding the behavior of the urban boundary over time. Each component in the property value has a corresponding component in the rents with the exception of the growth premium. This is because, as noted in the previous section, *expected* growth in location rent does not cause developers to delay development or demand a higher rent. However, as we noted previously, there is a growth premium in the asset value, for this incorporates the present value of the expected future growth in location rents.[9]

Notice in Exhibit 5-2 that both the growth premium and the irreversibility premium in the undeveloped land value grow dramatically as the urban boundary approaches. For likely realistic situations, almost all of the market value of undeveloped land parcels just beyond the urban boundary of a growing city consists of these two premiums. The irreversibility premium associated with uncertainty likely will be a significant part of the total undeveloped land value near the boundary.

The growth and irreversibility premiums represent what is often called the speculative value of undeveloped land. We can see from the discussion in this section that, in principle, such land value is based on real and rational considerations. While the irreversibility premium results in higher rents and higher urban densities, this is a rational response to uncertainty in real estate markets, leading to the efficient use of scarce construction capital, transportation resources, and land.

Depending on how fast the urban boundary is expanding outward, the growth and irreversibility premiums can cause undeveloped land values just outside the current boundary of urban development to grow at very high rates, making very high investment returns possible for speculative landowners. But such returns will also be quite risky and volatile, as a slight downturn in the urban growth rate can undercut the basis of the growth and irreversibility premiums that underlie the speculative land value.[10] Following the initial insights about the implications of option theory that were developed by Titman, Capozza, and others, subsequent scholarship provided a bit of a caveat. Professor Steve Grenadier's influential 2002 article suggested that sufficient competition among developers holding potentially substitutable development sites could drive the option premium value down to zero, diminishing all the

---

[8]The original Capozza-Helsley model has been further developed and explored in recent years. A contrasting view put forth by Steve Grenadier (RFS 2002) suggests that competition among landowners may drive away much of the option value. (See section 27.6 in Chapter 27 for more discussion.)

[9]Note that the rents modeled in Exhibit 5-1 are current "spot" rents, reflecting purely the current balance between supply and demand in the space market for the indicated locations in relation to the urban boundary. The rent one observes empirically in long-term leases does indeed often include a growth premium (depending on the lease terms; it is usually relatively small compared to the growth premium in land value).

[10]During the 1990s and early 2000s, for example, with inflation less than 3% per year, average returns of 15% to 30% per year were typically expected by land speculators, and achieved returns were often much higher. However, in the housing collapse after 2006 prices of developable land parcels often collapsed by as much as 80 percent or more, sometimes at least temporarily down to virtually no value at all.

EXHIBIT 5-1 Components of Property Rent Outside and Inside the Urban Boundary, Under Uncertainty

© OnCourse Learning

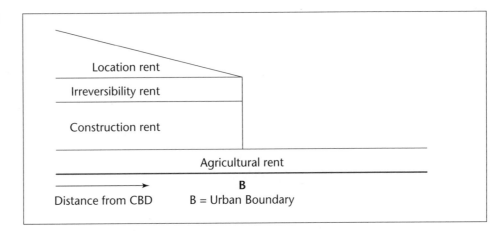

EXHIBIT 5-2 Components of Property Value Outside and Inside the Urban Boundary, Under Uncertainty

© OnCourse Learning

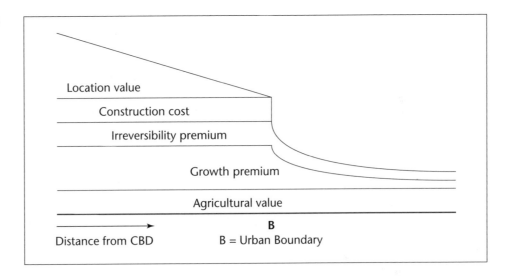

effects described above. More recently the theories have been tested empirically; the general conclusion so far seems to be that the option model is valid, but its effects are likely reduced in the circumstances Grenadier suggested.[11]

Extending the lessons of the simple monocentric city model we began in Chapter 4, we can summarize the effect of growth and uncertainty in a fifth principle, adding to the four already discussed in Chapter 4:

Principle 5:
Faster urban growth and greater uncertainty in that growth will tend to increase urban property values, with the uncertainty also suggesting that a smaller, denser city with higher equilibrium rents is optimal, as rational development is postponed while landowner/developers wait for higher rents to compensate for greater option value given up in irreversible development. However, this effect is diminished the more competition there is among developers and substitutable development sites.

---

[11]See for example (among others) studies listed in the bibliography by Cunningham (2006, 2007), by Schwartz & Torous (2007), and by Bulan, Mayer & Somerville (2009). (An earlier 1993 empirical test by Quigg had upheld the option model, but it did not test specifically against the Grenadier challenge.) Perhaps this could be one reason why property prices tend to remain lower in some rapidly growing cities, such as Dallas and Atlanta.

5.3 Let's Get Real: New Twists to the Old Model

The classical monocentric city model is great for developing a basic understanding of urban spatial economics. (Recall the description of Circlopolis in Chapter 4.) But real-world cities are much richer, more varied places than the homogeneous town of Circlopolis. Now that you have some of the basics down, let's consider some of these more realistic effects.

5.3.1 Density Variations and Heterogeneous Land Use

In the simple monocentric city model, we assumed a single, homogeneous land use, such as housing of a uniform density, throughout the city. Real-world cities have a variety of land uses (e.g., housing, commercial, industrial, etc.) and a range of densities (e.g., high-rise, low-rise, spread-out). What is the most productive way for these various land uses to locate and distribute themselves within the city?

The answer to this question is easy to observe. In most cities, we observe denser, more intensive land uses closer to the center. Taller buildings, packed closer together, are found in or near central points (such as the CBD or other major transportation nodes where transportation costs are minimized). But you now have the tools to understand *why* this is the case and how this happens.

Freely functioning land markets result in denser development and more productive use of land located closer to central points where transportation costs are minimized. Such a result makes sense from the perspective of maximizing profits or incomes, because it minimizes the aggregate transportation costs of the society for the given production and consumption allocation. How such a result comes about in long-run equilibrium in the land market can be seen in Exhibit 4-2 in Chapter 4, reproduced here as Exhibit 5-3. Recall that this exhibit depicts the bid-rent curves of three different land uses around a single central point. The equilibrium land rent gradient around a central point will be determined by the highest bid-rent curve at each location, as indicated by the thick line tracing out the highest bid-rent functions. The more productive land use with the greatest sensitivity to transportation costs (use *A* in the exhibit) will outbid other land uses near the center. Other things being equal, denser development will indeed be more productive per acre, because greater density means that more labor and physical capital (structures and machines) are applied to the production process per acre of land. Also, recall from our discussion of the monocentric

EXHIBIT 5-3 Bid-Rent Functions of Three Land Uses with Differing Productivity and Sensitivity to Transport Cost

© OnCourse Learning

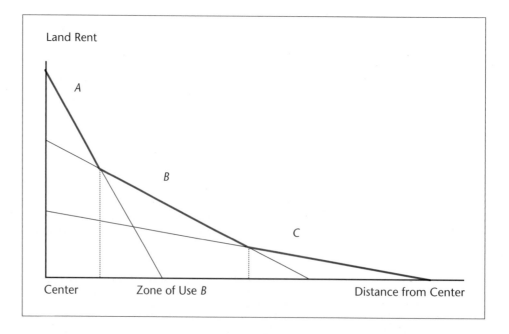

city that the rent gradient is proportional to density, other things being equal, because transportation costs per mile *per acre* are proportional to density. Thus, higher-density land uses will tend to be both more productive (at the central point) and characterized by steeper rent gradients.

So it is not just a coincidence that the density of development tends to decline as one moves away from a geographically central point or transportation node. It is a reflection of the fundamental economic principle that in a production process the input factors that are relatively scarce (and hence more expensive) should be used more sparingly and more productively. It is a basic fact of geometry (as well as geography) that central locations are scarcer than noncentral locations. If we combine this density result with the monocentric city model, we get the classical **concentric ring model of urban form**. First suggested by Ernest Burgess, of the famous Chicago School of Urban Geography, which flourished at the University of Chicago in the 1920s and 1930s, the concentric ring model is depicted in Exhibit 5-4. This model suggests that similar types of land uses will tend to locate at similar distances from the center of the city, resulting in concentric rings of similar land uses around the CBD. For example, denser, high-rise housing would tend to be located closer to the center than lower-density, low-rise housing.

The Burgess concentric ring model was a geographic model rather than an economic model like the monocentric city model. As such, Burgess's model was more complicated but less rigorous in some respects, including considerations other than just transportation costs and long-run equilibrium in the land market. In particular, the Burgess model considered the *dynamics of development,* including the effect of the chronological order in which different sections of the city are developed and the effect of the age of structures. His model also

EXHIBIT 5-4 Concentric Ring Model of Urban Land Use Structure (Burgess)
© OnCourse Learning

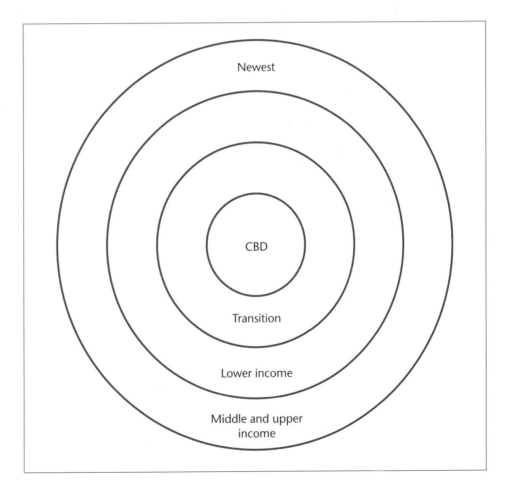

considered social factors characteristic in the United States in the twentieth century, such as the preference for greater lot sizes (lower residential densities) with increasing household income. In the Burgess model, the inner ring just outside the CBD was a transition zone or "gray area." This zone consisted of warehouses and industrial plants, uses that require good access to transportation, especially rail transport, which tended to be focused in or near the CBD at that time. This inner ring is viewed as a zone in transition, evolving into the expanding CBD at its inner edge and merging with low-income, high-density housing for the factory workers on its outer edge. As the city expands outward, this next ring consists of older and therefore less desirable houses than those in the outer, newest ring of the city, which consists of the lower-density middle- and upper-income housing.

The Burgess model explained many of the major features of the typical industrial city of mid-twentieth century America. Most notable was the tendency of higher-income residential neighborhoods to be located farther from the center. This is a somewhat curious phenomenon not found in many other countries. As noted in the previous chapter, higher-income households should have higher value of time and therefore greater transportation costs per mile per person, leading to a steeper rent gradient. Higher-income households should also have a greater ability to pay for housing. These two facts by themselves would lead higher-income neighborhoods to tend to be located closer to the center of the city, as is indeed typical in the cities of many other countries. So how does it happen that higher-income residential neighborhoods tend to exist farther from the center in U.S. cities?

Here is a basic answer. Recall that lower densities reduce the transportation cost per acre and thereby reduce the rent gradient. If upper-income people desire enough larger lot sizes or have a strong enough preference for low-density neighborhoods, then this density effect can more than offset the transportation cost effect, resulting in an equilibrium location of higher-income households farther from the center. Furthermore, if higher incomes lead households to want to purchase newer houses, then this will also tend to force the higher-income neighborhoods farther from the center, at least in a city that has been growing rapidly for some time (as most twentieth-century cities were). This is because development proceeds from the center outward, leaving inner neighborhoods full of older housing stock. (Of course, in time that stock may be renewed, and if the city ceases population growth and household formation, eventually all neighborhoods could have similar-age housing structures.) Social and political issues related to crime, quality of education, and racial or ethnic diversity have also been factors affecting U.S. cities, which are characterized by municipal political boundaries that separate central cities from their surrounding newer suburbs.

While the concentric ring model captures some important elements of urban form, it also leaves much unexplained. Not long after Burgess came up with his model, another Chicago geographer came along with an alternative model, which is pretty much the opposite of the Burgess model. Homer Hoyt was not only a first-rate academic, but also a successful real estate investor and famous for developing the **sector model of urban land use**.

According to the sector model, similar land uses do not all lie at a similar distance from the center of the city, but rather cluster along rays or in pie-shaped wedges emanating from the center. Again, the theory is based on the phenomenon of cities growing outward from their centers. Hoyt noted that once a particular type of land use becomes predominant in a particular direction from the center, or on a particular "side of town," then new development tends to continue that land use in the same direction outward from the center as the city grows. For example, early on it became established in such East Coast cities as Boston and Philadelphia that the west side of town was the fashionable side where the upper-income residents tended to locate. As those cities grew in all directions, the west side continued to be the fashionable and upper-income side, extending farther and farther from the center.

The Hoyt model is depicted in Exhibit 5-5. Hoyt's theory was that some land uses are more compatible with each other and tend to be found in adjacent sectors. Thus, lower-income housing would more likely be found adjacent to industrial development than would high-income housing. He also suggested an environmental cause of some location patterns, with high-income residential areas tending to be located upwind from heavy industrial zones.

EXHIBIT 5-5 Sector
Model of Urban Land Use
Structure (Hoyt)
© OnCourse Learning

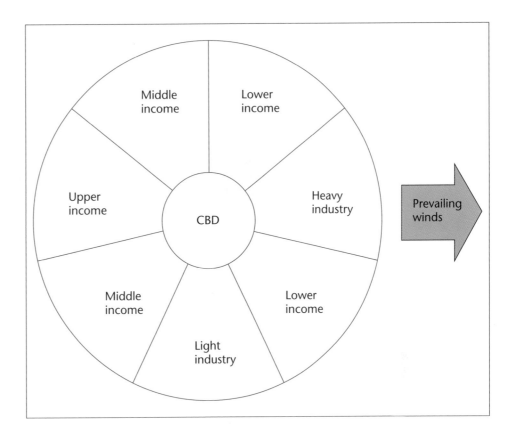

The concentric ring model and the sector model are diametrically opposite one another in their view of urban structure. Yet both clearly contain some of the essence of the truth. Most cities are partly explained by both perspectives.

5.3.2 Effect of Land Use Boundaries

Both the concentric ring model and the sector model of urban form and land use recognize that similar land uses tend to "clump together" in cities. For example, we speak of residential neighborhoods, commercial districts, and industrial zones. And we speak of high-income neighborhoods, middle-income neighborhoods, and low-income neighborhoods. In part, this is because similar land uses face similar transportation cost and locational needs. So, if one land use is the highest and best use at a particular site or location, that same general type of use will typically also be the highest and best use at nearby locations as well. Agglomeration economies and a preference for homogeneity may also play a role in some places. The natural tendency of similar land uses to coalesce is often reinforced by land use regulations in most cities, such as zoning regulations in U.S. cities. It is important to recognize that a natural consequence of districts that are relatively homogeneous in land use means that there will be land use *boundaries* between such districts. These boundaries affect the location rent and land value of the sites adjacent to them and nearby.

Certain types of land uses tend to be compatible and mutually supporting, bringing a synergy or increase in value to each district and use. Other types of land uses are incompatible and detract from the value of each other if they are located too closely. These are examples of what are known as spillover effects or locational externalities, as defined in Chapter 3. For example, residential neighborhoods benefit from having shopping opportunities nearby so that the residents do not have to travel too far to shop. There is thus a benefit in having certain types of commercial districts (those with stores useful to the residents, such as grocery

EXHIBIT 5-6 Effect of
Negative Externalities Near
a Land Use Boundary

© OnCourse Learning

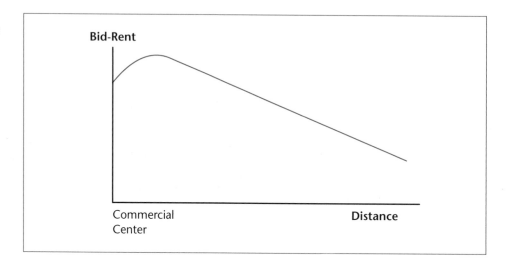

and convenience stores) near or within residential districts. On the other hand, heavy indus-trial zones—containing air or noise pollution generators, such as airports, or large commer-cial centers that generate high traffic volumes—are generally not compatible with most types of residential land use. Such land uses will tend to reduce the value of nearby residential homes.

Both a freely functioning land market and well-crafted zoning regulations will tend to separate incompatible land uses and draw compatible uses together, at least over the long run.[12] Recognition of such differences underlies both the concentric ring and the sector model of urban form (especially the latter).

Even **compatible land uses** may have local boundary effects that differ from the general effect, however. For example, residents may generally prefer to be located closer to shopping opportunities, as long as they are not so close that traffic congestion and noise reduces the quality of residential life. It may be nice to have a convenience store a block or two away, but not so nice to have the store right next to your backyard. Similar points may be made about schools and churches, or even parks, if the park presents safety or privacy concerns. This is an example of a **negative locational externality**. As a result of boundary effects such as these, location rents often are depressed near to a land use boundary, at least for one of the land uses (the one that is unfavorably affected, such as the residential use in the previous examples).[13]

This phenomenon is depicted in Exhibit 5-6, which shows the bid-rent function of a land use that benefits from accessibility to another land use at a boundary on the left edge of the horizontal axis of the graph. For example, the exhibit might depict the bid-rent of residential land use around a commercial center whose boundary is at the left edge of the graph. The bid-rent is lower near the land use boundary, then rises as distance eliminates the negative externality, then falls as further increasing distance reduces accessibility to the commercial center.

---

[12]Because these spillover effects involve externalities, a type of market imperfection, a completely free laissez-faire land market will generally not result in optimal land use, although it may come pretty close. In theory, a profit-maximizing monopolist owning all the land might do a better job, as all the spillover externalities would be internal-ized. Zoning and community land use controls are ways to improve upon the laissez-faire result while reflecting broader social and political concerns of the community and avoiding the dangers of power concentration in the hands of a monopolist.

[13]While location rent may be depressed by location near the boundary, location value may in some cases actually be increased, if the neighborhood is growing, as sites adjacent to the existing commercial center, for example, may offer the prospect of conversion from residential to more valuable commercial use.

5.3.3 Polycentric Cities

Up to now, our discussion of urban form has focused largely on single central locations or "monocentric" cities. While most cities do have a single dominant center known as the central business district (CBD) or downtown, real-world cities also have other important centers (often referred to as *urban subcenters* in the urban economics literature). For example, most metropolitan areas of a million or more population in the United States have other **major activity centers (MACs)** besides the CBD, which serve metropolitan-wide needs, such as airports, major medical centers, and sports or educational complexes. In addition, traditional cities are sprinkled with **neighborhood business districts (NBDs)** or centers (NBCs), which serve the needs of local communities. In the last half of the twentieth century, all U.S. cities have also developed large regional shopping malls in the suburbs, serving large segments of the metropolitan area. By the late twentieth century, some of the largest suburban commercial centers, particular those located on beltways and major interstate highway nodes, had developed into what Joel Garreau dubbed "edge cities," activity centers almost as large and multifaceted as many a traditional CBD.

Furthermore, some metropolises have never had a single very dominant CBD in the center. **Polynuclear cities** have not only subcenters, but also multiple major centers. Such cities range from "twins" such as Minneapolis-St. Paul, to multicentered conglomerates like the Los Angeles area, to clusters such as the Ruhr region in Germany.

Fundamentally, cities in the real world could never be perfectly monocentric because *different land uses have different and multiple central points* (locations where their relevant transportation costs are minimized). For example, recall the bid-rent example at the beginning of Chapter 4 regarding two land uses, a clothing factory and a grocery store. The clothing factory's central point (the maximum point of its bid-rent function) might be at the intersection of two interstate highways outside the center of town. The central point for the grocery store could be at the intersection of two commercial streets in the center of a residential neighborhood. Neither of these two central points is in the CBD of the metropolitan area. In fact, there might be several sites in the metropolitan area where either the factory or the store could be located with maximum productivity (minimum transport costs).

Thus, real cities are collections of major and minor central points within the metropolitan area. These tend to be related to one another in a more or less hierarchical manner much like Christaller's urban hierarchy model described in Chapter 3. Land values and rent gradients are, as always, determined in equilibrium by the usage with the highest bid-rent curve at each location, leading to land being used at its highest and best use in the long run. This is depicted schematically in Exhibit 5-7 for a cross-section through a city that has a dominant CBD but also major outlying centers as well. The land rents (which determine and reflect the land uses) are given by the heavy solid lines, the highest bid-rent functions over each point.

A general effect of polycentrism and especially the type of "edge cities" that seem to be becoming more common in the twenty-first century in many countries is a flattening of the

EXHIBIT 5-7 Rent Gradients in a Polycentric City

© OnCourse Learning

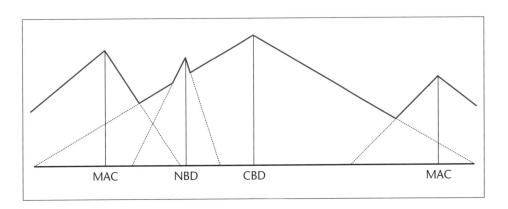

rent gradient. The development of multiple and mixed-use centers scattered throughout the metropolitan area has the effect of reducing the distance people need to travel, and this lowers transport costs per acre even without affecting transport costs per mile-traveled or reducing residential density. Along with the substitution of telecommunication and Internet/computing for physical travel, polycentrism appears to be a major way cities are evolving to deal with what would otherwise be rising transportation costs. But keep in mind that a relatively flat bid-rent surface does not necessarily preclude high land (location) values *within* the central places, as physical agglomeration remains a valuable human phenomenon.

5.3.4 Neighborhood Dynamics and Life Cycle

The simple monocentric city model considers only transport costs in a long-run equilibrium in which there is complete flexibility to change the built structures on the land. The age of the built structures or of the neighborhoods of the city is ignored in this simple model. On the other hand, both the Burgess and Hoyt models described previously recognized that land value and land use are indeed affected by the age of the built structures on the land. Older structures tend to be less productive, less desirable for users, and more expensive to operate or maintain. Yet even old structures usually have some value, and tearing them down is costly. It is usually cheaper to build new buildings on undeveloped land, or land on which the existing buildings are so old or outmoded that they have almost no further value (and by the time buildings get that old, there may be a stigma attached to the neighborhood). Undeveloped land, by its nature, tends to be located near or beyond the existing periphery of the urban area. Thus, neighborhoods on or near the periphery of the metropolitan area tend to have structures that on average are much newer than those in centrally located neighborhoods.

This unequal distribution of structural age in a city tends to be more pronounced in decades during and after major expansion, such as almost all U.S. cities experienced in the twentieth century. On the other hand, as we saw in Chapter 4, urban growth, especially if combined with growth in real incomes, should tend to increase the absolute value of all locations within the city. This includes the old, central neighborhoods, unless transportation cost reductions or social and political problems offset the advantages of centrality of location.[14]

This suggests a natural dynamic, or process of evolution, of neighborhoods within a city. Borrowing terminology from biology, this process is sometimes referred to as **neighborhood succession theory**. This theory differs from those we have previously examined in that it considers changes in land values and land uses in a single location (or part of a city, a neighborhood or district) across time. The previous models we have looked at focused on such changes across different locations within the entire city as of a single point in time. The typical life cycle of a neighborhood according to succession theory is depicted in Exhibit 5-8. Let us trace this model for a typical district, that of West Side in Anytown, USA.

At first a bucolic agricultural zone just beyond the edge of the expanding urban area of Anytown, West Side experiences an initial growth phase characterized by rapidly rising usage and land values as the area becomes ripe for urban development. (Usage value refers to the value of the typical highest and best use—the HBU—in the area of the neighborhood.) This phase begins at point *I* in time, represented on the horizontal axis in Exhibit 5-8. The West Side area is initially developed with low-density housing and within a generation is fully built up with such new houses. As development is completed, West Side's growth period and rapid rise in usage value and undeveloped land value ends, but the neighborhood enters a long period of maturity, in which values generally are maintained. Starting from point *II* in time, this mature period could continue indefinitely, with structures gradually being refurbished or replaced by new buildings as the original structures age, but the neighborhood retains its low-density residential character.

---

[14]In the long run, a stable city or one whose area is constrained would tend to have mixtures of new and old structures more evenly distributed across all neighborhoods, or might even have more new structures in the inner neighborhoods.

EXHIBIT 5-8
Neighborhood Succession
Model
© OnCourse Learning

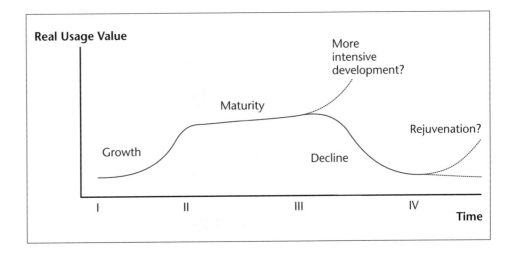

However, the evolution of the metropolitan area of Anytown as a whole may tend to put pressures on West Side that could cause it to evolve in either of two possible directions away from this stable maturity. This occurs at point *III* in time in Exhibit 5-8.

The happier possibility is that land value in West Side could rise again significantly. This might be caused by expansion of the overall geographic area of the Anytown metropolis, which could give West Side a greater location premium as the neighborhood becomes, relatively speaking, more centrally located in the metropolitan area. Or West Side might evolve into a new subcenter within the metropolis, perhaps due to its proximity to a major hospital or university or airport, for example. This type of evolution would tend to change the HBU in West Side, making redevelopment to more productive land uses profitable in the neighborhood, such as development of higher-density housing and/or commercial buildings.[15] Zoning or other political constraints might be applied to hold off such redevelopment, maintaining the original density but now with higher-valued houses, making the neighborhood over time a more exclusive, upper-income area. The profit incentive would argue strongly for redevelopment, however. This might cause dissension within the neighborhood between those favoring and those opposed to rezoning and new development. But we might view such dissension as a "good problem," which (we can hope) would be resolved through a fair and democratic process.

Alternatively, the unhappy possibility would see West Side entering into a period of decline. The Anytown metropolitan area might evolve in a manner that reduces West Side's value. Various economic, geographic, and sociopolitical factors could cause such decline. For example, intraurban transportation improvements could result in transport cost reductions that could reduce the location value of West Side. (Recall Exhibits 4-6 and 4-7 in Chapter 4.) As its structures age relative to newer neighborhoods, lower-income residents may move into West Side. Political boundaries based on historical accident may place West Side in a municipality with tax burdens that are high relative to income, with relatively poor-quality schools and social problems such as a high crime rate. Disinvestment may then ensue, in which West Side's buildings are allowed to age and deteriorate without capital replenishment. A negative spiral in terms of land value and property value could result, reflecting a lower-valued HBU for the area.

---

[15]Our previous discussion in sections 5.1 and 5.2 of land value just beyond the boundary of an expanding city is relevant to the value of property in West Side in this circumstance. West Side is now just beyond the boundary of an expanding higher-density or higher-value (per acre) land use, for example, just beyond the boundary of an expanding Burgess model "ring," or polynuclear subcenter. In such a circumstance, much of the value of property in West Side will be due to the redevelopment option value of land ownership rather than the value of the existing structures on the land. This option-based land value will contain the growth and irreversibility premia described in sections 5.1 and 5.2.

But this is not the end of the story. Of course, the decline could continue and gradually play out with West Side permanently stuck in a low-value status. However, it is also possible that in the decline in value lie the seeds of a turnaround. This is represented at point *IV* in time in Exhibit 5-8. With structures virtually completely deteriorated and property values depressed by the stigma of the neighborhood, redevelopment may now be rather inexpensive. If West Side has some favorable attributes that it can capitalize on, or if the Anytown metropolis evolves in a direction favorable for West Side, redevelopment or refurbishment of West Side could become profitable. For example, beginning in the 1970s and 1980s, many old, centrally located neighborhoods were revitalized through new investment (the term *gentrification* was coined). This process in the United States continued with greater momentum in the 1990s and early 2000s, especially in cities with growing economies attractive to large numbers of young, single professionals—centers of the knowledge-based economy. In recent years, the aging of the baby boom generation in the United States has also led many well-to-do "empty nest" households to move into attractive inner city neighborhoods. Vibrant immigrant populations have also turned around many central city neighborhoods.

Rigorously quantifying neighborhood-life-cycle effects on location value is difficult because it requires a very long time series of historical data on property prices. However, a few scholars have attempted such analysis, and one of the longest-run histories of location value is that compiled by Professor Piet Eichholtz in the Netherlands, for the Herengracht canal in Amsterdam. Exhibits 5-9A and 5-9B present a property price index for the Herengracht extending over three centuries, from 1628 to 1974. This index is based on repeat-sales of the same structures, and reflects the usage value of the Herengracht location. That is, it is in effect an index of the value of the highest and best use property at the location of the Herengracht.[16] The index in Exhibit 5-9A has been adjusted for inflation and thus reflects the actual purchasing power of the usage value of the Herengracht location. It therefore depicts the history of the Herengracht neighborhood's life cycle as it has unfolded into the last half of the twentieth century.

The Herengracht was first developed in the early seventeenth century, when it was on the outskirts of the city. It was then, and remarkably has remained throughout its history, a fine address. The Herengracht is also interesting because it is a circumferential canal, with all points along the canal remaining at a similar distance from the historical center of Amsterdam, about a half-mile away. It is thus a sort of natural "Burgess Ring." Furthermore, the buildings on the Herengracht have not changed very much, at least in external appearances. The original structures, three- to five-story townhouses that touch one another, have remained, or at least their type has remained, albeit with many updates, improvements, and reconstructions.

Note that while there were ups and downs, often reflecting wars, plagues, or alternative periods of prosperity and growth of the Dutch economy, the real value of the Herengracht simply cycled around a flat trend for almost three centuries, until the early twentieth century. During this long period, the population and radius of Amsterdam grew only slowly, and the HBU of the Herengracht remained residential. The only substantial and sustained increase in the Herengracht's real location value during the period covered by the historical index (up to 1972) is seen to be a relatively sudden jump in the early- to mid-twentieth century. This accompanied a great expansion in metropolitan Amsterdam that increased the centrality and therefore the location premium value of the Herengracht and altered its HBU from residential to commercial use. However, zoning regulations dampened the evolution of land use that would probably otherwise have occurred on the Herengracht during the mid- to late-twentieth century.

---

[16]Exhibit 5-9 is taken from P. Eichholtz and D. Geltner, *"Four Centuries of Location Value: Implications for Real Estate Capital Gain in Central Places,"* MIT/Maastricht Working Paper, 2004. This index is based on *all* property sales transactions on the Herengracht, not just those of residential parcels, and therefore reflects the effect on value of a change in use of a building. As the cost of capital improvements is not subtracted from the index, while the sale prices do reflect the value of such improvements, in effect this version of the Herengracht index traces the value of the location HBU over time. (This differs from the housing value Herengracht index published by Eichholtz in an earlier paper.)

EXHIBIT 5-9A
Herengracht Usage Value
Index, 1628–1974

Source: Eichholtz and Geltner
(2004).

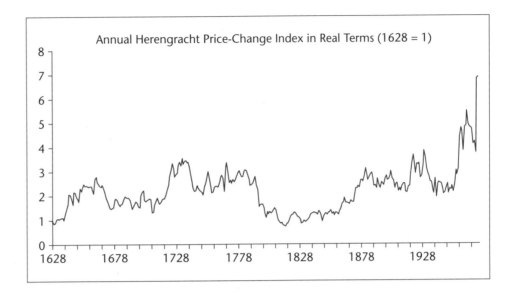

EXHIBIT 5-9B
Summary Statistics of
Herengracht Annual
Repeat-Sale Price-Change
Index

Source: Eichholtz and Geltner
(2004).

Period	Nominal			Real		
	Mean	**Standard Deviation**	**Signal/ Noise***	**Mean**	**Standard Deviation**	**Signal/ Noise***
1628–1974	1.28%	9.96%	2.20	0.56%	10.63%	2.35
1628–1699	1.00%	7.74%	1.04	0.59%	9.63%	1.29
1700–1799	0.13%	8.36%	1.94	−0.03%	10.35%	2.40
1800–1899	0.49%	8.09%	2.30	0.65%	8.95%	2.55
1900–1974	4.15%	14.61%	4.27	1.19%	13.70%	4.00

*Signal to Noise Ratio: Longitudinal standard deviation of estimated returns divided by the average standard error of the annual return estimates.

   The experience of the Herengracht is perhaps not typical of most neighborhoods, although it may be similar to many stable, fashionable neighborhoods in persistently success- ful cities. The Dutch are famous for the rigor and quality of their urban planning, and the Netherlands has had a generally successful economy since the Renaissance. With this in mind, it is interesting to note that the overall 347-year average annual gain in real location value on the Herengracht was only 0.56 percent. This value growth includes the effects of capital-improvement expenditures to develop or redevelop the structures and so is greater than the appreciation return that an investor would earn.[17] It is also interesting to note that the only substantial real gain in usage value after the canal's original development was associ- ated with an evolution of the HBU. This is consistent with our discussion of land value in sections 5.1 and 5.2 of this chapter. Major jumps in location value are associated with the advent and ultimately the exercise of the "real option" to develop or redevelop the land to a more productive use.

   From the perspective of real estate investors, neighborhood succession theory holds an important implication. Succession theory suggests two things about the course of location (or usage) rents and values over time, and both of these are illustrated in our Herengracht example. First, location rents and values will tend to remain nearly constant, in real terms,

---

[17]Investors must pay for capital improvements, and this cost detracts from the returns that would otherwise be implied by the change in property price depicted in the index.

over long periods of time, possibly indefinitely (once urban development has occurred in a neighborhood), even in successful locations. But second, the possibility exists of occasional, possibly relatively sharp or sudden changes in location rent and value, due to changes in the optimal role and function of the neighborhood within the metropolitan area (that is, changes in the neighborhood HBU). These changes may or may not be very easy to predict, and they can conceivably go in either a positive or a negative direction. As described in section 5.2, to the extent that a change in location rent is predictable, it will be reflected in advance by corresponding changes in land values as defined by the redevelopment option value of the property ownership. Normally, there will be at least one, but perhaps only one, positive "pop" in such land value for any given location (the Herengracht has had two), occurring at (and just prior to) the time when that location is reached by an expanding urban boundary, when development of urban land uses first becomes feasible on the site.

5.4 Property Life Cycle and the Effect of Building Structure Depreciation

Just as neighborhoods may be characterized by a succession of HBUs over time, individual properties (or sites) within the neighborhood experience their own characteristic life cycles. Even if the neighborhood is very stable, with an essentially constant characteristic HBU for the neighborhood, individual properties will pass through a repeating life cycle as the built structure on the site ages and eventually is replaced or rehabilitated. Like the neighborhood life cycle, the **property life cycle** is important for real estate investors to be aware of, as it is fundamental to the nature of the investment returns that can realistically be expected from a given property.

Real estate investors should bear in mind that fundamentally property value is the sum of two components: land value and structure value. But while understanding these two components is important conceptually, it is typically much easier to define and measure the sum, the property value, than either component alone. Indeed, the breakdown of the total property value into the two components will depend on the conceptual definition of the land value component.

There are two major perspectives on the definition of the land value component. The most traditional perspective is that of the appraisal and legal professions. We may define this as the "land appraisal value." From this perspective, the land value component of property value is how much the property would sell for if it had no structure on it, that is, the current market value of typical vacant land parcels similar to the subject property only without a structure. A more recent perspective is the way urban and financial economists define land value. From this perspective, the value of land ownership (distinct from ownership of a built structure) derives purely from the development or redevelopment option value that such ownership entails. This is consistent with the "real options" model of land value as a development option, as put forth by Titman (1985), Capozza and Helsley (1990), Williams (1991), and others (introduced in section 5.2).[18]

The relationship over time between a given parcel's property value and either of these two definitions of land value (keeping in mind that current "structure value" is simply the difference between the current property value and whichever definition of land value one prefers) is shown in the simple model of property life cycle presented in Exhibit 5-10. The exhibit presents a picture of a single location in the city across an entire history of continuous time, which is represented on the horizontal axis.

The discrete points in time when construction or major reconstruction of the structure on this site takes place are represented by the R symbols along the time axis. At those points in time, the structure is built or rebuilt to best serve the HBU of the site as of that point in time. This value of the newly developed or redeveloped property just after each development may be seen as tracing out the evolution of the usage value of the site over time, based on its

---

[18]This model will be presented in more depth in Chapter 27 of the text.

EXHIBIT 5-10
Components of Property
Value over Time
© OnCourse Learning

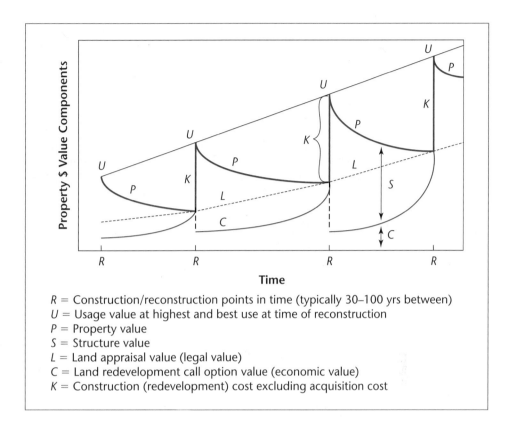

R = Construction/reconstruction points in time (typically 30–100 yrs between)
U = Usage value at highest and best use at time of reconstruction
P = Property value
S = Structure value
L = Land appraisal value (legal value)
C = Land redevelopment call option value (economic value)
K = Construction (redevelopment) cost excluding acquisition cost

HBU (as if vacant). This trend, indicated by the dashed line and the U symbols, is a good way to conceptualize the trend in the location value of the site.[19]

As depicted in Exhibit 5-10, the usage value of the site is growing continuously over time, as evidenced by the upward trend in the U values. Of course, this would not necessarily be the trend for any given site in the real world, especially if we measure value in real terms, that is, in dollars of constant purchasing power (i.e., net of general inflation). We have seen both in this chapter and the previous chapter how location value can either increase or decrease over time or remain constant for long periods.

As noted, the market value of the property at any point in time consists of the **structure value** plus the land value. Just after reconstruction, structure value makes up the bulk of the property value. But the structure value declines over time as the building depreciates, due to the effects of physical, functional, and economic obsolescence. **Physical obsolescence** refers to the structure physically wearing out as, for example, its roof deteriorates and begins to leak. **Functional obsolescence** refers to the effect of changing technology and changing tastes or user requirements on the optimal physical design of a new structure for the relevant HBU. (For example, major commercial structures may devolve from "class A" to "class B" status over a period of a few decades. In the 2000s, it began to be important in many markets for structures to be "sustainable" in some sense, in part to reduce the rate of functional obsolescence. See the boxed feature on page 97.) Finally, **economic obsolescence** refers to the fact that the nature of the structure may become unsuited to the HBU of the site as the HBU

---

[19]What we are calling "location value" reflects what the appraisal industry terms the "HBU as if vacant," the highest and best use to which the site would be developed if there were no existing structure on it. One should take care not to confuse this definition of location value with the value of the "location premium" component of property value described in our discussion of the monocentric city model in Chapter 4 and in sections 5.1 and 5.2 of this chapter. While the two concepts are related, "location value" here (as usage value) would also include the value of the structure (when new). (It should also be recalled that the simple version of the monocentric city model we were employing had only one urban usage of the land.)

evolves over time. For example, the HBU may evolve from low-density to higher-density residential use, or from residential to commercial use, so a single-family home would no longer be an economical use of the site, even though the house may be fine physically and functionally.

The other component of the property value is the **land value** (labeled L or C depending on the definition). As noted, the economic land value component consists only of the value of the **redevelopment option**, including the growth and irreversibility premia described in sections 5.1 and 5.2.[20] Defined this way, the land value component is very small just after redevelopment, because the building is then at the HBU for the site, so the profitability of further redevelopment, if any, is a long way off in the future.[21] Over time, the redevelopment option value component will grow if the structure depreciates physically or functionally, or if the HBU of the site as if vacant evolves and changes over time away from that which the current structure can serve (this latter is economic obsolescence, as described above). As investments, call options are much more risky than their underlying assets (in this case, the usage value of the built property), and hence require a much higher expected return. Furthermore, all of that return must be earned in the form of appreciation of the option value, as the option itself pays no dividend. Thus, the curve of the C value in the exhibit traces out an expected exponential growth that is quite rapid between the reconstruction points in time.

On the other hand, the appraisal or legal definition of land value is much less exciting. It tends to be a roughly constant percentage of the usage value of the site, as indicated by the L curve in the exhibit. This conception of land value grows at a much lower rate (if at all), and with much less volatility than the economic definition of land value.[22]

The total of land value plus structure value equals the property value at any point in time, labeled P in the exhibit. The optimal time for redevelopment will not occur until the entire value of the site equals its land value component alone; that is, the current structure has become worthless as such due to the value of the redevelopment option on the site.[23] At such points in time, both definitions of land value are the same, and this also equals the entire property value ($C = L = P$). In the exhibit, R is depicted as occurring when the old value of L or C equals the old value of P.

---

[20]As described in section 5.1, the growth premium component of the land value reflects the expected value of the location premium in the future rent from a new or redeveloped structure, beyond the redevelopment point in time. Note, however, that the value of any location premium associated with the *current* structure is reflected in the structure value component of the property value, as opposed to the land value component, as these concepts are being defined here. (This may appear to be inconsistent with the definition of land value in the context of the monocentric city model discussed in Chapter 4 and sections 5.1 and 5.2. But in fact, structural depreciation and redevelopment were not included in the basic monocentric city model, so this is a fine point that was not contemplated in the definition of land value employed in that model.) It should also be noted that the value of the current structure *as if* it would never be torn down represents an "opportunity cost" in any redevelopment of the site that would involve demolishing the existing structure. Even if this structure is no longer the HBU of the site, it would still typically be able to provide some future benefit flows. If the building is torn down, the future net cash flow it could have earned is forfeited. Analysis of option value in real estate will be discussed in more depth in Chapter 27. For the case of redevelopment (as opposed to initial development on vacant land), the option model has been refined by Amin and Capozza (1993) and Childs, Riddiough, and Triantis (1996).

[21]In financial option valuation terminology, the redevelopment option is *deeply* "out of the money" when the structure is new. This is because the value of the existing structure is part of the exercise price (or "strike price") of the option.

[22]Volatility is not depicted in Exhibit 5-10, which shows only the central tendency or expected trends over time. But recall from the residual theory of land value in Chapter 4 that most of the volatility in the property value will redound to the land value component.

[23]Note that this does not necessarily (or usually) imply that the existing structure could no longer earn positive net rents, only that such rents are insufficient to justify further delay of a more profitable redevelopment. The perspective taken here is consistent with traditional appraisal practice of charging against the structure any loss in property value due to economic obsolescence or divergence of the existing structure from the HBU as if the site were vacant. It should also be noted that in some cases it may be optimal to hold a site for some time purely for speculation, before beginning redevelopment, even after the existing building on it becomes essentially worthless. The new HBU for the site may evolve further in a favorable direction. If you develop too soon, you may miss such opportunity. This is analogous to the fact that it is not always optimal to exercise a call option as soon as it is "in the money." Also, we are ignoring here the demolition cost for the existing structure. Demolition is an additional cost of redevelopment that can delay the optimal timing of construction.

TOOLS TO MEASURE BUILDING SUSTAINABILITY

Investors may want to consider evidence of a building's "sustainability" when contemplating likely future real depreciation of the structure as noted in our discussion of property life cycle in section 5.4. But how can investors know about a building's sustainability? Some evidence can be provided by formal certifications, which began to be prominent in late in the 2000s decade. 1990 was the first year when any country took formal actions related to the environmental impact from buildings. That is the year when BREEAM was launched in the United Kingdom followed in 1996 by HQE in France and then LEED in the United States in 2000. LEED stands for "Leadership in Energy and Environmental Design", a set of standards that now apply to all types of buildings, interior space and even neighborhoods. LEED is administered by the United States Green Building Council, USGBC, an organization with over 165,000 members as of 2011. Each year the USGBC hosts a conference called "GreenBuild" where ideas, products, and technology are exchanged. The launch of LEED was followed quickly by CASBEE in Japan and later by DGNB in Germany, Green Star in Australia, and a variety of cross adoptions have followed in all industrialized nations.[1] Today variants of LEED are utilized in over 150 countries.

Each of these tools leads to an environmental based rating, i.e. Green Star uses a star rating from 1 to 6; LEED uses a scale that starts at simply "certified" then rises to Silver, Gold and finally Platinum, whereas BREEAM adopts a scale from pass to excellent.

LEED is based upon the design, construction, operation and maintenance of a building. The important elements within LEED, a point system that continues to evolve over time, include:

- **Sustainable Sites** which rewards mixed use, higher density and public transit accessible sites and discourages heat island effects and construction-related pollution.
- **Water Efficiency** which encourages rain water harvesting, water recapture, water saving appliances and water conserving landscaping.
- **Energy and Atmosphere** which is aimed at reducing energy consumption and the use of nonrenewable energy.

- **Materials and Resources** which is aimed at reducing the distance from which materials are brought to the construction site, reducing waste produced during construction, recycling waste from the construction site, and using renewable sustainable materials.
- **Indoor Environmental Quality** focused on air quality, the use of natural light and better acoustics.
- **Innovation in Design** provides bonus points for projects that use innovative technologies and strategies to improve a building's performance well beyond what is required by other LEED credits. This category also rewards projects for including a LEED Accredited Professional on the team to ensure a holistic, integrated approach to the design and construction process.
- **Regional Priorities** vary by location, so what is most important in the region may achieve extra bonus credits.
- **Awareness and Education** may also result in extra credits, based on reaching out to builders, tenants, local real estate professionals, building managers, to make the most effective use of green features within their building.

"Buildings represent a nexus of impacts and opportunities for people and the environment. We have ample documentation of the far-reaching consequences of buildings for energy use, water consumption, greenhouse gas emissions, human health, occupant productivity, and a myriad other factors. The magnitude of these impacts means that the design, construction, and operation of buildings also provide far-reaching opportunities to reduce negative impacts and ultimately strive to make active, positive contributions. This convergence of impacts and opportunities means that buildings must be central to any effort to address the sustainability of human activities," said Christopher Pyke, Ph.D., Director of Research at the United States Green Building Council, USGBC.

---

[1]See "International Comparison of Sustainable Rating Tools" by Reed, Richard, Anita Bilos, Sara Wilkerson, and Karl-Werner Schulte, *Journal of Sustainable Real Estate*, Vol. 1, 2009 available at www.josre.org.

Source: Quote excerpted from Christopher Pyke's message, "From the Director of Research at USGBC." © 2010 *The Journal of Sustainable Real Estate* 2(1): p. 11. Available at www.josre.org. Used with permission.

Typically, the structure value and the land value are bundled together and cannot be purchased separately.[24] Indeed, as noted, the breakout between these two components of property value at any point in time is practically and empirically difficult. But the combination of structure value and land value can be observed at any point in time as the total property value, the value of the bundle, *P*, indicated by the heavy line in the exhibit. The continuous change in *P* over time (between the reconstruction points) essentially determines the capital gain or loss that would be faced by an unlevered investor in the property during its period of operation between redevelopment events. The discontinuous jumps in property

---

[24]Some portion of the structure value may be "purchased" in the form of a long-term leasehold. The existence of long-term leaseholds encumbers the property to the potential detriment of the redevelopment option value component of the property value, possibly reducing the overall property value. [See Dale-Johnson (2001).]

value at the points in time of the reconstructions reflect the injection of new capital into the property via the construction process, indicated by the K symbols in Exhibit 5-10. Therefore, these jumps do not in themselves represent a capital gain for any investor. It is important to recognize that the capital gain (or loss) experienced by an investor in the property is represented by the change in P only between reconstruction points, not across construction points, in Exhibit 5-10.

Exhibit 5-10 shows how **depreciation of the structure** renders the growth rate of the property value (P) generally less than the growth rate of the location or usage value (U). This result is guaranteed by the fact that the value of the newly redeveloped property includes the construction cost component (K), over and above the site acquisition cost component.

This leads to a principle that is of fundamental importance in real estate investment analysis:

> The Depreciation Principle:
> *Over the long run, the change in location value provides a theoretical ceiling to the investment capital gain of the unlevered investor in stabilized property (that is property that is fully operational).*

As an example, suppose that redevelopment occurs once every 50 years, and at the time of redevelopment the old property (essentially just land value by then) is typically worth 20 percent of what the new, redeveloped property will be worth. This is equivalent to saying that site acquisition costs are 20 percent of the total project development costs. This means that during the 50 years between redevelopment events, built property value grows at an average rate of 3.2 percent per year *less* than the growth in location value of the site during that time.[25]

The preceding principle regarding property value carries an implication for the rents that can be charged by a property owner between major redevelopment events. To the extent that rents remain an approximately constant percent of property value, rents must also grow at a rate less than (or decline at a rate greater than) that of the location value of the site. In fact, the more fundamental direction of causality flows in the other direction. Property value declines below that of the potential HBU (that is, the HBU as if the site were vacant) fundamentally because the rent that the market will bear for the existing structure falls further and further below the rent of the potential HBU. Even if the HBU remains constant, the building must compete against newer, less functionally obsolete competitors.

5.5 Chapter Summary

This chapter and the previous chapter have taken you on an introductory tour through the inside of cities and into the basic structure of property value. This inside tour has complemented the overview tour of the system of cities presented in Chapter 3. The academic discipline primarily at work here, conducting these tours, has been urban economics, assisted ably by geography and, to some extent, sociology. The principles, tools, and insights raised in these tours are obviously important to making well-informed commercial property investment decisions. They relate especially to the ability to obtain a realistic impression of the long-run prospects for the space market relevant to particular locations. In the remaining chapter of Part II, we will zero in on commercial property market analysis at a less theoretical, more applied level typical of real estate business practice.

---

[25]Calculated as follows: $0.2 = 1 \times (1 + x)^{50} \rightarrow x = 0.2^{1/50} - 1 = -0.032$. If acquisition costs are 50% of development project value, and redevelopment occurs only every 100 years, then we have: $x = 0.5^{1/100} - 1 = -0.007$. Keep in mind that this refers to depreciation *only relative* to the evolution of the location value of the site, and applies on average over the entire property life cycle between redevelopment events. Although Exhibit 5-10 does not depict such a case, it is possible for property value to increase over time in real terms prior to redevelopment, if the land value component rises fast enough to more than offset the depreciation of the structure component. This will occur primarily only when either (a) the structure is nearly worthless, so that virtually the entire value of the property is in its redevelopment option value, or (b) there is a rapid positive change in the location value of the site.

KEY TERMS

growth premium
irreversibility premium
concentric ring model of urban form
sector model of urban land use
compatible land uses
negative locational externality
polycentric city

major activity center (MAC)
neighborhood business district
 (NBD)
polynuclear city
neighborhood succession theory
property life cycle
structure value

physical obsolescence
functional obsolescence
economic obsolescence
land value
redevelopment option value
structural depreciation

STUDY QUESTIONS

Conceptual Questions

5.1. How does the expected future growth rate of land rent affect the relationship between current land value and current land rent?

5.2. How does land provide its owner a "call option" that allows the owner to profit from uncertainty or volatility in future land rent?

5.3. How does uncertainty or volatility in future land rent affect current land value and land rent, all else being equal? As part of your answer, explain the notion of "value of waiting," why this leads to an "irreversibility" premium in land values, and the resulting implications for development timing and city size.

5.4. What are the fundamental determinants of (a) urban land value (i.e., inside the urban boundary) and (b) the value of undeveloped land just beyond the urban boundary? [Hint: Describe each component of land value, both inside and outside the urban boundary, as shown in Exhibit 5-2.]

5.5. Compare and contrast the Burgess concentric ring model with the Hoyt sector model of urban form. Which, if either one, do you think better describes most cities?

5.6. Draw a schematic picture of what the rent gradient looks like in a polycentric city.

5.7. What is meant by the term "edge city"?

5.8. What does neighborhood succession theory say about how the rate land values or rents will tend to grow over time within a given neighborhood?

5.9. Discuss the effect of land use boundaries on bid-rents and land values. Give an example of two land uses with negative locational externalities for at least one of the uses when the two uses are adjacent to one another.

5.10. Can you think of a city with a tight growth boundary or one with none? What types of prices do you observe in these two cities for a typical 2000 square foot home? Do you feel that density is important for a local government to control?

5.11. According to property life cycle theory, property value is the sum of the values of what two components? Describe each of these two components.

5.12. Describe the three forms or sources of depreciation experienced by a property structure as it ages. Is there anything an investor can do to prevent or slow down the rate of depreciation?

5.13. How do you know that property value must grow at a rate less than the growth rate in the location value of the site (on average over the long run between major redevelopment projects)?

5.14. When is it optimal (from an economic perspective) to demolish and redevelop a property?

5.15. Explain the difference in the evolution over time of *appraised (legal)* land value and *land redevelopment option (economic)* value of a site as illustrated in Exhibit 5-10.

5.16. **(Dynamics of Urban Form)** The simple monocentric city model presented in Chapter 4 is a long-run, static equilibrium model in which the past does not matter; in response to a change in income or population, the city is torn down and rebuilt in the new long-run equilibrium form. The explicit recognition in the current chapter of *time* (age) and the *durability* of real estate structures that depreciate over time means that a city is shaped by both its past and current market dynamics. Based on what you learned in this chapter about how cities grow as well as property and neighborhood life cycles, explain the economic logic underlying the following statements:

a. Cities tend to redevelop from the center outwards.

b. Older, growing cities offer significantly more redevelopment opportunities.

c. The density of housing falls with distance from the city center over time because of rising incomes and decreasing commuting costs, not because of a commuting cost-housing consumption tradeoff. [Assume housing is a "normal" consumption good, the demand for which increases with income. Also assume higher-income households demand higher-quality housing.]

d. Synthesize your answers to (a) through (c) and explain why many U.S. metropolitan areas are witnessing significant new housing construction at both the outer edges and the central city, with some redevelopment also taking place in so-called inner-ring suburbs.

Quantitative Problems

5.17. A downtown surface parking lot generates annual net cash flow of $180,000, and this is expected to grow indefinitely at 3% per year. Based on the current use and current capital market conditions you feel that investors require a 12% return, which implies an initial income yield or cap rate of 9% (12% − 3%).

a. What is the indicated current use value of the property? [Remember that value equals net rent divided by cap rate.]

b. A developer recently paid $4.5 million for the site. What is the implied cap rate associated with this deal? Explain why the sale price differs significantly from the current use value you calculated in (a).

5.18. Consider two undeveloped land sites. At site 1, the highest and best use (HBU) is a warehouse that would cost $1 million to build (exclusive of land cost) and would then generate annual net rents of $150,000, which are expected to grow at 3% per year. At site 2, the HBU is an apartment building that can generate net rents of $800,000, projected to grow at 1% per year, with construction cost of $5 million. Suppose investors buying built properties (that is, properties already developed and in operation) require an initial annual return (in the form of current net income) of 12% minus the expected annual growth rate in the net income, as a percent of the investment cost. For example, they would want an initial yield or cap rate of 9% for the warehouse (12% − 3% = 9%). Suppose the land value for site 1 is $1 million and the land value for site 2 is $2 million. On which of these sites (1, 2, both, or neither) is it currently profitable to undertake construction? Show your reasoning.

5.19. Suppose site acquisition costs typically equal 30% of total development project costs, and 30 years typically elapse between major redevelopment on a given site. By what percent per year does the property value grow *less than* the growth rate of the location value of the site?

REAL ESTATE MARKET ANALYSIS

LEARNING OBJECTIVES

After reading this chapter, you should understand:

⟲ What is meant by real estate market analysis and what types of business decisions it can usefully assist.

⟲ The key elements and quantitative variables involved in market analysis.

⟲ Some of the major types of data sources for conducting market analyses.

⟲ The difference between simple trend extrapolation and a structural market analysis.

⟲ The major steps in conducting a structural analysis of the real estate space market.

⟲ The implications for space market dynamics and cyclicality when market participants cannot or do not base decisions on forward-looking forecasts of the space market.

The preceding chapters discussed the underlying economic and geographic forces that govern urban land values and location patterns. Successful real estate professionals base their decisions on knowledge of these fundamental patterns. In addition to such general and fundamental knowledge, however, real estate professionals typically use a set of practical analytical tools and procedures that relate fundamental principles to the decision at hand. These practical research procedures are often collected under the label of **real estate market analysis**, the subject of this chapter. Market analysis is typically designed to assist in such decisions as:

- Where to locate a branch office
- What size or type of building to develop on a specific site
- What type of tenants to look for in marketing a particular building
- What the rent and expiration term should be on a given lease
- When to begin construction on a development project
- How many units to build this year
- Which cities and property types to invest in so as to allocate capital where rents are more likely to grow
- Where to locate new retail outlets and/or which stores should be closed

Market analysis has as its objective the quantitative or qualitative characterization of the supply side and demand side of a specific space usage market that is relevant to the given decision. For example, we might perform a market analysis for retail space in the Boston CBD (central business district) or for luxury apartment units south of Market Street in downtown San Francisco. Although real estate market analysis techniques and data sources differ somewhat by market sector or property type, all real estate market analysis shares some basic features. This generic core is the focus of the present chapter.

6.1 General Features of Real Estate Market Analysis

As noted, real estate market analysis seeks to quantify and forecast the supply and demand sides of specific space usage markets. Practical market analysis must be simple enough, and based on realistic data, so that it can be applied relatively quickly and inexpensively, and easily communicated and understood in the real world of business practice. Most market analysis is thus characterized by rather direct, common sense procedures. This section will sketch some typical market analysis considerations and procedures.

6.1.1 Purpose of Market Analysis

Real estate market analysis is performed for a wide variety of purposes and in varying contexts to assist with different types of real estate decisions. Some market analyses focus on specific microlevel decisions, while others focus on broader and more general characterizations of real estate markets. Specific microlevel analyses focus on individual building sites or individual users of real estate. For example, a developer might want to examine the feasibility of building a particular type of development on one or more specific sites. This is sometimes referred to as "feasibility analysis" or "site analysis" for a real estate development.[1]

The second type of analysis, general characterization of a real estate market, has as its purpose quantifying and forecasting the supply of and demand for space, typically including the forecast of future rents and vacancies in a particular geographic real estate **market segment**. You may recall from Chapter 1 that real estate space usage markets are segmented by both property type and geographic location. Thus, the definition of a relevant real estate market normally specifies a geographic scope and property type. For example, a market analysis might focus broadly on the office market in metropolitan Chicago or more narrowly on the market for class A office buildings in downtown Chicago. Such general market characterizations provide information that is useful for making a number of different decisions having to do with that market or comparing that market with other markets.

Clearly, the purpose of the market analysis will strongly dictate the type of analysis approach to be taken. The variety of typical uses of market analyses makes it impossible to present an exhaustive or general procedure. Rather, we will here consider a general framework that is applicable for most examples of general market characterization.

6.1.2 Market Supply and Demand Variables and Indicators

The typical general market analysis will focus on a few variables, or indicators, that quantitatively characterize both the supply and demand sides of the real estate space market, as well as the balance between these two sides (the market equilibrium). Following is a typical list of the market descriptive variables:

- Quantity of new construction started
- Quantity of new construction completed
- Absorption of new space
- Vacancy rate
- Rent level

---

[1]Development project feasibility analysis will be discussed further in Chapter 28.

The quantity of new **construction starts** and/or **completions** is a fundamental indicator of real estate markets. As described in Chapter 2, construction represents the addition of new supply to the stock of space available in the market. Of course, construction takes time, typically anywhere from a few months to build a simple house to a few years to build a large commercial complex. The new supply does not enter the market until the construction is complete, although preleasing may commit tenants in advance. In some older markets, it is also important to consider demolition or conversion of old structures, as well as construction of new buildings, to arrive at the net addition of space supply in the market.

The second key market indicator is space **absorption**. This refers to the amount of additional space that is occupied per year. Absorption can be thought of as an indicator of the activity on the demand side of the space market, just as construction is an indicator of activity on the supply side. It is useful, however, to distinguish between gross and net absorption in the market.

Gross absorption measures the total amount of space for which leases were signed during the year, regardless of where the tenants came from. This is a good measure of the volume of rental transaction activity, a very relevant measure of the demand for leasing brokerage services. However, some tenants would be moving from one site to another within the same market, so the signing of their lease would imply vacating one space in the market, as well as occupying another space in the same market. This would not imply a growth in the overall amount of occupied space in the market and thus would not signify growth in the overall demand for space in the market.

A better measure of demand growth is **net absorption**, which is simply the net change in the amount of occupied space in the market. This is the more relevant number to compare to the net amount of construction completed during the same period of time. Comparing net construction completed to net absorption indicates whether demand and supply are growing at the same rate, with resulting implications for changes in the balance between demand and supply in the market. When net absorption exceeds net construction completions, vacancy declines in the market, and when construction exceeds absorption, vacancy rises. The relationship between the quantity of vacant space at the end of a period and the quantity of net construction completions and net absorption during the period is indicated by the following equation:

$$(vacant\ space)_t = (vacant\ space)_{t-1} + (construction)_t - (net\ absorption)_t$$

The **vacancy rate** refers to the percentage of the stock of built space in the market that is not currently occupied. To compute the vacancy rate, one must know two more fundamental quantities: the total stock of space in the market and the amount of space that is currently vacant. For current and historical data, these quantities are determined by inventorying and surveying public records and landlords and are often compiled by brokerage firms and consulting firms or data firms that sell real estate market information.

To be more accurate, the vacancy rate should include all space that is currently unoccupied and available for occupancy, including space that may be currently under lease but available for subleasing. The vacancy rate is one indicator that reflects the current balance between supply and demand in the market (the other is the current market rent level). Vacancy is thus an equilibrium indicator rather than an indicator of either the supply side or the demand side alone. Vacancy rate data are usually more widely available and more reliable than the other equilibrium indicator, rents.

It is important to keep in mind that in a typical real estate market it is normal for some vacancy to exist. Fundamentally, this is because it does not make economic sense for landlords to rent space to the first potential tenant that comes along, no matter what rent that tenant is offering to pay. Similarly, it does not make sense for tenants to rent space in the first building they find, no matter what is the rent there or how suboptimal the location. Both the space owner (landlord) and space user (tenant) suffer costs when tenants move (such as lost rent incurred by the landlord when the space is vacant and moving expenses incurred by the tenant who moves). This is why leases are typically signed committing both parties for some period of time (especially in commercial property markets, where leases are often for multiple years). Therefore, for both the supply and demand sides of the market, profits will be maximized if firms take some time to search for better deals. This search time results in space being held vacant, waiting (in effect) for better deals to show up. Thus, zero vacancy in a market would probably indicate suboptimal behavior on the part of decision makers.[2]

Another rational reason for vacancy in a market is growth in the demand side and the variable and unpredictable nature of that growth. Supply typically has to be added in a "lumpy" manner, because buildings must be built of a certain size in order to be economical, considering construction and land costs. Because of the time it takes to build, construction decisions must be made in the absence of perfect information about the future balance of supply and demand in the market at the time when the building will be completed. This also leads naturally to some excess space being provided in the typical real estate market from time to time. It also suggests, in combination with our previous point about optimal search, that it may be profitable to maintain some inventory of available space. This "inventory model" of vacancy tends to be more important in markets where demand is growing faster and with more volatility, or ups and downs in the growth rate.

For these reasons, real estate markets are characterized by what is sometimes called a **natural vacancy rate**, which is the vacancy rate that tends to prevail on average over the long run in the market, and which indicates that the market is approximately in balance between supply and demand. When vacancy is below the natural rate, it is said that the market is a sellers' or landlords' market or that the rental market is tight, with demand exceeding supply in some sense. When the vacancy rate is above the natural level, the market is said to be a buyers' or tenants' market (or overbuilt), with the supply of available space exceeding the current level of demand. *When vacancy is below the natural rate, rents will tend to be driven up (and new development will tend to occur). When vacancy is above the natural rate, rents will tend to be driven down.*

The natural vacancy rate is not the same for all markets. As noted, it tends to be higher in faster-growing, more volatile markets and in markets where there are fewer regulatory or geographical constraints on new development. Whatever the natural vacancy rate (and it is usually difficult to know precisely what it is in any given market), the actual vacancy rate will tend to cycle over time around this natural rate.

The final, and in some respects, most important market indicator is the current **market rent**, which refers to the level of rents being charged on typical new leases currently being signed in the market. Of course, rents on specific leases will vary according to the specific nature of the site and space being rented and to the terms of the lease. It is therefore important to control for such variations when trying to measure trends in rents across time. This makes reliable quantification of market rents rather difficult. It is also usually important to control for the effect of general inflation, to examine the trend in *real rents*. This is because real rents are what really matter (reflecting purchasing power or opportunity cost) and because real rents reflect the actual physical and economic balance between supply and demand in the space market. Another factor to keep in mind is that *asking rents*, which may typically be reported in surveys of landlords, may differ from the *effective rents* actually being charged new tenants. The concept of effective rent (discussed more fully in Chapter 30) includes the monetary effect of concessions and rent abatements that landlords may sometimes offer tenants to persuade them to sign a lease. For example, a landlord may quote a rent of \$10/SF but then offer the first year rent-free if the tenant signs a 5-year lease. Yet the rent may be reported in a survey or a casual inquiry as \$10. Effective rents tend to be private information.

In summary the five variables described in this section form a basic quantitative overview of the space market, including how the balance between supply and demand in the market changes and the sources of those changes on both the supply and demand sides. Exhibits 6-1 and 6-2 show the results of historical analyses of the office space markets in three major metropolitan areas of the United States during the 1980s through 2010. Exhibit 6-1 shows construction completions, net absorption, and vacancy in New York, San Francisco,

---

[2]See Appendix 30C on the CD for additional discussion of this topic.

and Atlanta, expressed as a percent of the existing stock of office space in each market. (The construction and absorption percentages are expressed in annual rates, even though the time periods on the horizontal axis are quarters, so you can get an idea about the magnitude of annual growth rates.)

The three metropolitan office markets depicted in the exhibits were selected because they demonstrate the kind of variety that can exist across space markets. New York represents a very large and mature office market. While it may have large amounts of construction measured in absolute terms (its total stock of commercial office space is in the neighborhood of 500 million square feet according to CoStar Group, the source of the data in the exhibits), New York's growth in demand and new construction is relatively small as a percent of the existing stock, averaging less than 1 percent per year. Exhibit 6-1 reveals that New York has recently experienced three major down cycles in its office market, with negative net absorption (absolute decline in the amount of occupied space): most severely in the late 1980s and early 1990s, then again in the early 2000s, and again after the financial crisis of 2008. San Francisco was a much more volatile market than New York during the period shown, with faster growth (construction averaging 2.5 percent of existing stock per year), but a huge negative shock to demand after the dot.com crash of the early 2000s. Atlanta has tended to be the most rapidly growing of the three markets, with annual growth averaging some 4 percent of stock per year over the 25 years and in the 1980s exceeding 10 percent per year. (In general, the 1980s was a peak period for office development in the United States.) But Atlanta presents the highest vacancy rates. As noted, the natural vacancy rate tends to be greater in faster-growing cities that have relatively weak constraints on new supply, that is, where it is relatively easy and inexpensive for developers to build new space.

All three of the space markets shown in the exhibits display substantial variation in the balance of supply and demand, as indicated by the variation in the vacancy rate and the rents shown in Exhibit 6-2. The rents in the exhibit are the average reported asking rents for new leases, in dollars per square foot per year. Exhibit 6-2 displays "real rents," that is, net of inflation (expressed in constant 2011 dollars). In general, the variation in both vacancy and rents appears strongly cyclical, though some markets are more cyclical than others, and the cycle is not necessarily the same across the markets.[3] New York's vacancy cycle is less prominent (less amplitude) than the other two cities, but Atlanta displayed the least cyclicality in rents. The exhibit thus suggests that rents were less sensitive to vacancy in Atlanta. This would reflect greater **price elasticity** of supply in Atlanta (i.e., a small increase in rents evokes a large and fast response in new development thereby preventing rents from rising further).

Exhibit 6-2 graphically displays the fundamental point noted earlier that rents tend to move inversely to vacancy. If we take the average vacancy over the 1982–2011 period covered in Exhibit 6-1, we would estimate the "natural" vacancy rate as about 11 percent in New York, 13 percent in San Francisco, and closer to 18 percent in Atlanta. There is some evidence in all three cities that this natural vacancy rate has been gradually increasing in recent decades (though this might simply evidence better data collection about true vacancy). The differences in the long-run average real level of asking rents (in 2011 dollars: $51/SF in New York, $36/SF in San Francisco, and $25/SF in Atlanta) reflects the basic principles of urban form introduced in Chapter 4. Atlanta faces the greatest availability of land, a full 360-degree development arc, and far lower density than either New York or San Francisco, hence, a flatter rent gradient and

---

[3]It should also be noted that just because a metro area tends to be strongly cyclical in one space market segment does not necessarily mean it will be strongly cyclical in other segments. For example, during the period shown in Exhibit 6-2 New York displayed much less cyclicality in apartment rents than in office rents. We will explore the cyclicality question in section 6.2 of this chapter, and on this point the reader may also wish to review the previous discussion of the "real estate system" in Chapter 2. It should also be kept in mind that any cycle in a space market will not necessarily be exactly echoed in the corresponding property asset market. Asset values reflect the present values of investors' expected future cash flows, discounted to reflect time value of money and risk aversion. To some extent space market cycles can be (or should be) predictable in advance by asset market participants, which would mitigate their impact on changes in asset values since predictable rent changes would smooth out in the present value. On the other hand, asset values may be moved substantially by factors in the capital market that are not reflected in the space market, such as changes in interest rates, risk aversion, and liquidity. (See previous discussion in Chapter 2 and relevant further discussion in Chapters 7, 12, and 22.)

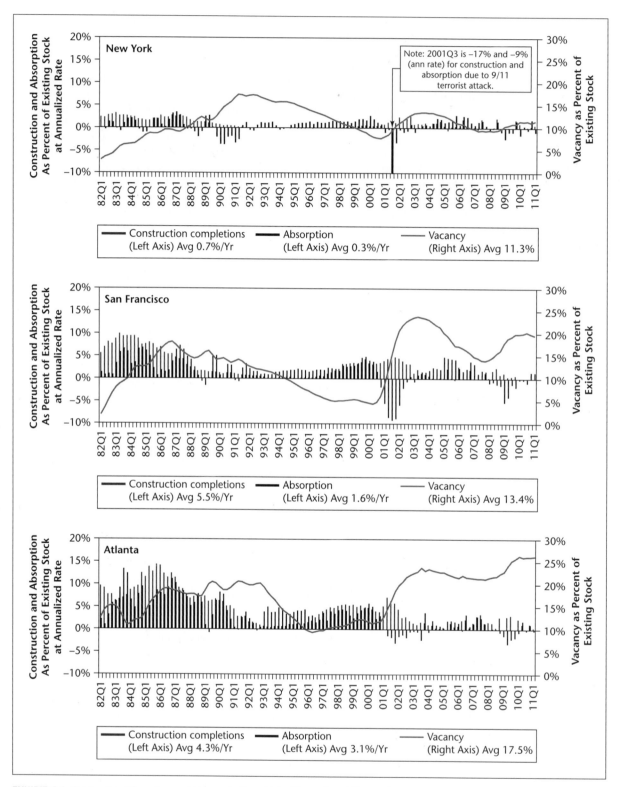

EXHIBIT 6-1 Construction, Absorption, and Vacancy in Three Major Metropolitan Office Markets, 1982 to 2011

Source: Based on CoStar data.

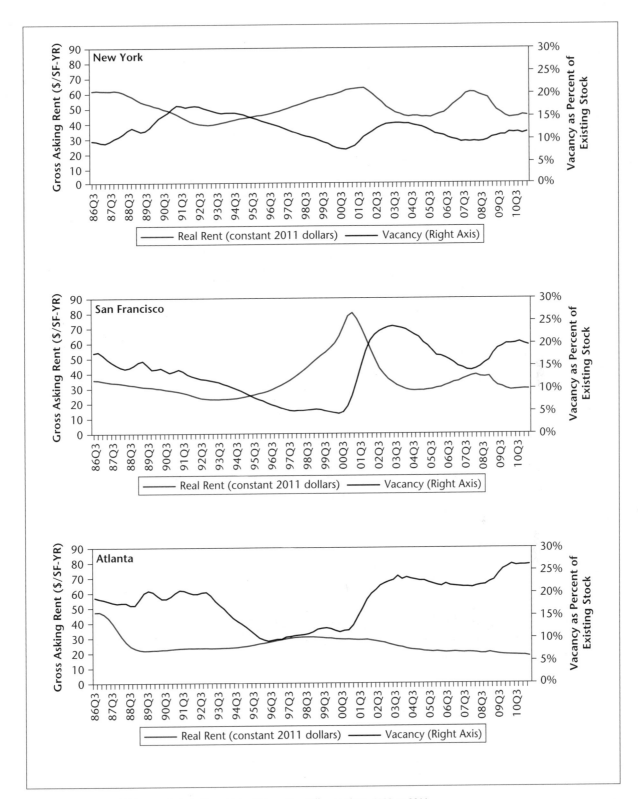

EXHIBIT 6-2 Rents and Vacancy Cycle in Three Major Metropolitan Office Markets, 1982 to 2011

Source: Based on CoStar data.

lower central place location premiums. New York is by far the largest of the three metros in population, which we noted in Chapter 4 tends to increase location premia.

The particular analyses in Exhibits 6-1 and 6-2 are purely historical, but forecasts of the space market are also regularly conducted by real estate consulting and information-vending firms, as well as by the research staffs of the major brokerage firms and investment-management firms.

The five basic variables described in this section can often be combined or added to other data to provide indicators that are useful for gazing into the future and attempting to draw some conclusions about where a market is headed. For example, if you take the current amount of vacant space in the market, plus the amount of any new construction started but not yet complete, and divide that sum by 1/12th the annual net absorption, you get an indicator known as the **months supply**. The formula is presented here:

$$MS = \frac{Vacancy + Construction}{Net\ absorbtion/12}$$

The months supply (MS) is an indicator of how long it will take (in months) for all of the vacant space in the market to be absorbed (driving the market down to a zero vacancy rate). For such interpretation of the MS formula, one would have to assume (1) the rate of new demand growth continues as indicated by the net absorption rate, and (2) there is no new construction in the market other than what has already been started. The months supply can be compared to the length of time (in months) that it takes to complete the typical construction project. If the months supply is less than the construction time, then the market can support additional new construction. If (as we suggested earlier) it is not practical for the market to go all the way down to zero vacancy, or if there is likely to be demolition or abandonment of existing occupied space in the market, then the market can handle additional new construction, even when the months supply is somewhat greater than the average construction-project duration. However, if the months supply extends far beyond the average construction-project duration, then the indication is that the market is oversupplied and there will be continued downward pressure on real effective rents.

6.1.3 Defining the Scope of the Analysis

In any space market analysis, one must know or define the subject market. While national aggregations are of interest for studying the entire industry, to be relevant to specific business decisions, it is usually necessary to define the market more specifically and functionally. Generally market analysis focuses at the metropolitan level or even narrower, such as a quadrant or neighborhood of a metropolitan area (e.g., the North Dallas Market or the South Atlanta Market). A metropolitan region forms an overall functional market area that can usually be usefully subdivided into several **submarkets**. The CBD (or downtown) of the metropolitan area is typically considered one market area, and the suburbs are divided into several markets by geographic sector, sometimes including inner and outer rings. Typically, each market area has one or a few major transportation nodes and major activity centers.

Finally, space markets tend to segregate by property "quality", often labeled as class A, class B, or (sometimes) class C (and others). Class A are the premium properties that tend to be newer and have more amenities or better design and features. The exact definitions of such quality market segments tend inevitably to be dynamic and fuzzy. Such market segments are also related to one another in that there is normally a "trickle down" of older class A properties into class B supply, and some potential tenants may want to move from one class to another (typically up to a higher class if and when rents are depressed). But the quality market segments are very real in that different potential tenants are naturally at different price points in the rental market.

As an example of a specific sub market analysis, Exhibit 6-3A shows a map of the metropolitan area of Atlanta divided into 42 office sub markets. The exhibit also shows how these submarkets can be consolidated into 10 major submarkets. While many potential office tenants would need to be located specifically in one of these market areas, other tenants—for example, a large national firm moving an initial branch office to Atlanta from outside the metropolitan area—might consider several different submarkets to be equally appropriate for their needs. So

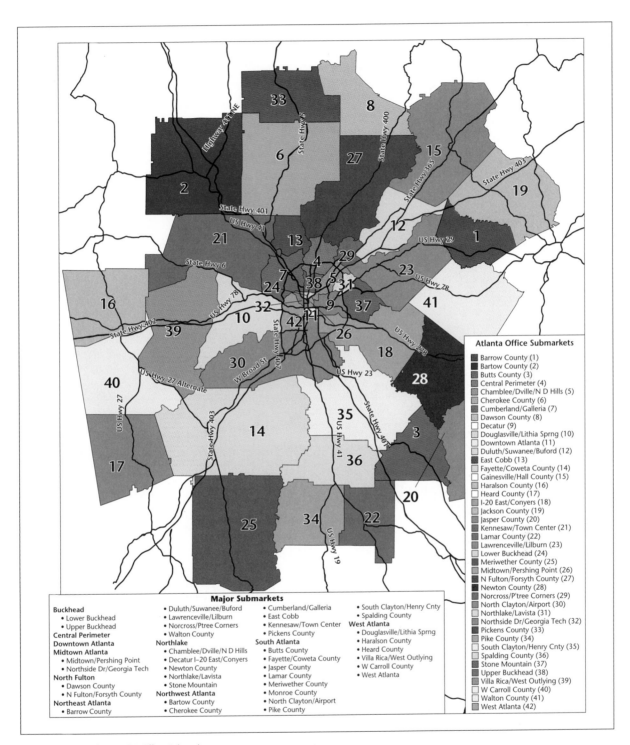

EXHIBIT 6-3A Atlanta MSA Office Submarkets

Source: CoStar Property, used with permission.

to some extent one must consider the entire metropolitan area as a single market, although the geographically distinguishable submarkets within the metro area are also relevant.

It is also interesting to note in Exhibit 6-3B the difference in rents between the class A and class B quality market segments. While information about class B rents may be less

Class A Market Statistics

Market	Existing Inventory		Vacancy			YTD Net Absorption	YTD Deliveries	Under Const SF	Quoted Rates
	# Blds	Total RBA	Direct SF	Total SF	Vac %				
Buckhead	46	15,136,275	2,546,080	2,732,620	18.1%	409,649	0	0	$26.14
Central Perimeter	79	20,717,900	3,433,301	3,672,549	17.7%	524,075	300,000	300,000	$21.83
Downtown Atlanta	30	16,428,027	2,960,675	3,269,055	19.9%	(212,230)	0	0	$19.44
Midtown Atlanta	40	16,275,244	2,722,405	2,923,162	18.0%	274,272	0	450,000	$26.17
North Fulton	113	16,678,599	2,539,667	2,758,154	16.5%	(5,149)	0	72,310	$19.69
Northeast Atlanta	69	8,386,917	1,434,935	1,459,613	17.4%	116,233	67,500	344,476	$19.92
Northlake	23	3,371,463	451,495	454,958	13.5%	(75,833)	0	290,000	$20.07
Northwest Atlanta	83	17,949,924	2,758,250	2,846,632	15.9%	(122,782)	0	0	$21.57
South Atlanta	22	1,645,906	377,640	411,771	25.0%	15,741	0	0	$20.16
West Atlanta	1	71,500	0	0	0.0%	0	0	0	$0.00
Totals	506	116,661,755	19,224,448	20,528,514	17.6%	923,976	367,500	1,456,786	$21.97

Class B Market Statistics

Market	Existing Inventory		Vacancy			YTD Net Absorption	YTD Deliveries	Under Const SF	Quoted Rates
	# Blds	Total RBA	Direct SF	Total SF	Vac %				
Buckhead	86	4,797,941	820,644	847,587	17.7%	8,050	0	0	$18.92
Central Perimeter	256	9,560,549	2,604,334	2,684,364	28.1%	84,617	16,000	0	$18.05
Downtown Atlanta	147	15,059,769	1,249,348	1,250,658	8.3%	(38,992)	0	0	$14.46
Midtown Atlanta	134	6,419,880	885,651	936,071	14.6%	84,056	0	0	$17.81
North Fulton	833	14,722,654	2,454,982	2,503,965	17.0%	134,143	2,400	0	$14.73
Northeast Atlanta	1,374	20,436,802	4,288,304	4,372,377	21.4%	99,853	22,200	23,504	$14.49
Northlake	674	18,646,450	2,081,709	2,136,103	11.5%	11,488	13,822	0	$16.94
Northwest Atlanta	1,113	21,682,629	4,044,095	4,088,813	18.9%	49,508	0	16,650	$15.73
South Atlanta	756	14,138,178	1,719,928	1,779,284	12.6%	59,354	0	41,145	$16.62
West Atlanta	191	2,540,934	300,831	300,831	11.8%	57,362	40,000	40,000	$15.28
Totals	5,564	128,005,786	20,449,826	20,900,053	16.3%	549,439	94,422	121,299	$15.96

EXHIBIT 6-3B Atlanta Space Market Data Consolidated Into 10 Major Submarkets, Mid-Year 2012

Source: CoStar Property, used with permission.

complete and accurate than that about class A, many markets exhibit differences similar to what is shown in this case for Atlanta, with class B rents typically about two-thirds to three-quarters that of class A rents.[4]

Apart from geographical scope, the temporal range of the analysis must also be defined—that is, what period of time is to be covered. Historical analysis can give important insights into and perspective regarding the dynamics of a market. But many market analyses also try to provide explicit future forecasts, since decisions are forward-looking in time. A 5- to 10-year future horizon is usually desirable, although data problems and random events often make forecasting much beyond three years rather unreliable. If the market tends to be cyclical (see section 6.2), the length of that cycle and the market's current position within the cycle should be considered. Some rental market cycles tend to be longer than ten years, and it can be important to understand if one is likely to be near a peak or bottom.

6.1.4 Trend Extrapolation versus Structural Analysis

Another threshold issue in defining a market analysis is the type of analysis approach required. In this regard, it is useful to distinguish two broadly different types of approaches (but keep in mind that a hybrid involving elements of both is often most useful). The two approaches may be labeled **simple trend extrapolation**, and **structural analysis**. With simple trend extrapolation, one looks directly at the market supply and demand variables of interest and extrapolates these variables into the future based purely on their own past historical trends. For example, one would obtain data on the historical vacancy rate and rents in the market and project the future vacancy rate and rents based on the historical trend.

This approach can take advantage of time-series statistical techniques. As noted earlier, real estate space markets tend to have a lot of inertia and to be rather cyclical. This potentially allows for considerable ability to forecast at least a few years into the future, based just on past trends. Indicators such as the months supply described earlier can be useful for making near-term forecasts. Formal time-series econometric techniques also can often be usefully applied to this type of forecasting.[5] However, in common business practice, more informal or heuristic procedures are often used to make the projection, or the formal models are combined with judgment that is more intuitive.

The structural approach to market analysis, on the other hand, attempts to model the *structure* of the market by identifying and quantifying the underlying determinants of the variables of interest. This requires explicit quantification and forecasting of both the supply side and the demand side of the market, so that equilibrium indicators such as the vacancy rate and rent can be projected by forecasting the supply and demand sides separately and comparing the two forecasts. Depending on the depth at which the structural analysis is done, this may include developing a model of the determinants of space usage demand in the market (a demand model), and forecasting these underlying sources of demand. For example, demand for office space usage is driven fundamentally by the amount of office employment in the area, while the demand for retail space is driven by the

---

[4]Recall our point in section 5.4 of the previous chapter about functional depreciation of structures. If a building devolves from class A to class B over a 30-year period, and the latter rents are two-thirds of the former, then this implies a 1.3%/year real depreciation rate relative to top-of-the-market class A rents. If class A rents are just keeping up with inflation, then the subject property would experience 1.3%/year less value growth than inflation provided the property's cap rate remained unchanged. Such real depreciation would reflect an effective decline in the real value of the structure, assuming the land or location value was keeping up with inflation.

[5]The most basic techniques include autoregression, in which the market variable of interest (such as the vacancy rate) is regressed on its own past values to estimate a relationship across time. If designed properly, autoregression and more general univariate models, such as autoregressive integrated moving average (ARIMA), can capture cyclicality and lagged effects. Relatively user-friendly statistical software packages for personal computers are available to facilitate this type of forecasting. If data permit, more sophisticated techniques such as transfer function analysis, vector autoregression, or vector error correction models can be employed, potentially encompassing variables from the asset market, such as property yields and capital market factors, as well as structural variables from the space market itself.

level of real per capita disposable income and the regional population. A structural model should also consider the supply side of the market. At a minimum, this consideration must include an examination of current new and planned construction and demolition in the market.[6]

6.1.5 Major General Tasks in Conducting a Basic Short-Term Structural Market Analysis

Here we review the major steps and tasks involved in conducting a structural market analysis at a very basic level, a level that will often suffice for short- to medium-term forecasts of space market conditions (up to about three years in the future). Exhibit 6-4 presents an overview of the tasks involved in a typical analysis of this type. Eight separate tasks are identified. Notice

EXHIBIT 6-4 Generic Framework of a Basic Short-Term Structural Market Analysis for Real Estate

© OnCourse Learning

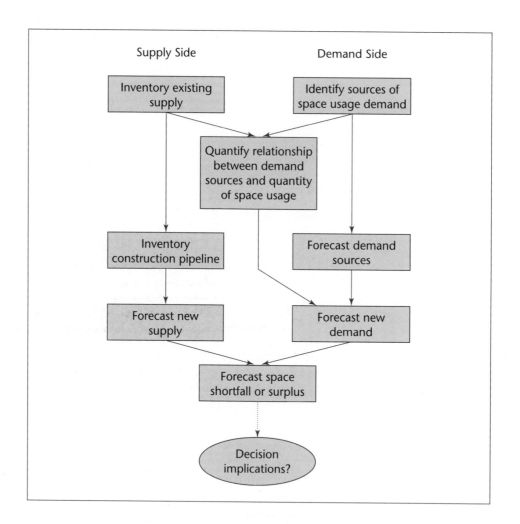

---

[6]A more sophisticated structural analysis would include a formal system of models of market equilibrium between supply and demand. This requires estimating formal models of both demand and supply, including some representation of the price elasticities of both demand and supply, and the response lags in both these sides of the market. *Price elasticity* relates how much the amount of space supplied (or demanded) responds to a given change in the rental price in the market. The *lags* relate to how much time elapses between a rental price change and the resultant change in demand or supply responding to that price change. This type of formal structural analysis will be described in more detail in section 6.2.

EXHIBIT 6-5

Major Demand Drivers by
Property Type

© OnCourse Learning

Property Type	Demand Drivers
Residential single family (Owner occupied)	• Population • Household formation (child-rearing ages) • Interest rates • Employment growth (business and professional occupations)
Residential multifamily (Apartment renters)	• Population • Household formation (non–child-rearing ages) • Local housing affordability • Employment growth (blue collar occupations)
Retail	• Aggregate disposable income • Aggregate household wealth • Traffic volume (specific sites)
Office	Employment in office occupations: • Finance, Insurance, Real Estate (FIRE) • Business and professional services • Legal services
Industrial	• Manufacturing employment • Transportation employment • Airfreight volume • Rail and truck volume
Hotel & convention	• Air passenger volume • Tourism receipts or number of visitors

that the tasks involve analysis of both the supply and demand side of the market, with three tasks focusing on each side of the market separately and two tasks integrating across the two sides.

The first steps in the structural market analysis are to inventory the existing supply of space and to identify the fundamental sources of the demand for space usage in the relevant market. Supply inventories are available from local brokerage firms, local planning agencies, and commercial firms specializing in providing this type of data. The fundamental sources of demand are the drivers of the need for space usage in the market. Some typical indicators of these **demand drivers** that are relatively easy to quantify and are often used in demand studies for different types of property are indicated in the table in Exhibit 6-5. Population projections are published by the Census Bureau. Employment data by occupation are published by the Bureau of Labor Statistics and Bureau of Economic Analysis of the federal government, including regional breakdowns and future projections.[7] Most state governments also publish such data, as do many local planning commissions and chambers of commerce. Income information by type and region is published by the Bureau of Economic Analysis and the Census Bureau, as well as state and local sources and private commercial sources. Geographic Information Systems (GIS) technology makes possible more geographically precise use of such information.

The next step in the structural market analysis is to relate the underlying demand sources to the amount of real estate space usage demand. In some cases, this will be straightforward because of the nature of the market. For example, there should be approximately a one-to-one correspondence between the number of households and the number of housing units demanded (except for special markets such as student housing). But in other markets, it will be necessary to relate, for example, the number of square feet of space required to the number of employees of a given occupation. This can be done by comparing the square footage of various types of

---

[7]The Standard Industrial Classification (SIC) system for classifying industries was discussed in Chapter 3 and may also be useful here. Note that in 2002 the U.S. Census Bureau replaced the previous SIC codes with a new industrial classification system designed to be integrated with those used in Canada and Mexico. The new system is called the NAICS, and is described on various Web sites.

space identified in the supply stock inventory to the number of employees of various occupations identified in the demand side analysis. For example, it might be determined that the average office worker uses 200 square feet of space under typical market conditions.[8] (The appendix on the CD presents a discussion and recent data about office space demand.)

Next, one must develop forecasts of future demand for and supply of space in the relevant market. On the demand side, the sources of demand previously identified must be projected based on the extrapolation of past trends or judgment about the evolution of the local economic base.[9] Combined with the relationship between demand sources and space usage, this will result in a projection of the amount of space demand at various times in the future.

On the supply side, this step involves inventorying the construction pipeline, that is, identifying all projects currently under construction, as well as projects that are in various stages of planning. This information could be found by researching construction permits issued by local governments, information that is public. Also, local business and financial newspapers typically announce major construction projects that receive financing. However, not all projects that are planned will actually be built, so the quantification of the construction pipeline will involve some judgment or estimation. In older neighborhoods or regions, it will be important to also estimate the amount of demolition and abandonment of existing occupied space in this step of the analysis. The result of this step is a projection of net new space to be added to the market at various times in the future.

The end result of a basic structural analysis such as we are describing here is some projection of the future relationship between supply and demand in the market. In the near term (say, one to three years in the future), this type of analysis can be fairly accurate and result in a quantitative projection of the magnitude of space supply shortfall or surplus. What tends to trip up some such analyses in the real world are unexpected downturns in the underlying economy or the failure to foresee a turning point in a market cycle. Analysts should probably be on their guard against getting caught up in prevailing conventional assumptions or extrapolations of recent past trends, and conclusions should be elaborated on by including sensitivity analyses of the effects on forecasts of changes in underlying assumptions.

With this in mind, market supply/demand balance projections may have various decision implications. For example, it might appear that within three years there will be a demand for a million more square feet of office space in a certain market than is currently in the construction pipeline. If typical projects are around 500,000 square feet, then this would suggest a possible need for two new such projects. Alternatively, the projection might indicate that excess supply will continue in the market even after three years, with no need for new projects.

In general, projected tightening of the market (as indicated by a growing space shortfall) should lead to higher rents and lower vacancy rates, and a projected surplus of supply will lead to rising vacancy rates and falling rents. This relates not only to construction and development decisions but also to other types of real estate decisions. Leasing decisions can be enlightened by such a market analysis as well. For example, a landlord may hesitate to commit to a long-term lease at a low rent if the market is projected to tighten. Investment in existing structures will appear more profitable the greater the projected future space supply shortfall (other things being equal, in particular, the price of the property), for this would imply better prospects for future rental growth or greater ease of leasing currently vacant space.[10]

---

[8]Keep in mind that when markets are soft and rents are low, tenants expecting growth may lease more space than they need, inflating the apparent square feet of space per employee. The reverse may happen when markets are tight and rents are high.

[9]See Chapter 3, section 3.4.

[10]As noted previously, the ability to predict space market variables such as rents and vacancy does not necessarily imply an ability to predict property investment total returns, as asset prices may already reflect predictable movements in the space market. However, real estate asset markets are not perfectly efficient, and practitioners widely believe that those who can predict the space market best will have greater opportunities to earn higher investment returns. [See, for example, Miles (1997) and Miles & Guilkey (1998).] In any case, a space market in its "cycle" does affect the nature of the investment performance of real estate assets (such as the relative magnitude of current income versus capital growth), even if it does not affect the ex ante total return. Specific space markets are often at different places in their cycles at the same time, so there is clearly a rationale to use space market analysis to help guide investment allocation among alternative markets.

*6.2 Formal Model of Space Market Equilibrium Dynamics and Cyclicality[11]

To help the interested reader gain a basic familiarity with formal space market equilibrium forecasting, this section will present a simplified numerical example of a system of articulated supply, demand, and construction models with price response elasticities and **lags**.[12] Such a system of models is useful not only to help you get an idea of how more sophisticated real estate market forecasting is done, but also to derive some classical principles of real estate market dynamics, such as the potentially cyclical nature of many real estate space markets. (The general type of model examined here is often called a **stock-flow model**.)[13] Formal modeling of the type described here can allow a more rigorous and explicit quantitative forecast of future rents and vacancies and facilitate longer-term forecasts.

Here, our simple dynamic model of a space market is represented by a system of six linked equations that reflect the relationship among supply, demand, construction, rent, and vacancy over time. The equations are linked by the fact that the output from each equation represents input in another equation, forming across all six equations a complete representation of the market equilibrium over time. The system will allow the simulation and forecast of rents, vacancy, construction, and absorption in the market each year.

The first two equations reflect the supply side of the market. Equation (1) is a model of the development industry, relating construction completions (new additions to the supply of space in the market) to rents prevailing in the market at the time when the construction projects are started.

$$C(t) = \begin{cases} \varepsilon R(t - L), & \text{if } R(t - L) > K, \\ 0, & otherwise \end{cases} \tag{1}$$

$C(t)$ is the amount of new space completed in year t. $R(t - L)$ is the rent prevailing in the market in year $t - L$. Because construction takes time, there is a lag between when construction decisions are made (when the rents that trigger that decision are observed) and when new supply is completed.[14] This lag is expressed in the model by the parameter L, which is the length of time it takes to complete the typical construction project in the market. There is also a "trigger rent" (like the replacement cost rent discussed in Chapter 1), above which new construction will start and below which no new construction will start. This trigger rent level is indicated by K. The supply elasticity is reflected by the parameter ε, which determines the amount of new construction started per dollar by which the current rent exceeds the trigger rent. Greater values of ε indicate that development responds more elastically to rents; that is, more new supply will be built for each dollar that rents rise above the trigger level.

Equation (2) simply states that the total stock of space supply in year t, labeled $S(t)$, equals the previous year's stock, $S(t - 1)$, plus the new construction completed in year t.

$$S(t) = S(t - 1) + C(t) \tag{2}$$

Two more equations portray the demand side of the space usage market. Equation (3) is the demand model, relating the amount of space that potential users would currently

---

[11]Sections indicated with a preceding asterisk in the section number cover more advanced or analytically difficult material. Students with relatively little economics or quantitative background may want to skip or skim these sections.

[12]The model presented here is simple enough for a student with only basic computer spreadsheet skills to enter the formulas into a spreadsheet and play around with the parameters of the model to see the effect on the resulting dynamic behavior of the market.

[13]The development of this type of model for real estate markets has been associated with researchers such as Kenneth Rosen, William Wheaton, and, more recently, Patric Hendershott, among others. Though first developed for office markets, these types of models can be applied to any real estate market sector. While a comprehensive literature review is beyond the scope of this book, some seminal articles are cited in the reference list at the end of Part II. See in particular Ibanez and Pennington-Cross (2011) for a review as well as a survey overview applying the modeling to 34 major metropolitan areas and four space market sectors.

[14]Note that this model thus assumes that developers are unable to forecast changes in rents.

like to occupy, $D(t)$, to the current rent level, $R(t)$, and the current level of underlying need, $N(t)$.[15]

$$D(t) = \alpha - \eta R(t) + \tau N(t) \tag{3}$$

The measure of need reflects the fundamental sources of space usage demand discussed in the previous section. For example, for office markets, $N(t)$ might be measured by the number of office employees working in the market. The three parameters, α, η, and τ, calibrate the demand model. The parameter α is a constant or "intercept" for the model. The response sensitivity parameter η reflects the price elasticity of demand, while the parameter τ reflects the "technology" of space usage, reflecting the quantity of space usage demanded per unit of underlying need. For example, if $N(t)$ is the number of office employees, then τ would represent the number of square feet per employee.

We assume it takes one year for space users to implement or realize the level of space usage demand they desire (due, for example, to time required to find the necessary space and move into it or, in the case of reductions in space demand, to vacate space and get out of leases). So equation (4) simply equates the amount of space actually occupied at time t, $OS(t)$, to the demand in the previous year, $D(t-1)$. The previous year's demand is just the output of equation (3) applied in the previous year.

$$OS(t) = D(t-1) \tag{4}$$

The fifth equation in the system simply reflects the definition of the vacancy rate, $v(t)$, as the fraction of the currently available stock of space that is currently unoccupied.

$$v(t) = [S(t) - OS(t)]/S(t) \tag{5}$$

Note that the variables on the right-hand side of equation (5) are outputs from equations (2) and (4).

Finally, the system is made complete by equation (6), which represents landlord- and tenant-rental-pricing behavior. Landlords are assumed to raise or lower rents in response to perceived contemporaneous vacancy rates.[16] In particular, if current vacancy rates are above the natural vacancy rate for the market, labeled V, then landlords will reduce rents. If current vacancy rates are below the natural rate, then landlords will raise rents. The sensitivity of rental response to vacancy-rate deviations from the natural rate is reflected in the response parameter λ. It is assumed that it takes a year for landlords to respond effectively to changes in the market (perhaps due to difficulty of accurately observing the market or sluggish response to the market).

$$R(t) = R(t-1)(1 - \lambda\{[v(t) - V]/V\}) \tag{6}$$

The above six equations present a complete dynamic system of the real estate space market, including market supply, demand, and construction. By quantifying the parameters in the equations, the decision-relevant characteristics of the market equilibrium can be simulated through time. In a realistic application, such a model would be specified and calibrated using econometric techniques. It is also possible to build explicit links to the capital market into the model, for example by relating the trigger rent, K, to capital market parameters such as real interest rates [see Hendershott (1995)].

To see how such a model of the real estate space market can simulate the functioning of the market over time, consider an office market that starts off with an employment level of 70,000, a stock of 20 million SF of built space, a vacancy rate of 10 percent (equal to its natural vacancy rate), and a rent level of $20/SF. Now suppose this market is characterized by system parameters with the following numerical values:

---

[15]Thus, space users also do not forecast rents in this model.

[16]As with the other actors in this model, landlords do not forecast future rents.

- Supply sensitivity $\varepsilon = 0.3$
- Demand sensitivity $\eta = 0.3$
- Technology $\tau = 200$ SF/employee
- Demand intercept $\alpha = 10$ million SF
- Rent sensitivity $\lambda = 0.3$
- Construction lag $L = 3$ years

Exhibit 6-6 shows the 40-year evolution of rents, vacancy rate, and construction in such a market, if the employment level grows steadily at a rate of 1 percent per year. The left-hand vertical scale in the exhibit shows the equilibrium level of rent (in $/SF), the vacancy rate (in percent), and the level of office employment in the market. The right-hand vertical scale measures the amount of new construction in millions of square feet. The graph traces the annual levels of each of these variables, starting from the steady state described earlier.

The cyclical nature of the resulting market dynamics is obvious in this model. With the response and lag parameter values cited, this space market has a cycle of approximately 11 years. This **real estate cycle** exists even though there is no cycle, just steady growth, in the underlying source of the demand for space usage (employment) and even though there is no "lumpiness" in the provision of new space (buildings can be built in any size). The example depicted in Exhibit 6-6 demonstrates several features that tend to characterize real estate space market cycles.

- The real estate cycle may be different from and partially independent of the underlying business cycle in the local economy.
- The cycle will be much more exaggerated in the construction and development industry than in other aspects of the real estate market, such as rents and vacancy.
- The vacancy cycle tends to lead the rent cycle slightly (vacancy peaks before rent bottoms).
- New construction completions tend to peak when vacancy peaks.

The existence of a "built-in" cycle in the real estate space market, and indeed the specific features of the cycle noted, can be seen to result from several characteristics of the model

EXHIBIT 6-6 Simulated Space Market Dynamics
© OnCourse Learning

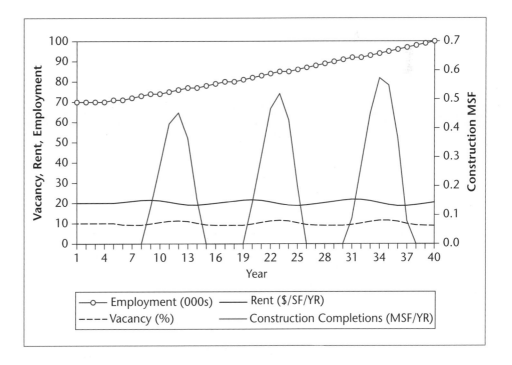

described here. The particular response sensitivities and lags determine the cyclicality of the market and, more fundamentally, the myopic or adaptive nature of the behavior of the market participants tends to produce cyclicality. In this model, the market participants (developers, landlords, and tenants) base their decisions on present and past information rather than on forecasts of the future. Actual behavior in realistic markets is not as simple as that depicted in this model. As noted in Chapter 2, market participants do try to forecast the future, especially through the role that the real estate asset market plays in the overall system and also given the prevalence of long-term leases in many markets (though such leases can also exacerbate cyclicality by dampening responsiveness in rental price and space occupancy). Nevertheless, the simple model shown here probably does capture an important part of real estate market behavior, since market participants may not always put as much effort into basing decisions on future forecasts as they should, and even if they did, those forecasts would never be perfect.[17]

6.3 Chapter Summary

This chapter presented the objectives, scope, and major elements involved in real estate space market analysis, as this type of analysis can help in making specific real estate decisions, including investment decisions. The elements and tools used in market analysis are based on the more fundamental urban economic and geographic principles discussed in the previous chapters. But market analysis needs to focus at a more specific level. Market analysis of this type is designed above all to be practical in a business or public policy decision-making environment. This means the analysis procedures must be simple enough to be understood and applied by practitioners, and they must be usable with data that are realistically available. In this closing chapter of Part II, we left the more academic or theoretical realm of the preceding three chapters. If real estate market analysis does not help decision makers in a timely manner, it will not usually be useful in the real world. However, in this chapter, we also saw how an articulated system of supply and demand models of the space market (including the construction industry) can be used to reveal some general patterns in the dynamics of these markets.

This chapter concludes Part II, the part of this book that is based primarily on urban economics and focuses primarily on the space market component of the real estate system defined in Chapter 2. The remainder of this book will focus primarily on topics most relevant to the asset market component of the system, and will be based primarily on financial economics as the major underlying academic discipline.

KEY TERMS

real estate market analysis	vacancy rate	price elasticity
market segment	natural vacancy rate	lags
construction starts	market rent	demand drivers
construction completions	months supply	stock-flow model
absorption	submarkets	real estate cycle
gross absorption	simple trend extrapolation	
net absorption	structural analysis	

---

[17]See Wheaton et al. (2001) and Ibanez & Pennington-Cross (2011). The latter's overview of 34 metro areas and four usage sectors suggests that space market cyclicality is highly variable across markets. Some markets appear to be much more cyclical and volatile than others, and response rates vary widely both in the short run and the long run. Overall, office markets tend to exhibit more cyclicality than other usage types. See also Chapter 27 later in this book (section 27.6) for a discussion of an alternative theory of real estate cycles based on option valuation theory that does not involve myopic or irrational behavior.

STUDY QUESTIONS

6.1. What is the difference between a microlevel market analysis and a general characterization of a real estate market?

6.2. What are the two dimensions normally involved in defining a relevant real estate market?

6.3. Name and define the major supply and demand variables and indicators of market balance for real estate space usage markets.

6.4. In computing the market vacancy rate, how should one treat space that is leased but unoccupied and available for sublease?

6.5. Why is it normal for there to be some vacancy even in a healthy, well-functioning real estate market?

6.6. What is the relationship among the current market vacancy rate, the natural vacancy rate, and the direction of change in market rents?

6.7. What characteristics of a market are associated with a higher natural vacancy rate?

6.8. What is the difference between asking rent and effective rent?

6.9. Why is net absorption a better measure of demand growth in a market than gross absorption?

6.10. Discuss how you can use the months supply measure of vacant space in a market, combined with knowledge of the typical length of time to complete construction projects, to judge whether the market is likely to be able to absorb additional new construction.

6.11. Suppose a certain market has 1 million SF of currently vacant space, 2 million SF of space under construction, and annual absorption of 1.5 million SF. What is the months supply in this market? If the average project takes two years to complete, would you say this market is oversupplied, meaning that there is no need to pursue any new development projects?

6.12. What would happen if more firms start to allow workers to work at home? Or share non-dedicated space at the office, so no one has private space? If we slowly move from 200 square feet per worker to 100, do you think the market can absorb this decline with economic growth and the need to replace obsolete space?

6.13. Can you think of some firms that are providing more space per worker and more amenities? What is the purpose of such changes?

6.14. Discuss the following statement: In a complete market analysis, one must always consider an entire metropolitan area, even if one is really only interested in one part or subregion within the metropolis.

6.15. Discuss the differences between and relative merits of trend extrapolation and structural analysis as a way of conducting a market analysis.

6.16. Describe the eight basic tasks typically required in a structural analysis of a real estate space usage market.

6.17. Describe the major quantifiable drivers of demand for the principal types of real estate.

*6.18. Use a spreadsheet to build the simple stock-flow model of a real estate market as described in section 6.2. Extend the simulation out for at least 50 years. Assume a constant rate of growth of underlying need. (You can access such a spreadsheet on this book's Web site.) Now vary the parameters that calibrate the system (elasticities, sensitivities, lags) and see how the resulting dynamics of the market change. Discuss your findings.

*6.19. What are the major features characterizing cycles in the real estate space usage market according to the basic stock-flow model?

*6.20. What is meant by myopic or adaptive behavior by market participants in the stock-flow model?

6.21. Do you think some cycles for a given property type are faster or slower in some markets?

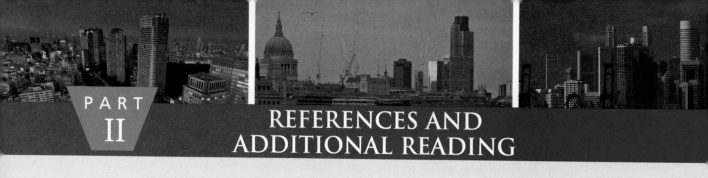

Chapter 3: Central Place Theory and the System of Cities

Batty, M. 2008. The size, scale, and shape of cities. *Science* 319(5864): 769–71.

Christaller, Walter. 1933. *Central Places in Southern Germany.* Trans. C. W. Baskin. London: Prentice-Hall, 1966.

Gabaix, X. 1999. Zipf's laws for cities: An explanation. *Quarterly Journal of Economics* 114(3): 739–67.

Goetzmann, W., and S. Wachter. 1995. Clustering methods for real estate portfolios. *Real Estate Economics* 23(3): 271–310.

Guilkey, D. 1999. How good are MSA forecasts? *Real Estate Finance* 15(4): 27–42.

Krugman, Paul. 1995. *Development, Geography, and Economic Theory.* Cambridge, MA: MIT Press.

Losch, A. 1940. *The Economics of Location,* trans. Fischer, Yale University Press, New Haven, 1954.

Mueller, G. 1993. Refining economic diversification strategies for real estate portfolios. *Journal of Real Estate Research* 8(1): 55–68.

Nitsch, V. 2005. Zipf zipped. *Journal of Urban Economics* 57(1): 86–100.

Soo, K. T. 2005. Zipf's Law for Cities: A Cross-Country Investigation. *Regional Science and Urban Economics* 35(3): 239–63.

Chapters 4 and 5: Inside the City

Albouy, D., and N. Seegert. 2011. Optimal city size and the private-social wedge." 46th Annual AREUEA Conference Paper (January 7, 2011). Available at SSRN: http://ssrn.com/abstract=1716938.

Alonso, William. 1964. *Location and Land Use.* Cambridge, MA: Harvard University Press.

Amin, K., and D. R. Capozza. 1993. Sequential Development. *Journal of Urban Economics* 34: 142–158.

Brown, R. L., and D. Achour. 1984. The pricing of land options. *Urban Studies* 21(3): 317–323.

Bulan, L., C. Mayer, and C. T. Somerville. 2009. Irreversible investment, real options, and competition: Evidence from real estate development. *Journal of Urban Economics* 65(3): 237–51.

Burgess, Ernest. 1925. *The City.* Chicago: University of Chicago Press.

Capozza, D., and R. Helsley. 1990. The stochastic city. *Journal of Urban Economics* 28: 187–203.

Childs, P. D., T. J. Riddiough, and A. J. Triantis. 1996. Mixed uses and the redevelopment option. *Real Estate Economics* 24: 317–39.

Clapp, J. M., and T. Lindenthal. 2009. Option value created and destroyed by the big bang in the Berlin housing market, 1978–2007. (November 19, 2009). Available at SSRN: http://ssrn.com/abstract=1537397.

Cunningham, C. R. 2006. House price uncertainty, timing of development, and vacant land prices: Evidence for real options in Seattle. *Journal of Urban Economics* 59(1): 1–31.

Cunningham, C. R. 2007. Growth controls, real options, and land development. *Review of Economics and Statistics* 89(2): 343–358.

DiPasquale, D., and W. Wheaton. 1996. *Urban Economics and Real Estate Markets.* Englewood Cliffs, NJ: Prentice Hall.

Dixit, Avinash, and Robert Pindyck. 1994. *Investment Under Uncertainty.* Princeton, NJ: Princeton University Press.

Garreau, Joel. 1994. *Edge City: Life on the New Frontier.* New York: Doubleday.

Grenadier, S. R. 2002. Option exercise games: An application to the equilibrium investment strategies of firms. *Review of Financial Studies* 15(3): 691–721.

Han, S. S. 2005. Polycentric urban development and spatial clustering of condominium property values: Singapore in the 1990s. *Environment and Planning* A 37(3): 463–81.

Hoyt, Homer. 1939. *The Structure and Growth of Residential Neighborhoods in American Cities.* Washington, DC: Federal Housing Administration.

Mills, E. 1973. Notes on new urban economics. *Bell Journal of Economics* 4(2): 593–601.

Muth, Richard. 1969. *Cities and Housing.* Chicago: University of Chicago Press.

Quigg, L. 1993. Empirical testing of real option-pricing models. *Journal of Finance* 48(2): 621–40.

Quigley, J. M., N. Kok, and P. Monkkonen. 2010. Geography, regulation and the value of land. (November 29, 2010). 46th Annual AREUEA Conference Paper. Available at SSRN: http://ssrn.com/abstract=1717032

Schwartz, E., and W. Torous. 2007. Commercial office space: Testing the implications of real options models with competitive interactions. *Real Estate Economics* 35(1): 1–20.

Titman, S. 1985. Urban land prices under uncertainty. *American Economic Review* 75: 505–14.

Von Thunen, Johann. 1875. *The Isolated State in Relation to Land Use and National Economy.* Schmaucher Zarchlin, Berlin.

Wheaton, W., M. Baranski, and C. Templeton. 2009. 100 years of commercial real estate prices in Manhattan. *Real Estate Economics* 37(1): 69–83.

Williams, J. 1991. Real estate development as an option. *Journal of Real Estate Finance & Economics* 4(2): 191–208.

Chapter 6: Real Estate Market Analysis

Clapp, John. 1993. *Dynamics of Office Markets.* AREUEA Monograph Series No. 1, Washington, DC: Urban Institute Press.

Dale-Johnson, D. 2001. Long-term ground leases, the redevelopment option, and contract incentives. *Real Estate Economics* 29(3): 451–84.

ERE-Yarmouth Investment Research. 1997. *Real Estate Outlook.*

Guilkey, D. 1999. How good are MSA forecasts? A review of the major supply- and demand-side information providers. *Real Estate Finance* 15(4): 27–42.

Hendershott, P. H. 1995. Real effective rent determination: Evidence from the Sydney office market. *Journal of Urban Economics* 12: 127–35.

Hendershott, P. H., B. D. MacGregor, and R. Tse. 2002a. Estimation of the rental adjustment process. *Real Estate Economics* 30(2): 165–83.

Hendershott, P. H., B. D. MacGregor, and M. J. White. 2002b. Explaining real commercial rents using an error correction model with panel data. *Journal of Real Estate Finance and Economics* 24(1&2): 59–87.

Hendershott, P. H., C. M. Lizieri & B. D. MacGregor. 2010. Asymmetric adjustment in the City of London office market. *Journal of Real Estate Finance and Economics* 41(1), 80–101.

Ibanez, M., and A. Pennington-Cross, 2012. Commercial property rent dynamics in U.S. metropolitan areas: An Examination of office, industrial, flex and retail space. *Journal of Real Estate Finance and Economics,* forthcoming 2012.

Miles, M. 1997. A foundation for the strategic real estate allocation: The space market index. *Real Estate Finance* 14(3): 23–30.

Miles, M., and D. Guilkey. 1998. A tactical look at the space market index. *Real Estate Finance* 14(4): 39–46.

Miller, N., and M. Sklarz. 1986. A note on leading indicators of housing price trends. *Journal of Real Estate Research* 1(1): 99–109.

Mueller, G., and S. Laposa. 1994. The paths of goods movement. *Real Estate Finance* 11(2).

Rosen, K. 1984. Toward a model of the office sector. *Journal of the American Real Estate & Urban Economics Association (AREUEA)* 12(3): 161–69.

Shilling, J., C. F. Sirmans, and J. Corgel. 1991. Natural office vacancy rates: Some additional evidence. *Journal of Urban Economics* 31: 140–43.

Wheaton, W. et al. 2001. Real estate risk: A forward looking approach. *Real Estate Finance* 18(2).

Wheaton, W. 1987. The cyclic behavior of the national office market. *Journal of the American Real Estate and Urban Economics Association (AREUEA)* 15(4): 281–99.

Wheaton, W., and R. G. Torto. 1988. Vacancy rates and the future of office rents. *Journal of the American Real Estate and Urban Economics Association (AREUEA)* 16(4): 430–36.

Wheaton, W., R. Torto, and P. Evans. 1997. The cyclic behavior of the Greater London office market. *Journal of Real Estate Finance and Economics* 15(1): 77–92.

Williams, J. T. 1997. Redevelopment of real assets. *Real Estate Economics* 25(3): 387–407.

Some References on Sustainability in Real Estate Investment Considerations

Eichholtz, P., N. Kok, and J. M. Quigley. 2010. Doing well by doing good? Green office buildings. *American Economic Review* 100(5): 2492–2509.

Fuerst, F., and P. McAllister. 2011. Green noise or green value? Measuring the effects of environmental certification on office values. *Real Estate Economics,* 39: 45–69.

Goering, J. 2009. Sustainable real estate development: The dynamics of market penetration. *Journal of Sustainable Real Estate* 1(1): 167–201.

Harrison, D. M., and M. J. Seiler. 2011. The political economy of green office buildings. *Journal of Property Investment and Finance* 29(4/5): 551–65.

Harrison, D. M., and M. J. Seiler. 2011. The political economy of green industrial warehouses. *Journal of Sustainable Real Estate* 3(1).

Jaffee, D. M., R. Stanton, and N. E. Wallace. 2010. Energy factors, leasing structure and the market price of office buildings in the U.S. *Fisher Center Working Papers,* November 30, 2010.

Miller, N. G., D. Pogue, Q. D. Gough, and S. M. Davis. 2009. Green buildings and productivity. *Journal of Sustainable Real Estate* 1(1): 65–89.

Miller, N., J. Spivey, and A. Florance. 2008. Does green pay off? *Journal of Real Estate Portfolio Management* 14(4): 385–400.

Pivo, G., and J. D. Fisher. 2010. Income, value, and returns in socially responsible office properties. *Journal of Real Estate Research* 32(3): 243–70.

PART

III

BASIC FINANCIAL ECONOMIC CONCEPTS AND TOOLS

Perhaps the most fundamental characteristic of real estate is that it is long-lived. After all, land underlies all real estate, and land "lives" forever, practically speaking. When we combine this longevity with the fact that real estate can generally produce benefits of some type for some people, we arrive at the essence of why financial economics is important for understanding real estate. Financial economics is the branch of economic science that focuses on the capital markets, that is, markets for capital assets. Capital assets are claims to potential future benefit flows that can be measured in monetary terms. Real estate assets are therefore capital assets. One cannot understand real estate without knowledge of financial economics.

The heart of financial economics is the systematic study of how markets for capital assets function and thereby determine the prices of such assets, giving monetary value to such things as real estate assets. Fundamentally, financial economics is concerned with how capital markets weigh the timing, risk, and other attributes of the possible future cash flows from different types of assets to determine what these assets are worth in the market today, that is, at what price they trade or could be traded. Closely related to this issue (indeed, a part of it) is

the matter of how these asset market values change over time.

In Part III, we begin the in-depth study of the financial economics of real estate that is the main focus of this book. Orienting ourselves within the real estate system presented in Chapter 2, in Part III (and most of the remainder of this book through Part VII) we will be focusing primarily on the real estate asset market and the broader capital markets of which it is a part. Part III covers some basic background material and fundamental building blocks. If we may permit ourselves the analogy: Parts III and IV together will present the building blocks and the foundation on which the rest of the structure will be built.

Chapter 7 presents an introduction and overview (continuing from the introduction in Part 1), situating real estate in the context of the broader capital markets and giving the reader some perspective of the recent history of real estate as an investment asset class. Chapter 8 presents the major mathematical formulas used in converting multiyear cash flow streams to present value and computing returns on investments, the essential tools in the study and practice of financial economics as applied to real estate. Chapter 9 presents the fundamentals of the measurement of investment performance.

REAL ESTATE AS AN INVESTMENT: SOME BACKGROUND INFORMATION

CHAPTER OUTLINE

LEARNING OBJECTIVES

After reading this chapter, you should understand:

➲ The basic structure and functioning of the investment industry.

➲ The nature of investor objectives, constraints, and concerns.

➲ The major types of investment products and vehicles and the difference between an underlying asset and an investment product.

➲ The major similarities and differences in the investment products based on real estate as opposed to other classical industrial or service corporations as underlying assets.

➲ The four major traditional investment asset classes and their characteristic differences.

➲ The investment performance of the major asset classes in recent decades, at a broad-brush and general level.

➲ Some of the major historical trends and events that have influenced real estate investment performance in recent decades.

How much do you already know about the investment industry in general? How much do you already know about commercial real estate in particular as an investment? Unless you can answer *quite a bit* to both of these questions, this chapter will provide some useful background that will help you to understand the subsequent chapters in this book. We won't go into any deep academic theories or methods in this chapter, but we will present some of the very basic information practitioners deal with every day, directly or indirectly, in the investment business. This chapter is divided into two major sections. The first discusses the investment industry, beginning with the most fundamental underlying consideration—investors' objectives and concerns. The second section presents real estate as one investment asset class among several, and compares real estate investment performance to that of the other major asset classes at a broad-brush level, including a brief history of recent real estate investment trends.

7.1 Investment Industry, and Real Estate's Role Therein

The word *industry* carries a variety of specific meanings. We often think of factories and the production or distribution of physical goods when we hear the word *industry*. In this sense, you may not think of investment activity and the professional management of investment as an industry because you don't see any smokestacks or physical products. But this would be misleading. More broadly, the word *industry* refers to purposeful work and diligence, and in economics, the term is used to refer to a branch of economic activity or trade. In this sense, the investment business is a major industry in the United States in which much value is added and income earned. An introduction to some aspects of this industry is a very good place to begin a serious study of commercial real estate as an investment, and that is the purpose of this first section of this chapter. We begin with the most fundamental element in this industry: investors.

7.1.1 Investor Objectives and Concerns

Investors buy and sell capital assets, thereby making up both the demand and supply side of the capital markets. Through the process of buying and selling, investors determine the market values of capital assets, that is, the prices at which these assets trade. In deciding the prices at which they are willing to trade, investors consider the fundamental characteristics of the assets' future cash flow prospects. Investors also consider the nature of the capital markets in which the assets trade and how the functioning of those markets may affect the prices at which assets can trade as well as the cost and timeliness of such trading. In Part I of this book, we introduced you to these basic considerations when we presented the space and asset markets and the real estate system. Now let's focus in more depth on the players in this game, the investors. Naturally, investors view considerations about real estate cash flow and asset values and tradeability from the perspective of their own objectives and constraints.

With this in mind, consider the question, *Why do people invest?* Investment is the act of putting money aside that would otherwise be used for current consumption expenditure.[1] Why would someone do that? At the individual level, people may find themselves with more money than they currently need for consumption, or they may have a future objective for which they are willing to sacrifice some current consumption.

Consider a dual-income couple in their 20s. They may want to save for a down payment on a house. This might involve an investment horizon of, say, three to five years. Now consider a couple in their mid-30s. They may want to begin saving for their children's college tuition. This might involve a horizon of 10 to 15 years. Another couple in their mid-40s might want to save for their own retirement, with an investment horizon of over 20 years. Finally, consider a retired couple in their 60s or 70s. They may have assets they have accumulated over their working lives and now may want to begin drawing current income out of these assets, or even drawing down the principal value of the assets to bolster their spendable income during their retirement years.

All of these individuals may differ not only in their investment time horizons, but also in their preferences for risk-taking in their investments. Virtually all investors would prefer a safe investment to a risky one, other things being equal. But other things are not equal; in particular, investments vary in their risk and trading characteristics, with riskier assets generally offering higher returns on average in a well-functioning capital market. (They have to, otherwise no one would buy them.) Some investors are willing to take on more risk in order to expect a higher return on average. Other investors prefer the opposite. What are

---

[1]In this context, we could use the word *save* as well as the word *invest*. But of course, money that is saved "goes somewhere." In effect, savings *is* investment, and it is the investment aspect that is of concern to us in this book.

the major **investment objectives** and the major constraints or concerns faced by most investors? At a fundamental level, it is useful to distinguish two different and mutually exclusive types of investment objectives:

- The **growth** (or **savings**) **objective**, which implies a relatively long time horizon with no immediate or likely intermediate need to use the cash being invested.
- The **income** (or **current cash flow**) **objective**, which implies that the investor has a short-term and ongoing need to use cash generated from the investment.

Investors with the growth objective can put money away for a relatively long period of time. The investment need not pay out any cash unless and until it is sold and need not be sold in the near term. If the investment does generate income in the meantime, this might be plowed back into investment so as to maximize the growth of the accumulated capital over the investment time horizon. This objective is typical of young to middle-aged individuals, of wealthy individuals of all ages, and of institutions such as pension funds of growing companies that expect to experience more cash inflow than outflow liabilities for many years into the future. Many endowments or sovereign wealth funds are also in this category for much of their investment.

On the other hand, investors with the income objective need to consider how much cash the investment will generate initially, as well as how this cash flow stream may change over time. Normally, an investor with a current income objective would tend to look for an investment with a high current cash payout rate, that is, the fraction of investment value that is typically paid out to the investor each year (e.g., in the form of interest coupons, dividends, or net rental payments). Investors with an income objective would typically include retired individuals and institutions such as endowment funds or pension funds or life insurance companies with a larger number of retired members or policyholders than current contributors.

It may be said that all investors have either a savings or an income objective. In some cases, the same investor may define both of these objectives for different parts of a wealth portfolio. But in addition to these objectives, investors also face one or more of a set of typical constraints or concerns. The following list summarizes the major constraints and concerns that affect most investors, particularly in the real estate asset market:

- **Risk**: The possibility that future investment performance may vary over time in a manner that is not entirely predictable at the time when the investment is made.
- **Liquidity**: The ability to sell and buy investment assets quickly at full value and without much affecting the price of the assets.
- **Time Horizon**: The future time over which the investor's objectives, constraints, and concerns are relevant.
- **Investor Expertise** and **Management Burden**: How much knowledge, ability, and desire the investor has to manage the investment process and the investment assets.
- **Investor Size**: How "big" the investor is in terms of the amount of capital in need of investment.
- **Capital constraint**: Whether the investor faces an absolute constraint on the amount of capital he or she has available to invest, or can obtain additional capital relatively easily if good investment opportunities are available (e.g., from stockholders or depositors).

Some of these issues have already been mentioned. We noted that investors dislike risk. Real estate investors are no different from other investors in that, other things being equal, they will prefer less risky investments.

Similarly, investors like liquidity. Other things being equal, investors will pay more for (or equivalently, accept lower returns from) assets that are more liquid. Liquidity gives investors flexibility to move capital in or out of the investment and to respond to news and perceived opportunities. Different investors have different needs for, or preferences for, liquidity, just as they do for risk avoidance. Liquidity is potentially a major constraint or concern in real estate investment, because property assets can require a long time to sell at full value compared to publicly traded stocks and bonds, for example. As noted in Chapter 1, private asset markets are generally less liquid than public markets, and private real estate markets may be more cyclical, with possibly extended periods of reduced liquidity.

Investors' time horizons obviously affect both their ability to bear risk and their need for liquidity, or tolerance for illiquidity. Another particular concern in traditional real estate investment, as distinguished from securities, is the need for specialized expertise and the ability to bear some management burden when investing in property assets.

Finally, in real estate investment, as in other types of investment, the nature of the opportunities and challenges differs according to the size of the investor. For example, larger investors may face lower costs per dollar invested due to economies of scale, and they may face a broader range of alternatives. They may also face greater ability to hire professional managers, both for their investments in general and for the operation of any properties they own. On the other hand, larger investors may have less liquidity, as the weight of their capital may tend to influence asset prices when they move it around.

Many large investors, and virtually all small investors, typically face some sort of "capital constraint," a limit to the amount of funds they can invest in any period of time. This means that they may sometimes have to forego investing in profitable opportunities, and it means that anything they do invest in prevents them from investing in something else. Such investors need to make certain they are ordering their priorities correctly so as to choose the best overall combination of investments available to them at a given time.

7.1.2 Implications of Investor Heterogeneity

A key implication of the range of differing investment objectives and constraints is that *investors are heterogeneous*—they have different personal goals and lifestyles, they are at different points in their life cycles, and they have different amounts of wealth and earned income. The ideal investment for one investor will not be the same as the ideal investment for another investor. Furthermore, many investment decisions are not made by individuals as such, but by institutions: banks and life insurance companies; funds, such as pensions, endowments, sovereign wealth, and mutual funds; and investment intermediaries such as private equity investment management funds. Like individuals, investment institutions also are a heterogeneous lot. They have different constituencies, different liabilities, different levels or types of expertise, and they are subject to different types of regulations and legal constraints. Institutions also come in all sizes, from small to very large. All of this affects their investment objectives and constraints, as described previously.

One implication of **investor heterogeneity** is that this lays the foundation for a market in investment products. Different products can be tailored to different objectives and constraints, and heterogeneity means that some investors will want to buy when other investors want to sell, thereby creating liquidity in the asset marketplace. Beneath investment products (possibly many layers of them) lie underlying physical or productive assets that generate profits and cash flow by adding value in the economy.

7.1.3 General Structure of Investment Products and Vehicles

At a broad-brush level, the investment industry matches heterogeneous investors (sources of financial capital) with heterogeneous productive assets (physical capital). This is done by the development of investment institutions, products, and vehicles. In this system, it is useful to distinguish underlying assets from investment products or vehicles. **Underlying assets** refers to the directly productive physical capital, such as an office building or an industrial or service corporation. Such a corporation is in fact a collection of physical, human, and legal assets and relationships organized into a system that can produce net cash flow over time through the production and sale of goods or services. In contrast to underlying assets, **investment products** or **vehicles** are typically (though not necessarily) one or more levels removed from the underlying assets, but they are based on the underlying assets. While investment products and vehicles are not themselves directly productive in the physical as opposed to purely financial sense, they have direct or indirect claims on, and sometimes commitments to, the directly productive underlying physical assets. Investment vehicles may or may not have governing authority over the underlying assets. And the investment products (the investment industry) add value by matching and connecting sources and uses of capital.

Perhaps the best way to understand this system is to look at a picture. Exhibit 7-1 schematically depicts the way the investment industry works in the classical and traditional structure of U.S. industry, using a fictitious industrial corporation, ABC Widgets Corporation, as the underlying asset. The box at the bottom of the diagram depicts ABC Widgets, the underlying asset, a collection of physical and human resources that generates a cash flow stream by the production and sale of widgets. For the investment industry, underlying assets such as ABC Widgets Corporation are the "raw material" on which investment products are based. The "finished products" are vehicles in which investors can directly place their money, or financial capital.

The first layer of investment products are those based most directly on the cash flow of the underlying asset. This layer would be represented by common stocks and corporate bonds issued by the underlying corporation. In traditional corporate finance for large industrial and service corporations, these basic investment products are usually publicly traded in a relatively liquid secondary market, such as the stock exchange. In essence, the claims to ABC's cash flows are partitioned into two classes of investment products that have different risk and return characteristics.

ABC corporate bonds are the senior claims, meaning that they will be paid first, and they are for a fixed contractual amount with a finite expiration or maturity.[2] All of these features make ABC bonds relatively low risk for most investors. Traditional bonds provide a relatively high current income yield to their investors, as this represents the entire expected total return to the bonds.

EXHIBIT 7-1 Underlying Assets versus Investment Products, an Example from Traditional Corporate Finance

© OnCourse Learning

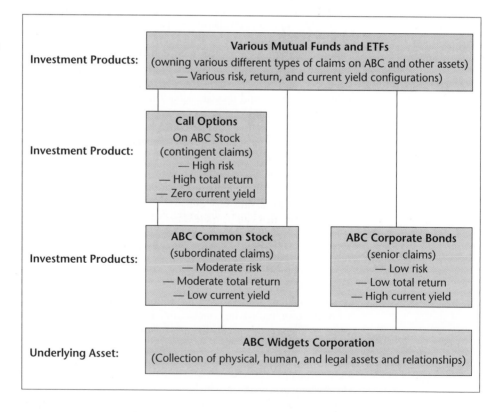

---

[2]Corporations also make use of privately held debt, such as bank debt or privately placed bonds, but we assume ABC has no such debt as it is not depicted in Exhibit 7-1.

By contrast, ABC's common stock is the residual (subordinated) claim on ABC's cash flow, with no contractual guarantee of the amount the stockholders will receive. ABC's stock represents the equity in the ABC Corporation, perpetual-lived claims with governing authority over the corporation, and they present the typical investor with more risk, but the prospect of higher returns on average over the long run, than ABC's bonds. If ABC is a large, well-established firm, then its stock may be viewed as having moderate investment risk. Such a firm would normally pay regular dividends, providing stockholders with at least a small current yield on their investment, with the bulk of their total return coming in the form of expected growth in share price over time. This share price represents the present value of the expected future stream of dividends.

This first level of investment products—stocks and bonds—has been the mainstay of corporate finance and the investment industry in the United States since the nineteenth century. But particularly in recent years, additional layers and types of investment products have been developed based on the stocks and bonds. Some of these secondary products are specialized claims, such as contingent claims, that pay off only under certain circumstances and otherwise expire worthless.

The archetypal examples of this type of product are the standardized "call and put options" that are publicly traded on the Chicago Options Exchange and elsewhere. Options are an example of a derivative investment product in that they are derived from other products, in this case common stocks. For example, an ABC call option would allow its holder to purchase a certain number of shares of ABC stock at a specified price on or prior to a specified date. For such a product, the underlying asset is another investment product, namely the common stock of ABC Corporation. Call options are typically very high risk, because they are effectively levered to a high degree and they may end up being worthless if the underlying asset's share price never rises above the exercise price at which the option allows purchase of the stock. The expected return on long positions in call options is very high, but that is because the risk is very high, and there is no income yield at all while holding the option.[3]

Another type of investment product that has become very important in recent decades is the mutual fund and its more recent refinement, the Exchange Traded Fund (ETF). A typical mutual fund or ETF is a diversified pool of stocks and/or bonds. Such funds allow investors to invest indirectly in a large number of different stocks or bonds simply by purchasing a share in the fund. Mutual funds and ETFs are quite varied, with different objectives and different risk and return profiles.[4]

The main point of the system of investment products built upon the underlying asset of ABC Widgets Corporation, as depicted in Exhibit 7-1, is to allow investors with different risk and return objectives all to be satisfied investing, directly or indirectly, in the same underlying asset. By defining different types of claims on future cash flows, ABC Widgets can offer investors products with very different risk and return characteristics, indeed, risk and return characteristics that can be quite different from those of the underlying asset itself. ABC Widgets' future cash flow stream may be a perpetual, low-risk, slightly variable stream, while its bonds are very low-risk, finite-lived, fixed streams; its stock shares are moderate-risk, perpetual assets with substantial price volatility; and its call options are very high-risk, short-lived "bets." An investor in a mutual fund owning some shares of ABC will barely notice the individual or unique effect of ABC in his returns.

---

[3]Though not depicted in the exhibit, there are contingent claims on corporate bonds as well, for example, the "credit default swaps" that grew enormously in usage during the 2000s. CDSs pay only when and if the corporation suffers a "credit event" on its bonds, for example, if the bonds' credit rating is downgraded or if the corporation defaults on the bonds. CDS's can thus be used to provide corporate bond investors with a type of insurance for their investment (at a cost, of course, as the party selling the CDS must be paid regular payments over the life of the CDS).

[4]A key difference between a mutual fund and an ETF is that the latter is itself directly traded on the stock exchange, whereas traditional open-end mutual funds are not traded but rather offer very quick and transparent redemption at values based on the current market values of the publicly-traded securities held by the fund.

We see how investor heterogeneity drives the investment industry. We also see how the entire system is built ultimately on underlying physical assets, producers of cash flow streams from the production and sale of goods and services, the "raw material" in the investment industry.

Let's carry this analogy a bit further. If the only type of ore that existed were iron ore, we could produce quite a variety of different types of finished products out of steel, but we could not produce any products of aluminum or copper or tin. The existence of a variety of different ores (raw materials) allows the production of more and a broader variety of finished products. This is the case also in the investment industry. A greater range and variety of underlying physical assets allows a greater variety of investment products, with a greater range of risk and return characteristics and potential for diversification of investment portfolios. This allows more types of investors in greater numbers to be served through the investment process and increases the effectiveness and efficiency of the allocation of financial capital to underlying physical assets.

This is where real estate comes into the picture. Real property assets are underlying assets in the investment industry, comparable to, but different from, the industrial and service corporations that characterize traditional corporate finance and investments.[5] Because real estate is different, it presents unique opportunities. The investment industry based on real estate underlying assets, and the variety of real estate investment products and vehicles, is growing and evolving rapidly. Traditionally, the investment system for real estate has been a bit different from that of industrial corporations, although recent evolution has brought the two systems closer together.

Exhibit 7-2 depicts the investment system for a typical collection of real estate underlying assets, say, a group of shopping centers developed and owned by a single family, the Grump brothers. Like underlying physical assets of any type, these real properties produce a stream of cash flow from the production and sale of goods or services, in this case, built space and location for operations by retail tenants.

Unlike the situation for the typical large industrial corporation, however, in the traditional real estate system it is possible for investors to *own directly the underlying physical assets*. This is indicated in Exhibit 7-2 by the line linking the underlying asset at the bottom with the investors represented by the box at the top of the diagram. But note that this box is divided into two types of investors, large and small. Underlying physical assets are large entities, typically worth millions of dollars each.[6] It is generally not possible for small individual investors who are not very wealthy to own whole commercial properties directly.[7] But it is possible for wealthy individual investors, as well as investment institutions (such as pension funds or life insurance companies), to own large commercial properties or portfolios of properties directly. And there is a market in which such underlying physical assets trade directly, namely, the private property market that we introduced in Chapter 1. This is a key difference between the investment system for real estate and that for typical industrial and service corporations: the direct tradability of the underlying physical assets in a well-functioning private market.

---

[5] Real estate is "different," in the most fundamental sense, in the same way that each type or class of underlying physical asset is different. In a mathematical sense, real estate values and cash flows are *statistically independent*; that is, they do not change over time in ways that are perfectly correlated with any one or combination of other classes of underlying assets. More specific aspects of real estate's uniqueness have been mentioned in Part I of this book, and will be covered in more depth in this and subsequent chapters.

[6] In fact, individual real estate assets are usually not worth as much as individual whole corporations, which is one reason that it is possible to have direct ownership of whole real estate assets. In the example in Exhibit 7-2, we are talking about a collection or portfolio (perhaps a "chain") of numerous individual shopping centers managed as a single underlying asset, and this, of course, greatly builds up the value. This portfolio or chain of centers may easily be worth as much as a typical medium-size corporation traded on the stock exchange.

[7] Of course, small commercial properties and apartments are not that expensive, and it is possible for individuals of modest wealth to get into real estate investment at this so-called "mom and pop" end of the business. Indeed, this is how many great real estate investment firms got their start. But while this book is quite relevant in principle to such small-scale investment, it is not our primary focus.

EXHIBIT 7-2 Real Estate Example of the Investment System

© OnCourse Learning

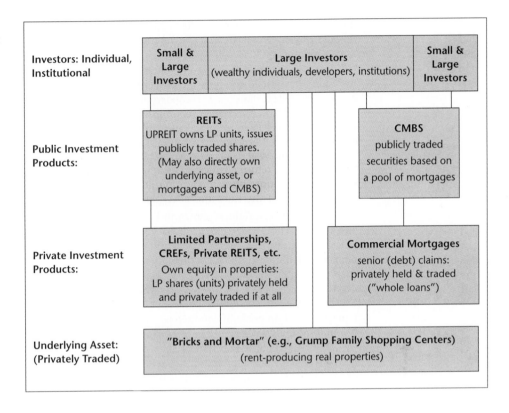

| Investors: Individual, Institutional | Small & Large Investors | Large Investors (wealthy individuals, developers, institutions) | Small & Large Investors |

Public Investment Products:

REITs — UPREIT owns LP units, issues publicly traded shares. (May also directly own underlying asset, or mortgages and CMBS)

CMBS — publicly traded securities based on a pool of mortgages

Private Investment Products:

Limited Partnerships, CREFs, Private REITS, etc. — Own equity in properties: LP shares (units) privately held and privately traded if at all

Commercial Mortgages — senior (debt) claims: privately held & traded ("whole loans")

Underlying Asset: (Privately Traded)

"Bricks and Mortar" (e.g., Grump Family Shopping Centers) (rent-producing real properties)

As with the stocks and bonds that form the backbone of corporate finance, a "first layer" of traditional real estate investment products has been around for a long time. Best known of these are the commercial mortgages, which are debt products, loans secured by the underlying real property assets. Commercial mortgages are comparable to corporate bonds in that they represent senior claims on the property cash flows and they provide investors with a finite-lived, contractually fixed cash flow stream. Unlike typical corporate bonds, commercial mortgages traditionally have not been broken up into small homogeneous shares or units that are traded in public exchanges. Instead, the traditional procedure has been to keep each mortgage as a "whole loan," which was typically held to maturity by the originating institution (such as a life insurance company or bank) or occasionally traded privately in a negotiated deal for the whole loan in its entirety.

There are also investment products designed to enable **passive investors** to invest in real estate equity. Passive investors are those who do not wish to be deeply or directly involved in the management and operation of the underlying real estate assets. They may lack the necessary specialized expertise or the time and resources required by such management, yet they value the risk and return characteristics of commercial real estate equity. For example, passive investors in real estate equity are often interested in real estate's ability to diversify an investment portfolio that otherwise consists largely of traditional corporate stocks and bonds. A variety of real estate passive equity investment products have been developed over the years. Some of the most prominent include real estate limited partnership units (RELPs), **commingled real estate funds** (CREFs or unit trusts), and **private REITs** (**real estate investment trusts** whose shares are not traded publicly). These investment vehicles are similar to corporate stock in that they provide their investors with an ownership interest in the underlying asset, often leveraged. However, these real estate equity vehicles differ from corporate stock; in some cases, they have rather limited governance authority over the assets, and they are not traded in liquid public exchanges.

Indeed, a common and prominent feature of the first level of real estate investment products shown in Exhibit 7-2, the traditional level, is that these products are privately traded, if traded at all, not traded on public exchanges like stocks and bonds. While secondary markets do exist to some extent in which some of these products can be traded, in the United States such secondary markets have never developed much and generally lack liquidity.

In fact, we have noted that in contrast to other industries, the major traditional market for trading real estate equity is the property market in which the underlying physical assets are directly traded, rather than secondary markets for the first-level equity and debt products shown in Exhibit 7-2. Although the property market is a **private market**, in which individual buyers and sellers have to "find" each other and negotiate deals privately, this is a highly developed and well-functioning asset market.

As with the corporate side of the investment industry, recent decades have seen the development of significant new real estate investment products and vehicles. Most notable for commercial property was the "securitization revolution" of the 1990s, which saw a tremendous development of publicly traded investment vehicles, represented by the second level of investment products shown in Exhibit 7-2, the REITs (real estate investment trusts) and **CMBS (commercial mortgage-backed securities)**. This has linked Wall Street (traditional mainstream corporate finance and investment) to Main Street (traditional real estate finance and investment) much more closely than ever before and provided a major new source of capital for commercial real estate. CMBS and REITs were introduced and briefly described in Chapter 1, and we will say only a little bit more about them here.

In essence, CMBS are debt products, while REITs are equity products.[8] CMBS are typically based on pools of commercial mortgages. Different classes of securities are usually issued from the same underlying pool. Some classes are more risky than others, and different classes have different typical maturities. This allows a variety of risk and return patterns to be created for the different CMBS classes based on the same underlying pool of mortgages. In this way, investors with different risk preferences and investment horizons can be served.

Publicly traded REITs, on the other hand, are usually perpetual ownership vehicles that typically specialize in investing in, and often actively developing and managing, portfolios of commercial property equity. They are usually levered, issuing either "entity-level debt" backed by the REIT as a whole (such as bonds) or mortgages backed by specific properties owned by the REIT ("property-level debt"). Traditional REITs directly own underlying physical real estate assets. In the 1990s, a new type of REIT structure known as the umbrella partnership REIT, or UPREIT, was pioneered. By the end of the 1990s, many of the largest REITs were UPREITs. As depicted in Exhibit 7-2, an UPREIT does not directly own the underlying "bricks and mortar," but rather owns units in a partnership, which in turn owns the underlying physical properties either directly or indirectly. The purpose of this complicated arrangement is to allow property owners to "sell" their properties to the REIT without incurring a taxable event.[9] By the early 2000s, REITs had grown to represent important shares of the major commercial investment property market sectors, as depicted in Exhibit 7-3. REITs were particularly dominant in the regional shopping mall sector but held important positions in major cities in the other major property-type sectors as well.

---

[8]However, REITs can invest in mortgages, and some REITs specialize in this activity, or in buying CMBS. These are known as mortgage REITs. However, even mortgage REITs typically behave like equity rather than debt, in part because they tend to be highly leveraged, so the debt on the liability side of their balance sheets largely offsets the debt-like characteristics on the asset side of their balance sheets. On the other hand, as we will see in Chapter 20, the bottom (least protected against default) classes of CMBS may have more characteristics of real estate equity than debt, as there is a high chance that the security owners will end up owning the properties collateralizing the mortgages via the default and foreclosure process.

[9]Successful individual real estate developers and investors own many properties that are worth much more than their current book values. If they sold these properties, they would realize a large capital gain and owe large income taxes on that gain. This is what would happen if they sold their properties to a REIT either for cash or common equity shares of the REIT. However, if you exchange an interest in one partnership for an interest in another partnership, the form of ownership does not change, and the IRS considers that no taxable event has occurred. An UPREIT can "pay" for properties it acquires by giving the seller units in the umbrella partnership, rather than cash or common shares. These umbrella partnership units may be convertible over time into equity shares in the REIT, giving their owner flexibility over when and whether to realize the taxable event. If the conversion occurs after the death of the original owner, then the cost basis is stepped up, and little or no capital gains tax may be owed.

EXHIBIT 7-3 REIT
Ownership Share of U.S.
Institutional Property Asset
Market, 2003

Source: Hess and Liang (2004).

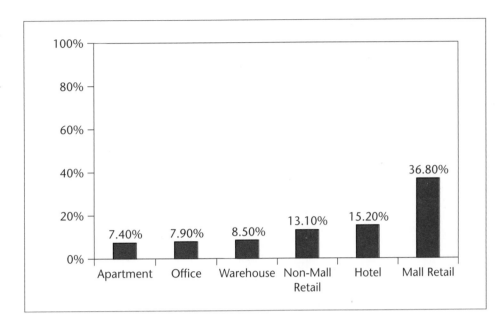

REITs typically present their investors (stockholders) with risk and return characteristics similar to those of levered investment in the underlying physical real estate, but with some important differences. First, REIT shares are small, enabling small individual investors to participate in commercial property investment.[10] Second, REIT shares are usually publicly traded, and therefore they provide the typical investor with more liquidity than direct investment in privately traded underlying real estate assets. Third, unless the investor purchases a large proportion of all the REIT shares, the investor will have little management burden, as the job of managing the properties will be done by the REIT's professional management. (This is analogous to buying stock in an industrial firm but not having to be actively involved in the management of that firm, as the firm has a full-time professional management team.) Fourth, REITs are typically rather actively managed firms that may engage in buying and selling of properties as well as property development, not just passively holding and operating a static portfolio of properties.[11] Thus, the risk and return characteristics of the REIT reflect the risk and return characteristics of the REIT's management, including the stock market's perception of their abilities and future opportunities, as well as the nature of their existing portfolio of properties.

A final difference between the investment performance of REITs and direct investment in underlying real estate assets is due simply to the fact that REITs trade in the stock market. As a result, REIT share values reflect the functioning and valuation of the stock market rather than that of the direct property asset market. It is unclear to what extent this affects REIT risk and return, but as noted in Chapter 1, the stock market is likely more informationally efficient than the private property market. Thus, REIT share prices probably respond more

---

[10]This was the original purpose Congress had in mind in establishing the REIT investment vehicle as a tax status in 1960. As noted in Chapter 1, REITs avoid corporate-level income tax by conforming to certain requirements that ensure that REITs remain, in essence, a purely real estate investment vehicle.

[11]REITs are encouraged by the tax code not to be too "active." They must pay out 90 percent of their accrual accounting-based earnings (not their cash flow) each year as dividends, or they will lose their REIT tax status and be forced to pay corporate income tax. This may put some constraint on their ability to retain cash for discretionary activity without having to go to the capital market. Also, REITs must typically hold most of their assets for at least four years, which prevents rapid turnaround and "merchant building." Nevertheless, these provisions effectively do not prevent most REITs from considering a substantial range of rather active management strategies. (See Chapter 23 for more discussion.)

EXHIBIT 7-4 End-of-Year Public versus Private Asset Market Commercial Real Estate Values (Indexes set to have equal average values 1974–2010.)

© OnCourse Learning

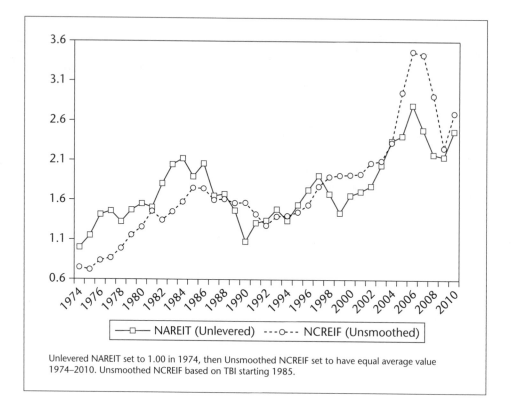

Unlevered NAREIT set to 1.00 in 1974, then Unsmoothed NCREIF set to have equal average value 1974–2010. Unsmoothed NCREIF based on TBI starting 1985.

quickly and completely to news relevant to their value. Some researchers also believe that the stock market is subject to fads or overreaction, leading to excess volatility, at least in the short run.

As a result of the development of the REIT industry during the 1990s, commercial real estate equity is now traded in two major asset markets: the private property asset market in which the underlying physical assets are traded directly; and the public stock exchange in which REIT shares are traded. Both of these asset markets are well-functioning, very highly developed markets. This situation is rather unique to real estate. It would be as if, in addition to being able to buy shares in automobile manufacturing companies, investors could also directly buy and sell stamping plants, engine factories, and vehicle assembly plants, or perhaps even individual machines, parts inventories, and design labs—in short, all the physical assets of an automobile company.[12] There are some implications of this unique double-market environment for real estate investment, which we will come back to in subsequent chapters in this book. For now, the main point is simply for you to realize that this dual market situation exists. Exhibit 7-4 shows one way to depict these two parallel markets. The exhibit traces the changes in implied values of commercial property assets in the two markets. It shows two indices of asset value—one from the National Association of Real Estate Investment Trusts and the other from the National Council of Real Estate Investment Fiduciaries. The NAREIT index is based on the share prices of REITs. The NCREIF

---

[12]If REITs were only very passive investors in existing fully operational properties, then they would be comparable to closed-end mutual funds that invest in portfolios of stocks, with the closed-end fund's shares trading separately in the stock market. To some extent, REITs are indeed like closed-end stock funds, only they invest in real estate assets instead of stocks. But most of the newer and larger REITs, especially those formed during the 1990s and more recently, are much more actively managed, deeply and directly involved in the operation and management of their properties, and often in the development of new buildings as well. Such firms are more similar to a vertically integrated industrial or service corporation specializing in providing built space to tenants than they are like mutual funds that simply buy and sell existing assets.

index is based on the transaction prices of large commercial properties held directly by institutional investors.[13] The two indices trace broadly the same picture over time. However, the REIT share prices seem to have some tendency to lead the private market valuations in time, by registering turning points and trends a bit sooner. On the other hand, the REIT-based index appears a bit more volatile in the short run, with some ups and downs that prove to be transient and not echoed in the private market. Sometimes one market seems to value real estate more than the other market, although which one has the higher valuation varies over time. The great asset market "bubble" of the mid-2000s was perhaps more pronounced in the private market than in the REIT market.

Let us now summarize the modern real estate investment system depicted back in Exhibit 7-2. The defining characteristic of this system is that the underlying assets are real properties. Real property is unique, presenting risk and return characteristics not exactly like those of the whole industrial and service corporations that form the underlying assets in traditional corporate finance.[14] Unlike typical corporate finance, real estate underlying physical assets trade directly in a well-functioning, albeit private, asset market. As always, the investment industry creates investment products and vehicles that enable a variety of risk and return patterns to be carved out of the same underlying assets, so that heterogeneous investors can be better served, and capital can flow more efficiently and effectively to real estate. As always, equity products and debt products are prominent in the investment system. In recent years, publicly traded vehicles have been developed that significantly increase the liquidity, and perhaps the informational efficiency, in the real estate investment industry. By the early 2000s, approximately 20 percent of the value of commercial real estate in the United States was held or financed directly or indirectly by these public market debt and equity vehicles, REITs and CMBS, including a larger percentage of some higher-end property types. This creates a unique double-market environment for real estate, unlike what prevails for other types of underlying assets.

7.2 Real Estate as an Asset Class

Do you recall what we said about the importance of having different types of underlying physical assets, so that greater quantity, variety, and range of alternatives can be offered to heterogeneous investor groups? We noted that commercial real estate is a unique class of underlying assets. What we want to do in the remainder of this chapter is to put ourselves in the shoes of investors, scanning the big picture of the investment universe available to them to see the nature and role of real estate as one of several major investment asset classes. We will review the historical, empirical investment performance of the major asset classes. To simplify matters at this broad-brush level, we will consider the main traditional form of

---

[13]Exhibit 7-4 is based on the NAREIT All-REIT index of share price capital returns and the NCREIF index of same-property price changes. The NAREIT index has been "unlevered" using aggregate REIT industry balance sheet statistics provided by NAREIT (the National Association of Real Estate Investment Trusts, Washington). The NCREIF index (published by the National Council of Real Estate Investment Fiduciaries, Chicago), which is already unlevered, has been "unsmoothed" to remove the effect of appraisal lag. (The problem of "appraisal lag" is discussed in Chapter 25.) This is done by employing the transaction price based version of the NCREIF Index (TBI) from 1984, and prior to that, the NCREIF Index (and predecessor commingled fund indices) are unsmoothed by reverse engineering (see Chapter 25). Because the starting value of an index is arbitrary, no generality is lost by setting the starting values of these two indices so that their average value levels across time are equal. One would expect a relationship like this to hold on average over the long run, or else all the assets would tend to be held in only one form or the other (whichever provided the highest valuation). It should be noted that NCREIF properties benefit from large capital improvement expenditures whose effects are reflected in the price trend, while REIT properties are managed and culled typically more to optimize net income generation. (The chart does not depict total investment returns, only capital gains in nominal prices.)The result is pictured in Exhibit 7-4. Thus, this is only an approximate and broad-brush picture: it demonstrates the basic nature of the relationship between the two types of asset markets for real estate equity investment, but it is not a completely "apples-to-apples" comparison.

[14]At the level of the underlying physical assets, this same statement could probably be made about any major segment or class of assets; for example, airlines are different from banks.

institutional real estate investment, that is, the direct unlevered investment in large-scale commercial property (the so-called "core" of private real estate investment portfolios).

7.2.1 Four Major Investment Asset Classes

Traditionally, four major asset classes are identified in the core of the investment universe for portfolio planning.

- Cash (T-bills)
- Stocks
- Bonds
- Real estate

Although classification at this level is necessarily somewhat stylized and simplified, these four classes make a useful taxonomy for several reasons. First, each presents unique typical characteristics regarding the objectives and constraints that concern investors. Second, substantial empirical historical data are publicly available regarding the investment performance of each of these asset classes, including time series of periodic total returns. Third, each of these four classes is large enough in magnitude to support substantial capital flow into or out of the asset class without great disruptions to markets and industries. Fourth, each of these asset classes is "investable." In other words, asset markets and investment vehicles exist, enabling passive institutions and/or individuals to buy and sell assets in each of these classes.[15] The approximate aggregate value of the assets in each of the four classes is shown in Exhibit 7-5, as of the early 2000s.[16] Real estate equity represented a little over one quarter of the total $64 trillion investable asset pie.[17]

The table in Exhibit 7-6 presents a qualitative characterization of the typical investment performance expectations of each of the four asset classes. The table qualitatively describes each of the asset classes along five dimensions of investment performance.

- Risk
- Average total return on investment
- Average current yield (current income as a fraction of investment value)
- Average growth (capital return or growth in investment principal value)
- Relative degree of inflation protection (positive correlation of investment returns with unexpected changes in inflation)

---

[15]Other, less "investable," asset classes can be defined conceptually, such as "human capital" and small, privately held businesses. But it is difficult to invest in such other classes, and difficult to quantify their magnitude.

[16]The real estate asset class total value of approximately $17 trillion depicted in Exhibit 7-5 includes residential as well as commercial property, but it includes only "pure-play" equity value. The value of mortgages and of corporate real estate (property held by publicly traded, non-real-estate companies) is excluded in the real estate share in the exhibit, but included in the bond and stock shares, respectively. The total value of underlying real estate assets including these components would be some $27 trillion. Commercial property in the United States is less than one-third the total of the underlying real estate asset value, on the order of $8 trillion. The source of the estimates in Exhibit 7-5 is Miles & Tolleson (1997), adjusted and updated by the authors' estimates based on FRB statistics. Exhibit 7-5 differs from Exhibit 1-8 in Chapter 1 primarily because private debt (other than mortgages) is not classified as "investable" in Exhibit 7-5, and so is not included in the "pie."

[17]Lists of asset classes often include international equity as a fifth asset class. However, from a broader perspective, *all* of the three risky asset classes (stocks, bonds, and real estate) may include international as well as domestic investment. In addition, many professionally managed portfolios now include relatively small allocations to so-called "non-core" or "alternative" investment asset classes. These are arguably "styles" of investment vehicles rather than asset classes, and include such categories as hedge funds and private equity investment funds. While real estate may play a role in some of these alternative types of vehicles, it is also true that within the real estate portfolio itself there are now both "core" and "non-core" components, with the latter including such investment vehicles as "opportunity funds" that specialize in development projects, operating companies, or other "turnaround" type investments, through relatively illiquid private vehicles. By contrast, the real estate "core" includes high quality, stabilized, income-producing properties, typically relatively new and with low vacancy (at least when they are initially purchased for investment).

EXHIBIT 7-5 Approximate Aggregate Value of Asset Classes, USA Early 2000s (in trillions of dollars)

© OnCourse Learning

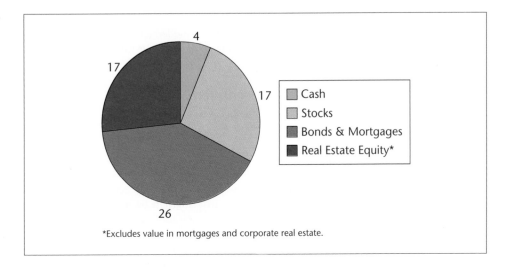

*Excludes value in mortgages and corporate real estate.

EXHIBIT 7-6

Stereotypical Characterization of Major Investment Asset Classes

© OnCourse Learning

Investment Concern	Stocks	Real Estate*	Long-Term Bonds[†]	Cash (T-Bills)
Risk	High	Moderate to Low[‡]	Moderate to Low[‡]	Lowest
Total Return	High	Moderate	Moderate	Lowest
Current Yield	Low	High	Highest	Moderate
Growth	High	Low	None	None[§]
Inflation Protection	L. R. Good	Good	Bad	Best (if reinvested)

*Unlevered institutional quality commercial property (fully operational, "stabilized").
[†]Investment grade corporate or government bonds.
[‡]Low risk for investors with long-term horizons and deep pockets, so they can hold the assets to maturity or until prices are favorable. Moderate risk for investors fully exposed to asset market price volatility.
[§]Unless the investment is rolled over (reinvested), in which case there is no current yield.

Exhibit 7-6 clarifies what we mean when we say that each asset class offers investors unique investment performance attributes. None of the four classes substantially duplicates any of the others in what it provides for investors. Together, they present a wide range of possibilities.

Real estate has an important role in the overall picture as one of these four major asset classes. Note in particular that in the risk and return dimensions, unlevered investment in real estate tends to fall between stocks at one extreme and cash (or short-term bonds such as T-bills) at the other extreme. In this regard, real estate is much like long-term bonds. Unlike bonds, however, real estate provides some capital growth and relatively good inflation protection. On the other hand, the contractual and finite nature of bond cash flows enables investors who can buy and hold bonds to maturity, without having to sell them in the bond market, to greatly reduce the risk in their investment (at least in nominal terms).[18]

Another important and defining characteristic of the four major asset classes is that they do not all "move together" in their investment performance. That is, they do not always tend

---

[18]Real estate investors who can have a long-term and flexible holding horizon also can greatly reduce the risk. Most of the return for such investors will come in the form of the relatively stable and predictable real estate rents. Such investors may also be able to take advantage of the greater degree of asset price predictability in the real estate market (see Chapter 12). Note also that real estate is fairly categorized as low to moderate risk only in the absence of substantial leverage (see Chapter 13).

to all do well at the same time, or all do poorly at the same time. The correlation among their periodic returns is generally only moderately positive. This means that investors can diversify their portfolios by allocating across the four asset classes.[19]

7.2.2 Historical Investment Performance

Exhibit 7-7 presents a broad-brush historical, empirical picture of the investment performance of the four asset classes since 1969. The exhibit shows what one dollar of investment at the end of 1969 would have grown to by the end of each of the following years in each of the four asset classes. Exhibit 7-7 assumes that any income generated by the investment was plowed back into the investment, so that the values shown represent the compounded accumulation of the total returns. In addition to the four asset classes, Exhibit 7-7 shows the effect of inflation by tracing the Consumer Price Index (CPI), indicating the number of dollars necessary in each year to purchase what one dollar could have bought in 1969.

Over the historical period shown in Exhibit 7-7, the champion performer was the stock market. For every dollar invested at the beginning of 1970, the investor in the stock market would have $49.56 by the end of 2010. A similar investment in real estate would have grown to $42.95, while an investment purely in long-term bonds would have grown to $30.12. The

EXHIBIT 7-7 Historical Performance of Major Investment Asset Classes, Compared to Inflation (CPI), 1969–2010

© OnCourse Learning

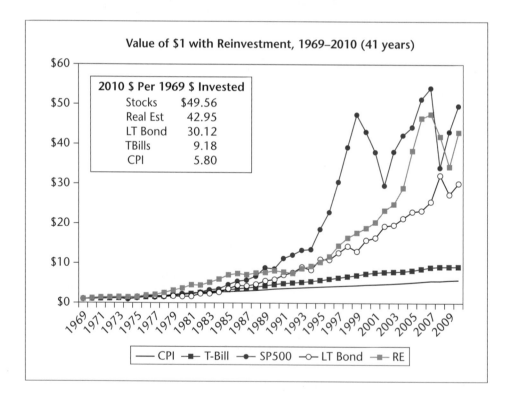

[19]Suppose we measure the stock market by the S&P 500 and the real estate market by the NCREIF-based TBI (transaction based index), then for the 36 calendar years between 1975 and 2010, the total investment returns in those two asset classes were both positive in 24 of the years (67 percent), and in 11 of the remaining 12 years one asset class was up when the other was down (6 years real estate up and stocks down, 5 years stocks up and real estate down). In only one of those 36 years were both real estate and stocks down (2008). Of course, 1975-2010 is a particular slice of history, but it seems that years in which both stocks and real estate provide negative total returns are quite rare, probably associated with exceptionally major economic or financial crises. Of course, bonds can provide a further stabilizing and diversifying element in an investment portfolio.

lowest return was provided by U.S. Treasury bills, that is, a continuously rolled-over reinvestment in the short-term notes of the government, similar to a typical money market fund. Such investment would have grown to only $9.18 per dollar of original investment. All four of the asset classes "beat inflation;" that is to say, they provided their investors with a positive "real" return, increasing the purchasing power of their invested dollars. The CPI indicates that it would have taken $5.80 to buy at the end of 2010 what $1.00 bought at the beginning of 1970.[20]

While the historical results shown in Exhibit 7-7 are broadly consistent with the relative total return expectations noted in Exhibit 7-6, it is important to realize that investment performance is always risky to some extent. This means that performance, in both absolute and relative terms comparing across the asset classes, varies over time in ways that are never perfectly predictable. For example, during most of the first half of the historical period shown in Exhibit 7-7, it was not the stock market, but rather real estate that posted the best overall performance, as seen in Exhibit 7-8A. Although a rally in the stock market in 1989 put that asset class in first place as of that year (ending with $8.90 to $7.73 in real estate for each $1.00 invested at the end of 1969), just a year earlier it was real estate that was still ahead in the cumulative total return. During the decade of the 1970s, both bonds and stocks struggled with a combination of weak economic growth and troublesome inflation.[21]

During the second half of the overall 1970–2010 period, depicted in Exhibit 7-8B, the stock market experienced one of the greatest bull markets ever during the 1990s, quintupling nominal value on a cumulative total return basis, only to bump into a rather traumatic crash during 2000–2002, associated with the bursting of the "dot.com bubble." That crash negated 38 percent of the S&P 500 index cumulative value during the three years 2000–2002. The market then rebounded to peak again in 2007 only to crash again in the financial crisis of 2008, a year in which the market again lost 37 percent.

Earlier in this historical period, there had also been a crash in commercial real estate markets. On a calendar year basis from a peak at the end of 1985 to a trough at the end of 1992, the TBI lost 27 percent in nominal same-property asset pricing. However, the relative gradualness of the decline, coupled with real estate's relatively high cash yield payout rates, resulted in a peak-trough loss of only 8 percent on a cumulative total return basis in that property market crash. But the more severe crash associated with the more recent financial crisis and recession hit real estate harder, losing on a calendar year basis 28 percent in cumulative nominal value even with income.

The overall result for the 1989–2010 period was that for each dollar invested at the beginning of this period the stock market investor would have $5.57 and the real estate investor $5.56 by the end of 2010, a virtual tie. The bond market investor would have done almost as well with $5.37. This was a generally good period for bonds due to generally falling long-term interest rates, first due to declining inflation expectations bringing down nominal interest rates and then during the 2000s due to declining real interest rates as much of the growth in global liquidity found its way to dollar-denominated investments. The low interest rates of

---

[20]Quantitative performance histories such as those portrayed in Exhibit 7-7 must be interpreted cautiously. It is difficult to measure investment performance in a way that is exactly comparable across asset classes, and there is always a question of what "index" best represents the specific investments or opportunities faced by a given investor. The numbers in Exhibit 7-7 are based on the following indexes. For the stock market, we have used the Standard & Poor's 500 Index, which consists of 500 relatively large stocks. For bonds, we have used an index of long-term U.S. Treasury bonds. Both the stock and bond index returns, as well as the Treasury bill returns, are as computed by Ibbotson & Associates in their annual *Stocks, Bonds, Bills & Inflation Yearbook*. The real estate returns shown here are based on previously noted transaction price-based version of the NCREIF index (TBI), and prior to 1984 on unsmoothed versions of the NCREIF Property Index and predecessor commingled fund indices, in order to correct for appraisal smoothing to provide an index that is more comparable to the other three.

[21]Long-term bonds performed relatively poorly over the 1970–1989 period due to rising inflation and resulting rising nominal interest rates over much of that historical period. As noted in Exhibit 7-6, bonds are negatively affected by inflation. However, it must also be recognized that the historical periodic returns examined in this section assume, in effect, that investors sell and reinvest their portfolios at the end of each year. This results in an investor in long-term bonds being subject annually to the vagaries of the bond market, which was generally unfavorable during the 1970s. In reality, many investors in long-term bonds would not sell their investments so frequently, but would instead hold onto their bonds until maturity, taking in the coupon interest income as their return on investment.

EXHIBIT 7-8A
Performance of the Major
Asset Classes, 1969–1989
© OnCourse Learning

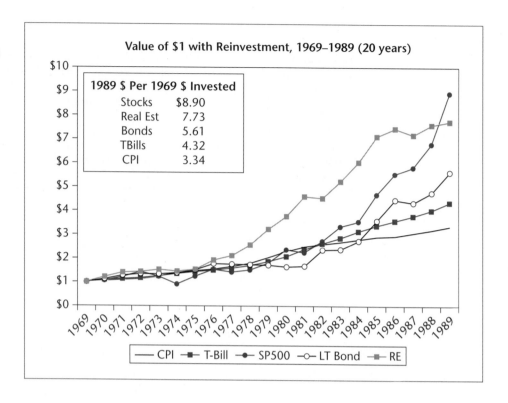

EXHIBIT 7-8B
Performance of the Major
Asset Classes, 1989–2010
© OnCourse Learning

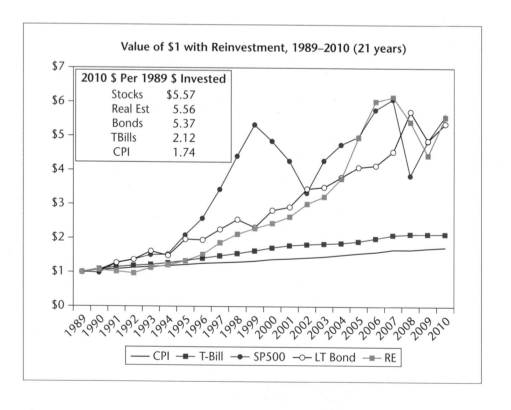

EXHIBIT 7-9

Historical Statistics on
Annual Returns, 1970–2010

© OnCourse Learning

Statistics On Annual Returns, 1970–2010 (41 Years)

Asset Class	Average Total Return	Standard Deviation	Average Income Return	Average Appreciation Return
T-Bills	5.60%	3.10%	5.60%	0.00%
G Bonds	9.26%	11.73%	7.74%	1.52%
Real Estate	10.15%	10.86%	6.40%	3.74%
Stocks	11.56%	17.91%	3.46%	8.10%
Inflation	4.42%	3.07%		

this period explain why money invested only in (rolled-over) T-bills would have grown only to $2.12 from 1989 to 2010, barely more than the relatively small effect of inflation, which caused $1.74 worth of 2010 dollars to equate to each 1989 dollar

The table in Exhibit 7-9 summarizes the 1970–2010 annual investment performance history shown in Exhibit 7-7, in the form of some basic statistical measures. The first column of Exhibit 7-9 indicates the average annual total return, the growth in investment value from both capital value appreciation and income paid out to the investor (such as dividends, interest, or rent). The second column indicates the annual standard deviation in these yearly total returns during the 34-year history considered. This standard deviation is a measure of the variability across time in the returns, also known as the volatility of the investment. This is a basic way to measure the risk in the investment asset class. Volatility is reflected in the "bumpiness" or propensity for "up and down" movement or cycles in the historical charts of index values. The last two columns on the right in the table break the average total return into two components. The income return is the average current income paid out to the investor each year by the investment, as a fraction of the investment value at the beginning of each year. The appreciation return is the average annual capital gain or percentage growth in asset value.[22]

The historical statistics presented in the table in Exhibit 7-9 are depicted graphically in the bar charts in Exhibits 7-10A and 7-10B. Exhibit 7-10A shows the average total return and breaks out the two components: average current income and capital appreciation. Notice that the bulk of the return on investment in stocks comes typically in the form of capital gain or share price appreciation. By contrast, virtually all of the return to bonds over the long run is from the income paid by the bond interest.[23] Commercial real estate typically derives its return from both asset value appreciation and current net rental income, although the bulk of the return to unlevered investments in fully operational properties comes from net rental income.[24] The dashed horizontal line in Exhibit 7-10A is the average inflation rate over the

---

[22]These various measures of investment performance will be defined more rigorously and discussed in more depth in Chapter 9. The allocation of the entire total return of T-bills to the income component is somewhat arbitrary, as T-bill investors can easily convert current income to growth by rolling over the maturing T-bills into the purchase of new bills. Note that the average annual investment appreciation return to unlevered institutional quality real estate was some 68 basis points (0.68 percent) less than the average inflation rate over the same historical period. This reflects the real depreciation of property even after capital-improvement expenditures (as the real estate income return component here is a cash flow based number net of capital expenditures). This reflects the depreciation principle we introduced in Chapter 5 as well as the evolution of location premium as described in our discussion of location value in Chapters 4 and 5.

[23]This is because prior to the maturity of the bonds, bond values vary inversely with currently prevailing market interest rates, and interest rates tend to be mean-reverting: as likely to go up as down over time. However, during the particular historical period covered in the exhibit, interest rates went down a bit more often than they went up, and more so than investors had been expecting, giving bonds a slight positive average appreciation return for that period.

[24]Capital appreciation would be a larger component of real estate return during periods of higher inflation. On average, over the historical period represented in Exhibits 7-10a and 7-10b, inflation was not sufficiently high to cause the appreciation return component to approach the income return component in magnitude. Use of financial leverage can change the nature of real estate investment returns, skewing more toward growth rather than income, as will be discussed in Chapter 13.

1970–2010 period. Note that it is less than the total returns provided by any of the four asset classes but slightly more than the appreciation return rate for the unlevered institutional quality real estate represented by the NCREIF/TBI index.

Exhibit 7-10B shows the volatility, the annual standard deviation in the asset periodic returns across time. We noted that this is a basic way to measure the risk in an investment, because it indicates the range of variability in the investment performance outcomes across time. Comparing Exhibits 7-10A and 7-10B reveals an important point. Note that the average total return shown in Exhibit 7-10A corresponds closely to the magnitude of volatility shown in Exhibit 7-10B relatively speaking. This is the classical relationship between *risk and return*, in which *greater risk is associated with greater average returns over time*, and lower average returns are associated with more stability in those returns across time.

EXHIBIT 7-10A Average Annual Total Return, 1970–2010

Sources: NCREIF, MIT, Ibbotson.

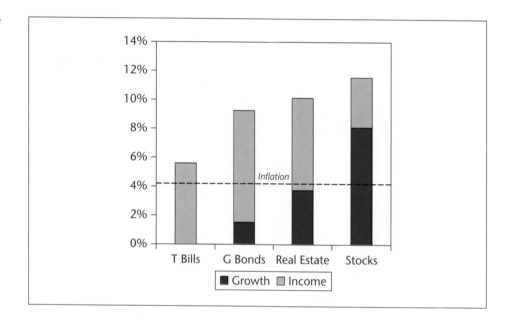

EXHIBIT 7-10B Annual Volatility, 1970–2010

Sources: NCREIF, MIT, Ibbotson.

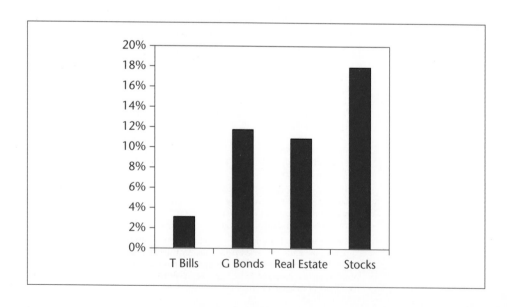

Exhibits 7-10A and 7-10B reveal the actual realization of these expectations during the 1970–2010 period at the broad-brush level of the four major investment asset classes.[25]

7.3 Perspective on the U.S. Institutional Property Market

With the preceding fundamentals in mind, let us now take a practical perspective on the U.S. institutional property market. In this section we will give you some historical background and a summary of the major players and sources of real estate investment capital as of the early twenty-first century. This is the kind of perspective and basic background information that practitioners in the industry all share and which therefore underlies typical thinking and decision making. It is therefore an important part of the introduction of the student to the industry.

7.3.1 Brief History of Commercial Real Estate Investment during Recent Decades

Exhibit 7-11 depicts the "roller coaster ride" in commercial property values in the United States over the 1970–2010 period. The cyclical-looking picture presented in the exhibit is annotated to indicate some of the major events and developments that affected institutional investment and asset valuation in the commercial property market.

Exhibit 7-11 indicates "same-property" price evolution based on the transaction prices of properties bought and sold by investors. It does not include including income reinvestment. As such, it traces a rough picture of average property market values over time for large

EXHIBIT 7-11 The "Roller Coaster Ride" in U.S. Institutional Commercial Property Prices over Recent Decades

Sources: Moody's/REAL, TBI, and author's estimates.

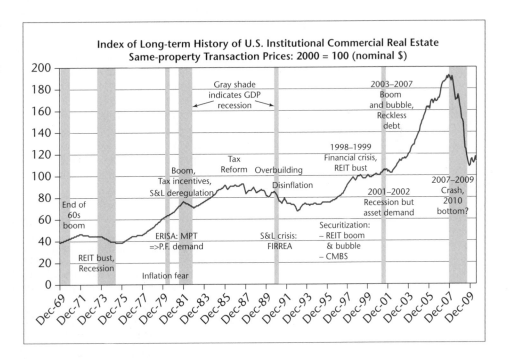

---

[25]A slight exception is apparent in the historical period represented here, in that real estate has a slightly higher average return than bonds even though it has less volatility. However, as noted previously, many bond investors need not face the type of annual periodic volatility measured here, as they may hold their bond investments to maturity. This effectively reduces the risk implied by the bond volatility in the exhibit.

commercial properties of the type invested in by institutions such as life insurance companies, banks, and pension funds (as will be discussed in the next section).[26]

The history begins on the heels of strong commercial property performance during the long period of economic growth of the 1960s (notwithstanding a minor recession at the end of that decade), including a boom fueled in part by REIT investment in the late 1960s and first years of the 1970s. The typical REIT in this early period was a mortgage REIT, highly levered by money borrowed on a short-term basis at low interest rates financing investment made on a long-term basis in mortgages at higher fixed interest rates. Then government deficit spending during the Vietnam War combined with the first Arab Oil Embargo of 1973–1974 to lead to an unprecedented rise in inflation combined with a simultaneous deep economic recession. (Periods of GDP recession are indicated in Exhibit 7-11 by the shaded gray bands.) This was the beginning of the so-called **stagflation** of the 1970s.[27] This cut demand for commercial property space usage just as short-term nominal interest rates soared in response to the new inflation. These movements placed the mortgage REITs in a classical interest rate squeeze in which they had to refinance their short-term debt at new interest rates that exceeded the interest on the long-term mortgages they were holding. This resulted in bankruptcies in the REIT sector. The simultaneous contractions in both the space and asset markets led to a crash in commercial property prices during 1972–1975, when commercial institutional investment property typically lost almost 20 percent of its nominal value (and even more of its real inflation-adjusted value).

With the economic recovery of the mid to late 1970s, commercial property really took off as an investment. Stagflation kept the stock and bond markets in the doldrums (and the stock market had a long memory with regard to its experience with REITs in the early 1970s), but inflation fears actually helped fuel investor demand for real estate, which was perceived as a good hedge against the inflation danger. Furthermore, 1974 saw the passage by Congress of the **Employee Retirement Income Security Act (ERISA)**, which stimulated a boom in institutional investment in commercial property. ERISA required that defined-benefit pension funds be "funded;" that is, capital had to be invested for the long term so that there would be sufficient money in the funds to cover future pension benefit liabilities promised by the pension plans. While the law did not extend to defined-contribution plans, ERISA did take account of some theoretical developments in financial economics of the 1950s and 1960s known as Modern Portfolio Theory (MPT). This theory suggested that defined-benefit plan sponsors should diversify their investments broadly, so as to minimize risk and maximize return per unit of risk. This led ERISA to suggest, in effect, that pension fund investments should be broadly diversified, effectively including consideration of real estate as an alternative investment in addition to the traditional pension asset classes of stocks and bonds. This resulted in a vast new source of capital flowing into commercial property investment, as defined-benefit pension fund contributions mushroomed with the bulge of the baby boom generation entering the labor force.

With inflation fears and the growth in institutional investors bolstering real estate investment demand, the commercial property markets barely skipped a beat with the sharp

---

[26]Exhibit 7-11 depicts nominal (current value) dollars. It is spliced together from several sources: the monthly Moody's/REAL Commercial Property Price Index (CPPI, a repeat-sales index) from 2001–2010; the quarterly transaction price based version of the NCREIF Index (TBI) produced by MIT to cover the period 1984–2000; the NCREIF Property Index unsmoothed to correct for appraisal smoothing (see Chapter 25) for the period 1978–1984, and predecessor commingled fund indices prior to that and similarly unsmoothed (both these latter at annual frequency) as in the earlier exhibits. All of these indices essentially attempt to reflect same-property transaction price evolution of institutional quality property (unlevered, and reflecting the effect of capital improvement expenditure but also the "real depreciation" of structures noted in Chapter 5). Exhibit 7-11 therefore reflects typical property price evolution as experienced by investors, but it is not exactly the same as an average market price index (which would reflect new buildings renewing the stock), nor does it include the income or effect of reinvestment of property income on total investment returns.

[27]Normally, it is more common for higher inflation to be associated with economic boom times rather than recessions, and for recessions to be associated with declines in inflation. The 1974 recession was different because it was caused largely by real cost increases on the supply side of the macroeconomy, due to the U.S. economy's dependence on imported oil, rather than by a reduction in aggregate demand. The troublesome combination of a stagnant economy and inflation was dubbed *stagflation*.

back-to-back recessions of 1980–1981. (Unlike the recession of the early 1970s, property markets were not significantly overbuilt in the early 1980s, so there was little excess supply of built space.) Yet more real estate investment incentives were provided by the tax cut of 1982 ushered in by the new Reagan administration. This tax law enhanced previous provisions that provided generous depreciation allowances and tax shelters for wealthy investors, which benefited real estate. Also during the 1980s, the deregulation of the savings and loan industry allowed these institutions to invest in commercial mortgages for the first time, thus opening up another new (and inexperienced) source of capital for commercial property. Deregulation and tax incentives combined with the economic recovery of the mid-1980s and the continued flow of institutional capital into real estate, resulted in a continuation of the boom in commercial property prices through the mid-1980s. We have seen in Chapter 2 how the combination of rising rents in the space market and compressing cap rates (falling yields, that is, rising price/income multiples) in the asset market can lead to a price spiral and "bubble" mentality in the commercial property market.

By the mid to late 1980s, the huge accumulated flow of capital to commercial real estate had stimulated a building boom of historic proportions. Financial capital was converted to physical structures by the development industry, especially into office buildings, shopping malls, and hotels. Much of this development was driven or supported by tax incentives that distanced the investor from the underlying economic costs and benefits of the physical real estate that was being built, resulting in many bad projects that found themselves with few tenants. Furthermore, the savings and loan and commercial banks that financed much of the new construction operated in an environment of "moral hazard," in which government deposit insurance divorced their source of capital from the risks of its investment.[28]

In 1986, a sweeping tax reform act removed virtually all of the special tax incentives from which real estate had benefited. Also, by the late 1980s, the inflation rate was down sharply, and inflation appeared to be under control, undercutting the "inflation fear" source of real estate investment demand. And by the late 1980s, the extent of overbuilding in the space market was becoming obvious, as was the financial crisis in the overextended savings and loan industry, which had loaned vast sums in commercial mortgages backed by economically weak building projects. The commercial real estate asset market began to falter. The stock market drop and economic recession of 1990 were the straws that broke the camel's back (even though it was a mild and short-lived recession). Amid crumbling financial institutions awash with bad mortgages, the bottom fell out of the commercial property market in the early 1990s. Traditional sources of capital for commercial real estate, such as banks, life insurance companies, and pension funds, dried up completely. Indeed the capital flow from such sources turned negative, with lenders refusing to refinance loans that came due and even trying to sell existing mortgages. Commercial real estate asset prices fell 30 to 50 percent in the span of two years in most of the major property markets, the largest drop in property values in the United States since the Great Depression. (In contrast, the housing market was not hit nearly so hard at that time, with the exception of a few overheated cities.)

The bottom for commercial properties was finally reached in 1992 and 1993, with a flood of new capital coming into real estate. The money came first from opportunistic "vulture funds" and "grave-dancers" financed by wealthy individuals. This was followed rapidly by the public capital markets as a new source of money in the form of an unprecedented expansion of the REIT industry, as well as the development of an entirely new industry in the form of commercial mortgage-backed securities (CMBS). In 1993 alone, 50 new REITs issued initial public offerings (IPOs) of stocks, raising over $9 billion, more than three times the largest previous annual total.[29] During this period, it was not uncommon to be able to

---

[28]The term *moral hazard* was coined in the insurance industry to describe a situation in which one party controls the risks (in this case, the financial institutions), while another party pays the price of the downside outcome from a risky decision (in this case, the U.S. government, via the Deposit Insurance Corporations).

[29]Of the total of $147 billion raised through the public capital markets by REITs in the first 37 years of their history from 1961 through 1997, $108 billion was raised during the five years from 1993 through 1997, while some $200 billion in CMBS were issued from 1992 through 1998 (a source that had virtually not existed at all before then).

buy large new commercial properties for a small fraction of their construction cost (although such properties were often largely devoid of tenants!).

The remarkable development of securitization in the public capital markets as a source of real estate investment money during the 1990s powered the recovery of the commercial property investment market during most of the remainder of that decade (until 1998) and greatly changed the real estate investment industry, as described in Section 7.1. The development of both the debt and equity sides of this market was stimulated by government actions. For example, the CMBS industry had its roots in the **Financial Institutions Recovery, Reform, and Enforcement Act** of 1989 (**FIRREA**) passed by Congress to bail out the savings and loan industry. FIRREA set up the Resolution Trust Corporation (RTC), a government corporation charged with rapidly selling huge quantities of bad commercial mortgages that the government had taken from defunct banks and thrifts. FIRREA also imposed risk-adjusted capital requirements on financial institutions, giving them an incentive to hold assets in a publicly traded ("securitized") form, such as CMBS, rather than as whole loans. Necessity being the mother of invention, the means to tap the public debt market was found via the CMBS vehicle.

REITs also were given a boost by tax reforms in the late 1980s and early 1990s that gave them greater management flexibility and facilitated institutional investment in REIT stock. This, combined with the invention of the umbrella REIT (UPREIT) structure and the great need for liquidity among commercial property owners in the early 1990s, led to the takeoff of the REIT revolution in 1993.[30] For the first time in history, large quantities of prime commercial property equity were being transferred from traditional private ownership to ownership by publicly traded specialized real estate investment corporations in the form of REITs.

By the mid-1990s, the traditional sources of capital, especially the pension funds and commercial banks, were also back in the real estate investment business in a big way. With the long economic boom of the 1990s, excess supply in the space markets was gradually filled up with tenants, further bolstering the confidence of conservative investors. The commercial property market was fully recovered by the end of the decade. There was also some evidence that the REIT and CMBS markets were improving the efficiency of the capital markets in playing their role as a negative feedback loop, or regulator of overall capital flow to the real estate system, as we described in Chapter 2. A sharp pullback in the REIT and CMBS markets occurred during 1998 as a result of Russian and Asian sovereign debt defaults and follow-on financial strains in the United States, including a fiasco with the hedge fund Long Term Capital Management that briefly threatened to bring down the entire financial system. This pullback in the REIT and CMBS markets temporarily cut off a part of the money flow to new real estate development projects, thereby heading off what had begun to appear to some as the beginning of a new round of overbuilding in some markets.[31]

The early years of the new century were very good for commercial and investment real estate asset markets, even though a comparatively mild national recession in 2000–2001 cut badly into demand for many types of commercial space usage and undercut rents in most space markets. After a substantial fall in REIT prices during 1998–2000, which had relatively little impact on the private property market, REIT shares soared with the bursting of the high-tech "dot.com bubble" in 2001 and a resulting counter-flow of investors into an asset class that provided cash flow, dividends, and tangible assets—the opposite of many of the ephemeral dot.com stocks that had recently crashed. More broadly, the mainstream professional

---

[30]The pioneering UPREIT IPO was that of Taubman Centers, Inc., a chain of regional shopping malls run by the Taubman brothers, in the fall of 1992.

[31]During the early to mid-1990s, REITs had been able to purchase existing properties in the property market at prices that appeared to be "bargains" from the perspective of the stock market where REITs trade. So capital flowed rapidly into REITs and through them into the property market as REITs purchased existing buildings. By around 1997, property market values had recovered to the point that there were no longer "bargains" from a REIT valuation perspective. This removed the easy growth opportunities that REITs had enjoyed, and REIT investors in the stock market reacted accordingly, repricing REITs as income stocks rather than growth stocks. This resulted in a fall in REIT share prices and a temporary cut-off of capital flow as new REIT stock issues were canceled. This type of process will be discussed further in Chapters 12, 20, and 23.

investment establishment on Wall Street seemed finally to be recognizing both direct private investment in real estate as well as REITs and CMBs as legitimate elements in the core of the institutional investment portfolio. The bursting of the dot.com bubble seemed to erase the stigma of real estate being an "informationally inefficient" asset class (and the memory of the early 1990s real estate crash), just as it erased the idea that the "informationally efficient" stock market could not be susceptible to "irrational exuberance" with its attendant corrections. The resulting boost in investor demand for real estate kept asset prices up, even as underlying space markets were tumbling and property income declining.

Real estate income yields (cap rates) fell to historically low values in the early 2000s, but not so low *relative* to bond yields, which were also very low by that time. The result propelled property prices to new heights with the economic recovery during 2003–2005. By 2007 institutional commercial real estate asset valuations were at levels never before seen relative to rents and relative to their long-run trend (as evident in Exhibit 7-11), especially in the private property market. Yet property investors were comforted by the relative lack of overbuilding in the space market and by similarly high valuations (low yields) in the other major asset classes as the stock market peaked (for a second time in seven years) and bond market yield spreads compressed, as vastly increased global liquidity (due in part to the take-off of such emerging giants as China and India) sent waves of money into U.S. investments of all types. Once again a type of "bubble mentality" similar to the early 1970s and late 1980s took hold in the commercial property markets, including lax lending practices and buyers aiming for quick profits only from "flipping" properties into rising prices after a short hold. But this time (in contrast to the late 1980s) the much larger housing market was in more perilous shape than the commercial property market, and the general financial overextension was not just in real estate but extended throughout most of the financial sector and also included the federal government and much of the corporate sector.

During 2006 and through most of 2007 commercial property investors lulled themselves into thinking that commercial real estate was remote from troubles with the excessive pricing, reckless lending, and overbuilding that were becoming apparent in the U.S. housing market by mid-2006. The housing market was propelled by new types of easy-credit home mortgages (which were easily securitized and sold into the booming bond market) and low interest rates maintained too long by the Federal Reserve after the recovery from the 2001 recession. The Case-Shiller home price index peaked after a death-defying run-up of 126 percent from 2000 to 2006. The subsequent collapse in the housing market (at first deceptively gradual until late 2007), and therefore in the debt that the housing sector supported, exposed the entire financial system that had grown unprecedentedly interconnected and far too leveraged, not least the federal government itself.[32] Complex new financial instruments such as credit default swap derivatives and privately issued multilayered securities, including many based on residential and commercial mortgages, created a sense of a highly efficient risk allocation by a very sophisticated market. While that may have been true in important respects, the way the securitization and derivatives industry was operating was in fact spinning a web of systemic risk with too much leverage dependent on underlying assets that had become badly overvalued.

Few people recognized or acted on such concerns in the euphoria of the 2005–2007 peak. (Nearly $200 billion worth of CMBS loans were issued in just the first half of 2007, as much as were issued during all of the 1992–1998 period!) And of course it is difficult for any one player or part of an integrated system to go against the tide. For example, many life insurance companies had gotten badly burned in the early 1990s and therefore perhaps had a better institutional memory than other players. When they refused to relax loan underwriting standards as aggressively as CMBS loan originators were doing, the life insurance lenders

---

[32]There could have been some déjà vu by this time, as the Bush Administration repeated the Johnson Administration's 1960s mistake of not raising taxes to cover war expenditures (Iraq in the 2000s echoed Viet Nam), which combined with tax cuts to fuel a ballooning federal debt even during a period of economic growth when a government should not engage in deficit spending. In the 1970s the result was inflation, but in the 2000s the economy was less prone to inflation and the temptation was politically irresistible to simply borrow to finance the deficit given the strong demand for U.S. government debt (in part from burgeoning foreign sovereign wealth funds largely in Asia and the Middle East).

got largely shut out of the commercial mortgage lending market during its peak—an event that subsequently redounded to their advantage.

The result was a global financial crisis and resulting economic recession more severe in the United States than any since the Great Depression and a general collapse in prices across all asset classes. Investors panicked (with reason) and fled risk of any kind for the safe harbor of U.S. Treasury Bills (whose yields actually went slightly negative for a time as their prices were bid up!). Commercial property was not at all immune. On a calendar year basis the TBI price index dropped 35 percent from the end of 2006 to the end of 2009 (a 28 percent loss after accounting for income generated by the properties during that period), completing commercial real estate's third major asset market pricing cycle in a half century (with prior bottoms in 1975 and 1992). This latest crash was steeper and faster than the previous ones, and even the NCREIF Property Index rammed its valuations down much harder and quicker than in the 1990s. (In late 2008 and early 2009, NCREIF member fund managers and accountants sometimes overruled appraisers in making property valuation reports into the index, as the appraisers had little hard price evidence to work from amid virtually paralyzed markets for large properties.)

With newly reawakened memories of the previous cycle, commercial property market participants reacted a bit differently than in the 1990s. Many more bad commercial mortgages were held onto longer by lenders and CMBS problem loan managers ("special servicers"), invoking a policy of "pretend and extend." Instead of dumping large quantities of bad loans and underlying troubled properties onto the market at once (which arguably led to a "negative bubble" in the early to mid-1990s—prices lower than they needed to be), creditors this time sought to work out solutions with borrowers or to hold onto properties until the market recovered somewhat. There still remained a vast amount of global cash, now chastened and more risk averse, seeking solid investments or in some cases hunting like "vultures" for bargain deals from distressed sellers. And although employment was especially hard hit and slow to recover, undercutting the demand side of the real estate space markets, a favorable point was that the U.S. commercial property market had not been badly overbuilt in the 2000s, in contrast to the 1980s (and in contrast to the single-family housing market in the 2000s). This fact, along with the speed and depth of the asset market pricing correction by 2009 and the quantity of global money seeking solid or bargain investments, sowed the seeds of a rapid recovery of sorts in the commercial property market in 2010. Nevertheless, the economic recession was particularly deep and long lasting after the 2008 collapse, as is typical of financial-triggered recessions with their attendant need for subsequent de-leveraging (and exacerbated by the central role that the housing sector has played in the U.S. economy since the mid-twentieth century).

As in the 1990s, the recovery in the commercial property market was once again led by private equity funds and REITs seeking to buy distressed assets at bargain prices or to place capital into safe, income-generating and potentially inflation-hedging assets. But in the context of an anemic underlying economy and vast need for de-leveraging, the recovery of 2010–2011 was mixed, volatile, and tentative, with the institutional property market split into major segments with very different price points for distressed versus "trophy" assets. In the private property market some indices of large, strongly-leased properties in prime locations with nondistressed ownership and supply-constrained space markets ("trophies" of the type that appealed to risk-averse investors) indicated price recoveries in excess of 30 percent above the 2009 bottom by 2011 (barely 10 to 20 percent below 2007 peak values). On the other hand distressed assets continued to sell at prices 50 percent or more below peak 2007 values (some 40 percent below otherwise similar trophy properties).[33]

---

[33]This was an example of major segmentation largely centered in the asset market, something, which we noted in Chapter 1, is less common than segmentation in the space market. This type of segmentation in the asset market was sustainable, at least for a while, because in the economic climate of the time trophy assets were relatively scarce compared to the investor demand for very solid investments, while distressed properties embodied major problems with either their tenancy, their ownership or indebtedness, and/or their physical condition, often combined with a weak underlying local space market.

In the public market, REITs had fallen earlier and farther than private market asset prices. (In part this is an apples-to-oranges comparison as REIT shares are levered while property price indices track asset prices not levered equity in the properties). But REITs then staged a huge recovery starting in the spring of 2009 after experiencing their worst losses ever. The NAREIT equity REIT share price index, after falling from a level of 649 in January 2007 to 186 in February 2009 (pegged to 100 in 1971 in nominal terms), bounced back to 427 by December 2010. By 2010 REITs were major buyers using capital freshly raised in the somewhat recovered stock market and bond market where interest rates had fallen back to low levels. The new-issue CMBS market, which had dried up completely in 2009, attempted a small and chastened recovery in 2010 with some $11 billion in new issuance that year (very conservatively underwritten, and most of it privately placed rather than IPOs). But large quantities of troubled commercial mortgage debt remained outstanding; overdue or "underwater" loans (that is, loans on properties now worth less than the loan balance) posed a large cloud hanging over the commercial property market as it entered the second decade of the twenty-first century. There were also unresolved regulatory issues related to the new Basel-III international banking accords and the Dodd-Frank financial reform act in the United States that sought to prevent a future financial meltdown of the type that occurred in 2008 but that raised thorny problems of implementation in what remained a very complex investment industry.

Exhibit 7-11 traces over 40 years of U.S. commercial real estate asset market pricing history. It is a story that is interwoven with the economic and financial history of the United States and the world and with what was going on in the underlying space markets through time. Note, however, that GDP recessions in the macroeconomy (indicated by the gray-shaded bars in the exhibit) do not always engender major asset price corrections in the private property market. GDP recessions do tend to hit the commercial property space markets and especially the development industry (see Exhibit 2-1 in Chapter 2). However, the market for existing stabilized assets can sometimes ride through recessions if the supply side of the space market is not greatly overbuilt going into the recession and if the capital markets remain strong, or if real estate is viewed by investors as a hedge or relative "safe harbor" in whatever economic storm is brewing at the time (e.g., as a hedge against inflation in the early 1980s, or as a transparent provider of solid earnings in the crash of the "zero-earnings" tech stocks of 2001). Yet somehow it seems that the commercial property asset market finds it hard to avoid a cycle of over-pricing and subsequent major correction (on the order of 30 percent or more loss of peak value in real terms) at least once within every couple of decades. History suggests that the tendency to this type of long (more than a decade) cycle is strong in the property market, perhaps stronger or more apparent in the private property market than in the publicly-traded securities markets, even though since the 1990s the private market has been strongly linked to and influenced by the more informationally efficient securities markets (via both REITs and CMBS).

7.3.2 Sources of Debt and Equity Capital

The above-described history was experienced by most practitioners in the commercial real estate investment business today, and so forms part of their implicit understanding. Exhibits 7-12 and 7-13 quantify another basic aspect of the U.S. commercial property landscape that practitioners know implicitly and which therefore is an important part of an introduction to the business for newcomers. These exhibits describe the sources of the money that flows into institutional property investment.

Recall from Chapter 1 that the total stock of commercial property in the United States is probably worth $8 or $9 trillion, based on estimates from CoStar Group. However, probably less than half of this stock is actively traded as investment product among large-scale institutions. Within this institutional segment, several hundred billion dollars worth of property typically changes hands in an average year. For example, the data firm Real Capital Analytics (RCA), tracking property sales of $5 million and up, recorded a precrash peak of $513 billion traded in 2007. But trading volume is very cyclical, and this dropped to an extreme postcrash low of only $55 trillion in 2009. If we take the midrange of around $300 billion as average in

EXHIBIT 7-12 Buyer Composition of Investors into U.S. Institutional Commercial Real Estate, 2005–2010

Source: Real Capital Analytics Inc.

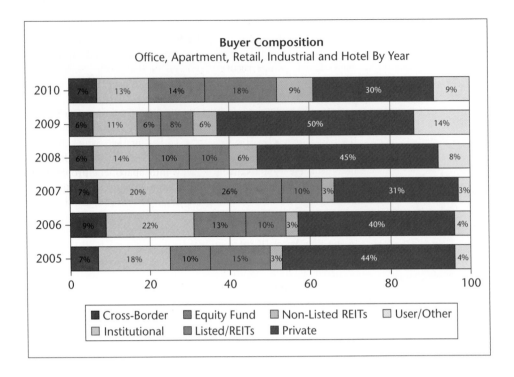

EXHIBIT 7-13 Sources of Debt Capital for Various Types of U.S. Institutional Property Investment, 2010

Source: Real Capital Analytics Inc.

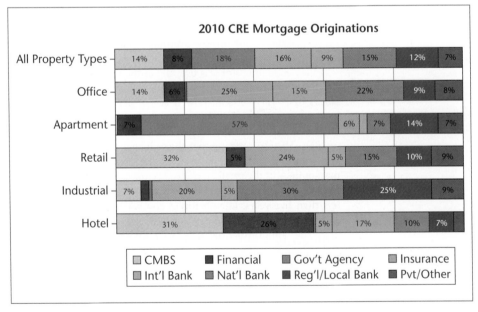

a healthy market as of the early 2000s, and assuming an average holding period of 10 years, then this implies about \$3 trillion of institutional scale investment property in the United States.[34] Probably half or more of this is financed by commercial mortgage debt, with a somewhat larger share being debt-financed at the time of initial purchase. (The average

---

[34]Studies at CoStar Group indicate that among actively traded properties, perhaps less than one fifth have values greater than \$5 million but account for well over two-thirds of the transaction dollar volume. (See Peng et al., 2010.) See Chapter 11 for evidence about the difference in price performance between the smaller "non-institutional" properties and the larger institutional properties, based on CoStar data.

loan-to-value ratio tends to decline subsequent to initial purchase with loan amortization and nominal property value appreciation.)

Exhibit 7-12 shows the pattern of the source of equity capital among buyers of $5 million+ properties during 2005–2010 according to RCA, a period encompassing the peak of the boom and the bottom of the crash and initial post-crash year. The largest single source was private investors, relatively small, typically locally oriented often family-based enterprises. These types of investors are more prominent among smaller properties and secondary markets. They got relatively eclipsed during the peak of the boom, but remained in the game better than the big players during the worst of the crash. In part this is because they were able to employ "relationship lending" from local commercial banks, and also because they were relatively heavily into apartment properties that could tap money from the federal housing agency lenders, Fannie Mae and Freddie Mac ("Government Sponsored Enterprises," or GSEs), during the financial crisis when other capital sources were paralyzed.

At the other end of the spectrum are the large institutions and equity funds, private non-bank sources of money that have large-scale real estate investment expertise. These intermediaries often place capital on behalf of pension and endowment funds. They tend to focus more on larger properties in top tier or "gateway" metropolitan areas.

In between are REITs, led most characteristically by the publicly listed firms that often provide vertically integrated real estate investment products and services as described earlier. These firms can tap the fast-responding and informationally efficient public stock market as well as the bond market, for external capital, and can sometimes arbitrage pricing differences between the public and private markets (see Chapters 12 and 23). Most REITs are specialized by property type and/or target locations. Private (or "nonlisted") REITs come in two types. One is the "incubator REIT" that may serve as a convenient vehicle for private equity real estate investment, aiming ultimately at going public either by an IPO or a buy-out by a pre-existing public REIT (perhaps, when/if the terms are right). The other is a type of investment product aimed at small individual investors, typically sold through brokers, often aimed at retirement and estate planning, typically oriented toward providing a fixed annual income. Rounding out the picture are direct foreign investors and owner-occupiers (space users).

Typically of equal magnitude or greater than the buyers' equity money is debt capital coming in the form of commercial mortgages. The sources of this capital are indicated in Exhibit 7-13 by property sector. While this is a dynamic issue that evolves over time, the exhibit gives a snapshot as of a particular year, 2010. At that time, as is typical, bank sources dominate in mortgage lending, with a wide range of types of banks. Traditionally small- to medium-sized local and regional banks have specialized more in commercial property lending than the larger national and international banks, relatively speaking. These are the classical sources of "relationship lending," and in the case of the smaller regional banks have been particularly important for smaller properties. Bank loans tend to be shorter in duration, often less than five years. Life insurance companies and other financial institutions (such as funds and investment management vehicles) were able in 2010 to focus on the larger, more prime properties and top-tier locations, as CMBS was still struggling to come back from its collapse during the financial crisis.[35] In 2010 apartment property finance was still heavily dependent on a unique source of lending only available to residential properties in the form of loans from the GSEs.

7.4 Chapter Summary

This chapter has presented some very basic background information about commercial real estate assets as an investment class. We highlighted the similarities and differences between real estate and the other major traditional investment asset classes, stocks and bonds in particular. We noted important recent developments in the public capital markets and the REIT and CMBS industries in particular as well as the current major sources of capital. We put this

---

[35]In 2010, Exhibit 7-13 indicates that CMBS lending was particularly focused on retail and hotel properties. But this is not always or necessarily the case.

information in some historical context and provided some summary quantification of typical investment performance in recent decades based on empirical evidence. You should now have a working knowledge of the basic commercial real estate investment products and vehicles and the recent history that sets the stage for today's real estate investment world. This knowledge will be useful as you pursue subsequent chapters in this book or undertake a career in the industry.

KEY TERMS

investment objective
growth (savings) objective
income (current cash flow) objective
risk
liquidity
time horizon
investor expertise
investor management burden
investor size

capital constraint
investor heterogeneity
underlying asset
investment product (vehicle)
passive investors
commingled real estate funds (CREFs)
private REITs (real estate investment trusts)

private markets
commercial mortgage-backed securities (CMBS)
stagflation
Employee Retirement Income Security Act (ERISA)
Financial Institutions Recovery, Reform, and Enforcement Act (FIRREA)

STUDY QUESTIONS

7.1. Describe the two major, generally mutually exclusive, objectives of investors.

7.2. Characterize the following investors as to whether their major investment objectives are likely to be savings or income. What would be a likely typical investment horizon for each investor?

    a. A graduate student in her mid-20s

    b. A fading rock star in his mid-20s who has saved several million dollars over the past five years

    c. A dual-income professional couple in their mid-30s, with two children

    d. A 40-year-old just-retired major league baseball player who never went to college but has saved up several million dollars and owes large annual alimony payments

    e. A retired couple in their late 60s.

7.3. What are the major constraints and concerns faced by most investors?

7.4. What are the major differences between real estate and traditional industrial corporations regarding the structure and nature of the investment products and vehicles based on these underlying assets, and the asset markets in which these entities trade?

7.5. In the traditional commercial real estate investment structure, what is the significance of the fact that it is possible for investors to own the underlying physical assets directly, and that these assets are not too large? Suppose there was a well-functioning, highly active market for blast furnaces or automobile stamping plants. How would this help, say, Inland Steel, or Ford Motor Company, to know whether it makes sense to build a new blast furnace or stamping plant?

7.6. Consider the left (equity or ownership) side of the "Real Estate Example of the Investment System" in Exhibit 7-2. Explain what investors are gaining and what they are losing in terms of investment attributes as they move from owning the underlying asset, to owning limited partnership units, to owning shares in a publicly traded REIT that owns the underlying asset(i.e., what are the tradeoffs)?

7.7. The questions below relate to the following statement: "Investment returns of (public) REITs appear to exhibit traits of both publicly traded common stock and private real estate market performance, with public stock market influences dominating in the short run and real estate market dynamics in the longer term. REIT returns display greater volatility than private real estate returns, though much of this added volatility is transitory or short-lived." [Hint: See the discussion about REITs in relation to Exhibit 7-2.]

    a. What explanations have been proposed to address the difference in the investment performance of REITs versus direct property in the short run?

    b. What are the linkages between securitization, liquidity, and asset value volatility? Provide two potential explanations for the higher short-run volatility of REIT returns, compared to direct property.

    c. Why might the public REIT market be a leading indicator of the private real estate asset market?

7.8. What are the four major traditional investment asset classes? Based on typical examples of each class, rank-order the classes by

    a. expected total return

    b. current income yield

    c. capital value growth

    d. risk

    e. inflation protection ability

    (When considering risk, assume that the investor is fully exposed to the asset price volatility in the periodic returns to the asset class.)

7.9. Which asset class gave the best historical (ex-post) investment performance (based on average total return) during the 1970s through to mid-1980s period? Which class gave the best performance over the 1986–2003 period?

7.10. Suppose an investor placed $5 million into each of two investment funds at the beginning of 1970. All investment earnings were reinvested. One fund invested in commercial real estate and produced a performance like that portrayed for real estate in Exhibit 7-8. The other fund invested in common stocks and produced a performance like that indicated for the stock market in Exhibit 7-8.

    a. How much did the investor have in each of the two funds at the end of 1989?

    b. What was the real purchasing power in each of the two funds, measured in dollars of 1969 purchasing power?

    c. Now repeat your answers to (a) and (b) only assuming the initial $5 million investment was made at the beginning of 1989 until 2010 and use 1989 dollars as the measure of constant purchasing power.

    d. Why was 1986 a significant year for the income-property sector?

7.11. What is the apparent historical relationship between average investment performance (total return) and the riskiness of the investment as measured by volatility?

7.12. The crash in prices of institutional grade commercial property in the United States during 1989–1992 was the worst since the Great Depression.

    a. Make an argument that this crash was largely due to unique historical events during the preceding decade.

    b. Now make a counterargument suggesting that such swings are likely to recur.

7.13. What are the major institutional sources of capital for commercial real estate in the United States today? How has the relative importance of different sources been changing in recent years?

7.14. Explain how the real estate depression and capital crunch of the early 1990s was the spark for the growth in public market involvement in, and the securitization of, commercial real estate, on both the debt and equity sides. What role did the federal government play in stimulating the growth of public real estate markets, again on both the debt and equity sides?

7.15. Explain why the increased securitization of commercial real estate, on both the debt and equity sides, could make real estate markets less susceptible to boom and bust cycles. What happened in 1998 that helps support this line of reasoning?

7.16. Given what you now know about investor objectives and constraints, the historical performance of the major investment asset classes, as well as the more mainstream acceptance of real estate investment in recent years, think about the impact of the aging baby boom generation on investor demand for real estate going forward. Do you think the movement of boomers into retirement age implies that the real estate asset class will continue to attract significant capital relative to other asset classes? Support your answer with sound economic reasoning, based on what you learned in the chapter.

PRESENT VALUE MATHEMATICS FOR REAL ESTATE

CHAPTER OUTLINE

On the Accompanying CD:
Business Calculator Keystrokes and Excel® Examples

LEARNING OBJECTIVES

After reading this chapter, you should understand:

⊃ The basic formulas and procedures for converting typical real estate future cash flow and risk patterns to present value, given the appropriate discount rates.

⊃ The origin or derivation of these formulas, in such a way that you can apply them with some flexibility to new situations.

⊃ How to invert the present value formulas to compute the implied return or the time until a future value is received.

⊃ How a typical business or financial calculator works to make these calculations quick and easy.

I f someone offered you a choice between $10,000 today or $10,000 one year from now, which would you choose? It is a fundamental fact of financial economics that dollars at one time are not equivalent to dollars at another time. This is not just because of inflation. Due to the real productivity of capital, and due to risk, future dollars are worth less than present dollars, even if there were no inflation. In real estate investment analysis, we constantly need to compare dollars at different points in time. Present value mathematics consists of the formulas, procedures, and techniques for making such comparisons and evaluations. This chapter will present some of the most basic and commonly used of these tools.

Please keep in mind that the focus of this chapter is on the mechanics—the formal mathematical formulas. In order to know how to use these formulas properly in real estate investment analysis, you need to know the right numbers to plug into the formulas. This requires combining economics with mathematics, which we will explore in later chapters.

For the purposes of this chapter, present value formulas can be grouped into two classes: single sums and multiperiod cash flows. The single-sum formulas are the most basic building blocks, as the multiperiod formulas are all built up as sums of the single-sum formulas. So we will begin this chapter with single-sum formulas, and then advance to multiperiod formulas in the second half.[1]

8.1 Single-Sum Formulas

Single-sum formulas refer to situations in which only two points in time are considered. Typically, one of these two points is the present. A single cash flow or monetary value is posited at one of the two points in time, and the task is to determine the value it equates to at the other point in time.

8.1.1 Single-Period Discounting and Growing

The simplest sort of present value problem is single-period discounting or growing. Let's go back to the choice between $10,000 today versus one year from today. We no doubt agree that we would all choose the $10,000 today. But suppose the choice is $10,000 today versus $11,000 in one year, or $12,000, and so on. Clearly, there is some value greater than $10,000 that we would prefer to take in one year. How high that "indifference point" is depends on several things. For example, we would want to consider how much interest we could earn on a one-year deposit in a bank. If we could earn 5 percent simple interest on a one-year certificate of deposit (CD), then $10,500 in one year would be equivalent to $10,000 today, because $10,000 \times 1.05 = 10,500$. However, we might require a promise of more than $10,500 in a year in exchange for our $10,000 today if we view the future promise as being more risky than a bank CD. In effect, we might want more than a 5 percent expected return to get us to forgo the present cash. Suppose we wanted a 10 percent expected return "risk premium" on top of the 5 percent we could earn at the bank, for a total expected return of 15 percent in order to entice us to forgo our $10,000 today in exchange for a cash sum promised next year. Then $11,500 is our indifference point, because

$$\$10,000 + (15\% \times \$10,000) = \$11,500$$

or equivalently

$$\$10,000 \times (1 + 0.15) = \$11,500$$

Now suppose that we know our required expected return percentage (say, 15 percent, as in the previous example), and we know the amount that is being promised one year from

---

[1]If you are already familiar with these formulas and procedures, you can safely skip this chapter. The only thing we do here that is a little different from the typical coverage is that we present the underlying geometric series formula from which the regular multiperiod (annuity and perpetuity) present value formulas are derived. This will give the reader some additional depth and flexibility and enable us to show how to develop formulas for the present values of buildings with long-term leases, a common problem in commercial real estate.

now. So, the question is, how much are we willing to forgo today in exchange for the promised sum in one year? We can find this present value by simply inverting the previous formula and solving for the present value rather than for the future value. For example, if $11,500 is being offered in one year, then we could determine that we are willing to pay $10,000 today by dividing the expected future amount by one plus the expected return, as follows:

$$\$10,000 = \frac{\$11,500}{1 + 0.15}$$

Assuming that 15 percent is our required expected return (opportunity cost of capital), any offer of more than $11,500 next year would be preferred over holding on to our $10,000 today, while any offer of less than $11,500 would be rejected in favor of keeping our $10,000 today.

In the previous example, the $10,000 amount is the *present certainty equivalent*, often more simply referred to as the **present value**, of the *future expected sum* (or **future value**) of $11,500 in one year, based on a simple annual expected return of 15 percent. In general, if we let *PV* represent the present value, *FV* represent the future value, and *r* represent the simple expected return, then the formula for discounting future values to present value is:

$$PV = \frac{FV}{1 + r} \tag{1a}$$

and the corresponding formula for growing a present value to its future equivalent is:[2]

$$FV = (1 + r)PV \tag{1b}$$

Using formula (1a), you could answer the question of how much cash in the present would equate to $10,000 promised money in one year, under the 15 percent required return assumption of the previous numerical example. The answer would be $PV = \$8,695.65 = 10,000/1.15$. When solving for present value given the future value, the problem is one of **discounting** rather than **growing**, and the required expected return percentage in the denominator acts as the **discount rate**. Discounting is merely the inverse of growing.

8.1.2 Single-Sums over Multiple Periods of Time

The problem in the previous section involved only a single period of time, with the return or discount rate expressed as a simple rate per the amount of time in that period. For example, if everything in the earlier numerical example were the same except that the waiting period between the present cash and the future payment were two years instead of one year, then the formulas would still apply only we would have to interpret the 15 percent return as a simple biennial rather than annual return, that is, a return over two years instead of one year.

Now suppose there is more than one period of time between the time of the *PV* amount and the time of the *FV* amount, yet we want to express the return per unit of time in each period. For example, suppose the future payment is promised in two years and we want to obtain 15 percent simple annual return *each* year. If you put, say, $100 in a one-year CD at 15 percent simple annual interest, you would have $115 = (1.15 \times \$100)$ after one year. If you took that $115 and put it in another 15 percent CD again the second year, your $115 would

---

[2]This is the first of many formulas you will encounter in this chapter. Most people don't like memorizing formulas, so business calculators are sold that effectively "translate" these formulas into keystrokes that are entered in a pretty intuitive manner. We have included the keystrokes for business calculators for all of the problems presented in this chapter, in the PowerPoint© Lecture Notes file for this chapter available on the CD accompanying this book. The CD also has an Excel© file for this chapter with the formulas for all of the odd-numbered study questions at the end of this chapter, which cover all of the types of problems presented in the chapter.

grow to $132.25 = (1.15 \times \$115)$ after the second year. In other words, $100 growing at 15 percent simple annual interest compounded annually for two years is

$$(1.15)(1.15)100 = (1.15)^2 100 = 132.25$$

Note that this is more than the $130 you would have if you simply took the original $15 interest and multiplied by two. This is because you earn interest on interest (or return on return) whenever the interest or return is compounded (that is, computed and credited to the principal in the account). This process is known as **compounding** or compound growth.

It is easy to see by extension of this reasoning that if we were dealing with three years instead of two, we would have

$$(1.15)(1.15)(1.15)100 = (1.15)^3 100 = 152.09$$

So, by inductive reasoning, we can see that the general formula for equating present and future value across multiple periods with compounding once per period is given by

$$PV = \frac{FV}{(1+r)^N} \tag{2a}$$

for discounting a future sum to present value and:

$$FV = (1+r)^N PV \tag{2b}$$

for compounding a present sum forward to its future equivalent, where r is the simple interest or discount rate (or expected return) *per period*, and N is the number of periods between the present and the future time when the future sum is to be received.

The previous formulas are the building blocks for classical present value and mortgage mathematics. In modern practice, these formulas are normally applied using a calculator or spreadsheet. For example, the right-hand side of (2a) would be keyed in a spreadsheet as $FV/(1+r)^N$, where FV, PV, r, and N represent the cell addresses of the relevant future sum, present value, simple interest rate per period, and number of periods, respectively.

In case you need to solve for the compound growth rate or the length of time until the future value will be received, the previous formulas can be algebraically inverted to solve for r or N:

$$r = \left(\frac{FV}{PV}\right)^{1/N} - 1 \tag{2c}$$

$$N = \frac{\ln(FV) - \ln(PV)}{\ln(1+r)} \tag{2d}$$

where ln(.) refers to the natural log.

8.1.3 Simple versus Compound Interest

From the discussion in the previous section, you can see that there is more than one way to define how the **interest rate** (or equivalently, the rate of return, or the discount rate) is measured per period when there is more than one period between the PV cash flow and the FV cash flow. For example, go back to the example in the previous section in which we started out with $100 in the present and grew this to $132.25 after two years. We saw how this growth could be expressed as a per annum (or annual) rate of 15 percent, using annual compounding, because $(1 + 0.15) \times (1 + 0.15) = 1.3225$. But it would also be possible to take the total return increment over the two years, the 32.25 percent, and simply divide this by two and express the return as 16.125 percent per annum. This latter definition is called simple interest, because it does not include the effect of compounding.

The important point to remember is that how we define the interest or return per period does not affect the actual dollars that we have at the two points in time. The definition is merely a matter of convention. Whether we call it 15 percent per year compounded annually, or

16.125 percent per year simple interest, it is still $132.25 starting out from $100 two years earlier. You do have to be careful to understand the definition being used in a given context, and you must be consistent (e.g., don't compound simple interest in formulas to compute future sums).

8.1.4 Effective versus Nominal Rates

In the example in the previous section the compound interest rate was computed assuming the interest was compounded once per year (annual compounding). But, in fact, interest may be compounded at any **frequency**. Often, interest is compounded more frequently than once per year. For example, suppose 7.5 percent semiannual interest were compounded over a year (i.e., twice). After one year, you would have $(1.075)(1.075) = 1.155625$ times whatever amount you started with. As you can see, 7.5 percent compounded semiannually would be equivalent to a little over 15.56 percent simple annual interest or interest compounded annually. Nevertheless, in terms of the conventions of measurement and quoting of interest rates, the 7.5 percent compounded semiannually would usually be referred to as 15 percent per annum interest, compounded semiannually. The term **effective annual rate** (or **EAR**) would be used to refer to the 15.5625 percent actual yield.

In real estate applications, cash flows often occur at monthly intervals. For example, rents and mortgage payments are usually scheduled at monthly intervals. As a result, monthly interest rates are often actually applied in calculations, but rates are quoted in what is called nominal per annum terms. Under the convention of quoting rates in nominal per annum terms, the simple per-period rate (which is the rate that is actually applied in calculations) is multiplied by the number of periods in a year for the purpose of quoting the rate in per annum terms. For example, a simple interest rate of 1 percent per month would typically be referred to as a 12 percent per annum rate (i.e., the nominal per annum rate), even though the effective rate or EAR is $(1.01)^{12} - 1 = 12.6825\%$. The EAR is defined as the actual annual yield corresponding to the nominal rate defined previously, given the simple per-period rate compounded at the end of each period. The relationship between effective and nominal rates is shown in the following formulas:

$$EAR = (1 + i/m)^m - 1 \tag{3a}$$

$$i = m[(1 + EAR)^{1/m} - 1] \tag{3b}$$

where i is the nominal annual rate, m is the number of compounding periods per year, and $i/m = r$ is the actual simple interest rate being applied per compounding period. In the previous example, we had $i = 12.00\%$, $EAR = 12.6825\%$, $r = 1.00\%$, and $m = 12$. The nominal annual rate i is sometimes referred to as the **equivalent nominal annual rate** (**ENAR**).

As a result of this naming convention, when applying the present value and future value formula (2) described previously, one usually works in nominal terms by expanding the simple per-period interest rate compounded once per-period (r) and the number of basic periods of time (N) as follows, consistent with the earlier definitions:

$$r = i/m$$

$$N = m \times T$$

where i is the nominal annual rate of interest (e.g., 12 percent in the previous example), m is the number of compounding periods per year (e.g., 12 in the example of monthly compounding), and T is the length of time between when the PV and FV cash flows occur *measured in years*. Recast in nominal per-annum terms (allowing for a compounding frequency different from yearly), the present value formulas for single sums become as follows:

$$PV = \frac{FV}{\left(1 + \frac{i}{m}\right)^{mT}} \tag{4a}$$

$$FV = PV\left(1 + \frac{i}{m}\right)^{mT} \tag{4b}$$

$$i = m\left[\left(\frac{FV}{PV}\right)^{1/(mT)} - 1\right] \tag{4c}$$

$$T = \frac{\ln(FV) - \ln(PV)}{m\ln(1 + i/m)} \tag{4d}$$

Most calculators designed especially for business applications allow the user to set the value m so the calculator knows the number of compounding periods per year, and the user can then enter the interest rate in its nominal annual form (that is, you enter i and T rather than r and N; e.g., in the previous example you would enter 12 for the interest rate rather than 1 or .01, and enter the number of years between the PV and FV cash flows, rather than the number of months). The calculator then automatically divides i by m to determine the rate per period to apply in the formulas. On the other hand, microcomputer spreadsheet financial formulas typically require as direct inputs the rate per period (r) and the number of periods (N). In order to work in nominal annual terms, the user must therefore have the spreadsheet calculate r and N from i, m, and T in other cells of the worksheet, and have these other cells serve as the inputs to the present value formulas.

8.1.5 Bond Equivalent and Mortgage Equivalent Rates

As noted, rent is usually collected monthly and mortgage payments are usually made monthly, so nominal rate (i, or the ENAR, using the earlier labels) based on the previous formulas with $m = 12$ is the most common way interest rates or yields are quoted in real estate. Nominal rates defined this way are sometimes referred to as **mortgage equivalent rates**.

Meanwhile, over on Wall Street, traditional corporate bonds and long-term government bonds are designed to pay interest semiannually, that is, twice per year.[3] In fact, classical bonds had coupons corresponding to each of the promised semiannual interest payments, which the bondholder would clip off and turn in at a bank to receive the payment in cash. Because of this, in the bond market, rates are typically quoted with $m = 2$ in formula (3). Nominal rates based on $m = 2$ are thus referred to as **bond equivalent** or **coupon equivalent rates.**

Thus, real estate rates and bond rates are quoted in different ways. This was fine as long as Wall Street and Main Street did not interact very directly. But nowadays many mortgages are combined in pools and sold in the bond market, and bond market yields largely determine mortgage market yields. People dealing with mortgages need to be able to convert readily between mortgage equivalent and bond equivalent yields. This is done by *equating the effective annual rate (EAR)*. For example, we noted that a bond equivalent rate of 15 percent corresponds to an EAR of 15.5625 percent, found by plugging $i = 0.15$ and $m = 2$ into formula (3a). Now plug this 15.5625 percent EAR into formula (3b) with $m = 12$ to find that the mortgage equivalent rate of 14.551655 percent corresponds to the bond equivalent rate of 15 percent. Mortgage equivalent rates are lower than their corresponding bond equivalent rates because the increased frequency of compounding results in faster growth. If the mortgage equivalent rate were 15 percent, this would correspond to a bond equivalent rate of 15.4766 percent and an EAR of 16.07545 percent. [Plug $i = 0.15$ and $m = 12$ into formula (3a) to obtain the EAR, which you then plug into formula (3b) with $m = 2$.] As always, this type of operation is easily done using financial calculators by changing the value in the "periods per year" register, without the need to memorize the formulas. You simply substitute the appropriate value for m in the "periods per year" register. (See Questions 8.11 through 8.20 at the end of this chapter.)

---

[3]The terms *semiannual* and *biannual* are equivalent, both referring to twice per year. The term *biennial* is different, referring to once every two years.

*8.1.6 Continuously Compounded Interest Rates

The extreme limit of frequent compounding of interest is **continuous compounding**. Many bank accounts, CDs, and other financial instruments employ continuous compounding, and many interest rates are quoted in continuously compounded terms. Continuous compounding is also mathematically convenient for many types of analyses, especially those involving advanced mathematics, and so is often used in sophisticated studies.[4] In continuous compounding, the interest is literally compounded every instant.

Computing continuously compounded interest rates and continuously compounded growth or discounting is easy using the natural logarithm and the base of natural logs (the latter is known by the mathematical symbol e, which stands for a value approximately equal to 2.7183, and is available as a special key on most business calculators and in all spreadsheet software). The continuously compounded equivalents corresponding to the various forms of formulas (2) or (4) are shown as formula (5), where T is the amount of time in years (including fractional parts of a year) between the PV and FV cash flows, and k is the *per-annum* continuously compounded rate (of growth or discount, i.e., the continuously compounded interest rate).

$$PV = FV/e^{Tk} \tag{5a}$$

$$FV = PVe^{Tk} \tag{5b}$$

$$k = \frac{\ln(FV) - \ln(PV)}{T} \tag{5c}$$

$$T = \frac{\ln(FV) - \ln(PV)}{k} \tag{5d}$$

8.2 Multiperiod Problems

The formulas described in section 8.1 are the basic building blocks. They deal with only one future cash flow. Of course, real estate is a long-lived asset that typically produces cash flows for many periods, or indeed infinitely into the future. The present value of any stream of discrete cash flows can be computed using the previous formulas by simply computing the present value of each future sum and then adding all these present values together. For example, suppose $10,000 will be received in two years and another $12,000 will be received in three years. Suppose the interest rate applicable to the payment two years from now is 10 percent, and the rate applicable to the payment in three years is 11 percent (all compounded annually). Then, the present value of the future cash flow stream consisting of these two payments is $17,038.76, computed using formula (2) as follows:

$$PV = \frac{\$10,000}{(1+0.10)^2} + \frac{\$12,000}{(1+0.11)^3} = \$8,264.46 + \$8,774.30 = \$17,038.76$$

Of course, such a procedure gets tedious when there are many future cash flows. This is one reason it is often useful in real estate investment analysis to be able to express the present value of a multiperiod future cash flow stream using a simplified formula. Another reason is that such simplified formulas may enable interesting relationships to become apparent. For example, they can reveal the basic nature of the relationship among the current yield or income return, the expected average future **growth rate** of the cash flows, and the discount rate or required expected total return on a long-lived commercial property with a regular pattern of cash flow generation.

---

[4]Continuous compounding enables one to convert complex multiplicative expressions into simple additive expressions using natural logs. Additive expressions are much easier to work with mathematically. For example, if r_t is the simple rate of return in period t, then at the end of two periods, $FV = (1 + r_1)(1 + r_2)PV$, but if r_t is the continuously compounded rate of return in period t, then $\log(FV) = \log(PV) + r_1 + r_2$, where $\log(.)$ is the natural log. The ending log value is simply the beginning log value plus the sum of all the continuously compounded periodic returns.

Relatively simple formulas for present value relationships can usually be found if the future cash flow stream has a regular pattern. While the cash flow streams of real buildings will not usually be so regular, they can often be well approximated (or "modeled") by regular patterns that enable simple present value formulas to be computed. These simple multiperiod formulas are the subject of this section of this chapter.

*8.2.1 Geometric Series Formula

In the real world, cash flow streams often all occur at equal intervals of time, and all change over time at a constant rate (even if that rate is zero). Such a regular stream of cash flow is known as an **annuity** if the stream has a finite life (finite number of cash flows), or a **perpetuity** if the stream is infinite. Many important real estate cash flows are of this type (such as mortgages and leases). Other real estate cash flows can be reasonably approximated by annuities or perpetuities (e.g., the net cash flow from an apartment building may be modeled as a constant-growth perpetuity). So, these are very important.

In order to explain how to value annuities and perpetuities, we think it is best to begin with first principles: a famous mathematical formula known as the **geometric series formula**. This is not just for your cultural benefit. If you understand the geometric series formula, you will have a greater depth of knowledge that will give you more flexibility to solve a wider range of real estate problems in the real world. For example, you will be able to develop a simple analytical formula for the value of a building that rents out its space in long-term leases, a typical and fundamental situation in commercial real estate. This will enable you to analyze such issues as the optimal lease term, or the trade-off between lease term and rent levels or rent growth rate. So bear with us a moment as we delve into some classical mathematics. At first this may seem complicated and abstract, but we will soon get to a very simple formula that you will be able to apply in a variety of practical real estate situations.

Suppose we have a sum consisting of N terms, each of which is exactly d times the value of the preceding term, and whose first term has the value a. Another term for d is the **common ratio**. Label the value of this sum S.

$$S = a + ad + ad^2 + \cdots + ad^{N-1}$$

Now multiply this sum by the common ratio, d:

$$Sd = ad + ad^2 + ad^3 + \cdots + ad^N$$

Now subtract Sd from S:

$$S = a + ad + ad^2 + \cdots + ad^{N-1}$$
$$-Sd = \quad - ad - ad^2 - \cdots - ad^{N-1} - ad^N$$

The intermediate terms all cancel out in the subtraction, leaving:

$$S - Sd = a - ad^N$$
$$= (1-d)S = a(1-d^N)$$

Thus,

$$S = a(1-d^N)/(1-d) \tag{6a}$$

Formula (6a) is the geometric series formula. It says that the sum of the series equals the first term times the quantity one minus the common ratio raised to the power of the number of terms, all divided by the quantity one minus the common ratio.

Now note that if $d < 1$, then $d^\infty = 0$, so if the series is infinite (as in a perpetuity), then the value of the sum simplifies to

$$S = a/(1-d) \tag{6b}$$

These simple formulas can be used to address a wide range of real estate problems. Some of the most important examples are discussed in the following sections.

8.2.2 Present Value of a Level Annuity in Arrears

Perhaps the most widely used application of the geometric series formula is to compute the present value of a **level annuity** in arrears, which is a series of equal payments made at the *end* of every period starting one period from the present. This type of cash flow stream defines the classical mortgage, with monthly payments. For example, a 30-year mortgage is a level annuity in arrears with $N = 360$.

To see how this problem is an example of the geometric formula, let's take a specific example. Suppose there are 240 payments left on a mortgage that has monthly payments of $1,000 each. How much is the mortgage worth today if the opportunity cost of capital (discount rate) is 12 percent per year (actually, 1 percent per month) and the next payment on the mortgage is due one month from now?

We can set up this present value as the sum of a sequence of present values of single-sums, using formula (2):

$$PV = \frac{\$1000}{1.01} + \frac{\$1000}{1.01^2} + \frac{\$1000}{1.01^3} + \cdots + \frac{\$1000}{1.01^{240}}$$

Here, the first term is $a = 1,000/1.01$. The number of terms is $N = 240$. And the common ratio is $d = 1/1.01$, because each term is that factor times the previous. Now if we substitute these values of a, d, and N into the geometric formula (6a) we arrive at

$$PV = \frac{a(1-d)^N}{1-d} = \frac{(\$1000/1.01)[1-(1/1.01)^{240}]}{1-(1/1.01)}$$

$$= \frac{\$1000[1-(1/1.01)^{240}]}{0.01} = \$90,819$$

This famous case of the geometric formula is often written as

$$PV = PMT\frac{1-1/(1+r)^N}{r} \tag{7a}$$

or alternatively as

$$PV = PMT\left(\frac{1}{r} - \frac{1}{r}\frac{1}{(1+r)^N}\right)$$

where *PMT* is the level cash flow payment amount, and r is the effective simple interest rate *per payment period*.

The ratio of the present value of the annuity to the amount of each payment, *PV/PMT*, is often referred to as the "annuity factor," or the "present value interest factor for an annuity" (PVIFA).[5] As we can see from formula (7a), the annuity factor is a function only of the interest rate r and the number of payment periods N: $[1 - 1/(1+r)^N]/r$. You multiply the periodic payment amount by this factor to arrive at the present value of the cash flow stream.

Keep in mind that the underlying formula that is equivalently expressed in (7a) is

$$PV = \frac{PMT}{1+r} + \frac{PMT}{(1+r)^2} + \frac{PMT}{(1+r)^3} + \cdots + \frac{PMT}{(1+r)^N} \tag{7}$$

From this expansion, we can see that the annuity formula is an application of the geometric series formula, with $a = PMT/(1+r)$ and $d = 1/(1+r)$. We also see how formula (7) is built up as a series of applications of formula (2). It should be clear that an underlying assumption is that the simple effective interest rate per payment period (r) is being compounded at the end of every payment period. Thus, for example, if the payment period is monthly

---

[5]For constant-payment mortgages, this is also known as the mortgage constant, the ratio of the mortgage payment to the initial principal loan amount.

and $r = 1\%$, then the nominal interest rate would typically be quoted as 12 percent, and the effective annual rate would actually be 12.6825 percent, based on formula (3a).

Expressed in terms of the nominal annual rate, the annuity formula becomes

$$PV = PMT \frac{1 - \left(\frac{1}{1 + \frac{i}{m}}\right)^{(Tm)}}{\frac{i}{m}} \tag{7b}$$

where the variables are all defined as before.

8.2.3 Present Value of a Level Annuity in Advance

Sometimes the cash flows arrive at the *beginning* of each period, rather than at the end. This is particularly common for rent payments in long-term leases. For example, suppose a 20-year ground lease has a fixed net rent of $1,000 per month paid at the beginning of the month. What is the value of this lease when it is signed if the opportunity cost of capital is 12 percent per year (1 percent per month)? We have

$$PV = \$1000 + \frac{\$1000}{1.01} + \frac{\$1000}{1.01^2} + \cdots + \frac{\$1000}{1.01^{239}}$$

This is the same as the previous problem only multiplied by 1.01. Here, the first term is $a = 1,000$, but otherwise this problem is identical to the previous one (N is still 240, the number of terms on the right-hand side, or the total number of payments, and the common ratio, d, is still 1/1.01). So, the lease is worth

$$PV = \frac{a(1 - d^N)}{1 - d} = \frac{(\$1000)[1 - (1/1.01)^{240}]}{1 - (1/1.01)}$$

$$= \left(\frac{1.01}{0.01}\right)\$1000[1 - (1/1.01)^{240}] = \$91,728$$

To convert formula (7a) to give present value with payments in advance, you simply multiply the right-hand side of (7a) by the factor $(1 + r)$, or equivalently by $[1 + (i/m)]$, to remove one period's discounting from the present value calculation. Thus, the annuity present value formula for payments in advance is given by formula (8a) (keeping in mind that $r = i/m$ and $N = mT$ in the usual convention).

$$PV = PMT(1 + r) \frac{1 - 1/(1 + r)^N}{r} \tag{8a}$$

The annuity formula is much more commonly used assuming payments in arrears than in advance. Business calculators typically have a button that allows one to set the calculator for payments either in arrears or in advance (the default setting is normally payments in arrears). Spreadsheet software formulas also typically provide an optional indicator to convert present value formulas to payments in advance, with the default being for payments in arrears.

8.2.4 Present Value of a Constant-Growth Annuity in Arrears

The annuities we have just considered were level payment annuities; that is, all their periodic cash flows were equal. Now let's relax that assumption by allowing all the periodic cash flows to grow (or shrink) at the same rate. That is, each cash flow is the same multiple of the previous cash flow. The present value of such a stream of cash flow will clearly also be an application of the geometric series formula. For example, consider a 10-year lease providing for annual payments at the ends of the years. The initial rent is $20/SF but that rent will grow at a rate of 2 percent per year each year thereafter. What is the present value of the lease, per SF, assuming an opportunity cost of capital of 10 percent per year?

To solve this problem, first set up the underlying present value problem as a series of formula (2) type single-sums:

$$PV = \frac{\$20}{1.10} + \frac{(1.02)\$20}{1.10^2} + \frac{(1.02)^2\$20}{1.10^3} + \cdots + \frac{(1.02)^9\$20}{1.10^{10}}$$

This allows us to see clearly that the first term is $a = 20/1.10$, the number of terms on the right-hand side (number of periodic payments) is $N = 10$, and the common ratio is $d = (1.02/1.10)$. Plug these values into formula (6a) to get

$$PV = \frac{a(1 - d^N)}{1 - d} = \frac{(\$20/1.10)[1 - (1.02/1.10)^{10}]}{1 - (1.02/1.10)}$$

$$= \$20\frac{1 - (1.02/1.10)^{10}}{0.10 - 0.02} = \$132.51$$

So, the lease is worth \$132.51/SF.

This case of the geometric formula is referred to as the **constant-growth annuity**, and in general it is often written as

$$PV = CF_1\left(\frac{1 - [(1 + g)/(1 + r)]^N}{r - g}\right) \tag{9}$$

where CF_1 is the value of the *initial* cash flow (periodic payment), g is the growth rate *per period* in the cash flows, and r is as always the discount rate per payment period.[6] Note that in the special case where $g = 0$, the constant-growth annuity formula collapses to the level payment annuity formula, as it should.

8.2.5 Present Value of a Constant-Growth Perpetuity

Now consider an infinite sequence of cash flows, a perpetuity in which each periodic payment is a constant ratio times the previous payment. For example, suppose an apartment building has 100 identical units that rent at \$1,000 per month with building operating expenses paid by the landlord equal to \$500 per month. On average, there is a 5 percent vacancy. You expect both rents and operating expenses to grow at a rate of 3 percent per year (actually, 0.25 percent per month). The opportunity cost of capital is 12 percent per year (actually, 1 percent per month). How much is the property worth?

Once again, to solve this problem we first set it up as a fundamental series of single-sums based on formula (2). The initial monthly net cash flow is $500 \times 100 \times 0.95 = \$47,500$. Thus, the underlying present value problem is

$$PV = \frac{\$47,500}{1.01} + \frac{(1.0025)\$47,500}{1.01^2} + \frac{(1.0025)^2\$47,500}{1.01^3} + \cdots$$

This allows us to see clearly that the first term is $a = 47,500/1.01$ and the common ratio is $d = 1.0025/1.01$. As this is a perpetuity, we apply the simpler version of the geometric formula (6b) instead of (6a), so we have

$$PV = \frac{a}{1 - d} = \frac{\$47,500/1.01}{1 - (1.0025/1.01)} = \frac{\$47,500}{0.01 - 0.0025} = \$6,333,333$$

The building is worth \$6,333,333.

---

[6]Standard business calculators typically do not have a g key to compute growing annuities. However, you can "trick" your calculator to do this type of problem using the standard keys, by simply defining the interest rate as $1/d - 1$ [that is, $(1 + r)/(1 + g) - 1$]. You then enter the initial cash flow (undiscounted) as *PMT*, set the calculator to assume payments in advance (beginning-of-period payments, as if the problem were not in arrears, even though it is), compute the *PV*, and then divide the answer by $1 + r$ to get it back in arrears. For example, in the previous problem, enter the interest rate as 7.84314% ($= 1.10/1.02 - 1$), enter 20 into *PMT*, 10 into *N*, 0 into *FV*, and compute $PV = 145.76$, which when divided by 1.10 will give 132.51.

This case of the geometric formula is written in general notation as

$$PV = \frac{CF_1}{r-g} \tag{10}$$

with the variables defined as before, and it is referred to as the **constant-growth perpetuity** formula.

8.2.6 Some Basic Economic Implications of the Perpetuity Formula

The constant-growth perpetuity formula is often taught in introductory finance as a famous and simple way to compute the fundamental value of a share in a company's common stock. The formula is referred to as the *Gordon Growth Model*, in which CF_1 is the current annual dividend payment per share, g is the expected long-term average annual growth rate in the company's dividends (presumably the growth rate in the company's earnings per share), and r is the stock market's required expected annual total return from investing in the stock (including consideration of how risky the stock is). For example, if a company currently pays $1 per share in quarterly dividends ($4/year), has a track record of providing consistent long-term average growth in dividends of 5 percent per year, and the market requires an average annual total return (including both dividends and capital gain) of 12 percent, then the stock should be worth $4/(0.12 − 0.05) = $4/0.07 = $57.14 per share. Presumably (according to the model), if the stock is currently selling for less than that, then it is a good buy.

In general, the constant-growth perpetuity model represents a basic way to understand the value of any infinitely lived income-producing asset, as a relationship among the current level of net cash flow produced by the asset, the likely long-term average rate of growth in that cash flow, and the expected annual total return required by investors in the asset. As such, this model is broadly applicable to commercial property and provides a basic under-standing of the cap rate, defined as the current annual income divided by the value of the property. For example, the constant-growth perpetuity model reveals that the apartment building described earlier would have a cap rate of 9 percent (12% − 3%) (this is $r − g$ on a per-annum basis). In other words, the apartment would sell for a price approximately 11 times its annual net income (that is, 1/0.09). In fact, the building's annual net income is $570,000 ($47,500 × 12). Dividing this by the $6,333,333 estimated value implies the cap rate of 9 percent. Thus, the perpetuity model reveals that the cap rate for a building like this equals investors' expected total return minus their expected annual long-term growth rate in the building's net income.

*8.2.7 Introducing Long-Term Leases

While some types of commercial real estate, such as apartment buildings, do not make much use of long-term leases, most types of commercial property use leases that last several years or more. For example, leases in office or warehouse buildings are often 3 to 10 years long. Within each lease, once the lease is signed, the cash flows specified in the lease have relatively low risk because the tenant is contractually obligated to make the lease payments. (From the perspective of the risk of the rental cash flows, once the lease is signed, it is much like a loan to the tenant, or a bond issued by the tenant.) On the other hand, prior to the signing of any given lease, the cash flows that the building can earn under such future leases are less certain, which makes them more risky, for it is not known exactly what rent a landlord will be able to charge. Furthermore, within each lease the growth rate in the rent will often be known for certain, while between leases the growth rate will depend on conditions in the rental market.

Thus, to model the cash flows of a building subject to long-term leases, we really need to consider two different growth rates and two different discount rates. One set of rates applies *within* leases (the **intralease rates**), and the other set of rates applies *across* leases (the **inter-lease rates**). At first glance, this would seem to complicate the present value calculation greatly. However, the geometric series formula enables us to obtain a relatively simple formula for the present value of such a building. The present value calculation is broken down into two steps. Each lease is a constant-growth annuity whose present value as of the time of lease signing can be determined using formula (6a), and the building as a whole is a constant-growth perpetuity whose value can be determined using formula (6b). In effect, the building is a "perpetuity of successive annuities." Consider the following example.

A space will lease out in 10-year leases successively in perpetuity. The leases have annual rent payments at the beginnings of the years. Each lease will be for a constant rent once that lease is signed, but new leases will be signed at rent levels reflecting annual growth in market rent. This growth is expected to be 1 percent per year, but this is an uncertain, risky growth expectation. So the expected rent in each successive lease will be 1.01^{10} times the previous lease's rent, although this is not guaranteed. Once a lease is signed, the opportunity cost of capital for computing the PV of that lease as of the time of its signing is 6 percent per year, reflecting the relatively low risk of the contractually fixed rental payments. However, between leases or prior to lease signings, the opportunity cost of capital is 11 percent per year, reflecting the greater risk associated with not knowing for certain what the future market rent will be. The initial lease is expected to be signed (and first rent received) one year from now, with an annual rent of $10/SF. What is the value of this property per SF?

In the first step of solving this problem, we compute the present value of the first lease when it is signed, as a level annuity in advance. We have $a = 10$, $N = 10$, $d = (1/1.06)$:

$$PV(Lease\ 1) = \frac{a(1-d^N)}{1-d} = \frac{\$10(1-1/1.06^{10})}{1-1/1.06}$$
$$= \$10\left(\frac{1.06}{0.06}\right)(1-1/1.06^{10}) = \$78.02/SF$$

The present value of this first lease as of today is this expected value at signing (one year from now) computed above, divided by 1.11 (because this is a risky value—we do not know for sure the lease will be signed with a rent of $10/SF). Thus, the present value of the first lease as of today is $78.02/ 1.11 = $70.29/SF. This is the value of the first term in the perpetuity of successive annuities that represents the present value of the property as a whole. Thus, this is the value of a in the perpetuity formula (6b) for calculating the building's value.

In the second step of solving this problem, we need to identify the common ratio, d, to apply in the perpetuity problem. In this case, $d = (1.01/1.11)^{10}$, because there are 10 years (the lease term) between each expected lease signing, and we expect market rents to grow at a rate of 1 percent per year in this rental market. In other words, if we let PVL_j represent the value of the jth lease at the time of its signing, then the perpetuity that represents the building value is given by the following infinite series of single-sums:

$$PV(building) = \frac{PVL_1}{1.11} + \frac{(1.01)^{10}PVL_2}{1.11^{11}} + \frac{(1.01)^{20}PVL_2}{1.11^{21}} + \cdots$$

Note that the larger interlease discount rate of 11 percent is used here because we are discounting *across leases*, that is, across time prior to the signings of the future leases we are evaluating. (This is in contrast to the computation of the values, at signings, of each lease, in which the smaller intralease discount rate is applied in the annuity formula.) Thus, the value of the property is

$$PV(building) = \frac{a}{1-d} = \frac{PVL_1/1.11}{1-(1.01/1.11)^{10}} = \frac{\$70.29}{1-(1.01/1.11)^{10}} = \$115.05/SF$$

So, the building is worth $115.05/SF.

Note that this is a substantially different value than if we employed the simple constant-growth perpetuity formula to the initial $10/SF rent level as if there were no long-term leases: $PV = CF_1/(r-g) = \$10/(0.11-0.01) = \$10/0.10 = \$100/SF$.

The use of the long-term leases, while delaying the growth in cash flow to only once every 10 years, reduces the risk of the cash flows sufficiently in this case so that the present value of the space is substantially greater than it would be if only short-term leases were employed. The ability to apply the underlying geometric series formula flexibly as in this problem enables one to analyze questions involving long-term leases, such as the trade-off between lease term, rental level, and building value.

8.2.8 Summarizing the Present Value of Geometric Cash Flow Streams

All of the previous problems have really only used a single underlying formula, the geometric series formula (6). The general procedure has been to set up the underlying present value problem as a sequence of single-sums, so that it is clear what is the first term on the right-hand side of the equation (the value a), what is the common ratio between those terms (d), and what is the number of terms (N). In complex problems, such as when more than one long-term lease is involved, this procedure should be applied in more than one step, building up the overall present value problem. The following list summarizes the application of formula (6) to the basic simple cases:

- For the level perpetuity or annuity, $d = 1/(1 + r)$ where $r =$ interest rate per period.
- For constant-growth perpetuity or annuity, $d = (1 + g)/(1 + r)$.
- For cash flows in arrears (at ends of periods), $a = CF_1/(1 + r)$.
- For cash flow in advance (at beginnings of periods), $a = CF_1$.
- For annuities, $N =$ number of periods.
- For perpetuities, $N =$ infinity and d must be <1 (so, $d^N = 0$).

8.2.9 How to Convert Annuities to Future Values

All of the previous examples were present value problems in which we were converting a future cash flow stream to present value. In some cases, it is useful to do the reverse: convert a stream of cash flows into a future value as of a terminal point in time, by growing the cash flows to the terminal point. In fact, this can be done still using the same geometric formula. For example, consider the future value of an annuity of $100/month in arrears (paid at the ends of the months) for 12 months at 12 percent per annum (compounded monthly, actually 1 percent per month). As always, the first step is to set the problem up as a sequence of single-sums based on formula (2), in this case formula (2b). Here we have

$$FV = \$100(1.01)^{11} + \$100(1.01)^{10} + \cdots + \$100$$

So the first term is $a = 100\,(1.01)^{11}$, the number of terms is $n = 12$, and the common ratio is $d = 1/1.01$. Thus,

$$FV = \frac{\$100(1.01)^{11}[1 - (1/1.01)^{12}]}{1 - (1/1.01)} = \$1{,}268.25$$

In general, the future value problem simply represents $(1+r)^N$ times the present value problem. For example, if the following gives the present value:

$$PV = \frac{CF_1}{1+r} + \frac{CF_2}{(1+r)^2} + \cdots + \frac{CF_N}{(1+r)^N}$$

then multiplying both sides of the equation by $(1 + r)^N$ will give the future value as in formula (11):

$$
\begin{aligned}
(1+r)^N PV &= (1+r)^N \frac{CF_1}{1+r} + (1+r)^N \frac{CF_2}{(1+r)^2} + \cdots + (1+r)^N \frac{CF_N}{(1+r)^N} \\
&= CF_1(1+r)^{N-1} + CF_2(1+r)^{N-2} + \cdots + CF_N = FV
\end{aligned}
\tag{11}
$$

8.2.10 Solving for the Cash Flows

If the present value can be expressed as a function of a single periodic payment amount, such as the level payment in an annuity or the initial cash flow in a growth annuity or perpetuity, then it is straightforward to invert the present value formula to solve it for the cash flow. For example, the following formula inverting (7a) tells the level payment amount (*PMT*) that is required to produce a given present value, given the number of payments and the interest rate:

$$PMT = PV \frac{r}{1 - 1/(1 + r)^N} \tag{7c}$$

For example, a borrower wants a 30-year, monthly-payment, fixed-interest mortgage for $80,000. As a lender, you want to earn a return of 1 percent per month, compounded monthly. You agree to provide the $80,000 up front (i.e., at the present time), in return for the commitment by the borrower to make 360 equal monthly payments in the amount of $ 822.89 each, starting with the first payment due in one month. The required monthly payment of $822.89 is found as

$$822.89 = 80{,}000 \frac{0.01}{1 - 1/(1.01)^{360}}$$

8.2.11 Solving for the Number of Payments

Similarly, it is possible to invert the previous formulas to find the number of payments or length of time required for a given cash flow stream to produce a given present value. For example, to find the number of specified level payments required to pay off a given amount at a given interest rate, formula (7) can be solved for *Tm*:

$$Tm = -\frac{\ln\left(1 - \frac{i}{m}\frac{PV}{PMT}\right)}{\ln\left(1 + \frac{i}{m}\right)} \tag{7d}$$

where ln(.) is the natural logarithm. In the case of the growth annuity, formula (9) is solved for *N*:

$$N = \frac{\ln\left(1 - \frac{PV}{CF_1}(r - g)\right)}{\ln\left(\frac{1+g}{1+r}\right)} \tag{9a}$$

8.2.12 Combining the Single Lump Sum and the Level Annuity Stream: Classical Mortgage Mathematics

The typical calculations associated with classical mortgage mathematics can be solved using one or the other or a combination of the single-sum formulas described in section 8.1 and the annuity formulas just described. This is because the classical mortgage is constructed as an annuity with the contractual principal as the *PV* amount.[7] To calculate the monthly payments on a loan of a given amount, you simply apply the annuity formula solved for the payment as in (7c). To calculate how much you can borrow given a specified level of monthly payments for a specified number of years, you apply the present value annuity formula (7a). To calculate the remaining outstanding loan balance (*OLB*) at any point in time (i.e., after a given number of payments), the annuity formula also applies. The *OLB* equals the present value of the remaining loan payments discounted at the loan's contractual interest rate, so you apply the annuity formula (7a) to determine the *PV* with *N* equal to the number of

---

[7]Note that the contractual principal of a loan is not necessarily exactly equal to the amount of cash the borrower will receive from the lender at the time the loan is disbursed. This is due to the possible presence of discount points of prepaid interest or loan application fees and other expenses that may be taken out of the loan disbursement. Nevertheless, the borrower's debt obligation at the time the loan is taken out equals the entire contractual principal amount.

payments not yet made. The *PV* amount so determined equals the *OLB* on the loan. In other words, after *q* payments have been made on a loan that has a monthly payment amount of *PMT* and originally was for *T* years at a rate of *i*, the *OLB* is given by

$$OLB = PMT \frac{1 - \left(\frac{1}{1+\frac{i}{m}}\right)^{(Tm - q)}}{\frac{i}{m}} \qquad (7e)$$

For example, the $80,000, 12%, 30-year mortgage we noted earlier with the monthly payments of $822.89 would have an outstanding loan balance after 10 years of payments equal to $74,734.39, based on the following calculation:

$$74,734.39 = 822.89 \frac{1 - 1/(1.01)^{240}}{0.01}$$

The classical mortgage is "fully amortizing," meaning that the regular monthly payments completely and exactly pay off the entire contractual principal over the course of the maturity of the loan. But many loans are not fully amortizing. They may amortize, for example, at a 30-year rate but have a maturity of only 10 years, which means that the outstanding loan balance is due after 10 years. An extreme version of this would be a loan that does not amortize at all, also known as an interest-only loan. Interest-only loans are common particularly among commercial mortgages.

In the case of partially amortizing or nonamortizing loans, the cash flow stream from the mortgage consists of the combination (or sum) of an annuity plus a single lump sum payment at the end. The annuity portion consists of the interest plus any partial amortization, while the single sum at the end consists of the remaining principal at the time of maturity of the loan. In the case of an interest-only loan, the annuity is purely interest (each payment equaling the per-period simple interest rate times the contractual principal), while the single-sum liquidating payment at the end equals the entire contractual principal amount.

Using our previous labels and formulas (i.e., *FV* represents the single-sum amount and *PMT* represents the regular periodic payment amount), a wide variety of mortgages can be represented by the following formula:

$$PV = \left(\frac{PMT}{(1+r)} + \frac{PMT}{(1+r)^2} + \cdots + \frac{PMT}{(1+r)^N} \right) + \frac{FV}{(1+r)^N} \qquad (12)$$

where, as always, $r = i/m$, the simple per-period interest rate, and $N = Tm$, the total number of periods in the maturity of the loan. In formula (12), the first part on the right-hand side in the parentheses is the annuity part, and the last term on the right is the single sum. For example, a 12% interest-only loan for $80,000 would have $PMT = \$800$ and $FV = \$80,000$, which would give $PV = \$80,000$ at the 12% nominal annual rate ($r = 12\%/12 = 1\%$), for any loan term (any value of N).

8.2.13 How the Present Value Keys on a Business Calculator Work

Business calculators typically have two sets of keys or functions that are useful in solving present value problems: the mortgage math keys and the discounted cash flow (DCF) keys. The former are designed specifically to deal with the type of level annuity and single-sum problems discussed in section 8.2.12 and represented by formula (12). The DCF keys are designed to enable present value and **internal rate of return (IRR)** calculation of a more general stream of future cash flows. The IRR and DCF valuation will be defined and discussed in Chapters 9 and 10, while mortgages will be discussed further in Part VI. The focus of the present chapter is only on the mathematical mechanics and the functioning of the typical business calculator.

The mortgage math keys are the quickest way to solve problems that can be set up with some combination of a stream of level regular cash flows plus at most one additional lump sum cash flow at the end of the level stream. There are typically five mortgage math keys corresponding to the five variables in formula (12): *PV*, *FV*, *PMT*, *N*, and r.[8] The mortgage math keys work by solving formula (12) for the value of the variable whose key has been pressed, given the values that currently reside; the registers of the other four variables in the formula. Note that, as per formula (12), the calculator assumes that the last one of the regular annuity cash flows whose amounts are specified in the *PMT* register occurs at the same time (*N* periods in the future) as the single lump sum amount represented in the *FV* register.

Note also that formula (12) can be rewritten to equate to zero as follows:

$$O = -PV + \left(\frac{PMT}{(1+r)} + \frac{PMT}{(1+r)^2} + \cdots + \frac{PMT}{(1+r)^N} \right) + \frac{FV}{(1+r)^N}$$

In this form, it is seen clearly that the sign of the *PV* amount will normally be opposite to that of the *PMT* and *FV* amounts. From the lender's perspective, the *PV* amount represents an up-front cash outflow, while the other amounts are the future debt service payments that provide cash inflows. Thus, it makes sense that calculators represent amounts entered into the *PMT* and *FV* registers as being of opposite sign to amounts calculated in the *PV* register, and vice versa.[9]

8.2.14 IRR and Multiperiod DCF Formula

The DCF keys on the calculator are designed to solve a more general present value problem. If the future cash flows are not well described by the equal payments of a level annuity plus at most one lump sum at the end, then the DCF keys must be used to compute present values or internal rates of return (IRR). The DCF keys allow all the future cash flow amounts to be different.

Consider an arbitrary stream of cash flows occurring at the ends of each of a consecutive sequence of uniform-length time periods (net cash flow amounts labeled CF_0, CF_1, CF_2, etc., occurring in time periods labeled 0, 1, 2, and so on, where period 0 is the present). These cash flow amounts are entered into the calculator cash flow registers, which are often labeled something like CFj or C0, C1, and so on. The DCF keys solve the equation in formula (13) for either the *NPV* value or the *IRR* value:

$$NPV = CF_0 + \frac{CF_1}{(1+IRR)} + \frac{CF_2}{(1+IRR)^2} + \cdots + \frac{CF_T}{(1+IRR)^T} \quad (13)$$

where *T* is the number of future periods encompassed in the analysis (beyond the present).[10]

---

[8]As noted, in many cases you can enter the payment frequency per year in the calculator, and then you can enter the interest in nominal annual terms, and the calculator will automatically compute $r = i/m$.

[9]An exception is when using the mortgage math keys to compute the terminal value (*FV*) of a level stream, as in formula (11). For such problems, set $PV = 0$ in the calculator and solve for *FV*. The *FV* amount represents the terminal (compound growth) value of the payments, with *FV* being opposite in sign to *PMT*, as in formula (11) set equal to zero. Note that in general there is no algebraic analytical formula to solve formula (13) for the IRR. The calculator must find the answer by a repetitive trial-and-error process through which it iterates to an answer that is acceptably close to solving the equation.

[10]Note that equation (13) is the most general formula for the present value of an arbitrary stream of discrete future cash flows assuming a constant discount rate. (If the cash flows occur at irregularly spaced points in time, one can simply define the smallest common time divisor as the period, and have $CF_t = 0$ between the cash flow receipts.) An even more general formula would allow for time-varying discount rates, as follows:

$$NPV - CF_0 + \frac{CF_1}{(1+r_1)} + \frac{CF_2}{(1+r_2)^2} + \cdots + \frac{CF_T}{(1+r_t)^T}$$

where r_t is the time-weighted average multiperiod return from time zero to time *t*. It is useful to note that even in this most general form, the present value equation is "homogeneous of degree one" in the cash flows. That is, if all the cash flow amounts on the right-hand side of the equation are multiplied by any constant *a*, then the left-hand side NPV is also multiplied by that same constant. More formally: if $NPV = f(CF)$, then $aNPV = f(aCF)$, where $f( )$ is the present value equation, *CF* here is an arbitrary vector of cash flows, and *a* is a scalar constant. This is simply a consequence of the distributive law of multiplication and addition: $a(b+c) = ab + ac$, but it allows great computational convenience in working with present values. For example, the ability to use tables of "annuity factors," and the ability of lenders to publish loan interest rates applicable to loans of varying amounts, is a consequence of this homogeneity property.

To solve for the *IRR*, the *NPV* is by definition assumed to be zero, and the amount in the CF_0 register must be of opposite sign to the bulk of the values in the other CF_j registers (j = 1,..., T).

For example, you would typically enter the up-front investment amount as a negative number representing cash outflow in register CF_0, such as the price of the property, while the subsequent cash flows would be largely positive representing the net cash dividends or rental payments received from the investment. If the discount rate were then specified (typically in the interest key of the calculator), then this discount rate would be used in place of the *IRR* rate in formula (13) and the formula would be solved to determine the net present value (*NPV*) of the project. Alternatively, if you press the *IRR* register, the calculator will compute the value of the IRR.[11] Finally, if you specify an amount of zero for the CF_0 register, then pressing the *NPV* key will compute the present value (corresponding to the *PV*, or gross present value) of the future stream of cash flows (in arrears). Note that in this case the *NPV* register does not in itself compute a *net* present value, as we have 0 in the present cash flow.

8.3 Chapter Summary

This chapter has presented the major formulas and procedures that are most useful for the calculation and analysis of the present value of the types of cash flow streams most commonly found in commercial real estate. Included in this are the important inverses of the present value formulas, that is, formulas for calculating implied returns, terminal values, and the time (or number of payments) until a certain present or future value is achieved. We have focused on the formal mechanics of the basic formulas, leaving the economic reasoning and analysis necessary for the correct application of these formulas largely to be covered in later chapters.

KEY TERMS

single-sum formulas
present value
future value
discounting
growing
discount rate
interest rate
compounding
growth rate
compounding frequency

effective annual rate (EAR)
equivalent nominal annual rate
   (ENAR)
mortgage equivalent rate
bond equivalent (coupon equivalent)
   rate
continuous compounding
annuity
perpetuity
geometric series formula

common ratio
level annuity
constant-growth annuity
constant-growth perpetuity
intralease rate
interlease rate
internal rate of return (IRR)
calculator registers (N, I, PV, PMT,
   FV, NPV, IRR, CF)

STUDY QUESTIONS

8.1. What is the present value of an offer of $15,000 one year from now if the opportunity cost of capital (discount rate) is 12% per year simple interest?

8.2. What is the present value of an offer of $14,000 one year from now if the opportunity cost of capital (discount rate) is 11% per year simple interest?

8.3. What is the present value of an offer of $15,000 two years from now if the opportunity cost of capital (discount rate) is 12% per year compounded annually?

8.4. What is the present value of an offer of $14,000 two years from now if the opportunity cost of capital (discount rate) is 11% per year compounded annually?

[11]In some calculators, the IRR may be reported on a per-period basis, so that, for example, if the periods were months, you would have to multiply the computed IRR by 12 to obtain the nominal per-annum rate.

8.5. What is the future value of $20,000 that grows at an annual interest rate of 12% per year for two years?

8.6. What is the future value of $25,000 that grows at an annual interest rate of 11% per year for two years?

8.7. What is the present value of an offer of $15,000 one year from now if the opportunity cost of capital (discount rate) is 12% per year nominal annual rate compounded monthly?

8.8. What is the present value of an offer of $14,000 one year from now if the opportunity cost of capital (discount rate) is 11% per year nominal annual rate compounded monthly?

8.9. What is the future value of $20,000 that grows at a nominal annual interest rate of 12% per year, compounded monthly, for two years?

8.10. What is the future value of $25,000 that grows at a nominal annual interest rate of 11% per year, compounded monthly, for two years?

8.11. What is the effective annual rate (EAR) of 8% nominal annual rate compounded monthly?

8.12. What is the effective annual rate (EAR) of 6.5% nominal annual rate compounded monthly?

8.13. What is the effective annual rate (EAR) of 8% nominal annual rate compounded semiannually?

8.14. What is the effective annual rate (EAR) of 6.5% nominal annual rate compounded semiannually?

8.15. If the bond equivalent rate is 10%, what is the corresponding mortgage equivalent rate?

8.16. If the bond equivalent rate is 6%, what is the corresponding mortgage equivalent rate?

8.17. If the mortgage equivalent rate is 10%, what is the corresponding bond equivalent rate?

8.18. If the mortgage equivalent rate is 6%, what is the corresponding bond equivalent rate?

8.19. What is the effective annual rate (EAR) of 8% nominal annual rate compounded continuously?

8.20. What is the effective annual rate (EAR) of 6.5% nominal annual rate compounded continuously?

8.21. If you invested $15,000 and received back $30,000 five years later, what annual interest (or growth) rate (compounded annually) would you have obtained?

8.22. If you invested $40,000 and received back $100,000 seven years later, what annual interest (or growth) rate (compounded annually) would you have obtained?

8.23. In Question 8.21, what nominal annual rate compounded monthly would you have obtained?

8.24. In Question 8.22, what nominal annual rate compounded monthly would you have obtained?

8.25. In Question 8.21, what continuously compounded rate would you have obtained?

8.26. In Question 8.22, what continuously compounded rate would you have obtained?

8.27. If you invest $15,000 and it grows at an annual rate of 10% (compounded annually), how many years will it take to grow to $30,000?

8.28. If you invest $20,000 and it grows at an annual rate of 8% (compounded annually), how many years will it take to grow to $40,000?

8.29. In Question 8.27, suppose the 10% is a nominal annual rate compounded monthly.

8.30. In Question 8.28, suppose the 8% is a nominal annual rate compounded monthly.

8.31. In Question 8.27, suppose the 10% annual rate is compounded continuously.

8.32. In Question 8.28, suppose the 8% annual rate is compounded continuously.

8.33. A real estate investor feels that the cash flow from a property will enable her to pay a lender $15,000 per year, at the end of every year, for 10 years. How much should the lender be willing to loan her if he requires a 9% annual interest rate (annually compounded, assuming the first of the 10 equal payments arrives one year from the date the loan is disbursed)?

8.34. A real estate investor feels that the cash flow from a property will enable her to pay a lender $20,000 per year, at the end of every year, for eight years. How much should the lender be willing to loan her if he requires a 7.5% annual interest rate (annually compounded, assuming the first of the eight equal payments arrives one year from the date the loan is disbursed)?

8.35. In Question 8.33, suppose the lender wants the 9% as a nominal annual rate compounded monthly?

8.36. In Question 8.34, suppose the lender wants the 7.5% as a nominal annual rate compounded monthly?

8.37. In Question 8.33, suppose that not only will the interest be compounded monthly, but the payments will also arrive monthly in the amount of $1,250 per month (the first payment to arrive in one month)?

8.38. In Question 8.34, suppose that not only will the interest be compounded monthly, but the payments will also arrive monthly in the amount of $1,666.67 per month (the first payment to arrive in one month)?

8.39. In Question 8.37 (with 120 equal monthly payments of $1,250) suppose the borrower also offers to pay the lender $50,000 at the end of the 10-year period (coinciding with, and in addition to, the last regular monthly payment). How much should the lender be willing to lend?

8.40. In Question 8.38 (with 96 equal monthly payments of $1,666.67) suppose the borrower also offers to pay the lender $90,000 at the end of the eight-year period (coinciding with, and in addition to, the last regular monthly payment). How much should the lender be willing to lend?

8.41. You are borrowing $80,000 for 25 years at 10% nominal annual interest compounded monthly. How much must your monthly payments be if you will completely retire the loan over the 25-year period (i.e., what is the level payment annuity with a present value of $80,000)?

8.42. You are borrowing $125,000 for 30 years at 9% nominal annual interest compounded monthly. How much must your monthly payments be if you will completely retire the loan over the 30-year period (i.e., what is the level payment annuity with a present value of $125,000)?

8.43. At a nominal annual interest rate of 10% compounded monthly, how long (how many months) will it take to retire a $50,000 loan using equal monthly payments of $500 (with the payments made at the end of each month)?

8.44. At a nominal annual interest rate of 8.75% compounded monthly, how long (how many months) will it take to retire a $100,000 loan using equal monthly payments of $750 (with the payments made at the end of each month)?

8.45. A tenant offers to sign a lease paying a rent of $1,000 per month, in advance (i.e., the rent will be paid at the beginning of each month), for five years. At 10% nominal annual interest compounded monthly, what is the present value of this lease?

8.46. A tenant offers to sign a lease paying a rent of $2,500 per month, in advance (i.e., the rent will be paid at the beginning of each month), for seven years. At 9% nominal annual interest compounded monthly, what is the present value of this lease?

8.47. A building is expected to require $1 million in capital improvement expenditures in five years. The building's net operating cash flow prior to that time is expected to be at least $20,000 at the end of every month. How much of that monthly cash flow must the owners set aside each month in order to have the money available for the capital improvements, assuming the equal monthly contributions placed in this "sinking fund" will earn interest at a nominal annual rate of 6%, compounded monthly?

8.48. A building is expected to require $4,250,000 in capital improvement expenditures in three years. The building's net operating cash flow prior to that time is expected to be at least $200,000 at the end of every month. How much of that monthly cash flow must the owners set aside each month in order to have the money available for the capital improvements, assuming the equal monthly contributions placed in this "sinking fund" will earn interest at a nominal annual rate of 5%, compounded monthly?

8.49. A landlord has offered a tenant a 10-year lease with annual net rental payments of $30/SF in arrears. The appropriate discount rate is 8%. The tenant has asked the landlord to come back with another proposal, similar in every way except with rent that steps up annually at a rate of 3% per year, in return for a lower starting rent. What should the landlord's proposed starting rent be?

8.50. A landlord has offered a tenant a five-year lease with annual net rental payments of $20/SF in arrears. The appropriate discount rate is 10%. The tenant has asked the landlord to come back with another proposal, similar in every way except with rent that steps up annually at a rate of 5% per year, in return for a lower starting rent. What should the landlord's proposed starting rent be?

8.51. An apartment building can be well represented as producing net rent of $10/SF annually in arrears, with expected annual growth over the long run of negative 1% per year (that is, a decline of 1% per year). Use the constant-growth perpetuity formula to estimate the apartment building's value (per SF) if the required annual expected total return from the investment is 10%.

8.52. An apartment building can be well represented as producing net rent of $7.50/SF annually in arrears, with expected annual growth over the long run of 1% per year. Use the constant-growth perpetuity formula to estimate the apartment building's value (per SF) if the required annual expected total return from the investment is 12%.

8.53. Suppose a certain property is expected to produce net operating cash flows annually as follows, at the end of each of the next five years: $15,000, $16,000, $20,000, $22,000, and $17,000. In addition, at the end of the fifth year we will assume the property will be (or could be) sold for $200,000.
   a. What is the NPV of a deal in which you would pay $180,000 for the property today assuming the required expected return or discount rate is 11% per year?
   b. If you could get the property for only $170,000, what would be the expected IRR of your investment?

8.54. Suppose a certain property is expected to produce net operating cash flows annually as follows, at the end of each of the next five years: $35,000, $37,000, $45,000, $46,000, and $40,000. In addition, at the end of the fifth year, we will assume the property will be (or could be) sold for $450,000.
   a. What is the NPV of a deal in which you would pay $400,000 for the property today assuming the required expected return or discount rate is 12% per year?
   b. If you could get the property for only $375,000, what would be the expected IRR of your investment?

*8.55. A 100,000-SF space is expected to rent in five-year fixed-rent leases successively in perpetuity (annual payments at the beginnings of the years). You expect the first lease will be signed one year from now, with the first rent payment to be received at that time. The second lease will begin five years after that, the third five years later, and so on. The rent in each lease is constant, but between new lease signings the rent is expected to grow at a rate of 2% per year. The rent on the first lease is expected to be $20/SF per year. To compute the present value of each lease as of the time of its signing, use a low discount rate of 8% per year, reflecting the fact that the cash flows under the lease are contractually fixed. However, prior to the signing of each lease, the amount of the rent for that lease is uncertain and risky, so a 12% rate is appropriate for discounting lease values back to present value prior to lease signings. Use the level annuity formula embedded in a constant-growth perpetuity formula to compute the present value of this 100,000-SF space. [Hint: Recall the $S = a \; (1-d^n)/(1-d)$ geometric sum formula. This is a level annuity in advance embedded in a constant-growth perpetuity.]

*8.56. A 250,000-SF space is expected to rent in 10-year fixed-rent leases, successively in perpetuity (annual payments at the beginnings of the years). You expect the first lease will be signed one year from now, with the first rent payment to be received at that time. The second lease will begin 10 years after that, the third 10 years later, and so on. The rent in each lease is constant, but between new lease signings the rent is expected to grow at a rate of 1% per year. The rent on the first lease is expected to be $15/SF per year. To compute the present value of each lease as of the time of its signing, use a low discount rate of 6% per year, reflecting the fact that the cash flows under the lease are contractually fixed. However, prior to the signing of each lease, the amount of the rent for that lease is uncertain and risky, so a 10% rate is appropriate for discounting lease values back to present value prior to lease signings. Use the level annuity formula embedded in a constant-growth perpetuity formula to compute the present value of this 250,000-SF space. [Hint: Recall the $S = a \; (1-d^n)/(1-d)$ geometric sum formula. This is a level annuity in advance embedded in a constant-growth perpetuity.]

MEASURING INVESTMENT PERFORMANCE: THE CONCEPT OF RETURNS

CHAPTER OUTLINE

LEARNING OBJECTIVES

After reading this chapter, you should understand:

↺ What is meant by investment returns and how to quantify both period-by-period total returns and IRRs.

↺ The two major components of the total return, and why they are important.

↺ The characteristic features of the main types of returns, and when it is best to use each type.

↺ What is meant by risk in investment, how to quantify risk, and how it relates to returns.

↺ How to account for inflation in return measures.

↺ The NCREIF Property Index (NPI) and how the NPI return formula is derived.

N ow that you are equipped with some basic background information and tools from the two preceding chapters, you are ready to begin mastering the basic building blocks of real estate investment analysis, beginning in this chapter with a consideration of how return and risk are measured. Of course, the problem of measuring investment performance is common to all types of investment, not just real estate, so much of what we will cover in this chapter is identical to what you will find in any introductory corporate finance or investments textbook. Here, we will make sure the application of these concepts to real estate is made clear, and we will cover some considerations and conventions that apply uniquely or particularly to real estate investment analysis.

9.1 Investment Returns: Basic Definitions and Classification

Recall from Chapter 7 that underlying the variety of investors and investment goals are two fundamental types of objectives, what we called income and growth (or savings). We also noted several typical constraints and concerns investors have, including most prominently the question of *risk* in the investment. What we want to do now is to build on these concepts to define a way to *quantify investment performance*: How well is the investment doing for the investor? To this end, the concept of investment **returns** is very useful. Returns are the measure of investment performance both at the micro-level of individual properties and deals and at the macro-level of the overall investment strategy (the big picture of real estate as an asset class among others in the capital markets). Indeed, we will see how this concept may be defined and measured in ways that will allow us to quantify not only the overall end result or average investment performance over time, but also the nature and amount of risk in the investment.

Return is how we measure profit in an investment endeavor. In essence, the return on an investment is *what you get, minus what you started out with, expressed as a percentage of what you started out with.*

For example, if you invest $100 and end up a year later with $110, then you have made a 10 percent return. If you end up with only just your original $100, you have a zero percent return, and if you end up with only $95, you have a return of negative 5 percent.

Investors typically quantify measures of return either by looking backward or forward in time.

1. Looking backward in time, **ex post** (i.e., realized, historical) returns are used to measure past performance, which is useful
   - to estimate future performance (to the extent the future can be predicted from the past);
   - to judge the past performance of investment advisors or managers; and/or
   - to understand the current investment environment and "mood," as it is a product of recent past experience.
2. Looking forward in time, **ex ante** (i.e., expected) returns are used to quantitatively express future performance expectations, which are directly relevant for making investment decisions in the present, for these decisions will have their wealth impact for the investor as a result of what transpires in the future.

9.1.1 Two Fundamental Types of Return Measures

It is useful to distinguish two major types of return measures: **period-by-period** (or **periodic**) **returns**, and **multiperiod returns**. We will consider each of these in turn.

Periodic returns are usually quantified as simple **holding period returns (HPR)**. They measure what the investment grows to *within* each single period of time, assuming that all cash flow (or asset valuation) occurs only at the *beginning* and *end* of the period of time (i.e., no intermediate cash flows). Periodic returns are measured separately over each of a sequence of regular and consecutive (relatively short) periods of time (typically daily, monthly, quarterly, or annually). For example, in 2008 the return on the S&P 500 index of stocks was a most disappointing negative 37 percent, but in 2009 it bounced back nicely with a very pleasing 26.5 percent return, followed by 15.1 percent return in 2010. Periodic returns can be averaged across time to determine the **time-weighted return (TWR)**, so called because a given rate of return that is earned over more periods or during a larger fraction of the overall time interval will figure more strongly in the overall average return.

The second general type of return measure, the multiperiod return, gives a single inherently multiperiod return number for a relatively long-term period of time during which there can be cash flows into or out of the investment at intermediate points in time. The most widely used multiperiod return measure is the **internal rate of return (IRR)**. Unlike period-by-period returns, the IRR can be computed without having to know the capital value of the investment at intermediate points in time. This makes the IRR more convenient to compute for real estate investments that are not regularly and frequently reappraised (or "marked to market"). Although the multiperiod return usually covers more than one year, it is generally quoted as a per-annum (i.e., per-year) rate. For example, we might determine that a certain investor earned a 12 percent return per year over the 3-year period from the beginning of 2011 through the end of 2013. The IRR is a **money-weighted** (or dollar-weighted) **return** because it reflects the effect of having different amounts of money invested at different periods of time during the overall lifetime of the investment.[1]

9.1.2 Advantages and Disadvantages of Periodic and Multiperiod Return Measures

In modern real estate investment analysis, both period-by-period and multiperiod return measures are widely used. Each type of return measure has several advantages and disadvantages, or strengths and weaknesses, for different applications.

In real estate, period-by-period returns are more relevant at the macro-level and in examining portfolios of investments. Periodic returns allow real estate investment performance to be quantified on the same type of metric that is used for the main components of most institutional portfolios, stocks and bonds. Investment classes that do not have good measures of their periodic returns are traditionally considered marginal or "noncore" components of such portfolios. Periodic returns also facilitate the measurement of the risk in investment performance by making possible the quantification of the variability of returns over time (asset "volatility"). For macro-level and portfolio analysis, real estate performance must be compared with that of other types of assets over the same interval of time, both in regard to risk and return, and it is important to observe the **comovement** of different assets. That is, we need to know how different asset classes tend to move either together or differently over time. Periodic returns allow this type of analysis to be done. Similarly, periodic returns are particularly useful for tracing the historical ups and downs of asset markets, identifying turning points, and discerning time trends in the markets.

Period-by-period returns are also more appropriate for evaluating or comparing the performance of investment managers who have no control over the timing of capital flow into or out of the investments they manage. This is because periodic returns and the time-weighted averages computed from them are insensitive to the timing of capital flows into or out of the investments whose returns are being measured. (This is not true of money-weighted returns.) Many investment managers or institutions lack control over capital flow timing. For example, a pension fund must invest all the money that flows into it from active employee member contributions each year, and it must draw out each year sufficient money to pay the pension benefit liabilities it faces for retired members. These are functions of demographics and employment policies of the pension plan sponsor and are not under the control of the investment manager.

On the other hand, the IRR is the classical measure of investment return at the micro-level of individual properties and development projects. For this purpose, the IRR has two great advantages. First, it does not require knowledge of market values of the investment asset at intermediate points in time. (This is in contrast to the periodic return, which cannot be computed without such intermediate asset value knowledge.) In real estate, the typical investment is held for several years, and we typically do not know the exact capital value of the investment asset except at the beginning and end of the investment holding period when the property is bought and sold. But we do know the cash flows generated by the asset each period, which is what we need to compute the IRR. In such circumstances, a money-weighted multiperiod return such as the IRR may be the only type of total return that can be quantified.

The other advantage of the IRR is just the opposite of that of the TWR regarding the effect of the timing of capital flow. Just as there are times when one does not want the return measure to be influenced by the timing of capital flow into or out of the investment, so there are times when one does want precisely this. In particular, a money-weighted, purely internal return measure such as the IRR will give a fairer and more complete picture of the performance of an investment manager who does have responsibility and control over the timing and amounts of cash flow into and out of the investment vehicle.

---

[1]Hybrid return measures that combine some elements of both time-weighted and money-weighted returns are also possible. (See for example D'Alessandro, 2011.)

In the remainder of this chapter, we will develop your understanding of each of these two types of return measures in greater depth, with particular emphasis on real estate investment applications.

9.2 Periodic Returns

In traditional real estate investment analysis, and even today at the "mom and pop" level of small commercial properties, periodic returns are not computed or considered. Yet modern real estate investment at the institutional level could not function without the widespread use of periodic returns. These types of returns are the bread and butter of the world of Wall Street. The ability to compute real estate periodic returns is fundamental to the linking of Wall Street and Main Street, which was a seminal development of the last decades of the twentieth century in the real estate investment industry. Periodic returns for real estate are necessary to elevate real estate to the status of an investment asset class that can compete in the multiasset institutional portfolio alongside the classical investment classes of stocks and bonds, asset classes for which a wealth of periodic return data exist.

There is another reason for learning how to relate the periodic return measure to real estate in some depth, even at the micro-level. Because of the simplicity of its definition and construction, the simple HPR is a powerful conceptual tool and an elegant pedagogical device. It can be very useful for building your understanding of the nature of real estate investment performance. For all of these reasons, in this section, we will present the periodic return measure formally and in some depth and relate its computation to a basic definition of investment risk.

9.2.1 Formal Definition of the Periodic Return

It is time to introduce the most widely used quantifiable definition of the period-by-period return, the simple holding period return, and describe how this return measure may be broken out into various components that are separately important to investors.

The most basic and complete measure of periodic return is called the **total return**, because it includes both the change in the capital value of the asset during the period and any income paid out by the asset to the investor during the period. We will use the symbol r_t to refer to the total return during period t. (The periods most commonly used for real estate period-by-period returns are quarters, with some use also of either monthly or annual periods.) The formula for the total return during period t is

$$r_t = (CF_t + V_t - V_{t-1})/V_{t-1} \tag{1}$$

In formula (1), CF_t represents the net amount of cash flow or income paid out to the investor in (owner of) the asset during period t, and V_t represents the market value of the capital asset as of the end of period t. Note that formula (1) can also be written as

$$r_t = [(CF_t + V_t)/V_{t-1}] - 1$$

In formula (1), the assumption is that CF_t occurs entirely at the *end* of period t. The HPR assumes a passive, zero cash flow investment *within* each period of time, with valuations at the beginning and end of each period. It is as though the asset were bought at the beginning of each period and then sold at the end of each period. The lack of cash flow prior to the period end may not exactly match reality, however. For example, a stock may pay out its quarterly dividend in the middle of the calendar quarter. In practice, the periods used for computing the sequence of periodic returns are defined as intervals of time short enough so that the exact timing of the cash flow within the period makes little numerical difference. Usually, quarterly or shorter intervals will do the trick in this regard. If not, then approximations are typically employed, such as time-weighted investment, which will be described shortly.

NUMERICAL EXAMPLE OF PERIOD-BY-PERIOD RETURN COMPONENTS IN REAL ESTATE

Property value at end of 2013 = $1,000,000
Property net rent during 2014 = $100,000
Property value at end of 2014 = $1,010,000

What is 2014 r, g, y?

$$y_{2014} = \frac{\$100,000}{\$1,000,000} = 10\%$$

$$g_{2014} = \frac{\$1,010,000 - \$1,000,000}{\$1,000,000} = 1\%$$

$$r_{2014} = 10\% + 1\% = 11\%$$

The period-by-period total return can be broken down into two components, known as the **income return** and the **appreciation return**. These are relevant for the two major types of investment objectives we noted in Chapter 7, income and growth.

The income return, which is also often referred to as the **current yield** (or "cash yield" or "cash-on-cash"), we will label y_t for period t, and define it as

$$y_t = CF_t / V_{t-1} \tag{2}$$

Thus, the income return equals the cash flow paid out to the asset owner during period t, as a fraction of the value of the asset at the beginning of the period. The appreciation return is also referred to by a variety of other labels, such as **capital return**, capital gain, price-change component, or growth. We will symbolize it by g_t for period t, as given by

$$g_t = (V_t - V_{t-1}) / V_{t-1} \tag{3}$$

Thus, the appreciation return is the change in the asset market value during period t, as a fraction of the asset market value at the beginning of period t.

Note that the income and appreciation return components sum to the total return, during the period:

$$r_t = y_t + g_t \tag{4}$$

Thus, the income and appreciation returns represent components of the total return. Clearly, *the income return component is more directly relevant to the income objective of investors, while the appreciation return component is more directly relevant to the growth objective.*

The total return is the most important measure of the periodic return because it is more complete than either the growth or income component alone. Furthermore, it is generally possible to convert growth into yield or vice versa within the total return, *but it is not possible to increase the sum of the two components* (that is, the total return). For example, to convert growth into yield, one sells a portion of the investment, thereby "cashing out" some or all of the capital gain. To convert yield into growth, one reinvests some or all of the received income, either in the same asset or in a different asset.

The total return is thus the fundamental statistic for measuring period-by-period investment returns. However, it is important to realize that in the case of direct investment in real property assets, it may be more difficult or expensive to convert between yield and growth than is the case with investments in financial securities such as stocks and bonds (or REITs). For example, it may be difficult or unwise to reinvest income from a property back into improvements in that property, as the property may not need improvement, or improvement of the property would not yield sufficient future payback in the form of rental increases or building operating expense reductions. (Of course, income from the property could be invested in other assets.) Similarly, it may be difficult or impossible to sell a part of a property or a partial interest in a property in order to convert capital gain into realized income. (Another possibility would be to borrow against the increased equity the property provides as

A NOTE ON RETURN TERMINOLOGY

Unfortunately, return terminology can get confusing, as different branches of the investment industry use the same terms to mean different things, and different terms to mean the same things.

Income return (CF_t/V_{t-1}) is typically called current yield or dividend yield or just yield in stock market terminology. However, particularly in the bond market (but also in real estate), the word *yield* (often clarified as *total yield* or *yield to maturity*) is also used to refer to the internal rate of return (IRR), which is a multiperiod measure of the *total* return.

In real estate, people often define the income return as: NOI_t/V_{t-1}, where *NOI* is the net operating income generated by the property. This is the definition employed in the NCREIF index and essentially also in the IPD indices. On an annualized basis, such an NOI-based income return is essentially equivalent to what is often referred to as the OAR or cap rate (short for overall rate, or capitalization rate, sometimes also referred to as "return on assets," or ROA). But in principle (and to be more comparable to stock market definitions), the income return should be defined based on cash flow distributable to the investor. This would

normally be the NOI less any internally-raised capital improvement expenditures.* That is, $CF_t = NOI_t - CI_t$, where CI_t is the capital improvement expenditures during period *t*. For example, a $100,000 property with net operating income of $10,000 and capital expenditures of $2,000 would have a cap rate of 10 percent but current cash yield of 8 percent. Sometimes this problem is dealt with by "expensing" the average level of capital improvement expenditures as a "capital reserve" expense item, so the NOI is then computed net of normal capital expenditures. Capital improvement expenditures typically average 1 to 2 percent of property value per year, over the long run, for most types of buildings.

---

*Young et al. (1995) point out that as long as the money spent on capital improvements is generated by the property itself, subtracting such expenditures from the "income" and not from the "appreciation" results in return component definitions most comparable to those applied in the stock market. In contrast, capital expenditures raised externally (from new debt or equity investment) should be subtracted from appreciation rather than income (where appreciation is the ending property value minus the beginning value).

© OnCourse Learning

a result of gain in value, but this will increase the risk of the remaining investment.) Because conversion between yield and gain is more difficult or costly for real estate assets, investors often are more concerned about the individual return components in the case of real estate assets than they are for financial securities such as stocks.

The formulas given previously make it clear that in order to calculate the period-by-period returns and components, one must know (or estimate) the value of the property at the beginning and end of each period of time, with the periods defined as fairly short intervals, such as years or quarters. While most individual investors do not go to the trouble or expense to reappraise and record property values so frequently, institutional investors and fiduciaries such as pension funds may indeed require frequent reappraisals for the purpose of "marking to market" the values of investors' assets and indeed to enable the tracking of the period-by-period returns. Indices of period-by-period capital returns may also be computed statistically using transactions price data from a large sample of individual properties at least some of which are bought and sold each period.[2] As a result, a growing amount of period-by-period return data is available for real estate.

9.2.2 Time-Weighted Investment

The simple HPR formula described earlier, which assumes all cash flow occurs at the ends of the periods, works well enough in the securities market where public asset price quotes enable periodic returns to be computed typically on a monthly or daily frequency. In fact, it usually works fine as a very close approximation even for quarterly returns, common frequency for some major real estate indices. But the longer the period, the greater the inaccuracy caused by the fact that not all cash flows actually occur only at the ends of the periods. A method is needed to deal with intermediate cash flows (e.g., monthly cash flows within quarterly periodic returns).

---

[2]Examples as of 2012 in the United States included the Moody's/RCA Commercial Property Price Index (CPPI) and the CoStar Commercial Repeat-Sales Index (CCRSI), as well as the transactions based version of the NCREIF Index (TBI). Statistical techniques for such computations, such as repeat-sales price indices, will be discussed in Chapter 25.

The general approach to address this problem is to compute the internal rate of return (IRR) within each period assuming the asset was bought at the beginning of the period and sold at the end, with other cash flows occurring whenever they actually occurred within the period. As the exact computation of the IRR is inconvenient, in practice this approach is implemented for our present purposes by an adjustment to the simple HPR, known as time-weighted investment. This involves the replacement of the simple V_{t-1} denominator in the HPR formula with a time-weighted denominator.[3] The time-weighted adjustment to the HPR formula is shown in formula (5), for the return within each period (the subscript t is omitted for simplicity).

$$r = \frac{EndVal - BegVal + \sum CF_i}{BegVal - \sum w_i CF_i} \tag{5}$$

where $\sum CF_i$ refers to the sum of all net cash flows occurring in period t, and w_i is the proportion of period t remaining at the time when net cash flow i was received by the investor. (Note that cash flow from the investor to the investment is negative; cash flow from the investment to the investor is positive.)

For example, consider an asset that was worth $100 at the beginning of the calendar quarter, still worth $100 at the end of the quarter, and paying out $10 to the investor only at the end of the first month of the quarter. The simple HPR for the quarter would be computed as $(100 - 100 + 10)/100 = 10.00\%$. The exact IRR for the quarter is 10.70 percent (not annualized), computed as

$$0 = -100 + \frac{10}{1 + IRR/mo} + \sum_{j-2}^{3} \frac{0}{(1 + IRR/mo)^j} + \frac{100}{(1 + IRR/mo)^3}$$

$$\Rightarrow IRR/mo = 3.4469\%$$

$$\Rightarrow IRR/qtr = (1.034469)^3 - 1 = 10.70\%$$

The HPR computed with the time-weighted denominator is 10.71%, computed as

$$r = \frac{100 - 100 + 10}{100 - (2/3)10} = \frac{10}{93.33} = 0.1071 = 10.71\%$$

9.2.3 NCREIF Index Return Formula

The most widely used index of institutional commercial property periodic returns in the United States is the NCREIF Property Index (NPI). The NPI is published quarterly by the National Council of Real Estate Investment Fiduciaries, an industry association whose data-contributing members include the major real estate investment advisory firms providing management services to tax-exempt investors, primarily pension and endowment funds. The NPI is based primarily on regular appraisals of the properties in the index, which by the early 2000s included approximately 6,000 properties worth more than $250 billion. The index represents property level (that is, unlevered) total returns, including breakdowns of the income and appreciation components as described earlier. It is published at both the aggregate level and with numerous sectoral and market breakdowns, by both property type and geographic region. The historical series begins in 1978 for the aggregate index and major subindices.[4]

The NPI uses a time-weighted investment formulation to compute its quarterly returns, which are value-weighted aggregates across all the properties in the index each quarter. The

---

[3]The derivation of this adjustment is explained in Giliberto (1994). It is a mathematical approximation of the IRR.

[4]Similar indices are published in other countries, especially by the Investment Property Databank (IPD), a London-based firm that publishes indices for the United Kingdom and many other countries in the EU, Asia, Pacific, and elsewhere, as well as international aggregates. IPD also publishes a U.S. index similar to the NPI but based on a slightly different database of properties and slightly different return computation conventions more consistent with IPD's other international indices.

exact NCREIF formula uses a time-weighted denominator that is based on the assumption that one-third of the property's quarterly NOI is received at the end of each month within the quarter, and that any capital improvement expenditures (CI) or partial sales receipts (PS) occur at the midpoint of the quarter. The formula is presented as:

$$r_{NPI} = \frac{EndVal - BegVal + (PS - CI) + NOI}{BegVal - (1/2)(PS - CI) - (1/3)NOI} \tag{6}$$

Note that one-third of the quarterly NOI is subtracted out of the denominator as a result of the time-weighting process. This term actually derives from the following calculation of the $\sum w_i CF_i$ term

$$(1/3)NOI = (2/3)(1/3)NOI + (1/3)(1/3)NOI + (0)(1/3)NOI$$

reflecting the three assumed monthly payments of the NOI.[5] To construct the index, these individual property returns are weighted by the share of their values within the total aggregate NCREIF property valuation at the beginning of each period and then the weighted returns are summed across all the properties within the database at the beginning of the period. Properties sold within the period have an *End Val* of zero but the transaction sale price is entered as the partial sale (*PS*) value in the formula.

NCREIF reports the quarterly NPI returns broken down into income and appreciation components. These are defined as follows:

$$
\begin{aligned}
g_{NPI} &= \frac{EndVal - BegVal + (PS - CI)}{BegVal - (1/2)(PS - CI) - (1/3)NOI} \\
y_{NPI} &= \frac{NOI}{BegVal - (1/2)(PS - CI) - (1/3)NOI}
\end{aligned}
\tag{6a}
$$

Note that NCREIF defines the income return based on the NOI without subtracting capital improvement expenditures. Instead, NCREIF subtracts capital improvement expenditures from the end-of-period asset value in computing the numerator of the appreciation return.[6] Assuming that most capital expenditure is internally financed from the net operating income generated by the properties, this causes the NCREIF appreciation return to typically understate the amount of price appreciation in the property market, and the income return to overstate the current cash yield. (It does not affect the total return.) The NPI income return is more like a quarterly "earnings/price" ratio, and the appreciation return reflects purely property market pricing effects (as estimated by appraisers) net of capital improvement effects.[7]

9.2.4 Real versus Nominal Returns

In order to understand fully the meaning of the return measures we have just described, you need to understand the role of **inflation** in return measures, and the difference between a real and a nominal return.

Inflation is the gradual loss of purchasing power of the dollar (or any currency unit) as prices of the same goods and services rise over time. When we speak about inflation, we usually are referring to general inflation, which describes the rise in prices across an average

---

[5]A more typical assumption is that operating income is received uniformly throughout the period, or at the midpoint of the period (or the midpoint of each month within the period). This results in the coefficient on the NOI term in the denominator being (1/2) rather than (1/3). The (1/2) coefficient is used, for example, by the IPD indexes. All such return formulas (based on the time-weighted investment formula) are referred to generally as "Dietz" return measures, named after Peter Dietz, a pioneering financial economist.

[6]This convention is typical in the computation of private real estate market periodic returns. It is also employed by the IPD in many countries outside the United States (although accounting conventions and property management practices can result in smaller capital expenditures in some countries, so that this entire issue has less impact).

[7]However, NCREIF provides an option on its Web site (in the members data query screen) for users to download the NPI return components "reconstituted" with the income component based on cash flow rather than NOI and the appreciation component including the effect of capital improvement expenditures. This is referred to as the "cash flow based" return components.

"market-basket" of all goods and services in the economy. The most widely employed measure of general inflation in the United States is the Consumer Price Index (CPI), which is published monthly by the Bureau of Labor Statistics in Washington. If the CPI rises from 150 in December 2013 to 155 in December 2014, then we would say there was 3.33 percent inflation in 2014 (as $(155 - 150)/150 = 0.0333$). This means that, on average (or, for the "average" consumer), prices are 3.33 percent higher in December 2014 than they were a year earlier. Put another way, the real purchasing power of the dollar shrank by 3.33 percent in 2014. That is, it requires $1.0333 in 2014 to buy what $1.00 bought in 2013.

What may matter most to investors is the **real return**, which is defined as the return net of inflation. A real return is a return measured in constant-purchasing-power dollars. On the other hand, returns are generally actually observed and reported using "current" dollars, that is, dollars of whatever purchasing power prevails at the time when the dollars are transacted. Returns in current dollars are often called **nominal returns**, to distinguish them from real returns. Thus, nominal returns include inflation, while real returns are adjusted for inflation so that they reflect the actual purchasing power return net of inflation. Unless it is clearly stated otherwise or obvious from the context, returns are normally quoted and reported in *nominal* terms. It is then up to the user of the return information to make the inflation adjustment.

Let's go back to our hypothetical example in which the CPI at the end of 2013 is 150 and at the end of 2014 it is 155, so there was 3.33 percent inflation during 2014. Suppose a property that was worth $1,000,000 at the end of 2013 (in current 2013 dollars) is worth $1,020,000 at the end of 2014 (in current 2014 dollars). The property also generated $80,000 in net cash flow during 2014 (assume all of this cash flow occurred at the end of the year). In nominal terms, the total return would be computed as

$$r_{2014} = \frac{80,000 + (1,020,000 - 1,000,000)}{1,000,000} = 10.00\%$$

which includes 8 percent income component and 2 percent appreciation. To get the real return, we divide the 2014 dollar amounts by the ratio of the 2014 to 2013 cost of living, 1.0333, so as to express all components of the return in dollars with the same purchasing power, namely year 2013 dollars. The computation of the real returns is shown in the box on the following page.

You should note several points about this computation. First, the real growth or appreciation is negative, reflecting a real depreciation (negative appreciation) of 1.29 percent; the property value would have had to increase to $1,033,300 just to keep pace with inflation. Second, the real total return is some 3.55 percent less than the 10 percent nominal return. This difference is greater than the 3.33 percent inflation, because of the effect inflation has not only on the $1,000,000 base capital as of the beginning of the period, but also on the incremental earnings represented by the $80,000 income and $20,000 nominal capital gain. Third, note that the effect of inflation is much smaller in the income return component than it is in the appreciation return component or total return, in percentage terms. This is because the income is generally at least an order of magnitude smaller than the property value when measured in dollar terms over a short interval of time (such as a year). Thus, inflation is often ignored in the current yield component of real estate investment. Fourth, note that the commonly used shortcut of simply subtracting the inflation rate from the nominal appreciation or total return gives answers that are approximately correct, to the nearest whole percent (as long as the amount of inflation is small).

Finally, you should note that inflation can be negative, during periods of deflation, when the purchasing power of the currency increases over time. All of the previous procedures still apply, only with negative percentages for the inflation (subsequent CPI levels lower than prior levels).

9.2.5 Measuring Risk in Returns

One of the things investors are most concerned about in making investments is *risk*. As real estate is well known to involve risk, understanding how risk is related to returns is a basic part of understanding real estate investment. In traditional real estate investment analysis

---

EXAMPLE OF REAL VERSUS NOMINAL RETURN

2013 property value = $1,000,000
2014 net rent = $80,000
2014 property value = $1,020,000
2014 inflation = 3.33%

What is the *real r, y,* and *g* for 2014?

Real $g = (1,020,000/1.0333)/(1,000,000 - 1 = -1.29\% \approx 2\% - 3\% = -1\%)$
(versus nominal $g = +2\%$)

Real $y = (80,000/1.0333)/(1,000,000 = +7.48\% \approx 8\%)$
(versus nominal $y = 8\%$ exactly)

Real $r = (1,100,000/1.0333)/(1,000,000 - 1 = +6.46\% \approx 10\% - 3\% = 7\%)$
(versus nominal $r = 10\%$)

$y + g = +7.74\% + (-1.29\%) = 6.46\% \approx 8\% - 1\% = 7\%$

---

and at the "mom and pop" level, risk is largely ignored quantitatively and addressed only qualitatively. Such an approach will not work in the modern institutional investment environment, however. We need to be able to quantify the risk in real estate investment, and to quantify it in a way that is comparable to the way risk is measured in the other major investment asset classes. In recent decades, this is beginning to be done with increasing sophistication, based on the use of real estate periodic returns data.

In principle, we can think about investment risk and define it formally in various ways. For example, one intuitive definition would be that risk is the probability that the investors will lose all of the capital they invest. For example, if you take out a mortgage to buy a property, and later you cannot make the mortgage payments and the bank forecloses on your loan and fails to sell the property for more than you owe on the loan, then you would have lost all the capital you put into the property. This, however, is a rather extreme and narrow definition of risk, relevant only to the specific problem of default risk on levered investments. We might also consider risk as the possibility of losing *any* of the original invested capital. For example, if you pay $100,000 for a property free and clear of any debt, and a year later the property has earned $5,000 in net income, but you cannot then sell the property for more than $90,000, then you would have lost 5 percent of your investment value (at least on paper, as of that point in time). Or we could define risk as some combination of the probability of loss and the likely severity of loss if it occurs.

All of these notions of risk are related to the range in the possible future returns that the investment might earn, or to the degree of deviation or dispersion of those returns around the ex ante expected return. The most widely used statistical measure to quantify such dispersion is known as the **standard deviation** of the probability distribution of the future return possibilities. This measure of investment risk is also known as **volatility**. The greater is the standard deviation in the possible return (for a given future time horizon), the greater will usually be the risk defined in any of the previous ways. Thus, a good general way to think about and quantify risk in investments is depicted in Exhibit 9-1. The horizontal axis represents all the possible values that the return on some investment could have over some given future time horizon. The vertical axis measures the probability associated with each possible future return value.

If the future return could be known exactly in advance, then there would for certain be only one point on the horizontal axis, the known certain future return, which would have a probability of 100 percent. In this circumstance, the subsequently realized return (ex post) would for certain exactly equal the expected return (ex ante). This would be a *riskless* asset, and is depicted in Exhibit 9-1 for the asset labeled *A* which has a sure

EXHIBIT 9-1 Risk and
Expected Return as Future
Return Probability
Distributions: Three Assets
© OnCourse Learning

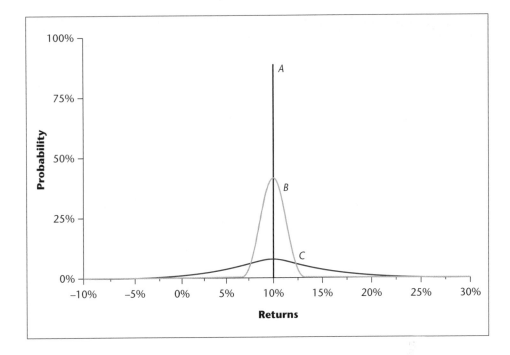

return of 10 percent. The standard deviation of the probability distribution of asset *A*'s return is zero.

The asset labeled *B* depicts an investment asset with a little bit of risk. The future return is not known for certain in advance; there is some range of possible values. The ex post realized return will not necessarily exactly equal the ex ante expectation. For asset *B*, the expected return is again 10 percent, but now the standard deviation is 1 percent. The probability distribution pictured in Exhibit 9-1 has the typical bell shape of what is called the normal (or Gaussian) distribution. Most analysts consider that this shape is not a bad approximation of the general shape of the typical return distributions of real estate and other major capital assets.[8]

The normal distribution is symmetrical, which means the realized returns are as likely to be above as below the mean or expected value, which is also the single most likely value. With the normal distribution there is about a two-thirds chance that the realized return will lie within one standard deviation of the mean. So in the case of asset *B* this means there is only about one chance in three that the realized return would fall outside the range of 9 to 11 percent. Although no extreme return value is completely ruled out by the normal distribution, as you can see in the graph, there appears to be effectively no chance of asset *B*'s return falling below 7 percent or above 13 percent during the given time interval covered in this example.

The asset labeled *C* in Exhibit 9-1 depicts a more risky investment asset. The expected return is again 10 percent, but now the standard deviation is 5 percent, implying a one-third chance that the return could fall below 5 percent or above 15 percent, and we see that the effective outer range of future possibilities appears to extend from −3 percent (a loss), to +23 percent. There is only a 1 percent chance that the realized return would lie beyond this range.

To place this quantitative measure of investment risk in some practical perspective, there is good evidence that the standard deviation of the return distribution of a typical individual

---

[8]But it is only an approximation. Actual returns (in many types of investments, including real estate) tend to have "fat tails," with more probability of extreme events (especially on the down side) than is indicated by the normal distribution. See Young and Graff (1995). While the normal distribution is still widely used for analytical purposes, it is good to keep in mind this caveat.

HOW VOLATILE ARE COMMERCIAL PROPERTY ASSETS?

Volatility is a very basic measure of the risk of assets from an investment perspective. It is very easy to observe empirically and measure the volatility of assets that are traded as securities on public exchanges, such as stocks and bonds (including REITs). It is much more difficult to measure the volatility of assets that are rarely (and privately) traded, such as commercial properties. Nevertheless, research undertaken in the academic community starting in the late 1980s and more recently large electronic databases of commercial property transaction prices such as those compiled by CoStar Group and Real Capital Analytics Inc (RCA), have given us a pretty clear idea about the quantitative magnitude of real estate volatility measured in a manner roughly comparable to that of stocks and bonds.

The evidence regarding the magnitude of real estate volatility is of various types. For individual property volatility, early evidence came from studies applying option pricing theory to real estate. Option theory allows the implied volatility of built property assets to be derived from the prices of mortgages or land. Studies of this nature include Quigg (1993); Ciochetti and Vandell (1999); and Holland, Ott, and Riddiough (1998), among others. Additional evidence is in Geltner, Graff, and Young (1994). These studies all estimate individual property annual volatility approximating, or effectively in excess of, 15 percent. A more direct measure comes from the large transaction price databases such as RCA's and CoStar's. For example, analysis of the dispersion of repeat-sales returns residuals from the Moody's/RCA Commercial Property Price Index (CPPI) suggests that individual property investments experience idiosyncratic drift (volatility uncorrelated with the market index) at the rate of approximately 12 percent per year. This is in addition to a non-temporal price "noise" standard deviation of approximately 15 percent per transaction (see Chapter 25 for further explanation). Such idiosyncratic volatility would be combined with the systematic market volatility as measured by an index to give total individual asset volatility.

Evidence on the volatility of diversified portfolios of many properties, or the volatility of aggregate indices of commercial

real estate ("market volatility" as distinct from individual asset volatility), comes primarily from studies of the historical periodic returns to such portfolios or indices. The annual volatility of the periodic total returns was 8.2 percent in the NCREIF Property Index (NPI) of unlevered commercial property during 1978–2010 and 18.9 percent in the NAREIT Index of equity REIT total returns during 1972–2010.

As noted in Chapter 7, the NPI is based on appraised values, and most academic researchers are convinced that it tends to artificially "smooth" the true property returns, suggesting that the actual volatility was greater than the 8.2 percent indicated by that index. This is supported in various academic studies and by the transactions price based version of the NPI (known as the TBI), which had annual total return volatility during the 1985–2010 period of 11.4 percent (as published by MIT). Annual volatility in the Moody's/RCA CPPI during 2001-2010 was 14.1 percent, but that was a particularly volatile decade, and econometric based indices such as the CPPI or TBI may display some excess volatility due to statistical noise (as described in Chapter 25). Inertia in the private property market, as evidenced by positive serial correlation at the annual frequency in indices such as the NPI, TBI, and CPPI, implies that volatility would increase more than proportionately in private real estate returns measured over longer intervals. (Three times in the past 50 years, commercial property values have dropped market-wide by more than 30 percent in real terms—a phenomenon of "fat tails.") On the other hand, the use of leverage and other characteristics of REITs suggests that passive holdings of diversified portfolios of individual properties should be less volatile than the 18.9 percent annual volatility recorded by the NAREIT index.

In summary, it would seem that annual volatility of 10 percent is a conservative (lower bound) but reasonable estimate for commercial property private market volatility for well diversified portfolios or indices. We combine this with the aforementioned 12 percent idiosyncratic drift volatility, we arrive at an estimate of typical individual property annual volatility of around 16 percent (as $\sqrt{0.10^2 + 0.12^2} = 15.6\%$).

© OnCourse Learning

real estate investment (say, a fully leased income property) is in excess of 15 percent per year. A diversified portfolio of many individual real estate assets would have a smaller standard deviation, but probably still be around 10 percent per year, or more, depending on how the returns are measured. (See the feature at the top of this page.) This compares to annual volatility of around 30 percent for a typical individual stock, and more than 15 percent for diversified investments in large stocks as represented by an index such as the S&P 500.[9]

We are thus able to quantify both the expected return and the risk in that return for investments by using statistics about the probability distributions of their future return possibilities. The expected return is represented by the mean of the distribution, and the risk is

---

[9]Some recent historical quantitative evidence on volatility was presented in Chapter 7. As a point of interest, among approximately 60 individual U.S. REIT stocks publicly listed in 2010 that had also been continuously listed since 2000, the (unweighted) average annualized volatility during that decade was approximately 35 percent.

represented by the standard deviation of the distribution. The main point to understand in this definition of risk and return is that risk is represented by the range or deviation of the possible future return outcomes around the prior expectation of the return, which may be thought of roughly as a best guess (that is, an unbiased guess, neither optimistic nor pessimistic). This definition of investment risk therefore raises an interesting corollary: the more risky (higher standard deviation) the asset, the greater also is the "upside" possibility. That is, given two assets with the same expected return, the more risky asset will typically have a greater chance of returning a larger profit than the less risky asset could. This may partly explain why more trading and investor interest surrounds more volatile assets.

9.2.6 Relationship between Risk and Return

Investors are *risk averse*. For example, suppose two assets are available to investors, both identical in every respect (including, in particular, the fact that they have the same expected return ex ante), except that asset *A* is less risky (has a lower standard deviation of return), while asset *B* is more risky (as in the depiction in Exhibit 9-1). No investor would want to buy asset *B* faced with this choice, and indeed any investor holding *B* would prefer to sell it and buy *A*. Thus, the price of asset *A* would be bid up, and the price of *B* would be bid down. This process would act to increase the expected return on *B* and decrease the expected return on A (relative to the prices one would have to pay to obtain them).[10] In equilibrium (that is, when supply and demand balances for both assets), the riskier asset must offer a higher mean return (ex ante) than the less risky asset.

This is perhaps the most fundamental point in the financial economic theory of capital markets: that expected returns are (and should be) greater for more risky assets. This point is depicted in Exhibit 9-2. This same point is also described algebraically in the following equation:

$$[E[r]_t] = r_{f,t} + E[RP_t] \tag{7}$$

where $E[r_t]$ is the expected total return of a given asset over future period t, $r_{f,t}$ is the return one could earn during period t from investing in a riskless asset (such as U.S. government Treasury bills), and $E[RP_t]$ is the expected **risk premium** that investors require on an ex ante basis for investing in the given asset. The expected risk premium is proportional to the amount of risk investors perceive to be involved in investing in the given asset.

In Exhibit 9-2, risk (as perceived in the investment marketplace) is measured on the horizontal axis, and expected total return (ex ante, going forward) is measured on the vertical axis. The idea is that by investing in a riskless asset, investors can achieve a sure return equal to the rate labeled r_f. This **risk-free interest rate** compensates investors for the pure **time value of money**, the fact that investors are allowing someone else (in this case the government) to use their money for some period of time. Risky assets must offer a higher expected return in order to compensate investors for taking on risk when they buy these assets. The difference between the risk-free interest rate and the expected return on a risky asset is the expected risk premium, which is seen in the graph to be proportional to the amount of risk in the asset.

The picture presented in Exhibit 9-2 might be called financial economics in a nutshell. It is perhaps the single most important idea to remember from this book. It is an idea that is so simple and obvious that it never evokes arguments from students in an academic setting, yet it seems to be much more difficult for people to keep in mind when they get out in the real world. People investing in real estate commonly believe, implicitly if not explicitly, that they are getting a higher ex ante return *without* assuming greater risk. We will see how the risk/return trade-off depicted in Exhibit 9-2 enters at a fundamental level into almost every aspect of investment analysis and decision making as the later chapters of this book unfold. So, always keep Exhibit 9-2 in mind.

---

[10]We will have more to say about the link between asset prices and returns in the next chapter. Suffice it to say here that a lower price for an asset implies, other things being equal, a higher expected return for the investor.

EXHIBIT 9-2 Financial
Economics in a Nutshell:
Risk and Return
© OnCourse Learning

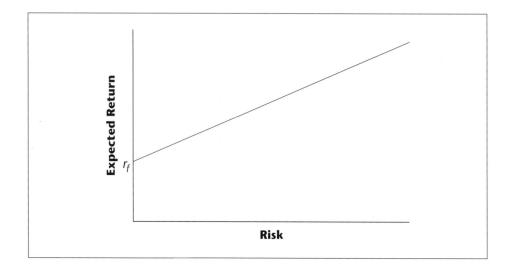

9.2.7 Summarizing Periodic Returns: Synthesizing the Three Ways to Break Down the Total Return

This is perhaps a good time to pause and step back, to synthesize some of what we have learned about periodic returns. The HPR is an elegant measure of investment performance, capturing a rich depth of attributes that matter to investors in a simple way that allows quantitative measurement. Notice in particular that we have identified three different ways in which the periodic or time-weighted average total return can be broken down into two components: income plus growth, risk-free rate plus risk premium, and real return plus inflation premium. These are summarized here:

$$r = y + g$$
$$r = r_f + RP$$
$$r = R + (i + iR) \approx R + i$$

where i refers to the inflation rate and R refers to the real total return.

9.3 Multiperiod and Money-Weighted Returns

Suppose you want to know the return earned over a multiperiod span of time, expressed as a single average annual rate. There are two widely used approaches for computing such a measure. One is simply to take the average of the periodic returns across the time span in question. This will produce a *time-weighted* average return (TWR). The other approach is to compute an inherently multiperiod return, most often the IRR, which is a *money-weighted* average return. These two approaches will be discussed in this section.

9.3.1 Time-Weighted Average Return

The average of consecutive period-by-period returns across time is referred to as a time-weighted average return for the overall interval of time. The term *time-weighted* comes from the fact that, for example, if the periodic returns are 10 percent, 10 percent, and 13 percent in each of three consecutive years, then the arithmetic average return across the three periods is 11 percent per year (the 10 percent is weighted twice as much as the 13 percent). As noted, the time-weighted average return is *independent of the magnitude of capital invested at each point in time*. It is therefore *not affected by the timing of capital flows into or out of the investment.*

We can compute the time-weighted average return from a series of periodic returns in two ways. The simple or **arithmetic average** indicates the central tendency of the individual periodic returns, and is computed as the sum of the individual periodic returns divided by the number of periods. In the previous example, $(10\% + 10\% + 13\%)/3 = 11.00\%$. In contrast, the **geometric average** reflects the effects of **compounding**, or the earning of return on return. This is also referred to as **chain-linking** the returns. In the previous example, the geometric mean would be computed as follows:

$$(1.10 \times 1.10 \times 1.13)^{\wedge}(1/3) - 1 = 10.99\%$$

(In this example, it makes little difference, but in practice, the two measures can be significantly different.)

Each of these methods of computing the time-weighted average has some advantages and disadvantages that make it more appropriate than the other for certain purposes. The arithmetic mean is characterized by the following attributes:

- The arithmetic mean is *always* at least as great as the geometric mean (e.g., if the geometric mean is negative 5 percent, the arithmetic mean might be negative 4 percent), the more so the greater is the volatility in the periodic returns series. The two measures are equal only if there is no volatility at all.
- The arithmetic mean has "superior statistical properties" in the sense that it provides the best estimator of the true underlying return tendency each period and therefore provides the best forecast of the return for any one future period (assuming that the future is governed by the same underlying return generating process as the past).
- The arithmetic mean return components (income and appreciation) sum to the arithmetic mean total return.

These attributes of the arithmetic mean can be contrasted with the following attributes of the geometric mean:

- Because the geometric mean reflects compounding of returns, it better represents the average growth rate per period during the overall time span so as to reflect the relation between the amount of value the investor ends up with and the amount they started with (assuming reinvestment).
- The geometric mean is independent of the volatility of the periodic returns (given the beginning and ending values of the investment). The geometric mean return components (income and appreciation) do not sum to the geometric mean total return. (A complicated "cross-product" term involving interaction of the two components is left out of the compounding of the individual components.) Indeed, the geometric mean income return is of questionable economic meaning, although the geometric mean appreciation return can represent the average growth in asset value or price.

Considering the previous attributes, it is not surprising that the arithmetic mean is most widely used in forecasts of future expectations and in portfolio analysis. On the other hand, because of the geometric mean's direct relation to ending value as a multiple of beginning value, it is not surprising that the geometric mean is most widely used in historical performance measurement and in the evaluation of investment managers. For this purpose, it is also an advantage of the geometric mean that it is more independent of the volatility of the periodic returns.[11] In general, the geometric mean tends to be used more often by professional practitioners and accounting professionals, while the arithmetic mean tends to be used more often by academics and economists.[12] The arithmetic and geometric means are more similar

- the less volatility there is in the periodic returns, and
- the more frequent the returns (shorter the return periods)

---

[11]For a given geometric mean performance, the arithmetic mean will be larger the greater is the volatility in the periodic returns. Thus, an investment manager can score a higher arithmetic mean simply by holding in more volatile assets.

[12]Academics are prone to avoid the whole issue of geometric versus arithmetic means by simply working with continuously compounded returns (log differences), in which the distinction between the two types of means effectively disappears. (The sum of the log differences divided by the number of return periods is the same as the log of the ratio of ending to beginning value levels divided by the length of time between them.)

In the extreme, if there is no volatility at all (constant returns), or the length of the return periods approaches zero (continuous compounding), the arithmetic mean will exactly equal the geometric mean across time.

9.3.2 Internal Rate of Return (IRR)

The IRR is the classical and traditional measure of investment performance in real estate. It is needed in two situations. Since investments in real property are usually held for a long period of time, several years at least, most property owners do not want to go to the expense of regularly appraising the value of their property when they are not planning to sell it. Thus, at the micro-level of individual properties and deals, it is often impossible to calculate the period-by-period returns necessary to compute a time-weighted average. In contrast, the IRR can be calculated easily with data that the property owner will almost always have available. It requires only (1) the price the property was bought for, (2) the net cash flow generated by the property during each period since it was bought, and (3) an estimate of what the property is currently worth (or what it was sold for).

The IRR is also useful because it is a money-weighted average return, as contrasted with a time-weighted average. As noted earlier, a money-weighted return reflects the effect of the magnitude of capital invested during each period. As a result, it captures the effect of capital flow *timing*. If an investor tends to enter an investment just before it does well and exit the investment just before it does poorly, the IRR earned by that investor will improve accordingly, above the TWR on the underlying investment. The reverse occurs if the timing is unfavorable. Thus, if it is appropriate to measure the effect of capital flow timing on the investment performance, then the IRR is a better measure than the TWR. Similarly, if it is not appropriate to include such effects (such as when the manager being evaluated does not have responsibility or control over timing), then the IRR is not an appropriate performance measure. In the real world, many situations are rather ambiguous in this regard. An investment manager may have some influence over capital flow timing, but not complete freedom. In classical investment analysis in the securities industry, the time-weighted average return has been generally considered to be more appropriate in most investment management situations. However, each case may be considered on its own merits.

The formal definition of the IRR is as follows. Let *PV* represent the amount that was invested in year 0 (e.g., 2013), and let CF_t refer to the net cash flow in year t (e.g., $t = 1$ refers to 2014, $t = 2$ refers to 2015, and so on). It is important to note that the net cash flow during intermediate years may be generated either from operation of the asset or partial sales, that is, disposition of part of the asset. Intermediate cash flows may also reflect subsequent investments after the initial purchase or construction of the property (for example, capital improvement expenditures are negative cash flows from the investor/owner's perspective). The sign of cash flows must be defined consistently. For example, cash outflows (from the investment to the investor) are positive, while cash inflows (from the investor to the investment) are negative. Now define an investment holding period or "horizon" such that in year *N* the investment is assumed to be completely liquidated (i.e., sold). Then CF_N includes both any net operating cash flow during year *N* as well as the "salvage" value or net sale proceeds from the final disposition of the property (this latter cash flow is usually referred to as the "reversion" in real estate parlance). Then the IRR is defined by the following equation:

$$PV = \frac{CF_1}{(1 + IRR)} + \frac{CF_2}{(1 + IRR)^2} + \cdots + \frac{CF_N}{(1 + IRR)^N} \tag{8}$$

In general, it is not possible to solve an equation such as (8) algebraically to determine the IRR analytically. It is necessary to solve the equation "numerically," that is, by trial and error. For some patterns of cash inflows and outflows across time, it will be mathematically impossible to compute an IRR (the IRR will not exist), or the IRR may not be unique (more than one value may solve the equation). Such cases are pretty rare in practice, generally involving situations in which there is more than one reversal of sign in the cash flow stream.

This may occur in redevelopment or turnaround projects, for example, in which an initial investment is followed by positive cash flow that is then followed by large cash outflows for redevelopment and then more positive cash inflow after the redevelopment.[13]

To better understand how the IRR is a money-weighted average return across the time span it covers, consider our previous numerical example in which we postulated three consecutive years in which an investment produces periodic returns of 10 percent, 10 percent, and 13 percent. We noted previously that this gives the investment a time-weighted average return of 11 percent. Now suppose you put $100 into the asset earning these returns at the beginning of the first year. At the end of the first year, you would have $110, and by the end of the second year, your investment would have grown another 10 percent to $121 (equal to $110 × [1 + 10%]). At that point in time, suppose you decide to put an additional $200 of new capital into the asset. So you have $321 in the investment at the beginning of the third year, when it earns 13 percent. You end up with $362.73 at the end of the third period ($321 × [1 + 13%]). Your net cash flows are − $100 at the beginning of year 1, − $200 at the beginning of year 3, and + $362.73 at the end of year 3. This cash flow stream can be computed using the previous formula to have an IRR of 11.69 percent. The IRR is higher than the time-weighted return because more capital was tied up in the investment during the year when the higher (13 percent) periodic return was earned.

On the other hand, suppose instead of investing more at the beginning of year 3 you had disinvested part of your capital at that point in time, say, by selling half of your $121 investment. Then the cash flow stream would have been − $100 at time zero, + 60.50 two years later, and then + 68.37 at the end of year 3. This stream has an IRR of 10.60 percent, which is not only less than the IRR with the previously considered favorable cash flow timing, but also less than the underlying investment's time-weighted return of 11 percent.

Finally, suppose you were completely passive after your initial $100 investment, taking nothing out and putting no more into the investment. Your cash flow stream would then have been − $100 at time zero and + $136.73 at year 3 (100 × 1.1 × 1.1 × 1.13). This stream has an IRR of 10.99 percent, exactly equal to the geometric mean time-weighted average return for the underlying investment during those three years.

The IRR is referred to as an *internal* rate because it includes only the returns earned on capital *while it is invested in the project* (or with the manager who is being evaluated). Once capital is withdrawn from the investment, it no longer influences the IRR. This is in fact what makes the IRR a money-weighted return.

It is also important to note that the IRR gives a measure of the total return that was achieved by the investment: from initial income flow, subsequent growth (or decline) in income flow, and finally capital value appreciation (or decline) as reflected in the sale price (or terminal value) of the asset at the end. The IRR reflects both the initial cost of the investment and any subsequent capital invested, as the IRR is based on *net* cash flows in each period. It is a purely cash-flow-based measure that does not differentiate between investment and return on or return of investment. The IRR does not indicate *when* the return was generated within the overall span of time the investment was held (e.g., would the return per annum have been higher or lower if the asset had been held half as long?). It is therefore not useful for computing statistics such as co-movements among assets or volatility of returns across time.

Some other aspects of the IRR may help to build your intuition about it, particularly in relation to the time-weighted return. First, as we saw in the previous example, *if there are no*

---

[13]The problem may also arise in computing IRRs realized by investors in funds that draw in and pay out cash over time. In such cases, while a unique IRR may not be determinable, there will often (though not always) exist only one IRR that is reasonable. In any case, a reasonable "cost of capital" can always be posited by the analyst and a single net present value (NPV) determined for the project at that capital cost. (More about this in the next chapter.) Also, various types of "adjusted IRRs" have been developed in the financial management literature to facilitate computation of an explicit return, although any of these require additional assumptions that inevitably involve some subjectivity and judgment. (See for example Altshuler and Magni, 2011.)

A NOTE ON IRR TERMINOLOGY

In the real estate appraisal business, the IRR is often called the "total yield." In real estate investment and appraisal, the expected IRR looking forward into the future when making an investment is often called the "going-in IRR." In the bond business, the IRR is simply called the bond yield. The yield to maturity (YTM) is the IRR assuming the bond is held to maturity.

---

intermediate cash flows, the IRR will exactly equal the time-weighted geometric mean return (no cash placed into or taken out between the beginning and end of the investment). Second, there is a special theoretical case of regularity in both the space and asset markets in which the IRR and periodic return are the same. Suppose (1) regular intermediate cash flows grow at a constant rate every period, and (2) the asset value always remains a constant multiple of the current periodic cash flow. Then the IRR will exactly equal the sum of the initial cash yield rate plus the growth rate ($IRR = y + g$), and the IRR will exactly equal both the arithmetic and geometric time-weighted mean return ($IRR = r$).[14] (The growth rate, g, here applies identically to both the cash flows and the asset capital value.) This special case is equivalent to a constant-growth perpetuity, which as we saw in Chapter 8 has a present value of $PV = CF_1/(r - g)$, and a current yield equal to the inverse of the constant multiple: $y = CF_1/PV$.

9.4 Chapter Summary

This chapter has continued to develop your basic set of tools and building blocks for real estate investment analysis by defining investment returns in some depth and detail. We defined two types of returns at a specific, quantitative level: periodic returns (the HPR), which underlie time-weighted average returns (TWR), and money-weighted multiperiod returns (in particular, the IRR). The strengths and weaknesses, and the major uses, of each of these types of returns were described. We also showed how the periodic return could be used to define components of return, as well as investment risk in a way that can be measured quantitatively, as the volatility, or range of variability, in these returns over time. The next chapter will use what we have presented here to show how real estate investments can be analyzed and evaluated quantitatively at the *micro*, or individual asset, level.

KEY TERMS

returns	comovement	volatility
ex post	total return	risk premium
ex ante	income return	risk-free interest rate
period-by-period (periodic) returns	appreciation return	time value of money
multiperiod returns	current yield	arithmetic average return
holding period returns (HPR)	capital return (gain, growth)	geometric average return
time-weighted return (TWR)	inflation (general, CPI)	chain-linking (compounding)
internal rate of return (IRR)	real return	returns
money-weighted return	nominal returns	
(dollar-weighted return)	standard deviation	

---

[14]The combination of constant-growth cash flows and constant-multiple asset value implies that the periodic returns are constant across time, so there is no volatility, allowing the arithmetic and geometric means to equate in the periodic returns.

STUDY QUESTIONS

Conceptual Questions

9.1. Describe the two fundamental types of return measures.

9.2. Explain the difference between *time-weighted* and *dollar-weighted* multiperiod return measures.

9.3. In what situations (or applications) is it most advantageous to use periodic returns? When does it make the most sense to employ multiperiod return measures?

9.4. How can the NCREIF Property Index (NPI) periodic return formula be viewed as the calculation of the internal rate of return for properties in the index?

9.5. Consider two real estate investments. One offers a 10% expected return with volatility of 10%; the other offers a 15% expected return with volatility of 20%. Is it possible to say, from just this information, which one is the better investment? (Hint: Consider Exhibit 9-2.)

9.6. Describe three ways to break the total nominal return down into two components. (Provide formulas, and label your variables.)

9.7. What is wrong with the following statement: Time-weighted average return is particularly well suited to measuring real estate investment performance for investors who actively try to time the market when buying and selling properties.

9.8. Explain the difference between *arithmetic* and *geometric* time-weighted average return.

Quantitative Problems

9.9. Suppose the Sam Sell Select Fund buys a property at the end of 2005 for $11,250,000 on behalf of its wealthy investor clients. At the end of 2006, the fund sells the property for $12,500,000 after obtaining net cash flow of $950,000 at the end of 2006. Suppose inflation during 2006 was 3.5% and government bonds yielded 5%. Consider the simple holding period returns for the 2006 calendar year period. Compute the following return measures (to the nearest basis point).

   a. The nominal income return

   b. The nominal appreciation return

   c. The nominal total return

   d. The ex post risk premium

   e. The real appreciation return (using the exact definition)

   f. The continuously compounded nominal total return

   g. The continuously compounded nominal appreciation return

9.10. The real estate investment advisor to the Tired Old Firemen's Pension Fund is faced with a possible property acquisition that will cost $4,200,000. The advisor feels that in one year this property will face the following subjective probabilities. There is a 25% chance for an optimistic scenario or "upside" outcome, in which case the property will be worth $5,000,000. There is a 25% chance of a pessimistic scenario or "downside" outcome, in which case the property would be worth $3,750,000. And there is a 50% chance of an expected scenario or "most likely" outcome, in which case the property will still be worth $4,200,000 next year. Using simple HPRs, compute the following.

   a. The expected appreciation return

   b. The standard deviation of the possible appreciation return (Note: If you use Excel on this, use STDEVP rather than STDEV because this is not a sample—it is your complete subjective probability distribution. The range on which to apply STDEVP would include four cells, two for the "most likely" outcome.)

9.11. In the fourth quarter of 2005, the NCREIF Property Index (NPI) total return for the Boston metropolitan area was 4.47% (this is a quarterly return, not per annum). This was based on 165 properties having, as shown in the following table, an aggregate appraised (market) value of $10,254,210,187 at the beginning of the quarter and $10,209,681,774 at the end of the quarter. The drop in appraised value does not imply a decrease in property values in this case, as investors sold partial ownership interests in properties (partial sales) in the index generating aggregate proceeds of $414,134,757. The properties produced $160,072,817 in net operating income and absorbed $81,264,596 in capital improvement expenditures during the quarter. Using the data provided and the NCREIF return formulae given in the chapter, answer the following questions.

NPI Data for Boston (End of Quarter)

	Total Return	Income (NOI)	Capital Exp. (CI)	Market Value	Partial Sales (PS)
2005 Q3				$10,254,210,187	
2005 Q4	4.47%	$160,072,817	$81,264,596	$10,209,681,774	$414,134,757

a. What would the quarterly total return for Boston have been if the NPI used the simple HPR formula (with just the beginning asset value in the denominator) instead of a time-weighted investment value in the denominator? (Note how little difference this would make in basis points, even multiplying by four to factor up to annual from quarterly rates.)

b. Recall that NCREIF defines the income return based on the NOI without subtracting capital improvement expenditures. Instead, NCREIF subtracts capital improvement expenditures from the end-of-period asset value in computing the numerator of the appreciation return. NCREIF reported an income return for Boston in 2005.4 of 1.60% and an appreciation return of 2.87%. Verify these two numbers [i.e., calculate the income & appreciation return components using equations (6a)]. Now compute how different the two return components (in part b) would be if the income return were defined on a cash flow basis with capital expenditures subtracted and if appreciation return were defined on an asset price change basis using just ending asset value without subtracting capital expenditures. How big a difference would this change have made in Boston in 2005 if you factored your answer up by a multiple of four, to put it in per annum instead of quarterly terms? (Report your answer in basis points.)

9.12. The following table gives the NPI total return for a 3-year (12-quarter) period for Boston and San Francisco.

YYQ	Boston	San Francisco
2003.1	0.0024	0.0141
2003.2	0.0098	0.0050
2003.3	0.0082	0.0078
2003.4	0.0156	0.0296
2004.1	0.0325	0.0429
2004.2	0.0181	0.0248
2004.3	0.0427	0.0421
2004.4	0.0655	0.0309
2005.1	0.0301	0.0439
2005.2	0.0361	0.0393
2005.3	0.0520	0.0433
2005.4	0.0487	0.0447

Compute the following quarterly statistics for both cities to the nearest basis point, and answer the subsequent questions. (Hint: We suggest using a computer spreadsheet.]

a. The arithmetic average return (use the AVERAGE function in Excel)

b. The standard deviation of the return ("volatility," use STDEV in Excel)

c. The geometric mean return (you can use the Excel statistical function GEOMEAN, but you have to add unity to each return in the series, and then subtract unity from the GEOMEAN result, or just apply the geometric mean return formula directly by compounding the returns in the spreadsheet)

d. Why are the arithmetic means higher than the geometric means?

e. Based on the geometric mean, and factoring up to a per-annum rate, by how many basis points did San Francisco beat Boston during this period?

f. Now compute the quarterly Sharpe ratio for each city based on the geometric mean you computed in (c) and the volatility you computed in (b). The Sharpe ratio is a measure of risk-adjusted return performance, defined as the risk premium divided by the volatility. Assume that the average quarterly return to Treasury Bonds during the period in question was 1.50%. Which city had the better Sharpe ratio?

9.13. A common type of real estate investment vehicle used by institutional investors is known as a "unit fund" or "open-end" commingled fund (CREF). Investors can put capital into, and withdraw capital out of, such funds on the basis of the appraised value of the assets in the fund, which are reappraised regularly and frequently. Thus, if the assets are appraised at $10 million, and you invest $100,000, you have a 1% share, entitling you to 1% of the net cash flow and proceeds from sales within the fund. Now consider a "passive" buy-and-hold strategy over a 3-year period in such a fund. Suppose you invest $200,000 in the fund at the end of 2004, to obtain two "units" (i.e., shares). During 2005, the fund pays $5,000 per unit from net rental income, and at the end of 2005 is reappraised to a net asset value of $98,000 per unit. During 2006, the fund pays $10,000 per unit in net rental income, and the appraised value at the end of 2006 surges to $112,000 per unit. Finally, during 2007, the fund pays out $7,000 in net income, and at the end of 2007, the assets of the fund are sold in the real estate market and liquidated for net cash proceeds of $118,000 per unit. Use your calculator or a computer spreadsheet (the latter will be faster and more reliable) to answer the following questions, reporting your answers to the nearest basis point.

a. Assuming that appraised value accurately reflects market value (opportunity cost) of the assets at intermediate points in time, what are the period-by-period total returns for each of the three years the investment was held (2005, 2006, and 2007)?

b. Based on these period-by-period returns, what is the geometric average annual total return during the 3-year holding period of the investment (2005–2007)?

c. What is the internal rate of return (IRR, per annum) of the investment over its 3-year holding period?

d. Which of these two average returns over the 3-year life of the investment tells exactly what the profit would have been per original dollar invested if the investor had taken the cash paid out plus proceeds from liquidating his units at the end of each year and used all (and only) this cash to immediately purchase units (and fractions thereof) in the fund again for the following year (i.e., so that there was no cash flow into or out of the investment except at the beginning and end of the 3-year period)?

9.14. Suppose that the investor in the above question 9.13 at first was cautious, buying only one unit at the end of 2004. Then a year later, he felt that the market would rebound in 2006 after its poor performance in 2005. So he made an additional capital contribution to buy one more unit at that time. Then, with the great performance of the fund in 2006, he decided to cash out one of his units at the end of 2006 (assume the fund would purchase the unit back for its appraisal-based value as of the end of 2006).

a. Calculate the investor's IRR.

b. Why is this IRR higher than that calculated in the previous question, and also higher than the mean period-by-period return to the fund over the 2005–2007 period?

    c. Why is the time-weighted HPR a better measure for judging the performance of the fund, and the IRR a better measure for judging the performance of the investor in this case?

    d. Under what conditions would the IRR not be a fair measure of the investment decision maker's ex post performance?

9.15. Consider two assets: an apartment building in town and a raw land parcel on the fringe of the metropolitan area. Assume the raw land produces no income but owes 1% of its value per year in property taxes, while the apartment has a current yield (cap rate) of 8%. Assume also that the value of the raw land is more risky than that of the apartment building. Which of these two assets is likely to have a higher appreciation return component? Why? Now prove (using simple algebra and basic investment economic logic) that the raw land must have an ex ante expected appreciation rate at least 9% greater than that of the apartment building. [Hint: Use your answer to Question 9.6.]

9.16. Using the standard deviation, quantify the risk in a property investment whose total return one year from now will be either +20% or −5%, with equal probability. What is the mean or expected return?

Altshuler, D. and C. A. Magni. 2011. Why IRR is not the rate of return for your investment: Introducing the AIRR to the real estate community. Working paper presented to the NCREIF Research Committee, July 2011.

Bank Administration Institute. 1968. *Measuring the Investment Performance of Pension Funds for the Purpose of Inter-Fund Comparison.* Park Ridge, IL: Bank Administration Institute.

Brealey, R. and S. Myers. 1996. *Principles of Corporate Finance,* 5th ed., ch. 3. New York: McGraw-Hill.

Ciochetti, B. A. and K. Vandell. 1999. The performance of commercial mortgages. *Real Estate Economics* 27(1): 27–62.

D'Alessandro, J. 2011. A new measure for the investment management industry: The Time & Money Weighted Return (TMWR). *Journal of Performance Measurement,* 63–74.

Fisher, J., D. Geltner, and R. B. Webb. 1994. Value indices of commercial real estate: A comparison of index construction methods. *Journal of Real Estate Finance and Economics* 9(2): 137–164.

Geltner, D. 1993. Estimating market values from appraised values without assuming an efficient market. *Journal of Real Estate Research* 8(3): 325–346.

Geltner, D., R. Graff, and M. Young. 1994. Random disaggregate appraisal error in commercial property: Evidence from the Russell-NCREIF Database. *Journal of Real Estate Research* 9(4): 403–419.

Giliberto, M. 1994a. The inside story on rates of return. *Real Estate Finance* 11(1): 51–55.

Giliberto, M. 1994b. The inside story on rates of return II: Commercial mortgages. *Real Estate Finance* 11(2): 10–13.

Hess, R. and Y. Liang. 2004. Strategies of focus & opportunity. *Prudential Real Estate Investors (U.S.) Research Report, August 2004.*

Holland, S., S. Ott, and T. Riddiough. 1998. Uncertainty and the rate of commercial real estate development. MIT Center for Real Estate Working Paper.

Mahoney, J., J. Murphy, and S. Keogh. 1998. The internal rate of return and institutional performance measurement for real estate portfolios. *Real Estate Finance* 15(2): 63–72.

Miles, M. and N. Tolleson. 1997. A revised look at how real estate compares with other major components of the domestic investment universe. *Real Estate Finance* 14(1).

Peng, R., A. Florance, M. Huang, N. Miller, and K. Case. 2010. An introduction to CoStar repeat-sale price indices. Paper presented to the American Real Estate Society, April 2010.

Quigg, Laura. 1993. Empirical testing of real option-pricing models. *Journal of Finance* 48: 621–639.

Young, M., et al. 1995. Defining commercial property income and appreciation returns for comparability to stock market-based measures. *Real Estate Finance* 12(2): 19–30.

Young, M. and R. Graff. 1995. Real estate is not normal: A fresh look at real estate return distributions. *Journal of Real Estate Finance and Economics* 10(3): 225–260.

REAL ESTATE VALUATION AND INVESTMENT ANALYSIS AT THE MICRO-LEVEL

Part IV continues our presentation of the basic building blocks of real estate investment analysis begun in Part III. In Part IV, we are going to focus very intensely on what we will call the micro-level. To see what we mean by this, consider an analogy between real estate and rain forests. Two types of scientists study rain forests. At the micro-level, biologists study the individual species of plants and animals, learning how they live, reproduce, and evolve over time. At the macro-level, ecologists study the big picture—how all the individual species relate to one another. In Part IV, we are going to be like the biologists, studying how individual real estate assets get their values in the asset market, and how investors may view and evaluate individual deals. From a decision-making perspective, Part IV is about the most fundamental micro-level decision: what properties or projects you should invest in.

The basic plan is as follows. Chapter 10 will present the fundamental concepts and tools of the evaluation of micro-level investment decisions, the basics of risk and return in the context of the analysis of individual investment transactions, projects, and deals. Chapter 11 will cover the nuts and bolts of real estate cash flow proformas, or projections of future expected cash flows generated by real estate assets, and how to discount those cash flows to present value. Chapter 12 will discuss some issues unique to real estate, issues that begin to bridge the micro- and macro-levels, such as the implications of the simultaneous existence of the REIT market and the direct property market for real estate assets. But our focus in Chapter 12 will still be at the micro-level. These are topics that are at the same time advanced because of their subtlety and complexity, yet still basic because of their omnipresence and importance in making rational real estate investment decisions.

THE BASIC IDEA: DCF AND NPV

CHAPTER OUTLINE

LEARNING OBJECTIVES

After reading this chapter, you should understand:

➲ The relationship between investor return expectations and asset prices.

➲ The DCF valuation procedure and how to use it.

➲ The relationship between DCF and ratio shortcut procedures such as direct capitalization.

➲ The NPV investment decision rule (including the hurdle rate).

A t the micro-level of real estate investment activity, the level at which deals are made, the primal question can usually be summed up as, How much is the asset worth? Each side in a potential deal will almost always be willing to "do the deal" at *some* price. So the question boils down to, at *what* price? In other words, how much is the asset worth? What we want to do in this chapter is to answer this question in a way that gives you a solid basis from which you can use your reasoning abilities to deal with the range of situations the real world may present. To do that, we begin with the link to the fundamental investor objectives and concerns we talked about and learned how to quantify in Part III.

10.1 Relation between Return Expectations and Property Values in the Asset Market

Here we are at the beginning of Chapter 10 saying that the focus of the action in the deal is on the asset value. Yet, we just devoted the entirety of Chapter 9 to a description of investment *returns*, and we made a big deal about how earning returns is the objective of investment. Do we have a disconnect here?

Not really. But it is clear that in order to understand fundamentally what is going on at the micro-level in most real estate activity, we need to establish the link between the expectation of returns, which motivates investors, and the prices or values of assets, which is the issue they are most directly grappling with in the day-today business of real estate investment. In essence, this "missing link" can be summed up in the following precept:

The prices investors pay for properties determine their expected returns, because the future cash flow the properties can yield is independent of the prices investors pay today for the properties.

To make this point more concrete, consider the following simplified example. Suppose it is reasonable to expect that a certain property can produce in the upcoming year a net rental income of $10,000 and will be worth $105,000 at the end of the year. Then, if we pay $100,000 for the property today, our expected total return at the time of the purchase is 15 percent. This is determined as the $10,000 rent plus the $5,000 capital gain ($105,000 less the $100,000 price we paid), expressed as a fraction of the amount invested (i.e., the price we paid). On the other hand, if we pay $105,000 today, the expected return is only 9.52 percent ($10,000, plus no capital gain, divided by the $105,000 investment amount). If we could get the property today for $95,000, our expected return would be 21.05 percent over the coming year ($10,000 rent, plus $10,000 gain in investment value from $95,000 to $105,000, as a fraction of the $95,000 initial investment).

Thus, the expected return is inversely related to the price of the asset, because the expected future cash flows from the asset (including the resale) *remain the same*, no matter how much you pay today for the asset. They remain the same *because they are determined by factors that are independent of how much you pay today for the asset.* Future rents are determined by supply and demand in the space market. The resale price you can reasonably expect is determined by the future rents the next buyer can expect going forward and by the opportunity cost of capital (the next buyer's required expected return) at the time of your resale. Neither of these factors—neither the equilibrium in the space market nor that in the capital market—is influenced by the price you pay today for the property.

Don't play the "Greater Fool."

In the classroom, this precept may seem terribly elementary and obvious. Students never argue against it when we teach it in an academic environment. But out there in the real world, a kind of "fog of war" descends over the field of the deal-making battle. There is often pressure to close a deal, and that makes participants susceptible to wishful thinking. The seller won't budge below $10 million. I know the first year's income will be $1 million, and I know my fund's target return is 12 percent, so it must be reasonable to expect that the property will be worth $10,200,000 a year from now (as that will give me the 12 percent return).

This type of reasoning is so tempting, and so easy to slip into in the heat of battle, that it is not at all uncommon. Indeed, it is sometimes even put forth as an explicit principle of real estate investment, known as the **Greater Fool Theory**. According to this theory, you don't need to worry about paying too much for a property because, even if you have been foolish and paid too much, it is unlikely that you are the stupidest person in the market. Thus, you can always count on finding a greater fool who will pay at least that much again and rescue your ex post return!

In truth, we cannot deny that it may sometimes be possible to "luck out" in this manner. But if you have gone to the trouble to get this far in this book, then you probably already agree with us that the Greater Fool Theory is hardly a sound systematic basis on which to make good real estate investment decisions.[1]

Apart from its hazards at the individual level, widespread application of the Greater Fool Theory would lead, by definition, to a disconnection between asset prices and the underlying fundamental cash flow generation potential of those assets. Such a disconnection is the definition of an asset price "bubble," in which prices grow over time only because each buyer expects such growth, unrelated to the underlying physical productive potential of the assets. Most finance students have heard about the famous Tulip Bulb Bubble in seventeenth-century Holland, in which the equivalent of hundreds of thousands of dollars were paid for single tulip bulbs. Closer to hand, many practitioners regard the pricing many real estate assets attained during 2007 as reflecting some sort of bubble. Of course, bubbles have a tendency to burst. When they do, it is the practitioners of Greater-Fool-Theory investing who get burned, who prove themselves to have been the greatest fools after all.

10.2 Discounted Cash Flow Valuation Procedure

Remembering the fundamental link between asset prices and returns, based on underlying operating cash flow potential as described in section 10.1, can help prevent you from becoming the latest victim of the real estate market's famous boom and bust cycles. To apply this pricing principle in practice, the basic investment valuation framework known as multiperiod **discounted cash flow** valuation (or just **DCF** for short) has gained wide acceptance in recent decades, both in academic circles and in professional practice.

DCF is probably the single most important quantification procedure in micro-level real estate investment analysis. In essence, the procedure consists of three steps:

1. Forecast the expected future cash flows.
2. Ascertain the required total return.
3. Discount the cash flows to present value at the required rate of return.

Mathematically, these three steps can be summarized in the following equation, letting V represent the value of the property today:

$$V = \frac{E_0[CF_1]}{1 + E_0[r]} + \frac{E_0[CF_2]}{(1 + E_0[r])^2} + \cdots + \frac{E_0[CF_{T-1}]}{(1 + E_0[r])^{T-1}} + \frac{E_0[CF_T]}{(1 + E_0[r])^T} \tag{1}$$

where: CF_t = Net cash flow generated by the property in period t

$E_0[r]$ = Expected average multiperiod return (per period) as of time zero (the present), the **opportunity cost of capital (OCC)** for this investment, expressed as the **going-in IRR**[2]

---

[1] We will refine this point in Chapter 12. Uncertainty surrounding exactly how much any real estate asset is worth can make it rational for a subsequent buyer to indeed be influenced to some extent by what the previous price was. And there is growing evidence in the field of "behavioral economics" that even seasoned and professional business people are psychologically prone to make systematic mistakes, such as "anchoring" value estimates onto prior prices. But this does not change the fundamental rationality and sensibleness of the principle enunciated here that it is best to base value estimation primarily on the asset's objective capability to generate operating net cash flow.

[2] Note the similarity in form between equation (1) and the equation that defined the internal rate of return (IRR), equation (8) in Chapter 9. Thus, the IRR is indeed the type of return measure that is usually used in DCF analysis.

$T =$ The terminal period in the expected investment holding period, such that CF_T would include the resale value of the property at that time, in addition to normal operating cash flow

To clarify the basic mechanics of this procedure, consider the following simple numerical example. The subject property is an office building with a single lease. Suppose the present time is the end of the year 2013. The building has a six-year net lease that provides the owner with $1,000,000 at the end of each year for the next three years (2014, 2015, 2016).[3] After that, the rent steps up to $1,500,000 for the following three years (2017 through 2019), according to the lease. At the end of the sixth year (2019), the property can be expected to be sold for ten times its then-current rent, or $15,000,000. Thus, the investment is expected to yield $1,000,000 in each of its first three years, $1,500,000 in each of the next two years, and finally $16,500,000 in the sixth year (consisting of the $1,500,000 rental payment plus the $15,000,000 "reversion" or sale proceeds). In this way, we have quantified an *expectation* of the multiperiod future cash flow stream this property can generate.

Now suppose that, after considering the relative risk and current expected returns of real estate versus stocks and bonds, and of this particular office building versus other types of real estate, you figure that 8 percent per year would be a reasonable expected average total return (the "going-in IRR") for an investment in this property. In other words, 8 percent is the opportunity cost of capital (OCC) for this property, what you could expect to earn from other investments of similar risk to this building. Then the value of the property is found by applying the DCF formula (1) as follows:

$$15,098,000 = \frac{1,000,000}{(1.08)} + \frac{1,000,000}{(1.08)^2} + \frac{1,000,000}{(1.08)^3} + \frac{1,500,000}{(1.08)^4}$$
$$+ \frac{1,500,000}{(1.08)^5} + \frac{16,500,000}{(1.08)^6}$$

We see that the estimated market value of the property is $15,098,000 as of the present time (year 2013). This price will yield an expected average total return of 8 percent for the buyer. If the price were less than this, say, $14 million, the buyer would get an ex ante (going-in) return greater than 8 percent (namely, 9.6 percent at the $14 million price, computed as the IRR on the $14 million investment, assuming the given expected future cash flow stream). This would be a better deal for the buyer but a bad deal for the seller, assuming the 8 percent going-in IRR well reflects capital market expectations for returns on this type of investment. If the price were greater than the indicated value, say, $16 million, then the expected return for the buyer would be less than 8 percent, indeed only 6.8 percent at the $16 million price, and this would presumably be a bad deal for the buyer and a good deal for the seller.

With the basic idea of the DCF procedure in mind, let us spend a little time refining your understanding of how to apply this procedure to real estate, and honing your ability to use this tool in a practical way.

10.2.1 Match the Discount Rate to the Risk: Intralease and Interlease Discount Rates

In the DCF valuation procedure, the discount rate serves to convert future dollars into their present value equivalents. This requires accounting for both the time value of money and the risk in the expected future cash flows. Recall from Chapter 9 that the total return (which we labeled r) can be broken into a risk-free interest component and a risk premium component: $r = rf + RP$. The risk-free interest rate component accounts for the time value of money, and

---

[3]A net lease is one in which the tenants pay the operating expenses of the building, so in this example we will assume the rent equals the net cash flow to the landlord. Note more generally that the cash flow for each period is the *net* difference between any cash flowing from the investment to the investor, minus any cash flowing from the investor to the investment.

Year	1	2	3	4	5	6	7	8	9	10
CF_t	$1	$1	$1	$1.5	$1.5	$1.5	$2	$2	$2	$22

EXHIBIT 10-1 Hypothetical Office Building Net Cash Flows

© OnCourse Learning

the risk premium component accounts for the risk.[4] This means that a higher discount rate should be applied to more risky cash flows, because such cash flows effectively have a higher cost of capital in the asset markets.[5]

An important application of this principle to commercial property investment analysis relates to properties with long-term leases, in particular, many office and industrial buildings in the United States. Cash flows within signed leases are fixed contractual obligations of the lessee (tenant), and therefore do not subject the landlord to rental market risk (except in the case of tenant default). Such projected cash flows should thus normally be discounted at a lower rate within the lease (that is, subsequent to the signing of the lease). The relatively low discount rate used to convert cash flows across time *within* leases may be referred to as the **intralease discount rate**. Conversion of projected future cash flows or values to present value across time prior to when the future values are contractually fixed would be made using a higher **interlease discount rate** that reflects the property's rental market risk. The interlease discount rate would normally apply to determine the present value both of the future long-term leases not yet signed (discounted to present from the time of their projected future signing), as well as of the residual or **reversion cash flows** representing projected proceeds from future resale of the property.

To clarify this point, let us extend our previous numerical example of the office building. When applying DCF analysis in the real world of commercial property analysis, it is more common to use a ten-year projection of future cash flows than the six-year projection we used before. Suppose that the existing net lease in the building expires at the end of the sixth year, but we wish to do a ten-year DCF valuation. Suppose further that our expectation as of today about the net rent this property can earn for the four years following expiration of the existing lease (years 7 through 10) is $2 million per year and that we expect the property would sell at the end of year 10 for $20 million. Thus, the ten-year expected cash flow projection for this property is given by the table in Exhibit 10-1.

The first six of these annual cash flows are relatively low risk because they are already contracted for with an existing tenant. The last four cash flows, corresponding to years 7 through 10, reflect our expectations about the most likely annual rent that would be signed at the end of year 6 (beginning of year 7) for a *multiyear lease beginning at that time*. Once that lease is signed, the risk within the years covered by the lease will be low, like the risk in the first six cash flows.

Because of this, the four annual $2 million expected cash flows from the second lease, covering years 7 through 10, should in principle be discounted at the low intralease discount rate back to a "future present value" as of the beginning of year 7 (the time the second lease is expected to be signed, six years from now). Once the "future present value" of the second lease is calculated as of its signing, then this amount should be discounted back to time zero at the higher interlease discount rate.

---

[4]Implicitly if not explicitly, classical financial economics bases the DCF asset valuation model on the existence of a "twin asset," or "replicating portfolio," whose payoffs will be identical to the subject investment in all possible future states of the world, and this replicating portfolio is traded in the capital market at a current price that reflects an expected return of $E[r]$. Hence, $E[r]$ is the OCC for the subject investment.

[5]Note that it is not necessary to use a larger discount rate merely because a risky cash flow will be received further in the future. The discounting process itself accounts for the fact that risk compounds over time. The risk premium in the discount rate should reflect the amount of risk per unit of time. (See also the presentation of the certainty equivalence discounting method in Appendix 10C on the CD accompanying this book.)

With this more sophisticated perspective, assuming the OCC relevant for the intralease discount rate is 7 percent, and the interlease rate is 9 percent, we arrive at a present value of $18,325,000 as our value estimation for our office property, as follows:[6]

$$\$18{,}325{,}000 = \sum_{t=1}^{3} \frac{\$1}{(1.07)^t} + \sum_{t=4}^{6} \frac{\$1.5}{(1.07)^t} + \left(\frac{1}{(1.09)^6}\right)\left(\sum_{t=1}^{4} \frac{\$2}{(1.07)^t}\right) + \frac{\$20}{(1.09)^{10}}$$

10.2.2 Blended IRR: A Single Discount Rate

At this point, we should pause and point out that the matching of discount rates to cash flows is not always done in current practice. It is more typical to apply a single blended OCC to all the property's projected net cash flow. In part, this may be due to laziness on the part of practitioners. But there is often some justification for this practice. For one thing, many buildings with long-term leases have many different spaces all with leases that expire at different times. It gets quite tedious and time consuming to rigorously apply the approach described in the preceding section.

Another consideration is that it is often not precisely clear what the different discount rates should be. For one thing, property net cash flows may not be entirely fixed even during periods covered by leases. The leases may be "gross leases" that only fix the rental revenue, leaving the landlord exposed to risk in the operating expenses of the property. Or the leases may include percentage rents or indexed rent which will vary according to future contingencies. And there may be some risk of tenant default. Uncertainty over the correct discount rates takes some of the motivation out of the desire to be methodologically correct. Finally, if a property has a pattern of lease expirations over time that is typical for buildings of its type, then one may apply a single **blended IRR** rate as a legitimate shortcut. The legitimacy of this shortcut depends on the rate having been derived from observation of the values of buildings similar to the subject property, so that the blended rate indeed represents the opportunity cost of capital, the expected return on investments of comparable risk.

To see how this works, let's return to our numerical example. We can compute a single blended rate of return that discounts the ten expected future cash flows in Exhibit 10-1 to the "correct" present value of $18,325,000, simply by computing the IRR for this cash flow stream. The IRR is 8.57 percent. If our building were typical of a class of similar buildings regarding the time and risk pattern of its lease expirations and cash flows, then we would tend to observe a blended rate of around 8.5 percent being widely applied in the market, as a shortcut to value buildings such as ours, using the DCF procedure. We could then take that blended rate observed in the market and apply it to our building's projected future cash flows to arrive at the same value estimation of $18,325,000, as follows:

$$\$18{,}325{,}000 = \sum_{t=1}^{3} \frac{\$1}{(1.0857)^t} + \sum_{t=4}^{6} \frac{\$1.5}{(1.0857)^t} + \sum_{t=7}^{10} \frac{\$2}{(1.0857)^t} + \frac{\$20}{(1.0857)^{10}}$$

10.2.3 Unbundling Cash Flows: An Example

As noted, the use of separate, explicit interlease and intralease discount rates is not widespread in current DCF valuation practice. We have introduced the concept here partly for pedagogical reasons, to deepen your understanding of the fundamental sources of commercial property value and to build your intuition about how to apply the DCF technique. How precisely it is necessary or possible to match discount rates with different risks in the cash flow components is always a judgment call. In the real world, separate rates are typically used only when special circumstances exist, such as when a building has a long master lease or other atypical lease expiration pattern. However, as the capital markets develop for real estate, it becomes more and more possible to **unbundle** real estate cash flow components and sell

---

[6]A good source to estimate the OCC to determine the appropriate intralease discount rate would typically be the tenant's borrowing rate, the rate at which the tenant could borrow money from a bank or from the bond market, for a loan of similar duration to the lease. A simple approach to estimating the interlease discount rate is presented in Appendix 10B on the CD accompanying this book.

different components in the capital markets.[7] This suggests that differential discounting may become more widespread in property valuation. For example, in the 1990s, securities backed by leases began to be sold in the bond market (these were often called LOBS, for "lease obligation backed securities"), and this trend has grown in recent years as part of the "asset backed security (ABS)" or "structured finance" business. In the modern investment industry, one person's shortcut can be another person's gold mine, and a lost opportunity to the "shortcutter." Consider the following example.

Suppose there is another office building just like the one we valued earlier, except that its existing lease has seven years left on it rather than only six years. In other words, the expected cash flows in this second building are the same as the expected cash flows in the previous building (including a contractual net rent step-up to $2 million in year 7 of the existing lease in the second building). The only difference is the time of lease expiration and therefore the risk in the year 7 cash flow projection. Now suppose the original building is more typical of what prevails in the market, so that a familiarity with the market for these types of buildings would suggest that a blended rate of 8.57 percent would be applicable in a ten-year DCF valuation of the property.

Now we will suppose that the second building, the one with the longer lease, is owned by an old investor by the name of Peter Shortcut. Mr. Shortcut applies the typical blended rate to his building's projected cash flows to arrive at his value estimation of $18,325,000, as in the formulation in the previous section. Mr. Shortcut is now approached by a young whipper-snapper investment ace named Sue Marketwise, who offers Shortcut $18,350,000 for the property. Peter Shortcut snaps up the offer, thinking he's copped a bargain from a young, inexperienced investor. Meanwhile, Ms. Marketwise takes the property and sells the existing lease for $7,083,000 to investors who are glad to accept a 7 percent expected return on these low-risk cash flows, and who therefore compute the value of the lease as follows:

$$\$7,083,000 = \sum_{t=1}^{3} \frac{\$1}{(1.07)^t} + \sum_{t=4}^{6} \frac{\$1.5}{(1.07)^t} + \frac{\$2}{(1.07)^7}$$

Ms. Marketwise then sells the property (subject to the lease assignment) to other Investors, perhaps in an "opportunity fund," who are glad to accept a 9 percent expected return for the rental market and residual value risk (with a 7 percent return on the second lease payments once that lease is signed).[8]

These investors therefore pay Marketwise $11,319,000 for the property, based on the following calculation:

$$\$11,319,000 = \left(\frac{1}{(1.09)^7}\right)\left(\sum_{t=1}^{3} \frac{\$2}{(1.07)^t}\right) \frac{\$20}{(1.09)^{10}}$$

Marketwise realizes $18,402,000 ($7,083,000 + $11,319,000) in total from unbundling and selling the property. Her investment was only $18,350,000. She therefore nets a profit of $52,000. Had Peter Shortcut been less lazy and applied the appropriate risk-adjusted discount rates to his property's actual projected cash flows, instead of using the blended rate, he would have realized that the property was worth $18,402,000, based on the following calculation:

$$\$18,402,000 = \sum_{t=1}^{3} \frac{\$1}{(1.07)^t} + \sum_{t=4}^{6} \frac{\$1.5}{(1.07)^t} + \frac{\$2}{(1.07)^7} + \left(\frac{1}{(1.09)^7}\right)\left(\sum_{t=1}^{3} \frac{\$2}{(1.07)^t}\right) + \frac{\$20}{(1.09)^{10}}$$

Armed with this knowledge, old Mr. Shortcut might have bargained a bit more shrewdly with Ms. Marketwise and obtained a higher price from her.

---

[7]See, for example, R. Graff (1999).

[8]Opportunity funds are investment vehicles for real estate investors who are seeking higher returns by placing capital into more risky investment opportunities. Such a fund would certainly lever up their investment in this case, to reach a higher target return than 9 percent, but the 9 percent starting point will give them more positive leverage to do this with than the 8 percent return on the complete property. (See Chapter 13 for the definition of "positive leverage.")

10.3 Ratio Valuation Procedures: Direct Capitalization and GIM as Shortcuts

The use of a single blended discount rate in the DCF procedure may be considered a bit of a shortcut. But if you are interested in shortcut valuation techniques, an even *shorter* shortcut is widely used in practice. This is known as **direct capitalization**, which we defined and described way back in Chapter 1. Now that you understand the DCF approach, let's revisit this shortcut and see how it relates to multiperiod analysis.

With direct capitalization, the property's initial year net operating income alone is divided by the cap rate to arrive at an estimate of the property value. The *multiyear cash flow projection is skipped*. As an example, consider again our previous $18,325,000 office property. If this property were typical of a class of similar properties whose current income and sales prices could be observed easily in the market, then we would tend to observe cap rates for sales of such properties around 5.46 percent, as this is our property's first year net income divided by its current value (1/18.325 = 5.46%). Thus, we could estimate our property's value by inverting this equation, dividing the $1 million initial year's income by 0.0546, a shortcut to arrive at our value estimate of $18,325,000.

Another shortcut valuation procedure is to apply the **gross income multiplier (GIM)** to the gross income of the property rather than applying the cap rate to the net income.[9] The GIM is particularly useful for valuing small properties where one can estimate the gross revenue with relative ease and reliability, based simply on observation of the prevailing gross rents in the relevant space market, combined with knowledge about the size and rentable space in the subject building. Information on the building's operating expenses and, hence, net income, may be more difficult to obtain, or viewed with more suspicion, as its only source may be the current property owner who is trying to sell the building. Both the cap rate and the GIM are examples of **ratio valuation**; in which a single year's income or revenue from the property is multiplied (or divided) by a ratio to arrive at an estimate of the current asset value of the property.

10.3.1 Relationship of the Cap Rate to the Total Return

Shortcut procedures certainly have their place in practice, but as *causal* models of asset value they tend to be simplistic and awkward, or incomplete and sometimes misleading, compared to the multiperiod DCF procedure. For example, even though our example property's value of $18,325,000 may be estimated by the use of, or expressed in terms of, a 5.46 percent cap rate, this does not imply that its value is *caused by* investors' simply wanting an initial current income yield of 5.46 percent. Rather, investors care (or *should* care) about a more complete multiperiod total return perspective on their future investment performance, as represented in the DCF procedure. It is more accurate to think of the longer-term total return perspective represented by DCF as *causing* the property value of $18,325,000. The cap rate of 5.46 percent is then best viewed as merely a reflection of the more fundamental DCF valuation. Don't mistake the reflection for *the real thing!*[10]

---

[9]As an example, suppose that the $18,325,000 property we have been previously talking about charged the tenants in the current lease a *gross* rent of $1,500,000, with $500,000 annual operating expenses, to result in the current net income of $1,000,000. Then this property would have a GIM of $18,325,000/$1,500,000 = 12.2. If this were typical of the market, we could observe this GIM in the marketplace and estimate our building's value by multiplying its current gross income by the GIM.

[10]As an historical aside, the term *cap rate* has its origins in the appraisal profession, where it was originally viewed as something more akin to the discount rate in the multiperiod DCF, hence, the term *capitalization rate*. In the days before personal computers, appraisers needed a mathematical shortcut to collapse the multiperiod problem into a simple calculation. In effect, ways were devised to calculate cap rates so they would equate to a full-blown multiperiod DCF valuation, with some regularity assumptions. A famous and widely used example was the Ellwood Formula. In this traditional appraisal use, cap rates were indeed viewed as causal, determining the market values of properties given their initial (or stabilized) NOIs. More commonly nowadays, even appraisers simply observe cap rates empirically in the marketplace, by observing property NOIs and transaction prices. As such, cap rates clearly are caused by market value, rather than themselves causing value, especially in a world in which PCs make solving the explicit multiperiod problem very easy for anyone to do.

Year	1	2	3	4	5	6	7	8	9	10
A	$1.000	$1.000	$1.000	$1.000	$1.000	$1.000	$1.000	$1.000	$1.000	$15.286
B	$1.000	$1.020	$1.040	$1.061	$1.082	$1.104	$1.126	$1.149	$1.172	$25.582

EXHIBIT 10-2 Annual Net Cash Flow Projections for Two Identical-Risk Buildings ($ millions)

© OnCourse Learning

For example, consider the two buildings whose ten-year future expected cash flows (including resale) are portrayed in the table in Exhibit 10-2. Building A and building B both have the same current net annual cash flow of $1 million, and we will assume that they both have the same risk. Should they both be valued using the same cap rate? As their current incomes are the same, this would imply that the two buildings have the same current value. But surely no investor would be foolish enough to pay the same price for these two buildings. Any rational investor would be willing to pay more for building B because its future cash flows are expected to grow more than building A's. But how much more would you pay for B than for A? In order to answer this question, you would undoubtedly prefer to consider your expected *total* return and to apply a multiyear DCF valuation.

Since these two buildings have identical risk, investors would require the same expected total return, $E[r]$, for each building. Suppose this required return is 7 percent per year. Then applying the multiyear DCF formula (1) tells us that building A is worth $14,286,000, while building B is worth $20,000,000. In other words, building A has a cap rate of 7 percent while building B has a cap rate of 5 percent. This is fundamentally because the investor requires a 7 percent total return for the multiperiod investment, given the amount of risk involved. Thus, both buildings' values, and hence their cap rates, are determined by application of the multiperiod procedure.

This example also points out the relationship among the cap rate, the expected long-term growth rate in the building's cash flow and value, and the investor's required total return. The two buildings in Exhibit 10-2 happen to be perfect examples of constant-growth perpetuities with constant valuation multiples, where the cash flows grow at a constant rate (2 percent in the case of building B) and the asset value is always a constant multiple of the current cash flow. Recall from Chapter 9 that this corresponds to the regularity assumptions in which the IRR equates to the time-weighted average total return, which can be broken down exactly into the sum of a current yield component and a capital gain or growth component. In other words, Exhibit 10-2 corresponds to the case in which $V = CF_1/(r - g)$. For building A, $g = 0$ percent, so its value is $V_0^A = \$1/0.07 = \$14.286$ million. For building B, $g = 2$ percent, so its value is $V_0^B = \$1/(0.07 - 0.02) = \$1/0.05 = \$20$ million. The cap rate in both cases is given by the current yield component of the total return: $y = r - g$.

Real world buildings do not exactly match the regularity assumptions of the constant-multiple, constant-growth perpetuity, although they often come close, making this a decent model to build intuition about property value. Thus, the model of the cap rate as approximately equaling the investor's required total return less the expected long-run growth rate (in both income and property value) is useful as a basic conceptualization. We applied this model in Chapter 1 when we presented the cap rate as being largely determined by three factors: interest rates, expected growth, and risk. Expanding the previous model of the cap rate, using the breakdown of r described in Chapter 9, we see that $y = r - g = rf + RP - g$, where rf is the risk-free interest rate and RP is the risk premium in the required total return.

This relationship holds both in nominal and in real terms, at least as a close approximation for many buildings. Expected inflation is a component of both the expected total return (r) and the expected growth rate (g). Thus, inflation largely cancels out in the $r - g$ formula. This model therefore suggests that cap rates, or property price/income multiples, should be relatively insensitive to changes in inflation expectations. This relates to the fact noted in Chapter 7 that real estate is generally perceived as a good hedge against inflation risk.

Note that there is a case in which the cap rate and the total return discount rate in the DCF are indeed the same: when $g = 0$, that is, when the building is expected to have essentially level nominal cash flows and level nominal value. This situation will be widespread, at least as an approximation, when the inflation rate approximately equals the real annual rate at which buildings depreciate.[11]

10.3.2 Empirical Cap Rates and Market Values

If the cap rate is not by itself the fundamental determinant of property value, it is nevertheless quite useful as a way of measuring empirically observed property prices in the real estate asset market. Similar to the way bond prices are quoted as yields, real estate asset prices are often quoted as **empirical cap rates**.

When used to infer or estimate the value of a specific subject property, the cap rate is, in effect, a way of quoting the price of the property as its value per dollar of current income, except that the inverse of this ratio is used. Viewed from this perspective, the direct capitalization procedure is just a way to translate the observable net income of a subject property into its current expected market value, under the prevailing conditions in the real estate market, with no fundamental causality implied. While this approach is quite handy and very widely employed, two dangers must be kept in mind, both due to the skipping of the explicit multiyear cash flow forecast for the subject property.

First, buildings may appear superficially similar, yet have different long-run future cash flow forecasts in relation to their current income. We saw this in our previous example of building A and building B. The cap rate that is empirically observed in the marketplace must be taken from buildings that are similar to the subject property not only regarding risk, but also regarding the occupancy and rental growth expectations, lease histories and expiration patterns, and need for capital improvement expenditures. One property may be dominated by leases that were signed five years ago and are about to expire, while the similar property that sold last month across the street has all new leases. In short, anything that could cause the DCF valuation to differ between the subject building and the buildings whose cap rates are observed in the market could cause direct capitalization to be misleading as a method of valuing the subject property.

Another consideration is that by allowing the investor to skip the multiyear forecast of operating cash flows, direct capitalization exposes the investor to greater danger of being swept up in an asset market pricing bubble. In a bubble, asset market prices get disconnected from realistic consideration of the underlying ability of the assets to generate operating cash flow over the long run. If direct capitalization simply divides current income by the ratio of current income to price in the existing market, it will yield implied asset values that simply reflect any current bubble in the market. Recall that part of the benefit of the DCF procedure lies precisely in forcing the analyst to go through the exercise of thinking realistically about the property's fundamental ability to generate net cash flow from its operation over the *long-term* future.[12]

---

[11]The real depreciation rate of built property in the United States is typically 1 percent to 2 percent per year, largely due to aging and obsolescence of the built structure. The factors determining the growth rate in land or location value were discussed in Part II. Care must also be taken regarding how the cap rate is measured. As noted in Chapter 9, the cap rate is often measured as NOI/V, without subtracting realistic long-run capital expenditure requirements from the NOI. This will overstate the cap rate defined strictly as the net cash flow yield (y).

[12]This danger in direct capitalization is related to the difference between market value and investment value. These differing concepts for valuing real estate assets will be discussed in Chapter 12. For now it suffices to recognize that direct capitalization based on empirically observed market prices, when applied correctly, yields an estimate of the property's market value. This value may differ from the investment value the property would have to a given investor who would hold the property for a long time without selling it in the property market. To quantify investment value, a long-term approach such as DCF is necessary. In most cases, however, the two concepts of value should be approximately the same, as market values should reflect investment values, which in turn reflect the long-term DCF perspective.

10.4 Typical Mistakes in DCF Application to Commercial Property

Students and practitioners should be aware of a few mistakes or peculiarities in the way the DCF method is often applied to commercial real estate. Generally, the mechanics of the DCF procedure are carried out correctly (that is, the "math all adds up"). But all too often there is a **GIGO** problem. This stands for "Garbage In, Garbage Out." The point is, a valuation result can be no better than the quality of the cash flow and discount rate assumptions that go into the right-hand side of the DCF valuation formula (1).

If one is trying to use the DCF to come up with a realistic and unbiased estimate of property value, then the forecasted cash flows and the required return should be *realistic* expectations, neither optimistic nor pessimistic. In principle, the cash flow forecast should come from a careful examination of the space market in which the property is situated, as described in Parts I and II of this book, as well as consideration of the existing leases and vacant space in the building. The required return (the **discount rate**) should generally be found by considering the capital markets, including the likely total returns and risks offered by other types of investments competing for the investor's dollar. The required expected total return ($E[r]$), serving as the discount rate, should be thought of as the opportunity cost of capital and should represent the going-in IRR investors could expect from alternative investments of similar risk. In practice, time and resource limitations will often prevent in-depth, formal analysis of these inputs. But why would one use unrealistic or biased numbers, given the available and relevant public information? Let us briefly consider three types of GIGO mistakes that are prevalent in the application of DCF to commercial real estate. The first is intentional misleading, the second is excessive laziness, and the third is a (perhaps more forgivable) failure to pay sufficient respect to the cyclical tendency of the commercial property asset market.

10.4.1 If Your Case Lacks Merit, Dazzle Them with Numbers

The full-blown DCF procedure might look rather fancy, simply because it involves a lot of numbers and mathematical formulas. The procedure itself can sometimes be used as a smoke screen to draw attention away from the underlying assumptions, or the reasonableness of the input numbers on the right-hand side of the equation. In fact, the correctness of the math can hide biased assumptions aimed, for example, at making the property look better (more valuable) than it really is. Here are some illustrative examples of such assumptions, which either may not be stated explicitly or be hidden in the fine print:

- The existing leases will all renew with 100 percent probability, implying no need to forecast an expected revenue loss from vacancy between leases and no need to forecast needed capital improvement expenditures to retain or attract tenants.
- Inflation is projected at 3 percent per year even though recent inflation experience, and average economic forecasts, has inflation running at barely over 2 percent per year.
- The current market rent applicable for the subject building is based on leases recently signed for other buildings that are nearby but newer than the subject property and which have greater appeal in the space market than the subject property, or the rent projections may be benchmarked on leases either in the subject building itself or other buildings but that contained concessions offered to the tenants at the time of signing that are not reflected in the subject property future cash flow projections.

The point is that it is easy for analysts with a vested interest in one side or the other of a valuation argument to purposely develop their DCF analysis with a view through rose-tinted lenses. The idea is to hide their bias in the sheer mass of numbers and formulas presented in the analysis. The lesson: don't be taken in by this intentional form of GIGO.

10.4.2 Excessive Laziness

A second widespread and implicit form of GIGO in the application of DCF to commercial property occurs when overly simplistic (or downright incorrect) assumptions get taken up into the conventional wisdom and then are applied pretty much as a matter of course in the typical DCF valuation (e.g., We all know cash flows grow with inflation, don't we?). If it would require expensive and time-consuming custom-tailored studies to debunk these assumptions, one could forgive their use in routine work (such as regular appraisal of properties) or in the heat of battle (when the pressure is on to "do a deal"). But in many cases it would take no such expensive or time-consuming studies, just an application of common sense and some basic urban economics (as described in Parts I and II of this book) to improve upon (or debunk) the conventional assumptions.

What is particularly insidious about these types of mistakes is that they could never become widespread or endure so long, except that, in the right-hand side of the DCF valuation formula (1), *the mistakes in the numerators and denominators cancel out!* The result is a reasonably accurate indication of the present value of the property. This is important because in a well-functioning property market, DCF assumptions that give unrealistic present values would be easy to spot as silly assumptions: the implied property values would seem unrealistic (for example, by comparison of the implied subject property cap rate with those of other comparable sales or prevailing market yields).

In essence, here is what goes on in a typical form of conventional-wisdom GIGO. The property net cash flow in the numerators is forecasted either too high on average, or to grow over time at a rate that is unrealistically high. For example, forecasted capital improvement expenditures will be unrealistically low, or the projected resale price may be unrealistically high, or the rent the building can charge will be assumed to grow at the expected rate of general inflation. This last assumption is often easy to pass off as being reasonable, until you realize that it ignores the likely real depreciation of the building as it ages in its life cycle. Such excesses in the cash flow forecasts would lead to obvious overvaluation of the property, except that they are offset by the use of an unrealistically high expected total return as the discount rate in the denominators. For example, 3 percent per year expected growth in rents along with a 10 percent discount rate will typically give about the same property valuation as 1 percent annual growth with an 8 percent discount rate.[13]

So what?, you say. If we get the right present value for the property anyway, then what's the problem? In fact, there are two problems, and both of them are serious. For one thing, investors develop false expectations about returns. The discount rate is the multiperiod expected total return on the investment. If it is unrealistically high, investors are living in a fairy tale world in which they think they are going to get higher returns than they actually will, on average. They may also be misled into expecting greater growth in their capital over time than is in fact realistic. Unrealistic return expectations could cause investors to make incorrect allocations of capital between alternative types of investments, or to make financing decisions that do not have the effect they think they will.[14]

A second problem is that the use of "fairy tale numbers" undercuts the credibility of the DCF valuation framework. Market participants and analysts lose faith in the ability of DCF to tell them anything useful, because they corrupt it with misinformation. It becomes a "mere proforma" exercise made to satisfy a formality or act as window-dressing. You wouldn't buy a good car and then run it on impure gasoline that will corrode the engine. So, don't use GIGO assumptions on the right-hand side of the DCF valuation equation, even if you can (apparently) get the "right" property valuation. Such a valuation may be "right" only in the sense that it seems consistent with the current property market, as indicated by observed transaction price cap rates. If the market is currently overvalued, this GIGO-based way of using DCF will not protect you from investing at the wrong time. Recall that one reason for using the multiperiod analysis is to provide some check against the possibility of an

---

[13]Recall the constant-growth perpetuity model: $V = CF_1/(r - g)$.

[14]Suppose an investor thinks a property presents an expected return of 10 percent, and the investor can take out a long-term mortgage on the property at an 8 percent interest rate. One reason the investor might be interested in the mortgage is because he believes he will have "positive leverage," due to the 200 basis-point spread between the expected return on the underlying property and the contractual cost of the debt. But if the realistic expected return on the property is only 8 percent instead of 10 percent (reflecting more realistic cash flow growth assumptions), then the positive-leverage argument is either not realistic or greatly exaggerated. (The issue of positive leverage will be discussed further in Chapters 13 and 19.)

overheated asset market that is likely to suffer a correction or fall back in the near- to medium-term future.

10.4.3 Watch Out for the *Cycle*

This brings us to a third major type of mistake in the application of the DCF process. It has not been applied very effectively in the role noted in that last point above: to help prevent investors from overpaying at the peak of the asset market pricing cycle. This is perhaps a much more understandable and forgivable mistake than the other two. After all, in a fully rational world and completely efficient asset market there should not be a predictable asset pricing cycle. Current asset prices should fully incorporate any relevant information, including any predictable future market-wide pricing movements. And until recently there was not enough hard quantitative data about the history of commercial property prices in the United States to say anything very clearly or strongly or quantitatively about the cyclical tendencies in the market. But we don't think this is an excuse any longer (especially for institutional real estate investment). Analysts and investors ought to think very carefully about cycles in making the projections on the right-hand-side of the DCF valuation formula (1). Both space market cycles (in rent and occupancy) and asset market cycles (in cap rates, as relevant for the terminal cap rate or "going-out" cap rate used in the DCF to project the property resale price) should be noted explicitly in the DCF assumptions.

We admit that exactly *how* to account for cycles in the DCF analysis is problematical. Space market cycles vary in duration and amplitude and from market to market. Yet for a given market one can look at the history, try to make some judgment as to whether one is near a peak or a trough in the relevant rental market, and then perform market analyses such as we described in Chapter 6. On the other hand, asset market cycles probably tend to be more nationwide in scope (if not global), due to the fungibility of capital (and the asset market cycle may or may not coincide with a space market cycle or economic business cycle). We have seen in Chapter 7 how the private market asset pricing cycle has at least for the past half century been remarkably regular with a total period of between 15 and 20 years including a down-phase that tends to be quicker and shorter than the up-phase.[15] The asset market cycle should be considered in the DCF when thinking about the projected resale price. The horizon of the cash flow analysis might be reconsidered (perhaps a proforma longer than the conventional ten years should be employed, if the typical asset market cycle is longer than that). And at a more conceptual level, the meaning of the implied DCF valuation should be more carefully and explicitly considered and spelled out, as to whether it relates to current market value or long-term investment value; that is, whether it reflects transient cyclical valuation effects or more purely a long-term sustainable valuation (the terms "market value" and "investment value" in this context will be discussed in Chapter 12).

10.5 Underwriting Haircuts

Apart from the kinds of mistakes described in the previous section, there is another important peculiarity in the way DCF analysis is often employed in the commercial real estate industry. We use the word "peculiarity" rather than the word "mistake," because in haircutting (or "giving the DCF a haircut") the analyst is deliberately making conservative assumptions about the projected future cash flows (that is, projecting such cash flows deliberately "erred on the low side"), rather than trying to make unbiased realistic assumptions. More rarely, the analyst may also (or alternatively) deliberately make a conservative assumption about the discount rate (employing a high hurdle rate). The result, quite intentionally, is to come up with a low estimate of the current value of the property. Low-side estimates of future cash flow may also be an objective in their own right of such "underwriting assumptions" in the proforma.

---

[15]See section 7.3.1 and Exhibit 7-11.

The purpose of this type of deliberate "erring" on the down side is to help to protect against making an investment mistake. It is particularly the province of (and traditionally derives from) the commercial mortgage lending industry. (The process of approving and issues a commercial mortgage is traditionally referred to as "underwriting" the loan.) In the lending industry the investors (those providing the money for the loan) generally want to make a conservative (low-risk) type of investment and as a result are not asking for a very high return in the form of interest payments. And they are generally not in as good a position as the borrower (the equity investor/owner in the property) to know realistically the unbiased expectations for the property's future cash flow and valuation potential. Nor will they have direct control over the operational management of the property. It is natural and appropriate for such investors to want to quantify a conservative perspective on the property value and its future debt servicing capacity (based on its projected operating net cash flow).

While underwriting haircuts are a legitimate and understandable tool and application of DCF, they can raise some problems, primarily because they deliberately seek not to reflect objective, unbiased reality. This can tend to divorce the investment analysis process from rigorous empirically-based and objective information about the property and the market. The analytical process can "float off" in its own world in which it can lose its moorings.

Suppose a lender's "underwriting criteria" call for a projected terminal ("going-out") cap rate (for purpose of projecting future property value on resale or loan maturity) no lower than, say, 9 percent and a discount rate no lower than 10 percent. But suppose the real property market provides actual rates of 7 and 8 percent, respectively (i.e., the underwriting criteria are conservative, as they are meant to be). Then, other things being equal (in particular, the property's projected cash flows), the underwriting assumptions will imply property value below the current market value. Yet the borrower must pay the market value for the property, and is in the market for a loan to help finance that purchase. The lender is, after all, in the lending business; lenders make money from lending, not from not lending. You can see the pressure to ignore the underwriting criteria. And since those criteria are not based in the current property market reality anyway, it is hard not to ignore them! If company rules prevent them from being ignored, then something has got to give. The easiest thing to give might be the cash flow projection in the DCF right-hand-side numerators. The loan will still "pencil out" if the projected cash flows are high enough. And those projections are only estimates anyway. Who is to say the property rents won't grow with inflation (sounds reasonable, after all)? Who is to say the required capital improvement expenditures won't end up being minimal after all?

You see where we're headed. The underwriting haircut, originally intended to protect the investor from making a bad investment, is starting to simply aid and abet the types of mistakes we described in the previous section: mistakes that actually tend to support careless or sloppy investment or excessive payment for property.

We don't want to imply that underwriting haircuts are a mistake. They certainly have their usefulness. But they need to be carefully and diligently applied, not with complacency, and not in the absence of rigorous realistic objective analysis of the property and the market. Lenders cannot force the market to be as conservative as they might like it to be, but they can operate with transparency and with more explicit knowledge and statement of what the realistic return expectations and risks are. If such knowledge and transparency permeates throughout the system, the industry may be less prone to damaging cycles than it has been in the past.

10.6 Capital Budgeting and the NPV Investment Decision Rule

The DCF valuation procedure described in the preceding sections can be combined naturally with a very simple and intuitive investment decision rule known as the **net present value** (or **NPV**) rule.

In this section, we will consider in some depth the application of the NPV rule to commercial real estate investment decisions. Let's begin by making sure we have a clear definition of what is meant by this decision rule. The NPV of an investment project or a deal is defined as the present dollar value of what is being obtained (the benefit) minus the present dollar value of what is being given up (the cost).[16]

For example, recall once again the office building described in section 10.2 that was worth $18,325,000. If the present owner offered the property for sale at $15 million, then from the seller's perspective the NPV of the deal would be $3,325,000. This is computed as the $15 million cash that would be received in the present from the sale (the benefit of the deal for the seller) minus the $18,325,000 present value of the asset, which is being given up in the sale (the cost of the deal to the seller). From the buyer's perspective, the NPV would be exactly the opposite, + $3,325,000, as the $15 million sale price is what is given up, and the property worth $18,325,000 is obtained from the deal.

To make good micro-level investment decisions, here is what the NPV rule says to do:

NPV Investment Decision Rule

1. Maximize the NPV across all mutually exclusive alternatives.
2. Never choose an alternative that has: NPV < 0.

Following this rule, combined with careful (*realistic*) application of the DCF valuation procedure (avoiding the GIGO mistakes) would protect the seller in the previous example from making the mistake of offering the property for sale for $15 million. It would also clarify and quantify the value of the deal from the buyer's perspective.[17] The first part of the rule would help the potential buyer to choose, for example, between two mutually exclusive investments in which, say, the other alternative was a project worth $2 million whose cost was $1 million. It would make more sense to buy the $18,325,000 property at $15 million (NPV = +$3,325,000) than the $2 million property at $1 million (NPV = +$1,000,000), provided one has to choose between these two.[18]

The beauty of the NPV rule lies in its elegance, simplicity and intuitive appeal. The power of the NPV rule derives from the fact that it is based directly on the fundamental **wealth maximization** principle. In effect, the NPV rule says nothing more, and nothing less, than "Maximize your wealth." The corollary to this is that any rule other than the NPV rule will violate the wealth maximization principle. In effect, if you do not follow the NPV rule, you will be "leaving money on the table." This is expressed symbolically here:

Wealth Maximization → *NPV rule*

To clarify the link between the DCF valuation procedure and the NPV decision rule, it may be helpful to express the NPV for the typical commercial property investment decision as follows:

$$\begin{array}{l} \text{If buying}: \ NPV = V - P \\ \text{If selling}: \ NPV = P - V \end{array}$$

---

[16]In the public sector, this type of analysis is often referred to as benefit-cost analysis. The idea is the same, only the benefits and costs are measured in terms of their social values rather than private wealth.

[17]The second part of the rule (never choose investments that have NPV < 0) is actually encompassed in the first part of the rule. It is virtually always possible to do something with NPV = 0 no matter how much money you have available to invest (including the possibility of "doing nothing," e.g., buying Treasury bills), so that there is practically always a zero-NPV alternative that is mutually exclusive to any investment. Hence, maximizing the NPV across mutually exclusive alternatives logically implies never doing a deal with NPV < 0.

[18]Note that this is in spite of the fact that the second project offers a 100 percent "profitability ratio" while the first project only offers a 22.2 percent "profitability ratio." Remember, the two projects here are *mutually exclusive*: you have to do one *or* the other; you cannot do both. This type of absolute mutual exclusivity arises, for example, between two alternative ways to develop the same land parcel, or between developing the land today versus waiting and developing it next year. With this absolute type of mutual exclusivity, the wisdom of the NPV rule is obvious: would you rather have $3,325,000 or $1,000,000? But hold on, you say, the first project uses up $15,000,000 of my capital; the second project only $1,000,000, leaving me with $14,000,000 more still available to invest. You may have a good point there, for example, if you face a rigid capital availability constraint and have other positive NPV opportunities available, or if the flexibility provided by retaining more liquidity would be valuable. Considerations such as these can be difficult to quantify. The NPV Rule is best when comparing alternatives that are not too different in scale and nature. As always, reason and common sense must be given the last word.

Where: V = Value of property at time zero (e.g., based on DCF)

P = Selling price of property (in time-zero equivalent \$)

This makes it easy to see that the NPV rule is simply saying that you should maximize the value of what you are getting minus the value of what you are giving up, assuming these values are computed in an "apples versus apples" manner, adjusting for time and risk. The role of the DCF procedure is to make the necessary adjustment for time and risk.

10.6.1 NPV Rule Corollary: Zero-NPV Deals Are OK

The following corollary to the NPV decision rule is often overlooked in practice:

Zero-NPV deals are OK!

A deal does not have to have a large positive NPV to make sense. Zero-NPV deals are not zero-profit deals, in the sense that, if the discount rate accurately reflects the opportunity cost of capital, it includes the necessary expected return on the investment. This return is the normal amount of "profit" that would be required for an investment of this nature. Zero NPV simply means that there is not supernormal profit expected. A zero-NPV deal is only "bad" if it is mutually exclusive with another deal that has a positive NPV.

Related to this point, notice that, if the NPV is defined on the basis of the *market value* of the asset in question, then the NPV on one side of the deal (e.g., that of the seller) is just the negative (or opposite sign) of the NPV on the other side of the deal (e.g., that of the buyer). **Market value**, which we will label *MV* for short, is by definition *the price at which the property is expected to sell in the current asset market*. This is therefore also the price a buyer must expect to pay to obtain the property. Thus, from this perspective:

$$NPV(Buyer) = V - P = MV - P$$
$$NPV(Seller) = P - V = P - MV = -NPV(Buyer)$$

Now if both the buyer and the seller are applying the NPV rule, then they both require $NPV \geq 0$. But as we saw in the earlier equations, this requirement can only be satisfied simultaneously on both sides of the deal if $NPV = 0$. That is

(i) $NPV(Buyer) \geq 0 \rightarrow -NPV(Seller) \geq 0 \rightarrow NPV(Seller) \leq 0$

(ii) $NPV(Seller) \geq 0 \rightarrow -NPV(Buyer) \geq 0 \rightarrow NPV(Buyer) \leq 0$

(i) and (ii) together $\rightarrow NPV(Buyer) = NPV(Seller) = 0$

Thus, as long as we are evaluating the NPV on the basis of market values, then a zero NPV is actually what we would expect.

In practice, investment decision makers often only like to do deals that appear to have a substantial positive NPV. This desire may not be very realistic, however, when the deal is evaluated from a market value perspective. The impression of widespread achievement of large positive NPVs may be more illusory than real in typical commercial real estate investing. Fundamentally, this is because real estate assets usually trade in well-functioning markets, where there is plenty of competition among potential buyers and sellers and among different but similar properties.

Several factors may make it appear that real estate investments have large positive NPVs when in actuality they do not. For example, the discount rate or cost of capital may be taken to be the cost of borrowed funds, which is lower than the full opportunity cost of capital because it ignores the higher risk (hence higher required return) equity component. Another common mistake is that cost components are left out of the equation. For example, the investor's own time and resources spent finding the deal and managing the project, or the property ownership responsibility, may be left out of the analysis or not fully priced. In development projects, the true opportunity cost of the land may be ignored in the NPV calculation or included only at its historical cost rather than current market value. Yet the use of the land is clearly an opportunity cost of the development (due to the irreversibility of the construction project), and the value of that opportunity cost is the current market value of the land including the effect of any permitting, assemblage, or improvements the developer has added, which may be considerably greater than the land's historical cost.

The fact that the expected NPV of a typical real estate investment deal is approximately zero has an important practical implication. It suggests that if you analyze a deal and find that it appears to offer a large positive NPV based on market values (relative to the amount of investment involved), then you should first double-check your analysis and information. An apparently large positive NPV would typically imply that either you or the opposite party in the transaction has made a serious mistake. Make sure it is not you![19]

10.6.2 Choosing among Alternative Zero-NPV Investments

How is an investor to decide among alternative deals if they all seem to present an NPV of zero, evaluated honestly? There are two major answers to this question. The first has to do with the difference between "market value" and "investment value." This difference will be discussed in depth in Chapter 12. The point here is that it is possible for NPV to be substantially positive for a given investor for a given deal when evaluated from that investor's personal investment value perspective, even when the assets are priced fairly at market value such that the NPV of the deal is zero from a market value perspective. This normally requires that at least one party on one side of the deal has some unique ability to profit from the real estate that is being traded.

The second way investors may rationally decide among alternatives that have equal (zero) NPVs is similar to the kinds of investment decisions that investors in the stock market must make all the time. In the stock market, it is taken as virtually self-evident that the efficiency of the market gives transactions a zero NPV from a market value perspective. Investors typically have other objectives and constraints besides maximizing NPV, which leads them to select some stocks over others. For example, in real estate, investors may have portfolio objectives, such as to increase exposure to some types of properties or decrease exposure to other types (e.g., for diversification purposes). Or investors may feel that they know more than the market does about the long-term value or worth of a given asset. In real estate, certain investors may feel that they have greater expertise or ability or can operate more efficiently in some real estate markets or in managing certain types of real estate assets. (Recall that, unlike investors in the stock market, investors in the direct property markets can obtain operational control and responsibility of the assets they invest in. This brings both opportunities and potential burdens that must be considered regarding the specific assets available.) Investors may also have target investment amounts and property sizes (this may reflect a desire to minimize administrative costs or overhead of the macro-level investment entity). They may prefer doing business with certain parties, either on the opposite side of the deal or as joint venture partners with them. Another consideration is that, while two alternatives both may realistically present the same (zero) NPV, the *quality* of the information about one of the alternatives may be better, thereby presenting the investor with less uncertainty.[20] All of these provide reasons to choose one available asset over another when they both present equal (zero) NPVs.

Appendix 10A at the end of this chapter also provides a way to parse or "attribute" the expected going-in investment return (IRR) in a manner that may help to distinguish between alternative investments. This can help investors match investment opportunities with their

---

[19]The conditions under which it would be reasonable to expect a large positive NPV are discussed in Chapter 12. An obvious filter that is widely employed in practice is to ascertain how long an apparent bargain has been available in the market. One would not expect substantially positive NPV opportunities, measured on the basis of market value, to wait around very long in a well-functioning market. By definition, such opportunities should get snapped up quickly. If you have found a deal that is abnormally good-looking but has been available for quite a while, your suspicions should rightly be raised. Presumably, a lot of other people have shied away from the deal for some reason. What is the reason? That reason is probably that the deal does not really present an NPV bargain.

[20]"Uncertainty" in this context is not the same thing as "risk." The latter refers to the "known unknowns," the understood possibility of the future turning out to be different from one's prior expectations. The former refers to "unknown unknowns," what you don't even know that you don't know! Risk can at least in principle be quantified and explicitly considered by investors; uncertainty cannot.

CAN SELLERS TAKE ADVANTAGE OF "INSIDE INFORMATION" TO GET POSITIVE NPVS?

Property owners sometimes claim that they know more about a building they have owned for a number of years than any potential buyer could know and that this gives them an information advantage in negotiating a sale price, enabling them to earn a positive NPV in the sale transaction. The problem with this reasoning is that it falls into the well-worn *the-other-guy-is-stupid* thought trap. Sure, a seller knows more about his building. But potential buyers are well aware of their information disadvantage in this regard. They discount the price they are willing to offer accordingly, based on the likely or average level of "unseen problems" for buildings like the subject property. They also build contingencies into the offer and employ their own inspectors of

various types, and they may demand covenants or warranties in the sale. The situation is much like that in the used-car market. "Lemons" are more common in the used-car market than in the car population as a whole. Buyers are aware of this and discount the prices they are willing to pay accordingly, or they require warranties from the seller. Furthermore, with long-lived assets such as real estate, any buyer (or seller) at one point in time will be (or was) a seller (or buyer) of the same property at another point in time. This does not mean that owners are never able to take advantage of their inside information, but it does mean that, on average over the long run, sellers do not earn positive NPVs any more than buyers do.

© OnCourse Learning

---

preferences for different return attributes (e.g., income vs. growth), or with their perception of their strengths and capabilities as asset managers or property operators.

Finally, it should be remembered that, just because the *expected* (and average or typical) NPV of a real estate investment is zero, this does not imply that you can *assume* that the NPV is zero, without doing an honest and conscientious "due diligence" analysis. Real estate assets are not homogeneous securities being traded in highly efficient exchanges where the dissemination of public information and the trading on private information are highly regulated. Both buyers and sellers sometimes make pricing mistakes, and in the direct property markets of real estate investments, the old expression *caveat emptor* still applies to a greater degree than in the securities markets.

10.6.3 Hurdle Rate Version of the Decision Rule

An alternative version of the NPV decision rule—preferred by many decision makers—expresses the decision rule in terms of the investment's expected return (typically a single blended IRR rate) rather than in terms of its NPV. The IRR version of the investment decision rule is as follows:

1. *Maximize the difference between the project's expected IRR and the required return.*
2. *Never do a deal with an expected IRR less than the required return.*

As always, the required return is the total return including a risk premium reflecting the riskiness of the investment, the same as the discount rate that would be used in the DCF valuation of the investment described in section 10.2. This required return is referred to as the **hurdle rate**. The first part of the rule ensures that projects with the highest returns will be selected first. The second part ensures that no projects will be selected that do not at least cover their opportunity cost of capital on an ex ante basis.

In most typical circumstances, the IRR version of the investment decision rule will give the same decision result as the NPV version of the rule. That is, if the investment under consideration passes the NPV test with NPV ≥ 0, then it will also pass the IRR test with IRR $\geq E_0(r)$.[21] However, the two versions of the rule will not necessarily give the same rank-ordering of potential investment projects, and this can be important for decision making if some of the projects are mutually exclusive. Mutual exclusivity occurs if the investor cannot do both projects: implementing one project rules out the possibility of implementing

---

[21]Recall from Chapter 8 that in some circumstances the IRR of an investment cannot be calculated, or is not unique. In such cases, it may be impossible to apply the hurdle rate rule based on the IRR. Modifications of the IRR (such as the financial management rate of return—FMRR) have been promoted to deal with this problem, but such procedures require additional assumptions. The simplest recourse is to apply the NPV rule, as the NPV can always be calculated and will always give the correct answer.

DO INVESTORS USE THE HURDLE RATE RULE INSTEAD OF THE NPV RULE?

Sometimes investors claim that they use the hurdle rate rule instead of the NPV rule. If this is really true, then they are not maximizing their wealth. As successful investors in the long run are, virtually by definition, those who maximize their wealth, it is probably not entirely accurate that these investors use the hurdle rate rule instead of the NPV rule. It is likely that they routinely employ the hurdle rate rule, but in those rare circumstances in which the hurdle rate and NPV rules would give a different answer, the most successful investors probably implicitly apply the NPV rule instead, due to its wealth implications. Although it is intuitive to think in terms of returns, ignoring the NPV can lead to muddled thinking. When you focus uniquely on the return, it is tempting to want to allocate your money to investments that provide the highest return. But this may be unwise if the high-return investments are also of greater risk or prevent you from making larger investments that would actually increase your present wealth more.

the other. A typical situation in which this occurs is with real estate development on a particular parcel of land. Preclusion may also occur if the investor faces an overall constraint on the amount of capital available to invest. The general rule in these cases is that one should select whatever feasible combination of projects has the highest NPV, as this will maximize the wealth of the investor.

If the IRR rule is properly applied, the main source in practice of potential disagreement between the NPV rule and the IRR rule is differences in scale between mutually exclusive projects. For example, consider two mutually exclusive one-year projects, alternative candidates for the same parcel of land, both with a 10 percent hurdle rate (opportunity cost of capital). Project A is a \$15 million investment presenting a 15 percent going-in IRR, while project B is a \$5 million investment presenting a 20 percent going-in IRR. The NPV of project A is:

$$1.15(\$15M)/1.10 - \$15M = \$17.25M/1.10 - \$15M = +\$682,000.$$

The NPV of project B is:

$$1.20(\$5M)/1.10 - \$5M = \$6M/1.10 - \$5M = +\$455,000.$$

In general project A is preferable (wealth maximizing), even though it presents the smaller IRR.[22]

Another consideration is that, even though the IRR rule is usually valid when properly applied, it is not uncommon in practice for the IRR rule to be misapplied, in that investors simply seek the project that presents the highest IRR, without considering possible differences in risk. The NPV rule is less susceptible to this weakness, as it forces an explicit determination of the opportunity cost of capital (the discount rate).

10.7 Chapter Summary

This chapter presented the basic concepts and procedures for commercial property valuation and investment analysis at the micro-level, that is, the level of individual properties or projects. In this chapter, we started with the concept of investment returns from Chapter 9 and related the returns investors are interested in to the asset values they are grappling with in micro-level deals. We presented the multiperiod DCF method as the basic tool in this process, although we also discussed shortcuts in the valuation context such as direct capitalization. Finally, we related asset valuation to investment decision making by considering the NPV rule. The following chapters will elaborate on the basic concepts introduced here.

---

[22]Suppose the investor has a total of \$15 million of equity capital available to invest. With project B, she could still invest \$10 million in Treasury bonds (or in the stock market, for example). With project A, she has blown all her capital. But investments in Treasury bonds (or in stocks) are generally zero NPV, leaving her wealth unchanged. To maximize her wealth, she must put all \$15 million into project A.

Appendix 10A Micro-Level Investment Performance Attribution: Parsing the IRR

One of the salient characteristics of investment in the private property market is that individual assets are typically held by investors for relatively long periods of time. For example, investors typically hold income properties 5 to 10 years. This is due in part to the relatively high transaction costs in buying and selling property. It is also due to the ability and desire of many direct real estate investors to earn investment returns through successful operational management of the properties they invest in, rather than simply from "trading" (that is, buying and selling assets). Real estate, with its long individual asset holding periods, contrasts with investment in the stock market, for example, where so-called "active" portfolio managers often change their positions in individual assets (that is, the stocks of individual firms) much more frequently.

Another feature of real estate assets is that they tend to be "cash cows" compared to the typical stock market investment. This feature interacts with the long holding period to magnify the importance of operational income generation in the overall investment return.

Both of these features, long individual asset holding periods and income-based returns, make the internal rate of return (IRR) typically a more interesting investment-performance measure in real estate than in the stock market. Recall from Chapter 9 that the IRR can be calculated over a long, multiyear holding period for an investment in a given property, and it provides a meaningful quantification of the investment performance of that asset. The IRR thus can be computed either *ex ante* (at the outset of the investment), where it measures *expected* performance, or *ex post* (at the end of a holding period), where it measures the realized return on the investment.

In either use of the IRR, it is sometimes of interest for diagnostic or analytical purposes to break the IRR down into components that add up to the total IRR and represent, formally speaking, different "sources" of the total return. This process is sometimes called "parsing" or "partitioning" the IRR, and it may be viewed as a type of micro-level **performance attribution**, because it attributes the overall investment performance to the components that make up the IRR.[23]

IRR attribution is usually broken down into three components: (1) initial-cash-flow yield (IY), (2) subsequent-cash-flow change (CFC), and (3) yield change (YC, or "valuation change") between the beginning and end of the holding period. IRR attribution is not an exact science, in part because there are interaction effects among the return components, and also because the attribution result is sensitive to the length of the holding period. Nevertheless, micro-level return attribution can provide interesting insights into the source and nature of the overall multiperiod return.

To see how IRR attribution can be done, consider the following simple example. A property is bought at an initial cash yield of 9 percent and held for ten years. Net cash flow generated by the property grows at a rate of 2 percent per year for each year during that holding period, at the end of which the property is (or could be) sold at a yield of 10 percent based on the upcoming (year 11) operating cash flow projection. The cash flows from this ten-year investment are presented in the first three rows of the table in Exhibit 10A-1. The first row is the net operating cash flow (net of capital expenditures); the second row is the capital flow; and the third row is the overall cash flow (the sum of the two previous rows).[24]

The first step in performance attribution is to compute the overall actual IRR and the initial yield. These act as the two reference points on which the cash flow growth

---

[23]Macro-level performance attribution, that is, analysis of the performance of a professional investment manager or of an actively managed portfolio of many individual properties, will be discussed in Chapter 26.

[24]The initial capital outflow of $11.11 million reflects the initial yield of 9 percent. The terminal capital inflow is the proceeds from property resale at a price reflecting the 10 percent yield on the projected year-11 operating cash flow.

Year

	IRRs	0	1	2	3	4	5	6	7	8	9	10	11
(1) Actual Oper.CF			1.0000	1.0200	1.0404	1.0612	1.0824	1.1041	1.1262	1.1487	1.1717	1.1951	1.2190
(2) Actual Capital CF		−11.1111										12.1899	
(3) Actual Total CF (= 1 + 2)	10.30%	−11.1111	1.0000	1.0200	1.0404	1.0612	1.0824	1.1041	1.1262	1.1487	1.1717	13.3850	
(4) Init.Oper.CF constant			1.0000	1.0000	1.0000	1.0000	1.0000	1.0000	1.0000	1.0000	1.0000	1.0000	1.0000
(5) Capital CF @ Init.Yld.on(4)		−11.1111										11.1111	
(6) Init.CF @ Init.Yld (= 4+5)	9.00%	−11.1111	1.0000	1.0000	1.0000	1.0000	1.0000	1.0000	1.0000	1.0000	1.0000	12.1111	
(7) Capital CF @ Init.Yld.on(1)		−11.1111										13.5444	
(8) Actual Oper. CF @ Init.Yld (= 1 + 7)	11.00%	−11.1111	1.0000	1.0200	1.0404	1.0612	1.0824	1.1041	1.1262	1.1487	1.1717	14.7395	
(9) Capital CF @ ActualYld.on(4)		−11.1111										10.0000	
(10) Init.CF @ Actual Yld (= 4 + 9)	8.32%	−11.1111	1.0000	1.0000	1.0000	1.0000	1.0000	1.0000	1.0000	1.0000	1.0000	11.0000	
Initial Yield Component (= (6)IRR)	9.00%												
CF Growth Component* (= (8)IRR−(6)IRR)	2.00%												
Yield-Change Component** (= (10)IRR−(6)IRR)	−0.68%												
Interaction Effect (= (3)IRR−sum (components))	−0.02%												

*Based on initial yield.
**Based on initial CF level.

EXHIBIT 10A-1 Example Property Investment Cash Flow

© OnCourse Learning

and yield-change components will be defined. The overall actual IRR is based on the actual operating and capital cash flows depicted in the third row of the exhibit. The actual IRR is 10.30 percent. The **initial yield component (IY)** is then defined simply as the net cash flow yield that was obtained in the first year of the investment, based on the purchase price. As noted, this is 9.00 percent ($1,000,000/$11,111,100). Note that it is equivalent to compute the initial yield as the IRR over the holding period based on the actual purchase price but holding the cash flows constant at the initial level, and assuming the terminal yield remains the same as the initial yield. This is seen in row 6 in the exhibit, which is the sum of rows 4 and 5.

The next step is to compute the **cash flow change return component (CFC)** defined on the initial yield. This is the IRR increment to the initial yield that would be caused purely by the actual change in cash flows over time, holding the other two factors constant, in particular, holding the initial cash flow at its actual level and holding the yield (valuation cap rate) constant at the initial going-in rate. The CFC is thus computed by figuring what the IRR would have been given the actual operating cash flows (in row 1) but with a terminal capital cash flow based on the initial yield of 9 percent rather than the actual terminal yield of 10 percent. A 9 percent terminal yield would have produced the capital cash flow indicated in row 7 in the exhibit. That is, if it were possible to sell the property at the end of year 10 for the same 9 percent yield as the property obtained at the beginning of the holding period, then the resale price would be $13.544 million, instead of the $12.190 million price that reflects the 10 percent yield actually obtained. This results in the 11.00 percent IRR indicated in row 8 (which is the sum of the row 1 and row 7 cash flows).[25] Then, the cash flow growth component is computed as 11.00% − 9.00% = 2.00%, the row 8 IRR minus the initial yield (row 6 IRR).

Finally, we compute the **yield-change (YC) component** as the IRR increment of the pure effect of a change in valuation yield over the given holding period on a constant cash flow level equal to the actual initial cash flow. In other words, the YC component is based on what the overall property cash flows would be if the initial net operating cash flow remained constant throughout the holding period, but the yield changed as it actually did between the initial purchase and the resale. In that case, the operating cash flows would remain at their initial level of $1,000,000 per year (as indicated in row 4), and the resale price of the property at the actual terminal yield of 10 percent would then be $10,000,000 (as indicated in row 9). This would result in the overall cash flows indicated in row 10 (the sum of rows 4 and 9), which provide an IRR of 8.32 percent on the initial purchase price of $11.11 million. This is the IRR that would result if there were no growth in property net operating cash flow, but the yield changed as it actually did from 9 to 10 percent between the initial purchase and the subsequent resale. The yield-change component (YC) is then computed as −0.68 percent = 8.32 percent − 9.00 percent, the difference between the row 10 IRR and the initial yield (or row 10 IRR minus row 6 IRRs).

Now note that the three IRR components defined earlier do not exactly add up to the overall total IRR: 9.00% initial yield + (−0.68%) yield-change effect = 2.00% cash flow growth effect = 10.32%. This is two basis points more than the total IRR of 10.30 percent. This difference may be thought of as an "interaction effect," or a combined effect of the cash flow growth and the yield-change effect based on the initial yield and cash flow level.[26]

---

[25]The row 8 IRR in Exhibit 10A-1 happens to be an example of the special case noted in Chapter 9 in which the IRR exactly equals the sum of the initial yield and the constant-growth rate (of both the cash flows and the asset value). This is a peculiarity of the simple numerical example depicted here. In general, of course, property cash flows will not necessarily grow at a constant rate every year during an investment holding period (either ex post or ex ante, due in part to the effect of long-term leases and capital expenditures). So the equating of the IRR to the sum of initial yield and the overall growth rate is the particular result in this example.

[26]The interaction effect will not always be as small as it appears in the numerical example in Exhibit 10A-1. However, within the property-level IRR the yield-change and cash flow growth interaction effect is a second-order effect and, therefore, tends to be less important than it often is in macro-level portfolio performance attribution as described in section 26.1.3.

This method of defining the three components of the IRR gives a logical, common-sense result, For example, it is clear in this case that the CFC component should be +2 percent, as the cash flows do in fact grow at exactly that rate every year in this simplified illustration. Similarly, it makes sense that the YC component should be negative in this case, as the yield increased between the going-in rate and the going-out rate. The magnitude of this increase, from 9 percent to 10 percent would be sufficient to cause a roughly 10 percent decline in value (e.g., the actual $12.19 million terminal value in row 2 is 90 percent of the $13.54 million terminal value in row 7 that would have prevailed had the yield not fallen). But this 10 percent decline in value is spread over the ten-year investment, and when discounting and compounding is considered, it makes sense that the IRR impact would be a bit less than 1 percent per year, as indicated by the −0.68 percent YC component we computed. It is also desirable that the method of parsing the IRR results in components that add up very nearly to the exact total IRR, which we see is the case in this simple example.

It is important to keep in mind that the attribution of IRR components represents only a *formal* breakdown of the sources or determinants of the IRR. That is, they are simply a mathematical decomposition of the overall IRR, with no necessary correspondence to, or implication regarding, what the investor did, or what the property market did, over the period covered by the IRR computation. For example, the reasons the yield increased from 9 percent to 10 percent, or the property operating cash flows grew an average of 2 percent per year, are not addressed by the formal analysis.

Nevertheless, this type of logical performance attribution, if used carefully, can provide interesting investment insights. In Chapter 26, we will see how this type of property level investment performance attribution can be applied ex post to help diagnose why or how an investment manager or asset manager achieved the investment performance that they did. (This is particularly useful when the performance attribution can be *benchmarked* against a relevant "universe" of similar properties and/or similar types of investors.) The three performance attributes defined here can be related to the four fundamental investment-management functions at the property level: property selection, acquisition transaction execution, operational management (during the holding period), and disposition transaction execution.[27]

Alternatively, the type of performance attribution described in this appendix can be used in an ex ante ("going-in" or forward-looking) perspective based on the prospective investment's proforma cash flow projection (including reversion). When used in this ex ante way, the performance attribution is usually less about diagnosing management strengths than about understanding where the projected return from an investment is expected to come from. This can be helpful in at least two ways: (1) to help judge the reliability in the expected return projection (e.g., CFC or YC components may be viewed as less reliable than the IY component in many cases), and (2) to help relate the investment to the investor's return component preferences (see section 10.6.2). For example, some investors may prefer short-term and continuing-income yield as presented by the IY attribute, while other investors may prefer longer-term growth in the income yield as presented by the CFC component, or even longer-term growth in capital value without intermediate payback as presented by the YC component. As noted, such preferences may be based either on ultimate investment objectives, or on the investment manager's perception of her particular strengths (or weaknesses) as an asset manager or property operator. For example, a property investor/operator may feel that they have particular ability to enhance returns through operational improvements that enhance the CFC or YC components. In any case, such ex ante analysis can help to match investor preferences to investment alternatives, when all investment alternatives appear to present an equal NPV (given that typically NPV = 0 measured on a market value basis, as noted in section 10.6.1).

---

[27]This use of property level IRR performance attribution is discussed in D. Geltner (2003) and in T. Feng and D. Geltner (2011).

KEY TERMS

returns and values
expected cash flows (numerators)
Greater Fool Theory
discounted cash flow (DCF)
opportunity cost of capital (OCC)
going-in IRR
intralease discount rate
interlease discount rate
reversion cash flow

expected returns (denominators)
blended IRR
unbundled cash flows
direct capitalization
gross income multiplier (GIM)
ratio valuation
empirical cap rates
GIGO
discount rate

net present value (NPV)
wealth maximization
market value
hurdle rate
performance attribution
initial yield component (IY)
cash flow change return component (CFC)
yield-change component (YC)

STUDY QUESTIONS

Conceptual Questions

10.1. What is the relationship between the ex ante return on an investment and the price for the asset paid by the investor?

10.2. What is the Greater Fool Theory? How can the multiperiod DCF valuation procedure help to protect investors from falling victim to this theory?

10.3. What is the relationship between the discount rate that should be used in the DCF procedure and the cash flows that are being discounted?

10.4. When is it most important to "unbundle" a property's cash flows to apply different discount rates to different cash flow components?

10.5. What is wrong with the following statement: Property X is worth $10 million in the market today because it produces $1 million of annual net income, and cap rates in the relevant property asset market are currently 10 percent.

10.6. What is meant by the term *GIGO* in reference to the practical application of the DCF valuation procedure for commercial property? What are some typical mistakes in the numerators? What about in the denominators?

10.7. What is the approximate relationship among the cap rate, the discount rate, and the long-run average growth rate in property cash flow and value?

10.8. Starting with your answer to Question 10.7, write the investor's required return as the sum of the risk-free rate plus a risk premium to establish the approximate relationship between the cap rate, interest rate, risk premium and growth rate in property cash flow. Then answer the following questions:

   a. How are cap rates affected by interest rates? Does an increase in the risk-free rate imply higher cap rates? (Hint: There is no mention of "all else equal.")

   b. Many analysts have taken to defining the spread between the cap rate and the risk-free rate as a risk premium. What is wrong with this practice? Under what conditions does this lead to the perception of a high-risk premium being incorporated into property values, when in fact the opposite is true?

10.9. What is wrong with the following statement: Investors typically overstate both the numerators and denominators in applying the DCF approach to commercial property, with the two types of errors largely canceling each other out, so that there is really no harm done by this type of mistake.

10.10. What fundamental principle underlies the NPV investment decision rule? (Hint: What is the relation between NPV and the investor's wealth?)

10.11. Why is a zero-NPV deal OK? Where is the profit for the investor in a deal in which NPV = 0?

10.12. Why is the NPV of the typical deal zero when evaluated from a market value perspective?

10.13. Describe at least two other considerations besides NPV that can allow investors to choose among alternative investments that have the same NPV.

10.14. Describe at least two problems that can be encountered in using the hurdle rate version of the NPV investment decision rule, and how those problems can be resolved.

Quantitative Problems

10.15. Consider a property with expected future net cash flows of $25,000 per year for the next five years (starting one year from now). After that, the operating cash flow should step up 20 percent, to $30,000, for the following five years. If you expect to sell the property 10 years from now for a price 10 times the net cash flow at that time, what is the value of the property if the required return is 12 percent?

10.16. In the previous question, suppose the seller of the building wants $260,000.

a. Should you do the deal? Why or why not? (Hint: What would be the net present value of the deal for the buyer at $260,000?)

b. What is the IRR if you pay $260,000? How does this compare to the required return of 12 percent?

c. What is the IRR if you could get the seller to accept $248,075 for the property? What is the NPV at that price?

10.17. Suppose that the required return on the property in Question 10.15 is 11 percent instead of 12 percent. What would the value of the property be? By what percentage has this value changed as a result of this 100-basis-point change in the required return? (Note the sensitivity of property value to small changes in the expected return discount rate used in the denominators of the right-hand side of the DCF valuation equation.)

10.18. Go back to the property in Question 10.15 with the 12 percent required return. What is the value of the property if the cash flow steps up 25 percent in year 6, to $31,250, instead of the original assumption of 20 percent? By what percentage has this roughly 1 percent per year change in the rent growth assumption (25 percent over five years instead of 20 percent over five years) changed the property value? [Note the sensitivity of property value to small changes in the percentage growth in expected cash flows in the numerators of the right-hand side of the DCF valuation equation.]

10.19. (**Bit of a challenge**) Consider a property that is expected to produce a constant net operating income (NOI) of $150,000 per year in perpetuity. An investor who is considering purchasing the property plans to hold it for 10 years. The investor expects the property to appreciate by 100 percent (double in value) over this period. The discount rate is 15 percent. *What is the maximum price an investor should be willing to pay for the property?*

10.20. An apartment complex has 1,000 units of which on average 100 are vacant at any given time. Per unit, the rent is $400 per month, and the operating expenses are $1,800 per year (per occupied unit). If you expect both rents and expenses to grow at 3 percent per year, the required return is 12.5 percent, and the building value is expected to remain a constant multiple of its net income, then what is the NPV of a deal to buy the property for $25 million? [Hint: Use the perpetuity formula: $PV = CF_1/(r - g)$.]

10.21. What is the IRR of the deal in Question 10.20? (Hint: Just invert the perpetuity formula and solve for r.)

10.22. (**Excel**) Answer Question 10.20 using discounted cash flow (DCF) analysis in Excel instead of the shortcut perpetuity formula approach (i.e., convince yourself that the shortcut formula works). Set up a basic 10-year cash flow projection in which property income (NOI) grows by 3 percent each year and the year 10 sale price is calculated as year 11 property income divided by the 9.50 percent cap rate (the perpetuity formula assumes that the ratio of property income to value is constant, and hence the "terminal" or "sale" cap rate is identical to the "going in" or first year cap rate). Determine the NPV assuming an asking price of $25 million. [Use the "=NPV(...)" financial function to estimate the property value (i.e., PV) based on year 1 through year 10 cash flows. Then subtract the asking price.]

10.23. The following table shows two 10-year cash flow projections (in $ millions, including reversion) for the same property. The upper row is the projection that will be presented by the broker trying to sell the building, and the bottom row is the realistic expectations. Suppose that it would be relatively easy for any potential buyers to ascertain that the most likely current market value for the property is about $10 million.

a. What going-in IRR (blended rate) will equate the presented cash flow projection to the observable $10 million present value (as of year 0)?

b. What rate will equate the realistic projection to that same present value?

c. What is the most likely amount of "disappointment" in the ex post rate of return earned by an investor who buys this property believing the broker's cash flow projection (i.e., the difference in presented versus realistic return)?

Year	1	2	3	4	5	6	7	8	9	10
Presented	$1.0000	$1.0300	$1.0609	$1.0927	$1.1255	$1.1593	$1.1941	$1.2299	$1.2668	$14.7439
Realistic	$1.0000	$1.0100	$1.0201	$1.0303	$1.0406	$1.0510	$1.0615	$1.0721	$1.0829	$12.1399

10.24. The buildings in a certain warehouse market are characterized by net cash flow projections like the one shown in the following table, based on net leases of five years' duration. In this market, properties are typically evaluated using a going-in IRR of 10.50 percent (blended rate). Thus, the typical property sells for a cap rate of about 8.25 percent. You have the opportunity to purchase a property with these same typical cash flow projections, at the typical cap rate or going-in IRR. However, your building is entirely covered by a 10-year lease with a AAA-credit tenant who can borrow money at 6 percent.

a. How much is this lease worth (for example, if it could be sold into a LOBS pool)?

b. Assuming that the appropriate interlease and reversion discount rate is 12 percent, what is your NPV from this deal?

Ten-Year Cash Flow Projection ($ millions)										
Year	1	2	3	4	5	6	7	8	9	10
Operating	$1.0	$1.0	$1.1	$1.1	$1.2	$1.2	$1.3	$1.3	$1.4	$1.4
Reversion										$14.0
CF	$1.0	$1.0	$1.1	$1.1	$1.2	$1.2	$1.3	$1.3	$1.4	$15.4

10.25. Suppose a property worth $10 million in the marketplace provides an initial annual gross income of $2 million and a net income of $1 million. What is the GIM, and what is the cap rate prevailing in the property market for this type of property?

10.26. The projected cash flows (including reversion) are shown in the following table for property A and property B.

a. If both properties sell at a cap rate (initial cash yield) of 10 percent, what is the expected total return on a 10-year investment in each property?

b. If the 10 percent cap rate represents a fair market value for each property, then which property is the more risky investment (and how do you know)?

c. What is the annual growth rate in operating cash flows for each building during the first nine years?

d. How is this growth rate related to the cap rate and the investor's expected total return (IRR) in each property?

				Annual Net Cash Flow Projections for Two Properties ($ millions)						
Year	**1**	**2**	**3**	**4**	**5**	**6**	**7**	**8**	**9**	**10**
A	$1.0000	$1.0100	$1.0201	$1.0303	$1.0406	$1.0510	$1.0615	$1.0721	$1.0829	$12.1399
B	$1.0000	$0.9900	$0.9801	$0.9703	$0.9606	$0.9510	$0.9415	$0.9321	$0.9227	$9.9573

*10.27. **(based on Appendix 10A)** A 10-year property investment is characterized by the net cash flow stream indicated in the following table (including initial investment and reversion at the end of year 10). Compute the following:

   a. Overall total IRR
   b. Initial cash yield component
   c. Cash flow growth component
   d. Yield-change component
   e. Interaction effect [Hint: Base your answers to (c) and (d) on the initial yield and initial cash flow level.]

Year	**0**	**1**	**2**	**3**	**4**	**5**	**6**	**7**	**8**	**9**	**10**	**11**
(1) Actual Operating CF		$1,000	$1,005	$950	$1,010	$1,015	$1,020	$800	$1,025	$1,030	$1,036	$1,041
(2) Actual Capital CF	−$12,500	$0	$0	$0	$0	$0	$0	$0	$0	$0	$12,244	
(3) Actual Total CF (1 + 2)	−$12,500	$1,000	$1,005	$950	$1,010	$1,015	$1,020	$800	$1,025	$1,030	$13,279	

CHAPTER

11

NUTS AND BOLTS FOR REAL ESTATE VALUATION: CASH FLOW PROFORMAS AND DISCOUNT RATES

CHAPTER OUTLINE

LEARNING OBJECTIVES

After reading this chapter, you should understand:

⊃ The components and terminology of the typical commercial property investment cash flow projection proforma.

⊃ Some major practical considerations in making realistic commercial property cash flow projections.

⊃ Some major practical considerations in estimating the appropriate opportunity cost of capital to use as the discount rate in DCF valuation of commercial property.

C hapter 10 laid out the basic framework for investment valuation at the micro-level. In this chapter, we will explore the details of how these tools are typically applied to commercial real estate. The DCF valuation problem can be thought of conceptually as involving two major analytical steps: (1) forecasting the future expected net cash flows from the property, and (2) determining and applying the appropriate opportunity cost of capital as a discount rate. We will treat each of these steps in turn in this chapter.

All of the discussion in this chapter is at what may be called the "property-before-tax" (PBT) level. That is, we are examining cash flows and valuation at the property level, as distinguished from the level of the owner of the property equity. The PBT level is most appropriate for analyzing the market value of property assets. Thus, the analysis here does not consider funds borrowed against the property, debt service payments, or income taxes, which are matters to be treated in subsequent chapters.

11.1 Proformas and Cash Flow Projection

In this section, we turn to the forecasting of the property cash flows. This task is so basic that a special term has evolved to describe the document that lays out the cash flow projection. It is called a **proforma**. The Latin origin of this word (it means "for form") suggests that this cash flow forecast document may be produced more for appearance's sake or as a formality than as a serious step in analysis and evaluation. Indeed, we would be less than honest if we did not admit that this is often the case in practice, as lenders and outside investors will typically require a proforma as a matter of course before a deal can be considered. But the proforma, or the cash flow forecast that makes it up, should be taken seriously. Going through the exercise of trying to estimate unbiased, realistic forecasts of a property's future cash flow generation potential is fundamental to sound decision making. With this in mind, let's look at the nuts and bolts of a typical real estate proforma.

Cash flows are typically projected for a reasonably long period of time (10 years is the most common). This is because real properties are long-lived and most investors hold properties for long periods (in part in order to minimize the effect of transactions costs on returns). Even if the owner expects to sell the property shortly, the resale value of the property (i.e., the price any potential buyer would be willing to pay for it) is fundamentally dependent on the ability of the property to generate operating income over the long term, so a long horizon is still necessary for a solid evaluation. Long-horizon forecasts also have the salutary effect of forcing the analyst to grapple with difficult issues regarding where the rental market is headed. (Most of the value of most buildings is derived from the building's earning potential *after* the current leases expire.)

The importance of going through the proforma construction exercise is particularly obvious in the case of commercial properties with long-term leases. It may also be useful for apartment properties, however, as it makes explicit the long-term rental-and-expense growth rate assumptions that underlie the value of the property.

Broadly speaking, two categories of cash flows should be represented in a complete proforma for real estate investment analysis: the **operating cash flows** and the **reversion cash flows**. The former refers to cash flows that result from normal operation of the property and therefore accrue to the owner of the property regularly throughout the period the property is held as an investment. In contrast, reversion cash flows occur only at the time of, and due to, the sale of all or a portion of the property asset.

The table in Exhibit 11-1 shows in general form the typical line items in a proforma for an income-producing property. A brief discussion of each of these items will be helpful.

11.1.1 PGI and Market Rent Projection

The top line item in the operating cash flows is the primary potential source of property revenue, the cash it could earn if it were fully rented. This item is typically labeled potential revenue or **potential gross income (PGI)**. In practice, this item is also often referred to as

Operating (all years):

Potential gross income (PGI) = (Rent/SF) × (Rentable SF) =	PGI
− Vacancy allowance = − (Vacancy rate) × (PGI) =	− v
+ Other Income (e.g., parking, laundry) =	+ OI
− Operating expenses* =	− OE*
Net operating income =	NOI
− Capital improvement expenditures** =	− CI**
Property-before-tax cash flow =	PBTCF

Plus reversion (only last year and when partial asset sales occur):

Property value at time of resale =	V
− Selling expenses (e.g., brokers' fees) =	− SE
Property-before-tax cash flow =	PBTCF

*Major operating expense categories:

- Largely fixed costs (insensitive to occupancy level):
    Property taxes
    Hazard insurance
    Property security
    Property management
- Largely variable costs (sensitive to occupancy level):
    Utilities
    Building and grounds maintenance and routine repairs

[Note: Some or all of the expenses may be reimbursed from tenants to landlords or paid directly by tenants based on "net" or "expense stop" leases. In this case, an additional revenue line item for the landlord, typically entitled "expense reimbursements," may appear in the proforma.]

**Major capitalized expenditures:

- Leasing costs:
    Tenant build-outs or improvement expenditures (TIs)
    Leasing commissions to brokers
- Property improvements:
    Major repairs
    Replacement of major equipment (e.g., HVAC, elevators)
    Major remodeling of building, grounds, and fixtures
    Expansion of rentable area

EXHIBIT 11-1 Typical Line Items in a Proforma for Income Property

© OnCourse Learning

the **rent roll**, especially in properties with long-term leases. This refers to the fact that in properties with long-term leases the current PGI is often enumerated by explicitly listing each lease and potentially leasable space in the property. The PGI is determined by multiplying the amount of rentable space (e.g., square feet) by the rent per unit of space (e.g., rent per SF).[1]

For space covered by existing long-term leases, projection of the PGI will involve two rather different sorts of calculations. As long as an existing lease will be in effect, the revenue

---

[1]In the case of apartment properties, the apartment unit itself is often the spatial unit used. For example, the rent roll for a building with 100 similar apartment units would be calculated by multiplying the average expected rent per unit times the 100 units in the building. Also note that the rentable building area (RBA) is generally a bit less than the gross building area (GBA), especially in multi-tenant buildings (due to common areas such as lobbies and hallways, for example). As described more fully in Appendix 6 on the CD, regarding the measurement of building area, a recent survey indicates that in multitenant office buildings in the United States the RBA/GBA ratio (known as the "efficiency ratio" of the building) averages about 94 percent. So called "assignable space" (which is what the office tenant can actually use to assign to employees) averages only some 84 percent of RBA, an important consideration when relating required RBA to number of employees.

is a function of the contractual rent terms in that lease. Once the existing lease expires, and for any space not covered by existing leases, the revenue will be a function of future leases that will likely be signed. Thus, projecting the rent roll in the proforma becomes primarily an exercise in examining and understanding the existing (aka "vintage") leases and in forecasting the rental market in which the property is situated. As noted in previous chapters, the latter requires consideration of both supply and demand in the space market, as well as the subject building's particular circumstances.

Estimating the current and future market rent levels applicable to the space in the subject building is crucial to property valuation. Because of their importance, these rental assumptions are often listed explicitly in the proforma table. They are often presented in a "supra line item" placed above the PGI line in the table to emphasize the fact that much of the PGI projection, especially in future years, is derived from the market rent level projection.

In any proforma projection, it is important to recognize that the future is inherently uncertain. We cannot predict the relevant future rent levels with anything like perfect accuracy, but for an analysis to be well done, forecasts should be realistic and unbiased.

The realism of the assumption about current market rent can be checked by examining recent leases signed for the building and comparing them with recent leases signed in similar buildings. This is known as a **rent comps analysis** (short for "comparable" buildings) and is a standard procedure of commercial appraisers.

Projection of future change in market rents going forward in principle involves analysis of supply and demand in the relevant space market, as discussed in Parts I and II of this book. However, in typical current practice, the initial market rent relevant to the subject building is often simply projected to grow at a constant rate, often what is expected to be the general inflation rate. This may be modified if the local rental market is perceived as being temporarily "out of equilibrium."[2]

But you would do well to be skeptical of this practice. Even apart from temporary cyclical considerations, the simplistic assumption that rents will grow at the inflation rate is often unrealistic, even for the long-run average trend. Recall the effect of functional and economic obsolescence and the real depreciation of the building over the property life cycle that we discussed in Chapter 5. Especially if the subject structure is not already very old (essentially fully depreciated) and if it is located in a stable or growing market in which new structures are built from time to time, the subject building must compete against these newer structures in the same market. This will tend to force it to lower its rents relative to the "top of the market" rent level. And recall our discussion in Parts I and II how fundamental spatial and urban economic forces of supply and demand can lead even the rents commanded by new "top of the market" properties to not necessarily increase faster than inflation or even in some circumstances to decline in real terms.[3] Because of these considerations, in many cases, it is more realistic to assume that the market rent effective for a *given* (i.e., *aging*) building will tend to grow typically at annual rates one to two percentage points *less than* inflation, over the long run.

For example, Exhibit 11-2 shows the growth rate of net operating income (NOI) compared to the Consumer Price Index (CPI) of general inflation, over the 1978–2010 period, within the NCREIF Index properties. As described in Chapter 10, these are relatively large, prime properties owned by institutional investors and professional investment managers (approximately 6,000 properties as of 2010). The NOI growth depicted in the exhibit is "same-property" growth of the type experienced by property-owning investors.[4] Note that

---

[2]Recall our discussion in Parts I and II about supply and demand in the space market, and the interaction of the space and capital markets via the development industry, including our discussion about cyclicality in the space markets in Chapters 2 and 6. Market rents may temporarily rise above or fall below long-run equilibrium levels, making it realistic to expect them to fall back or pop up to the long-run equilibrium level in real terms. Cyclicality can vary substantially across different space markets (see Ibanez and Pennington-Cross, 2011).

[3]In particular, recall our discussion in Chapter 1 of real estate's kinked supply function and in Chapter 4 about the determinants of a site's "location premium."

[4]The NCREIF Index is "same-property" not in the sense that it is a fixed static portfolio of properties, but in the sense that it is a quarterly index and within each quarter it tracks changes in the same properties between the beginning and end of the quarter. The mix of properties in the NCREIF Index does change over time, for example, including fewer apartment properties in the earlier years.

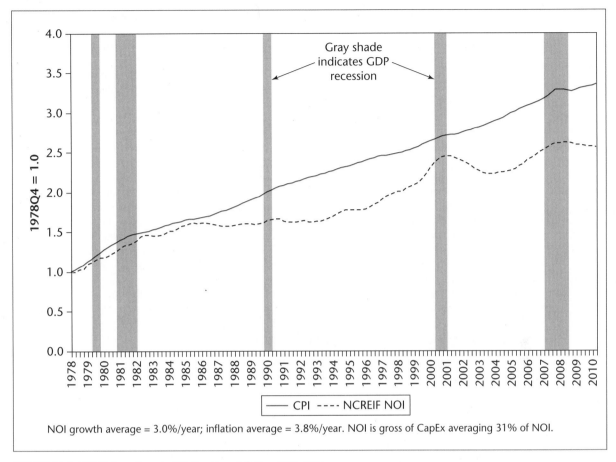

EXHIBIT 11-2 NCREIF Same-Property NOI Growth vs. Inflation, 1979–2011
© OnCourse Learning

the NOI of the NCREIF properties grew on average 0.8 percent per year *less* than inflation. This is in spite of the fact that the NCREIF properties benefit from a large amount of capital improvement expenditures, averaging some 31 percent of NOI over the period.[5]

A good way to gain some insight about the rental growth projection for a particular property is to examine the subject building's own past rental history and also that of other similar buildings in the market. Compare the rents charged in otherwise similar leases that were signed 5 to 10 years ago against the rents charged in more recent leases, *within the same buildings.*[6] Compute the average annual rental growth rate indicated by these comparisons. For example, if typical rent in leases signed 5 to 10 years ago was \$10/SF, and the typical rent in leases signed within the last three years was \$11/SF, then this suggests an average annual growth rate of approximately 1.6 percent, computed as $(11/10)^{[1/(7.5 - 1.5)]} - 1 = 1.6\%$. Then compare this average nominal growth rate with the average inflation rate over the same historical period. For example, if inflation averaged 3 percent per year during the period

---

[5]Note however that a decline in same-property real NOI can be caused not only by top-line potential gross rent (revenue) effects but also by a relative growth in operating expenses or by an increase in average vacancy, as NOI reflects the net effect of all of these factors. Also note that the decline in NOI relative to inflation tends to occur most strongly during and after periods of economic recession.

[6]In identifying the leases to examine, you will want to compare apples to apples as much as possible. Try to control for differences in the spaces or leases that might have significantly affected the rent, such as amenities, location within the building, size and contiguity of the space, length of the lease term, provisions for rent concessions, step-ups or expense pass-throughs, lease options, and so forth. No comparison will be perfect, but this exercise can be enlightening.

covered by the leases examined in the previous example, then the average *real* growth in rents was *negative* 1.4 percent per year, computed as $1.6\% - 3\% = -1.4\%$. In the real world, the result of such comparisons often indicates negative real growth in rents charged by existing buildings, especially in central locations.

Another approach to examine this same question is to compare the *current* rents charged by buildings of *different ages* in the local space market relevant to the subject building.[7] Try to compare buildings that were all considered "top of the market" at the time they were built. Notice the relationship between the rents charged by the newer buildings and those charged by older buildings. Suppose, for example, that buildings built within the past five years charge an average rent of $12/SF, while buildings over 10 years in age charge an average rent of $10/SF. Suppose the newer buildings average three years in age, and the older buildings average 15 years in age. Then this implies a decline of about 1.5 percent per year of age of the building in the market *real* rent relevant to a given building.

A rough method of computations is as follows: Take the ratio of the old building rents divided by the new building rents, in this case $10/12 = 0.833$. This represents the cumulative fall-off in rent associated with number of years of age difference between the new and old buildings, in this case 12 years, the difference between the 15-year average age and the three-year average age. Thus, the annual percentage fall-off in rent (below the top of the market, that is, the newest buildings in the market) is computed as $0.833^{1/12} - 1 = -0.015 = -1.5\%$. One typically finds results like this in U.S. markets for class A commercial properties in central locations.

11.1.2 Vacancy Allowance and EGI

Generally, we cannot realistically expect a property always to be fully leased and generating its entire PGI every year. The second line item in Exhibit 11-1, the **vacancy allowance**, accounts for the expected effect of vacancy in the net cash flow of the property. This line item is usually quantified in one of two ways. For properties with many short-term leases, such as apartment buildings, the vacancy allowance is typically accounted for as a percentage of the PGI. For example, suppose the average tenant remains in an apartment for five years, and the average apartment unit is vacant for three months between tenants. Then the total cycle for a unit is 63 months (60 months occupied, followed by three months vacant), so the average apartment is therefore vacant 3/63, or 4.8 percent, of the time, which could be rounded off to 5 percent. The vacancy allowance in the proforma would be computed as 5 percent of the potential gross revenue projection in each year.[8]

The second method of computing the vacancy allowance is to forecast explicitly the likely vacancy period that will be associated with each rental unit or space in the building, considering the expiration of each lease currently in the building. This method is more appropriate for buildings with long-term (i.e., multiyear) leases or buildings that currently have substantial vacancy that is expected to be filled up over some projected schedule.

With either method of vacancy calculation, the resulting projected overall long-term average vacancy percentage should be compared to available information about typical vacancy in the local market for similar buildings. If the projected vacancy rate for the subject building differs much from the typical vacancy in its market, this discrepancy should be either explained or corrected. It should be noted, however, that the vacancy in the space market, as discussed in Chapter 6, may tend to be higher on average (or at certain points in the cycle), than the average vacancy within stabilized "fully occupied" buildings, as the market vacancy includes very new and very old buildings that are not in what is known as a "stabilized" occupancy condition (meaning that they are in the process of renting up, or perhaps emptying out prior to a major redevelopment). Once again we turn to the NCREIF

---

[7]The easiest way to conduct such a comparison is to use the current asking rents quoted by property managers and leasing brokers. As always, try to control for lease term and quality of space.

[8]If the apartment market is currently oversupplied, a larger vacancy allowance percentage might be applied in the near-term years of the proforma projection. Similarly, if the apartment building currently has a vacancy level different from the long-term average, the first few years of the proforma projection should reflect this fact.

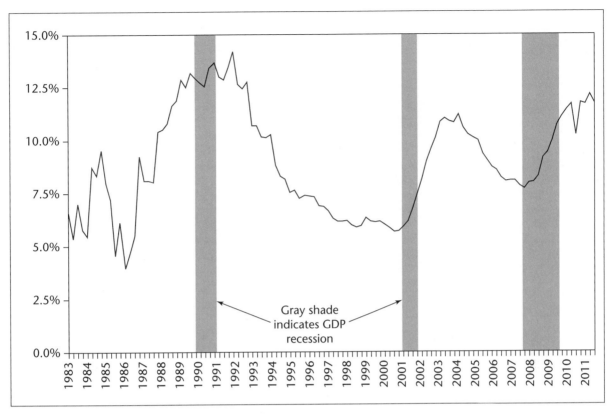

EXHIBIT 11-3 Average Reported Vacancy among NCREIF Properties, 1983–2011

© OnCourse Learning

Index database as an illustration of typical stabilized properties. Exhibit 11-3 shows the average vacancy rate among NCREIF Index properties during 1983–2011. The overall long-run average across that period was 9 percent, cycling between less than 5 percent and over 13 percent, with peaks lagging after the ends of economic recessions (as occupancy tends to reflect employment, which tends to be a lagging effect of recessions).[9]

It should also be noted that the realistic vacancy allowance tends to increase over time as buildings age. Other things being equal, older buildings face a higher likelihood that existing tenants will not renew, and/or that there will be a longer vacant period between tenants in a given space. Especially during times of excess supply in the space market, tenants may tend to "move up" from older to newer buildings when their leases expire. For example, Exhibit 11-4 shows historical data for office buildings in major U.S. office space markets. The exhibit shows the average building vacancy rate minus the average market vacancy rate for the submarket in which the building is located, for two different vintages of buildings, over time. As time progresses (the horizontal axis) and these two cohorts of buildings age, their average vacancy rates increase relative to that of their submarkets (the upward slope of the lines in the chart). Note that in the early years of a building's life (first 15–20 years) it tends to have vacancy lower than the average of the submarket within which it is located. It is also of interest that the exhibit suggests that a type of "plateau" is reached when the buildings are 20–30 years old in which the younger (1980s vintage) cohort no longer has lower vacancy (relative to the submarket) than the older (1970s vintage) buildings, as evidenced by the elimination of the difference between the two lines. This suggests an age when a

---

[9]Note the greater degree of over-building in the space market prior to the 1990 recession, indicated by the run-up in average NCREIF vacancy even before the recession.

EXHIBIT 11-4 Difference Over Time between Building Vacancy Minus Average Submarket Vacancy (within which the buildings are located) for Two Vintages of Buildings Based on Year of Construction

Source: CBRE/Torto Wheaton Research, "Overview & Outlook," winter 2004.

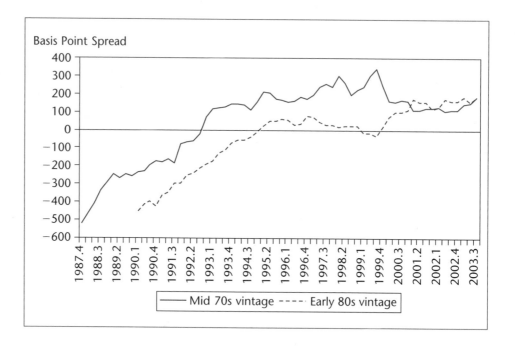

building becomes "no longer new" (shall we say, "middle-aged"), when institutional quality commercial buildings built originally as "class A" have likely devolved more toward "class B."[10]

Subtracting the vacancy allowance line item amount from the PGI provides a projection of what is often referred to as the **effective gross income (EGI)** for the property in each year in the proforma. However, many properties have other sources of earning income besides the rental of their space for the occupancy of tenants, for example, revenue from the operation of vending machines or laundry machines in apartment buildings, and revenue from parking operations or billboard or antenna rental in office or retail buildings.[11] These sources of income are typically referred to as **other income**, represented by the third line item in Exhibit 11-1.

11.1.3 Operating Expenses

The next major category in the proforma is **operating expenses**. This heading will include a number of regularly occurring, specific expense line items associated with the ongoing operation of the property. Typical major categories include property management and administration, utilities, insurance, regular maintenance and repair, and property taxes. Note that charges for depreciation expenses are *not* included among the operating expenses. This is because the property proforma statement is a cash flow statement rather than an accrual income statement, and depreciation expenses are not a cash outflow per se. The occurrence of real depreciation of the property over time (whether due to physical, functional, or economic obsolescence) will be reflected in the cash flows (and hence in the proforma statement) in one or a combination of several possible ways. These include: (1) lower real rents and

---

[10]See earlier discussions in Chapters 5 and 6, concerning functional depreciation and the difference between "class A" and "class B" (or between "institutional" versus "noninstitutional" property). We noted in Chapter 6 that this transition may be accompanied by a decline in the rent the building can charge, often by about a third. However, there is evidence that better quality buildings in relatively supply-constrained locations may retain higher status longer. (See also the recent literature on the effect of "sustainable" or "green" architecture, listed in the Part II bibliography.)

[11]A recent development is the advent of the possibility of using building roof space for solar energy collection using photovoltaic arrays for electricity generation that can be used not only by the building itself but sold by the landlord into the public electric grid. This is of course particularly intriguing for buildings with large roof areas such as warehouses and retail malls, and in locations with high solar radiation such as the south and west of the country.

higher vacancy allowances over time (as previously noted); (2) higher operating expenses; (3) higher capital improvement expenditures; or (4) lower resale value (higher terminal cap rate applied) in the reversion cash flow at the end of the period covered by the proforma.[12] Also, income taxes are not included in the operating expenses because such taxes are attributable to the owner/investor, not to the property itself.

It should also be noted that for purposes of investment analysis, property management expenses should be identified and charged as an operating expense (i.e., *above* the NOI bottom line), *even if the owner/investor will be managing the property itself*. The time and energy of whomever is performing this job reflects the **property management opportunity cost**. In the case of owner/managers (or "self-management"), it is important not to confuse return on the *financial* capital invested in the property with return on *human* capital or labor invested in property management. After all, investment in other forms of capital such as stocks or bonds would not generally require a management input on the part of the investor. So comparisons among investment alternatives will be biased in favor of real estate if this cost is not subtracted from the real estate yield.

In general, the cost of property management in cases of self-management can be quantified by the opportunity cost defined by the fee that would be charged by a professional property manager to manage the subject property. For small properties, this is often in the range of 5 percent to 10 percent of the EGI per year. Management costs are usually lower on a percentage basis for larger properties, due to economies of scale. For example, management costs of large-scale class A office properties are typically in the 2 percent to 3 percent range.

It is often useful to describe a property's operating expenses in terms of either **fixed** or **variable costs** (or, some line items may be best described as a combination of the two). Fixed expenses, in principle, are unaffected by the level of occupancy in the building. They will remain at the same level (at least in the short run, say, for a year or so) no matter how vacant or full the building may be. Property taxes and insurance charges are typically in this category. Variable expenses occur in direct proportion (more or less) to the level of occupancy. For example, in a building that is half-vacant, utility expenses may be only a little over half what they would be when the building is full.

Class A properties often have so-called **net leases** in which the tenants pay all or most of the operating expenses. Other leases provide for partial reimbursement of some or all operating expense line items. For example, landlords and tenants often negotiate **expense stops**, in which tenants pay all operating expenses above an agreed-on base level, which typically reflects the level of operating expenses per SF when the lease was signed. When operating expenses are expected to be reimbursed by tenants, these reimbursements will typically appear as additional cash flow line items in the proforma, as positive inflows in the landlord's favor, partially offsetting the operating expense outflows.

11.1.4 Net Operating Income

The **net operating income (NOI)** results from the subtraction of the operating expenses from all the sources of revenue previously discussed (rental revenue net of vacancy allowance, other income, and expense reimbursements). NOI is the most widely used indicator of the net cash flow or operating profit generation ability of the property. This is in spite of the

---

[12]While depreciation per se is never deducted from the income reported in the property NOI, in some cases, as noted earlier, a "reserve for capital improvement expenditures" is deducted as a regular amount each year. Fundamentally, of course, capital improvement expenditures act to mitigate the effect of depreciation in a real physical sense. Deduction of a capital reserve from the operating income is particularly common in the appraisal profession when attempting to arrive at a "stabilized NOI" that is meant to reflect a (forward-looking) typical amount of net cash flow the property can provide per year, on average over the long run. In contrast, property managers often work with operating budgets and capital budgets that are deliberately separate and distinct, with capital expenditures not "reserved" out of the NOI bottom line in the operating budget. In part, this is because the owner may choose to finance capital improvements "externally" rather than from the cash flow generated by the property's operations. Care must be taken in working with proforma statements and NOI figures to ascertain whether the NOI is net of such a capital reserve deduction, and if so, whether the deduction is realistic and complete.

fact that a more complete and accurate measure of net cash flow would subtract necessary capital improvement expenditures routinely made on the property. However, because of the irregular and discretionary nature of the timing of many capital improvement expenditures, the NOI is typically a more stable and easily quantified number than the actual net cash flow after capital expenditures. As a result, in common usage, NOI is often treated as virtually the same thing as the property's net cash flow, and property investment current yield or income return measures (such as the cap rate) are often quantified as the current NOI divided by the current property value. While convenient and often sufficient, such a practice does risk ignoring the potentially important impact of capital improvement expenditures.

11.1.5 Capital Improvement Expenditures

This brings us to the next line item in Exhibit 11-1, **capital improvement expenditures**. In general, this item refers to major expenditures providing long-term improvements to the physical quality of the property, required to maintain or add to the value of the property.[13] Examples would be replacing the heating, ventilation, and cooling (HVAC) system; replacing a roof; adding a parking lot or repaving an existing one; adding new landscaping; or other such investments.

In addition to capital improvements to the building as a whole, there are often capital expenditures associated with the signing of specific long-term leases. Such **leasing costs** include **tenant improvement expenditures** (TIs) and **leasing commissions** paid to leasing brokers (including tenant reps). TIs are a major category of capital expenditures in many buildings with long-term leases. This refers to customized physical improvements, including finishings, partitionings, and decorations, provided at the time of lease signing to the space the tenant will occupy. To some extent, these may be viewed as **concessions** the landlord offers the tenant to get the tenant to sign the long-term lease. In the United States, it is not uncommon for the landlord to incur some level of TI expenditures even just to get an existing tenant to stay and sign a new lease when their existing lease expires. TIs may be managed and paid for directly by the landlord, or the landlord may simply provide the tenant with an allowance amount, which the tenant then spends as it deems fit. There may also be some TIs paid for by the tenant in some cases, which do not therefore enter into the property cash flow proforma.

From a cash flow timing perspective, the characteristic of capital improvement expenditures that distinguishes them from regular operating expenses is that capital expenditures occur less frequently, at irregular intervals of time. General capital expenditures are also characterized by considerable flexibility and discretion on the property owner's part as to exactly when to make the expenditure and how much to spend, while leasing costs are linked to the dates when leases are projected to expire.[14] In the property management business, projected capital expenditures will typically be presented in a separate proforma, as part of a capital budget for the property. But for investment analysis purposes, capital expenditures must be consolidated into the overall property proforma.

Even though the NOI is often thought of as the operating bottom line in property level analysis, it is important to recognize that capital expenditures are, in fact, neither a minor nor a trivial determinant in the net cash flow of the property. On average over the long run, capital improvement expenditures typically equal 1 percent to 2 percent of the property

[13]If a capital expenditure does not add to the value of the property *relative to* what that value would be without the expenditure (as of the time of the expenditure), an increment in value at least equal to the cost of the expenditure, there is no rational business justification for making the expenditure at that time. (The usual NPV rule introduced in Chapter 10 applies.) Generally, capital improvements add to property value either by increasing the future rent that can be charged or by decreasing the future operating expenses (or both), relative to a baseline that would occur without the expenditures.

[14]It is often possible to borrow much or all of the expenditure amount. However, such financing considerations are usually left out of the property proforma, as they represent a separate issue from the valuation of the property. The method in which capital improvements are financed does not generally change the value of the property because such financing transactions rarely have a significantly nonzero NPV.

value per year (typically around 10 percent to 20 percent of the NOI).[15] This percentage will of course tend to be less in new buildings and greater in middle-aged buildings. (Very old buildings may be nearing redevelopment and so are not worth major capital improvement expenditures.)

It is also important to recognize that accounting procedures vary as to what is classified as a capital improvement as opposed to operating expense. For example, as noted, commissions paid to leasing brokers are often classified as capital improvement expenditures, even though such expenditures are generally not rare or discretionary and they are typically financed from the cash flow generated by the building. GAAP accounting rules allow some discretion in the treatment of capital expenditures. At one extreme, some landlords treat almost all capital expenditures as current expenses (taken out above the NOI "bottom line").[16]

11.1.6 The Bottom Line: PBTCF

As noted, viewing the NOI as the bottom line of cash flow available for distribution from building operations can be somewhat misleading. The more realistic picture of the free-and-clear cash flow available to the owners of the property (before debt service and income taxes are taken out) is represented by the NOI less the capital improvement expenditures, the **property-before-tax cash flow (PBTCF)**. This is identified in Exhibit 11-1 as the overall operating bottom line.[17]

11.1.7 Reversion Cash Flows

In addition to the operating cash flows described above, reversion cash flows must be included in the proforma in any year when all or part of the property is expected to be sold. In most cases, reversion cash flows will appear only in the last year of the proforma, as the entire property is expected to be sold at once. Indeed, for investment analysis purposes, a proforma should always include reversion cash flows in the last year of the proforma; otherwise, a major part of the value of the property will be left out of the analysis. At the property-before-tax level, the reversion cash flows consist simply of the expected resale price of the property at the projected future point in time, net of selling expenses (such as brokers' fees and transaction costs).

An often-heard complaint about the projection of future selling price is that it is an exercise in "crystal ball gazing." But remember that cash flow projections are not expected to be without error ex post, only unbiased ex ante. The fact that future cash flows will differ from prior projections is merely a reflection of the fact that real estate is risky, and this risk is treated in the denominator of the DCF procedure by the use of the risk-adjusted discount rate that reflects the market opportunity cost of capital for the investment (see section 11.2 below). With this in mind, clearly, the projection of future resale value is one of the most

---

[15]The fractions are larger than this among the NCREIF Index properties, though these tend to be prime "institutional" quality properties that may take larger than average capital expenditure or may reflect some degree of renovation or rehabilitation.

[16]Another difference that must be considered between accrual based income statements that may be used for income tax or reporting purposes versus a cash flow based proforma that is more relevant for investment analysis is that rental concessions such as rent rebates and rent holidays are sometimes "accrued," that is, spread out over the life of the lease rather than reflected in the years when the rent cash flows are actually reflected.

[17]An additional line item of expense not included here may sometimes be appropriate. If the property is not a fee-simple ownership ("freehold") but rather is a leasehold that requires regular payments on a ground-lease (a long-term lease by the landowning lessor to the operating leasehold property owner lessee), then such ground-lease payments should be recognized as an obligation of the leasehold property. In the United States such lease payments are usually subtracted out below the NOI in a manner comparable to capital expenditures or financing costs analyzing the equity cash flow to the property owner. But in principle the leasehold "property value" can be evaluated separately apart from other equity financing considerations. Such leasehold "property value" is of course not the entire value of the property as a perpetuity. The latter would also include the value of the ground lease to its lessor-landowner. In any case, the cash flow and valuation impacts of a ground leases should not be ignored if it exist. These can tend to make the leasehold property less valuable and more risky, as effectively the leasehold is at least a slightly reduced and levered version of the entire property as if in fee-simple ownership. (See further discussion in Chapter 14 and 27.)

important and useful exercises in the proforma analysis. In a typical ten-year DCF valuation, the projected reversion accounts for well over one-third of the total present value of the property.[18]

Generally, the best, as well as most widely used, method for forecasting the resale price of the property is to apply direct capitalization to the end of the proforma projection period. Typically, the analyst projects the NOI of the property one more year beyond the proforma horizon. For example, in a 10-year analysis, the NOI would be projected for an 11th year. The year-11 NOI would then be divided by an assumed **reversion cap rate** (also known as the **going-out cap rate**, or **terminal cap rate** or **resale cap rate**) to forecast the expected market value of the property at the time of reversion at the end of the 10th year. If the NOI projection is realistic, and the cap rate assumption is realistic, then this should provide a realistic projection for the selling price.[19]

This procedure helps protect the investor against temporary real estate market bubbles and the Greater Fool fallacy, as described in Chapter 10. In the first place, by placing the reversion fairly far into the future (e.g., 10 years), the relative magnitude of the reversion value component in the overall present value of the property is sharply reduced. (It is usually well below one-half the total present value.) This serves to mitigate the effect of mistakes or bias in the projected reversion value, such as the reflection of the current asset market cycle (e.g., a possible bubble?) in the reversion amount being circularly reflected back in the derived present value of the property. Second, by using projected direct capitalization based on NOI, the reversion forecast is based on a projection of the fundamental ability of the property to earn operating cash flow in the rental market, rather than a simple extrapolation of the current investor's purchase price of the property.[20]

In applying this procedure, the projected reversion will be quite sensitive to the assumed going-out cap rate. It is normally most realistic to project a going-out cap rate at least equal to, or slightly higher than, the **going-in cap rate** (that is, the cap rate at the time of purchase), based on typical market cap rates. This is because, as buildings age, they usually become more risky or less able to grow the rents they can charge (or more prone to needing capital improvement expenditures). So cap rates of older buildings tend to be higher than those of otherwise similar newer buildings.[21] However, prevailing cap rates will depend on the nature of the market at the time, and the cap rate relevant to a given building will depend on its particular circumstances regarding, for example, existing tenants and leases and the need for capital improvements.

---

[18]The magnitude of the reversion component in the present value of the property is of course very sensitive to the length of the horizon in the DCF analysis, for example, 5 years versus 10 years versus 20 years. As this horizon is often fundamentally somewhat arbitrary, focusing on how much of the present value is attributable to reversion is not necessarily a very meaningful exercise, or says more about the DCF model being employed than about the property itself. Note that pushing the reversion DCF horizon farther out so that the reversion amount is in the more distant future does not in itself require a higher discount rate to reflect the fact that the more distant future is more uncertain than the nearer term. The discounting process itself reduces the present value of a future sum exponentially as a function of the time until receipt of the future sum, and thusly reflects greater uncertainty as a function of time (measured in present dollar value as a fraction of the future expected dollar value). The discount rate should only change as a function of the time horizon if there is a discontinuity in the *rate* at which risk accumulates over time, such as between versus within long-term lease contracts or before versus after exercise of a construction option.

[19]In direct capitalization, the cap rate is divided into the upcoming year's NOI, that is, the first year of NOI subsequent to the valuation date of the property. If the year-11 NOI is atypical in a major way (such as due to lease expiration in a large proportion of the building's space), reversion may be estimated by applying the terminal cap rate to a "stabilized" NOI projection reflecting a more typical or average year for the building, or alternatively the DCF horizon may be extended another year or two.

[20]An alternative procedure for forecasting reversion value, growing the initial purchase price of the property at some specified growth rate, obviously does not protect the investor in this respect. Any mistake in the initial purchase price would simply be projected onto the reversion forecast, as per the Greater Fool Theory.

[21]As buildings age, they tend to gradually evolve from "class A" quality to "class B" quality, with the resulting required expected investment return risk premium evolving from that of "Institutional Quality" to "Noninstitutional Quality" real estate, as noted in Chapter 5 and as will be described in section 11.2 below (and further discussed in Chapter 22). Other things being equal, this phenomenon will tend to cause the going-out cap rate to exceed the going-in rate.

For example, if the asset market is particularly "exuberant" at the time of purchase, the going-in cap rate will tend to be abnormally low, and such a low rate should probably not be projected for the reversion. Alternatively, at the bottom of an asset market cycle cap rates might be abnormally high. We noted in Chapter 7 that in the private property market the asset value cycle has tended to be 15 to 20 years long. This suggests it might be best to extend the horizon of a DCF valuation to 15 or 20 years instead of the more conventional 10 years, as that way the property may be likely to be in the same phase of the asset market at the resale point as it is today, so the assumption of a going-out cap rate similar in magnitude to the going-in rate would be more realistic. If the investor is trying to use the DCF analysis to genuinely and realistically grapple with asset market cyclicality then, as noted, a longer DCF horizon will allow a valuation based more on fundamentals (operating cash flow) that is less susceptible to bias by current asset market conditions.[22]

Another possibility has to do with a cycle in the rental market. Consider the case in which a building has a large existing lease that was signed when the rental market was "hot" several years ago, but that lease will soon expire in a space market characterized by lower rents. The building's going-in cap rate will appear abnormally high, reflecting the large initial revenue from the vintage lease divided by a present asset value that reflects the likely lower rents in the future. In such a circumstance, it might be appropriate to project a going-out cap rate lower than the going-in rate.

11.1.8 Summary of Cash Flow Projection

The previous sections have provided a general overview of the cash flow projection process. For typical properties with a conventional 10-year proforma horizon, the implied present value or property valuation will be most sensitive to assumptions about the growth rate in future rents, the magnitude of the projected resale price (often a function of the assumption about the terminal cap rate), and the opportunity cost of capital that is applied as the discount rate, which will be discussed in section 11.2. Sometimes the assumption about the average vacancy rate can also have a large impact (especially for apartment properties). As suggested in the boxed feature on page 242, it is wise to perform some sensitivity analysis on the cash flow assumptions. To make the cash flow projection process more concrete, the CD and electronic resources of this book provides a simple numerical example for a hypothetical property. (See Appendix 11A on the student CD.)

11.2 Discount Rates: The Opportunity Cost of Capital

Recall that the DCF valuation procedure consists of numerators and denominators on the right-hand side of the valuation equation [formula (1) in Chapter 10]. The preceding section focused on the numerators, the cash flow projection. To complete the picture, we need to give some more attention now to the denominators. In particular, we need to consider the "**discount rate**" used in property level valuation, what we labeled $E[r]$ in the formula.

The basic conceptual idea behind the DCF discount rate was already discussed in Chapter 10. The discount rate is the multiperiod, dollar-weighted average *total* return expected by the investor, in the form of a going-in IRR. It is therefore an ex ante return measure. As it is a total return, the discount rate includes a risk premium (which we labeled RP) on top of the **risk-free rate** (which we labeled r_f). This risk premium should reflect the amount of risk in the cash flows that are being discounted. There must always be this relationship between the denominators and numerators in a DCF valuation: the denominators must reflect the risk that is in the numerators. For this reason, we noted that in some cases it is desirable to separate the property's cash flows into components that are characterized

---

[22]See the discussion in Chapter 12 about the difference between the "market value" and "investment value" of the property.

HOW ABOUT SOME "SENSITIVITY ANALYSIS" AND "SIMULATION"?

Now that you see all of the assumptions and forecasts that go into projecting the future cash flows that are so fundamental in evaluating a real estate asset, you must be asking yourself a question like the following: *Since we can't possibly know many of these inputs very certainly, what will happen if we are wrong about some of the projections?*

The most fundamental point to think about in addressing this question is to recognize that in asking this question you are simply confronting the fact that real estate assets are risky investments. But, of course, you already knew that. And we pointed out in Chapter 10 that the fundamental way we deal with this fact is in the discount rate that we use to bring our cash flow projections back to present value. The main point of the cash flow proforma is that the projections should be "unbiased," that is, "most likely" or "expected" amounts.

Having said that, it is nevertheless very tempting in some circumstances to go back and ask questions like: Even though I think it most likely the market rents will grow on average at 2 percent per year, how would it change my proforma and my valuation if they grow only at 1 percent per year (or zero percent, or even negative 1 percent, for example)? Quantitatively exploring questions like this is called "**sensitivity analysis**," and it can indeed be a useful exercise. The *Argus* cash flow analysis software mentioned previously and included on the book's accompanying CD can be helpful in performing sensitivity analysis. Such analysis tends to be most useful for examining specific contingencies, often related to the financial structuring of an investment in a real estate asset. For example, how low a rental growth rate will still enable the property's projected terminal reversion value to exceed a projected outstanding loan balance at that time on a mortgage used to finance the property acquisition?

If one also attaches subjective probabilities to the possible future parameters (e.g., 40 percent chance the rental growth rate will be 2 percent, 30 percent chance it will be zero percent, and 30 percent chance it will be 4 percent, probabilities that are consistent with an expectation of 2 percent growth), then the sensitivity analysis can be expanded to a "**simulation analysis**" of the question of interest about the property, in which subjective (ex ante) probabilities can be attached to outcomes.

While simulation analysis, and especially sensitivity analysis, can be useful investment analysis tools in real estate, we will not focus in depth on them in this book. Other books are more specialized in this subject. (See for example: Roger J. Brown, *Private Real Estate Investment: Data Analysis & Decision Making*, Academic Press Advanced Finance Series, 2006.) We do include an example of sensitivity analysis in Chapter 15 when we discuss project level capital structure (section 15.3.3).

Our only caveat in the use of simulation tools is that the generation of impressive statistics based on subjective probabilities and models of the relevant structural relationships (e.g., between rent growth, and expense growth and interest rates) can present an *appearance* of knowing more than you actually do. Don't kid yourself. In the face of real risk and uncertainty, humility is always a virtue, and the parsimony of the fundamental economic model we are working with brings some useful elegance to our analysis. That parsimony is the idea that the discount rate fully captures the valuation implications of the risk and uncertainty, and the discount rate is the opportunity cost of capital, which derives from equilibrium in the capital markets including the market where the subject asset trades. The capital market cares about risk. Do you know more than the market knows?

by different risk, for example, existing lease cash flows versus residual cash flows. More often, however, at least in current practice, a single "blended" discount rate is applied to the entire net cash flow of the property, especially if the property has a typical multitenant occupancy and lease expiration pattern. What we want to do in this section is to focus at a more practical level, to provide some guidance about how to determine what is a reasonable rate to use in the DCF valuation of typical commercial properties.

A good place to begin is to recall the answer to the basic question, Where do discount rates come from? The DCF discount rate is meant to be the **opportunity cost of capital (OCC)** for the subject investment. It is the return investors could typically expect to earn (on average) in other investments of similar risk to the subject investment. This is what is required to get investors to be just willing to invest in the subject property. If the expected return in the subject property is lower than that of similar-risk investments, no one would want to invest in it; if the expected return in the subject property is higher than that in similar-risk investments, then there will be a stampede of investors wanting to sell other investments and use the money to buy it, which would drive up the price of the subject property until this price offered a return similar to the other investments. (Recall the inverse relationship between the current price of the asset and its expected return.) As "other investments," by definition, are traded in the capital markets, we can therefore say that discount rates "come from" the capital markets (including both public and private asset markets).

11.2.1 General Observations about Real Estate Discount Rates

This concept of the OCC is all well and good in principle, but what can we say in practice about how to determine the specific numbers to use in analyzing real estate investments? Two steps are involved in answering this question. First, we need to be able to draw empirical conclusions about the typical rates of return investors expect from different types of investments. Second, we need to make some judgment about the relative risk of the property we are interested in, as compared to other investments whose ex ante returns we think we can observe empirically.

Two of the characteristics that define a well-functioning asset market are that there is sufficient volume of trading of assets and sufficient information about transaction prices and asset income yields so that investors can make reasonably informed judgments about the ex ante returns prevailing in the market. Clearly, public stock and bond markets provide a wealth of historical information that helps investors to estimate reasonable return expectations. As stocks and bonds are part of the overall investment universe in which real estate competes, information about stock and bond returns is also relevant for forming real estate return expectations. In addition, the private real estate asset market functions sufficiently well to provide direct empirical evidence about expected returns for most types of real estate.

It is important to recognize that equilibrium expected returns vary over time in asset markets, therefore, discount rates employed in a DCF valuation should similarly vary over time if one is trying to represent current market valuations. Time-varying return expectations happen in real estate markets as well as in the stock and bond market. Generally speaking, when asset prices are "high" (in the sense of historically high price/income multiples), then realistic return expectations going forward are "low" (and *vice versa*). This may be because the real risk-free rate changes over time with the relative supply and demand for capital, or it may be because investors' risk perceptions or preferences change over time. However, *stated* return expectations may change less than actual realistic return expectations based on realistic cash flow forecasts.[23]

In general, it is useful to recall what was noted in Chapter 9 about the two ways of breaking out a total investment return r:

(1) $r = r_f + RP$

(2) $r = y + g$

where r_f is the risk-free interest rate, RP is the risk premium relevant for the subject asset, y is the current annual income cash yield payout rate from the asset, and g is the expected growth rate or capital gain component in the total return.[24] In principle, both of these perspectives should agree and add up to the same total return rate: r. In practice, breakout (1), $r_f + RP$, can often be more easily applied to represent a normative or "equilibrium model" of what the expected return *should* be (realistically), whereas breakout (2), $y + g$, may be more easily inferred from direct and current empirical evidence about prices and incomes in the asset

---

[23]We described in Chapter 10 how unrealistic discount rates can be applied to unrealistic cash flow forecasts such that the two errors cancel out in the DCF exercise, to arrive at an accurate valuation of the subject asset in the current market. See also section 22.1.2 for further elaboration regarding time-varying discount rates.

[24]Since we're generally employing a multiperiod return measure (as real asset investments typically have a multiyear time horizon), the g component may be thought of as consisting of both the cash flow change (*CFC*) and yield change (*YC*) components in the IRR attribution breakout components described in Appendix 10A of the preceding chapter.

marketplace. Thus, in practice the two perspectives do not always agree, and when they don't, this can have implications about where one is in the real estate asset market pricing cycle. (More about this shortly.)

With the above general considerations in mind, let's try to give you some more specific and practical advice about discount rates.

11.2.2 Putting in Some Numbers: The Risk-Free Rate

As the OCC consists of two components, the risk-free rate plus the risk premium ($r_f + RP$), let us begin by considering how we should quantify the risk-free component in the context of a multiyear, forward-looking IRR.

For a short-term investment, the traditional choice to use for r_f is the current T-bill yield, the return expected on investments in the government's short-term debt. Such investments have virtually no interest-rate risk and traditionally have virtually no default risk. However, the typical real estate investment is long term. As noted, the typical DCF analysis will be performed over a 10-year horizon, with the discount rate being a single, blended IRR that represents a long-term OCC. Current T-bill yields may reflect transient market conditions and efforts by the Federal Reserve Bank to control the economy through monetary policy, in addition to the capital market's supply of and demand for short-term money.

In this context, the relevant risk-free component for use in a long-term real estate investment's OCC is not the current T-bill yield but rather the *average* T-bill rate expected over the long-term investment horizon. A relevant number is this regard is the current yield on long-term Treasury bonds, such as the 10-year T-bond. But it is important to recognize that long-term T-bonds are not riskless, and their yields reflect some risk premium in the investment marketplace. To adjust for this, a simple approach is to subtract from the current long-term T-bond yield the typical or average "yield curve effect," that is, the *difference* between the yield on long-term and short-term government debt that typically prevails in the capital market. This is typically 100–200 basis points between 3-month and 10-year U.S. Treasury securities.[25] Thus, for example, if 10-year Treasury bonds are currently yielding 4.5 percent, one might subtract about 150 basis points from this yield to reflect an average expected risk-free rate of about 3 percent during the next 10 years.

11.2.3 Putting in Some More Numbers: Historical Evidence on the OCC for Institutional Commercial Property

With the above general considerations in mind, let's begin by building on what we learned in Chapter 7 about the historical returns to different broad classes of assets, to shed some light on what are typically appropriate rates to use in discounting real estate cash flows. In particular, we will focus now on the risk premium (*RP*) component within the $r_f + RP$ model of the OCC. Exhibit 11-5 reproduces a part of Exhibit 7-9 and computes the historical **risk premiums** ("excess returns" over T-bills) associated with the total returns on stocks, bonds, and real estate. This has been done in Exhibit 11-5 by treating the return to Treasury bills as the risk-free rate (r_f) and subtracting this from the average annual total returns earned by each of the other three asset classes over the same period of time.

From this exhibit, we see that, during the 1970–2010 period, the risk premium on the sorts of institutional quality commercial properties represented by the NCREIF index averaged 4.55 percent (or 455 basis points). The risk premium on long-term bonds was 366 basis points, while the risk premium on stocks was the highest, at 596 basis points.

If these historical risk premiums represent current expectations, then we can apply them to the projected Treasury bill yield as we described it in the previous subsection to derive

---

[25]Over the period 1926–2010, the average annual difference between the yield on the 10-year U.S. Treasury Bond and the return on the 30-day Treasury Bill was 1.64% (164 basis points).

Asset Class	Total Return	Volatility	Risk Premium
T-Bills	5.60%	3.10%	NA
G Bonds	9.26%	11.73%	3.66%
Real Estate	10.15%	10.86%	4.55%
Stocks (S&P 500)	11.56%	17.91%	5.96%

EXHIBIT 11-5 Historical Return, Risk, and Risk Premiums, 1970–2003

Source: Based on data from NCREIF, Ibbotson, TBI.

current expected total returns. For example, if the projected average Treasury bill yield is 3 percent, then adding an approximately 4 percent risk premium to this risk-free rate would suggest an expected total return for institutional quality commercial real estate of about 7 percent, going forward on investments made as of some time when 10-year T-bond yields are in the 4 to 5 percent range as described above. If T-bond yields were in the 6 to 7 percent range, then the real estate OCC would be more like 5% + 4% = 9%.

Of course, it must be recognized with this approach that the historical results in Exhibit 11-4 are **ex post risk premiums**, not **ex ante expectations**. They represent the realization of what actually did happen during one sample of time (1970–2010), not necessarily what investors were expecting *would happen* when they made their investments (in the sense of what was realistically implied ex ante in the prices they were paying), nor necessarily what investors currently are expecting. Nevertheless, to the extent that the future is not expected to be too radically different from the past, historical results such as those in Exhibit 11-5 do provide important information relevant to forming current expectations, especially regarding the asset class as a whole.[26]

11.2.4 Another Perspective: Survey Evidence

In addition to historical empirical evidence, another way to get an idea about investors' expected returns on real estate investments is simply to *ask them*, at frequent intervals. Several national real estate information firms regularly survey the investment community and publish the average stated returns investors say they expect going forward. In addition, brokerage and appraisal firms, as well as commercial mortgage underwriters, usually have a working familiarity with the discount rates that are currently being used for specific types of property in specific types of locations.

The results of a widely used national survey of investor return expectations, presented in Exhibit 11-6 for the 1992–2010 period, will serve to illustrate this type of survey-based evidence about investor return expectations. Exhibit 11-6 shows the reported values of the PwC Yield Indicator (PYI), a national survey-based measure of professional investors' expected total returns (free-and-clear going-in IRRs) on unlevered investments in institutional quality commercial property.[27]

The PYI pertains to the same types of property, and is based on the same types of institutional investors, as the **NCREIF Property Index (NPI)** we considered previously for the historical record. For purposes of comparison, Exhibit 11-6 also shows the historical cumulative average annual total return to the NPI since its inception (at the end of 1977) up to each year indicated in the exhibit. Thus, in Exhibit 11-6, the PYI indicates investors' stated *expected* property-level returns going forward in investments as of the year indicated,

---

[26]Additional perspective on long-term expectations can be obtained from modeling the equilibrium risk premiums in the capital markets, as will be discussed in Chapter 22.

[27]The PYI (formerly Korpacz Yield Indicator—KYI) is published quarterly in the PwC Real Estate Investor Survey, by PricewaterhouseCoopers, LLP. Similar information is published by other firms.

EXHIBIT 11-6 Backward-Looking vs. Forward-Looking Total Returns in the U.S. Institutional Property Market: NCREIF vs. PwC

© OnCourse Learning

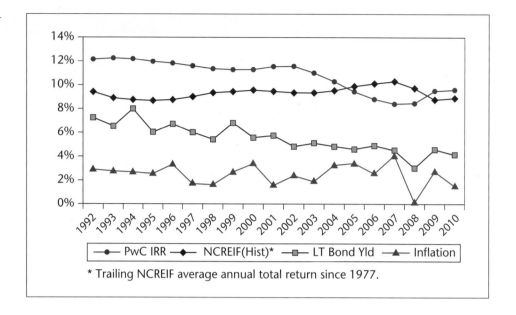

* Trailing NCREIF average annual total return since 1977.

while the NPI indicates actual average ex post property performance as of that same year (since 1978). Exhibit 11-6 also shows current long-term government bond yields, and the current inflation rate, as of each year. The bond yield, like the PYI, is a current ex ante measure, although the nature of bonds enables this to be an objective measure based on current bond market prices and the yields to maturity implied by those prices.

11.2.5 Getting an Indication of Realistic Total Return Expectations by Observing Current Cap Rates in the Property Market

In addition to historical information from sources such as NCREIF or IPD, and survey information such as described above, a third approach to estimating current expected returns in the property market is to start by observing the cap rates (or current yields) that are prevailing in the relevant property market. It is easier to objectively and empirically observe the cap rates at which properties trade than it is to observe the ex ante total returns investors are expecting in those trades. All you need to observe cap rates empirically is information about transaction prices and the likely net operating income (NOI) of the traded properties. Because of this, investors polled in surveys may tend to state their going-in cap rate expectations more realistically than their going-in IRRs. Or you can compute your own estimate of current average cap rates if you have access to transaction price data.[28] This approach of basing the OCC estimation on current cap rate evidence can therefore be a way to apply the $y + g$ model of the OCC suggested in section 11.2.1 as a means of inferring the current expected returns actually (and realistically) prevailing in the marketplace.

The cap rate itself is not directly the same as the going-in IRR we need for the DCF denominators (OCC), but the cap rate and the IRR are closely related, as noted in Chapter 10. In particular, at least as an approximation, we can invoke the **constant-growth perpetuity model** (introduced in Chapter 8). Recall that this implies that the current yield equals the long-run expected total return minus the long-run expected average growth rate in the property net cash flow and value. Turning this relationship around, we can derive at least an

---

[28]Information on transaction price-based cap rates in the institutional commercial property market is becoming more available, from sources such as NCREIF, Real Capital Analytics, CoStar, and others.

EXHIBIT 11-7 Stated Going-in IRRs, Cap Rates, and Inflation

© OnCourse Learning

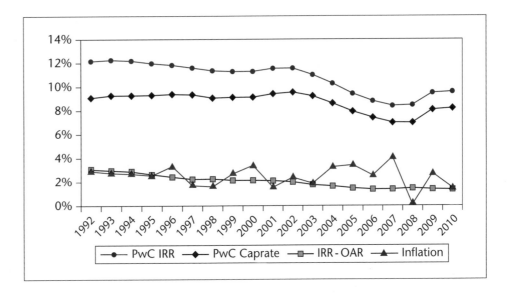

approximate indication of the expected *total* return (or discount rate) from observations about current cap rates, by adding realistic growth expectations onto the cap rates:

$$E[r] = E[y] + E[g] \approx (Cap\ Rate) + E[g]$$

With this in mind, Exhibit 11-7 presents both IRR and cap rate information from the PwC survey.[29] However, it is important to note that the cap rates reported in the survey, as is typical of cap rates quoted in the industry, are based on property NOI, not the property PBTCF that reflects actual cash flow net of capital expenditures (as described in section 11.1). But the $E[y]$ that matters for computing the $E[r]$ in the above formula should be the actual net cash flow yield. Thus, we need to adjust the survey-based cap rates downward by typically about 100 to 200 basis points to reflect this difference (as discussed in section 11.1.5). If the survey reported cap rate is 7 percent, the relevant $E[y]$ rate in the formula above might be 5 percent to 6 percent.

The $E[g]$ component in the above formula can be estimated from typical rent growth rates in the space market in which the property is situated, net of the "real depreciation" effect discussed in section 11.1.1 (and recall more fundamentally the principles introduced in Chapter 5). The $E[g]$ component should also reflect the effect of likely "cap rate creep," as the going-out cap rate will tend to exceed the going-in cap rate in a long-term investment on average, bringing down slightly the realistically expected going-in IRR, in spite of capital improvement expenditures on the property (as described in section 11.1.7). Thus, in a typical property market where rents are expected to grow over the long term at, say, a projected CPI inflation rate of 3 percent/year, one might reduce the realistically applicable $E[g]$ rate in the formula above by 100 to 200 basis points to perhaps 1.5 percent.[30]

Putting the realistically adjusted $E[y]$ and $E[g]$ components together as in the above formula, we obtain a realistic going-in IRR of, for example (based on the previously noted 7 percent empirically observed cap rate):

$$E[r] = E[y] + E[g] = 5.5\% + 1.5\% = 7\% = OCC$$

Specific numbers might differ for specific property markets based on the survey evidence about the perceived cap rates. But note that in a circumstance where inflation is low, say,

---

[29]Another expression for cap rate is "overall rate," often abbreviated as "OAR."

[30]Recall from Appendix in Chapter 10 that the IRR can be parsed into three major additive components: the initial cash yield (which corresponds to the realistic $E[y]$ component here), and two growth components: the cash flow change effect and the yield change effect, which together determine the $E[g]$ component here.

3 percent or less per year, the realistic expected total return often ends up being very similar to the NOI-based cap rate, after you consider the effect of capital improvement expenditures and the real depreciation of the property. (In the present example the resulting OCC turns out to be *exactly* the same as the observed cap rate.)

Yet the survey-based numbers in Exhibit 11-7 indicate that investors in the U.S. institutional property market tend to state that they *perceive* that they will get a total return somewhat *greater* than the cap rate. (Note that **overall rate** or **OAR** is another term for cap rate.) The IRR-OAR line in Exhibit 11-7 is positive, not zero, and though it has been declining in recent years, it remained well over 100 basis points in 2010. On a subjective, ex ante basis, investors may be expecting less capital improvement expenditures, or more inflation or growth in rents, or less real depreciation in their buildings, than seems to be borne out on average for institutional real estate in the United States, based on the other evidence discussed particularly in Parts I and II of this book and earlier in the present chapter. This may be part and parcel of the "typical mistakes" or "underwriting perspective" noted in our discussion of the use of the DCF technique in Chapter 10 (see section 10.5). We noted there that investors often overestimate cash flow growth in the numerators and offset this by applying unrealistically high discount rates (going-in IRRs) in the denominators. This is also suggested in Exhibit 11-6, where the going-forward stated nominal IRR expectations approximately equal or even exceed the long-term historical NPI total returns, even though the latter occurred during a period when inflation averaged higher than current inflation expectations (implying investors expecting higher real estate returns than historically achieved, in real terms).

11.2.6 Double Checking: Two Perspectives on the OCC Estimate

We have now suggested how to quantify two different perspectives on estimating the OCC for real estate investments. The "risk premium approach" is given by the $r_f + RP$ sum of the risk-free interest rate plus appropriate risk premium. The "cap rate approach" is given by the $y + g$ sum of the current realistic income and growth components. In practice, the former approach can often more easily reflect an underlying normative or equilibrium theory perspective, that is, what the OCC *should* be, while the latter approach is more directly based on or observable from current empirical evidence in the property asset marketplace, in particular, the cap rates at which properties are trading. In principle, and often in practice, these two perspectives agree; they give the same OCC number. But it is a very useful exercise to try to quantify the OCC from both perspectives. Doing so not only helps to hone the accuracy and reliability of the resulting estimate, but it also deepens your (the investor's) understanding about a very fundamental question: what is the investment return on the property asset about which you're making an investment decision.

Sometimes these two perspectives on the OCC differ, and this can raise a "red flag." As an example, let us look at data typical of what is widely available in the real estate investment industry. For illustrative purposes, we will consider data published by Real Capital Analytics Inc. (RCA), though there are other sources out there in the marketplace. According to RCA as of August 2007, the peak month of the asset market cycle of the 2000s decade, the nationwide average cap rate among sales that month of core institutional commercial properties was 6.44 percent.[31] Thus, with inflation expectations running around 3 percent, the "cap rate approach" described in section 11.2.5 might have led one to a realistic OCC or going-in IRR estimate for a typical institutional core property investment of:

$$r = 6.44\% - 1.5\% + 3\% - 1.5\% = 6.44\%$$

But at that same time, 10-year Treasury Bonds were yielding an average of 4.67 percent. Thus, based on the "risk premium approach" described in sections 11.2.2 and 11.2.3, and

---

[31]This was based on approximately 1200 sales of apartment, industrial, office, and retail properties of greater than $5,000,000 value. (Source: Real Capital Analytics.)

assuming a typical 400 basis points RP assumption (based on historical average institutional real estate performance), we would estimate an OCC of:

$$r = 4.67\% - 1.5\% + 4\% = 7.1\%$$

The two approaches differ, with the risk premium approach suggesting a higher OCC than the cap rate approach. The difference is not huge, and perhaps it can be dismissed, as no doubt it largely was back in 2007 (if it was even noted at all). After all, there is plenty of fuzziness in many of the numbers and assumptions going into this analysis. But if the difference is real and meaningful, what it implied was that the then-current (2007) asset prices underlying the observed transaction based cap rates were providing a realistic expected return going-forward *less* than what the risk premium model was at the same time suggesting they should have been providing. In other words, U.S. commercial property prices were on average too high. This would imply that they might be in for a fall, which of course is what certainly did happen, shortly after that time.

Role the clock forward to December 2009, the bottom of the subsequent trough in asset prices. At that time the same data source was stating an average transaction based cap rate of 7.88 percent,[32] with 10-year T-bonds yielding 3.59 percent. Thus, at that time the two approaches (holding other assumptions the same) were giving on average:

Cap rate approach:	$r = 7.88\% - 1.5\% + 3\% - 1.5\% = 7.88\%$
Risk premium approach:	$r = 3.59\% - 1.5\% + 4\% = 6.09\%$

Once again the two approaches are disagreeing, only now the difference goes in the opposite direction, with the more normative risk premium approach suggesting a *lower* OCC than the more empirical cap rate approach. You might say that inflation expectations in December 2009 would have been reduced below 3 percent in the recession, or that the market was requiring a risk premium higher than the more conventional 4 percent assumption due to extreme risk aversion in the aftermath of the financial crisis of 2008. But even so, the suggestion is apparent in the difference between these two approaches that property prices by December 2009 had fallen too low, that they were primed for a rebound, which is exactly what happened in 2010 among the sorts of larger institutional properties measured here.

Our point is not that real estate valuation or investment analysis can be as precise or as easy as suggested by this exercise. Our point is that it can be useful to go through an exercise like this, and to *think about* the results you get, mindful of the tendency of the property asset market to be somewhat cyclical. Real estate investment analysis is always a mixture of both "science" and "art."

11.2.7 Variation in Return Expectations for Different Types of Property

The preceding section gave some idea about how to quantify realistic discount rates at a broad-brush level, that is, for typical **institutional quality commercial property**. This has traditionally been considered to include large, fully operational, income-producing properties of high-quality construction in high-quality locations (so-called class A or premium properties). But, as different types of commercial property have different amounts of investment risk, the appropriate discount rate should differ accordingly across property types. In this regard, the type and location of the property, though not to be ignored, is often less important than two other dimensions that govern the perceived ex ante risk and return of the property: the *size* of the property (as measured by its value) and its operational or life cycle status.[33]

As far as perceived risk and return are concerned, "large" properties may be defined as those that typically interest major institutional equity investors. For example, by the early

---

[32]Based on 537 sales nationwide, of the same types of properties as noted above.

[33]This issue will also be discussed in Chapter 22, where we speculate that the difference noted here may be akin to the effect of the "Fama-French" factors of size and book-to-market ratio noted in the stock market.

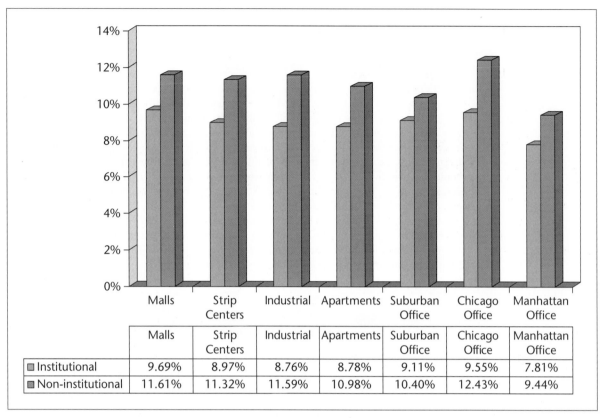

	Malls	Strip Centers	Industrial	Apartments	Suburban Office	Chicago Office	Manhattan Office
Institutional	9.69%	8.97%	8.76%	8.78%	9.11%	9.55%	7.81%
Non-institutional	11.61%	11.32%	11.59%	10.98%	10.40%	12.43%	9.44%

EXHIBIT 11-8A Investor Total Return Expectations (IRR) for Various Property Types
Source: PwC Real Estate Investor Survey, 2nd quarter 2011.

2010s, the average individual property in the NCREIF index was worth over $40 million. Large institutions (including REITs) are the primary equity investors in such properties, and these institutions have traditionally perceived such properties, when they are "stabilized" (or fully operational, that is, fully leased, or nearly so), as being relatively low risk. As many of these institutions tend to be conservative regarding their risk preferences, such properties are viewed as real estate investment **portfolio core properties**. Smaller, older, or less fully utilized properties, as well as development or redevelopment projects are viewed as being more risky by these investors and as such are often referred to as noninstitutional or noncore properties.[34]

Exhibits 11-8a and 11-8b show the typical differences in expected total returns and cap rates across different types of commercial property in the early 2000s, once again based on the PwC survey.[35] Expected returns and stated cap rates for noninstitutional properties are typically at least 100 to 200 basis points greater than those for otherwise similar institutional properties. This difference reflects a greater ex ante risk premium applied by investors in noninstitutional property.

---

[34]Institutions also invest in some such noninstitutional properties (usually larger ones), but they are often classified in a different component of the portfolio as "opportunistic" or "alternative" (or simply referred to as "noncore") investments, aimed at earning high returns by knowingly taking on higher risk.

[35]For additional evidence on institutional property cap rates from a different source, see Exhibit 1-11 in Chapter 1, based on actual transaction prices rather than surveys. Empirical cap rate information of various types (based on transactions, appraisals, or surveys and estimates) are available from a number of industry sources, including (among others) NCREIF, Real Capital Analytics, CoStar, Real Estate Research Corporation.

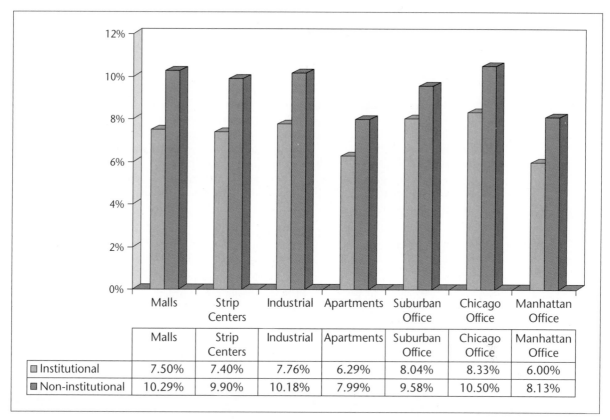

	Malls	Strip Centers	Industrial	Apartments	Suburban Office	Chicago Office	Manhattan Office
Institutional	7.50%	7.40%	7.76%	6.29%	8.04%	8.33%	6.00%
Non-institutional	10.29%	9.90%	10.18%	7.99%	9.58%	10.50%	8.13%

EXHIBIT 11-8B Investor Cap Rate Expectations for Various Property Types

Source: PwC Real Estate Investor Survey, 2nd quarter 2011.

There is some debate as to whether this differential in risk premiums is justified by the actual difference in the amount of investment risk. It is not clear, for example, why size per se should affect the risk. On the other hand, properties that are less fully occupied, or in need of major development or redevelopment investment, or that are occupied by tenants that are less creditworthy, will clearly carry greater uncertainty about their future net cash flow generation potential and about the quality of information available about the property.[36]

It also seems likely that the private property asset markets are somewhat **segmented**, or characterized by different investor **clienteles**. Smaller-scale individual investors tend to dominate the asset market for the smaller noninstitutional properties, while large financial institutions and REITs dominate in the institutional asset market. These different investor clienteles may have different risk perceptions and preferences. For example, small investors may not be able to diversify their portfolios as well as large institutions can, exposing them to more risk from property investments. If this is so, and the typical clientele investors are the marginal investors in each market segment, then asset market prices in that segment will reflect each clientele's risk perceptions and preferences. This could

---

[36]This is not just greater purely random volatility. It is likely that the greater downside in noninstitutional property would tend to coincide temporally with slumps in the macroeconomy, while the upside would coincide with economic booms. Thus, it may be difficult to fully diversify away the added risk in noninstitutional property. A similar effect is noted in the so-called small-cap and the book/market equity ratio factors in the stock market. Small stocks and those with relatively high book/market equity ratios tend to require higher expected returns, on average. This issue is discussed in more depth in Chapter 22.

explain higher expected returns for noninstitutional properties (see further discussion in Chapter 22).

Certain types of property investments are traditionally considered more risky than the major core types of commercial properties portrayed in Exhibit 11-7. For example, hotel properties, especially if they are not luxury hotels in prime locations, will typically command risk premiums 100 to 300 basis points above those of the four major core property types (office, industrial, retail, and apartment). In part, this may be due to the lack of leases governing their rents. At the extreme for real estate return expectations (on unlevered investments), raw land is reputed to command total return expectations typically in the 15 percent to 30 percent range. Such real estate generally produces little or no current positive cash flow, and its value depends entirely on the NPV of future construction that can be built on it. As noted in Part II, this gives raw land investment performance characteristics like those of call options, similar to that of a highly levered investment in the underlying asset (the future building on the site).

11.3 Chapter Summary

Chapter 11 put the flesh on the bones of the micro-level investment valuation framework laid out in Chapter 10 by getting down to the specifics of cash flow projection and discount rate determination in the DCF process. Keep in mind that at this level of specificity, things change over time, and each deal must be considered anew. Nevertheless, in this chapter, we tried to present a way of approaching the quantification of real estate valuation parameters and showed how to characterize realistic base assumptions. The burden of proof lies with those who claim assumptions significantly different from these.

KEY TERMS

proforma
operating cash flows
reversion cash flows
potential gross income (PGI)
rent roll
rent comps analysis
vacancy allowance
effective gross income (EGI)
other income
operating expenses
property management
 opportunity cost
fixed costs
variable costs
net leases

expense stops
net operating income (NOI)
capital improvement expenditures
leasing costs
tenant improvement
 expenditures (TIs)
leasing commissions
concessions
property-before-tax cash flow
 (PBTCF)
reversion cap rate
going-out cap rate
terminal cap rate
resale cap rate
going-in cap rate

discount rate
risk-free rate
sensitivity analysis
simulation analysis
opportunity cost of capital (OCC)
risk premiums
ex post risk premiums
ex ante expectations
NCREIF property index (NPI)
constant-growth perpetuity model
overall rate (OAR)
institutional quality commercial
 property
portfolio core properties
capital market segments and clienteles

STUDY QUESTIONS

Conceptual Questions

11.1. Define net operating income (NOI) for commercial real estate assets (formula), and state the three typical recipients of this cash flow.

11.2. What is the difference between the net operating income and the property's before-tax cash flow (PBTCF)?

11.3. What are the major categories of capital improvement expenditures (CI)? How do capital expenditures differ from regular operating expenses?

11.4. Describe the two different ways investors might account for capital improvement expenditures in multiyear proformas.

11.5. Consider the projection of the reversion value in a multiyear DCF valuation.

   a. What should be the typical expected relationship between the going-in cap rate and the going-out (reversion or terminal value) cap rate projected for the resale of the property at the end of the expected holding period (i.e., should you usually expect the going-out to be less than, equal to, or greater than the going-in)?

   b. Why?

   c. How is your answer related to projected capital improvement expenditures during the holding period?

   d. How is your answer related to the state of the property market at the time of purchase of the property at the beginning of the holding period (factors that affect the going-in rate)?

11.6. What items should be included in the operating expenses but taken out before computing the property NOI?

11.7. Why should you subtract management expenses before determining the property NOI even if you are managing the property yourself?

11.8. What does it mean that "discount rates come from the capital markets"?

11.9. Why is it more difficult to determine discount rates to employ in valuing assets traded in private markets compared to public markets?

11.10. Outline the three approaches discussed in section 11.2 to determine the appropriate discount rate or opportunity cost of capital in property valuation. Highlight the pros and cons of each.

11.11. Provide two explanations suggested to justify a higher ex ante risk premium in the discount rate used to value noninstitutional class property relative to institutional property.

Quantitative Problems

11.12. A tenant has a gross lease with an "expense stop" of $2.75/SF. If the building has 200,000 SF of leasable space, reimbursable operating expenses of $750,000, and the tenant rents 25,000 SF, then how much does the tenant owe the landlord in expense reimbursements (the total dollar amount)?

11.13. Show a 10-year proforma projection of the operating NOI and net property-before-tax cash flow (PBTCF) for a three-unit apartment house in which (a) each unit currently (year 1) rents for $300/month; (b) rents are projected to grow at 3 percent per year; (c) the average tenant will remain three years, and then the apartment will be vacant an average of three months before the next tenant moves in; (d) operating expenses are currently estimated at $1,500 per unit per year (including management expenses), expected to escalate at 3 percent per year; (e) you anticipate needing to replace kitchen appliances for $1,000 per unit in year 3; and (f) you anticipate having to replace the single roof for $2,500 in year 5.

11.14. A 150,000-SF office building has a triple-net lease providing a constant rent of $20/SF per year. (With a triple-net lease, you can assume the rent equals the net operating cash flow.) The lease has five years before it expires (i.e., assume the next payment comes in one year, and there are four more annual payments after that under the present lease). Rents on similar leases being signed today are $22/SF. You expect rents on new leases to grow at 2.5 percent per year for existing buildings. You expect to release the building in year 6 after the current lease expires, but only after experiencing an expected vacancy of six months, and after spending $10/SF in tenant improvements (TIs). After 10 years, you expect to sell the building at a price equal to 10 times the then-prevailing rent in new triple-net leases. Based on survey information about typical going-in IRRs prevailing currently in the market for this type of property, you think the market would require a 12 percent expected return for this building.

    a. What is the NPV of an investment in this property if the price is $30 million? Should you do the deal?

    b. What will be the IRR at that price?

    c. What is the cap rate at the $30 million price?

11.15. Consider the building described in Question 11.14. Suppose everything is the same except that, since the time the current lease was signed, the market for office space has softened. Rents on new leases are lower now and will be only $18/SF next year instead of the $20/SF that prevailed when the current lease was signed. Furthermore, suppose that the current lease has only one more year until it expires, instead of five. You expect to release in year 2, and again in year 7, with six months of vacancy and $10/SF in capital expenditures each time, as before. You still expect growth of 2.5 percent per year in new-lease rental rates, starting from the expected year-1 level of $18.

    a. What is the value of the property under the required return assumption of Question 11.14?

    b. What would be the NPV of the deal from the buyer's perspective if the owner wants to sell the building at a cap rate of 10 percent based on the existing lease?

    c. What would be the cap rate for this building at the zero-NPV price?

    d. Why is the market value cap rate so different in this case than in the case presented in Question 11.14?

11.16. You are a financial analyst constructing a multiyear proforma to value a potential property acquisition. As part of the analysis, you are considering the most likely scenario for a certain space for which the current tenant's lease will expire at the end of 2008. You estimate the following: the probability the existing tenant renews is 50 percent; if the tenant renews, you will need to spend an estimated $5/SF to upgrade the space; should the tenant not renew, it will take $15/SF to modernize the space for a new tenant; and you expect there will be six months of vacancy. Leases in this property are "triple-net" with the owner responsible for operating expenses associated with vacant space. Reimbursable building level operating expenses are expected to be $5.50 in 2009, while market rent for triple-net leases is expected to be $14/SF. What is the expected property before-tax cash flow forecast (on a per square foot basis) you will put in year 2009 of your proforma for this space?

11.17. It is late November and you are undertaking an investment analysis of an office property that your firm is considering purchasing at the end of this year. The property has 80,000 SF of leasable space currently occupied by two tenants each leasing 40,000 SF. Both tenants have triple-net leases; all operating expenses are passed through to tenants. The owner pays operating expenses associated with vacant space. Current "market" rent is $20/SF on a triple net basis (for leases signed today). Operating expenses for the property are currently $6/SF per year.

    Tenant #1: has 15 years left on a long-term, fixed payment lease with annual rental payments at $15/SF (constant for the next 15 years). This firm has a strong AAA credit rating.

    Tenant #2: lease expires at the end of the next year and calls for fixed rental payments at $18/SF. As part of your analysis therefore, you have to estimate vacancy allowance and tenant improvement expenditure line items for year 2. You feel that the probability of the existing tenant renewing its lease is 80 percent. If they do not renew, you anticipate four months of vacancy and that your firm will have to spend $10/SF to modernize the space for the next tenant. If, on the other hand, the existing tenant renews, your firm will not spend any money on tenant improvements for this space (note, both your vacancy allowance and TI numbers are expected values in the sense they reflect the probability of nonrenewal). Assume any lease signed will have at least a five-year term and fixed rental payments and that the next tenant would lease the full 40,000 SF.

a. Determine the "market value" of the property assuming a five-year holding period with a sale at an anticipated terminal cap rate of 9 percent and selling expenses of 3 percent. Market rents are expected to grow by 2 percent per year, and the typical investor requires a 10.5 percent total return (market going-in IRR).

b. Briefly explain in what sense the 10.5 percent required IRR is a "blended" required rate of return and why it might actually be difficult to infer the appropriate discount rate to employ here from recent market activity (i.e., survey and recent transaction information).

12

ADVANCED MICRO-LEVEL VALUATION

CHAPTER OUTLINE

LEARNING OBJECTIVES

After reading this chapter, you should understand:

⊃ The relationship between investment value (IV) and market value (MV) in the asset market, and how to use both of these concepts in real estate investment decision making.

⊃ The circumstances that make substantially positive NPV investment opportunities realistic.

⊃ The investment implications of imperfect price discovery in the real estate asset market.

⊃ The implications, for equity investors at the micro-level, of the simultaneous existence of two types or levels of real estate asset markets: the property market and the REIT market.

⊃ The difference between firm-level REIT cost of capital and the micro-level opportunity cost of capital applicable to REIT valuation of individual properties at the micro-level.

C hapters 10 and 11 introduced you to the basics of doing investment analysis and evaluation at the micro-level of individual deals, or transactions, involving commercial property. The material presented there is essentially standard corporate finance and investments fare applied to real estate. However, to be a more sophisticated user of such methods in the real estate arena, you should be aware of some additional issues and concepts relating to the unique situation of real estate.

In particular, the commercial real estate investment environment has three salient characteristics that differ from the typical corporate capital budgeting environment or the typical securities investment environment, the focus of most mainstream finance textbooks.

1. Unlike the typical corporate environment, a well-functioning market usually exists for the underlying physical assets that are being considered, namely, commercial buildings (as opposed to, say, pharmaceutical labs or microchip plants).

2. Although the commercial real estate asset market is a well-functioning market, it is not as informationally efficient in some sense as the market for publicly traded securities, such as the stock market in which most industrial corporations trade (and in which REITs trade as well), with implications for price discovery as this relates to asset values and investment strategy.

3. In addition to the private real estate asset market, there also exists a large market for publicly traded REIT shares in the stock exchange. Thus, parallel asset markets, or two levels of asset markets, are both relevant for real estate investment.

The major issues raised by these three differences are the subject of the present chapter. These are rather subtle issues, relating to basic economic and valuation theory, and their subtlety makes them worthy of advanced students, such as yourselves. So, fasten your seatbelts!

12.1 Market Value and Investment Value

Up to now, we have been defining and measuring NPV on the basis of the market value of the assets involved in the deal, with market value defined as the expected price at which the assets would sell currently in the private real estate asset market. We noted that such a definition of NPV is possible because that market is a well-functioning market for the assets in question, the property market. Now we need to think about this in a little more depth.

In some sense, we have been treating real estate asset values in much the same way as stock market analysts treat stock values.[1] But investors in stocks can buy and sell very quickly and easily, at very low transaction costs, without assuming any management burden of the assets they are purchasing. As a result, stock market investors typically hold onto a given stock for a relatively short period of time, often only a couple of years or less for many stocks for many traders. On the other hand, when you buy a commercial property, it is typically something you are investing in for the long haul; average holding periods for institutional investors are typically between five and ten years and often longer.

In this respect, real estate investing is more like corporate capital budgeting than it is like stock market investing. Corporations make decisions to allocate their capital to long-lived projects to produce real goods and services over a long period of time, such as a new chemical plant or a line of consumer products. But the corporate capital budgeting situation is a bit different from the real estate situation, too, for the previously noted reason that there is typically no well-functioning market for the underlying assets in which the corporation is investing.

Because real estate straddles these two worlds (securities investments and corporate capital budgeting), we need to be careful in how we apply the classical principles and methodologies developed in these two fields. In this regard, the first thing we must do is pursue the concept of *value* in a bit more depth.

To begin, let us be clear what we mean by **market value** (which we will sometimes abbreviate as **MV**), and why this concept is important and useful in real estate investment analysis. Market value is the *expected price* at which the asset can be sold in the current property market. In other words, if we put a property up for sale, we don't know for sure exactly what price we can get. It depends in part on who we find as an opposite party in the deal. We may find someone who is particularly enthusiastic about the property, or, on the other hand, we may end up having to deal with a really tough negotiator. The market value can be thought of as the most likely price at which we will do a deal, prior to a deal actually being done. It is the ex ante expectation (or the mean of the probability distribution) of the possible prices.[2]

---

[1]The stock market analogy helps us to see why the NPV of a typical deal is zero. When investors buy and sell stocks, such trading is not generally perceived as involving positive or negative NPV for the participants.

[2]The concept of market value also must entail a commitment to sell (or buy) the property reasonably quickly, regardless of the current market conditions. Otherwise, we could make MV out to be unrealistically high (or low), and just say we will wait as long as it takes to find someone willing to pay (or accept) that price. In effect, we would be saying that we will wait until the *market moves* in our favor (if it ever does). This would be analogous to a stock market investor placing a "limit order" to sell (buy) a given stock at a specified price above (below) the current market price of the stock. The real estate concept of MV is meant to be analogous to the market price of the stock, not some investor's limit order price.

As thusly defined, the market value is a very important and useful measure of value because it reflects the current opportunity cost or **opportunity value** of the investment in the asset. That is, any investor has the ability at any time to either purchase or sell the asset for a price close to its market value (and with the actual ex post transaction price as likely to be above as below the market value). In effect, as well as any single number can represent, the investor gives up the opportunity to retain or receive the MV in cash when she decides instead to purchase or continue holding the asset.

Although market value, and an NPV estimation based on MV, is always useful and of fundamental importance in decision making, one can conceptually define and measure commercial property value another way, and calculate an NPV based on this second concept of value. This second definition of value is what is referred to in the real estate profession as the **investment value** (which we will sometimes abbreviate as **IV**).[3] The investment value of a property is its value *to a particular owner,* who would be owning and operating the asset *for a long period of time,* and explicitly not planning to sell the asset for a long period of time. As IV is defined with respect to a specified investor, and investors differ in their ability to generate and use future cash flow and value from the asset, so IV values may differ for different investors for the same asset as of the same point in time. In contrast, the MV is, in principle, the same for a given asset for all investors as of a given point in time.[4] You can think of the distinction between MV and IV in rough terms as follows:

$$MV = \text{What you can sell the asset for today}$$
$$IV = \text{What the asset is worth to you if you don't sell it for a long time}$$

IV is a private or subjective valuation of a party; MV is an objective value exogenous to any one party, in principle.

In classical corporate capital budgeting, because there is typically no well-functioning market for the underlying physical assets, IV is the *only* way one can measure the value of the relevant assets, and the only basis on which one can calculate the NPV of proposed projects.[5] In real estate, the property market enables the MV perspective also to be quantified (for individual physical assets). However, we can still define the IV perspective for real estate deals as well. Indeed, some real estate deals involve assets or financial arrangements so unique that it would be very difficult to estimate accurately the relevant market values. Even when we can estimate MV accurately, the IV perspective is still relevant to investment decision making in real estate, as we will see in the following sections.

12.1.1 How to Measure Investment Value

In quantifying investment value, one should use the same multiperiod DCF technique described in Chapters 10 and 11. Indeed, in practice the multiperiod perspective is often more important in quantifying IV than MV. Although, in principle, multiperiod DCF analysis underlies the determination of MV at a fundamental level, estimating the current MV for a given type of property may often be done by the shortcut of simply observing the

---

[3]Investment value is especially well defined in the appraisal profession, where it is closely related to such other definitions of value as "inherent value" or "usage value." The appraisal industry distinguishes these concepts carefully from those of market value (or "exchange value"). Another term sometimes used in a manner similar to investment value is "intrinsic value." Like inherent value, intrinsic value highlights the value placed on real property by users of the property, in contrast to investment value, which highlights more explicitly the value of the property for a nonuser owner (an investor). However, there is considerable overlap in meaning across all the "i" valuation concepts: inherent, intrinsic, and investment. (See Appendix 12A at the end of the chapter for further elaboration on concepts of value.)

[4]Although two people may disagree in their estimate of MV, conceptually only one true MV exists at any given time.

[5]In classical capital budgeting theory, it is assumed that IV at the level of the corporation's underlying assets will be reflected rapidly in the MV of the corporation's stock, due to the informational efficiency of the stock market. Thus, for a publicly traded firm, IV at the level of the firm is traditionally taken to be virtually equivalent to MV at the level of the firm's investors. While this classical conception ignores such issues as asymmetric information between managers and investors, it probably provides a useful approximation of reality for most publicly traded firms most of the time (including REITs).

transaction prices of similar assets (for example, as reflected in prevailing cap rates). But IV, which is based on the assumption of a long-term holding of the asset, can only be determined by going through a full long-term projection of net cash flows.[6]

Because IV is specific to a particular owner or user of the asset, the cash flows should reflect how that owner or user would manage and operate the asset, including synergy or spillover effects with the owner's other assets and operations, and also the owner's particular income tax situation. Thus, the actual cash flow amounts forecasted on the right-hand side of the DCF formula may differ from one investor to another in computing IV. In principle, the investor's after-tax cash flows are discounted at market after-tax discount rates.[7]

In theory, the discount rate applied in the denominators of the DCF calculation may also differ from one investor to another in the computation of IV. However, care must be taken not to abuse this theoretical possibility in practice. Discount rates for computing IV should not be "pulled from the air" or made up on an ad hoc basis on the claim that a given investor has "unique risk preferences." Remember that discount rates reflect the time value of money and the price of risk. All investors have access to the capital markets, and so all investors face the prices of time and risk available in that market. Going beyond the market in this regard is stepping out on very soft sand.[8] Therefore, as a matter of good practice, even when we are computing IV, discount rates should still reflect an **opportunity cost of capital (OCC)** based on the capital market. Thus, we should always analyze the capital market (including the property market itself) in order to determine the relevant price of risk and time value of money.[9] Only if the investor would (realistically) operate the subject property in a unique way, so that its cash flows would be perceived *by the capital market* to be of different risk than that of the typical operation of such a property, can one legitimately employ a different discount rate risk premium than the property market would apply. Such a situation is rare and difficult to quantify with rigor. Thus, the main focus in questions of IV differing from MV should normally be on the numerators of the DCF valuation, the expected future cash flow generation, rather than on the denominators.[10]

---

[6]An exception to the need for a long horizon in the analysis sometimes occurs in the case of raw land and development projects. It is sometimes appropriate for an IV analysis horizon to end with a projected sale of the completed new structure.

[7]Income tax considerations will be treated in more depth in Chapter 14.

[8]For example, to apply a "personalized" risk premium, in principle it is necessary to quantify the investor's utility function or risk preferences, given his overall wealth portfolio and consumption patterns. Such analysis is rare in practice and usually considered beyond the reasonable scope of the definition of investment value. Indeed, for an investment entity that has more than one individual owner, there is fundamental theoretical ambiguity about how to aggregate preferences across the different owners. (Economist Kenneth Arrow won a Nobel Prize in part for his discovery of an "Impossibility Theorem," that individual preferences cannot be aggregated into a rational "social welfare function" describing aggregate utility.)

[9]In general, this implies that the relevant OCC both for determining MV and IV will reflect the risk and time preferences of the *marginal* investors in the relevant part of the capital market, based on the market model that will be presented below in section 12.1.3 and Exhibit 12-1. This point will be made more concrete in Chapter 14 in our discussion of after-tax investment valuation in section 14.3.

[10]In traditional corporate capital budgeting, the investment decision-making entity is a publicly traded corporation, acting on behalf of its shareholders. In such circumstances, the derivation of the appropriate discount rates purely from the capital market is obvious, because the capital market will determine the corporation's share price, and hence its shareholders' wealth impact of any corporate investment decisions, based on the market for the firm's equity shares. This same argument applies in real estate to the case of investment by publicly traded entities such as REITs. However, in real estate investment, property assets can be held directly by individuals or private entities. It is in such circumstances that personalized IV discount rates can be contemplated, at least theoretically. For example, a private investor whose personal wealth is uniquely and necessarily tied to Chicago apartment property may place a low investment value on the purchase of an additional Chicago apartment due to its failure to provide any diversification in her constrained portfolio. In effect, an additional Chicago apartment is a more risky investment to her than to the typical investor. However, such considerations are normally addressed at the macro-level of investment strategy, as part of the investor's portfolio policy, as they are difficult to quantify at the micro-level in terms of the investment value of specific assets. (Portfolio theory will be addressed in Chapter 21.)

12.1.2 Joint Use of IV and MV in Decision Making

As it is common in real estate to be able to compute reasonable estimates of both IV and MV, we need to consider how these two perspectives of value relate to each other in making rational investment decisions. Recall that the basic investment decision rule is to maximize your NPV across all mutually exclusive alternatives, and to never do a deal with a negative NPV. But in applying this rule should you use the NPV based on market value or based on investment value?

To answer this question, you first need to compute the NPV both ways, so you know what sort of situation you face. If the deal looks like it passes the NPV criterion no matter which way you compute it, then there is no philosophical issue, though it is still useful to know both values, in particular as they both can be useful in the process of negotiating the deal and in understanding the way in which you can "create value."

Suppose you are an investor interested in buying a particular asset or project, and you differ from the typical marginal investor in the market for such assets. Then your IV can differ from the MV of the asset, and in this case you can face one of two interesting situations that require some thought: either $NPV_{MV} \gg 0 \gg NPV_{IV}$ or $NPV_{IV} \gg 0 \gg NPV_{MV}$ where "$\gg$" means "substantially greater" (net of transaction costs).

In the first situation, the deal makes sense from a market value perspective but not from an investment value perspective. This implies that you could do the deal and then reverse it almost immediately in the marketplace and almost certainly make some money. As noted in Chapter 10, such situations are no doubt rare in practice and must be presumed to result from some "error" on someone's part. The wealth-maximization principle would suggest that you should go ahead and do the deal even though from your personal perspective it has $NPV_{IV} < 0$. However, apart from the importance of looking such "gift horses" very carefully "in the mouth," there is an important question of business strategy here. The fact that $NPV_{MV} > NPV_{IV}$ by an apparently significant margin suggests that the type of deal in question here is not the type that you specialize in or for which you have particular expertise. It is by definition a type of deal for which you are not as well suited as the typical marginal investor in the market (as such marginal investors determine the MV). In other words, this is not the type of deal that conforms with what is (or should be) your main business strategy. In such a circumstance, you need to think carefully about whether it really makes sense for you to get distracted by pursuing the deal. (Perhaps you can pass it on to someone else in return for some share of the positive NPV, without spending much of your own firm's resources on the deal?)

Now consider the second interesting situation, in which the deal makes sense from an investment value perspective but not from a market value perspective. For example, you would have to buy the relevant asset(s) for more than their market value (or if you were a seller, you would have to sell for less than market value) in order to obtain the positive NPV that you believe you can create from your own personal IV perspective. Should you make such a deal?

There are two philosophies in answering this question. For convenience, we can term one the "conservative philosophy" and the other the "liberal philosophy" (though these terms have no implications regarding political philosophy). The conservative philosophy says "no," you should not make the deal. You should never pay more than MV for something (or sell for less than MV), because, after all, why should you? The definition of MV is that you should be able to buy (or sell) at that price. For example, if the seller does not sell to you, then he cannot expect to get more than MV for the asset from anyone else, so why should you reward him with a windfall just because you are able to do something unique with the property or use it in some particularly advantageous way because of your unique circumstances? Bargain the seller down to where his price equals MV (and hence $NPV_{MV} = 0$), or else walk away from the deal.

On the other hand, the liberal philosophy says "yes," make the deal, even if necessary at $NPV_{MV} < 0$, as long as the deal meets the investment decision criterion on the NPV_{IV} basis. Since this rule does require you to obtain as high an NPV as possible (across all mutually exclusive alternatives), it presumes that you will bargain the seller down to as low a price as possible (or if you are the seller, bargain a purchaser up to as high a price as possible). Once you have done that, the idea is that it would be foolish (not wealth-maximizing) to walk away from a deal that presents a positive NPV from your investment value perspective (that is, based on what you realistically can do with it or on what your unique circumstances are).

Of course, there may be a considerable gap between your IV and the MV for the subject asset. Even under the "liberal" philosophy, should you really be willing to pay all the way up to your IV for the asset? The NPV rule says you should try to get the asset for as low a price as possible, but how low is low enough? The answer to this question, from a rational or normative perspective, is the subject of a field of economics known as "optimal search theory." According to this theory, logically enough, the answer depends on how sure you are or how clearly you can determine what exactly is the actual MV of the asset, and of course it also depends on how much you want the asset, how costly it is for you to continue searching for alternative assets, and so forth. Optimal search theory suggests that you may think about how high you are willing to pay (up to a maximum of your IV for the asset) in terms of a "reservation price" which you set privately (secretly for yourself), below which you will stop searching or negotiating and buy the asset. In general, the less certain you are about what the MV of the asset is, the lower (more conservatively) you would set your reservation price (farther below your IV). On the other hand, the more certain you are about the MV, the closer to that perceived MV (less above it) you will set your reservation price (assuming your IV remains above the MV).[11]

Real estate deals can have substantially positive (or negative) NPV when computed from the IV perspective. This could occur even though the deal is done at market value so that it has a zero NPV from the MV perspective. Indeed, viewed from the IV perspective a deal can produce a positive NPV for both sides of the transaction, due to unique circumstances affecting one or both parties. This is because IV is personal, in the sense that it relates to a specific owner or investor and is divorced from the market in the sense that the asset is presumed to be held off the market for a long period of time. In fact, finding situations in which the IV-based NPV is positive for both sides of the deal is one of the main objectives of much real estate investment activity.

Unique characteristics of the investor and the property, or the relationship between the two, can cause IV to differ from MV for a given investor. Let's look at an example. KrazyLoPrices Inc. Discount Warehouse has built a booming business at its store at 9999 Consumption Boulevard and is now in need of expansion space and more parking capacity. It would also hate to see its main competitor, EvenLowerPrices Ltd., open up one of its mega-stores across the street. In such a situation, the vacant lots adjacent to and across the street, at 9997 and 9998 Consumption Boulevard, are likely worth more to KrazyLo than they are to any other party. In other words, $IV > MV$ for those lots for KrazyLo.

In general, when $IV > MV$, it makes sense to buy, build, or hold (whichever is relevant). On the other hand, when $IV < MV$, it makes sense to sell if you already own, and not to buy if you don't yet own the property, as would be the case, for example, if KrazyLo somehow lost its ability to make a profit at the Consumption Boulevard location.

An important difference between real estate and securities is that unique, whole assets are traded in the property market (along with their governing authority and operational responsibility). This creates a certain "lumpiness" in the property market and makes it difficult to know exactly what the MV is of a given asset at any given time. With this in mind, a notion that is often used in practice to help conceive of MV and relate it to IV is that of the **second-most-motivated buyer**. The maximum price this buyer would be willing to pay (the IV to this buyer) is taken to be the MV for the property. The most-motivated buyer is the one who has the highest IV for the property. For example, the most creative and entrepreneurial developer with the greatest expertise regarding how to use a given site

---

[11]We will note optimal search theory again in Appendix 12A at the end of this chapter, and we will provide a simple example of a particular optimal search model (for landlord tenant search) in Appendix 30C in the electronic resources of Chapter 30.

(or most ability to profit, like KrazyLo in the previous example) can probably purchase that site for a positive NPV viewed from his own IV-based perspective. The IV of the site for this "best" developer is greater than it is for any other developer, and hence greater than the MV of the site.[12]

If there is not much heterogeneity or uniqueness in the properties or the potential investors, then the IV of the most-motivated and second-most-motivated buyers will be very similar. But if the most-motivated buyer would place a much higher IV on the property than would the second-most-motivated buyer, then it may be possible to sell the property for more than its market value (based on the "liberal" philosophy noted above).

One implication of the difference between IV and MV is that you need to be aware that the opposite party in a transaction may have some idea about the magnitude of *your* IV in the deal. They will naturally try to negotiate a price above MV, closer to your IV, in order to take advantage of this knowledge if they can. For example, the owner of 9997 and 9998 Consumption Boulevard will certainly know that her lots are worth more to KrazyLo than to anyone else, that is, more than their MV. The question is how much more? This is where careful investigation and negotiating skill can pay off (on either side). If you are dealing with unique assets or financial arrangements, then you may have little recourse to competing players as alternative opposite parties in the deal. But the other side may have little recourse as well. Obviously, it is important to keep IV information confidential and to apply sound negotiation principles when dealing in such a situation.[13]

This brings us back to our starting point about the difference between real estate and securities investment on the one hand, and between real estate and corporate capital budgeting investment on the other hand. The more lumpiness and uniqueness there is among assets and investors, the more difficult it will be to estimate market values accurately, and the more likely it will be that investors' IVs could greatly differ from any estimate that could be made of MV. This is the situation in which real estate investment analysis converges toward corporate capital budgeting analysis in some respects, and IV tends to become the only relevant value perspective.[14] The more homogeneous the assets and the investors are, the easier it will be to estimate market values, and the less likely it will be that IV differs much from MV for most of the active participants in the market. This is the situation in which real estate investment analysis converges toward classical securities investment analysis, and MV becomes the dominant valuation perspective.[15] Much commercial real estate investing occurs somewhere between these two extremes.

---

[12]The positive NPV the best developer can obtain in this circumstance is attributable to "entrepreneurial profit." Note, however, that it is possible to view this model as well from the other side, in which the subject asset's MV is based on what the second-most-motivated *seller* would be willing to accept. More broadly, one would expect in general that the transaction price (if there is to be a successfully consummated transaction) must be greater than or equal to the IV of the most-motivated seller and less than or equal to the IV of the most-motivated buyer, of and for similar sites or assets. The ex ante expectation of what this transaction price will be is the MV of the property. Suppose we have two competing sellers and two competing buyers, with their IVs ordered as follows: $IV^{S1} < IV^{S2} < IV^{B2} < IV^{B1}$, where "S1" is the most-motivated seller, "S2" is the second-most-motivated seller, "B1" is the most-motivated buyer, and "B2" is the second-most-motivated buyer. Then the best guess for the transaction prices of the asset, P, is that it will lie between the IVs of the second-most-motivated parties: $IV^{S2} < P < IV^{B2}$. Since this best guess for P is, by definition, the MV of the assets in question, this is the basis for the "second-most-motivated" rule.

[13]See Appendix 12B: *Negotiation and Risk Management in the Real Estate Contracting Process*, located on the CD accompanying this book. Appendix 12B presents in some depth negotiation principles that are quite important for the points raised in section 12.1 regarding the difference between investment and market values in real estate. For example, the concept of second-most-motivated buyer (or seller) can be related to the negotiation value referred to as the "BATNA"—Best Alternative to a Negotiated Agreement, if you are negotiating with the "best" opposite party in the conception presented here.

[14]An important difference between classical corporate capital budgeting and real estate investment in the United States is that real estate investment typically operates in a very different income tax environment. This will be treated in Chapter 14.

[15]An important difference between classical securities investment analysis and real estate investment analysis is that the real estate asset market, at least the private market for directly held property, is less informationally efficient than the securities market, as we noted previously and will be discussed in section 12.2.

12.1.3 The Asset Market Model with Marginal and Intramarginal Investors: How to Get Positive NPV

We noted that the investment value NPV of a given deal for a given investor is typically determined by the difference between the MV and IV of the asset for the investor. We can deepen our understanding of both IV and MV and derive some additional practical insight by examining how these two valuation measures operate in a well-functioning property market. A useful concept in this regard is the distinction between **marginal** and **intramarginal investors** in the market.

The chart in Exhibit 12-1 presents a schematic picture of a well-functioning property market.[16] The horizontal axis represents the annual volume of trading in the asset market (e.g., number of properties bought and sold). The vertical axis represents the prices of properties (e.g., per square foot). The downward-sloping demand function shows the amount of assets potential buyers would like to purchase, based on their perceived investment values. Investors with the highest IVs would become active in the market first, even at relatively high prices. At lower prices, additional buyers would enter the market. So, the demand function is downward-sloping. The upward-sloping supply function shows the amount of assets potential sellers (that is, existing owners of the assets) would like to sell, based on *their* perceived investment values. At low prices, only a few sellers would be willing to do deals. More sellers enter the market at higher prices that exceed more owners' investment values, producing the upward-sloping supply function shown in the chart.[17]

Market value is determined by **asset transaction market equilibrium**. The equilibrium price is that which equates supply and demand. This is the price at which IV is the same for both buyers and sellers who are on the margin. By definition, the equilibrium market price (the expectation of which is the MV of the assets in this market) produces $NPV = 0$ computed on both an IV and MV basis for the marginal participants in this market. Exhibit 12-1 shows how the IV of the marginal investors determines or underlies the market prices. *MV equals the IV of the marginal participants in the asset market.*

IV will differ from MV (and this will enable positive NPV deals to be done, measured on the basis of IV, by trading at MV prices) *only for intramarginal market participants,* those that are to the left of the equilibrium point in the diagram. These are market participants for whom (and deals in which) the IV for the buyer differs from the IV for the seller, for the same asset. By definition, this requires that the sellers and buyers in these deals are different from each other in some way that is important to the investment value of the asset.

We can distill from this analysis some practical conclusions about how you can know whether you are likely to be able to do a substantially positive NPV deal measured on the basis of your IV, in a well-functioning market. We see that positive NPV deals are *intramarginal* deals. Our market model gives us a way to recognize such deals. A necessary characteristic of intramarginal deals is that the principal parties on the two sides of the deal must be *different* in some important way regarding their ability to profit from the asset, at least going forward and on an after-tax basis. This type of difference is a necessary, although not sufficient, condition of positive investment value NPV deals. (Such a difference by itself is not sufficient to ensure a positive NPV because you still have to make sure you are not making a pricing mistake in negotiating the deal.)

In practice, the two most common sources of positive investment-value NPVs are probably income tax status and operational advantages in controlling the real productive capacity

---

[16]Deeper understanding of the nature of this model of the asset market can be obtained by reading Appendix 12A at the back of this chapter.

[17]As described in the Appendix 12A, the demand and supply functions may be influenced by search behavior including the setting of "reservation prices" (at which parties will stop searching and consummate transactions). This can cause the demand and supply functions to be "flatter", more price-elastic, than would be implied by the underlying investment values, and this price-elasticity may vary over time (sometimes quickly and radically). But fundamentally the demand and supply functions reflect the investment values potential buyers and sellers place on the individual properties potentially in the asset market, and there is evidence that prices and trading volume are interconnected in the private property market in a manner that suggests lack of perfect price elasticity (i.e., the demand is downward-sloping and supply upward-sloping supply, as indicated in the exhibit). In private property markets trading volume and prices tend to move together, with changes in volume slightly leading changes in prices.

EXHIBIT 12-1 Relation
between Investment Value
(IV) and Market Value (MV)
in a Well-Functioning Asset
Market

© OnCourse Learning

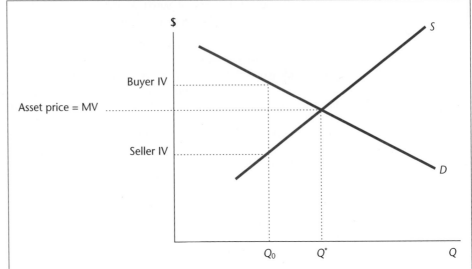

$ = Property prices (vertical axis)
Q = Volume of investment transaction per unit of time
Q_0 = Volume of transactions by investors with more favorable circumstances, hence would
enter market at less favorable prices (i.e., intramarginal market participants, e.g., investors
with different tax circumstances than marginal investors in the market)
Q^* = Total volume of property transactions, including marginal investment (investors on
margin are indifferent between investing and not investing in property)
Note: Prices, and hence market values (MV), are determined by the IV of the marginal
investors (the investors for whom NPV = 0 on both an IV and MV basis).

of the property.[18] Often, the latter source involves some sort of quasi-monopolistic position
that gives the investor some advantageous market control. For example, a developer's ownership of adjacent sites might give it unique ability to profit from a certain type of development
on a given parcel of land, due to synergy and spillover effects. Another typical type of potentially profitable situation occurs when the owner of the property would also be the primary
user of the property, and the property has a unique fit in the real productive process of this
owner (as in our KrazyLo example earlier).

In fact, the type of uniqueness associated with substantially positive NPV opportunities
often requires some sort of construction or redevelopment of a property. The market tends to
reward, at least temporarily, those who are first with a good idea. **Entrepreneurial profits**
are the supernormal return on successful business creativity, in real estate as in any other
industry. Be the first to invent and produce some new "super-senior-housing" formula for a
fast-growing demographic segment that has latent demand for such a product and you will
make a bundle, at least for a while (until other copycat developers build enough competing
units to drive rents and prices down to the normal profit level).

12.2 Danger and Opportunity in Market Inefficiency

The necessity to deal simultaneously with IV and MV measures of value in making investment decisions is one result of real estate's unique asset market characteristics. Now we
want to consider the implications of the fact that informational efficiency and price discovery

---

[18]A third possible source, "quasi-arbitrage" between the market for REIT shares in the stock market and the private
(direct) market for property assets, will be discussed in section 12.3. There may also be circumstances in which the
financing arrangements for a deal generates advantageous results for one or more parties to the transaction, apart
from anything having to do with the underlying physical productivity of the asset.

HOW BIG IS RANDOM NOISE?

How much "randomness" is there in commercial property prices or estimates of market value? Are individual transaction prices or appraisal estimates of individual property values widely dispersed around the "true" property market values? Or is the distribution very tight, with little randomness?

This question is difficult to answer because it is essentially an empirical question, yet a key ingredient we need for the answer is empirically unobservable, *in principle*, namely, the true market value. However, we can say something. First, statistical and experimental techniques do allow indirect estimation of the relative magnitude of the random valuation component, the "standard error" in property value estimates. For example, two academic researchers, Julian Diaz and Martin Wolverton, conducted an experiment in which professional appraisers independently estimated the market value of the same asset, as of the same point in time, based on the same information about the property and its market. The resulting value estimates had a standard deviation of around 5 percent of the average estimate of property value. This agrees with statistical estimates of the magnitude of transaction price noise in the housing market, published by Professor Goetzmann of Yale. Statistical analysis of the NCREIF Property Database suggests an average error magnitude in the range of 5 percent to 15 percent.* Second, theory tells us something about what to expect about the magnitude of random noise. In particular, we believe that noise should be greater for assets that are more unique, and for assets trading in "thinner," less active markets. In such circumstances, there is less information on which to base estimates of value.

More recently in the United States major transactions-based indices of commercial property prices have been published that provide more direct empirical evidence about the "deal noise" magnitude question, and these suggest that the upper end of the above-noted range may be relevant. The histogram shown in

Exhibit 12-2 gives a typical picture. This shows the distribution of the residuals from the property price model that underlies the TBI index produced at the MIT Center for Real Estate, spanning the 1984–2010 period. This price model is based largely on the recent appraised values of the properties sold from the NCREIF Index database recently before their sale. The residuals are the differences between the actual sale prices and the prices predicted by the regression model (the latter being similar to the appraised values but corrected for biases such as appraisal lag). The histogram in Exhibit 12-2 has a standard deviation of $+/-15$ percent of the property value and an average absolute deviation of $+/-11$ percent.**

----

*The Diaz-Wolverton experiment is reported in Diaz and Wolverton (1998). Goetzmann's estimates are found in Goetzmann (1993). The 10 percent estimates are described in Geltner (1998). Geltner & Goetzmann (2000) indicate a range of 7 percent to 15 percent for random error in individual appraisals in the NCREIF database. A much lower estimate of average error (around 3 percent) comes from a study by Richard Graff and Mike Young of simultaneous "external" and "internal" appraisals of the properties in a major investment advisor's portfolio. [See Graff and Young (1999).] However, it is likely that the external and internal appraisals in the Graff-Young study were not completely independent of one another, as they both may have had access to the prior appraised values of the properties. This could provide a common anchor for the two appraisals, which would reduce the apparent dispersion in value estimations. Additional evidence on random dispersion in appraisal estimates was reviewed in England by Crosby, Lavers, and Murdoch (1998). They suggested an average error magnitude on the order of 10 percent.

**The standard deviation is based on the squares of the individual deviations and is therefore larger than the average absolute deviation. The "bell shape" of the histogram in Exhibit 12-2 shows that the random price noise is approximately normally distributed. However, there is a slight positive skew, indicating that the distribution is closer to lognormal, which is typical of asset price dispersion.

© OnCourse Learning

differ in the private real estate asset market compared with the public exchanges on which securities such as stocks and bonds are traded. Two aspects of these types of **informational inefficiency** considerations are important. One is the presence of **random noise** in the asset valuation and pricing process. The other is the presence of more inertia and predictability in real estate's periodic investment returns than one finds in securities returns.

12.2.1 Valuation Noise

Real property markets are characterized by infrequent, privately negotiated deals in which whole, unique assets are traded. These are private search markets for whole assets, rather than the public auction markets for homogeneous shares that characterize the securities industry. In a private whole-asset market, it is difficult to know at any given time the precise market value of any given asset. A potential buyer or seller of the office building at 100 North Main Street cannot simply pull out her smartphone and look up the latest trade price for a share of ownership in the building. She would have to do some research to estimate the current market value of a given real estate asset, or pay someone else to do such research for her. And even then she wouldn't be sure of the exact MV. Furthermore, to actually purchase 100 North Main, the buyer will have to go through a bidding and negotiation process the exact price outcome of which will not likely be known in advance.

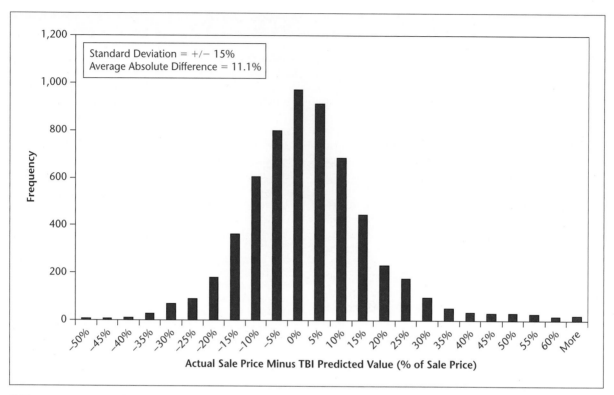

EXHIBIT 12-2 Histogram of Predicted Sale Price Error
Source: Authors' analysis based on NCREIF data.

In this scarcity of price information lies both danger and opportunity of a type not present in stocks or bonds investing. We can define this danger and opportunity in terms of the NPV and valuation concepts we have been using. In investing in real estate, while the *expected* NPV is approximately zero when measured on an MV basis, *this is not guaranteed.*

> *In real estate investment in the direct (private) property market, it is possible to do deals with substantially positive, or negative, NPVs, measured on the basis of market value.*

In part, this is because parties to transactions sometimes make mistakes. They may fail to discover or consider adequately some knowable information relevant to the market value of the property. But even when neither side in a deal makes a mistake, the nature of the real estate market is somewhat random. Market values can never be observed definitively, but only estimated. Both sides in a deal may have done their homework adequately and equally well. Neither party may have made any mistake in the sense that they both made reasonable use of all the information and resources available to them at the time when the deal was made. Yet one side gets the better deal. If we could step back after the dust settles and have the deal reviewed by an impartial panel of experts (individually or collectively), with all the information available to the panel, the judgment of the panel would sometimes be that one side got the better deal, relative to the market value at the time.[19]

How can this happen? In some cases, one party will have better information. They may not have investigated the deal any harder or more diligently than the other side, but they just "lucked out" by happening to discover something about, say, expansion plans of a potential tenant or an adjacent property owner. If such information is not private (in the sense that it can be verified by anyone), then it is arguably relevant to the market value of the property,

---

[19]It is important to recognize that individual transaction prices are not the same as market values. Appendix 12A, at the end of this chapter, describes in more depth the difference between transaction prices and market values.

particularly as it may be revealed once the deal is closed. In other cases, one side will simply be a better negotiator than the other side. A third possibility is that one side may be under some sort of duress, or greater pressure to close the deal. Perhaps a seller is in need of cash to pay creditors. Perhaps an investment manager on the buy side of a deal will lose credibility if she is unable to place all the capital her client wants invested by the end of the year.

To guard against the danger of substantially negative NPV deals evaluated from an MV perspective, financial institutions engaged in commercial real estate investment, as well as investment managers acting as fiduciaries, mandate specific predeal investigation and analysis procedures, often referred to as **due diligence** (which sometimes includes the hiring of a professional appraiser). Investors typically also try to learn something about the motivations of the parties on the other side in the deal, as best they can. As noted in the previous section, negotiation skill is important in real estate investment (see Appendix 12B on the CD). Another implication of real estate's "fuzzy" or "noisy" values is that it may be optimal to wait longer or until there is sort of "buffer" beyond the expected outcome of whatever decision one is making. A basic tenet of rational search theory is that when uncertainty surrounds the value of the object being traded, parties on both sides should err on the side of caution (that is, buyers should place a *lower* reservation price and sellers a *higher* reservation price, thereby increasing the difficulty of making deals).[20]

It is important to note that the flip side of the negative NPV danger is the positive NPV opportunity. Because MV is the same for everyone, in principle, whenever one side does a negative-NPV deal from an MV perspective, the other side of the deal gets a positive NPV deal from the MV perspective (by definition). Part of the uniqueness and excitement of real estate investing lies in the presence of this danger and opportunity. This is different from investing in stocks and bonds. And it is different from corporate capital budgeting. Real estate investors can often reap a reward for individual investigation and research efforts more easily than can investors in more efficient markets. As noted in the boxed feature on page 265 and illustrated in Exhibit 12-2, individual property price noise appears to be large in magnitude, perhaps on the order of $+/-15\%$ standard deviation around the MV. This suggests that acquisition and disposition transaction execution at the individual property level can be an important determinant of real estate investment performance.

12.2.2 Asset Market Predictability

To the extent that MV-based nonzero NPVs are an essentially random occurrence, their effect on the investor may be greatly reduced if the investor is well diversified, investing in many different individual properties. Random errors (on both the positive and negative side) tend to average out over the long run and across many deals. But another result of market inefficiency can have a more systematic effect. As noted in previous chapters, informational efficiency in asset markets refers to the tendency of prices to reflect quickly and fully all relevant information or news. Markets with high informational efficiency, like the stock market, are characterized by asset price changes that are difficult to predict in advance. Although private property markets are generally well-functioning, efficient markets, the nature of price discovery and information aggregation in whole-asset private search markets implies that asset prices move more slowly in response to the arrival of news, only **partially adjusting** within a given short- to medium-time horizon. This results in future asset market price movements at a broad level being more predictable than they are in the stock market (even if they are less precisely knowable at the micro-level of individual assets).[21]

As with random noise, the **predictability** result of inefficiency brings both danger and opportunity. The opportunity is that investors can take advantage of the predictability to

---

[20]Again, see Appendix 12A. Also see Childs, Ott, and Riddiough (2002a, 2002b) who obtain a result in asset valuation and development not unlike what is suggested in this text for optimal leasing behavior in Appendix 30C of Chapter 30.

[21]Some studies documenting and quantifying the predictability in private real estate asset market returns include the following: Barkham and Geltner (1995), Case and Shiller (1990), Case and Quigley (1991), Gyourko and Keim (1992), among others. The major transactions-based commercial property price indices, such as the Moody's/RCA CPPI and the NCREIF-based TBI, demonstrate considerable positive autocorrelation at the annual frequency.

CAN PREDICTABILITY CAUSE IV TO DIFFER FROM MV?

It is sometimes suggested that predictability in the real estate asset market can cause investment value to differ from current market value for assets and investors in general. The idea is that if the property market is somewhat predictable, then it will at least sometimes be possible to predict, not with certainty but with relatively high probability, that asset MVs will be headed in one direction or the other over the medium to long run. For example, when asset price/earnings multiples appear to be very high or very low by historical standards, or asset price indices indicate an historically anomalous run-up or crash in price levels, this may be an indication that the asset market is either "overheated" (as in a bubble), or temporarily excessively depressed (sometimes referred to as a "negative bubble"). As IV is based on long-run holdings, the long-run forecast of MV (together with the future operating cash flows the asset will generate) is more relevant to IV than the current prevailing MV. This is a different concept of IV than the traditional definition, which is based on

differences among individual investors. In this case, the argument is that IV in general differs from MV in the same way for *all* investors in the market as of a given time. In this conception, the current market is viewed as "mispricing" assets, viewed from a long-run perspective and the (market-wide) IV would represent a more sustainable or noncyclical level for prices.

While this conception of IV and MV is interesting, it raises questions that are very difficult to answer rigorously, from both a conceptual and empirical perspective. For example, it suggests not only that the asset market is inefficient, but also that market participants are acting generally irrationally or suboptimally in paying (or accepting) prices equal to the current market values. But asset prices may be abnormally low because risk is abnormally high, from an ex ante perspective. Sellers may be forced by creditors to accept low prices. It is therefore not clear what the practical implications of this concept of IV should be. Nevertheless, this is an intriguing, even if somewhat nonstandard, use of the IV concept.

© OnCourse Learning

attempt to buy low and sell high. Investors in real estate probably have a greater opportunity for **market timing** than do investors in securities.[22]

Taking advantage of real estate asset market predictability may not be as easy or profitable as it may first appear, however. For one thing, real estate asset markets are far from completely predictable. While they are almost certainly not as informationally efficient as the securities market, and hence more predictable than such markets, real estate asset markets are not terribly inefficient either, and hence cannot be fully predicted.

Second, **transaction costs** in buying and selling assets directly in the property market are much greater than those in the securities market. Such costs can remove much of the profit investors could otherwise obtain from trading on predictable asset movements.[23] Transaction costs can be mitigated by holding real estate investments for long periods of time because this spreads out the transaction costs over many periods of return. But long holding periods also mitigate the per-annum percentage profit that can be earned from timing the ups and downs of the market. This is because long holding periods also spread out over more years of investment the "windfall" gain from successful timing, and also because the farther in the future one tries to predict, the less accurately it is possible to predict, even for relatively predictable markets. Investment returns over long holding periods will often be more sensitive to how well the property is managed during the holding period than to the timing of when the property was bought or sold.

Finally, at least at the individual property level, the randomness of transaction noise, as described in the preceding section, may swamp much of the advantage of market timing, or in any case can add greatly to the risk of short-term investments.

For all these reasons, most real estate investors cannot generally or systematically make **supernormal profits** due to the predictability of real estate asset market prices. Indeed, we can be almost certain that supernormal profits are not widespread because there are no major

---

[22]See, for example, Geltner and Mei (1995), Stevenson (2002), and Marcato and Key (2005), Plazzi, Torous, and Valkanov (2010).

[23]Typical "round-trip" (i.e., buying and selling) transaction costs in real estate are on the order of 5% to 10% of asset value. Costs include brokerage, legal, and administrative fees, as well as the cost of the search and any research and investigation undertaken by the investor directly. [Marcato and Key (2005) estimated trading costs in the United Kingdom at 7.5% round-trip, though he claims this estimate is meant to be on the high side.] In contrast, transaction costs for dealing in the securities market are on the order of one-third to one-tenth this magnitude (sometimes much less, and tend to move down with technological developments in securities trading).

barriers to investors of many types entering the real estate market, either directly or indirectly.[24] If supernormal profits were widely and easily available, investors would be drawn toward real estate and would reallocate their investments toward real estate and away from other asset classes. This would bid up real estate asset prices (and bid down other asset prices) to levels at which supernormal profits were no longer generally available in real estate.[25]

But this does not mean that, as a real estate investor, you can afford to ignore the predictability of real estate returns. That would be foolish, not only because you might miss upside opportunities, but because you could get stuck on the losing end of the cyclical swings in the property market. Inertia in the property markets means that when asset prices start rising, they often have a tendency to continue to rise for several years. Similarly, when prices start to fall, they may have a tendency to continue to fall for several years. Wary investors try to avoid buying near the peaks of such **cycles**, and selling near the troughs. In traditional real estate practice, probably the single greatest cause of investors being forced to sell into a down market is the use of large amounts of debt to finance real estate investment. Investors with low to moderate levels of debt can usually ride out prolonged downswings.[26]

It should be noted that in the twenty-first century the investment industry has begun to develop vehicles to enable indirect or synthetic trading of claims that can represent the private commercial property market at a broad level. Beyond REITs (which were developed earlier and will be discussed below and in Chapter 23), these vehicles include derivatives, such as property price index swaps or futures, and credit default swaps (CDS) based on market baskets of CMBS bonds (such as the CMBX). Similar products also exist for the housing market. Such synthetics can at least in principle do two things that traditionally made profiting from trading on the cyclicality in the private property market difficult: they can greatly reduce the transactions costs of trading, and they can allow short selling (selling first and buying later). Indeed, such vehicles were used by a few shrewd (lucky?) investors to make legendary fortunes during the property market crash of 2008–2009 (in both housing and commercial property).[27] But the development and use of these types of investment vehicles remains in a formative stage, with the relevant regulatory landscape in flux. The traditional considerations described above regarding predictability and cyclicality in the property market remain overwhelmingly relevant particularly for smaller or conservative investors.

---

[24]Recall our discussion in Chapter 7 about the variety of real estate investment products and vehicles, and the incentives facing the investment industry to develop new such products and vehicles to allow investors to place capital directly or indirectly in real estate assets.

[25]Marcato and Key (2005) claim to find super normal profits from momentum trading in direct private real estate in the United Kingdom, even after allowing for transaction costs. However, once the effects of appraisal smoothing are fully accounted for, it appears that the magnitude of any super normal profits may be rather small. Even if it is possible to earn high ex ante returns by using the predictability in the private property market, such returns would not necessarily represent supernormal profits. Property prices may be depressed because the market perceives real estate as being more risky than usual, or prices may be inflated because the market perceives real estate to be less risky than usual. Who is to say the market is wrong, ex ante?

[26]The causes of large amounts of net real estate investment just prior to and during the peak of the *cycle* are more of a mystery. Of course, it is always easier to identify the peak *after* the market has turned, but even so, behavioral and institutional problems may cause excess investment around the market peak. For example, analysts have identified a phenomenon labeled the Santa Claus effect, in which investment and financial institutions tend to reward asset classes that have performed well in the recent past by increasing capital allocations to those types of investments, and punish investment managers who have done poorly in the recent past by removing capital allocation from them. [See Mei (1996).]

[27]These exploits were the subject of a popular book by Michael Lewis, "The Big Short" (W.W. Norton, 2010), and the hedge fund founder John Paulson famously made the greatest annual personal income in the history of Wall Street (over $3 billion) in 2008 in part by betting against the housing market using such vehicles. In principle the ability to sell short can also be used conservatively, to hedge real estate risk exposure and manage risk. Real estate investment synthetics and derivatives will be discussed in more depth in Chapter 26 in the part of this text that focuses at the macro-level of real estate investment, as such vehicles are much less effective at relating to individual property investments than to large portfolios or entire markets of properties.

*12.3 Dueling Asset Markets: The REIT Market and the Property Market

This brings us to the third characteristic feature of real estate asset markets that holds implications for the application of basic investment analysis tools at the micro-level. This is the existence of not one, but two types or levels of asset markets that are relevant for real estate asset valuation: the private direct property market and the public market for REIT shares. This situation was noted in Chapter 7, but up to now (since Chapter 10) our micro-level valuation discussion has focused on the private direct property market alone. What are the implications of the simultaneous existence of the REIT market?

Broadly speaking, at least three major questions of interest to real estate investors are raised by the existence of parallel asset markets. One is the question of which asset market to use in making real estate investments: public, private, or both (and how to manage the allocation between the two). A second question is the possibility of "**arbitrage**:" could it be possible to trade between the two asset markets to make profits on real estate investments (e.g., assemble a portfolio of properties acquired in the private market and take them public as a new REIT or as part of a preexisting publicly traded REIT that acquires them, or go the other way and take a public REIT private or sell properties from a public REIT to private investors)?[28] The third question concerns asset valuation and underlies the previous question. Do the two asset markets value differently the same underlying physical assets as of the same point in time, and, if so, which market's value is "correct"?

Obviously, all three of these questions are related to one another, and all are important. However, the third question most directly concerns us at the micro-level of individual asset valuation and investment analysis at the level of individual property transactions. As this is our focus in the current chapter, we will largely put off the other two questions until Part VII. Therefore, our focus here is on the third question, and in particular on its first part: Do the REIT market and the private direct property market value the same underlying physical assets differently as of the same point in time?

In common parlance and on the basis of the casual empiricism frequently heard among practitioners in the real estate investment industry, the answer to this question would clearly be yes. Industry investment analysts commonly refer to price/earnings multiples as being different in the REIT market versus the private property market, and this is typically taken as evidence that the two markets are evaluating the same properties differently. More careful analyses attempt to quantify the **net asset value** (NAV) of REITs by evaluating REIT property holdings as they would currently be valued in the private market and subtracting the value of the REIT's debt liabilities to arrive at an equity valuation based on the private market. Then this NAV (per share) is compared to REIT share prices in the stock market, and a **premium** or **discount** to NAV is computed, implying (or at least suggesting) a **differential valuation** of the same assets in the two markets.

Exhibit 12-3 shows the history of public versus private market pricing at the macro-level, based on average monthly share price premium to NAV (or P/NAV) at the aggregate level,

---

[28]We place the term *arbitrage* in quotes here because we do not mean the classical academic finance definition in which, strictly speaking, arbitrage refers to trades that generate immediate profits with no risk at all. That is, transactions aimed at capitalizing on security mispricing across markets or specific securities (so-called arbitrage opportunities) in which net investment is zero but expected cash payoff is positive. It is not generally possible to construct rigorous arbitrage trades in real estate as it is in the bond or options markets, for example. Transactions involving the direct property market cannot possibly be executed fast enough, or at prices certain enough in advance, to allow completely riskless trading. The term *arbitrage* as employed here, and also generally implied when real estate market participants talk of arbitrage is thus an approximation, and better thought of in terms of trades or transactions that aim to capitalize on potential states of imbalance between public and private real estate markets. Such trades are based on the quest for "super-normal profits" in positive NPV investment actions (buy or sell), and by their very nature will work to restore equilibrium over time. See *Real Estate Capital Markets Arbitrage,* by Prudential Real Estate Investors Research, October 2001, for industry perspective on arbitraging public versus private market real estate pricing. We examine the role of arbitrage, and also the limits of it, in explaining observed dynamics of REIT pricing relative to underlying property NAV (i.e., the REIT share price premium to NAV) in more detail in Chapter 23 that covers RIETs in detail.

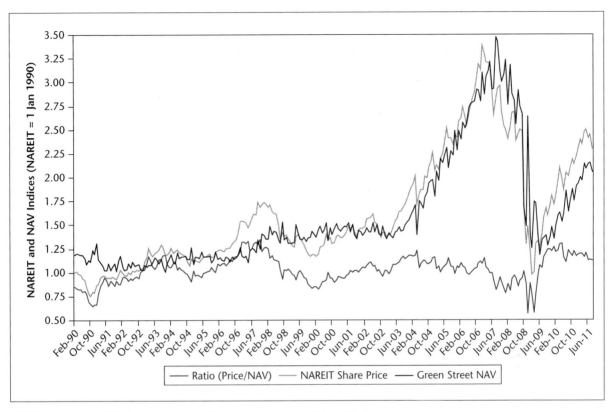

EXHIBIT 12-3 Equity REIT Share Prices versus Private Property Net Asset Values (NAVs)

Source: Authors' calculations based on the NAREIT equity REIT share price index and REIT sector average premium to NAV data provided by Green Street Advisors.

Notes on Exhibit 12-3. Green Street Advisors estimates the net asset value (NAV) on a monthly basis for each of the roughly 65 to 70 larger market capitalization REITs they follow. The firm provided us with a monthly series of average premium to NAV based on the firms in their coverage universe, where premium to NAV is defined as the dollar difference in REIT share price and underlying NAV divided by NAV. To compute the NAV series in the exhibit, we combined the Green Street premium to NAV series with the NAREIT equity price index (set equal to 1 in Jan. 1990) to back out an "implied" NAV index as follows: NAV index = NAREIT index/(1 + premium to NAV). The ratio of the equity REIT price index to NAV, Price/NAV, is shown in the exhibit rather than the percent premium to NAV, simply to facilitate displaying all three lines on the same graph. The ratio of P/NAV equals 1 + Premium to NAV.

according to Green Street Advisors, a leading firm that produces REIT NAV data.[29] The main point in Exhibit 12-3 that concerns us at present is that there is significant fluctuation over time in the ratio of share price to NAV that appears to be mean reverting. REIT share values tended to be below their NAVs, as evidenced by Price/NAV values less than one, during the early 1990s and again in the late 1990s and early 2000 and in the peak of the 2007 bubble and early stages of the 2008–2009 property crash, while the opposite relationship characterized most of the 1993–1998 period, much of the first half of the 2000s decade, and the period of recovery just after 2009.

---

[29]A similar but slightly different perspective on this same point is provided in Exhibit 7-4 back in Chapter 7. Note that the P/NAV ratio in Exhibit 12-3 reflects the effect of leverage in the REITs covered by Green Street. In general leverage would tend to exaggerate the P/NAV differences from 1.0, in other words, implied unlevered property valuation differences would be less than those in the exhibit. (Exhibit 7-4 is constructed much more crudely entirely at the aggregate level, based on unlevered property market prices and de-levered aggregate REIT price index returns.) While conceptually straightforward, NAV estimation, like appraisal in general, is not an exact science, since the analyst must perform a mass appraisal on the properties or groups of properties owned by the REIT. REIT NAVs are estimated by various firms and sometimes by the REITs themselves, and there are typically some differences in the estimates. See "An Inexact Science" by Art Gering in *Real Estate Portfolio Magazine,* November/December 2002 published by NAREIT. In Chapter 23, we will delve deeper into the mechanics of NAV estimation and the use of NAV as a tool for valuing REIT shares.

12.3.1 Valuation at the Micro-Level

Although interesting at the macro-level, the type of broad-brush aggregate relationships depicted in Exhibit 12-2 can be misleading if you attempt to apply them directly at the micro-level to individual asset valuation. We need to be more careful in order to answer the question of whether, or to what extent, the two asset markets imply differential valuation at the micro-level.

First off, it is important to recognize that we are not technically comparing "apples-to-apples" in Exhibit 12-3. REIT NAVs are derived based on a static portfolio of existing properties or assets in place. REIT share prices, as determined in public stock market, reflect the market's assessment of the net present value of the REIT's firm-level (also referred to as "entity level") management. REITs are not static portfolios of properties, and management may be able to generate growth opportunities beyond the existing asset base or generate profits from property trading (that is, selling existing properties at positive NPV as we noted in section 12.2 is conceptually possible based on the dispersion in property prices around MV) or provision of property management or related services. Perhaps management can even generate some value by financing or by arbitraging any underlying difference that does exist on the private and public market valuations of property.

To be more precise, what in fact do we mean when we ask whether the REIT market and the private direct property market could imply different valuations of the same physical assets at the same point in time? Effectively, if REITs can generally purchase and sell properties at prices equal to the prevailing market value in the private property market without such actions causing any change in REIT share prices, then there is no differential valuation between the two markets at the micro-level. If, on the other hand, REIT purchase or sale of assets at the prevailing private property market MV would cause a change in REIT share prices, then a valuation differential currently exists.

This definition helps to clarify when, and under what conditions, we are likely to observe differential valuation at the micro-level. Differential valuation implies positive-NPV opportunities for REITs based on investment value (i.e., a public-private market arbitrage opportunity). As suggested by the asset market model in section 12.1, such opportunities can only occur when the relevant REITs are intramarginal participants in the private property asset market. Although such opportunities may occur idiosyncratically for any given REIT at any given point in time for a given specific property (as discussed in section 12.1), in order for such opportunities to imply general, market-wide differential valuation between the REIT and property markets, such positive opportunities would have to be widespread, accruing generally to all (or most) REITs at the same time. In such circumstances, we would typically observe REITs very actively dealing in or with the private property market, and primarily on *one side* of the property market, either tending only to buy or tending only to sell.[30]

Another way of stating the previous result is to say that differential pricing exists at the micro-level only in markets and for properties in which the investment value for REITs differs from the investment value for the *marginal* participants in the private market: $IVR_R \neq IV_P$.

Let us clarify how the two markets work in tandem in this regard by considering a simple example. Suppose that at some point in time REIT market valuation exceeds

---

[30]There will always be idiosyncratic deals and idiosyncratic REITs, but the aggregate net trading of the industry as a whole would be clearly on one side of the market (at least for segments of the industry where the differential valuation is clear). REITs do face some regulatory constraints, such as a four-year holding rule that might dampen the intensity of the arbitrage trading and therefore the speed of adjustment to apparent arbitrage opportunities. But REITs have been adept and finding ways to profit from arbitrage opportunities in either direction. For example, when private market valuations are above public market valuations, apart from privatizing the entire REIT or selling off numbers of its assets, a REIT may set up a private equity fund and place REIT properties into the fund in return for private equity capital investment into the fund at private market based valuations, while the REIT still effectively retains operational control and indirect partial ownership of the properties. (In effect, the REIT goes into the private equity real estate investment management business.)

private property market valuation such that, in general, $NPV_R = IV_R - MV_P > 0$. That is, such positive opportunities for REITs arise not just idiosyncratically for a few properties or a few REITs, but are widespread. Stock market investors will in such circumstances recognize that REITs face widespread positive NPV opportunities simply from buying existing properties in the property market. The stock market will capitalize this expected positive NPV "growth opportunity" in the share prices of REITs, driving up share prices to reflect the value not only of the REITs' existing in-place assets but also of the expected future NPVs the REITs will obtain from future property purchases. The result will be a high price/earnings multiple for REIT shares, making it easy for REITs to raise additional equity capital in the stock market to finance property market purchases.

But this process sows the seeds of its own destruction: This is how speculative markets work to provide a negative feedback loop in the real estate system and development cycle. As REITs raise capital that they apply to making purchases in the property market, competition among REITs drives prices in the private property market up to the level at which $NPV_R = IV_R - MV_P = 0$, in other words, until $MV_P = IV_R$. At this point, REITs are no longer intramarginal participants in the property market, and their positive NPV growth opportunities are gone. The stock market will recognize this (perhaps even foresee it coming in advance), and will down-value REIT shares accordingly, so that REIT share prices now only reflect the value of the REITs' in-place assets. (The present value of a future $NPV_R = 0$ opportunity is, of course, just zero.) This will result in REIT price/earnings multiples falling to levels more typical of their long-run historical average.[31] There they will remain until something changes either in the REIT market or the private property market to perturb the equilibrium again.

12.3.2 What about Informational Efficiency?

We have noted that the stock market in which REIT shares trade is more informationally efficient than the private property market in which whole individual properties trade directly. Thus, temporary differences between REIT and private market property valuations may occur due purely to this difference in the trading arena and resulting informational efficiency between the two asset markets. In particular, REIT share prices may respond more quickly to news relevant to property values (for example, news about the real macroeconomy or about interest rates). Such price changes do not in themselves reflect fundamental differences in valuation between the private and public markets. The two markets would (in principle) agree about the value implications of the news. The private market merely takes longer to reflect these (same) value implications.[32]

This possibility bears upon the second part of the question we set out to answer at the beginning of section 12.3, namely, if the two asset markets do imply a different value for the same asset as of the same point in time, *which valuation is "correct"*? In truth, there may be no complete or definitive answer to this question. In a sense, both markets are "correct" from

---

[31]Let MV_R be the market value of a REIT's existing in-place assets as valued by the stock market. Let $NPV_R = IV_R - MV_P$ be the value of the REIT's growth opportunities, and let D_R be the value of the REIT's existing debt liabilities. Then if there are N shares of the REIT's equity outstanding, the share price of the REIT in the stock market is $(MV_R + NPV_R - D_R)/N$. If the growth opportunities disappear (i.e., $NPV_R = 0$), then the REIT's share price must adjust to $(MV_R - D_R)/N$. If NPV_R had been positive and now is zero, then this adjustment represents a fall in share price. Note that such adjustment in share price occurs even though the expected total return required by stock market investors for investing in the REIT has not necessarily changed at all. The disappearance of positive NPV_R opportunities, for example, may have resulted purely from a bidding up of prices in the property market, that is, a rise in MV_P. In this sense, the adjustment in REIT share prices may reflect *no change at all in the REIT's opportunity cost of capital*. What has changed is the allocation of the expected total return between the expected growth (or capital gain) component and the current cash yield component.

[32]The reason is the previously noted difficulty in equating general publicly available news to its exact quantitative implications for the values of specific individual real property assets in the absence of a continuously functioning "auction" market for homogeneous shares of each individual property. Private markets have less ability to aggregate information across individuals and "learn from themselves" through the observation of transaction prices. (See Appendix 12A at the end of this chapter for additional elaboration.)

their own perspectives, or from the perspective of their marginal investors. Nevertheless, to the extent that the value difference is due purely to differences in informational efficiency, it is tempting to conclude that the REIT valuation is, shall we say, "more correct" (in the sense that it reflects more up-to-date information). On the other hand, we have noted that the stock market may overreact to news (or fall to its own behavioral weaknesses), leading to subsequent price "corrections" and excess volatility. This can result in the two markets sometimes presenting a tortoise and hare relationship to each other. In short, it is wise to be cautious about making judgments as to which market valuation is "more correct" in this sense.[33]

12.3.3 Micro-Level Risk Is in the Property, Not in the REIT

Before leaving this section, we should note a point that is relevant to the micro-level consideration of REIT and property valuation, and which often causes some confusion among practitioners. The point can be summed up by the following general statement: *Risk resides in the asset, not in the investor.* This simply reflects that the relevant OCC for evaluating a given property is an OCC that reflects the risk in *that* property. This point no doubt seemed innocuous enough when we presented it in Chapter 10, where we were thinking purely in terms of a private property market perspective.

But now suppose we have two REITs: REIT A has an average cost of capital of 10 percent, while REIT B has an average cost of capital of 12 percent, in both cases based on their total return performance history in the stock market. To simplify this illustration, we will also assume that neither of these REITs has ever employed any debt.[34] Does REIT A's lower average cost of capital imply that it can use a lower discount rate in estimating its present investment value for property X, an office building in San Francisco? In other words, can REIT A "afford to pay" a higher price for property X than REIT B can because of REIT A's lower average cost of capital?

The answer is, probably not. Any REIT's overall cost of capital reflects the average risk of all of its assets. This may or may not be the same as the risk of property X. In general, the *marginal* (or incremental) cost of capital relevant to investment in a given asset may differ from the *average* cost of capital of the firm as a whole. The most likely explanation for REIT A's lower historical cost of capital is that REIT A's assets have historically been less risky than REIT B's. This may be because REIT A invests in less risky properties, or it may be because REIT B tends to undertake more new construction and development projects. (Development is inherently more risky than in-place bricks and mortar, even though the type of property may be the same once built.)

In general, REIT A's lower historical cost of capital *at the firm level* does not imply that it can afford to pay more for property X *at the property level.* Assuming both REIT A and B face the same incremental future cash flow stream from property X (including any spillover or synergistic effects on their other properties), the investment value of property X is the same for both REITs. If either REIT pays more than this value, its stock price per share will be diluted. If either REIT can get property X for less than this IV, its stock price will be enhanced. For either REIT, the OCC relevant for evaluating the investment value of property X is the property X OCC, not the REIT's average OCC. Of course, the REIT's firm-level average OCC may give a good indication of property X's OCC, but only to the extent that the REIT's other assets (on average or in the aggregate) are similar in risk to property X.[35]

---

[33]The relation between public and private markets at the macro-level will be discussed further in Chapter 23.

[34]In subsequent chapters, we will see how such firm-level cost of capital estimates can be calculated as a weighted average cost of capital (WACC) for the firm.

[35]Stock market analysts or the REIT's investors might question the corporate strategy involved in purchasing a property that has substantially different risk characteristics from the typical properties in the REIT's portfolio, but there could well be a good strategic reason for such purchase.

If you follow this reasoning, then you should be able to see more easily through the following two fallacies that are common in real world practice: (1) REIT A can borrow money at 6 percent while REIT B has to pay 8 percent interest on its debt; therefore, REIT A can afford to pay a higher price for property X. (2) REIT A has a price/earnings multiple of 12 while REIT B's multiple is only 10. Therefore, REIT A can afford a higher price for property X. You should now realize that neither the interest rate on a firm's debt, nor its earnings yield (or inverse price/earnings multiple) is generally equivalent to the expected total return on the firm's underlying assets (the firm's average OCC). Furthermore, as we just noted, even the firm's average OCC is not necessarily the relevant OCC for computing its investment value for a given asset.[36]

12.3.4 Summarizing the Dueling Markets: Going from the Micro to the Macro Perspective

To summarize the discussion in this section, we can make a couple of qualitative generalizations about the micro-level valuation implications of the existence of real estate's two "dueling" asset markets. First, asset valuation differences at this level are not impossible, and indeed are probably not uncommon, based on differences both in cash flow expectations and in the opportunity cost of capital. Second, at least at the micro-level, such differences will probably tend to be small more often than not, with large differences tending to be short-lived, and therefore less permanent than some proponents may believe. Third, at least over the very long run, valuation differences should tend to average out so that neither market structure provides permanently higher or lower values. Otherwise, all assets would tend to gravitate toward one ownership form or the other.

A final question that we should touch briefly on relates back to Exhibit 12-3 and the professional practitioners' focus on short-run measures such as current yields and price/earnings ratios. If micro-level differences in valuation are relatively small and transient, why do we see relatively large differences in macro-level valuations such as those portrayed in Exhibit 12-3? The answer to this question obviously lies in the difference between the micro- and macro-levels. As noted in section 12.3.1, REIT share prices reflect not only their existing in-place assets, but also their entity-level capital structure (such as the degree of leverage), and their future **growth opportunities** as represented by their ability to make positive NPV acquisitions, developments, and dispositions. Financial management and growth opportunities are highly sensitive to the nature and quality of entity-level REIT management. REIT share prices, and REIT risk and return, reflect these macro-level variables as well as the aggregate of all their existing micro-level asset holdings. This certainly explains some of any apparent discrepancy between REIT and private property market valuation statistics.

12.4 Chapter Summary

You can now unfasten your seatbelts. We have landed. Chapter 12 dealt with some very deep and subtle issues. This is the kind of thing you have to read more than once, and think about for a while. We sympathize. But the topics addressed here are obviously important and fundamental. Although they are of academic interest, they also carry important implications for real world investment decision making. Furthermore, it is in these unique characteristics of real estate that some of the most exciting opportunities in real estate investment can be found. If you study this chapter carefully, you should come away with a deeper and more accurate understanding of and insight into micro-level real estate investment decision making and how real estate asset markets work. Smart people can make use of such a level of knowledge in the real world!

---

[36] A firm's debt is usually, by construction, less risky than the firm's underlying assets. (See Chapter 13 and Part VI.) A firm's earnings/price ratio is akin to its current cash yield, $E[y]$, except that some of the earnings are typically held back to finance growth and not paid out in dividends, resulting in the earnings/price ratio typically being larger than the current dividend yield.

Appendix 12A Basic Valuation Concepts: Transaction Prices, Market Values, and the Model of the Asset Market

Valuation theory has a long history in economics and the appraisal profession. Becoming familiar with some of the basics of this theory should help to build your intuition and understanding of value in real estate. In this appendix, we will define and distinguish between several different concepts of value and price.

The most primal concept of value is what is often termed **inherent value**. This refers to the value of an object (in our case, a commercial property) to a given owner or user of the object, in the absence of any consideration of the market value or exchange value of the object. Inherent value represents the maximum amount a given person would be willing to pay for a good. From the perspective of a *user* of the property, inherent value is the **usage value** of the property. This would apply, for example, to owner/occupiers as in the case of some corporate real estate, in which ownership and usage are not separated. From the perspective of an *investor* in a property, defined as a nonuser owner, inherent value is essentially the same as what we have been calling investment value (IV).[37]

Now consider two populations of potential user owners or investors for a given type of property. One population already owns such property, while the other population does not. These two populations are represented in Exhibit 12A-1a. The left-hand distribution consists of potential buyers of this type of property (current nonowners), and the right-hand distribution is that of potential sellers (current owners of such property).[38] The horizontal axis measures inherent value (say, in dollars per square foot) for the type of property in question, while the vertical axis shows the number of parties in each population having the inherent value indicated on the horizontal axis.

Now suppose these two populations are able to interact and trade examples of this type of property among themselves. For a price corresponding to any given value on the horizontal axis, we would have a number of willing buyers equal to the area underneath the buyer curve to the right of the given price. We would also have a number of willing sellers equal to the area underneath the seller curve to the left of the given price. The entire potential buyer population would be willing to pay at least the amount A for this type of property, while no buyer would be willing to pay more than D. No current owner of this type of property would be willing to sell for less than B, while all owners would be willing to part with their property for the amount E.

If potential buyers and potential sellers randomly find each other, we would observe some transactions, for there is some overlap of the two distributions. All transactions would occur within the price range between B and D. **Transaction prices** are the prices at which deals are actually done, the prices at which examples of the type of property in question change hands. While inherent values are very difficult if not impossible to observe empirically, transaction prices can be observed empirically, and can thus be thought of as objective information (in contrast to inherent values, which may be more subjective in nature). If we observe many transactions, we would expect that the frequency distribution of transaction prices (a histogram of such prices) would have a shape similar to the triangular region that is simultaneously underneath both curves between B and D.[39]

If the property market functioned as a well-ordered double auction, with the auctioneer calling out prices and bidders (both buyers and sellers) revealing their true inherent values, C is the price at which the market would clear, the "equilibrium price." C is thus the value at

---

[37]As noted, the terms *inherent value, intrinsic value,* and *investment value* have a fair amount of overlap in common usage. But in general, the former two terms have more of a usage value connotation, while investment value refers more specifically to values for nonuser owners, landlords rather than owner/occupiers.

[38]For the potential sellers, the inherent value may be interpreted as the *minimum* price at which they would be willing to sell the property *if* they could not sell at a higher price.

[39]That is, the transaction price frequency distribution would resemble the intersection of the areas underneath the two inherent price distributions with only a few deals observed around the extreme prices of B and D and many deals observed with prices similar to C.

EXHIBIT 12A-1a Buyer
and Seller Populations,
Inherent Value Frequency
Distributions

© OnCourse Learning

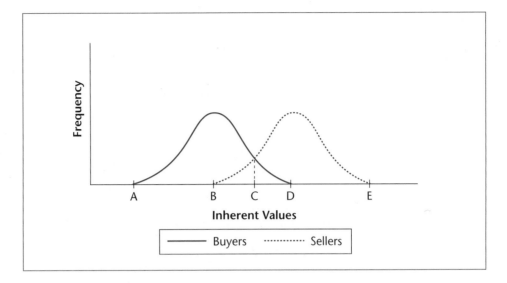

EXHIBIT 12A-1b Buyer
and Seller Populations,
Reservation Price Frequency
Distributions

© OnCourse Learning

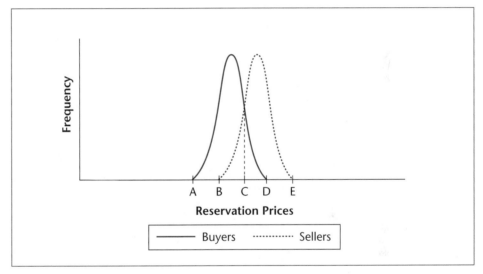

which there are as many willing buyers as there are willing sellers (the area to the right of C under the buyer curve equals the area to the left of C under the seller curve). In a well-ordered auction market with perfect inherent value information revelation, *all* the transactions for this type of property would take place at the price C, and this price would maximize the aggregate consumer or producer surplus from the usage of this type of property.[40]

In real property markets, however, we do not have perfect auction markets to reveal the equilibrium value C. But we do usually have reasonably active and well-functioning asset transaction markets. The potential buyers and potential sellers of a given type of property can observe (more or less easily and accurately) the prices at which transactions of that (or similar) type of property occur from time to time. Such observation gives potential market participants some information about the equilibrium value (C in our diagram). This allows market participants to put some range around the likely equilibrium value. Potential buyers and sellers rationally use such transaction price information in determining their **reservation prices**, the prices at which they will stop searching any further for a willing partner and will

[40]Economic "surplus" in this context refers to the net value or utility obtained by the producer or consumer as a result of trade—IV minus price for buyers, price minus IV for sellers.

agree to trade. Reservation prices are based on inherent values but also incorporate information about the market, the perceived likely equilibrium value.[41]

Rational buyer reservation prices will be no higher than, but in some cases may be lower than, inherent values. Seller reservation prices will be no lower than, but in some cases may be higher than, inherent values. Potential buyers who see evidence from the market that their inherent values are above the equilibrium value will tend to reduce their reservation prices below their inherent values, because no one should want to pay more than necessary, and because the market informs people about values. Sellers who perceive the equilibrium price to be above their inherent values will tend to raise their reservation prices above their inherent values, because no one should want to sell for less than necessary. At the other end of the inherent value distributions, nonowners whose inherent values are well below the range of observable transaction prices will effectively drop out of the potential buyer pool. Owners whose inherent values are well above the observed transaction price range will similarly drop out of the potential seller distribution.[42]

This causes reservation price distributions to be tighter, less spread out, and closer to the true equilibrium value C than the underlying inherent value distributions. This difference between the reservation price distributions of the effective potential market participant pool on the one hand, and the underlying inherent value distributions on the other hand, is the effect of the market "teaching itself about itself" through the information *revealed by transaction prices observable through the functioning of the market itself.*[43] In the financial economics literature, this process is often called **price discovery**. The more numerous and frequent the transactions, the more alike or homogeneous the individual properties or assets in the market, and the easier it is to observe quickly and accurately the transaction prices, the tighter and closer to C will be the reservation price distributions. This is because the information revealed by the observed transactions will be more directly relevant to the valuation of the other assets in the market. This is sometimes referred to as the effect of **market density**.[44]

---

[41]Reservation prices are also based on the cost of the searching process and the amount of uncertainty. The more difficult and costly it is to find potentially suitable properties (or buyers), the higher (lower) will be the optimal reservation price for buyers (sellers) of a given type of property, other things being equal. The more uncertainty, the lower (higher) the reservation price for buyers (sellers). Reservation prices also reflect the degree of urgency or pressure (sometimes referred to as "motivation") to conclude a transaction. Rational search theory has become a well-developed field in economics since the 1970s, and has led to the 2010 Nobel Prize in Economics for Peter Diamond, Dale Mortensen, and Christopher Pissarides. A simple example is presented in Appendix 30C in the electronic resources for Chapter 30. (The example there is of optimal landlord asking rent, but the same type of model could be applied, on the opposite side of the market—demand rather than supply—to optimal investor reservation price for an asset purchase.) There may also be less rational, more behavioral components in the formation of reservation prices, reflecting theories associated with another Nobel Prize (awarded to Daniel Kahneman in 2002). Several economists and psychologists (including Amos Tversky, Richard Thaler, Herbert Simon, among others) have developed theories such as "anchoring", "loss aversion", and the "disposition effect" (among others) which suggest that parties might overly bias their reservation prices in response to such considerations as the price the property was purchased for or how much value it has gained since it was bought. (See for example in the Part IV bibliography such articles as: Genseove and Mayer (2001), Crane and Hartzell (2011), Bokhari and Geltner (2011), Yavas and Wang (1995), among a growing body of literature.)

[42]In other words, in both cases they will simply stop (or never start) searching for opposite parties to a potential transaction.

[43]The astute reader will realize that this mechanism of market self-learning through transaction price observation holds implications for our previous assertion at the beginning of Chapter 10: that the price at which an investor can expect to sell a property in the future is *independent* of the price paid for the property in the past by the investor. In fact, in a market of thinly traded unique assets, the price paid by the current owner may indeed rationally have some relevance in the future as an indication of value for the property. However, this relevance diminishes with the passage of time, and in any case would be far from determinative. What we asserted in Chapter 10 is *essentially* true in the context of that chapter, and provides the best guidance for rational and prudent investment decision making.

[44]Note that an implication of this is that when there is less price discovery, more uncertainty about what the market equilibrium value is, there is likely to be less overlap between the buyer and seller reservation price distributions, and hence less scope for trading, and therefore less turnover or "liquidity" in the market. Conversely, greater liquidity is associated with better or easier price discovery (which in turn can stimulate liquidity in a virtuous spiral). The positive feedback loop represented by the relation between liquidity and price discovery can cause the property market to have more tendency toward boom and bust cycles, at least as regards trading volume.

Let's consider an extreme case, in which homogeneous shares of the same asset are traded continuously in a double-auction market open to the public and always full of numerous buyers and sellers, and in which all transaction prices are reported immediately and publicly, similar to what goes on in a public stock exchange. In such an extreme case, buyer and seller reservation price distributions might effectively collapse onto the single value of C, the market-clearing equilibrium value. Then (but only then, in such a hypothetical extreme case), the unique observed transaction price would exactly equal the equilibrium value of the asset, as of the time of the transaction. This would be an extreme case of maximum overlap between buyer and seller reservation prices and hence maximum trading volume or liquidity, due to the elimination of any uncertainty about what is the market value of the assets being traded.[45]

Exhibit 12A-1b illustrates a more realistic case of reservation price distributions for property markets. The scale on the horizontal axis is meant to be the same as that in Exhibit 12A-1a, so that the narrower frequency distributions in Exhibit 12A-1b indicate that the reservation price distributions shrink the transaction price distribution range from what it would be with no market information available to buyers and sellers. More and better transaction price information improves reservation price formation and asset price discovery and thereby improves liquidity in the market. The observable transaction price range from B to D around C is narrower in Exhibit 12A-1b than it is in 12A-1a based only on the inherent value distributions. This is the effect of market density, and is related in both cause and effect to liquidity and price discovery. In the typical property market situation depicted in Exhibit 12A-1b some dispersion of observed transaction prices around the equilibrium value still occurs because the market is not sufficiently dense and liquid to eliminate all such dispersion. (This is in principle—and with some oversimplification—a key difference between private property markets and public securities markets like the stock market including the REIT market.)

Now it is important to recognize that the value C in this model is what is normally defined as the *market value*, or the exchange value of the type of property in question.[46] Recognizing that Exhibit 12A-1b represents a snapshot of the property market as of one point in time, we see that even if several transactions were occurring at precisely that point in time, these observable transaction prices would be merely "drawings" from the transaction price distribution (which ranges between B and D). No single transaction price necessarily equals C, nor is there even any guarantee that the average among the observed transaction prices will necessarily exactly equal C. We thus arrive at a fundamental principle of the valuation of thinly traded objects:

Observed transaction prices are dispersed around the contemporaneous market value.

This principle underlies the application of modern statistics to the empirical study of market values in real estate. It suggests a statistical-based definition of market value as the mean of the ex ante (i.e., potential) transaction price distribution as of a given point in time. This allows us to employ basic statistical inference and sampling theory, for example, to enlighten the process of estimating market values. In particular, we may assume that the arithmetic average of randomly observed transaction prices is a statistic whose ex ante mean is the market value (C).[47] The standard deviation of this statistic is $(1/\sqrt{n})$ times the standard

---

[45]In the context of this simple asset market model, it is only in this extreme case of complete buyer and seller overlap that asset price and trading volume are unrelated to each other (complete demand and supply price elasticity, as will be explained shortly).

[46]Recall that, as we are talking about a type of property, this value would probably be measured in some normalized units, such as dollars per square foot or dollars per dollar of current income (the inverse of the cap rate or current yield). At the micro-level of individual assets one must of course account for specific unique features of individual properties in their valuations.

[47]Here we are assuming that all observed transactions occur as of a single point in time (a snapshot of the market). Obviously, as market values change over time, a sample of observed transaction prices occurring at different points in time will each be drawn from the potential price distribution centered around the (longitudinally varying) market value as of the time each transaction occurred. Such a sample mean would then represent a type of "moving average" of market values across time. The implications this holds for real estate price index time-series return and risk statistics will be discussed in Chapter 25.

deviation of the potential transaction price distribution, where n is the number of transaction price observations.[48] This is sometimes referred to as "the square root of n rule." The general implication of this statistical perspective is that the average of the observed transaction prices, at a single point in time, is a statistically unbiased estimate of the true market value, C, as of that point in time, and the more transaction observations we include in computing this average, the more precise will be our estimate.[49]

We should also note at this point the relationship between the reservation price frequency distributions in Exhibit 12A-1b and the asset market supply and demand functions in Exhibit 12-1 in the main body of this chapter. The supply function in Exhibit 12-1 is the cumulative distribution under the sellers' reservation price frequency distribution in Exhibit 12A-1b, and similarly the demand function in 12-1 is the cumulative distribution under the potential buyers' reservation price frequency distribution in 12A-1b. The horizontal axis in Exhibit 12A-1b corresponds to the vertical axis in Exhibit 12-1 (the graphs are transposed). The market value (MV) on the vertical axis in Exhibit 12-1 corresponds to the market-clearing equilibrium price "C" on the horizontal axis in Exhibit 12A-1b. The equilibrium quantity of trading on the horizontal axis of Exhibit 12-1 (Q*) reflects the area of overlap simultaneously under both the buyers' and sellers' reservation price frequency distributions (the intersection of those two sets) in Exhibit 12A-1b.

Reservation price distributions that are more spread out horizontally in Exhibit 12A-1b, as when there is less liquidity and less price discovery or a thinner market, correspond to demand and supply functions in Exhibit 12-1 that are steeper and exhibit less price elasticity. Conversely, tight, narrowly spread reservation price frequency distributions in Exhibit 12A-1b resulting from a denser more liquid market with greater price discovery will correspond to less steeply rising or falling, more price-elastic, supply and demand functions in Exhibit 12-1.

In the extreme, if both reservation price frequency distributions collapsed onto the single price C (as in our simple conception of a perfectly functioning stock market), there would be infinite price elasticity and asset prices would not be influenced by or related to trading volume. In reality, such a condition is not perfectly true even in the stock market (though some classical models of the stock market assumed it so), and in the private property market we observe more relationship between price and trading volume, typically with volume and price moving together pro-cyclically, and often with changes in volume slightly leading changes in price in time.

KEY TERMS

market value (MV)	random noise (in asset valuation)	net asset value (NAV)
opportunity value	due diligence	discount/premium to NAV
investment value (IV)	partial adjustment (of asset prices to news)	differential valuation (across asset markets)
opportunity cost of capital (OCC)		
second-most-motivated buyer	predictability (inertia in asset price movements)	growth opportunities (for REITs)
marginal investors		inherent value
intramarginal investors	market timing	usage value
asset transaction market equilibrium	transaction costs	transaction price
entrepreneurial profit	supernormal profits	reservation price
informational inefficiency (in asset markets)	cycles	price discovery
	arbitrage	market density

[48]For the mean of the potential transaction price distribution to equal exactly the equilibrium value C, we require that the mean of that distribution equal its median, that is, that the distribution be symmetrical, which in turn requires that the buyer and seller reservation price distributions are symmetrical in their relevant tails. In this case, the mode of the transaction price distribution, or single most likely price, will also coincide with C.

[49]We assume here that each transaction is independent of the others, and that the transacting properties are all identical, or that errors induced in adjusting the observed prices for differences in the properties are independent. Vandell (1991) presented a more detailed analysis of optimal selection and weighting of comparable property transactions. A statistical procedure known as hedonic regression can also be used for this purpose.

STUDY QUESTIONS

12.1. Why is market value (MV) an important way to conceive of, and measure, asset value for investors in commercial real estate?

12.2. Why is investment value (IV) an important way to conceive of, and measure, asset value for investors in commercial real estate?

12.3. Suppose a certain site has a McDonald's restaurant on it (equipped with the usual golden arches, etc.). As a McDonald's, the site can generate $50,000 per year, net cash. In any other use it can only generate at most $40,000 per year, and it would cost $20,000 to remove the golden arches. Assuming a 10% required return:

    a. What is the market value of this property?

    b. What is its investment value to McDonald's? (Hint: Use the perpetuity formula: $V = CF/r$.)

12.4. In Question 12.3, assume that the property is currently owned by McDonald's.

    a. What is McDonald's expected NPV from selling the property, evaluated from an MV perspective?

    b. What is McDonald's expected NPV from selling the property, evaluated from an IV perspective?

12.5. Now assume that the property described in Question 12.3 is owned by someone other than McDonald's, a "typical" real estate investor by the name of Bob.

    a. What is Bob's expected NPV from selling the property, evaluated from an MV perspective?

    b. What is Bob's expected NPV from selling the property, evaluated from an IV perspective?

    c. What if Bob tries to sell the property to McDonald's?

12.6. What are the general (and defining) characteristics of marginal participants in an asset market?

12.7. Describe a characteristic indicator that a property market is currently in equilibrium?

12.8. What are the general necessary conditions for a real estate investment transaction to involve substantial positive NPV for at least one side of the deal without involving negative NPV for the other side?

12.9. If a certain property is put up for sale, there is a 50% chance it will sell for $900,000 and a 50% chance it will sell for $1,100,000.

    a. What is the market value of this property?

    b. What is the standard deviation of the random noise in this property's price as a percentage of its market value?

    c. If the property sells for $900,000, what was the ex post NPV from the market value perspective for the seller and the buyer?

    d. If the property sells for $1,100,000, what was the ex post NPV from the market value perspective for the seller and the buyer?

    e. What is the ex ante NPV from the market value perspective?

12.10. Name at least three sources or causes of real estate transaction prices deviating around the market value of the asset.

12.11. Suppose two identical properties are traded in two different asset markets: property A in a relatively inefficient or sluggish market and property B in a more efficient market. When news arrives relevant to asset value, property A's market value will move only halfway to the new value in the first period, and the rest of the way in the next period. Property B's value will move all the way to the new value in the first period. At the beginning of period 0, both properties are worth $1,000. Then news arrives that implies they should be worth 10% more.

    a. In the absence of any further news, how much will property A and property B be worth at the end of period 1 and period 2?

b. In the absence of transaction costs, and assuming you can borrow $1,000 for two periods at $50 interest, how much money could you make (and how could you make it) by trading between the two properties across the two markets? (Assume that at the beginning of the dealing you do not own either property, and at the end you cash out completely, paying back any loaned money.)

c. Suppose the transaction costs are 3% of property value each time you either buy or sell a property (but loan transactions are free). Now what is your profit or loss from the same transactions as in (b)?

12.12. Why is it difficult for real estate investors to make supernormal profits from market-timing investments even though the property market is somewhat sluggish with relatively predictable short-run movements in asset prices?

*12.13. Describe a general indicator of the existence of differential valuation of (the same) real estate assets between the private property market and the REIT market. (Hint: What would we expect to see in the nature of the parties to the transactions in the private property market?)

*12.14. a. What are the two fundamental sources of possible differential valuation of real estate assets between the private property market and the REIT market?

b. How might REITs in general be able to influence property cash flows in ways that private owners could not?

c. How might the risk perceptions and preferences of the average investor in the stock market differ from those of the average investor in the direct private property market?

*12.15. Why is it unlikely that large differences in valuation would persist for long periods of time between the private property market and the REIT market?

*12.16. (**based on Appendix 12A**) What is the difference among inherent value, reservation prices, transaction prices, and market values? Define and contrast each of these conceptions or measures of value.

*12.17. (**based on Appendix 12A**) What is meant by the term *price discovery*? Why is price discovery likely to be more efficient in "denser" asset markets?

PART IV

REFERENCES AND ADDITIONAL READING

Adams, P., B. Kluger, and S. Wyatt. 1992. Integrating auction and search markets: The slow Dutch auction. *Journal of Real Estate Finance and Economics* 20(3): 239–254.

Barkham, R. and D. Geltner. 1995. Price discovery in American and British property markets. *Real Estate Economics* 23(1): 21–44.

Bender, A., E. Jani, and M. Hoesli. 2006. Monte Carlo simulations for real estate valuation. *Journal of Property Investment and Finance* 24(2): 102–122.

Bokhari, S. and D. Geltner. 2011. Loss aversion and anchoring in commercial real estate pricing: Empirical evidence and price index implications. *Real Estate Economics* 39(4): 635–670.

Brealey, R. and S. Myers. 1996. *Principles of Corporate Finance*, 5th ed., New York: McGraw-Hill, chs. 2, 4–6.

Brown, R. J. 2006. *Private Real Estate Investment: Data Analysis and Decision Making.* Academic Press, Advanced Finance Series.

Case, B. and J. Quigley. 1991. Dynamics of real-estate prices. *Review of Economics and Statistics* 73(1): 50–58.

Case, K. and R. Shiller. 1990. Forecasting prices and excess returns in the housing market. *AREUEA Journal* 18(3): 253–273.

Childs, P., S. H. Ott, and T. J. Riddiough. 2002. Optimal valuation of claims on noisy real assets: Theory and an application. *Real Estate Economics* 30(3): 385–443.

Clayton, J., D. C. Ling, and A. Naranjo. 2009. Commercial real estate valuation: Fundamentals versus investor sentiment. *Journal of Real Estate Finance and Economics* 38(1): 5–37.

Colwell, P. F. and H.J. Munneke. 2006. Bargaining strength and property class in office markets. *Journal of Real Estate Finance and Economics* 33(3): 197–213.

Crane, A. and J. Hartzell. 2009. Is there a disposition effect in corporate investment decisions? *Evidence from real estate investment trusts.* Working Paper. The University of Texas at Austin.

Crosby, N., A. Lavers, and J. Murdoch. 1998. Property valuation variation and the "margin of error" in the UK. *Journal of Property Research* 15(4): 305–330.

D. Geltner. 2004. IRR-based property-level performance attribution. *Journal of Portfolio Management* 138–151.

Diaz, J. and M. Wolverton. 1998. A longitudinal examination of the appraisal smoothing hypothesis. *Real Estate Economics* 26(2).

Downs, A. 1994. Public, private market valuations do diverge. *National Real Estate Investor* 36(13): 20.

Feng, T. and D. Geltner. 2011. Property-level performance attribution: Investment management diagnostics and the investment importance of property management). *Journal of Portfolio Management* 35(5): 110–124.

Fisher, J., D. Gatzlaff, D. Geltner, and D. Haurin. 2003. Controlling for the impact of variable liquidity in commercial real estate price indices. *Real Estate Economics* 31(2): 269–303.

Fisher, J., D. Gatzlaff, D. Geltner and R. Haurin. 2004. An analysis of the determinants of transaction frequency of institutional commercial real estate investment property. *Real Estate Economics* 32: 239–264.

Fisher, J., D. Geltner, and H. Pollakowski. 2007. A quarterly transactions-based index of institutional real estate investment performance and movements in supply and demand. *Journal of Real Estate Finance and Economics* 34(1): 5–33.

Geltner, D. 1989. Estimating real estate's systematic risk from aggregate level appraisal-based returns. *Real Estate Economics* 17(4): 463–481.

Geltner, D. 1993. Estimating market values from appraised values without assuming an efficient market. *Journal of Real Estate Research* 8(3): 325–346.

Geltner, D. 1997. The use of appraisals in portfolio valuation & index construction. *Journal of Property Valuation & Investment* 15(5): 423–447.

Geltner, D. 1998. How accurate is the NCREIF Index as a benchmark, and who cares? *Real Estate Finance* 14(4).

Geltner, D. and J. Mei. 1995. The present value model with time-varying discount rates: Implications for commercial property valuation and investment decisions. *Journal of Real Estate Finance & Economics* 11(2): 119–136.

Geltner, D. and W. Goetzmann. 2000. Two decades of commercial property returns: A repeated-measures regression-based version of the NCREIF Index. *Journal of Real Estate Finance and Economics* 21(1): 5–21.

Genesove, D. and C. Mayer. 2001. Loss aversion and seller behavior: Evidence from the housing market. *Quarterly Journal of Economics* 166: 1233–1260.

Giliberto, S. M. and A. Mengden. 1996. REITs and real estate: Two markets reexamined. *Real Estate Finance* 13(1): 56–60.

Goetzmann, W. 1993. The single family home in the investment portfolio. *Journal of Real Estate Finance & Economics* 6(3): 201–222.

Graff, R. 1999. Changing leases into investment-grade bonds. *Journal of Real Estate Portfolio Management* 5(2): 183–194.

Graff, R. and M. Young. 1999. The magnitude of random appraisal error in commercial real estate valuation. *Journal of Real Estate Research* 17: 33–54.

Gyourko, J. and D. Keim. 1992. What does the stock market tell us about real estate returns. *Real Estate Economics* 20(3): 457–486.

Hoesli, M., E. Oikarinen, and C. Serrano. 2011. The long-run dynamics between direct and securitized real estate. *Journal of Real Estate Research* 33(1): 73–103.

Ibanez, M. and A. Pennington-Cross. Commercial property rent dynamics in U.S. metropolitan areas: An examination of office, industrial, flex and retail space. *Journal of Real Estate Finance and Economics*, forthcoming.

Lin, Z. G. and K. D. Vandell. 2007. Illiquidity and pricing biases in the real estate market. *Real Estate Economics* 35(3): 291–330.

Ling, D. and A. Naranjo. 1999. The integration of commercial real estate markets and stock markets. *Real Estate Economics* 27(3): 483–516.

Linneman, P. 1997. Forces changing the real estate industry forever. *Wharton Real Estate Review* 1(1): 1–12.

Liu, C., D. Hartzell, T. Grissom, and W. Grieg. 1990. The composition of the market portfolio and real estate investment performance. *Real Estate Economics* 18(1): 49–75.

Marcato G. and T. Key. 2005. Direct investment in real estate—Momentum profits and their robustness to trading costs. *Journal of Portfolio Management* 55 + Sp. Iss. SI.

Mei, J. 1996. Assessing the "Santa Claus" approach to asset allocation. *Real Estate Finance* 13(2): 65–70.

Mei, J. and A. Lee. 1994. Is there a real estate factor premium? *Journal of Real Estate Finance & Economics* 9(2): 113–126.

Plazzi, A., W. Torous, and R. Valkanov. 2010. Expected returns and expected growth in rents of commercial real estate. *Review of Financial Studies* 23(9): 3469–3519.

Riddiough, T., M. Moriarity, and P. Yeatman. 2005. Privately versus publicly held asset investment performance. *Real Estate Economics* 33(1): 121–146.

Stein, J. 1995. Prices and trading volume in the housing market: A model with down-payment effects, *The Quarterly Journal of Economics* 110(2): 379–406.

Stevenson, Simon. 2002. Momentum effects and mean reversion in real estate securities. *Journal of Real Estate Research* 23(01/02): 47–64.

Vandell, K. 1991. Optimal comparable selection and weighting in real property valuation. *Real Estate Economics* 19(2): 213–239.

Vogel, J. 1997. Why the new conventional wisdom about REITs is wrong. *Real Estate Finance* 14(2).

Wheaton, W. 1998. Vacancy, search and prices in a housing market matching model, *Journal of Political Economy* 98(6): 1270–1292.

Williams, J. 1995. Pricing real assets with costly search. *Review of Financial Studies* 8(1), 55–90.

Yavas, A. and S. Yang. 1995. The strategic role of listing price in marketing real estate: Theory and evidence. *Real Estate Economics* 23(3): 347–368.

Yavas, A. and Y. Yildirim. 2011. Price discovery in real estate markets: A dynamic analysis. *Journal of Real Estate Finance and Economics* 42(1): 1–29.

PART

V

COMPLETING THE BASIC INVESTMENT ANALYSIS PICTURE

In Parts III and IV, we introduced the fundamental financial economic principles and procedures underlying the valuation of real property, including the basics of investment analysis at the micro-level of individual properties. In Part V, we will add to that picture by introducing two additional considerations that are often important in considering commercial real estate investments: debt and income taxes. These topics are a bit more advanced, in the sense that they build on the basic foundation presented in the previous chapters. However, these topics are not any more difficult to master than what we have already come through, and our treatment here will remain at a practical level. With the incorporation of debt and taxes, we address the necessary concomitant to the investment decision covered in Part IV. There, you learned how to decide which property to invest in. Here, you learn how to finance and structure such an investment.

The topics considered in Part V differ from our previous focus in that they relate to the *owners* of properties, rather than to the properties themselves per se. That is, we are shifting focus from the property level to the investor level, the individuals or institutions who are considering real estate investments. One implication of the owner perspective is that the issues addressed in Part V sometimes go beyond the consideration of a single property to encompass a broader perspective of the investor's decision making, based upon the investor's overall financial position, which may include a portfolio of many properties as well as different types of investments such as stocks and bonds. Nevertheless, our primary focus in Part V will remain at the micro-level, on the analysis of individual properties and deals. (We will reserve most of our treatment of broader, macro-level issues primarily for Part VII.)

CHAPTER

13

USE OF DEBT IN REAL ESTATE INVESTMENT: THE EFFECT OF LEVERAGE

CHAPTER OUTLINE

LEARNING OBJECTIVES

After reading this chapter, you should understand:

⊃ What is meant by the term "leverage" and how the use of debt financing affects the leverage of the equity investment.

⊃ How leverage affects the equity investor's expected total return, and the income and appreciation components of that return.

⊃ How leverage affects the risk in the total return to equity, and therefore the market's required risk premium in the ex ante return.

⊃ The weighted average cost of capital formula (WACC) and how this formula can be useful in quantifying leverage effects in theory, and in making practical approximations.

⊃ What is meant by the term "positive leverage," and the conditions that result in such leverage.

⊃ How the use of debt, and its effect on leverage, enables the same underlying real property asset to serve investors with different objectives and concerns.

The use of debt financing is very widespread in real estate investment. Indeed, real estate is famous as a source of collateral for vast amounts of debt. In the early 2010s, there was over $3 trillion in commercial mortgage loans outstanding in the United States (including loans backing CMBS), as well as additional real estate debt in the form of entity-level bank loans, bonds issued to REITs, and others.[1] Indeed, individuals and taxable investors and REITs typically use large amounts of debt, and even cash-rich tax-exempt institutions sometimes employ mortgage financing.

In order to help you develop a sophisticated understanding of the use of debt in real estate investment, we will be examining this topic in this and the next two chapters. Here we will present the basics of leverage. Chapter 14 will introduce the effect of income taxes and their

---

[1]See section 7.3.2 and Exhibit 7-13 for a discussion of the sources of commercial mortgage financing in the United States.

interaction with debt in the investment, and Chapter 15 will treat broader issues of capital structure, including the use of various types of financing at the project level. All of these chapters will consider the role of debt in real estate investment primarily from the borrower's perspective, the property equity investor, although this will occasionally require consideration of what is happening to the lender as well. (Real estate debt viewed primarily from the perspective of the lender, or debt holder, will be the main focus of Part VI.)

As noted, the present chapter will focus on the effect of **leverage** on the investment performance of the equity position. The use of debt to finance an equity investment creates what is called "leverage" in the equity investment, because it allows equity investors to magnify the amount of underlying physical capital they control (which may also magnify the risk and return performance of the equity). It is important to understand this effect thoroughly. In this chapter, we will largely ignore income tax considerations related to debt, to focus on the pure effect of leverage.

The effect of leverage on equity investment is fundamental to all investment analyses, not just real estate analyses. However, leverage as a topic per se is often skimmed rather lightly in corporate finance textbooks (as distinct from the broader question of corporate capital structure) because it is argued that stockholders can lever up or down "on their own account" (either by borrowing money or investing in bonds). They do not need the corporation in whose stock they are investing to do their levering for them.

This argument is as applicable to REITs as it is to other publicly traded firms, but REITs control only a fraction of all commercial property investment. In real estate, it is not uncommon for individual or institutional investors to effectively own the underlying productive assets directly, with no corporate-level entity involved in the investment decision-making process. Furthermore, even when the direct owner of the real estate equity is a corporate or partnership entity, it is important to understand how leverage affects the risk and return performance of that investment entity. The effects of leverage at the entity level are likely to have important implications for the strategic and tactical management of the entity. In addition, the ultimate individual investor/owners of a real estate investment entity need to understand leverage in order to determine whether to adjust their personal leverage on their own account in response to the entity leverage. With this in mind, the present chapter will start out at a very elementary level and take you up through a level at which you can apply some basic analytical tools that are quite useful in real world practice.

THE "BIG PICTURE"

Before we get into the nuts and bolts of leverage, however, let's step back for a minute and introduce the use of debt in its broader context in real estate investment, to consider the forest rather than the individual trees. Do you recall the point we made early in Chapter 7 about **heterogeneous investors**? This fundamental fact permeates all aspects of investment, including the issue of debt financing for real estate investments. Indeed, at a broad-brush level, it may be said that a fundamental reason for the widespread use of mortgage debt in income-property investment is the diversity among investors.

Recall that different individuals, as well as different types of institutional investors, have different objectives and constraints governing their investment decisions. Some investors want growth, while others want income. Some are willing to take on considerable risk in pursuit of high returns, while others are willing to sacrifice high returns in order to keep their investments safe and liquid. Some have specific future liabilities they are responsible for paying. Also, access to capital, and the resulting availability of one's own funds to invest, varies greatly across investors. This variety among investors results in a need for a variety of **investment products**, as we called them in Chapter 7.

In this chapter, we will see how leverage provided by mortgage debt allows the same underlying income-generating physical asset to offer very different types of investment products that can satisfy the needs of investors with very different types of objectives and constraints. A moderate-risk, underlying real estate asset presenting moderate growth and moderate yield may support high-risk equity investment with high growth and a low current yield, as well as low-risk debt investment with zero growth and a high current yield. In fact, mortgages are distinguished from real estate equity not only, or not necessarily, by differences in risk and return. Mortgages allow relatively "passive" investment, in which the investor does not have to manage the property. And mortgages provide a contractually fixed, finite maturity cash flow stream that may be ideal for an investor with a fixed investment horizon or a future liability to plan for.

Because of the various ways in which mortgages differ from real estate equity from an investment perspective, the pool of investors who are potentially able and willing to invest (directly or indirectly) in real estate (i.e., to provide capital toward the purchase of property) is increased by the use of debt. This tends to increase property values and/or the efficiency of the allocation of capital to real estate. At a very fundamental and big-picture level, this is what is going on in the widespread use of debt in real estate investment. At this level, real estate debt, and therefore the use of leverage, exists in virtually all countries, including many emerging markets. Now with this in mind, let's get down to the nitty-gritty of understanding how leverage works.

13.1 Basic Definitions and Mechanics of Leverage

A good way to understand the effect of leverage on the real estate equity investor's (that is, the debt borrower's) position is by analogy to the physical principle of the lever. This principle was first explicitly formulated by the ancient Greek mathematician and mechanical engineer Archimedes (287–212 BCE) who lived in Syracuse on the island of Sicily and was famous for his designs of catapults and siege machines, among other clever devices. To illustrate the principle of the lever, Archimedes supposedly made the statement: "Give me a place to stand, and I will move the Earth." He meant this literally, although he would also need an incredibly long-armed lever and a place to put the fulcrum!

In fact, the analogy between financial and physical leverage is very helpful. This analogy is depicted in Exhibit 13-1. The upper panel depicts a physical lever. The weight that can be balanced or lifted at the end of one arm of the lever equals the weight at the end of the other arm times the ratio of the lengths of the two arms. In the example shown, a 200-pound man balances a 500-pound weight by standing at the end of an arm that is two and one-half times longer on his side of the pivot point than it is on the other.

The analogy to financial leverage is direct and provides important insight into the effect on investment. This is represented in the bottom panel in the exhibit. An investor purchases a $10 million apartment property using, say, $4 million of her own money and $6 million borrowed in a mortgage backed by the property as collateral. The leverage ratio in this case is $10 million divided by $4 million, or 2.5. Just as physical leverage enables 200 pounds of force to lift 500 pounds of weight using a lever with a leverage ratio of 2.5, so financial leverage enables the equity investor to purchase (and "own" or *control*) an asset whose value is 2.5 times greater than the amount of equity capital invested. With financial leverage, the **leverage ratio (LR)** is defined as the total value of the underlying asset divided by the value of the equity investment: $LR = V/E = (L + E)/E$, where V is the asset value, L is the loan value, and E is the equity.[2]

The word **equity** actually has its roots in the notion of balance, and thereby recalls the physical leverage analogy. Investors' equity is their ownership share; in an accounting balance sheet, it equals $V - L$ (assets minus liabilities). Equity normally gives its owners primary governing control over the underlying asset, as long as they live up to their requirements under their debt obligation. On the other hand, the debt receives a senior, or preferred, claim on the underlying asset's cash flow and value. As a balancing compensation for giving up that senior position, the equity gets the **residual claim**, that is, the claim to the entire residual value in the investment, or all the remaining cash flow and value after subtracting the debt holder's claim.[3] Thus, equity value equals the underlying property value minus the mortgage value. In the case shown in Exhibit 13-1, the property value is $10 million and the debt is worth $6 million, so the equity is worth $4 million.

---

[2] Other common symbols meaning the same thing are "A" or "P" for the underlying property asset (instead of "V"), and "D" for the value of the debt (instead of "L").

[3] We are speaking here of *private sector* claims on the property. Of course, government gets the first claim, in the form of property taxes.

EXHIBIT 13-1 Analogy of Physical Leverage and Financial Leverage
© OnCourse Learning

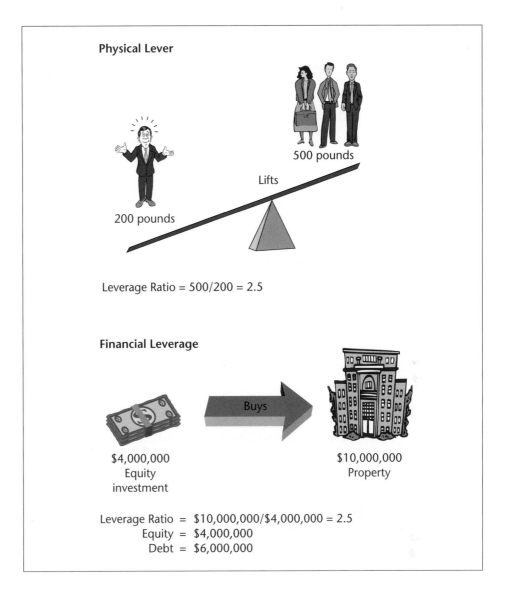

LEVERAGE RATIO VERSUS LOAN-TO-VALUE RATIO: A NOTE ON TERMINOLOGY

It is important to recognize that the term "leverage ratio," as we are here defining it (labeled *LR*), is not the same as the **loan-to-value ratio (LTV)**, though the two are related. In particular, if *V* is the value of the underlying property, *E* is the value of the equity, and *L* is the value of the loan (such that $V = E + L$), then the *LR* is $V/E = V/(V - L)$, while the *LTV* is L/V. The greater the *LTV*, the greater the *LR*, but the relationship is not linear:

$$LR = 1/(1 - L/V) = 1/(1 - LTV); LTV = 1 - (1/LR).$$

For example, an *LTV* of 50 percent corresponds to an *LR* of 2, while an *LTV* of 75 percent corresponds to an *LR* of 4. Increasing the *LTV* by a factor of one-half in this case results in a doubling of the leverage ratio. It is important to keep the difference between *LR* and *LTV* in mind, because in real estate practice leverage is typically spoken of in terms of the *LTV*, whereas equity investment risk and return performance is more directly related to the *LR*, as we will see.

© OnCourse Learning

Management Incentive Effects

It is important to note that this arrangement generally results in a *compatible matching of governance and incentive*. Equity's governance of the asset gives it the greater ability to influence the total value of the underlying asset (e.g., by management actions), while its residual claim causes any increment in this value to accrue to the value of the equity. If the equity owners manage the property well, they will reap the benefit; if they manage it poorly, they will suffer the loss (at least up to a point). Thus, by giving the equity owner the primary management control, the value of the underlying asset (the property) will likely be maximized, thereby maximizing the productivity of the physical capital.[4]

Leverage can be tempting, but *watch out!*

You can see how tempting leverage can be for the property equity investor. If you are the property equity investor, you do get to use "other peoples' money" to buy something you largely control and from which you can take all the profit (after you pay what you owe to the lender). But look back at that picture of the physical lever: It is like an extremely off-center seesaw offering a different ride for each side. The person riding on the long-arm side (the property equity investor) will bounce wildly up and down; the person on the short-arm side only bounces a little. The person riding the long-arm side of the seesaw can crash onto the ground with devastating force. In real estate investment, excessive use of leverage is the main cause of excessive losses and bankruptcy.

Leverage is also tempting for the lenders as well. The money they're lending to you is probably also largely borrowed from depositors, bondholders, insurance policy-holders, or even the government! The temptations of leverage are not limited to commercial real estate, but extend to housing and indeed throughout the capital markets, for corporations and funds of many types.[5] As a result, capital markets have a tendency toward excessive use of leverage and toward "systemic" risk caused by interconnected chains of debt through which a failure in one part of the system can rapidly propagate to other parts at first seemingly remote.

Governments and the investments industry itself attempt to police these tendencies, for example by requiring banks to restrain the amount that they borrow (ceilings on their own leverage ratios). But the capital markets are such a fast-growing, dynamic, technologically-changing, and entrepreneurial arena that the system sometimes, inevitably, gets out of control. We have noted in Chapters 2 and 7 how this happened with devastating results in 2008, but that was only the most recent (and widespread and serious) financial crisis. Commercial property asset markets have suffered more localized "crashes" at least once every couple of decades in the United States, and in each case excessive leverage has played a major role and claimed its latest crop of equity investor victims.[6]

13.2 Effect of Leverage on the Risk and Return to Equity

Now let's drill deeper in our quantitative analysis and consider the effect leverage has on the expected return and the risk of the investment from the perspective of the equity investor. We will consider the expected return first and then the risk.

---

[4]Obviously, maximization of the underlying property value is also in the interest of the debt holder, as it minimizes default risk. While the equity/debt incentive alignment works well in normal circumstances (e.g., when the debt is not too large relative to the current property value), there are circumstances in which the incentives can get out of alignment and cause a conflict of interest between equity and debt holders to the detriment of overall underlying property value. Such "agency costs" are ignored in the present chapter but will be treated in Chapter 15.

[5]There may be additional issues associated with use of leverage by homebuyers. This text is focused on commercial and investment real estate as a business enterprise, not on home buying or consumer finance. Homeowners potentially risk not only equity investment losses, but personal bankruptcy or loss of their home, and they may lack the type of expertise and financial knowledge that investors do (or should) have. And owner-occupied housing is a much larger segment of the national wealth and of the demand underlying the national economy (the GDP), implying greater spillover effects or systemic risk.

[6]See additional reading in the bibliography of Part V. A good starting point might be Jim Clayton's 2009 article in the *Journal of Real Estate Portfolio Management*. Excessive leverage in the housing sector was arguably the largest single cause of the great financial crisis of 2008 and subsequent recession.

13.2.1 Effect on the Expected Return

We can see the essence of the effect of leverage on the equity investor's expected return by continuing the previous example for another year. Suppose, in particular, that by the end of the subsequent year our $10,000,000 apartment property has increased 2 percent in value, to $10,200,000, and meanwhile also has provided $800,000 in net cash flow during the year. Thus, the underlying property has provided a 2 percent appreciation return or growth, and an 8 percent income return, for a total return of 10 percent. This is the return applicable to an all-equity investment in the property free and clear of debt, that is, an *unlevered* investment ($LR = 1$; $LTV = 0$).

But what about the levered investor? Suppose the mortgage is an interest-only loan at 8 percent (no amortization of principal), so $480,000 of interest must be paid as "debt service" from the $800,000 cash flow generated by the property, ($8\% \times \$6,000,000 = \$480,000$). This leaves only $320,000 cash flow remaining for the equity investor ($\$800,000 - \$480,000 = \$320,000$). The capital position of the equity investor at the end of the year consists of the asset, which is now worth $10,200,000, minus the $6,000,000 liability still owed to the mortgage lender, for a net capital value of $4,200,000. However, the equity investor only invested $4,000,000 of her own money; the rest was obtained from the mortgage. Thus, the return on the leveraged equity investment is 13 percent, consisting of 8 percent in the income component ($\$320,000/\$4,000,000$) and 5 percent in the appreciation component (the $200,000 increase in equity value from $4,000,000 to $4,200,000, as a fraction of the $4,000,000 invested).

These results are summarized in the table in Exhibit 13-2. Notice that the substantial leverage used in this case ($LR = 2.5$; $LTV = 60\%$) has the effect of substantially increasing the expected return.[7] This is because the equity investor has been able to borrow money at an interest rate lower than the expected return on the property (8 percent is less than 10 percent). It is also important to note that, in this case anyway, the increase in the expected return has come entirely in the form of an increased appreciation component, with no change in the income component.

At first, this sounds great. It sounds like a free lunch: the investor has increased her total return expectation simply by using other people's money! But rarely do we get something for nothing in the real world. In fact, this brings us to the other side of the effect of leverage on the equity investment.

EXHIBIT 13-2
Typical Effect of Leverage on Expected Investment Returns

© OnCourse Learning

	Property	Levered Equity	Debt
Initial value	$10,000,000	$4,000,000	$6,000,000
Cash flow	$800,000	$320,000	$480,000
Ending value	$10,200,000	$4,200,000	$6,000,000
Income return	8%	8%	8%
Appreciation return	2%	5%	0%
Total return	10%	13%	8%

---

[7]When considering the effect of leverage on the risk and return performance of the investment, we are implicitly holding constant the total amount of capital to be invested by the equity investor. This is why we typically measure the effects of leverage using return percentages rather than absolute dollar amounts. For example, in the case of our apartment building example, we are implicitly assuming, in effect, that the equity investor has a total net wealth of $4,000,000 available to invest at the present time. Thus, the benchmark of comparison for the equity investor is the levered $4,000,000 investment in the $10,000,000 property versus an unlevered (all-equity) investment in a similar but smaller $4,000,000 property. The expected total return for the unlevered investment is thus $10\% \times \$4,000,000 = \$400,000$, while that for the levered investment is $13\% \times \$4,000,000 = \$520,000$.

13.2.2 Effect on the Risk in the Return

Under normal circumstances, *if leverage increases the ex ante return on the equity, then it will also increase the risk in that equity.* How does leverage increase the equity investor's risk? To answer this question, let us continue our previous numerical example based on the $10 million apartment building.

Suppose at the time the investment decision must be made, we do not know exactly what the future will bring for this property. This is of course a realistic assumption reflecting the fact that the underlying asset is risky. To simplify the picture for purposes of illustration, let us say that we can represent the risk in the property by defining two possible future scenarios, each of which is equally likely to occur. We will call the first scenario the optimistic scenario. If this scenario unfolds, the property will increase in value over the coming year to $11,200,000, a 12 percent increase in value (10 percent more increase than the expected growth of 2 percent), and the property will also generate $900,000 in net cash flow for the year ($100,000 more than the expected amount of $800,000). The pessimistic scenario envisions a reduction in property value over the coming year to $9,200,000, a decline of 8 percent (which would be 10 percent lower growth than the +2 percent expectation), and the generation of only $700,000 in net cash flow by the building during the year ($100,000 less than expected).[8] These are the only two possible future eventualities. Let us furthermore assume that, *no matter which of these two scenarios actually occurs,* if the investor has taken out the 8 percent loan, she will still owe $480,000 in interest and $6,000,000 in principal on the loan.

Exhibit 13-3 then quantifies the return components that would prevail in each of the two scenarios under these assumptions, and it indicates the range in these returns between the optimistic and pessimistic outcomes. This range is a way to quantify the risk in the investment. Greater range indicates more uncertainty about the future returns, including a potentially worse downside outcome. For example, without leverage, the pessimistic scenario will result in a total return on the property equity over the coming year of −1 percent. But with the 60 percent LTV loan, the levered equity total return would be −14.5 percent if the pessimistic scenario occurs. Thus, leverage magnifies the downside loss by 13.5 percent in this case.

Exhibit 13-3 indicates that the ranges in the equity return components increase by a factor of 2.5 as we move from the unlevered (underlying property) to the levered equity position.[9]

	Property (*LR* = 1)			Levered Equity (*LR* = 2.5)			Debt (*LR* = 0)		
	OPT	PES	RANGE	OPT	PES	RANGE	OPT	PES	RANGE
Initial value	$10.00	$10.00	NA	$4.00	$4.00	NA	$6.00	$6.00	NA
Cash flow	$0.90	$0.70	±$0.10	$0.42	$0.22	±$0.10	$0.48	$0.48	0
Ending value	$11.20	$9.20	±$1.00	$5.20	$3.20	±$1.00	$6.00	$6.00	0
Income return	9.0%	7.0%	±1.0%	10.5%	5.5%	±2.5%	8.0%	8.0%	0
Appreciation return	12.0%	−8.0%	±10.0%	30.0%	−20.0%	±25.0%	0.0%	0.0%	0
Total return	21.0%	−1.0%	±11.0%	40.5%	−14.5%	±27.5%	8.0%	8.0%	0

OPT = Outcome if optimistic scenario occurs.
PES = Outcome if pessimistic scenario occurs.
RANGE = Half the difference between optimistic scenario outcome and pessimistic scenario outcome.
Note: Initial values are known deterministically, as they are in present, not future, time, so there is no range.

EXHIBIT 13-3 Sensitivity Analysis of Effect of Leverage on Risk in Equity Return Components, as Measured by Percentage Range in Possible Return Outcomes ($ values in millions)

© OnCourse Learning

[8]Note that if each of these scenarios is viewed as having a 50 percent chance of occurring, then the ex ante means, or expected values of the returns (looking forward in time), equal the returns discussed in Exhibit 13-2.

[9]Under the 50/50 probability assumption, the range in the return over the coming year is identical to the standard deviation of the probability distribution of the future return. The ranges depicted in Exhibit 13-3 are centered around the mean (or expected) returns shown in Exhibit 13-2. Recall also that to see the dollar effect of leverage, we must hold constant the total amount being invested. Holding the amount invested by the equity investor constant, the ranges in the absolute dollar outcomes would be magnified by the same multiple as the percentage returns (in this case, 2.5).

WHO BEARS DEFAULT RISK?

In our discussion of the effect of leverage on the risk in the borrower's equity, we have noted only the effect of leverage on the *range* of investment outcomes for the borrower. Of course, from the perspective of periodic returns, this effect is closely related to volatility. The volatility in the equity's periodic returns will generally be increased with more leverage. What we have not mentioned, however, is **default risk**. Some people claim that when equity investors borrow more money, they increase their default risk, and that this is a form of risk separate from what we described here by the effect of leverage on the range or volatility in the future equity return. If the equity investor is levered, she can lose *all* of her investment (that is, a capital return component of −100 percent) if she defaults on the loan. The argument is, therefore, the greater the leverage, the greater the probability of such default.

If you think it through carefully, however, you should see that this type of default risk is either already included in (the downside of) the range effect we described previously, or else it is actually a risk borne by the lender, not the borrower. Thus, it is conceptually incorrect to think of default risk as an additional component of risk borne by the borrower, apart from the range-magnification effect we described.

To see this, consider once again the $10,000,000 apartment building. Suppose the range of outcomes was ±$5,000,000 in the property value and ±$500,000 in the cash flow, instead of ±$1,000,000 and ±$100,000 as before. In this case, the downside scenario leaves the equity investor holding a property worth $5,200,000 generating $300,000 of income, against a mortgage on which $6,000,000 of principal and $480,000 of interest is owed. Suppose first that the equity investor could not default on the loan (presumably because the loan allows the lender "recourse" to other assets the borrower has, which are sufficient to cover the debt obligation). In that case, the equity investor would be subject to the full downside capital loss of $4,800,000 (compared to the initial property value of $10,000,000), which would represent a levered capital return of −120 percent, computed as ($5,200,000 − $6,000,000 − $4,000,000)/$4,000,000. This is just the effect of leverage on risk that we already described, because the 120 percent loss is 2.5 times the 48 percent loss in the (unlevered) property value. (It fell in value from $10,000,000 to $5,200,000.)*

Now suppose the equity investor can effectively default on the loan, giving up the property to the lender (who has no further recourse to the borrower's other assets). In that case, the equity investor loses (shall we say, "only") 100 percent of her initial capital. The ability to effectively default ("limited liability," as with a "nonrecourse" loan) has actually reduced the magnitude of the equity investor's loss, from 120 percent to 100 percent of her original investment (the loss is reduced from $4,800,000 to $4,000,000, a savings of $800,000 for the borrower). The ability to default allows the borrower, at her option, to pass some of the potential loss (in some scenarios) over to the lender. That is why default risk is a risk borne by lenders, not by borrowers.**

---

*There would also be a −4.5 percent return in the income component, compared to +3 percent without leverage. Compared with the ex ante income return expectation of 8 percent, the downside result in the income return is 5 points less without leverage, but 12.5 points less with leverage.

**In addition, $180,000 additional cash outflow in interest payments would also be avoided by the borrower: a total savings to the borrower of 24.5 percent of her original equity is passed on as loss to the lender through the default process. Default risk from the perspective of the lender will be discussed in Part VI.

© OnCourse Learning

For example, the range in the total return between the optimistic and pessimistic scenarios is ±11 percent with no leverage, and ±27.5 percent with the 60 percent LTV loan. The 2.5 factor magnification of the outcome range holds not only for the total return but also for *each component* of the total return (current income as well as appreciation). The factor 2.5 is also the leverage ratio for a 60 percent LTV loan. It is not a coincidence that the underlying property risk is magnified by a factor equal to the leverage ratio in this case. In this example, the debt is effectively riskless because the debt investor gets the same return (8 percent) no matter which future scenario occurs. *When debt is riskless, the risk in the equity return is directly proportional to the leverage ratio (LR).*

Of course, debt in the real world, especially long-term debt, is not riskless. We saw in Chapter 7 that long-term bonds may have a periodic return **volatility** as high as that of unlevered property equity. However, treating the debt as though it were riskless can often be a useful analytical device from the perspective of the borrower, for the purpose of seeing how the debt affects the risk in the levered equity position. This is because the borrower is contractually obligated to pay the debt service amounts specified in the loan, no matter what happens to the property value or the rents it can earn. Furthermore, the equity investor often intends to hold the property investment and its debt at least until the maturity of the loan.[10] In that case, the volatility in the market value of the debt (usually due primarily to fluctuations in interest rates) would not be relevant to the equity investor. The situation faced by the equity investor is then indeed similar to what is depicted in Exhibit 13-3.[11]

13.2.3 Risk and Return: The Security Market Line

We have now seen, at least for our simple apartment building example, the effect of leverage on both the expected return and the risk in the return for the equity investor.[12] Exhibit 13-4 puts these two effects together and demonstrates the effect on the risk premium in the ex ante equity return, under our previous assumption that the mortgage is riskless. Consistent with that assumption, the 8 percent return on the mortgage includes no risk premium. In that case, the risk premium in the levered equity return is directly proportional to the leverage ratio, LR. The underlying property asset (or equivalently an unlevered equity investment) has a leverage ratio of 1 and a risk premium of 2 percent (the difference between the property's 10 percent expected return and the mortgage's 8 percent return). With the 60 percent LTV loan, the levered property equity investment has a leverage ratio of 2.5 and a risk premium of 5 percent (the difference between the 13 percent expected return on the levered equity and the 8 percent mortgage return), which is 2.5 times the 2 percent risk premium on the unlevered property.

This proportionality of the risk premium and the leverage ratio makes sense when the debt is riskless because, as we saw previously, in that case the equity risk is also directly proportional to the leverage ratio. Thus, the equity risk premium is simply remaining proportional to the risk.

Note that the expected total return, $E[r]$, does *not* increase proportionately with the risk. (The 13 percent expected total return on the levered equity is only 1.3 times the 10 percent expectation on the unlevered investment, even though there is 2.5 times the risk.) This is because the ex ante total return includes the risk-free rate (compensation for the time value of money) as well as the risk premium (compensation for risk). Only the risk premium component of the total return need increase with the added risk brought on by the leverage.

Now let us suppose, more realistically, that the mortgage is not riskless.[13] In this case, the 8 percent interest rate on the mortgage includes a risk premium for the debt investor. For example, suppose that T-bills are yielding 6 percent, the risk-free rate of return. Then the 8 percent mortgage has a 2 percent risk premium, the 10 percent expected return on the unlevered property represents a 4 percent risk premium, and the levered equity with the 60 percent LTV loan has a 7 percent risk premium, based on the difference between its expected return of 13 percent and the 6 percent risk-free rate. This situation is depicted in Exhibit 13-5.

---

[10]This is particularly true for commercial mortgages, which often have a maturity of only 5 to 10 years. Transaction costs often make it inadvisable to sell property more frequently than that as a general rule.

[11]The main simplifications in our numerical example are the existence of only a single period of time (the present and next year), and of only two possible future scenarios (with even the downside scenario not involving the property going "underwater", that is, property value below the loan balance). In the real world, one would want to consider a multiperiod measure of return (such as the IRR) and a probability distribution of many possible future outcomes (including some underwater). This requires a more involved mathematical analysis, including a *sensitivity analysis* and more sophisticated metrics such as "value at risk" (VaR), which would attempt to quantify the probability of the lender losing specified amounts of the loan investment. Nevertheless, the general qualitative impacts on risk to the equity investor will normally be quite similar to what is depicted in Exhibit 13-3 (as measured by the standard deviation of the equity investor's ex post realized IRR, for example).

[12]It should be noted that in some types of real estate investment the above-described effects of leverage are inherent in the operational characteristics of the investment even without the use of financial leverage (in the form of debt financing). See, in particular, our discussion of land and development investment in Chapters 27 and 29.

[13]As will be discussed in more depth in Part VI, a mortgage typically has two major sources of risk from the perspective of the mortgage investor. One source is purely related to interest rates prevailing in the capital market. A fixed-interest rate mortgage's present value will vary inversely with prevailing interest rates (that is, the risk-free interest rate, such as that on Treasury bonds), and this makes the mortgage a somewhat risky investment for the mortgage holder. The other source of risk for the mortgage lender is the possibility of default by the borrower on the loan and loss of value in the collateral backing the loan (the property). This source of risk is clearly related to the real estate markets and in particular to the property that is collateral for the loan.

EXHIBIT 13-4 Effect of Leverage on Investment Risk and Return

© OnCourse Learning

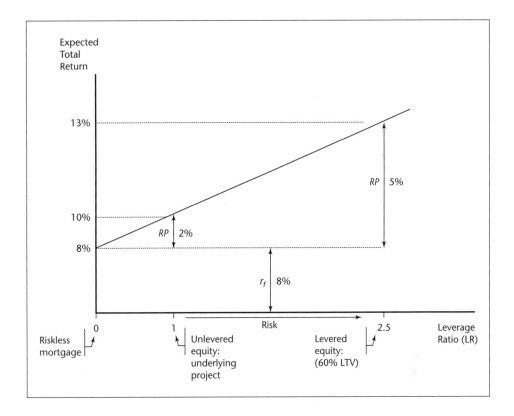

EXHIBIT 13-5 Effect of Leverage on Investment Risk and Return: A Risky Debt Example

© OnCourse Learning

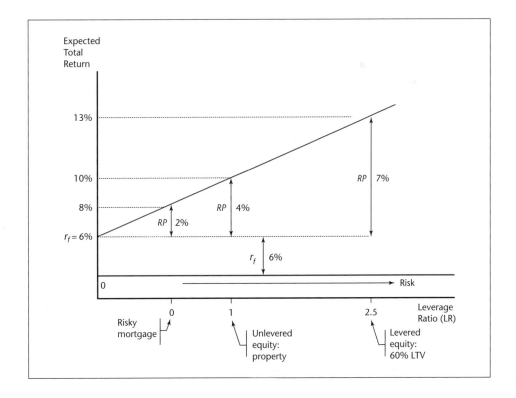

When the debt is not riskless, the equity risk premium is no longer directly proportional to the leverage ratio. (The 7 percent risk premium on the levered equity is only 1.75 times the 4 percent risk premium on the unlevered property, even though the leverage ratio is 2.5 times that of the unlevered property.) However, the equity risk premium is still a linear function of the leverage ratio. The exact nature of that function will be discussed in the next section, in which we introduce the WACC formula. For now, the important point is that, regardless of whether the debt is riskless, the ex ante equity risk premium will normally be *directly proportional* to the amount of risk in the equity, where risk is defined *in the way that the asset market cares about it*. This is indicated by the second horizontal axis in Exhibit 13-5, parallel to and above the axis measuring the leverage ratio. This top horizontal axis measures risk as defined by the capital markets. By definition, the zero point on this axis corresponds to the 6 percent risk-free rate of return, the rate of return that includes zero risk premium. If we assume that the property and debt are both obtained at prevailing market rates of expected return (reflecting fair market value of the property and of the debt, respectively), then this guarantees that the ex ante equity risk premium will be directly proportional to its risk as defined by the capital market.

Another way of saying this is to say that the equity ex ante risk premium *per unit of risk* (as defined by the capital market) will remain constant no matter how large or small a loan the equity investor takes out to buy a property. This result holds as long as the loan is unsubsidized and the property is bought at fair market value. By definition, this equity risk premium per unit of risk equals the **market price of risk**.[14] This is another way of saying that there is no free lunch in the normal use of leverage. Leverage affects the ex ante equity risk premium in just such a way that the benefit of the additional expected return is exactly offset by the cost of the additional risk, as evaluated by the capital market.[15]

The relationships between risk and expected return described here and depicted in Exhibits 13-4 and 13-5 reflect what in capital markets theory is referred to as the "Security Market Line" (SML), the function that reflects the capital market's price of risk and relationship between risk and expected return that results from the general equilibrium in the trading among all types of assets in the capital market, including commercial properties. In traditional mainstream investments courses the SML is primarily applied to and within the stock market, and the capital assets being considered are stocks. In the present context the "securities" consist of debt (in the form of the mortgage), a property asset (the underlying property collateralizing the loan), and the levered equity investment in the property. These may not be "securities" in the sense that they have not been securitized (broken up into numerous small homogeneous shares or units that are publicly traded on the stock exchange), but they are capital assets that are tradable in the same overall capital market in which stocks also trade. No insurmountable barrier prevents stock market investors from investing in mortgages or property (levered or unlevered). And no insurmountable barrier prevents real estate investors from also (or instead) investing in the stock market or bond market. Hence, assuming a reasonable degree of integration among all these branches of the capital market, the SML that applies to

---

[14]The market price of risk is, by definition, the ex ante risk premium per unit of risk implied in the market prices of assets.

[15]Here we are speaking of market values, "MV" in the terminology introduced in Chapter 12. (Investment value, "IV," considerations of the use of debt will be discussed in Chapter 14.) Note that if the property is purchased at below market value, providing an MV-based positive NPV to the buyer, then the ex ante equity risk premium will be more than proportional to the leverage ratio (assuming market rate debt). However, the debt transaction itself will still be zero NPV as long as the debt is at market interest rates. In other words, leverage at market interest rates leaves the dollar magnitude of the equity investment NPV unaffected. This results in any nonzero NPV being a larger fraction of the equity investment as the amount borrowed is increased.

levered equity investment in real property also applies to stock market investment and vice versa.[16]

Note that in Exhibits 13-4 and 13-5 we have not defined exactly *how* the risk on the (upper) horizontal axis is defined and measured or quantified. This is a subject we will address in Chapter 22. In the current context, for practical purposes when analyzing real estate investment risk at the micro-level of individual properties, it may often be useful and legitimate to simply define a numéraire quantity of risk as that in the subject underlying risky asset, the unlevered property asset, and set this amount of risk (however much risk is in the property) as being equal to "one unit" of risk on the horizontal axis. The levered equity in that underlying asset is essentially a "derivative" of the underlying property asset, with risk essentially *like* the risk in the underlying asset, only *more* of it.[17]

13.3 A Useful Formula: The WACC

To quantify the effect of leverage on equity risk and return, a formula known as the **weighted average cost of capital (WACC)** is often useful. The WACC formula is given here:

$$r_P = (LTV)r_D + (1 - LTV)r_E \tag{1}$$

where r_P is the return on the underlying property free and clear; r_D is the return to the debt on the property; r_E is the return on the levered equity in the property; and LTV is the loan-to-value ratio: L/V.[18]

For example, suppose the LTV ratio is 60 percent, and the return to equity is 13 percent, while the return on the debt is 8 percent. Then the previous formula provides a return on the underlying property equal to 10 percent. These numbers should seem familiar. Our numerical example in the previous section was simply an example of the WACC formula. And the "security market lines" in Exhibits 13-4 and 13-5 were also simply graphical expressions of this same formula.

The WACC formula is derived directly from the basic accounting identities and the definition of the simple holding period return (HPR):

Assets = Liabilities + Owners' Equity
Property Cash Flow = Debt Cash Flow + Equity Cash Flow

---

[16]We shall nuance and qualify this point in our discussion of equilibrium asset pricing and REITs in Chapters 22 and 23, and recall our point in section 12.3 of the last chapter that the stock market trading REIT shares and the private property market trading whole property assets may not always agree on asset values at the micro-level, a possibility due to lack of perfect integration between those two branches of the capital markets. And please note, again, that in the present chapter we are focusing at the before-tax level on market values (MVs) as defined in section 12.1 of the previous chapter.

[17]Derivatives are characterized as having perfect or near-perfect correlation between their returns and those of their underlying assets. What's good for the property will almost always be good for the equity in the property, and vice versa (usually). The returns to the property and to the equity in the property will generally move up or down together over time. This gives them the same "type" of risk. The fact that the levered equity return moves *more* than the underlying property return (recall our seesaw metaphor), reflects the amount of risk but typically does not imply a substantially different *type* of risk. Thus, the SML model tends to work well for analyzing leverage and the investment risk impact of financing at the micro-level.

[18]In many corporate finance texts, the WACC is defined on an after-corporate-income-tax basis, in which the return to the corporation's debt, r_D, is multiplied in the WACC formula by $(1 - T_c)$, where T_c is the marginal corporate income tax rate. However, in most real estate applications there is effectively no double taxation, either because the real estate investment is made directly without a (taxable) corporate ownership layer (e.g., partnership, LLP, etc.), or because the investment is being made by a corporation that is exempt from corporate-level income tax, such as a REIT. Thus, in effect, $T_c = 0$ for most real estate applications, so our definition of the WACC is not really inconsistent with the corporate finance textbook definition. In other words, we are working here at the before-tax level for the ultimate investor, which is typically equivalent to an after-tax level at the corporate level for most real estate holdings. Taxes will be treated in the next chapter.

Thus, the WACC is valid for the HPR whenever these identities hold, including for *simple* returns.[19] However, in practice, the formula is applied over positive spans of time over which a multiperiod return measure is used, such as the IRR. In this case, the WACC formula holds exactly only if all the variables in it, the LTV ratio and the returns, remain constant, which is rarely ever the case.[20] This causes the formula to lose exactness in typical applications. It will be less exact when it is applied over longer periods of time, during which there can be greater fluctuations in the variables. Nevertheless, the WACC formula is a useful approximation when applied with common sense to periodic returns and to ex ante multiperiod returns over time horizons when the variables are not expected to fluctuate too greatly.

One of the nice things about the WACC is that it is quite intuitive and therefore easy to learn. Since the claims on the property net cash flow consist of the debt claim and the equity claim, the property value, and hence the return on the property, must consist of a debt share and an equity share. In the WACC formula, the return to each component is simply weighted by that component's share of the underlying property asset value.

13.3.1 The WACC and REIT Cost of Capital

The WACC formula as expressed in equation (1) shows the return to the underlying asset isolated on the left-hand side of the equation, and the LTV and returns to debt and equity on the right-hand side. This is the intuitive way to memorize the formula, and also the convenient way to apply the formula when it is easier to observe empirically the return on the levered equity than it is to observe the return on the underlying physical assets. This is in fact the typical situation in corporate finance, in which we can empirically observe the return on corporate equity by examining the history of the corporation's stock returns. This situation is also relevant to applying the WACC formula to REITs, whose equity is publicly traded. The return on a REIT's stock is the return to its levered equity, r_E.

For example, suppose REIT A can borrow at 6 percent, while REIT B has to pay 8 percent interest on its debt. Doesn't this imply that REIT A has a lower cost of capital than REIT B? We can use the WACC to answer this question. Suppose REIT A has a debt/equity ratio of 3/7 (implying LTV = 30 percent), while REIT B has a debt/equity ratio of unity (LTV = 50 percent). Suppose both REITs have an expected return to their equity of 15 percent. Then formula (1) tells us

$$WACC(A) = (0.3)6\% + (0.7)15\% = 12.3\%$$
$$WACC(B) = (0.5)8\% + (0.5)15\% = 11.5\%$$

The weighted average cost of capital for REIT A's assets is 12.3 percent, compared to only 11.5 percent for REIT B's assets. Apparently, REIT B holds less risky property assets than REIT A does (or REIT B tends to be less involved in risky development projects, for example). REIT B's debt is more costly probably because REIT B is more highly levered than REIT A, causing its debt to have more default risk. REIT B's lenders must be compensated for this risk by obtaining a higher interest rate on their loans.[21]

---

[19]That is, where all cash flows and values are registered as of only two points in time, the beginning and end of the "period" (of whatever temporal length) over which the return is defined as the simple ratio of the ending value divided by the beginning value less unity. (See Chapters 8 and 9 for more discussion of return measures.)

[20]For example, the LTV changes as the market value of the property and of the debt change over time. Changes in the LTV also cause changes in the expected returns to debt and equity (*ceteris paribus*), as changes in the LTV affect the relative risk of the equity and debt.

[21]REIT B's debt may also be more costly if it is has a longer-term average maturity than REIT A's debt and the yield curve in the debt market is upward-sloping. Or perhaps REIT A's debt is largely floating-rate while REIT B's is fixed-rate. Indeed, quantifying the cost of debt capital is a bit more complex than suggested in this simple example. The yield curve, as well as default risk premiums and the relationship between stated yields and expected returns on debt, will be discussed in Chapters 18 and 19.

13.3.2 Use of the WACC in Direct Property Investment

In applying the WACC formula to the private property market and to direct investments in commercial real estate, it is often more convenient to turn formula (1) around and solve it for the equity return. This is because it is often easier in practice to observe empirically or estimate the return on the underlying property than it is to estimate directly the return on the levered equity. So we would invert the WACC formula to solve for the return on the levered equity:

$$r_E = (r_P - LTVr_D)/(1 - LTV) \tag{2}$$

In this way, the more observable parameters are all on the right-hand side of the equation.

For example, suppose we can observe in the property market that the expected total return on a certain type of property is 10 percent, and that mortgages are available at 8 percent interest and a 60 percent LTV ratio. Then the expected total return on the equity invested in such property using a 60 percent LTV ratio mortgage would be 13 percent:

$$13\% = [10\% - (0.60)8\%]/[1 - (0.60)]$$

(Again, it is no coincidence that the numbers are familiar from our previous discussion.)

13.3.3 The WACC and Return Components

The WACC formula can be applied to any additive components of the total return, such as the yield (y) and the growth (g), or the **risk premium (RP)** that we introduced in Chapter 9. You just have to be consistent, applying the formula to only one component at a time within the equation. For example, if we apply the WACC to the current yield component of the return, then we can obtain the following formula for the **equity cash yield**:

$$y_E = (y_P - LTVy_D)/(1 - LTV) \tag{3}$$

This is sometimes known as the equity yield formula. If the current yield on the property is 8 percent, and the cash yield on the debt is 9 percent, then with an LTV ratio of 50 percent the initial cash yield on the levered equity investment will be 7 percent. This is often referred to as the **cash-on-cash return** on the investment. Note that in applying the formula in this way, the current yield on the loan may not be the same as the interest rate on the loan. The loan's current yield is its annual debt service as a fraction of the loan amount, so if the debt service includes amortization of principal then the loan current yield will be greater than its interest rate.[22]

13.3.4 The WACC and Risk

As the WACC formula is applicable to any additive component of total return, we can apply it to the risk premium (RP). For example, expressing the WACC formula in terms of the leverage ratio instead of the LTV ratio, the ex ante risk premium in the levered equity investment is given by the following formula:

$$RP_E = RP_D + LR(RP_P - RP_D) \tag{4}$$

The equity risk premium equals the debt risk premium plus the leverage ratio times the spread between the property and debt risk premiums. Formula (4) specifies the linear

---

[22]The loan interest rate (or "yield to maturity") represents the total return to the loan (assuming it is held to maturity and does not default). We can represent the appreciation return component of the loan as the percentage change in the loan balance due. (This is a "book value" definition, ignoring changes in the market value of the debt as might be caused, for example, by changes in interest rates or in the LTV.) The loan appreciation rate would therefore be negative for an amortizing loan. As the appreciation rate plus the current cash yield rate always sum to the total return, this implies that the current yield in an amortizing loan will exceed its contractual interest rate or total yield. For a classical constant-payment amortizing loan, the cash yield is given initially by the "mortgage constant," or annuity factor, introduced in Chapter 8 and discussed in more depth in Chapter 17.

relationship between the risk premium and the leverage ratio noted in our discussion of Exhibit 13-5.[23] In the present context it describes the SML relevant for the property, the debt, and the levered equity investment. Formula (4) also demonstrates that if the debt is riskless ($RP_D = 0$), the equity risk premium is directly proportional to the leverage ratio (Exhibit 13-4), as formula (4) then reduces to:

$$RP_E = (LR)(RP_P)$$

As noted, risk in the equity investment (as measured by the capital market) will be directly proportional to the equity risk premium if both the property and debt are obtained at prevailing market prices, whether the debt is riskless or not.

13.4 Positive and Negative Leverage

In the real estate investment industry, the term **positive leverage** is often used. It refers to the situation in which leverage will increase the equity investor's return. **Negative leverage** is less widely spoken of (perhaps because it is a less happy circumstance), but it would imply the opposite: leverage decreasing the equity investor's return. These terms are most often applied in an ex ante sense, referring to return expectations going forward for the investor.

The condition for positive leverage is the following:

Whenever the return component is higher in the underlying property than it is in the mortgage loan, there will be positive leverage in that return component.

The condition for negative leverage is of course just the opposite: whenever the property return component is lower than the corresponding debt component. When the property and debt have the same expected return, leverage is neutral, leaving the equity return unaffected. These conditions follow directly from the WACC formula, as seen clearly in the leverage ratio version of the formula:

$$r_E = r_D + LR(r_P - r_D) \tag{5}$$

The equity return equals the debt return plus the leverage ratio times the difference between the property return and the debt return.[24] If this difference is positive (property return is greater than debt return), then more leverage will increase the equity return. If this difference is negative, then just the opposite will occur. As noted in the previous section, formula (5) can be applied to any component of the total return.

Consider the previous apartment building investment as an example. The income return component was 8 percent in both the underlying property and the debt, so leverage was neutral in the income return component, leaving the equity investor's expected income return unchanged by the amount of leverage. The property appreciation was 2 percent, which was greater than the zero appreciation in the loan amount (recall that the loan was interest-only, with zero amortization), so there was positive leverage in the appreciation return component. The total return in the underlying property was 10 percent, and the

---

[23]Note that this linearity assumes that the debt risk premium, RP_D, remains constant over the relevant range in the leverage ratio. As high values of LR will result in greater default risk in the loan, typically implying a higher risk premium in the debt, formula (4) must be adjusted accordingly (The debt and equity expected returns will normally always remain on the SML, but at varying risk points on the upper horizontal axis relative to the leverage ratio; sufficiently high LTVs will move the debt to the right on that axis while thereby mitigating to some extent the rightward movement of the equity, as the debt investor comes to share more of the underlying property risk while the limited liability equity investor pushes more of that risk off onto the debt investor.).

[24]Once again, we are simplifying by treating the debt return as a constant over the relevant range of the leverage ratio. In reality, sufficiently higher LR will result in a higher r_D. At the extreme, a 100 percent LTV ratio (infinite LR) must imply that r_D equals r_P and r_E is then undefined, for at that point the debt holder effectively owns the property as the equity holder has no value at all. This is clearly seen by substituting 100 percent for LTV in formula (1):

$$r_P = LTVr_D + (1 - LTV)r_E = 1r_D + (1 - 1)r_E = r_D$$

total return to the loan investor was 8 percent, resulting in positive leverage in the total return.

13.5 Effect of Leverage on Growth and Yield

We can apply the WACC formula to examine the differential effect of leverage on the income and appreciation components of the expected return. This is shown in Exhibit 13-6 based on the WACC, for typical numerical values.[25] The major point to notice is that, for typical values of the relevant return variables, leverage *shifts the investor's return relatively away from current income and toward capital gain.* This occurs whether the cash-on-cash leverage is positive or negative. The fundamental reason is that the property-minus-loan differential is usually greater in the appreciation return than in the income return. In other words, usually:[26]

$$g_P - g_D > y_P - y_D$$

In the example in Exhibit 13-6, $g_P - g_D$ is +3 percent, and $y_P - y_D$ is either +1 percent (in the top panel, with the 6 percent loan) or −1 percent (in the bottom panel, with the 8 percent loan). In either case, the growth differential exceeds the yield differential. Let us review how these differentials are computed.

The property growth rate of 2 percent equals the difference between the 10 percent total return and the 8 percent current yield or cap rate on the property ($g_P = r_P - y_P$). The loan growth rate is the negative of its amortization as a fraction of the current outstanding loan balance. This can be seen as the difference between the loan's current cash yield and its total return as represented by the loan interest rate ($g_D = r_D - y_D$).[27] The current cash yield of the loan is its annual debt service as a fraction of its outstanding loan balance. Initially, this will equal the **mortgage constant (MC)**, the annual annuity factor used to compute the loan payments.

In Exhibit 13-6, we have two loan scenarios, one in which the loan interest rate is 6 percent, resulting in positive leverage in the cash-on-cash yield for the equity investor, and the other in which the loan interest rate is 8 percent, resulting in negative leverage. In both cases, however, the loan amortizes initially at a rate of 1 percent per year, as indicated by the difference between the mortgage constant and the loan interest rate. (The 6 percent loan has a 7 percent MC, while the 8 percent loan has a 9 percent MC.) Thus, the initial growth rate differential between the property and the loan is +3 percent [computed as: $g_P - g_D = 2\% - (-1\%) = 2\% + 1\% = 3\%$].[28]

The difference between the property yield of 8 percent and the loan current cash yield (or mortgage constant), which is either 7 percent or 9 percent, determines whether the loan will present the equity investor with positive or negative leverage in the cash yield. With the 6 percent loan, the leverage is positive, while with the 8 percent loan the leverage is negative.

---

[25]Exhibit 13-6 makes the same simplification as before, that the loan interest rate remains the same across the various LTV ratios considered. In principle, one would expect the interest rate to be higher in loans with higher LTV ratios. However, in practice the mortgage industry has not always been that finely tuned. Furthermore, the loan expected return would be less sensitive to the LTV than the loan's contractual interest rate would be, because the loan's expected return is net of expected losses should the loan default, and it is the loan's expected return that is actually the more relevant number for risk/return investment analysis (see Chapters 18 and 19 for more on this point).

[26]The condition noted here applies to the absolute percentage difference between g and y. The condition for leverage to shift the *relative g/y* ratio toward g is: $g_D/y_D < g_P/y_P$.

[27]For our purpose here, we can ignore origination fees and other sources of the loan's total yield, and we can assume market value equals book value for the loan. Returns to debt investment will be discussed in more detail in Part VI.

[28]In the absence of refinancing, assuming a standard constant-payment amortizing mortgage, the loan balance will decline gradually over time while the loan payments remain the same, so the loan amortization rate as a fraction of the remaining loan balance will grow over time.

EXHIBIT 13-6

Typical Relative Effect of Leverage on Income and Growth Components of Investment Return (numerical example)

© OnCourse Learning

Property total return (r_P): 10:00%
Cap rate (y_P): 8.00%

Positive cash-on-cash leverage:
Loan interest rate (r_D): 6.00%
Mortgage constant (y_D): 7.00%

		Equity return component:		
LR	**LTV**	y_E	g_E	r_E
1	0%	8.00%	2.00%	10.00%
2	50%	9.00%	5.00%	14.00%
3	67%	10.00%	8.00%	18.00%
4	75%	11.00%	11.00%	22.00%
5	80%	12.00%	14.00%	26.00%

Negative cash-on-cash leverage:
Loan interest rate (r_D): 8.00%
Mortgage constant (y_D): 9.00%

		Equity return component:		
LR	**LTV**	y_E	g_E	r_E
1	0%	8.00%	2.00%	10.00%
2	50%	7.00%	5.00%	12.00%
3	67%	6.00%	8.00%	14.00%
4	75%	5.00%	11.00%	16.00%
5	80%	4.00%	14.00%	18.00%

Thus, we see that in the top panel of Exhibit 13-6 the equity yield (y_E) rises the more leverage is applied (as indicated by the leverage or loan-to-value ratios shown in the left-hand columns). In the bottom panel, the equity cash yield falls the more leverage is applied. In both cases, however, the equity appreciation return increases with leverage, and rather substantially.[29]

The return component effects of leverage indicated in Exhibit 13-6 have been computed using the WACC formula presented in section 13.3. For example, in the case of a 67 percent LTV with the 6 percent loan in the top panel, we have

$$\text{Total}: \quad 10\% = (67\%) \times 6\% + (33\%) \times 18\%$$
$$\text{Yield}: \quad 8\% = (67\%) \times 7\% + (33\%) \times 10\%$$
$$\text{Growth}: \quad 2\% = (67\%) \times (-1\%) + (33\%) \times 8\%$$

The levered equity total return is 18 percent, consisting of 10 percent current yield and 8 percent growth.

Note that, even in the case of positive cash-on-cash leverage, where the equity yield rises with leverage, the equity appreciation return rises even faster, resulting in a *relative* increase in the growth component within the equity total return. Thus, leverage has the effect of shifting the total return relatively away from current income and toward growth, even when income leverage is positive. While this will not necessarily always be the case, it is typical.

---

[29]In Exhibit 13-6, the equity appreciation return increases more than proportionately with the leverage ratio, because the loan amortization results in negative growth in the loan value.

IS THERE ALWAYS POSITIVE LEVERAGE IN THE TOTAL RETURN?

Investors usually assume that positive leverage will exist, at least on an ex ante basis in the total return. In fact, such positive leverage is not guaranteed, for two reasons.

First, the equity investor may overpay for the property. As noted in Chapter 12, real estate markets are "thin" and not perfectly efficient, so such pricing mistakes are possible. If the equity investor pays more than fair market value for the property, his realistic ex ante return (on an unlevered basis) will have a risk premium less than what the market requires, and possibly less than that in the mortgage, even though the mortgage may be less risky than the property.

Second, it is possible for the mortgage to be riskier than the underlying property, when risk is defined by the capital markets. It is thus possible for the ex ante return on the mortgage to exceed that on the underlying property, even though both the mortgage and property are obtained at market value. Particularly when dealing with more than one asset class (here we have two: real estate and debt), the "type" of risk, or the relevant definition of "risk" as it matters in the capital markets (and hence, as it is reflected in return expectations) is probably not well represented by a one-dimensional measure such as the volatility. The mortgage clearly has *different* risk from the underlying property, but not necessarily *less* risk from this perspective. For example, suppose the major source of risk that the market cared about was uncertainty in the future inflation rate. The nominally fixed cash flows in a fixed rate mortgage would then make such a mortgage riskier, in terms of real (inflation-adjusted) value, than the property whose rent and value will likely be able to adjust to unexpected increases in future inflation.

In fact (as is discussed in more depth in Chapter 19), empirical evidence in the form of historical periodic returns suggests that, from the perspective of the capital markets, long-term fixed rate commercial mortgages may be only a little less risky than typical institutional quality commercial property. During the 1972–2010 period, the volatility in the Giliberto-Levy Commercial Mortgage Price Index (GLCMPI) was 8.1 percent versus 10.5 percent in the NCREIF Index of commercial property, after adjusting for inflation and "smoothing."* The "beta" of the GLCMPI with respect to the stock market was greater than that of the NCREIF index.[†] Also, the average total return in the GLCMPI was 8.7 percent per year (net of credit losses), while that in the NCREIF index was only 50 basis points greater, at 9.2 percent, only a small amount of positive leverage. Of course, such average ex post historical returns may not coincide with typical ex ante expectations during the historical period, or with reasonable going-forward expectations today. The general downward trend in interest rates during the 1972–2010 period may have caused the historically realized mortgage returns to overstate the going-in expectations.

On a going-forward basis, most investors view mortgages as less risky than the underlying property, and on an ex ante basis mortgage yields usually appear to be lower than realistic IRRs on commercial property, although not necessarily much lower. Ex ante yields on mortgages are relatively easy to observe, and they typically give long-term fixed rate commercial mortgages realistic risk premiums on the order of 150 to 300 basis points above T-bills, when the yield curve has its most common slightly upward-sloping shape.[‡] While *realistic* ex ante returns on commercial property are more difficult to observe (as we noted in Chapter 11), a typical reasonable range for institutional quality commercial properties is on the order of 400 basis points above T-bills. The ex ante return spread between property and mortgages (the degree of positive leverage) will tend to be greater in noninstitutional property, or with shorter-term or adjustable rate loans.[§] On the other hand, positive leverage will tend to be less, other things being equal, when long-run inflation expectations are high or rising.

In summary, the existence and degree of positive leverage in the ex ante total return depends on the specifics of the loan, the property, and the state of the capital markets and the macroeconomy.

---

*"Smoothing" here refers to the effect of appraisals and lagged valuations in artificially damping the apparent risk in the NCREIF index as described in Chapter 25. Both GLCMPI and NCREIF returns are computed annually net of inflation.

[†] As will be discussed in Part VII, "beta" is a measure of nondiversifiable risk for an investor whose wealth is invested in the stock market.

[‡] The yield curve reflects the difference between interest rates on long-term versus short-term debt. As will be explained in Chapter 18, realistic ex ante returns on mortgages are a bit less than their stated yields or interest rates, as one must take into account the probability of credit losses as a result of default. Mortgage risk and ex ante risk premiums will be discussed further in Chapter 19.

[§] In principle, the spread should also be increased for sufficiently low LTV ratios, as this should lower the market's required default risk premium in the mortgage ex ante return.

© OnCourse Learning

13.6 Chapter Summary

Let us summarize what we have learned in this chapter about leverage and the use of debt to finance the equity real estate investment. In general, we see that debt financing, and the resulting leverage, has three major effects:

1. *Under the typical assumption that the loan is less risky than the underlying property, leverage will increase the ex ante total return on the equity investment by increasing the risk premium in that return.*

2. *Under the same relative risk assumption as above, leverage will increase the risk of the equity investment normally proportionately with the increase in the risk premium noted in (1).*

3. *Under the typical situation of nonnegative price appreciation in the property and nonnegative amortization in the loan, leverage will usually shift the expected return for the equity investor relatively away from the current income component and toward the growth or capital appreciation component.*

We have also seen how all three of the effects noted qualitatively here can be quantified, in many cases to a useful approximation, by use of the WACC formula. The trade-off implied by the first two points implies that the use of leverage does not normally affect the NPV of the equity investor's position, assuming the debt is unsubsidized. And we noted that excessive leverage appears to be an all-too-common reason why real estate investors get into trouble. Nevertheless, debt is a tremendously useful source of capital for real estate investment. The previously noted risk and return effects of leverage allow underlying real estate property assets to attract capital from a variety of investors. Some investors prefer equity's management control and growth potential even though it may have greater risk. Others prefer the more passive role, contractually fixed cash flows, and finite maturity of mortgages. In the big picture, this differentiation improves the choices available to investors and the overall efficiency of the capital markets.

KEY TERMS

leverage	management incentive effects	equity cash yield
heterogeneous investors	volatility	cash-on-cash return
investment products	default risk	positive leverage
leverage ratio (LR)	market price of risk	negative leverage
equity	weighted average cost of capital	mortgage constant (MC)
residual claim	(WACC)	
loan-to-value ratio (LTV)	risk premium (RP)	

STUDY QUESTIONS

Conceptual Questions

13.1. How does the use of fixed cost debt financing create "leverage" in the equity position of an income-property investment?

13.2. What is the difference between the leverage ratio (LR) and the loan-to-value ratio (LTV)? How much greater property value can be purchased with a 75% LTV than with a 50% LTV? What is the LR associated with each of those two LTVs?

13.3. What is the relationship between the leverage ratio (LR) and the loan to equity (L/E) ratio?

13.4. What is meant by the preferred or senior claim of debt?

13.5. How does the equity investor's ability to control property management align the interests and incentives of the debt and equity investors in normal circumstances, so as to maximize total property value? (Hint: What are the implications of the fact that equity has the "residual" claim on property value?)

13.6. What is wrong with the following statement: Only a fool would invest in real estate without financing most of the purchase with a mortgage; borrowing allows you to increase your expected return by using other people's money!

13.7. What is the relationship between the leverage ratio and both the risk and the risk premium in the equity investor's return, assuming that debt is riskless?

13.8. Without assuming riskless debt, what is the relationship between the ex ante equity risk premium and the amount of risk in the equity investment, measuring risk as it is defined by the capital markets and assuming that both the property and debt are obtained at market value? How is this relationship affected by the degree of leverage (amount of debt)?

13.9. **a.** How does leverage affect the equity investor's ex ante risk-adjusted return, or the expected risk premium per unit of risk, assuming the property is bought at fair market value and the debt is unsubsidized?

b. How does leverage affect the NPV of the equity investor's investment if the property is bought at a price *different from* its fair market value, assuming the loan is at the market interest rate and the investor has unlimited equity capital available to invest?

13.10. Identify what is wrong with the following statements: Real estate investors who use debt financing have a significant advantage when interest rates are low. The cheaper cost of debt allows these investors to outbid pension funds and other investors who typically do not employ financial leverage for property acquisitions.

13.11. Why doesn't the equity investor's expected total return increase proportionately with risk?

13.12. That famous real estate investor, Bob, has $1,000,000 of his own equity capital available to make a real estate investment. He finds a bargain, a property with a market value of $1,100,000 that he can buy for $1,000,000.

a. By how much can Bob enhance his net wealth by leveraging his purchase of this bargain property using borrowed money to finance at least part of his investment?

b. Now suppose the bargain property is twice as large, worth $2,200,000, and Bob can buy it for $2,000,000, but he still has only $1,000,000 of his own capital available. In these circumstances, how much more can Bob increase his net wealth by using leverage, assuming he could borrow at least up to a 50% LTV ratio?

13.13. What is the underlying conceptual basis of the WACC formula shown in equation (1)?

13.14. Derive the WACC formula in terms of first-year property, equity investor and lender yields (i.e. current income yield components of return). [Hint: Start with the identity *Property cash flow = Debt cash flow + Equity cash flow*, which you can write as PBTCF = DS + EBTCF. Divide each side by V, and then multiply DS by (L/L) and EBTCF by (E/E). You should have no trouble finishing from here.]

13.15. Discuss the following statement: There is *always* positive leverage with respect to the *total* return (ex ante).

13.16. With respect to the *income component* of the before-tax ex ante return, when will there be positive leverage, and when will there be negative leverage?

13.17. How is the expected income return component related to the LTV ratio, the property cap rate, and the mortgage constant on the loan (on a before-tax basis)?

13.18. Write the WACC formulas for equity cash yield, y_E, and total equity return, r_E, shown in equations (3) and (5), respectively, using (L/E) instead of LTV or LR to measure financial leverage. Substitute out for either LTV or LR by writing them in terms of (L/E). Explain how these versions of the equations help one to understand the conditions for positive and negative leverage.

13.19. Show that with riskless, fixed-rate debt the variability of the equity investor's return is equal to the leverage ratio times the variability of the property returns, where variability is measured by standard deviation of returns. [Hint: Take the variance of both sides of equation (5) and then the square root to obtain standard deviations. You will need the following statistical result: if X and Y = cX are random variables with "c" a constant, then Variance(Y) = c^2Variance(X).] How much more variable are ex ante equity investor returns relative to ex ante property returns if the investor obtains a mortgage with a 75% LTV?

13.20. Suppose you want to increase the income component of your return from your real estate equity portfolio but you do not want to sacrifice the appreciation component.

What must you look for? If you can't find a loan with positive leverage in the equity yield, what trade-off must you accept?

13.21. How does leverage usually affect the relative magnitude of the income and appreciation components in the equity investor's expected return?

13.22. Does increasing leverage (borrowing a larger fraction of the property value) usually primarily increase the expected income component of the return or the appreciation component? Why? [Hint: Use the WACC formula and assume that $E[g_D]$ is usually either zero or negative, less than $E[g_P]$, while $E[y_D]$ is usually positive and around the same magnitude as $E[y_P]$.]

13.23. How does leverage enable the same underlying asset to serve the investment objectives of different types of investors? What are the two types of investment products that result from the use of debt financing of real estate investment?

*__13.24.__ **(Effect of Leverage with Floating Rate Debt)** Consider the case of (riskless from a default perspective) variable or floating rate debt. Show that the volatility of the equity return to a property investment financed with floating rate debt could be less than the volatility of the equity return if the same property was financed with the same amount of fixed-rate debt. Derive and interpret the conditions under which this can happen. [Hints: This is an extension of Question 13.19 to the variable rate debt case; the debt yield, r_D, is now random variables. You need to use the following statistical result: if X and Y are random variables, with standard deviations σ_X and σ_Y, and $Z = aX + bY$, with "a" and "b" constants, then $Var[Z] = a^2 Var[X] + b^2 Var[Y] + 2ab\sigma_X\sigma_Y\rho_{XY}$, where ρ_{XY} is the correlation coefficient between X and Y.]

Quantitative Problems

13.25. Suppose you expect that one year from now, a certain property's before-tax cash flow ($PBTCF = NOI - CI$) will equal only $15,000 per year under a plausible pessimistic scenario or as much as $25,000 per year under a plausible optimistic scenario. If you borrow an amount such that the loan payments will be $10,000 per year (for certain), then what is your *range* of expected income return component (equity yield) under the no-leverage and leverage alternatives, assuming that the property price is $200,000 and the loan amount is $100,000?

13.26. a. If the cap rate on a certain property is 12% and loans are available at an 11% mortgage constant (where $MC = DS/LOAN$), then what is the expected income component of your before-tax return (i.e., first return on equity or cash-on-cash return) if you borrow 80% of the property price?

   b. What if you only borrow 50%?

13.27. A property is being acquired today for $100. The cap rate, or return on assets, is 7.5%, and the investor can obtain a mortgage for 75% of the property purchase price with an annual mortgage constant (MC) of 6.25%.

   a. What is the leverage ratio associated with this transaction? What is the loan-to-equity ratio?

   b. What is the investor's expected first-year return on equity (cash-on-cash return)? Compute this two different ways: (i) directly using the definition of equity cash yield = EBTCF/E; and (ii) using the WACC formula approach.

13.28. An investor is considering the purchase of a property for $1 million. Based on the $1 million price, the property has a cap rate of 10.5%. The investor can obtain an interest-only mortgage loan at 8.0%. Suppose the investor borrows 75% of the price to acquire the property. What is the maximum price the investor could pay for the property before debt financing has a neutral effect on the equity cash yield?

13.29. a. Answer part (a) of Question 13.26, only now with respect to the growth component of the equity return, assuming the loan interest rate is 10% and the expected total return on the property is also 10%.

   b. What if the property cap rate were 9% instead of 12%?

13.30. The figures in the following table depict the before-tax cash flow projection for a typical 10-year holding period for a levered investment in a property whose current market value is $5 million, for which a $3 million interest-only 10-year mortgage would be the typical financing mechanism at a market interest rate of 8%. What is the market's implied required going-in 10-year IRR for the levered equity investment?

Year	0	1	2	3	4	5	6	7	8	9	10
Prop. Inc.		450,000	454,500	459,045	463,635	468,272	472,955	477,684	482,461	487,286	492,158
Debt Svc.		−240,000	−240,000	−240,000	−240,000	−240,000	−240,000	−240,000	−240,000	−240,000	−240,000
Prop. Sale	−5,000,000										5,523,111
Loan	3,000,000										−3,000,000
Equity CF	−2,000,000	210,000	214,500	219,045	223,635	228,272	232,955	237,684	242,461	247,286	2,775,269

13.31. a. Assuming riskless debt, if the loan-to-value ratio is 80%, approximately how much more risk will there be in the equity return than if the LTV ratio were 60%? Put another way: If the return to equity can vary per year within a range of ±20% with a 60% LTV ratio, then within what range can it vary with an 80% LTV ratio?

    b. How much larger should the market's required risk premium be in the required return to equity with 80% debt as compared to 60% debt?

13.32. A certain real estate limited partnership (LP) advertises that it has a target of matching the stock market in total return for its limited partner investors, before taxes. (Suppose that the stock market risk premium is expected to be 7%.) The conservative office and warehouse properties that the partnership plans to acquire typically command risk premiums in their before-tax expected returns of about 3%. Assuming riskless debt, what loan-to-value ratio must the LP plan to maintain in its property investments in order to have a good chance of meeting its stated target?

13.33. Answer Question 13.32 assuming the risk-free interest rate is 5% and the debt would have an interest rate of 7%.

CHAPTER

14

AFTER-TAX INVESTMENT ANALYSIS AND CORPORATE REAL ESTATE

CHAPTER OUTLINE

LEARNING OBJECTIVES

After reading this chapter, you should understand:

⊃ How to extend the micro-level commercial property cash flow proforma projection to the level of the equity investor's after-tax cash flows.

⊃ The major impacts income taxes have on the investor's cash flows, including the basic effects of tax shields on the after-tax cash flows and investment returns of the levered equity investor.

⊃ A rigorous economic framework for analyzing and evaluating after-tax levered equity investment at the micro-level.

⊃ How to analyze the buy-versus-lease decision by a profitable taxed corporation.

I n the last chapter, we began to step beyond pure property-level analysis to investor-level analysis by considering the effect of leverage on the equity investment. In this chapter, we extend this progression with a basic consideration of how the owner's income tax obligations may affect the cash flows and investment valuation decisions discussed in Part IV. We will see how income tax effects interact with the possible use of debt financing in the equity investment, although we will not assume that debt financing will necessarily be employed.

The first two sections of this chapter present the basic nuts and bolts of after-tax levered equity investment at the micro-level, including a simple numerical example. Section 14.3 will then take you to a deeper level, showing how a rigorous economic framework can be applied to give you a more sophisticated understanding and perspective of what is fundamentally going on in real estate investment at the micro-level, including the effect of both debt and taxes and their interactions. This will tie back to basic concepts introduced in Chapters 12 and 13. Finally, section 14.4 will apply this same framework to the classical corporate real estate decision of whether to own or lease the space needed for their operations, viewed from a financial economic perspective.

It should be noted that many of the specific considerations in sections 14.1 and 14.2 are relevant particularly to the income tax and accounting provisions of the United States. Indeed, they reflect the specific provisions prevailing as of the time of writing the current edition of this book. Tax laws and accounting conventions change from time to time, and the decade of the 2010s promises to be a particularly dynamic period. Other countries of course have different laws and conventions. But at a more general level, the basic principles and ideas of this chapter should be broadly applicable, in other countries as well as the United States, and even as specific provisions change (and one must therefore adjust the specific applications of the basic principles).

It is at this deeper and more general level that section 14.3 is most relevant. While most of the material in section 14.3 is not found in traditional real estate finance texts, it represents a straightforward application to real estate of basic tenets of mainstream financial economics as applied to the fields of corporate finance and investments as taught in advanced MBA programs throughout the world. The framework presented in these sections is simply the application at the equity after-tax level of the three fundamental and powerful economic principles that have guided us throughout this text and that will continue to do so: (1) the operation of real estate investment within well-functioning asset markets that tend toward equilibrium; (2) the concept of opportunity cost based on the relevant markets; and (3) the wealth-maximization decision principle. We will endeavor to make the explication of the methodology applying these principles more concrete by carrying forward into section 14.3 the simple numerical example of section 14.2. If you venture all the way through section 14.3, you will certainly be fully engaging your brain, but isn't that what makes graduate school so much fun after all?

14.1 General Effects of Income Taxes and Debt

To begin, it is important to understand how a property owner's income tax obligation reduces the net after-tax cash flow received by that investor, and how certain expenses can provide what is termed a *tax shield* for taxable investors. To see how this works, we need to consider the difference between **property-level before-tax cash flows** and **owner-level after-tax cash flows**.

This requires consideration of some basic differences between accrual accounting and cash flow accounting. Accrual accounting is designed to register income and expenses when they are "accrued," that is, when they are legally owed.[1] On the other hand, cash flow accounting is designed to register cash inflows and outflows when they actually occur for the property owner. Even though, as always, we primarily care about cash flows, the owner's accrual-based income statement is relevant, because in the United States, the owner's income tax obligation on commercial property income is based on accrual accounting, and income taxes themselves, of course, a cash flow item.

Recall first from Chapter 11 that the typical property-level before-tax cash flow statement identifies the net operating income (NOI) from the property, as well as a bottom-line

---

[1]You can view accrual accounting as simply the standard type of accounting taught in basic accounting courses and used in corporate accounting. Many of its fundamental procedures and principles famously have their origins in the Italian Renaissance.

property-level before-tax net cash flow (PBTCF), which consists of the NOI less any capital improvement expenditures. This cash flow statement differs in several respects from the accrual statement on which the owner's income tax obligations are computed. Three differences are usually most important: depreciation expense, capital expenditures, and debt amortization.

Depreciation Expense. Depreciation expense is not deducted from the cash flow bottom line because depreciation expense is not a cash outflow, but rather reflects (in theory) the presumed accrual of losses in property value over time. While in reality property often does not lose nominal value over time (typically due largely to the effect of inflation), IRS tax rules still allow property depreciation expenses related to the built structure on the property to be accrued for purposes of calculating net income from the property for the purpose of computing the owner's income tax obligation. On the other hand, at the time of property resale, the capital gains income tax obligation will be based on the difference between the sale price and the **book value** of the property (referred to in U.S. tax rules as the "adjusted basis" of the property), with the latter reflecting the **accumulated depreciation** expenses during the period of ownership.[2]

Capital Expenditures. Capital expenditures are deducted from the cash flow bottom line because these are cash outflows. In contrast, on an accrual basis such expenditures would not be fully charged as expenses in the year they are made, but rather would be capitalized into the book value of the asset and then depreciated gradually over the life of the improvement. Thus, capital expenditures do not (much) reduce the income tax obligation of the property owner in the year they are made, even though they do reduce the owner's net cash flow that year.

Debt Amortization. If the owner has financed the property by taking out a mortgage or debt associated with the property acquisition, the cash flow to the owner is reduced by the entire amount of the debt service payments to the lender, including both the interest component of the debt service and the **debt amortization** component (repayment of principal). From an accrual perspective, however, only the interest portion of the debt service payment is charged as an expense against the owner's taxable income, as any portion of the debt service that is used to pay down principal is viewed as a reduction of the owner's debt liability, which is not an expense.

All three of these general effects of income taxes and debt on the property owner's operating cash flow are depicted in Exhibit 14-1A. Starting from the property NOI, the exhibit shows two branches of further calculations. The right-hand branch is accrual-based, and the left-hand branch is cash flow-based. In the right-hand branch, the owner's income tax obligation is calculated based on taxable income, which removes the accrual items of debt interest and depreciation expenses from the NOI. The income tax obligation thusly calculated from accrued income is itself a cash outflow item, which is removed from the NOI along with the entire debt service (principal amortization as well as interest) and any capital improvement expenditures, to arrive at the equity-after-tax cash flow (EATCF) at the bottom of the left-hand branch in the diagram. The EATCF is the bottom line that is of ultimate interest to the property owner.[3] The right-hand branch simply shows how the tax item is computed.

In addition to these effects on operating income, during years when there is reversion cash flow (e.g., typically when the property is sold), the owner must pay **capital gains tax** (CGT) on the difference between the net sale proceeds and the book value (or adjusted basis) of the property. This is shown in Exhibit 14-1B.[4]

---

[2]Note, however, that the capital gains tax may be deferred by using the sale proceeds to buy a similar property (referred to as a section 1031 "like-kind" transfer).

[3]As Professor Stewart Myers once said in a 1984 class when explaining why cash flows are more relevant for investment analysis than accounting-based income: "You can't buy beer with accrued net income."

[4]The capital gains tax will be discussed in more detail in the numerical example that follows.

EXHIBIT 14-1A Equity-After-Tax Cash Flows from Operations

© OnCourse Learning

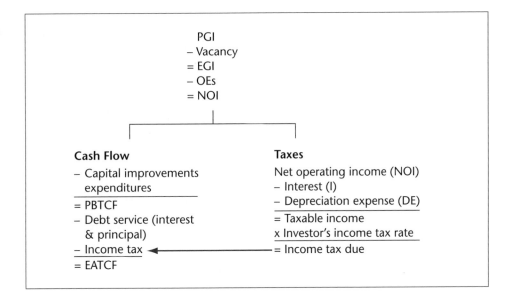

PGI
− Vacancy
= EGI
− OEs
= NOI

Cash Flow

− Capital improvements expenditures

= PBTCF
− Debt service (interest & principal)
− Income tax ◄
= EATCF

Taxes

Net operating income (NOI)
− Interest (I)
− Depreciation expense (DE)
= Taxable income
× Investor's income tax rate
= Income tax due

EXHIBIT 14-1B

Computation of CGT in Reversion Cash Flow

© OnCourse Learning

Net sale proceeds (NSP)
− Adjusted basis
= Taxable gain on sale
× CGT rate
= Taxes due on sale

where the adjusted basis or net book value is calculated as

Original basis (total initial cost)
+ Capital improvement expenditures
− Accumulated depreciation
= Adjusted basis

14.2 Numerical Example of After-Tax Proforma

The effect of these accrual-based income tax considerations can best be seen by recourse to a simple numerical example. Exhibit 14-2 depicts a 10-year proforma statement for an apartment property investment being contemplated by an individual investor who faces (including both federal and state taxes) a 35 percent marginal tax rate for ordinary income and a tax rate for long-term capital gains income that includes a 15 percent rate on the "economic gain" (essentially, any positive difference between sale price minus purchase price) plus a 25 percent rate on accumulated depreciation expense "recapture."[5] The property could be purchased for $1 million, with a depreciable cost basis of $800,000, reflecting the fact that IRS rules allow only the building structure, equipment, and fixtures on the property to be depreciated, not the land component of the property value. The rationale behind the non-depreciability of land is that land does not physically "wear out" as a structure does, and

---

[5]These rates prevailed at the federal level in the United States from 2002, but are subject to change and the reader should check current tax laws and make adjustments as appropriate.

"location value" (as described in Part II) is traditionally considered to be at least as likely to increase as decrease over time.[6]

14.2.1 Basic Equity Cash Flow Calculations

The cash flow projection in Exhibit 14-2 picks up largely where our description of property cash flow proformas left off in Chapter 11. In this example, the NOI of the apartment property is projected to start out at $60,000 in the first year, and then grow at a rate of 1 percent per year to a level of $65,621 in year 10. As described in Chapter 11, this NOI is a property-level operating income figure net of all operating expenses, including property taxes and management expenses.

Depreciation of the property value over time is not considered an operating expense (and, as noted, may not actually occur for a properly maintained building in an environment with even modest inflation). However, the IRS allows depreciation expense to be charged against taxable income. As of the early 2000s, the IRS rules for residential income property such as this apartment building allowed **straight-line depreciation** based on a 27.5-year lifetime for the building.[7] This means that the property owner can charge an annual expense against the property's NOI equal to 1/27.5 of the cost basis of the property. In this case, this allows a depreciation expense of $29,091 per year, as seen in the next line in the proforma, as $800,000/27.5 = $29,091.[8]

The proforma in Exhibit 14-2 assumes that the investor will take out a loan to finance 75 percent of the purchase price of the property. This $750,000 mortgage will have an interest rate of 5.5 percent, and requires that $2,000 of the principal balance be paid back ("amortized") each year in annual payments in arrears (that is, at the ends of the years). Thus, as the initial loan balance is $750,000, the 5.5 percent interest rate requires $41,250 in interest to be paid in year 1 ($750,000 × 0.055). The total **debt service** payment owed by the property owner to the bank that year, however, is $43,250, including the $2,000 principal amortization, which will bring the new loan balance down to $748,000 at the beginning of year 2. Thus, in year 2 the interest owed is $41,140 (calculated as 5.5 percent of $748,000), and the total debt service is $43,140. For income tax purposes, the property

---

[6]In other words, there has been an assessment that $200,000 of the $1 million property value is due to the land component. (See Chapter 5, section 5.4 for more depth of discussion concerning land value and structure value components of property value.) It should be noted that if the property asset that was purchased for $1 million is actually only a leasehold (also called a "ground lease," as distinct from a perpetual "freehold" of the property), then in most circumstances the entire $1 million purchase price could be depreciated under U.S. tax law (not just the $800,000 structure value). In other words, in effect, the leasehold is presumed for tax purposes to not include land value. See Appendix 14A for more discussion of the treatment of leasehold properties.

[7]The IRS *depreciable life* for nonresidential commercial buildings was 39 years as of the early 2000s and through the publication of the third edition of this book. Residential structures, such as apartment investments, could be written off over 27.5 years. Also, capital improvements, such as roofs or heating/cooling systems, made to the building can usually be depreciated over a different lifetime than the building as a whole, often 5 to 15 years. Investments that help a building to attain a LEED rating (see text box in Chapter 5) such as photovoltaic solar cells and new lighting systems or raised floors could be eligible for faster write-offs. Depreciation of the leasehold in the case of ground leases would generally be over the lesser of either the structure depreciation lifetime (27.5 or 39 years) or the remaining lifetime of the lease. In the interest of simplicity, we have ignored this in the present numerical example, though in reality, so-called "cost segregation" can be a method to reduce the tax obligation of the property. Cost segregation can apply not only to new capital improvements, but existing components of the building. Usually 5 percent to 20 percent of the building value can be separated off for faster write-off than the 27.5- or 39-year life for the building as a whole.

[8]Most closing costs incurred in the property acquisition (ignored in this example) can be written into the depreciable cost basis (including loan "points," which can be amortized over the life of the loan). Some components of the property equipment such as HVAC or kitchen appliances may be depreciated more rapidly than the building life. Tenant improvement expenditures paid by the landlord to finish out or improve spaces associated with specific long-term (multiyear) leases are "amortized" (depreciated) over the maturity of the building (27.5 or 39 years), but may be completely written down when/if the tenant leaves or terminates the lease. Some leasing costs, such as broker commissions, may be amortized (depreciated) over the life of the lease. All of these subtleties are ignored for clarity of exposition in this example.

Property Purchase Price (Year 0):	$1,000,000		Unlevered	Levered
Depreciable Cost Basis:	$800,000	Before-tax IRR:	6.04%	7.40%
Ordinary Income Tax Rate:	35.00%	After-tax IRR:	4.34%	6.44%
Capital Gains Tax Rate:	15.00%	Ratio AT/BT:	0.719	0.870
Depreciation Recapture:	25.00%			

TRADITIONAL FORMAT

Operating Accrual Items	Year: 1	2	3	4	5	6	7	8	9	Oper. Yr. 10	Reversion Item	Rever. Yr. 10	Total Yr. 10
NOI	$60,000	$60,600	$61,206	$61,818	$62,436	$63,061	$63,691	$64,328	$64,971	$65,621	Sale Price	$1,104,622	
− Depr. Exp.	$29,091	$29,091	$29,091	$29,091	$29,091	$29,091	$29,091	$29,091	$29,091	$29,091	− Book Val.	$809,091	
− Int. Exp.	$41,250	$41,140	$41,030	$40,920	$40,810	$40,700	$40,590	$40,480	$40,370	$40,260			
= Net Income (BT)	($10,341)	($9,631)	($8,915)	($8,193)	($7,465)	($6,730)	($5,990)	($5,243)	($4,490)	($3,730)	= Book Gain	$295,531	$291,801
− Inc. Tax	($3,619)	($3,371)	($3,120)	($2,867)	($2,613)	($2,356)	($2,096)	($1,835)	($1,571)	($1,305)	− CGT	$73,421	
= Net Income (AT)	($6,722)	($6,260)	($5,795)	($5,325)	($4,852)	($4,375)	($3,893)	($3,408)	($2,918)	($2,424)	= Gain (AT)	$222,111	$219,686

Adjusting Accrual to Reflect Cash Flow

	Year: 1	2	3	4	5	6	7	8	9	Oper. Yr. 10	Reversion Item	Rever. Yr. 10	Total Yr. 10
− Cap. Imprv. Expdtr.	$0	$0	$50,000	$0	$0	$0	$0	$50,000	$0	$0			
+ Depr. Exp.	$29,091	$29,091	$29,091	$29,091	$29,091	$29,091	$29,091	$29,091	$29,091	$29,091	+ Book Val.	$809,091	
− Debt Amort	$2,000	$2,000	$2,000	$2,000	$2,000	$2,000	$2,000	$2,000	$2,000	$2,000	− Loan Bal.	$730,000	
= EATCF	$20,369	$20,831	($28,704)	$21,766	$22,239	$22,716	$23,198	($26,317)	$24,173	$24,667	= EATCF	$301,202	$325,868
+ Inc. Tax	($3,619)	($3,371)	($3,120)	($2,867)	($2,613)	($2,356)	($2,096)	($1,835)	($1,571)	($1,305)	+ CGT	$73,421	
= EBTCF	$16,750	$17,460	($31,824)	$18,898	$19,626	$20,361	$21,101	($28,152)	$22,601	$23,361	= EBTCF	$374,622	$397,983

CASH FLOW COMPONENTS FORMAT

Operating Cash Flow Items	Year: 1	2	3	4	5	6	7	8	9	Oper. Yr. 10	Reversion Item	Rever. Yr. 10	Total Yr. 10
NOI	$60,000	$60,600	$61,206	$61,818	$62,436	$63,061	$63,691	$64,328	$64,971	$65,621	Sale Price	$1,104,622	
− Cap. Imprv. Expdtr.	$0	$0	$50,000	$0	$0	$0	$0	$50,000	$0	$0			
= PBTCF	$60,000	$60,600	$11,206	$61,818	$62,436	$63,061	$63,691	$14,328	$64,971	$65,621	= PBTCF	$1,104,622	$1,170,243
− Debt Svc.	$43,250	$43,140	$43,030	$42,920	$42,810	$42,700	$42,590	$42,480	$42,370	$42,260	− Loan Bal.	$730,000	
= EBTCF	$16,750	$17,460	($31,824)	$18,898	$19,626	$20,361	$21,101	($28,152)	$22,601	$23,361	= EBTCF	$374,622	$397,983
− Tax on NOI	$21,000	$21,210	$21,422	$21,636	$21,853	$22,071	$22,292	$22,515	$22,740	$22,967	Tax Mkt. Gain	$693	$23,661
+ DTS	$10,182	$10,182	$10,182	$10,182	$10,182	$10,182	$10,182	$10,182	$10,182	$10,182	− Acc. DTS	($72,727)	($62,545)
+ ITS	$14,438	$14,399	$14,361	$14,322	$14,284	$14,245	$14,207	$14,168	$14,130	$14,091			$14,091
= EATCF	$20,369	$20,831	($28,704)	$21,766	$22,239	$22,716	$23,198	($26,317)	$24,173	$24,667	EATCF	$301,202	$325,868

EXHIBIT 14-2 Example After-Tax Income and Cash Flow Proformas

© OnCourse Learning

owner (debtor) may charge against taxable income the *interest component only* of these debt service payments, as **interest expense**, as indicated in the third line of the proforma.[9]

14.2.2 Accrual-Based Income and Tax Shelter

This brings us to the fourth line, which is the owner's net income from this property investment as recorded by the owner for income tax reporting purposes. Note that in year 1 (and indeed for all of the projected years) this taxable net income is a negative number. The $60,000 NOI from the property is reduced first by the $29,091 depreciation expense and then by the $41,250 interest expense to leave a net taxable income of negative $10,341. If the property owner has other positive taxable income from other appropriate sources, then this **tax loss** of $10,341 on the apartment building can be deducted against this other income, thereby reducing the owner's overall taxable income. This will save the owner income taxes in the amount of her income tax rate times the taxable income deduction, in this case $3,619 (calculated as 35 percent times $10,341). This is referred to as a **tax shield** or **tax shelter**, because it allows other income that would otherwise be taxable to avoid paying taxes.

The IRS has put some limits on the ability to use property tax losses to shelter other income. These limits change as tax rules change, but they tend to apply most severely to higher income investors. In any case, *property income* (from other properties the investor might own that are producing positive taxable income) can always be sheltered by tax losses on a given property. Tax losses can also be carried forward from one year to the next when the investor's total taxable income is negative.[10]

The proforma in Exhibit 14-2 assumes that the investor can use all of the tax shelter this apartment property can provide in each year. Even on an after-tax basis, reflecting any savings from tax shelter, the net income is negative by $6,722 in the first year. (After-tax net income is simply the before-tax income minus the income tax, but as a tax shelter is counted as "negative taxes" because it saves that amount in taxes, after-tax income will be greater, that is, less negative, than before-tax income whenever taxable income is negative, and the property owner can use the tax shelter.)

So why would the investor even contemplate such an investment? Part of the answer lies in the potential for profit in selling the property later. But the more important and more fundamental reason lies in the difference between accrual-based taxable income and actual current cash flow. The importance of this difference is seen in the rest of the proforma in Exhibit 14-2. In the lines below the Net Income (AT) line in Exhibit 14-2, we adjust the accrual-based accounts to reflect current cash flow, in the traditional format.

14.2.3 After-Tax Operating Cash Flow

Looking at these Operating Cash Flow items in Exhibit 14-2, we first subtract any capital improvement expenditures that were not expensed. These typically include expenditures for large physical improvements to the building or its equipment, such as installing a new

---

[9]If the property were a leasehold (instead of a freehold as in the present example), and if the ground lease required regular ground rent payments, then those rental payments could also be deducted entirely from the property owner's taxable income similarly to the interest on the loan. Indeed, such ground rent payments imply that the ground lease is acting in the role of providing some financing for the property purchase, similar in this respect to a loan (assuming relatively fixed ground rent not based on the property net income, and with resulting leverage implications as discussed in Chapter 13 and electronic Appendix 14A to this chapter).

[10]Property rental income is classified by the IRS as "passive" income, and all sources of a taxpayer's passive income are pooled for tax reporting purposes. However, above certain overall income limits, losses from passive income cannot be deducted from "active" income (e.g., from wages) or "portfolio" income (e.g., from financial investments). As of the early 2000s, losses could be carried forward as much as five years.

roof or new windows. These are cash outflows. In the example apartment building in Exhibit 14-2, the owner is projecting such expenditures of $50,000 in year 3 and year 8.[11]

The next step in going from accrual to cash flow accounting is to add back the depreciation expense we previously subtracted, because (as noted) this is not a cash outflow. On the other hand, we must subtract the debt principal amortization, which is indeed a cash outflow.

This brings us to the **equity-after-tax cash flow (EATCF)** to the levered equity owner in Exhibit 14-2. This is the most important bottom-line number for the property owner, assuming that the tax shelter is indeed useful. To arrive at the **equity-before-tax cash flow (EBTCF)**, we simply add the income tax back into the EATCF. This is the last line in the traditional format in Exhibit 14-2. In years when there is negative income tax payment from the property (i.e., when the property is a net tax shelter), which will occur when there is a tax loss from the property (the property's taxable income is negative), the EATCF will be larger than the EBTCF.

Below the traditional format in Exhibit 14-2, we have presented an alternative method of calculating the same cash flows. This cash flow components format is simpler than the traditional format in some respects and illustrates more clearly the components of the after-tax cash flows. In particular, this presentation explicitly highlights the tax shield components of the cash flow, including a separation of the portions of the tax shields attributable to depreciation and to interest expense. In this approach, the EBTCF is calculated first, directly from the PBTCF and the debt service. Then the income tax, as if there were no tax shields, is computed by applying the ordinary income tax rate to the NOI. Finally, the **depreciation tax shields (DTS)** and **interest tax shields (ITS)** are directly and separately computed and added back in to arrive at the EATCF. For operating cash flows, the DTS equals the depreciable cost basis divided by the **depreciable life** times the owner's ordinary income tax rate.[12] The ITS equals the loan interest expense times the owner's ordinary income tax rate.[13] This cash flow components format can be useful for analytical purposes, because each line item is a cash flow stream, and some of these components have different risk characteristics.

Notice that the cash flows in Exhibit 14-2 look to be quite a bit more positive than the accrual-based net income figures described previously. The first year's after-tax cash flow is $20,369, which is 8.15 percent of the equity investment of $250,000 (the $1 million purchase price less the $750,000 loan). The impact of the tax shields combined with the fact that the depreciation expense is not a cash outflow causes the net cash flow from the property to be larger than the accrual-based net income.

While the cash flows are generally larger than the net income, they are also less smooth over time. As noted in Chapter 11, this is because of the effect of capital expenditures, which tend to be "lumpy," occurring in large amounts at irregular and occasional points in time. However, this lumpiness effect is magnified in the equity bottom line, due to the effect of debt adding financial leverage to the operating cash flow of the building. In the case of our example apartment building, the cash flow proforma reveals years in which the equity owner will experience substantial negative net cash flow, much larger negative amounts in a single year than appear in the accrual-based net income figures. (Note that this is in some contrast to the unlevered PBTCF bottom line indicated in the lower panel of Exhibit 14-2, as no projected negative years occur prior to debt service payment.) The owner must plan for and budget for such negative years, and the lender should also be aware of the stress such years

---

[11]Because major capital improvement expenditures are "lumpy" across time, that is, occur at somewhat infrequent and irregular intervals and amounts, many proforma operating statements include a regular, relatively constant amount each year as a "reserve" item, instead of projecting the specific lumpy expenditures. This stabilizes the annual cash flow, making it easier to work with the numbers. However, the annual reserve is not really a cash outflow to the owner, as even if such cash is actually placed aside in a separate sinking fund account, it is still owned by the investor and earns interest for the investor. On the other hand, large capital expenditures may be financed with borrowed funds, which will smooth the cash flow impact over time.

[12]$10,182 - 0.35 \times (\$800,000/27.5)$

[13]For example, for the first year, $14,438 = 0.35 \times \$41,250$

can put on the borrower's ability to service the debt, unless adequate precautions and preparations are made.

While some types of capital expenditures are somewhat discretionary and can be postponed, or perhaps financed with loans or paid for gradually, other types of capital expenditures cannot be delayed and must be paid for up front. For example, the expiration of long-term leases may require major expenditures to bring in a new long-term tenant.

14.2.4 After-Tax Reversion Cash Flow

Recall from Chapter 11 that the last year of a proforma cash flow projection for investment analysis must include not only the normal operating line items for that year but also the so-called reversion items associated with the (presumed) resale of the property at the end of the year. Hence, in year 10 Exhibit 14-2 depicts both operating and reversion components, which are then summed to present the year-10 total bottom-line figures for net income and net cash flow (in the far right-hand column). The reversion items are labeled and quantified in the two columns immediately to the left of the last column in the exhibit.

Reversion calculations begin with the projected resale price (net of projected selling expenses such as broker and legal fees). In the apartment building example in Exhibit 14-2, this projected sale price is $1,104,622. (This is a 1 percent per year increase from the $1 million initial purchase price, based on the assumption that the net operating income is projected to grow at that rate, and that the asset market's required yield, or cap rate, will remain the same for this building, that is, at 6 percent based on NOI, reflecting a mature, stable market and good upkeep of the building.)

Based on current law, the projected capital gains tax (CGT) owed upon sale consists of two components. The first part is based essentially on the difference between the resale price and the gross book value, that is, what we paid for the building plus capital improvement expenditures. In the present example, we are paying $1 million for the property today, and we are projecting another $100,000 in capital improvement expenditures ($50,000 in each of years 3 and 8), for a total of $1.1 million gross investment. If the resale price exceeds this gross cost basis, we will owe 15 percent of that difference as capital gains tax. In this case, this results in only $693 of tax $[0.15 \times (\$1,104,622 - \$1,100,000)]$.

The second component of the CGT consists of the accumulated depreciation recapture. In the present example where we have charged depreciation expense only on the $800,000 original purchase depreciable "structure value," the accumulated depreciation over the 10-year projected holding period is $290,910 (10 years × $29,091 per year).[14] Any portion of this accumulated depreciation that is recovered in the resale price will be subject to the "recapture tax," at a rate of 25 percent. This results in taxes of $72,727, calculated as: 0.25 × $290,910. Thus, the total projected CGT is $693 + $72,727 = $73,421 (including round-off).[15]

Once the CGT is determined, the reversion cash flows are straightforward to calculate. The before-tax reversion for the equity owner is simply the projected property sale proceeds of $1,104,622 (net of any selling expenses, which are here ignored) less the projected outstanding loan balance on the mortgage, which in this example is $730,000 (the original $750,000 loan amount less 10 years' worth of annual $2,000 amortization payments). This leaves an equity-before-tax reversion cash flow of $374,622. If we then subtract the projected capital gains income tax obligation of $73,421 (as calculated previously), we arrive at the equity after-tax reversion cash flow of $301,202 (including rounding). As noted, the complete

---

[14]In a more complete and realistic example, there would also be accumulated amortization of capital improvement expenditures, including leasing costs and tenant improvements for buildings with long-term leases. These accumulated amortization charges may also be subject to the recapture tax.

[15]Note that in the cash flow components format at the bottom of Exhibit 14-2 the tax on the economic gain is included in the "Tax on NOI" component line item, while the recapture tax on the accumulated depreciation is included in the depreciation tax shields (DTS) component line item. This groups cash flows of similar risk together, and separates cash flows of different risk. Depreciation charges are based on historical costs that are essentially fixed and hence relatively low risk going forward. Resale proceeds, like property NOI, are based on future market values that are more risky.

year-10 cash flow includes both the operating and reversion components, as shown in the last column of Exhibit 14-2.[16]

It is important to note that under current IRS rules, payment of the capital gains tax can be deferred by the use of so-called "like kind exchanges," in which the investor invests the proceeds of the property resale into a new "like-kind" investment. The original cost basis carries forward into the new investment. Such exchanges under section 1031 of the Internal Revenue Code were facilitated in the early 2000s by approval of the ability to use tenancy-in-common (TIC) funds to effect the like-kind transfer. This enables individual investors who had owned their investments in the tenancy-in-common form of ownership (many small "mom and pop" property investors) to exchange their investment for units in a TIC fund which invests in a portfolio of properties. The investor can retire from direct management responsibility while obtaining a diversified investment and also deferring capital gains tax payment. The down side is that the TIC fund involves an additional layer of management which takes a portion of the investment earnings. Also, the investor is under time pressure to make the like-kind exchange, as current IRS rules (as of the early 2000s) only allow six months to close the exchange (and only 45 days to identify the exchange, with the investor not allowed to take possession of the original property resale proceeds in between the two investments). TIC funds also typically may lack liquidity. (Several TIC funds launched during the 2000s decade suffered major losses in the crash of 2008-09.)

14.2.5 Cash Flow Components Analysis and Projected Total Return Calculations

Now that you are familiar with the basic mechanics of after-tax proforma construction, we can begin to do some investment analysis. A good way to begin this is to recast and expand the proforma cash flow projection as we have done in Exhibit 14-3 below for our apartment property example presented previously in Exhibit 14-2.

Exhibit 14-3 presents the same cash flow components as in the bottom panel of Exhibit 14-2 (described in section 14.2.3), only transposed so the years run down the columns, and with a few added columns to help with investment analysis. Investment cash outflow components corresponding to the subsequent cash inflow components are indicated as negative amounts in the "year zero" (investment decision time) row at the top of the columns. Reversion and operating cash flows are combined in the terminal year-10 row, so that we can apply a spreadsheet IRR function directly to the cash flow range in each column to compute the IRR associated with any cash flow component.[17]

Separating the investment cash flows into components in this manner can be helpful for investment analysis because it highlights the different sources and nature of the various cash flow components, and it groups the cash flows into component streams of similar risk. For example, the unlevered property-based cash flows in columns (4), (5), and (7) contain moderate risk. The contractual or debt-like cash flows in columns (6), (9), (10), and (13) contain relatively less risk. The levered equity cash flows in columns (11) and (12) contain the most risk. When we compute the going-in IRRs presented by each of these columns, you can see that the lower-risk cash flows present lower returns (apart from the effect of income taxes).

Using the net cash flow figures in the proforma, it is possible to calculate the overall projected internal rate of return (IRR) for the investment in the apartment property. Assuming an up-front investment of $1 million in cash and ignoring the debt-based components of the cash flow projection, one can calculate the unlevered returns, also known as property-level or free-and-clear returns. At a before-tax level, this is done by applying the IRR function to the PBTCF stream in column (4) of Exhibit 14-3. This indicates that this asset presents a

---

[16]The reversion EATCF is also found from the accrual-based gain by adding back the non–cash flow item (the "book value," which is the gross cost basis minus the accumulated depreciation and amortization) and subtracting the cash outflow item (loan balance), as shown in the traditional format in the upper panel of Exhibit 14-2.

[17]You can see the year-10 operating and reversion components separately by reference back to the cash flow components format panel in the bottom of Exhibit 14-2, where the two components of year 10 are indicated separately.

Apprec.Rate =	1.00%
Yield =	6.00%
Income Tax Rate =	35.00%

Bldg.Val/Prop.Val =	80.00%
Depreciable Life =	27.5 years
CGTax Rate =	15.00%
DepRecapture Rate =	25.00%

Loan =	$750,000
Int =	5.50%
Amort/yr =	$2,000

Year	(1) Prop.Val	(2) NOI	(3) CI	(4) PBTCF	(5) tax w/out shields	(6) DTS	(7) (4)−(5)+(6) PATCF	(8) LoanBal	(9) Loan DS	(10) ITS	(11) (4)−(9) EBTCF	(12) (7)−(9)+(10) EATCF	(13) (9)−(10) LoanATCFs
0	$1,000,000			($1,000,000)			($1,000,000)	$750,000	($750,000)		($250,000)	($250,000)	($750,000)
1	$1,010,000	$60,000	$0	$60,000	$21,000	$10,182	$49,182	$748,000	$43,250	$14,438	$16,750	$20,369	$28,813
2	$1,020,100	$60,600	$0	$60,600	$21,210	$10,182	$49,572	$746,000	$43,140	$14,399	$17,460	$20,831	$28,741
3	$1,030,301	$61,206	$50,000	$11,206	$21,422	$10,182	($34)	$744,000	$43,030	$14,361	($31,824)	($28,704)	$28,670
4	$1,040,604	$61,818	$0	$61,818	$21,636	$10,182	$50,364	$742,000	$42,920	$14,322	$18,898	$21,766	$28,598
5	$1,051,010	$62,436	$0	$62,436	$21,853	$10,182	$50,765	$740,000	$42,810	$14,284	$19,626	$22,239	$28,527
6	$1,061,520	$63,061	$0	$63,061	$22,071	$10,182	$51,171	$738,000	$42,700	$14,245	$20,361	$22,716	$28,455
7	$1,072,135	$63,691	$0	$63,691	$22,292	$10,182	$51,581	$736,000	$42,590	$14,207	$21,101	$23,198	$28,384
8	$1,082,857	$64,328	$50,000	$14,328	$22,515	$10,182	$1,995	$734,000	$42,480	$14,168	($28,152)	($26,317)	$28,312
9	$1,093,685	$64,971	$0	$64,971	$22,740	$10,182	$52,413	$732,000	$42,370	$14,130	$22,601	$24,173	$28,241
10	$1,104,622	$65,621	$0	$1,170,243	$23,661	($62,545)	$1,084,037	$730,000	$772,260	$14,091	$397,983	$325,868	$758,169
IRR of above CF Stream =				6.04%			4.34%		5.50%		7.40%	6.44%	3.58%

EXHIBIT 14-3 Cash Flow Components Investment Analysis of the Example Apartment Property

© OnCourse Learning

EXHIBIT 14-4
Apartment Example Going-in
IRR Estimates
© OnCourse Learning

10-year Going-in IRR:	Property (Unlevered)	Equity (Levered)
Before-tax	6.04%	7.40%
After-tax	4.34%	6.44%
AT/BT	434/604 = 72%	644/740 = 87%
→ Effective Tax Rate	100% − 72% = 28%	100% − 87% = 13%
With ordinary income tax rate = 35%, CGT rate = 15%, Recapture tax rate = 25%.		

property-level before-tax (PBT) going-in IRR of 6.04 percent per year over the projected 10-year holding period. At the after-tax level, we apply the IRR function to the PATCF stream in column (7), which reflects what the cash flow after income taxes would be without any debt on the property. The result is a property-level after-tax going-in IRR of 4.34 percent.

To calculate the levered equity return based on the $250,000 up-front cash investment and the $750,000 loan, we use the EBTCF and EATCF streams in columns (11) and (12) of Exhibit 14-3, for before-tax and after-tax returns, respectively. The result is levered equity-level going-in IRRs of 7.40 percent and 6.44 percent before-tax and after-tax, respectively.

The calculated IRRs are summarized in Exhibit 14-4. Note that the before-tax returns are higher than the after-tax returns, because income taxes take away some of the investor's investment earnings.[18] Note also that the levered equity returns are higher than the unlevered property-level returns, due to the effect of positive leverage (as we described in Chapter 13). The equity returns are not greatly above the unlevered returns in this case, because there is not a great deal of positive leverage, as the loan faces a 5.5 percent return and the property barely a half point above that at 6.04 percent.[19] Note, however, that the after-tax return expectation for the levered equity is not as much reduced below the before-tax return as is the case without leverage. This reflects the levering of the tax shield effects, primarily the depreciation tax shields.

In this case, without leverage the after-tax return is 72 percent of the before-tax return (4.34%/6.04%), reflecting an "effective" tax rate of 28 percent in the 10-year going-in IRR (the difference between 4.34 percent and 6.04 percent is 28 percent of 6.04 percent: 1 − 0.72 = 0.28). This effective 28 percent tax rate is a blend of the 35 percent **ordinary income tax** rate, the 15 percent capital gains tax rate, and the 25 percent recapture rate. The effective tax rate on the IRR reflects the fact that some of the total return is achieved through the receipt of ordinary income, and some through the realization of capital gain. It also reflects the effect of the depreciation tax shield and the length of the projected investment horizon (10 years).

With leverage, the effective tax rate is reduced in this example to only 13 percent (comparing the 6.44 percent return to the 7.40 percent return in the same manner as we compared the 4.34 percent and 6.04 percent returns above). This reduction in the effective tax rate occurs for two reasons. For one thing, the leverage shifts the composition of the investor's IRR relatively away from ordinary income and toward the capital gain component, which is more lightly taxed (15 versus 35 percent). More important, however, the leverage magnifies the effect of the depreciation tax shields. It should also be kept in mind that the lower

---

[18]This is typical, but in real estate does not necessarily always have to be the case, as sufficient tax shelter can sometimes be provided to actually cause after-tax returns to exceed before-tax returns. That would be most common in cases where tax incentives are provided as a means for subsidizing the investment, such as with affordable (or "social") housing or historical preservation properties or properties able to take advantage of government programs of financial stimulus for alternative energy or energy efficiency.

[19]However, as will be discussed in Chapter 19, this amount of positive leverage may not be exceptionally low for high-quality real estate investments with long-term fixed-rate debt, based on realistic projections (see sections 10.4 and 10.5 in Chapter 10 for discussion of typical biases in property DCF analyses that can tend to make leverage appear more positive than it really is).

effective tax rate on the levered investment, while appealing, does not necessarily imply that the use of debt financing brings any positive NPV in itself. Remember that leverage brings added investment risk to the equity, and this added risk can easily offset the greater return expectation, viewed either from a before-tax or after-tax perspective. (The relationship between debt financing and NPV will be discussed in depth in section 14.3.5.)

14.3 After-Tax Equity Valuation and Capital Budgeting

What you have seen up to this point in this chapter is the nuts and bolts of forecasting cash flows and investment returns at the equity after-tax level of micro-level real estate investments. These nuts and bolts are, of course, very essential, but they lead to a basic question: *So what?* What should the investor (or *potential* investor) make of these forecasts? What are the implications for investment decision making? Our example apartment investment offers a realistic after-tax levered ex ante return of 6.44 percent. Is that good enough? How do you know? To answer questions like this, we must delve deeper and apply our trusty economic framework to help us analyze and understand the investment market context in which the individual micro-level decision is embedded. Indeed, we can use this context and framework to gain a more rigorous perspective and understanding about what is fundamentally going on in the real estate investment market, an understanding that can be used to make more educated investment decisions. Indeed, you will be able to see through and beyond some widely held conventional notions. We will suggest a theoretically grounded investment analysis procedure that is no more difficult to apply than what is typically done in current practice.

As noted at the outset of this chapter, section 14.3 will extend the numerical example we have just presented in 14.2 to demonstrate concretely how we can apply three basic economic principles to analyze micro-level real estate investment at the levered equity after-tax level. The principles are: (1) the concept that real estate investment decision making operates within a well-functioning asset market that tends toward equilibrium and for which such equilibrium provides a normative framework for valuation; (2) the concept of opportunity cost based on the relevant asset market; and (3) the wealth-maximization decision principle which led us fundamentally to the NPV decision rule in Chapter 10.

In Chapter 10, we introduced the DCF method and the NPV decision rule at the property level (prior to considering the use of debt) and on a before-tax basis (prior to considering the property owner's income tax).[20] Our focus then was (rather implicitly) on the estimation of market value (MV), a term we defined more explicitly in Chapter 12 along with another concept: investment value (IV). But the DCF and NPV procedures can also be applied at the after-tax level for specified equity investors who may or may not use debt financing. Indeed, we noted in section 12.1 that the concept of investment value is applied in principle at the after-tax level of a specified owner of the given property. This will provide the starting point for our equity after-tax investment analysis in this section.

14.3.1 After-Tax DCF in General

To compute investment value, the first step is to discount the projected equity-after-tax bottom line from the after-tax proforma [the EATCF row in Exhibit 14-2 or column (12) in Exhibit 14-3]. This results in an estimate of the present value of the investor's levered equity in the property, including consideration of the income-tax-shield effects. (Be sure to include the after-tax equity reversion in the terminal year.) Add this equity present value to the amount of any loan the equity investor will be receiving for the property purchase to arrive

---

[20]In corporate finance textbooks, DCF valuation and capital budgeting analysis are applied at the after-tax level. However, in the typical corporate context, the taxes being considered are corporate-level income taxes only. The typical textbook application is actually at a before-tax level from the perspective of the ultimate investors, the shareholders of the corporation. In real estate, taxed corporate-level entities rarely hold the property, so our before-tax presentation in Chapter 10 was actually consistent with the typical corporate finance textbook presentation viewed from the perspective of the ultimate investors.

at an estimate of the total investment value of the property to the equity investor. This represents the maximum price the investor would be willing to pay for the property, if he had to. (But don't forget our discussion in Chapter 12 about optimal search strategy and the buyer's "reservation price." You normally should not have to pay much more than MV, even when your IV substantially exceeds the asset MV.) The value for the property computed in this way may then be compared to the price at which the property can be obtained (or sold for) in the property market, to arrive at the NPV of the deal for the equity investor from an investment value perspective.

In evaluating the investor's equity in this way, it is important to be consistent in the treatment of the numerator and denominator within the basic DCF operation. The following rule must be heeded carefully:

Discount equity-after-tax cash flows at the appropriate equity-after-tax discount rate.

The appropriate discount rate for levered equity cash flows will normally be greater than that for property-level free-and-clear cash flows, for the reason presented in Chapter 13 that the levered position is normally more risky for the equity investor and so requires a greater risk premium in the expected total return. On the other hand, the discount rate for after-tax cash flows is usually less than the discount rate for before-tax cash flows because the after-tax opportunity cost of capital reflects the paying of income taxes on investment returns.

Correctly quantifying the effect of equity leverage and the effect of income taxes in the opportunity cost of capital can be quite difficult in practice. We know that the amount one must add to the before-tax risk premium in the required expected total return is usually greater, the greater the leverage. *But how much greater?*[21] We know that the after-tax required return is likely to be lower than the before-tax required return for a taxable investment. *But how much lower?* For example, the effective tax rate on the total return is a function of the proportion of the return that will be received as ordinary income as opposed to capital-gains income, and also of the likely holding period of the investor.[22] It is often difficult in practice to account explicitly and properly for all of these considerations to estimate an appropriate after-tax discount rate for the levered equity cash flows.

Many traditional real estate investment texts simply ignore this problem by suggesting, in effect, that the investor chooses the discount rate he wishes to employ. After all, at the equity after-tax level we are focusing on investment value (IV), not market value (MV), so why shouldn't we use the investor's own perception of his OCC?

Of course, the investor cannot just "make up" any discount rate he likes without invalidating the realism of the entire investment analysis. No investor can "make the market." We all must deal in the market of the real world that reflects the equilibrium between many investors on the supply and demand sides. For this reason, it also is not rigorous for the investor to use a "personalized" OCC as the discount rate for determining IV. As explained in section 12.1 of Chapter 12, even for IV analysis, the OCC comes from the capital market, not from any particular investor. The OCC must reflect the capital market's price of time and of risk, because any investor can always access the capital market to trade investment payoffs in the time and risk dimensions. This OCC will reflect the after-tax perception

---

[21]The WACC formula described in Chapter 13 gives some idea of the effect of leverage on the required equity return, but remember that the WACC formula is only an approximation in the IRR over multiperiod spans of time. For an investor looking at a 10-year holding horizon, the WACC approximation may not be accurate enough. And it may be difficult to quantify the appropriate inputs to the WACC formula at the after-tax level.

[22]The *effective* capital gains tax rate is less than the nominal rate due to the effect of deferral of the capital gains tax until the gain is actually realized at the time of the resale of the property (or even later with like-kind reinvestment). This effect, in turn, is a function of the growth rate in property value and the length of time the property is held before its resale. Suppose investment value grows at 10 percent for 10 years. With a capital gains tax rate of 20 percent (and ignoring depreciation for exposition), the after-tax capital available is $(1.10)^{10} - 0.20[(1.10)^{10} - 1] = 2.274994$, which is equivalent to $(1.08567)^{10}$. Thus, the effective after-tax growth rate is 8.57 percent per year, which is 85.7 percent of the before-tax growth rate, implying an effective tax rate of $100 - 85.7 = 14.3$ percent, instead of 20 percent. This effect can be further enhanced by the use of like-kind exchange to defer the payment of CGT beyond the time of resale of the subject property. (See section 14.2.4.)

and preferences for time and risk of the *marginal* investors in the relevant part of the capital market, in this case the subject property asset market.

But if this is the rigorous approach in principle, it is nevertheless difficult to implement in practice, because it is difficult to observe empirically after-tax returns to equity. Such information is proprietary and varies across individual investors. This makes levered after-tax returns much more difficult to observe than the property-level returns (before accounting for debt or taxes). Property-level returns can usually be inferred at least to a reasonable approximation from widely available market information, and then used to compute MV.

We cannot get around this problem simply by focusing on the expected return, rather than the NPV of a deal, by "backing out" the IRR implied by a given price. Even if the price is a fair market value for the asset, at the after-tax level we are focusing on investment value for the subject investor, not just market value for the asset. Without some more rigorous framework and analysis we cannot know whether the backed-out levered after-tax IRR is "good" or "bad" for the subject investor.[23]

14.3.2 Shortcut for Marginal Investors

The preceding discussion has pointed out a fundamental practical difficulty in computing investment value. It is often difficult to know the correct discount rate to apply. Fortunately, a shortcut is often possible. As noted in Chapter 12, in many cases it may be safe to assume that investment value and market value are virtually identical. In particular, this is true by definition for marginal investors in the property market.

Our discussion in section 12.1.3 suggested that you should usually be skeptical about the notion that you are "intramarginal" (that is, *not* a marginal investor), unless it is clear that you can do deals at market value with investors who are substantially different from you in their ability to use the type of property in question. In general, if you are on the buy side and cannot clearly point to some substantial advantage that you have over other successful and typical buyers in the market for the type of property in question, then you probably should not assume that you are intramarginal. If you are on the sell side (that is, you already own the property) and cannot clearly point to some substantial disadvantage in owning the property that you face compared to other typical and active sellers in the market for the type of property in question, then you probably should not assume that you are intramarginal.

If you are not intramarginal, then you are marginal, and that means that your IV equals the MV in the market. (You may want to look again at the asset market model in Exhibit 12-1.) In that case, you can work with property-level before-tax cash flows (PBTCF) rather than the equity-after-tax cash flows (EATCF) when doing valuation and capital budgeting analysis. And you can use the property-before-tax level OCC as the discount rate you apply to the PBTCF. This shortcut approach, in effect *assuming* that IV = MV, is widely used in the real world of real estate investment practice (implicitly if not explicitly). We will label this "shortcut" the **property-before-tax (PBT) approach**.

For purposes of estimating market value explicitly, the PBT shortcut is doubly sound. Not only is this approach simpler, but by avoiding the need to estimate the marginal tax rates and holding periods and leverage of the marginal investors in the property market, it avoids the danger of making mistakes in estimating these parameters. In a well-functioning property asset market, it is generally easier to make reliable empirical observations regarding the market values of the before-tax numbers (both the cash flows and the expected returns), so mistakes are less likely at the PBT level.

As an example of this approach, consider again our apartment property in Exhibit 14-2. Suppose we can reliably estimate through observation of the property market that the current

---

[23]Consider a simple example. Suppose a tax-exempt pension fund examined the same levered apartment investment deal we considered in section 14.2 and Exhibit 14-3. The pension fund's levered after-tax going-in IRR would be 7.40 percent, not 6.44 percent, because the pension fund pays no income taxes. (Column 11 rather than column 12 in Exhibit 14-3 would describe the pension fund's equity investment returns.) But this still might not be a good deal for the pension fund, because they might do better on a risk-adjusted basis with less leverage, since they cannot use the interest tax shields that are appealing to most borrowers.

market return (10-year going-in IRR) for such properties is 6.04 percent on a before-tax, property-level basis.[24] Then working at the PBT level, we can ascertain that $1 million is the current market value for the property. Now suppose our example investor in Exhibit 14-2 is typical of the type of investor on the margin in the market for that type of property.[25] Then we know by definition that $1 million is the investment value of the property for this investor. In this way, we do not need to estimate the after-tax levered opportunity cost of capital for this investor. Indeed, we do not even need to estimate the investor's EATCFs in order to estimate her IV.

Had we somehow known that 6.44 percent was the investor's after-tax levered opportunity cost of capital, we could have applied this rate to the investor's EATCFs, and added in the $750,000 loan value assuming that the loan IV = MV also for this investor (i.e., assuming that the investor is also marginal in the debt market) to arrive at the same $1 million investment value. But this would be a longer and more difficult route, especially because, as noted previously, we would not know that 6.44 percent was the correct discount rate. And once we know that $1 million is the MV of the property, we can "back out" that 6.44 percent is the levered after-tax OCC to the equity investor given the loan and anticipated holding period. But knowing this IRR in this way does not solve the original valuation or investment decision problem.

Notice that what enables us to use this PBT shortcut is the fact that a well-functioning market exists for the underlying physical assets involved in real estate investment decisions. In our apartment example, the fact that we can "observe" (directly or indirectly) that $1 million is the current market value of this property enables us to avoid having to work at the after-tax level.

Although the PBT shortcut is very useful and widely applied, remember that in principle it applies to market value, and therefore to investment value only for the typical marginal investor in the market for the type of property in question. What can we do to estimate investment value for intramarginal investors?

*14.3.3 Evaluating Intramarginal Investment Value

Before we answer this question, perhaps we should step back and think a minute about why it might be useful to quantify investment value for intramarginal investors. After all, such investors should be able to trade at market value prices like anyone else. But while this is true, we suggested in Chapter 12 that knowledge of IV can still be useful for intramarginal investors. At a very basic level, such knowledge tells the investor which side of the market they should be on. (For example, if IV < MV, you should be selling, not buying.) At a more nuanced level, the magnitude of the difference between IV and MV gives the intramarginal investor an idea about how strongly they should want to do the deal or type of deal in question. From an IV perspective, the expected NPV of selling equals MV − IV, and that of buying equals IV − MV. As MV in real estate is never known precisely for any given asset, knowledge of the magnitude of this IV-based NPV (as a percentage of gross value) is

---

[24]In practice, this would probably be typically done by applying the market's observable 6 percent cap rate to the projected first year NOI of $60,000. The 10-year DCF of the PBTCF is the more fundamental perspective, however, and should be considered, as we discussed in Chapter 10.

[25]How would we know this? In practice, this is not an "exact science," but in principle you are looking for the after-tax cash flows (and leverage and holding period) for investors on the buy side who are least advantaged and yet still actively and successfully buying properties of the subject type, and/or for investors on the sell side who are least disadvantaged in owning the property and yet are still actively and successfully selling properties of the subject type. Often, such marginal investors would be viewed as "typical" investors in the market, because they would be both buying and selling, so their after-tax equity proformas would be typically used by brokers and investment analysts to characterize the market (albeit perhaps with some "rose-tinting," as described in sections 10.4 and 11.2). For example, in our apartment property illustration, we have employed income tax rates, debt leverage ratio, and holding period that typify high-income individuals subject to personal income taxes on their investment earnings, reflecting the fact that such investors are less advantaged than tax-sheltered investors, and yet such high-income taxed investors are typically active on the buy side in many apartment investment markets.

HOW ARE PENSION FUND CONTRIBUTIONS EFFECTIVELY TAX-EXEMPT?

Consider $1,000 of pretax (i.e., gross) income at time zero. You first have to pay taxes on this income at time zero before you can do anything with it. If the tax rate is 30 percent, you have $700 of disposable income left over to invest. Suppose you can invest at a pretax rate of return of 10 percent (e.g., you buy a government bond that yields 10 percent). If your investment is not tax sheltered, then you have to pay taxes of 30 percent each year on your investment earnings that year. This makes the effective after-tax rate of growth of your money 7 percent $[(1-0.3) \times 10\% = 7\%]$, not 10 percent. Therefore, after N years, you will have $700(1.07)^N$ of disposable cash available to spend, with no more taxes owed at that time. On the other hand, if you could have invested your $700 time-zero disposable income in a vehicle that was tax-sheltered, then you would have been able to earn the entire 10 percent return without paying taxes, so your disposable cash in year N would have been $700(1.10)^N$, which is obviously greater than $700(1.07)^N$ (and this difference is more, the greater is N).

Now consider the way pension fund contributions work. We start with the same $1,000 of pretax gross income at time zero. If you put that in a pension fund at time zero you won't have to pay taxes on it at time zero because pension contributions are deductible from your taxable income. So you can invest the entire $1,000 rather than just $700. Furthermore, earnings in the fund are tax exempt as long as you leave them in the fund. So your money will grow at the full 10 percent rate during the N years, after which time you will have $1,000(1.10)^N$ in the fund. However, when you take your money out of the pension fund in year N, you do then have to pay taxes on all the money you withdraw from the fund. Thus, your after-tax disposable cash in year N from your pension investment is $(1-0.3) \times \$1,000(1.10)^N = \$700(1.10)^N$, which is the same as if you had been able to make a time-zero investment of your regular after-tax disposable income in a tax-sheltered vehicle that did not have to pay taxes on its investment returns. Thus, the combination of tax-deductible contributions up front, plus tax-sheltered growth while the investment is in the fund, makes pension investments effectively exempt from tax, as though the investment returns were not taxed.

© OnCourse Learning

useful private information entering into a deal negotiation or a bidding auction for an asset. Indeed, for some more unique types of real estate assets or deals, it can hardly be said that a "market" even exists for very close substitutes. Thus, both for big picture strategic investment policy making (which side of the market to be on) and for tactical transaction decision making (how strongly to negotiate or how aggressively to bid or how to structure the deal), knowledge of IV can be important.

Alas, to evaluate investment value for intramarginal investors, there is no shortcut that allows us to avoid estimating the investor's after-tax cash flows. We must use the investor's personalized cash flows in the numerators of the DCF valuation. (Indeed, the exercise of trying to quantify these can be useful in itself, as we argued in Chapter 10.) Yet, as described above and in Chapter 12, we also must use an appropriate OCC from the relevant capital market. This must reflect the after-tax return expectations of marginal investors in that market, for investments of similar risk as the subject investment. Fortunately, a very useful procedure exists to facilitate this type of analysis, and the procedure is valid both for marginal and intramarginal investors. We turn to this procedure in the next section.

*14.3.4 Value Additivity and the APV Decision Rule

In this section we introduce a simple and intuitive procedure for dealing with the interaction of investment and financing decisions at the after-tax level, which is the essence of our subject in section 14.3. Recall when we introduced the cash flow components format of the equity after-tax proforma projection in the bottom panel of Exhibit 14-2: we suggested this type of parsing of cash flow by component could be useful for investment analysis, because different components of the future cash flow stream have different risk characteristics. This components format was carried forward into Exhibit 14-3 (only transposed). Now we will extend and formalize this approach by giving it the name of the **value additivity principle**, the idea that the value of the property must equal the sum of the values of all the (private sector) claims on the property's cash flows.

Perhaps the simplest and most basic (and most widely used) application of this principle is to break out and value separately (and then add back together) the value of the property cash flows and the debt cash flows (or any financing-related cash flows) associated with a levered equity investment. In this case, the value additivity approach dovetails very nicely with the PBT shortcut we described in section 14.3.2, and in this context value additivity underlies an investment decision procedure often referred to as **adjusted present value**, or **APV**. The APV procedure dates back to the early 1970s in corporate finance and is attributed originally to Professor Stewart Myers. It can be as useful for real estate investment analysis as it is for corporate capital budgeting.

The APV procedure is an extension of the basic NPV analysis procedure described in Chapter 10. APV allows the NPV procedure to include explicitly the effect of financing in evaluating a real estate investment deal. From the equity investor's perspective, the deal may be considered the *combination* of the property purchase as if it were free and clear of debt and the financing arrangements.

More formally, the APV of a deal is defined as follows:

$$APV = NPV(Property) + NPV(Financing) \tag{1}$$

In equation (1), *NPV(Property)* is the NPV of the property transaction as if there were no debt. *NPV(Financing)* is the net value of the financing arrangements. Typically, financing involves the use of debt, and if we are evaluating the APV from the perspective of the property purchaser we should think of the *NPV(Financing)* term as the NPV of the borrowing transaction, from the perspective of the equity investor (the borrower).

The APV investment decision rule states that the traditional NPV decision criterion should be applied to the APV, that is, to the NPV of the deal as a whole including its financing component. This APV must be maximized across mutually exclusive alternatives and always be nonnegative in order for the deal to make sense from a wealth-maximization perspective. As with NPV, we would expect that market equilibrium would tend to drive the typical APV to zero when evaluating deals from a market value perspective, and also from an investment value perspective for marginal investors in the market.

As the debt market is usually rather competitive and efficient, the *NPV(Financing)* term will usually have a value of zero from a MV perspective, assuming unsubsidized, market-rate financing of typical "commodity-like" debt products (as would typically be obtained, for example, from a bank or other private financial institution or by issuing bonds in the public market). In these conditions, therefore, the NPV of the equity investment (using debt) is the same as the NPV of an all-equity investment in the property without using debt, evaluated from the perspective of market value, that is, $APV = NPV(Property)$. This is the condition in which the PBT shortcut described in section 14.3.2 is typically applied.

On the other hand, if subsidized financing is involved in the deal, such as some seller-provided loans or government-assisted financing, then the NPV of the financing part of the deal can be substantially positive to the buyer/investor, even viewed from a market value perspective.[26] In this case, the APV can exceed the NPV to an all-equity investment in the property. The PBT shortcut may still be useful for quantifying the *NPV(Property)* component of the APV, but the *NPV(Financing)* component must be valued separately and added to the *NPV(Property)* to obtain the total deal value for the equity investor.

It is important to note that the APV procedure (like the NPV) can be applied from either the MV or IV perspective. From the IV perspective, one needs to consider whether the investor (for example, the property purchaser) is marginal or intramarginal not only in the property market for the subject asset, but also in the debt market for the financing aspect of the deal. Positive or negative net value can occur in either component of the overall deal, particularly from an IV perspective because of differential income tax effects. This raises a topic that is very important in real estate investment, and perhaps somewhat misunderstood in some current practice in the United States: the after-tax valuation of debt financing from the point of view of the property investor (borrower).

---

[26]Obviously, the flip-side of this point is that a seller should offer cut-rate financing only if it would otherwise be impossible to sell the property at as high a price (in the same period of time). From a MV perspective, the value of the *NPV(financing)* term in the APV formula is the same magnitude for the seller as for the buyer, only opposite in sign, as for the seller financing the two parties are simply on the opposite side of the same before-tax cash flows.

*14.3.5 After-Tax Valuation of Debt Financing

In this section, we want to consider how to evaluate rigorously the use of debt financing from a market value and an investment value perspective, that is, both before-tax and after-tax. We have previously made the point that use of debt to finance a real estate investment does not automatically bring any positive NPV component in itself. The effect of positive leverage gearing up the total expected return to the equity is offset by the increase in risk, we said. However, this will always be exactly true only from the market-value perspective and the investment-value perspective (that is, after-tax) only of marginal borrowers in the debt market. From an investment value perspective more generally, use of debt may be either positive or negative in its NPV impact on the investment, depending on the investor's tax situation.[27]

To see this, let us consider a simple stylized hypothetical debt market. In this market, all loans are perpetual, and the prevailing market interest rate on mortgages is 4 percent. For every $100 that you borrow to finance a property acquisition, you will pay $4 interest at the end of every year forever. In addition, there is a market for tax-exempt debt, such as notes issued by state and local governments ("municipal bonds," or "munis"), where the prevailing market interest rate is 3 percent. Because equilibrium must exist across the markets for mortgage investment and municipal bond investment, the market interest rates in these two markets tell us that marginal investors in the debt market (marginal lenders) face an effective tax rate on mortgage interest income of 25 percent. This is the tax rate that leaves investors indifferent between a 4 percent return before-tax in the mortgage market and the 3 percent return they can get tax-free in the municipal bond market. Thus, we can readily observe that in the mortgage market the OCC is 4 percent before tax and 3 percent after tax.[28]

First consider how we would represent the market value (MV) of a mortgage in this market framework, using DCF valuation. The market value of $100 worth of debt would be, by definition, $100, based on the following DCF equation, which discounts the before-tax cash flows of the mortgage at the market's before-tax OCC of 4 percent (recalling the perpetuity formula):

$$MV = \frac{\$4}{1.04} + \frac{\$4}{1.04^2} + \cdots = \frac{\$4}{0.04} = \$100$$

Now let's consider how this MV compares to the investment value (IV) of the debt liability obligation associated with this mortgage for three intrepid real estate investors who want to borrow $100 to help finance a real estate investment. The first investor is Mary. Mary is like the typical marginal investor in the debt market in that she faces a marginal tax rate of 25 percent on her investment income. To compute Mary's investment value of her mortgage interest obligations, labeled IV_M, we discount her after-tax cash flows at the market's after-tax OCC of 3 percent:

$$IV_M = \frac{(1 - .25)\$4}{1.03} + \frac{(1 - .25)\$4}{1.03^2} + \cdots = \frac{\$3}{0.03} = \$100$$

Mary can deduct the $4 of interest expense each year from her taxable income, thereby saving $1 in taxes each year as a result of her borrowing the mortgage (25% × $4 = $1, leaving her an after-tax interest cash outflow of only $3 each year). Mary's IV_M exactly equals the MV of the mortgage, because Mary is like the marginal investors in the debt market. Thus, the loan for her is a zero-NPV transaction, giving her $100 of cash up front in return for a future interest liability obligation that has a present value IV_M to her also of exactly $100.

The next investor is Abner. Abner is "tax-advantaged." He faces only a 20 percent marginal income tax rate on investment earnings, instead of the 25 percent rate faced by Mary and the marginal investors in the debt market. (Perhaps this is because Abner has

---

[27]The statement, and the analysis to follow in this section, presumes that the investor does not borrow "to excess." That is, we assume that capital structure is not sub-optimal in the sense of borrowing so much that financial distress or agency costs detract from the value of the overall investment. The question of optimal capital structure will be discussed in Chapter 15.

[28]In the real world, it is typical in the United States for municipal bonds to be priced at yields that are about three-quarters the yield of similar-maturity, similarly rated, corporate bonds, although this ratio does vary somewhat over time and should logically reflect changes in tax policy.

lower taxable income or lives in a state with no state-level income tax.) Of course, Abner faces the same market value as Mary or anyone else, so he will also receive $100 up front in the loan. But Abner's investment value of the subsequent loan liability, labeled IV_A, is different from Mary's because of his different tax status. Abner's IV_A value of his obligations is computed by discounting his "personalized" after-tax cash flows of the loan, at the market's after-tax OCC:

$$IV_A = \frac{(1 - 0.20)\$4}{1.03} + \frac{(1 - 0.20)\$4}{1.03^2} + \cdots = \frac{\$3.20}{0.03} = \$107$$

Abner can only save $0.80 in taxes each year as a result of the mortgage, because his tax rate is only 20 percent, leaving him with after-tax interest payments of $3.20 per year. Thus, for Abner, borrowing to finance his real estate investment is actually a negative NPV deal. He obtains $100 cash up front, but incurs an obligation that has an investment value to him of negative $107, for an IV-based NPV of negative $7.

Just the opposite case is provided by our third investor, Clarence. Clarence is tax-disadvantaged as an investor, perhaps not unlike a profitable "C corporation," which in effect subjects its investors to double taxation on investment earnings, once by the corporate income tax, and then by the personal income tax that is applied to realized investment income. For simplicity in this example, let's say Clarence faces a 30 percent tax rate. Thus, the investment value of the loan payment obligations Clarence incurs, labeled IV_C, is given by:

$$IV_C = \frac{(1 - 0.30)\$4}{1.03} + \frac{(1 - 0.30)\$4}{1.03^2} + \cdots = \frac{\$2.80}{0.03} = \$93$$

Thus, for Clarence, borrowing to finance his real estate investment is a positive NPV proposition. Apart from whatever leverage objectives he may have or other reasons to want to use debt to finance his real estate investment, the debt financing by itself provides a positive NPV viewed from Clarence's investment value perspective, even though it is unsubsidized (market rate) debt.

What we have just discovered is summarized graphically in our asset market model framework originally introduced in Exhibit 12-1 of Chapter 12, here for the present debt market example in Exhibit 14-5. Mary is a marginal borrower, while Abner and Clarence are both intramarginal, on opposite sides of the market. Borrowing to finance a real estate transaction normally is zero-NPV from a market value perspective (unless the debt is subsidized, non–market rate). From an investment value perspective, it is also zero NPV for investors who face

EXHIBIT 14-5 Market Value and Investment Value of Debt for Marginal and Intramarginal Investors Based on Tax Bracket

© OnCourse Learning

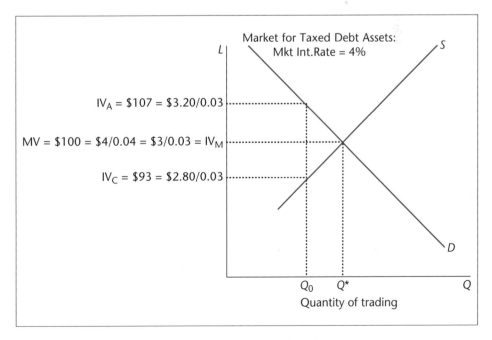

a marginal tax rate similar to the marginal investors in the debt market (which we suggested has traditionally been around 25 percent in the United States). For investors facing a lower tax rate, such as our tax-advantaged investor Abner, borrowing is negative NPV. (For example, this might be the case for many lower or even moderate income home purchasers.) But for investors facing an effectively higher tax rate than the marginal investors in the debt market, borrowing is itself a positive NPV transaction.

It is important to note, however, that even for high-tax-bracket investors, the magnitude of the positive NPV from debt financing is probably not very large compared to the size of the loan, and much less than the value of the interest tax shields (ITS) associated with the loan. For example, the present value of the ITS for each of our three investors is calculated below:

$$PV(ITS)_M = \frac{(0.25)\$4}{1.03} + \frac{(0.25)\$4}{1.03^2} + \cdots = \frac{\$1.00}{0.03} = \$33$$

$$PV(ITS)_A = \frac{(0.20)\$4}{1.03} + \frac{(0.20)\$4}{1.03^2} + \cdots = \frac{\$0.80}{0.03} = \$27$$

$$PV(ITS)_C = \frac{(0.30)\$4}{1.03} + \frac{(0.30)\$4}{1.03^2} + \cdots = \frac{\$1.20}{0.03} = \$40$$

Interest tax shields are worth most to the high-tax-bracket borrower, Clarence. But even to the low-tax-bracket borrower, Abner, they are worth 27 percent of the amount of the loan (in this perpetual loan scenario). Nevertheless, this does not make the loan a positive NPV transaction for Abner, and even for Clarence the NPV of the loan is only 7 percent of the loan value, compared to the ITS being worth 40 percent of the loan value. Of the present value of the ITS tax savings to these borrowers, $33 is offset by taxes paid by the marginal lender in the debt market. It is only the net effect of tax shields that remains in the private sector that redounds to the investment value in the private sector.

In a market-rate (unsubsidized) borrowing transaction, from an investment value (after-tax) perspective, it makes sense to think of the NPV for the borrower as being equal to the negative of the NPV to the government as a result of the loan. In the present example, the government will continue to receive $1 per year in income taxes from the marginal lender in the debt market, which has a present value of $33 (at the market after-tax OCC of 3 percent). It is only to the extent that the borrowing transaction results in a net change in the government's take that there can be net value created or lost in the private sector as a result of the borrowing transaction. And it is only to this extent that the borrowing transaction can have a non-zero NPV to the borrower, even from an IV perspective.[29]

Because this point may seem a bit counterintuitive, and is not widely understood in current real estate investment practice, it may be worth considering it a bit further. One way that investors may trick themselves into thinking that interest tax shields (and therefore borrowing to finance a real estate investment) are more valuable than they really are is by forgetting the dictum that after-tax cash flows should be discounted at *after-tax* discount rates. For example, Abner might look at the loan in our example as follows:

$$NPV(Financing)_A = 100 - \left(\frac{(1-0.20)4}{1.04} + \frac{(1-0.20)4}{1.04^2} + \cdots\right)$$

$$= 100 - \frac{3.20}{0.04} = 100 - 80 = +20$$

But it is inconsistent and wrong to discount after-tax cash flows at a before-tax OCC. This perspective ignores what is happening on the other side of the debt market, and will

---

[29]Value cannot be created from nothing. If no net value remains in the private sector (as a result of the borrowing transaction), then asset valuations in the private sector cannot gain overall as a result of the borrowing transaction. Positive net values in the property market (accruing to borrowers) would have to be offset by negative net values in the debt market (for lenders). But that would not be consistent with equilibrium across the two markets (property and debt). Prices would be bid up in the property market and bid down in the debt market (interest rates bid up) until there is zero net value in both markets (on the margin). Thus, effectively, the lender passes through the taxes of the *marginal* investor in the debt market to the borrower in the property market.

make it appear that even a low-tax bracket investor such as Abner would make a positive-NPV investment by borrowing money, when in fact that is not true.[30]

As you can see, correctly applying the APV procedure to separately value the NPV of the property and financing components of a real estate investment can help investors to avoid thinking that borrowing to finance the transaction is more valuable than it actually is. Excessive debt got real estate investors into big trouble in the 2008–2009 property market crash, as it did in previous market downturns (and as it did to many home-buyers as well). Of course, debt financing can be extremely useful, and in some cases quite valuable. We only want investors to think carefully and rigorously about its use. The APV procedure can be helpful in this regard. (We will note some other concerns about debt financing in our broader discussion of capital structure in Chapter 15. See also sections 7.4 and 12.2.)

The above analysis hopefully clarifies the interaction between the value of debt financing and the investor's tax rate for unsubsidized (market-rate) loans. But what about the case where the real estate investor can take advantage of seller financing or government-subsidy programs that enable borrowing at below-market interest rates?[31] In such cases, the debt will have a positive NPV for the borrower, viewed from both the MV and the IV perspectives. This can be quantified using the same methodology as we have been employing consistently in this section.

For example, suppose a seller offers a perpetual loan like the ones we have been considering, at a below-market interest rate of, say, 3.5 percent, when the market interest rate is 4 percent as we described above. Then, the NPV of the loan to the borrower from the market value perspective is:

$$NPV(MV) = \$100 - \left(\frac{\$3.50}{1.04} + \frac{\$3.50}{1.04^2} + \cdots\right) = \$100 - \frac{\$3.50}{0.04} = \$100 - \$88 = +\$12.$$

From the seller's perspective, the MV is just the opposite, negative \$12. In equilibrium in the market, the APV of the property-plus-loan deal will be driven by competition down to zero, which suggests that the property component of the deal alone will sell at a price \$12 more (per \$100 of subsidized loan) than it otherwise would. This would result in the overall MV-based APV of the deal as follows:

$$APV = NP(Property) + NPV(Financing) = -\$12 + \$12 = 0.$$

Thus, if you evaluate each component of the deal separately, the property component itself (without any debt) will appear to be selling at a price that results in a negative NPV. (Otherwise, why would the seller offer such financing?)

From an investment value perspective, the subsidized loan NPV calculations are shown below for all three of our previous borrowers:

$$NPV(IV_M) = 100 - \left(\frac{(1-0.25)3.50}{1.03} + \frac{(1-0.25)3.50}{(1.03)^2} + \cdots\right) = 100 - \frac{2.63}{0.03} = 100 - 88 = +\$12.$$

$$NPV(IV_A) = 100 - \left(\frac{(1-0.20)3.50}{1.03} + \frac{(1-0.20)3.50}{(1.03)^2} + \cdots\right) = 100 - \frac{2.80}{0.03} = 100 - 93 = +\$7.$$

$$NPV(IV_C) = 100 - \left(\frac{(1-0.30)3.50}{1.03} + \frac{(1-0.30)3.50}{(1.03)^2} + \cdots\right) = 100 - \frac{2.45}{0.03} = 100 - 82 = +\$18.$$

---

[30]Another common mistake is to apply *each* investor's own personalized after-tax OCC as the discount rate. For example, Abner would discount the loan's after-tax cash flows at a rate of $(1 - 0.20)4\% = 3.2\%$. This seems intuitive at first, as it does represent Abner's after-tax OCC on a similar investment. However, as described in section 12.1 when we introduced the concept of investment value, it makes more sense in computing IV to take the OCC *from the capital market*. If one applies each investor's own personal OCC to each investor's own personal after-tax cash flows, then a market-rate loan will *always* have an NPV of zero, from an IV perspective, for *all* investors no matter what their tax situation is. This violates the spirit and meaning of "IV," which should quantify a higher value for tax-advantaged investors than for tax-disadvantaged investors on the buy side, and correspondingly lower values for tax-advantaged investors and higher values for tax-disadvantaged investors on the sell side (as in the case of borrowers in a loan transaction).

[31]For example, some government programs allow real estate projects to be financed using tax-exempt municipal bond debt.

Note that the loan has a positive NPV from the IV perspective of all of our borrowers, though less so for the tax-advantaged investor and more so for the tax-disadvantaged investor, as before.

It should also not surprise you that the NPV of the subsidized loan viewed from the IV perspective differs from that of the MV perspective for all but the marginal borrower. Regarding the implications of this for how much more each investor should be willing to pay for a property that comes with subsidized debt, recall our discussion in section 12.1.2 about the two philosophies for dealing with the situation in which MV and IV carry different NPV investment-decision implications, and consider the entire package including both the loan and the property it is attached to.

For example, in the case of Abner, a conservative approach would suggest that he should not pay more for the property than the lesser of $7 more than his IV of the property, or $12 more than the MV of the property (per $100 of subsidized loan amount), with the latter case presuming that the loan is transferable (and ignoring transactions costs). The more aggressive philosophy would allow Abner to pay up to the maximum of those two amounts. The $12 MV of the loan deal is relevant for Abner only if the loan is transferable, because that, in theory, enables him to buy the property with the loan and then turn around and remarket the property together with its subsidized financing for a price equal to the property MV plus the loan's $12 NPV.[32]

*14.3.6 Example Application of APV to Marginal Investor

Let us now bring together the points from the preceding two sections to see how they can be used to analyze a typical investment property market, by returning once again to our apartment property example. Back in section 14.3.2, we discussed how we could derive an estimate of the market's after-tax OCC for the levered equity investment from knowledge of the property's market value and assumptions about the characteristics of the typical marginal investor. Assuming the cash flows in Exhibit 14-3 are representative of the marginal investor in the market for our apartment building that has a market value of $1 million, our estimate of the equity after-tax OCC was 6.44 percent for the 10-year IRR, resulting in the $250,000 valuation of the equity.

Now let us suppose that while this investor is indeed marginal in the property market, she is intramarginal in the debt market. In particular, let's suppose that our apartment property investor is in a higher marginal income tax bracket than the marginal investor in the debt market. This will make our apartment investor intramarginal on the "sell" (i.e., borrow) side of the debt market, not unlike Clarence in the example in the previous section, obtaining some positive NPV from borrowing. To be more specific, let us suppose that by comparison of market yields in the municipal bond market and the corporate bond and mortgage markets, we can ascertain that the marginal investor in the mortgage market faces an effective tax rate of 25 percent on investment income. This compares with the 35 percent tax bracket for ordinary income faced by our marginal apartment investor, relevant for evaluating debt interest tax shields. Exhibit 14-6 shows how we can use this knowledge of the after-tax OCC of debt combined with our APV = 0 equilibrium condition to derive the implied investment value for the marginal investor of the property itself without any debt.

First, we compute the NPV of the loan component of the marginal investor's deal. If the loan's interest rate is 5.5 percent, then the implied after-tax OCC for this debt investment is $(1 - 0.25) \times 5.5\% = 4.13\%$. If the mortgage were issued by a tax-exempt municipality, it would presumably trade at a 4.13 percent yield in the municipal bond market. We discount our apartment investor's personalized after-tax debt service cash flows (reflecting

---

[32]For finite duration loans, the NPV of subsidized loans will be less than what is implied in the present perpetuity example and, from the IV perspective, will differ from the MV perspective, even for the marginal borrower. As the loan term becomes short, the NPV of a subsidized loan from an IV perspective converges toward (1-T) times the NPV of the loan from a MV (before-tax) perspective, where "T" is the borrower's tax rate. This suggests that sellers might not achieve a property price above property market value to the full extent of the MV-based NPV of the loan subsidy. The deal might appear favorable to the buyer on a before-tax basis but be just zero-NPV on an after-tax basis.

Start with the known after-tax OCC of debt observable from muni bond market. (Here, 4.13%, based on 25% marginal tax.)

Apprec.Rate =	1.00%
Yield =	6.00%
Income Tax Rate =	35.00%
Debt Mkt Margl Tax Rate =	25.00%

Bldg.Val/Prop.Val =	80.00%
Depreciable Life =	27.5 years
CGTax Rate =	15.00%
DepRecapture Rate =	25.00%

Loan =	$750,000
Int =	5.50%
Amort/yr =	$2,000

IV(loan liability) @4.13% = −$717,119

Year	(1) Prop.Val	(2) NOI	(3) CI	(4) PBTCF	(5) tax w/out shields	(6) DTS	(7) (4)−(5)+(6) PATCF	(8) LoanBal	(9) Loan DS	(10) ITS	(11) (4)−(9) EBTCF	(12) (7)−(9)+(10) EATCF	(13) (9)−(10) LoanATCFs
0	$1,000,000			($1,000,000)			($967,119)	$750,000	($750,000)		($250,000)	($250,000)	($717,119)
1	$1,010,000	$60,000	$0	$60,000	$21,000	$10,182	$49,182	$748,000	$43,250	$14,438	$16,750	$20,369	$28,813
2	$1,020,100	$60,600	$0	$60,600	$21,210	$10,182	$49,572	$746,000	$43,140	$14,399	$17,460	$20,831	$28,741
3	$1,030,301	$61,206	$50,000	$11,206	$21,422	$10,182	($34)	$744,000	$43,030	$14,361	($31,824)	($28,704)	$28,670
4	$1,040,604	$61,818	$0	$61,818	$21,636	$10,182	$50,364	$742,000	$42,920	$14,322	$18,898	$21,766	$28,598
5	$1,051,010	$62,436	$0	$62,436	$21,853	$10,182	$50,765	$740,000	$42,810	$14,284	$19,626	$22,239	$28,527
6	$1,061,520	$63,061	$0	$63,061	$22,071	$10,182	$51,171	$738,000	$42,700	$14,245	$20,361	$22,716	$28,455
7	$1,072,135	$63,691	$0	$63,691	$22,292	$10,182	$51,581	$736,000	$42,590	$14,207	$21,101	$23,198	$28,384
8	$1,082,857	$64,328	$50,000	$14,328	$22,515	$10,182	$1,995	$734,000	$42,480	$14,168	($28,152)	($26,317)	$28,312
9	$1,093,685	$64,971	$0	$64,971	$22,740	$10,182	$52,413	$732,000	$42,370	$14,130	$22,601	$24,173	$28,241
10	$1,104,622	$65,621	$0	$1,170,243	$23,661	($62,545)	$1,084,037	$730,000	$772,260	$14,091	$397,983	$325,868	$758,169
IRR of above CF Stream =				6.04%			4.76%		5.50%		7.40%	6.44%	4.13%

Then back out the value of the property without debt using the APV = 0 equilibrium condition for marginal investor.

0 = APV + NPV(prop) + NPV(loan) = (X − $1,000,000) + ($750,000 − $717,119);
→X = $967,119 = IV(prop);
→AT(unlevered)OCC = 4.76%

EXHIBIT 14-6 Apartment Property Example Valuation by Components for Marginal Investor
© OnCourse Learning

her 35 percent tax rate) shown in column (13) of Exhibit 14-6.[33] Discounted at the 4.13 percent OCC, we determine that the present value of the loan obligation payments is $717,119 from the IV perspective of this investor. Thus, the investor obtains $750,000 cash up front from the loan, in return for a liability that has a present value of $717,119, resulting in an IV-based NPV of the loan of positive $32,881.

Given that the apartment investor portrayed in Exhibit 14-6 is marginal in the property market, we know that the APV of the deal must equal zero. Hence, the NPV of the property component of the deal without any debt must be negative $32,881. Given that the market value of the property is $1 million , this implies that the investment value of the property to the marginal investor must be $967,119 without any debt. The result will be:

$$\begin{aligned} APV &= NPV(Property) + NPV(Financing) \\ &= (\$967,119 - \$1,000,000) + (\$750,000 - \$717,119) \\ &= -\$32,881 + \$32,881 = 0. \end{aligned}$$

Knowing that the property by itself without any debt is worth $967,119 to the marginal investor in the property market implies that the market's after-tax *unlevered* OCC is 4.76 percent, the IRR of an investment of $967,119 that returns the property-level after-tax cash flows shown in column (7) of Exhibit 14-6. This compares to the property-level before-tax OCC of 6.04 percent that we noted back in section 14.2.5 and Exhibit 14-3.

Note that this does *not* imply that one could buy the property for $967,119 if one did not take out a loan. The market price of the property is $1 million and this is its equilibrium value in the marketplace. The implication is that if you face a personal tax rate above 25 percent on your marginal income (from such a property investment), then the acquisition at market value will be negative NPV from your IV perspective *unless* you take out a loan.

This information can now be used to help us dissect the apartment deal for the typical marginal investor using valuation by components and value additivity. In Exhibit 14-7, we have presented the same cash flow components as in Exhibit 14-3, only now we are grouping these into two categories: those that are relatively risky, because they are subject to the volatility of the property and rental markets, and those that are relatively safe or fixed, because they are essentially contractual or statutory. The former category includes the PBTCF and the tax without shields in columns (4) and (5). The latter includes the depreciation tax shields and the loan cash flows in columns (6) and (13). Together, these two categories add up to the total after-tax cash flows of the equity investor.

To value the investment by components, we discount each type of cash flow stream at the market OCC that is appropriate for its type of risk, and then add back together the resulting component present values. As we are dealing here with after-tax cash flows, we use after-tax discount rates. Assuming the investor is typical on the margin in the market, the IRRs shown at the bottom of the cash flow columns in the exhibit are the market's after-tax OCC rates appropriate for each cash flow component. Thus, the relatively risky cash flows are discounted at the 4.76 percent rate that is the IRR on the PATCFs in column (4),[34] while the relatively safe cash flows are discounted at the 4.13 percent rate that is the IRR on the loan after-tax cash flows in column (13). The risky cash flows thus have a present value of $933,257. The relatively safe cash flows have a value of $683,592, negative to the investor. The net difference of $249,664 is essentially the same as the $250,000 value of the equity that is implied by discounting the EATCFs directly lumped together at their market

---

[33]Recall that the interest component of the debt service is, for example in the first year: $750,000 × 0.055 = $41,250, thereby providing interest tax shield cash flow of $41,250 × 0.35 = $14,437.50 (in col. 10), resulting in first year loan ATCF (outflow) for the equity investor of the total debt service (col. 9) $43,250 (including amortization) minus the ITS of $14,437.50, which equals the $28,812.50 in column 13 (as rounded).

[34]Indeed, for the reasons noted in the previous section, it will often be easier, and less prone to error, to quantify *NPV(Property)* and *NPV(Financing)* separately and add these two components, rather than attempting to quantify directly the NPV of the levered equity. At a minimum, the APV approach provides a good check on any direct quantification of the levered equity value. In particular, direct evaluation of *NPV(Equity)* should not generally imply violation of the APV = 0 rule for MV-based valuations, unless there is a clear reason to believe that this rule does not apply. (See section 14.3.4.)

	Apprec.Rate =	1.00%
	Yield =	6.00%
	Income Tax Rate =	35.00%
	Debt Mkt Margl Tax Rate =	25.00%

	Bldg.Val/Prop.Val =	80.00%
	Depreciable Life =	27.5 years
	CGTax Rate =	15.00%
	DepRecapture Rate =	25.00%

	Loan =	$750,000
	Int =	5.50%
	Amort/yr =	$2,000

Year	(1) Prop.Val	(2) NOI	(3) CI	(4) PBTCF	(5) tax w/out shields	(6) DTS	(7) (4)−(5)+(6) PATCF	(8) LoanBal	(9) Loan DS	(10) ITS	(11) (4)−(9) EBTCF	(12) (7)−(9)+(10) EATCF	(13) (9)−(10) LoanATCFs
0	$1,000,000			($1,000,000)			($967,119)	$750,000	($750,000)		($250,000)	($250,000)	($717,119)
1	$1,010,000	$60,000	$0	$60,000	$21,000	$10,182	$49,182	$748,000	$43,250	$14,438	$16,750	$20,369	$28,813
2	$1,020,100	$60,600	$0	$60,600	$21,210	$10,182	$49,572	$746,000	$43,140	$14,399	$17,460	$20,831	$28,741
3	$1,030,301	$61,206	$50,000	$11,206	$21,422	$10,182	($34)	$744,000	$43,030	$14,361	($31,824)	($28,704)	$28,670
4	$1,040,604	$61,818	$0	$61,818	$21,636	$10,182	$50,364	$742,000	$42,920	$14,322	$18,898	$21,766	$28,598
5	$1,051,010	$62,436	$0	$62,436	$21,853	$10,182	$50,765	$740,000	$42,810	$14,284	$19,626	$22,239	$28,527
6	$1,061,520	$63,061	$0	$63,061	$22,071	$10,182	$51,171	$738,000	$42,700	$14,245	$20,361	$22,716	$28,455
7	$1,072,135	$63,691	$0	$63,691	$22,292	$10,182	$51,581	$736,000	$42,590	$14,207	$21,101	$23,198	$28,384
8	$1,082,857	$64,328	$50,000	$14,328	$22,515	$10,182	$1,995	$734,000	$42,480	$14,168	($28,152)	($26,317)	$28,312
9	$1,093,685	$64,971	$0	$64,971	$22,740	$10,182	$52,413	$732,000	$42,370	$14,130	$22,601	$24,173	$28,241
10	$1,104,622	$65,621	$0	$1,170,243	$23,661	($62,545)	$1,084,037	$730,000	$772,260	$14,091	$397,983	$325,868	$758,169
IRR of above CF Stream =				6.04%			4.76%		5.50%		7.40%	6.44%	4.13%

PBTCF & tax w/out shields are relatively high risk: OCC = 4.76%.

DTS & loan ATCF are relatively low risk (legally fixed): OCC = 4.13%.

EXHIBIT 14-7 Apartment Property Example Cash Flow Components Grouped by Risk Category
© OnCourse Learning

333

after-tax levered OCC of 6.44 percent, as we saw regarding the investment value for the marginal investor described in section 14.3.2 and Exhibit 14-3.

When we are dealing with market value, or investment value for marginal investors, the value additivity and valuation by components approach of Exhibit 14-7 should, in principle, produce exactly the same equity value as direct valuation of the equity as represented in column (12) of Exhibit 14-3 and the market value as discussed in section 14.3.2. If there is a discrepancy between these two approaches, this suggests some sort of disequilibrium or "super normal" profit opportunity across the markets for property and debt. In reality, of course, real estate valuations cannot be determined so precisely. Combined with trading costs, this prevents minor valuation discrepancies from being immediately "arbitraged" away. Nevertheless, the two approaches are useful as a crosscheck on one another to determine normative valuation. Furthermore, this valuation by components procedure can be applied in more complex circumstances to evaluate more uniquely structured financial arrangements, for example with more than one layer or type of debt, provided one can come up with a reasonable estimate of the appropriate OCCs to apply as discount rates. To pursue this framework further to see how it can be applied to estimate the IV for an intramarginal investor (such as a tax-exempt pension fund), see Appendix 14B on this book's CD or electronic resources.

14.4 Corporate Real Estate: The Own-versus-Rent Decision

In the real estate investment industry, the term "corporate real estate" refers to real estate owned by non-real estate corporations or companies, that is, firms that are not primarily in the business of real estate development or investment. In most countries, this includes a large amount of commercial and industrial property. A very important question in corporate real estate management is the **buy-versus-lease** (or, more generally, **own-versus-rent**) **decision**. Broadly, this is the question of how much space, and *which* space, should the company *own* as opposed to *rent*. A corporation may face this question from either the buy or sell side, as the possibility of engaging in sale-leaseback transactions for space the company already owns enables consideration of the sale of corporate property without giving up the necessary usage and control of the space.

There are many considerations in answering the own-versus-rent question, both at a macro policy level and at the micro-level of specific space decisions. Many of these considerations are beyond the scope of this text.[35] However, there is an important financial economics component to the buy-versus-lease question. Whatever other considerations are important in a given own-versus-rent question, it is at a minimum also a micro-level real estate investment decision. Should the corporation invest in a given real property asset (that it would use) or not (and therefore rent the space)?

Viewed from this perspective, we hope it is clear that the after-tax levered equity investment analysis framework we have presented in this chapter in section 14.3 is quite relevant to analyzing the corporate own-versus-rent decision. Indeed, from this perspective, holding the underlying real estate investment economics neutral (i.e., assuming market value pricing), the impact of the decision on the value of the corporation will be driven by the particular income tax situation that the corporation's investors face. Assuming that the real estate in question would be purchased (or sold, in the case of a sale-leaseback) at fair market value (zero NPV transaction from a market value perspective), the NPV from an investment value perspective will essentially equal the negative of the change in the present value of the future tax revenues the government can expect to receive as a result of the property tenure status. The framework presented in section 14.3 when applied to a corporate own-versus-rent question will show this impact.[36]

The details of the application of this methodology in this context are presented in Appendix 14C on the CD accompanying this book (where there is also an example spreadsheet application).

---

[35]Commercial leases are discussed from a property owner's perspective in Chapter 30. For a broader perspective from the corporate users' side, see, for example, O'Mara (1999).

[36]This perspective dates back to Lewellen, Long, and McConnell (1976), and Myers, Dill, and Bautista (1976).

Here in the text, we will content ourselves with enumerating the key guiding principles of the own-versus-rent evaluation:

- Discount after-tax cash flows at after-tax discount rates to compute NPV.
- Include both levels of taxation: corporate and personal.
- Discount cash flow components at OCC rates reflecting their risk (not always at the corporate WACC).

These principles can be applied using the *valuation by components* and *adjusted present value* (APV) procedures described in section 14.3. This will provide a coherent framework that ensures consistency of the own-versus-rent evaluation with equilibrium (market) pricing within and across the three asset markets relevant to the decision: the property market, the bond market, and the stock market in which the corporation's shares (do or could) trade. The inclusion in the analysis framework of both levels of taxation, corporate and personal, is more obviously necessary in the case of real estate than other types of corporate assets, because real estate assets trade directly in a well-functioning asset market in which the marginal participants typically face less overall taxation than investors in profitable taxed corporations. (Recall our analysis of the bond market in section 14.3.5 in which we likened our "tax-disadvantaged investor" to a corporation that results in double-taxation to its investors.)

When these principles are applied to the typical own-versus-rent decision of a profitable taxed corporation in the United States under the tax rules prevailing in the early 2000s, the result is typically that it is better for the corporation to lease than to own, from a tax perspective. However, the magnitude of the value impact is typically rather small when one also considers the effect of property ownership on the corporation's debt capacity (recall that borrowing is a positive NPV transaction for the tax-disadvantaged investor). And there are particular circumstances where the evaluation can turn out the other way, depending on the specific parameters of the micro-level decision, such as the duration of the anticipated corporate usage of the space, the magnitude of depreciation allowances that can be used, the price/rent multiple in the current property market, and both the expected capital gains and capital gains tax rates (among other factors). It is also important to recognize that other considerations besides the narrow tax-based financial considerations considered here can be important in the final decision about corporate ownership of a given space.[37] If a corporation should decide that it wants to reduce its exposure to real estate market investment risk while continuing to own its corporate real estate, a new mechanism for accomplishing this is beginning to be marketed in some countries, in the form of real estate index return swaps, an investment derivative product that allows hedging of commercial real estate property market risk. This innovation will be discussed in Chapter 26.

14.5 Chapter Summary

Chapter 14 extended the basic micro-level investment analysis and evaluation framework of Part IV to the equity-after-tax level, going from PBTCFs to EATCFs. While equity after-tax analysis is in principle a straightforward extension of the framework presented in Part IV, in practice it is often complicated and difficult to know exactly the correct cash flow and discount rate assumptions to apply. Fortunately, the widespread existence of a well-functioning property market often makes it possible in real estate practice to take a shortcut around these difficulties by working at the PBT level and using the APV rule. More generally, we saw how fundamental economic principles can be applied to develop a rigorous

---

[37]For example, Fisher (2004) analyzes a sample of corporate sale-leaseback decisions to show that the classical theory of the firm model of corporate control over proprietary processes in part explains the preference for long-term versus short-term leases. Direct ownership of the space or longer term leases are used only when the space has more unique characteristics that particularly benefit the lessee corporation, and sale-leasebacks increase shareholder value when the real estate is not specialized to the corporation, as signaled by relatively short-term leases.

framework within which real estate investment can be analyzed and understood at the equity after-tax level, including a rational micro-level investment decision methodology, and application to the corporate real estate own-versus-rent decision. In presenting this framework, Chapter 14 continued our progression, begun in Chapter 13, from the property level to the owner level of analysis, by adding the basics of income tax considerations in the investment analysis. As always, the methodology presented in this chapter is simply a reasonably practical manner to apply three abiding principles: (1) wealth maximization as the objective of the decision; (2) opportunity cost as the basis for quantifying wealth impacts; and (3) the relevant markets (capital, property, debt) provide the source and evidence regarding what are the true opportunity costs. The next chapter will now turn to examine in more depth the issue of capital structure, the method of financing, real estate investment.

KEY TERMS

property-level before-tax cash flows
owner-level after-tax cash flows
depreciation expense
book value
accumulated depreciation
capital expenditures
debt amortization
capital gains tax (CGT)

straight-line depreciation
debt service
interest expense
tax loss
tax shield or tax shelter
equity-after-tax cash flow (EATCF)
equity-before-tax cash flow (EBTCF)
depreciation tax shields (DTS)

interest tax shields (ITS)
depreciable life
ordinary income tax
property-before-tax (PBT) approach
value additivity principle
adjusted present value (APV)
buy-versus-lease (or own-versus-rent) decision

STUDY QUESTIONS

Conceptual Questions

14.1. What is the difference between the property's before-tax cash flow and the equity before-tax cash flow?

14.2. How does depreciation shield real estate investors from taxation?

14.3. How can your after-tax cash flow be higher than your before-tax cash flow in a real estate investment?

14.4. Why is the distinction between operating expenses and capital expenditures an important one from the IRS's perspective?

14.5. Two rookie real estate investors are having a heated discussion about how to calculate annual equity after-tax cash flow (EATCF) on an income-property investment. The two agree that $EATCF = EBTCF − income\ tax$, and that $income\ tax = (taxable\ income) \times (tax\ rate)$, but are at odds over the calculation of taxable income. Investor #1 believes that $taxable\ income = EBTCF + principal + CI\ reserves − depreciation$, whereas investor #2 feels this is incorrect and argues that $taxable\ income = NOI − interest − depreciation$. Who is correct? Explain.

14.6. What are the two components of "taxes due on sale" for a taxable investor selling an income property? Explain how each is determined.

14.7. What is meant by the adjusted present value (APV) approach to extending the NPV rule to encompass project financing? What is the relationship of the APV technique to the value additivity principle?

14.8. In valuing income property rigorously with discounted cash flow analysis, is it necessary for "marginal" investors to use after-tax cash flows? Why or why not? What about "intramarginal" investors?

14.9. Explain whether the following statement is true or false and why: One reason to borrow money to finance a real estate investment is that you obtain valuable interest tax shields that save you from paying some taxes you would otherwise owe.

14.10. a. Why do the interest tax shields associated with debt financing have a positive value for the typical profitable corporation but not for the typical taxed individual investing directly in the property market?

b. Answer the same question in part (a) but for REITs.

14.11. If income taxes were the only consideration, would you expect to find profitable taxed corporations owning much of their own real estate? Why or why not?

Quantitative Problems

14.12. The NOI is $850,000, the debt service is $600,000 of which $550,000 is interest, the depreciation expense is $350,000, and the income tax rate is 35%.

a. What is the before-tax cash flow to the equity investor (EBTCF) if there are no capital improvement expenditures or reversion items this period?

b. What is the after-tax cash flow to the equity investor if the income tax rate is 35%?

14.13. A nonresidential commercial property that cost $500,000 is considered to have 30% of its total value attributable to land. What is the annual depreciation expense chargeable against taxable income?

14.14. Determine the acquisition cost of an apartment property if the annual depreciation deduction will be $170,000, assuming 20% of the cost is allocated to land and 80% to structure at the time of purchase.

14.15. Consider the following information for the first year of a proposed property acquisition: effective gross income (EGI) is estimated to be $1.5 million; operating expenses are $450,000; $25,000 will be put into a capital improvement reserve account; the investor has a 35% marginal tax rate. The property is going to be acquired with a 65% loan to value ratio mortgage, interest-only with a 10-year term and 6% interest rate. The acquisition cost implies an 8.4% going-in cap rate, based on first-year NOI. It is anticipated that 25% of the acquisition cost will be allocated to land for tax purposes. Depreciation is straight-line over 39 years. Determine the first-year equity after-tax cash flow (EATCF).

14.16. Ten years ago, an investor acquired a property for $14 million. At the time of acquisition, the land value was estimated to be $2.1 million. The depreciation (cost recovery) period for the building is 27.5 years with depreciation being straight-line. Each year since she acquired the property, the investor has set aside $100,000 in a capital reserve account. The estimated current market value of the property is $20 million. If the investor were to sell the property today, what would be her total federal income taxes due at sale assuming that depreciation recapture is taxed at 25% and capital gains at 15%? For simplicity, assume that the entire amount in the capital reserves account would be spent now, immediately before the property sale. Selling expenses will be 4% of the sale price.

14.17. Consider an apartment property that costs $400,000, of which $300,000 is structure value (the rest is land). Suppose an investor expects to hold this property for five years and then sell it for at least what he paid for it (without putting any significant capital into the property). If the investor's marginal income tax rate is 35%, and depreciation recapture is taxed at 25%, what is the present value, as of the time of purchase, of the depreciation tax shields obtained directly by this investor during the five-year expected holding period (including the payback in the reversion)? Assume taxes are paid annually, with the first tax payment due one year from present, and assume that DTS for this investor are effectively riskless, and the investor's after-tax borrowing rate is 5%.

14.18. Consider a commercial (nonresidential) property that costs $1 million with an initial before-tax yield of 9% (based on NOI) and an expected growth rate of 2.5% per year (in income and value). Ignoring capital improvements and selling expenses, develop a 10-year proforma for before-tax and after-tax property and equity cash flows. The relevant tax rates are 35% on annual operations, 15% for capital gains, and 25% for depreciation recapture. Assume mortgage financing of 75% of the property price with a 10% interest-only loan, and that land is worth 20% of the property value.

    a. Use the proforma to determine the ex ante before-tax IRR of the unlevered property investment.

    b. Use the proforma to determine the after-tax IRR of the unlevered property investment.

    c. Use the ratio of the ATIRR calculated in (b) divided by the BTIRR calculated in (a) to determine the after-tax borrowing rate for the investor (by applying this ratio to the loan rate).

    d. Apply the after-tax borrowing rate you just calculated to determine the present value of the DTS during the projected 10-year holding period (including the payback of the DTS in the reversion).

    e. Compute the implicit PV (DTS) component in the reversion resale price of the property by treating the present value of the DTS you computed in (d) as a constant-growth perpetuity that recurs once every 10 years with a growth rate of 2.5% per year and a discount rate to present value equal to the ATIRR you calculated in (b).

    f. Add the answers to (d) and (e) to arrive at the total component of DTS in the value of the property, as a percentage of the property value.

    g. Compute the before-tax ex ante IRR of the levered investment in this property.

    h. Compute the after-tax ex ante IRR of the levered equity in this property.

    i. Compute the ratio of the AT/BT in the levered IRR, and note the difference between this ratio and the unlevered equivalent. Do you think this is an argument for debt financing for this property investment for this investor?

14.19. (APV Decision Rule) A seller has offered you a $1.5 million interest-only seven-year loan at 6% (annual payments), when market interest rates on such loans are 7%. You face a 35% marginal income tax rate.

    a. Basing your decision on market values, how much more should you be willing to pay for the property than you otherwise think it is worth, due to the financing offer?

    b. Answer the same question only now basing your answer on investment value rather than market value. You may assume that the investor is typical of the marginal investors in the property market, and faces a tax rate similar to that of marginal investors in the bond market.

15

REAL ESTATE INVESTMENT CAPITAL STRUCTURE

CHAPTER OUTLINE

LEARNING OBJECTIVES

After reading this chapter, you should understand:

➲ What is meant by capital structure and the major pros and cons for the use of debt financing of real estate equity investments for different types of investors.

➲ What is meant by an equity capital constraint and how this can affect the value of debt financing.

➲ The relationship between the use of debt financing and such considerations as management incentives, investor liquidity, and inflation.

➲ The costs of financial distress and how these are affected by the use of debt.

➲ Typical capital structures used in micro-level real estate investment (project-level financing).

C hapter 15 continues our exploration of the role of debt in the real estate equity investment, begun in the preceding two chapters, and moves beyond simple debt to consider some other typical types of finance vehicles used in real estate project finance. In this chapter, we will consider both the big picture of why different types of investors might want to (or not want to) employ debt and other similar vehicles to finance their real estate investments, as well as examine more "nuts and bolts" of how micro-level capital structure (project finance) is typically done in the global institutional real estate investment business. These questions are traditionally considered in corporate finance under the topic of **capital structure**, which is classically defined as the relative use of debt versus equity financing of publicly traded corporations, including the closely related question of how much financing should be externally sourced versus internally generated from retained earnings. Our purpose in the present chapter is to examine this topic particularly from the perspective of real estate investment and real estate investors. (Additional discussion relevant particularly to REITs capital structure will be addressed in Chapter 23.)

As usual, some of the peculiar aspects of real estate, and the context in which real estate investment typically occurs, bring some unique considerations regarding capital structure. For example, much real estate investment is made directly, that is, by **ultimate investors** themselves or via relatively passive pass-through vehicles such as partnerships or funds. Thus, we will focus here primarily at the micro-level of individual deals or projects, which is the level at which capital structure and financing is often addressed in the real estate investment business. Also, the nature of the underlying physical assets—which are relatively easy for outsiders to observe, understand, and evaluate (thanks in part to a well-functioning direct market for these assets)—has implications for the use of secured debt and other such project financing vehicles. It is interesting to see how various types of investors and investment vehicles can be combined to structure the financing of complex deals, such as large scale real estate development projects, so as to allocate to each class of investor the type of risk and return they are seeking for their investment in combination with the type of control and incentives that will facilitate the successful investment outcome of the overall project. Finally, we will briefly address changes in typical deal-financing structures before and after the financial crisis and property market collapse of 2008–2009.

The plan of attack in Chapter 15 is to first survey the major issues relevant to the use of debt in real estate investment, and then to focus on the nuts and bolts of more complex capital structures. We have already discussed some of the important issues regarding the use of debt in our discussion of leverage in Chapter 13 and in our analysis of equity after-tax investment in Chapter 14. There we noted that real estate equity is a very different investment product from real estate debt, and some of these differences are magnified by the use of leverage. For example, the use of debt financing will typically increase the risk and average total return in the equity investment, especially the growth component of that return. These characteristics may be appealing to certain investors. Our discussion in Chapter 14 also treated at the micro-level the classic mainstay of corporate finance capital structure analysis, the relationship between debt financing and the investor's income taxes, suggesting there that the tax-based value of debt financing may be less than is often believed.

In this chapter, we will introduce some further considerations. We will begin with a consideration of the implications of equity capital constraints. This topic is often skipped or lightly passed over in corporate finance textbooks. Large publicly traded corporations do not usually face a constraint on their availability of equity capital for financing good investments. But this topic is worthy of consideration for many real estate investors. Next, we will introduce several other issues that can be important, such as the costs of financial distress and the roles of liquidity, management incentives, and inflation. Finally, we will zero in on the nuts and bolts level again, this time presenting typical complex capital structures that gained prominence for project-level finance in the institutional investment world before the financial crisis of 2008, including more types of capital than just straight equity and straight debt.

15.1 Debt When There Is an Equity Capital Constraint

Large publicly traded corporations can almost always raise capital rather easily to finance positive NPV investment opportunities, and they usually have a choice of raising either equity capital or debt capital. For example, equity capital can be raised in the public markets through new stock issuance, or it can be raised privately through joint ventures. Individual investors and tax-exempt institutions, on the other hand, may not have this kind of freedom. If they want to expand their investments beyond what their own equity can provide, debt may effectively be their only alternative. Even their ability to borrow money may be sharply constrained unless the debt is secured by tangible assets such as real estate.

In such cases, debt financing represents a way to break through an **equity capital constraint**. But why would this be valuable? Why should investors *want* to invest more capital than they already own by themselves? Apart from the leverage issue already discussed (i.e., to move up and out along the security market line to an investment position of greater expected return but greater risk), there are two reasons: (1) to take advantage of positive NPV investment opportunities and (2) to diversify their holdings of risky assets. Let's consider each of these in turn.

15.1.1 Debt to Obtain Positive Equity NPV

Although positive NPV opportunities may be rare when evaluated from a market value (MV) perspective, we suggested in Chapter 12 (and to some extent in some circumstances in Chapter 14) that positive NPV opportunities may be available from an investment value (IV) perspective for entrepreneurial or tax-advantaged developers and investors. Furthermore, the "lumpiness" of real estate investment, typically requiring the purchase of "whole assets," often presents investors with capital requirements greater than their available equity. In short, but for the use of debt financing, they would have to forgo positive NPV opportunities.

Related to this point is a consideration that is often particularly important at the level of small-to moderate-scale individual real estate entrepreneurs. This is the possibility of *leveraging the investor's own "human capital."* The point is that for some investors, the effect of leverage can extend beyond the leveraging of their financial capital invested in commercial property. It can also leverage their human capital in the form of their property management or development abilities.

In general, the term **human capital** refers to productive abilities and skills, or valuable expertise, that individuals have acquired that can be used to generate income. Such income, the "return" on human capital, is typically in the form of wages or salaries or other earned income, but in general it may come in any form of wealth enhancement. Some individuals possess human capital in their ability to manage or develop commercial property. For such individuals, acquisition of such property is not only an investment of their financial capital, but also a means to obtain a return on their human capital. By owning or developing property, they effectively guarantee themselves some degree of employment as property managers or developers. In the presence of the previously noted constraints and difficulties involved in the acquisition of equity capital, the use of debt financing allows such individuals to purchase larger physical quantities of property than would otherwise be the case. This allows them to perform more property management or development services and thereby obtain more return on their human capital.

Although small companies are most likely to face a capital constraint, larger companies can also use debt to lever property management or real estate development human capital within the firm. Real estate operating companies (REOCs) and vertically integrated REITs that are quite large in scale often argue, in effect, that their unique real estate skills enable them to "create value."

How would the leveraging of human capital show up in the quantitative DCF and NPV mechanics we described in previous chapters? In practice, it may be difficult to distinguish this component. However, in principle, the present value of the return on human capital should show up as a component in a positive NPV calculation of an appropriate deal at the micro-level, evaluated from the IV perspective. Investors' human capital gives them a unique ability to profit from a given investment. One way to account for this is to define multiple "profit centers" for the firm, some of which derive from operations as distinct from passive investment. Thus, the property "operating expenses" that are pure cash outflows from the investment perspective may contain an element of profit from the operational perspective. This is most obvious when the firm engages in property or development operations "for fee" for other property owners, but it may also be a component of investment profitability for particular investors.

Recall from our discussion of IV and MV in Chapter 12 that the NPV of a property acquisition equals IV − MV when evaluated from an IV perspective. And recall that, at the level of individual deals, it is often most practical to think of MV as being determined by what the second-most-motivated buyer is willing to pay. In this circumstance, it may be the human capital of the first-most-motivated buyer that elevates her IV above the MV cost of the acquisition. In this framework, the cost of acquiring the relevant human capital has already been paid (i.e., it is a "sunk cost" in economics terminology). Thus, the return on this capital in the form of the unique ability to earn additional income from the property investment represents a positive component in the investor's NPV.[1]

Now assuming this human capital return (measured in dollars) is proportional to the physical size or dollar value of the property investment, the positive NPV component due to human capital will be greater the larger the underlying property investment. Hence, to the extent that equity capital availability is constrained below the level of exhaustion of the investor's human capital, debt financing enables additional positive NPV to be realized.

15.1.2 Debt and Diversification

It can be valuable to break through a capital constraint on real estate equity investment for another important reason. The use of debt financing may be the only way equity-constrained investors can *diversify their real estate investments*. Due to the previously noted lumpy nature of direct real estate investment in the private property market, where whole assets must be purchased, even a moderately large amount of equity capital may only be sufficient to purchase one or a few individual properties. However, mortgages can typically be obtained for large fractions of the total value of the underlying property, enabling debt capital to stretch the investor's equity significantly, facilitating diversification across a greater number of individual properties. For example, without the use of debt, $10 million worth of equity can only purchase two $5 million properties. With the use of 75 percent LTV ratio debt, the same $10 million equity can be diversified across eight different $5 million properties.

Diversification is theoretically a desirable part of any investment strategy, no matter how risk averse or aggressive the investor is. Diversification is a rare phenomenon in economics in that it offers a type of "free lunch." Diversification allows you to increase your expected return without increasing your risk, or vice versa, to reduce your risk exposure without reducing your expected return.[2]

An important point should be kept in mind regarding the diversification argument for the use of debt. Any diversification financed by debt should generally be in the form of equity investments in *risky* assets, such as property or stocks. In general, it does not make sense to finance "diversification into bonds" by the use of debt. Do not "*borrow in order to lend.*" If you are simultaneously borrowing money to finance a real estate investment while you are investing in bonds or mortgage-backed securities, then you are just canceling out one position with the other, while paying the **banker's spread** (the difference between the borrowing and lending interest rate).[3]

15.1.3 Limitations on the Equity Constraint Argument for the Use of Debt

Clearly, there is a powerful argument for the use of debt financing in real estate equity investment if that is the only way the investor can realize a positive NPV equity opportunity or diversify his equity investments. But how widespread are genuine constraints on the supply of equity capital, particularly when positive NPV equity investment opportunities are available? The existence of such constraints would seem to reflect a shortcoming in the capital

---

[1]The "sunk cost" aspect of human capital gives it much the same nature as that of a call option, including the ability of its owner to exercise the option when it is favorable to do so as we described in Chapter 5. Option theory applications to real estate will be discussed further in Part VIII.

[2]This will be discussed in more depth in Chapter 21.

[3]There may be a temptation to borrow at a low interest rate and invest in a debt instrument that pays a higher interest rate. But the higher interest rate will normally reflect greater risk. Such a strategy is not diversification, but merely leverage, similar to what was described in Chapter 13. (See the discussion of bond economics in Chapter 19.)

markets. Getting rid of such shortcomings provides profit opportunities in the investments industry. Has somebody missed an opportunity here?

In fact, constraints on equity capital are probably not as widespread as is often assumed in real estate, even for relatively small individual investors. Comingled real estate investment funds, limited partnerships, tenancy-in-common funds, and syndications of various types, in addition to both private and public REITs, are among the many types of vehicles that are widely used to funnel equity capital into commercial real estate. Real estate entrepreneurs are adept at setting up partnerships and corporations of various types, including limited partnerships in which the "outside" equity capital providers have very little control over property or asset management. This may be difficult for very small individual investors just starting out, but once a track record of successful investment can be shown, it is much easier to obtain equity partners.

REITs and large publicly traded firms are not the only ones with virtually unconstrained access to equity capital, especially if positive NPV equity opportunities are available. Indeed, access to equity capital may depend more on the track record of the seeker than on the way in which its equity is traded, although there is probably a bias in favor of large size. Unsuccessful REITs have little ability to raise equity by issuing new shares, but large firms can probably make more small mistakes before investors sour on them.

Nor is it necessary even for small real estate investors to use debt in order to diversify their real estate investments across numerous individual properties. Diversified real estate equity investment vehicles, ranging from publicly traded REITs to private unit trusts and partnerships, exist as alternatives to debt-financed diversification. Therefore, the diversification argument for debt financing is not a "pure" argument in favor of the use of debt. It must involve other considerations, such as control or information sharing, or the type of income tax considerations described in Chapter 14. This suggests once again that positive NPV equity opportunities and human capital considerations are likely to be involved.

To summarize, equity capital is rarely completely constrained in an absolute sense when positive NPV opportunities are available. Rather, there may be issues of management **control and governance** and of information revelation and sharing that may convince some investors not to look for additional equity partners at a time when they face a given positive NPV opportunity. This may be perceived as an "effective equity constraint." In other circumstances, however, an absolute equity constraint may indeed be said to exist. Pension funds may be an important example of this, as discussed in Chapter 14.

15.2 Other Considerations Regarding the Role of Debt in Real Estate Investments

In addition to the previously described considerations of leverage and risk/return preference-matching (Chapter 13), income tax considerations (Chapter 14), and dealing with capital constraints or management control concerns (this chapter), several other considerations are important in the overall picture of the role of debt in real estate investment. Some of the major such considerations will be described in the present section.[4]

---

[4]Some considerations that are prominent in corporate finance are left out of the following discussion, such as the possible "signaling" roll of the use of debt finance, and the resulting "pecking order" theory suggesting a preference for debt finance over external equity. It is not clear that such considerations are as important for real estate due to the different tax and investment holding environments, as discussed earlier. Empirical evidence regarding the pecking order for REITs is mixed. Ghosh, Nag, and Sirmans (1997) found some evidence that REITs prefer external equity to debt, contrary to the traditional pecking order in taxed corporations. On the other hand, an earlier study by Howe and Shilling (1988) found evidence of a preference for debt. More recent studies still find mixed evidence (e.g., Feng, Ghosh, and Sirmans, 2007).

15.2.1 Debt as an Incentive and Disciplinary Tool for Management

One argument for the use of debt in real estate investment is that leverage can actually be a tool to help give incentive or discipline to property asset managers (**management incentive**).[5] This argument differs in a fascinating way from our previous discussion in that it is based on human behavioral considerations that go beyond the classical economic assumption of rational behavior. In particular, the idea is that real estate equity investors, as owner/managers of property, behave irrationally (or anyway, suboptimally) when they are faced with lower levels of risk and reward in their investment. Here is how the argument goes.

You have seen how debt increases the risk and return potential in the property equity owner's position. Indeed, as it is typically possible to borrow large fractions of the underlying property value, risk and reward can be greatly magnified through the use of debt. At least as an approximation, an equity investment with a 75 percent LTV loan will have *four times* the risk and reward potential of an unlevered position in the property, and *twice* the risk and reward even of a 50 percent LTV investment (100 percent debt/equity ratio). Yet property investments with 75 percent LTV ratios are not considered abnormally risky, and they are not at all uncommon in the real world.[6] If such highly levered equity is not abnormally risky, imagine how little is the risk in the underlying property assets free and clear of debt. Without debt, much commercial property apparently presents very low risk, with correspondingly low reward potential.

Property's low level of risk and reward potential is particularly noticeable in comparison with other productive underlying physical assets that require active management, such as the typical industrial or technology and service corporations that trade on the major stock exchanges. Furthermore, the argument continues, it is relatively easy and straightforward to manage properties. Compared to managing, say, a high-tech firm or multinational industrial corporation, there is limited scope to the creative possibilities of what can be done, or how the income-earning capability of the underlying assets can be made to grow. Managers can't usually make major mistakes, apart from doing obviously stupid things. Indeed, this characteristic of real estate is probably a major reason lenders are willing to loan such a high percentage of the underlying asset value in real estate.

In short, in the absence of leverage, the argument goes, real estate is a bit *boring*. Properties by themselves are not likely to attract the best and brightest management talent, people willing to work hard and take risks in order to advance up a long-run career path. With so little risk and so little scope for management impact, this argument suggests that property owner/managers would get a bit lazy over time. They might tend to let opportunities to improve the profitability of the underlying properties slip by. They might not notice or pursue an opportunity that only improves returns by, say, 1 percent or they might overlook or fail to correct a mistake that damages returns by only 1 percent.

But sufficient leverage can change this picture, according to the argument. Leverage (and lots of it) can make these stodgy underlying assets very interesting, even exciting. As we have seen in Chapter 13, sufficient leverage can turn low-risk, low-growth underlying assets into high-risk, high-growth investments from the perspective of the equity owner/manager of the property. This can turn those 1 percent impacts into 4 percent impacts (e.g., with 75 percent LTV ratio debt). Little things start becoming more noticeable. Managers start facing much more incentive to pay attention to details and opportunities. If you "borrow to the hilt," gearing the equity up to leverage ratios of three or four, then those cozy cash flow margins become much thinner. Managers have to stay on their toes and occasionally get quite creative to make the necessary profits and avoid losing their equity by default. In other words, *debt is what makes real estate exciting* (at least for fully operational, up-and-running properties)! And this excitement makes property owner/managers do their jobs more efficiently and

---

[5]The argument presented here lacks widespread support in the academic literature, although it is hinted at in such articles as Jensen (1986).

[6]Mortgages with 75% LTV ratios are regularly issued on institutional commercial properties by conservative lending institutions such as life insurance companies and pension funds, without recourse to the borrower guaranteeing the loan (that is, the loan is backed only by the property collateral).

effectively. This, in turn, enhances the productivity and the value of the underlying real physical assets. In short, through the use of debt, real value is potentially created.[7] If the amount of debt is right, not too little and not too much, this could increase the size of the total pie, for both debt and equity investors.[8]

This argument in favor of debt applies in principle both to small individual entrepreneurs and to large corporations and institutions such as REITs. It is relevant both in the management of individual property assets and portfolios of assets, at both the property management and asset management levels.

15.2.2 Debt and Liquidity

We have shown how the WACC model can be used to quantify how debt increases the risk of the equity investment. But there is another cost of debt that is closely related to the increase in risk, but more difficult to quantify, although it is no less real. Debt generally results in a *loss of liquidity* by the equity investor.

Why is this a problem? Well, it may not be, for an investor who is very liquid overall, or for one who only borrows a small fraction of the underlying property value. But it is often possible to borrow large fractions of the value of income-producing properties. Such debt can result in a serious loss in liquidity for the borrower. **Liquidity** in this context refers to one's ability to convert one's net worth quickly into cash without suffering a loss of value. Investors have liquidity when the value of their assets, especially of their readily marketable assets such as cash and securities (sometimes called "liquid assets"), comfortably exceeds the value of their liabilities. *Liquidity is desirable for investors because it provides* **decision flexibility**.

In general, lack of liquidity, or illiquidity, is one of the major concerns about direct real estate investment in comparison with stocks and bonds, for example. While the typical investor can sell stocks or bonds virtually immediately at full value, it may take months to sell a commercial property at full value. However, *provided you have not already borrowed much against a property you own*, you can generally convert much of the equity value of a real estate investment into cash relatively quickly and at relatively little transaction cost without selling the property at all by taking out a mortgage on it. Thus, one way to at least partially "cure" the illiquidity problem in real estate investments is not to lever the initial purchase of the property, holding the debt capacity "in reserve" for a time when it is more needed. In other words, *if you don't borrow now, you can borrow later*.

Keeping debt as low as possible gives the investor strategic and tactical decision flexibility and control. This is particularly important in the face of inefficiency in asset markets.

---

[7]The authors of this text have personal first-hand experience and exposure to this type of issue. We have seen particularly entrepreneurial landlords come up with ingenious custom-tailored innovations that work in specific situations. An example might be an office landlord in Atlanta who provides his tenants with bowling and baseball leagues and picnics, at very little cost but tremendous impact in that particular case in terms of tenant retention and reduced turnover. The wife of one of the authors used to manage leases in a Kentucky shopping mall. Entering a situation that had previously been institutionally managed, she could easily observe and analyze the cannibalization of sales when similar tenants were allowed to lease too much space, and fought against leasing agents who were incentivized only to get leases signed and fill space. The mix mattered a lot and when a manager is well motivated to be strategic they can avoid some mistakes that will cause some tenants to not make it. A leasing manager might bring in a soft play area that boosts the percentage rents the landlord collects from children-oriented nearby tenants. Even picking the right Santa Claus at Christmas can have an impact! Complacency may be widespread in property management, but there is great scope for enterprise and innovation where it is sufficiently motivated. A particularly important example of how property management could be improved, but often is not, is in the area of energy efficiency and "green" building. For example, a 2011 study by one of the authors of this text focused specifically on LEED renovated properties (see Chapter 5 for the definition of the "LEED" designation in the United States). The sample of over 300 properties were upgraded both for energy and water efficiency and environment. On average these properties saw rent premiums of about 7 percent over non-LEED counterparts of the same age and size and location after the upgrades. The returns varied but were generally positive NPV. Yet most property owners still do not consider these types of retrofits.

[8]Although it would be very difficult to quantify this effect in practice, in principle this argument implies the existence of a general positive NPV component to the use of debt to finance real estate equity investment (or perhaps a negative NPV result from failure to use debt). But this argument may apply only up to a point, for it is counteracted by the potential costs of financial distress, as we will discuss shortly.

We have noted in previous chapters how property market prices sometimes "bubble up" above their fundamental values, and sometimes "crash" below their true value. Such cyclicality may make property markets more predictable than security markets.

As we noted in Chapter 12, there is both danger and opportunity in real estate asset market inefficiency and predictability. Those who maintain liquidity are likely to be more able to take advantage of the opportunity and are less likely to fall victim to the danger. The principal danger, of course, is that one may pay too much for a property and then be forced to sell it at the bottom of the cycle. The most likely reason an investor would be forced to sell when the market is bad is that his creditors are demanding payment and the investor lacks sufficient cash (i.e., liquidity) to come up with the money owed. On the other hand, a more liquid investor will be able to take advantage of bargain buys when the market is down. Indeed, this point applies even apart from cyclical opportunities in real estate markets. Favorable investment opportunities in the form of individual positive NPV opportunities do not tend to wait around for long, and even with the use of debt the investor still must typically come up with some equity cash. Taking advantage of such opportunities requires liquidity. This, in turn, requires keeping indebtedness low.

While the liquidity argument against the use of debt applies to all investors in principle, it is certainly less important for investors who by their very nature tend to be highly liquid, such as pension funds of growing corporations, for example. Also, this argument may not be as applicable to individual investors making real estate investments via relatively liquid vehicles such as REITs. On the other hand, the liquidity argument does apply at the entity level of the REITs themselves, as they are investing directly in the relatively illiquid private property market.

While flexibility argues for minimizing the use of debt as a general policy, there is another side of the coin in the relationship between debt and liquidity in real estate investment. The illiquidity of property itself, combined with the ability property affords to borrow secured debt at high loan-to-value ratios, enables debt to play a useful role in allowing investors to partially liquefy their real estate investment holdings without actually selling these equity investments. Mortgages can be a useful vehicle to "cash out" a large portion of the capital gains an investor has incurred over the years in a property investment, while still holding onto the investment. However, it must be remembered that this practice brings with it the leverage and loss of flexibility (i.e., the ability to do the same thing at a later date) previously discussed.

15.2.3 Cost of Financial Distress

The argument in section 15.2.1 about the incentive benefits of debt suggests that human behavioral characteristics may cause debt to actually add real value to the underlying property investments. This is a controversial idea because it is difficult to quantify or prove, and it goes against the classical economic assumption of rational human behavior (in some sense). On the other hand, another argument, which is much less controversial, points out that debt, at least at a sufficiently high LTV, brings deadweight costs onto the underlying property investment. This potential cost of debt is often referred to as the **costs of financial distress**, or **COFD** for short.

There are two fundamental sources of COFD. One is the deadweight burden of **third-party costs**, such as legal and administrative fees, in the event of default, **foreclosure**, or **bankruptcy** caused by the existence of the debt. These legal and administrative costs are potentially a burden to both the equity and debt investor. The second source of COFD is the **agency cost** associated with conflicts of interest that can arise between the equity and debt investors at high LTV ratios. This cost is well described in most corporate finance texts. Because of the existence of **limited liability**, equity investors with highly levered positions face little downside risk from highly risky investments on the part of the corporation, thereby exposing the corporation's debt holders to most of the downside. The result can be a skewing of incentives to the detriment of the overall value of the firm (that is, to the sum of both debt and equity value). In the case of real property, for example, equity investors may lose their incentive to seek good long-term tenants and to maintain or upgrade the property in the optimal manner.

Both the third-party costs of default and foreclosure, and the agency costs, arise in an expectational or probabilistic sense ex ante, well before they might materialize in actuality. The mere possibility of their occurrence affects the present value of the debt and equity. Although such costs fall largely on debt holders ex post (when and if they ever actually occur), their ex ante impact at the time a loan is taken out falls on the equity investor, as lenders factor in the expected COFD in the interest rates and origination fees they charge to issue debt.

As a result of these considerations of the cost of financial distress, we can say for certain that 100 percent debt financing (even if it were possible) would *never* be optimal, even for the borrower (at least in a well-functioning debt market).[9] How much less than 100 percent is the optimal level of debt depends on the relative strengths and importance of the likely costs of financial distress and the other pros and cons of debt we have been discussing in this chapter.

In this regard, it is important to note that fully operational commercial real estate assets (so-called "stabilized" assets) are probably able to take on higher levels of debt than other more management-intensive or more volatile underlying assets without raising a significant expectation of financial distress costs. As we noted in section 15.2.1, fully operational real estate assets are relatively low in volatility and their management is relatively straightforward, presenting managers with relatively little opportunity to make major mistakes. The relative simplicity of property and asset management also makes it easy for outside investors, such as debt holders, to observe and monitor the quality of such management. This *transparency* reduces the potential conflict of interest between equity and debt investor and enables a larger fraction of underlying asset value to be borrowed before COFD becomes significant.

This is probably a major reason debt/equity ratios are higher for mortgage loans secured by real property than for debt backed by the typical publicly traded industrial or service corporation. This point is illustrated in Exhibit 15-1, which traces the total "value of the firm" (or value of the underlying asset) as a function of the ratio of debt value divided by total firm value (or LTV ratio). The solid line represents the typical industrial or service corporation traded on the stock exchange, while the dashed line represents a typical fully operational real property asset. The value of the firm equals the underlying asset value free and clear of debt, minus the present value of any expected future costs of financial distress: $V - COFD$.

EXHIBIT 15-1 Effect of Expected Costs of Financial Distress (COFD) on the Value of the Firm and on Property Value

© OnCourse Learning

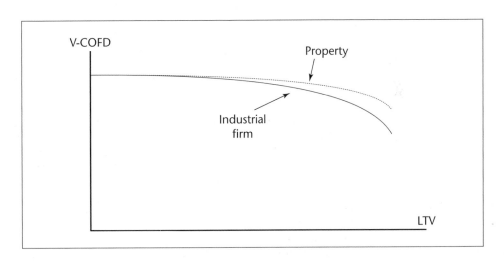

[9]In real estate investment circles one sometimes hears stories about "100 percent debt financing." In fact, 100 percent debt financing for individual projects is generally a sort of illusion. Either a significant (hidden) equity contribution is in fact being made (perhaps "in kind"), or the lender is counting on recourse to the borrower's other assets and income-earning ability. Otherwise, why would the lender accept relatively low debt-like returns for an investment that contains at least as much risk for the lender as an all-equity position in the underlying asset, which offers higher risky-asset return expectations? If the apparent 100 percent financed project actually displaces borrowing capacity on the part of the owner of the project, then effectively only a portion of the project debt is actually backed by the project itself; the rest is backed by the borrower/owner of the project. In this sense, the financing is not really 100 percent.

Real estate typically allows a greater LTV ratio before the COFD factor becomes important. Traditionally, commercial mortgages have often been made at LTVs up to 75 percent, whereas the debt-to-asset ratios of most publicly traded corporations (other than financial institutions) tend to remain around or below 50 percent, except as a result of corporate distress.

15.2.4 Debt and Inflation

During the 1970s and early 1980s, when the investment community was very concerned about **inflation**, the popular "get-rich-quick" literature on real estate investment touted the benefits of debt financing as a way to make money off inflation. The more you borrow, the more money you make just from inflation, and real estate provides more ability to borrow than any other type of investment. After all, when you borrow money in an inflationary environment, the dollars you pay back to the lender are worth less than the dollars you originally borrowed, due to the effect of inflation eating away the purchasing power of the dollars.

You probably already see the fallacy in this argument. Like the simplistic conventional wisdom about the tax advantages of debt no matter the borrower's tax rate, this inflation-based argument for debt ignores the lender side of the debt market. It implicitly assumes either that lenders are stupid, or that they don't have as good ability to forecast inflation as borrowers do. Neither of these assumptions is true. Lenders factor the expected rate of inflation into the interest rate at which they are willing to lend. The total dollars you pay back to the lender are more than the dollars you borrow, due to the interest you pay. The market interest rate in the debt market, whether it be for mortgages or bonds, is sufficient to cover the expected level of inflation and still provide lenders with a real return.

Now, once a fixed rate loan is made, it is indeed true that if inflation turns out to be higher than had been expected, the borrower will be rendered better off, and the lender worse off. But this is ex post, not ex ante, and the borrower has no ability to control or influence the subsequent inflation rate. Inflation is just as likely to turn out to be lower than had been expected at the time when the loan was made, which would make the borrower worse off and the lender better off. It is the ex ante expectations that are relevant for making the decision about the use of debt, and those expectations do not favor either the borrower or the lender in the debt transaction.

Nevertheless, it is important to understand the effect of inflation on the borrower's ex post position, and how this alters real estate's natural inflation-hedging ability. In general, rents and property values tend to move with inflation. When inflation turns out to be greater than had been previously expected, rents and property values are able to be greater than they otherwise could be, *measured in nominal terms*. This makes real estate act as an inflation hedge, protecting the investor against unanticipated increases in inflation.[10]

This inflation-hedging quality of real estate equity is magnified by the use of fixed rate debt, to the point that inflation can actually become a positive risk factor in the levered equity. That is, unanticipated surges in inflation may actually *improve* the levered equity real estate return net of inflation. This can be a valuable effect for investors who are particularly exposed to possible harm from unanticipated increases in inflation. For example, if the investor is likely to lose her job as a result of a surge in inflation, or if her wealth is trapped in assets that tend to be particularly negatively affected by inflation, then the "inflation-reversing" effect of financing real estate investment with fixed rate debt could be attractive.[11]

---

[10]Remember: real estate is a risky asset, even measured in real terms, net of inflation. Thus, real estate is not a "perfect" hedge against inflation. Real estate returns in the private property market tend to be positively correlated with inflation, but not perfectly correlated. Also keep in mind that unanticipated changes in inflation are usually correlated with events in the real macroeconomy and in monetary policy. These events often have an impact on the real value of property. For example, an unanticipated upsurge in inflation may trigger tighter monetary policy and signal slower-than-anticipated future real growth in the economy. Such "news" would be negative for most real estate values, in real terms.

[11]On the other hand, don't forget our dictum: Don't borrow in order to lend, as the net result is the payment of the banker's spread. If the investor's portfolio is overly sensitive to inflation due to heavy concentration in long-term fixed rate bond investments, it would generally make more sense to reduce the bond exposure rather than to borrow money while still holding onto the bonds.

EXHIBIT 15-2

Example of Effect of Inflation on Ex Post Levered Equity Appreciation Returns with One-Year Loan

© OnCourse Learning

Scenario:	Ex Post−	Ex Ante	Ex Post+
Inflation:	**0%**	**2%**	**4%**
Values*			
Property:			
Yr. 0	$100	$100	$100
Yr. 1	$99	$101	$103
Debt balance payable:			
Yr. 0	$60	$60	$60
Yr. 1	$60	$60	$60
Levered equity:			
Yr. 0	$40	$40	$40
Yr. 1	$39	$41	$43
Appreciation %			
Nominal returns			
Property:	−1.0%	1.0%	3.0%
Levered equity:	−2.5%	2.5%	7.4%
Nominal deviation from *ex ante*			
Property:	−2.0%	0.0%	2.0%
Levered equity:	−5.0%	0.0%	5.0%
Real returns			
Property:	−1.0%	−1.0%	−1.0%
Levered equity:	−2.5%	0.5%	3.3%
Nominal deviation from *ex ante*			
Property:	0.0%	0.0%	0.0%
Levered equity:	−2.9%	0.0%	2.8%

*Real depreciation rate = 1%/yr.

Of course, the inflation effect cuts the other way when inflation turns out to be less than previously expected. Then nominal real estate equity returns turn out to be lower than previously expected, and the use of fixed rate debt will magnify this effect, leading to a lower real return than had been expected.

These effects are illustrated numerically in Exhibit 15-2. The exhibit portrays a property initially worth $100 in an environment in which inflation over the next year is anticipated to be 2 percent and the property is expected to depreciate 1 percent in real terms. The middle column of figures reflects these ex ante expectations. The two other columns show alternative inflation scenarios, one in which inflation turns out to be 2 percent less than anticipated, and the other in which inflation turns out to be 2 percent greater than anticipated. The property itself is assumed to be a "perfect" inflation hedge, in the sense that it retains its same *real* value no matter what happens to inflation. The exhibit shows the effect on the levered equity of the presence of a 60 percent LTV ratio one-year loan whose principle is payable at the end of the first year.[12]

---

[12]We may assume the loan interest is paid from the property operating cash flow, which is not depicted in the exhibit.

Notice that the property value grows 1 percent less than the inflation rate in all scenarios, producing a −1 percent real return. The real deviation of the ex post return from the ex ante expectation is zero in all scenarios for the unlevered property, as seen in the second-to-last row in the table. This reflects our "perfect hedge" assumption. On the other hand, the property growth is magnified in the levered equity, allowing it to provide a slightly positive real return under the ex ante scenario, and magnifying its positive covariance with inflation. The levered equity will lose 2.5 percent in real value if the low-inflation scenario materializes, or gain 3.3 percent if the high-inflation scenario occurs. In real terms, the levered equity loses (or gains) when inflation turns out to be lower (or higher) than anticipated, even though the unlevered property real return is invariant across inflation scenarios. The levered equity's real deviation from its ex ante expectation is approximately ± 3 percent, positively correlated with the inflation outcome.[13]

Thus, the example in Exhibit 15-2 shows how leverage can increase the covariance between the ex post nominal return and inflation and introduce positive correlation between the ex post real return and inflation. This **reverse-inflation risk** may be useful to some investors, or a needless increase in risk to other investors. It is a factor to consider, but not a general argument in favor of debt financing applicable to all investors.

15.3 Project-Level Capital Structure in Real Estate

As noted, much real estate finance occurs at the micro-level of individual investments in properties, projects, or "deals." As a result, much "capital structure" in real estate occurs at this micro-level. In part, this is because much real estate investment is still done directly by individuals or small entrepreneurial firms. But it is also because of the nature of real estate assets. As we have pointed out before, the relatively simple, tangible, and "transparent" nature of property assets as investments makes them ideal candidates for secured debt and other types of project-level financing, in which external investors need to feel confident that they know what is going on in the investment even if they don't have direct management control or highly specialized expertise. The law governing real property rights also facilitates this type of finance, at least in Anglo-Saxon "common law" countries.[14]

In general, the prevalence of project-level finance does not alter the basic principles and considerations that we have raised in the preceding sections of this chapter and Chapters 13 and 14 regarding capital structure and the use of debt. The classical micro-level real estate finance deal consists simply of an equity-owning investor taking out a mortgage loan secured by the property, and our previous discussion in this chapter as well as the analysis framework presented in Chapters 13 and 14 can be applied to this model. In recent years, however, the capital markets have become more sophisticated in custom-tailoring investment vehicles to a more diverse range of investors. Combined in some cases with a growing prevalence of larger, more complex property investment projects, such as those including development phases and/or multiple individual assets, the result has been a growth in more complex capital structures, even at the micro-level. Financing considerations peculiar to development project investments will be addressed in Chapter 28, and mortgages will be addressed from an investment perspective in Part VI. Here, however, it will be worth our while to point out some of the major types of financing and capital structures currently or recently used for real estate investments in the United States and indeed, internationally within the global institutional investment community.

Broadly speaking, the additional financing arrangements consist of investment vehicles that are intermediate or "hybrid" between the classical first-lien mortgage and the classical pure undifferentiated residual equity. These include both subordinated debt and preferred

---

[13]Note that the results portrayed in Exhibit 15-2 are well approximated by the WACC formula described in Chapter 13. Slight deviations from this formula reflect the fact that a positive span of time (one year) is covered in Exhibit 15-2, during which time the LTV ratio changes, which makes the WACC formula an inexact approximation.

[14]See Lynn Fisher, "Renegotiation in the Common Law Mortgage and the Impact of Equitable Redemption," Journal of Real Estate Finance and Economics 32.1 (2006): 61–82.

equity vehicles (with and without "convertibility" or equity call option features), as well as differentiation among "classes" of investors within the residual equity ownership entity itself. The overriding purpose of developing these types of more complex capital structures is to facilitate two related objectives:

1. To match the risk and return (and holding horizon or liquidity) preferences of different types of investors, thereby attracting capital from more or larger pools of investors; and
2. To match appropriately investment performance incentives with the governance structure of the operational control and authority in the project, so as to optimize the management of the project and thereby minimize agency costs and maximize underlying project value for all parties.

15.3.1 Enriching the Traditional Capital Structure Plate

Some of the more widely used vehicles and mechanisms of project-level capital structure include subordinate types of debt (often called "mezzanine") preferred equity, and differentiated residual equity classes with investment return "hurdles" and "promotes."[15] These are described below.

Multiple-Note Mortgages   It used to be that a mortgage was always a single undifferentiated note. While this is still largely the case, the twenty-first century has witnessed the advent of multiple-note mortgages. Typically they originate with very large first-lien (senior) mortgages. Splitting a mortgage into two or more separate notes allows separate investors (or owners) of the same mortgage. The splitting may be done either "horizontally" or "vertically." With horizontal splitting the two notes are identical in terms of seniority and interest (referred to as "pari passu"). Sometimes one note will be securitized and the other held privately, or the two notes will both be securitized but into different CMBS (commercial mortgage-backed securities) pools, as the entire loan might be too large for any one pool. In the case of vertical splitting, there may be an "A" note and a "B" note, with the former having precedence in claims over the latter. In effect, the B-note becomes much like a "second mortgage" or subordinate debt, though it is structured as a note on a single underlying mortgage. Sometimes the A-note will be securitized and the B-note held privately. Multiple-note mortgages, while an important innovation, do not fundamentally affect the equity investor as much as the other types of vehicles listed below.

Mezzanine Debt   So-called "mez debt" is a somewhat vaguely defined term whose meaning can vary. It refers to an investment vehicle structured as a loan and senior to equity but subordinated to other debt that is senior to it. In some cases mez debt is secured directly by real property assets and includes a "lien"[16] on the underlying property, but subordinated to other specified senior investment vehicles (typically including a first mortgage that might be a construction loan for a development investment and/or a permanent loan for a stabilized investment). In this case mez debt is essentially like a "second mortgage" or other such subordinated mortgage. However, in the early 2000s the term "mez debt" came to be applied particularly to loans not necessarily secured directly by property assets but rather made to an investment entity (which in turn owned property assets encumbered by senior mortgage debt). In general, mez debt investors are not entitled to receive return of or on their

---

[15]Another hybrid vehicle, "participating mortgages," will be discussed in an appendix to Chapter 18. In brief, a participating mortgage, which is often a first-lien note, gives the debt holder some participation in the collateral property's equity cash flow or property value appreciation or at least the upside thereof, in return for a lower base interest rate or other considerations for the borrower.

[16]A "lien" is a construct of Anglo-Saxon common law that gives a creditor potential real property ownership rights, for example, in the event of default on the loan enabling the creditor to take ownership of the property. More than one lien may be attached to a property, in which case the liens have a priority normally based on chronological order but able to be subordinated to subsequent liens, as in the case of mez debt that might be arranged prior to a permanent first-lien mortgage. Classical mortgage terminology and covenants will be discussed in Chapter 16.

investment until after senior debt holders are fully compensated for what is owed them. On the other hand, if not all capital is invested at once, mez debt capital is typically "drawn" or placed into the investment *before* the senior debt capital. In this way, the mez debt investment provides a buffer of capital exposure helping to protect the senior debt investors. In particularly large and complex deals there may be more than one layer or type of mez debt. Mez debt typically carries interest rates considerably above those of first mortgages, and usually the interest that is not paid out currently accrues and accumulates with compounding (interest is earned on interest not yet paid out).

Preferred Equity   Preferred equity is similar to mez debt in that it provides a contractually stated dividend or yield payment in the form of a "guaranteed" return. But preferred equity is normally subordinated to debt on the property or investment entity (including mez debt). Preferred equity normally has no formal lien on the underlying real estate. On the other hand, as the name implies, preferred equity precedes common (or residual) equity in priority of claims. Preferred equity obtains its returns usually purely in the form of a preferred dividend (no appreciation of principal or capital paid in). Sometimes the preferred return not paid out currently accumulates with (or without) compounding, as with debt. In capital structures where there is both mez debt and preferred equity, usually the preferred equity goes in before, and comes out after, the mez debt capital, and the preferred equity return is higher than the mez debt interest rate. While mez debt typically has a maturity or explicit principal payback horizon, this is not generally the case for preferred equity. The preferred equity holder may or may not have some say in whether or when the underlying assets are to be sold (leading to pay back of investment principal).

Common (or Residual) Equity   This is normally the property ownership entity that has the operational management responsibility and primary governing control of the project, at least unless and until there is a default of the senior obligations. (Secured senior debt in particular, by virtue of its lien and loan covenants, can take over control in the event of default.) Common equity has no guaranteed or contractual return and receives only the residual cash flow generally after the other senior investment vehicles have been paid their preferred returns. (However, a variety of specific arrangements are possible; for example, common equity is sometimes entitled to return of its paid-in capital with zero return prior to preferred equity being paid its preferred return.)

Differentiated Equity Partners (Classes)   It is typical particularly in larger real estate investments for the common equity ownership entity to have more than one investor, organized as a partnership or corporation. In such a "**joint venture**," it is common for the investors to be differentiated according to what they bring into the deal and what they want to get out of it. For example, an entrepreneurial investor may essentially bring operational management ability and the deal itself (e.g., in a development, the land with entitlements and permits, as well as the project design), while a money partner brings most (or sometimes, *all*) of the required equity cash but lacks the ability or desire to manage the operation of the project or property. To reflect such differing contributions and investment objectives, it makes sense to define different "classes" of partners or stockholders in the ownership equity entity. A typical arrangement will grant operational management control primarily to what we will label the "**entrepreneurial partner,**" (or "manager") while the "**money partner**" will often retain primary control over major capital decisions (financing and asset buy/sell decisions). The entrepreneurial partner may or may not subordinate some of its equity claim to that of the money partner (though the entrepreneurial partner may also take a fee for service). A very common arrangement splits the equity entity's overall cash flow (net of fees) among the partners on a "**pro rata pari passu**" basis (proportionately relative to their capital contributions) up until the equity entity achieves a certain "**preferred**" or "**hurdle**" **return** (specified either on a cumulative current or a look-back IRR basis, or both); beyond that hurdle return, the cash flow split is differentiated so as to provide the entrepreneurial partner with a proportion greater than its capital contribution (either on a current or back-end basis). This is called a "**promote**," and surpassing the preferred return hurdle is referred to as "earning the promote."[17] Such structures provide the partner charged with operational management more incentive to make the project a success. As such success benefits not only the managing partner but all of the investors in the project, it is crucial to provide this kind of incentive. The promote structure may also provide some degree of "reward" for putting the deal together in the first place.

One of the characteristics of project-level capital structure is that two investment management considerations are to some extent blended together: that of capital structure per se (in particular the nature and degree of leverage), and that of project management and governance, including the very important considerations of incentives compatibility and mitigation of potential conflicts of interest among the various investors. The structuring of the equity partnership vehicle is more about the latter considerations, while the use of extra intermediate or hybrid finance vehicles with claim priority between that of the traditional first-lien mortgage and traditional equity is more about the capital structure issue. In general, both mez debt and preferred equity vehicles were part of the evolution to ever greater degrees of leverage in property investment during the mid-2000s "bubble." Coming on top of traditional first-lien mortgages, they brought in new types of real estate capital providers, typically from the nonbank financial sector (such as private equity funds), and allowed ever thinner slices of real estate equity investment to buy and control underlying property assets with very little cash investment. After the financial crisis and property crash of 2008–2009, use of these types of vehicles diminished in favor of a simpler structure that was more transparent (and more traditional). But use of intermediate financing did not cease altogether, as it can provide valuable benefits. And while extra layers in the capital structure probably tends to be driven by the desire for greater leverage, the overall degree of leverage can be kept down by reducing the LTV of the first-lien mortgage and reducing the "thickness" (amount of financing) in the intermediate layers, thereby keeping the overall LTV to a safe level (including all layers of financing other than the residual equity). One lesson from the crash, however, was that complexity itself can have a cost, as it can obfuscate the picture of the investment and confound the control of the project. Too many layers of finance can be like too many cooks in the kitchen!

15.3.2 Numerical Example of Multi-Tiered Project Capital Structure

To see more concretely how this type of project level capital structure and joint venture equity structuring works, let us return to our simple apartment property example from Chapter 14. Only now, let us consider not just the simple first-lien mortgage and undifferentiated equity considered there, but let us also include some of the vehicles and arrangements noted in the previous section.

To add a bit more richness to the example, let us also further suppose that the investment is actually a development project to build the apartment building, rather than an investment in a pre-existing stabilized building.[18] In particular, let us suppose that the completed property, which, as you recall, is projected to be worth $1 million , will take a year to build. The development phase involves land purchased up front for $200,000, as well as construction, which will be financed entirely by a first-lien construction loan that will be due upon project completion in one year, with a contractual balance owed at that time of $750,000, including accrued interest as well as principal.

---

[17]Typical preferred return hurdles have been in the range of 6 percent to 12 percent, with the promote share to the entrepreneurial partner typically ranging from 10 percent to 50 percent. There may also be "claw-back" or "hold-back" provisions that allow the money partner to retrieve some promote that had been paid to the managing partner if subsequently the deal performance turns out badly after it had previously been good enough to provide some promote. Another type of arrangement gives the money partner a senior position ahead of the manager up until the preferred return is earned but then allows the manager to have a "catch-up" period in which he gets *all* of the cash flow until he also has made the preferred return, followed then by a promoted split structure. Yet another structure is more complex, in which there may be two (or more) hurdles. This is more typical in business entities that are not just for the purpose of a single investment but allocating money to a portfolio of several properties. For project level finance and joint ventures, hurdles are typically specified based on IRR metrics. However, in the case of co-mingled funds with many investors and many properties it is generally presumed that the manager does not have control over investment timing, in which case hurdles and promotes are typically based on time-weighted returns (see section 9.3 in Chapter 9).

[18]As will be described in Part VIII, the term "stabilized" in this context refers to a property whose construction and lease-up is complete, or any property that is largely leased up to the extent of its normal profitable operation.

We will define the time when the land must be purchased as the end of "year 0," and the time one year later when the construction will be complete and the construction loan paid off as the end of "year 1." For simplicity, we will (as before) lump all cash flows into annual end-of-year amounts, and we will ignore any start-up partially leased phase, picking up with the projected stabilized operating cash flows of the property as in Exhibits 14-2 and 14-3 of the previous chapter, only now with those stabilized cash flows starting at the end of year 2 (instead of year 1 as in Chapter 14). Note that by coming in at the development phase, the apartment property can be obtained for a total of $950,000 (including $200,000 land cost up front plus $750,000 construction cost, including financing cost a year later), even though the completed building will (let's assume) indeed be worth $1 million upon completion at the end of year 1. The $50,000 difference represents "entrepreneurial profit" for the development phase, reflecting the extra risk involved in a development project compared to the purchase of a preexisting stabilized property.[19]

We will continue to assume, as before, that the $750,000 first-lien permanent loan already described in Chapter 14 will be used to finance the investment after construction, replacing (and paying off or "taking out") the construction loan at the end of year 1. As you may recall, this loan carries a 5.5 percent interest rate and amortizes (pays down principal) by the fixed amount of $2,000 per year.

Let us now assume that the equity investment and ownership of this project will consist of two differentiated partners. A relatively passive money partner will contribute 90 percent of the equity cash requirement (that is, $180,000 of the $200,000 land price at year 0), while an entrepreneurial partner will contribute the rest of the cash and have operational management control of the project and the property. The arrangement between these two partners specifies that the money partner will receive an annual preferred return of 6 percent, with any unpaid current return accumulating forward with annual compounding. Any positive net operating cash flow from the property (after the debt service has been paid) will go first to provide the money partner with her preferred 6 percent return (as current as possible) but then any extra operating cash flow after that will be split 50/50 between the two partners (even though the money partner contributes 90 percent of the equity capital and the entrepreneurial partner only 10 percent). Reversion cash flow from net resale proceeds (after debt repayment) will go first to provide the money partner with her preferred 6 percent return. Any remaining reversion cash available after that upon termination will go first to pay back the entrepreneurial partner for his capital contribution (with zero return) and next will be split 50/50 between the two partners.

Note that the arrangement described in this illustration does *not* provide for a pro rata pari passu split of residual cash flow up to the earning of the 6 percent preferred return. Thus, this structure combines the senior/subordinate aspect of the "preferred equity" intermediate capital structure layer (between the mortgage and the residual equity) described in section 15.3.1 with aspects of the return hurdle-with-promote joint venture arrangement described at the end of that section. This hybrid structure has consequences for the entrepreneurial partner that we shall see shortly. Exhibit 15-3 presents a visual depiction of the cash flow "waterfall" implied by the arrangement. The exhibit highlights both the "horizontal" splitting of cash flows in the senior/subordinate arrangement characteristic of capital structure slices or "tranches," as well as the "vertical" cash flow splitting characteristic of residual equity classes. It also shows graphically how the arrangement is slightly different in this example between operational and reversion (asset sale proceeds) cash flows, with an extra layer of horizontal splitting in the reversion, to give the managing partner some priority in at least getting their capital investment back.[20]

---

[19]See Chapters 28 and 29 for more depth on this point.

[20]While the structure described here could well exist in particular circumstances in the real world, we are using it here more for pedagogical purposes (not suggesting that it would be very typical). We are doing this in order to make a point about fairness and incentive considerations in cash flow splits arrangements, and in order to demonstrate capital accounting for the senior intermediate portions of the capital structure. In effect the money partner in this deal has assumed two roles, that of a preferred equity investor, and that of a joint venture partner, and is taking much of their joint venture partnership return through their preferred equity vehicle.

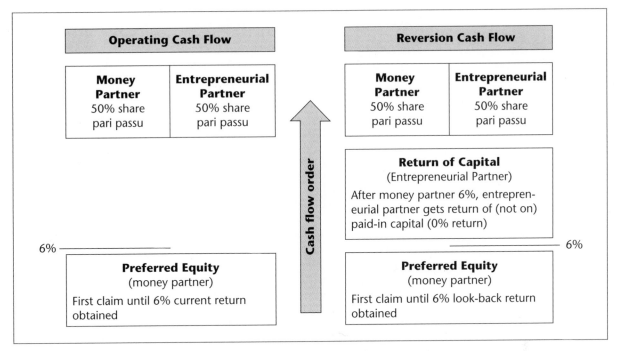

EXHIBIT 15-3 Apartment Example Waterfall Illustration
© OnCourse Learning

Exhibit 15-4 summarizes the projected cash flows of this project quantitatively at the before-tax level for the development phase and a projected 10-year holding horizon of stabilized operations after completion of construction, through year 11. (Negative cash flows, or cash outflows, are indicated by parentheses.) The items under years 0 and 1 in the upper left portion of the exhibit represent the development phase, including the $200,000 land purchase at "time zero" and the $750,000 construction loan repayment at the end of year 1. The next section of the exhibit shows the 10-year stabilized operating phase of the investment occurring in years 2 through 11 starting with the property-level before-tax cash flows (PBTCF) in the top row and moving down through the (undifferentiated) EBTCF from the previous chapter's Exhibit 14-3, including the $750,000 permanent mortgage used at year 1 to repay the construction loan, and including property resale reversion and loan pay back in year 11. (Recall that the PBTCF is low in years 4 and 9 due to projected capital improvement expenditures, and this causes the EBTCFs to actually be negative in those years, requiring additional capital contribution.)

The section just below the EBTCF line in Exhibit 15-4 is the preferred equity **capital account**. This section shows in simplified form how senior portions of the intermediate capital structure layers are accounted for in the proforma cash flow projection.[21] As the money partner in this case is entitled to a senior preferred return, we must keep track of what is owed to this partner separately. For example, in year 1, this partner earns $10,800 of preferred return based on the 6 percent preferred rate times her $180,000 balance at the beginning of the year.[22] As the project produces no net equity cash flow in year 1, this return cannot be paid currently to the money partner, and so it accumulates into the money partner's capital account balance going forward, which now becomes $190,800.

In year 2, the 6 percent preferred return therefore is $11,448, including 6 percent on the unpaid return of the previous year. As year 2 is projected to yield EBTCF in excess of this amount, the entire $11,448 current return is projected to be paid in year 2. In addition, any

---

[21]The Excel file for this chapter on the accompanying CD shows the detailed formulas used in this capital account.

[22]In the real world, this type of accounting would typically be done at a monthly frequency.

Calendar Years Ending:	Year 0	Year 1	Year 2	Year 3	Year 4	Year 5	Year 6	Year 7	Year 8	Year 9	Year 10	Year 11
Project Cash Requirements as Proposed:												
Site Acquisition	200,000											
Hard & Soft Development Costs		750,000										
Total Development Phase Cash Requirements	(200,000)	(750,000)										
Development Phase Total Equity Funding	200,000											
Development Phase Debt Funding(Construction Loan)		750,000										
Construction Loan Repayment		(750,000)										
Proposed Permanent Loan Amount (Take Out)		750,000										
Operating PBTCF			60,000	60,600	11,206	61,818	62,436	63,061	63,691	14,328	64,971	65,621
Reversion PBTCF			0	0	0	0	0	0	0	0	0	1,104,622
PBTCF			**60,000**	**60,600**	**11,206**	**61,818**	**62,436**	**63,061**	**63,691**	**14,328**	**64,971**	**1,170,243**
Permanent Loan Debt Service			(43,250)	(43,140)	(43,030)	(42,920)	(42,810)	(42,700)	(42,590)	(42,480)	(42,370)	(42,260)
Permanent Loan Repayment												(730,000)
Permanent Loan Debt CFs			(43,250)	(43,140)	(43,030)	(42,920)	(42,810)	(42,700)	(42,590)	(42,480)	(42,370)	(772,260)
Operating EBTCF			16,750	17,460	(31,824)	18,898	19,626	20,361	21,101	(28,152)	22,601	23,361
Reversion EBTCF			0	0	0	0	0	0	0	0	0	374,622
EBTCF			**16,750**	**17,460**	**(31,824)**	**18,898**	**19,626**	**20,361**	**21,101**	**(28,152)**	**22,601**	**397,983**
Preferred Equity Capital Account:												
Preferred Return Allocation:												
Beginning Equity Investment Balance	0	180,000	190,800	185,498	180,000	219,442	213,710	208,642	208,642	208,642	246,497	238,685
Annual Preferred Investment	180,000	0	0	0	28,642	0	0	0	0	25,337	0	0
Preferred Return Earned	0	10,800	11,448	11,130	10,800	13,166	12,823	12,518	12,518	12,518	14,790	14,321
Preferred Return Paid	0	0	(11,448)	(11,130)	0	(13,166)	(12,823)	(12,518)	(12,518)	0	(14,790)	(14,321)
Payment of previous earned			(5,302)	(5,498)	0	(5,732)	(5,068)	0	0	0	(7,812)	(4,707)
Accrued But Unpaid Preferred Return	0	10,800	0	0	10,800	0	0	0	0	12,518	0	0
Ending Equity Investment Balance	180,000	190,800	185,498	180,000	219,442	213,710	208,642	208,642	208,642	246,497	238,685	233,978
Reversion Preferred Allocations:												
Allocation to Satisfy Preferred Return Requirement												(233,978)
Allocation to Return Subordinated Investment Requirement												(25,998)

(Exhibit continues on next page)

EXHIBIT 15-4 Apartment Property Example Cash Flows, Splits, and Returns

Annual CF approximations for purpose of checking fairness splits	IRR	Year 0	Year 1	Year 2	Year 3	Year 4	Year 5	Year 6	Year 7	Year 8	Year 9	Year 10	Year 11
Project-Level Cash Flows*:													
Construction Phase	25.00%	(200,000)	250,000										
Operational Phase	6.04%		(1,000,000)	60,000	60,600	11,206	61,818	62,436	63,061	63,691	14,328	64,971	1,170,243
Both Phases	6.54%			60,000	60,600	11,206	61,818	62,436	63,061	63,691	14,328	64,971	1,170,243
Debt Investor Cash Flows:	5.50%		(750,000)	43,250	43,140	43,030	42,920	42,810	42,700	42,590	42,480	42,370	772,260
Equity-Entity-Level Cash Flows (EBTCF):**													
Construction Phase	25.00%	(200,000)	250,000										
Operational Phase	7.40%		(250,000)	16,750	17,460	(31,824)	18,898	19,626	20,361	21,101	(28,152)	22,601	397,983
Both Phases	9.09%		0	16,750	17,460	(31,824)	18,898	19,626	20,361	21,101	(28,152)	22,601	397,983
Preferred-Partner-Level Cash Flows:													
Construction Phase (if sell on completion)	16.89%	(180,000)	210,400										
Both Phases	8.13%	(180,000)	0	16,750	17,044	(28,642)	18,898	18,759	16,440	16,810	(25,337)	22,601	312,496
Subordinated-Partner-Level Cash Flows:													
Construction Phase (if sell on completion)	98.00%	(20,000)	39,600										
Both Phases	14.62%	(20,000)	0	0	416	(3,182)	0	868	3,921	4,291	(2,815)	0	85,487

* Sometimes referred to as "Asset Level."

**To the LLC joint venture partnership as a whole.

EXHIBIT 15-4 (Continued)

© OnCourse Learning

remaining EBTCF is used to pay off as much as possible of the unpaid previously earned preferred return. Since the year 2 EBTCF is $16,750, the difference between that and the previously-noted $11,448, which is $5,302, can be used to reduce the unpaid previously-earned preferred return of $10,800. This reduces the balance carried forward into year 3 to $185,498. Note that the preferred return not paid currently accrues and accumulates (including in this case compounding, that is, earning return on return).

Operating cash flows will be applied to reduce the preferred equity balance down to just the amount of actual equity contribution with zero return, which is initially $180,000. This is projected to occur by the end of year 3. In fact, the year 3 projected EBTCF of $17,460 would be sufficient to cover not only the $11,130 then current preferred return (6% × $185,498) plus the remainder of the unpaid previously earned preferred return ($5,498) but also to have $832 left over. According to the joint venture partnership agreement this residual amount would then be split 50/50 to the two partners, thus providing in year 3 a projected positive operating cash flow to the entrepreneurial partner of $416. The money partner of course would receive a much larger cash flow that year of $17,044 (consisting of $11,130 + $5,498 + $416).

Additional equity capital "draws" in years 4 and 9 are projected, due to the negative EBTCF in those years caused by the projected need for major capital expenditures. Those draws will add to the cumulative preferred equity balance carried forward for the money partner that is not to be repaid from operating cash flows. For example, the projected entity-level EBTCF in year 4 is negative $31,824. Ninety percent of this amount, $28,642, will be drawn from the money partner and added to his preferred equity account balance, bringing it up to $208,642. This is the balance, as of the end of year 4, which is earmarked to be paid back from property resale reversion funds upon termination of the investment. As we saw before, the preferred equity account balance also includes carried forward any earned but unpaid returns, for example $10,800 earned in year 4, bringing the balance carried forward into year 5 up to $219,442.

By the end of the 10-year holding period, the capital balance projected in the money partner's preferred account is $233,978. This represents the money partner's share of the initial equity capital outlay of the joint venture, as well as of the subsequent draws of operating capital expenditure requirements in years 4 and 9 (as well as any previously earned unpaid current returns still not paid off by that time, of which in this case there are not projected to be any). This balance is net of current returns paid from operations. Based on the hybrid senior/subordinate structure of this deal, the money partner's preferred equity gives her a senior position to claim this balance upon resale of the property. The money partner will thus have first claim on the reversion cash flow projected in year 11 until her projected preferred capital balance of $233,978 is fully paid off. The intended result of the preferred equity capital account rows in Exhibit 15-4 is to pay the money partner her 6 percent preferred return insofar as possible with priority over the entrepreneurial partner's receipts. As the projected reversion EBTCF in year 11 is $374,622, it is expected that the preferred capital balance will indeed be paid off at that time (as would normally be the case in a forward projection).

The next claim on the partnership's reversion cash flow in the terminal period is that of the entrepreneurial partner's original and subsequent capital investment (with zero return) of $25,998 (including his original $20,000 investment plus his share of the negative equity cash flow, years 4 and 9 due to major capital improvement investments). In the present agreement, this amount is to be paid as much as possible from reversion cash flow. As the total reversion projected for year 11 is $374,622, which is more than $25,998 in excess of the $233,978 that must be paid to the money partner, the expectation is that the entrepreneurial partner will indeed be paid back their $25,998 capital contribution from the reversion in year 11.

The bottom section of Exhibit 15-4 summarizes all of the cash flows for all of the parts of the capital structure, including the effect on the equity partners of the differentiated splits reflecting the promote for the entrepreneurial partner. Going-in IRR expectations are computed in the first column at each level and for each investor. These IRRs are computed separately for the development phase investment alone (assuming sale of the property for

$1 million upon completion of construction at end of year 1) and for the combined development and stabilized 11-year holding period (sale of property at end of year 11). The IRR is also computed separately for just the 10-year stabilized investment holding period (assuming purchase of the property at its opportunity cost of $1 million at the end of year 1) at the level of the underlying project (unlevered property level) and at the level of the ownership entity (undifferentiated levered equity level).

Consider first the project level, at the top of this section of the exhibit. This level ignores the permanent loan to consider the underlying asset investment performance directly.[23] The development phase of the investment involves the $200,000 land purchase up front, followed by property sale for $1 million minus the $750,000 construction costs (including construction loan interest) at year 1, for an expected return of 25 percent. Such a high expected return reflects the high risk in the development phase (as will be discussed in depth in Chapters 28 and 29). The 10-year operational-phase investment alone (assuming purchase for $1 million at the end of year 1) provides a going-in IRR of 6.04 percent at this unlevered property level. (Recall that this is the same PBT level IRR we noted for this apartment property in Chapter 14.) The "blended" going-in IRR for the combined 11-year development and stabilized investment is slightly higher, at 6.54 percent, reflecting the greater risk of the development phase that is included.[24]

The next line in Exhibit 15-4 is the cash flow of the permanent mortgage lender, the first lien holder who is willing to accept a relatively low 5.5 percent return for the relatively low risk and finite maturity of this investment.[25] This investor will provide $750,000 of so-called "permanent" financing (three-quarters of the total requirement for the stabilized property) and has the most senior claim to the project's cash flows. If this claim is not met, the mortgage holder can declare the borrower (in this case the joint venture equity partnership) in default and invoke a foreclosure sale or take control of the property (see Chapter 16).

The next section of Exhibit 15-4 shows the cash flows and expected returns at the level of the equity ownership entity, the joint venture as a whole undifferentiated between the two partners.[26] At the equity entity level we see the effect of the leverage caused by the permanent mortgage. For the 10-year stabilized investment, the levered equity IRR goes up to 7.40 percent, reflecting the positive leverage caused by a 5.5 percent loan against a property yielding 6.04 percent, as discussed in Chapters 13 and 14. The blended IRR for the combined development and stabilized investment goes up to 9.09 percent for the undifferentiated levered equity.[27]

This brings us down to the analysis of the JV **cash flow splits** including the manager's promote at the level of the differentiated equity partners, and here we are also including the preferred equity return to the money partner that we kept track of above in her preferred capital account.

Consider first the money partner. She contributes 90 percent of the equity investment, or $180,000 of the $200,000 land purchase at time zero (and also 90 percent of the subsequent capital improvement cash requirement during the stabilized phase). Considering only the development phase, the property would be sold upon completion for $1 million at the end of year 1, and the $750,000 construction costs and loan paid off then, leaving $250,000 reversion for the two partners to split. The money partner gets first claim, up until she receives $190,800 (1.06 × $180,000). Then, the entrepreneurial partner gets his $20,000 investment back. The remaining $39,200 [$250,000 − ($190,800 + $20,000)] is then split 50/50 between

---

[23]The construction loan is still included, in part because the construction costs must in any case be paid for, and construction loans are a ubiquitous method of such payment, even among investors who do not intend to use leverage in the longer-term stabilized phase of the investment. (See Chapter 28.)

[24]In the combined investment, there is no sale or purchase of the property at year 1, merely the pay back of the construction loan.

[25]See Part VI for in-depth discussion of mortgage investment.

[26]Here we are treating the money partner's preferred equity as part of the joint venture, though in some cases it would be more appropriate to treat it separately as another line item between the debt and the residual equity entity.

[27]In the combined investment, the cash flow in year 1 is zero, because there is no sale or purchase of the property at that time and the payback of the construction loan is exactly offset by the taking out of the permanent mortgage.

the two partners, giving the preferred partner a total of $210,400 ($190,800 + $19,600). This provides a 16.89 percent expected return on the $180,000 investment, not as high as the 25 percent return expectation on the development project as a whole, but the money partner is assuming less risk due to her preferred position.

For the 11-year combined development and stabilized investment, the preferred partner is looking at an 8.13 percent expected return, again somewhat less than the 9.09 percent of the project as a whole, but this reflects her lower-risk preferred position and still provides a higher expected return than a similarly levered nonpreferred investment purchasing an already stabilized property (which we saw would be 7.40 percent).

We have already described how the partners' cash flow splits are determined during typical operating years (see our earlier discussion of years 2, 3, and 4). Picking up now where we left off in the terminal year 11, we see as follows. From the entity-level operating EBTCF that year of $23,361, the money partner receives her senior preferred return of $14,321 plus $4,707 to pay off the remaining unpaid previously earned current return as described previously, and then she receives 50 percent of the remainder, for a total of $21,195 (consisting of $14,321 + $4,707 + $2,167) from year-11 operations. From the entity-level reversion of $374,622, the money partner gets the first $233,978 to pay off the balance in her preferred equity capital account. The next $25,998 of the reversion goes to the entrepreneurial partner to pay back his equity investment, leaving an additional 50 percent of $374,622 − ($233,978 + $25,998), or $57,323 additional for the money partner from the reversion. This gives the money partner a total of $312,496 (computed as: $21,195 + $233,978 + $57,323) in year-11 cash flow.

The entrepreneurial partner's cash flows and expected returns are presented in the bottom two rows of Exhibit 15-4. As the entrepreneurial partner is the residual claimant, his cash flows may be easily calculated as the difference between the undifferentiated equity entity level EBTCF minus the preferred-partner cash flows described in the preceding paragraphs.[28] Note that the entrepreneurial investor faces the highest expected returns: 98 percent for the development phase alone, or 14.62 percent per annum for the 11-year combined levered investment. It is appropriate that the entrepreneurial partner receive the highest going-in returns, because his investment is in the riskiest position.

As noted, the arrangement in our apartment project example here does not provide for the classical hurdle-with-promote structure, in which all equity cash flows are shared pro rata pari passu until the specified hurdle return. Nevertheless, the 50/50 sharing after the preferred return does provide the entrepreneurial partner with a strong incentive to achieve superior performance in the project. In fact, the example structure combines a sort of "stick" with the usual "carrot." The "stick" is that the entrepreneurial partner does not earn *any* return at all until after the money partner makes her 6 percent. The "carrot" is that after that point, since the entrepreneurial partner gets 50 percent of the residual cash flow while having invested only 10 percent of the equity capital, he can make a very high return if the project performs sufficiently well.

The expected returns on the investment in this example apartment project are summarized in the table below.

Going-in IRR to:	For Development Phase (1 Year)	For Both Phases (11 Years)
Underlying Project	25.00%	6.54%
Undifferentiated Equity Entity	25.00%	9.09%
Preferred Equity Partner	16.89%	8.13%
Residual Equity Partner	98.00%	14.62%

---

[28]For example (and as a check), in year 11 the entrepreneurial partner's cash flow consists of, first, $2,167 as his 50% share of the excess operating cash flow that year, then $25,998 as his return of capital invested, and finally $57,323 as his 50% share of the excess reversion cash flow, for a total of $85,487.

The question now naturally arises as to whether these expected returns are *fair* to all the parties in this capital structure, and whether they provide appropriate incentives to both parties under a range of possible scenarios.[29] Should the entrepreneurial partner really receive expected returns so much higher than the money partner? On the other hand, has the entrepreneurial partner given away too much to the money partner, perhaps by excessively exposing himself to downside outcomes through the "stick" referred to earlier, by not taking a pro rata share until the money partner earns a 6 percent return? The following section will present a simple approach to begin to examine this type of question.

15.3.3 Analyzing Project-Level Capital Structure: An Example Application of Sensitivity Analysis

In principle, we know how to examine the question of the fairness of project finance and capital structure arrangements such as that described for our apartment example in the previous section. Each investor or class of investors (each of which might involve a combination of components or investment entities or "vehicles" in the capital structure) should earn an expected return going into the investment equal to the market opportunity cost of capital (OCC) for investments with similar risk characteristics. As discussed in depth in Chapters 12 and 14, the market OCC provides a zero net investment value for the marginal investors in the market. The result will be to provide each investor with an expected return risk premium that is directly proportional to the relative amount of risk that their position in the capital structure exposes them to, as the capital market perceives and values such risk.

In practice, however, it may be very difficult to ascertain what the appropriate market OCC for any particular component of a complex and unique capital structure is, such as the preferred and residual equity components and splits in our previous apartment example. In effect, there may not be a functioning "market" for unique pieces of privately held project-level capital structure, hence, no way to observe "market" return expectations. Nevertheless, some insight can be obtained by the use of artful and honest **sensitivity analysis**.

Fundamentally, the idea is to make use of the fact that the various pieces of the capital structure of the same underlying asset can often be viewed largely as *derivatives* of the underlying asset. Thus, their investment performance is highly correlated with each other and with the underlying asset, so that the *relative* amount of risk in each piece, as the capital market would view and evaluate such risk, can be ascertained by modeling the performance of each piece as a function of the performance of the underlying asset. We offer the following "binomial" analysis as a simple example of this type of approach.[30]

Returning to our apartment investment example of the previous section, the first step is to compose hypothetical "optimistic" and "pessimistic" future scenarios for the underlying project in order to determine "upside" and "downside" ex post IRR results for all of the pieces of the capital structure. The simplest way to do this is to alter the assumptions or projections about future rents, rental growth rates, and yields (cap rates) in the relevant apartment market. The idea is to produce upside and downside IRR outcomes that are roughly

---

[29]For simplicity, we will here ignore the debt component, assuming that any loans are at market interest rates in a competitive debt market, implying that the debt's expected return is fair and that the use of such debt does not alter the fairness of the equity returns. This is a reasonable assumption from a market value perspective, but recall our discussion in section 14.3 of Chapter 14 regarding after-tax investment value. If the two equity partners face different income tax situations (e.g., the money partner might be a tax-exempt institution and the entrepreneurial partner might be a taxable corporation), then from an IV perspective the two partners might not benefit equally from the debt. Nevertheless, we will assume that the borrowing decision has already been made and for whatever reasons (e.g., perhaps related to our discussion in earlier sections of the present chapter) is agreeable to both parties.

[30]The approach presented here is informal. More sophisticated or formal approaches could be considered, such as a multi-nominal simulation: three or more different outcomes, with probabilities attached to each and "relative risk" defined based on standard deviation or alternatively, on downside half-deviation. From an economics perspective, a more rigorous approach in principle will often be a real options based model (see Chapters 27 and 29). Nevertheless, the fundamental nature and basis of any such analysis is illustrated in our simple example here, which is the attempt to quantify the risk in any part of the capital structure not in an absolute sense but *relative* to the risk in the underlying asset by making use of the *derivative* nature of the pieces of the capital structure.

symmetrical above and below the going-in (expected) IRR computed at the underlying project level in the preceding analysis, and which reflect plausible positive and negative future scenarios.[31]

This has been done in Exhibits 15-5a and 15-5b by varying:

- The initial apartment rents such that the year-2 NOI is either $63,000 or $57,000 instead of the proforma (expected) assumption of $60,000. (This results in year-1 completed building values of either $1,050,000 or $950,000, instead of the $1,000,000 base case assumption.)
- The annual NOI growth rate beyond year 2 either up to 2 percent or down to zero percent instead of the base case assumption of 1 percent.
- The year-11 terminal yield (going-out resale cap rate) either down to 4.5 percent or up to 7.5 percent from the base case assumption of 6.0 percent.

The optimistic or upside scenario is defined by the simultaneous occurrence of the favorable outcome on all three of the above dimensions, while the pessimistic or downside scenario is similarly composed of the combined occurrence of the unfavorable outcome on all three dimensions.

The impact of these two scenarios is then traced through to the resulting hypothetical *ex post* IRRs achieved at each level or component of the capital structure, and thus for each investor, as seen in the lower portion of the two exhibits. For example, instead of the expected or base case going-in IRR of 25 percent for the development phase investment, the optimistic scenario results in a 50 percent return, while the pessimistic scenario results in a zero percent return, at the underlying project level. This results in upside return outcomes of 30.78 percent for the preferred partner and 223 percent for the residual partner in the development phase and in downside returns of 6 percent for the preferred partner and *negative* 54 percent for the residual partner. This compares to expected (going-in or base case) development phase returns of 16.89 percent and 98 percent, respectively, for the preferred and residual partners.

In order to relate the risk that is implied by this scenario analysis to the expected returns of each party going into the investment, we need to subtract the risk-free interest rate from the going-in expected returns to compute the expected risk premia. For example, supposing the risk-free interest rate (e.g., as proxied by the T-bill yield) is 3 percent, this implies that for the development phase investment the preferred partner faces a 13.89 percent (computed as: 16.89% − 3%) risk premium, while the residual partner faces a 95 percent risk premium. Taking the absolute range between the scenario upside and downside outcomes as a measure of relative risk, the two partners face development phase risk of 24.78 percent (computed as: 30.78% − 6%) and ±277 percent [computed as: 223% − (−54%)], respectively, for the preferred and residual partner. Dividing these ex ante risk premia by the simulated relative risk, we get a risk premium-to-risk ratio of 0.56 (computed as: 13.89/24.78) for the preferred partner and 0.34 (computed as: 95/277) for the residual partner.[32]

In principle, at least as a starting point, one might expect that these two ratios should be approximately equal, implying the same expected return risk premium *per unit of risk* (equal "risk-adjusted" returns, for a common "price of risk") across the two partners, at least if the risk model implied by our scenario sensitivity analysis is a reasonably complete and unbiased representation of the *relative* amount of risk that matters in the capital markets. The fact that the residual partner is looking at a risk premium-to-risk ratio considerably below that of the preferred partner suggests that the residual partner may not be getting a "fair" deal in the proposed capital structure, at least relative to the preferred partner. See Exhibit 15-6, in

---

[31]While ex post returns distributions for individual pieces of the capital structure are often rather asymmetric, an assumption of symmetric probability around the underlying asset return is usually pretty reasonable for income-generating real estate assets. There will, however, be exceptions to this general guideline.

[32]These ratios are akin to what is known in investment management analysis as "Treynor Ratios," the risk premium per unit of risk where risk is measured by a one-dimensional metric reflecting how the capital market prices risk in the asset market. Here we are taking the absolute range of our scenario analysis outcomes as a proxy for the risk metric, *relative to* the risk in the underlying asset (the apartment property in this case).

which the straight line reflects the price of risk, that is, the ex ante risk premium per unit of risk in the underlying asset, implying that in principle the going-in expected returns of all parties should lie on that straight line.[33] Perhaps the lack of a pro rata pari passu provision prior to the 6 percent hurdle, in combination with the height of the 6 percent preferred return hurdle (along with the 50/50 residual cash flow split provision), puts the residual partner at too much of a disadvantage.

Of course, this is only a suggestion, not in itself a definitive analysis, because there are aspects of risk and the investors' objectives and concerns that are not included in the above model and analysis. For example, in practice it is common for the entrepreneurial partner, assuming he is serving effectively as the operational manager of the investment, to take "asset management fees" (or "developer fees" if it is a development project) off of the top of any equity cash flow to the joint venture. (Sometimes some of these fees are even paid for out of the construction loan.) These fees may be structured in various ways, and for institutional investment are typically on the order of 1 percent of the invested capital per year. While such fees should be interpreted at least in part as a fee for service (not a return on financial investment), they serve to increase the revenue and reduce the risk position of the managing partner.[34]

It should also be noted that the partners' risk quantification described by the simple ratios computed here apply only *relative to* the price of risk provided by the underlying investment. For example, if the underlying investment is a positive NPV proposition, meaning that it provides an ex ante return premium in excess of the market price of risk, then even a partner who obtains a lower risk premium to risk ratio (below the straight line in Exhibit 15-6) might be looking at a "fair" return in the sense that it is providing at least equal to the market price of risk.[35]

Finally, it should be noted that a very important additional dimension to analyzing capital structure regards the incentive ramifications for the various participants. This is particularly true regarding the joint venture arrangements and the implications for the equity partners. It is important to consider what sort of incentives each party will face under various scenarios, including substantial upside and substantial downside outcomes that differ sharply from the initial expectations. This can be particularly important in the event of downside outcomes, and especially in the case of development projects, which will depend on the managing partner continuing to perform to bring the project to as successful a conclusion as possible even though things have not worked out as originally anticipated and hoped. While such incentive considerations are not unrelated to the sort of "fairness" considerations noted above, they do present an important additional type of consideration. For example, incentive considerations no doubt underlie much of the rationale for the widespread use of pro rata pari passu arrangements which give the managing partner equal returns to the money partner in downside scenarios even though the managing partner receives a promote that gives him much higher returns in the upside.

---

[33] Note that the line in Exhibit 15-6 may not be the relevant "security market line" (SML), which would reflect the *market's* price of risk for the underlying asset. If the underlying asset is being obtained at a price that differs from its market value (nonzero NPV acquisition), then the slope of the line through the underlying asset expected return in Exhibit 15-6 would differ from the *market's* price of risk. As suggested earlier, the line in Exhibit 15-6 is like a "Treynor Ratio" of the underlying asset.

[34] They may be subject to different income tax treatment than the cash flow splits.

[35] In addition, there are other important considerations not addressed in this example. In general, the same types of agency costs we described earlier regarding COFD in section 15.2.3 regarding debt can also potentially cause problems in equity joint venture splits. Asymmetry in the managing partner's incentives needs to be seriously considered. Some of the important considerations not addressed in this simple example include questions of control over major capital decisions (including control of the resale decision, which is typically done via some sort of "buy/sell agreement" that specifies how either equity partner can buy out the other's interest, as well as and the value of the borrower's "put option" that the equity joint venture has to potentially default on the debt in downside scenarios (effectively limiting the liability of the joint venture, as will be described in Chapter 16). It should also be noted that there are alternative ways to define the relative risk measure. For example, particularly if the capital structure results in asymmetrical outcomes for one or more investors, it may be appealing to define the relative "risk that matters" as only the downside half-range (the deviation of the pessimistic outcome below the going-in expected return).

Calendar Years Ending:	Year 0	Year 1	Year 2	Year 3	Year 4	Year 5	Year 6	Year 7	Year 8	Year 9	Year 10	Year 11
Project Cash Requirements as Proposed:												
Site Acquisition	200,000											
Hard & Soft Development Costs		750,000										
Total Development Phase Cash Requirements	(200,000)	(750,000)										
Development Phase Total Equity Funding	200,000											
Development Phase Debt Funding (Construction Loan)		750,000										
Construction Loan Repayment		(750,000)										
Proposed Permanent Loan Amount (Take Out)		750,000										
Operating PBTCF			63,000	64,260	15,545	66,856	68,193	69,557	70,948	22,367	73,815	75,291
Reversion PBTCF			0	0	0	0	0	0	0	0	0	1,706,592
PBTCF			**63,000**	**64,260**	**15,545**	**66,856**	**68,193**	**69,557**	**70,948**	**22,367**	**73,815**	**1,781,883**
Permanent Loan Debt Service			(43,250)	(43,140)	(43,030)	(42,920)	(42,810)	(42,700)	(42,590)	(42,480)	(42,370)	(42,260)
Permanent Loan Repayment												(730,000)
Permanent Loan Debt CFs		750,000	(43,250)	(43,140)	(43,030)	(42,920)	(42,810)	(42,700)	(42,590)	(42,480)	(42,370)	(772,260)
Operating EBTCF			19,750	21,120	(27,485)	23,936	25,383	26,857	28,358	(20,113)	31,445	33,031
Reversion EBTCF			0	0	0	0	0	0	0	0	0	976,592
EBTCF			**19,750**	**21,120**	**(27,485)**	**23,936**	**25,383**	**26,857**	**28,358**	**(20,113)**	**31,445**	**1,009,623**
Preferred Equity Capital Account:												
Preferred Return Allocation:												
Beginning Equity Investment Balance	0	180,000	190,800	182,498	180,000	215,536	204,736	204,736	204,736	204,736	235,122	222,838
Annual Preferred Investment	180,000	0	0	0	24,736	0	0	0	0	18,102	0	0
Preferred Return Earned	0	10,800	11,448	10,950	10,800	12,932	12,284	12,284	12,284	12,284	14,107	13,370
Preferred Return Paid	0	0	(11,448)	(10,950)	0	(12,932)	(12,284)	(12,284)	(12,284)	0	(14,107)	(13,370)
Payment of previous earned	0	0	(8,302)	(2,498)	0	(10,800)	0	0	0	0	(12,284)	0
Accrued But Unpaid Preferred Return	0	10,800	0	0	10,800	0	0	0	0	12,284	0	0
Ending Equity Investment Balance	180,000	190,800	182,498	180,000	215,536	204,736	204,736	204,736	204,736	235,122	222,838	222,838
Reversion Preferred Allocations:												
Allocation to Satisfy Preferred Return Requirement												(222,838)
Allocation to Return Subordinated Investment Requirement												(24,760)

(Exhibit continues on next page)

EXHIBIT 15-5A Apartment Property Example Cash Flows, Splits, and Returns, Optimistic Scenario

Annual CF approximations for purpose of checking fairness of splits	IRR	Year 0	Year 1	Year 2	Year 3	Year 4	Year 5	Year 6	Year 7	Year 8	Year 9	Year 10	Year 11
Project-Level Cash Flows*:													
Construction Phase	50.00%	(200,000)	300,000										
Operational Phase	9.54%		(1,050,000)	63,000	64,260	15,545	66,856	68,193	69,557	70,948	22,367	73,815	1,781,883
Both Phases	10.59%	(200,000)	(750,000)	63,000	64,260	15,545	66,856	68,193	69,557	70,948	22,367	73,815	1,781,883
Debt Investor Cash Flows:	5.50%		(750,000)	43,250	43,140	43,030	42,920	42,810	42,700	42,590	42,480	42,370	772,260
Entity-Level Cash Flows (EBTCF)**:													
Construction Phase	50.00%	(200,000)	300,000										
Operational Phase	15.66%		(300,000)	19,750	21,120	(27,485)	23,936	25,383	26,857	28,358	(20,113)	31,445	1,009,623
Both Phases	18.81%	(200,000)	0	19,750	21,120	(27,485)	23,936	25,383	26,857	28,358	(20,113)	31,445	1,009,623
Preferred-Partner-Level Cash Flows:													
Construction Phase (If sell on completion)	30.78%	(180,000)	235,400										
Both Phases	14.96%	(180,000)	0	19,750	17,284	(24,736)	23,834	18,834	19,571	20,321	(18,102)	28,918	610,536
Subordinated-Partner-Level Cash Flows:													
Construction Phase (If sell on completion)	223.00%	(20,000)	64,600										
Both Phases	33.70%	(20,000)	0	0	3,836	(2,748)	102	6,550	7,286	8,037	(2,011)	2,527	399,087

* Sometimes referred to as "Asset Level."
**To the LLC joint venture partnership as a whole.

EXHIBIT 15-5A (Continued)

© OnCourse Learning

Calendar Years Ending:	Year 0	Year 1	Year 2	Year 3	Year 4	Year 5	Year 6	Year 7	Year 8	Year 9	Year 10	Year 11
Project Cash Requirements as Proposed:												
Site Acquisition	200,000											
Hard & Soft Development Costs		750,000										
Total Development Phase Cash Requirements	(200,000)	(750,000)										
Development Phase Total Equity Funding	200,000											
Development Phase Debt Funding												
(Construction Loan)		750,000										
Construction Loan Repayment		(750,000)										
Proposed Permanent Loan Amount (Take Out)		750,000										
Operating PBTCF			57,000	57,000	7,000	57,000	57,000	57,000	57,000	7,000	57,000	57,000
Reversion PBTCF			0	0	0	0	0	0	0	0	0	760,000
PBTCF			**57,000**	**57,000**	**7,000**	**57,000**	**57,000**	**57,000**	**57,000**	**7,000**	**57,000**	**817,000**
Permanent Loan Debt Service			(43,250)	(43,140)	(43,030)	(42,920)	(42,810)	(42,700)	(42,590)	(42,480)	(42,370)	(42,260)
Permanent Loan Repayment												(730,000)
Permanent Loan Debt CFs		750,000	(43,250)	(43,140)	(43,030)	(42,920)	(42,810)	(42,700)	(42,590)	(42,480)	(42,370)	(772,260)
Operating EBTCF			13,750	13,860	(36,030)	14,080	14,190	14,300	14,410	(35,480)	14,630	14,740
Reversion EBTCF			0	0	0	0	0	0	0	0	0	30,000
EBTCF			**13,750**	**13,860**	**(36,030)**	**14,080**	**14,190**	**14,300**	**14,410**	**(35,480)**	**14,630**	**44,740**
Preferred Equity Capital Account:												
Preferred Return Allocation:												
Beginning Equity Investment Balance	0	180,000	190,800	188,498	185,948	229,532	229,224	228,787	228,214	227,497	273,079	274,834
Annual Preferred Investment	180,000	0	0	0	32,427	0	0	0	0	31,932	0	0
Preferred Return Earned	0	10,800	11,448	11,310	11,157	13,772	13,753	13,727	13,693	13,650	16,385	16,490
Preferred Return Paid	0	0	(11,448)	(11,310)	0	(13,772)	(13,753)	(13,727)	(13,693)	0	(14,630)	(14,740)
Payment of previous earned			(2,302)	(2,550)	0	(308)	(437)	(573)	(717)	0	0	0
Accrued But Unpaid Preferred Return	0	10,800	0	0	11,157	0	0	0	0	13,650	1,755	1,750
Ending Equity Investment Balance	180,000	190,800	188,498	185,948	229,532	229,224	228,787	228,214	227,497	273,079	274,834	276,584
Reversion Preferred Allocations:												
Allocation to Satisfy Preferred Return Requirement												(30,000)
Allocation to Return Subordinated Investment Requirement												0

EXHIBIT 15-5B Apartment Property Example Cash Flows, Splits, and Returns, Pessimistic Scenario

(Exhibit continues on next page)

Annual CF approximations for purpose of checking fairness of splits	IRR***	Year 0	Year 1	Year 2	Year 3	Year 4	Year 5	Year 6	Year 7	Year 8	Year 9	Year 10	Year 11
Project-Level Cash Flows*:													
Construction Phase	0.00%	(200,000)	(950,000)										
Operational Phase	3.22%		57,000	57,000	57,000	7,000	57,000	57,000	57,000	57,000	7,000	57,000	817,000
Both Phases	3.14%	(200,000)	(750,000)	57,000	57,000	7,000	57,000	57,000	57,000	57,000	7,000	57,000	817,000
Debt Investor Cash Flows:	5.50%		(750,000)	43,250	43,140	43,030	42,920	42,810	42,700	42,590	42,480	42,370	772,260
Entity-Level Cash Flows (EBTCF):**													
Construction Phase	0.00%	(200,000)	200,000										
Operational Phase	−11.74%		(200,000)	13,750	13,860	(36,030)	14,080	14,190	14,300	14,410	(35,480)	14,630	44,740
Both Phases	−10.58%	(200,000)	0	13,750	13,860	(36,030)	14,080	14,190	14,300	14,410	(35,480)	14,630	44,740
Preferred-Partner-Level Cash Flows:													
Construction Phase (If sell on completion)	6.00%	(180,000)	190,800										
Both Phases	−8.85%	(180,000)	0	13,750	13,860	(32,427)	14,080	14,190	14,300	14,410	(31,932)	14,630	44,740
Subordinated-Partner-Level Cash Flows:													
Construction Phase (If sell on completion)	−54.00%	(20,000)	9,200										
Both Phases	−100.00%	(20,000)	0	0	0	(3,603)	0	0	0	0	(3,548)	0	0

* Sometimes referred to as "Asset Level."

**To the LLC joint venture partnership as a whole.

*** "−100%" is a label for "total wipe out", not a literal IRR.

EXHIBIT 15-5B (Continued)

© OnCourse Learning

EXHIBIT 15-6 Framework for Evaluating Fairness of Capital Structure Terms

© OnCourse Learning

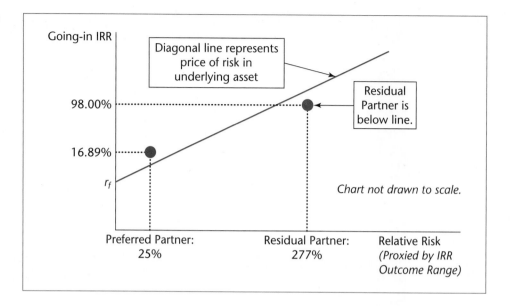

15.4 Chapter Summary

This chapter reviewed the value of debt financing of real estate equity investments from the perspective of the equity investor. In this chapter, we broached the question of optimal capital structure (the share of debt versus equity) in real estate investment, but we did not attempt to offer a definitive answer to this question. We instead sought to clarify the major issues and considerations that are important for designing finance strategy for various types of real estate investors. These issues lie on both sides of the argument for the use of debt and affect different types of investors in different ways. The treatment of capital structure in this chapter should be viewed in combination with our discussion of leverage in Chapter 13 and of tax considerations related to the value of debt from the equity investor's perspective in Chapter 14.

The obvious overall result of a comprehensive consideration of the pros and cons of debt is that, on balance, some investors find it more profitable to borrow, while others find it more profitable to lend. This result applies both to real estate investors and to investors at large. The debt market equilibrates these two positions in the aggregate, with the resulting interest rates and yields that are observed in that market. (In Part VI, we will move to a consideration of mortgages from the lender's perspective.)

To summarize Chapter 15 and Part V, clearly, no single "correct" capital structure exists for all real estate investments or all investors. However, it does appear likely that relatively "transparent" and stable, low-volatility investments such as most income-producing properties can optimally support higher levels of debt than can more managerially complicated, higher-risk underlying assets such as many industrial and service corporations. The widespread use of large amounts of debt in real estate investment (over $3 trillion outstanding for commercial mortgages in the United States) suggests that this is so. On the other hand, casual empiricism suggests that the major reason why real estate investors get into trouble usually has to do with excessive debt (at least, with the advantage of hindsight). Both the equity investors (borrowers) and the debt investors (lenders) suffer in this repeating play. Perhaps the conventional wisdom "hypes up" the advantages of debt a bit more than is really warranted. So, be careful!

KEY TERMS

capital structure
ultimate investors (individuals)
equity capital constraint
human capital
IV-based NPV
diversification (and debt)
banker's spread
control and governance issues
management incentives
liquidity
decision flexibility
costs of financial distress (COFD)

third-party costs
foreclosure
bankruptcy
agency costs
limited liability
ex ante costs (probabilistic expectations)
inflation
hedging inflation risk
real returns
reverse-inflation risk
multiple-note mortgages

mezzanine debt
preferred equity
common (or residual) equity
differentiated equity partners (classes)
joint venture
entrepreneurial partner
money partner
pro rata pari passu
promote (hurdle and preferred return)
capital account
cash flow splits
sensitivity analysis

STUDY QUESTIONS

Conceptual Questions

15.1. What is "human capital," and in what sense does debt financing allow small- to moderate-scale real estate entrepreneurs to "leverage their own human capital"?

15.2. Why does the ability to leverage positive-NPV opportunities and the ability to diversify property investments make an argument in favor of borrowing for investors that face a constraint on their supply of equity capital but not for investors that are not so constrained (such as REITs or open-end funds)?

15.3. Discuss the following statement: One reason to borrow money to finance a real estate investment is to reduce your risk exposure. If you borrow $80,000 and put up only $20,000 of your own money to buy a $100,000 property, you have less of your own money at risk, particularly if you take the extra money that you would otherwise have put in the property and put it in a safe investment such as CDs or Treasury bonds instead.

15.4. What types of investors or investment entities are likely to truly face a serious equity capital constraint? How does the issue of governance and control of the underlying asset interact with the capital structure question so that it may appear to some investors that they face an equity constraint?

15.5. Explain why constraints on equity capital are probably not as widespread as is often assumed in real estate, even for relatively small individual investors.

15.6. How can it make sense for a pension fund, which is tax-exempt, to borrow money to finance a real estate equity investment?

15.7. Describe the management incentive argument for the use of debt financing in real estate. Why might this argument be more relevant for understanding the use of debt by equity real estate investment trusts (REITs) than for project-level finance decisions by private real estate entrepreneurs? [Hint: Why might REIT investors (i.e., shareholders) want REIT managers to employ debt financing?]

15.8. What is the relationship between debt and liquidity, and why is liquidity valuable for investors? Are there considerations peculiar to real estate that affect the value of liquidity? If so, what are they?

15.9. Describe the two fundamental sources of the costs of financial distress (COFD). How is the COFD related to the ex ante cost of debt capital faced by the borrower at the time of the financing decision?

15.10. Is the expectation of future inflation a reason for real estate equity investors to borrow money to finance their real estate investments? Explain why or why not.

15.11. (**Putting it all together**). Chapters 13 through 15 provide a comprehensive exploration of the role of debt financing in equity real estate investment. Based on material presented in these three chapters, discuss the pros and cons of borrowing to finance real estate investments. As part of your answer, describe at least two considerations that would always be a negative for debt for any investor, and at least two considerations that would always be positive for virtually any investor. In addition, explain how leverage, taxes, liquidity, and inflation considerations might lead some investors to prefer borrowing and others to avoid borrowing.

15.12. What is mezzanine debt? Why is mezzanine debt referred to as an intermediate or hybrid parts of the project-level capital structure or capital stack?

15.13. What does each partner bring to the deal in a typical real estate development joint venture arrangement between a local entrepreneur and national capital source? What does each partner expect to get out of the deal?

15.14. Describe the pro rata pari passu arrangement with a "promote" for determining the allocation (or split) of overall equity cash flows to the equity partners. What is the purpose of the "promote"?

Quantitative Problems

15.15. Believe it or not, Bob has amassed quite a lot of human capital in the form of his property management expertise. For every 100,000 SF of property Bob manages, he can earn $20,000 per year of net "wages," over and above what he could earn doing anything else with his time. Over Bob's expected remaining active lifetime, these earnings amount to a present value of $200,000 for every 100,000 SF he manages permanently. Bob has the capacity to manage up to 1,000,000 SF of property at any given time. However, Bob likes to work on his own, and so he prefers to manage his own properties rather than hiring himself out as a third-party manager. (This is more efficient and allows Bob more freedom and flexibility to use his expertise to the maximum.) The types of properties Bob knows how to manage cost $50/SF and come in buildings of 100,000 SF each. Suppose Bob has access to over $100 million of equity capital, consisting of his own wealth and that of some partners whom he feels comfortable with and that he knows they will not interfere with his property management practices.

   a. What is the value to Bob of being able to borrow up to 80% of the value of any properties he buys?

   b. Now suppose Bob can access only $10 million of equity without jeopardizing his ability to control management. What is the value to Bob of being able to borrow up to 60% of the value of any properties he buys? What is the value to him of being able to borrow up to 80% of property value?

15.16. Consider the numerical example of a multi-tiered capital structure in section 15.3.2. Suppose that the time zero cost of the land is not $200,000 but $220,000 and that the relatively passive equity money partner contributes 85% of the equity cash requirement rather than 90%. These are the only two parameters of the deal that change. Recalculate the figures in the preferred equity capital account as well as the cash flows to the preferred and subordinated equity partners in years 1 through 4. That is, revise the numbers in Exhibit 15-3 for these years. Do this first by hand, and then check your answers using the Excel worksheet for this chapter on the accompanying CD.

15.17. (**Hybrid Financing with a "Lookback" IRR**) An investor acquires a property with expected operating cash flows (PBTCF) shown below. In addition to a senior permanent mortgage loan, the capital structure includes a mezzanine loan with the following features: $15 million loan, 10-year term, 1% upfront fee, 7% annual interest and annual payments. Payments are interest-only payments in years 1 through 5. Principal payments, in addition to interest, start in year 6 and are specified as a function of PBTCF as follows: year 6 = 10% of property operating PBTCF, year 7 = 20%, years 8, 9, and 10 = 25% of PBTCF. In addition, at the end of year 10, the investor must make a lump sum payment such that the mez lender receives a 14% internal rate of return on the mez loan investment. This lump sum includes the principal or balance owing on the loan plus a bonus to bump the expected total return to 14%. Based on this information and the property cash flows, show the expected loan cash flows and determine the size of the lump sum and the bonus that must be paid. [Hints: Answer this in Excel either using trial and error with the "=IRR()" function or alternatively using the "Solver" tool. Note that the mez lender's initial time zero investment is $14.85 million because of the upfront 1% fee, though interest payments are based on the full $15 million principal amount]

	1	2	3	4	5	6	7	8	9	10
PBTCF	6,746	9,894	10,505	11,283	11,780	12,348	12,920	13,438	14,201	14,694

Ahern, T., Y. Liang, and N. Myer. 1998. Leverage in a pension fund real estate program. *Real Estate Finance* 15(2): 55–62.

Altshuler, D., and R. Schneiderman. 2011. Overpayment of manager incentive fees – When preferred returns & IRR hurdles differ. *Journal of Real Estate Portfolio Management* 17(2): 182–89.

Brealey, R., and S. Myers. 1996. *Principles of Corporate Finance*, 5th ed. New York: McGraw-Hill, Chapters 13–14 and pp. 17–19.

Brounen, D., and P. Eichholtz. 2005. Corporate real estate ownership implications: International performance evidence. *Journal of Real Estate Finance and Economics* 30(4): 429–45.

Cannaday, R., and T. Yang. 1996. Optimal leverage strategy: Capital structure in real estate investment. *Journal of Real Estate Finance and Economics* 13(3): 263–71.

Carey, S. A. 2006. Real estate JV promote calculations: Recycling profits. *Real Estate Finance Journal* (summer 2006).

Childs, P., D. Mauer, and S. Ott. 2005. Interactions of corporate financing and investment decisions: The effects of agency conflicts. *Journal of Financial Economics* 76(3): 667–90.

Childs, P., S. Ott, and T. Riddiough. 1997. Leasing risk, financing risk and capital structure decisions. Real Estate Research Institute (RERI) Working Paper (WP-64).

Clayton, J. 2009. Debt matters (more than it should): Leverage, liquidity and property valuation. *Journal of Real Estate Portfolio Management* 15(1).

Cooper, I. and K. Nyborg. 2008. Tax-Adjusted Discount Rates with Investor Taxes and Risky Debt. *Financial Management* 37(2): 365–379.

Esifeldt, A., and A. Rampini. 2009. Leasing, ability to repossess, and debt capacity. *Review of Financial Studies* 22(4): 1621–57.

Feng, Z., C. Ghosh, and C. F. Sirmans. 2007. On the capital structure of real estate investment trusts (REITs). *Journal of Real Estate Finance and Economics* 34(1): 81–105.

Fisher, L. 2004. The wealth effects of sale and leasebacks: New evidence. *Real Estate Economics* 32(4).

Gau, G., and K. Wang. 1990. Capital structure decisions in real estate investment. *Real Estate Economics* 18(4): 501–21.

Geltner, D. 1999. Debt and taxes: A pension fund investment perspective. *Real Estate Finance* 16(3).

Ghosh, C., R. Nag, and C. F. Sirmans. 1997. Financing choice by equity REITs in the 1990s. *Real Estate Finance* 14(3): 41–50.

Hardin, W., and M. Hill. 2008. REIT dividend determinants: Excess dividends and capital markets. *Real Estate Economics* 36(2): 349–69.

Howe, J., and J. Shilling. 1988. Capital structure theory and REIT security offerings. *Journal of Finance* 43(4): 983–93.

Jaffe, J. 1991. Taxes and the capital structure of partnerships, REITs, and related entities. *Journal of Finance* 46(1): 401–7.

Jensen, M. 1986. Agency costs and free cash flow, corporate finance & takeovers. *American Economic Review* 26: 332.

Khandani, A., A. Lo, and R. Merton. 2009. Systemic risk and the refinancing ratchet effect. MIT Sloan Research Paper No. 4750-09, Harvard Business School Finance Working Paper No. 1472892.

Kok, N., N. Miller, and P. Morris. 2011. The economics of green retrofits. Working Paper, Burnham-Moores Center for Real Estate, University of San Diego.

Lewellen, W., J. Long, and M. McConnell. 1976. Asset leasing in competitive capital markets. *Journal of Finance* 31(5): 787–98.

Maris, B., and F. Elayan. 1990. Capital structure and the cost of capital for untaxed firms: The case of REITs. *Real Estate Economics* 18(1): 22–39.

McDonald, J. 1999. Optimal leverage in real estate investments. *Journal of Real Estate Finance and Economics* 18(2): 239–52.

Miller, N., and P. McKeown. 1979. Optimizing the distributions of limited partnership returns. *Real Estate Economics* 7(3): 393–409.

Modigliani, F., and M. Miller. 1958. Cost of capital, corporation finance and the theory of investment. *American Economic Review* 48(3): 261–97.

Myers, S., D. Dill, and A. Bautista. 1976. Valuation of financial lease contracts. *Journal of Finance* 31: 799–819.

Myers, S. 1974. Interactions of corporate finance and investment decisions: Implications for capital budgeting. *Journal of Finance* 29: 1–25.

O'Mara, M. 1999. *Strategy & Place: Managing Corporate Real Estate and Facilities for Competitive Advantage.*, New York: The Free Press.

Rutherford, R. C. 1990. Empirical evidence on shareholder value and the sale-leaseback of corporate real estate. *Real Estate Economics* 18(4): 522–29.

Sirmans, C. F., and B. A. Slade. 2010. Sale-leaseback transactions: Price premiums and market efficiency. *Journal of Real Estate Research* 32(2): 221–42.

Slovin, M. B., M. E. Sushka, and J. A. Polonchek. 1990. Corporate sale-and-leasebacks and shareholder wealth. *Journal of Finance* 45(1): 289–99.

Yan, A. 2006. Leasing and debt financing: Substitutes or complements? *Journal of Financial and Quantitative Analysis* 41(3): 709–31.

MORTGAGES FROM AN INVESTMENT PERSPECTIVE

In Part V, we discussed real estate debt from the perspective of the equity investor, the borrower. We pointed out that, from the broader perspective of the capital markets and the investment industry as a whole, the borrowing transaction creates two different types of "investment products" from the same underlying real asset: levered property equity and debt secured by the property. Each of these two products appeals to different types of investors. Investors who are more risk averse, possibly more tolerant of inflation risk, and who need more current income from their investments, or who want an asset with a specified finite lifetime and do not want to be involved in property management, find real estate debt to be an appealing type of investment product. The debt market equates the supply (borrowers wanting debt capital) and demand (debt investors) in the market for debt products of all types, including mortgages, which are debt products backed by real estate assets. (Or one can look at it the other way, the borrowers representing the "demand" for financial capital—money—while the lenders provide the "supply" of such capital.)

The debt market as a whole is arguably the largest, deepest, and most technically sophisticated of all the branches of the capital markets. It includes both short- and long-term U.S. government debt, international bonds, corporate and municipal bonds, commercial paper, both residential and commercial mortgages, and asset-backed securities, including both residential and commercial mortgage-backed securities (MBS). In the United States alone, by the early 2010s there were over $36 trillion worth of tradable debt assets outstanding, over a third of which were based directly or indirectly on real estate. These included some $2.5 trillion worth of directly held commercial mortgages (whole loans), plus well over a half-trillion dollars' worth of commercial mortgage-backed securities (CMBS). Before the 2008 financial crisis and recession, more than $200 billion of commercial mortgages were issued in the United States in a typical year.

Even if your primary focus is on equity investment in real estate, you need to have some depth of familiarity with the debt side of the picture, that is, with real estate debt from the perspective of the debt investor. Not only is such perspective necessary to deepen and round out the understanding of the equity investor, but also real estate debt provides a large and important set of professional career opportunities for graduate students in the real estate field. Many major real estate investors, such as pension funds and life insurance companies, deal simultaneously in both equity and debt products as investors.

With this in mind, the five chapters in Part VI will introduce the basic concepts, terminology, and methodologies useful for understanding and dealing with real estate debt from the debt investor's perspective. We have two primary specific objectives in this part. First, we want you to understand enough of the debt investor's typical perspective and concerns so that you, as an equity investor (or working for an equity investor), can be an effective partner, either on the same or opposite side of a deal with a debt investor. Second, we want to extend your understanding of real estate debt sufficiently so that you can be somewhat creative in putting together real estate financing packages, whether you are working from the equity or debt investment side. To this end, Chapters 16 and 17 will present mortgage fundamentals (most of which are in fact relevant to both residential and commercial loans). Chapters 18 and 19 will then delve in more depth into the underlying economics of the debt market in general, and commercial mortgage investment and underwriting in particular. Finally, Chapter 20 introduces some basic concepts and tools used in the CMBS industry (and we will note some of the considerations in that industry in the aftermath of the 2008–2009 financial crisis, which affected the CMBS market severely).

MORTGAGE BASICS I: AN INTRODUCTION AND OVERVIEW

LEARNING OBJECTIVES

After reading this chapter, you should understand:

⊃ The legal and financial structure of mortgages.

⊃ The major different types of real estate mortgages in the United States and how the mortgage industry works.

⊃ The major legal terms and legal characteristics of mortgages.

⊃ The nature and costs of the foreclosure process and the workout process as a way to avoid foreclosure.

T he classical form of real estate debt is the **mortgage**, a loan secured by real property as collateral. The word *mortgage* comes from two Middle English words (which are actually French in origin): *gage* meant an obligation or commitment (as in our modern word *engaged*), while *mort* referred to death or dying. Hence, it was a "dying commitment," that is, a commitment that was not permanent but had a finite lifetime. In return for present value obtained, a landowner committed himself to pay compensation in money or in-kind over a period of time in the future, but not forever. As land was the direct source of most wealth in medieval times, it was natural to secure the mortgage with a pledge of real property. Thus, mortgage lending is one of the oldest forms of debt recognized in Anglo-Saxon law.

In the present chapter, we will focus on the basic legal and financial structure of the mortgage; fundamental terminology and concepts that apply to virtually all mortgages, residential as well as commercial; and to standard fixed rate and adjustable rate loans as well as other more exotic species. As always, our focus is primarily on loans on commercial property, although at the basic level of this chapter, all mortgages have much in common. We begin with an introductory overview of the different types of mortgages and branches of the mortgage industry.

To begin, let us note the magnitude and importance of mortgage lending in real estate investment. Mortgages are traditionally the largest source of financial capital for most real estate purchases and investment in the United States. Exhibit 16-1 provides an overview as of 2011. Panel A shows that the majority of the $13.5 trillion U.S. mortgage debt outstanding was secured by owner-occupied homes, with $3.1 trillion commercial mortgages outstanding. Of the approximately $10.4 trillion residential loans (mostly on single-family homes), almost $6 trillion was held by Government Sponsored Enterprises (GSEs) and agencies, dominated by Fannie Mae (FNMA) and Freddie Mac (FHLMC) including the securitized mortgage pools sponsored by those agencies. Almost $3 trillion was held by commercial banks and savings institutions ("thrifts") or credit unions. Over $1 trillion was securitized in loan pools sponsored by private asset backed securities (ABS) issuers other than the GSEs, a relatively new development since the late 1990s.

Panel B of Exhibit 16-1 portrays the capital structure of commercial property, focusing on so-called "institutional" assets (relatively larger properties), as estimated by Property & Portfolio Research (a division of the CoStar Group). Note that over half of the capital invested in such property is in the form of debt. The "public debt" component in Panel B refers to debt that has been securitized, meaning that tradable bonds have been issued backed by pools of commercial mortgages. This component is over $1 trillion outstanding and includes commercial mortgage backed securities (CMBS) as well as the commercial mortgages held by publicly traded entities such as Fannie Mae and Freddie Mac (loans on apartment properties) and mortgage REITs.

Panel C of Exhibit 16-1 shows the sources of the capital as measured by who is holding the $3.1 trillion of commercial mortgages outstanding as of 2011. Exhibit 16-2 shows the evolution of the capital sources since 1978. The largest source includes commercial banks and savings institutions, including many small to medium sized local and regional banks. These institutions typically specialize in construction loans and short-term loans on completed properties. Of the $3.1 trillion total, almost $800 billion were construction loans as of 2011, most of this from among the $1.5 trillion held by banks and similar depository institutions. Construction and short-term commercial mortgages are often part of the banks' traditional "relationship lending" business, in which the bank cultivates a local business as a client for various services including as a borrower from the bank, and the bank then tends to hold such loans in the bank's own asset portfolio. Banks and such depository institutions tend to be particularly important in lending to smaller commercial properties and those in smaller communities. Nonbank sources of capital are more important for the larger properties.

Life insurance companies (LICs) are also a major source of commercial mortgages, and they tend to focus on larger properties and longer-term loans (typically 5–10 years in maturity). The LIC-sourced component of the Panel C pie chart are so-called "**whole loans**" (not securitized), retained in the LIC's own portfolios, though life insurers also sometimes sell loans into pools for the CMBS market (and sometimes invest in CMBS securities themselves). Exhibit 16-2 reveals that over the past several decades the role of life insurers as holders of whole-loan commercial mortgages has declined relatively speaking in the United States, though it remains large and important, especially for larger properties in prime locations. Exhibit 16-2 shows that the decline in LIC share has largely been taken up by the advent of the CMBS industry.

The CMBS component of Panel C represents over $600 billion of securities backed by commercial mortgage pools (down from a peak of over $800 billion before the 2008 financial crisis), including many medium-sized "conduit loans" issued by various originators (including commercial and investment banks). CMBS lending grew rapidly from its inception in the mid-1990s and became a major source of financing for medium to large size commercial properties before the financial crisis. The near-collapse of this industry in 2008–2009 was a major element in the commercial real estate crash of that period, and the industry has been a focus of attempts at reform and recovery since then, including aspects of the Dodd-Frank Wall Street Reform and Consumer Protection Act of 2010.

Both Panel C of Exhibit 16-1 and Exhibit 16-2 reveal that during the 2000s the GSEs assumed a larger and important role in providing debt capital to multifamily housing. Particularly in the aftermath of the 2008 financial crisis these were the only major sources of commercial mortgage credit still available. As noted, however, the long-term future of these agencies is in doubt as of 2011.

EXHIBIT 16-1 Overview of U.S. Mortgage Debt Outstanding as of 2011

Panel A
U.S. Mortgages Outstanding, 2011 $13.5 trillion

Sources: FRB, CoStar Group Inc.

Panel B
U.S. Institutional Commercial Real Estate Capital Structure, 2011 $4.1 trillion

Source: CoStar Group Inc.

Panel C
U.S. Commercial Mortgages Sources, 2011 $3 trillion outstanding

Source: CoStar Group Inc.

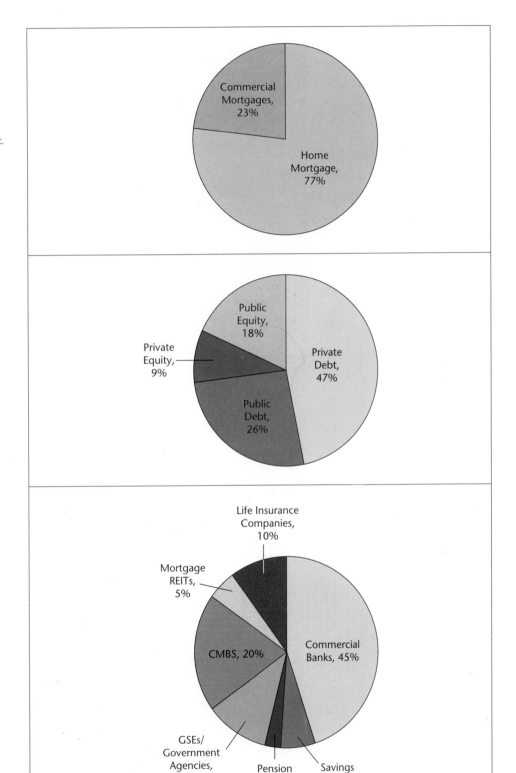

EXHIBIT 16-2 U.S. Commercial and Multifamily Mortgages Share of Outstanding Balance Held by Various Capital Sources, 1978–2011

Source: Federal Reserve Board.

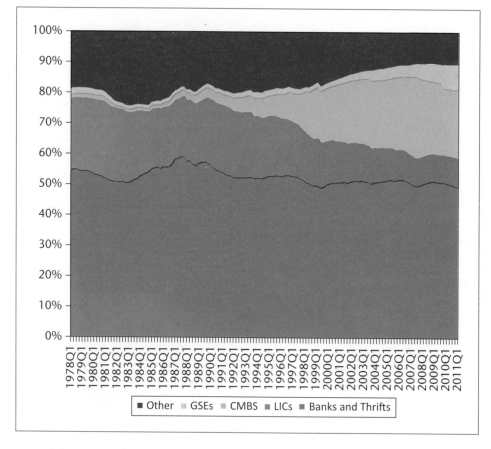

Exhibit 16-3 shows the quarterly magnitude of the net flow of capital into commercial mortgages (including multifamily) from 1978 to 2011, including the share that was CMBS. The flow of mortgage capital into commercial real estate has been famously cyclical, tending to peak in the big property booms just before the big crashes. This is seen in Exhibit 16-3

EXHIBIT 16-3 U.S. Commercial and Multifamily Quarterly Mortgage Flows, 1978–2011 (Change in Balance Outstanding)

Source: Based on data from the Federal Reserve.

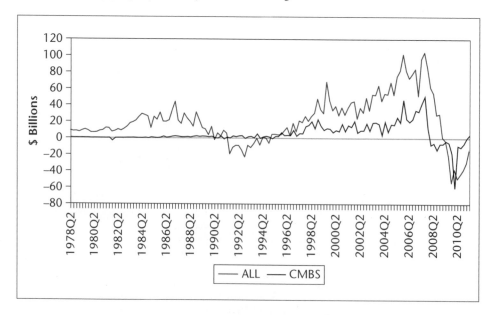

during the 1980s and again in the 2000s. At the peak of the 2000s property boom, mortgage capital was flowing into U.S. commercial real estate at an annual rate of over $300 billion, and well over $100 billion of that was through the CMBS industry. By that time CMBS loans included a relatively small number of large loans on prime properties as well as a very large number of smaller- to medium-sized loans on typical commercial properties. The CMBS industry combined these very different types of loans and properties into a type of mortgage pool known as a "fusion," because it included both types. Exhibit 16-3 graphically shows how in the crashes following the booms the flow of mortgage capital actually becomes negative in the United States, as lenders retrench and seek to reduce their real estate exposure, selling and marking down the mortgages they hold and not refinancing all the debt that is paid off. These huge flows of debt capital, in both directions, both reflect, and cause, the property pricing cycles that we described back in section 7.3 of Chapter 7.

16.1 Basic Typology of Mortgages and Overview of the U.S. Mortgage Industry

While we can categorize mortgages in many ways, Exhibit 16-4 presents a simple typology useful for characterizing the mortgage industry in the United States in the early twenty-first century. Broadly speaking, mortgages are divided into **residential mortgages** and **commercial mortgages**. The former are secured by owner-occupied single-family homes, the latter by income-producing property.[1] Residential and commercial loans make up two distinct branches of the industry and are typically administered separately. These two sides of the business differ in several respects:

- Individual residential loans are much smaller on average, but much more numerous, than commercial loans.
- Residential owner-occupied properties generate no income, so the lender depends on the individual borrower's income to service the loan, while commercial loans can be serviced from the income produced by the property securing the debt.
- Residential borrowers are usually not financial or business professionals and are typically in the market for a loan only occasionally (on average about once every 5–10 years), while commercial borrowers are typically commercial or financial entities staffed by business professionals with much greater financial expertise than the typical homeowner.
- Commercial properties tend to be more unique, while single-family homes tend to be relatively homogeneous.
- Social and political concerns, and the resulting government involvement, are much greater regarding residential loans than commercial loans, including different statutory and common laws governing foreclosure and bankruptcy for residential versus commercial loans.

As a result of these differences, the residential mortgage business has become a "mass production," fairly standardized industry, while commercial mortgages (particularly for larger loans) remains more of a "custom shop," where individual loans are crafted and negotiated, to some extent, one deal at a time (although this is less true in the CMBS part of the industry). Also, the federal government established an extensive regulatory oversight that has helped to standardize the residential mortgage business. Residential mortgages are generally considered part of the "consumer finance" industry, rather than business or investment finance, and as such are also treated differently under the Dodd-Frank Act. Our main focus in this text is on commercial real estate investment.

Within each of these two main branches of the industry are further subbranches and categories of loans. For example, residential mortgages are traditionally divided into

---

[1]In fact, most lenders include in the residential category loans backed by multifamily dwellings up to four units per apartment (often with the borrower living in one of the units). Loans on larger apartment buildings and complexes are usually treated and classified as commercial mortgages.

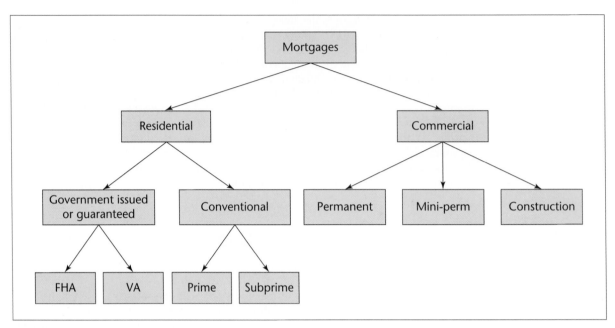

EXHIBIT 16-4 Typology of U.S. Mortgages
© OnCourse Learning

government-insured and conventional loans. The former category includes Federal Housing Administration (FHA) and Veterans Administration (VA) loans, in which the federal government insures the lender against loss in the event of default and foreclosure. This enables these loans to be made for larger fractions of the underlying asset value (indeed, VA loans have traditionally been able to cover 100 percent of the house value). Conventional loans have no government-provided default insurance. However, private mortgage insurance is often purchased, enabling loan-to-value (LTV) ratios up to 95 percent of the house value. (Without insurance, conventional loans are typically limited to no more than 80 percent LTV.)[2]

Loan standardization and the widespread availability of default insurance, and the related efforts of the federal government starting in the 1930s and continuing into the 1970s, helped to establish an extensive and well-functioning **secondary market** for residential mortgages in the United States. A secondary market is one in which mortgages are bought and sold by third parties. The **primary market** is where the loans are **originated** and issued initially. In the primary market, the lending institution or mortgage company issuing the mortgage is the buyer of the loan, in the sense that it is providing the money up front in return for the promised future cash flows (i.e., taking the long position in the mortgage as an investor). The borrower is the seller of the loan, in the sense that it is receiving the money up front, in effect taking a short position in the mortgage as an investor. Once issued, however, the mortgage itself is a capital asset, a claim on a stream of future cash flows, and this asset can be traded (if properly constructed legally), that is, sold by the original issuer to a third party, who may then sell it again to another party, and so forth. This is the secondary market. The development of such a market for home mortgages was pioneered in the United States as a means to promote home building and home ownership coming out of the Great Depression and World War II. By using money derived from the bond market and providing liquidity for such investors, the secondary market has

---

[2]Loans above 80 percent LTV without insurance or where the credit of the borrower is questionable are referred to as subprime loans. These include loans with less documentation, called No-doc loans or Alt-A loans, issued prior to 2008.

facilitated the supply of financial capital to housing and in turn helped to transform American society and landscape.

In the case of residential mortgages, the secondary market experienced extensive **securitization** beginning in the early 1970s. That is, not only was there a secondary market for individual mortgages (which had become dominated by Fannie Mae and Freddie Mac), but large numbers of individual mortgages were pooled with large numbers of small homogeneous securities (like shares of stock, or "units") being sold into the bond market, based on the underlying mortgage pool. Holders of these securities receive shares of the cash flows received by the pool of underlying mortgages. In fact, most residential mortgages in the United States are not retained by their original issuing institution, but rather are sold into the secondary market to be securitized largely as MBS.

By contrast, several barriers inhibited the development of a secondary market for commercial mortgages for many years. Commercial properties tend to be larger and more heterogeneous than houses, and they do not benefit from government-support programs such as FHA insurance. The lack of standardization and default protection, combined with the smaller number and scale in the commercial mortgage industry, made securitization difficult. However, in the early 1990s, and encouraged by the successful securitization of troubled loans after the RTC (Resolution Trust Corporation) took over many troubled financial institutions, widespread securitization of commercial mortgages took off with the development of the **commercial mortgage-backed securities (CMBS)** industry, though with some notable differences from residential loan securitization. As commercial loans lack default insurance, bond-rating agencies had to develop the ability to classify CMBS securities according to their default risk in a manner that enabled the bond market to price such securities effectively. The growth of CMBS has led to more standardization in commercial mortgages, but still not nearly as much as in residential loans. Up until the early 2000s most conventional residential mortgages were financed by capital from Fannie Mae and Freddie Mac. These GSEs were private corporations, but chartered by the federal government, and it was widely believed that the government provided an unofficial but implicit guarantee for them. This enabled them to obtain capital at lower cost, in effect, an implicit government subsidy for housing. Indeed, in the financial crisis of 2008, the government did bail out these two institutions, and at that point they were taken into receivership and became effectively owned by the government. As of the writing of this edition of this text, the long-term future of Fannie and Freddie is in doubt, though they continued to provide the major source of financing for the crippled housing market after the crash of 2008 including financing for multifamily housing. Because of the GSEs dominance and pioneering role in providing a secondary market for mortgages and in securitization, Fannie and Freddie long provided a de facto source of standardized underwriting guidelines and procedures for conventional residential mortgages, thereby strongly influencing how, and in particular, *how carefully*, mortgages were issued, attempting to filter out borrowers who would have trouble paying the debt.

Beginning primarily in the late 1990s and blossoming in the early to mid-2000s, private sources of finance for conventional residential mortgages entered the market in a big way, for the first time providing major competition to Fannie and Freddie. These private issuers included major Wall Street investment banks as well as specialized private mortgage companies. The private mortgage providers were responding in part to a huge growth in liquidity, that is, in money seeking investment opportunities, resulting from the prosperity of the 1990s, the maturing of the baby boom generation, and unprecedented global economic development. Housing in the United States looked like a very solid investment, as it had never suffered a really serious or widespread downturn since the 1930s. The new private financing sources of residential mortgages took a large share of the market by the mid-2000s. With competition to place capital, lending became aggressive and underwriting standards weakened, even at Fannie and Freddie. The private capital sources were more innovative in developing and promoting new types of residential mortgages that targeted borrowers with lower credit ratings, that is, higher risk borrowers. The new loans included so-called "subprime" loans and "Alt-A" no-documentation loans which relied upon stated household income without any verification process. In part this type of activity was encouraged by government policy under both the Clinton and G. W. Bush administrations who wanted to see home owner-ship expand. It did, reaching near 69 percent of all U.S. households at the peak in 2006. Many renters and lower income households became homeowners and this was felt to be a good thing.

Most of the new higher-risk home mortgages originated by the private institutions were "conduits," meaning that they were always intended to be immediately sold by the originators into the ABS market where they would be pooled and securitized and issued into the bond market. This was one reason why the originators of the loans did not worry too much about how careful they were being in their loan origination and underwriting processes. When the housing price bubble burst beginning in 2007 many of the resulting securities col-lapsed. To make matters worse, many of these securities had been hedged by derivatives issued on them, in the form of "credit default swaps" (CDS—where one party contracts to pay another party for losses as a result of defaults on bonds). And those derivatives had been issued by other private financial institutions that had insufficient capital to cover the losses caused by the housing collapse, which the industry had not foreseen.

Developments that were individually not bad (even good for some people), interacted in a devastating form of "systemic risk." The individual developments included: low interest rates (due to the large supply of financial capital and also for a while due to Federal Reserve policy); new and innovative mortgages and securitization methods and products that helped to match supply and demand of capital and reduce the transactions costs of borrowing, including refinancing; and the rise in home prices with the great housing boom of 2000s.[3] Bond rating agencies, upon which bond investors had always relied to help them gauge risk, totally missed the true risk of potential losses within the housing market, and this further compounded the problem as many homeowners kept refinancing and driving up loan-to-value ratios such that there was little real equity paired with the mortgage debt in the sub-prime markets. The resulting financial crisis was the most severe since the 1930s, literally threatening the entire global financial and economic system in late 2008 and early 2009, and leaving the United States and many other rich countries with a massive debt-overhang reces-sion, a type of recession the United States had not seen since the 1930s, that is particularly difficult to recover from, as it requires a massive delevering process that undercuts aggregate demand in the economy.

Although residential mortgages, and especially the new subprime types with more risk, were the prime trigger of the financial crisis, the underlying context was excessive leverage in many financial sectors, including in commercial real estate. Commercial property also suffered a price crash in 2008–09, and commercial mortgages suffered great distress, with the CMBS industry virtually drying up in 2009.

Within the commercial mortgage industry, an important division occurs between so-called **permanent loans** and **construction loans**. The latter are made specifically for the purpose of financing a construction project (which may be either to build single-family homes or income-producing buildings). Once the building is complete, the loan is supposed to be paid off. Permanent commercial mortgages are long-term loans designed to finance a completed, fully operational income property. Both the real estate economics and the finan-cial nature of these two branches of the business are quite distinct. Construction loans are relatively short term, typically one to three years in duration, while permanent commercial mortgages are typically five to ten years in duration (sometimes much longer). In construc-tion loans, the cash is disbursed from the lender to the borrower gradually, as the project progresses, sometimes with limited or no payments from the borrower to the lender until the project is complete, when the entire loan is due together with any accrued interest that hasn't been paid currently. In permanent loans, the cash is typically disbursed from the lender to the borrower all at once up front and traditionally was paid back with interest

---

[3]Each of these three phenomena were arguably not bad in themselves. Low interest rates reduce the cost of capital. Matching risk and return objectives improves investment and capital allocation efficiency. Rising home values benefits existing homeowners (which were the majority of all households). Yet the interaction of these three "not bad" phe-nomena created a spiral that led simultaneously to excessive debt and a bubble in asset prices. (See Khandani, Lo, and Merton (2009).)

gradually over the life of the loan. A feature of the mortgage market during the 2000s was the advent of interest-only loans (in both residential and commercial markets), in which no principal was paid until after a period of time, in some cases equal to the entire maturity of the loan (for commercial mortgages).

Construction loans have extensive default risk, as the underlying building does not yet exist when the loan is made. However, they have relatively little **interest rate risk**, which is the risk that the value of the loan will fall in the secondary market as a result of a rise in interest rates in the bond market. The fact that construction loans are of short duration, and often made at **floating interest rates** (interest rates that move with the prevailing shorter-term interest rates in the bond market), protects construction loans from interest rate risk. On the other hand, permanent loans have less default risk (as they are typically secured by a fully operational property), but they often have considerable interest rate risk for the investor (unless they are **adjustable rate mortgages**, or ARMs).

As a result of these differences, construction loans and shorter-term permanent loans are traditionally issued by commercial banks and thrift institutions, while longer-term commercial mortgages are often placed with life insurance companies and pension funds and with the GSEs (for multifamily mortgages). Banks and thrifts are **depository institutions** whose liabilities are of short duration (depositors can remove their money largely on demand). They need to match these short-term liabilities with short-term assets, such as construction loans. Life insurance companies and pension funds tend to have liabilities of much longer duration (based on life insurance policies and pension benefit obligations), often with a high degree of predictability in their future cash outflow requirements. Such institutions need to match these long-term liabilities with stable and dependable long-term cash inflows, such as permanent mortgages can provide.

Because of the extensive default risk in a construction project, the construction lender must be very familiar with the local real estate space market and the local real estate developers and construction firms . Commercial banks and thrift institutions have extensive systems of local branch offices that can develop this kind of expertise. Permanent lenders buying whole loans are often large national and international institutions, far removed from Main Street. However, they usually work through **mortgage bankers** and **mortgage brokers** who have local expertise in the local real estate industry in order to place their mortgage capital.[4]

In the traditional functioning of the commercial mortgage industry, construction and permanent lenders often work as a team to provide construction finance. The construction lender will not commit to provide the construction loan until a permanent lender has agreed to provide a permanent loan on the completion of the project. In this case, the permanent loan is referred to as a **take-out loan**, as it is used to pay off (or "take out") the construction loan. In the event a construction loan is made with the possibility of extension into the operational period of the property, it is called a "mini-perm."[5]

Until the last years before the financial crisis, only permanent commercial mortgages were securitized. But by 2006 some construction loans were being securitized in a new type of vehicle known as a **collateralized debt obligation** (CDO). Construction loans are more vulnerable to economic downturns than permanent mortgages, and the new CDOs were decimated in the post-2008 financial crisis.

---

[4]Mortgage bankers issue loans but do not generally hold onto them as long-term investments, rather selling them immediately to long-term investors such as life insurance companies and pension funds. Mortgage brokers do not issue loans, but screen loan applicants and bring candidates to the issuing institutions.

[5]Sometimes a third type of loan is used to bridge the construction loan and the permanent loan. This may be necessary for projects built "on spec," that is "speculative" developments, in which few if any tenants for the building have committed themselves in advance to lease space in the completed building. For such projects, there may be an extensive lease-up period between the completion of the construction and full or nearly full occupancy of the building. The construction lender may want to be paid when the project is physically complete, but the permanent lender may not be willing to disburse funds until the building is substantially occupied. Bridge financing is sometimes referred to as a "mini-perm" loan, and it may be provided by either the permanent lender or the construction lender. Construction finance, and the analysis of the financial feasibility of development projects, will be treated in more depth in Part VIII of this book.

A NOTE ON TERMINOLOGY: EE VERSUS OR

Mortgage terminology is often rather arcane. Two widely used terms that are often confusing to new students are *mortgagee* and *mortgagor*. The mortgagee is the lender, and the mortgagor is the borrower. Here's a way to help remember these: the borrower is the property *owner*. *Owner* begins with an *O*, so the *or* ending is appropriate. The same trick works for the terms *lessor* (the landlord, or property owner) and *lessee* (the tenant or renter).

© OnCourse Learning

16.2 Basic Legal Concepts and Terminology for Mortgages

Whether residential or commercial, permanent or construction, all mortgages are based on certain fundamental legal concepts and structures. Mortgages also typically involve a number of specific provisions and terms that may sound rather like "legalese," but you must be familiar with them in order to work with real estate debt at a practical level. In this section, we will introduce some of these basic considerations.

16.2.1 Legal Structure of Mortgages

A mortgage is **secured debt**, which means that specified collateral can be used by the debt holder, or **mortgagee**, to obtain the funds owed if the borrower, or **mortgagor**, fails to pay what is owed under the loan. In a real estate mortgage, the collateral is real property. The mortgage consists technically of two separate but connected legal documents: a **promissory note** and a **mortgage deed**.

The promissory note establishes the debt. It is a written, signed contract between the borrower and lender. In this contract, one legal person (the mortgagor) promises to pay another legal person (the mortgagee) the cash flow amounts specified in the loan, in return for the loan.

The mortgage deed, also known sometimes as a **security deed** or a **deed of trust**, secures the debt by conveying, or potentially conveying, the ownership of the collateral from the borrower to the lender. In essence, if the borrower fails to live up to the terms and conditions specified in the promissory note, then the mortgage deed enables the lender to acquire the collateral property for purposes of obtaining what is owed. The mortgage deed should be recorded in the title recording office appropriate to the specified property. The date it is recorded will, in the absence of contravening factors, establish the priority that the lender has in his claim to the collateral property.

There are two types of legal bases for the lender's claim on the collateral property. In most states, mortgages are governed by what is called the **lien theory**: the mortgagee holds a lien on the collateral property. This gives her the right to take the property to force a foreclosure sale in the event the borrower fails to perform under the promissory note, but it does not give the lender the title to the property. In contrast, in a few states mortgages are governed by what is called the **title theory**.[6] Under this theory, the mortgagee holds the ownership title to the collateral property until the borrower is released from the promissory note commitment (normally by the loan being paid off). The borrower technically only retains the right of use and possession of the property, as long as the provisions of the promissory note are kept. In title theory states, the lender can generally take possession of the property more quickly and easily in the event of default.

The essential relationship between the borrower and lender regarding the note and deed is portrayed in Exhibit 16-5. In return for cash up front the borrower gives the lender a note and deed. When the loan is paid off, the lender releases the borrower from the note and returns the deed.

---

[6]The title theory states are Alabama, Georgia, Maine, Maryland, Mississippi, New Hampshire, Pennsylvania, Rhode Island, and Tennessee.

EXHIBIT 16-5 Mortgage Deed Relationships
© OnCourse Learning

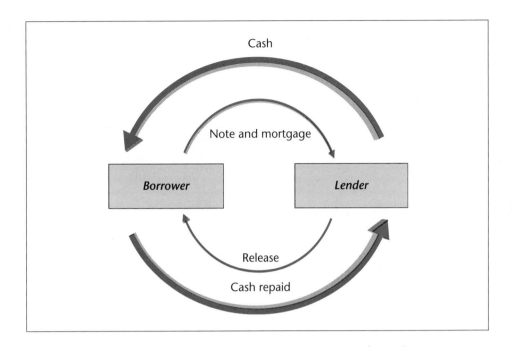

EXHIBIT 16-6 Deed of Trust Relationships
© OnCourse Learning

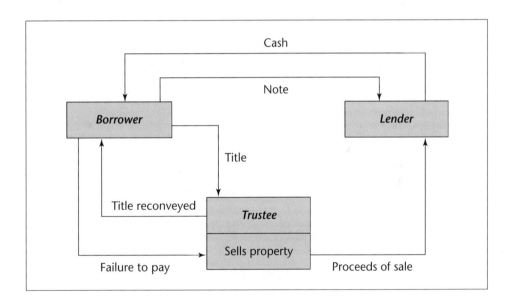

In some states, the legal structure of the mortgage is more complicated, based on a deed of trust, as depicted in Exhibit 16-6. In this case, a third party known as the trustee is involved in the mortgage, in addition to the borrower and lender. When the money is loaned, the borrower gives the ownership title of the property to the trustee, who holds the title for the benefit of the lender during the time the loan is in effect. If the loan is paid off, the trustee returns the title to the borrower. If the borrower defaults, the trustee has the power to sell the property on behalf of the lender, using the proceeds of the sale to compensate the lender for what is owed under the loan. In this case, the trustee has what is called the **power of sale**. In some states, the mortgagee has the power of sale even without the deed of trust arrangement. In other states, only a court can actually sell the collateral property in foreclosure, in what is called a **judicial sale**.[7] In general, the foreclosure sale process tends to be a bit quicker and less administratively costly in power-of-sale states.

16.2.2 Priority of Claims in Foreclosure

As noted, if the borrower defaults on his obligations under the promissory note, the lender can force a **foreclosure** sale of the collateral property and use the proceeds from that sale to obtain what is owed. But there may be more than one claimant to the foreclosure sale proceeds. Anyone with a lien on the collateral property has a claim. There may be more than one mortgage on the property, and there may be others with liens apart from mortgage lenders. For example, the local property tax authority can place a lien on a property if its owner has not paid the property tax due on the property. Also, a construction firm that has done work on the property can place a lien on the property if it was not paid in full for the work performed.

When property has multiple lien holders, the claimants are arranged in a "pecking order" of priority that is generally established by the date of recording of the lien, with the following exceptions:

- Property tax liens come first.
- Sometimes mechanics' liens can take priority over others.
- Explicit subordination clauses can reduce priority.
- Bankruptcy proceedings may modify debt holder rights.

Property tax liens are entitled to take first position no matter when they were recorded. Statutory provisions often give construction firms a certain window of time in which to record mechanics' liens after work was performed and not paid for. These liens can take priority over other liens recorded prior to the end of the relevant window of time. A loan may have a subordination clause that explicitly subordinates it to other loans issued later. This is common in mortgages provided by sellers, for example. Finally, if the borrower has declared bankruptcy, even secured creditors may have their claims altered by the bankruptcy court, especially in the case of commercial mortgages.

Apart from these exceptions, the priority of claims in foreclosure goes according to the date of the recording of the lien, which would normally be the date when the mortgage was issued. The first mortgage is the most **senior debt** in position, and would normally be the outstanding loan that was made first. If the owner subsequently took out a second mortgage, it would be subordinate to the first mortgage, an example of junior debt. There could be a third mortgage, a fourth, and so on. Senior claims must be fulfilled completely before any remaining available proceeds from the foreclosure sale are applied to the next highest claimant in the pecking order.

For example, suppose $9 million is owed on a first mortgage, $2 million is owed on a second mortgage, and $1 million is owed on a third mortgage. The collateral property sells in foreclosure for $10 million. The first mortgagee will receive the entire $9 million she is owed. The second mortgagee will receive the remaining $1 million from the sale, half of what he is owed. The third mortgagee will receive nothing.

It is important to note that this pecking order prevails no matter which lien holder actually brought the foreclosure suit in court. Subordinate lien holders will have their liens extinguished by the foreclosure suit, provided they are included in the suit and properly notified thereof in advance. For this reason, junior lien holders who stand to gain or lose the most in the foreclosure process are most likely to actually bring the foreclosure suit. This is described by the dictum: Redeem up, foreclose down.

Take the previous example as a case in point. If it is known that the current market value of the property is approximately $10 million, then the foreclosure suit would most likely be brought by the second mortgage holder, as he is most on the margin regarding

---

[7]The major states in which judicial sales predominate for commercial mortgages are Connecticut, Delaware, Florida, Illinois, Indiana, Kansas, Kentucky, Louisiana, New Jersey, New York, North Dakota, Ohio, Pennsylvania, South Carolina, and Wisconsin.

whether he will obtain his full principal or not. Lien holders can bid for the property in the foreclosure sale and use their claim as payment. For example, the second mortgagee could bid $11 million for the property and use his claim to pay $2 million of this. He would then have to pay the first mortgagee the full $9 million owed on the first mortgage, but the second mortgagee now controls the property and can make sure it is sold for as high a price as possible. The first lien is extinguished by the suit and the payment of the $9 million (this is the "redeem up" part of the dictum). The third lien is extinguished merely because the third lien holder was included in the suit and properly notified in advance (this is the "foreclose down" part of the dictum). If the second mortgagee sells the property for $10 million, he would be left with $1 million, or half of what he was owed under his loan.

The lien holder bringing the suit must identify any junior lien holders and include them in the foreclosure suit. The suit will not extinguish any validly recorded liens not included in the suit. The purchaser of the property in the foreclosure sale could end up owning the property subject to a lien that had been junior and now is senior, a danger of which any astute bidder would be aware.

16.2.3 Typical Mortgage Covenants

The deed and note in a mortgage will typically include a number of clauses and **covenants** detailing the agreement between the borrower and lender at the time the mortgage is issued. The rights and duties of both parties should be specified clearly. Over the years, a number of clauses and covenants have become common in many mortgages. Familiarity with these terms will increase your practical understanding of how mortgages work.

Promise to Pay   This clause is in every mortgage and means just what it says. The borrower promises to pay the lender the principal, interest, and penalties specified in the promissory note.

Order of Application of Payments   This clause establishes the order in which any payments received from the borrower will be applied to the various components of the debt. In particular, the standard order is as follows:

> **First:**   Expenses
> **Second:**   Penalties
> **Third:**   Interest
> **Fourth:**   Principal

If the lender has had to incur any expenses to which he is entitled to be recompensed by the borrower, the borrower's payments will be used for this purpose first. Any funds left over from the borrower's payments will next be applied to pay off any penalties the borrower has incurred under the agreed terms of the debt. Then, interest owed will be paid. Finally, if any money from the payment is left over, it will be applied to reduce the outstanding principal balance of the loan.

Good Repair Clause   This clause requires the borrower to maintain the property in reasonably good condition. This clause is usually coupled with another: the lender's right to inspect, which enables the lender to enter and inspect the property from time to time (generally with prior notice and at the borrower's convenience) to verify that the property is being properly kept up. These clauses help the lender to make sure that the value of their collateral is being maintained.

Joint and Several Liability   This clause provides that, when there is more than one signatory to the loan, each individual signing the debt is completely responsible for the entire debt.

Acceleration Clause   In general, an **acceleration clause** allows the lender to "accelerate" the loan, that is, to make the entire outstanding principal balance due and payable immediately under certain conditions. Acceleration clauses may be used for several purposes in the mortgage agreement. One is in case of default by the borrower, such as if the borrower fails to make the payments required in the loan. This enables the lender to obtain the entire remaining loan balance through the foreclosure sale process, rather than just the delinquent payments, penalties, and expenses. Another common use of the acceleration clause is to effect a due-on-sale provision.

Due-on-Sale Clause   This enables the lender to accelerate the loan whenever the borrower sells the property.[8] This is particularly valuable to the lender if market interest rates have risen since the time the loan was issued, enabling the lender to reinvest at a higher yield the capital that had been tied up in the loan. In any case, without such a clause, the lender could end up with a borrower responsible on the note who no longer owns the property securing the loan. This could cause a loss of incentive by the borrower to repay the loan. The due-on-sale clause does not force the lender to accelerate the loan on the sale of the property; it merely gives the lender that right. There may be times when the lender would be pleased to have the loan continue in effect after a sale, perhaps with the new property owner taking over the loan.

The process of changing borrowers is known as **loan assumption**.[9] In the absence of a due-on-sale clause, the lender will not generally be able to effectively block assumption of the loan by a new buyer of the property.[10] Such assumption can be valuable for both the original borrower and the new buyer of the property if interest rates have risen since the time the loan was issued. In effect, it enables the purchaser of the property to obtain a below-market-interest-rate loan, which should enable the seller of the property to sell it for a higher-than-market price. Most conventional residential mortgages in the United States have due-on-sale clauses in them, but FHA and VA loans do not, and many commercial mortgages do not.

Borrower's Right to Reinstate   This clause allows the borrower to stop the acceleration of the loan under default, up to a point in time just prior to the actual foreclosure sale, upon the curing of the default by the borrower (that is, the payment of all sums due).

Lender in Possession Clause   This clause gives the lender the automatic right of possession of the property in the event the borrower defaults on the loan. This enables the lender to control the leasing and maintenance of the building prior to completion of the foreclosure process. Sometimes this can help the lender to mitigate the "running down" or loss in value of the property during a prolonged foreclosure process.

Release Clause   In all loans, the borrower will be released from the debt and the lender is required to return the mortgage deed and extinguish his lien on the property when the loan is paid off according to the terms of the promissory note. (This is referred to as defeasance or reconveyance.) In some cases, there will be additional specific release clauses, for example, freeing specified parts or amounts of the original collateral property upon the paying off of portions of the debt principal. This is useful when the original collateral will be sold off gradually in parts or parcels, as in the case of housing tract developments and subdivisions. In another use, an original borrower may be released from the debt when the mortgage is assumed by another debtor.

---

[8]Usually, the due-on-sale clause is written such that any transfer of a substantial beneficial interest in the property triggers the acceleration provision. Thus, the due-on-sale requirement cannot be avoided by use of land contracts or other such procedures in which the title does not initially change hands.

[9]One situation in which assignment is useful is when the original borrower is having trouble servicing the debt, not due to problems with the collateral property, but to problems from other sources. By selling the property and assigning the loan to the new owner, the health of the debt can be restored.

[10]Even without a formal assumption of the mortgage, the borrower (seller of the property) will often be able to keep the original loan in effect through the use of a "wraparound" second mortgage. The seller issues a second mortgage to the buyer for an amount that covers the payments on the first mortgage.

Prepayment Clause   This provision gives the borrower the right (without obligation) to pay the loan off prior to maturity.[11] This can be valuable for the borrower when interest rates fall below the contract rate on the loan, as it enables the borrower to refinance the mortgage at lower interest rates by paying off the old loan with the proceeds from a new, lower-interest-rate loan. (Of course, lenders understand this possibility when they issue the mortgage in the first place and charge an interest rate sufficiently high to compensate for the value of this option they are giving the borrower.) Unless a prepayment clause is explicitly stated in the mortgage agreement, the borrower does not have the right to pay the loan off early, that is, prior to its originally stated maturity. Virtually all residential mortgages in the United States have prepayment clauses.[12] Many commercial mortgages do not have prepayment clauses, or have such clauses that only kick in after a period of several years. (This is often referred to as a "lockout" or, confusingly, as the borrower being "locked in" to the loan.) Often, commercial loans technically permit prepayment, but set prepayment penalties so high as to effectively eliminate the value for the borrower of refinancing the loan at a lower rate.[13] This eliminates prepayment risk for the lender, which is the risk that the loan will be paid off at the borrower's discretion before the loan's contractual maturity. This is an important consideration because many debt investors want to use their investments precisely for the purpose of matching the maturity of liabilities with that of their assets, and so they buy debt assets with a view toward holding them to maturity.[14] Sometimes prepayment penalties kick in after a lockout period and then diminish with a sliding scale approaching the loan maturity.

During the 2000s the evolution in the CMBS industry was toward conduit loans having what is called **defeasance** provisions. This provided that the borrower could pay off the mortgage but only by providing setting up a series of (typically) U.S. Treasury bond securities that would assure the mortgage holder (the CMBS trust) receives all of the payments that the borrower would otherwise have made under the loan. This actually improved the situation for the mortgage holder, because they received the same cash flows as they otherwise would have, only now with the credit quality of U.S. government bonds. Obviously this process was costly to the borrower, and so would only be worthwhile if the borrower faced a strong incentive to get out of the mortgage obligation.[15]

Subordination Clause   As noted previously, this is a provision making the loan subordinate to other loans that the borrower obtains, that is, lower in claim priority for the lender in the event of foreclosure, even though the other loans may have been recorded subsequent to the loan in question.[16] Subordination clauses are often used in seller loans and subsidized

---

[11]This is broadly the same type of option that exists in callable corporate bonds. In effect, it gives the borrower a *call option on a bond*, in which the bond has cash flows equivalent to the remaining cash flows on the callable debt, and the exercise price of the option is the outstanding loan balance (plus prepayment penalties, i.e., what one would have to pay to retire the debt).

[12]Government regulations require that adjustable rate residential mortgages permit prepayment without penalty. Most fixed rate residential loans also allow prepayment with little or no penalty.

[13]This still gives the borrower some flexibility, but removes the interest rate risk for the lender. For example, the prepayment penalty may be specified to be sufficient so that the lender's original contract yield is maintained over the original contract maturity of the debt, called yield maintenance, even though the lender would have to reinvest the prematurely prepaid principal at market interest rates below that contractual yield for the remainder of the original loan's lifetime. Yield maintenance based on the present value of the remaining loan term is often based on the presumption that the paid-off loan proceeds are reinvested in Treasury bonds of a specified duration so that the lender assumes zero yield risk when prepayment occurs.

[14]If they can do this, they also avoid exposure to interest rate risk in the sense that they would have to reinvest their capital at lower interest rates prior to the end of their investment target horizon.

[15]In the 2000s the incentive was not usually merely to obtain a lower interest rate mortgage, but rather to obtain a *larger* mortgage, thereby "cashing out" some of the increased equity in the property resulting from the rapidly growing property values during the unprecedented commercial property price boom of the 2004–2007 period. (Or the defeasance might have been associated with a property sale that was similarly motivated by the run-up in prices.) In many cases the properties that were "defeased" during the peak of the 2000s boom subsequently became "distressed assets" after the crash of 2008–2009.

[16]Recall that claim priority is normally established by the date of recording of the mortgage deed. The subordination clause overrules this priority.

financing to enable the recipient of such financing to still obtain a regular first mortgage from normal commercial sources.

Lender's Right to Notice   This is a provision in junior loans (i.e., subordinate loans, such as second mortgages) requiring the borrower to notify the lender if a foreclosure action is being brought against the borrower by any other lien holder. Junior lien holders may wish to help cure the borrower's default on the other loan or help work out a solution short of foreclosure. This is because junior lien holders will stand to lose much more in the foreclosure process than senior lien holders, due to their being lower in the pecking order for the foreclosure sale proceeds.[17]

Future Advances Clause   This provides for some or all of the contracted principal of the loan to be disbursed to the borrower at future points in time subsequent to the establishment (and recording) of the loan. This is common in construction loans, in which the cash is disbursed as the project is built. Even though some of the loan principal is not disbursed until later, the priority of the lien applying to all of the principal is established based on the time of the initial recording of the mortgage.

Exculpatory Clause   This removes the borrower from responsibility for the debt, giving the lender no recourse beyond taking possession of the collateral that secures the loan. Without an exculpatory clause, the lender can obtain a deficiency judgment and sue the borrower for any remaining debt owed after the foreclosure sale (i.e., in the event the foreclosure sale proceeds are insufficient to recompense the lender for all that is owed). Loans containing exculpatory clauses are known as **nonrecourse loans**. They are common in the commercial mortgage business in the United States, especially for borrowers that have a solid track record of past performance.[18]

16.3 Default, Foreclosure, and Bankruptcy

Although the majority of real estate loans are repaid in full without incident, problems are not uncommon. On average, over 15 percent of long-term commercial mortgages in the United States end up facing serious default, and a foreclosure, bankruptcy, or workout situation, at some point before the maturity of the loan.[19] Technically, a **default** occurs whenever the borrower violates any clause or covenant in the mortgage agreement. However, many

---

[17]This provision would enable the junior mortgagee to find out about the foreclosure action earlier than would necessarily occur when she is officially joined in the foreclosure suit. Recall our example in the previous section in which there were three lien holders. The third lien holder might want to cure the borrower's default on the other loans to prevent the foreclosure sale in which the third lien holder stands to lose his entire claim. Perhaps the property market will turn around or the property itself can be turned around so that it would be worth more than $12 million, instead of the current expected value of $10 million. At $12 million, there would be enough value to make whole even the third lender.

[18]Even in the absence of an explicit exculpatory clause, commercial mortgages can often be made effectively nonrecourse by use of "single-asset" borrowing entities that have limited liability, such as a corporation that owns nothing other than the property that is being financed by the mortgage. However, astute lenders wanting to avoid a nonrecourse loan situation can require the parent holding company or an individual with large net worth to sign the note with joint and several liability, or they may require additional collateral for the loan. On the other hand, an opposite situation can occur. The lender may want protection against possible borrower bankruptcy and loan modification "cramdown" during a Chapter 11 bankruptcy proceeding (see next section). A "bankruptcy-remote" single-asset entity is set up to borrow the loan. However, as CMBS lenders to General Growth Properties found out after 2009, care must be taken that the bankruptcy-remote borrowing entity really is sufficiently independent of any larger corporation such that the larger corporation's bankruptcy does not jeopardize the mortgagee's claim on the property.

[19]Data on permanent loans issued by life insurance companies between 1972 and 1992 indicate a lifetime cumulative default rate roughly between 10 percent and 25 percent, depending on the nature of the property asset market in the years subsequent to the issuance of the loan. Default is most likely during the third through seventh year of the loan's lifetime. See Esaki, l'Heureux, and Snyderman (1999). Their working definition of a serious default is payment delinquency greater than 90 days. The incidence and cost of commercial mortgage foreclosure will be discussed in more depth in Chapter 18.

defaults are not serious in that they do not pose a threat to the lender's yield-to-maturity and are ignored by the lender. Serious defaults generally have to do with failure to make the stipulated loan payments.

When faced with a default by the borrower, lenders have a number of possible actions they can take. Broadly speaking, these can be categorized as being either **litigious** or **nonlitigious** in nature. The former involve the courts and formal legal proceedings that can lead ultimately to foreclosure. If lenders delay or avoid this course of action, they are said to be exercising **forbearance**. As a general rule, lenders prefer to resolve problems without recourse to litigious actions, if possible, thereby saving legal expenses and retaining more flexibility to deal with the borrower in a less formal, less adversarial, and often more expeditious manner.

When nonlitigious options are insufficient, lenders face several types of judicial actions they can take through the courts. As a first step, they can *sue for specific performance* under the promissory note. This involves getting a court to officially require the borrower to perform some specific act (such as fix a default). This is often used as a "shot across the bow," warning the borrower how seriously the lender views the default.[20] A second level of recourse is for the lender to sue for damages under the promissory note, without invoking the mortgage deed. This is less expensive and administratively involved than the third step, which is to invoke the mortgage deed to bring a foreclosure action.

The foreclosure process allows a forced sale of the collateral property, with the proceeds being used to compensate secured creditors for what is owed them, insofar as possible. Any remaining proceeds from the foreclosure sale, after payment of debts and expenses, go to the borrower, but there is normally nothing left over by that point. Foreclosure is generally regarded by both lenders and borrowers as a last resort because it is expensive and slow and represents a rather public type of failure of the loan for both parties.

If the foreclosure sale does not provide funds sufficient to pay the secured debt holders all that they are owed, the holders of remaining nonextinguished debts can obtain a **deficiency judgment**. This allows the lender to sue the borrower for the remainder of the debt, provided the mortgage did not contain an exculpatory clause (as previously described). However, in practice, deficiency judgments are often of limited value, as the borrower may by this time have little other assets or income that can be attached, or the borrower may declare **bankruptcy**.

Bankruptcy on the part of the borrower is in fact a major danger to commercial mortgage lenders prior to foreclosure, even if the collateral property securing the loan contains sufficient value and income-generating ability to service the debt. The most serious threat to secured lenders such as mortgage holders is what is known as **cramdown**, which may occur under a **Chapter 11** filing by the borrower for protection from creditors.[21] The idea behind Chapter 11 is to allow a potentially salvageable business to continue operating while it works itself out from under excessive debt. Under Chapter 11, all of the borrower's creditors are lumped together, and they all may be forced to accept a restructuring of their debts, including secured lenders whose collateral might be sufficient to service their loans by themselves. In effect, healthy properties could be used to bail out sick properties or businesses at the expense of the holders of mortgages on the healthy properties. In effect, a restructuring of the mortgage is forced by the bankruptcy proceeding onto the lender (crammed down the lender's throat, as it were). Because of this, the mere possibility or threat of bankruptcy can be a weapon used by borrowers against lenders.[22]

---

[20]To some extent, the litigious and nonlitigious tracks can be pursued in parallel, in a kind of "good cop/bad cop" routine.

[21]A declaration of bankruptcy under Chapter 7 is of less concern to secured lenders, as this involves complete liquidation of all of the borrower's assets, with secured debt holders obtaining the proceeds of any sale of collateral assets in much the same manner as under the foreclosure process.

[22]Cramdown is of sufficiently widespread concern among commercial mortgage lenders that an industry exists providing insurance specifically against the possibility of cramdown. In some cases, lenders require borrowers to pay for this type of insurance before they will commit to the loan, or as part of a workout agreement restructuring a loan. As noted, another technique that is applicable to loans on individual properties held by large multiproperty borrowers is the formation of a "bankruptcy-remote" borrowing entity for each loan on each property.

16.4 Nonlitigious Actions and Workouts

As noted, lenders generally view foreclosure as a last resort and prefer to address loan problems before they get to that point (and before a Chapter 11 declaration can cause them to lose negotiating leverage). If applied in a timely and deft manner, nonlitigious actions can often obtain the most successful resolution of loan problems.

16.4.1 Costs of Foreclosure

The value of nonlitigious solutions to debt problems may be viewed as the avoidance of the costs of foreclosure. Foreclosure involves a variety of costs, nearly all of which are **deadweight burdens**, that is, a loss to one or the other side of the loan without a commensurate gain on the other side. In Chapter 15, we noted that as a part of the "costs of financial distress" (COFD), even the possibility of such costs can reduce the value of levered equity in property ownership, making excessive debt undesirable from the borrower's perspective. When they actually occur, foreclosure costs can be quite large as a fraction of the property value and the loan balance. They include the following:

- Third-party costs in the form of legal and administrative expenses such as court costs will typically be on the order of 10 percent of the loan balance, and can be much more.
- Deterioration of the property during the foreclosure process is common. The borrower has little incentive to maintain the property well during this period, and lenders and courts lack property management skills. The problem with commercial property is not just the physical maintenance and repair, but also tenant relations and leasing.
- Revenue may be lost by the property, and interest payments lost to the lender, while capital is still tied up in the loan, during the time taken by the foreclosure process, which is typically close to a year in length, sometimes more.[23]
- Both the borrower and the lender can suffer negative reputation effects from the foreclosure process, which is a very public procedure.
- Lenders will usually have to write down officially the value of the assets on their books as a result of a foreclosure, whereas book values may be maintained to some extent, at least for a while, if foreclosure can be avoided. Writing down assets can cause lenders problems with reserve requirements and other regulations.

The magnitude of these and other costs can easily exceed 25 percent to 35 percent of the outstanding loan balance in total.[24]

16.4.2 Nonlitigious Actions

To avoid such costs, lenders commonly employ several nonlitigious actions when faced with problem loans. One such option is a transfer of the loan to a new borrower. This solution is most common when there is no major problem with the property, but only with the original borrower, perhaps due to problems in the borrower's other holdings or business ventures. A variation on this is to negotiate a "short sale," whereby the lender allows the borrower, threatening default, to sell the property on the borrower's own. While the sale must be approved by the lender, it is understood that the price will likely be below the mortgage balance. The lender, in effect, permits the seller to do its own marketing under the presumption that the selling price will be higher than if the property were sold as an REO ("real estate owned") property directly from the lender. Short sales became very common in the residential market after 2008 and fairly common in the commercial industry as well in 2009–2011. Another

---

[23]Studies by Brian Ciochetti (1996) of foreclosures on permanent commercial mortgages issued by insurance companies indicate an average length of the formal foreclosure proceeding of 9.1 months, after an average of 3.5 months of payment delinquency, for a total of 12.6 months.

[24]The Esaki-l'Heureux-Snyderman study (1999) found an average loss severity of almost 38 percent as a fraction of the outstanding loan balance, among loans that were liquidated in foreclosure. This figure includes lost interest as well as principal and expenses.

common type of nonlitigious resolution to a mortgage problem is the procedure known as **deed in lieu of foreclosure**. In this case, the borrower simply gives the property to the lender in return for the lender releasing the borrower from the debt. The result is virtually the same as a foreclosure, but without the legal expense and delay. This benefits the lender, who stands to lose most from such expense and delay. On the other hand, the borrower benefits because a deed-in-lieu is not as public and does not stain the borrower's reputation as much as a formal foreclosure. The deed-in-lieu is a useful device when both sides agree that nothing can be done to save the loan.

A third approach is for the lender and borrower to work together to **restructure** the loan, to bring new equity partners into the deal, or otherwise creatively "work out" the problem. Indeed, this process is sufficiently common that the verb has become a noun: it is referred to as a **workout** of the loan.

16.4.3 Workouts

Workouts occur in infinite varieties, with varying degrees of good or bad feelings among the parties, and with the possibility of litigious action always waiting in the wings. The basic ingredients are typically some combination of a rescheduling or forgiveness of some debt, often in return for the lender obtaining either some equity participation in the property or a greater yield in the long run. For example, the loan term may be extended, or a repayment "holiday" provided. Sometimes a nonrecourse loan may be restructured with more recourse or use of additional capital, or new equity or debt partners may be brought into the deal. This may involve an assumption of all or part of the debt by the new partner. Some firms and individuals specialize in helping with real estate loan workouts, acting as advisors, brokers, and mediators to the principal parties. There is even scope for entrepreneurial profit in the workout process, provided the underlying property has good long-term potential.

An important consideration for the lender in mortgage restructurings is the presence of other lien holders on the property. If the subject loan is modified sufficiently, it may be deemed by the courts to be a new loan and may thereby lose its seniority among the other preexisting liens. Also, courts may invalidate a restructuring of one loan that excessively burdens other lien holders on the same property. The cooperation of all lien holders is usually necessary in a major workout.

16.5 Limited Liability and Foreclosure Costs: The Borrower's Put Option and Strategic Default

Now that you understand basically how mortgages work, let's draw on financial economics to deepen your understanding of mortgages as investments. Obviously, the basic idea in a mortgage is to provide the investor with a reliable cash flow stream, and this is normally what happens—a bit boring perhaps, but useful. When borrowers or loans get into trouble, however, the nature of the investment can change drastically. Investors are aware of this as a possibility (with some probability of occurrence) long before it occurs in reality. Two features of the typical commercial mortgage are of particular importance in this regard and can interact to cause additional ramifications. We are speaking of **limited liability** on the part of the borrower and the existence of significant costs associated with the foreclosure process.

16.5.1 Limited Liability and the Borrower's Put

Many commercial mortgages are nonrecourse loans. In effect, the only thing the lender can take in the event of default and foreclosure is the property collateral securing the debt. The fact that this property may be worth less than the outstanding balance on the loan gives the borrower a type of option known as the **borrower's put option**. Options always

EXHIBIT 16-7 Value (*M*) of a $100 Mortgage at Maturity as a Function of the Underlying Property Value (*V*)

© OnCourse Learning

PANEL A Without Limited Liability

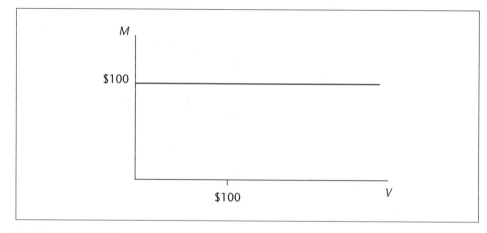

PANEL B With Limited Liability (showing effect of borrower's put)

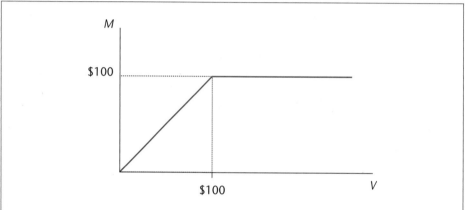

have a positive value to their holders, so this option has some value to the borrower. However, this value is taken from the lender.

In general, a put option gives its holder the right without obligation to sell a specified underlying asset at a specified price. In the case of a nonrecourse mortgage, the underlying asset is the collateral property, and the borrower's ability to default on the loan effectively gives him the ability to sell the property to the lender at a price equal to the outstanding loan balance.[25] By defaulting on the loan, the borrower is said to "put" the property to the lender, thereby ridding himself of a liability equal, at least in book value, to the outstanding loan balance. The lender loses an asset with this same book value. Of course, the borrower loses, and the lender gains, the value of the property.

This situation is depicted in Exhibit 16-7 as of the time of maturity of a $100 loan. The horizontal axis represents the value of the underlying property securing the loan. The vertical axis represents the value of what the lender obtains. If there were no limited liability, the lender would receive $100 no matter what the value of the property, as depicted in Exhibit 16-7, Panel A. With the existence of limited liability (as with the nonrecourse loan), the lender faces the situation depicted in Exhibit 16-7, Panel B. As long as the property is worth more than the outstanding loan balance, the lender will receive the whole amount due ($100). If the property is worth less than the loan balance, the borrower would maximize her own wealth by defaulting on the loan and putting the property back to the lender. The lender then receives only the value of the property, which is less than the loan balance. For

---

[25]To be more precise, the exercise price equals the current market value of a default-free version of the mortgage. This may differ from the outstanding loan balance ("par value" of the loan) if market interest rates have changed since the loan was issued. To simplify the basic point here, however, we can ignore this interest rate effect.

example, if the property were worth $90, the lender would receive value that is $10 less than the $100 owed. If the property were worth only $80, then the gap would be $20.

The difference between the loan value to the lender without limited liability (as in Exhibit 16-7, Panal A) and its value with limited liability (Exhibit 16-7, Panel B) is the value of the put option to the borrower. To the lender, this is obviously a negative value, or cost. Of course, lenders are aware of this possibility when they issue the loan, and mortgage investors in general are aware of the borrower's put option whenever they make investments. Mortgage prices, and the resulting yields in the mortgage market, reflect the existence of the borrower's put option. This is why mortgage yields are higher than equivalent-maturity U.S. government bonds, which lack default risk. On a probabilistic basis, the greater are the expected losses from the borrower exercising the put option (i.e., the greater the **credit risk** or expected credit losses in the loan), the higher will be the contractual yield the mortgage lender or investor will require.[26]

16.5.2 Foreclosure Costs and Strategic Default

In the previous example, there were no costs of foreclosure. If the property was worth $90 when the borrower defaulted, then the lender obtained $90 worth of value on his $100 debt. In reality, the lender can only take the property by going through the legal process of foreclosure. As noted, this is a time-consuming and expensive process. This gives the nonrecourse borrower additional potential leverage over the lender and suggests the possibility of the borrower engaging in **strategic default** behavior. This refers to the borrower deliberately defaulting on the loan for the purpose of forcing the lender into a workout to the borrower's advantage, even though the collateral property is generating sufficient income to service the debt and has a current market value likely in excess of the outstanding loan balance.[27]

How can such behavior be in the borrower's interest? The presence of the deadweight burden of foreclosure costs can make it so. Consider a simple numerical example involving a nonrecourse mortgage. There is only one cash flow left on the loan, due one year from now, in the amount of $10,600,000. The value of the underlying property at that time is currently uncertain, but has the following three possibilities:

- Scenario I: $13 million
- Scenario II: $11 million
- Scenario III: $9 million

If foreclosure occurs, the costs of foreclosure will amount to $2 million of deadweight burden (legal and administrative expenses paid to third parties). As the loan is nonrecourse, the lender would have to bear all of these costs in the event of foreclosure, although they could be recouped from the property sale proceeds.

Considering only the previous facts, it is easy to see what a wealth-maximizing borrower would do in each scenario. In scenario I, the borrower would not default. To default on the loan would be irrational because the lender could take the $2 million costs of foreclosure plus the debt balance from the foreclosure sale proceeds, leaving the borrower with a net of only $400,000 ($13,000,000 − $10,600,000 − $2,000,000). On the other hand, by not defaulting, the borrower nets the full $2.4 million difference between the property value and the loan balance. Thus, the NPV consequence of a decision to default would be −$2 million. In effect, the borrower would needlessly pay the costs of foreclosure if he defaulted.

Now skip to scenario III, the case in which the property is worth only $9 million, which is less than the outstanding loan balance. (Such a circumstance is referred to as the loan being "under water" or an **underwater loan.**) In this case, it would be rational for the borrower to default, exercising his put option as described previously. If the borrower does

---

[26]Chapters 18 and 19 will discuss in more depth the impact of credit risk on commercial mortgage interest rates and expected returns. Chapter 27 will present a simple binomial model of "real option" value that can be used to value the mortgagee's put option. Although the specific application presented in Chapter 27 is to a "call option" instead of a "put option" (the option to buy, rather than to sell, the underlying asset), the same type of model can be applied to a put option.

[27]The term *strategic default* was used in a 1994 article by Riddiough and Wyatt, demonstrating how such borrower behavior could be consistent with equilibrium pricing in the mortgage market.

not default, then he must pay the full $10.6 million loan balance. As the property is only worth $9 million, the decision not to default would have a negative NPV consequence of $1.6 million. (Alternatively, you can view the decision to default as having a positive NPV impact of $1.6 million relative to its only alternative.)

This would be an example of classical **rational default**, when defaulting on the loan is a positive NPV action that maximizes the NPV to the borrower across all the mutually exclusive alternatives available to him and hence satisfies the basic micro-level investment decision rule presented in Chapter 10.[28] Note that under scenario III, default would be rational even if there were no deadweight costs of foreclosure. The borrower might simply give the lender a deed in lieu of foreclosure in these circumstances. Otherwise, the $2 million foreclosure costs would be absorbed by the lender, paid out of the property sale proceeds as the loan is nonrecourse, and the lender would net only $7 million of the $10.6 million owed.

Finally, consider the intermediate case, scenario II, in which the property is worth $11 million. In this case, the loan is not under water: the property is worth more than the outstanding loan balance. However, it is not worth more than the sum of the outstanding balance plus the foreclosure costs. This is the situation in which strategic default becomes a possibility. The borrower can credibly threaten the lender with default, given the nonrecourse nature of the loan, and probably force the lender into a workout deal in which the debt is restructured to the borrower's advantage. Suppose, for example, that the borrower defaults on the loan and offers the lender the following workout deal. If the lender refrains from foreclosing on the property, the borrower will pay the lender $9.1 million, instead of the $10.6 million owed. Why would the lender take such a deal? Because by avoiding the $2 million deadweight burden of the foreclosure costs, the lender will be better off by $100,000. The borrower, of course, ends up $1.5 million better off than if he did not default. In effect, the two parties have split the $1.6 million difference between the loan balance and the net value of the property in foreclosure, with the borrower getting the bulk of this difference because of his ability to force the lender to absorb up to $1.6 million worth of foreclosure costs if he defaults.

The action described for the borrower in scenario II would be an example of a strategic default. In this case, the borrower did not have to default on the loan. The property was generating sufficient cash and value to service the debt. But by defaulting (or credibly threatening default), the borrower was able to improve her position by forcing the lender into a workout.

Of course, the real world is more complicated than the simple example described here. For one thing, both sides have **reputation effects** to consider. If the lender accepts the borrower's offer, the word may get out, and other borrowers with other loans may be tempted to play the same game with the lender. If instead the lender calls the borrower's bluff and forecloses, he may develop a reputation as a "tough guy" who will not play such games. After all, if the lender forecloses in response to the borrower's default, the lender may lose up to $1.6 million compared to what was owed under the loan, but the borrower also would lose $400,000 compared to the case in which the borrower did not default. The borrower would also suffer the negative reputation effects of foreclosure, which could harm her future ability to borrow funds.[29] So the borrower may indeed be bluffing. In any case, the borrower would probably agree to pay quite a bit more than $9.1 million to the lender in order to avoid formal foreclosure.

In practice, borrowers and lenders address workout situations in a variety of ways in the commercial mortgage business. In part, this may depend on the size of the loan and whether it is being held in the portfolio of the original lender. A portfolio lender may have more flexibility than the "special servicer" entity that governs the foreclosure decision in a CMBS pool of conduit loans.[30] While problem loans raise the specter of the deadweight costs of foreclosure, once a loan or borrower is in trouble, both opportunities and further dangers

---

[28]In general, it is not necessarily rational for the borrower to default as soon as the loan is under water if the loan is not yet mature. However, in the present simple example, the loan is due.

[29]Ciochetti and Vandell (1999) estimated that typical default transaction costs in permanent commercial mortgages average 5 percent and 15 percent of the outstanding loan balance for the borrower and lender, respectively.

[30]See Chapter 20 for discussion of CMBS conduit loans and the role of the special servicer.

are presented from that point, with the resulting scope for creativity and entrepreneurship. Even as a mere possibility, actions such as strategic default need to be considered by lenders and mortgage investors in a probabilistic sense, for they can affect investment prospects and values.

16.6 Chapter Summary

This chapter introduced the real estate mortgage and the U.S. mortgage industry. Although our focus was primarily on commercial loans, we presented underlying legal and financial structures, terminology, and salient features that are common to most mortgages in the United States. Although the majority of loans never cause problems, we discussed the nature of the default, foreclosure, and workout processes, as these possibilities always exist in a probabilistic sense and must be considered by investment decision makers.

KEY TERMS

mortgage	mortgagee	default
whole loans	mortgagor	litigious and nonlitigious actions
residential mortgage	promissory note	forbearance
commercial mortgage	mortgage deed	deficiency judgment
secondary mortgage market	deed of trust (security deed)	bankruptcy
primary mortgage market	lien theory	cramdown
origination (issuance) of loans	title theory	Chapter 11 bankruptcy
securitization	power of sale	short sale
commercial mortgage-backed securities (CMBS)	judicial sale	deadweight burden
permanent loans	foreclosure	deed in lieu of foreclosure
construction loans	senior and junior debt	restructuring loans
interest rate risk	covenants	workout of loans
floating interest rates	order of application of payments	limited liability
adjustable rate mortgages (ARMs)	acceleration clause	borrower's put option
depository institutions	due-on-sale clause	credit risk (credit loss)
mortgage bankers	loan assumption	strategic default
mortgage brokers	wraparound loan	underwater loans
take-out loan	prepayment clause	rational default
collateralized debt obligation (CDO)	defeasance	reputation effects
secured debt	subordination clause	
	nonrecourse loans	

STUDY QUESTIONS

16.1. What determines whether a mortgage is classified as residential or commercial in the United States?

16.2. What are the major differences between the residential and commercial mortgage business in the United States?

16.3. Why is it that large commercial mortgage borrowers can often negotiate a customized loan from the issuer, while us small-fries trying to buy a house have to take a standard model?

16.4. When Bob takes out a mortgage to buy a $10 million apartment building, is that transaction occurring in the primary or secondary mortgage market? Is Bob's position short or long in the debt asset?

16.5. Why are commercial banks predominant in the issuance of construction loans, while life insurance companies and pension funds are a larger presence in the permanent loan market? (Hint: Recall the maturity matching principle.)

16.6. What are the two parts (or legal documents) required in any mortgage? Under what circumstances does the mortgage deed convey title to the property?

16.7. What is a nonrecourse mortgage loan? Why do you think most permanent commercial mortgage loans are nonrecourse but residential mortgages as well as construction loans tend to be recourse?

16.8. a. Which states would you expect to have slightly lower mortgage interest rates: title theory states or lien theory states? Why?
b. Answer the same question regarding power of sale versus judicial sale.

16.9. Bob is the mortgagee in a mortgage recorded on 1/31/1996 on the property at 1000 North Main Street in the amount of $7,500,000. Sue has a mortgage on the property for $1,000,000, recorded on 2/28/1998. Piet has a third mortgage for $500,000, recorded on 3/31/2000. The property sells in foreclosure for $9,000,000, and there are $1,000,000 in costs to third parties.
a. How much does each lien holder receive?
b. Which of the three lien holders is most likely to bring the foreclosure suit, and why?
c. How do your answers to (a) and (b) change if Sue's mortgage has a subordination clause in it and Piet's does not?

16.10. Why might a first mortgage holder not have the first priority on the proceeds from a foreclosure sale?

16.11. What is meant by the expression, "Redeem up, foreclose down"?

16.12. a. What is the normal order of application of payments in a mortgage?
b. How does this order affect the remaining balance after an annual $1 million payment is made (on time) on a mortgage with 10 percent simple annual interest and an outstanding balance of $8 million just prior to the payment (i.e., what is the new balance after this payment is made)?
c. Suppose the payment was late by one day, and the loan provisions call for a late-payment penalty fee of $10,000.

16.13. Bob and Piet are 50/50 joint venture partners in a property investment in which they have borrowed $10 million and both signed the mortgage. Apart from the real estate investment, Bob has a net worth of $10 million, while Piet's net worth is 50 cents. They default on the loan when the property is worth $8 million. Assuming foreclosure expenses of $1 million, what are Bob's and Piet's respective net worths after the foreclosure, assuming the loan had a joint-and-several-liability clause but no exculpatory clause?

16.14. What is meant by acceleration of a loan? Name two common applications of acceleration clauses in a mortgage agreement.

16.15. When (and why) is it most valuable to the borrower for a loan *not* to have a due-on-sale clause in it?

16.16. Bob is the mortgagor on a $5 million, 6 percent, interest-only first mortgage on the property at 1000 North Main. The loan has another five years to run before it comes due, and it has no due-on-sale clause. Since Bob bought the property, it has increased in value from $7 million to $10 million, while interest rates have increased from the 6 percent that had prevailed to 8 percent today. Sue now wants to buy the property from Bob for $10 million, but she has only $2 million available for a down payment and can only afford 7 percent interest on an $8 million loan. Describe how Bob can clench this deal by extending Sue a wraparound loan as a second mortgage.

16.17. Other things being equal, would you expect a lender to demand a higher interest rate on a loan with an exculpatory clause in it? Why?

16.18. What is cramdown? When does it occur?

16.19. Why might a lender employ forbearance, or avoid instituting a formal foreclosure procedure with a borrower in default?

16.20. Describe the nature and magnitude of the typical deadweight costs of foreclosure for commercial properties.

16.21. What are some of the specific options available to borrowers and lenders in a work-out process? (Hint: Describe various ways in which loan terms can be altered and/or additional equity capital injected into the property.)

16.22. Why are deficiency judgments often of relatively little value to the lender, even though the borrower has no exculpatory provision?

16.23. Why might a borrower give the lender a deed in lieu of foreclosure?

16.24. What is the relationship between the borrower's limited liability and the value of the borrower's put option?

16.25. What is strategic default, and how is it related to limited liability and the costs of foreclosure?

16.26. Suppose $10,600,000 is due and payable on a nonrecourse mortgage, and the property securing the loan is only worth $9,000,000. What is the value to the borrower of her put option?

16.27. Consider a nonrecourse mortgage with one payment of $10,600,000 due one year from now. The uncertain future is characterized by the following scenarios and probabilities:

Scenario I (70 percent probability): Property worth $13,000,000

Scenario II (20 percent probability): Property worth $11,000,000

Scenario III (10 percent probability): Property worth $9,000,000

If foreclosure occurs, the costs paid to third parties will be $2 million. U.S. government bonds maturing in one year are yielding 6 percent. If investors would require an expected return risk premium of 1 percent, what would this loan sell for today if scenario III would result in a deed-in-lieu and scenario II would result in a strategic default in which the difference between the borrower's and lender's extreme positions is split 50/50? What would be the loan's nominal yield, and what would be the present value cost of the credit risk?

MORTGAGE BASICS II: PAYMENTS, YIELDS, AND VALUES

LEARNING OBJECTIVES

After reading this chapter, you should understand:

⊃ How to compute mortgage payments and balances for a variety of different types of loans, and how to creatively design your own customized loans.

⊃ How to compute mortgage yields, and how to use mortgage yields to evaluate mortgages.

⊃ The nature of the refinancing and prepayment decision, including the ability at some level to quantitatively evaluate this decision from a market value perspective.

The preceding chapter introduced you to the basic legal structure of the mortgage, how mortgages work. In this chapter, we will pick up from there, and also from the present value mathematical principles introduced in Chapter 8. Our objective here is to hone your understanding of how to compute loan payments, values, and yields, so that you can use this ability to creatively design and structure loans and effectively analyze debt investments. While the material in this chapter is rather technical and quantitative, it is also extremely practical and useful. Furthermore, it is much more fun than it used to be because much of the drudgery of formula memorization and number crunching is automated nowadays through the use of electronic calculators and computer spreadsheets. This makes it easier for you to concentrate on the (more important) underlying economics.

17.1 Calculating Loan Payments and Balances

The most basic thing you need to be able to do to handle a mortgage (whether as borrower, lender, or investor) is to know how to compute loan payments and balances given the loan terms. In fact, you already have the tools to do this, based on what you learned in Chapters 8 and 16. Chapter 8 presented the relevant present value mathematical formulas and gave you some practice with the basic calculations. Chapter 16 presented the relevant legal structure. Now let's put the two together and see how we can be more creative.

17.1.1 Four Basic Rules

You may recall from Chapter 16 that one of the basic clauses present in all mortgages is the order of application of payments clause. This clause stipulates that payments received are applied to interest before principal. From this clause and the basic terms of the mortgage agreement, we derive the **four basic rules** for calculating loan payments and balances.

- Rule 1: The interest owed in each payment equals the applicable interest rate times the outstanding principal balance (i.e., the **outstanding loan balance**, or **OLB** for short) at the end of the previous period: $INT_t = (OLB_{t-1})\, r_t$.
- Rule 2: The principal amortized (paid down) in each payment equals the total payment (net of expenses and penalties) minus the interest owed: $AMORT_t = PMT_t - INT_t$.
- Rule 3: The outstanding principal balance after each payment equals the previous outstanding principal balance minus the principal paid down in the payment: $OLB_t = OLB_{t-1} - AMORT_t$.
- Rule 4: The initial outstanding principal balance equals the initial contract principal specified in the loan agreement: $OLB_0 = L$.

The following abbreviations are being used:

$$L = \text{Initial contract principal amount (the loan amount)}$$
$$r_t = \text{Contract simple interest rate applicable for payment in period } t$$
$$INT_t = \text{Interest owed in period } t$$
$$AMORT_t = \text{Principal paid down in the period } t \text{ payment}$$
$$OLB_t = \text{Outstanding principal balance } after \text{ the period } t \text{ payment has been made}$$
$$PMT_t = \text{Amount of the loan payment in period } t$$

The first of these rules derives from the basic nature of the mortgage agreement, that the borrower agrees to compensate the lender for the use of the lender's money by paying interest. The second rule is the order of applications clause. (Under normal circumstances, we can ignore the expenses and penalties portion of the clause.) The third and fourth rules follow directly by definition. Together, these four rules define a complete mathematical system for determining all payments and the outstanding balance due on the loan at any point in time.[1]

It is important to note that the first rule refers to the **contract interest rate**, that is, the rate stipulated in the loan agreement, applied as a simple interest rate *per payment period* specified in the mortgage. Thus, if the mortgage specifies monthly payments, then the applicable interest rate is the simple monthly rate, which is conventionally defined as the nominal per-annum rate stipulated in the loan, divided by the number of payment periods per year specified in the loan. For example, a 12 percent loan with monthly payments actually applies a simple interest rate of 1 percent due at the end of each month.[2] Using the notation from Chapter 8: $r = i/m$, where i is the nominal annual rate and m is the number of payment

---

[1]If the borrower pays more than the required payments, these rules imply that the excess will effectively reduce the OLB below what it would otherwise be. This will not necessarily reduce the amount of the subsequent required payments, but it will result in the loan being paid off earlier, according to rules 2 and 3. Note also that the four rules as stated here assume simple interest compounded on the dates each payment is due, which is the typical way interest is computed in mortgages in the United States. In principle, it is possible to use other methods. For example, interest could be compounded continuously even though payments are due only at one or more discrete points in time. Whenever interest is compounded, the principal balance on the loan is adjusted to include the compounded interest. If interest is compounded more frequently than it is paid, the resulting compound growth in principal is known as "accretion of principal." Prior to payment due dates, interest not yet compounded to principal accrues on a pro rata basis as simple interest owed proportionate to the fraction of the time between the last and next compounding date. Interest accrued but not paid at the time a payment is due is generally added to the principal balance at the time the payment is due (as implied by rules 2 and 3, considering that $AMORT_t$ can be a negative number). Thus, the four rules can be applied to the case in which interest is compounded more frequently than payments are due, simply by treating the payment periods defined here (indexed by the t subscripts) as corresponding to the interest-compounding periods in the loan, rather than as the actual payment-due periods.

[2]Recall from Chapter 8 that this implies an effective annual rate (EAR) of $(1.01)^{12} - 1 = 12.68\%$, compounding the simple monthly rate at the monthly frequency.

periods per year. Also, keep in mind that the contract interest rate in the loan does not necessarily equal the yield prevailing in the current mortgage market.

Similarly, the "initial principal" referred to in rule 4 is not necessarily equal to the net cash flow proceeds obtained by the borrower from the lender at the time the loan is made. For example, prepaid interest (points) or origination fees may be deducted from the cash paid up front by the lender to the borrower.

17.1.2 Applying the Rules to Design Loans

The four rules described earlier practically cry out to be entered as formulas in the cells of a computer spreadsheet, from which you can use your creativity in designing a loan with payment and repayment patterns to your liking. Let's examine a few of the more famous patterns.

Interest-Only Loan   ($PMT_t = INT_t$, or equivalently: $OLB_t = L$, or $AMORT_t = 0$, for all t) This is the oldest and most basic pattern of loan payments. In the **interest-only loan**, there is no amortization of principal: the outstanding loan balance remains constant throughout the life of the loan, and the entire original principal must be paid back by the borrower in a lump sum at the loan's maturity date. As a result, the regular loan payments consist purely of interest. If the interest rate is fixed at a constant rate, then the regular payments will be fixed and level. This is the classical payment pattern of long-term corporate and government bonds, and it is not uncommon in commercial mortgages in the United States (with the difference that bond payments are traditionally semiannual whereas mortgage payments are monthly).

The payment and interest profile of the interest-only loan is depicted graphically in Exhibit 17-1, for an example $1 million, 30-year loan at 12 percent interest with monthly payments. The table below the chart shows the first and last scheduled payments. As 12 percent nominal annual interest equates to a simple monthly interest rate of 1 percent, the interest and payment amounts due each month on this loan are $10,000. The last payment (at the end of month number 360) is $1,010,000, including the last month's interest and the entire original principal. The amounts in the cells of the loan schedule table are computed using the appropriate formulas from the previously described four basic rules, as indicated at the top of the table columns.[3]

The interest-only loan is very straightforward and easy to understand. It has the advantage to the borrower of regular payments that are less than those of an otherwise equivalent amortizing loan. Some borrowers may view as an advantage the fact that the entire regular payment is tax-deductible.[4]

On the other hand, because principal is not paid down, the interest-only loan maximizes the total dollar magnitude of interest paid over the lifetime of the loan, as compared to amortizing loans. Because of the repayment spike at the loan's maturity, the weighted average time until the loan payments are made is greater than that for an amortizing loan of the same maturity. This may have some negative implications for some debt investors. For example, if the loan has a fixed interest rate, it will make the present market value of the loan more sensitive to movements in market interest rates.[5] The repayment spike at the end also con-

---

[3]Note that the four rules are applied as formulas in *three* of the four necessary columns in the spreadsheet (one column corresponding to each of the four variables: OLB, PMT, INT, and AMORT). If the rules were applied in formulas in *all four* columns, the system would be "circular." Instead, one of the four columns is defined based on the defining characteristic of the loan type. For example, in Exhibit 17-1, we have chosen to define the PMT column based on the $PMT_t = INT_t$ (for all t) criterion of the interest-only mortgage. (Alternatively, we could have chosen to define any one of the other three columns based on the loan type definition, such as $AMORT_t = 0$ or $OLB_t = OLB_{t-1}$.)

[4]Recall from Chapter 14 that only the interest portion of the debt service payment is tax deductible. However, recall from Chapter 15 that the tax-shelter value of debt to the borrower is often largely illusory, as much (if not all) of the taxes saved through the deduction are paid indirectly by the pass-through of the marginal lender's taxes in the form of the difference between the market yield on taxed bonds and that on tax-exempt bonds.

[5]In general, the present values of cash flows that are more distant in the future are more sensitive to the average per-period discount rate than are the present values of more near-term cash flows. For example, the PV of $110 one year from now declines only from $100 to about $99 if the interest rate increases from 10% to 11 percent ($110/1.10 versus $110/1.11). However, the PV of a perpetuity of $10 per year declines from $100 to about $91 with the same change in the interest rates ($10/0.10 versus $10/0.11).

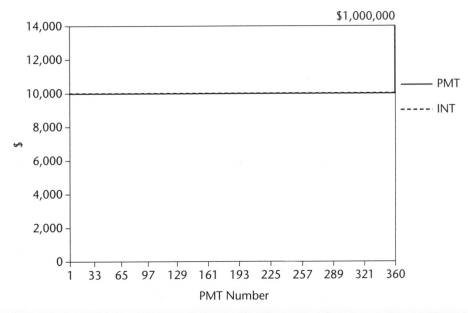

Month	Rules 3 & 4 OLB (Beg)	PMT	Rule 1 INT	Rule 2 AMORT	Rules 3 & 4 OLB (End)
0					$1,000,000.00
1	$1,000,000.00	$10,000.00	$10,000.00	$0.00	$1,000,000.00
2	$1,000,000.00	$10,000.00	$10,000.00	$0.00	$1,000,000.00
3	$1,000,000.00	$10,000.00	$10,000.00	$0.00	$1,000,000.00
...	...	...	...	...	...
358	$1,000,000.00	$10,000.00	$10,000.00	$0.00	$1,000,000.00
359	$1,000,000.00	$10,000.00	$10,000.00	$0.00	$1,000,000.00
360	$1,000,000.00	$1,010,000.00	$10,000.00	$1,000,000.00	$0.00

EXHIBIT 17-1 Interest-Only Mortgage Payments and Interest Component ($1 million, 12%, 30-year, monthly payments)
© OnCourse Learning

fronts the borrower with the need to either refinance the loan or sell the property when the loan matures. This can cause problems if either the property or the debt market is not favorable at that time. Indeed, this is the major problem with the interest-only loan, and the major motivation for the development of amortizing loans.

Constant-Amortization Mortgage (CAM) $(AMORT_t = L/N,$ all $t)$ The simplest way to solve the problem of the repayment spike at the end of the interest-only mortgage is to pay down a constant amount of principal in each loan payment. This results in a **constant-amortization mortgage**, or **CAM**. Such loans were used for a time in the 1930s when interest-only loans were causing havoc during the Great Depression (many a family farm was lost when the mortgage came due) and when persistent deflation resulted in declining rents and land values. As can be seen in Exhibit 17-2, the CAM is characterized by a declining payment pattern. As the loan balance is reduced by a constant amount each period, the interest owed falls by a constant amount as well.

The payments on a CAM are computed by dividing the initial principal by the number of payments to compute the amortization amount per period, and then applying rule 2 to compute the total payment due each period as the sum of the amortization and the interest

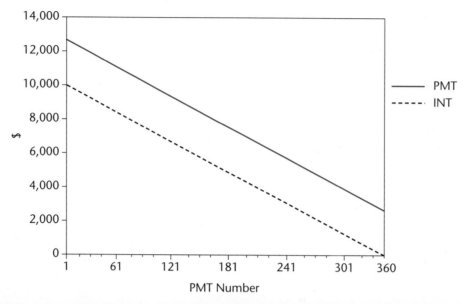

Month	Rules 3 & 4 OLB (Beg)	Rule 2 PMT	Rule 1 INT	AMORT	Rules 3 & 4 OLB (End)
0					$1,000,000.00
1	$1,000,000.00	$12,777.78	$10,000.00	$2,777.78	$997,222.22
2	$997,222.22	$12,750.00	$9,972.22	$2,777.78	$994,444.44
3	$994,444.44	$12,722.22	$9,944.44	$2,777.78	$991,666.67
...	...	...	...	...	...
358	$8,333.33	$2,861.11	$83.33	$2,777.78	$5,555.56
359	$5,555.56	$2,833.33	$55.56	$2,777.78	$2,777.78
360	$2,777.78	$2,805.56	$27.78	$2,777.78	$0.00

EXHIBIT 17-2 Constant-Amortization Mortgage (CAM) Payments and Interest Component ($1 million, 12%, 30-year, monthly payments)
© OnCourse Learning

computed based on rule 1. Thus, for our $1 million, 30-year example loan, the amortization each month is $2,777.78, computed as $1,000,000/360. Therefore, the first payment is $12,777.78, considerably higher than the $10,000 interest-only payment. After the first payment, the loan balance is reduced to $997,222.22 by the application of rule 3, which in turn slightly reduces the amount of interest owed a month later in the second payment. This pattern continues until, after the 100th payment in our example, the CAM payment is less than that of the interest-only loan and continues to decline linearly to the end of the loan maturity. The outstanding loan balance also declines linearly.

In an economy free of persistent deflation, the declining payment pattern in the CAM is an undesirable characteristic for many borrowers, and for many debt investors as well. From the borrower's perspective, it causes the initial loan payment to be excessively high, and does not well match the loan payment pattern with the likely income generation pattern of the underlying property that is being financed with the mortgage. From the perspective of the typical mortgage investor, the CAM likely requires an inconvenient (and possibly expensive) reinvestment of capital each period as the mortgage is amortized. For this reason, CAMs are not widely used in the United States today, although there may be unique circumstances in which such loans would be appropriate.

The Constant-Payment Mortgage (CPM) ($PMT_t = PMT$, a constant, for all t) This brings us to the classic. The **constant-payment mortgage** solves many of the problems of both the interest-only loan and the CAM. Its constant payments make budgeting easy for both the borrower and lender, and tend to match well the typical pattern of rent growth in mature income properties. It provides flexibility in the trade-off among payment level, amortization rate, and maturity. If the loan is fully amortizing (as is typical with residential mortgages), the CPM avoids the problem of the repayment spike at the loan's maturity, and if the amortization rate is slow enough, the payments are not much higher than with an interest-only loan (although this requires very long-term debt). A "hybrid" payment pattern can be obtained by setting the maturity of the loan shorter than the amortization rate. This results in a **balloon payment** at maturity, but the size of the balloon can be reduced by increasing the payment level (faster amortization).[6] Although a CPM need not necessarily have a fixed interest rate (the amortization can vary according to rules 2 and 3), it is most common to combine the CPM payment pattern with a contractually fixed interest rate for the life of the loan.

The payments on the CPM are determined using the annuity formula applied with the contractual interest rate, the initial contractual principal, and the number of payment periods specified in the contractual amortization of the loan: $PMT = L/[(1 - 1/(1 + r)_N)/r]$. Then rule 1 is applied to determine the interest components, and rule 2 is applied to back out the amortization component each period.

Continuing our $1 million, 12 percent, 30-year example in Exhibit 17-3, this results in a constant monthly payment of $10,286.13. This is barely more than the $10,000 payment on the interest-only loan, although it fully pays off the debt. Of course, 30 years is a long time, and if the loan is paid off prior to that time, a large liquidating payment may be required. As evident in the chart in Exhibit 17-3, in the early years of the CPM almost all of the payment consists of interest, so the outstanding loan balance declines very slowly. (The dashed line showing the interest component in the chart traces a pattern corresponding to that of the outstanding loan balance, as with any fixed interest rate loan the interest is always a constant fraction of the outstanding balance.) In our example, after 15 years (180 payments), the remaining balance is still $857,057.13, less than 15 percent of the principal having been paid down in the first half of the loan life. In the later years of the fully amortizing CPM, the principal is paid down rapidly, as indicated by the sharp falloff in the interest line in the chart. As a result, in the later years of a CPM, only a fraction of the payment consists of interest expense, which sharply reduces the tax deductibility of the debt service.

Graduated Payment Mortgage (GPM) ($PMT_{t+s} > PMT_t$, for some positive value of s and t) Just as the declining payment pattern of the CAM was appropriate for a deflationary environment, a loan with a growing payment pattern would often be most appropriate in a strongly inflationary environment.[7] Such a loan is represented by the **graduated payment mortgage (GPM)**. The typical GPM has a fixed interest rate, but its payments increase over time. This is done in order to allow the initial payments to be lower than they otherwise could be. The GPM is useful not only in inflationary environments in which high interest rates make CPM mortgage payments hard to afford, but also for dealing with loans on income properties that are in turnaround, development, or workout situations, in which their ability to generate net rent is expected to increase over time. GPMs may also be useful for first-time homebuyers, whose incomes can be expected to grow.

The most straightforward way to set up a GPM would be to simply use the constant-growth annuity formula introduced in Chapter 8, rather than the level annuity

---

[6]A basic trade-off in all mortgages is between the payment level and the amortization rate. Other things being equal, faster amortization implies higher payments.

[7]Another approach for dealing with inflation is the price level adjusted mortgage (PLAM). In a PLAM, the value of the outstanding balance is adjusted periodically using an index of purchasing power such as the CPI. This enables the interest rate charged on the loan to approximate the real interest rate, rather than the nominal interest rate which includes an inflation premium.

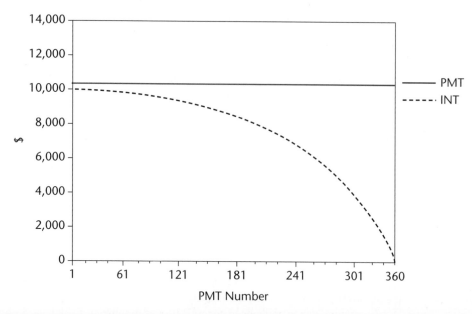

Month	Rules 3 & 4 OLB (Beg)	Rule 2 PMT	Rule 1 INT	AMORT	Rules 3 & 4 OLB (End)
0					$1,000,000.00
1	$1,000,000.00	$10,286.13	$10,000.00	$286.13	$999,713.87
2	$999,713.87	$10,286.13	$9,997.14	$288.99	$999,424.89
3	$999,424.89	$10,286.13	$9,994.25	$291.88	$999,133.01
...	...	...	...	...	...
358	$30,251.34	$10,286.13	$302.51	$9,983.61	$20,267.73
359	$20,267.73	$10,286.13	$202.68	$10,083.45	$10,184.28
360	$10,184.28	$10,286.13	$101.84	$10,184.28	$0.00

EXHIBIT 17-3 Constant-Payment Mortgage (CPM) Payments and Interest Component ($1 million, 12%, 30-year, monthly payments)
© OnCourse Learning

formula.[8] However, in practice, it is inconvenient to have the payment changing every month. It makes more sense to have the payment step up at regular intervals, such as once per year. Also, it is often not necessary or practical to have the payment growing throughout the entire life of the mortgage. Four or five annual steps during the first part of the life of the loan usually accomplish the desired objective of improving the affordability of the loan for the borrower and matching the loan payment pattern with the ability of the underlying property or borrower to service the debt.

Exhibit 17-4 depicts our standard example $1 million, 12 percent, 30-year loan as a GPM with four step-ups of 7.5 percent each. Thanks to the GPM structure, the initial monthly payment can be reduced to $8,255.76, well below the $10,286.13 of the equivalent CPM. However, after three step-ups, the payment in the fourth year, at $10,256.10, exceeds that of the interest-only loan, and after the fourth step-up, the payments level off for the remainder of the loan at $11,025.31, considerably above the CPM payment level.

---

[8]If g is the growth rate per payment period, then recall from Chapter 8 that the constant-growth annuity formula relates the initial payment (PMT_1) to the initial principal (L) as follows:

$$PMT_1 = L \left/ \left(\frac{1 - [(1+g)/(1+r)]^N}{r - g} \right) \right.$$

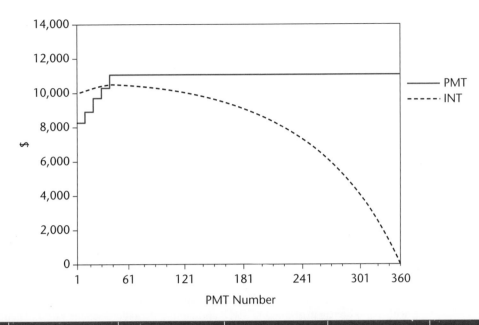

Month	Rules 3 & 4 OLB (Beg)	Rule 2 PMT	Rule 1 INT	AMORT	Rules 3 & 4 OLB (End)
0					$1,000,000.00
1	$1,000,000.00	$8,255.76	$10,000.00	($1,744.24)	$1,001,744.24
2	$1,001,744.24	$8,255.76	$10,017.44	($1,761.69)	$1,003,505.93
3	$1,003,505.93	$8,255.76	$10,035.06	($1,779.30)	$1,005,285.23
...	...	...	...	...	...
12	$1,020,175.38	$8,255.76	$10,201.75	($1,946.00)	$1,022,121.38
13	$1,022,121.38	$8,874.94	$10,221.21	($1,346.28)	$1,023,467.65
14	$1,023,467.65	$8,874.94	$10,234.68	($1,359.74)	$1,024,827.39
...	...	...	...	...	...
24	$1,037,693.53	$8,874.94	$10,376.94	($1,502.00)	$1,039,195.53
25	$1,039,195.53	$9,540.56	$10,391.96	($851.40)	$1,040,046.92
26	$1,040,046.92	$9,540.56	$10,400.47	($859.91)	$1,040,906.83
...	...	...	...	...	...
36	$1,049,043.49	$9,540.56	$10,490.43	($949.88)	$1,049,993.37
37	$1,049,993.37	$10,256.10	$10,499.93	($243.83)	$1,050,237.20
38	$1,050,237.20	$10,256.10	$10,502.37	($246.27)	$1,050,483.48
...	...	...	...	...	...
48	$1,052,813.75	$10,256.10	$10,528.14	($272.04)	$1,053,085.79
49	$1,053,085.79	$11,025.31	$10,530.86	$494.45	$1,052,591.34
50	$1,052,591.34	$11,025.31	$10,525.91	$499.39	$1,052,091.95
...	...	...	...	...	...
358	$32,425.27	$11,025.31	$324.24	$10,701.05	$21,724.21
359	$21,724.21	$11,025.31	$217.24	$10,808.07	$10,916.15
360	$10,916.15	$11,025.31	$109.16	$10,916.15	$0.00

EXHIBIT 17-4 Graduated Payment Mortgage (GPM) Payments and Interest Component ($1 million, 12%, 30-year, monthly payments; 4 annual steps of 7.5%)

© OnCourse Learning

An important feature of GPMs is revealed by the arc of the interest component line in the chart in Exhibit 17-4 (the dashed line). Notice that this line rises first, before it begins to fall. As the interest is a constant proportion of the outstanding loan balance, the curve of this line indicates that the OLB rises for a while in the GPM. Initially, the payments are less than the interest owed ($PMT_t < INT_t$), resulting in **negative amortization** ($AMORT_t = PMT_t - INT_t < 0$). This may be of concern to lenders, as it runs some risk that the loan-to-value ratio (LTV) could rise above its initial level, unless the property value increases as fast as the loan balance.[9]

To compute the payment and balance schedule of a GPM, you apply the loan graduation terms to the initial payment to compute each subsequent payment once the initial payment is known (e.g., step-ups of 7.5 percent once every 12 months for the first four years). Once the payment in each period is determined in this manner, you proceed as usual using the four rules: deriving the interest component from the application of rule 1, backing out the amortization using rule 2, and going forward with the outstanding balance using rule 3.

The only trick is determining the amount of the initial payment. This is done by repetitive application of the level annuity formula, recognizing that each step in the GPM is a level annuity, and the present value of all the GPM payments is just the sum of the present values of all of the steps. In our example, each step has a periodic payment value 7.5 percent higher than the previous step, and the present value of the annuity corresponding to that step must be discounted back to time zero from the point at which the step begins, one year later than the previous step.

For example, let $PV(r,N,PMT)$ represent the present value of the N-period level annuity with periodic payment amount PMT and simple periodic discount rate r. Then the present value as of time zero of the first annual step in our 12 percent example loan is $PV(0.01,12, PMT_1)$ where PMT_1 is the initial payment level. The time-zero value of the payments in the second step is: $PV(0.01,12,PMT_2)/1.01^{12}$, where PMT_2 is the second payment level. But we know that $PMT_2 = 1.075(PMT_1)$. Now recall that the annuity formula is proportional to the payment level, that is, $PV(r,N,PMT) = PV(r,N,1) \times (PMT)$. Thus, the present value of the second step is: $(1.075PMT_1/1.01^{12})PV(0.01,12,1)$. Therefore, the present value (as of time zero) of the entire GPM in our example can be written as

$$L = PMT_1[PV(0.01,12,1)$$
$$+ (1.075/1.01^{12})PV(0.01,12,1)$$
$$+ (1.075^2/1.01^{24})PV(0.01,12,1)$$
$$+ (1.075^3/1.01^{36})PV(0.01,12,1)$$
$$+ (1.075^4/1.01^{48})PV(0.01,312,1)]$$

where L is the initial contract principal ($1 million). It suffices merely to invert this formula to solve for the initial payment value, PMT_1 ($8,255.76 in our example). While this formula may seem a bit daunting, it is easily built up in steps, and easily typed into the appropriate cell in a computer spreadsheet.

Adjustable Rate Mortgage (ARM)　($r_t \neq r_{t+s}$ for some s and t) Another way to improve the affordability of a mortgage for a borrower is to allow the contract interest rate in the loan to adjust periodically to changes in the interest rates prevailing in the debt market. This reduces the interest rate risk for the lender (or mortgage investor), making a lower interest rate possible.

The advantage of the ARM in reducing the initial interest rate is particularly strong for long-term mortgages during times when a steeply upward-sloping **yield curve** is prevailing in the bond market. The yield curve depicts the yield on bonds as a function of their maturity. With a steeply upward-sloping yield curve, short-term bonds are priced with a much lower yield than long-term bonds. This tends to occur when inflation is expected to increase in the long term, or when short-term real interest rates are temporarily depressed due to stimulative government monetary policy and/or low current demand for short-term capital (as during a macroeconomic recession). Although the ARM may be a long-term mortgage, it is

---

[9]Recall from Chapter 16 that lenders can get into trouble when a loan threatens to go "under water" (LTV > 100%), or even when it is still slightly "above water." Presumably, the danger of negative amortization causing an increase in the LTV is less of a concern in inflationary times, as with sufficient inflation the nominal value of the property would tend to rise even if its real value were remaining the same or falling.

like a chain of short-term fixed rate loans linked together, because the interest rate can be adjusted at relatively short intervals.[10] The ARM can therefore be priced similar to short-term debt, with an interest rate based on the short-term end of the yield curve.

Continuing our previous numerical example, Exhibit 17-5 depicts a hypothetical $1 million, 30-year ARM that might be available at the same time as the 12 percent loan we examined in the previous examples. This ARM has an initial interest rate of 9 percent, and the applicable interest rate adjusts once every year (12 payments), based on the prevailing interest rates on U.S. Treasury bonds with a one-year maturity, plus a constant **margin** to reflect the greater default risk in the mortgage.[11] In this case, the one-year government bond is serving in the role of what is called the **index** for the ARM because it is governing the applicable interest rate on the ARM.[12]

Ex ante, it is impossible to know for certain what the future payments on the ARM will be beyond the initial year because it is impossible to forecast with certainty what the prevailing market yields will be for the index on the loan. Of course, a forecasted payment schedule can be computed based on an *assumed* forecast of future bond rates. Ex post, the actual payment and balance history of the ARM is likely to look jagged, as in Exhibit 17-5, which assumes a particular (hypothetical) history for the government bond rate.

The interest rates applicable over the life of an ARM are likely to vary both up and down over time; however, they may tend to be higher on average than the initial interest rate, for two reasons. First, if the yield curve is steeply upward-sloping when the loan is issued, market yields even on short-term debt (such as the loan index) will tend to rise in the years after the loan is issued.[13] Second, the initial rate on the ARM may be what is called a **teaser rate**. A teaser rate is an initial rate less than the current value of the index-plus-margin for the loan at the time the loan is issued. If the initial rate is a teaser, then the applicable rate on the loan will rise even if market interest rates (as represented by the rate on the loan index) remain the same.[14]

Although the applicable contract interest rate may vary unpredictably in the ARM, the loan will certainly fully amortize over its 30-year lifetime because the four rules will always be applied to determine the payments. To see how this works in practice, consider the payment and balance history depicted in the lower panel of Exhibit 17-5. The initial interest rate on the loan is 9 percent. This gives the loan an initial monthly payment of $8,046.23, found by applying the level annuity formula, $PMT(r,N,PV)$, with $r = 9\%/12 = 0.75\%$, $N = 30 * 12 = 360$, and $PV = L = \$1,000,000$, the initial principal. After 12 payments and the application of the four basic rules, this leaves a remaining balance of $993,168.

Now at the one-year anniversary of the loan, suppose that the one-year U.S. Treasury bond yield turns out to be 8.99 percent. If the ARM has a margin of 200 basis points, then the applicable interest rate on the ARM will adjust from its previous 9 percent rate to a new rate of 10.99 percent. This is computed as the observed index rate on the anniversary date (8.99%) plus the 2 percent margin.[15] The payment for the second year of the ARM is then

---

[10]Short-term commercial loans, such as construction loans, often have a "floating" interest rate, which may adjust frequently. Long-term ("permanent") loans typically adjust no more frequently than once per year.

[11]ARMs also often have "caps" or "ceilings," placing limits on how far the applicable interest rate in the loan can adjust in any one move, or over the lifetime of the loan.

[12]The index on an ARM must be a publicly observable rate that is not subject to manipulation by the lender. The most widely used index for residential loans is the U.S. Treasury bond with maturity corresponding to the adjustment interval in the ARM. Other widely used indexes include cost of funds indices (COFI) relevant to the lender and the London Interbank Borrowing Rate (LIBOR).

[13]An abnormally steep yield curve is usually an indication that the capital markets are predicting a rise in future short-term interest rates. On the other hand, if the yield curve is slightly upward-sloping, with long-term rates, say, 100 to 200 basis points above short-term rates, then it will usually be approximately correct to forecast future short-term interest rates at a constant level equal to the current short-term rates. (See Chapter 19 for an explanation of the yield curve.)

[14]For example, suppose the current one-year T-bond is yielding 8% and an ARM with a one-year adjustment interval has a 2% margin. If the initial interest rate on the ARM were 9%, this would be a teaser rate, 1% below the fully indexed rate. In this case, even if the market interest rate remains at 8% for the T-bond, the ARM rate will rise to 10% at the first adjustment time.

[15]Sometimes the relevant rate is specified as the *average* yield observed on the index during some window of time, such as the month prior to the anniversary date of the loan. This reduces the borrower's risk somewhat, as it tends to mitigate the danger associated with the anniversary date of the loan happening to fall at the time of a brief spike in market interest rates.

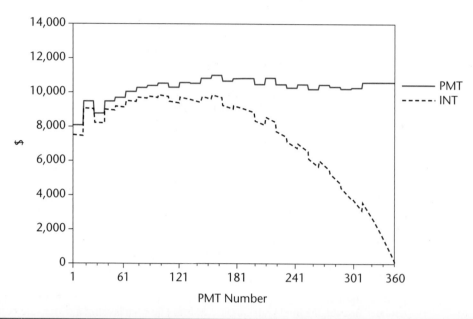

Month	Rule 3 & 4 OLB (Beg)	PMT	Rule 1 INT	Rule 2 AMORT	Rule 3 & 4 OLB (End)	Applied Rate
0					$1,000,000.00	
1	$1,000,000.00	$8,046.23	$7,500.00	$546.23	$999,454	0.0900
2	$999,454	$8,046.23	$7,495.90	$550.32	$998,903	0.0900
3	$998,903	$8,046.23	$7,491.78	$554.45	$998,349	0.0900
...	...	...	...	...	...	...
12	$993,761	$8,046.23	$7,453.21	$593.02	$993,168	0.0900
13	$993,168	$9,493.49	$9,095.76	$397.73	$992,770	0.1099
14	$992,770	$9,493.49	$9,092.12	$401.37	$992,369	0.1099
...	...	...	...	...	...	...
24	$988,587	$9,493.49	$9,053.81	$439.68	$988,147	0.1099
25	$988,147	$8,788.72	$8,251.03	$537.68	$987,610	0.1002
26	$987,610	$8,788.72	$8,246.54	$542.17	$987,068	0.1002
...	...	...	...	...	...	...
358	$31,100	$10,605.35	$356.61	$10,248.74	$20,851	0.1376
359	$20,851	$10,605.35	$239.09	$10,366.26	$10,485	0.1376
360	$10,485	$10,605.35	$120.23	$10,485.12	0	0.1376

EXHIBIT 17-5 Adjustable Rate Mortgage (ARM) Payments and Interest Component ($1 million, 9% initial interest, 30-year, monthly payments; one-year adjustment interval, possible hypothetical history)

© OnCourse Learning

computed as $PMT(r,N,PV)$ with $r = 10.99\%/12 = 0.9158\%$, $N = 29 * 12 = 348$, and PV = $993,168, the outstanding loan balance at the beginning of the second year. This gives a monthly payment during the second year of $9,493.49. This type of procedure is applied at each anniversary date or adjustment time in the loan.[16]

ARMs typically have at least slightly lower overall average expected yield-to-maturity than otherwise similar **fixed rate mortgages (FRMs)**. This is because the yield curve is typically at least slightly upward-sloping, even in the absence of inflation fears or expansionary monetary policy. Of course, this does not imply that the borrower is getting something for nothing, for the borrower absorbs the interest rate risk that the lender avoids.[17]

In our numerical example, the initial interest rate and payment is considerably lower in our 9 percent ARM than in the traditional fixed rate CPM. (Recall that the fixed rate loan was at 12 percent, with the CPM payment at $10,286.13, versus an initial payment of $8,046.23 for the ARM.) However, with this much of a difference between their initial interest rates, it is not unlikely that the applicable interest rate and payment on the ARM will rise to levels above that of the equivalent FRM at some point during the life of the loan. For example, the bottom of the lower panel in Exhibit 17-5 reveals that in the last year of the life of our example ARM the applicable interest rate turned out to be 13.76 percent, which resulted in monthly payments that year of $10,605.44, considerably above those on the corresponding FRM.[18]

Your Customized Loan   The types of mortgages and payment patterns previously described include the most common ones prevailing in the United States during the 1990s, but they obviously do not exhaust the possibilities. With a computer spreadsheet and the four basic rules, you can easily become a creative "financial engineer" and develop your own type of loan and payment pattern. Such creativity may not do you much good in trying to get a mortgage on your house, but remember that the commercial mortgage business is less standardized and often allows more customization and negotiation. Particularly in dealing with unique properties or investment circumstances, such as developments, turnarounds, and workouts, it may be useful to be able to be creative in designing loan terms and financing packages.

17.2 Loan Yields and Mortgage Valuation

Investors, as we know, are interested in returns. This is no less true for debt investors than it is for equity investors. In the debt market in general, and in the mortgage market in particular, investment returns are generally referred to as **yields**.[19] Now that you know how to compute loan payments and balances, you can easily learn how to compute loan yields. From there, it is a short step to loan valuation.

---

[16]In principle, it is possible for the payments in the ARM to be fixed even though the applicable interest rate varies. In this case, changes in the interest rate cause changes in the amortization of the contractual principal remaining on the loan, resulting either in changes in the loan maturity or the size of the balloon payment due at maturity. Fixed-payment ARMS are rare, however, in part because of the danger of "negative amortization" noted previously.

[17]Indeed, as will be discussed in Chapter 19, interest rate risk is fundamentally *why* the yield curve is most commonly slightly upward-sloping. Fully rigorous comparison of ARM versus otherwise similar fixed rate mortgages requires use of option theory. The relevant seminal articles are by Kau, Keenan, Muller, and Epperson (1990 and 1993), listed in the Part VI bibliography.

[18]The ARM may have a prepayment clause in it entitling the borrower to refinance. (U.S. government regulations require residential ARMs to have the prepayment option.) However, the ARM payments will tend to fall when prevailing market interest rates fall, which reduces the value to the borrower of refinancing at that time. When market interest rates fall, the ARM rate will tend to automatically adjust downward as well. Thus, the prepayment option is typically less valuable in an ARM than it is in a FRM. As this option is less valuable to the borrower, so it is less costly to the lender. This is another aspect of the lender's reduced interest rate risk, which enables the ARM interest rate to be lower than rates on otherwise identical FRMs.

[19]Recall from Chapter 9 that terminology in the bond and mortgage market is a bit different from that in the stock and equity market. Yield in the equity market typically refers to the income component of the periodic total return, or the current income or dividend value as a fraction of the current asset value. "Yield" in the debt markets typically refers to a multiperiod measure of the total return.

17.2.1 Computing Mortgage Yields

The yield of a loan generally refers to its internal rate of return (IRR). Most commonly, this IRR is computed over the full remaining potential life of the loan, as if the loan would not be prepaid and the investor would hold the loan to maturity. To be more precise, this should be referred to as the **yield-to-maturity (YTM)** of the loan, although in common parlance, unless it is specified otherwise, the simple word *yield* usually refers to the YTM.

As an example, consider a $1 million, 30-year CPM with an 8 percent annual interest rate. Such a loan would have monthly payments of $7,337.65. The IRR of this loan computed as a simple monthly rate is found by solving the following equation for r.

$$0 = -\$1,000,000 + \sum_{r=1}^{360} \frac{\$7,337.65}{(1+r)^t}$$

Of course, the answer is $r = 0.667\%$, which equates to the nominal annual rate of $i = rm = (0.667\%)(12) = 8.00\%$. We know this because of how we determined the payment amount of $7,337.65, by using the annuity formula with a nominal annual rate of 8 percent.[20] In this case, therefore, the YTM of the loan is identical to its contract interest rate.

The yield on a mortgage will not always equal its interest rate. Suppose the previous $1 million loan had a 1 percent **origination fee**. This means that the lender charges the borrower 1 percent of the loan amount up front, just to grant the loan. Such charges may also be referred to as prepaid interest or discount points (or just points, for short). They are normally quoted in **points** (a point in this sense refers to a percentage point of the outstanding loan balance).[21] With a one-point origination fee, the lender will actually disburse to the borrower only $990,000, even though the contractual principal (L) and the initial outstanding loan balance (OLB_0) is $1 million.[22] In this case, the YTM on the loan is found by solving the following equation for r.

$$0 = -\$990,000 + \sum_{r=1}^{360} \frac{\$7,337.65}{(1+r)^t}$$

The answer is $r = 0.6755$ percent, or a nominal annual rate of 8.11 percent. The effect of the origination fee is to increase the mortgage YTM by 11 **basis points** (or 0.11 percent) over the stated contract interest rate in the loan.

Another way in which the YTM of a loan can differ from its contract interest rate is through the effect of the mortgage market on the value of the loan. Suppose the originator of this mortgage got the commitment and terms to this loan locked in a month before the closing of the loan transaction. During that month yields dropped in the mortgage market, so that the loan originator has an offer to sell this mortgage as soon as it closes for a value of $1,025,000. The buyer of the loan in the secondary market is, in effect, offering to pay more for the loan than its current contractual outstanding balance ($1 million), or **par value**. In effect, the mortgage market has caused the market value of the loan to differ from its par value or contractual OLB. The loan originator can make an immediate profit of $25,000, or $35,000 including the one-point origination fee. The buyer of the mortgage is, in effect, offering to make an investment in this mortgage with a YTM of 7.74 percent, found by solving the following equation for r (and multiplying by 12).

$$0 = -\$1,025,000 + \sum_{r=1}^{360} \frac{\$7,337.65}{(1+r)^t}$$

Contractual Interest Rates versus YTMs In general, the YTM of a loan will differ from the loan's contractual interest rate whenever the current actual cash flow associated with the

---

[20]In this book, we will round monthly payments to the nearest cent, and present or future lump-sum values to the nearest dollar. A more exact monthly payment computation for a precise 8.00% yield is $7,337.645739. In practice, the final payment on the loan would be adjusted slightly to make up for the effect of rounding.

[21]The term *basis points* refers to one hundredth of a percent. One hundred basis points equals one point or 1%.

[22]As soon as the borrower signs on the dotted line, he legally owes $1 million, even though he receives only $990,000.

acquisition of the loan differs from the current outstanding loan balance (or par value) of the loan. At the time of loan origination in the primary market, this will result from discounts taken from the loan disbursement. In the resale of the loan in the secondary market, the YTM will reflect the market value of the loan regardless of the par value or contractual interest rate on the loan.

APRs and Effective Interest The YTM from the lender's perspective at the time of loan origination is often referred to as the **annual percentage rate**, or **APR**. This term is used in consumer finance and residential mortgages, where it has an official definition based on the Truth-in-Lending Act.[23] In common parlance, the YTM at the time of loan issuance is also often referred as the **effective interest rate** faced by the borrower. However, it is important to recognize that the borrower may face additional transaction costs associated with obtaining the loan that are not reflected in the APR or YTM. In particular, costs for items that are required by the lender but paid to third parties, such as appraisals and title insurance, are not included in the APR calculation. These costs may differ across lenders, so the actual lowest cost of capital for the borrower will not necessarily come from the lender with the lowest APR.

YTMs and Expected Returns The YTM of a loan may differ from the investor's expected total return (and therefore also from the borrower's expected cost of capital) for two reasons. First, the YTM computed as before ignores the possibility of default on the loan by the borrower. The contractual cash flows specified in the loan agreement are assumed in computing the yield. More realistically, there is normally some ex ante probability that default will occur at some point in the life of the loan. This causes the realistic ex ante mean return faced by the investor to be less than the default-free YTM, which is the way loan yields are measured and quoted in the market.[24]

Second (even ignoring the possibility of default), if the loan has a prepayment clause or a due-on-sale clause, then the borrower may choose to pay the loan off before its maturity. This is common in residential mortgages, and not uncommon in commercial mortgages. The yield (IRR) over the realistic expected life of the loan (until the borrower prepays) will differ from the YTM whenever there is a **prepayment penalty** and whenever the YTM differs from the contractual interest rate on the loan.

At the time of loan origination in the primary market, the YTM differs from the contractual interest rate only due to disbursement discounts, so the expected yield to the lender (or effective interest rate to the borrower) generally *increases* the shorter the time until the realistic prepayment horizon. This effect is magnified if there is also a prepayment penalty.

As an example, let's return to our previous $1 million, 30-year, 8 percent loan with the one-point origination fee. We saw that its YTM at origination was 8.11 percent. Now suppose the borrower is expected to prepay the loan after 10 years. The yield of the loan with an expected prepayment horizon of 10 years is 8.15 percent, computed by solving the following equation for r (and multiplying by 12).[25]

---

[23]See Federal Reserve Board, Regulation Z, 12 C.F.R. 226 as amended. This regulation does not apply to most commercial mortgages. Note that the APR is generally rounded to the nearest eighth of a point.

[24]Default risk will be discussed in more depth in the next chapter. Keep in mind, however, the basic principle introduced in Chapter 16, that the value of the loan to its holder equals the value of an otherwise equivalent default-free loan (such as a government bond) minus the value of the borrower's put option represented by the borrower's limited liability. Thus, option valuation theory can be used to value default-risky debt, and the YTMs observed in the debt market reflect such valuation.

[25]Recall from Chapter 8 that a business calculator solves the following problem [equation (12) in Chapter 8]:

$$0 = -PV + \sum_{t=1}^{N} \frac{PMT}{[1 + (i/m)]^t} + \frac{FV}{[1 + (i/m)]^N}$$

Thus, to solve the problem on a business calculator, first enter the contractual loan terms ($N = 360$, $i = 8\%$, $PV = 1000000$, $FV = 0$, and compute $PMT = -7337.65$). Then change the number of payments to that in the expected horizon ($N = 120$) to compute the OLB as $FV = -877247$, *before* changing the amount in the PV register to reflect the fee: $PV = 990000$. It is important to change the amount in the PV register last, just before computing the yield using the i register. This is a general rule. For example, if the loan had also had a prepayment penalty, it would be important to compute the amount of the prepayment penalty with the original contract principal in the PV register, and include the prepayment penalty in the FV register amount, before changing the value in the PV register to reflect any disbursement discount.

$$0 = -\$990{,}000 + \sum_{t=1}^{120}\frac{\$7{,}337.65}{(1+r)^t} + \frac{\$877{,}247}{(1+r)^{120}}$$

The resulting 8.15 percent yield is more realistic than the 8.11 percent YTM if this loan would in fact more likely be repaid in 10 years. The 8.15 percent yield is also the YTM of a 10-year mortgage with a 30-year amortization rate. Such a loan would have a mandatory balloon payment of $877,247 at the end of its 10-year maturity.[26]

The shorter the prepayment horizon, the greater the effect of the disbursement discount on the realistic yield of the mortgage. Prepayment penalties cause a similar (though slightly smaller) effect. The effect is hyperbolic, not linear, with the impact on the yield much greater the shorter the prepayment horizon. This is seen in Exhibit 17-6a, which shows the effect on the yield of a 30-year, 8 percent mortgage caused by various different prepayment horizons and loan terms. For example, with one point of disbursement discount the yield would be 8.25 percent over a five-year horizon, or 8.55 percent over a two-year horizon. If the loan

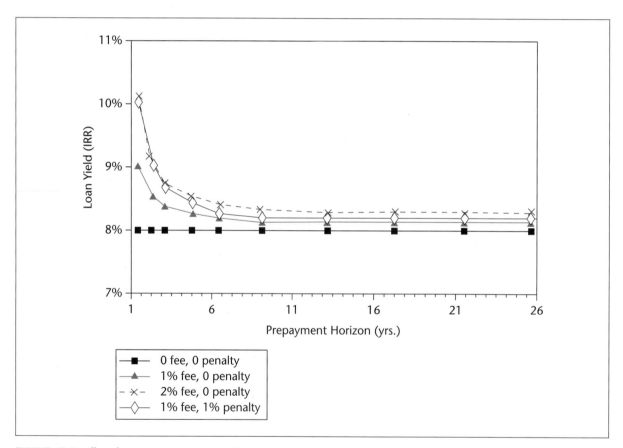

EXHIBIT 17-6a Effect of Prepayment on Loan Yield (8%, 30-year)
© OnCourse Learning

[26]The OLB on the loan can be computed on a business calculator in either of two ways. You may enter the number of payments *already made* in the N register and then compute the future value (FV) of the loan (with the initial principal amount in the PV register). Alternatively, with the loan's original liquidating payment at maturity in the FV register (zero for a fully amortizing loan), it is equivalent to enter the number of payments *yet to be paid* in the N register, and then compute the present value (PV). That these two approaches are mathematically equivalent can be seen by manipulating the mortgage math calculator equation [equation (12) in Chapter 8]. Letting q be the number of previous payments and Tm be the original number of payments in the fully amortizing loan maturity, it is equivalent to solve this equation either for PV with $N = Tm - q$ and $FV = 0$, or for FV with $N = q$ and $PV = P$, the original contract principal.

Loan Terms	Prepayment Horizon (yrs.)						
	1	**2**	**3**	**5**	**10**	**20**	**30**
0% fee, 0 pen	8.00%	8.00%	8.00%	8.00%	8.00%	8.00%	8.00%
1% fee, 0 pen	9.05%	8.55%	8.38%	8.25%	8.15%	8.11%	8.11%
2% fee, 0 pen	10.12%	9.11%	8.77%	8.50%	8.31%	8.23%	8.21%
1% fee, 1% pen	10.01%	9.01%	8.67%	8.41%	8.21%	8.13%	8.11%

EXHIBIT 17-6b Yield (IRR) on 8%, 30-year CP-FRM

© OnCourse Learning

had two points of disbursement discount instead of one, its yield over the 10-year horizon would be 8.31 percent instead of 8.15 percent. If it had one point of prepayment penalty instead of the additional point of disbursement discount, the 10-year yield would be 8.21 percent.[27]

17.2.2 Why Points and Fees Exist

In the commercial mortgage industry, origination fees are often charged to compensate mortgage brokers who find and filter loan applications for the financial institutions who supply the long-term capital. In general, loan originators face overhead and administrative costs that may be attributed to the loan origination process per se, and which therefore differ from the opportunity cost of the capital that is being invested in the loan. While the latter cost accrues over the life of the loan, the former cost is sunk at the time the loan is issued. Up-front fees are a way for the loan originator to make some profit while providing some disincentive against early prepayment of the loan by the borrower. (Recall the hyperbolic relation between the yield and the prepayment horizon when there is a disbursement discount.) Up-front fees can also be used as a trade-off against the level of the regular loan payment: greater origination fees and discount points allow lower regular loan payments for the same yield. This results in the familiar **mortgage menu** typically offered by residential lenders, in which discount points are traded off against the interest rate on the loan.

For example, suppose the originator of the previously described $1 million mortgage with the 30-year amortization rate expects (or requires) that the loan will be paid back in 10 years (i.e., with a balloon payment and no penalty). The following combination of disbursement discount points and contract interest rate will all provide the same 8.15 percent 10-year yield, with the resulting indicated difference in the monthly payments.

Discount Points	Interest Rate	Monthly Payment
0	8.15%	$7,444.86
1	8.00%	$7,337.65
2	7.85%	$7,230.58
3	7.69%	$7,124.08

---

[27]It is computationally useful to note that when the disbursement discount and prepayment penalty are quoted in points, that is, as a fraction of the outstanding loan balance or par value of the loan, then there is no need to know the dollar magnitude of the loan or its payments in order to compute its yield. You can substitute any convenient loan amount (such as $1) to compute the yield for any loan so described. This is a consequence of the fact that the present value equation is homogeneous of degree one in the cash flows, as noted in Chapter 8.

At the other end of the loan's lifetime, prepayment penalties are rare in residential mortgages in the United States, but are more widespread in commercial mortgages. They are used to discourage prepayment, in effect, by reducing the net value of the borrower's prepayment option. In the extreme, prepayment penalties may be set so high as to effectively eliminate the value of this option.[28]

17.2.3 Using Yields to Value Mortgages

Now that you know how to compute mortgage yields, you can use this knowledge as a valuation tool. Investors buy mortgages (or issue them as loan originators) in order to earn returns, as with any other investment. We have seen how the mortgage yield is related to the return the mortgage investor can expect. As with any investment, the return (and therefore the yield) is an inverse function of the price of the asset (holding the future cash flows constant). For a given loan (i.e., a given set of contractual future cash flows), a given yield will therefore correspond to a certain price, and vice versa. In effect, yields become a convenient way to measure and quote the prices of mortgages prevailing in the debt market. By applying the relevant market yield to a given mortgage, you can ascertain the market value of that mortgage, what it is likely to sell for in the secondary market. In general, for a given required yield, you can determine how much a specified mortgage is worth.

As an example, consider once again our $1 million, 8 percent, monthly-payment, 30-year-amortization, 10-year-maturity balloon loan. How much is this loan worth at closing if the market yield at that time is 7.50 percent? The answer is $1,033,509, computed as[29]

$$\$1,033,509 + \sum_{t=1}^{120} \frac{\$7,337.65}{(1.00625)^t} + \frac{\$877,247}{(1.00625)^{120}}$$

This is just the inverse of the yield calculation problems we did in the last section. There, we knew the present cash flow value (the PV amount), and solved for the implied return. Now we know the required return, so we must solve for the implied present value. This is nothing more (or less) than a DCF valuation problem similar to those we introduced in Chapter 10, only now we are valuing a debt asset rather than an equity asset.[30] The discount rate is the yield observed in the debt market for loans with similar risk and payment timing patterns as the subject loan. The implied loan value is that at which the loan can be traded with NPV = 0 based on market value.[31]

Similarly, if both the yield and the worth of the mortgage are specified, you can determine the required payments and hence the contract interest rate and/or discount points that are required for a given par value or contractual principal amount. For example, suppose the market

---

[28]The prepayment penalties described in this chapter are defined as a simple, constant amount of "points" (basis points) throughout the life of the loan, that is, a dollar amount that is always a constant proportion of the current outstanding loan balance. However, in commercial mortgages, it is common for prepayment penalties to be defined based on "yield maintenance" provisions. This approach, which causes the prepayment penalty to be a function of current market interest rates, is demonstrated in the Excel file for this chapter in this book's accompanying CD, and will be discussed further in Chapter 20 regarding CMBS.

[29]Here, the market yield (discount rate) has been quoted as a **mortgage-equivalent yield** (MEY), so the nominal annual rate of 7.50% corresponds to a simple monthly rate of 7.5%/12 = 0.625%. In practice, the mortgage market and bond market are tightly integrated, and market yields are usually quoted in bond- or **coupon-equivalent terms** (BEY or CEY). Yields quoted in bond terms must be converted to MEY before application to monthly cash flows. In the previous example, if the market yield is 7.5% MEY, then the observed market yield in the bond market (for a bond of equivalent risk and maturity) must be 7.62% BEY, as $[1 + (0.0762/2)]^2 = [1 + (0.075/12)]^{12}$. See Chapter 8 for a discussion of mortgage-equivalent and bond-equivalent yields and effective annual rates (EARs).

[30]As noted, one difference here is that the contractual cash flows are used in the numerators on the right-hand side of the valuation equation. In Chapter 10, the realistic *expectations* of the cash flows in each period were used in the numerators. Considering the probability of default, the contractual cash flow amounts are generally higher than the realistic expectations of these cash flows. Thus, the discount rate (the market yield) in the corresponding denominators is gross of the expected credit loss to the lender in the event of default.

[31]With reference to Chapters 12 and 15, note that the valuation described here computes the market value (MV) of the loan, which equates to the investment value (IV) only for marginal investors.

yield on the day of closing of the 8 percent, $1 million loan is 8.5 percent instead of 7.5 percent. How much must the loan originator charge the borrower in the form of discount points if the lender is not to do a negative NPV deal from her perspective, based on market value?

To answer this question, we solve the same type of loan valuation equation as before, to see that the loan will be worth $967,888 on closing:[32]

$$\$967,888 + \sum_{t=1}^{120} \frac{\$7,337.65}{(1.0070833)^t} + \frac{\$877,247}{(1.0070833)^{120}}$$

As this value is $32,112 less than the initial principal, that is the amount by which the lender must discount the up-front disbursement. In other words, 3.2112 points of prepaid interest or origination fees must be charged.[33]

17.3 Refinancing Decision

If a loan has a **prepayment option**, the borrower can choose to pay the loan off early to take advantage of favorable interest rate movements, **refinancing** the old loan with a new, cheaper loan. This refinancing decision can be evaluated by comparing two loans, the existing ("old") loan and a "new" loan that would replace it. Traditionally, this comparison is made using the classical DCF methodology we have just been describing. In this section, we will first present this traditional approach, then we will explore something important that is left out of the traditional picture, namely, the prepayment option value in the old loan.

17.3.1 Traditional Refinancing Calculation

The traditional approach involves a simple DCF valuation of the two loans. Here we will label the DCF-based present values of the two loans $PV(CF^{OLD})$ and $PV(CF^{NEW})$, for the old and new loans, respectively. The $PV()$ function here refers to the DCF procedure, and CF^{OLD} represents the *remaining* cash flows in the old loan. CF^{NEW} represents the future cash flow stream in the new loan (after its initial disbursement to the borrower). In order to make an apples-to-apples comparison, both loans must be evaluated over the same time horizon (including the same remaining term on the loan), and for the same loan amount.[34] Furthermore, both loans must be evaluated using the current opportunity cost of capital as the discount rate. With the two loans evaluated in this manner, the **NPV of refinancing** for the borrower is defined as the value of the old liability minus the value of the new liability, quantified as $PV(CF^{OLD}) - PV(CF^{NEW})$, less any transaction costs the borrower faces in the refinancing deal.

This procedure is equivalent to calculating the net incremental difference in cash flows each period under the new loan compared to the old, and summing the present values of these periodic savings to the borrower. Using the same discount rate (the current opportunity cost of capital), the difference in the present values of the cash flows equals the present value of the differences in the cash flows:[35]

$$PV(CF^{OLD}) - PV(CF^{NEW}) = PV(CF^{OLD} - CF^{NEW})$$

---

[32]8.5%/12 = 0.70833%

[33]This shows how leaving the final determination of the loan origination fee flexible until the closing can enable the latest changes in the secondary mortgage market to be reflected in the loan terms.

[34]This condition is necessary in order to avoid mixing two distinct decisions: the refinancing decision and a decision to change the degree of leverage on the equity investment. The importance of keeping these two decisions separate can be seen by recourse to an extreme example. Suppose a $1 million loan is to be refinanced with a $500,000 loan. The borrower will be getting rid of an old liability that has twice the magnitude of the new liability. Simply comparing the values of the two liabilities, it would appear that the borrower would be approximately $500,000 better off no matter what the difference in interest rates! Obviously, this would be misleading from the perspective of evaluating the refinancing decision per se. To isolate the NPV of this decision alone, we hold constant for analysis purposes the amount of debt in comparing the old loan with its replacement loan. Of course, in practice, the investor may choose to change the amount of debt at the same time as the refinancing.

[35]This identity follows directly from the distributive law of multiplication and addition: $ab + ac = a(b + c)$.

Normally, the savings from refinancing will occur in the regular monthly payments, while the last cash flow in the analysis time horizon may involve an incremental cost to the borrower, as the new loan may at that time have a larger outstanding balance than the old loan would have had.

To implement this DCF procedure in practice, we need to define specifically how to determine the common time horizon applied to both loans, the amount of the new loan, and the discount rate. The common time horizon should be the expected time until the old loan would be likely to be paid off in the absence of refinancing, which at the latest is the maturity date of the old loan.[36] This may be earlier than the maturity of the replacement loan, in which case the replacement loan must be evaluated with expected cash flows corresponding to such early prepayment of the replacement loan. In order to keep the amount of debt constant, the new loan should be evaluated for an amount such that the actual cash disbursement the borrower receives is just sufficient to pay off the old loan exactly. Thus, if the new loan has a disbursement discount, then the contractual principal borrowed on the new loan must exceed the current OLB plus prepayment penalty on the old loan. Finally, the opportunity cost of capital used as the discount rate in the analysis should be determined as the yield on the new loan, computed over the common time horizon. If the new loan has any disbursement discounts, or if the new loan has a prepayment penalty and the common time horizon is prior to the new loan's maturity, then this discount rate will, of course, exceed the contract interest rate in the new loan.

Shortcut Procedure   The preceding conditions on the discount rate and the amount of the new loan imply that a shortcut exists to quantify the difference between the new and old loan values. In effect, *we do not need to quantify the amount of the new loan or its payments.* Defining the opportunity cost of capital as the yield on the new loan assures that $PV(CF^{NEW})$ equals the cash disbursement to the borrower on that loan. And the condition on the new loan amount requires that this cash disbursement must equal the amount required to pay off the old loan, an amount we will label OLB^{OLD}. Thus, the conditions described above imply $PV(CF^{NEW}) = OLB^{OLD}$. The refinancing NPV can thus be redefined (apart from transaction costs) as: $PV(CF^{OLD}) - OLB^{OLD}$.

This result has an important conceptual implication. Fundamentally, the refinancing decision *is not a comparison of two loans.* Rather, it is a decision simply regarding the old loan: *Does it make sense to exercise the old loan's prepayment option?* It does not matter whether the old loan would be paid off with capital obtained from a new loan, or additional equity, or some combination of debt and equity. Thus, the refinancing decision is simply a comparison of the current liability value of the old loan with the cash that would currently be required to pay off the old loan. A new loan is necessary in the analysis only as a (possibly hypothetical) source for ascertaining the current relevant opportunity cost of capital.

An Example NPV Calculation   The best way to understand the traditional refinancing valuation is to consider a specific numerical example. Let's go back to our previously described 8 percent, $1 million mortgage with 30-year amortization and 10-year maturity at origination. Suppose this loan was issued four years ago and has a prepayment option with a penalty of two points. Suppose that if not refinanced, this loan would probably be held to its maturity, six more years. Now suppose that new loans are available today with a maturity of six years at an interest rate of 7 percent, with one point of disbursement discount up front, and an amortization rate of 30 years. What is the net value of refinancing the old loan at this point in time (apart from transaction costs)?

Step 1: Old Loan Liquidating Payment   Let's begin by calculating what it would take to pay off the old loan today. The outstanding balance on the old loan after four years (48 payments) is $962,190, and when we add two points of prepayment penalty this gives a liquidating payment of $1.02 \times \$962,190 = \$981,434$.[37] This is the amount we labeled OLB^{OLD}.

---

[36]It may be earlier than the maturity if the loan has a due-on-sale clause.

[37]$\$962,190 = PV(0.08/12, 26 * 12, 7337.65) = FV(0.08/12, 48 * 12, 7337.65)$, where $\$7,337.65 = PMT(0.08/12, 30 * 12, 1000000)$

Step 2: Opportunity Cost of Capital Now let's compute the relevant cost of capital as the yield on the new loan over the remaining maturity on the old loan. We don't need to know the loan amount to do this. The loan would have monthly payments based on a 360-month level annuity at a simple interest rate of 7%/12 = 0.5833% per month. For every dollar of loan amount, this is a monthly payment of 0.006653 dollars: $PMT(0.07/12,30*12,1) = 0.006653$. The balloon at the end of the six-year maturity on the new loan would be $0.926916 per dollar of loan amount:

$$PV(0.07/12,24*12,[PMT(0.07/12,30*12,1)])$$
$$= FV(0.07/12,6*12,[PMT(0.07/12,30*12,1)]) = 0.926916$$

Considering the one-point disbursement discount up front, this gives the new loan a yield over the six-year horizon of 7.21 percent, as[38]

$$\$0.99 + \sum_{t=1}^{72} \frac{\$0.006653}{[1+(0.0721/12)]^t} + \frac{\$0.926916}{[1+(0.0721/12)]^{72}}$$

This would be the yield (or effective interest rate) no matter what the amount of the new loan. Thus, 7.21 percent is the current opportunity cost of capital (OCC) relevant to our refinancing calculation.

Step 3: Present Value of the Old Loan Liability Now let's compute the present value of the old loan's remaining cash flows using the 7.21 percent OCC we just computed in step 2 as the discount rate. The old loan has regular monthly payments of $7,337.65 and a balloon payment of $877,247 at its maturity six years from now (10 years from the issuance of the loan).[39] Thus, the present value of this liability to the borrower is now $997,654, computed as[40]

$$\$997,654 + \sum_{t=1}^{72} \frac{\$7,337.65}{[1+(0.0721/12)]^t} + \frac{\$877,247}{[1+(0.0721/12)]^{72}}$$

This is the value we labeled $PV(CF^{OLD})$. Traditionally, this amount is viewed as the present value of the benefit of the refinancing to the borrower, as it is taken to represent the current value of the liability that would be removed by paying off the old loan.

Step 4: Computing the NPV Now we can compute the traditional NPV of refinancing to the borrower before considering transaction costs. This is simply the present value of the benefit computed in step 3 less the amount of the liquidating payment computed in step 1:

$$NPV = \$997,654 - \$981,434 = \$16,220$$

This is the value of $PV(CF^{OLD}) - OLB^{OLD}$, including the prepayment penalty in OLB^{OLD}.

The Long Route: Specifying the New Loan Let's confirm that this shortcut gives us the same NPV as if we specified the replacement loan amount. From step 1, we know we need $981,434 of cash disbursement from the new loan in order to pay off the old loan. As the new loan has a one-point disbursement discount, we would have to borrow $991,348 as the initial contractual principal in the new loan, computed as $981,434/0.99. At 7 percent interest, this gives the new loan a monthly payment of $6,595.46 and a balloon of $918,896 after six years.[41] We already know from step 2 that the yield on this new loan, over the six-year horizon, is 7.21 percent, including the effect of the one-point disbursement discount. Now, what is the present value of this new loan discounted at the 7.21 percent rate? Of course, it is $981,434! The yield, by definition, is the discount rate that causes the loan's future cash flows to have a present value exactly equal to its time-zero cash disbursement.[42]

---

[38] $0.0721 = 12*RATE(6*12,0.006653,0.99,0.926916)$

[39] $\$877,247 = PV(0.08/12,20*12,7337.65) = FV(0.08/12,10*12,7337.65)$

[40] $\$997,654 = PV(0.0721/12,6*12,7337.65,877247)$

[41] $\$991,348 = PV(0.07/12,6*12,6595.46,918896)$

[42] $\$981,834 = PV(0.0721/12,6*12,6595.46,918896)$

Thus, we can immediately confirm that the difference in the two loan values is $997,654 − $981,434 = $16,220. In other words, $PV(CF^{OLD}) − PV(CF^{NEW}) = PV(CF^{OLD}) − OLB^{OLD}$. We don't need to deal with the new loan, except as a means to ascertain the relevant current cost of capital.[43]

*17.3.2 What Is Left Out of the Traditional Calculation: Prepayment Option Value

According to the traditional analysis performed earlier, our example loan should be prepaid, as long as the transaction costs involved in obtaining the necessary capital are less than $16,220. Suppose, for example, that such transaction costs would be $10,000 (approximately 1 percent of the amount of capital required).[44] Then the NPV of paying off the old loan would be $16,220 − $10,000 = $6,220. However, something important has been left out of this analysis. We have ignored the value to the borrower of the prepayment option in the old loan. The DCF-based valuation of the old loan liability, $PV(CF^{OLD})$, did not account for the positive value of this option as an asset to the borrower.

That the prepayment option has a positive value to the borrower can be seen in the previous calculations. We have determined that by exercising this option today the borrower could increase the market value of its net wealth by $6,220, even after transaction costs. Clearly, the prepayment option is worth *at least* this much. But in paying off the old loan, the borrower extinguishes this prepayment option. An option no longer exists after it is exercised.[45] The loss of this option is therefore a cost to the borrower if they prepay the old loan. How much is this option worth?[46]

To develop some basic intuition about the nature and value of the prepayment option, let's extend our previous example. In that example, current market interest rates are 7 percent. But what will interest rates be a year from now? We don't know for sure. But suppose we can characterize the future of interest rates one year from now by the following probabilities:[47]

5% with 50% probability
9% with 50% probability

We can calculate what the NPV of paying off the old loan would be under each of these two future interest rate scenarios. This is done simply by repeating the traditional DCF valuation procedure described in the previous section, only with the old loan advanced one more year into the future, and using the future interest rate scenarios as the basis for determining the OCC in each case. With five years paid off on the old loan, its outstanding balance would be $950,699, and its required liquidating payment including prepayment penalty would be $969,713. Under the 5 percent market interest rate scenario, the yield on a new loan would be

---

[43]We also arrive at the same answer if we evaluate the incremental savings of the new loan versus the old within each period. The old-loan minus new-loan monthly payment is $7,337.65 − $6,595.46 = $742.19. The old-loan minus new-loan balloon payment after six years is $847,247 − $918,896 = $41,649. The present value of these incremental cash flows is $16,220:

$$\$16,220 + \sum_{t=1}^{72} \frac{\$742.19}{[1 + (0.0721/12)]^t} - \frac{\$41,649}{[1 + (0.0721/12)]^{72}}$$

[44]These transaction costs would typically include third-party fees such as appraisal and title insurance costs that might not be included in the loan origination fee, or investment banker fees (in the case of equity capital). In addition, the borrower should consider his or her own costs involved in searching for replacement capital.

[45]It is true that a new loan used to replace the old loan might also have a prepayment option. But this option will have very little current value because the new loan is at the market interest rate. Furthermore, the borrower would have to pay for a prepayment option in a new loan (the presence of such an option is one reason the yield on a new loan would be as high as it is), whereas the borrower already owns the option in the old loan.

[46]As noted in Chapter 16, the prepayment option is a call option on a bond-like asset whose value is $PV(CF^{OLD})$ and whose exercise price is OLB^{OLD}.

[47]Historically, the annual standard deviation of the yield on long-term government bonds has been on the order of 200 basis points, the standard deviation our interest rate probability function assumed here. Thus, this numerical example, though crude, is not out of the ballpark for realistic implications.

5.24 percent (with five years' maturity instead of six, and a 30-year amortization rate). Applying this discount rate to the old loan's five years of remaining cash flows to maturity gives a $PV(CF^{OLD})$ value of $1,062,160. This results in an NPV of loan prepayment of $1,062,160 − $969,713 = $92,448 prior to transaction costs, or $82,448 net of these costs, under the 5 percent interest rate scenario.

Similar calculations reveal that under the 9 percent interest scenario, prepaying the old loan would have a *negative* NPV to the borrower of $75,078 (including the $10,000 transaction cost). With market interest rates at 9 percent, it would obviously not make sense for the borrower to pay off an 8 percent loan. However, a basic characteristic of options is that they provide their owner with a *right without obligation*. The borrower does not have to prepay the old loan just because he has the option to do so. Obviously, if the 9 percent interest rate scenario occurred, the borrower would not exercise the prepayment option on the 8 percent loan.

Considering the previous analysis, we can see that the prepayment option in the old loan provides the borrower with the following **contingent values** one year from now:

$82,448 in the 5% scenario

$0 in the 9% scenario

These values are contingent because they depend on which interest rate scenario actually occurs. However, given the 50 percent probability for each scenario, we can compute the expected value, as of today, of the prepayment option next year. It is[48]

$$(50\%) * (\$82,448) + (50\%) * (0) = \$41,224$$

How much is this expected future value worth today? To find out, we must discount it to present value using a risk-adjusted discount rate that reflects the amount of risk in the prepayment option value. Such options tend to be quite risky. Witness the large range in possible value outcomes next year between the two scenarios: $82,448 versus nothing. Thus, we should use a high discount rate. Suppose, for example, the market would require a 30 percent expected return for investing in such an option.[49] Then the present value of the prepayment option today (given our future interest rate scenario) is $31,711 ($41,224/1.30).

If the prepayment option is worth anything like this much, then clearly it would not make sense to pay off the old mortgage today. Prepayment today, when interest rates are 7 percent, has an NPV of $6,220, as we have seen, ignoring the option value. Not prepaying today, but rather waiting until next year to see what happens with interest rates, has an NPV of $31,711, ignoring the current payoff value. These two possibilities are mutually exclusive. We cannot both pay off the old loan today and wait until next year and see if we prefer to pay it off next year instead. Each course of action rules out the other. Recall the basic NPV investment decision criterion: *Maximize the NPV across all mutually exclusive alternatives.* Thus, the classical NPV criterion tells us that we should choose the wait-and-see alternative, given the interest rate scenario we have assumed here. The $31,711 NPV is preferable to the $6,220 NPV.

We can also obtain this same result by properly including the prepayment option value in the valuation of the old loan. The prepayment option value is positive to the borrower, but negative to the lender.[50] Labeling $C(Prepay)$ as the market value of the prepayment option, and $D(Old)$ as the market value of the old loan, we have

$$D(Old) = PV(CF^{OLD}) - C(Prepay) \qquad (1)$$

---

[48]Actually, the expected value of the option next year is at least this great, as we have ignored any possibility that the option might be even more valuable if it were not exercised in the 5% scenario.

[49]Rigorous option value theory uses arbitrage arguments to avoid having to estimate this discount rate. However, it is not uncommon for call options to provide expected returns well in excess of 20% even when they are "in the money."

[50]The holder of the short position in the loan holds the long position in the prepayment option. Similarly, the holder of the long position in the loan holds the short position in the prepayment option.

The market-value-based NPV of old loan prepayment, from the borrower's perspective, is therefore:

$$NPV(Prepay) = D(Old) - OLB^{OLD} - TC \tag{2}$$

where *TC* is the borrower's transaction costs in the deal.

Equation (2) simply says that when the market value of the existing loan exceeds the cash that would be required to pay off that loan (including the transaction costs), then refinancing will have a positive impact on the borrower's net wealth. As the market value of the old loan already incorporates the value of the prepayment option (which reflects the possible value of waiting to prepay the old loan later), paying off the old loan will be currently optimal for the borrower whenever equation (2) is positive. Combining (1) and (2), we see that

$$NPV(Prepay) = PV(CF^{OLD}) - C(Prepay) - OLB^{OLD} - TC \tag{3}$$

This makes it clear that the *C(Prepay)* component is left out of the traditional refinancing analysis. Because option value is always positive, the traditional, purely DCF-based approach will be biased in favor of refinancing, tending to give too high a value for the NPV in equation (3). In fact, because of the value of the prepayment option, it will never be optimal to pay off a loan as soon as market yields drop just a little bit below the interest rate on the old loan.

It is important to recognize that in a highly liquid debt market, *D(Old)* could be observed empirically from the prices (yields) of traded bonds or mortgage-backed securities, and these prices would include the value of the *C(Prepay)* component. However, most commercial mortgages are unique and held privately as whole loans, not securitized or traded on the bond market. It is often difficult to find a liquid asset closely comparable to a given mortgage.[51] This makes it necessary to evaluate the prepayment option component explicitly in order to obtain a precise computation of the market-value-based NPV of loan prepayment.

The fully rigorous evaluation of this option is a pretty technical affair, requiring the use of option theory. While we will present an option model in Chapter 27 of this text, we should tell you right now that the fully rigorous application of option theory to mortgages is more complex than what can be handled by the model we will present there. This is because a mortgage valuation model that considers both the "call" option to prepay and the "put" option to default (that was described in Chapter 16) must consider two independent underlying "state variables": the bond-like asset that is the remaining value of the subject mortgage, and the equity-like value of the real estate collateral securing the mortgage. The fundamental model to address this problem was developed by Kau, Keenan, Muller, and Epperson in a 1992 paper in the *Journal of Money, Credit & Banking.*[52]

If you don't want to get that technical, in practice a simple rule of thumb is often applied to deal with the prepayment option value effect. When yields on new loans get to around 200 basis points below the interest rate on the old loan, prepayment likely makes sense, even considering the prepayment option value. However, if not much maturity is left on the old loan, or if one has good reason to believe that market interest rates may fall further in the near future, then it may still not make sense to pay off the old loan.[53] On the other hand, if the loan has a long time remaining before maturity, or if one has good reason to believe that interest rates are about as low as they will go, then it may make sense to refinance, even if current interest rates are less than 200 basis points below the old loan rate.

---

[51]What is needed is comparability in the contract interest rate, maturity, prepayment ability (including penalties), and default risk. Similar size of the loan may also be important if there are economies of scale in prepayment transaction costs.

[52]Hilliard, Kau, and Slawson (1998) present a useful simplified approach based on an expanded version of the "binomial model" that we will present in Chapter 27.

[53]Also, a substantial prepayment penalty or abnormally large transaction costs can eliminate the value of prepayment to the borrower.

17.4 Chapter Summary

Building on Chapters 8 and 16, this chapter presented the basic nuts and bolts for quantifying mortgage cash flows and yields. We saw how to apply this knowledge in loan valuation and in addressing related decisions such as refinancing. The procedures and methods presented here are as relevant for residential loans as for commercial loans, and as important to borrowers as they are to lenders.

KEY TERMS

four basic rules of payments and balances
outstanding loan balance (OLB)
contract principal (L)
interest owed (INT)
amortization of principal (AMORT)
payment amount (PMT)
contract interest rate (r)
interest-only loan
constant-amortization mortgage (CAM)
constant-payment mortgage (CPM)
balloon payment

graduated payment mortgage (GPM)
negative amortization
adjustable rate mortgage (ARM)
yield curve
margin (in ARM)
index (in ARM)
teaser rate
fixed rate mortgage (FRM)
yield (IRR)
yield-to-maturity (YTM)
origination fee
discount points
basis points

par value
annual percentage rate (APR)
effective interest rate
prepayment penalty
mortgage menu
mortgage-equivalent yield (MEY)
bond- or coupon-equivalent yield (BEY, CEY)
prepayment option
refinancing
NPV of refinancing
contingent value

STUDY QUESTIONS

Conceptual Questions

17.1. Describe the four basic rules for computing loan payments and balances.

17.2. What are the major advantages and disadvantages of interest-only loans for both borrowers and lenders, as compared to amortizing loans?

17.3. In what type of economy might a CAM be most useful? What are the major problems with CAMs in a non-deflationary economy?

17.4. What advantages do CPMs have over CAMs and interest-only loans?

17.5. Describe the general relationship among the amortization rate, maturity, regular payment, and balloon payment in a CPM.

17.6. What are the advantages and disadvantages (for both the borrower and lender) of a GPM, as compared to an otherwise similar CPM? Under what circumstances (economic and property-specific) will a GPM be most useful?

17.7. What are the major advantages and disadvantages of ARMs from the borrower's and lender's perspective? How does an ARM subject the lender to less interest rate risk than does a CPM? In what economic circumstances (e.g., interest rate environment) will ARMs be most useful?

17.8. What are the conditions in which the YTM will equal the contract interest rate on the mortgage?

17.9. At the time of loan issuance in the primary market, what can we say in general about the relationship between the YTM and the contract interest rate if the loan has disbursement discount points?

17.10. a. What is the difference between the quoted YTM and the expected return (going-in IRR) for the typical mortgage investors? (Hint: Describe two sources of difference.)
   b. When will the expected return (over the realistic prepayment horizon) exceed the YTM in a default-free loan?

17.11. What is the APR, and how is it related to the YTM?

17.12. a. What are some of the major reasons up-front points and fees are so common in the mortgage business?

b. What is the major reason for the existence of prepayment penalties?

17.13. a. How can the refinancing decision be evaluated as a comparison of two loan values?

b. How must you define the new loan (or replacement loan) in such an analysis?

c. Why is the refinancing decision not, fundamentally, a comparison of two loan values? What is it instead?

17.14. What is the relevant opportunity cost of capital to use as the discount rate in a refinancing evaluation?

17.15. Why is it important to keep the loan amount constant between the old and new loan in a refinancing analysis?

17.16. What is left out in the traditional DCF-based valuation of the refinancing decision?

17.17. a. Why might it not make sense to refinance a loan with a prepayment option as soon as the market yield on new loans dips below the contract rate on the old loan?

b. How is the prepayment option value incorporated in the classical NPV investment decision criterion applied to the refinancing decision?

17.18. Describe the rule of thumb commonly applied in practice to deal with the effect of the prepayment option on the refinancing decision.

Quantitative Problems

17.19. Consider a $2 million, 8%, 30-year mortgage with monthly payments. Compute the first three payments and the loan balance after the third payment for each of the following loan types: (a) interest-only, (b) CAM, (c) CPM.

17.20. Compute the mortgage constants for the interest only and CPM mortgages in 17.22. [The annual mortgage constant (MC) is the annual debt service per dollar loan amount, or MC = (12 * PMT)/LOAN.]

17.21. Consider a $2 million, 8%, 30-year GPM with monthly payments and two annual step-ups of 10% each (one after the first 12 payments, and the other after the 24th payment).

a. What is the initial monthly payment on this loan (prior to the first step-up)?

b. What is the final monthly payment level (after the second step-up)?

17.22. Consider a $2 million, 30-year amortization ARM with monthly payments and annual interest adjustments. The initial interest rate is 6%. The index for the loan is one-year U.S. Treasury bonds, currently yielding 5.5%. The loan has a margin of 250 basis points.

a. Is the loan's initial interest rate a teaser rate? How do you know?

b. If one-year T-bonds remain at 5.5%, what will be the applicable interest rate for this mortgage after the first year?

c. What are the initial monthly payments on this loan?

d. Assuming T-bonds remain at 5.5%, what will be the monthly payments after the first year?

e. Under that assumption (and assuming no discount points), what is the forecasted yield-to-maturity on this loan at the time it is issued, assuming it has no discount points?

17.23. Consider a $120,000, 25-year amortization ARM with monthly payments and annual interest rate adjustments. The initial interest rate is 6.5%. The index for the loan is one-year U.S. Treasury bonds, currently yielding 4.75%. The loan has a margin of 250 basis points, and *interest rate caps* of 2% per year at each adjustment and 4% over the life of the loan. It is expected that one-year bond yields will increase to 6.25% over the second year (at the end of year 1) and to 8% during year 3 (at the end of year 2).

a. Compute the payments and balances over the first three years. [Hint: With interest rate caps in effect, the contract rates in year 2 and beyond equal the minimum of the following three quantities: (i) index + margin (i.e., rate in the absence of caps); (ii) previous period rate + annual adjustment cap; (iii) initial period rate + life-of-loan cap.]

b. Assuming a loan origination fee of 2 points paid up front, determine the yield (effective cost) assuming a three-year holding period. (Hint: Use your "cash flow" keys and solve for the IRR.)

17.24. Consider a $2 million, 8% CPM with monthly payments. What is the regular monthly payment and the balloon payment amounts in each of the following cases?

a. Fully amortizing, 25-year loan

b. 25-year amortization, 10-year balloon

c. 15-year amortization, 10-year balloon

d. What are the major disadvantage and advantage of the 15-year amortization-rate 10-year loan in part (c) as compared to the 25-year amortization-rate 10-year loan in part (b)?

17.25. Consider a $2 million, 7.5%, 30-year mortgage with monthly payments. What is the YTM of this loan under the following circumstances?

a. No points, fully amortizing

b. Two points of disbursement discount, fully amortizing

c. Two points of disbursement discount, eight-year maturity with balloon

17.26. Consider a $2 million, 7.5%, 30-year mortgage with monthly payments and an expected realistic prepayment horizon of eight years. What is the contractual yield (effective interest rate) at issuance over the expected life of the loan under the following circumstances?

a. No points or penalties

b. One point of disbursement discount

c. Two points of disbursement discount

d. Two points of disbursement discount plus one point of prepayment penalty

17.27. Consider a $2 million, 7.5%, 30-year mortgage with monthly payments and an eight-year maturity with balloon.

a. How much is this loan worth at issuance if the market YTM for such loans is 7.125% BEY?

b. If instead the market yield is 7.875%, how many disbursement discount points must the lender charge to avoid doing a negative NPV deal?

17.28. A lender wants to achieve a 7.5% yield (MEY) on a 30-year amortization, monthly-payment loan with an eight-year maturity with balloon. How many disbursement discount points must the lender charge under the following circumstances?

a. Contract interest rate is 7.25%.

b. Contract interest rate is 7.0%.

17.29. a. As a borrower, which of the following two 25-year, monthly-payment loans would you choose if you had a 15-year expected prepayment horizon: 6% interest rate with four points, or 6.75% interest with one-half point?

b. Suppose your prepayment horizon was five years.

17.30. You work for an investment company that is considering the purchase of a "seasoned" mortgage loan that was originated two years ago. The original principal amount of the loan was $2 million, and it has an interest rate of 8%, a 15-year term and amortization period, monthly payments, and no prepayment penalty. You decide to value the loan based on the assumption that the loan is held to full maturity (i.e., there is no prepayment). Since interest rates have fallen somewhat in the past year, you offer a price based upon a required return or yield to maturity of 7.25%.

a. What price do you offer for the loan package (i.e., under your assumptions, what is the current market value of the loan)? Compare this to the current OLB or "book value" of the loan, and explain the difference.

b. Assume you purchase the loan at the price you determined in part (a) and that interest rates continue to fall afterwards, and as a result, the borrower prepays the mortgage 14 months from today. What yield or IRR will you have realized?

c. Consider the situation in part (b). Determine the size of the prepayment penalty ($ amount) that would have ensured that you earned a yield (or IRR) of 7.25%.

17.31. Five years ago, you took out a $120,000, 30-year mortgage at 9% interest, with no pre-payment penalty. Today you can get a 25-year mortgage at 7% with 2 points in closing costs. Assuming you plan to be in your house another five years, determine the NPV of refinancing (ignoring option value considerations). Do the calculation twice, once using the traditional refinancing calculation and then again using the shortcut (or comparison of OLB and market value approach). Of course, your answer should be the same for each.

17.32. (**Excel Exercise**) An insurance company is negotiating contract terms on a commercial mortgage loan with a potential borrower. The loan in question is a monthly payment, 20-year amortization, fixed rate balloon loan with a seven-year term (i.e., maturity), an annual interest rate of 5.85% and 1.5 points of disbursement discount.

a. The yield to the lender assuming the loan is held to the end of the term (assume a loan amount of $100). You should do this first with your financial calculator and then replicate your calculations in Excel; create a spreadsheet that takes the mortgage contract terms (amount, rate, etc.) as inputs and then use financial functions [=PMT(), =FV(), etc.] to calculate PMT and OLB. Show the mortgage cash flows from month zero to month 84 in a single column, and use the =IRR() function to solve for the yield to the lender.

b. Now suppose the borrower wants to modify the loan cash flows as follows: payments are interest-only for the first two years in the life of the loan, and then amortized payments start in the first month of the third year, with a 20-year amortization period [hence, payments in years 3 through 7 are the same as those you calculated in the original loan in part (a)]. The lender agrees but only if the borrower promises to make a lump sum payment, in addition to the OLB at the end of year 7, such that the lender's yield (IRR) is 6.5%. Determine the size of the lump sum payment. You should do this in the Excel spreadsheet you created for part (a). Specifically, add another column, make the required changes to the PMTs and OLB(84), and determine the additional lump sum required to make the IRR equal 6.5%.

*17.33. (**Prepayment Option**) Three years ago, you obtained a 10%, $6 million, monthly-payment mortgage with 20-year amortization and an eight-year maturity. (The loan thus matures five years from now, with a balloon payment.) This loan has a prepayment clause, but stipulates a three-point prepayment penalty on the outstanding balance. Today, it would be possible to obtain a similar mortgage at 8% interest with a one-point origination fee up front and 20-year amortization.

a. Assuming transaction costs would be $60,000, and the current value of the prepayment option in the old loan is $150,000, what is your NPV for paying off the old loan today?

b. If you could reduce the transaction costs to $50,000, should you pay the loan off immediately?

*17.34. (**Wraparound Loan**) Consider the same old loan as in Question 17.36, only now suppose interest rates have risen instead of fallen, so that similar loans today would carry a 12% interest rate. Suppose further that the old loan has no due-on-sale clause, and you want to sell the property that is collateral on the loan. A buyer is willing to pay $10 million for the property, but has only $2 million available, and does not feel comfortable with the payments on an $8 million mortgage at 12%, although he would do the deal at 11.5% with a 30-year amortization rate and a five-year balloon.

     a. What would be your yield on your investment in a wraparound loan meeting the seller's specifications?

     b. Why are you able to get an expected return on this investment so much in excess of the current market rate of 12%?

*17.35. **(Yield Maintenance)** A commercial mortgage is written for $1 million at 8% with 30-year amortization and a 10-year balloon payment. A yield-maintenance (YM) prepayment penalty is included as follows. If the borrower pays the loan off early, she must pay the lender an amount such that if the lender reinvests the proceeds (including the prepayment penalty) in U.S. Treasury bonds maturing on the same date as the original maturity of the mortgage, the lender will receive the same 8% mortgage-equivalent YTM on the loan's outstanding balance as she would have received in the mortgage over the remaining time until the loan's original maturity. Now suppose the borrower prepays the loan after seven years. Suppose that on that date three-year government bonds are yielding 6% (bond-equivalent yield). How much prepayment penalty must the borrower pay? Compute your answer based on coupon-equivalent yield, converting the mortgage MEY to its equivalent BEY. (This is an example of a *Treasury flat yield maintenance* prepayment structure with the remaining cash flows discounted at the then prevailing Treasury yield with no added margin or spread. In principle, it is identical to the *defeasance* premium associated with prepaying a CMBS conduit loan. Additional details on different prepayment penalty structures and their evolution as CMBS have become a major force and are provided in Chapter 20, specifically in the text box, "Call Protection in CMBS Bonds: Defeasance.")

*17.36. **(Yield Maintenance)** A commercial mortgage is written for $1 million at 8% with 30-year amortization and a 10-year balloon payment. A yield-maintenance prepayment penalty is included as follows. If the borrower pays the loan off early, he must pay the lender the present value of the remaining contractual payments on the loan discounted at the then-prevailing rates on T-bonds of a maturity equivalent to the remaining time on the loan, plus a margin of 50 basis points. (The difference between MEY and BEY is ignored, that is, the BEY T-bond rate plus margin is applied directly, to the remaining monthly cash flows in the loan as if it were a MEY rate.) Now suppose the borrower prepays the loan after seven years. Suppose that on that date three-year government bonds are yielding 5.50%. How much prepayment penalty must the borrower pay?

COMMERCIAL MORTGAGE ANALYSIS AND UNDERWRITING

CHAPTER OUTLINE

LEARNING OBJECTIVES

After reading this chapter, you should understand:

⇨ How to quantify the effect of default risk on the expected returns to commercial mortgages.

⇨ How commercial mortgage underwriting procedures are related to default risk.

⇨ The major traditional procedures and measures used in commercial mortgage underwriting in the United States.

T he previous two chapters familiarized you with the fundamentals of mortgages, basic concepts and considerations that are relevant to both borrowers and lenders, for both residential and commercial mortgages. In this chapter, we will focus more specifically on issues that are most relevant to commercial mortgage lenders and investors. (Of course, an appreciation of the lender's perspective can also be very useful to borrowers who must negotiate with lenders.) This chapter is divided into two main parts. After an introduction discussing some quantitative aspects of default risk, we will describe the nuts and bolts of typical commercial mortgage underwriting.

18.1 Expected Returns versus Stated Yields: Measuring the Impact of Default Risk

The previous chapter described in depth how to compute the yield-to-maturity (YTM) for a mortgage. We noted that the yield computed in this way is a **contract yield**, or what is often referred to as a **stated yield**, as distinct from a realistic **expected return**. The former is based on the contractual cash flow terms of the mortgage, while the latter recognizes the realistic probability of default and foreclosure. To distinguish these two measures of return, in the present chapter, we will use the abbreviation YTM to refer to the contract yield, and $E[r]$ to refer to the expected return (which may also be referred to as the *expected yield* or *ex ante yield*).[1]

In practice, quoted yields are always contract yields, and people work with contract yields when designing and evaluating mortgages. However, for mortgage *investors*, whether they are loan originators or buyers in the secondary market, realistic expected returns are the more fundamental measure for making investment decisions. The difference between the stated yield and the expected return quantifies the impact of the default risk in the ex ante return that the lender cares about.

Let's look at a quick and simple numerical example to clarify some basic terminology. Consider a three-year, annual payment, interest-only (nonamortizing) mortgage, with no fees or disbursement points up front. This mortgage is originated for $1 million at a 6 percent interest rate. This 6 percent rate will be the mortgage's contractual interest rate or "**coupon**" (rate) throughout the life of the loan and no matter what happens in the bond market, and the equation below describes these contractual terms on the loan:

$$\$1,000,000 = \frac{\$60,000}{1.06} + \frac{\$60,000}{1.06^2} + \frac{\$1,060,000}{1.06^3}$$

Suppose the bond market suddenly changes and prevailing interest rates drop a whole point so that immediately after being issued this mortgage now commands a price of $1,027,232. The same mortgage with the same contractual cash flows would have a market yield or YTM of 5 percent, reflecting the bond market. This would be expressed in its prevent value DCF equation as follows:

$$\$1,027,232 = \frac{\$60,000}{1.05} + \frac{\$60,000}{1.05^2} + \frac{\$1,060,000}{1.05^3}$$

This means that the mortgage at its current market price presents investors with a 5 percent expected return (in the form of a going-in IRR) *provided* it pays all three of its annual cash flows according to contract as indicated in the equation. But suppose in the third year the lender was not able to obtain the $60,000 interest payment, but only recouped the $1 million principal amount. The realized IRR on that three-year cash flow stream would be 3.10 percent. Note that we solved for the 3.1 percent yield, which matched all the cash flows received with the initial investment of $1,027,232:

$$\$1,027,232 = \frac{\$60,000}{1.031} + \frac{\$60,000}{1.031^2} + \frac{\$1,000,000}{1.031^3}$$

Finally, suppose that there is a 90 percent chance that the loan will pay off as contracted, including all three annual interest payments and return of principal, and a 10 percent chance that it will default in the third year as described above, with these two possibilities exhausting all possible outcomes of the loan. Then the *expected return* (what we will label $E[r]$) on the loan investment at the $1,027,232 price, based on these two cases shown above and their corresponding probabilities, would be:

$$E[r] = (0.9)5.00\% + (0.1)3.10\% = 4.81\%$$

The 19 basis-points difference between the 5 percent contractual YTM (on the 6 percent coupon loan) and the 4.81 percent expected return on the loan is due to the possibility of default on the loan. This difference is obviously important for investors (and indeed for borrowers as well). The sections that follow will introduce you to this consideration in more depth.

18.1.1 Yield Degradation and Conditional Cash Flows

In the commercial mortgage business, shortfalls to the lender as a result of default and foreclosure are referred to as **credit losses**. The effect of credit losses on the realized yield as compared to the contractual yield is referred to as **yield degradation**. To understand how to

---

[1]Note that the use of $E[r]$ in this context is consistent with our previous use of this label in Parts III–V of this book where it referred to the mean of the probability distribution of the future return.

quantify the difference between stated and expected yields in mortgage investments, let's begin by examining yield degradation with a simple numerical example, using our previous simple three-year loan example, with some slight modifications.

Suppose the loan is for $100 at an interest rate of 10 percent, such that the contractual cash flows call for two annual payments of $10 followed by $110 at the end of the third year. As there are no points or origination fees, the contractual YTM on this loan at origination is 10 percent. Therefore, at the end of the third year, the realized yield on the loan will also be 10 percent if there is no default.

Now suppose that the borrower makes his first two payments but defaults when it comes time for the third payment. The lender takes the property and sells it immediately, but is only able to get 70 percent of what is owed, or $77. In this case, the credit loss is $33, and 70 percent is referred to as the **recovery rate**, or alternatively, a **loss severity** of 30 percent. The result would be a realized yield on the mortgage of −1.12 percent, computed as the IRR on the actual cash flows to the lender:

$$0 = -\$100 + \frac{\$10}{1 + (-0.0112)} + \frac{\$10}{[1 + (-0.0112)]^2} + \frac{\$77}{[1 + (-0.0112)]^3}$$

The yield degradation is 11.12 percent, as the realized yield of −1.12 percent is this much less than the contract yield of 10 percent. The yield degradation is how much the lender loses compared to what she was supposed to get, measured as a multiperiod lifetime return on the original investment.

From an ex ante perspective, analyzing the mortgage beforehand, we would refer to this 11.12 percent yield degradation as a **conditional yield degradation**. It is the yield degradation that will occur *if* the loan defaults in the third year, and *if* the recovery rate is 70 percent. The 70 percent recovery rate is also a conditional rate, conditioned on the default occurring in the third year. Thus, ex ante, the 11.12 percent yield degradation is *conditional* on these events or assumptions.

Suppose the default occurs in the second year, with 70 percent recovery. In this case, the realized yield would be −7.11 percent, as

$$0 = -\$100 + \frac{\$10}{1 + (-0.0711)} + \frac{\$77}{[1 + (-0.0711)]^2}$$

The yield degradation would therefore be 17.11 percent. This points to an important fact. Other things being equal (in particular, the conditional recovery rate), *the conditional yield degradation is greater, the earlier the default occurs in the loan life.* Lenders are hit worse when default occurs early in the life of a mortgage. (This has important implications for construction loans, which are inherently shorter term in duration. If there is default in a construction loan, it will be before very many years into the lender's investment.)

Now let's consider the relation among the contract yield, the conditional yield degradation, and the expected return on the mortgage. After all, the expected return is most relevant to the mortgage investor at the time when the decision is made to invest in the loan (i.e., to issue the loan). In other words, it is an unconditional ex ante measure, so we must specify the ex ante probability of default and the expected conditional recovery rate or loss severity and derive the unconditional expected return from that. As in our introductory example, suppose that at the time the mortgage is issued, there is a 10 percent probability of default in the third year with 70 percent recovery and no chance of any other default event. Thus, there is a 90 percent chance the loan will return the contract yield, and a 10 percent chance it will return that yield less the third-year conditional yield degradation of 11.12 percent. Under these circumstances, the expected return at the time the mortgage is issued is approximately 8.89 percent, computed as:

$$
\begin{aligned}
E[r] = 8.89\% &= (0.9)10.00\% + (0.1)(-1.12\%) \\
&= (0.9)10.00\% + (0.1)(10.00\% - 11.12\%) \\
&= 10.00\% - (0.1)(11.12\%)
\end{aligned}
$$

Thus, we can express the expected return as equal to the contract yield (labeled *YTM*), minus the product of the default probability (labeled *PrDEF*) times the conditional yield degradation (labeled *YDEGR*):

$$E[r] = YTM - (PrDEF)(YDEGR)$$

*18.1.2 Hazard Functions and the Timing of Default

In this example, we simplified the problem of computing the expected return by assuming there is only one point in the life of the mortgage when default can occur. In reality, default conceivably can occur at any point in time. This possibility is represented by what is known as a **hazard function**. The hazard function tells the conditional probability of default at each point in time given that default has not already occurred before then. As an example, let's return to the simple three-year loan again. Suppose that the hazard function representing the conditional probability of default in each year is given in the following table:

Year	Hazard
1	1%
2	2%
3	3%

This means that there is a 1 percent chance of default in the first year (i.e., at the time of the first payment), a 2 percent chance in the second year *if the loan has not already defaulted in the first year*, and a 3 percent chance in the third year if the loan is still in effect by then.

Once we know the hazard function for a mortgage, we can compute the cumulative and unconditional default and survival probabilities, as shown in the following table.

Year	Hazard	Conditional Survival	Cumulative Survival	Unconditional PrDEF	Cumulative PrDEF
1	0.01	$1 - 0.01 = 0.9900$	$0.99 \times 1.0000 = 0.9900$	$0.01 \times 1.0000 = 0.0100$	0.0100
2	0.02	$1 - 0.02 = 0.9800$	$0.98 \times 0.9900 = 0.9702$	$0.02 \times 0.9900 = 0.0198$	$0.0100 + 0.0198 = 0.0298$
3	0.03	$1 - 0.03 = 0.9700$	$0.97 \times 0.9702 = 0.9411$	$0.03 \times 0.9702 = 0.0291$	$0.0298 + 0.0291 = 0.0589$

The **conditional survival probability** in each year is 1 minus the hazard for that year. It is the probability the loan will not default in that year, given that it has not defaulted prior to that year. The **cumulative survival probability** is the probability that the loan has survived (not defaulted) through the given year. This is the product of all the previous conditional survival probabilities (including the given year). The **unconditional default probability** is the probability, as of the time of loan origination, that default will occur in a given year. It equals the hazard in that year times the cumulative survival probability through the end of the previous year.[2] This is an unconditional probability because it does not depend on the conditioning assumption of the loan not having yet defaulted prior to the given year. The cumulative default probability is the probability, as of the time of loan origination, that the loan will have defaulted during or prior to the given year. It equals the sum of the unconditional default probabilities up to and including the given year, and it also (equivalently) equals one minus the cumulative survival through the given year.

Thus, the probability that the loan will default at any time during its life is the **cumulative default probability** through the end of the loan maturity, or (equivalently) the sum of all the unconditional default probabilities across all the years in the loan life. With hazards of 1 percent, 2 percent, and 3 percent, the ex ante probability that Bob will

---

[2]The unconditional default probability can also be computed as the difference in the cumulative survival probability at the beginning and end of the given year (e.g., $0.0291 = 0.9702 - 0.9411$).

default at some point in the life of his three-year loan is 5.89 percent (computed as $0.0589 = 0.0100 + 0.0198 + 0.0291 = 1 - 0.9411$).[3]

For each year in the life of the loan, a conditional yield degradation can be computed, conditional on default occurring in that year, and given an assumption about the conditional recovery rate in that year. For example, we saw that with our previous example 10 percent loan, the conditional yield degradation was 11.12 percent if default occurs in year 3, and 17.11 percent if default occurs in year 2, in both cases assuming a 70 percent recovery rate. Similar calculations reveal that the conditional yield degradation would be 22.00 percent if default occurs in year 1 with an 80 percent recovery rate.[4]

Defaults in each year of a loan's life and no default at all in the life of the loan represent mutually exclusive events that together exhaust all of the possible default timing occurrences for any loan (analyzing at the annual frequency). For example, with the three-year loan, it will either default in year 1, year 2, year 3, or never. Thus, the expected return on the loan can be computed as the contractual yield minus the sum across all the years of the products of the *unconditional* default probabilities times the conditional yield degradations. This is simply a generalization of formula (1):

$$E[r] = YTM - \sum_{t=1}^{T}(PrDEF_t)(TDEGR_t)$$

where $PrDEF_t$ is the unconditional default probability in year t, $YDEGR_t$ is the conditional yield degradation in year t, and there are T years in the life of the loan.

For example, given the previously stated hazard function (1 percent, 2 percent, and 3 percent for the successive years) and conditional recovery rates (80 percent, 70 percent, and 70 percent for the successive years), the expected return on our example 10 percent mortgage at the time it is issued would be

$$\begin{aligned} E[r] &= 10.00\% - [(0.0100)(22.00\%) + (0.0198)(17.11\%) + (0.0291)(11.12\%)] \\ &= 10.00\% - 0.88\% \\ &= 9.12\% \end{aligned}$$

The 88-basis-point shortfall of the expected return below the contractual yield is the **ex ante yield degradation** in Bob's mortgage. This might also be referred to as an **unconditional yield degradation**. It reflects the ex ante credit loss expectation in the mortgage as of the time of its issuance.[5]

18.1.3 Yield Degradation in Typical Commercial Mortgages

How large is the ex ante yield degradation in typical commercial mortgages in the United States? To answer this question, we need to know something about the hazard function that is typical of commercial mortgages. Surprisingly enough, there was relatively little publicly available information on this subject until the 1990s.

---

[3]Note that this is less than the sum of all the individual hazards, which would be 6.00%.

[4]This is computed as $(80\%) \times \$110/[1 + (-0.12)] = \$100$, so -12% is the conditional return, and -12% is 22% less than the contractual yield of 10%. Note that in computing the conditional yield, the conditional recovery rate is applied to the OLB at the time of the default, in this case $\$110$. This reflects the fact that the lender would accelerate the loan in the event of default so that the entire outstanding balance would be due at that time, including interest owed. It is likely that a greater proportion of the loan balance could be recovered from a foreclosure in the first year, as there is less time for the property to have lost value subsequent to loan issuance. So it is plausible to assume a recovery rate of 80% in the first year if the subsequent rate is 70%.

[5]An alternative method of computing the expected return may be employed. Instead of taking the average across the IRRs associated with each future scenario, we could compute the IRR of the average cash flow across the future scenarios. Instead the average IRR: $E[r] \equiv E[IRR(CF)]$ as above, we could define and compute the expected return as the IRR of the average cash flow: $E[r] \equiv IRR(E[CF])$. The values are not exactly the same, though they are usually similar (with the average cash flow method indicating a few basis points less yield degradation than the average IRR method). The average cash flow method is implicitly assumed in calculations of expected returns for property equity investments and in standard DCF applications as introduced in Chapter 10. However, the "average IRR" method described in the text here makes sense from an "investment manager's perspective," where investor preferences are defined on returns achieved.

Since then, a growing number of studies have contributed to our ability to analyze commercial mortgages rationally. Initially the major data source used for the most high pro-file studies in the institutional commercial property investment industry was the record of mortgages issued by members of the American Council of Life Insurers (ACLI). We noted in Chapter 16 that life insurance companies were the major traditional source of debt capital for long-term loans on larger, stabilized properties. The ACLI data goes back into the 1970s, thus presenting a long history that, importantly, included a couple of major down cycles in the commercial property market (mid-1970s, late-1980s). Another data source is the Federal Reserve Board and other government regulators of banks and depository institutions. However, banks and thrifts tend to specialize in short-term and construction loans, as well as in smaller properties many of which might be considered below the "institutional" invest-ment threshold.[6] A challenge was posed by the fact that a new and rather different major source of capital for commercial mortgages arose in the 1990s in the form of the CMBS industry. Of course, there was at first no historical database of the performance of CMBS loans. CMBS investors tended to infer from the most similar seeming source of data with a long history, that of the ACLI. But we now have a wealth of data on CMBS loan performance, most interestingly in the aftermath of the financial crisis and recession of 2008–2010.

Exhibit 18-1 portrays the empirical hazard function found in an influential study that was updated several times, initially by Snyderman, Esaki, and others at the investment bank-ing firm of Morgan Stanley.[7] The study examined defaults through 2002 in almost 18,000 individual commercial mortgages issued from 1972 through 1997 by major life insurance companies that are members of the ACLI.[8] Note that the hazard function is characteristically humpbacked. The probability of default immediately after loan issuance is relatively low, but rises rapidly, peaking in the early to middle years of the loan life, before falling off in the later years. Constant-payment loans are most likely to get into trouble roughly during the third through seventh year of the life of the loan.[9] In the ACLI data, the hazard probabilities peak at 1.8 percent in the sixth year and fall off rapidly after the seventh year. The implied mean time until default (if it occurs) is about seven years.

Exhibit 18-2 portrays the cumulative survival function implied by the hazard probabili-ties in Exhibit 18-1. The implied cumulative lifetime default probability is slightly under 16 percent. Almost one in six commercial mortgages issued by life insurance companies in the United States during the 1972–1997 period defaulted.[10] However, as of the time of the study in the mid-2000s, a much smaller fraction of commercial mortgages issued after 1990 had defaulted. But that favorable record turned out to have been rather misleading in terms of the subsequent experience for CMBS loans.

It is very important to note that historical default rates have varied widely depending on when the loans were issued. This was clear even based on the ACLI data available in the 1990s, as is depicted in Exhibit 18-3. The bars in the exhibit indicate the cumulative lifetime default rates for ACLI loans issued in each of the years 1972–1997, as compiled in the Esaki et al. study. The line in the graph traces the relative level of institutional commercial property values, based on the NCREIF index.[11]

---

[6]You may want to look back at Exhibit 16-2 and the discussion thereof in the introduction to Chapter 16.

[7]The original study was by Mark Snyderman in 1991. The reference for the version reported here is Howard Esaki, "Commercial Mortgage Defaults: 1972–2000," *Real Estate Finance* 18(4), winter 2002. This version represented the state of the long-run empirical evidence regarding commercial mortgage default behavior as the CMBS industry went into the major boom period of the mid-2000s.

[8]The ACLI publishes data on loan defaults in the *ACLI Quarterly Survey of Mortgage Loan Delinquencies and Foreclo-sures*. In the study, a loan was considered to be defaulted if it was reported as being more than 90 days delinquent. Most such loans are ultimately foreclosed or restructured or liquidated in some manner.

[9]It would seem reasonable to expect that loans with large balloon payments, such as interest-only loans, would tend to run into trouble when they come due, although the Esaki study finds little historical empirical evidence of this.

[10]Esaki et al. (1999) reported that the default rate on loans with at least ten years of seasoning (defaults through 1997 on loans issued through 1987) was 18.1%.

[11]The NCREIF index appreciation value levels in Exhibit 18-3 have been "unsmoothed" by the authors and extended back in time using additional data, as described in Chapter 7.

EXHIBIT 18-1 Typical
Commercial Mortgage
Hazard Rates

Source: Based on data from
Esaki et al. 2002.

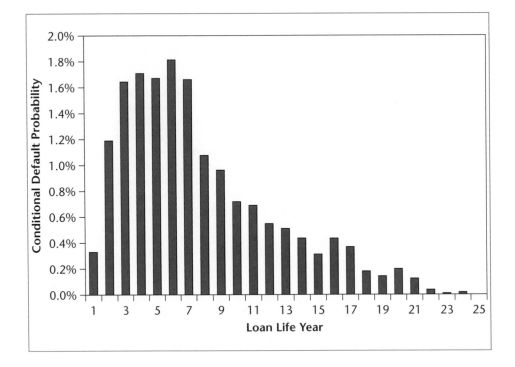

EXHIBIT 18-2 Typical
Commercial Mortgage
Survival Rates

Source: Based on data from
Esaki et al. 2002.

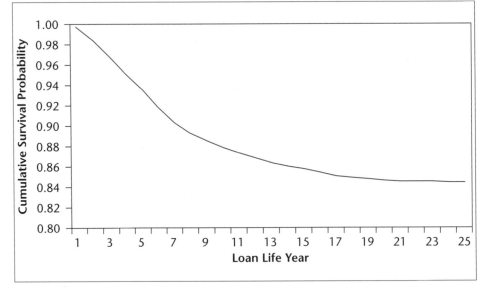

The historical lifetime default rates shown in Exhibit 18-3 are relatively low on cohorts of loans issued in years when property values were relatively low. For example, loans issued in the mid to late 1970s had lifetime default rates around 10 percent. Of the loans issued in 1992, for example, less than 5 percent had defaulted through the end of 2002. On the other hand, loans issued when property values were relatively high, such as the early 1970s and mid-1980s, had much higher lifetime default rates, peaking at almost 28 percent for loans issued in 1986. When property values were relatively low, mortgage issuers granted only relatively small loan amounts, and subsequent rises in property values made default relatively rare. When property values were relatively high, larger loans were issued and there was an increased probability that subsequent falls in property market values would put the loans

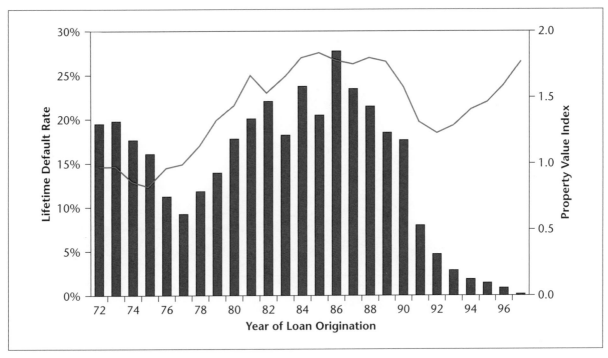

EXHIBIT 18-3 Lifetime Default Rates and Property Values
Sources: Based on data from Esaki, et al. 2002 and NCREIF Index.

"under water," that is, the outstanding loan balance (OLB) would be greater than the value of the property collateral securing the loan.

As noted previously, this type of behavior has been described as a "Santa Claus approach," in which borrowers are rewarded (that is, loaned more capital) when they have done well and penalized (given less capital) when they have performed poorly, during the recent past. Indeed, if real estate markets are cyclical, and the LTV ratios at which lenders will grant loans are constant, then this could result in the type of default rate cyclicality suggested in Exhibit 18-3.The cycle will be only further exacerbated if lenders are actually more aggressive, as by effectively relaxing their underwriting standards, during periods when the property market is booming (and perhaps pull back to excessive conservatism just after having been "burned" in a down cycle). Of course, boom periods practically by definition correspond to times when large quantities of financial capital are flowing into the property market, normally including a large share of debt capital in the form of commercial mortgages. Thus, the system may be structured to support boom-and-bust pattern.

The good performance on loans issued in the early 1990s was due, in part, to the fact that underwriting standards became much stricter and lending was very conservative in the immediate aftermath of the great commercial property "crash" of the late 1980s and early 1990s. Through the rest of the 1990s, lending was generally conservative. The other part of the very favorable outcome for the early 1990s loans was the strong rental market during the late 1990s, followed by the boom in property asset market values in the early 2000s (e.g., see Exhibit 7-11 in Chapter 7 for a history of commercial property values). The late 1990s and early 2000s was a "forgiving" period in commercial mortgage lending.

Ironically, the very good performance of the mid-1990s cohorts of loans may have helped to lull the capital market into complacency. After all, there had been what seemed at the time a major global financial crisis in 1998, and a major stock market crash and recession in 2001–2002, and commercial mortgage performance came through those crises in pretty good shape. Many players in the industry may have been able to convince themselves that the new system, which balanced traditional "relationship" and portfolio lending from life

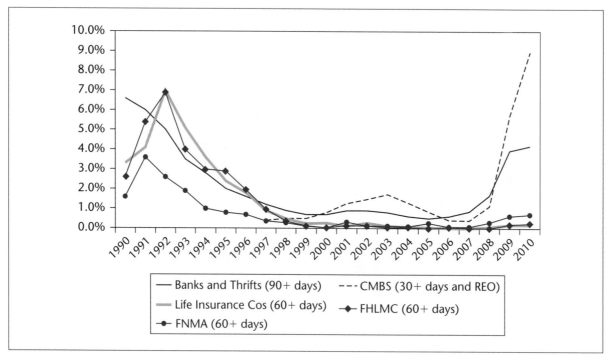

EXHIBIT 18-4 Default Rate in Outstanding Loans by Lender: 1990–2010*

*Excluding construction loans.

Source: Mortgage Bankers Association.

insurance companies and commercial banks with securitized conduit lending via the CMBS industry, provided a highly efficient machine. By the mid-2000s loan underwriting was became very aggressive again, especially in the new CMBS conduit segment of the market.

Exhibit 18-4 shows the history from 1990 through 2010 of the current default rate on loans outstanding by various types of lenders. The current default rate is not exactly the same thing as either the lifetime cumulative default rates by loan issuance cohorts shown in Exhibit 18-3 nor the longitudinal profile of loan lifetime hazard rates shown in Exhibit 18-1. Current default rates give a picture of how *all* the loans outstanding as of a given time are performing (or you can think of it as how the average such loan is performing). For example, Exhibit 18-4 indicates that in the early 1990s mortgages issued by life insurance companies were experiencing default rates of around 7 percent, as measured by the percentage of loans that were delinquent in payment by 60 days or more. If such a default rate were to continue for 10 years on all remaining loans (like an annual hazard rate), then at the end of 10 years only $(1 - 0.07)^{10} = 48\%$ of the loans would still be "alive," a cumulative default incidence of 52 percent. But of course such a high default rate did not persist, and we saw in Exhibit 18-3 that in fact the cumulative lifetime default incidence on the worst-performing cohort of ACLI loans (those issued in 1986) was actually less than 28 percent. But you can see how the current default rate gives a type of glimpse at the current instantaneous hazard rate facing the currently outstanding mortgages.

With this in mind, look at the picture presented by Exhibit 18-4. As bad as the previous commercial mortgage default performance was in the early 1990s in the aftermath of the commercial property down cycle at that time, the new CMBS loans were experiencing equally bad default performance by 2010 in the aftermath of the then-latest down cycle. By 2011 the delinquency rate for the worst-performing cohort of loans issued during the 2007 peak of the bubble was up to 12 percent.[12] Banks were also suffering severely by 2010, although still at

---

[12]As compiled by Moody's Investors Service "Delinquency Tracker Report" of November 2011, based on loans 60+ days delinquent or in foreclosure or REO status. By this definition the overall average CMBS loan delinquency rate in 2011 was over 9%.

rates below their peak default performance in the previous cycle. Interestingly, in the down cycle of the 2000s the life insurance companies (LICs) were experiencing much less loan distress than the other major lenders (other than the two government-sponsored enterprises that were restricted to apartment loans on moderate-income-oriented multifamily rental housing). In part, it reflects differences in policies and procedures and in reporting of default rates, but this also may have been because LICs had learned a hard lesson in the previous down cycle and did not get quite as aggressive in their underwriting as the CMBS conduit lenders in the peak of the 2005–2007 boom. As a result, the LICs were somewhat "squeezed out" of the market during the peak of the bubble years, to their subsequent benefit.[13]

Default probabilities are not the only type of information necessary to estimate the typical magnitude of ex ante yield degradation in commercial mortgages. We also need information on conditional recovery rates or loss severities once default occurs. This type of information is more difficult to obtain, although more is becoming available all the time. Losses generally result to the mortgage holder even if an actual foreclosure does not happen as a result of the default. As described in Chapter 16, actions following loan default range from loan workouts to "deed in lieu" or "short sales" to formal foreclosure.[14]

The Esaki et al. study reported that about 55 percent of defaulting loans (defined as 90+ days delinquent in payment) were foreclosed or liquidated, 40 percent were restructured, 3 percent became delinquent again, and only 2 percent fully recovered. Among liquidated loans, the average conditional recovery rate was 69 percent (or equivalently, 31 percent loss severity). This included the effects of foreclosure expenses as well as lost interest and principal based on the *reported* value of the property at the time of foreclosure. However, a more detailed study by Ciochetti (1998) tracked 308 foreclosed mortgages from "cradle to grave," including the period subsequent to foreclosure when the property was owned by the lender (as "real estate owned"— REO). The loans had all originated between 1974 and 1990. Ciochetti found that while the average recovery was 57 percent based on reported property value as of the time of foreclosure (which resulted in 6.5 percent conditional yield degradation), the average recovery was only 34 percent through to the final disposition of the collateral property by the lender (equivalent to 10.6 percent conditional yield degradation in his loan sample).

In the more recent down cycle, in which CMBS loans have been in some respects the biggest problem within the institutional property market, the loss severity experience may be even worse. Evidence reported by Moody's Investors Service (based in part on data from the CMBS data collection firm Trepp) indicated average loss severities of almost 40 percent by

---

[13]The default rates shown in Exhibit 18-4 are not exactly comparable across the different types of lenders, in part because they have been defined differently in terms of the length of delinquency. For example, in the Mortgage Bankers Association report that Exhibit 18-4 is based on, CMBS default is defined by 30+ days of delinquency or REO status (real estate ownership taken over by the lender), whereas the bank and thrift default rate is defined by 90+ days of delinquency. However, there tends to be a very high correlation among delinquency duration (i.e., once a loan goes delinquent it tends often to continue to do so). It should also be recognized that the different types of lenders in Exhibit 18-4 tend to specialize in different types of commercial properties, which may therefore subject them to different severities of market conditions. For example, banks tend to focus on smaller properties and shorter-term loans (even apart from construction loans). Another reason for the "apples-versus-oranges" comparison across the different lenders in Exhibit 18-4 has to do with different policies and procedures regarding the treatment and recording of loans where the borrower is in trouble. In particular, portfolio lenders and relationship lenders (including most notably life insurance companies and banks) adopted more flexible policies with their borrowers that allowed the lenders to avoid recording loans as delinquent or nonperforming after the 2008–2010 down cycle than was the case for CMBS loans or indeed for the portfolio lenders themselves during the previous down cycle. (The new behavior became known as "pretend and extend," and it helped the relationship lenders to avoid experiencing losses that would have been even worse.) It should also be noted that, while many loans from banks and thrifts are construction loans, which are a rather different and more risky and cyclical type of product, these have been excluded from the figures portrayed in Exhibit 18-4.

[14]In this context, the term "short sale" refers to a situation in which the borrower in default and the lender mutually agree to sell the property, generally due to market conditions at a price below what is owed on the loan, after which the lender takes all of the proceeds from the sale, but the lender then releases the borrower without formal foreclosure or seeking a deficiency judgment. This is similar to the "deed in lieu" except that in the latter case the borrower does not sell the property and the lender might hold onto the property for a while as REO (real estate owned) hoping for the market to improve. This is much more possible in commercial (income producing) real estate than with owner-occupied houses.

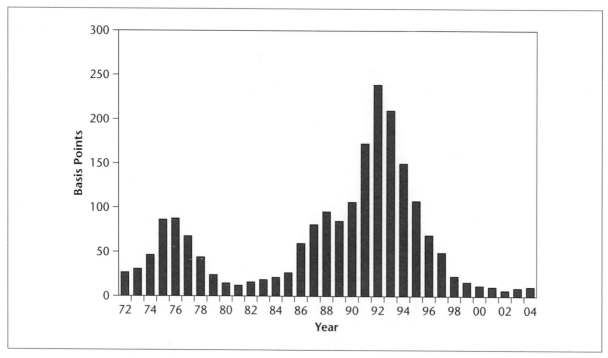

EXHIBIT 18-5 Commercial Mortgage Credit Loss as Fraction of Par Value
Source: Based on data from GLCMPI—John B. Levy & Co.

2011, with the loss severities on the three loan cohorts from the peak of the boom (issued in 2006, 2007, and 2008) being 53 percent, 49 percent, and 56 percent as of 2011.[15]

Default probabilities and conditional recovery statistics can be combined to provide estimates of conditional and ex ante yield degradation for typical loans.[16] Such information can be used in the construction of indices of the periodic returns to commercial mortgages, based on synthetic portfolios of typical mortgages. Such an index of commercial mortgage whole loan investment performance is the Giliberto-Levy Commercial Mortgage Performance Index (GLCMPI), which is based largely on ACLI loan performance data.[17] The GLCMPI includes estimates of the magnitude of credit losses suffered in the index total return each quarter as a fraction of the OLB of all loans. On an annualized basis, these credit losses provide an approximate indication of the magnitude of the **ex post yield degradation** realized by the aggregate portfolio of outstanding loans during each year.

Exhibit 18-5 shows the magnitude of annual credit losses in the GLCMPI over the 1972–2004 period (measured in basis points of outstanding par value). As we would expect, credit losses are higher during downturns in the commercial property asset market (mid-1970s, early 1990s). Credit losses peaked at almost 240 basis points in 1992, but were as low as 6–9 basis points during the boom years of the early 2000s, only to rise to close to 100 basis points again by 2010. Ex post realizations of credit loss are certainly more volatile than expectations

---

[15]Moody's Investors Service, "US CMBS Loss Severities, 2Q 2011 Update," Special Report, September 8, 2011.

[16]As noted, not all defaulting loans are foreclosed, as some defaults are worked out, as described in Chapter 16. However, lenders usually still suffer losses in such cases. In addition, lenders suffer some losses from loan delinquencies that are not classified as defaults (e.g., delinquencies of less than 90 days).

[17]The GLCMPI was originally published by John B. Levy & Company, Richmond, Virginia and was taken over by the Investment Property Databank (IPD) in 2011.

IS IT SURPRISING THAT SO MANY COMMERCIAL MORTGAGES DEFAULT?

No borrower plans to default on a loan when he or she takes it out. Lenders seem to go to lots of trouble to try to avoid making loans that will default. So is it surprising that about one out of every six long-term commercial mortgages in the United States defaults? Perhaps not, when you go back to fundamentals.

One of those fundamentals is *volatility* in the property market. Recall in Chapter 9 we suggested that the typical individual commercial property probably has an annual volatility in excess of 15 percent (and this doesn't include "deal noise" as described in Chapter 12). This means that the annual standard deviation in a typical property's appreciation return (or change in value) is at least about 15 percent of its initial value, including market risk and idiosyncratic risk. Now recall that the normal probability distribution has about one-third of its total probability beyond one standard deviation from its mean. This implies that about one-sixth of the probable value outcomes are at or below one standard deviation *below* the mean outcome. Suppose the expected (i.e., mean) property value a year from now is the same as the current property value. Then 15 percent annual volatility implies that there is about a one-sixth chance that a given property will be worth, one year from now, 85 percent or less of its current value. Now suppose property values follow a "random walk" through time. In other words, suppose property values change randomly across time, like stock market values. (Whether the value rose or fell during the past year does not tell you anything about whether it will rise or fall next year, like the flipping of a coin.) Then it is a mathematical fact that the volatility grows with the square root of the time over which it is measured. The biennial volatility would be $\sqrt{2}$ times the annual volatility; the decennial volatility would be $\sqrt{10}$ times the annual volatility, and so forth.*

Now we know from the Esaki et al. study that the typical commercial mortgage default occurs about seven years into the life of the loan. Thus (somewhat simplistically speaking), the relevant volatility for determining default frequency is the seven-year volatility, not the annual volatility. If the annual volatility is 15 percent, then the seven-year volatility is $\sqrt{7}$ times this amount, or 40 percent. Without any expected appreciation in the property value, there would be about a one-sixth chance that a given property would be worth, seven years from now, only 60 percent of its current value, or less. Even if the property is expected to appreciate at, say, 2 percent per year, this will increase the expected value in seven years only to about 15 percent above the current value, so there would still be a one-sixth chance that the property would be worth only 75 percent of its current value, or less, after seven years. The standard loan-to-value (LTV) ratio required by mortgage issuers has traditionally

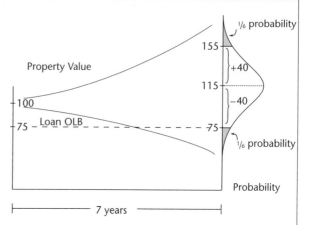

been 75 percent. If loans don't amortize much and borrowers tend to default whenever the loan is "under water" (that is, when the property is worth less than the loan balance), then the 75 percent LTV criterion suggests a typical default probability of about one-sixth. (See illustration above.)

Of course, this analysis is highly simplified, and many commercial mortgages amortize their principal over time. But, on the other hand, in a low-inflation environment, many properties may tend to appreciate at less than 2 percent per year, and we are not considering "deal noise" here (possible mispricing as of any given point in time). And while it may not make sense to default on a loan just because its par value is under water, the reason the property has lost value is likely to be because its rental income has dropped, which may force the borrower to default. You can see the basic point: *Empirically observed default rates in commercial mortgages are consistent with empirical evidence about property volatility.*[†] The average property may not be as risky as the average stock (whose annual volatility is typically around 30 percent), but when you lend 75 percent of a property's value, you are asking for, well, about a one-sixth chance of running into a default at some point in the life of the loan).

---

*If property values do not follow a purely random walk, but rather have some inertia, as would be the case in a sluggish or informationally inefficient asset market, then the volatility actually increases *more than* the square root of the measurement time interval. So the analysis here would be conservative in that regard, suggesting even greater chance of default.

[†]Ciochetti and Vandell (1999) studied this question much more rigorously. Their estimate of the individual property annual volatility implied by the empirical evidence on commercial mortgage values and default rates is about 17 percent, assuming property values follow a random walk.

© OnCourse Learning

beforehand. However, averaged across a long span of time, ex post credit losses provide some indication of the typical ex ante yield degradation in permanent commercial mortgages in the United States. The average annual credit loss in the GLCMPI during the 1972–2004 period was 62 basis points.[18] Construction loans would be expected to contain greater ex ante yield degradation than permanent loans because of their short maturities and likely greater conditional loss severities.

18.2 Commercial Mortgage Underwriting

Underwriting is the word used to describe the process commercial mortgage originators go through to decide whether to issue a proposed mortgage. As noted in Chapter 16, this process can be much more involved than taking out a typical home mortgage. Commercial mortgages are often negotiated, and the terms of the loan may be customized to reflect the unique circumstances presented by the borrower, the lender, and the collateral property. This is less true with CMBS conduit loans, which are necessarily more standardized and commoditized. But even with conduits there is often some room to maneuver or to choose among competing originators. The larger the loan is, the more it is worthwhile to spend time and energy in this negotiation and customization process. For typical commercial mortgages of several million dollars, procedures are generally fairly standardized. Even for larger loans, in the tens of millions of dollars each, standard underwriting criteria are issued by the institutions supplying the mortgage capital.

In this section, we will describe typical commercial underwriting criteria and how the underwriting process works in a normative sense. That is, our focus and perspective is on how the process is *supposed* to work. But keep in mind that, as we discussed in the preceding section, there may be times when market pressures cause the system, in effect, to "bend" the rules, even if on paper the rules may not appear to change that much. Even then, the process still utilizes the same metrics that we will discuss in this section.

What Underwriting Is All About To begin, you should recognize the normative purpose of underwriting. In principle, the purpose of underwriting is *to make default a rare event*. We noted in the previous section that, on average, about one in six long-term commercial mortgages in the United States defaults, or at least did so during the last quarter of the twentieth century. Is this one-sixth rate "rare enough"? Well, it could be, provided lenders are being adequately compensated for the risk. As with all investments, such compensation occurs in the magnitude of the ex ante total returns, or yields, the lenders can realistically expect when they issue the loans. Thus, more broadly and fundamentally, underwriting has as its purpose to ensure that lenders are getting the expected return they want at the time they make the loan. The tighter the underwriting criteria are, the lower will be the probability of default and the lower will be the ex ante yield degradation, thereby raising expected returns toward the contractual yield rates.

Of course, lenders cannot operate outside the market. Suppose a lender tried to set underwriting guidelines so tight that the ex ante yield degradation would be eliminated altogether. This would make the mortgage like a default-free bond. If the lender then tried to charge an interest rate above the yield on default-free government bonds, then she would probably find it difficult to make the loan. Borrowers conforming to such tight underwriting criteria could shop around among competing lenders to get a lower interest rate.

---

[18]The GLCMPI also estimates periodic total returns on commercial mortgages both with and without adjustment for credit loss. The average per-annum adjusted return over the 1972–2004 period was about 90 basis points lower than the average unadjusted return. This number is greater than the 62 basis-point average credit loss because the denominator in the holding-period returns (HPRs) adjusts over time to reflect changes in the current market value of the mortgage. This value declines prior to loan default, as the current loan-to-value ratio typically rises and debt service coverage ratio typically falls, increasing the loan's default risk and thereby lowering its market value. In contrast, the denominator in the credit loss calculation remains at the par value of the loan (its contractual OLB). For this reason, in principle, the average credit loss over time probably provides a better indication of the magnitude of ex ante yield degradation.

In fact, most real estate borrowers cannot (or do not want to) conform to underwriting standards so tight as to eliminate default risk. As a result, mortgage lenders have to monitor the market constantly and modify their underwriting criteria accordingly, if they want to play the game (that is, issue commercial mortgages). Loan originations must satisfy both sides of the deals, and as with any market, prices (that is, ex ante yields) reflect an equilibrium in which, on the margin, both sides are just willing to do business. Thus, in principle, underwriting criteria ensure that the realistic expected return to the lender is high enough, but not too high, so that it includes just the ex ante risk premium required by the market.

The Two Foci of Underwriting—Borrowers and Properties When examining a mortgage loan application, a lender's attention is naturally focused on two subjects: the borrower and the proposed collateral property. In the commercial mortgage business (in contrast to the residential business), the more important of these two foci is normally the property. As noted, many commercial mortgages are nonrecourse, and even when recourse is technically available beyond the collateral property to the borrower, there is often little of value the lender can get. Furthermore, with a commercial mortgage (unlike a residential loan), the borrower will rely principally on the collateral property itself, being an income property, to provide the cash to service the loan. If the property is sufficiently lucrative in comparison with the loan requirements, then the loan will probably turn out all right even if the borrower is a bit weak.

Nevertheless, the borrower is still an important consideration even in commercial mortgages. On the downside, a borrower who gets into trouble on other businesses or properties other than the collateral property may use the collateral property as a "cash cow" to bail out his other losses, perhaps to the detriment of a loan on the healthy collateral property. Borrowers of commercial mortgages also can wreak havoc on secured lenders by filing for protection under Chapter 11 of the bankruptcy law. So lenders need to examine the nature of the borrowing entity and any parent or related firms and holding companies in order to ascertain the financial health of the relevant borrowing entity.

On the upside, borrowers on commercial mortgages (more so than residential borrowers) are often potential repeat customers. Commercial borrowers are often wealthy individuals, businesses, or institutions that are permanently in the real estate investment business in one way or another. If they are successful, they will be needing capital regularly for other projects and investments. It makes good business sense for lenders to cultivate such customers. Thus, the reputation and future business prospects of the borrower are important considerations for the lender. The mortgage lending business is very competitive in the United States, and a lender may relax underwriting criteria to some extent to cultivate or retain a borrower with good future potential.

18.2.1 Basic Property-Level Underwriting Criteria

Although information about the borrower is important, the primary attention when putting together the nuts and bolts of a specific deal typically focuses on several traditional criteria relating to the property that is to be the collateral in the loan. These criteria focus on two major aspects of the property: asset value and income flow. The value of the property relates naturally to the value of the loan, while the magnitude of the property's income flow is more directly relevant to the amount of periodic debt service that will be required by the loan.

Initial Loan-to-Value Ratio (ILTV) The **initial loan-to-value ratio** (ILTV) is the classical asset-value-based underwriting criterion. It is defined as the initial loan value (the contractual principal amount of the loan) divided by the current market value of the collateral property:

$$LTV = L/V$$

The ILTV ratio is an important underwriting criterion for obvious reasons. Commercial property market values display **volatility**, which means they can go down as well as up over time.

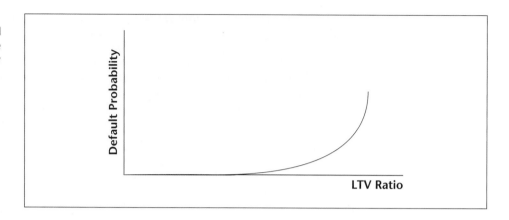

EXHIBIT 18-6 Typical Relationship between Initial LTV Ratio and the Ex Ante Lifetime Default Probability on a Commercial Property Mortgage
© OnCourse Learning

A lower initial LTV ratio will reduce the probability that at some point during the life of the loan the property will be worth less than the OLB. Although default will not necessarily occur as soon as the property is worth less than the loan balance, if the property value falls far enough below the OLB, default will certainly be rational (i.e., wealth maximizing) for the borrower. Thus, the initial LTV ratio is directly related to the ex ante default probability in the loan. Indeed, because the current market value of the property reflects the entire future income stream the property can generate, the ILTV is arguably the most fundamental and important single underwriting criteria, as it reflects both asset value considerations (directly) and income coverage considerations (indirectly) in a single summary measure.[19]

For typical levels of commercial property volatility, the relationship between default probability and the initial LTV ratio on a long-term commercial mortgage looks something like the curve shown in Exhibit 18-6. Note that this relationship is highly nonlinear.[20] Default probability is very low and nearly constant over a wide range of low values of the LTV ratio, but then increases sharply over higher LTV ratios.

The greater the volatility in the collateral property value is, the lower will be the initial LTV ratio corresponding to a given ex ante default probability. Typical commercial mortgage underwriting criteria in the United States have traditionally required the ILTV ratio to be equal to or below 75 percent. ILTV limits on property types that are viewed as more risky, such as raw land, will be set lower than this.[21] As noted in Chapter 15, an LTV ratio of 75 percent implies a much higher leverage ratio or debt/equity ratio than is typical in the stock market. Nevertheless, during periods of rapid price inflation and during real estate booms there is often strong pressure on lenders to relax this traditional limit. The traditional limit may also be exceeded if extra guarantees and credit enhancements are included in the loan, such as extra collateral, recourse provisions, cramdown insurance, and so forth.[22]

In estimating the market value of the property (V), lenders will generally require their own independent appraisal, and if the loan is to finance a property purchase, they may take

[19]On the other hand, the difficulty of estimating precisely the market value of the property may render the LTV a "fuzzier" measure than income-based measures, as current income can often be observed more reliably than property value. Recall in Chapter 12 we noted evidence of institutional property price dispersion around predicted values on the order of a 15% standard deviation (though valuation error for specific individual properties may be less than this).

[20]In fact, this curve would typically have a hyperbolic shape very much like how we described the relationship between the "leverage ratio" and the LTV back in Chapter 13: LR = 1/1−LTV.

[21]Although stated limits rarely exceed 75% or 80%, competitive pressures in the property and lending markets have likely on occasion pushed the effective (honestly stated) limit to well beyond 75%, with consequences in terms of subsequent default rates that were discussed in section 18.1. Credit rating agencies rating CMBS bonds have devised more conservative and rigorous LTV metrics that during the peak bubble year of 2007 sometimes approached or exceeded 100%, though it should be noted that these metrics are deliberately conservative.

[22]It should be noted that if property value tends to increase over time in nominal terms due to inflation, and the borrower does not add to the debt on the property, then the average LTV ratio over time will tend to be less than the initial ratio.

the property value to be whichever is lower between the appraisal and the agreed-on purchase price of the property. In practice, the loan terms may be effectively agreed on before an independent appraisal is conducted, and lenders may often rely for decision-making purposes on their own informal estimate of property value. In any case, at least two methods of estimating property value are often employed, direct capitalization and multiyear DCF valuation (as described in Chapter 10). In keeping with principles of conservative underwriting, lenders would use the lower of the two values indicated by these two approaches for underwriting purposes. In some cases lenders will set general guidelines governing their in-house valuation procedures, such as placing lower bounds on the capitalization rate and/or the discount rate that can be employed in the valuation.[23]

While the LTV ratio criterion is applied most stringently as of the time of loan issuance, it is also often forecasted over the life of the loan based on a projection of the property NOI and direct capitalization. Of particular concern, of course, is the projected LTV ratio at the time of loan maturity if the loan is not fully amortizing. The lender needs to be able to expect that the property value will well exceed the OLB on the loan at that time.

Debt Service Coverage Ratio (DCR) As the LTV ratio is the basic asset-value-based underwriting criterion, so the DCR is the classical income-based criterion. The **debt service coverage ratio (DCR)** is defined as the collateral property's annual net operating income (NOI) divided by the annual debt service required by the loan:

$$DCR = NOI/DS$$

The debt service (*DS*), of course, includes both the periodic interest payments and any amortization of principal called for in the loan terms. This ratio clearly makes sense as an underwriting criterion, for the NOI generated by the property is normally the primary source of cash to service the loan.

A typical standard for the DCR would require that this ratio must equal or exceed 120 percent. To reduce the risk of a cash flow squeeze, the lender wants some buffer, provided by the excess of the required DCR above 100 percent. The DCR criterion may be raised higher for types of property that appear more risky, or during times when lenders are more risk averse. On the other hand, lower DCR hurdles may be accepted during times of rapid inflation, or when the loan market is "hot." A projected temporary violation of the DCR hurdle for one or two years may be tolerated if there is a solid projection of sufficient debt service coverage during the other years of the loan life. Taken together, the LTV ratio and the DCR are the two most widely used underwriting criteria. However, other measures are also commonly examined.

Break-Even Ratio (BER) The **break-even ratio** (BER) is another widely employed income-based underwriting criterion that is usually not used instead of the DCR but as a supplemental requirement that must also be met. The BER is most simply defined as the sum of the annual debt service and property operating expenses divided by the potential gross income:

$$BER = (DS + OE)/PGI$$

The BER gives the occupancy ratio of the building (one minus the vacancy rate) below which there will be insufficient net operating income to cover the debt service. If the BER is greater than 100 percent, then the property investment will be a net cash flow drain on the borrower (even without considering any necessary capital improvement expenditures on the property). This would obviously be a dangerous situation from the lender's perspective, so underwriting

---

[23]For example, a lender may state that cap rates no lower than 9% must be employed in conducting a direct capitalization valuation. Of course, all such rigid criteria must bend to the market, as noted previously, assuming the lender really wants to be in the mortgage business. In other words, a stated standard of a 9% cap rate floor may look nice on paper, but if the cap rates currently prevailing in the property market are 8%, then the lender will not be able to issue many mortgages unless it either informally relaxes its cap rate floor or otherwise relaxes its LTV limit.

criteria will typically require the BER to be less than some fraction well below 100 percent. A typical BER limit might be on the order of 85 percent or less. Sometimes the maximum BER criterion is stated as the average occupancy rate prevailing (or expected to prevail) in the space market in which the property is situated, or that rate less some buffer.[24]

Equity-Before-Tax Cash Flow (EBTCF) As noted in Chapter 14, the **equity-before-tax cash flow (EBTCF)** is the cash flow bottom line for the equity investor on a before-tax basis, reflecting the need for capital improvement expenditures on the property. The EBTCF equals the NOI less debt service and capital improvement expenditures:

$$EBTCF = NOI - DS - CI$$

If this measure is projected to be negative for any year during the life of the loan, this raises an obvious underwriting red flag, as the borrower faces a potential negative cash flow in any such year. While the EBTCF measure is arguably more relevant in principle than the DCR, it is often relatively difficult for the lender to estimate and project future CI needs. Furthermore, CI expenditures tend to be somewhat discretionary in their amount and timing, and the property owner may be able to finance some types of CI expenditures by the use of additional debt. As a result, the DCR criterion is more widely employed in practice than the EBTCF measure, although both are often examined. The EBTCF measure is particularly relevant for certain types of property, such as properties in need of improvement and properties that employ long-term leases in which major tenant improvement expenditures (a component of CI) may be required of the landlord whenever a lease expires.[25]

Loan Yield After the 2008–2009 financial crisis many lenders and CMBS credit rating agencies began to consider another metric, known as the "**loan yield**" (or sometimes the "loan cap rate"), defined as the property's current NOI divided by the loan amount (or the remaining balance due on the loan, to update the measure as the loan amortizes). The rationale behind this metric is that it relates the loan amount to a property-pricing metric that would become relevant should the borrower default and the lender take over the property as "real estate owned" (REO). For example, suppose a property has a cap rate (NOI/Value) of 8 percent and a lender makes a 75 percent LTV loan on the property. The loan yield would be $8\% \frac{}{0.75} = 10.67\%$. This suggests that if the lender took over the property in foreclosure, then it could recoup the amount owed to it on the loan provided it could sell the property at a cap rate of 10.67 percent or lower. (Keep in mind that price is inversely related to cap rate.) This gives the lender an indication that if prevailing market cap rates rose from 8 percent to 10.67 percent the loan would still be recoverable (assuming the property's NOI held up, and ignoring costs of foreclosure and sales). The loan yield doesn't really provide any more information than the LTV, as it merely suggests that the property market could take a tumble in terms of its pricing per dollar of NOI equivalent to 25 percent (as 1/0.1067 is 75% of 1/0.08) and still cover the loan, which is exactly what is implied by the LTV of 75 percent. But people dealing with the property market often tend to think in terms of cap rates as the metric to track asset pricing, so it is an intuitive measure in that regard (even though it may

---

[24]A more complete and sophisticated formula for the BER would recognize that some expenses are essentially fixed no matter what is the occupancy in the property, while other expenses are variable. Defining "FC" as the fixed costs and "VC" as the variable costs (such that the total operating expenses can be expressed as the sum: $OE = FC + VC$), and assuming that VC is directly proportional to the occupancy in the building, then we have:

$$BER = (FC + DS)/(PGI - VC)$$

where VC is defined based on full occupancy (that is, VC*Occ is the actual variable cost component of the OE given an occupancy rate of Occ where Occ varies from 1.00 at full occupancy to zero at 100% vacancy). If the property is also subject to a ground lease (i.e., the property holding is actually a leasehold not a fee-simple ownership) and the ground lease requires regular annual payments, then add the amount "GL" to the numerator in the BER formula, where "GL" is the amount of the ground lease rental payment.

[25]In some cases, lenders attempt to define the NOI used in the DCR ratio to be net of recurring capital expenditures, such as leasing costs (commissions and TIs).

be a heroic assumption to presume that the property NOI would remain the same in such circumstances).

Multiyear Proforma Projection Although lenders typically scrutinize the ratio criteria described earlier (LTV, DCR, BER, and loan yield) most carefully for the initial year of the loan, they generally should require and examine a multiyear cash flow projection for the property and debt service, extending to the maturity of the loan. Borrowers usually supply such proforma projections, but lenders should take these with a grain of salt and attempt to double-check the assumptions. Lenders may examine any or all of the criteria noted previously for all the years in the proforma, not just the initial year.[26]

The above list summarizes the major commercial loan underwriting metrics, the use of which in traditional underwriting is meant to be conservative and is often how they are in fact employed. As noted, even during the relatively rare periods when there is strong market pressure to "bend the rules," that is, to make loans that are more risky than they should be (or than on paper they claim to be), the same metrics are still usually employed formally. During such times, the incentives for aggressive underwriting may be greater among originators who intend not to keep the mortgages but to "flip" them to a conduit pool in the secondary market. (It is widely believed that this occurred during the 2006–2007 bubble.) Securitization of mortgage pools sets up layers of structure between the ultimate investors in the bonds and the underlying individual borrowers in the loans (as will be described in Chapter 20), which makes it more difficult for originators who are not intending to keep "skin in the game" to resist pressures to be overly aggressive. But such market-wide systemic pressures can sometimes then reverse, after a crash, when lenders may become excessively conservative.

18.2.2 Variables and Loan Terms to Negotiate

Commercial mortgages present a potentially large array of possible loan terms and variables that can be negotiated. A partial list would include the following:

- Loan amount
- Loan term (maturity)
- Contract interest rate
- Amortization rate (in the extreme up to interest-only loans)
- Up-front fees and points
- Prepayment option and back-end penalties
- Recourse vs. nonrecourse debt
- Collateral (e.g., cross-collateralization)
- Lender participation in property equity

All such items can affect the risk and expected return in the loan. The number of these variables presents considerable flexibility and scope for creativity in the loan negotiation process. Typically, one or more of these items will matter more to one side of the deal than to the other side. As with any negotiation, much of the art of putting together a successful deal lies in finding a combination that maximizes both sides' preferences. This requires an understanding of the trade-offs—most fundamentally, how changing the loan terms and variables affects the ex ante risk and return on the loan from the perspective of both the borrower and lender. On the basis of previous discussions in this chapter and Chapters 16 and 17, you should have a good idea about the nature of this trade-off for some of the items listed. For example, we saw in Chapter 17 how reducing the amortization rate in the loan (i.e., longer amortization) can reduce the annual debt service (thereby increasing the DCR ratio) without changing the contract interest rate. Ultimately, the giving and taking in a successful negotiation results in ex ante risk and return expectations in the loan that conform to the market and to the desires of both sides of the deal.

---

[26]See Chapters 11 and 14 for more detailed descriptions and discussion of the proforma.

18.2.3 Numerical Example of the Normative Underwriting Process

It's our favorite real estate investor, Bob, once again. This time, Bob wants to buy an existing fully operational 100,000-SF single-tenant office building in Iowa, and he has come to your firm, Sioux City Capital (Sioux for short), requesting a $9,167,000 purchase-money mortgage. Bob's mortgage broker has put together a package indicating that Bob will be paying $12,222,000 for the property, so that the requested loan would have an ILTV of 75 percent. Bob wants a 10-year interest-only nonrecourse loan. He is willing to accept a lockout loan that does not permit prepayment. You must decide whether to grant this loan as requested, reject it out of hand, or try to negotiate a modified loan.

To begin to answer this question, you first look at the capital markets to see what sort of contractual interest rate you would have to charge for a typical loan of this nature. You note that 10-year U.S. Treasury bonds are currently yielding 6 percent. You also note that in the commercial mortgage market spreads on nonrecourse 10-year lockout loans with a 75 percent ILTV are currently running at 200 basis points CEY. From this information, you can compute that the mortgage would have to carry a 7.87 percent interest rate (MEY).[27]

Next, you consider the underwriting criteria Sioux is currently employing for loans of the type Bob wants. Given the fact that Sioux City Capital is actually a mortgage bank rather than a portfolio lender, Sioux will not be investing in Bob's mortgage on a long-term basis themselves. Rather, they will be placing into Bob's mortgage the capital of a large international life insurance company with whom Sioux has an ongoing relationship. It is this ultimate capital provider (who probably does intend to hold Bob's mortgage for the long term) whose underwriting criteria must be met. Unlike Sioux, this life insurance company does not know anything about Bob or the local real estate market, but they do know what sort of risk and return they are looking for in their commercial mortgage portfolio. Based on these considerations, they have specified the following underwriting criteria that Sioux will have to meet in any loans they issue:

1. Maximum ILTV $\leq$ 75%
2. Maximum projected terminal LTV $\leq$ 65%
3. In computing LTV: (a) apply direct capitalization with initial cap rate no less than 9%, terminal cap rate no less than 10%; (b) apply multiyear DCF valuation also for ILTV with discount rate no less than 10%; and (c) use the lower of the two ILTVs computed.
4. Minimum DCR $\geq$ 120%
5. Maximum BER $\leq$ 85% or average market occupancy less 5%, whichever is lower
6. Consider need for capital improvements and avoid negative EBTCF projections.

With these requirements in mind, you examine Bob's loan request in some detail, applying your own knowledge of the space market in which Bob's property is situated. Bob's mortgage broker has submitted a package of information with the loan application including the following information about the property:

1. 100,000-SF fully leased single-tenant office building
2. Good-credit tenant (not a publicly traded corporation) signed 10-year net lease three years ago.
3. The lease has current net rent of $11/SF per year (annual payments at ends of years), with step-up provisions to $11.50 in year 5 (two years from now) and $12.00 in year 8 (five years from now).

---

[27]Note that spreads are quoted on Treasury bonds of equivalent maturity to the mortgage loan (although see also discussion in Chapter 20 about use of LIBOR swaps in this role in the CMBS conduit loan market). Also, recall that mortgage and bond market yields must be equated on an effective annual rate (EAR) basis. Thus, the 200-basis-point spread implies that the mortgage must have a bond-equivalent yield of 8.00% (the 6.00% T-bond yield plus the 200-basis-point CEY spread). This equates to an EAR of 8.16%, which is therefore the loan interest rate that equates to the current capital market requirements. The monthly payments in the mortgage require a mortgage-equivalent yield of 7.87%, computed as $\{[(1+0.08/2)^2]^{(1/12)}-1\}\times 12 = 0.0787$. This is the rate we will use in the present illustration.

4. Current rents in the relevant space market are $12/SF for new 10-year leases (with no concessions), and are expected to grow at a rate of 3 percent per year (e.g., will be $12.36 one year from now, $16.13 in 10 years).

The broker has also submitted the cash flow proforma projection shown in Exhibit 18-7A. In this proforma, the broker has assumed a 75 percent probability of renewal for the tenant at the beginning of year 8, and has assumed that if the tenant does not renew there will be a three-month vacancy period. The broker has not included any provision for capital improvement expenditures and has assumed a 9 percent terminal cap rate to estimate the reversion value of the property at the end of year 10.

After examining this proforma and making some inquiries, you develop an alternative proforma projection for Bob's property that you feel is more realistic. You agree that the current market rent is $12/SF, but you decide to reduce the expected rent growth rate assumption from 3 percent to 1 percent per year for Bob's building. Even though rents for new buildings in the space market might grow at 3 percent, Bob's building will be aging and becoming more obsolete in that market, so you feel that 1 percent is a more realistic expectation. After some investigation, you decide that the tenant, though not a publicly traded corporation, is a stable company that presents good credit risk. You decide to accept the broker's assumptions about this tenant's renewal probability and the vacancy downtime in the event of non renewal, but you believe that some leasing expenses will be involved even if the tenant does renew. You decide to project year-8 leasing commission fees of $2/SF if the tenant renews and $5 if they do not renew. You also decide that it would be realistic to project tenant improvement expenditures of $10/SF if the existing tenant renews and $20/SF if a new tenant moves in. Finally, you decide that a 10 percent terminal cap rate would be a more realistic projection than the broker's 9 percent assumption considering that the building will be 10 years older by then.

Your modified proforma is shown in Exhibit 18-7B, including the implied underwriting income ratios, the DCR and BER, given the $9,167,000 interest-only loan that Bob wants, assuming the 7.87 percent interest rate currently required by the mortgage market.[28] It appears from Exhibit 18-7B that Bob's loan request will satisfy Sioux's income-based underwriting criteria. The initial DCR is 152 percent, well above the 120 percent minimum requirement, and the projected DCR is even higher in future years as the rent in the existing lease steps up and the space turns over at a higher projected market rent.[29] Your familiarity with the space market makes it clear that the initial BER of 60 percent is well below the average space market occupancy rate less 5 percent.[30]

Unfortunately, Bob's loan proposal as it stands has several problems. One is apparent in the cash flow projection. It appears that there could well be a sharply negative EBTCF in year 8, the year the existing lease expires. The EBTCF is projected to be negative by over $1 million in that year.[31] This problem can probably be dealt with, however. Single-tenant buildings, or properties in which a large proportion of the space is under leases that all expire near the same time, commonly face this type of occasional negative cash flow. Much of the problem is due to the need for capital improvement expenditures. The borrower may be able to finance some of this need. More to the point, there is ample positive EBTCF projected prior to the

---

[28] The monthly debt service on the interest-only loan is calculated as $(0.0787/12) \times \$9,167,000 = \$60,120$. Thus, the annual debt service is $12 \times \$60,120 = \$721,443$. (As with many numerical examples in this book, slight numerical discrepancies in equations are due to round-off.)

[29] The initial DCR of 152% is calculated as $1.1 million NOI for year 1 divided by the $721,443 debt service.

[30] The BER in Exhibit 18-7B has been calculated based on the projected market rent, rather than the property's rent based on the existing lease. This makes sense as the underwriting criterion compares the BER to the average occupancy rate in the market. Thus, the 60% BER for year 1 in the proforma is found as the $7.21443/SF debt service divided by the $12.12/SF projected market rent for that year.

[31] The projected cash flow in year 8 reflects the mean or expectation across the renewal scenarios. It is calculated as follows. The vacancy allowance per SF is $(1 - 75\%) \times (0.25 \times \$12.99) = \$0.81/SF$. This is the nonrenewal probability $(1 - 75\% = 25\%)$ times the conditional loss from vacancy that will occur if the tenant does not renew. This is expected to be three months of vacancy, or 25% of the income from a year that could otherwise earn the projected market rent of $12.99/SF. The expected lease commission is $(75\%)(\$2/SF) + (1 - 75\%) \times (\$5/SF) = \$2.75/SF$. The expected tenant improvement expenditure is $(75\%)(\$10/SF) + (1 - 75\%) \times (\$20/SF) = \$12.50/SF$.

Year	1	2	3	4	5	6	7	8	9	10	11
Market rent (net)/SF	$12.36	$12.73	$13.11	$13.51	$13.91	$14.33	$14.76	$15.20	$15.66	$16.13	$16.61
Property rent (net)	$11.00	$11.50	$11.50	$11.50	$12.00	$12.00	$12.00	$15.20	$15.20	$15.20	$15.20
Vacancy allowance	$0.00	$0.00	$0.00	$0.00	$0.00	$0.00	$0.00	$0.95	$0.00	$0.00	$0.00
NOI/SF	$11.00	$11.50	$11.50	$11.50	$12.00	$12.00	$12.00	$14.25	$15.20	$15.20	$15.20
NOI	$1,100,000	$1,150,000	$1,150,000	$1,150,000	$1,200,000	$1,200,000	$1,200,000	$1,425,116	$1,520,124	$1,520,124	$1,520,124
Reversion @ 9% cap										$16,890,268	

EXHIBIT 18-7A Broker's Submitted Proforma for Bob's Office Building

© OnCourse Learning

Year	1	2	3	4	5	6	7	8	9	10	11
Market rent (net)/SF	$12.12	$12.24	$12.36	$12.49	$12.61	$12.74	$12.87	$12.99	$13.12	$13.26	$13.39
Property rent (net)	$11.00	$11.50	$11.50	$11.50	$12.00	$12.00	$12.00	$12.99	$12.99	$12.99	$12.99
Vacancy allowance	$0.00	$0.00	$0.00	$0.00	$0.00	$0.00	$0.00	$0.81	$0.00	$0.00	$0.00
NOI/SF	$11.00	$11.50	$11.50	$11.50	$12.00	$12.00	$12.00	$12.18	$12.99	$12.99	$12.99
NOI	$1,100,000	$1,150,000	$1,150,000	$1,150,000	$1,200,000	$1,200,000	$1,200,000	$1,218,214	$1,299,428	$1,299,428	$1,299,428
Lease commission			$0	$0	$0	$0	$0	–$275,000	$0	$0	
Tenant improvements			$0	$0	$0	$0	$0	–1,250,000	$0	$0	
Reversion @ 10% cap										$12,994,280	
Less OLB										$9,167,000	
PBTCF	$1,100,000	$1,150,000	$1,150,000	$1,150,000	$1,200,000	$1,200,000	$1,200,000	–$306,786	$1,299,428	$14,293,709	
Debt service	–$721,443	–$721,443	–$721,443	–$721,443	–$721,443	–$721,443	–$721,443	–$721,443	–$721,443	–$9,888,443	
EBTCF	$378,557	$428,557	$428,557	$428,557	$428,557	$478,557	$478,557	–$1,028,229	$577,985	$4,405,266	
DCR	152%	159%	159%	159%	166%	166%	166%	169%	180%	180%	
BER @ market	60%	59%	58%	58%	57%	57%	56%	56%	55%	54%	

EXHIBIT 18-7B Sioux's Modified Proforma for Bob's Office Building and Loan Application

© OnCourse Learning

projected negative year, and the negative year is in the rather distant future by which time property appreciation should have reduced the danger of default. If necessary, some sort of sinking fund covenant might be included in Bob's mortgage to ensure that sufficient cash will be available to cover the projected shortfall in year 8.

A more serious problem in Bob's application is not apparent from the income analysis alone, but appears in the valuation analysis. If one applies a 9 percent going-in cap rate to the initial year's NOI of $1.1 million, the implied property value is $12,222,000, the same price Bob is apparently planning to pay for the property, and just sufficient to allow the proposed $9,167,000 loan to meet the 75 percent ILTV criterion. However, after investigating the relevant property market, you decide that realistic expected returns (going-in IRRs) for this type of property are well approximated by the 10 percent discount rate in your underwriting criteria. In any case, you do not see how you can apply a discount rate less than that in performing a DCF valuation of the property. At a discount rate of 10 percent, the 10-year projected property level cash flows (PBTCF) shown in Exhibit 18-7B (including the projected reversion) give a present value of only $11,557,000, which implies a 79 percent ILTV.[32] This violates the ILTV underwriting criterion.

As Bob's loan proposal does not fail your underwriting criteria by very much, you decide not to reject it out of hand, but rather to make a counterproposal. To meet the 75 percent ILTV limit in your underwriting criteria, you could offer Bob a slightly smaller loan of $8.7 million. However, without amortization, such a loan would still not meet the **terminal LTV (TLTV)** criterion of 65 percent. Dividing $8.7 million into the projected 10-year reversion value of $12,994,000 results in a projected TLTV of 67 percent. However, the smaller loan could have some amortization and still produce an annual debt service payment similar to what Bob was originally asking for with his larger interest-only loan. For example, if the loan amortized at a 40-year rate, then the balloon payment after 10 years on an $8.7 million loan would be $8,230,047, which implies a TLTV ratio of only 63 percent, less than the 65 percent limit. The annual debt service on such a loan would be $715,740 (with monthly payments), slightly less than the $721,443 Bob was originally proposing.

This shows how trade-offs among the loan terms can be manipulated to meet underwriting criteria. Bob might accept a counterproposal of a smaller $8.7 million loan with a 40-year amortization rate. If Sioux's underwriting criteria are competitive, and if your estimate is correct that the property market would not likely accept a realistic going-in IRR of less than 10 percent on a property like Bob's office building, then it should be difficult for Bob to find another lender that will lend any more than $8.7 million on the property.[33]

18.3 Chapter Summary

This chapter introduced you to the basics of commercial mortgages, largely from the lender's perspective. You should now have a feeling for how to analyze the default risk in such loans and how underwriting is carried out in the commercial mortgage origination industry. In the next chapter we will step back a bit to consider the broader economics of commercial mortgages from the perspective of the ultimate investors in such loans.

KEY TERMS

contract (stated) yield	credit losses	loss severity
expected return (ex ante yield)	yield degradation	conditional yield degradation
coupon (coupon rate)	recovery rate	hazard probability/function

---

[32]$9,167,000/$11,557,000 = 79.3%.

[33]Admittedly, these are two rather large ifs. The difficulty of being able to observe or estimate property market values precisely, combined with lenders' desire to be competitive in the mortgage lending business, probably goes some way in explaining why the default rate is as high as it is, and why it has been so much higher on loans issued during boom times.

conditional survival probability
cumulative survival probability
unconditional default probability
cumulative (lifetime) default
   probability

ex ante (unconditional) yield
   degradation
ex post yield degradation
underwriting
initial loan-to-value ratio (ILTV)
volatility

debt service coverage ratio (DCR)
break-even ratio (BER)
equity-before-tax cash flow (EBTCF)
loan yield
terminal LTV (TLTV)

STUDY QUESTIONS

Conceptual Questions

18.1. What is the difference between the contract (or stated) yield and the realistic expected return (ex ante yield) on a mortgage? Why is this difference important?

18.2. Ignoring multiple periods of time, what is the general relationship among the expected return, the contract yield (or YTM), the unconditional default probability, and the conditional yield degradation?

***18.3.** What is the hazard function for a mortgage? What is the relationship between the hazard function, the unconditional default probability, and the cumulative default probability?

18.4. What is the major purpose of underwriting in the commercial mortgage industry? What is the relationship between underwriting and the market for commercial mortgage assets?

18.5. What are the two major foci of the lender's attention in commercial mortgage underwriting? Which one of these is usually more important, and why?

18.6. What is the difference between value-based and income-based underwriting criteria? In what way could you consider that the value-based criteria are more fundamental or important?

18.7. What is the relationship of the initial loan-to-value ratio (ILTV) to the default risk in the loan? How is this relationship affected by the volatility in the underlying property?

18.8. Why do lenders need to consider multiyear cash flow projections rather than just the initial income of the property?

18.9. What potential problem would the projected equity-before-tax cash flow (EBTCF) reveal that the DCR or BER would not reveal?

Quantitative Problems

18.10. In a one-period world, if the conditional yield degradation is 10%, the unconditional default probability is 15%, and the lender wants an expected return of 8%, what contract yield must the loan carry?

18.11. Consider a three-year mortgage with annual payments in arrears. Suppose the probability of default is 1% in the first year and 5% each year thereafter given that default has not occurred previously.
   a. What is the hazard function of this loan?
   b. What is the unconditional default probability in year 2?
   c. What is the cumulative (or lifetime) default probability in this loan as of the time of its origination?

18.12. Suppose the loan in Question 18.14 is an 8% interest-only loan. If the conditional recovery rate is 75% in each year, what is the expected return on the loan?

18.13. Suppose 10-year Treasury bond yields in the bond market are 7.00% CEY (or BEY), and the mortgage market requires a contract yield risk premium of 175 basis points (CEY). If a property has a net operating income (NOI) of $400,000, and the underwriting criteria require a debt coverage ratio (DCR) of at least 125%, then what is the maximum loan that can be offered assuming a 30-year amortization rate and monthly payments on the mortgage?

18.14. Using the discounted cash flow (DCF) valuation method, what is the maximum loan that can be made on a property with the following annual net before-tax cash flow, assuming an 11.5% discount rate and underwriting criteria that specify a maximum loan/value ratio of 70%? Cash flows: $1 million in year 1, 1.1 million in years 2 through 4, 1.5 million in years 5 through 9, and $12 million in year 10 including reversion.

18.15. A property has an expected first-year NOI of $1 million. Recent sales of similar properties indicate that a first-year (or going-in) cap rate of 9.75% is reasonable for valuation purposes. A lender requires a minimum DCR (or DSCR) of 1.25 *and* will loan up to 70% of appraised value on a first mortgage. If the mortgage interest rate is 6.75%, payments are monthly, and the amortization period is 20 years, what is the maximum-sized loan the lender will advance?

*18.16. The boxed feature "Is It Surprising that So Many Commercial Mortgages Default?" presents a simplified way to compute a rough estimate of the likelihood of mortgage default as a function of property value volatility and the LTV ratio of the loan when it is issued. There it was argued that a 75% LTV ratio lending criterion would lead approximately to a one-sixth lifetime default probability. Use this same simplified approach, and the fact that about 5% of the normal probability distribution lies beyond two standard deviations from its mean, to estimate what LTV ratio lending criterion would be necessary to reduce the default probability to 1/40 (or 2.5%).

19

COMMERCIAL MORTGAGE ECONOMICS AND INVESTMENT

CHAPTER OUTLINE

LEARNING OBJECTIVES

After reading this chapter, you should understand:

⮑ The importance of the most basic concepts in bond investments and fixed-income portfolio management, such as duration, interest rate risk, and the yield curve.

⮑ The economics underlying commercial mortgage yields, that is, what drives investors' required expected returns on mortgages.

⮑ The nature of recent historical ex post total return (HPR) performance of U.S. commercial mortgages.

The previous chapter covered the nuts and bolts of commercial mortgage lending, focusing on loan origination, the primary market. Underlying this market, however, are the ultimate investors in commercial mortgages, including institutions that hold such loans in their portfolios and investors who deal in the secondary market for loans. In the secondary market commercial mortgages are often securitized in ways that are appealing to different types of investors. Indeed, commercial mortgages are part of the "debt market" broadly defined, which includes all types of bonds. In this chapter, we will consider the underlying economics of commercial mortgages within the context of the bond market and the overall capital market, including the investment performance of commercial mortgages and the roles such assets can play for different types of investors. We begin with a brief description of some fundamental considerations in the bond market, including duration, interest rate risk, the yield curve, and maturity matching. The second section relates these basic considerations to equilibrium expected returns in the commercial mortgage market and reviews ex post mortgage investment performance.

19.1 Some Basic Characteristics of Bonds

Broadly speaking, commercial mortgages are part of the bond market, the market for finite-lived assets with contractually fixed cash flows, also known as the debt market. To deepen your understanding of commercial mortgages from an investment perspective, you need to be familiar with a few basic characteristics of the bond market, characteristics that relate to all types of debt products, including commercial mortgages. In this section, we will discuss the concepts of duration, interest rate risk, the yield curve, and maturity matching.

19.1.1 Duration and Maturity

Recall that one of the defining characteristics of debt investments is the fact that their contractually fixed cash flows typically give the investor an explicit, finite **maturity** for their investment. For example, a 10-year mortgage will provide income and value for 10 years, and then it will expire.[1] This is a very useful attribute for certain investment purposes, such as covering or servicing a finite-lived obligation the investor may have, as in the case of a pension plan, for example. But maturity is also related to the sensitivity of the value of the debt to changes in market interest rates. You have no doubt noted previously that the present value of a more distant future cash flow is more sensitive to the discount rate than is the present value of a more proximate cash flow. Thus, the volatility of bond values, and the magnitude of interest rate risk for bond investors, is directly related to the maturity of the bond investment.

As an example, consider two zero-coupon 6 percent bonds currently worth $100 each.[2] Both the coupon rate (that is, the contract interest rate) and the current market yield are 6 percent, for both bonds, so they are selling at par value. Bond A has a maturity of five years, promising a single future cash flow of $133.82 in five years [$133.82 = $100(1.06)^5$]. Bond B has a maturity of 10 years, so its single future cash flow is $179.08 in 10 years [equal to $100(1.06)^{10}$]. Now suppose the relevant market yield suddenly changes to 7 percent. Thus, 7 percent becomes the opportunity cost of capital (OCC) at which the bonds' future cash flow must be discounted. However, the future cash flow amount is contractually fixed (as these are fixed rate loans). The present value of bond A therefore falls from $100 to $95.41 = $133.82/1.07^5$. But the PV of bond B falls farther, from $100 to $91.04 = $179.08/1.07^{10}$. The one-point increase in market yield (from 6 percent to 7 percent) caused the five-year bond to lose less than 5 percent of its value while the 10-year bond lost almost 9 percent.

Because the sensitivity of bond values to changes in market interest rates is very important for investors, we need to be able to measure it accurately. While the maturity of the bond gives some idea of this sensitivity, a more accurate measure is the **duration** of the bond. The duration is defined as the weighted average time (in years) until the bond's future cash flows will be received. The weighting is proportional to the component of each future cash flow in the present value of the bond. For zero-coupon bonds, the duration and maturity are the same because they have only one future cash flow (which therefore occurs at the maturity date). But for bonds that pay periodic interest, the duration, though generally a positive function of maturity, can differ significantly from the bond's maturity, especially for longer-term loans.

For example, suppose bond A and bond B, our five-year and 10-year loans from the previous example, were interest-only mortgages with annual payments, instead of zero-coupon bonds. Exhibit 19-1 demonstrates how we would compute the duration of each of these bonds and reveals that the five-year bond has a duration of 4.47 years, while the 10-year bond has a duration of 7.80 years.

The basic procedure for computing the duration of a mortgage with monthly payments is given in the following formula:

$$Duration = \sum_{j=1}^{N} t_j \left(\frac{CF_j/(1 + YTM)^{t_j}}{\sum_{i=1}^{N} CF_i/(1 + YTM)^{(t_i)}} \right) \Bigg/ 12 \qquad (1)$$

Here, t_j is the number of months until the jth cash flow is received, CF_j is the amount of the jth cash flow (including any balloon in the final payment), N is the total number of payments to

---

[1]Of course, if the debt instrument gives the borrower a prepayment option (callable debt), then the maturity is not precisely specified in the debt contract. However, many commercial mortgages do not permit prepayment (or charge high prepayment penalties).

[2]A "zero-coupon" bond does not pay out interest, but rather accrues interest over time, so that the only cash flow occurs at the maturity of the bond, and this cash flow includes the accumulated compounded interest accrued at the contract interest rate (which is still referred to as a coupon rate, even though the bond actually has no coupons per se). The interest accrual procedure is described in the four rules of loan payment and balance computation discussed in Chapter 17.

	Bond A (5-yr. maturity, 4.47-yr. duration)				Bond B (10-yr. maturity, 7.80-yr. duration)		
Year = t_j	CF_j	$PV(CF_j) =$ $CF_j/(1.06)^{\wedge}(t_j)$	$w = PV(CF_j)/$ $PV(Bond)$	$w \times t$	CF	$PV(CF_j) =$ $CF_j/(1.06)^{\wedge}(t_j)$	$w = PV(CF_j)/$ $PV(Bond)$	$w \times t$
1	$6.00	$5.66	0.0566	0.0566	$6.00	$5.66	0.0566	0.0566
2	$6.00	$5.34	0.0534	0.1068	$6.00	$5.34	0.0534	0.1068
3	$6.00	$5.04	0.0504	0.1511	$6.00	$5.04	0.0504	0.1511
4	$6.00	$4.75	0.0475	0.1901	$6.00	$4.75	0.0475	0.1901
5	$106.00	$79.21	0.7921	3.9605	$6.00	$4.48	0.0448	0.2242
6					$6.00	$4.23	0.0423	0.2538
7					$6.00	$3.99	0.0399	0.2793
8					$6.00	$3.76	0.0376	0.3012
9					$6.00	$3.55	0.0355	0.3196
10					$106.00	$59.19	0.5919	5.9190
Sum		$100.00	1.000	4.4651		$100.00	1.000	7.8017

EXHIBIT 19-1 Computation of Duration at Par Value for Two Interest-Only, 6% Coupon, Annual-Payment Mortgages

© OnCourse Learning

maturity, and *YTM* is the current market yield on the loan. The monthly weighted average time until cash flow receipt must be divided by 12 to put the duration in annual terms. Note that the summation in the denominator is just the current market value of the mortgage. If the current market yield equals the contract interest rate on the loan, then this market value will equal the current contractual OLB (or par value) of the mortgage.

It should be noted that the measure of duration computed in formula (1) is what is called **Macaulay duration**, named after Frederick Macaulay, who first coined the term in 1938. It is the most intuitive definition of the duration concept. However, a slightly different measure, often referred to as **modified duration**, is more commonly used in practice because it more closely approximates the relative sensitivity of bond values to changes in interest rates. Modified duration equals the Macaulay measure divided by $(1 + YTM)$.[3]

Exhibit 19-2 graphs the modified duration of a monthly-payment, 8 percent interest, 30-year amortizing mortgage, as a function of the maturity of the loan (that is, the year of its balloon payment or year of prepayment at par value). The solid curve in Exhibit 19-2 is typical of the relationship between maturity and duration for mortgages. The straight dashed line indicates the duration of a zero-coupon bond (which is the same as the maturity). Note that for short-term loans, maturity and duration are similar, but the mortgage duration tapers off for loans longer than about five years' maturity and is less than nine years even for a 30-year maturity mortgage. In general, duration is a function of the loan's maturity, its coupon rate (contractual interest rate), amortization rate, and the current relevant market yield. Greater maturity means greater duration, with the duration always being less than or at most equal to the maturity (in the case of zero-coupon loans). A greater coupon rate implies a lower duration as the annual cash flow is greater. Similarly, a greater amortization rate implies lower duration. Higher current market yield (prevailing interest rates) will reduce duration, as higher discount rates reduce the present value of near-term cash flows less than farther out cash flows.

The modified duration measure approximates the percentage change in the loan's value caused by a one-point change in the market yield. Thus, if we multiply the change

---

[3]Note that if the mortgage payments are monthly, then the YTM to use here is the monthly rate, applied to duration calculated in months. This will give the modified duration in months. Then divide by 12 to get the duration back to the annual terms in which it is normally quoted.

EXHIBIT 19-2 Duration
as a Function of Maturity
(30-year amortizing, 8%
monthly-payment, at par)
© OnCourse Learning

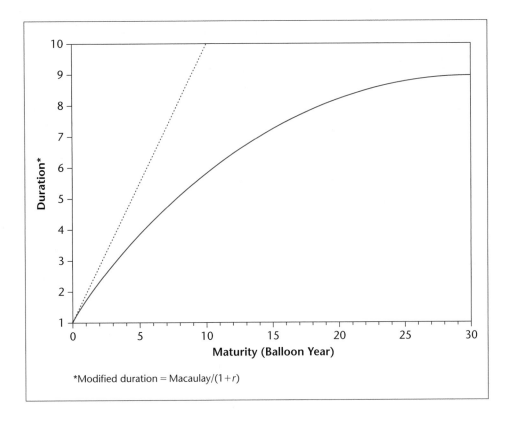

*Modified duration = Macaulay/(1+r)

in market yield by the duration, we get the approximate percentage change in loan value, as represented here:

$$\frac{\Delta D}{D} = -(Duration)(\Delta YTM) \tag{2}$$

where ΔD represents the change in current market value of the debt, and ΔYTM is the change in the relevant market yield. The sign is negative because bond values are inversely related to yields.

For example, consider our 6 percent, 10-year bond B in Exhibit 19-1. We computed its Macaulay duration to be 7.8 years at a 6 percent market yield. Its modified duration would thus be 7.36 years (7.8/1.06). Now suppose the relevant market yield moves up to 6.5 percent. Formula (2) would predict a loss of 3.68 percent in the value of bond B as $-(7.36) \times (0.5\%) = -3.68\%$. The exact new value of bond B is $96.41, found by applying the 6.5 percent yield in a full DCF valuation.[4] This is a loss of 3.59 percent, slightly less than what is indicated by formula (2). This is because the modified duration measure precisely indicates the percentage change in bond value only for infinitesimal changes in market yields. The approximation is less exact the greater is the change in the yield. Nevertheless, modified duration gives a useful picture of the sensitivity of bond value to market interest rates.[5]

---

[4]
$$\$96.41 = \sum_{j=1}^{10} \frac{\$6}{(1.065)^j} + \frac{\$100}{(1.065)^{10}}$$

[5]Debt values are nonlinear, declining functions of the relevant market yield. For noncallable debt, the curvature of this value function is convex; that is, it bends up away from the axes in a Cartesian graph. Because of this "convexity," bond values actually lose a bit less value when yields rise, and they gain a bit more value when yields fall, as compared to what is indicated by the modified duration measure in formula (2).

19.1.2 Interest Rate Risk and Preferred Habitat

Bonds typically have contractually fixed cash flows with seniority over equity claims on the underlying income-generating assets, and therefore are generally perceived as low-risk investments. Even so, bond investors are exposed to several types of risk. We already introduced the concept of default risk (or "credit risk") in previous chapters. But another type of risk exists to which even default-free government bonds are subject.[6] This is **interest rate risk**. Interest rate risk refers to the effect on the bond investor of changes in the interest rates that prevail in the debt market, known as **market yields**. Both short- and long-term interest rates change over time in ways that are difficult to predict. This is illustrated in Exhibit 19-3, which shows the history of yields on U.S. government bonds from 1926 to 2010. To better understand interest rate risk, let's consider how changes in interest rates can cause problems for two different types of bond investors.

Bob is our first investor (of course). He likes to trade bonds actively, buying and selling them frequently without waiting for them to mature. He does not have any particular future

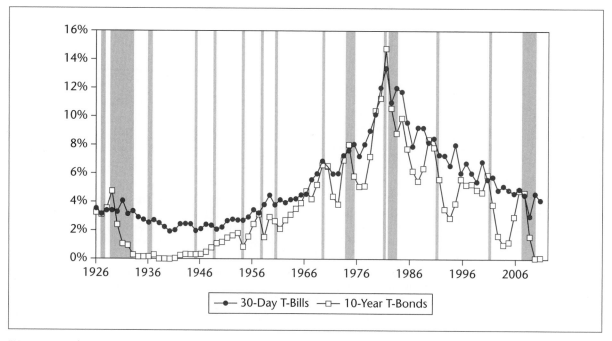

EXHIBIT 19-3 Short-term and Long-term U.S. Government Bond Yields, 1926–2010
Gray shaded vertical bands indicate periods of macro-economic recession (NBER designations).
Source: Based on data from Ibbostson Associates.

---

[6]In general economists regard U.S. government bonds as essentially free of default risk. This is not necessarily or generally true of all government debt, however. For example, government debt denominated in a foreign currency not controlled by the government issuing the debt is clearly and rather famously subject to default. Similarly, bonds issued by state and local governments within the United States are potentially subject to default. In recent years, there has even been some reason to doubt the security of U.S. Treasury debt, even though in principle the federal government could always "print money" (e.g., via actions taken by the Federal Reserve Bank) to cover its debts. But the government must obey the laws set by Congress, and Congress can set up legally binding debt ceilings and budget constraints that could conceivably require a default on Treasury bonds, in the event of severe political dysfunctionality in Washington. For example, the Congress could pass a budget that requires deficit spending, yet Congress could fail to raise the legal debt ceiling, thereby preventing the issuance of new debt necessary repay the maturing debt. The threat of just such an event during the summer of 2011 led one major bond credit rating agency to slightly downgrade the credit rating of U.S. Treasury debt. However, this downgrade was not accompanied by any uptick in Treasury bond yields in the marketplace, suggesting that the global bond market continued to perceive U.S. government debt as being very safe (or at least, safer than any other major liquid debt market).

horizon or target point in time when he needs to cash out of his bond investments. In his manner of investing, Bob is exposed to the volatility of bond market values caused by changes in interest rates. This is the type of volatility we have been dealing with in the previous section, in our discussion of duration. There we noted that longer-duration bonds have greater sensitivity to a given interest rate change. Thus, longer-duration bonds will tend to have more of the type of volatility that Bob must deal with.

We may call this investment strategy "bond trading." As Bob is risk-averse, he dislikes volatility (at least to the extent that the bond volatility reflects investment value comovements with the value of the rest of Bob's wealth portfolio[7]). Thus, Bob requires a higher expected return in order to induce him to invest in higher-volatility (longer-duration) bonds.

Now consider Sue. She has a specific target date at which she needs a specific amount of cash. In particular, Sue knows that she will need $1 million in five years, and she wants to set aside sufficient capital now to provide for that obligation. Sue faces several possible strategies to accomplish this objective.

The most obvious strategy for Sue would be to buy a zero-coupon bond maturing in five years. Suppose the market interest rate on such bonds is 6 percent (compounded annually). Then such a bond will sell for $1,000,000/1.06^5 = $747,258 today. Sue could invest this amount today and guarantee that she will have exactly the amount she needs in five years. She will face no risk (assuming the bond has no possibility of default). The fact that market interest rates may change between now and her five-year horizon is of no concern to her because she will certainly hold her bond to maturity, when it is contractually obligated to pay $1 million. This investment strategy is called **cash flow matching**. The investor's fixed future cash outflow obligations are exactly matched by future inflows that are contractually fixed.

But Sue faces at least two other alternatives. One would be to buy short-term bonds and plan to reinvest them when they mature. For example, suppose one-year bonds are yielding 6 percent. If she puts $747,258 into one-year bonds, she will have $792,093 (1.06 × 747,258) in one year. She could then reinvest that amount in a second one-year bond, and so forth, "rolling over" the short-term bonds for five years. With this **roll-over strategy**, however, Sue is exposed to interest rate risk. A year from now, one-year bonds may no longer be yielding 6 percent. Yields on such bonds may be either higher or lower than 6 percent. If they are lower, then Sue will have to reinvest at a lower yield. This may cause her to fail to meet her $1 million target in five years. For example, suppose interest rates fall to 5 percent in one year and remain there for the next four years for all maturities of bonds. Then the $792,093 that Sue got from her first-year investment would grow to only $962,794 by the end of the fifth year (792,093 × 1.05^4). She would fall short of her target by almost 4 percent.

A second alternative Sue could consider would be to invest in a bond whose maturity is longer than her target horizon, for example, a 10-year bond, and plan to sell this bond in five years, prior to its maturity. For example, if 10-year zero-coupon bonds are currently yielding 6 percent, then Sue could put $747,258 into such a bond, which promises a single contractual cash flow of $1,338,226 in 10 years. In five years, if yields on five-year zero-coupon bonds are 6 percent at that time, then this bond will have a market value of $1 million (1,338,226/1.06^5), which Sue could cash out by selling the bond. But this strategy also subjects Sue to interest rate risk. Suppose in five years market yields on five-year zero-coupon bonds are higher than 6 percent. Then the market value of Sue's bond at that time would be less than $1 million. For example, if interest rates are 7 percent, then her bond will only be worth $954,136 (1,338,226/1.07^5), a shortfall of more than 4 percent.

Which strategy should Sue employ? If market interest rates are the same on all maturities of bonds, then the answer is obvious. The cash flow matching strategy, buying a five-year zero-coupon bond, is clearly the best strategy because it eliminates the interest rate risk. We would say that a duration of five years is Sue's **preferred habitat** for her bond investments. That is the duration that matches the duration of Sue's liabilities, so it is the duration that she prefers for her bond investments, *other things being equal.*

---

[7]Portfolio considerations will be presented in depth in Chapters 21 and 22.

On the other hand, if interest rates on longer-duration bonds were sufficiently higher, then Sue could probably be induced to invest in bonds of longer duration than her preferred habitat. For example, suppose 10-year zero-coupon bonds were offering 7 percent interest, while five-year zeros were only offering 6 percent interest. Sue could either invest $747,258 in five-year bonds and meet her target risklessly or she could invest a smaller amount in 10-year bonds and expect to meet her target, albeit with some risk.[8] Similarly, if interest rates on short-term bonds were sufficiently higher than those on five-year bonds, then Sue could probably be induced to employ the roll-over strategy of investing in bonds of shorter maturity than her target.

19.1.3 The Yield Curve

You should now be in a position to understand a fundamental phenomenon of the bond market, the **yield curve**. This refers to the difference in the market yields of otherwise identical bonds of different maturities (or, more precisely, different durations). We mentioned the yield curve in previous chapters.[9] Now you can apply your understanding of interest rate risk to deepen your understanding of this important phenomenon. Essentially, the yield curve that is observed between short- and long-term Treasury bonds is due largely to two considerations: expectations regarding future short-term nominal interest rates and concerns about interest rate risk, as described in the preceding section.

Consider first the role of expectations about future short-term rates. If investors expect that rates on short-term bonds will be higher in the future than they are now, then they will naturally demand higher yields on long-term bonds than on short-term bonds. Otherwise, they could employ a roll-over strategy, investing only in short-term bonds, and expect to be better off at the end. There would be no investment demand for long-term bonds unless such bonds offered a higher yield than current short-term bonds. Similarly, if investors expect that rates on short-term bonds will be lower in the future than they are now, then borrowers will be able to extract lower interest rates on long-term loans than they could on current short-term loans. Otherwise, borrowers could expect to be better off by borrowing short term and planning to refinance when rates fall. There would be no borrowers willing to take capital from investors trying to issue long-term bonds. Investors would be willing to lend long term at lower rates because they would expect that otherwise they would probably have to roll over their investments at lower yields in the future. Such expectations can account for differences in yields between short- and long-term debt instruments. This is known as the **expectations hypothesis** for explaining the yield curve.

In recent history, a prime driver of differential expectations about short-term interest rates has often been inflation. Short-term interest rates will normally at least equal the current level of inflation prevailing at the time, as short-term lenders want to at least preserve the purchasing power of their capital.[10] But short-term *real* interest rates (net of inflation) are usually pretty low. Thus, when inflation is abnormally high, investors in the United States generally expect inflation to be lower in the long run, so short-term interest rates are

---

[8]For example, suppose Sue expects that in five years the market yield on five-year zeros will be 6 percent, the same as it is today. Then a 10-year zero that she bought today would have five years left on it, so she would require such a bond with a par value (at maturity) of $1,000,000 (1.06^5) = $1,338,226. A 10-year zero with such a par value would sell today at a 7 percent yield for $680,286 $(1,338,226/1.07^{10})$. Under these expectations, Sue faces a choice between investing $747,258 and meeting her five-year $1 million target for sure, or reducing her current investment by $66,972 (almost 9 percent), but then facing some possibly sleepless nights as she could not be sure she will exactly meet her target. (Of course, on the upside she might exceed her target if she has a longer-term bond and interest rates fall.)

[9]Most notably, in Chapter 11 (when we discussed the ex ante risk premium in the real estate OCC); in Chapter 13 (when we discussed the relationship of real estate and debt returns regarding the existence of positive leverage); and in Chapter 17 (when we discussed the rationale for adjustable rate mortgages and the forecasting of their YTMs).

[10]While this is normal, it is not always the case. If there is little demand from borrowers for short-term capital, and a lot of investors with money wanting a safe place to park it, the demand for "safe harbors" can cause real interest rates (net of current inflation) to actually be negative, as investors bid up the price of such safe and liquid short-term assets. This role has traditionally been played by U.S. Treasury bills, as we will discuss further shortly.

expected to fall. This is particularly true if the Federal Reserve Board (FRB or "Fed") can be counted on to adopt tight monetary policy to control inflation. Such policy drives up current short-term interest rates. On the other hand, when inflation is abnormally low, investors may expect that it will rise in the future, leading to higher future short-term interest rates. Also, when the economy is in a recession, the Federal Reserve tends to try to stimulate the economy by driving down current short-term interest rates (which may be low anyway due to lack of demand for capital). The FRB has considerable ability to influence current short-term interest rates but much less control over long-term rates.[11] If investors believe that the Fed is weak at controlling inflation, then long-term rates may rise due to fear of future inflation.

Expectations about future short-term interest rates are not the only influence on the yield curve. As noted, interest rate risk also plays a role. This role is more prominent when inflation is low and stable. Clearly, investors who actively trade bonds by selling them prior to maturity are subject to volatility that, for a given change in interest rates, is greater for longer-duration bonds. Risk aversion would generally lead such investors to require higher ex ante yields in long-term than in short-term bonds.

Related to interest rate risk, the preferred habitat of bond investors can drive the yield curve to assume various shapes. If more bond investors have short-term preferred habitats (because they have short-term obligations or prefer greater liquidity), then long-term bond yields will have to be higher than short-term bond yields in order to induce such investors to be indifferent between short- and long-term bonds. (Recall in our previous example that yields on 10-year bonds would have to be higher than yields on five-year bonds to get Sue, with her five-year horizon, to invest in 10-year rather than five-year bonds.) The borrowing side of the debt market may also complement this demand, if more borrowers tend to prefer longer-term debt, which puts them under less short-term refinancing pressure and thereby preserves *their* liquidity. In effect, other things being equal, borrowers have more liquidity if their debt is long term, while lenders have more liquidity if their debt investments are short term.[12] If the preferred habitat of borrowers is long term, and the preferred habitat of lenders is short term, then borrowers will be willing to pay the higher long-term interest rates that lenders require to get them to lend their capital long term.

This interest rate risk and habitat-based explanation for the yield curve is known as the **liquidity preference theory**. It seeks to explain why the yield curve typically is upward-sloping (i.e., long-term yields are typically greater than short-term yields).

Preferred habitat, liquidity preference, and interest rate expectations all interact to produce the yield curve observed in the debt markets. The yield curve constantly changes and is reported graphically in financial newspapers such as *The Wall Street Journal* and online.[13] Exhibit 19-4 depicts the yield curve during four rather different periods: the spring of 1993, the spring of 1995, the fall of 1998, and December 2011.

The curve for 1993 would be described as steeply rising, with long-term rates over 300 basis points higher than short-term rates. During that period, the economy was still viewed as

---

[11]FRB intervention to control long-term rates is rare, and can be less effective. But one thing the Fed can do is called "quantitative easing" (aka "QE"), in which the Federal Reserve Bank directly purchases long-term debt issued by the U.S. Treasury. In quantitative easing, the Fed is effectively "printing money" (not literally, but the effect is to increase the money supply). This can bring down long-term interest rates in the short term due to the direct effect on the demand for long-term Treasury debt. But it risks inflation in the longer term, and the fear of such inflation in the bond markets can undermine the direct effect, and may actually lead to higher rates in the future. Quantitative easing is therefore a tricky and delicate balancing act for the Fed to try to accomplish, though it probably successfully provided vitally needed liquidity during the financial crisis of 2008–2009, and at that time possibly helped to prevent the economy from slipping into a devastating deflationary spiral when there was genuine risk of a 1930s-style "Great Depression."

[12]Recall from Chapter 15 that one of the arguments we noted against the use of debt financing in real estate is its effect of reducing the liquidity of the borrower. Problems of illiquidity tend to become more immediate with short-term debt due to the imminent pressure to refinance. On the other hand, lenders have more flexibility to pursue other investment alternatives if their cash is not tied up long term.

[13]A great depiction of the history of the U.S. Treasury yield curve is published by the *Wall Street Journal* online as *The Living Yield Curve* (see: http://www.smartmoney.com/investing/bonds/the-living-yield-curve-7923/).

EXHIBIT 19-4 Yield Curve
U.S. Treasury Strips
© OnCourse Learning

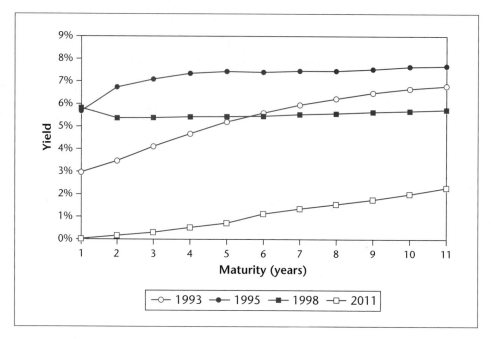

recovering from a recession. Federal monetary policy was generally expansionary (keeping short-term rates low), while investors expected greater inflationary pressures and/or greater demand for capital in the longer run as the economy recovered.

By 1995, the economy was fully recovered, and the FRB raised short-term interest rates to keep the economy from overheating, thereby reducing the long-run danger of inflation. By this time, inflation had been low and stable for some period, lending further credence to lower long-run inflation expectations. The slightly rising yield curve of 1995 is characteristic of a stable moderately growing economy with stable interest rate expectations.

The 1998 yield curve comes from the fall of that year, at which time there was consider- able fear that the U.S. economy was moving toward a recession, caused by an international financial crisis. The result was a flat (or even slightly inverted) yield curve, with long-term rates no higher (or even slightly lower) than short-term rates. If a recession occurred, demand for capital would be reduced, driving down future interest rates.

The 2011 yield curve is far below the others in levels, reflecting the secular decline in real interest rates for U.S. dollar-denominated investments that took place in the 2000s. But its general shape is much like that of the 1993 curve (i.e., continuously rising), although with somewhat less difference between the short- and long-term rates (225 basis-points differential instead of 382 basis-points). This may reflect the fact that it is difficult for nominal interest rates to fall below zero, while long-term prospects for the U.S. economy looked less robust in the early 2010s than in the early 1990s.

As noted, the most common type of yield curve is one that is slightly rising, with long- term yields some 100 to 200 basis points above short-term rates. However, a glance back at Exhibit 19-3 shows that there have been (relatively brief) periods when the yield curve has been inverted, with short-term rates above long-term rates. For example, during the late 1970s and early 1980s, energy price increases drove inflation to unprecedented peacetime levels, resulting in dramatically inverted yield curves. In fact, slightly inverted yield curves are often good leading indicators of impending recession in the macroeconomy, as they often occur when an overheated economy threatens to drive up inflation and leads the Fed to raise short-term interest rates to cool down the economy. (Recession did follow the inverted yield curves of the late 1970s but not that of 1998.) More generally, the yield spread, defined as the yield on long-term Treasury bonds minus the yield on short-term Treasury bonds, is positively correlated with future real economic growth. Exhibit 19-5 summarizes this discussion by presenting several characteristic yield curve shapes together with what they would typically be saying about the economy. And Exhibit 19-6 portrays a dramatic historical instance of how dynamic the yield curve can be.

EXHIBIT 19-5 Typical Yield Curve Shapes
© OnCourse Learning

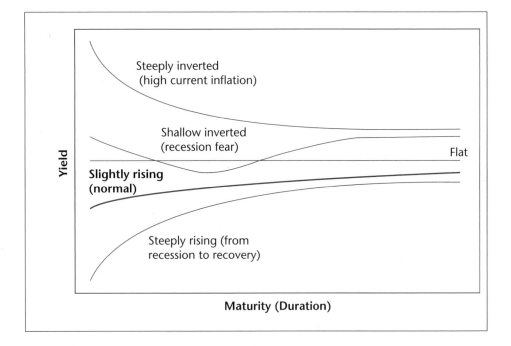

EXHIBIT 19-6 Yield Curve Changes During 2001
© OnCourse Learning

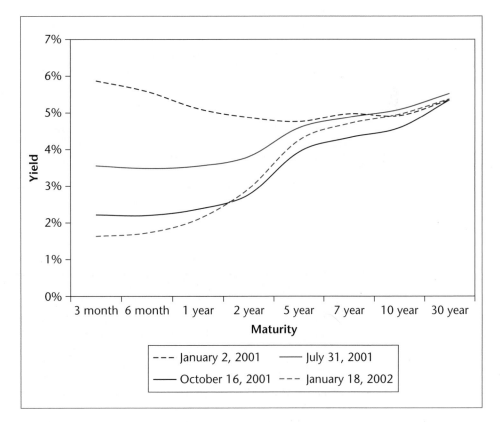

Such dramatic shifts in the yield curve occur occasionally as the economy swings from one regime to another, especially with the onset of recessions or financial crises. Entering 2001 the economy had been performing well, having weathered the 1998 financial crisis, though there was fear of overheating related to the "dot-com bubble" in the stock market and concern about the need for a "soft landing." This resulted in a slightly inverted yield curve declining from close to 6 percent at the short end to below 5.5 percent for 10-year maturities. By the summer of 2001 it was clear that the dot.com bubble had burst and there was strong evidence that the economy was slipping into recession, leading the Fed to ease up on short-term rates. By the end of 2001 the 9/11 terrorist attacks had shocked the world economy and financial system, bringing a threat of a more serious recession and leading the Fed to try to more strongly stimulate the economy by sharply dropping short-term interest rates. But, in an example of how it is more difficult for the Fed to control long-term rates, these remained stubbornly high. This was due in part to underlying demand for credit caused by robust growth in emerging markets and demand for real estate and consumer debt in the United States.

19.1.4 Maturity Matching and the Management of Fixed-Income Portfolios

What have the yield curve and interest rate risk to do with commercial mortgages? Such phenomena and considerations are basic to the motivations and decisions of the investors who ultimately supply the capital for mortgages, and they underlie or reflect much of the dynamics of the overall debt market. Commercial mortgages are a part of this market. To further your understanding of the roles commercial mortgages can play directly or indirectly for investors, we need to consider in more depth some of the concerns of investors in this market.

The Maturity-Matching Problem Let's begin by considering the problem of Simplified National Bank. The bank's balance sheet as of 6/30/2013 is depicted, in Exhibit 19-7A, with values measured in market values (which may differ from accounting book values). Simplified's assets consist of $100 million of commercial mortgages it has issued. Its liabilities consist of $90 million in deposits, leaving $10 million worth of stockholders' equity.

Simplified's mortgages all happen to be 10-year, zero-coupon loans at 6 percent. In other words, they provide for a total future cash flow of $179,084,770 on 6/30/2023. Simplified's deposits are all one-year certificates of deposit (CDs) yielding 5 percent. They promise payments totaling $94,500,000 on 6/30/2014. Now suppose news suddenly arrives that causes the entire yield curve to shift up by one point. One-year yields move from 5 percent to 6 percent, while 10-year yields move from 6 percent to 7 percent. The result for Simplified's stockholders is depicted in the market value balance sheet for the following day, depicted in Exhibit 19-7B.

Assets		Liabilities and Equity	
Mortgages:	$100,000,000	Deposits:	$90,000,000
		Equity:	10,000,000
Total Assets:	$100,000,000	Total L&E:	$100,000,000

EXHIBIT 19-7A Simplified National Bank Balance Sheet as of 6/30/2013
© OnCourse Learning

Assets		Liabilities and Equity	
Mortgages:	$91,037,616	Deposits:	$89,150,943
		Equity:	1,886,673
Total Assets:	$91,037,616	Total L&E:	$91,037,616

EXHIBIT 19-7B Simplified National Bank Balance Sheet as of 7/01/2013
© OnCourse Learning

Simplified's assets are reduced in value by about $9 million to approximately $91 million, while its liabilities are reduced in value by only about $1 million, to around $89 million.[14] Assets must balance against the total of liabilities and stockholders' equity. Thus, equity value falls by around $8 million, to less than $2 million. A one-point increase in interest rates has led to a 9 percent fall in asset value, a 1 percent fall in liability value, and an 80 percent fall in stockholders' equity value!

This is an example of the danger in what is known as a **maturity gap**. A maturity gap occurs when an investor's assets have greater weighted average duration than his liabilities. The maturity gap problem is exacerbated in lending institutions by the use of leverage. Many financial institutions tend to be extremely highly levered. (This is fundamental to the traditional business model of the classical depository financial institution.) In this case, the initial duration of Simplified's assets was 10 years, while the duration of its liabilities was one year, giving it a maturity gap of nine years. Simplified's equity value was initially 10 percent of its asset value, giving it an initial leverage ratio of 10. The combination of a maturity gap and leverage can greatly magnify interest rate risk.

Depository lending institutions tend to be susceptible to maturity gap problems because their deposits are their primary source of capital, and deposits tend to be of short duration.[15] Thus, such institutions tend to be highly levered with short-duration liabilities.[16] The duration of such an institution's equity is approximated by the product of its maturity gap times its leverage ratio.[17] For example, the 80 percent loss in Simplified's equity value due to a one-point rise in interest rates approximately equals its nine-year duration gap times its initial leverage ratio of 10.

Depository lending institutions are always looking for ways to deal with the maturity gap problem. One way is to make more short-term and fewer long-term loans, thereby reducing the maturity gap. This is one reason banks tend to like to hold construction loans in their asset portfolios more than long-term permanent mortgages. Permanent mortgages are among the longest duration of all bank loans. Another strategy is for banks to issue floating rate or adjustable rate loans. Such loans' values are not as sensitive to changes in market interest rates, because their contractual cash flows rise and fall with these rates. This is one reason banks are usually willing to make adjustable rate loans at lower interest rates than fixed rate loans. The interest rate sensitivity of a long-term adjustable rate loan may be no greater than that of a short-term fixed rate loan.

A third strategy for dealing with the maturity gap problem is to sell long-term loan assets into the secondary market rather than holding them in the institution's permanent asset portfolio. This approach has become very widespread in recent decades, first with residential mortgages and more recently with commercial mortgages. Ultimately, the bank becomes primarily only a loan originator, at least for some types of loans, rather than a long-term investor. The bank then makes its profits in the form of fees for services, rather than from the yield spread between their assets and liabilities. The services may include loan

---

[14]$179,084,770/1.07^{10} = \$91,037,616.\ \$94,500,000/1.06 = \$89,150,943.$

[15]Demand deposits such as checking and savings accounts are effectively near zero duration because depositors can move their funds out quickly if the interest rate offered by the bank on the deposits is not responsive to the market.

[16]High leverage is necessary for lending institutions because they must cover their administrative costs as well as make their profit from the narrow spreads between borrowing and lending rates. For example, suppose there is a 200 basis-point spread between borrowing and lending rates and administrative costs are 150 basis points. This leaves 50 basis points for profit. If the equity investors in the bank require a 10 percent return, then equity can be no more than 5 percent of total asset value (as 0.5% is 10% of 5%), implying a leverage ratio of 20.

[17]Using formula (2) and the $A = L + E$ accounting identity, we have

$$dur_E = -(\Delta E/E)/\Delta YTM = [(dur_A)A - (dur_L)L]/E = [dur_L + (dur_A - dur_L)(A/E)] \approx (dur_A - dur_L)(A/E)$$

where dur_A and dur_L are the durations of the firm's assets and liabilities, respectively, i.e., $(dur_A - dur_L)$ is the maturity gap.

origination and/or loan servicing. The latter refers to the administration of existing loans, including collection and distribution of loan payments.[18]

The maturity gap problem of depository institutions is probably one reason the liquidity preference theory usually works fairly well for explaining the yield curve. But one investor's problem is another investor's opportunity, for other types of financial institutions have long-duration liabilities. Chief among these are life insurance companies and pension funds. Such institutions typically have a long-duration preferred habitat as investors. They can often use long-term mortgages or bonds to implement something close to a maturity-matching strategy. Such institutions are therefore the natural investors in long-term loans, tending to hold such loans in their permanent asset portfolios. Such **portfolio lenders** traditionally provided most of the capital behind permanent commercial mortgages in the United States, until the advent of the CMBS industry in the 1990s.[19]

In addition to depository institutions and long-term portfolio lenders, other major categories of investors in the U.S. debt market include endowment funds, wealthy individuals, and foreign investors. Many of these investors have varied or flexible investment holding time horizons. Furthermore, duration habitat preference is not the only concern of bond investors. Although such investors tend generally to be more conservative than equity investors, there is nevertheless considerable range in risk preferences among debt investors. Some investors are willing to trade off interest rate risk and/or default risk for greater expected returns. Also, it must be recognized that investor risk perceptions are determined in many cases by an overall wealth portfolio perspective. Investors' overall wealth is typically invested in other types of assets besides just bonds, notably stocks. Bond risk differs from equity risk, and bonds can be used to diversify a stock portfolio. On the other hand, bonds typically carry more inflation risk than other types of assets, a particular concern to pension funds and others whose liabilities are adjusted to inflation.

Fixed-Income Investment Strategies Broadly speaking, investment management strategies for fixed-income portfolios can be classified as **trading-oriented** and **immunization-oriented strategies**. The former involve regular buying and selling of bonds prior to maturity. The latter seek to hold bonds to maturity.

Trading-oriented strategies include both active and passive approaches. The former seek to "beat the market" and earn superior risk-adjusted returns by employing superior interest rate forecasts, by finding debt products that are mispriced, or sometimes by engaging in arbitrage that may include hedging and the use of substantial leverage. The nature of bonds, with their precisely defined contractual cash flows, makes it possible to employ extremely high leverage ratios that can result occasionally in spectacular returns, but which can also expose large magnitudes of debt assets to financial risk. The basic objective of the active trading-oriented strategy is to trade in the bond market by buying low and selling high.

Passive approaches typically seek to minimize management expenses by investing in bond portfolios that closely replicate major indices of bond holding period returns. Passive strategies still require some bond trading, for example, to keep a constant average maturity, although passive strategies do not require as much trading as active strategies. Depending on the risk aversion of the investor, leverage may be employed in either active or passive trading-oriented strategies, in order to exploit yield spreads (e.g., borrowing at lower short-term rates in

---

[18]A fourth strategy for dealing with interest rate risk involves investment in derivative products that have negative interest rate risk, thereby hedging the lending institution's exposure. For example, in Chapter 20, we will describe a class of security known as an interest-only strip (or IO), based on mortgage loans sold into the secondary market. Certain IO securities can be used as interest rate risk hedges in some circumstances. More widely, lenders can use interest rate swaps to hedge interest rate risk, and credit default swaps to hedge default risk. Of course, the use of derivatives does not mean that the underlying risk has gone away. It merely means that the risk has been redistributed to other institutions that, presumably, are better able to withstand and use the type of risk in question. (Weaknesses in the functioning of some aspects of the derivatives market, particularly regarding credit default swaps, were painfully revealed during the financial crisis of 2008-09.)

[19]See our previous review of the commercial mortgage industry in the beginning of Chapter 16.

order to invest at higher long-term rates, in effect, purposely creating a maturity gap). All trading-oriented strategies are exposed to interest rate risk because in such a strategy bonds are often sold prior to maturity.

In contrast, immunization-oriented strategies seek to avoid interest rate risk. This can be done by avoiding the sale of bonds prior to maturity. Immunization-oriented strategies are more conservative than trading-oriented strategies and generally result in lower average investment returns. The cash flow matching technique described previously is an extreme example of immunization, possible when all future obligations can be predicted exactly in nominal terms (and when appropriate-maturity bonds can be found to match them). More typically, immunization is applied by matching the weighted average duration of assets and liabilities. This protects the investor's net wealth from most of the effects of interest rate swings.[20] It does not, however, protect against unexpected changes in inflation, if the investor's liabilities are adjusted to inflation. Immunization strategies are widely used, but are less popular than one might think, even among conservative institutions such as pension funds, probably because they provide low returns and therefore require high up-front cash investment in order to cover the future liabilities.

19.2 Commercial Mortgage Returns: Ex Ante and Ex Post

With some basic knowledge of bond investment in hand, you can now understand the fundamental determinants of commercial mortgage returns, both ex ante and ex post. The ex ante returns are the market yields looking forward (the required return expectations for marginal investors in the debt market), the yields that effectively determine bond prices in the debt market. Ex post returns are the returns actually realized by mortgage investors trading in the debt market. For broad-scale investment analysis purposes we typically measure ex post returns periodically by the **holding period returns** (**HPR**) achieved over time, reflecting the effect of changes in the market yield (and therefore in asset values) during each holding period. We begin with the former, ex ante returns.

19.2.1 Mortgage Yield: The Components of Ex Ante Returns

In this section, we want to integrate the debt investment economics you learned in the previous section with our quantification of default risk in Chapter 18 to summarize the overall components of commercial mortgage yields. This is important for borrowers because such yields represent their cost of debt capital and determine the amount that can be borrowed in return for a given pledge of future income. An understanding of ex ante yields is also important for mortgage investors because such yields represent their expected returns if they hold the mortgage to maturity, and changes in such yields cause either gains or losses in their realized returns if they do not hold to maturity. The better you understand mortgage market yields, the more rationally you can think about how such yields may change over time.

A good way to visualize the determinants of commercial mortgage yields is to build up the total yield as a stack of various components. This **contractual yield component "stack"** is represented in Exhibit 19-8. We will discuss briefly each component shown in the exhibit.

Real Risk-Free Rate This is the most basic part of the yield: the pure short-term time value of money (TVM) for constant-purchasing-power dollars, that is, the real short-term

---

[20]As noted, duration is not a perfect measure of interest rate sensitivity. Sophisticated immunization techniques also attempt to take account of convexity, shifts in the yield curve, and other issues. It is worthwhile to note also that a principle similar to duration matching, what is often referred to as **maturity matching**, is often applied to develop sound financing strategies for long-term equity investments. The idea is that assets should be financed with debt whose maturity corresponds to the expected lifetime of the asset (or more properly, the cash outflows for the debt service should correspond in time to the expected cash inflows from the asset). This avoids liquidity problems and interest rate risk for the equity investor.

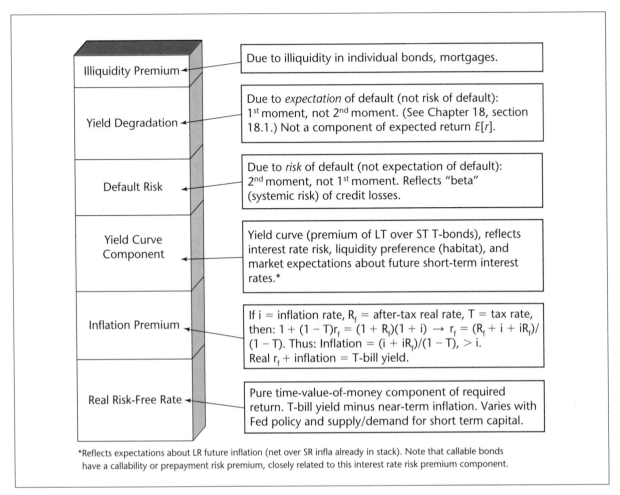

*Reflects expectations about LR future inflation (net over SR infla already in stack). Note that callable bonds have a callability or prepayment risk premium, closely related to this interest rate risk premium component.

EXHIBIT 19-8 Components of Commercial Mortgage Total Yield: The Contractual Yield Components Stack
© OnCourse Learning

value of what we have been labeling r_f in this book ever since Chapter 9.[21] For U.S. dollar-denominated investments this component is typically measured by the current T-bill yield minus the current inflation rate. It is typically in the neighborhood of 100 to 300 basis points, but it can vary widely with short-term capital supply and demand and in response to Federal Reserve Board monetary policy.[22]

---

[21]Recall we noted in section 11.2.2 that for long horizon investments such as most direct equity investment in real property it is more appropriate to think of the relevant risk-free rate (r_f) as reflecting the expected *average* of this short-term risk-free rate over the expected holding period of the investment. More on this shortly.

[22]This component can even appear to be negative at times as measured by U.S. Treasury Bill yields minus current inflation, when there is fear of financial crisis, as demand for a "safe harbor" for investors' money bids up the prices of U.S. T-bills. However, in the case of T-bill yields, this negative effect might more accurately be attributed to a negative "illiquidity premium," which is the top component on our yield stack, to be discussed shortly. In effect, due to U.S. T-bills' present role as a reserve currency depository and global safe harbor, T-bill prices reflect a positive "liquidity premium," which translates to a negative illiquidity premium in the expected return to holding T-bills. This issue is sometimes addressed by using a different benchmark as the measure of risk-free interest rates, the London Interbank Offering Rate (LIBOR). This is a private market rate that is nearly as risk-free as T-bills but not subject to the T-bills liquidity premium. Normally the LIBOR is only about 10 to 50 basis-points above the T-bill yield, but during times of crisis such it can be much higher. For example, during 2008-09 the LIBOR was often over 100 bps above Treasury yields and spiked briefly to over 400 bps above. The spread between LIBOR and comparable short-term T-bill yield is known as the "TED Spread" (Treasury minus Euro-Dollar).

Inflation Premium This is the premium due to the expected rate of inflation in the short term. It reflects the need of the investor to obtain the previously-described short-term real return measured in constant purchasing power. The inflation premium component is typically close to the recent past average rate of inflation, for example, 200 to 300 basis points in recent decades in the United States. The sum of the real risk-free rate and the inflation premium equals the short-term nominal risk-free rate, the short-term version of what we have labeled r_f, typically observed in the United States as the Treasury bill yield.[23] T-bill yields are essentially the same as their ex post returns, as they are very short-term instruments, so the history of these rates is well depicted in Exhibit 19-3. You can see that since the 1980s T-bill yields have fallen from double-digit levels (reflecting rampant inflation at that time) to as low as zero during financial crises and recessionary periods of the 2008–2011 years (similar to where it was during the deflation of the 1930s). From 1926 to 2010 the average T-bill yield was about 3.7 percent, and from 1980 to 2010, it was about 5.7 percent.

Yield Curve Component This component reflects the effect of the yield curve, as discussed in section 19.1.3. It reflects expectations about future short-term interest rates, as well as the effect of liquidity preferences and interest rate risk. Of course, interest rate expectations include the effect of long-term inflation expectations.[24] For a given mortgage, this component of the mortgage yield depends on the duration of the mortgage as well as on the current shape of the yield curve.[25] Usually, the yield curve is slightly upward-sloping, with long-term Treasury bonds yielding 100 to 200 basis points more than short-term T-bills. Fixed rate long-term (permanent) commercial mortgages are typically priced based on the long-term end of the yield curve (typically based on yields of Treasury bonds of the same maturity), and so would include a positive yield curve component in their YTMs. Adjustable rate loans can be priced based on the short-term end of the yield curve. Based on our discussion in section 19.1.3, the yield curve component of mortgage market yields varies over time in response to the outlook for the macroeconomy and long-term inflation fears. With a steeply upward-sloping yield curve, this component of mortgage yields may be 300 to 400 basis points or more. With an inverted yield curve, the yield curve component would be negative. As we are building up our "stack," Real r_f + Inflation Premium + Yield Curve Component = Long-Term Treasury Bond Yield (of similar maturity to subject mortgage).

While the expectations component of the yield curve varies widely with economic and financial cycles, in principle over the long run it should average out to around zero if expectations are rational, as it simply reflects the difference between the expected average future short-term T-bill yield and the current T-bill yield (assuming there is no long-run trend in T-bill yields). Thus, the long-run average magnitude of the yield curve probably tends to well approximate the liquidity preference and interest rate risk-based component of the yield curve, which seems likely to be more stable in principle. As noted, the long-run average yield curve upward slope is around 200 basis-points between T-bills and 10-year T-bonds. By subtracting this interest rate risk and liquidity preference component from the current T-bond yield, one can therefore arrive at an approximate estimate of the bond market's current expectation about the average future short-term T-bill yields over the maturity of

---

[23]Recall from Chapter 9 that $(1 + r) = (1 + R)(1 + i)$, where R is the real rate and i is the inflation rate. Thus, $r = R + i + iR$. The third term is usually ignored as it is very small. If investors require a nominal return sufficient to preserve a target after-tax real return, then we have $[1 + (1 - T) r] = (1 + R)(1 + i)$, which implies $r = [(1 + R)(1 + i) - 1]/(1 - T) = (R + i + iR)/(1 - T)$, where T is the tax rate and R is the *after-tax* target real return. This suggests that the Inflation Premium might in principle be somewhat larger than the actual current inflation rate.

[24]More precisely, the long-term interest rate expectations component includes the effect of any *difference* between long-run and short-run inflation expectations, as the latter are already included in the Inflation Premium component of the nominal T-bill yield that is already on our "stack."

[25]Prepayable mortgages lack definite maturity. This introduces what is known as prepayment risk, a risk that is closely related to interest rate risk, because prepayment is more likely when interest rates fall, forcing the lender to reinvest at a lower yield. As noted in Chapter 17, prepayment risk can be quantified and evaluated using option pricing theory. In general, callable bonds have higher yields than otherwise similar noncallable bonds, reflecting the cost to the investor of the prepayment option given to the borrower. The U.S. Treasury bonds on which the yield curve is computed are noncallable.

the bond. This is the rationale for the simple procedure we suggested back in Chapter 11 for estimating the risk-free rate (r_f) component of the opportunity cost of capital (OCC) for long-term real estate investments and property valuation (see section 11.2.2).

Default Risk   This component reflects the risk premium investors require in their expected total return due to the *risk* of default. (This is different from the effect of the *expectation* of default, which will be discussed next.) Recall that return risk refers to the phenomenon of realized ex post returns possibly varying *around* their expectation as of the time the investment was made. Risk is thus two-sided. Realized returns can be either above or below their prior expectations. Investors demand a risk premium in their ex ante returns because they dislike this uncertainty (they are risk averse). The risk that matters most to investors is the component of ex post return uncertainty that cannot be diversified away. Default risk is of this nature. Commercial mortgage borrowers tend to default more often when the economy is doing poorly, which is likely to be just when mortgage investors can least afford to experience an unpleasant surprise. Therefore, investors demand a risk premium because of the uncertainty associated with the possibility of loan default.[26] The **default risk premium** defined in this way, that is, as a component of the *expected return* to commercial mortgages, is probably typically in the neighborhood of 50 to 100 basis points.

Ex Ante Yield Degradation   This component reflects the effect of the *expectation* of default in the commercial mortgage. It is the difference between the *contractual* yield as if there were no possibility of default (the "stated yield") and the *expected return* including the realistic possibility of default. This component of the mortgage yield was discussed extensively in section 18.1 of the preceding chapter. There we noted that for typical long-term commercial mortgages in the United States, the ex ante yield degradation is probably in the neighborhood of 50 to 100 basis points on average.[27]

The sum of the default risk-based yield component, plus the ex ante yield degradation, equals the total default-based spread between quoted yields of commercial mortgages and those of similar-duration Treasury bonds. The two components together have typically averaged in the neighborhood of 150 to 200 basis points for commercial mortgages. For a given loan, both the expected yield degradation and the default risk premium component should in principle reflect the amount of default risk in the subject loan. For example, in 2011 in the secondary market for commercial mortgages loans with a loan-to-value ratio (LTV) of 50 percent would typically trade at yields about 25 basis-points lower than otherwise similar loans with the benchmark 75 percent LTV, while loans with 85 percent LTVs would require yields over 200 basis-points higher.

Illiquidity Premium   The final component of the typical commercial mortgage ex ante yield is an **illiquidity premium**. This is a component of the expected return premium necessary to compensate investors for putting their money in a relatively illiquid asset, that is, one that may be difficult to sell quickly at full value. Most commercial mortgages are not securitized but are held as whole loans. The secondary market for such loans, each of which is unique in some respects (including the nature of the property securing it), is thin, typically less well developed than the underlying property market. Although such illiquidity can pose problems for an investor, the types of investors that hold whole loans typically have deep pockets, that is, they have plenty of liquidity elsewhere in their wealth portfolios. Thus, the illiquidity of commercial mortgages is not of as much concern to them as you might think, and the illiquidity premium in commercial mortgages is typically fairly small, on the order of

---

[26]It should be noted that commercial mortgage default rates have more to do with the health of the commercial property sector than with the health of the macroeconomy as a whole. Although commercial property returns are positively correlated with such macroeconomic indicators as national consumption, this correlation is far from perfect. It is not clear how commercial mortgage default risk compares to that of corporate bonds in this regard. The systematic risk in empirical ex post commercial mortgage returns will be discussed in the next section.

[27]Recall that the average credit loss in the GLCMPI was 62 basis points during the 1972–2004 period.

20 to 50 basis points. The upper end of this range would apply to loans that are more unique or less appealing to large institutional investors.

The securitization of commercial mortgages, in the form of CMBS, resulted in whole loans being sliced up into different classes of securities, many of which are traded publicly, thereby acquiring greater liquidity. However, liquidity is far from perfect even for publicly traded corporate bonds, and investors in publicly traded securities may care more about liquidity than holders of whole loans, so they attach a greater premium to it. Furthermore, the securitization process, while it may result in a diminution of the illiquidity premium, brings additional layers of administration and servicing of the debt. This adds to the mortgage administrative costs, which places another layer onto the effective yield faced by loan originators and borrowers in the primary market. As a result, contractual yields on loans that are to be securitized are not obviously lower in general than yields on loans intended to be held whole by portfolio lenders.[28]

The sum of the top three components in our mortgage yield stack—Default Risk Premium + Expected Default Yield Degradation + Illiquidity Premium—equals the spread of the mortgage stated yield over the similar-maturity Treasury bond yield. This spread is often referred to as the mortgage "default risk premium." It is the basic comparison between mortgage interest rates and Treasury bond yields. As you can see, this spread really consists of separate default-related components: the risk premium plus the expected yield degradation, as well as a liquidity-based component. All three of these components together have typically averaged in the neighborhood of 150 to 250 basis points for commercial mortgages.[29] At the peak of the mid-2000s bubble the spread was sometimes slightly below that range, and at other times the spread over Treasuries has been much greater. For example, during and after the 2008–2009 financial crisis, yield spreads peaked at over 400 basis points. This reflected both increased risk aversion on the part of investors as well as illiquidity in the mortgage market, combined with a possible negative component in the Treasury bond yield. (Treasury yields were being driven down, reflecting Treasury bonds' role as a perceived "safe harbor" investment.) By 2011 spreads fell back to under 250 basis points.[30]

The sum of all six components in our stack gives the contractual yield prevailing in the commercial mortgage market. This is the yield that reflects the value of the mortgage asset in the debt market and that is used computationally to price mortgage loans (as we saw mechanically in Chapter 17). At the brick-and-mortar level, this prevailing yield is experienced by investors essentially as the interest rate they face for fixed-rate long-term commercial mortgages. The table in Exhibit 19-9 shows how the approximate values of the six components in our stack totaled up to typical mortgage market contract interest rates during different macroeconomic and financial "climates" prevailing at four periods of time during

---

[28]Exact apples-to-apples comparisons are difficult because the loans that are issued to be securitized typically differ in various respects (such as size, credit quality, and loan terms) from those that are not intended to be securitized. In theory, however, if there is an active primary market simultaneously in mortgages to be held whole in portfolios and in mortgages that are to be securitized in the secondary market, then the yields of both types of loans must be equal for the same type of loan. Otherwise, one side of the market would dry up (e.g., if yields were higher in loans not to be securitized, then borrowers would flock to the conduits issuing loans to be securitized, and vice versa—if yields were lower in loans not to be securitized then lenders would not issue such loans, that is, all loans would be securitized). In fact, the market has at times strongly favored one form or the other, for example, at the peak of the bubble in 2006–07 CMBS conduit lending tended to crowd out portfolio lending, and in the commercial property recovery after the financial crisis during 2010–11 portfolio lending tended to dominate CMBS lending.

[29]During 1989–2011 the average ACLI commercial and multi-family fixed-rate loan bond-equivalent yield at origination was 7.46 percent while the average long-term T-bond yield (based on the Ibbotson SBBI index) was 5.85 percent over that same period, for an average spread of 161 basis-points. However, this comparison does not exactly control for duration.

[30]Keep in mind that long-term Treasury bonds are not risk-free, as interest rate risk is reflected in the Yield Curve Component in our stack. Thus, the mortgage-treasury spread is not exactly the same as the expected return risk premium in the mortgage investment, indeed, for two reasons, not only the risk premium in the long-term T-bond but also the fact that the mortgage yield includes the expected yield degradation component above the mortgage's actual expected return.

	2010	2005	Late 1990s	1993
Real risk-free rate:	−2.00%	1.50%	2.50%	0.00%
Inflation premium:	2.00%	2.75%	2.50%	3.50%
Yield curve:	4.00%	0.50%	1.00%	3.50%
Default risk:	1.00%	0.50%	0.75%	1.00%
Yield degradation:	1.00%	0.50%	0.75%	0.50%
Illiquidity:	1.00%	0.25%	0.25%	0.50%
Total stated yield:	7.00%	6.00%	7.75%	9.00%

EXHIBIT 19-9 Approximate Commercial Mortgage Market Stated Yield Components at Four Historical Periods

© OnCourse Learning

the 1990s and early 2000s. The table depicts two earlier periods: the latter part of the 1990s when the economy was relatively stable, and 1993 when the commercial real estate market was still recovering from a recent major slump and the Fed had driven short-term interest rates sharply down to stimulate the macroeconomy out of a recession in the early 1990s. The year 1993 was also characterized by inflation expectations that were a bit higher than the latter period. By 2005, unprecedented worldwide liquidity (strong financial capital supply side pressure across all asset classes) had driven almost all components of the yield stack down to levels not seen in a generation.

By 2010, in the recessionary aftermath of the 2008–2009 financial crisis, Federal Reserve stimulative policy and global liquidity imbalances had driven U.S. T-bill rates literally to zero—an unprecedented level since the 1930s, when there had been major deflation in the dollar. The steep yield curve at that time reflected both the monetary stimulus policy and expectations for a future recovery. But the commercial mortgage market still suffered from a lack of liquidity (with CMBS barely beginning to recover) and investors, having been recently burned, were particularly risk averse and wary, leading to an abnormally high mortgage spread over long-term Treasuries.

The overall result was that commercial mortgage interest rates fell persistently from the early 1990s through the early 2000s, from around 9 percent to as low as 6 percent. Then with the financial crisis of 2008–2009 mortgage rates climbed a bit, but more recently have fallen to even lower rates. Most of the reduction in mortgage rates during the 1990s and until the financial crisis was due to compression in the expected return risk premium. If we define this premium as the difference between the overall mortgage yield net of the expected yield degradation component, minus the current nominal T-bill rate (that is: Yield Curve + Default Risk + Illiquidity Premium, which equates to expected return minus current risk-free rate: $E[r] - r_f$), then the investment risk premium fell from 5 percent in 1993 to 2 percent in the late 1990s to barely over 1 percent in 2005. After an upturn during the financial crisis, commercial mortgage interest rates again declined, but this time the driver was the extreme compression in the short-term nominal risk-free rate (the r_f component), rather than the risk premium. The 7 percent interest rate at the beginning of 2010 equated to a 6 percent risk premium! By 2011 mortgage interest rates were down to 5 percent for ACLI loans, but that still suggested a historically very high 4 percent expected return risk premium.

19.2.2 Ex Post Performance: The Historical Record

The yields described in the previous section are the market's ex ante stated yields, the contractual YTMs reflecting the before-tax expectations of the marginal investors in the mortgage asset market. For investors who hold their loans to maturity, these ex ante yields will indeed also equal their ex post realized yields, before taxes and in the absence of default or prepayment. However, for investors who sell mortgages prior to maturity, or for investors who compute the periodic returns to their mortgage portfolios by "marking to market" their portfolio values at the end of each period, realized ex post returns will typically differ from ex ante yields.

Computing HPRs for Mortgages   Ex post holding period returns (HPRs) are computed for bonds or mortgages just as they are for properties or stocks. Each periodic return consists of the cash flow within that period plus any change in the market value of the debt asset between the beginning and end of the period, all divided by the market value of the debt asset as of the beginning of the period. The periodic cash flow typically consists of regular debt service (both interest and principal amortization), although it would also include any prepayment of principal or loss recovery through foreclosure in the event of default. The change in market value of the debt asset reflects (1) changes in the contractual OLB (due to regular amortization and to prepayments or balloon payments) and (2) changes in the market value of the debt asset due either to changes in market interest rates or to changes in the perceived default risk of the loan.

The HPR formula for mortgages is represented symbolically in formula (3) below, for the return in period t:

$$r_t = \frac{CF_t + (V_t - V_{t-1})}{V_{t-1}} = \frac{(PMT_t + REC_t) + (D_t - D_{t-1})}{D_{t-1}} \tag{3}$$

where PMT_t is the regular debt service during period t, REC_t is the value of any prepayments or the net recovery in any foreclosures during period t, and D_t is the market value of any remaining debt as of the end of period t. In a mortgage index, this formula is aggregated across a large number of individual loans composing the index portfolio.[31]

Realized periodic total returns, as measured by the HPRs, are much more volatile than ex ante yields. The volatility of ex post mortgage total returns (like those of other bonds) derives primarily from changes over time in the *market value* of the debt asset (changes in $D_t - D_{t-1}$). As noted, such market value changes primarily reflect two effects: (1) changes in market interest rates and (2) changes in perceived default risk Apart from this volatility effect, the *average* level of ex post returns in a historical index reflects the effect of realized credit losses as a result of defaults in the loans that compose the index portfolio, as well as the effect of the general trend in market interest rates over the historical period being measured. For example, if market interest rates have been declining, then this will impart a positive component into the average ex post appreciation return component (via the $D_t - D_{t-1}$ component). Another difference to bear in mind between ex ante and ex post returns is that ex ante yields are multiperiod IRRs, while ex post periodic returns are typically reported as a series of HPRs.

With these differences in mind, we would expect mortgage HPRs to approximately equal ex ante yields on average over the long run, after adjusting as appropriate for credit losses and differences between IRRs and average HPRs.[32] Over the very long run, this expectation is indeed probably born out in practice. Although very long-term data are not available for mortgages, Exhibit 19-10 traces ex ante yields and ex post HPRs for long-term U.S. government bonds from 1926 through 2010. The ex ante yields (that is, the current yields observed in the bond market) are represented by the relatively smooth solid line, while the ex post HPRs are represented by the more volatile dashed line that oscillates around the ex ante yield. The striking volatility apparent in the HPRs is a manifestation of interest rate risk. Nevertheless, the average HPR is within a few basis points of the average ex ante yield for these default-free bonds over this long period of history.[33]

Over shorter periods of history, interest rates may trend in one direction, often reflecting swings in inflation or government fiscal and monetary policy. Such changes in interest

---

[31]In an index such as the GLCMPI, a simulated portfolio is used, composed of cohorts of typical loans. The loans in the index portfolio typically change from one period to the next, but by definition the HPR within each period is computed on the basis of a "static portfolio" (that is, the same loans) at the beginning and end of the period.

[32]Recall that the arithmetic time-weighted average HPR is a positive function of the volatility of the series. For normally distributed returns, the arithmetic mean approximately equals the geometric mean plus one-half the variance of the returns series. IRRs are essentially like geometric mean returns in this respect (although they are dollar-weighted rather than time weighted).

[33]Over the 1926–2010 period, the U.S. Treasury long-term bond geometric mean was 5.19 percent for the ex ante yield to maturity and 5.48 percent for the ex post annual HPR (based on Ibbotson Associates indices).

EXHIBIT 19-10 Yields
(ex ante) and HPRs
(ex post) on Long-Term
U.S. Government Bonds,
1926–2004

© OnCourse Learning

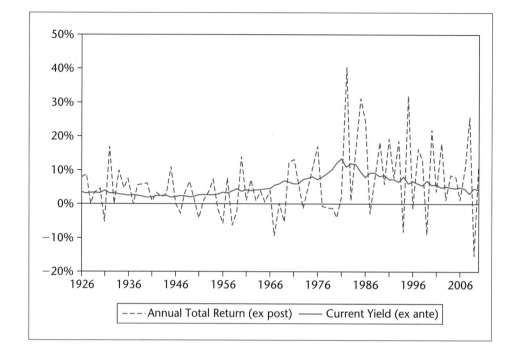

rates may not be completely anticipated by investors and therefore not fully reflected in ex ante yields. As interest rate changes are fully reflected in ex post returns, this can cause average ex post returns to differ from average ex ante returns over short to medium length historical periods. During periods of generally declining interest rates, such as the 1980s through early 2000s, ex post bond returns tended to exceed ex ante returns (at least for default-free bonds). The opposite was true in the preceding period of rising interest rates during the 1970s.

Historical Results for Commercial Mortgages   Exhibit 19-11 shows average prevailing contract yields and the annual ex post periodic total returns for long-term fixed rate commercial mortgages in the United States during the 1988–2010 period. Over this period the average stated yield was 7.81 percent, while the average ex post total return was 7.71 percent, as measured by the Giliberto-Levy Commercial Mortgage Price Index (GLCMPI)[34] The GLCMPI is adjusted to reflect credit losses due to defaults. During the 1988–2010 period, such losses were substantial due to the commercial property crash in the early part of that period.[35] Without including the effect of credit losses, the average GLCMPI return during 1988–2010 would have been 8.61 percent, considerably above the average contract yield. This reflects the effect of the generally declining interest rates during the 1988–2010 period.

Exhibit 19-12 presents a longer-term and broader view of ex post periodic return performance for institutional commercial property in the United States. The exhibit compares annual GLCMPI total returns (loss-adjusted) with those of the NCREIF Property Index, the S&P 500 Stock Index, long-term U.S. government bonds, and T-bills.[36] The Consumer

---

[34]Adjusting for volatility, the GLCMPI ex post average was 7.58 percent, while the stated yield is 7.80 percent. The stated yields in Exhibit 19-11 are taken from the PwC Real Estate Investor Survey.

[35]Recall that the GLCMPI is based on life insurance company (ACLI) originated mortgages. We noted in Chapter 18 that these loans suffered much less credit losses after the 2008–2009 financial crisis and recession than was the case for other types of commercial mortgages (notably those issued by banks and CMBS conduits).

[36]In Exhibits 19-12 and 19-13, the real estate returns are based on the transactions-based (TBI) version of the NCREIF Property Index and "unsmoothed" predecessors. (See Chapter 25 for further description.)

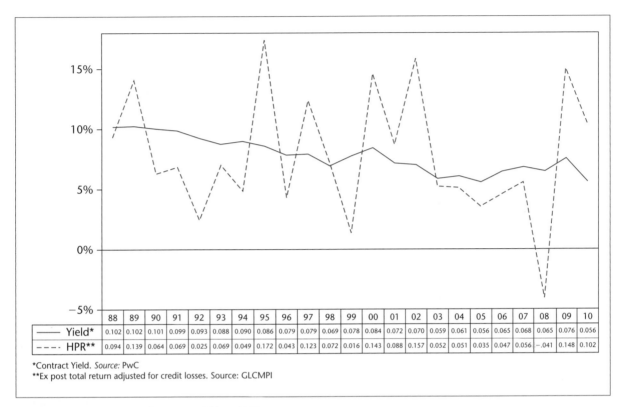

	88	89	90	91	92	93	94	95	96	97	98	99	00	01	02	03	04	05	06	07	08	09	10
—— Yield*	0.102	0.102	0.101	0.099	0.093	0.088	0.090	0.086	0.079	0.079	0.069	0.078	0.084	0.072	0.070	0.059	0.061	0.056	0.065	0.068	0.065	0.076	0.056
- - - HPR**	0.094	0.139	0.064	0.069	0.025	0.069	0.049	0.172	0.043	0.123	0.072	0.016	0.143	0.088	0.157	0.052	0.051	0.035	0.047	0.056	-.041	0.148	0.102

*Contract Yield. *Source:* PwC
**Ex post total return adjusted for credit losses. Source: GLCMPI

EXHIBIT 19-11 U.S. Commercial Mortgage Yields and HPRs
© OnCourse Learning

Price Index (CPI) is also shown. The chart indicates what one dollar invested at the end of 1971 would have grown to in each of the asset classes at the end of each subsequent year (with reinvestment of income). Exhibit 19-13 presents the historical statistics for the periodic total returns during this period. Commercial mortgages provided a time-weighted geometric average annual total return of 8.72 percent during this period, slightly more than the average long-term government bond return of 8.46 percent.[37]

It is important to note the evidence on the comovement between mortgages and other asset classes apparent in the correlation statistics in Exhibit 19-13. Such comovement is important in determining the effect of mortgages in a mixed-asset investment portfolio, and in determining the effect of leverage on real estate equity risk. The largest correlation among asset classes in Exhibit 19-13 is between mortgages and long-term bonds (59 percent). This reflects the fact that mortgages are essentially bond-like assets, whose HPR volatility is driven largely by interest rate movements.[38] Mortgages are also positively correlated with stocks, as represented by the S&P 500 index (+40 percent correlation), and negatively

[37]This 26-basis-point spread between mortgage and government bond returns does not necessarily imply that average mortgage ex post returns have failed to achieve the typical 50-to-100-basis-point ex ante default risk premium described in section 19.2.1. The long-term government bond index tracked here has a longer average duration than that of the GLCMPI, and the yield curve was upward-sloping on average during the 1971–2010 period. The average ex post return differential between mortgages and government bonds of similar duration was greater than 26 basis points during 1971–2010.

[38]The GLCMPI appears less volatile than the bond index in Exhibit 19-13. Once again, this difference is largely explained by the difference in average duration between the GLCMPI and the Ibbotson long-term government bond index. The bond index's longer average duration makes it more sensitive to interest rates. The GLCMPI duration was over seven years in the 1970s, but less than five years since the 1990s.

EXHIBIT 19-12 Year-End
Value of $1 (income
reinvested), 1971–2010
© OnCourse Learning

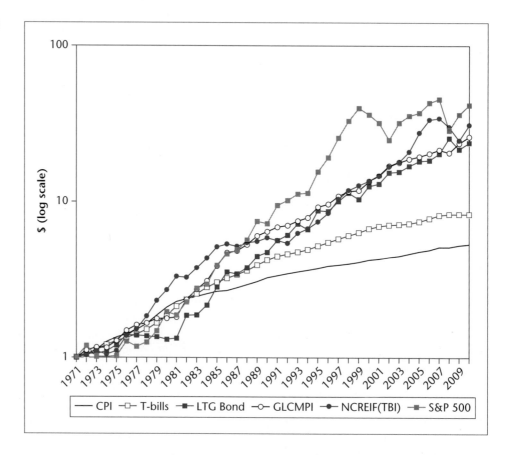

	CPI	T-bills	LT G Bond	GLCMPI[†]	NCREIF[‡]	SP 500
Geometric Mean	4.38%	5.56%	8.46%	8.72%	9.18%	10.04%
Arithmetic Mean	4.43%	5.61%	9.09%	8.94%	9.73%	11.68%
Volatility	NA	3.17%	12.00%	7.10%	10.96%	18.33%
Ex Post Risk Premium (arithmetic)	NA	NA	3.48%	3.34%	4.12%	6.07%
Sharpe*	NA	NA	0.29	0.47	0.38	0.33
Correlations:						
CPI	100%	65%	−34%	−28%	17%	−10%
T-bills	65%	100%	8%	12%	19%	9%
LT G Bond	−34%	8%	100%	59%	−1%	8%
GLCMPI	−28%	12%	59%	100%	3%	40%
NPI(uns)	17%	19%	−1%	3%	100%	19%
SP500	−10%	9%	8%	40%	19%	100%

*The Sharpe Ratio is equal to: (Mean − T-bill Mean)/Volatility, a measure of return adjusted for risk.
[†]Adjusted for credit losses.
[‡]TBI from 1985, NCREIF Unsmoothed (1-Step, See Chapter 25) prior to then.

EXHIBIT 19-13 Historical Annual Periodic Total Return Statistics, 1972–2004

Sources: Based on data from Ibboston Associates; John B.Levy & Co. and NCREIF

correlated with inflation (−28 percent). In both these respects, mortgages are very similar to long-term bonds.

It is perhaps a bit surprising that mortgages showed less correlation with real estate during the 1972–2010 period than they did with stocks. The annual GLCMPI and transaction-based NCREIF (TBI) index were effectively uncorrelated during this period. This probably largely reflects the differential response of property and fixed rate mortgages to changes in inflation expectations. As noted in previous chapters, commercial property is considered an inflation hedge, typically responding positively to increases in inflation. The opposite is true of fixed rate long-term debt. Thus, even though mortgages and underlying property might both respond in the same direction to unanticipated changes in *real* interest rates and to changes in property market fundamentals, their opposite response to unanticipated changes in inflation dampens their correlation. This means that leverage has a larger impact on the volatility of the levered equity investment than it would if mortgages and property were more highly correlated.[39]

Mortgage versus Property Risk and Return: Is There Positive Leverage? It is interesting to note in Exhibit 19-13 that commercial mortgage ex post total returns have averaged almost as high as those of underlying commercial property. Reflecting institutional real estate, the ACLI-based GLCMPI provided a 8.72 percent geometric average annual return over 1972–2010 versus less than 50 basis-points more, 9.18 percent, for NCREIF properties. This suggests that, from the perspective of average ex post HPRs (as opposed to ex ante expectations), borrowing did not generally provide much positive leverage for commercial property investors over the 1972–2010 period, at least for the types of institutional real estate represented by the NCREIF index.[40] Of course, the historical period covered by these statistics includes two commercial property market slumps and the long secular decline in interest rates from the early 1980s through the early 2010s. These historical phenomena probably caused average ex post HPRs to exceed average ex ante expectations in mortgages and to fall below such expectations in underlying property. This historical result may account for a relative lack of positive leverage ex post, without implying that positive leverage did not exist ex ante.

On the other hand, it may be that the capital markets viewed commercial mortgages as being practically as risky as underlying commercial property during the 1972–2010 period. As noted in Chapter 13 (in our discussion of leverage), although debt risk is different from property risk, it is not necessarily of less concern to the relevant marginal investors in the capital markets.[41]

In this regard, several points of comparison between the mortgage and property HPR statistics indicated in Exhibit 19-13 are worthy of consideration. On the one hand, the statistics suggest that commercial mortgages were less volatile than the underlying properties securing them (7 percent mortgage volatility versus 11 percent property index volatility). This point appears to suggest slightly less risk in mortgages than in the underlying property.

---

[39]The volatility of the levered equity position as a function of the leverage ratio (LR), the volatilities of the underlying asset and the debt (S_P and S_D, respectively), and the correlation between these two (C_{PD}) is

$$S_E = \sqrt{[(LR)S_P]^2 + [(LR-1)S_D]^2 - 2C_{PD}[(LR)(LR-1)S_P S_D]}$$

Thus, when the correlation between the underlying asset and the debt is positive ($C_{PD} > 0$), the periodic return volatility of the levered equity is reduced by the effect of the third term subtracted from under the square-root operator. This third term disappears in the case of zero correlation ($C_{PD} = 0$, as is approximately the case with commercial property and long-term fixed rate mortgages).

[40]The ex post average HPR perspective presented here is not exactly the same as the multiperiod return perspective of a borrow-and-hold investor who paid the loan off at par value. Nevertheless, the fact that the mortgage returns here are adjusted for credit losses, and our previous point that such average ex post returns tend to equal average ex ante mortgage return expectations in the long run, does suggest that there was, on average, very little positive leverage (ex post) in the total return on institutional quality commercial property during the 1972–2010 period.

[41]It seems likely that immunization-oriented debt market investors who experience buy-and-hold returns tend to be intramarginal, while the marginal investors who determine asset market prices may typically be more concerned with periodic returns, such as those represented by the GLCMPI.

On the other hand, mortgages were more positively correlated with stocks and bonds, and more negatively correlated with inflation, than were the underlying properties. This means that mortgages typically provided less portfolio diversification benefit, and greater exposure to inflation risk, than did underlying property.[42] Considering the foregoing, it seems plausible that the capital markets might have evaluated the risks of mortgages nearly as highly as those of institutional commercial property, on average during the 1972–2010 period. This would imply that even on an ex ante basis, long-term fixed rate debt would not have provided much positive leverage for equity investment in institutional quality commercial property.

19.3 Chapter Summary

In this chapter, we stepped back to give you some economic background relevant to the entire debt market, the branch of the capital market in which commercial mortgages are an integral part. By understanding such fundamental phenomena as interest rate risk, maturity matching, and the yield curve, you can better understand commercial mortgages and the role they play in the capital markets. We also completed in this chapter the picture of commercial mortgage investment risk that we began in Chapter 18, so that you now have a more comprehensive picture of what determines prices and yields in the mortgage market. Finally, we reviewed some evidence of the recent historical HPR investment performance of commercial mortgages in the United States. In so doing, we broached some of the macro-level portfolio concerns of mixed-asset investors, issues that we will pursue further in Part VII. In the meantime, we need to complete our picture of real estate debt by considering CMBS in the next chapter.

KEY TERMS

maturity	yield curve	holding period returns (HPR)
duration (Macaulay and modified)	expectations hypothesis	contractual yield component "stack"
interest rate risk	liquidity preference theory	maturity matching
market yields	maturity gap	default risk
cash flow matching	portfolio lenders	ex ante yield degradation
roll-over strategy	trading-oriented strategies	default risk premium
preferred habitat	immunization-oriented strategies	illiquidity premium

STUDY QUESTIONS

Conceptual Questions

19.1. Why is finite maturity important and useful to certain types of investors?

19.2. Define the term *duration*. What is the general relationship between duration and maturity? How is this relationship different for zero-coupon versus coupon bonds? How is it different for short-term versus long-term debt?

19.3. What is interest rate risk?

---

[42]This suggests that levered equity positions in real estate should make better inflation hedges and better diversifiers of a stock portfolio than unlevered property equity. Remember that the borrower has a negative (or short) position in the debt asset, while the lender or mortgage investor has the corresponding positive (or long) position. In a portfolio, the effect of the short position is just the opposite of the effect of the long position. Portfolio theory will be discussed in Part VII. For now, it suffices for you to realize that property's lower correlation with stocks and bonds gives it greater diversification benefit than mortgages in a mixed-asset portfolio that is long in bonds. On the other hand, mortgages are more useful than property for implementing immunization-oriented strategies such as maturity matching of assets and liabilities.

19.4. Interpret the *modified duration* number one obtains for a noncallable mortgage. What does it mean? How is it used? What is its relevance to asset selection and portfolio construction for financial institutions, in terms of the measurement and management of interest rate risk?

19.5. Describe the bond investment strategy known as cash flow matching. Give an example.

19.6. What is meant by the term *preferred habitat*? How is it related to the duration of a bond investor's liabilities?

19.7. What is the yield curve, and what are the two principal considerations of bond market investors that underlie the curve?

19.8. Suppose the bond market expects short-term interest rates to remain constant for the foreseeable future, yet we observe a rising yield curve in the bond market. What can you then say about the preferred habitats of borrowers versus lenders? What is the name for this theory to explain the typical upward-sloping shape of the yield curve?

19.9. Describe the typical macroeconomic current environment and future expectations associated with the following shapes of the yield curve: (a) steeply upward-sloping, (b) slightly upward-sloping, (c) shallow-inverted or flat, (d) steeply inverted.

19.10. What is a maturity gap? Why is this problem particularly acute in deposit-taking lending institutions that originate fixed rate mortgage loans? What does this mean for the types of real estate lending these institutions tend to specialize in?

19.11. How does *mortgage securitization* create opportunities for deposit-taking financial institutions to hedge interest rate risk without restricting the menu of choices available to borrowers?

19.12. What is a portfolio lender? What types of financial institutions are typically portfolio lenders for permanent commercial mortgages in the United States? What is it about the maturity of such institutions' liabilities that makes them natural candidates for this role?

19.13. What is the difference between trading-oriented and immunization-oriented strategies for managing fixed-income investments? What is the major type of risk trading-oriented strategies are exposed to? What is the major type of risk immunization-oriented strategies are exposed to if the liabilities are adjusted to inflation?

19.14. How do you think a bond portfolio manager might adjust the duration of her portfolio if she expects interest rates to increase?

19.15. What are the fundamental factors affecting the level of mortgage interest rates? Describe the six components of mortgage market contractual yields in the "stack" in Exhibit 19-8, as they relate to both adjustable and fixed rate loans. Discuss what different historical economic events and environment may have explained the difference between 1993, the late 1990s, and 2005 in each component of the stack as indicated in Exhibit 19-9.

19.16. Comment on the following statement: A borrower would be crazy to take out a long-term CPM (or FRM) during a period characterized by a steep yield curve. The large spread between FRM and ARM rates means that an ARM is a much better deal.

19.17. It is typically the case that interest rates on FRMs exceed those on ARMs. In what sense does this spread represent the cost of interest rate risk insurance from the borrower's perspective? How is the idea of FRMs as a means of hedging interest rate risk for borrowers consistent with the liquidity premium hypothesis explanation of the shape of the yield curve?

19.18. Why are ex post mortgage returns so much more volatile than ex ante expectations, as suggested in Exhibits 19-10 and 19-11?

19.19. What were the major statistical characteristics of ex post mortgage returns as represented by the GLCMPI during the last three decades of the twentieth century? Compare mortgages to private property equity, stocks, and bonds in regard to average ex post return and volatility.

19.20. What are the implications of the correlation statistics shown in Exhibit 19-13 regarding the role of mortgages, as compared to property equity, in a mixed-asset (stock and bond) portfolio? (Hint: Think about diversification potential and inflation risk.)

19.21. Discuss the following statement: There is some theoretical reason to believe, and some historical evidence to support, the hypothesis that long-term fixed rate mortgages often do not provide positive leverage in the total return to equity investment in institutional quality commercial property. (Hint: Describe the theory and the historical evidence, but also point out countervailing considerations and evidence that goes against the hypothesis.)

Quantitative Problems

19.22. What is the Macaulay duration of an eight-year, 10%, interest-only mortgage with annual payments occurring at the ends of the years? What is the modified duration of this same mortgage?

19.23. What are the Macaulay and modified durations of an eight-year, 10%, interest-only, monthly-payment mortgage?

19.24. Suppose market interest rates decline from 10% to 9%. What would the modified duration predict would be the percentage increase in value of the monthly-payment loan in Problem 19.25? What would be this loan's actual percentage increase in value?

19.25. Suppose a certain lending institution's assets have an average duration of five years and its deposits have an average duration of one-and-a-half years. Assume also that the market value of its equity is 5% of that of its assets. What is the approximate duration of the institution's equity?

19.26. Suppose half of a pension fund's liabilities have a duration of 15 years and half have a duration of five years. If the institution wants to immunize its net asset portfolio, what should be the average duration of its bond and mortgage investments?

*19.27. (**Forward Rates**) Assume there is no preferred habitat so that the expectations hypothesis is the only explanation for the shape of the yield curve. Suppose the yield on zero-coupon bonds maturing at the end of five years is 6.5% and the yield of zero-coupon bonds maturing at the end of four years is 6.25%. What is the bond market's implied expected short-term (one-year) interest rate, termed a "forward rate," four years in the future (that is, the one-year rate that is expected to prevail from the end of year 4 to the end of year 5)?

*19.28. (**Forward Rates as Estimates of ARM Index Values**) An investor who is a strong believer in the expectations theory of interest rates is considering financing a property acquisition with an adjustable rate mortgage having annual interest adjustments indexed to the one-year Treasury. She obtains the following *spot* yields on zero coupon U.S. Treasury securities:

Maturity	Yield
1 year	4.00%
2 year	4.95%
3 year	5.75%
4 year	6.33%

a. What are the "market's" implied forecasts of the one-year Treasury yield (estimated ARM index value) in Years 2, 3, and 4?

b. Now assume that liquidity preference plays a role in explaining the upward shape of the yield curve. Do your answers in part (a) overstate or understate the "true" estimated one-year Treasury yields? Explain.

CHAPTER

20

COMMERCIAL MORTGAGE-BACKED SECURITIES

CHAPTER OUTLINE

LEARNING OBJECTIVES

After reading this chapter, you should understand:

⊃ The basic outlines of the U.S. CMBS industry, including the typical structure of CMBS products and the role played by rating agencies.

⊃ What is meant by tranching, and how this is used to concentrate and stratify the default risk in CMBS.

⊃ What determines the market yields of CMBS, and why these yields have varied over time.

⊃ Some important considerations in the industry, such as moral hazard and adverse selection.

One of the most important and exciting developments in real estate finance during the 1990s was the emergence of a large and active secondary market for commercial mortgages, first in the United States and then, in the early 2000s, in Europe and Asia. The term Commercial Mortgage-Backed Securities (CMBS) refers to commercial mortgages that are pooled together and sold to investors, a type of process known as **securitization**. Many of these investors are in the bond market and, while not particularly looking to put their money into real estate, they are simply seeking a relatively safe and predictable stream of income from their investment. During the 1990s and until 2008 CMBS provided a relatively new and, in many respects, more efficient source of debt capital for real estate. This helped improve the liquidity and transparency of commercial real estate, as well as the integration of real estate with broader capital markets. CMBS also offered investors in the bond market a variety of new securities that could serve different types of investment needs and concerns.

CMBS products and the industry that produces and services them are inherently complex, and they became more so as the industry evolved, until the industry was decimated in the financial crisis of 2008–2009. As of the time of writing this edition, it is not clear exactly what the future of the industry will be, how large a role it will play, and exactly what the securities and the practices in the industry (and its regulation) will look like. But we think it likely that the industry will rise again, for it has the capability to bring unique advantages to real estate and to the capital markets. If the industry does not recover, then the lessons of its downfall will be all the more important to learn. In either case, it is worthwhile to dedicate a chapter of this book to CMBS. Our aim will be to introduce you to the basics of what CMBS are and how they work, as well as to provide you with some perspective on the history and lessons of this fascinating creature of the American financial industry.

20.1 What Are CMBS?

Commercial mortgage-backed securities (CMBS) are bonds backed by pools of commercial mortgages. CMBS securities provide claims to components of the cash flow coming from the underlying mortgages as the borrowers pay their interest and principal obligations. Exhibit 20-1 illustrates the commercial mortgage securitization process. Mortgage loans on individual commercial properties originated by lenders in the primary market are pooled together, usually by an investment banking firm, and transferred to a trust.[1] The trust then issues and sells a number of classes of bonds to investors to complete the securitization of relatively illiquid mortgage loans into securities, most of which can be relatively liquid (similar to the corporate bond market). The different classes of securities are known as **tranches** (*tranche* is French for "slice"). Each tranche is characterized by its priority of claim on the mortgage pool's cash flows and/or by the type of cash flows it has claim to (such as interest or principal payments). Bond rating agencies assign a credit quality rating to each bond class, varying from the highest-quality, low-risk investment grade (AAA at the first "spigot" in the "pipe" in the bottom right of Exhibit 20-1) down to low-quality, high-risk tranches rated well below investment grade (further down the pipe) or not rated at all (not shown in Exhibit 20-1).

The basic concept behind CMBS is the redistribution or reallocation of risk as well as of cash flow timing or maturity. Many securities backed by the pool of mortgage loans in a CMBS issue have higher credit quality than that of the mortgage loans in the pool, while other bonds in the CMBS issue are lower rated and are much more risky than the underlying loans. As we will see, this "**unbundling**" or "**partitioning**" of mortgage credit risk creates different securities that better match the needs of specific investor groups or clienteles, and this process creates value. We will delve deeper into this with a numerical example later in the chapter. For now you should recognize that, while the essential rationale for CMBS is the creation of value, competition in the marketplace nevertheless insures that in general no party is "getting something for nothing," in the sense that there remains the usual capital market trade-off between expected return and risk. The higher-rated CMBS bonds have lower risk because of their senior claims on the pool cash flow but they also carry lower interest coupons (see Chapters 16–19 for mortgage and bond terminology) and sell for high prices. The lower-rated bonds carry higher coupons and/or sell at a discount providing higher expected returns but also carry much greater risk of default and credit losses as these tranches are effectively *levered*, the more so the lower down they are in the "waterfall" or "cascade" (farther down the pipe in the lower right of Exhibit 20-1).

CMBS provide a vehicle by which investors in the bond (or so-called "fixed-income") market supply capital indirectly to mortgage borrowers. As with any security, CMBS are issued in relatively small, homogeneous units so as to facilitate trading by a large potential population of

---

[1]This is the structure that dominated in the 1990s and 2000s, and may well do so again. Typically, the trust elects to be a "REMIC" or real estate mortgage investment conduit, which is a pass-through entity that does not pay federal income tax. To qualify as a REMIC, the trust must comply with specific IRS rules governing REMICs designed to make it a passive investment vehicle with limited flexibility to modify the loan collateral in the trust unless a loan is in or near default. These rules have important implications for borrowers choosing between CMBS loans and whole loans originated by portfolio lenders. Other structures are possible, and may evolve in the future. For example, "covered bonds" can be issued by the sponsoring investment bank, instead of through a separate special-purpose trust as was the 1990s–2000s paradigm.

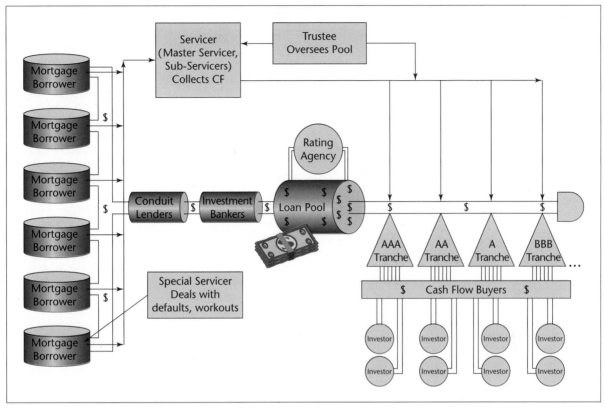

EXHIBIT 20-1 CMBS Securitization Process
© OnCourse Learning

investors. This population may include investors who do not wish (or are unable) to invest large sums of money in any given security, and/or it may include investors who have no particular expertise in real estate. This opens up the real estate market to *passive* investors who do not want to be involved in the management or operation of real estate assets; indeed, investors who ideally don't want to even have to worry about real estate market risks. Many such higher-rated CMBS are traded in relatively liquid public exchanges as part of the bond market. As is common with bonds, the market for a given individual security is likely to be rather thin, but the similarity within classes of securities is great enough to allow relatively efficient price discovery and resulting high levels of liquidity in the market.

Other CMBS tranches are privately placed initially and only traded privately thereafter, if at all, which may make them no more liquid (or even less liquid) than privately held whole loans.[2] Yet it is the very riskiness of some of these lower-rated securities that makes them attractive to certain investors with particular expertise in commercial real estate. Not only do the lower tranches carry higher coupons, but the credit risk in CMBS largely reflects commercial real estate market risk. This is exactly the type of risk in which certain investors have specialized expertise, making these securities a good fit for their portfolios. Of course, having expertise does not guarantee that one will never suffer losses.

---

[2]A famous (or should we say "infamous") exception was the development of "collateralized debt obligations" – CDOs – during the height of the boom in 2006–07, when lower-rated CMBS were re-securitized into a second (or even third) layer of pooling and tranching and securities issuance. This process proved disastrous in the financial crisis of 2008-09, as we will describe later in this chapter. It should also be noted that as the CMBS industry first began to recover after the financial crisis, during 2010–11, almost all of the CMBS deals were privately placed (including the top tranches) rather than the public offerings that had previously dominated the industry.

20.1.1 A Brief History of the CMBS Industry

The modern CMBS market got its start in the United States in the early 1990s.[3] As part of the Financial Institutions Reform, Recovery and Enforcement Act of 1989 (FIRREA), Congress established the Resolution Trust Corporation. The RTC was a federal government corporation established to liquidate the loan portfolios of thrifts and banks that had failed in the commercial property crash at the end of the 1980s. The RTC was faced with the task of selling large quantities of commercial mortgages (many of them nonperforming) very quickly. Traditional private sources of investment in commercial real estate debt were effectively unavailable at that time. These traditional institutions, such as commercial banks, life insurance companies, and pension funds, had just been "burned" in the crash. On the other hand, Wall Street was thriving and had spent the 1970s and 1980s cutting its teeth on residential MBS (RMBS), developing various procedures (in effect, a "technology") useful for securitizing large pools of mortgages. Key players and investors in the public capital markets perceived in the early 1990s that the commercial property market had overshot and fallen too far in the crash, relative to fundamental value. They also saw that the RTC was under great political pressure to sell assets quickly. These "grave-dancers" and bargain-hunters helped the RTC to give birth to a new industry—CMBS.

The key to this birth was the development by the traditional bond-rating agencies of the ability to rate the default risk of CMBS tranches. This was a particular innovation that had to be made for commercial mortgage securitization as distinguished from the residential mortgage securitization that had already been developed in the 1980s. At that time RMBS were based almost entirely on GSE-sponsored pools that provided mortgage insurance and pool-level insurance to effectively eliminate credit risk in the RMBS products of that day. Bond credit rating agencies had never before attempted to rate so-called "structured finance" products, that is, securities whose credit quality depended on a pool consisting of a multitude of individual underlying loans with many different individual borrowers and collateralized by many different underlying physical assets, and where furthermore the securities were stratified according to the tranching ("waterfall") system described in the previous section that results in varying degrees of leverage for all but the top tranche.

Never before had such a complex type of credit risk structure been rated by the bond agencies, and indeed, these agencies did not even have much experience with real estate markets at all as distinct from corporate and municipal sources of risk. It took some time for the rating agencies to gain confidence in their methods, and (more to the point) for the bond market to accept the validity of the ratings. So, at first, the ratings and the criteria for CMBS obtaining a high rating were quite conservative compared to what they would later become, and at first CMBS bonds were priced at a bit of discount, providing a return premium to investors compared to otherwise similar, and similarly rated, corporate bonds.[4]

But the eventual success of the rating process was crucial to the viability of the CMBS industry. As noted, many of the types of investors that are necessary to make a liquid public market function effectively are necessarily passive, particularly in the case of the bond market. Such investors lack the time, resources, and expertise to become involved in the risk assessment and management of either individual mortgages or pools of mortgages. When a CMBS tranche obtained a bond rating, investors who knew little or nothing about commercial real

---

[3]This was not the first major episode of commercial real estate in the U.S. bond market. A flourishing industry of commercial real estate bonds developed in the 1920s, only to crash and wither with the financial and economic turmoil of the 1930s. A fascinating review of the 1920s CRE bond industry and its performance and comparison to the modern CMBS industry is in Wiggers and Ashcraft (2012). They report that CRE bonds accounted for approximately 12% of all commercial property debt by the late 1920s.

[4]It is not clear that rating the credit risk of CMBS is inherently and necessarily more difficult than rating that of typical publicly traded corporations' bonds. After all, real estate assets are relatively simple and transparent physical assets that generally trade directly in a well functioning market, which helps to provide valuations for those assets. The typical individual corporation is generally more complex, dynamic, and management intensive, than the typical commercial property. But the bond rating agencies long history of rating corporate debt (since the early twentieth century) has given them time to build a substantial expertise, and has given the bond market time to gain a familiarity and confidence about the corporate bond rating process. Nevertheless, structured debt securities do pose unique and complicated ratings challenges. See White (2010).

estate felt comfortable working under the assumption that the default risk of that tranche was very similar to the default risk of any other bond with the same rating. This vastly expanded the pool of potential investors indirectly available for commercial real estate and thereby made the public market for CMBS viable.

20.1.2 Magnitude of the CMBS Industry and Its "Rise and Fall" (and Rebirth?)

The circumstances just described led to a very rapid development of the CMBS industry in the United States in the 1990s and, after some brief hiccups in the late 1990s and early 2000s, to even stronger growth culminating in a huge spurt in 2005–07. Then the new-issue CMBS industry collapsed in the financial crisis of 2008–2009. Currently there has been some recovery in the industry during 2010–2012, but it has been sporadic and incomplete, far below the earlier levels, and characterized by private placements of narrower, simpler products that attempt in various ways to address the problems that manifested themselves during the financial crisis and the property market crash. In the decade of the early 2010s the industry speaks in hopeful terms about a "version 2.0" of CMBS, but some claim we have at this point no more than a "version 1.5" and that may not be enough of an advance. In its heyday the CMBS industry played a large and important role in commercial property finance; CMBS provided such a seemingly useful "win-win" value-add proposition in allocating risk more efficiently that it seems likely the industry will figure a way to rebuild.

Exhibit 20-2 quantifies this history, showing the dollar value of CMBS bonds issued each year from 1990. It is apparent that the CMBS market really took off once the RTC finished its job of liquidating troubled loans and the Wall Street conduit model took over. (**Conduit loans** are mortgages issued with the intent of being securitized into CMBS pools; they became the bulk of the flow of capital and specialized in smaller loans that really brought "Wall Street" to "Main Street" by financing medium-sized commercial properties typically as small as $2.5 million.) There were pauses in CMBS growth in response to major negative shocks,

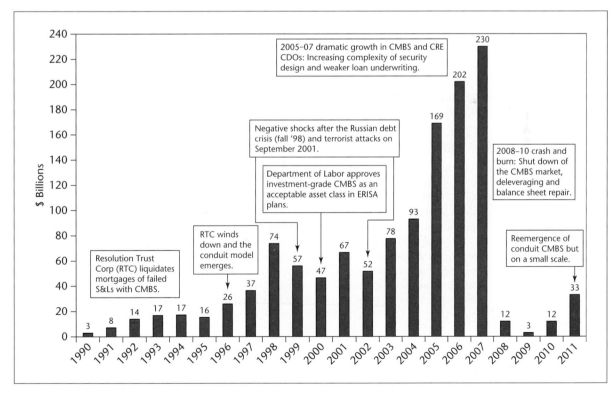

EXHIBIT 20-2 CMBS Issuance, U.S., 1990–2011

Source: Based on data from Commercial Mortgage Alert and Clodfelter (2005).

including the Russian debt crisis of 1998, the terrorist attacks in 2001, and the dot.com bust and ensuing recession. But the CMBS sector bounced back quickly after each of those, though not without some further developments and innovations (which will be noted later).[5] By the mid-2000s CMBS conduit lending had supplanted life insurance companies as the major source of long-term debt capital in the institutional property market. During the three peak years of 2005–2007, the net balance outstanding of CMBS loans grew by $345 billion in the United States, compared to less than $50 billion for life insurance companies. But from 2008 through the middle of 2011, CMBS loans net balances outstanding shrank by $117 billion, representing a net pullout of capital or a negative capital flow. Over the same period, the balance of loans held by life insurance companies shrank by only $15 billion. As of 2011, whole-loan portfolio lenders led by life insurance companies are able to outcompete CMBS in the United States, just the opposite of the situation in the mid-2000s.

20.2 CMBS Structure: Pooling, Tranching, and Subordination

We now turn to how CMBS work and, in particular, how value is created by **tranching** in the securitization process. The fundamental idea is that the different classes or tranches of bonds backed by a mortgage pool should be worth more as securities than the aggregate value of the mortgages in the pool as individual "whole loans." The whole has to be worth more than the sum of the parts, in general. This allows mortgages originated by CMBS conduits to be competitively priced and, therefore, attractive to borrowers on this dimension, and it allows the CMBS industry itself to make sufficient profit. The tranching of cash flow claim priority involves two primary dimensions: credit losses and loan retirement (or maturity). The former relates to the default risk in the securities; the latter relates to the securities' duration and interest-rate risk. (See Chapters 18 and 19 for an introduction to these two types of risk.) In CMBS the default-risk dimension is the more challenging, in part because most commercial mortgages have either lockout provisions that prohibit prepayment or significant prepayment penalties or "defeasance" provisions that mitigate or even eliminate prepayment risk. (See the boxed feature "Call Protection in CMBS Bonds: Defeasance" on page 491.) In addition to tranches prioritized by credit and maturity considerations, it is often the case that mortgage interest and principal cash flow components may be stripped from each other and assigned differently to the various classes, resulting in features in some securities that appeal to particular niches of investors. The best way to understand how tranching works is to consider a simplified numerical example.

20.2.1 A Simplified Numerical Example of Tranching

Consider a pool consisting of ten commercial mortgages, each with $10 million par value (that is, outstanding loan balance, or OLB) and a 10 percent coupon (contract) interest rate. (The "coupon" refers to the contract interest rate.) All ten mortgages are interest-only balloon loans with annual interest payments at the end of the year. All of the mortgages are nonrecourse, with lockouts preventing prepayment. Suppose further that five of the loans mature in exactly one year and the other five in exactly two years. Thus, the underlying pool is characterized by a total par value of $100 million, with a **weighted average maturity (WAM)** of 1.5 years and a **weighted average coupon (WAC)** of 10 percent.[6] Finally, suppose that the total value of all the properties collateralizing the pool loans is $142.857 million. Thus, the pool has a par value LTV ratio of $100 million divided by $142.857 million, or 70 percent. Now suppose that three tranches (classes) of CMBS securities are carved out of this pool and sold

---

[5]The reader may also wish to review the overall history of the U.S. commercial mortgage market presented in the introduction to Chapter 16, including the exhibits in that section which quantify the relative role of CMBS in the overall commercial property debt capital picture.

[6]In this simple example, all the loans are of equal value, so the "weights" are equal. More generally, the weighting is computed proportional to the par values, which typically vary across the loans in the pool.

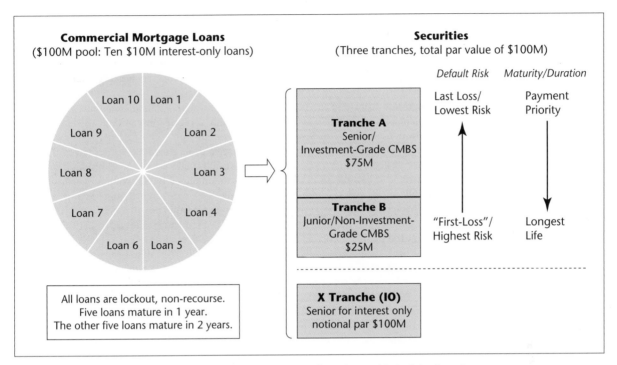

EXHIBIT 20-3 CMBS Mortgage Securitization Basics: Numerical Example of Tranching and Senior/Subordinate Structure
© OnCourse Learning

into the bond market, as shown in Exhibit 20-3, two tranches with claim to both interest and principal, and one interest-only class.

The first tranche is a senior class of securities we will call tranche A (or class A). This tranche has $75 million of the par value in the pool, or three-quarters of the total. (But note that this assignment of par value to the securities in the tranche does *not* imply that any particular mortgages are assigned to these securities, as the cash flow from *all* ten mortgages is first pooled and then the undifferentiated pooled cash is assigned to the securities.) Class A is, therefore, said to have credit support or subordination of 25 percent. This means that when (or if) any loans in the pool default and suffer loss in value, the total losses would have to exceed 25 percent of the entire par value in the pool, or $25 million, before the A tranche would lose any of its par value. The greater the degree of credit support for a tranche is, the less its default risk. In this case, as the pool LTV ratio is 70 percent, we can think of the property value underlying the mortgage pool as having to lose 47.5 percent of its value $(1 - [1 - 0.25] [0.70])$ before the value of the collateral underlying tranche A would be less than that tranche's par value. As tranche A is the safest $75 million of the pool par value (the top tranche), the underlying property value would have to fall to 52.5 percent of its initial value ($75M/$142.857M) before the A tranche would be underwater, that is, having less collateral value than its par value.[7] Since this tranche is the most senior one in the pool, this means that it has default risk similar to a mortgage with a 52.5 percent LTV ratio, which would be a very conservative mortgage. The most senior class of securities in a CMBS issue is the only class without "loan leverage," in that it cannot be wiped out unless or until the entire underlying mortgage pool is wiped out.

Another feature of this CMBS structure is that whenever a loan in the pool matures and pays down any principal balance, such principal repayment cash flow goes first entirely to tranche A and retires a corresponding amount of the tranche A par value. Thus, tranche A will be the first tranche to be retired. This gives class A the shortest weighted average

---

[7]In real world CMBS, most of the loans in the pool typically amortize, so the total par value in the pool is always gradually declining, paying off the most senior tranches first, then lower down the waterfall in order.

maturity and therefore the lowest interest-rate risk of all the securities issued from the pool. For example, tranche A's WAM is 1.33 years, while the overall pool average WAM is 1.5 years.[8] This type of payment structure, in which the most senior tranche is retired before subordinate tranches begin to receive principal payments, is termed a **waterfall** sequence. Waterfalls can also apply to other types of impacts on cash claims, such as credit losses in the mortgage pool, as we shall see shortly.

An important feature of the principal retirement waterfall is that over time, amortization and retirement of loan balances in the pool generally increases the amount of subordination (credit protection) in the CMBS structure. For example, after the first five loans pay off at their maturity at the end of year 1 in our illustrative deal, class A will then have 50 percent subordination instead of just 25 percent, as there will remain a total of $50 million of underlying pool principal balance and class A will still be protected by $25 million worth of subordination. Indeed, in cases where the underlying loans are amortizing (paying off some principal each period as well as interest), this increases the security of the CMBS in two ways. First, the LTVs in the underlying loans is reduced, making them safer. Second, the subordination in the pool is increased (as described in the preceding example).

Getting back to our illustrative example, the second class of securities issued from our underlying mortgage pool is assigned claim to the remaining $25 million of par value in the pool. This is a junior (or subordinate) class which we will call tranche B. In our simple example, tranche B is also what is called the **first-loss tranche** (or "B-piece"), because it bears the first and greatest exposure to credit losses due to defaults in the pool. Credit losses due to defaults in any of the mortgages in the pool are assigned to tranche B as long as tranche B still has some par value left that can be written down. While some mortgage defaults only result in lost or delayed interest payments, most defaults ultimately result in a loss of at least some if not all of the remaining principal owed on the loan. (Interest owed generally has priority over principal in the assignment of cash received, so ultimately losses tend to get assigned to principal, although not necessarily right away.) Any principal (loan balance or loan par value) that is written off is assigned to tranche B, meaning that the losses are subtracted from the par value of tranche B, thereby proportionately reducing its claim on subsequent interest cash flow. Only after the par value of tranche B is completely wiped out by mortgage principal write-offs will subsequent additional credit losses be assigned to the more senior tranche A.

At first glance, it might seem that our B tranche has about the same default risk as a 70 percent LTV mortgage, as that is the LTV ratio of the pool. But in fact the B tranche has much greater default risk than a 70 percent LTV whole loan. Referring to our terminology of Chapter 18, class B has about the same default *probability* as a 70 percent LTV loan, but it has much greater conditional *loss severity* in the event of default. In general, CMBS classes that are not the most senior in the issue have greater default risk than that of a whole loan with the same LTV ratio. Think of it like this: The B tranche is providing credit support for the A tranche, and it valiantly performs this role by potentially sacrificing itself. Suppose for example a $70 million mortgage is issued on a $100 million property; the loan subsequently defaults and only $50 million is recovered. The mortgage loses $20 million of its $70 million principal (par) value, or about 28.6 percent of its value. On the other hand, if our $100 million pool of loans loses $50 million of its par value due to loan defaults, then this would be more than sufficient to completely wipe out the B tranche.[9] This is what is meant when peo-

---

[8]The class A WAM of 1.33 years is computed as follows. The $100 million pool has $50 million of par value with a maturity of one year. As class A's par value exceeds that amount and class A is first in line to receive principal payments, $50 million of class A's $75 million par value has maturity of one year. The remaining $25 million of class A's par value will be paid off at the end of two years when the rest of the mortgage loans in the pool come due. Thus, of class A's $75 million of par value, $50 million or two-thirds of it has a maturity of one year, and $25 million or one-third of it has a maturity of two years, for a weighted average maturity of 1.33 years calculated as $(2/3) \times 1 + (1/3) \times 2 = 1.33$.

[9]Using the terminology of Chapter 18, tranche B faces about the same unconditional default probability as a 70% LTV loan, but it faces much greater conditional loss severity. Recall that the ex ante (or unconditional) yield degradation (the expected loss in yield due to default) equals, essentially, the unconditional default probability times the conditional loss severity. Another way to see this is to realize that tranche B in our example faces a default risk similar to a second mortgage equal to 17.5% of the value of a collateral property that also secures a first mortgage in the amount of 52.5% of property value.

ple refer to securities like those of tranche B as representing **levered debt**. The default risk is greater (possibly *much* greater) than that of a debt investment whose LTV ratio equals that of the underlying pool average LTV minus the amount of subordination protecting the security class. Investors need to be very careful about judging the amount of risk in levered debt securities, and bond credit rating agencies face difficult challenges in trying to quantify with precision exactly how much default risk is in such securities compared to other less complex debt securities.[10]

Not only is the first-loss tranche at the front of the line to get hit with defaults, but with the sequential-pay waterfall structure, it is also last in line to be retired at par value. Whenever loan balances are paid down or paid off by amortization or maturity of the loans, the cash receipts of principal are used to retire more senior tranches. Only after these are all retired will the first-loss tranche be entitled to receive payments of loan balances. Thus, the first-loss tranche not only carries the greatest default risk, but also the longest maturity and, therefore, the most interest rate risk. In our example, the WAM of the B tranche is two years, whereas the pool WAM is, as you recall, only 1.5 years.

Up to now, we have created a simple two-tranche security structure that highlights the fundamental point of CMBS, namely, the reallocation of risk and duration in the underlying mortgage pool among the different bond classes. The credit quality of the senior tranche is enhanced because the junior or subordinated class assumes a greater risk of loss.[11] Also, the senior tranche will be paid off sooner, giving it a shorter maturity or expected duration, which implies less interest rate risk and normally a lower yield in the bond market (assuming a typical upward-sloping yield curve, as described in Chapter 19). Since the senior bonds have higher credit quality than the average quality of mortgages in the CMBS pool, these bonds would sell at a price above par value (i.e., at premium) if the coupon rate on the class A bonds was set equal to the weighted average coupon (WAC) of the mortgages in the pool (i.e., all mortgage interest was simply passed through to tranche A and B bondholders). This would be because investors' required return (yield to maturity) for tranche A would be less than the coupon rate. Instead, the typical practice is to sell the senior bonds at par by setting their coupon rate lower than the WAC of the mortgages. This causes there to be "extra" interest left over in the pool—interest not assigned to the coupon rate of any par-valued class of securities. This "extra" interest can be "stripped" off (in our example, from tranche A) and sold as a separate security. This leads us to the third and final class to be carved out of our simple example mortgage pool.

---

[10]For example, suppose the underlying mortgage pool weighted average LTV ratio is 70%, and a particular class of subordinated securities has 10% subordination, meaning that 10% of the pool par value would have to be written off before any of the par value of this class is lost. You might quantify the LTV ratio of the subject class as 63%, equal to 70% minus 10% of 70% (that is: $63\% = (1 - 0.1) \times 70\%$), because the underlying property collateral value backing the mortgages would have to drop to 63% of its starting value before our subject class would be underwater. But as described above, unless this class of securities is the top (most senior) class in the CMBS issue, it will face greater loss severity and greater expected credit losses than a 63% LTV first-lien mortgage whole loan on similar property collateral. The extent of this "leverage" depends on the "thickness" of the tranche, how much more senior par value of classes of the CMBS issue is being "protected" by our 10% subordination tranche. For example, suppose the next more senior tranche had 14% subordination, giving it a nominal LTV ratio of $60\% = (1 - 0.14) \times 70\%$. Then underlying property value losses of 40% would completely wipe out the collateral protection for our levered tranche with its 10% subordination. Our 10% subordination class in this instance has 4% "thickness" in the pool, or 3% thickness in the underlying property collateral. The difference between 37% loss and 40% loss in the underlying property value could make all the difference in the world to our subject 10% subordination class of securities. And that 3% property value difference is a pretty small difference to try to analyze or predict with much precision in the commercial property market. Thus, thinness of classes makes credit risk analysis more difficult and less precise. In a similar vein, simply creating a more senior class will add to the default risk of all other classes even holding their subordination levels constant. For example, in our illustrative deal, if we created a "super-senior" A+ class with $50 million of par value, senior to our class A, then even though our class A would still have its 25% subordination, it would now be more risky, because it is "thinner" and it now protects the super-senior class that has 50% subordination. The creation of the super-senior class has not changed the default probability of the A class, but it has increased the conditional loss severity of that class. To retain the same credit rating, in principle our class A would now require more than 25% subordination.

[11]You may be wondering how the 25% subordination level was determined. This "line" is drawn by the CMBS bond rating agencies, and will be discussed further later in the chapter.

This last class of securities is labeled "class X" in our example, and it is an "interest-only" (or "IO") class. Such IO "strips" often are particularly appealing to certain niches of investors.[12] In our example CMBS, class X is assigned a par value equal to the entire underlying mortgage pool par value of $100 million. However, this is a "notional" par value for the IO securities, because class X actually has no claim on any principal payments made into the pool. Class X only has claim to interest payments. In our example, class X is assigned a coupon rate that varies across the two years of remaining life in the pool. Class X's coupon rate for the first year is 1.5 percent, and this is applied to the $100 million par value as of the first year. This gives class X a high priority claim (we'll say in our example class X has a claim on interest that is equal in seniority to that of class A) on $1.5 million of interest cash flow in the mortgage pool in the first year. For the second year class X's coupon rate drops to 1.0 percent, and this would be applied to the $50 million of par value that remains in the pool in the second year, giving class X a senior claim on $500,000 of interest cash flow that year.

20.2.2 Allocating the Credit Losses

To make sure you understand how the tranching and waterfall in our simple CMBS example works, let's carry the example forward in time. Suppose that all of the loans perform according to contract in the first year, but in the second year one of the remaining five loans defaults on its $1 million interest payment. The loan is sold or property is taken in foreclosure recovering net proceeds of $5 million. Thus, the pool is short $6 million of contractual cash flow in year 2, including $1 million of interest and $5 million of principal. Exhibit 20-4 shows how the ex post cash flows received compare in this case to the contract cash flows that had been scheduled for each tranche.

The $5 million recovered would be assigned first to interest owed on the loan (this is according to the normal priority in assignment of loan payments, first to interest owed then to principal). Thus, of the $5 million recovered on the bad loan, $1 million would be assigned to interest, leaving the pool "whole" in terms of interest cash flow with a total of $5 million in interest for the pool in year 2. The entire $6 million loss on the bad loan is then assigned to (taken out of) the par value of the lowest priority class, namely in this case tranche B. However, class B's par value is docked only after it is paid its owed coupon interest, since there is sufficient interest cash flow in the pool to do that. Thus, tranche B receives $2.5 million in interest (10 percent coupon on its going-in par value of $25 million) plus $19 million principal (after the $6 million write-down of its par value), thereby extinguishing the class after $21.5 million total cash flow to it in year 2 (versus the $27.5 million that class had been scheduled to receive). Investors in class A and class X (the IO tranche) bonds are unaffected by the default of the loan in the pool.

Clearly investors in the more junior tranche B bonds face considerably more risk than do investors in the senior tranches A and X bonds and, therefore, have a nontrivial probability of realizing a yield on investment that is significantly less than that expected based on the contract cash flows to maturity.[13] The relative risks, of course, directly impact the

---

[12]For example, there may be demand for CMBS IO tranches from banks and other financial institutions with short-term, variable rate liabilities. Such institutions may find IOs to be of value in matching the duration of assets and liabilities. IO securities lack the balloon payments of the par-value tranches, which can give them relatively short maturities.

[13]Note that, while the class X interest-only bondholders are unaffected by the default in this example because the total cash flow assigned to interest in the pool remained as scheduled, this would not necessarily always be the case. For example, in a longer-lived and more complex CMBS issue, as loans in the underlying pool default and are therefore extinguished early, the total amount of interest cash flow available in the pool will drop below what had been scheduled, and some of this loss may fall to the IO classes even if they have relatively high priority in the waterfall for interest cash flow. There are two separate waterfalls, one for interest and another for principal cash flow in the pool. Over time, credit losses may penetrate higher up the interest waterfall than up the principal waterfall in some cases, and the result can be that coupon payments owed on certain bonds may take a hit even though their par values have not been written down. The IO class, with no par value at all, is uniquely exposed because, even if it has high priority for whatever interest cash flow is in the pool, that cash flow will be reduced as loans are written off. While cash recoveries from any given mortgage may be assigned first to interest owed on *that* particular mortgage, that does not necessarily mean that other interest shortfall elsewhere in the pool caused by the previous write-down of other bad loans can be covered in this way.

CALL PROTECTION IN CMBS BONDS: DEFEASANCE

In residential MBS a big issue has generally been prepayment risk, the possibility of bonds paying off sooner than initially expected, as homeowners refinance mortgages when interest rates fall. But unlike residential mortgages, most commercial mortgage loan contracts contain covenants that restrict the borrower's ability to prepay. It is common to have outright (or "hard") **lockout** that prohibits prepayment over the early life of the loan. Historically, prepayment was often then permitted, but with a **penalty** to be paid to the lender. Penalties were either a **fixed percent of the remaining mortgage loan balance**, with the percent declining each year after lockout, or a **yield maintenance (YM)** charge equal to the present value of lost interest if the market rate was below the contract rate, making the lender "whole" in the sense of compensating for lost yield due to the early loan retirement. With YM, the present value of foregone loan payments would be calculated using a discount rate equal to the yield on a similar maturity Treasury plus a spread. The YM premium is the difference between this present value and the outstanding loan balance (OLB). The YM charge was conceptually straightforward but tended to be somewhat confusing in practice as different lenders used various "spreads" to discount future mortgage cash flows.

Prepayment represents a problem for CMBS since it results in the removal of loan collateral from the trust. This complicates the timing and nature of payments to bondholders, potentially impacts credit ratings of the tranches, and may affect the tax status of the trust. As a result, most conduit loans, which are designed from the outset to go into CMBS pools, came to not permit prepayment at all, as such. Instead, borrowers are given the option to "**defease**" future loan payments by replacing their loan with a portfolio of Treasury or agency securities, the cash flows of which replicate what the future cash flows of the mortgage would have been.* Defeasance became the dominant form of call protection in the CMBS world—typically permitted after a two-year lockout according to REMIC rules. It is similar in many respects to yield maintenance except that it is not technically prepayment, but a collateral substitution. From bond investors' perspective, the contract cash flows are unchanged and hence the bonds are completely call protected. Moreover, the pool collateral increases in credit quality (substituting Treasury securities for mortgages) which may in turn improve pricing of the CMBS. From the borrower's perspective, it provides the flexibility to exit the loan should that be optimal from a strategic or tactical perspective, such as to rebalance a portfolio or to access liquidity from growth in equity value.**

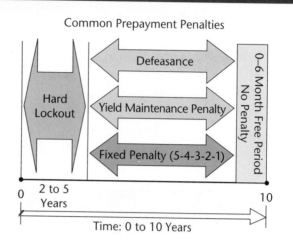

Common Prepayment Penalties

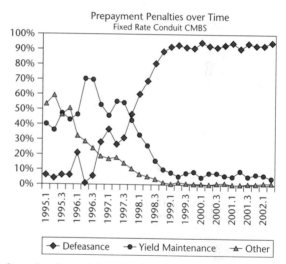

Prepayment Penalties over Time
Fixed Rate Conduit CMBS

Source: Bear Stearns & Co, reprinted by permission.

---

*M. Schonberger and D. Moliver, "Capital Markets: A Win-Win Solution," Urban Land, May 2002, provides a nice overview of the evolution of prepayment penalties and the emergence of defeasance to handle prepayment issues in CMBS.

**M. Dierker, D. Quan, and W. Torous (2005) suggested that prepayment of commercial mortgages was driven largely by the desire to access equity. They model defeasance as an option to exchange Treasuries in return for the underlying mortgage plus the liquidity benefits arising from accessing the accumulated equity in the property.

---

required returns and the expected yield degradation (as described in Chapters 18 and 19). This in turn affects the prices investors are willing to pay for the different classes of bonds, as reflected in the yields (the "YTMs," or yields to maturity) at which the bonds were sold. This is depicted in Exhibit 20-5, where it is presumed the bonds were issued at the end of "year 0."

EXHIBIT 20-4
Contract vs. Ex Post
(Realized) Cash Flows by
Tranche and Year
© OnCourse Learning

Class (Par $M, Coupon)	Cash Flow:	Year 1 Prin. + Int. = Total CF	Year 2 Prin. + Int. = Total CF
A (75, 8%)	Scheduled: Received:	50 + 6.0 = 56 50 + 6.0 = 56	25 + 2 = 27 25 + 2 = 27
B (25, 10%)	Scheduled: Received:	0 + 2.5 = 2.5 0 + 2.5 = 2.5	25 + 2.5 = 27.5 19 + 2.5 = 21.5
X (100, 1.5%, 1% yr 2)	Scheduled: Received:	0 + 1.5 = 1.5 0 + 1.5 = 1.5	0 + 0.5 = 0.5 0 + 0.5 = 0.5
Pool (100, 10%)	Scheduled: Received:	50 + 10.0 = 60 50 + 10.0 = 60	50 + 5 = 55 44 + 5 = 49

Class	Par Value	WAM	Credit Support	Coupon	YTM*	Realized Cash Flows			Realized (IRR)§
						Year 0†	Year 1	Year 2‡	
A	$75	1.33	25%	8%	8%	−$75.00	56.00	$27.00	8.00%
X (IO)	$100	1.25	NA	1.5%, 1%	8%	−1.82	1.50	0.50	8.00%
B	$25	2.00	0%	10%	12%	−$24.15	2.50	21.50	−0.34%
Pool	$100	1.50	NA	10%(WAC)	10%	−$100.97	60.00	49.00	5.44%
CMBS IRR	9.27%	<== Due to Added Value ==>					60.00	49.00	
Pool IRR	10.00%					−$100.00	60.00	49.00	6.16%

*YTM (yield to maturity) reflects pricing of bond classes as determined in the bond market at the time of the IPO.
†Year 0 cash flow is negative of initial market value as CMBS, proceeds from IPO (assumed Year 0). The value of each tranche is determined by taking the present value of contractual cash flows at the yield to maturity. For example, for tranche B,

$$Value = \frac{2.5}{1.12} + \frac{(25 + 2.5)}{1.12^2} = 24.15$$

‡Class B realized cash flow in Year 2 is $6.0 million less than contractual cash flow, due to credit losses.
§The realized yield is the IRR earned on the investment, ex post, assuming that investors paid "Value as CMBS" for each tranche. For tranche B investors,

$$24.15 = \frac{2.5}{1 + IRR} + \frac{19 + 2.5}{(1 + IRR)^2}, \Rightarrow IRR = -0.34\%$$

EXHIBIT 20-5 Summary of CMBS Example Bond Characteristics, Values, and Ex Post Realized Returns
© OnCourse Learning

20.2.3 Unbundling, Specialization, and Value Creation

The senior/subordinate structure, along with the stripping of excess mortgage interest in our example, creates three unique classes of securities that clearly differ in default risk and maturity and cash flow timing profile. This causes these securities to appeal to different types of investors. Recall that the basic principle of mortgage securitization is that the value of the securities sold to investors must be greater than the par value of the mortgage pool underlying the securities (i.e., there is value creation in the CMBS process[14]).

To see how this might work in our example, suppose that the 10 percent contract rate on the underlying mortgages happens to also be the current market interest rate for such loans.[15] Then it should certainly be possible to sell the class (tranche) A bonds at a yield

---

[14]This is really just another application of our NPV investment rule from Chapter 10.

[15]This would almost certainly be approximately true if the loans had all been recently issued, i.e., they were new (not "seasoned") loans. And this would typically be the case with conduit loans.

lower than 10 percent because of their default risk protection provided by the class B subordination (and probably also because of class A's shorter maturity).[16] For example, let us assume that tranche A bonds are issued with an 8 percent coupon rate and sell at par value in the CMBS market (hence, their yield to maturity also equals 8 percent). Let's assume also that tranche B bonds have a 10 percent coupon rate, equal to the minimum coupon in the underlying pool (which helps to insure that there will be sufficient interest in the pool to cover these bonds' coupons). Tranche B securities will sell at a discount to par value, given their greater default risk and longer expected maturity than the underlying pool. (Recall our point about "levered debt.") Let us suppose tranche B bonds sell at a 12 percent yield to maturity.

Having set the coupon rates on the par-valued tranches, we can quantify the expected cash flows to the IO tranche based on the difference between the 8 percent coupon in tranche A securities and the 10 percent coupon in the underlying pool. There will be $1.5 million of excess interest in the $100 million par value pool in the first year, due to the $75 million par value of class A securities requiring only the 8 percent coupon. ($75M × 10% − $75M × 8% = $7.5M − $6M = $1.5M.) Thus, class X thus gets a 1.5 percent coupon on a notional $100 million par value for year 1. In the second year the remaining $25 million of class A par value requires only $0.08 × 25M = $2M$ of interest while that much par value of the underlying mortgages should generate $0.10 × 25M = $2.5M$ of interest, allowing class X to have a 1.0 percent coupon on a remaining notional par value of $50 million in year 2. Because class X's claim on interest cash flow in the pool has high seniority, it will likely receive a high credit rating and therefore sell in the bond market at a relatively low yield. In this example we will assume class X sells at an 8 percent yield similar to class A.[17]

Exhibit 20-5 summarizes the three classes of CMBS issued from the mortgage pool. The important thing to notice is how tranching has *stratified and concentrated* the *default risk* and the *maturity* in the pool, resulting in different classes of securities that present investors with a wider variety of different levels and types of risk and cash flow timing than is available in the undifferentiated pool of underlying loans. Notice also that the *sum of the parts is worth more than the whole*. The underlying mortgages as whole loans have a current market value of $100 million, yet the CMBS issued from them sell for $100.97 million. How is this possible?

Part of the answer to this question is that the greater variety of securities in the CMBS tranches may be more useful to investors of different types than the undifferentiated whole loans. As noted, the CMBS present investors with a range of different maturities, default risks, cash flow profiles, and responsiveness to interest rate changes. Another part of the answer lies in the ability of relatively passive or distant investors to place their capital into the more senior CMBS tranches. For these investors, the need for local real estate expertise to help them understand the amount of default risk has been replaced by bond ratings.[18] The task of maintaining contact with the borrower and administering the collection of loan payments has been taken over by a **pool servicer**.[19] These changes allow investors who could not consider investing in whole mortgages directly to consider CMBS. Yet another source of value, at least for some tranches, is increased liquidity as compared to the underlying

---

[16]Recall from Chapter 19 that the yield curve is not always upward-sloping, so shorter maturity will not necessarily always warrant a lower yield. However, lower default risk will always allow bonds to be sold at a lower market yield. Bonds with a high credit rating such as the class A bonds would typically be more liquid than the underlying mortgages as whole loans, and this liquidity would also imply a lower yield as compared to the underlying loans.

[17]In our example pool, all the loans have prepayment lockout provisions meaning the bonds are fully "call protected" in that borrowers cannot prepay their loans. Hence, the only source of potential value reduction risk in the IO tranche would be loan defaults. But class X has a senior claim on interest, so this default risk would be viewed by the rating agencies as relatively low.

[18]For example, tranche A securities might receive a bond rating of A or above, indicating investment-grade securities, while tranche B securities might get a speculative-grade rating such as B or lower. We discuss bond ratings in the next section.

[19]There is frequently a master servicer with overall responsibility for the routine administrative work of collection and distribution of cash flows and reporting, and a primary or sub-servicer, often the mortgage banker or lender who sourced the loan, who maintains contact with the borrower and may be subcontracted by the master servicer to perform other loan serving duties as well. A third servicer, the special servicer, deals with loan defaults.

whole loans.[20] Finally, there are also efficiency gains and, hence, cost reductions due to the **specialization** by participants typically involved and **standardization** of process in specific components of the securitization process.

Look back at Exhibit 20-1, which summarizes the overall CMBS process. Fundamentally, loan capital flows from the bond market investors indicated at the bottom right of the figure to the real estate investors indicated at the left side of the figure. In return, interest and principal amortization payments flow from the real estate investors into the mortgage pool from which it is repackaged into the CMBS tranches that define the securities the bond market investors have bought. Intermediate agents such as investment banks, conduits, and bond-rating agencies (among others) make the whole process work, in effect, linking the underlying capital providers to the real estate investors. Of course, some cash flow and asset value is taken by these intermediaries as their compensation for the services they provide. The extra value created by the securitization process must be more than enough to cover these extra intermediate costs.

Typically, the investment-grade tranches that make up the bulk of a CMBS issue find ready buyers in the form of conservative institutions such as pension funds, life insurance companies, endowments, sovereign wealth funds, and bond mutual funds. On the other hand, the market for the more risky speculative and high-yield tranches (the so-called **B-pieces**) is much thinner and more specialized. There are relatively few **"B-piece" buyers**, and these tranches are generally privately placed rather than issued as publicly traded securities.[21] The major buyers and holders of the lower, non-investment-grade tranches are aggressive investors willing to take on risk for high expected returns and who typically have specialized knowledge and expertise regarding commercial property risk. Such investors have included, among others, the investment banks and conduits issuing the CMBS, the **special servicers** charged with taking over defaulted loans in the pool to attempt workouts with the borrowers (which are often divisions of experienced real estate investment companies), and specialized mortgage REITs.

Returning to our simplified CMBS example, Exhibit 20-5 quantifies how the basic structure plays out overall. The A tranche carries a lower coupon, 8 percent, and sells at par for an 8 percent yield, because it has relatively low risk and short maturity due to the structure of the waterfall with the subordination provided by the B tranche, which carries a 10 percent coupon (like the underlying mortgages) but sells at a discount to par, providing the bond investors with a higher yield (12 percent in our example, based on a price of $24.15 million for $25 million par value) to reflect the greater default risk and longer maturity. The extra interest stripped out of the pool made possible by the fact that most of the par value can sell at a yield (and coupon) lower than the underlying mortgages is used to produce an IO class of bonds which sells at a relatively low yield (8 percent) and provides additional proceeds of $1.82 million in the CMBS issue. The overall CMBS issue carries a weighted (or pooled) yield of 9.27 percent which is less than the 10 percent average yield of the underlying mortgages, enabling the CMBS issue to sell for $100.97 million when the underlying mortgages only cost $100 million.[22]

---

[20]Of course, the CMBS issue adds another layer of administration and transactions that must be paid for. Also, the quality of information available to bond-rating agencies about large mortgage pools is generally not as good as that available to portfolio lenders about individual mortgages and borrowers. These administrative cost and information disadvantages offset the advantages of CMBS, so that in the real world CMBS tend to be preferable to whole loans in some situations but not in others. And the relative advantages of CMBS versus portfolio lending has swung back and forth, most prominently in the mid-decade peak before the financial crisis of 2008–09 (when CMBS had a strong advantage) and the retrenchment after the crisis (when CMBS were moribund or could not compete with portfolio lending by life insurance companies and others). See Riddiough and Taira (2001) for an interesting early investigation of differences in the production and information environments of conduit versus whole loan lenders such as insurance companies.

[21]In the classical CMBS before the financial crisis, the B-piece buyer was also known as the Directing Certificate holder or Controlling Class. As a result of being in the first-loss position, these investors were able to exert significant influence over the structure of a CMBS deal before it went to market, even in some cases being given the right to "kick out" loans they did not like from the pool. A CMBS deal does not happen without a B-piece buyer. They also play an active role in loan monitoring during the life of the CMBS bonds.

[22]In the real world the dollar value difference would be greater, because the securities would be longer lived than the one or two years in the present example, and the deal would be more complex, enabling more possibilities for value creation by targeting particular niches in the bond market. The present example is simplified for illustrative purposes, but does contain the essence of the important features of classical CMBS. It should also be noted that other structures are possible. For example, one regulatory proposal attempting to implement the Dodd-Frank Act's requirement for securitizers to keep "skin in the game," would require the IO tranche (or some portion of it) to be retained by the issuing institution and placed in something like a first-loss position, in effect, to provide a type of pool insurance to the other bond classes.

CRE CDOS: A BRIDGE TOO FAR

A 1974 book by Cornelius Ryan (which became a movie in 1977) tells of the attempt led by British forces in September 1944 to bring an early end to World War II by outflanking German forces through southeastern Netherlands. The attack required the taking and holding of several bridges across the Maas and branches of the Rhine River. Though some bridges were taken, the attack failed when it could not secure all the necessary crossings, and the war endured cruelly for many more months. The battle plan had been very ambitious, requiring unprecedented use of airborne assaults. The title of this book, "A Bridge Too Far," has become an idiom for over-stretching, attempting to do more than is possible.

A famous (in fact *infamous*) example of this type of mistake occurred in the CMBS industry at the peak of the 2000s bubble. One way of looking at it is that the investment industry was making so much money and being so successful with tranching pools of mortgages, that they began to ask themselves: why stop with just one layer of securitization? The result was "Collateralized Debt Obligations" or CDOs. In fact, CDOs didn't start with commercial real estate, but with residential mortgages where they were much more prominent. But they soon spread to CRE. By 2006, CDO origination volume was approaching 20 percent of CMBS origination volume.

As we suggested in our previous simple example, the key to adding value in securitization is the subordination waterfall that enables a large fraction of the underlying pool capital to be resold as higher credit quality assets than the average credit quality of the underlying assets. If you can do this with mortgages, why not do it with CMBS based on mortgages? The essence of the typical CRE CDO was to take the lower-rated tranches of CMBS (together with possibly some other types of high yield commercial property loans, B-pieces of whole loans, some REIT debt, floating-rate and mezzanine debt, and even construction loans), pool all these assets, tranche them using the usual waterfall technology (thereby obtaining bond ratings), and then sell the resulting high-rated securities in the bond market. Such "alchemy" is possible in principle, because even a pool consisting entirely of risky assets will probably not completely default (will it?). These securitizations of the securitizations (and sometimes there was even a third rendition, known as "CDO-squareds") were used as balance sheet management devices by buyers of CMBS B-pieces (the lower-rated tranches), getting them off their balance sheets so they could buy more B-pieces. This may have undercut the incentive of the B-piece CMBS buyers to pay as much attention as they had been to the credit quality of the CMBS B-pieces, which was a lynchpin underlying overall CMBS credit quality. Thus we have an example of a type of "moral hazard" problem (see section 20.4).

In retrospect, it certainly seems as if the advent of these types of CDOs was perhaps a sign that things had gone too far. Hopefully you can see how even a simple single-layer CMBS is quite a complex set of securities, probably in itself difficult enough to analyze rigorously with precision for purposes of predicting default and loss probabilities for any given tranche. Imagine how much more complex and difficult to analyze were the CDOs. (And this is not even considering possible agency conflicts of interest, and the use of "synthetic" CDOs that were based purely on over-the-counter derivatives, without even having any actual assets underlying them, fully exposed to counter-party credit risk, which also began to occur in the peak year or two of the bubble.)

As with CMBS, the key to the viability of CDOs was the willingness of bond credit rating agencies to give CDO securities credit ratings (and ones that weren't too low for much of the par value). But this turned out to be "a bridge too far." Most CDOs suffered drastically and many were completely wiped out in the early stages of the financial crisis and recession, and the industry came to a complete halt by 2009.

Carrying our example through to its ex post outcome, we see that because of the default of the loan in year 2 as previously described, the ex post realized IRR over the entire pool is only 6.16 percent on its $100 million initial par value or 5.44 percent on its $100.97 million CMBS market value at issuance. However, both the A and X classes of bondholders receive their full 8 percent contract yields, thanks to the valiant sacrifices of the class B bondholders, who end up with a −0.34 percent IRR on their investment of $24.15 million.[23]

[23]The large impact on the investment outcomes due to a single loan defaulting is of course an artifact of this very reduced, simplified example, with only 10 loans and only two years of lifetime in the pool. Real world CMBS issues typically contain over a hundred loans and extend over ten years or more of bond maturity. In this simple example, the $6 million of credit losses on an original pool par value of $100 million represents a rather severe loss rate. However, as noted in Chapter 18, losses on CMBS in the wake of the financial crisis and so-called "Great Recession" were typically at this order of magnitude. The default rate in our example pool was 10% with a loss of 6% of pool par value. In 2011 Moody's estimated a 9% default rate on all outstanding CMBS loans with an average loss severity of 40% (which would suggest a loss rate of around 3.6%). For CMBS issued in the peak years of 2005–07 Moody's was projecting an ultimate loss rate of between 6.8% and 11.5% of original pool par value, somewhat worse than that in our simplified example. (Source: Moody's Investors Service, Special Report: US CMBS Loss Severities, Q3 2011 Update.)

20.3 CMBS Rating and Yields

As noted, the key to a well-functioning liquid public market in CMBS is the ability of distant, passive investors with no local real estate expertise to feel confident about the magnitude of default risk in the securities they are buying. Without such confidence, these investors will not place their capital into CMBS or will demand such a high yield as to make securitization unprofitable or uncompetitive. The only market for commercial mortgages would then be investors who have the specialized knowledge and expertise to evaluate the relevant credit risk on their own. The primary means by which nonspecialized bond investors derive confidence in the magnitude of default risk in CMBS has traditionally been the receipt of a credit rating for the securities from one of the established bond-rating agencies on Wall Street.

20.3.1 Bond Credit Rating

Exhibit 20-6 shows the major CMBS bond credit rating labels of two of these agencies: Moody's and Standard & Poor's.[24] Apart from the structured finance (sf) indicator (which will be explained shortly), these are the same credit rating labels as are applied within the entire bond market, most traditionally to corporate and government bonds. The idea behind the **bond credit rating** process is to provide investors with an objective and expert assessment of the approximate magnitude of default risk. In principle, any two bonds with the same credit rating (from the same agency) should have similar default risk.[25] The hierarchical labels are traditionally grouped into categories. The top four ranks of labels, from AAA through BBB using the S&P terms, are usually considered to be **investment grade**. Traditionally, this means that bonds of this credit quality are acceptable investments for conservative institutions. Some institutions may require the top rating of AAA form some of their investments.[26] Although traditional whole-loan commercial mortgages are generally not publicly traded and do not receive credit ratings, their market yields are often similar to that of corporate bonds rated BBB (or Baa) or between that of BBB and BB (especially for smaller loans).[27] The next two ranks, BB and B, are traditionally considered **speculative grade** or "high-yield," meaning that there is substantial probability of default. Traditionally in corporate bonds the single-B rated bonds have exhibited about a 50 percent incidence of default. Ranks lower than B, including nonrated bonds, are often termed junk bonds. Many of these bonds are in default, while for others there is simply not enough information for a rating agency to be willing to judge credit quality.

As noted, the traditional concept of bond rating held that the same rating should imply the same default risk, and hence presumably the same pricing in the bond market (same yield), holding other characteristics of the bond the same (such as maturity). The idea was that this should be the case whether the bond was a CMBS or a corporate bond or a

---

[24]Moody's and S&P have traditionally been the two largest of the four major bond-rating agencies. Fitch was the third largest and the Canadian firm, Dominion Bond Rating Service (DBRS), the fourth, and a relative newcomer to the U.S. CMBS sector. Subsequent to the financial crisis there have been new entrants into the business as both Morningstar and Kroll Bond Ratings were designated as "Nationally Recognized Statistical Ratings Organizations" (NRSROs) by the SEC, and Fitch surpassed S&P after 2011 to become the second largest rater of CMBS.

[25]In this context, the term default risk encompasses both the unconditional probability of default and the conditional loss severity in the event of default, in essence, the major factors that determine the magnitude of the expected losses (or ex ante yield degradation as defined in Chapter 18). Bonds are generally rated by more than one agency. In such cases, the ratings from the two agencies occasionally disagree. Ratings are reviewed and updated periodically or whenever a major event occurs that could affect creditworthiness.

[26]Because of such institutional requirements, there can be discrete break-points in demand for bonds, and therefore often in the prices and yields the bonds command. The AAA rating is of course most coveted, and there is a sharp break between BBB- and BB, that is, between investment grade and non-investment-grade.

[27]According to Stanton and Wallace (2010), during the 1938–1995 period the overall average default rate on 10-year corporate bonds rated Baa by Moody's (like BBB) was about 6%, and that on bonds rated Ba (like BB) was about 30%. Recall from Chapter 18 that the overall historical average default rate in ACLI commercial mortgages was about 16%.

EXHIBIT 20-6
Bond Ratings for CMBS
© OnCourse Learning

		Rating	
Moody's	**S&P**	**Structured Finance Indicator (Post 2008)***	**Meaning**
Aaa	AAA	(sf)	Highest quality, extremely safe
Aa1	AA+	(sf)	High quality investment grade
Aa2	AA	(sf)	
Aa3	AA−	(sf)	
A1	A+	(sf)	
A2	A	(sf)	
A3	A−	(sf)	
Baa1	BBB+	(sf)	Investment grade
Baa2	BBB	(sf)	
Baa3	BBB−	(sf)	
Ba1	BB+	(sf)	Medium to low quality, speculative grade
Ba2	BB	(sf)	
Ba3	BB−	(sf)	
B1	B+	(sf)	
B2	B	(sf)	
B3	B−	(sf)	
Caa1	CCC+	(sf)	Poor quality, some issues in default (speculative to "junk" grades)
Caa2	CCC	(sf)	
Caa3	CCC−	(sf)	
NR	NR	(sf)	Too little information or too risky to rate (generally "junk" grade)

*See explanation in text.

sovereign debt security, for example. But we also noted that "structured finance" products such as mortgage-backed securities (MBS) are more complex than traditional corporate or government bonds, and thereby pose some new and major challenges to rating agencies, as well as to bond market investors in interpreting or understanding the default risk. This is the reason for the new "sf" suffix that since the financial crisis has been attached to ratings of MBS. It is to signal to investors that the bonds being rated are structured finance, and therefore possibly the rating is not directly or exactly comparable to the same rating applied to traditional simple bonds such as classical corporate and government bonds.

The bond market has indeed priced MBS differently since the financial crisis. It is possible that if the ratings agencies had to attach such a suffix to CMBS rating when the industry was first trying to get started in the mid-1990s, the industry might never have taken off. The bond market needed a sense of comfort and familiarity about the default risk in these new types of bonds. But by the 2000s the CMBS industry was so large and established, and now it has so much of its own history and track record, that attaching a special suffix to MBS ratings is probably not harmful for the industry, and indeed may be realistic and beneficial, as it may encourage investors to evaluate CMBS bonds on their own merits based on their own performance history.

20.3.2 Credit Rating, Market Yields, and CMBS Structure

Look again at our simple hypothetical numerical example CMBS deal of section 20.2 with its three tranches. Viewing this as an initial offering, you can see how the profitability of the securitization process depends on how much of the overall par value in the underlying mortgage pool can be assigned to the senior class of bonds we labeled as the "A" class (or tranche). In the example, we were able to assign $75 million to this class by giving it "25 percent subordination," meaning that the junior tranches below A can absorb losses up to 25 percent of the original pool par value before the A tranche will take any loss.[28] If we had been able to give class A less subordination than that, then we could have assigned more of the bonds to the top class, for example, $80 million if we could have provided only 20 percent subordination (in which case class B would have had only $20 million of par). In that case, the deal would have been more profitable *provided* that we could still sell all the classes at the same yields in the bond market. In our example we assumed an 8 percent yield for classes A and X and a 12 percent yield for class B.[29] If we assigned $80 million to class A but then because that class now has less protection bond investors require an 8.5 percent yield, then we would end up worse off.[30]

Bond credit rating agencies decide how much subordination they require for a given credit rating within each CMBS issue. And the credit rating that a bond class receives generally largely determines the yield at which the bond market will price the securities. Thus, it would appear that the credit rating agencies determine the profitability or even the viability of CMBS. But the last word actually always goes to the market. If the market does not "believe" the rating agencies' ratings, then the market won't pay prices for the bonds that reflect those ratings. Then yields will rise and the deal won't work after all. And in the other direction, if the credit rating agency is more conservative than the bond market, then investors will bid up the bond prices, bringing down yields, putting the rating agencies under pressure (from the CMBS issuers) to reduce the subordination requirements. When you're in the bond business, it is, after all, very hard to ignore the bond market!

20.4 Lessons from the Financial Crisis

During the 15-year history of the CMBS industry from its birth in the early 1990s to its peak in 2007 two major phenomena shaped the evolution of the industry. The first was a learning process, as the new industry developed and CMBS became more familiar to all parties: issuers, investors, and the rating agencies. The second was a huge secular growth in the supply of financial capital. This second phenomenon did not just apply only to CMBS, but indeed to all of the capital markets, but CMBS was certainly no exception, particularly in

---

[28]This is the essence, but a slight over-simplification. As we noted in section 20.2, the pool cash flow is stripped into two separate waterfalls, one for interest and one for principal payments. Credit losses may be assigned differentially to those two waterfalls, such that a given class of bonds may suffer shortfalls in coupon interest payments before any write-down of its par value (or in some cases vice versa, as in the example with class B in section 20.2).

[29]Re-do Exhibit 20-5 with the new structure and you will see that the added profitability occurs in two ways. First, the additional $5 million of par in class A enables more interest to be stripped from the pool and applied to the IO class (due to the class A coupon being 8% while the underlying mortgage pool is paying 10%, with this difference now applied over $80 million par instead of just $75 million). This bolsters the amount of IO bonds that can be sold. Second, the reduction in the present value of the class B bonds will be less than the additional present value created in the class A bonds. This is because the class A bonds will sell at par value based on their (assumed) 8% market yield and their 8% coupon, raising the full $5 million additional par value as proceeds for the deal at issuance, whereas the class B bonds' present value will not drop by the full $5 million subtracted from their par value because these subordinated bonds sell at a discount to their par value (e.g., in Exhibit 20-5 we assumed a market yield of 12% on bonds with a 10% coupon).

[30]With the 8% coupon class A would then sell at a discount, for a value as CMBS of $79.5 million, and bringing the overall value of the issue down to $100.82 million compared to the original $100.97 million when we had 25% subordination for class A (and holding all else constant).

the 2000s. Both of these phenomena acted to make CMBS underwriting and credit rating less conservative or more aggressive, up until the financial crisis of 2008.

As the players gained more comfort and confidence with CMBS, they grew less conservative; they built in fewer buffers and they fine-tuned their risk analyses in ways that enabled higher ratings or higher pricing of bonds. All parties did this, including the rating agencies, as they adjusted their models and practices in ways that enabled less subordination to be required for a given credit rating holding underlying pool characteristics constant. But the CMBS industry was perhaps less mature, and more vulnerable, than it seemed at the time because it was such a new industry with relatively little performance (and short history of) data and because of the complexity of CMBS.

Look at Exhibit 20-7, which depicts the history of CMBS subordination levels up until the financial crisis. At first the rating agencies were very conservative. In the mid-1990s, when CMBS were a very new type of product (and often contained a lot of seasoned loans not originally issued as conduits), issuers typically had to provide around 30 percent subordination for AAA-rated bond classes (Moody's label Aaa). Even with this conservative subordination, CMBS bond prices were discounted by the market (yields carried a premium) compared to similarly-rated corporate bonds, because of the newness and uncertainty surrounding the industry.[31] This was a period of a rapid learning curve in the industry. To achieve the same Aaa level of credit rating, in 2000 the Aaa subordination had dropped to a

EXHIBIT 20-7 History of CMBS Subordination Levels, 1995–2008 (pre-crisis)

Source: Authors' correspondence with Moody's Investors.

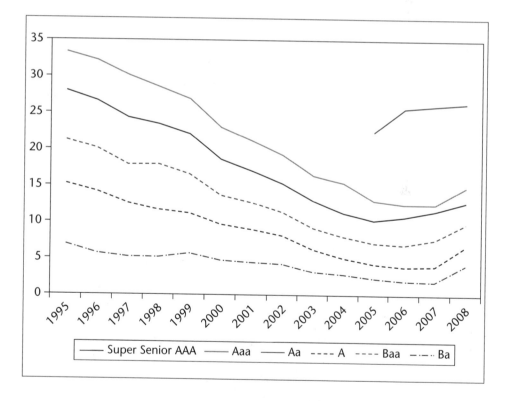

---

[31]Part of the reason for the yield penalty compared to corporate bonds may also have had to do with fear of agency problems in the complex structure of classes issued on the same underlying collateral. CMBS can be subject to conflicts of interest between senior and subordinate class bond holders which at the time appeared most likely to redound to the benefit of the subordinate class investors at the expense of the senior class investors. This was because typical rules and practices gave more control over dealing with problem loans to the subordinate classes. This type of potential conflict of interest does not arise with classical corporate bonds. It should also be noted that the early CMBS pools were different from later pools, with many more seasoned loans at a time period coming off of a recent downturn in the commercial property market at the end of the 1980s.

little over 20 percent; by 2004 it was under 15 percent; and by 2007 it was barely over 12 percent. But there were always lingering doubts about how much subordination was appropriate for the different credit ratings, particularly in the absence of actual historical experience with CMBS conduit loans during a major commercial property market downturn.

In the early years the ACLI historical data on the performance of life insurance company whole loans (that we described in Chapter 18) were influential in the CMBS industry, because this was the only available well-documented data source on commercial mortgage performance that spanned a major downturn in the commercial property market. Indeed, the commercial property "crash" of the late-1980s to early-1990s had been very severe, the worst since the Great Depression of the 1930s. This downturn was included in the ACLI historical database, and was viewed by many CMBS analysts as a likely "worst-case scenario." From 1986 through 1992 institutional commercial property prices had fallen on average almost 30 percent in nominal terms (over 40 percent in real terms) based on transactions prices of NCREIF properties (as tracked by the TBI index). In the ACLI loan performance database as it began to be analyzed during the late 1990s, the overall average loan lifetime default rate was about 15 percent with about 33 percent loss severity, for an overall average loss percentage of about 5 percent of original par value. For the worst-performing cohort of ACLI loans issued just before the late-1980s crash, the loans originated during 1986, the lifetime default rate was almost 28 percent with a 43 percent loss severity for an overall loss rate of about 12 percent.

By the early 2000s credit rating agencies were suggesting that investment grade CMBS bonds (Baa- or BBB-rating) should be protected against the "average" level of credit losses in commercial mortgages, which would suggest at least a little buffer above the 5 percent level of subordination based on the ACLI data.[32] And they were similarly suggesting that AA (or Aa) bonds should be protected against a repeat of the worst-case scenario, implying protection with some buffer above 12 percent subordination. This would have seemed at the time to have made the top, AAA (or Aaa), classes very safe indeed, provided the ACLI data and the 1980s commercial property crash were meaningful and relevant for CMBS in the 2000s.

We see in Exhibit 20-7 that at least this level of subordination was indeed applied on average by the rating agencies until about the year 2004. But the prevailing opinion in the early to mid-2000s was one of optimism, and that the markets had become more efficient since the crash of the late-1980s. This perception was bolstered by very good credit performance in commercial mortgages issued since the early 1990s, even through the financial crisis of 1998 and the recession of 2001 (which was very mild and in which, although some rental markets were hard hit, property asset values did not fall much if at all). People came to view the "worst-case scenario" of the ACLI 1986 cohort as increasingly unlikely, and the cyclical nature of commercial property prices was played down even in the face of the huge run-up in asset prices starting in 2004.

At that point, 2004, we see two ominous phenomena in Exhibit 20-7. First, the subordination levels dropped clearly below the previously stated criteria based on the ACLI loan performance data. Second, the bond market began to balk, or at least a part of it did. This was evidenced by the fact that the market began to demand (and be willing to pay for) what came to be called "super-senior" tranches of bonds. These were tranches that had even more subordination than what the credit rating agencies were willing to give the top rating to. There came to be two layers of AAA-rated classes, the classical senior tranche (which now came to be called "junior-seniors" or "AJ" classes) and the "super-seniors," which contained quite a bit more subordination than the regular AAA-rated bonds. This is evidenced in the chart in Exhibit 20-7 by the new "Super-Senior AAA" line that appears in 2005, above the Aaa line.[33] This was a rather blatant signal coming from the bond market that at least an important group of investors (the

---

[32]The buffer would be necessary at least in part because of "idiosyncratic risk," the fact that individual properties, and indeed individual loan pools, would exhibit performance dispersion around the average performance.

[33]The first "Super-Senior" bonds were launched in November 2004 with 20% subordination, and in May 2005 the "Super-Duper" class (dubbed "Dupers") was launched with 30% subordination.

most conservative ones) were becoming afraid of the subordination levels the rating agencies were providing, at least for the AAA (or Aaa) label. In part this was probably a reaction to the slipping below the historical ACLI-based criteria that had been touted, and in part it may have been a (rather astute) reaction to the run-up in property asset prices without any concomitant restraint or pull-back in loan underwriting standards in the primary market of loan originations. Proper recognition of cyclicality in the asset market would have dictated that either loan origination standards (such as LTVs and DSCRs in particular) or bond rating standards (in the form of subordination requirements) should be ratcheted up to more rigorous levels during the peak phase of the asset pricing cycle.[34] In fact, the opposite occurred, if anything, and indeed that is probably both a symptom and a partial cause of the bubble.[35]

This is seen dramatically in Exhibit 20-8, which depicts the average LTV ratio of CMBS conduit loans at issuance from 2003 through 2011. The bottom line is based on the reported LTV as underwritten by the loan issuers. The top line reflects the "haircut" that one of the credit rating agencies, Moody's, gave to the loans in their process of evaluating the quality of the loan pools underlying the CMBS issues. The haircut LTV is deliberately conservative, so it is not surprising that it lies above the underwritten LTV. But what is interesting is how

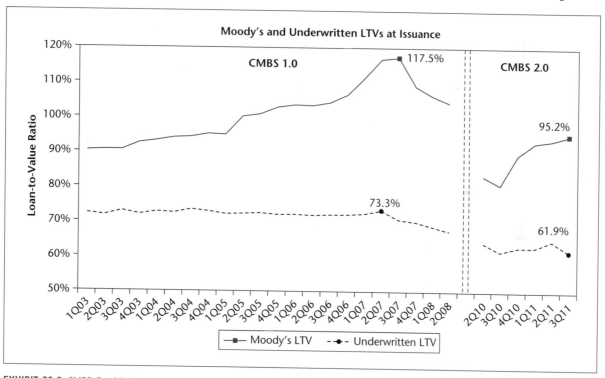

EXHIBIT 20-8 CMBS Conduit Loans LTVs at Issuance, as Underwritten by Issuers and as Haircutted by Moody's, 2003–2011
Source: Moody's Investors Service, Trepp LLC, September 2011. © Moody's Investors Service, Inc. and/or its affiliates. Reprinted with permission. All Rights Reserved.

---

[34]Apart from direct measures of loan underwriting such as average LTV and DSCR, there were other problems with the quality of the loan pools, including a sudden huge expansion in the use of interest-only loans. As illustrated in our earlier simple 3-tranche numerical example CMBS deal in section 20.2, loans that do not pay down principal before maturity reduce the credit quality of a mortgage pool in two ways, first at the individual loan level by making the loan less secure, and second at the pool level by reducing the rate of retirement of par value from the top of the bond stack.

[35]Clayton (2009) outlines how borrowers, lenders, appraisers and regulators alike were all lulled into complacency as property prices rose and price- and spread-based measures of risk provided false signals and ultimately pushed CMBS debt levels and property values to unsustainable heights. Arsenault, Clayton and Peng (2012) provide strong and robust empirical evidence of the feedback loop between mortgage supply and property values and the role it plays in real estate price cycles.

the gap widened and the haircut LTV rose to alarming levels well above 100 percent by the peak of the bubble in 2007. The period to the right of the break represents the so-called "CMBS 2.0," the new regime since the financial crisis, in which loan underwriting has again become very conservative.

Apart from the advent of the super-senior bonds, the investor (or "buy") side of the bond market did little to provide any warning or signal to put pressure on the rating agencies to get more conservative. Indeed, arguably the opposite was happening. Look at Exhibit 20-9, which shows the history of yield spreads (over comparable maturity LIBOR swaps) for AAA-rated CMBS bonds.[36] What would we expect this spread to be? LIBOR swaps are a very low-risk type of investment in terms of default risk, but they are not completely riskless. AAA-rated CMBS should also be very low risk. So we would expect this spread to generally be fairly small. The AAA CMBS-LIBOR spread depicts the bond market's perception of the amount of risk in the safest CMBS bonds. Higher yield spreads mean that the bond market is not willing to pay as much for CMBS, because investors are more afraid of default risk in the bonds.

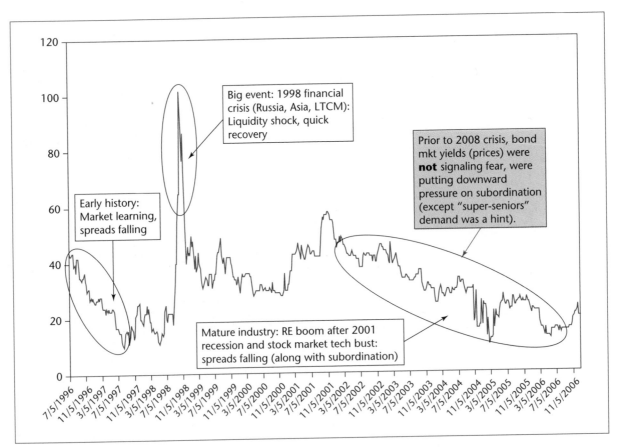

EXHIBIT 20-9 CMBS AAA Spreads over LIBOR Swaps, 1996–2006
© OnCourse Learning

---

[36]This is the way yields, or pricing, is typically quoted in the CMBS market. LIBOR swaps are the fixed interest rate version of the London Interbank Borrowing Rate, the rate charged on loans between banks. After the 1998 financial crisis LIBOR swaps became the primary benchmark for investment grade CMBS price quotes, rather than U.S. Treasury bonds, because LIBOR rates behave more like CMBS during liquidity crises, when U.S. Treasury securities play a "safe harbor" role, while other forms of private sector debt (including CMBS) do not exhibit this behavior.

The period from 1996 to 2006 shown in Exhibit 20-9 contains four regimes. At first, from 1996–1998, we were still in the start-up "learning" phase of the industry, and spreads were falling rapidly, from around 40 basis points to below 20. Then there occurred a sharp spike during the financial crisis of 1998, briefly up to 100 basis points. That financial crisis created a scary but short-lived liquidity crisis in the world bond markets that cut off the supply of capital to CMBS, in part because there loomed a threat of recession which would have undercut the demand for real estate. The resulting cut-back in the supply of financial capital to the commercial property market was viewed favorably at the time as an example of the informational efficiency of the public securities markets, putting the brakes on an incipient investment boom that might have got out ahead of demand. Spreads then rapidly recovered (more quickly in the senior bonds than in the more junior ones), back down to around the 30 to 40 bps level, although rising a bit above that during the 2001 economic recession which undercut rents in many space markets. There then occurred from 2002 through 2006 a long period of declining spreads, bringing them down to below 20 bps again, about as low as they ever got. This was the great real estate boom period, and the downward pressure on CMBS spreads (upward pressure on bond prices) reflected a bond market that was signaling strongly that investors were not very worried about default risk or the rating policies of the rating agencies (or anyway the equivalent of that, whether or not people would have said so at the time, considering that investors were willing to bid up CMBS bond prices).

It was in this environment that the great financial crisis of 2008–2009 hit, triggered not by CMBS or commercial real estate but by the housing sector and widespread excess leverage throughout the financial system, as well as other systemic structural weaknesses such as widespread use of over-the-counter bond credit default swap derivatives that were exposed to counter-party credit risk.[37] Commercial property prices plummeted, and the so-called Great Recession set in, deeper and longer than any since the Great Depression. Suddenly the CMBS industry was in a crisis the magnitude of which virtually no one had contemplated. Exhibit 20-10 portrays this history by a simple quantitative metric that is very dramatic. Exhibit 20-10 is the same CMBS AAA spread over swaps as we displayed in Exhibit 20-9, only now carried through to 2011. The previous dramatic spike in 1998 now looks like a tiny bump in the road, and 2008–2009 is a great mountain range! Briefly during the height of the crisis it was almost impossible to sell any CMBS securities other than the AAAs, and the quoted spreads for AAA bonds soared to over 1500 bps (briefly reducing their market value to barely 50 percent of face value). The new-issue CMBS market virtually shut down during 2009, and many investment banks laid off all of their CMBS trading staff. By 2010 a slight recovery began to form, with over $10 billion of new CMBS issued that year, and over $30 billion in 2011 (mostly in the first half of the year). These new "CMBS 2.0" deals were smaller and with simpler deal structures than before the crisis, and with some features to help assuage investors, such as LTV covenants in mortgages and new governance provisions that better balance the authority more equitably between senior and junior bondholders in the event of loans going bad.[38] They also had fewer, thicker tranches and higher subordination, back up to levels typical of 2002 or 2003, before the boom. For example, after a brief period of lower subordination in early 2011, rating agencies had to raise subordination for AAA bonds back up close to 20 percent by late 2011. Even so, the market still demanded super-senior tranches that had

---

[37]Credit default swaps (CDS) were a new type of derivative financial product that enabled parties to hedge, or purchase insurance, against defaults or credit losses in corporate bonds and other such debt securities, including RMBS and CMBS. The CDS is essentially a contract in which one party agrees to pay a counter-party a fixed fee in exchange for the counter-party agreeing to pay in the event of credit losses or defaults on the part of the underlying bond or MBS security (or a synthetic "basket" of such securities). Entities exposed to bond default risk, including banks and CMBS issuers, purchased the default insurance, but the counter-parties in many cases proved to have insufficient resources to make good on their contractual obligations once the financial crisis hit.

[38]Appraisal-based LTV covenants provide for appraisals of the underlying property collateral, with requirements that the borrower provide additional equity to pay down the loan balance if the LTV falls below a threshold level based on the appraisal. The new governance features give senior bondholders more authority over the special servicers who are authorized by the trust to deal with problem loans and borrowers.

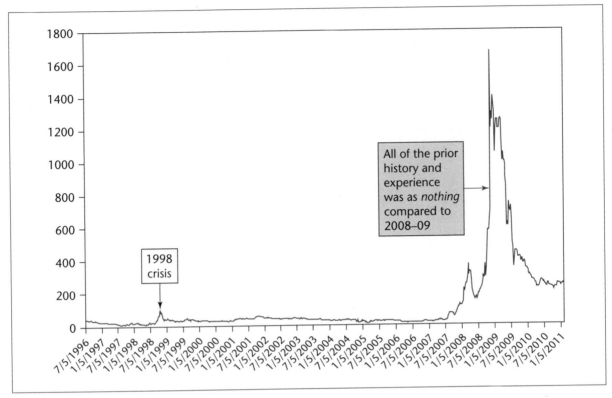

EXHIBIT 20-10 CMBS AAA Spreads to Swaps: 1996–2010
© OnCourse Learning

up to 30 percent subordination.[39] Yield spreads on the vintage AAA bonds based on the deals issued before the market correction remained over 200 bps (up to around 300 bps in the latter half of 2011), and even yields on the new CMBS issues were not much better: in late 2011 over 100 basis points for super-dupers and over 200 basis points for regular AAA.

As we write this edition it is not clear when or how (or even if) the bond market will lose its aversion to CMBS. Major uncertainties remain in the regulatory environment, including provisions in both the Basel III international banking regulations and in the Dodd-Frank financial reform act in the United States. For example, one provision of the Dodd-Frank law may require CMBS issuers to retain some sort of risk exposure to the bonds they sell ("skin in the game").[40]

From what you have learned about the way the CMBS industry works, you can see that it faces a type of squeeze. If credit rating agencies allow too little subordination and/or apply insufficient oversight of loan pool quality, then the bond market will not trust the ratings and discount the bonds accordingly, resulting in yields so high that CMBS issuers cannot compete with other types of lenders in the commercial mortgage market. If rating agencies require too much subordination then the securitization process becomes unprofitable for the securities

---

[39]As noted, most of the early recovery "CMBS 2.0" deals were privately placed rather than public offerings, suggesting a lingering caution or lack of appetite for CMBS in the broader public bond market.

[40]The shutdown of the CMBS market and departure of many key players during the credit crisis nearly led to the demise of the sector's key trade association, the Commercial Mortgage Securities Association (CMSA). Post credit crisis the CMSA has morphed into the Commercial Real Estate Finance Council (or "CREFC") that has adopted a broader mandate of fostering the growth and development of CRE debt markets in general including CMBS. Industry resources and developments, including the evolving regulatory environment for CMBS market, can be followed at www.crefc.org.

issuers. Either way, the viability of the industry is threatened: the root cause is fear on the part of investors or lack of confidence in the ability to fully know how much default risk is in CMBS bonds.

The challenge facing the CMBS industry is complicated by the possibility of two phenomena that are always a danger in any debt industry: **moral hazard** and **adverse selection**. In general, moral hazard exists when one party has control over an action or decision that affects the risk or well-being of another party. Adverse selection occurs when a relevant sample or selection tends to have unfavorable characteristics compared to the average characteristics in a population. For example, moral hazard can exist if loan issuers determine the amount of risk in the loans they issue by the underwriting standards they employ, but then this risk is immediately passed on to other parties if the originating loan issuers sell the loans into a CMBS loan pool, such that the loan issuers are no longer subject to the risk they have created.[41] Adverse selection can occur if, for example, CMBS are viewed by the bond market as being more risky, thereby requiring higher yields, which in turn requires that borrowers of CMBS conduit loans pay higher interest rates. The result could be that the best (lowest risk) borrowers and loans will go to competing non-CMBS types of lenders, namely, whole-loan portfolio lenders such as life insurance companies, leaving the CMBS industry able to place loans only to the more risky types of borrowers who must accept (and indeed deservedly should pay) higher interest rates.[42]

Both moral hazard and adverse selection can thrive in an environment of incomplete and asymmetric information, where borrowers and loan originators have more information about specific loans and borrowers than do CMBS issuers or rating agencies or bond market investors. Moral hazard and adverse selection can synergize with each other, as bond market investors' awareness of the existence of moral hazard can cause investors to require higher yields in CMBS bonds as compensation against moral hazard risk, and such higher yields force CMBS conduit loan originators into an adverse selection situation, which in turn incentivizes the loan issuers to sell off the loans quickly to lay off the risk onto other parties. The danger for the CMBS industry is that a stable equilibrium could conceivably result in which CMBS conduit loans become a type of "sub-prime" source of financing, catering during normal times only to less desirable borrowers, and potentially subject to highly cyclical supply and demand. Hopefully the industry will find a way to avoid this outcome through a combination of industry self-policing and self-regulation, as well as government regulatory incentives or frameworks such as what is envisioned in enlightened implementation of Dodd-Frank and Basel III.[43]

Though this is a difficult time for the CMBS industry, over the long run CMBS have two things in their favor. First, the financial crisis and Great Recession and their aftermath have provided a great historical experience from which more and better data on conduit loan performance will become available as all the loans issued before the crisis finally mature or are liquidated and we see how great the losses ultimately will actually be. This will help to reduce uncertainty and fear. Second, the fundamental reasons why the industry makes sense and how it can add value have not gone away. Hopefully our description in this chapter has helped you to understand what those reasons are, and in particular, how securitization allows the creation of debt products that are more liquid and custom-tailored to the needs of particular investors, including smaller and passive investors. With time, we will also be able to take a more complete and balanced look at how well or poorly the CMBS industry in fact performed through the worst financial crisis and economic recession in almost a century of U.S. economic history.

---

[41]This is the problem of lack of so-called "skin in the game." The problem can also exist at the level of the securities issuers.

[42]It should be noted that adverse selection is not just a danger with CMBS loans. It can potentially be a problem for any type of lender or type of loan that is less competitive, that is, less desirable from the borrower's perspective. If, for example, CMBS somehow became able to access more capital at lower cost than whole loan portfolio lenders, then the competitiveness balance might tip the other way and the portfolio lenders might be in greater danger of adverse selection.

[43]One example are the independent review boards that the rating agencies have set up since the financial crisis, in which the rating and subordination models are subject to review by presumably independent experts.

CMBS: FIXED-INCOME OR REAL ESTATE INVESTMENT?

It all depends. The biggest factor is whether the CMBS are investment-grade, rated BBB or above. "The investment-grade portion of the CMBS market is very, very much fixed-income," said Jeffrey Gandel, senior vice president and investment director at Fidelity Management Trust Co. "So Fidelity invests in the investment-grade portion of CMBS out of our investment-grade fixed-income group." Although Fidelity also views the below-investment-grade or high-yield sector as a fixed-income instrument, it is much more important to research the underlying collateral, and CMBS investment requires more real estate expertise. "So the below-investment-grade CMBS investments are made out of a team within our real estate group," says Gandel.

A focus on the underlying collateral is especially important for investors in below-investment-grade CMBS. "The B-piece guys are really looking for the weak link in the chain," say George Pappadopoulos, director of risk management and debt research with Property & Portfolio Research. "They're looking for which individual loans are really going to come up to bite them. So they're re-underwriting every single loan because even one default can mean a big difference in returns for them."

For a firm such as ARCap REIT, which purchases on a private-sale basis the bottom classes of newly issued transactions, CMBS are definitely real estate investments. "We are real estate-oriented investors, doing due diligence on 100 percent of the loans in each pool we purchase," says Leonard Cotton, chairman of ARCap REIT. The firm examines each loan portfolio with an eye toward understanding the underlying assets, making a determination as to how they will perform over the life of the loan and if the asset ultimately will be able to be refinanced at maturity.

Although examining collateral is crucial for investors at the bottom of the credit curve, Pappadopoulos notes quite a bit of focus is on underlying real estate fundamentals all the way up the tranche hierarchy. "You get to the triple-A and the investment-grade stuff and people are less concerned about it. They're looking at a lot of other factors," he says. "But that said, people still are cognizant of the real estate markets, even investment-grade spreads would widen as a result of it, not tremendously, not like the B-pieces or the double-Bs could." Investors do remember that real estate is the collateral of these bonds, explains Pappadopoulos.

"In addition, institutional investors have different goals for their CMBS investments, which can affect how they view the investment," says Tom Mattinson, senior vice president with GMAC Institutional Advisors. Life insurance companies attempt to invest in CMBS at higher yields than they can in alternative asset types, while pension funds are trying to outperform a benchmark, such as the Lehman Aggregate Index.

"Pension funds are kind of total-return oriented, so they are seeking to outperform a benchmark, typically," says Mattinson. "They will either look at CMBS as a real estate allocation or a fixed-income allocation, and to the degree you venture down the credit curve toward below-investment-grade CMBS, it tends to be more of a real estate allocation."

Life insurance companies typically regard CMBS as real estate, whether they are investment-grade or below-investment-grade. "It's typically an extension of what they're trying to do in mortgages," explains Mattinson. "Life insurance companies are significant mortgage investors because they like long-term paper that allows them to match their long-term liabilities. They're more oriented not toward total return but toward investing at a given credit level at the highest yield possible."

Source: Taken directly from L. Clodfelter, "The Evolution of CMBS: How Commercial Mortgage-Backed Securities Have Changed Real Estate," *The Institutional Real Estate Letter*, September 2005.

It is not clear that the industry won't come through looking fairly decent. The CMBS industry did not indulge in the extent of excesses that the residential mortgage industry did. Commercial real estate had learned a major lesson just a few years earlier in the crash of the late-1980s. The commercial space markets were not overbuilt when the recession hit. As of late 2011 Moody's was projecting ultimate losses in the most vulnerable peak 2007 and 2008 vintages of CMBS issues of no more than about 12 percent of the original par value. This is a huge rate of loss, but not significantly worse than the performance of the 1986 ACLI cohort of whole loans. It is enough to cause some severe losses in many AA classes and some losses in the regular ("junior") AAA classes of those peak-year CMBS issues, but the "super-seniors" seem pretty certain to ride through the worst financial and economic storm in nearly a century without any losses at all. And these made up a substantial fraction of all the CMBS bonds issued by value during the peak of the bubble. The industry was profitable with reasonably conservative levels of subordination in the late 1990s and early 2000s. It could be competitive again if bond investors could get to a comfort level that would bring yield spreads back to those that prevailed in most of the history shown in Exhibit 20-9. That, along with some regulatory clarity and stability, including a cooperative and constructivist partnership between government and industry, will surely see the CMBS industry rise again.

20.5 Chapter Summary

This chapter introduced you to the basics of CMBS, perhaps the most exciting recent development in the commercial real estate finance industry. While much of this chapter was given over to describing the basic nuts and bolts of what CMBS are and how they work, we also stepped back and presented the big picture. In a continuation of a theme that has run throughout the financial-economics parts of this book, we saw how CMBS can, when they work, serve the diverse needs of heterogeneous investors in the capital market. In serving such investors, CMBS open up a potentially vast source of capital for commercial real estate, a source that promises greater informational efficiency, at least in some respects, than the traditional sources. With this chapter, we complete Part VI, our focus on commercial mortgages. Now it is time to move back to the equity side of the picture, and up to the macro-level of strategic investment concerns, the level we have been dealing with on the debt side in both this chapter and the previous chapter.

KEY TERMS

securitization
commercial mortgage-backed
   securities (CMBS)
tranches, tranching
unbundling or partitioning
conduit loans
weighted average coupon (WAC)
weighted average maturity (WAM)
waterfall

first-loss tranche (or "B-piece")
levered debt
lockout
penalty
fixed percent of the remaining
   mortgage loan balance
yield maintenance (YM)
defease
pool servicer

specialization
standardization
B-piece buyers
special servicers
bond credit rating
investment grade
speculative grade
moral hazard
adverse selection

STUDY QUESTIONS

Conceptual Questions

20.1. Describe the essential structure of the CMBS industry: Who are the ultimate investors in CMBS? What branch of the capital market do CMBS trade in? What is the role of the conduit? The investment bank? The rating agency? The special servicer?

20.2. Explain the economics underlying commercial mortgage securitization. Specifically, explain the concept of *tranching* and how it can stratify and concentrate the default risk in the pooled mortgages, and why this is valuable.

20.3. Why are bond-rating agencies so vital in the CMBS market? What unique role do they play?

20.4. What is a B-piece buyer? How can these investors influence the composition of the mortgage loan pool underlying a CMBS issue? Could CMBS exist without B-piece buyers?

20.5. Under the traditional structure described in Section 20.2, what is the role of the interest-only (IO) tranche in the profitability of the CMBS issue for the investment bank?

20.6. Why is it, and how can it be, that the more junior CMBS tranches command stated yields that are higher than the expected returns to the underlying property equity that backs the credit of these securities? Why are junior CMBS tranches more risky than whole first mortgages with the same LTV ratios?

20.7. Why have CMBS bond rating agencies instituted a special suffix on their CMBS bond ratings, such as the "(sf)" shown in Exhibit 20-6, since the 2008 financial crisis? What does "sf" stand for and what does that suffix mean?

20.8. Based on the text box, "CMBS: Fixed-Income or Real Estate Investment?" answer the following: What types of investors would you typically expect to purchase bonds of the various credit classifications? Why do lower-grade CMBS yield spreads tend to react in a more exaggerated fashion than do senior tranches to bad news about the economy or the real estate market? In what senses does this make non-investment-grade bonds more informationally sensitive than investment-grade CMBS?

20.9. What is meant by the economic terms "moral hazard" and "adverse selection"? How do these phenomena enter into the CMBS industry?

Quantitative Problems

20.10. Suppose a CMBS mortgage pool has an average LTV ratio of 75%, and the senior tranche in the CMBS issue has 35% credit support. Approximately what LTV ratio in a first mortgage whole loan issuance would correspond to the same credit risk as the senior tranche of this CMBS issue?

20.11. A certain mortgage pool has $1 billion in par value. The senior (A) tranche has 30% credit support, and the next level (B) has 25% credit support. How much par value of securities was issued in the A tranche? How much par value was issued in the B tranche? How much par value will be lost by each tranche in each of the following scenarios:
a. 20% of the underlying pool par value defaults.
b. 27% of the underlying pool par value defaults.
c. 33% of the underlying pool par value defaults.

20.12. In a certain CMBS issue, $500 million of senior securities and $100 million of mezzanine securities are issued. The coupon on the senior securities is 7%, and that on the mezzanine is 9%. The average contractual interest rate in the underlying mortgage pool is 10%. Assuming annual interest payments and no par value retired or defaulted, how much residual interest will be available for an IO tranche from these two par-valued tranches at the end of the first year?

20.13. Consider a small, simplified CMBS deal based on a $100 million pool of commercial mortgages, comprised of 10 identical sized loans. Each mortgage is a five-year, 6.5% interest-only, annual payment balloon loan. The loans are all of similar credit quality on a stand-alone basis. Each loan has a 75% loan-to-value ratio and each of the 10 properties are valued at prices implying cap rates equal or close to 8.5%. The mortgage pool has been carved into two tranches or classes of bonds as follows:

Class/Rating	Par Value	Coupon	YTM
1/AAA	$80M	6.5%	4.0%
2/B	$20M	6.5%	?%

In this simplified world, both tranches have the same coupon as the underlying mortgages, and hence neither will sell at par.

a. Determine the implied loan-to-value (LTV) and debt coverage ratio (DCR) of the AAA class.

b. Determine the maximum yield to maturity or required return of investors in the B-rated securities that makes this deal work; that is, the YTM at which the total value of the securities equals the $100 million par value. Compare the yield you determine to the mortgage rate on the whole loans and the YTM required by investors in the AAA bonds and explain the differences. (Hint: First, value the AAA bonds, then back out the implied required value of the B-rated bonds, and then determine the YTM.)

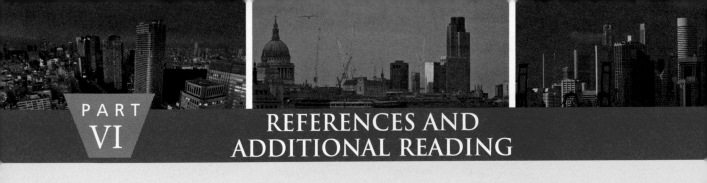

Ambrose, B., and A. Sanders. 2003. Commercial mortgage (CMBS) default and prepayment analysis. *Journal of Real Estate Finance and Economics* 26(2,3): 179–96.

Arsenault, M., J. Clayton, and L. Peng. Forthcoming. Mortgage fund flows, capital appreciation and real estate cycles. *Journal of Real Estate Finance and Economics*.

Bergsman, S. 2012. The mess that is CMBS: Delinquencies, special servicing and possible conflicts of interest plague the market. *The Institutional Real Estate Letter (North America)* 24(5).

Childs, P., S. Ott, and T. Riddiough. 1996. Property Diversification, Risk, and Return in CMBS Investment. Real Estate Research Institute Working Paper (WP-49).

———. 1996. The value of recourse and cross-default clauses in commercial mortgage contracts. *Journal of Banking & Finance* 20: 511–36.

Ciochetti, B. A. 1996. Loss characteristics of commercial mortgage foreclosures. Real Estate Research Institute Working Paper.

———. 1998. Investment loss characteristics associated with commercial mortgages. Real Estate Research Institute Working Paper.

Ciochetti, B. A., and K. Vandell. 1999. The performance of commercial mortgages. *Real Estate Economics* 27(1): 27–62.

Clayton, J. 2009. Debt matters (more than it should): Leverage, liquidity and property valuation. *Journal of Real Estate Portfolio Management* 15(1): 107–13.

Commercial Mortgage Securitization Association and Mortgage Bankers Association. 2004. *Borrower Guide to CMBS*.

Coval, J., J. Jurek, and E. Stafford. 2009. The economics of structured finance. *Journal of Economic Perspectives* 23(1): 3–25.

Dierker, M., D. Quan, and W. Torous. 2005. Valuing the defeasance option in securitized commercial mortgages. *Real Estate Economics* 33(4): 663-80.

Esaki, H., S. L'Heureux, and M. Snyderman. 1999. Commercial mortgage defaults: An update. *Real Estate Finance* 16(1): 81–86.

Fabozzi, F., and D. Jacob, eds. 1999. *The Handbook of Commercial Mortgage-Backed Securities*, 2nd ed. New Hope, PA: Frank J. Fabozzi Associates.

Geltner, D. 1993. Estimating market values from appraised values without assuming an efficient market. *Journal of Real Estate Research* 8(3): 325–46.

Giliberto, M. 1994. The inside story on rates of return II: Commercial mortgages. *Real Estate Finance* 11(2): 10–13.

Gordon, S. 2002. How to build a bond. *CMBS World*, Special Borrower Edition.

Hill, M. A., and R. D. Jones. 2002. A Miranda warning for potential conduit borrowers (or a checklist for loan officers). *CMBS World*, Special Borrower Edition.

Hilliard J. E., J. B. Kau, and V. C. Slawson. 1998. Valuing prepayment and default in a fixed-rate mortgage: A bivariate binomial options pricing technique. *Real Estate Economics* 26(3): 431–68.

Jacob, D. P., and J. M. Manzi. 2005. CMBS credit protection and underwriting standards. *The Journal of Portfolio Management*, Special Issue on Real Estate.

Kau, J. B., D. C. Keenan, Muller W. J., et al. 1992. A generalized valuation model for fixed-rate residential mortgages. *Journal of Money, Credit, and Banking* 24(3): 279–99.

Khandani, A., A. Lo, and R. Merton. 2009. Systemic risk and the refinancing ratchet effect. MIT Sloan Research Paper No. 4750-09, Harvard Business School Finance Working Paper No. 1472892.

Lancaster, B. 2001. The CMBS market, swap spreads and relative value, in *Investing in Commercial Mortgage-Backed Securities*. Frank J. Fabozzi (ed.), 211-16. New Hope, PA: Frank J. Fabozzi Associates.

Mei, J. 1996. Assessing the Santa Claus approach to asset allocation: Implications for commercial real estate investment. *Real Estate Finance* 13(2): 65–70.

Morgan Stanley. 2006. *Transforming Real Estate Finance: A CMBS Primer*, 6th ed.

Nomura Fixed Income Research. 2004. CDOs in plain English: A summer intern's letter home.

———. 2005. CMBS bond structure and its impact on performance.

———. 2006. The evolution of commercial real estate CDOs.

Polleys, C. 1998. An empirical investigation into CMBS pricing and the role of the rating agency. Real Estate Research Institute Working Paper.

Riddiough, T. 1994. Incentive issues and the performance of participating commercial mortgages. Real Estate Research Institute Working Paper (WP-21).

Riddiough, T., and K. Taira. 2001. Determinants of commercial mortgage choice, *Real Estate Finance*.

Riddiough, T., and S. Wyatt. 1994. Strategic default, workout, and commercial mortgage valuation. *Journal of Real Estate Finance & Economics* 9(1): 5–22.

Sanders, A. 2006. Commercial mortgage-backed securities, in *The Handbook of Fixed-income Securities*, Frank J. Fabozzi (ed.), 663–77. New York: McGraw-Hill.

Snyderman, M. 1990. A commercial mortgage performance index. *Journal of Portfolio Management* 16: 70–73.

———. 1999. Public debt: A new fact of the fixed income world. Presentation to the Association for Investment Management and Research Conference, Boston, November 1999.

Stanton, R., and N. Wallace. 2010. CMBS subordination, ratings inflation, and the Crisis of 2007–2009. NBER Working Paper No. 16206.

Sundaresan, S. 1997. *Fixed Income Markets and Their Derivatives*. Cincinnati, OH: South-Western College Publishing.

Vandell, K. 1992. Predicting commercial mortgage foreclosure experience. *Real Estate Economics* 20(1): 55–88.

Vandell, K., W. Barnes, D. Hartzell, D. Kraft, and W. Wendt. 1993. Commercial mortgage defaults: Proportional hazards estimation using individual loan histories. *Real Estate Economics* 21(4): 451–80.

Vogel, J. H. 2003. The amazing rise of commercial mortgage-backed securities: How an inferior product prevailed, *Real Estate Finance* 20(2): 15–20.

Vrchota, M., and S. Merrick. 2005. Large loans: Inclusion in fusion, what's the confusion? *CMBS World*, spring 2005.

White, L. J. 2010. The credit rating agencies. *Journal of Economic Perspectives* 24(2): 211–26.

Wiggers, T., and A. Ashcraft. 2012. Defaults and losses on commercial real estate bonds during the Great Depression Era. Federal Reserve Bank of New York, Staff Report no. 544, February 2012.

VII

MACRO-LEVEL REAL ESTATE INVESTMENT ISSUES

Recall the analogy we made at the outset of Part IV between real estate investment and a rain forest. There we said we were going to be like the botanists looking at individual trees rather than ecologists considering the entire forest. Indeed, most of this book up to now focused primarily at the micro-level of individual properties and deals. While some of the preceding material included broad background information and fundamental building blocks relevant to the macro-level (and more recent chapters went beyond a strict property-level focus*), nevertheless, the bulk of our attention on real estate equity investment so far has been at the micro-level.

That is about to change. Part VII will focus specifically on the major macro-level issues, concepts, and analytical tools. Here is where we study the forest as a whole rather than the trees. To be more precise, what we are referring to as the macro-level in real estate investment concerns the investor's decisions and management regarding many individual properties simultaneously, that is, aggregates of properties. The macro-level is also the level at which the investor's *overall portfolio* is considered, which is why it is often referred to as the portfolio level. At its broadest, this includes the investor's entire net wealth portfolio, including not just real estate but other investment asset classes as well, the so-called "mixed-asset portfolio." Indeed, it is at the macro-level that the interface between real estate and

other asset classes enters most directly into analysis and decision making. The macro-level is also a good place to talk more about REITs as investments. In a REIT, the decision-making entity (i.e., the firm) generally controls numerous individual properties.

The concept of a macro-level of real estate investment analysis and management really only dates from the last third of the twentieth century. Traditional real estate investment was effectively a purely micro-level endeavor. Indeed, the distinction between these two levels is somewhat unique to real estate. The concepts of macro-level investment decisions and activities, and macro-level valuation, for example, are a bit foreign to the fields of securities investments and corporate finance. Yet during the last two decades of the twentieth century, the macro-level of real estate investment analysis and decision making blossomed rapidly into a major component and force within real estate, with its effects permeating down to even small-scale micro-level transactions, not least because the macro-level is central to the growing link between Wall Street and Main Street. The macro-level is therefore also the level where we find many of the more modern and rapidly growing real estate professional career paths.

At a broad-brush level, and by way of an initial introduction, it is useful to think of three major types of macro-level real estate investment decision arenas: *strategic* policy formulation, *tactical* policy formulation, and policy *implementation*. Strategic investment

---

*For example, the last section in Chapter 12 (on the "dueling asset markets") touched on the relationship between the micro- and macro-levels of real estate investment. The type of financing and capital structure issues addressed in Part V are considered to be largely macro-level (that is, firm-wide) decisions in traditional corporate finance, although in real estate the prevalence of project-specific financing gives these issues a more micro-level flavor. The last chapters in Part VI addressed the role of mortgages from a broader, portfolio-level perspective.

policies define broad, overall allocations and long-run directions and objectives. Tactical policies seek to profit from shorter-term opportunities. Implementation concerns how to carry out policies of both the strategic and tactical type most effectively. For example, an analytical tool widely used at the strategic level is modern portfolio theory (MPT). A major concern at the tactical level is market timing and econometric forecasting of the space and asset markets. Major topics in implementation include the analysis and evaluation of the performance of investment managers and the crafting of incentive structures that align the interests of such managers with their investor clients. In all three of these decision areas, the macro-level cannot be divorced from the micro-level. Macro-level decisions are ultimately implemented at the micro-level, and the quality of the macro–micro link is a key to long-run success in real estate investment.

We will address all three of these macro-level decision arenas in Part VII, as well as the macro–micro link, by presenting some fundamental macro-level principles and analytical tools and showing how these relate to investment decision making. The major macro-level investment principles and analytical tools we will address include portfolio theory, equilibrium asset pricing theory, macro-level valuation and return measurement issues, and real estate investment management performance attribution and evaluation.

Part VII is organized into six chapters. Chapters 21 and 22 begin with a presentation of MPT and equilibrium asset pricing models, the classical tools and discipline for "top-down" real estate investment decision making, including particular consideration of the role of real estate in the mixed-asset portfolio. Chapter 23 then treats the REIT industry as a case of macro-level valuation of real estate by the stock market. Chapter 24 moves us to the global perspective with a treatment of international investment in real estate. In Chapter 25, we get down to a very fundamental nuts-and-bolts problem, that of dealing with the peculiarities and measurement errors inherent in real estate investment performance data, including the so-called appraisal smoothing problem and the development of transactions-based indices. Finally, Chapter 26 focuses on the investment policy implementation decision arena with a detailed look at the real estate investment management industry, including quantitative performance attribution and evaluation and a brief introduction to the new business of real estate derivatives.

REAL ESTATE AND PORTFOLIO THEORY: STRATEGIC INVESTMENT CONSIDERATIONS

CHAPTER OUTLINE

LEARNING OBJECTIVES

After reading this chapter, you should understand:

➲ What is meant by modern portfolio theory (MPT) and how to apply this theory using computer spreadsheets.

➲ The major strategic investment policy implications MPT holds for real estate at the broad-brush level of the overall mixed-asset portfolio.

➲ The usefulness of the riskless asset assumption and the meaning of the Sharpe-maximizing portfolio.

➲ The nature of institutional investment portfolios in the real world and the major practical considerations involved in applying portfolio theory to such investors.

T hroughout the financial economics part of this book, we emphasized two major concerns of investors: total *return* and the *risk* surrounding that return. In this chapter, we take our decision-making focus to the level of the investor's overall wealth, the portfolio level. But return and risk remain the major foci of our attention. In particular, this chapter will introduce you to a sophisticated body of principles and techniques known as **modern portfolio theory (MPT)**, or more generally, portfolio theory. Portfolio theory deals with the strategic decision of how best to allocate the investor's capital across a range of asset classes. To address this decision in a rigorous way, portfolio theory makes three major contributions: (1) it treats risk and return together in a comprehensive and integrated manner; (2) it quantifies the investment-decision-relevant implications of risk and return; and (3) it makes both of these contributions at the portfolio level, the level of the investor's overall wealth.

Before we begin, we should probably say a word or two about the nature of the material in this chapter. Modern portfolio theory (and its offspring, the capital asset pricing model, or CAPM for short) won a Nobel Prize for three of the most famous financial economists of all time: Harry Markowitz, William F. Sharpe, and John Lintner. This is sophisticated stuff. Portfolio theory contains a level of analytical rigor that makes it appear rather technical. If you don't like formulas and math, this will not be your favorite chapter in this book. But theories don't earn Nobel Prizes just for their technical impressiveness. Portfolio theory's elegance allows it to reveal, simply, some fundamental aspects of the world, aspects that cut right to the heart of good strategic investment decision making. This is why, from its inception, portfolio theory was used directly and widely in the real world of investment practice. This is not just ivory-tower academic stuff. It provides insights that are important for investment decision making at the broadest and most fundamental level. These insights are especially important for real estate, as we will see.

21.1 Numerical Example of the Portfolio Allocation Problem: Real Estate in the Mixed-Asset Portfolio

The best way to begin to learn about portfolio theory in a way that will be usable for you is to walk through a simple numerical example. Let's take the case of our favorite real estate investor, Bob. Bob was given the job of managing the $10 billion portfolio of a pension fund. He was told by the fund's board of trustees to come up with a recommendation on how to allocate their assets between three alternative investment asset classes: common stocks, long-term bonds, and commercial real estate. He was also told to

- "diversify the investments of the fund" so as to minimize risk as measured by the volatility in the fund's total portfolio value; and to
- meet a target long-term overall expected total return of 7 percent per annum for the fund.

What should Bob have done? (What would you have done in his place?)

In order to begin to answer this question in a rational and quantitative way, Bob realized that he had to ask himself what he expects the long-term average total returns would be in the future for the three asset classes he had to choose among: stocks, bonds, and real estate. In fact, this first step was a tough and very important part of the problem. Not surprisingly, Bob put in quite an effort to come up with what he thought were rather reasonable future average return estimates of 10 percent per year in the stock market, 6 percent in the long-term bond market, and 7 percent in commercial real estate.[1]

After expending such an effort to come up with ex ante return estimates that he was so proud of, Bob then rushed to a silly allocation recommendation that embarrassed him when he took it to the board of his pension fund client. He suggested a simple equal allocation of

---

[1]Bob based his reasoning on an examination of long-term historical return performance relative to "risk-free" Treasury bills, as well as current projections for inflation and short-term interest rates going forward into the future. In short, Bob conducted an analysis not unlike what we briefly described in Chapters 7 and 11. (See especially the discussion in section 11.2 regarding the estimation of real estate opportunity cost of capital.) To help quantify risk and the price of risk in different asset classes, Bob may also have used some insights from capital asset market general equilibrium pricing theory and practical stock value analysis tools (as will be described in a later chapter), as well as some lessons and tools from bond market economics (as described briefly in Chapters 18 and 19).

33.3 percent to each of the three asset classes. The board's independent consultant, Sue, immediately pointed out to Bob the problem with this suggestion. According to Bob's return expectations, his recommended allocation would overshoot the fund's 7 percent return target by 67 basis points. In particular, the portfolio expected return implied by Bob's suggested allocation was[2]

$$(0.333)10\% + (0.333)6\% + (0.333)7\% = 7.67\%$$

At first, Bob protested that such overshooting did not present a problem; after all, wasn't a 7.67 percent expected return better than a 7 percent expected return? But Sue retorted that the 7 percent target had been arrived at by considering *how much risk* the board wanted to take on in their investments, recognizing that in the capital markets, one can realistically obtain a higher ex ante return only by investing in assets that have more risk.

With that, Bob went back to the drawing board and came up with an allocation that exactly met the board's 7 percent target. In particular, Bob proposed to invest 22.5 percent of the fund in stocks, 67.5 percent in bonds, and 10 percent in real estate. The expected return to the fund would then be

$$(0.225)10\% + (0.675)6\% + (0.100)7\% = 7\%$$

But once again Bob was embarrassed by Sue (who actually seemed to take pleasure in his embarrassment). She asked Bob why this particular allocation was any better than the multitude of other possible allocations that would also exactly meet the 7 percent target.[3] Sue pointed her finger at Bob in front of the board and asked him whether this allocation minimized the expected **volatility** of the fund's overall portfolio ("as directed by the board," she rubbed it in). Bob could only stammer something about his intuitive feeling that it was "probably pretty close" to minimizing the volatility (but in fact he didn't really know). A meeting was scheduled for the following week, a week in which Bob burned a lot of midnight oil.

Bob realized that in order to be more rigorous in his recommendation, he would have to estimate the volatility of each of the three asset classes, as well as the correlation among their returns. This was necessary in order to compute the volatility that any combination of these three assets would have. Estimating these "second moment statistics" was even harder than estimating their expected returns.[4] Nevertheless, Bob came up with the following estimates for annual volatility, or standard deviation in the periodic returns across time:

- **Stock market annual volatility: 15%,** based on the historical investment performance of the S&P 500 index over the past few decades
- **Long-term bond annual volatility: 8%,** also based on historical performance, adjusted slightly downward because Bob expected interest rates might not be quite as volatile in the future as they had been in the last few decades
- **Real estate annual volatility: 10%,** based on the historical performance of the NCREIF index, adjusted slightly to account for the effect of appraisal smoothing, and considering evidence from some of the new transactions-based real estate indices
- **Correlation between stocks and bonds: +30%,** based on recent historical evidence and the understanding that both asset classes tended to respond in the same direction to macroeconomic news on such issues as economic growth, inflation, and real interest rates

---

[2]Note that the formula used here is essentially the same as the weighted average cost of capital (WACC) formula we described in Chapter 13. This and other formulas useful for computing portfolio statistics are described in Appendix 21 at the end of this chapter.

[3]Technically, what we have at this point is one linear equation with two unknowns: w_{ST} (10%) + w_{BN} (6%) + (1 − w_{ST} − w_{BN}) (7%) = 7%, where w_{ST} is the allocation to stocks and w_{BN} is the allocation to bonds. Mathematically, an infinite number of combinations of w_{ST} and w_{BN} would satisfy this equation. The solution $w_{ST} = 0.225$, $w_{BN} = 0.675$ is just one such solution.

[4]The distinction between "first moment" and "second moment" statistics is described in Appendix 21 at the end of the chapter.

EXHIBIT 21-1A

Bob's Risk and Return Expectations

© OnCourse Learning

	Stocks	**Bonds**	**Real Estate**
Expected Return ($E[r]$)	10.00%	6.00%	7.00%
Volatility	15.00%	8.00%	10.00%
Correlation with:			
Stocks	100.00%	30.00%	25.00%
Bonds		100.00%	15.00%
Real Estate			100.00%

- **Correlation between stocks and real estate: +25%,** based on historical evidence and the recognition that, although real estate market cycles have often appeared to be independent of the stock market, both real estate and stocks are dependent on the health of the underlying macro-economy and, as long-term assets, their values respond similarly to changes in real interest rates
- **Correlation between bonds and real estate: +15%,** a bit higher than the historical evidence, but perhaps more realistic for the future in which Bob expected inflation risk to be less than it had been in the available historical data[5]

Bob knew these estimates were "soft," and he was not extremely confident that they were correct. But he also knew that no one has a crystal ball and therefore no one could make perfect estimates. Nevertheless, decisions had to be made based on the best information available. He felt he could defend these estimates (even against Sue) because they were reasonable and realistic in the light of available historical evidence, plausible economic theory, and common sense. Bob's risk and return expectations for the three asset classes are summarized in the table in Exhibit 21-1A.[6] Perhaps more important from a political perspective, Bob actually got Sue to agree before the meeting with the board that these were plausible expectations.

Once Bob had come up with these risk and return expectations, the mechanics of computing the volatility of a portfolio consisting of any allocation across the three asset classes was actually quite easy, using the basic spreadsheet software that Bob had on his laptop computer. The first step was to compute a table of the **covariances** between each possible pair of assets. This was done using the information in Exhibit 21-1A, as indicated in the table in Exhibit 21-1B.

In this table, each cell is a covariance (or variance if the cell is on the diagonal).[7] For example, the middle cell in the top row of Exhibit 21-1B (covariance of stocks and bonds) is found from the data in Exhibit 21-1A as $0.0036 = (0.15)(0.08)(0.30)$.[8]

The next step in computing the portfolio variance was to multiply each of these covariances by the product of the "weights," or proportional shares of the total portfolio value, given to each asset class in Bob's proposed allocation. For example, in Bob's proposed allocation of 22.5 percent to stocks and 67.5 percent to bonds, the covariance of 0.0036 between stocks and bonds would be multiplied by the product of 0.225 times 0.675. Considering also

---

[5]The strongly negative correlation between real estate and bond returns during the 1970s and early 1980s heavily influenced the long-term historical evidence. However, this was a period of particularly high inflation risk that had a sharp negative impact on bond returns while actually stimulating investment in real estate as an inflation "hedge." Bob felt that a repeat of such a situation in the future was less likely than the common effect that changes in *real* interest rates would have on both bond and real estate returns, which would impart a positive correlation between the two asset classes.

[6]The actual historical annual correlation statistics for the three asset classes' periodic total returns as described in Chapter 7 for the 1970–2010 period were +30% between stocks and bonds, +17% between stocks and real estate, and −21% between real estate and bonds. Bob's adjustments from the historical annual data were meant to reflect likely long-run performance expectations going forward from the present time.

[7]As described in Appendix 21 at the end of the chapter, the variance in an asset's return is equivalent to its covariance with itself.

[8]In general, $COV_{ij} = S_i S_j C_{ij}$, where COV_{ij} is the covariance between assets i and j, S_i is the volatility (that is, the time-series standard deviation in the periodic total returns) of asset i, and C_{ij} is the **correlation coefficient** between the two assets' periodic returns.

EXHIBIT 21-1B

Bob's Covariance Expectations

© OnCourse Learning

	Stocks	Bonds	Real Estate
Stocks	0.022500	0.003600	0.003750
Bonds	0.003600	0.006400	0.001200
Real Estate	0.003750	0.001200	0.010000

EXHIBIT 21-1C

Bob's Weighted Covariances

© OnCourse Learning

	Stocks	Bonds	Real Estate
Stocks	0.001139	0.000547	0.000084
Bonds	0.000547	0.002916	0.000081
Real Estate	0.000084	0.000081	0.000100

the 10 percent allocation to real estate that Bob was proposing, this resulted in the table shown in Exhibit 21-1C.[9]

The final step in computing the volatility of Bob's proposed portfolio was simply to sum all of the **weighted covariances** in the nine cells in Exhibit 21-1C and take the square root of that sum.[10] This resulted in an expected portfolio volatility of 7.47 percent, based on Bob's risk and return expectations as indicated in Exhibit 21-1A, and Bob's proposed allocation weights of 22.5 percent stocks, 67.5 percent bonds, and 10 percent real estate.[11]

Once Bob had set up his electronic spreadsheet to compute the portfolio volatility, he realized that he could easily find the allocation that would indeed minimize the portfolio volatility, as the board of the pension fund wanted him to do (and Sue would surely demand). Bob found his ideal allocation using the **solver** utility in his spreadsheet software.[12] He told the solver to select an allocation across the three asset classes so as to minimize the value in the cell that computed the portfolio volatility, subject to the following constraints:

- The target return must be met:

$$\sum_{i=1}^{N} w_i E[r_i] = E[r_p],$$

where $E[r_p]$ is the target long-term return for the portfolio, w_i is the weight (proportion of total portfolio value) allocated to each asset class i, and $E[r_i]$ is the expected long-term return to each asset class.

---

[9]For example, looking again at the middle cell in the top row (stocks and bonds), the computation is $0.000547 = (0.225)(0.675)(0.0036)$. In general, the value in the cell in row i, column j of the weighted covariance table is $w_i w_j COV_{ij}$, where w_i is the proportional allocation to asset i within the portfolio (that is, the share of the total portfolio value invested in asset i).

[10]Of course, this is easily done in a spreadsheet simply by selecting the entire table as the range of cells to be summed.

[11]The variance of a portfolio is given by the following formula, as presented in the chapter appendix:

$$S_P^2 = \sum_{i=1}^{N} \sum_{j=1}^{N} w_i w_j COV_{ij}$$

where there are N assets in the portfolio, and

$$\sum_{i=1}^{N} w_i = 1$$

[12]Mathematically, the portfolio optimization problem described here is a type of constrained optimization problem that can be solved using a technique called quadratic programming. The solvers in general-purpose spreadsheets usually employ more general numerical solution procedures that can handle a wide variety of problems, including the portfolio problem described here. Spreadsheet solvers are usually adequate for handling portfolio problems with up to at least a dozen or so possible assets, while more specialized software is necessary for handling very large numbers of assets. Keep in mind that spreadsheet solvers iterate numerically to the constrained optimal solution. They may not provide an exact optimum. (An Excel® file template that uses the Solver to perform this optimization is available on the CD accompanying this book.)

● The allocation weights must all sum to unity:

$$\sum_{i=1}^{N} w_i = 1.$$

In addition, Bob added constraints requiring each asset allocation to be nonnegative because his pension fund client did not wish to take short positions (such as borrowing money) in any major asset class.[13]

As a result of this exercise, Bob found that an allocation of 16 percent to stocks, 48 percent to bonds, and 36 percent to real estate would meet the fund's 7 percent expected **return target** while minimizing its expected volatility at 6.89 percent, compared to the 7.47 percent volatility in Bob's previously suggested allocation.

Of course, this allocation is only ideal to the extent that Bob's risk and return expectations for the three asset classes, as summarized in Exhibit 21-1A, are accurate. However, Bob's confidence in this regard was raised by the fact that he had already gotten Sue to agree that these expectations were reasonable. Nevertheless, knowing that any such future expectations are only approximate, he thought it prudent to test the effects of changing his expectations within plausible bounds. Such **sensitivity analysis** was easy to do using his computer spreadsheet and solver, simply by changing the values in the input table (Exhibit 21-1A). For example, Bob was a bit unsure about his correlation assumptions for real estate, so he tested the effect of assuming that real estate was more highly correlated with the other asset classes: +50% with the stock market (instead of +25%) and +25% with long-term bonds (instead of +15%). The result was a variance-minimizing allocation of 17 percent stocks, 52 percent bonds, and 31 percent real estate.

Bob went back to the pension fund board with a recommended allocation that was relatively heavy in real estate and bonds and a bit light in stocks. Both the board and Sue seemed a bit uneasy about this suggestion, but they couldn't immediately find any flaw in Bob's approach or his conclusions. They had to admit that, if they didn't like his recommendation, they would have to go back to their own drawing boards and reexamine their stated objectives for the portfolio. For example, perhaps they did not really want to be so conservative as what was implied by their 7 percent return target. Or perhaps there was something important being left out of the picture, perhaps some element of risk that they weren't considering, or some cost of investment in one or more of the asset classes that was not being reflected in the directives they had given Bob.[14]

21.2 Basic Mean-Variance Portfolio Theory (MPT)

The preceding story of Bob and his three-asset portfolio allocation problem is an example of the application of what is called **mean-variance portfolio theory**. As noted in the beginning of this chapter, this theory is also sometimes referred to as modern portfolio theory (abbreviated as MPT), or Markowitz portfolio theory, for the economist who is largely credited with its development. In this theory the objective of the macro-level investment decision maker is taken to be the minimization of portfolio volatility (or variance) subject to an expected return target. In fact, this objective is mathematically equivalent to its "dual" description: the

---

[13]In a short investment position, the asset is sold (cash proceeds obtained) *before* it is bought (cash paid out). To prohibit short positions, constraints in the form of $w_i \geq 0$ must be entered in the solver for each possible constituent asset class i in the portfolio.

[14]In reality, most U.S. institutions consider more than just domestic stocks, long-term bonds, and real estate as the major asset classes in the core of their investment portfolios. In particular, "cash" (short-term debt, especially T-bills), small stocks, and international debt and equity are generally considered as major components. We will expand our consideration to include cash (T-bills) and small stocks later, and we have left out international investments to simplify this example. However, to be fair, it should be recognized that, if we were to expand stock and bonds to include separate international components, then we could in like manner (at least in principle) also expand real estate to include a separate international real estate component. Some U.S. institutions do invest directly in overseas real estate assets. Also, going beyond the traditional "core" asset classes, many investors now also include "alternative investments" such as commodities, private equity and hedge funds in their overall portfolios (usually in relatively small amounts). However, such alternative asset classes are difficult to include in classical portfolio theory because their periodic risk and return statistics are less reliable or meaningful than those of private real estate.

maximization of portfolio expected return subject to a volatility constraint. The numerical example in the preceding section demonstrated concretely what mean-variance theory does, how it is typically applied in the real world, and the basic mechanical steps for applying the theory using common computer spreadsheet software. Let us now step back and look at this theory from a broader and deeper perspective, so as to derive a more general understanding of how it can be useful to decision makers.

21.2.1 Investor Preferences and Dominant Portfolios

As risk and return are the two main issues portfolio theory is concerned about, a good place to begin is to consider a picture of the risk and return preferences of the investor. Exhibit 21-2 depicts risk and return on the horizontal and vertical axes of a rectangle, respectively. Each point in the rectangle is a different combination of risk and return. The investor's preferences are indicated by the indifference curves shown in the rectangle. These curves show how the investor judges the trade-off between risk and return for her investments. The investor is indifferent among portfolios that provide risk and return combinations that lie on the same indifference curve.

You can think of the indifference curves as contour lines on a map of a ski slope, representing a three-dimensional surface above the risk/return rectangle. Higher points on this surface indicate risk/ return combinations that are preferred by the investor. Other things being equal, investors generally prefer greater return and less risk. Thus, the investor preference surface is rising toward the upper left corner of the rectangle. The investor will prefer points farther to the "north" and "west" in the rectangle; points such as *P* will be preferred over points like *Q*.

EXHIBIT 21-2 Utility Preference Surface (indifference curves) of an Investor

© OnCourse Learning

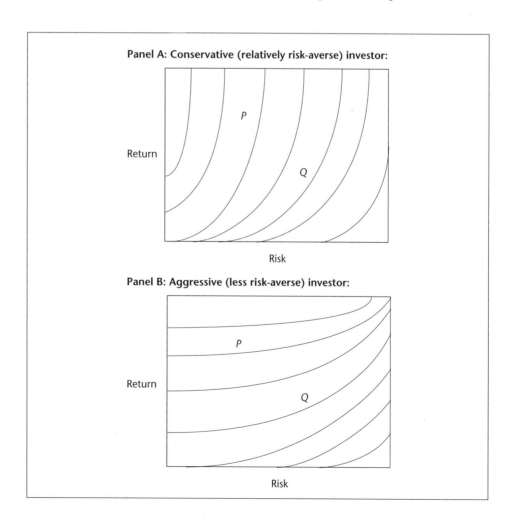

Panel A: Conservative (relatively risk-averse) investor:

Return

Risk

Panel B: Aggressive (less risk-averse) investor:

Return

Risk

The rectangle in the top panel in Exhibit 21-2 (panel A) depicts a conservative investor, one who is relatively more risk averse (less risk tolerant) in his investment preferences. Such an investor's indifference curves are steeply curved to the north in the risk/return rectangle, indicating that he must be compensated with a lot of additional return in order to be willing to take on a little more risk. This is seen by the fact that the curves move a considerable distance along the vertical (expected return) axis for each small increment along the horizontal (risk) axis.

In contrast, the rectangle in panel B of Exhibit 21-2 depicts a more aggressive investor, one who is relatively more risk tolerant. Such an investor's indifference curves are less steeply rising over the horizontal axis, indicating less need for additional expected return in more risky investments.

Suppose that points P and Q in Exhibit 21-2 represent the expected return and risk of two different portfolios, that is, two different allocations for the investor's wealth. Clearly, both the conservative and the aggressive investors depicted in Exhibit 21-2 would prefer portfolio P to portfolio Q. In fact, as long as investors are not actually "risk loving" (that is, as long as they do not actually prefer more risk to less, holding return constant), they will always prefer a point such as P to one like Q.

Now consider Exhibit 21-3. Here, the risk and return possibilities are divided into four quadrants emanating from portfolio Q. Any portfolio (such as P) that provides as much or more expected return than Q with as little or less risk, is said to *dominate* Q. This would be any portfolio providing risk/return combinations above and/or to the left of Q, that is, in the upper-left quadrant. Similarly, any risk/return combination in the lower-right quadrant would be *dominated by* Q. *Any* investor, no matter what her **risk preferences** (whether she is conservative or aggressive, as long as she is not actually risk loving), will prefer a **dominant portfolio** to a dominated portfolio.

In practice, and from a quantifiable perspective, mean-variance portfolio theory is used primarily to help investors avoid holding dominated portfolios. Portfolio theory is about moving investors from points such as Q to points such as P whenever possible, that is, moving up and/or to the left (or "northwesterly") in a standard risk/return diagram such as that in Exhibit 21-3.[15] Classical Markowitz portfolio theory has less to say (quantitatively) about choosing between Q and another portfolio that lies in either the quadrant to Q's northeast or the quadrant to Q's southwest. To rigorously make such a choice, we would need to know how to quantify the investor's risk preferences more completely than simply knowing that he is not risk loving.[16]

21.2.2 Portfolio Theory and Diversification

The expression "Don't put all your eggs in one basket" has been around a long time. Long before Harry Markowitz published his seminal paper on portfolio theory in 1952, people had an intuitive sense that they should not put too much of their total wealth into a single investment or type of asset. This might be referred to as intuitive diversification. It is common sense that if all (or nearly all) of your wealth is invested in only one type of asset, then

---

[15]For example, back in section 21.1, Sue's criticism of Bob's recommended allocation of 22.5% stocks, 67.5% bonds, and 10% real estate was based on the dominance argument. That allocation achieved no more expected return than the one Bob ultimately came up with (7%), but it had more volatility (7.47% instead of 6.89%).

[16]Some techniques have been developed to attempt to quantify investor preferences more precisely. For example, the investor may be guided through an exercise in which she states her preference for various combinations of stocks and bonds given various different expected returns and historical volatility patterns, in such a way that a "preference map" along the lines of what is depicted in Exhibit 21-2 can be constructed for the investor regarding various risk/return combinations. More commonly in the real world, however, this part of the portfolio allocation decision (that is, movement in a southwesterly or northeasterly direction in the risk/return diagram) is treated "heuristically" or nonquantitatively, which is to say for many investment institutions, politically. Implicitly, of course, some indication of the investor's preferences is inevitably revealed in the allocation policy he finally adopts. That the adoption process should be somewhat *political* actually makes *economic* sense. Although a Nobel Prize was given to Harry Markowitz for his development of portfolio theory, another Nobel Prize was given to economist Kenneth Arrow, in part for his development of what is called the "impossibility theorem." Arrow proved that it is mathematically impossible to define a so-called social welfare function that can be relied on to aggregate individual preferences into a single rational preference function. In effect, viewed from a very fundamental perspective, any investment decision-making institution that has more than one individual owner or beneficiary must employ some sort of political process to aggregate preferences effectively, so as to arrive at a common decision. Alas (but aren't you really glad), there is a limit to how far technocrats can take us.

EXHIBIT 21-3 Portfolio
Dominance
© OnCourse Learning

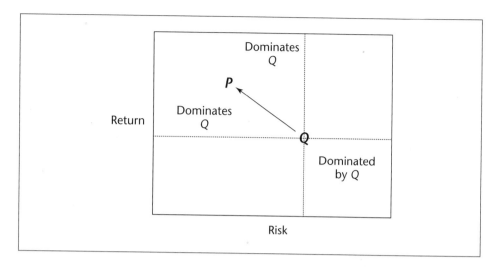

you are overly exposed to loss in the event of a downside event that randomly affects only that one type of asset. Portfolio theory adds to this primitive concept of diversification by quantifying the benefit of diversification in terms of portfolio risk and return, and by providing some rigorous (albeit somewhat simplistic) guidance as to exactly how to diversify, that is, *how many* eggs should you put in *which* baskets.

In this regard, it is important to understand that some combinations of assets are more valuable than others as far as their diversification effect is concerned. For example, Exhibit 21-4A shows a scatter-plot and regression line of the total annual returns to large and small stocks during the 1970–2010 period. Each point in the scatter-plot represents the annual periodic returns to large and small stocks in a given year. As you can see from the upward slope of the regression line, these two asset classes tended more often than not to move together in time. This tendency is quantified by their positive correlation coefficient of 71 percent.[17] On the other hand, look at the scatter-plot of bond and real estate returns for the same period shown in Exhibit 21-4B. These two asset classes were as likely to move in the opposite as the same direction during this period, as indicated by their correlation coefficient of zero percent.

Now look at the annual periodic total return histories for 1970–2010 shown in Exhibit 21-5. Exhibit 21-5A shows the returns to small and large stocks separately and to a portfolio consisting of 50 percent large stocks and 50 percent small stocks (the last represented by the solid line in the chart).[18] Small and large stocks were sufficiently positively correlated so that little reduction in volatility resulted from combining the two in a single half-and-half portfolio. The solid line moves up and down about as much as the two other lines. In fact, the volatility of small stocks was 23 percent, large stocks was 18 percent, and the 50/50 portfolio had a volatility of 19 percent. In contrast, Exhibit 21-5B shows that a 50/50 combination of real estate and bonds would have had noticeably less volatility than either pure portfolio alone. Note that the solid line between the two dashed lines jumps around noticeably less than either of the two dashed lines. The 50/50 portfolio had a volatility of only 8 percent, which was less than either the real estate (11 percent) or bond (12 percent) portfolios alone. In general, pairs of assets that do not move together provide greater diversification benefit when they are combined in a portfolio. The volatility of such assets tends to cancel out when they are combined in a portfolio.

21.2.3 Perceived Role of Real Estate in the Mixed-Asset Portfolio

Diversification is a very important consideration for real estate investment from a broad, mixed-asset portfolio perspective. After stocks and bonds, real estate comprises the third major asset class, representing a large amount of physical capital with unique risk and return

---

[17]The definition and meaning of the correlation coefficient is explained in Appendix 21 at the end of this chapter.

[18]Of course, the returns to the 50/50 portfolio simply lie midway between the returns to the two pure portfolios.

EXHIBIT 21-4A Scatter-Plot of Annual Large Stocks and Small Stocks Total Returns, 1970–2010 Based on S&P 500 and Ibbotson Small Stock Index
Source: Ibbotson.

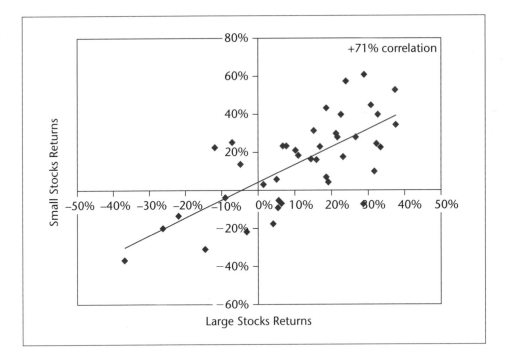

EXHIBIT 21-4B Scatter-Plot of Annual Real Estate and Bond Total Returns, 1970–2010 Based on Long-Term Treasury Bonds and Unsmoothed NCREIF
Source: Ibbotson, NCREIF, and authors.

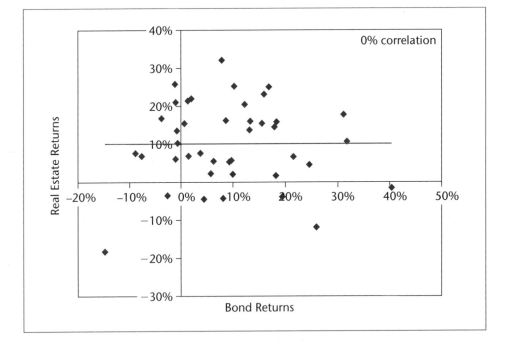

characteristics. As such, real estate gives investors the opportunity to diversify their portfolios more broadly than they could with only two major asset classes. This **diversification benefit** of real estate is a major reason for substantial inclusion of real estate in many large institutional portfolios.

For example, recall our numerical example in section 21.1. Bob ended up recommending a relatively large allocation to real estate in an "optimally diversified" portfolio (for a given return target). The large allocation to real estate in that example was clearly *not* due to real

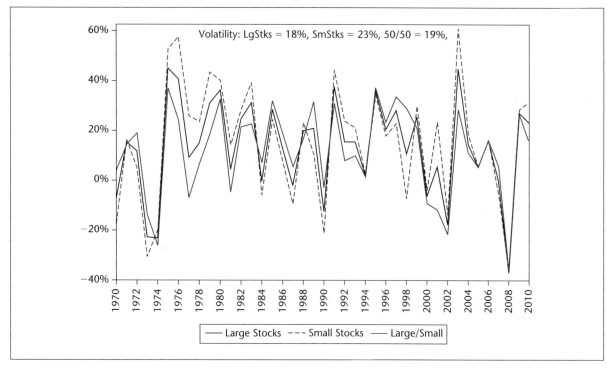

EXHIBIT 21-5A Annual Periodic Total Returns, Large and Small Stock, 50/50 Portfolio, 1970–2010

Source: Ibbotson, NCREIF, and authors.

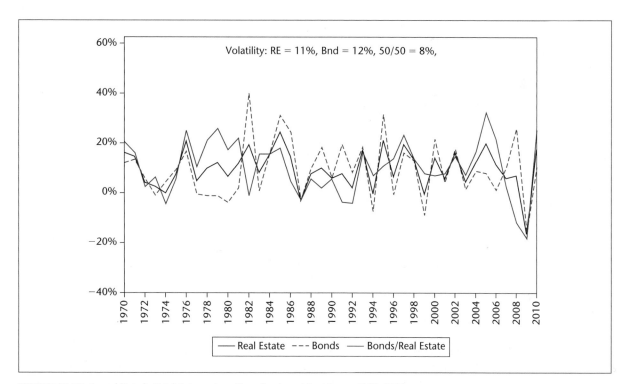

EXHIBIT 21-5B Annual Periodic Total Returns, Long-Term Bonds and Real Estate, 1970–2010

Source: Ibbotson, NCREIF, and authors.

EXHIBIT 21-6 Stock and Real Estate Returns, 1970–2011, 42 Yearly Total Returns to S&P 500 and NCREIF-based TBI

© OnCourse Learning

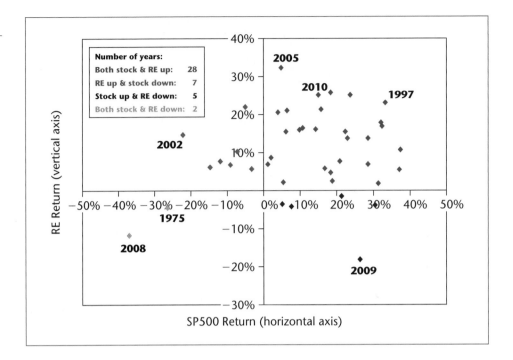

estate providing an exceptionally large expected return. (Recall that Bob estimated a real estate return of 7 percent, compared to 10 percent for stocks.) Nor was it because real estate was expected to provide exceptionally stable returns (that is, low volatility). (Recall that Bob estimated real estate volatility at 10 percent, compared to 15 percent for stocks and 8 percent for bonds.[19]) The reason it made sense to give real estate a large allocation in Bob's portfolio recommendation was primarily that it was not highly correlated with the other two asset classes.

Indeed, real estate's particularly low correlation with long-term bonds was especially useful in our example. By combining large and roughly equal amounts of real estate and bonds, the optimal allocation was able to reduce the portfolio volatility substantially. This is one reason stocks ended up with a relatively small allocation, even though they provided the highest expected return.

During and after the great financial crisis of 2008–2009, real estate asset values collapsed along with virtually all other asset classes during the financial crisis. Many real estate investors complained that real estate's vaunted diversification benefit had let them down just when they needed it most. While this was true, it should be placed in historical perspective. As Exhibit 21-6 reveals, in the 42 years from 1970 through 2011 there were only two years in which both real estate and stocks were negative in total returns: 1975 and 2008, a span of 33 years between the two episodes. And while rigorous quantitative data are not available prior to 1970, it seems likely that one would have to go back another 40 years or so to find another period when both real estate and stocks were negative together (probably during the Great Depression years of the 1930s). Diversification does not *guarantee* that asset classes will *always* move in opposite directions, only that they will tend to dampen out the volatility (average dispersion across time) in the portfolio's returns. It is a rare episode in which both real estate and stocks move significantly down together, but it can happen.

---

[19]It should be noted that there is an aspect of real estate returns that does tend to be relatively stable at least if the real estate investment is made without much debt financing. Real estate assets tend to provide a reliable income stream. This can be a very important consideration for an investment institution such as a pension fund, which needs to fund its pension payment obligations. However, classical MPT does not delve into this aspect as the MPT model does not drill down into the different components or characteristics of returns beyond simply their means, standard deviations, and correlations among the asset classes' total returns.

ANOTHER ROLE FOR REAL ESTATE

Mean-variance portfolio theory highlights real estate's role as a diversifier within the portfolio. This role makes sense from the MPT perspective, viewing the mixed asset portfolio as encompassing the investor's entire net wealth. From the perspective of a pension fund, however, or other such institution managing a portfolio of assets at least in part to meet future liability obligations, a somewhat different perspective may be warranted. The net wealth of the investor may be viewed as the asset portfolio minus the present value of future liability obligations (e.g., pension benefit payments to retirees). These obligations are generally largely contractually fixed (in the case of a "defined benefit" pension plan, for example). Managers of the fund must therefore consider two objectives, not only the risk and return optimization of the fund's assets, but also its need to meet obligations on the liability side. Management of the portfolio focusing on the liability rather than asset side of the balance sheet was discussed in Chapter 19, where we noted that immunization-oriented strategies may be more relevant than mean-variance optimization. Although bonds are particularly useful in such strategies, real estate also has a useful role on the liability side. In particular,

pension benefit obligations tend to be sensitive to inflation because of **cost-of-living adjustments (COLAs)** in the benefits. As noted in previous chapters, real estate is a relatively good inflation hedge, whereas long-term bonds are notoriously exposed to inflation risk. Thus, if real estate's major role on the asset side of the pension fund's balance sheet is as a diversifier, its major role to help with the liability side is often as an inflation hedge asset.*

———————

*That real estate assets provide a good inflation hedge is common sense based on the fact that real estate's value is based on a "real" physical product. (See also section 15.4.2 in Chapter 15 for the mechanics of how this can interact with debt finance.) However, the empirical evidence for how well or how strongly real estate returns are positively correlated with inflation is mixed. (See MacKinnon, 2011, for a good summary.) But inflation has been low and not very variable for the past three decades, the period from which almost all of the real estate investment return data exists. So, we don't have a very powerful empirical sample to study. Anecdotally, real estate performed well in nominal terms in the late 1970s and early 1980s when inflation was most problematical in U.S. history.

21.2.4 The Efficient Frontier

Now let's put together the general point about diversification we made in section 21.2.2 with the idea described in 21.2.1 about avoiding dominated portfolios. This synthesis is one of the most important ideas in portfolio theory: the efficient frontier.

To understand the concept of the efficient frontier, let's go back again to our numerical example from section 21.1. In particular, let's take Bob's risk and return expectations for the three asset classes, but let's ignore for the time being the constraint represented by the 7 percent return target. First, consider the risk and return opportunities facing Bob if he could only invest in one asset class, that is, if he could not diversify across asset classes but instead had to choose one "pure" portfolio, either stocks, bonds, or real estate. In that case, Bob would face the risk/return combinations indicated by the three points in Exhibit 21-6A. He could either get 6 percent expected return and 8 percent volatility by investing in bonds, or 7 percent return and 10 percent volatility in real estate, or 10 percent return and 15 percent volatility in stocks.

Notice that these three possibilities all lie generally in a northeasterly/southwesterly relation to one another in the risk/return diagram. No one possibility is dominated by any other. This is typical of the risk/return relationships we would expect among asset classes in a well-functioning capital market. But the possibilities shown in Exhibit 21-7A are highly constrained, not allowing any diversification across asset classes. Suppose we relax this constraint a little by allowing diversification across any *two* asset classes. This expands the risk/return possibilities to the three curved lines indicated in Exhibit 21-7B. Each curve represents the risk/return possibilities from mixing two asset classes, either stocks and bonds, stocks and real estate, or bonds and real estate. For example, the curve on the lower left, connecting the pure bond and pure real estate possibilities, represents risk and return combinations available from various allocations to bonds and real estate.

Now we see that certain pairwise combinations are dominated by others. Some points on each of the three curves lie to the northwest of some points on the other curves. For example, a portfolio containing 70 percent stocks and 30 percent real estate dominates a portfolio with 75 percent stocks and 25 percent bonds. The former has expected return of 9.1 percent

EXHIBIT 21-7A Three
Assets: Stocks, Bonds, Real
Estate (no diversification)
© OnCourse Learning

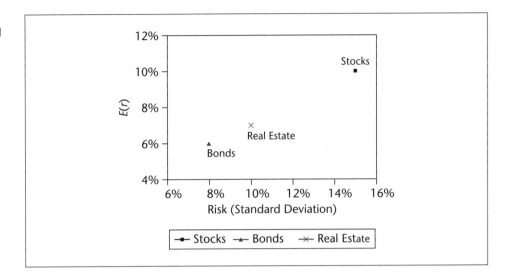

EXHIBIT 21-7B Three
Assets: Stocks, Bonds, Real
Estate (with pairwise
combinations)
© OnCourse Learning

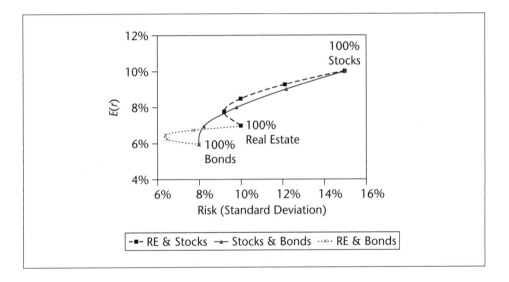

with volatility of 11.6 percent, while the latter has expected return of 9.0 percent and volatility of 12.0 percent, that is, a lower expected return with more risk. An investor with the risk and return expectations presented in Exhibit 21-1A should never hold a portfolio of 75 percent stocks and 25 percent bonds if he could invest in real estate instead of bonds.

It is interesting also to notice the shape of the three curves in Exhibit 21-7B. They all curve up and to the left as compared to a hypothetical straight line connecting the two endpoints of the curve (pure single asset class investments). This means that diversified mixtures of any two asset classes will provide some additional expected return for a given amount of risk, or less risk for a given expected return, between the risk/return limits implied by the undiversified (pure) investments (the endpoints of the curves). This favorable "bending" of the risk/return possibility curve is a mathematical result between any two assets or asset classes that are not perfectly positively correlated. This is important because in reality no two *underlying* assets (or asset classes) will ever be perfectly correlated. The result we see in Exhibit 21-7B is typical in this regard.

Note also that the curves involving real estate combinations (either with bonds or stocks) are more sharply bent to the left than the curve that represents stock and bond combinations.

EXHIBIT 21-7C Three
Assets with Diversification:
The Efficient Frontier
© OnCourse Learning

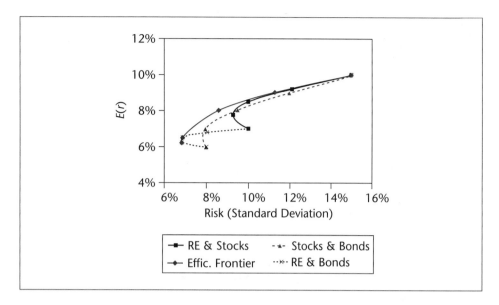

This is the effect of real estate's relatively low correlation with the other two asset classes, especially with bonds. In fact, among the three pairs depicted in Exhibit 21-7B, the most favorable bending is in the real estate/bond combinations. As you recall, Bob's estimates of the correlations among the asset classes was +15% between real estate and bonds, +25% between real estate and stocks, and +30% between stocks and bonds.[20]

Exhibit 21-7B still represents a constraint on the investor's ability to diversify, as diversification is limited to only two asset classes. Suppose we relax this restriction. With the possibility of diversifying across all three asset classes, many more risk/return possibilities open up. As no investor should want to hold any portfolios that are dominated, the set of interesting combinations of the three asset classes consists only of those that are not dominated. Any such portfolio is called an **efficient portfolio**, and the risk/return possibilities associated with the set of all possible efficient portfolios is called the **efficient frontier**.[21] Any portfolio on the efficient frontier is, by definition, not dominated by any other portfolio, and any non-dominated portfolio is on the efficient frontier. In other words, the efficient frontier consists of all asset combinations that maximize return and minimize risk.[22]

The efficient frontier for combinations among the three asset classes in our numerical example is shown in Exhibit 21-7C.[23] The heavy curved line marked with diamonds is the efficient frontier for stocks, bonds, and real estate given the risk and return expectations indicated in Exhibit 21-1A. This curved line represents the best risk and return possibilities, those that are farthest northwest in the diagram. Points farther to the north or west of the efficient frontier are not feasible. Now you see why this is called a frontier. The efficient frontier always has this characteristic curved shape, running generally from the southwest toward

---

[20]The reason for Bob's assumption of less correlation between real estate and bonds than between real estate and stocks is probably due fundamentally to the way the two asset classes respond differently to inflation. Also, real estate and stocks, being both equity, are more sensitive to the same fundamental real macro-economic characteristics such as GDP and employment growth.

[21]**Terminology alert:** Do not confuse *efficient* here with the sense of the term we previously used to describe the functioning of an asset market, that is, the concept of *informational efficiency*. An efficient portfolio is simply one that is not dominated by any other portfolio in its expected return and risk. This does not carry any implication regarding the informational efficiency of the asset markets in which its constituent assets trade.

[22]More precisely, for a given volatility, the efficient frontier maximizes the expected return, and for a given expected return the efficient frontier minimizes the volatility.

[23]Exhibit 21-9 and the other optimal portfolio results presented in this chapter have been calculated using a simple Excel® template that is a presented on the CD accompanying this book. You can use this template to try out your own risk and return expectations and perform sensitivity analysis on our results presented here.

the northeast in the risk/return diagram, bending upward and leftward relative to a straight line connecting the two endpoints.

Each point on the efficient frontier represents a unique combination of its possible constituent assets. In the case represented in Exhibit 21-7C, each point on the frontier represents a unique proportional allocation among stocks, bonds, and real estate.[24] Each point on the efficient frontier also corresponds to a unique risk/return combination. For example, as we saw in section 21.1, the point on the efficient frontier corresponding to an expected return of 7 percent entails a volatility of 6.89 percent and represents an allocation of 16 percent to stocks, 48 percent to bonds, and 36 percent to real estate (as Bob reported previously).

21.2.5 Bringing in Investor Preferences

Portfolio theory tells us that all investors should hold portfolios on the efficient frontier. Which portfolio on the efficient frontier any given investor should hold depends on the risk and return preferences of the investor. As noted, the efficient frontier is generally sloped from the southwest to the northeast in the risk/return diagram. A rational choice among different points on the efficient frontier can only be made by consulting the investor's preferences for risk and return. As we saw in the example in section 21.1, in practice these preferences are often expressed in terms of a target long-run rate of return for the portfolio, and within an institution this target may be selected by a more or less political process, often reflecting the policy needs and constraints of the institution.[25] In effect, investors who are more aggressive or risk tolerant specify higher return targets (knowing that the capital market will dictate that this will imply greater portfolio volatility), while conservative investors specify lower return targets.

This process is depicted in Exhibit 21-8. Both panels show the efficient frontier we just constructed based on the risk and return expectations in Exhibit 21-1A. The other curve shown in the figure is an indifference curve reflecting the investor's preferences. In particular, the indifference curve reflects the highest level of satisfaction (or "utility") the investor can achieve. Indifference curves that lie parallel to the curve shown would either be infeasible (to the northwest of the depicted curve) or indicative of lower levels of investor satisfaction (to the southeast of the depicted curve).[26] The indifference curve that is just "tangent" to the efficient frontier (i.e., the indifference curve that touches the efficient frontier at one and only one point) is the best the investor can do. In this sense, the investor's selected target return (on the vertical axis, or equivalently her corresponding target volatility on the horizontal axis) reflects the investor's risk/return preferences, as described in section 21.2.1.

The top panel, 21-8A, shows this result for a relatively conservative investor, indicating a target return of 7 percent. The bottom panel, Exhibit 21-8B, shows the result for a more aggressive investor, indicating a target return of 9 percent. The 9 percent target implies an

---

[24]In general, some of the efficient portfolios may have zero or negative allocations to one or more constituent assets. In the example we have been considering here, none of the allocations is negative because we have constrained our portfolio to avoid short positions (which gives the frontier a finite upper endpoint). The "no shorts" constraint is generally realistic for large institutional portfolios when considering allocation strategy across broad asset classes.

[25]A relatively sophisticated way to help make this decision which has become popular is called "Value at Risk" (VaR). In a VaR analysis a Monte Carlo simulation model is developed to simulate how the portfolio might perform over time (based on assumed expected returns and covariances specified for all of the candidate asset classes). Various different portfolio allocations are tested via the simulation model with a focus on what probability, based on the simulation results, is associated with a loss in portfolio value of a given specified magnitude. Of course, the VaR analysis is just as susceptible to the GIGO ("garbage in, garbage out") weakness as any analytical model. It may make the future appear less uncertain or more understood than it really is. A particular challenge is to capture the complete shapes of the future return distributions and covariances, including possible "fat tails" (nonnormal probability distributions that have greater probability of extreme outcomes than implied by normal probability) and covariances that increase to abnormal levels during financial crises. These types of problems are swept under the rug in classical MPT, which assumes stable and finite covariances. But at least the classical model may be less susceptible to lulling decision markers into a false impression of greater knowledge than they actually have, a problem that may have contributed to the bubble mentality in the mid-2000s decade.

[26]Recall that an indifference curve (also called an "isoquant") is like a contour line on a topographic map. No two indifference curves (representing different levels of utility of the same investor's preferences) can ever cross each other. So indifference curves mapping out an investor's preferences are parallel to each other, as in Exhibit 21-2.

EXHIBIT 21-8A Optimal
Portfolio for a Conservative
Investor (P = 7% target)

© OnCourse Learning

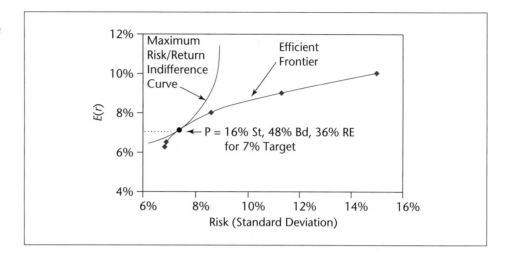

EXHIBIT 21-8B Optimal
Portfolio for an Aggressive
Investor (P = 9% target)

© OnCourse Learning

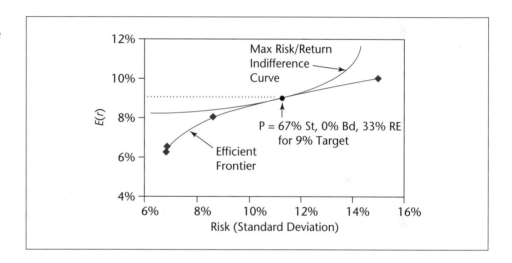

optimal portfolio volatility of 11.30 percent as compared to the 6.89 percent volatility implied by the 7 percent target. While the efficient portfolio for the 7 percent target had only 16 percent allocation to stocks, the efficient portfolio for the 9 percent target would have 67 percent allocation to stocks, based on the same risk and return expectations (those of Exhibit 21-1A). The 9 percent target has a 33 percent allocation to real estate, and zero percent to bonds.

21.2.6 Major Implications of Portfolio Theory for Real Estate Investment

Exhibit 21-9 shows another way to present the efficient frontier. This exhibit is what is called an "area chart," which shows how the optimal shares of the constituent asset classes change as a function of the investor's expected return target (i.e., as a function of the investors' risk preferences). The portfolio target rate of return is indicated now on the horizontal axis (instead of the vertical axis as before). The vertical dimension of the rectangle in Exhibit 21-9 stacks the efficient allocations to each asset class on top of each other to account for 100 percent of the investor's wealth. A vertical line is like a transept indicating the share of each asset class in the optimal (efficient frontier) portfolio corresponding to the given target return the vertical line intersects on the horizontal axis.

As before, Exhibit 21-9 is based on Bob's expectations as stated in Exhibit 21-1A. Notice that the optimal real estate share is rather large (over 30 percent) and stable for a broad range

EXHIBIT 21-9 Asset
Composition of the Efficient
Frontier (based on Exhibit
21-1A expectations)

© OnCourse Learning

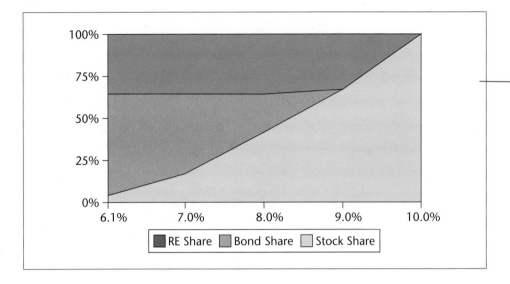

of conservative to moderately aggressive return targets (roughly from the minimum-variance target of just over 6 percent through at least 9 percent, which is not far below the maximum all-positive-weights portfolio return of 10 percent). The optimal share allocated to stocks rises steadily with the return target (i.e., with investor risk tolerance), first at the expense of bonds, and at more aggressive ranges at the expense of real estate. This makes intuitive sense, as real estate has a slightly higher expected return than bonds (though lower than stocks), and the correlation between real estate and stocks is here assumed to be slightly lower than that between bonds and stocks. Thus, throughout the broad conservative and middle range of the risk preferences, real estate makes up about one-third of the optimal portfolio, while the balance of the optimal portfolio goes from mostly bonds and some stocks at the conservative end to mostly stocks and some bonds at the aggressive end, given Bob's risk and return expectations of Exhibit 21-1A.

The above optimal allocation results are an important empirical and investment policy relevant conclusion from the application of modern portfolio theory at the broad-brush level across the three major underlying asset classes, with obviously important implications for real estate investment. Although the specific results summarized in Exhibit 21-9 depend upon the specific risk and return expectations of only one example investor (Bob's, of Exhibit 21-1A), those expectations are not implausible nor atypical, and similar optimal allocation results are obtained for other similar and similarly plausible expectations. In essence, if one divides the investment universe into only three underlying asset classes, then the role of each one of those asset classes will be generally fairly large, and the role of real estate, with its generally favorable risk/return expectations and low correlation to other asset classes, will tend to be greatest in the conservative to middle range of the risk/return preferences.

This is a tremendously important conclusion for real estate investment at the big picture macro-level. It says that real estate should occupy a prominent role in the average or overall investment portfolio. Of course, it may seem that we are "stacking the deck" in favor of real estate by allowing for only three asset classes in our analysis and making real estate one of those classes. How could we not find a large role for real estate? But "big pictures" are just that: they present the broadest outlines of reality. And the "biggest picture" in the investment world is, arguably, a three-asset-class world, with real estate one of those three. Recall our description of the overall capital markets and the investable universe in Chapters 1 and 7. Real estate in fact underlies roughly one-third of the overall capital market value (see Exhibit 1-8) and represents close to one-third of the professionally investable universe of asset classes in the United States (see Exhibit 7-5). One finds generally similar proportions in other countries. Stocks and bonds also each represent approximately similar proportions of the overall capital market value and the investable universe. Portfolio theory can provide an underlying explanation for this result![27]

21.2.7 Expanding the Asset Class Choice Set: The Role of REITs

What happens if we divide the investment universe more finely, among a greater number of asset classes? In general, the more asset classes we allow ourselves to choose among, the more diversification potential there is, and the better we can do. Assuming that the defined asset classes are not perfectly (or even very highly) correlated with one another, the identification of new, separate asset classes allows the efficient frontier to be expanded further to the north and west in the risk/return diagram, as we optimize the roles of the asset classes along the frontier.

The investment industry has of course responded over the years to this possibility, and in the real world of professional investment portfolio management there has been a long-term trend to specialize and identify more and more subcategories of investments as new asset classes or "subclasses." For example, the "equities" asset class, which was originally viewed essentially as a somewhat homogeneously perceived "stock market" populated by individual large-cap stocks perhaps divided into industry categories, has been divided into different investment "styles" or "factors" reflecting differences between large and small stocks and so-called "value" and "growth" stocks (as a function of whether they are relatively income-oriented or share price growth-oriented, respectively). There has also been an expansion to include international stocks as another dimension of distinction within the overall equities asset class (with this further subdivided between developed and emerging markets). Similar identification and differentiation of subclasses has occurred within the bond (or so-called "fixed-income") asset class, including differentiation along the duration dimension, the default risk dimension (such as investment grade versus high-yield—formerly referred to as "junk"—bonds), the currency denomination ("domestic" versus "foreign") dimension, and even according to the nature of the underlying collateral or backing of the bonds (e.g., asset-backed bonds, such as the real estate-based mortgage-backed securities, both residential and commercial, the latter as discussed in Chapter 20).

This differentiation phenomenon has also occurred within the real estate asset class, as REITs have come to be recognized as a separate subclass.[28] It is also possible to distinguish among different real estate investment styles based on the degree and nature of the use of leverage for property investment financing as well as on the "life cycle phase" of the property investments: development phase, stabilized operational phase, rehab/turnaround phase. For example, the major industry association tracking pension fund real estate investment in the United States, the National Council of Real Estate Investment Fiduciaries (NCREIF), now publishes regular quarterly investment performance indices for three different styles of real estate investment funds: "core," "value-add," and "opportunistic." However, all of these are subcategories within the *private* real estate market asset class, and the histories of their periodic returns are still relatively short.[29] Thus, at the broad mixed-asset-class level, the only

---

[27]Not only does real estate make up a large share of the *physical* capital stock in the economy, but real estate asset price dynamics and investment returns can be quantified in a relatively reliable manner somewhat comparable with those of stocks and bonds. This is fundamentally because real estate assets trade in a relatively well-functioning market. (More on this in Chapter 25.) Some other "asset classes" that have become prominent in many institutional portfolios in recent decades, such as private equity and hedge funds, are arguably more investment vehicles than asset classes at the fundamental level of the physical capital underlying them. And as noted previously their investment performance may be more difficult to reliably quantify than that of real estate.

[28]There is some debate whether REITs should be classified within the real estate or the stock market asset class, as they in fact reflect some characteristics of both. But this debate may be excessively "academic," if one applies portfolio theory as in principle it should be, at a single level to all available investment alternatives.

[29]And it is not clear that their characteristic investment performance differences reflect fundamentally much more than different degrees of leverage, either financial or operational, which therefore does not suggest that they should be treated as separate "asset classes".

major categories of real estate investments in the United States are arguably private direct property investments of the type represented by the NCREIF or IPD Indices, and REITs as represented by the FTSE/NAREIT Index (among other REIT indices).

To give you an idea how expansion of the asset class choice set affects the optimal portfolio allocation, let's consider a modest expansion from three to five asset classes. Suppose we add a "small stocks" category to our previous "stock market" category. And let's add REITs as a separate category to see the effect of allowing real estate investment either via the public stock market through REITs or via direct private investment. With these five asset classes, the table in Exhibit 21-10A might present plausible risk and return expectations as of the early 2000s (expectations that are consistent with those we were using previously for three asset classes in Exhibit 21-1A, taking our previous "stocks" class as being represented by "large stocks" and our previous "real estate" class as being represented by "direct private real estate investment").

Given the risk and return expectations of Exhibit 21-10A, the composition of the efficient frontier is as depicted in Exhibit 21-10B, which is an "area chart" comparable to Exhibit 21-9. As we should expect, the result is similar in its big picture to what we found before with three asset classes, only now there is a further subdivision within the two asset classes that we

	Large Stocks	Small Stocks	Bonds	REITs	Private Real Estate
Expected Return (E[r])	10.00%	12.00%	6.00%	10.00%	7.00%
Volatility	15.00%	20.00%	8.00%	15.00%	10.00%
Correlation with:					
Large Stocks	100.00%	60.00%	30.00%	45.00%	25.00%
Small Stocks		100.00%	0.00%	70.00%	25.00%
Bonds			100.00%	20.00%	15.00%
REITs				100.00%	40.00%
Private Real Estate					100.00%

EXHIBIT 21-10A Possible Risk and Return Expectations for Five Asset Classes
© OnCourse Learning

EXHIBIT 21-10B Asset Composition of the Efficient Frontier (based on Exhibit 21-10A expectations)
© OnCourse Learning

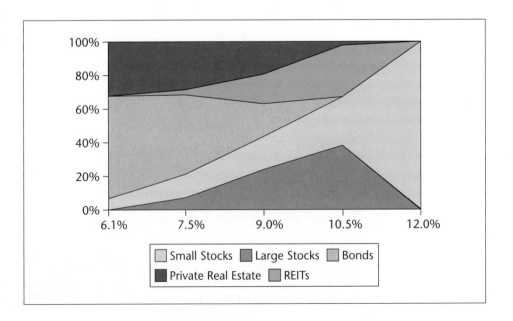

CAN MPT BE APPLIED *WITHIN* THE REAL ESTATE PORTFOLIO?

It is easy to see how, beginning in the 1970s, the real estate investment industry welcomed modern portfolio theory and its ERISA implications for planning capital allocations at the level of the broad, mixed-asset portfolio. For the first time, real estate was included, at least conceptually, as a vital part of the institutional investment picture, along with the traditional mainstays, stocks and bonds. By the 1980s, this enthusiasm had carried down to the level of the *real estate component* within the overall portfolio. Advocates argued that MPT could and should be applied *within* the real estate allocation, for example, to find the optimal mixture among different property types (e.g., office, retail, industrial, etc.) and/or geographic regions (e.g., the East, South, West, etc.).* What was being advocated, in effect, was a hierarchical or two-stage process. The investment institution would first use MPT to help decide how much capital to place in real estate as a whole and then use MPT again to help determine the optimal property segment allocation within the overall real estate budget.

While this type of hierarchical structure may make sense from an institutional management perspective for implementing strategic investment policy, there are a couple of problems in trying to apply MPT in this way. First, little conceptual basis exists for the application of MPT below the level of the entire wealth portfolio of the investor. A key tenet of MPT is that the investor cares about the risk and return in the entire portfolio, rather than any component of the portfolio in isolation. For example, suppose a property segment has little correlation with other property segments but high correlation with stocks and bonds. From the perspective of the real estate portfolio alone, such a property segment would look very appealing in an MPT framework. But from the perspective of the overall wealth portfolio, which includes large allocations to stocks and bonds, such a property segment would be much less appealing.

A second problem is practical in nature. It is very difficult to come up with the kind of highly refined yet reliable risk and return expectations by property segment that are necessary for the rigorous application of MPT within the real estate portfolio. As you can see from our discussion of MPT, one would need

good estimates of expected returns, volatility, and correlations among all pairs of property segments. For example, even if you only wanted to consider just four property types in just four geographic regions, you would need 16 return estimates, 16 volatility estimates, and 120 pairwise correlation estimates. Historical periodic returns data in the property market are just not good enough, nor is our knowledge of the determinants of future real estate returns, to permit very useful analysis at this level of detail.

For these reasons, rigorous application of MPT at the *within-real-estate* level is not very widespread in terms of detailed investment decision making. However, it is sometimes useful for conceptual purposes, for example, to understand the potential role a new type of real estate investment could play within the real estate portfolio. Also, less formal, common-sense-based diversification of the real estate portfolio is usually a wise strategy for large institutions.** Portfolio theory builds our intuition about how to think logically about such diversification. For example, portfolio theory suggests that property types whose uses tend to follow different economic cycles, or economic regions whose economic bases are distinct and relatively uncorrelated, would be relatively more valuable for diversification purposes. (Recall our discussion in Chapter 3 about the classification of geographic regions by economic base.) Even in such less formal application of portfolio theory intuition, however, it makes sense to consider the investor's overall wealth portfolio as the context for diversification, rather than just the real estate component of the investor's wealth.

---

*See, for example, Miles and McCue (1984).
**The most important argument *against* diversification in real estate investment is the need for specialized local expertise, both in the acquisition/disposition phases and in the property ownership/management phase. It may be difficult, especially for small investors, to acquire sufficient expertise efficiently in more than one local area or property type. The segmentation of real estate space markets, and lack of informational efficiency in property asset markets, then exposes "novices" or "outsiders" to greater risk at the micro-level, and this may more than offset the macro-level arguments for diversification.

---

broke into two subclasses, stocks and real estate. (Also note that the range of possible portfolio return targets has now expanded up to 12 percent, a new possibility afforded by the "small stocks" asset class.) Within the stocks class, large stocks dominate until the higher rather aggressive target return range where small stocks of necessity take over.

Within the real estate asset class, Exhibit 21-10B suggests that both REITs and direct private investment have important roles in the optimally diversified portfolio. As was alluded to in Chapters 7 and 12 (and as will be further discussed in Chapter 23), REITs are less similar to private real estate than one might at first suppose regarding their risk and return performance. While REITs and private real estate are substantially positively correlated, they are far from perfectly so, enabling the two forms of real estate investing to complement one another in the optimal portfolio. In the efficient frontier mapped out in Exhibit 21-10B,

REITs increase from a small to a large share as one increases the target return through the middle range of risk/return preferences, gaining at the expense of private real estate, and almost completely replacing private real estate in the more aggressive return target range, until REITs in turn get displaced by small stocks at the extreme aggressive end of the return target range.[30]

21.3 Allowing for a Riskless Asset: The Two-Fund Theorem and the Sharpe-Maximizing Portfolio

Portfolio theory as described in the preceding section provides an elegant and rigorous framework for thinking about strategic asset allocation at the level of the investor's overall wealth portfolio. It provides insight and builds intuition relevant to all investors. It is widely used in practice, particularly by large institutional investors such as **pension funds**.[31] However, an important consideration for many investors has not been included in the theory as presented so far. In particular, we have considered only *risky* assets as possible components of the portfolio. By risky assets, we mean investments whose returns cannot be predicted with certainty in advance, investments whose periodic returns are volatile. Yet it is often useful to envision another type of asset, a *riskless* (or *risk-free*) asset.

In principle, a riskless asset's return is known in advance for certain, and it is viewed as having no volatility in the realization of its periodic returns. In reality, of course, there is no such thing as a completely riskless asset. However, the concept of the riskless asset is a useful construct because it provides an interesting extension of the theory described previously.

One reason for the introduction of a riskless asset in portfolio theory is that this construct can *approximate borrowing or short-term lending* by the investor. Borrowing, or the use of debt to finance investment, can be represented by a short position in the riskless asset.[32] When the investor borrows money (in effect *levering* her overall wealth, as described in Chapter 13), she normally intends to pay back the loan without defaulting. Thus, from the investor's perspective, the return on the debt asset appears certain, providing some logic for treating the debt as riskless. On the other hand, many investors hold a certain amount of "cash" in their wealth portfolios, that is, investments in very short-term debt. This is most commonly in the form of U.S. Treasury bills (T-bills), although private sector "commercial paper" and other instruments are also used. The periodic returns on such short-term lending

---

[30]REITs have historically exhibited a very high positive correlation with small stocks, while providing a lower average return than typical small stocks (as represented for example by the Ibbotson Small Stock Index). REITs have themselves been small stocks during much of their history, though recently some REITs have moved into the mid-size category, and a few have joined the ranks of "large stocks" as indicated by inclusion in the S&P 500 Index. While many small stocks are growth oriented, REITs (and a number of other small stocks) would generally be classified as "value stocks," paying relatively high dividend yields and providing relatively low share price appreciation. Thus, REITs would be particularly highly correlated with a small stock value style index which might tend to usurp their role on the efficient frontier (although REITs would be included in such an index). For an interesting analysis and discussion of this issue, see Lee and Stevenson (2005). Both REITs and small-cap value stocks tend to dominate the upper target return range in classical MPT efficient frontiers much more so than their actual share of market value of investments in the real world. This is a reflection of so-called "Fama-French Factor premiums," which will be described in the next chapter. Stock market investors seem to demand a return premium for small stocks and stocks that have high book-to-market value ratios. Whatever reason exists for these extra return premia, they are not accounted for in classical MPT (and it is not clear that the same such rationale would exist for REITs as for other small-cap value stocks).

[31]As noted in Chapter 7, MPT inspired some of the language in the Employee Retirement Income Security Act of 1974 (ERISA), a federal law that is fundamental to the management of pension funds in the United States. This is one reason why defined benefit pension funds take MPT so seriously.

[32]Recall that a short position can be represented by a negative investment allocation. In the case of short positions, the investor receives cash when the position is taken and gives up cash when the position is closed or retired. This is in direct contrast to long positions, which are characterized by the fact that cash is given up at the time the investment position is taken, and cash is obtained when the asset is sold to close out the position. Thus, you can see how borrowing can be represented as a short position in a debt asset, just as lending is a long position in such an asset.

by the investor have very little volatility and virtually no default risk, and so may be viewed as an approximately riskless investment.

21.3.1 Two-Fund Theorem

While the riskless asset construct is useful as an approximation for borrowing and short-term lending, it has another, more technical use as well in portfolio theory. The riskless asset construct can be used as a sort of mathematical technique to simplify greatly the portfolio allocation problem. This simplification is known as the **two-fund theorem**, and it, too, is widely used in practice.

To see what the two-fund theorem means and how it works, you need to understand a basic mathematical fact. Recall from our discussion of Exhibit 21-7B that whenever two risky assets are less than perfectly positively correlated, the risk/return possibilities of combinations of those two assets lie along a curve that is bent upward and leftward in the risk/return diagram. But now suppose one of the two assets is riskless, that is, contains no volatility. In this case, the risk/return possibilities of combinations of the two assets will lie exactly on a straight line connecting the risk/return possibilities of each of the two assets alone.

This means that, in a risk/return diagram, the risk/return possibilities from a combination of a riskless asset and *any* portfolio of risky assets will lie along a straight line connecting the riskless asset's risk/return with the risky portfolio's risk/return. This is depicted in Exhibit 21-11A for combinations of a riskless asset with an interest rate of r_f and a risky portfolio with risk and expected return represented by point Q. All the risk/return possibilities lying on the straight line connecting r_f with Q are feasible by holding the portfolio Q combined with either long or short positions in the riskless asset. If the investor puts some of his wealth in the portfolio Q, and some in the riskless asset, then his risk and return will lie on the line segment between points r_f and Q, to the left of Q.[33] (The greater the share of his wealth in the riskless asset, the closer to r_f his expected return will be, and the farther to the left of Q on the straight line his risk and return will lie.) If the investor borrows money, then his risk and return will lie on the straight line to the right of Q.[34]

In Exhibit 21-11 the curved line represents the efficient frontier of risky assets described in the previous section. Thus, the risky portfolio Q is an efficient portfolio, in the absence of the possibility of investing in a riskless asset. Nevertheless, if it is possible to take positions in a riskless asset, no investor would want to combine such positions with Q. All of the risk/return possibilities on the straight line connecting r_f with Q are dominated by possibilities lying on the straight line connecting r_f with P, a different portfolio also lying on the efficient frontier of risky assets. This is depicted in Exhibit 21-11B. In fact, you can see by geometric reasoning that the possibilities on the straight line connecting r_f and P dominate any and all other feasible risk/return possibilities. P lies at the point on the risky asset efficient frontier (the curved line) that is just tangent to a straight line passing through r_f.[35]

This brings us to the two-fund theorem. According to this theorem, all investors (no matter what their risk preferences) will prefer combinations of the riskless asset and *a single particular* risky asset portfolio (the point P in Exhibit 21-11B). With the possibility of riskless

---

[33]This would be short-term lending, that is, taking a long position in the riskless asset.

[34]This would be taking a short position (placing a negative proportion of the investor's wealth) in the riskless asset. As the proportion of the investor's wealth in both the riskless asset and the risky portfolio must sum to unity, this implies that the proportion of the investor's wealth placed in the risky portfolio Q would exceed unity. In other words, borrowing enables the investor to place more than his total wealth in the risky portfolio, his own net wealth plus the amount he has borrowed against it. As the expected return to Q exceeds the risk-free rate of r_f at which he is borrowing, the resulting leverage is "positive" (to use the terminology introduced in Chapter 13), causing the investor's expected return to exceed r_Q, lying therefore to the right of Q on the straight line connecting r_f and Q.

[35]Any line northwest of P would not be feasible, as it would pass entirely through the infeasible region to the northwest of the risky asset efficient frontier. In other words, it would be impossible to find a risky portfolio to combine with the riskless asset to produce risk/return possibilities that lie on such a line. Any straight line through r_f that would run southeast of P would be dominated by the line through P.

EXHIBIT 21-11A Risk
and Return Possibilities of a
Combination of a Riskless
Asset with Return r_f and the
Suboptimal Risky Portfolio
with Expected Return r_q
© OnCourse Learning

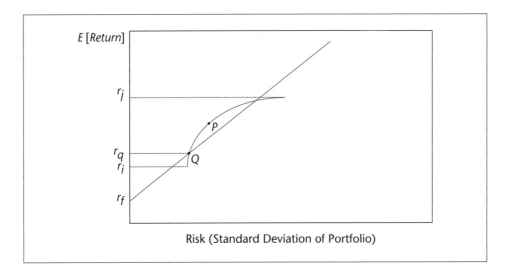

EXHIBIT 21-11B Risk and
Return Possibilities of a
Combination of a Riskless
Asset with Return r_f and the
Optimal Risky Portfolio with
Expected Return r_q
© OnCourse Learning

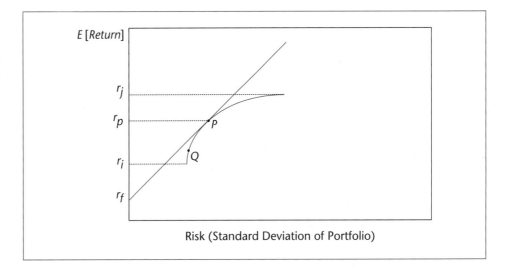

borrowing or lending, the optimal allocation among risky assets, P, is determined *not* by the investor's risk preferences, but only by her expectations about asset future returns. The investor's risk preferences can be met by adjusting the position in the riskless asset only, by either borrowing more (for more aggressive preferences) or lending more (for more conservative tastes), so as to meet the appropriate expected return target.

21.3.2 Sharpe-Maximizing Portfolio

How can we determine which combination of risky assets corresponds to the unique optimal allocation represented by point P in the two-fund theorem? The answer to this question is obvious in the geometry we just used to discover the theorem. The point P is the portfolio that maximizes the slope of a straight line connecting that portfolio's risk and return with the risk and return of the riskless asset. Of course, the riskless asset has zero risk, and its return is r_f. The risk (volatility) of the risky-asset portfolio is S_P, and its return is r_P. The slope of the line connecting these two points is thus: $(r_P - r_f)/S_P$. This is the risk premium of the risky asset portfolio divided by its volatility. This ratio is known as the **Sharpe ratio**, named after William F. Sharpe, who shared the Nobel Prize for portfolio theory. In the presence of a riskless asset, the optimal combination of risky assets is the one with the highest Sharpe ratio.[36]

While the two-fund theorem has an elegance that appeals to the aesthetic sense of academicians, it also has a simplicity and intuitive appeal that practitioners like. It is thus widely used in practice. As the Sharpe ratio is just the risk premium (what we have been labeling RP) divided by the risk (defined as volatility), it is a natural measure of **risk-adjusted return** and is widely (and somewhat informally) used as such by practitioners. The numerator of the Sharpe ratio measures the investor's compensation for risk, the excess return over what an investment in T-bills would provide. The denominator of the Sharpe ratio is the amount of risk in the investment as measured by the standard deviation of its periodic returns. If the Sharpe ratio is applied at the level of the investor's entire wealth portfolio, volatility is arguably the relevant measure of risk. Furthermore, the Sharpe ratio is unaffected by the investor's position in the riskless asset, either by borrowing or lending risklessly. Thus, it makes intuitive sense to want to find the risky asset allocation that maximizes the Sharpe ratio.

$$Sharpe\ ratio\ of\ P = \frac{r_p - r_f}{S_P} = \frac{RP_P}{S_P}$$

In considering the role of real estate in the optimal mixed-asset portfolio, the Sharpe-maximizing perspective sometimes reduces the real estate share for conservative investors, as compared to the perspective from classical MPT without a riskless asset. In general, the Sharpe-maximizing risky asset allocation tends to place lower weights in low-return asset classes, as compared to the variance-minimizing allocation with a conservative target return.

As an example, let us return again to Bob's three asset class portfolio allocation problem with the risk and return expectations in Exhibit 21-1A. To meet Bob's (rather conservative) 7 percent return target, recall that the variance-minimizing shares among the three risky asset classes were: 16 percent stocks, 48 percent bonds, and 36 percent real estate. Now suppose we can approximate the risk-free interest rate as being 3 percent. The Sharpe-maximizing risky asset allocation (P) would then consist of 27 percent stocks, 37 percent bonds, and 36 percent real estate. The relative proportion of stocks is considerably greater, and long-term bonds smaller, than in the 7 percent target variance-minimizing portfolio. However, this comparison is a bit misleading because this all-risky-asset Sharpe-maximizing portfolio is slightly too aggressive for Bob's client. This is seen by the fact that, without any investment in T-bills, the **Sharpe-maximizing portfolio** would have an expected return of 7.4 percent with 7.49 percent volatility (compared to 6.89 percent volatility in the 7 percent target all-risky-asset variance-minimizing portfolio).

To meet the 7 percent return target using the Sharpe-maximizing portfolio, we would have to allocate 90 percent of the investor's wealth to the Sharpe-maximizing risky asset portfolio and 10 percent to T-bills. The overall allocation would then be 25 percent stocks, 33 percent long-term bonds, 32 percent real estate, and 10 percent T-bills. The combined long- and short-term debt allocation (bonds and bills) would be 43 percent, slightly less than the 48 percent allocation to long-term debt alone in the variance-minimizing 7 percent target portfolio. Thus, the optimal 7 percent target portfolio from a Sharpe-maximizing perspective allocates considerably more weight to stocks (25 percent instead of 16 percent) and slightly less weight to both bonds (43 percent instead of 48 percent) and real estate (32 percent instead of 36 percent). In a sense, part of the reason the bond and real estate allocations are so high in the variance-minimizing portfolio is simply because the investor has specified a conservative return target, and real estate

---

[36]You can use the solver on a spreadsheet to find the Sharpe-maximizing allocation the same way as we described in section 21.1 to find the variance-minimizing allocation. Simply compute the Sharpe ratio of the portfolio in a cell of the spreadsheet using formulas A.1 and A.6 from Appendix 21, as before. Then, instead of telling the solver to minimize the portfolio variance, tell it to maximize the portfolio Sharpe ratio. You will no longer need the target return constraint in the solver. (The resulting optimal allocation will just be for the risky asset portfolio, P. You will have to lever this portfolio up or down using the riskless asset to meet a given target return.) Obviously, somewhere in the spreadsheet, you have to input the risk-free rate, r_f. The Sharpe-maximizing allocation will be different for different values of r_f. (An Excel® file template that uses the Solver to perform this optimization is included on the CD accompanying this book.)

	Return and Risk Expectations*			Portfolio Allocations	
	Return	**Volatility**	**Sharpe Ratio**	**Var.-Min.**	**Sharpe-Max.**
Cash (T-bills)	3.00%	NA**	NA	NA	10%
Bonds	6.00%	8.00%	0.38	48%	33%
Real Estate	7.00%	10.00%	0.40	36%	32%
Stocks	10.00%	15.00%	0.47	16%	25%
Var.-Min. Portfolio	7.00%	6.89%	0.58	100%	NA
Sharpe-Max. Portfolio	7.00%	NA**	0.59	NA	100%

*Also includes correlations:
Stock/Bond +30%, Stock/Real Estate +25%, Bond/Real Estate +15%.
**From the Sharpe-maximization perspective, T-bills are viewed as having zero volatility, but as this is not exactly true in reality, it would be misleading to calculate and show a Sharpe-maximizing portfolio volatility juxtaposed with that of the variance-minimized portfolio.

EXHIBIT 21-12 Comparison of Optimal 7%-Return-Target Portfolio Allocations, Variance-Minimization vs. Sharpe Ratio-Maximization

© OnCourse Learning

has a relatively low expected return! These differences between the Sharpe-maximizing and variance-minimizing perspectives are summarized in the table in Exhibit 21-12.[37] Note that, even though the optimal real estate allocation is reduced in the Sharpe-maximizing portfolio, it still retains a large share, given the indicated expectations.

21.3.3 Summary of the Implications of the Riskless Asset Construct

In this section, we have seen how the extension of the original Markowitz portfolio theory to include consideration of a riskless asset can be useful in several ways:

- It allows an alternative, intuitively appealing definition of the optimal risky asset portfolio, the one with the maximum Sharpe ratio.
- It can help to avoid "silly" portfolio recommendations that put too little weight in high-return assets just because the investor has a conservative target return (or vice versa).
- It provides a useful framework for accommodating the possible use of leverage or cash in the portfolio.

On the other hand, the riskless asset construct is an extension of the original model that adds an additional, not-quite-realistic assumption. The use of one form or the other of the portfolio model depends in part on taste, and in part on circumstances. In practice, both versions are widely used in the real world.

21.4 Some Broader Considerations in Portfolio Allocation

The preceding two sections introduced you to classical portfolio theory. Either with or without the riskless asset construct, this is the most widely used conceptual tool for considering macro-level investment allocation decisions in the framework of risk and return. It is an elegant and powerful theory for developing strategic insight about investment allocation. Furthermore, although the specific numbers we have been working with in this chapter are only examples, they are broadly consistent with typical expectations used in the real world.

With this in mind, it is of more than passing interest to note the similarity between the optimal real estate allocation share suggested in Exhibit 21-12 and the actual proportion real

---

[37]In Exhibit 21-12, T-bills are used as a proxy for the risk-free asset. As an example of the computation of the Sharpe ratio, the real estate ratio is computed as (7% − 3%)/10% = 0.40. Note that the Sharpe ratio of a portfolio is unaffected by its allocation to the risk-free asset.

estate represents in the total U.S. investable wealth indicated in Exhibit 7-5, way back in Chapter 7. While all of these numbers are soft, there is an important suggestion here of broad agreement between the normative perspective provided by portfolio theory and the empirical perspective provided by the actual asset class market valuations. Both perspectives seem to suggest that real estate is roughly between one-fifth and something less than one-half of the total pie.[38] This rough agreement suggests, at least at a very broad-brush level, that we have some combination of a good theory of asset allocation and an efficient capital market in the United States.[39]

Perhaps the largest group of centrally and professionally managed investment portfolios in the United States are those of defined benefit (DB) pension plans. As of 2010 there were some $6.6 trillion in DB pension funds. Of this, less than $350 billion (about 5 percent) was invested in real estate equity—considerably less than the MPT model we reviewed in this chapter would deem optimal. However, many pension funds are very small, and it may be difficult for them to find ways they are comfortable with for investing in real estate. Among members of the Pension Real Estate Association (PREA), which include most of the larger pension funds, the average real estate target allocation has been around 10 percent. Endowment funds, which are also centrally and professionally managed, often have higher real estate targets.

What is the reason for the seemingly rather low allocation of U.S. pension funds to real estate, at least as compared to the implications of classical MPT and compared to the weight of real estate physical capital in the overall investable universe? In their 2004 survey of U.S. pension and endowment funds, Dhar and Goetzmann note, "While modern portfolio theory provides a theoretical framework for [the investment allocation] process, in practice, allocation decisions must be made in an environment of incomplete information, changing estimates of return, and shifting definitions of the risk of investment ... Risk is a statistical input that is clearly defined and easily handled by modern portfolio theory. However, uncertainty is a lack of confidence about exactly what statistical inputs to use in the decision model. Our results suggest that uncertainty plays some role in decision-making."[40] This suggests that in order to understand institutional portfolio allocation decision making regarding real estate we need to take a broader view than what is provided by classical portfolio theory.

An alternative approach to explaining PF allocations might take a more behavioral or political approach combined with an apprehension of the implications of informational inefficiency in the private real estate asset markets. Recall our discussion in Chapter 12 about the investment implications of such inefficiency. We noted there that real estate markets are not able to provide the kind of protection public securities markets provide against doing negative NPV deals (measured from a market value perspective). Lack of **informational efficiency** means that real estate transaction prices are "noisy," that is, they are dispersed around the "true" market value of the properties being traded. There is a real danger of doing a bad deal, paying too much or selling for too little.

Now recall that space markets are segmented by property type and geographic area. And, of course, real estate asset values are strongly influenced by what happens in the space market in which the asset is situated (where real estate cash flows are ultimately determined). Therefore, to minimize the danger of "doing a bad deal" (i.e., incurring a negative NPV at the micro-level), you typically need good *local real estate expertise*. Pension funds lack such

---

[38]Exhibit 7-5 estimates the real estate equity asset class at around 27% of the total market value of the U.S. investable asset universe. The analysis in the previous sections of the present chapter suggest an optimal real estate allocation typically on the order of one-third (give or take 10% or so, depending on investor expectations and risk preferences) of a portfolio consisting of the same four asset classes: stocks, bonds, real estate, and cash. If we remove single-family housing from both the equity and debt categories of Exhibit 7-5 under the theory that housing is more a consumption good than an investment asset, then the commercial (or investment) real estate slice of the pie (including both debt and equity) remains about 16% of a total $44 trillion investable universe as of the early 2000s.

[39]If capital markets are efficient, then they should allow investors to implement their allocation goals. If the normative allocation theory is good (i.e., if it makes sense to people), then investors' allocation goals should generally reflect the recommendations of the theory. The conjunction of these two conditions (market efficiency and good normative theory) would therefore lead to the empirical observation that the "average portfolio" (as reflected in aggregate market value shares) resembles the normative recommendation from the theory.

[40]See also Bond and Slezak (2011).

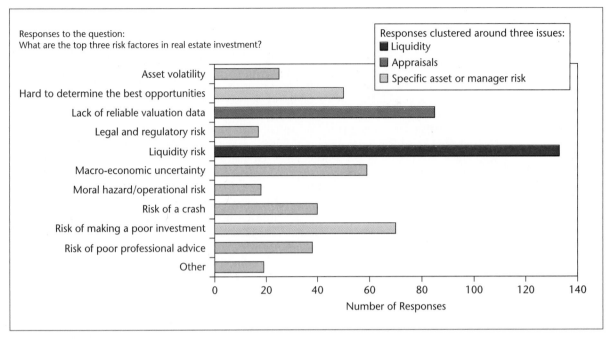

EXHIBIT 21-13 Top Risk Factors in Real Estate as Cited by U.S. Pension Funds
Source: Dhar and Goetzmann (2006).

expertise, and they know it. Sure, they can hire specialized real estate investment managers and local agents, but there may be agency problems in working with such third parties. This is similar in some respects to the situation we noted in Chapter 20 regarding the quantity and quality of information about CMBS compared to corporate bonds: When considering potential equity investment in real estate, many pension funds probably tend (rather understandably) to feel that they are at a relative disadvantage when dealing with privately traded real estate as compared to stocks and bonds.[41]

Exhibit 21-13 shows the responses the pension funds surveyed in the Dhar and Goetzmann study gave to the question, "What are the top three risk factors in real estate investment?" The responses clustered around three somewhat intertwined issues that tend to be prominent differences between private real estate versus traditional stocks and bonds as an asset class. These include concerns about **illiquidity**, the reliability or accuracy of asset valuations, and the need to hire specialized investment managers who will buy and operate a specific set of real physical assets whose performance may differ substantially from the broad asset class average represented by an index or benchmark.[42] Given the large physical capital base of commercial property that could support a larger pension fund investment, the nature of the investment concerns expressed in Exhibit 21-13 suggests that there may still be scope for the investment industry to develop new vehicles and tools to help address the concerns and allow real estate to play a larger role in pension portfolios. Promising vehicles and tools in this regard, such as REITs and derivatives (synthetic investment), will be discussed in subsequent chapters.

---

[41]Williams (1999) put forth a formal equilibrium model arguing along these lines, although his model was applied to a slightly different question, namely, why "noninstitutional" property typically commands higher expected returns than "institutional" property.

[42]Comparing individual real estate properties with individual stocks, it is not clear that specific asset risk (also referred to as "idiosyncratic risk"), deviations of individual assets away from broad indices or benchmarks, is any greater in real estate than in the stock market. However, because of the "lumpiness" of private real estate, in which whole assets must generally be purchased, there may be more difficulty in diversifying investment positions across as many different individual assets in the private real estate asset class compared to equities.

21.5 Chapter Summary

This chapter introduced you to the most famous and fundamental tool in macro-level real estate investment analysis, modern portfolio theory. This theory, including its extension using the riskless asset construct, provides the core discipline for rigorous strategic investment decision making. This is the level of decision making relevant to deciding broad, long-run capital allocation policies across the major asset classes. As real estate is one of the major asset classes, the perspective, intuition, and methodology we presented in this chapter are of vital importance to anyone seriously interested in real estate investment.

Appendix 21 A Review of Some Statistics about Portfolio Returns

At its root, portfolio theory is about the risk and expected return in a combination of individual assets. Risk and return are quantified using statistics that describe periodic returns series over time. Therefore, some basic statistics about periodic returns of portfolios are reviewed in this appendix. As portfolios are combinations of individual assets, it is also important to understand the relationship between time-series and cross-sectional return statistics as applied to real estate assets.

Cross-Sectional and Time-Series Return Statistics

Return statistics measure the central tendencies and dispersion in the returns to assets or portfolios (combinations of assets). The two types are defined here:

- *Cross-sectional* statistics are taken *across multiple individual assets, as of a single point in time.*
- *Time-series* statistics are taken *across multiple periods of time* (either for a single asset or portfolio, or for multiple assets or portfolios, but always measuring effects *across time*).

Although classical, formal portfolio theory makes direct use only of time-series statistics, both types of statistics are broadly relevant in the analysis and characterization of real estate portfolios. Furthermore, a good understanding of the distinction between these two types of return statistics is necessary to avoid confusion.

The best way to cement your understanding of the difference between these two types of statistics in practice is to consider a simple but concrete numerical example. Accordingly, let us consider two individual real estate assets (two properties), A and B. We will consider their investment performance as represented by their total periodic returns in each of two consecutive periods of time, year 1 and year 2. (To simplify the numerical example, we will assume that neither property generates any income in either year, so that their total returns are determined entirely by their change in value, or appreciation return.) The following table presents the value of each property at the beginning and end of each year:

Example Property Values

Time	Value	
	Property A	**Property B**
Beg. Yr. 1	$2,000,000	$1,000,000
End Yr. 1	$2,160,000	$1,060,000
End Yr. 2	$2,419,200	$1,123,600

Based on these values, we can compute property A's periodic returns as 8 percent and 12 percent, respectively, for year 1 and year 2.[43] Similarly, property B's return is 6 percent in both years.[44] Looking *across time* at each property in turn, we can see that property A's average return was 10 percent and property B's was 6 percent during the period of history

---

[43]($2,160,000 − $2,000,000)/$2,000,000 = 8%. ($2,419,200 − $2,160,000)/$2,160,000 = 12%.

[44]($1,060,000 − $1,000,000)/$1,000,000 = 6%. ($1,123,600 − $1,060,000)/$1,060,000 = 6%.

encompassed by years 1 and 2 together.[45] These time-series average statistics present a measure of the "central tendency" of the returns to each of these properties during that period. On the other hand, looking *across properties* within each year, we can see that the average return in year 1 was 7 percent and the average return in year 2 was 9 percent.[46] (Note that these cross-sectional average returns are *equally weighted* mean returns. The weight of each property's return in computing the cross-sectional average is identical, namely, 50 percent.)

We can also compute statistics of dispersion in the periodic returns, either across time or across properties. The simplest statistic of dispersion is the population standard deviation. This is computed as the square root of the equally weighted mean of the squared deviation of each return from its equally weighted mean. For example, by this measure the time-series dispersion in property A's return is $\pm 2\%$ around its mean of 10 percent, computed as

$$2\% = \sqrt{\left\{[(8\% - 10\%)^2 + (12\% - 10\%)^2]/2\right\}}$$

The cross-sectional dispersion in year 1 would similarly be measured as $\pm 1\%$ around its mean of 7 percent, computed as

$$1\% = \sqrt{\left\{[(8\% - 7\%)^2 + (6\% - 7\%)^2]/2\right\}}$$

The following table summarizes the individual periodic returns and the previously described mean and standard deviation statistics for our example. In the top left panel, the rows correspond to the two years, and the columns to the two properties. The cross-sectional statistics are presented to the right, and the time-series statistics at the bottom. (Note that property B's returns had zero percent standard deviation, indicating no dispersion during these two years, as the return was constant at 6 percent both years.)

Periodic Returns			Cross-Sectional Statistics		
Year	Property A	Property B	Year	Mean	St. Dev. (Pop.)
1	8.00%	6.00%	1	7.00%	1.00%
2	12.00%	6.00%	2	9.00%	3.00%

Time-Series Statistics		
Mean	10.00%	6.00%
St. Dev. (Pop.)	2.00%	0.00%

It is obvious from this simple numerical example that cross-sectional statistics and time-series statistics are very different animals. They are measuring conceptually different things. For example, you should see that it would be conceptually possible for there to be great cross-sectional dispersion within each period of time, yet the returns across time within all (or a combination of) properties could be constant, lacking any time-series dispersion (i.e., no volatility). Such a result would follow if each property always displayed a constant return, but that return was different for every property. Similarly, it would be possible for there to be no cross-sectional dispersion at all (all properties always having the same return within any given period of time), yet a portfolio consisting of all (or any combination of) such properties could have plenty of dispersion in its periodic returns over time (i.e., lots of volatility). All it would take to accomplish this result would be for each property's returns to vary across time.

Although portfolio theory uses time-series statistics, it is most concerned about such statistics for portfolios consisting of multiple individual assets. If each asset in the portfolio

---

[45]For property A: (8% + 12%)/2 = 10%. For property B: (6% + 6%)/2 = 6%. Recall from Chapter 9 that these are "arithmetic" means. Arithmetic means tend to be more widely used in portfolio theory. Property A's "geometric" mean return across the two years would be ($2,419,200/$2,000,000)$^{(1/2)}$ − 1 = 9.98%. Property B's geometric mean return is identical to its arithmetic mean, as it has no dispersion in its return over time: ($1,123,600/$1,000,000)$^{(1/2)}$ − 1 = 6%.

[46]For year 1: (8% + 6%)/2 = 7%. For year 2: (12% + 6%)/2 = 9%.

always had the same proportion of the portfolio's total value as every other asset, then the cross-sectional equally weighted mean returns such as those computed earlier would represent the portfolio's periodic returns. In practice, however, the value weights of the individual assets in a portfolio usually vary across the assets. For example, consider the portfolio consisting of property A and property B. The values of this portfolio at the beginning and end of each year are shown in the following table, along with the portfolio's periodic returns. The previously described time-series statistics are also computed for the portfolio, based on its periodic returns. The portfolio's time-weighted arithmetic mean return is 8.68 percent across the two years, and its volatility during that period was 1.35 percent.

Time	Property A	Property B	Portfolio	Return
Beg. Yr. 1	$2,000,000	$1,000,000	$3,000,000	
End Yr. 1	$2,160,000	$1,060,000	$3,220,000	7.33%
End Yr. 2	$2,419,200	$1,123,600	$3,542,800	10.02%
T.S. Mean				8.68%
T.S. St. Dev. (Pop.)				1.35%

Note that the portfolio returns of 7.33 percent and 10.02 percent in years 1 and 2, respectively, differ from the equally weighted average returns computed previously (7 percent and 9 percent). This is because the assets composing the portfolio had different returns and different value-based weights in the portfolio. The portfolio returns may also be referred to as the *value-weighted* average returns across the individual assets. For example, based on the asset values as of the beginning of year 1, property A has two-thirds of the portfolio value and property B has one-third because property A was worth $2 million at the beginning of year 1, when property B was only worth $1 million. Thus, the value-weighted average return across the two properties in year 1 is (2/3)8% + (1/3)6% = 7.33%.

In general, the return during period t to a portfolio consisting of N component assets is the value-weighted average return across all the assets:

$$r_{Pt} = \sum_{i=1}^{N} w_{it} r_{it},$$

where   (A.1)

$$\sum_{i=1}^{N} w_{it} = 1$$

where w_{it} is the proportion of portfolio value in asset i at the beginning of period t, and r_{it} is asset i's return that period.[47]

Time-Series Statistics Used in Portfolio Theory

As noted at the outset of this appendix, portfolio theory is essentially about the risk and return characteristics of portfolios. Such risk and return is quantified by statistics describing the period-by-period total returns to the portfolio, returns like those we just calculated for the portfolio in the simplified numerical example in the preceding section.[48] The statistics used directly in portfolio theory are therefore time-series statistics, that is, measures of central tendencies, dispersion, and comovement across time. In practice, any given historical period is normally taken to represent a sample of time. Thus, in practice, we usually use sample statistics rather than the population statistics used in the previous numerical example.[49]

---

[47]This is equivalent to the weighted average cost of capital (WACC) formula introduced in Chapter 13. As noted there, it applies to the simple holding period return (HPR).

[48]Recall from Chapter 9 that periodic returns are series of consecutive short holding period returns (HPRs) across time.

[49]The distinction between sample and population statistics is normally only a technical fine point in most of the practical applications we will consider. For example, as noted in formula (A.3), the formula for computing historical return variance (or volatility) is modified slightly from what was used in the previous numerical example.

Broadly speaking, we can group the statistics used in basic portfolio theory into two types. *First moment* statistics measure *central tendencies*, that is, the overall average or typical value of the return. *Second moment* statistics measure *dispersion* and *comovement*, that is, how returns vary over time and in relation to those of other assets. The classical first moment statistic used in portfolio theory is the mean, usually the arithmetic mean.[50] The major second moment statistics used in portfolio theory are the variance (and its square root, the standard deviation, or volatility) and the covariance (and its normalization, the correlation coefficient). These statistics are described here.

Mean   This is the average value of the returns across time. It represents expected performance (ex ante) or achieved performance (ex post). In general, for portfolio theory, the time-weighted mean is most relevant, for the reasons described in Chapter 9. Assuming the historical period from which the mean is calculated is a representative stretch of history, the historical arithmetic mean is the best estimate of the ex ante return, that is, what the return will be in any given future single period.[51] As noted in Chapter 9, the formula for computing the arithmetic mean of a series of T periodic returns ($r_1, r_2, \ldots r_T$) is as follows, where $\bar{r}$ is the ex post mean return:

$$\bar{r} = \left(\frac{1}{T}\right)\sum_{t=1}^{T} r_t \tag{A.2}$$

The ex ante return, or expected return, labeled $E[r]$, may or may not be taken to equal the ex post mean return from a given historical sample.[52]

Variance   This is the most widely used measure of the magnitude of dispersion about the mean.[53] In theory, it is the central tendency of the squared difference between the realized return and the ex ante mean return, $E[(r - E[r])^2]$. In practice, variance is often estimated statistically from a historical sample of periodic returns, using the following formula, where S^2 represents the variance:[54]

$$S^2 = \frac{\sum_{t=1}^{T}(r_t - \bar{r})^2}{T - 1} \tag{A.3}$$

Standard Deviation   This is the square root of the variance. Applied to a series of periodic asset returns as in portfolio theory, this measure is commonly referred to as the volatility. The advantage of this measure over the variance is that it is measured in units of returns rather than "squared returns." For example, if a return has an expected value of

---

[50]See Chapter 9 for a discussion of the differences between, and the relative advantages and disadvantages of, the arithmetic and geometric means. Recall also that when returns are defined as continuously compounded (or log differences), then the arithmetic mean is effectively the same as the geometric mean.

[51]The time-weighted geometric mean may be a better indicator of multiperiod average performance over an interval of time equal to that in the historical sample. (Recall that if the underlying returns are normally distributed, the arithmetic mean approximately equals the geometric mean plus one-half the variance in the returns.)

[52]The two most popular models for deriving ex ante return estimates in the stock market are the capital asset pricing model (CAPM) and the Gordon growth model. These will be discussed in Chapters 22 and 23.

[53]Other measures that are sometimes used in portfolio theory instead of the variance include most prominently the mean absolute difference (MAD) and the semivariance (based only on the left-hand tail of the return distribution, that is, only deviations *below* the mean are included). The former is less sensitive to a few "outlier" events, while the latter is arguably a better measure of how most investors view risk if returns are not symmetrically distributed. In practice, however, the traditional variance is still the most widely used measure of risk, and for many portfolio applications will give results similar to those obtained from other measures.

[54]Note that the sum of the squared differences from the mean are divided by *one less than* the number of observations in the time-series. This modification is necessary to remove bias from statistical estimators of second moments. In effect, this formulation of the variance estimator is treating the historical time-series as a sample drawn from a larger potential population of returns (including those that will occur in the future). In implementing this formula in an electronic spreadsheet (such as Excel), you need to use the "sample" (as opposed to "population") version of the formula: *VAR*( ) as opposed to *VARP*( ).

10 percent based on a 50 percent chance that it will turn out to be 15 percent and an equal chance that it will turn out to be 5 percent, its standard deviation or volatility is 5 percent, while its variance is 25 "percent-squared." As you can see, the standard deviation is a more intuitive measure than the variance.

As noted in previous chapters, the volatility is a basic measure of the risk of an investment. In particular, the volatility is often taken as the measure of the *total risk* in an investment (that is, including both the "idiosyncratic" or specific risk that can be diversified away and the "systematic" risk that cannot be diversified away). The volatility of an asset or portfolio is often used to measure the amount of risk an undiversified investor (that is, one who holds only that asset or portfolio) is exposed to.

The formula for estimating volatility from a historical series of periodic returns, labeled S, is as follows:

$$S = \sqrt{\frac{\sum\limits_{t=1}^{T} (r_t - \bar{r})^2}{T - 1}} \tag{A.4}$$

Covariance   This is the most widely used measure of pairwise comovement, that is, how the returns of two assets (or portfolios) move together across time. What the variance measures for a single asset's returns, covariance measures for a pair of assets.[55] The formula for computing the historical covariance between asset (or portfolio) i whose returns are $(r_{i1}, r_{i2}, \ldots r_{iT})$ and asset (or portfolio) j whose returns are $(r_{j1}, r_{j2}, \ldots r_{jT})$, labeled COV_{ij}, is as follows:[56]

$$COV_{ij} = \frac{\sum\limits_{t=1}^{T} [(r_{it} - \bar{r}_i)(r_{jt} - \bar{r}_j)]}{T - 1} \tag{A.5}$$

In terms of its economic significance in portfolio theory, the most important thing about the covariance statistic is the fact that the covariance between an asset and a portfolio is the component of that asset's variance that is not diversified away when the asset is added to the portfolio. Thus, covariance is basic to measuring the "systematic risk" in an asset, the risk that cannot be diversified away. This characteristic of covariance may help you to see the intuition in the following formula, which gives the time-series variance of a portfolio (S_P^2, the "volatility-squared" of the portfolio) as a function of the covariances of the returns to the N constituent assets in the portfolio and the weight (w_i, the share of the total portfolio value) invested in each asset i ($i = 1, \ldots N$):[57]

$$S_P^2 = \sum\limits_{i=1}^{N} \sum\limits_{j=1}^{N} w_i w_j COV_{ij} \tag{A.6}$$

In other words, the variance of a portfolio is the sum of the products of the weighted covariances of the individual constituent assets across all of the pairs of assets in the portfolio.[58]

---

[55]Indeed, covariance is a generalization of the variance measure, as one way to define the variance is as the covariance of an asset with itself.

[56]By comparing formula (A.5) with formula (A.3), you can see that COV_{ii}, the covariance of asset i with itself, is equivalent to the variance of asset $i : S_i^2$.

[57]Recall from formula (A.1) that the weights sum to one:

$$\sum\limits_{i=1}^{N} w_i = 1$$

[58]This is a summation of N^2 terms. Note, however, that $w_i w_j COV_{ij} = w_j w_i COV_{ji}$, and recall that $COV_{ii} = VAR_i = S_i^2$, the variance of asset i. Thus, formula (A.6) can also be expressed as a summation of $N + [(N^2 - N)/2]$ terms, including N terms in the variances of the assets and $(N^2 - N)/2$ terms that are twice the covariances of each different pair of assets in the portfolio:

$$S_P^2 = \sum\limits_{i=1}^{N} w_i^2 S_i^2 + 2 \sum\limits_{i=1}^{N} \sum\limits_{j=i+1}^{N} w_i w_j COV_{ij}$$

This is the formula that was used in the table in Exhibit 21-1C to compute the volatility of Bob's portfolio.

Cross-Correlation Coefficient   This statistic (referred to simply as the correlation for short) is a normalized measure of comovement. While the covariance is measured in units of "squared return" like the variance, the correlation ranges between negative unity and positive unity. The correlation (labeled C_{ij}) equals the covariance divided by the product of the standard deviations of the two variables:

$$C_{ij} = \frac{COV_{ij}}{S_i S_j} \qquad (A.7)$$

Note that the correlation coefficient has the same sign as the covariance, but it is bounded between -1 and $+1$.

Exhibit 21A-1 pictures what different correlations would typically look like in scatterplots of the two assets' returns. Exhibit 21A-1A depicts $+90\%$ correlation. Exhibit 21A-1B depicts -90% correlation. With *positive* correlation, the two assets' returns tend to move *together*: when one is up, the other tends also to be up; when one is down, the other tends also to be down. *Negative* correlation indicates that the two assets' returns tend to move *oppositely*: when one is up, the other is down. Zero correlation indicates a lack of systematic relationship between the two assets' returns. As the correlation approaches positive or negative 100 percent, the relationship between the two assets approaches a *deterministic* relationship in which the two assets move in lockstep (always either together or oppositely, lying on a perfectly straight line of either positive or negative slope[59]).

The correlation is important in portfolio analysis because it indicates how useful an asset (or a pair of assets) can be for purposes of diversification. The lower the correlation coefficient between two assets is, the better they can "diversify each other," in the sense that the greater will be the potential to reduce volatility by combining the two assets in a portfolio. In the extreme, two assets that are perfectly negatively correlated ($C_{ij} = -100\%$) can be combined to produce a portfolio that is completely riskless, in the sense of having zero volatility.

Autocorrelation   This is simply the correlation of an asset's (or portfolio's, or asset class's) returns with themselves lagged in time. The autocorrelation reflects the nature of the informational efficiency of an asset market, as discussed in previous chapters. For example, in general, zero autocorrelation is an indication of an informationally efficient asset market, in which prices quickly reflect full information (and therefore, returns lack predictability). Positive autocorrelation indicates a sluggish asset market that lacks perfect informational efficiency (prices only gradually incorporate new information). Negative autocorrelation indicates a "noisy" market (excessive short-run volatility, that is, a tendency for price overreactions that are subsequently "corrected").

Evidence suggests that private property markets display positive autocorrelation in the short to intermediate term. Public securities markets (including REITs) tend to show very little autocorrelation in general, though with some tendency toward negative autocorrelation in the intermediate run (perhaps offsetting some positive autocorrelation in the very short run).

When an asset has zero autocorrelation (over all lags), the variance in its return is directly proportional to the length of the time interval over which the return is measured. For example, annual periodic returns would have four times the variance of quarterly periodic returns. When an asset has positive autocorrelation, the long-run variance is more than proportional to the short-run variance, while the opposite is true with negative autocorrelation. Thus, private real estate volatility tends to increase *relative to* that of securities when returns are measured at lower frequency (longer periodic intervals). For example, quarterly private real estate returns generally appear quite a bit less volatile than quarterly stock market returns, but five-year-interval private real estate returns are probably about as volatile as five-year-interval stock market returns.

---

[59]The correlation indicates the sign of the slope but not its magnitude or steepness.

EXHIBIT 21A-1A
+90% Correlation
© OnCourse Learning

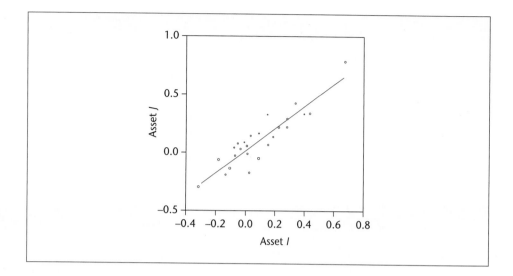

EXHIBIT 21A-1B
−90% Correlation
© OnCourse Learning

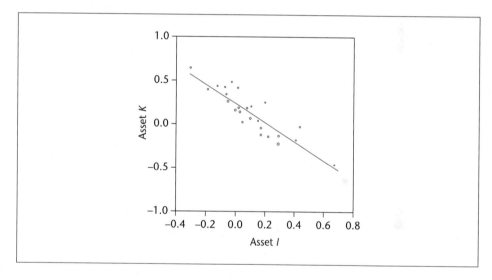

EXHIBIT 21A-1C
0% Correlation
© OnCourse Learning

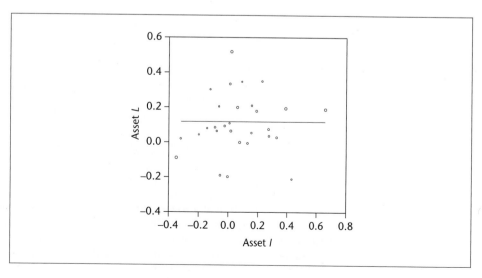

KEY TERMS

modern portfolio theory (MPT)
volatility (standard deviation of return)
covariances (between assets)
weighted covariances
correlation coefficient (between returns)
solver (in spreadsheet)
target return (for portfolio)

sensitivity analysis
mean-variance portfolio theory (Markowitz)
risk preferences (of investors)
dominant portfolio (domination)
diversification benefit
cost-of-living adjustments (COLAs)
mixed-asset portfolio
efficient portfolio

efficient frontier
pension funds
two-fund theorem
Sharpe ratio
risk-adjusted return
Sharpe-maximizing portfolio
informational efficiency
illiquidity

STUDY QUESTIONS

Conceptual Questions

21.1. In the example of Bob the investment manager in section 21.1, what would you say was the specific objective Bob ended up trying to serve in his portfolio allocation recommendation, and what constraint did he operate within?

21.2. Why should all investors, regardless of risk preferences, avoid holding *dominated* portfolios?

21.3. What does modern portfolio theory recommend besides not putting all one's eggs in one basket?

21.4. Why do investors invest in real estate? Answer this from a portfolio theory perspective, considering the trade-off between portfolio risk and return. (Hint: What is the primary role of typical income property real estate within the portfolio? Is it bought to achieve a high average return?)

21.5. Building off of your answer to Question 21.4, what is another role for real estate in helping to manage the portfolio of a defined benefit pension fund portfolio?

21.6. How are investor risk preferences reflected in typical portfolio theory application? (Hint: What is the role of the target return specified by the investor?)

21.7. Modern portfolio theory tells us that investors hold portfolios that lie on the efficient frontier and that efficient frontier portfolios change with investor's target required portfolio returns. Examine the role of real estate in optimal portfolios with different risk-return profiles by answering the following two questions:

    a. Explain how the optimal portfolio allocation or mix changes as we move from the more conservative to aggressive investor return expectations in a world with three major investment asset classes (stocks, bonds, and real estate) as shown in Exhibit 21-8.

    b. Consider the expanded five asset class investment universe that includes small cap stocks and REITs (Exhibit 21-9B). Does the inclusion of REITs into the asset class mix affect the optimal allocation to private real estate? If so, how, and in your opinion, why? Does there appear to be a role for both private real estate and REITs?

21.8. Discuss two fundamental, conceptual problems with the application of modern portfolio theory (MPT) to investment decision making within an investor's real estate portfolio. (See the text box titled "Can MPT Be Applied Within the Real Estate Portfolio?".)

21.9. How is the two-fund theorem useful in practical portfolio theory applications? What is the relationship between the two-fund theorem and the Sharpe-maximizing portfolio?

21.10. Available empirical evidence suggests that commercial real estate is an asset class that should be well represented in the mixed asset portfolios of institutional investors.

However, despite the perceived importance of real estate in mixed asset portfolios, pension funds typically allocate smaller shares to real estate than analysis based on Modern Portfolio Theory (MPT) predicts they should. Discuss why this might be so.

Quantitative Problems

21.11. You work for BSC Advisors, a major real estate investment manager. You are trying to convince a pension fund manager to allocate 10% of her portfolio to investment-grade income-property. Currently the fund is allocated 60% to stocks and 40% to bonds. Suppose you agree with Bob's asset class risk and return expectations shown in Exhibit 21-1A. Perform the following calculations, and then explain how you would use the results to persuade the pension fund portfolio manager to allocate funds to real estate. Be prepared to discuss the limitations of your analysis. {Help: A portfolio comprised of three asset classes ("1", "2" and "3") has expected return, $E[R_p]$, and standard deviation of returns (volatility), S_p, given by

$$E[R_p] = w_1 E[R_1] + w_2 E[R_2] + w_3 E[R_3] \text{ with } w_1 + w_2 + w_3 = 1, \text{ and}$$

$$S_p = \sqrt{w_1^2 S_1^2 + w_2^2 S_2^2 + w_3^2 S_3^2 + 2 w_1 w_2 S_1 S_2 C_{12} + 2 w_1 w_3 S_1 S_3 C_{13} + 2 w_2 w_3 S_2 S_3 C_{23}}$$

where the w_i are the portfolio weights for each asset class and the C_{ij} are the correlation coefficients between pairs of asset class returns.}

a. Determine the expected return and standard deviation of returns on the current portfolio (60% stocks/40% bonds).

b. Determine the expected return and standard deviation of returns on a portfolio comprised of 55% stocks, 35% bonds and 10% real estate.

21.12. Consider two portfolios. Portfolio A has an expected return of 10% and volatility of 8%. Portfolio B has an expected return of 9% and volatility of 7%. The interest rate on a risk-free investment is 5%. Which of the two risky portfolios is not on the efficient frontier? (Hint: Use the two-fund theorem.)

21.13. Consider again portfolios A and B from Problem 21.12. What would be the expected return to portfolio C that consists of a 50/50 weighting of A and B?

21.14. Consider again portfolio C from Problem 21.13. Assuming (very reasonably) that portfolios A and B are not perfectly positively correlated, will portfolio C's volatility be greater or less than halfway between A's and B's volatility (that is, 7.5%)?

EQUILIBRIUM ASSET VALUATION AND REAL ESTATE'S PRICE OF RISK IN THE CAPITAL MARKET

CHAPTER OUTLINE

LEARNING OBJECTIVES

After reading this chapter, you should understand:

➲ What is meant by equilibrium asset pricing models and how these tools are used in practice to aid macro-level investment decision making.

➲ The classical CAPM and its major theoretical and practical strengths and weaknesses.

➲ How the CAPM can be (or why it should be) applied to real estate and where it falls down in this regard, including a distinction between application at the overall multi-asset-class portfolio level and application at the more specific level within the private real estate asset class.

T he previous chapter introduced you to portfolio theory, the fundamental tool of **strategic investment decision making** at the macro-level. This chapter will build on portfolio theory to present a topic that is relevant and useful in principle for all three of the decision-making arenas noted in the Introduction to Part VII: tactical as well as strategic investment decision making, plus investment policy implementation. Our subject in this chapter will be equilibrium asset pricing models. Such models are typically built on the foundation of portfolio theory, but go beyond portfolio theory to provide a simplified representation of how the capital market perceives and prices risk (or other attributes of concern to investors) in the assets that are traded in the market. Intuitively, we know that assets that are riskier (in some sense that the capital market cares about) will trade in equilibrium at lower prices, so that they will provide higher expected returns.[1] Thus, asset pricing models at the macro-level are, in effect, models of the ex ante risk premium

---

[1]Recall the inverse relationship between asset value and expected return. (See, for example, Chapter 10.)

required by investors.[2] This means they can in principle be used to help forecast future long-run average returns.

This chapter will be presented in four parts. First we provide some introductory and threshold points in section 22.1. Then in section 22.2 we introduce the classical equilibrium asset pricing model in mainstream securities investments, the "CAPM." Section 22.3 applies this model at the overall level of the mixed asset class portfolio, stocks, bonds, and real estate. Finally, section 22.4 explores how, or whether, such modeling can be applied at a more granular level within the real estate asset class.

22.1 Introduction and Some Threshold Points

Before delving into the nitty-gritty of equilibrium asset price modeling itself, let us put this exercise in some perspective. This section will review the practical uses of the models, and then raise an important threshold point about the nature of the risk that is being modeled.

22.1.1 Practical Uses for Asset Price Theory

As noted, equilibrium asset pricing models have three major practical uses. First, asset valuation and tactical investment decision making are naturally linked because **tactical decision making** aims at profiting from short- to medium-term opportunities. This often involves identifying assets (or, more likely, asset classes, or *types* of assets or investment products) that are currently "mispriced" in some sense, such that there might be short- to medium-term opportunities in buying or selling. In order to know if something is mispriced, you need to have some idea about what its value should be when asset markets are in equilibrium. Asset pricing models give insight about what those equilibrium asset values and expected returns should be.

Equilibrium pricing models can also be useful for strategic investment decisions, that is, for more long run or permanent objectives for a given investor, in the following way. Suppose the model can identify a risk factor that is persistently and reliably "priced" in the capital market, but that a given investor is not concerned about. For example, say the capital market prices smaller properties in tertiary markets as though they are more "risky." In other words, such investments tend to provide an extra total return premium just because they are small and in tertiary markets. This would presumably be because the "average" investor (determining the equilibrium in the asset market) is persistently concerned about the particular risk in such assets (or their illiquidity, or some other negative attribute). If you as an investor don't share this concern that the average investor has, then the model has just given you a strategic reason to tilt your portfolio allocation a little bit extra towards smaller properties in tertiary markets. You would stand to earn an extra return over the long run (not *definitely* but *probably*, if the model is correct and the equilibrium is persistent) only by taking on an extra risk factor that you are not concerned about (in contrast to the average investor).

Finally, equilibrium asset price models provide a rigorous way to quantitatively adjust realized investment performance (ex post returns) for the amount of risk the investment was exposed to, based on the pricing of such risk in the capital market. In principle, this can enable a more fair and complete or correct evaluation of the performance of investment managers hired to implement investors' policies (including regarding risk exposure). If an investment manager did very well, but he did so by taking on a lot of risk, then perhaps a big part (or even all) of the high return he achieved was simply a compensation for risk exposure. Perhaps he wasn't "beating the market." Thus, asset pricing models can help to "benchmark" investment performance.[3]

---

[2]To put macro-level valuation in a broader context, note that the most widely used asset valuation model at the micro-level is the DCF model described extensively in Part IV. There, we noted the importance of the expected return risk premium in deriving the discount rate used in the denominators of the DCF valuation equation, and we noted that this risk premium reflects the opportunity cost of capital (OCC) as this is determined ultimately in the capital market. However, in Chapters 11 and 12, we stopped short of considering in depth *how* the capital market determines the expected return risk premium in the OCC. This is the question we turn to in the present chapter.

[3]This last topic will be addressed in Chapter 26, after we have covered more of the elements of macro-level real estate investment analysis.

EXHIBIT 22-1 The
Relationship between
Equilibrium Asset Price
Models and Investment
Policy
© OnCourse Learning

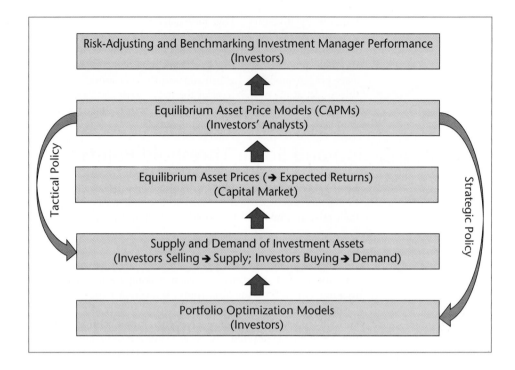

The context and roles of equilibrium asset price models are illustrated in Exhibit 22-1. Underlying investors' decisions are portfolio optimization models, a classical example of which (the MPT—Markowitz Mean-Variance Model) was described in the previous chapter. Investors decisions (which assets to buy and sell) lead to the pattern of equilibrium asset prices in the capital market. This equilibrium pricing is the subject of the asset price models (such as the classical "CAPM," which we will describe shortly) that seek to specify what are the equilibrium (or in some sense "fair market") expected returns to the various assets or asset classes. This information can then be used by investors: (1) to help inform their long-run strategic portfolio optimization policies due to differences between their preferences and the "average" market preferences (reflected in the equilibrium); (2) to help identify short to medium-term tactical opportunities due to mispricing in the market; and (3) to help evaluate or benchmark the performance of investment managers hired to implement the investors' strategic or tactical policies.

22.1.2 A Threshold Point: What Underlies Asset Risk?

Before we examine how to model the way asset risk is priced, let us step back briefly to consider the nature of that risk. The risk that matters to an investor in an asset is based on the risk in the *total return* that the asset provides. That is, what matters to the investor is both the income provided by the asset and the change over time in the value of the asset. Fundamentally, therefore, there are two sources of investment risk: cash flow risk, and asset-valuation risk. In the case of real estate assets, cash-flow risk derives from changes over time in the space market that cause changes in the rent the property can charge, as well as changes in operating expenses and capital improvement expenditures that also determine net cash flow. Asset-valuation risk reflects changes over time in the asset market that cause changes in the opportunity cost of capital applied by the asset market (the "discount rate" in the DCF procedure of Chapter 10), that is, changes in the equilibrium expected return required by investors.

While the space market and the asset's net cash flows are the fundamental source of property value, there is evidence that investment return risk in real estate assets, like that in the stock market, derives at least as much from changes in the asset market. Time variation in the discount rate may cause at least as much volatility in real estate investment returns as time variation in the property cash flow. This phenomenon in the stock market was first noted by the economist Robert Shiller in a famous 1981 article, "Do Stock Prices Move Too Much to Be Justified by Subsequent Changes in Dividends?" Shiller's answer was "yes," and although subsequent research has debated whether the word "*Justified*" in Shiller's title is, itself, *justified* (see section 22.4 below), there seems little doubt that a substantial part of the variation in asset prices is due to "revaluation" in the asset market, rather than to investors' revisions in their expected future cash flows.

A picture of this point is presented in Exhibit 22-2 (taken from research by Jianping Mei and David Geltner). The exhibit shows three lines. The line with solid square markers is the history of real estate present values based on a DCF model in which changes in both the future cash flows and the future discount rate are forecasted and used in the valuation.[4] This line closely tracks the actual market values of commercial property as represented by the NCREIF Index (unsmoothed). The similar line with diamond markers is the same DCF valuation model, only assuming a constant future

EXHIBIT 22-2 The Effect of Varying Cash Flow Expectations and Varying Return Expectations in a Present Value Model of Commercial Property

Source: Geltner and Mei (1995).

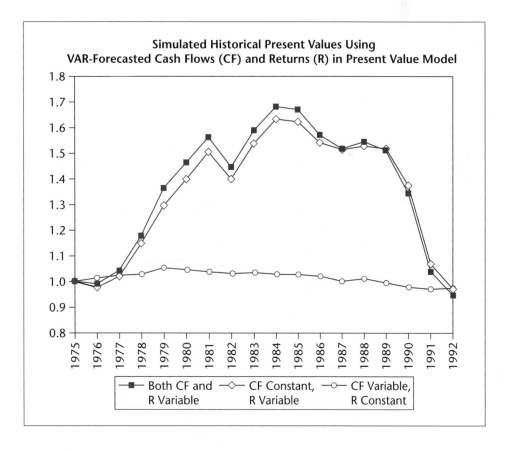

---

[4]In effect, instead of the constant "blended" discount rate presented in Chapter 10, the DCF valuation here forecasts the future OCC of real estate in each future period of time, and applies those future forecasted rates to discount the forecasted future cash flows in each period. For example, the PV of the cash flow two years hence would be, in essence: $E[CF2]/((1 + E[r_1])(1 + E[r_2]))$, where r_1 is the OCC in year 1 and r_2 is the OCC in year 2, and $E[.]$ represents forecasted values as of the present. (The actual model used in the study is a log-transformation.)

cash-flow level from each period going forward but including the forecasted time-varying discount rate in the valuation. The nearly flat line at the bottom, which does not much resemble what actually happened to commercial property values, applies the DCF model with a constant discount rate, but using the actual forecasted cash flows. While there was substantial variation in real estate cash flows, much of this variation was mean-reverting and predictable. Hence, the cash flow forecast does not change much from one period to the next, resulting in little change in asset present value unless the discount rate changes.[5]

Why is an understanding of this fundamental nature of real estate investment return risk important as you proceed to consider how that risk is priced? As you will see, the essence of the CAPM is that priced risk is not the isolated volatility of individual assets, but rather is related to the comovements of asset returns. When you realize that much asset value volatility derives from asset market valuation changes, you can appreciate how importantly asset markets, as well as space markets, can influence those all-important comovements that govern the risk that matters. For example, it is possible for real estate returns across different space markets to move together much more than the underlying space markets themselves may tend to move together. With this in mind, let us proceed to a presentation of the CAPM.

22.2 Review of Classical Asset Pricing Theory

In this section we will introduce and briefly review the classical equilibrium asset pricing model, **CAPM** (**capital asset pricing model**). It is such a famous and fundamental model that it is known traditionally simply as *the CAPM*.

22.2.1 From Portfolio Theory to the CAPM

The so-called Sharpe-Lintner CAPM is one of the most famous theories in all of financial economics (having earned Sharpe and Lintner a Nobel Prize). It grew out of, and is built on, the Markowitz mean-variance portfolio theory that we described in the previous chapter (MPT). So let's pick up where we left off in that chapter and see, in a simplified intuitive way, how we can extend MPT to develop a theory about how all assets in the market are priced. We can do this in four easy steps, as follows.[6]

Step 1: The Two-Fund Theorem   We begin with the basic assumptions of MPT, that investors want to maximize return and minimize risk in their wealth portfolios (i.e., they don't want to hold dominated portfolios), and we add the assumption described in Section 21.3 of Chapter 21 that a *riskless asset* exists. Recall that this leads to the two-fund theorem, which demonstrates that *all* investors (no matter what their risk preferences) should want to hold *the same* portfolio (i.e., the same relative weights) of risky assets, as long as those investors have the same risk and return expectations.

Step 2: Common Expectations   Remember that asset markets (especially securities markets such as the stock market) are known to be pretty efficient, that is, asset prices are pretty good at reflecting all publicly available information relevant to their values. Thus, any one investor will not usually have better information than the market as a whole concerning the values of assets or their future expected returns. Thus, everyone will converge to having the same expectations regarding risks, returns, and values. Combined with the two-fund theorem, this will lead everyone to want to hold the same portfolio (relative weights) of risky assets,

---

[5]This type of finding has been largely confirmed, and extended and nuanced, in a more recent study by Plazzi, Torous and Valkanov (2010). They find a less dominant role for expected return variation, but still a very substantial role, in the determination of total return variation over time.

[6]The CAPM can be derived in several different ways, depending on what simplifying assumptions one wishes to make. The approach presented here corresponds closely in spirit (although not in analytical rigor) to the original development of the model.

which will therefore be empirically observable as the **market portfolio**, the aggregate of all risky capital assets. The relative weight placed on each asset (or asset class) in this market portfolio corresponds to the current market value of each asset as a fraction of the aggregate market value. This market portfolio thus reflects the overall wealth portfolios of all investors.[7]

Step 3: Only Covariance with the Market Matters   Now recall that a basic tenet of portfolio theory is that all investors care only about the risk (variance or volatility) in their *overall* wealth. The variance of any individual component of that wealth does not matter per se. Since, by our reasoning in steps 1 and 2, all investors hold the same portfolio, the market portfolio, the only risk that matters to investors in any given asset is how that asset affects the risk in the market portfolio. But it is a fact of basic statistics that the marginal contribution of each asset to the variance of a portfolio is directly proportional to the covariance of the asset's periodic returns with the portfolio's periodic returns. Thus, the only risk that matters to investors in an asset can be quantified by that asset's covariance with the market portfolio.[8]

Step 4: Asset Pricing and Expected Returns   As all investors hold their entire wealth in the market portfolio (plus or minus a riskless asset), the variance in the market portfolio quantifies the risk that all investors are exposed to. Therefore, the risk premium in the expected return to the market portfolio, divided by the variance in the return to the market portfolio, quantifies the "price of risk," that is, the market's required expected return risk premium *per unit of risk* (variance). Multiplying this price of risk by the amount of risk in each asset (that is, the risk that matters to investors, the asset's covariance with the market) gives the market's required risk premium in each asset's expected return:

$$E[r_i] = r_f + RP_i = r_f + COV_{iM}\left(\frac{E[r_M] - r_f}{S_M^2}\right) \tag{1a}$$

where $E[r_i]$ is the market's equilibrium required expected return to asset class (constituent of the market portfolio), $E[r_M]$ is the market's equilibrium required expected return to the market portfolio as a whole, r_f is the risk-free interest rate, COV_{iM} is the covariance between asset class i and the market portfolio, and S_M^2 is the variance (volatility squared) of the market portfolio.

That does it: four steps. Formula (1a) is the Sharpe-Lintner CAPM. We have simplified a bit in order to present a less technical (hopefully more intuitive) derivation of this Nobel Prize–winning theory. But this is the complete model. It is important to understand where it comes from because such understanding can enable you to recognize both how it *can* be useful and circumstances in which it *cannot* be validly used.

The Sharpe-Lintner CAPM is usually expressed in a slightly different form than formula (1a). The more familiar formula uses a more intuitive measure of risk called **beta**. Beta simply

---

[7]A simplified way of presenting essentially this same step in the model's derivation is to posit the concept that the entire capital market can be represented by a single "representative investor" who holds the market portfolio and who determines the pricing in the market.

[8]Recall that the variance of the portfolio is the sum of all the pairwise weighted covariances among the portfolio's constituents:

$$VAR_P = \sum_{I=1}^{N}\sum_{J=1}^{N} w_i w_j COV_{ij}$$

Thus, the marginal contribution of any one constituent to the overall portfolio variance, per unit of weight of the constituent in the portfolio is:

$$\partial VAR_P / \partial w_i = 2\sum_{J=1}^{N} w_j COV_{ij} \equiv 2COV_{iP}$$

The doubling (multiplication by two) drops out in the comparison of the *relative* amount of risk contributed by each constituent. So the relative risk that matters is completely quantified by the covariance with the market.

normalizes the asset's risk as a fraction of the overall average or market risk (variance in the market):

$$Beta_{iM} = \frac{COV_{iM}}{S_M^2} \tag{2a}$$

Using beta, the CAPM as expressed in formula (1a) becomes

$$E[r_i] = r_f + RP_i = r_f + Beta_{iM}(E[r_M] - r_f) \tag{1b}$$

In words, the CAPM says that an asset's expected return risk premium is directly proportional to its beta. Any asset's risk premium equals its beta times the **market price of risk**, which is observable as the expected return risk premium on the market portfolio, that is, the expected return on all investors' overall wealth over and above the risk-free interest rate.

As indicated in Exhibit 22-3, the CAPM provides financial economists and investment practitioners with a rigorous foundation for, and a way to formalize and quantify, the **security market line (SML)**, the relationship between risk and return that we first introduced way back in Chapter 9 where we called it "financial economics in a nutshell."

It is interesting to note that a mathematically equivalent way to express beta is as the correlation between asset class i and the market, multiplied by the ratio of asset i's volatility divided by the market portfolio's volatility:

$$Beta_{iM} = \frac{S_i}{S_M} C_{iM} \tag{2b}$$

This makes it clear that the risk premium in an asset's required expected return is directly proportional not only to its risk as measured by the asset's own volatility (S_i), but also to its correlation with the market wealth portfolio (C_{iM}). An asset can be quite volatile, yet it still may not provide or require a high expected return if it is not highly correlated with the market. On the other hand, even an asset with relatively low volatility may command a relatively high risk premium if it is highly correlated with the market because in that case it does not provide investors with much diversification benefit in their wealth portfolios. Risk is defined by the *interaction* of the asset's own volatility and its correlation with the "market," that is, with investors' wealth portfolios.

EXHIBIT 22-3 The CAPM in Graphical Form (the Security Market Line)

OnCourse Learning

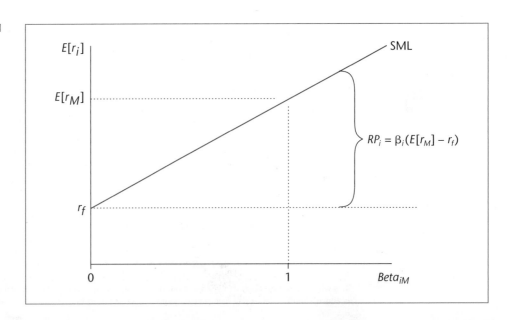

22.2.2 The Main Point in the Basic CAPM

The main investment insight provided by the CAPM is the *irrelevance of, and therefore lack of compensation for, diversifiable risk*. The CAPM suggests that, as covariance with the market portfolio is the only risk that matters to the capital market, it is therefore the only risk that will be priced in equilibrium. Risk that cannot be diversified away is referred to in asset pricing theory as **systematic risk**. Diversifiable risk, that is, the component of an asset's own total variance in excess of its covariance with the market, is referred to as the asset's **specific** (or **idiosyncratic**) **risk**.

$$S_i^2 = COV_{iM} + VAR[\varepsilon_i] \tag{3}$$

where $VAR[\varepsilon_i]$ is the variance of asset i's idiosyncratic return component.[9] Since idiosyncratic risk can be diversified away, it does not matter to the investor.

Particularly after our discussion of portfolio theory in Chapter 21, you can probably see that this point about nonpricing of diversifiable risk is actually broader and deeper than the specific Sharpe-Lintner CAPM itself. No matter how the risk that matters to the capital market is defined, whether it is well measured by the traditional CAPM beta or not, it is only such risk that will be priced, by definition. Under the (rather reasonable) assumption that virtually all investors can diversify away risk that is very specific to any one asset or group of assets, it therefore follows that specific risk will not be priced.

An important investment strategy is implied by this result: investors should generally not hold undiversified portfolios. Since investors are not compensated by the market (in the form of expected return) for exposing themselves to specific risk, they should get rid of all such risk by diversifying their wealth portfolio. Indeed, strictly speaking, the Sharpe-Lintner CAPM says that you should not hold any portfolio other than the "market" (scaled down to your wealth, of course, and levered up or down to conform to your risk preferences).

22.2.3 Isn't the CAPM Wrong?

At this point, students often cry foul. "The CAPM can't be right," they say, "it's based on false assumptions." Indeed it is. There is no such thing as a truly riskless asset. Markets are not perfectly efficient. Not all investors share the same expectations about the future. And we do not all hold the same portfolios (that is, relative risky asset weights in our wealth investments). Thus, *obviously*, the CAPM is "wrong" in the sense that it is not a *complete* description of reality of equilibrium asset pricing. Good empirical tests should be able to detect this fact, and indeed they do.[10]

In an important sense, however, this criticism misses the point, not only about the Sharpe-Lintner CAPM, but also about the fundamental nature and purpose of equilibrium asset price modeling in general, and indeed (if we may wax poetic), about the purpose of virtually all scientific theory. By this criterion of "wrongness," Newtonian physics is wrong, as it is built on simplified (false) assumptions that ignore the relativity of time and space. Yet who can deny that we learn a lot that is quite useful from the Newtonian model, both at a practical level and at a deeper, more fundamental level. Virtually all industrial and engineering advances up to at least the middle of the twentieth century were based purely on Newtonian physics. Like Newtonian physics, the CAPM continues to be used widely in practice, not only by academics, but also by professionals in the investment industry.

What the CAPM loses as a result of its unrealistic assumptions, namely, the ability to model the world completely, is more than made up for by what the model gains by these assumptions, namely, the ability to simplify the world so that we can understand it better. The elegance in the basic CAPM enables us to obtain insights that we could not from a more complex model.

---

[9]By definition, idiosyncratic risk is the component of the asset's volatility that is not correlated with anything else. In a time-series statistical regression of asset i's periodic returns onto the market portfolio's periodic returns, would be the variance of the *residuals* from the regression (sometimes referred to as the errors because they are the difference between the returns predicted by the regression and the actual returns of asset i).

[10]In a strict sense, the CAPM has been "flunking" empirical tests at least since the early 1970s, when famous studies by Black, Jensen, and Scholes (1972) and Fama and MacBeth (1973) were published. More recently, particularly influential such studies were published by Fama and French (1992) and Black (1993).

So, let's consider the value and usefulness, as well as the limits and shortcomings, of the CAPM from a more sophisticated perspective. In so doing, we can begin to see how it may be modified or extended particularly to improve its relevance for real estate.

22.2.4 Strengths and Weaknesses in the Basic CAPM

The CAPM, like any valuation model, can be viewed from either a normative or descriptive perspective. From the normative perspective, the model is addressing what *should* be, under the given assumptions. From this perspective we can gain what might be called wisdom, insight that improves our understanding. For example, the general point about the nonpricing of diversifiable risk is a key insight. The extreme suggestion that all investors should hold the same portfolio no doubt goes too far. But the suggestion that all investors should diversify their wealth is a good prescription and is seen to hold widely in reality.

From a descriptive perspective, the CAPM is addressing what *is*, out there in the real world. From this perspective, we hope to gain a practical tool to predict what will happen, a model of cause and effect in the real world. In this respect, the CAPM, while not perfect, is useful in practice. Empirically, beta is not the whole story for explaining expected returns, but it is a big part of the story.

The CAPM is useful in practice presumably because the model's assumptions, while simplifications of reality, are not terribly far from the truth. Although asset markets are not perfectly efficient, they are reasonably efficient most of the time (especially securities markets such as the stock market). Although all investors do not hold the same expectations or the same portfolios, most investors hold fairly similar expectations and fairly similar portfolios (especially large institutional investors).[11] As a result, the CAPM works well enough to be useful, at least at a broad-brush level, or with some fairly simple enhancements. Indeed, beta has become virtually a household word on Wall Street and is regularly estimated and reported as a matter of course by stock analysts. It is especially widely used in the equity mutual fund business.

On the other hand, the hopes that were originally held for the basic Sharpe-Lintner CAPM have not been completely fulfilled. We now recognize that a substantial part of the cross-section of expected returns across assets within the stock market is not well explained by beta. Other risk factors, reflected in such indicators as the size of a firm and its book/market value ratio (the so-called "Fama-French factors"), have a strong influence on expected returns apart from a stock's beta with respect to the stock market.

Nevertheless, it is important to keep in mind several caveats before excessively discounting the value of the basic CAPM. First, although beta (with respect to the stock market) is not the whole story about risk premiums within the stock market, it is an important part of the story. For example, once one controls for such other factors as firm size and book/market value ratio, beta describes a large portion of the remaining variation in average ex post returns to portfolios of stocks. Second, the additional risk factors that matter to the market apart from beta (e.g., the risk factors captured in such characteristics as firm size and current yield) may not *negate*, as much as they *refine*, the theoretical underpinnings of the basic CAPM.

For example, small firms and firms with high current yields or high book/market value ratios are often most susceptible to catastrophic failure in the event of macroeconomic downturns or capital market crises.[12] Exposure to this kind of risk may not be well measured by

---

[11]The development and tremendous growth of passive "index funds" in the mutual fund industry was originally stimulated and largely motivated by the efficient market hypothesis and the type of reasoning that is reflected in the CAPM.

[12]It is easier for a small firm to go completely out of business, in part because small firms may have less bargaining power with their creditors. Also, among the population of firms listed on the stock exchange, small firms and firms with relatively high book/market value ratios will tend more often than other types of firms to be distressed in some manner, or recovering from recent distress. This is because, in general, the stock exchange tends to attract firms that are relatively large and typically have a growth-oriented business strategy. The smaller-cap, lower-multiple stocks on the exchange therefore tend to include a larger proportion of "fallen angels." Such firms tend to be more vulnerable to crises or negative shocks in the real economy or the financial markets than are larger, more highly priced firms.

firms' covariances with respect to the stock market.[13] Yet it is difficult for investors to diversify away such risk exposure because the downside outcomes are correlated with the overall economy and the capital market broadly defined. So investors demand an additional risk premium for this type of risk exposure, for fundamentally the same reason that they demand a risk premium for beta, namely, difficulty of diversifying away risk in their wealth or welfare. Thus, we see that in its more fundamental implications, such as the nonpricing of diversifiable risk, the basic CAPM remains largely intact.[14]

22.3 Applying the CAPM to the Private Real Estate Asset Class as a Whole

The CAPM has relevant application to real estate investment in at least two different contexts or foci. Perhaps the most obvious application is to REITs and other real estate firms within the stock market. REITs will be addressed in detail in Chapter 23, but as regards the applicability of the CAPM to REITs within the stock market (with risk defined with respect to stock market risk factors), a couple of points should be noted. First, REITs tend to be low-beta stocks. Second, the CAPM seems to predict REIT returns in a similar manner, and as usefully, as it is applied to most other sectors of the stock market in general. Since many REITs are small-cap or high book/market stocks, one implication is that REITs tend to command relatively high expected returns even though their betas tend to be relatively low.

The more challenging and unique application of the CAPM to real estate, however, is to direct investment in the private property market. Even within this focus on privately traded real estate, it is useful to distinguish two further levels at which one might try to apply the CAPM. At a more specific level, one could try to apply the CAPM *within* the private real estate asset class, for example, to quantify risk and expected return differences between different types of property in different locations. Application at this "sectoral" level will be the subject of the next section in this chapter. But at a more macro-level, one could try to apply the CAPM broadly to the mixed-asset portfolio as a whole, encompassing private real estate as one of the major asset classes. It is to this macro-level application that we turn our attention in the present section.

22.3.1 Brief History

By the 1970s and 1980s, the CAPM was so popular and widely used in the investment industry that many began to wonder why it was not being applied to real estate investment decision making. Inspired by MPT, institutional investors wanted to apply the same sophisticated investment analysis tools to private market real estate investment as to the rest of their mixed-asset portfolio, which consisted largely of stocks and bonds. In particular, as real estate was a "risky asset," a form of equity, it seemed that the CAPM should apply to real estate as well as it did to stocks.

---

[13]In part, this may be because such risk may not be "normal" (that is, represented by a Gaussian probability distribution) in a statistical sense, as it may be due to large, discrete events rather than continuous incremental change or news. In a sense, this type of risk may be more akin to event risk or default risk in corporate bonds or mortgages than to beta or covariance-based measures of risk. As we discussed in Chapters 18 and 19, default risk is typically measured by multiperiod average return measures such as yield degradation (either ex ante or ex post), rather than by periodic HPR-based risk measures such as beta.

[14]See Fama and French (1992, 2004) for more depth of discussion. We will also return to this issue in Section 22.4. It should be noted that it is also possible that investors "overreact" in some irrational or "behavioral" manner to some characteristics of some investments, such as small firm size and high book/market ratio, causing such investments to be chronically undervalued and hence to provide higher returns than what would be rationally warranted. (Shiller's "excess volatility" that was first noted in his 1981 article that we previously cited began a line of inquiry about so-called "behavioral," as distinct from "rational," models of the stock market.) In this case, the classical CAPM (without the Fama-French extension) may represent a sort of normative model of what "should" be in a rational world rather than what actually is in the real world.

The problem was that when analysts calculated the beta for portfolios of commercial properties, they typically came up with zero, or even a negative number. It seemed that, according to the CAPM, real estate required little or no risk premium in its expected return, perhaps even a negative risk premium. Yet, real estate was clearly perceived in the capital market as a risky asset and seemingly offered a considerable risk premium in its expected return, typically around half as high as the stock market's risk premium.[15]

Of course, some people jumped on this discovery as an indication that real estate was a bargain, providing supernormal expected returns after adjusting for risk.[16] Others, viewing the glass as half empty, warned that this was evidence that the CAPM was fundamentally flawed as a model because it did not work for a major risky asset class such as real estate. Perhaps the simplifying assumptions in the CAPM made it too incomplete as an equilibrium model in the broader context of different asset classes.[17] Or perhaps capital markets were highly *segmented*, with the real estate asset market operating virtually isolated from the stock and bond markets, with different types of investors holding different types of wealth portfolios.[18]

There was probably some merit to both sides of the 1980s debate about the CAPM's applicability to private real estate. In any case, history would soon silence the debate through the painful lesson of a major crash in commercial property prices at the end of the decade. By the early 1990s, it seemed far-fetched to argue either that real estate presented little risk or that its returns evidenced an excessive risk premium, at least ex post.[19]

22.3.2 Broadening the Market Portfolio and Correcting for Smoothing

In fact, there is some evidence in support of the basic Sharpe-Lintner single-factor CAPM in application to private real estate at a broad-brush level across asset classes. But we must be more careful in how we define and measure the market portfolio and how we compute real estate periodic return statistics. Consider the market portfolio first.

According to the CAPM theory, as we described its derivation in section 22.2.1, the market portfolio should represent *all* the wealth of *all* investors, in other words, the aggregate wealth in the economy as a whole. Yet the CAPM is traditionally applied using the stock market alone as the "proxy" for this overall wealth portfolio or risk benchmark. Clearly the stock market alone is not adequate as a market proxy when we are trying to quantify the risk in an asset class that is not even included in the stock market, such as private real estate.

---

[15]See the previous discussions of real estate ex post and ex ante returns in Chapters 7, 11, and 19.

[16]Of course, those who adopted this response often stood to gain from selling real estate, or from the expansion of the role of real estate in institutional investment portfolios. However, claiming that real estate had negative risk and presented a return/risk bargain did not necessarily help to overcome skepticism within the target investment community. Many Wall Street-oriented investment decision makers were shy of real estate, in part because of a traditional image of Main Street as an unsophisticated arena where hucksters and snake-oil salesmen pushed property deals onto gullible investors in an inefficient asset market. Negative risk? Come on...

[17]An example of a well-thought-out presentation of this perspective was the New Equilibrium Theory (NET) put forth by Ibbotson, Diermier, and Siegel (1984). The idea was that investors had other concerns besides just risk defined as the volatility of their wealth. (Recall our discussion of investor concerns at the outset of Chapter 7.) In particular, investors no doubt dislike illiquidity, and so in equilibrium, assets with less liquidity than securities could command an expected return premium (e.g., an illiquidity premium) higher than that of more liquid securities of similar risk. The total expected return premium over T-bills would be built up of several layers corresponding to various types of "disutility" investors perceived in different types of assets. Although not as formally developed as the CAPM, this type of approach reflects long-held investor perceptions in the capital markets. (See also our discussion in Chapter 19 about bond yields.)

[18]In the extreme, this could imply that real estate might have its own market portfolio, and that a real estate CAPM might apply within the real estate market, with beta calculated with respect to this different market portfolio.

[19]Ironically, this "crash" turned out to have presented investors at the bottom of the property market in the early 1990s with, indeed, a return/risk bargain (for buyers going forward from the trough, anyway as long as they got out before the *next* crash in 2007–2009).

The other problem with early attempts to apply the CAPM to real estate had to do with the type of data that were being used to calculate the real estate beta. As noted in Chapter 9, periodic returns time-series data are necessary to calculate comovement statistics such as correlations and beta. Such data are readily available for individual stocks and for the stock market as a whole, based on highly liquid market values reflected in, for example, daily closing prices of stocks. In the case of privately traded real estate, however, the traditional periodic returns data were based on appraised values of properties, such as the NCREIF Property Index (NPI) in the United States.

Appraisals are estimates of property values typically derived by appraisers who are trained to "look backwards" in time to find prices of "comparable properties" that were sold in the past. Furthermore, indices or portfolios aggregating the appraised values of many individual properties may include properties that are not reappraised every period. Thus, many valuations in the index or portfolio may be "stale."

The result is that, compared with a more liquid contemporaneous market value index such as the stock market, real estate periodic return indices tend to be *lagged* and *smoothed* across time. This results in a tendency to underestimate the covariance between real estate and indices such as the stock market.[20]

Suppose we correct both of these problems, that is, the data problem and the market portfolio definition problem, and then apply the basic single factor CAPM at the broad level of the three major risky asset classes that we considered in Chapter 21: stocks, bonds, and real estate. In particular, let's suppose that an overall national wealth portfolio (NWP) consisting of equal one-third shares of stocks, bonds, and real estate would well approximate the theoretical market portfolio that the CAPM requires in principle.[21]

Now to compute our asset class risk and return measures according to the CAPM, let's use the example risk and return expectations we employed in Chapter 21. These expectations are repeated in Exhibit 22-4A.

In Chapter 21, we attributed these expectations to our investment hero, Bob. Although they are only example numbers, recall that they were developed with some care to be broadly reasonable and representative of typical expectations as of the early 2010s, with an assumed risk-free interest rate of 3 percent. Furthermore, the real estate second moments in these expectations (real estate's volatility and its correlations with the other asset classes) attempt to take account of, and correct for, the type of data-smoothing problems we described before.[22]

EXHIBIT 22-4A

Typical Risk and Return Expectations

© OnCourse Learning

	Stocks	Bonds	Real Estate
Expected Return ($E[r]$)	10.00%	6.00%	7.00%
Volatility	15.00%	8.00%	10.00%
Correlation with:			
Stocks	100.00%	30.00%	25.00%
Bonds		100.00%	15.00%
Real Estate			100.00%

---

[20]Smoothing and other real estate periodic returns data issues will be discussed in more depth in Chapter 25.

[21]As described in Chapter 7 (Exhibit 7-5), the complete "pie" of the investible wealth in the United States is probably characterized by weights not too different from this assumption. The exact weights in Exhibit 7-5, aggregated within the three risky asset classes only, are 28% stocks, 43% bonds, and 29% real estate.

[22]In addition to the smoothing issue per se, these expectations probably also reflect a somewhat longer-term perspective than one might get just by looking at annual frequency historical periodic returns data. Historical evidence suggests that over short intervals (such as quarters or years) there is less positive correlation (and perhaps more negative correlation) than what is presented here between real estate and the other asset classes.

We can use the expectations in Exhibit 22-4A to compute the covariances between each asset class and the NWP that we are using as the CAPM market portfolio. For example, the covariance between real estate and the NWP is 0.004983, computed as follows:[23]

$$COV[r_{RE}, r_m] = COV\left[r_{RE}, +\frac{1}{3}r_{ST} + \frac{1}{3}r_{BN} + \frac{1}{3}r_{RE}\right]$$

$$= \frac{1}{3}COV[r_{RE}, r_{ST}] + \frac{1}{3}COV[r_{RE}, r_{BN}] + \frac{1}{3}COV[r_{RE}, r_{RE}]$$

$$= \frac{1}{3}S_{RE}S_{ST}C_{RE,ST} + \frac{1}{3}S_{RE}S_{BN}C_{RE,BN} + \frac{1}{3}S_{RE}^2$$

$$= \frac{1}{3}(0.10)(0.15)(0.25) + \frac{1}{3}(0.10)(0.08)(0.15) + \frac{1}{3}(0.10)^2$$

$$= 0.004983$$

Similarly, the covariances with the market portfolio are 0.009950 and 0.003733 for stocks and bonds, respectively. The variance of our equally weighted market portfolio is $S_M^2 = 0.006222$.[24] Thus, we can compute the beta of each of our three asset classes with respect to the overall mixed-asset market portfolio as follows:

$$Beta_{ST} = 0.009950/0.006222 = 1.60$$
$$Beta_{BN} = 0.003733/0.006222 = 0.60$$
$$Beta_{RE} = 0.004983/0.006222 = 0.80$$

Now we see that the real estate beta appears to be rather reasonable. With a beta with respect to the NWP of + 0.80 compared to the stock market's NWP beta of 1.60, real estate has half the risk of the stock market, according to the CAPM, and long-term bonds have just a little bit less risk than real estate. These betas are pretty much in line with the return expectations shown in Exhibit 22-4A, which are broadly consistent with typical expectations in the real world.

To clarify this point, note that, by the expectations in Exhibit 22-4A, the market portfolio has an expected return of 7.67 percent.[25] Now recall that these return expectations are based on an assumed risk-free rate of 3 percent. Plugging the betas into the basic CAPM gives the following expected returns for each of the three major asset classes:

Stocks: $3.00\% + 1.60(7.67\% - 3.00\%) = 10.46\%$
Bonds: $3.00\% + 0.60(7.67\% - 3.00\%) = 5.80\%$
Real Estate: $3.00\% + 0.80(7.67\% - 3.00\%) = 6.74\%$

As seen graphically in Exhibit 22-4B, the basic theoretical CAPM fits pretty well these risk and return expectations. The real estate expected return of 7 percent is just slightly above the CAPM security market line prediction of 6.74 percent (perhaps reflecting the need for an extra illiquidity premium compared with securities). The bond expected return of 6 percent is also slightly above the CAPM prediction of 5.80 percent.[26] The stock market expected return of 10 percent is slightly below the predicted SML. While the expectations we are using here are just example numbers (Bob's estimates), they are broadly reasonable

---

[23]Some basic algebraic properties of the covariance statistic are useful to keep in mind: $COV[aX, bY] = abCOV[X, Y]$, and $COV[X, (Y + Z)] = COV[X, Y] + COV[X, Z]$, where a and b are constants and X, Y, and Z are random variables.

[24]Computed using formula (A.6) from the Chapter 21 appendix: $(1/9)[0.0225 + 0.0064 + 0.01 + 2(0.0036 + 0.00375 + 0.0012)] = 0.006222$.

[25]This is computed as $(1/3)10\% + (1/3)6\% + (1/3)7\% = 7.67\%$.

[26]It is interesting to note the similarity in risk and return between bonds and commercial property. This similarity was also touched on in our discussion in Chapters 13 and 19 regarding commercial mortgage returns and the question of positive leverage in commercial property investment. In Chapter 19, in particular, we noted some reasons mortgages and other long-term debt instruments might be viewed by the capital market as having nearly as much risk as (or conceivably even more risk than) underlying commercial property assets, where risk is defined "as it matters" to the capital market.

EXHIBIT 22-4B Bob's Expectations and the CAPM Prediction

© OnCourse Learning

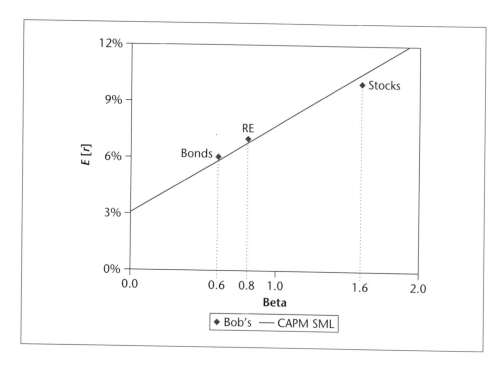

and in line with typical real world perceptions in the early 2010s (relative to a risk-free rate of 3 percent).

In summary, the basic single-beta Sharpe-Lintner CAPM arguably works, in essence, at a broad-brush level *across* the asset classes. This is a level that is useful for broad strategic and tactical investment policy making for managers responsible for mixed-asset portfolios, that is, portfolios that potentially include all the major asset classes. It also is a level that is relevant for adjusting for risk the investment performance of managers or portfolios that encompass more than one broad asset class, for example, a real estate investment manager whose job includes allocation between direct private market investment and REIT equity investment.[27]

22.4 Attempting to Quantify Risk and Return within the Private Real Estate Asset Class

Can we apply the CAPM beyond the broad-brush asset class level to quantify risk and model the market's ex ante risk premiums at a more narrow and specific level within the private property market, for example, to quantify differences in the risk and return expectations for different types of property in different geographic locations? In other words, assuming "rational expectations" (that investors' ex ante return expectations tend to actually manifest themselves in ex post investment performance *on average and in the long run*), can the CAPM, or perhaps a similar but slightly enhanced equilibrium asset pricing model, explain the cross-section of the long-run average returns across sectors or market segments within the overall private real estate asset class?

In general it seems to be more difficult to apply the basic CAPM *within* asset classes than *across* them. This is true not only for real estate but also for the stock market. The classical single-beta CAPM does not explain much of the variation in ex post returns across portfolios of individual stocks within the market.

[27]Specific quantitative methods for using the CAPM to adjust portfolio returns for risk are presented in all major graduate-level investments textbooks. See, for example, Bodie, Kane, and Marcus (1999), ch. 24. A single-index model like the basic CAPM allows a Treynor-type measure to be employed for risk adjustment.

A dramatic picture of this is seen in Exhibit 22-5, which reproduces a famous graph from an article by Eugene Fama and Kenneth French.[28] The figure in Exhibit 22-5 differs markedly from Exhibit 22-4B. Each point in Exhibit 22-5 represents the long-run (1963–2003) average return and beta (with respect to the stock market) for one of ten portfolios defined by their average book/market value ratios. If the simple single-factor CAPM held, then all the portfolios should theoretically plot along the straight upward-sloping line shown in the figure. In fact, the portfolio risk/return points do not bear any relationship to the CAPM security market line. Instead, they plot very nicely according to their book/market value ratios (indicated by the portfolio label numbers), with portfolios that have lower market values (relative to the book or historical cost values of their net assets) tending to earn higher returns. So-called "value stocks," the type that are preferred by investors of the "value style," which typically have higher book/market ratios, provided higher returns during the 1963–2003 period, no matter what their beta was. In other words, "growth stocks" (typically having lower book/market ratios) were priced at a premium by the stock market, providing a persistently lower return (again, no matter what their beta).

Fama and French thus expanded the traditional CAPM to include in addition to the market beta two new "risk" factors as determinants of the expected return: the book/market ratio factor noted in Exhibit 22-5, and a "small stock" factor representing the "size" of the stock in terms of its market capitalization. In the case of the stock market, the empirical prominence of the Fama-French factors has led to the widespread acceptance and use of this "Three Factor Model." The additional risk factors are referred to as "HML" (for high-minus-low book/market ratio portfolio returns) and "SMB" (for small-minus-big stock portfolio returns). It remains controversial among academic financial economists whether the Fama-French factors are important because of some sort of irrationality or "behavioral" phenomenon on the part of stock market investors, or whether the extra two factors in fact proxy for rational forms of risk perhaps as described in section 22.2.4.

The situation appears to be similar within the private real estate asset class. If anything, we are even less able to draw conclusions about causality and systematic patterns in real

EXHIBIT 22-5 Stock Market Historical Fama-French Book/Market Value Portfolios Return versus Beta

Source: Reproduced from Fama and French (2004), Figure 3.

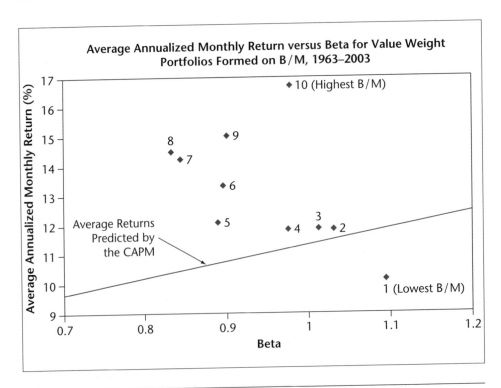

Average Annualized Monthly Return versus Beta for Value Weight Portfolios Formed on B/M, 1963–2003

---

[28]The version shown here is from Fama and French (2004).

EXHIBIT 22-6 Risk and
Return within Private
Institutional Commercial
Property, 2000–2011:
NCREIF Subindices Based
on Size and Sector

Source: Based on data from
Jones (2012).

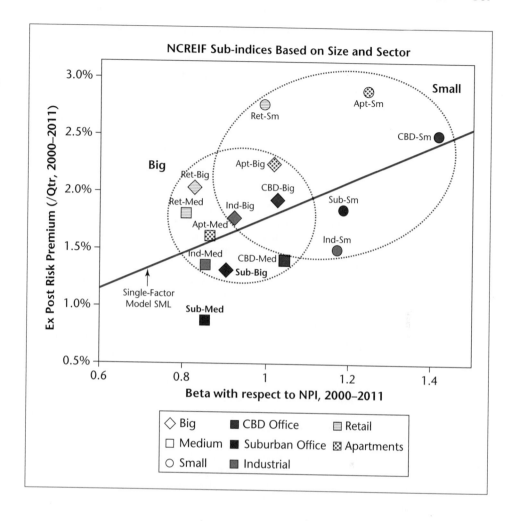

estate risk and return because there is much less historical data quantifying risk and return
performance than in the stock market. As an example of the type of behavior one finds,
Exhibit 22-6 summarizes some results from an examination of portfolios or subindices of
NCREIF properties during 2000–2011.

Exhibit 22-6 shows the risk and return performance of 15 mutually exclusive and
exhaustive subindices of the NCREIF Property Index (NPI). The 15 subindices are differentiated along two dimensions—property size (value) and usage type sector. The five sectors
are CBD office properties, suburban office properties, industrial, retail, and apartment properties. The three breakouts by size have value cutoffs that vary by sector, so as to keep
approximately one-third of all the NCREIF properties within each size category: small,
medium, and big.[29] The vertical axis plots the subindices' average quarterly ex post total
return risk premia (over T-bills) during 2000–2011 (45 quarters of data). The horizontal
axis plots the subindices' betas with respect to the NPI, effectively their traditional CAPM
type systematic risk with respect to the institutional investment property market represented
by NCREIF (the large tax-exempt investment institutions in the United States, primarily

---

[29]For example, within the CBD office sector, which tends to have the largest or most valuable properties, the "small"
category consisted of properties below $40,000,000 in appraised value and the "big" category was properties over $110
million. At the other extreme, NCREIF industrial properties are much less pricey and the "small" threshold was below
$7 million with the "big" threshold being above $18 million.

pension and endowment funds, invested in real estate largely through specialized investment managers).[30]

If the classical single-factor CAPM well modeled the real estate risk and return in Exhibit 22-6 (and assuming that among NCREIF properties the beta with respect to the NPI is generally proportional to the beta with respect to the overall national wealth portfolio as described in the previous section), then we should see all the points representing the subindices plot along a straight upward-sloping line similar to the single-factor Security Market Line (SML) indicated in the exhibit. In fact, the subindices' risk/return performances are rather scattered, though not as perversely related to the CAPM as appeared to be the case with the stock market in Exhibit 22-5. In Exhibit 22-6 we do see some hint of a positive relationship between the average 2000–2011 returns and the betas. In fact, a statistical regression of the 15 risk premia onto their betas yields a strongly statistically significant positive coefficient on beta (with a value equal to 1.6 percent per quarter, reflecting the generally robust performance of commercial property investments over the 2000–2011 period). This provides some evidence in favor of the CAPM. However, the "R-square" of the regression is only 27 percent, meaning that most of the variation in the subindices returns is not explained by their betas.[31]

What if we try to expand the asset pricing model in the spirit of the Fama-French extra factors that seem to be so helpful in explaining the cross-section of stock returns?[32] In particular, let's add a size factor similar to the Fama-French SML factor, represented by the difference between the small property minus big property returns (each period). Another factor that institutional real estate investors claim is important is the metropolitan "tier" where the property is located. Top-tier cities disproportionately attract foreign capital, are relatively constrained in their physical supply elasticity, and may be more liquid for large investors such as NCREIF members. Labeled as "major" markets, during the 2000–2011 period measured in Exhibit 22-6 these were considered to include New York, Los Angeles, Chicago, San Francisco, Washington D.C., and Boston. The industry then defines a "secondary" tier of cities that are also major targets for domestic institutional investors.[33] All other locations are categorized as "tertiary" markets for large institutional investors. The metro tier factor is thus constructed as the "major" minus "tertiary" returns (MMT). Finally, investors seem to be sensitive to the usage type sector directly, so we can define "dummy variables" representing the five property type sectors in Exhibit 22-6.

Now regress the 15 subindices average 2000–2011 returns onto an expanded set of risk factors including their betas, their size and market tier loadings,[34] and property type sector dummy variables.[35] The result is that the R-square of the regression rises to over 90 percent,[36] with an insignificant intercept, so that the "risk" factors now explain most of the variation in

---

[30]The smoothing and lagging present in the NPI has little impact on the betas of components of the NPI with respect to the NPI itself, because the smoothing and lagging is essentially the same on both sides of the regression and thus cancels out in the estimation of the beta. Furthermore, it is plausible to assume that the betas of NPI components with respect to a broader market indicator such as the NWP described in the previous section would be proportional to their betas with respect to the NPI. Such proportionality is all we need for the CAPM to apply in theory.

[31]Of course, some of the dispersion of individual portfolios around the SML would always be expected, reflecting the realization of idiosyncratic risk in portfolios that are not perfectly diversified. But a risk factor that only explains a small portion of long-run average returns is not very useful.

[32]The study described in this paragraph is presented in Jones (2012), and is an extension of earlier work reported in Pai and Geltner (2007). There is a large and ever growing academic literature on the quest to model real estate risk and return, much of which is listed in the bibliography at the end of Part VII.

[33]For the study described here, applying to the 2000–2011 period, the "secondary" cities were defined as Atlanta, Miami, Dallas, Houston, Phoenix, Denver, San Diego, Seattle, Minneapolis, and Philadelphia.

[34]The term "loadings" here refers to the equivalent of "beta" only with respect to the extra factors returns instead of with respect to the market returns. For example, a subindex's size loading is determined by a longitudinal regression of the time series of the index returns (2000–2011) onto the time series of the factor returns (such as the SML returns during 2000–2011).

[35]For example, the apartment dummy variable equals one for the three (different size-based) subindices that are apartment properties, and zero for the other 12 subindices.

[36]Adjusted R-square over 85%.

returns. The market beta (with respect to the NPI) remains highly statistically significant, as are the betas with respect to both property size and metro tier, with positive signs (meaning that smaller properties, and "major" metros, have positive risk premia). In addition, at least some of the property type sector dummies are significant, most notably the apartment sector which commands a strong positive return premium.

We thus seem to have an asset pricing model that was rather effective at explaining the cross section of NCREIF property returns during 2000–2011. But there are several problems with drawing any major conclusions from such a study. For one thing, it is just one slice of the private real estate asset class. When we slice the NCREIF properties in different ways, for example, creating the subindices based on metro tier rather than on size, or when we go beyond the NCREIF population of properties to a broader representation of commercial investment properties such as those underlying the Moody's/RCA Commercial Property Price Index (CPPI), or if we look at an earlier historical period within the NCREIF Index, the model does not perform as well.

A particular concern regards asset pricing factors that do not clearly make sense from the perspective of risk or other plausible concerns that investors might have. Two such factors stand out in the investment property performance results of recent decades. One is the metro tier factor in which the major markets out-perform the tertiary markets (MMT). If this reflects the rational pricing of a systematic risk factor, then it implies that investors regard the major markets as being more risky (or less liquid, or some other negative attribute from an investment perspective) than the tertiary markets. The other anomalous risk factor is the apartment effect. Do institutional investors really perceive large-scale apartment properties as more risky or less liquid than other types of property? Neither of these risk factors seems to make sense as such, and most investors would not claim them to be risk factors. This is borne out by surveys of investors' *stated* return expectations. Look again at Exhibit 11-8A back in Chapter 11, which shows the return expectations from the PwC investor survey. Typical of such surveys, Exhibit 11-8A does not suggest investors expect larger returns from apartments or properties in major markets, particularly among the larger "institutional" properties of the type in the NCREIF population.

When a risk/return analysis produces results that fit well empirically but do not make sense theoretically, one suspects an idiosyncratic historical result, a purely ex post return result rather than the reflection of a persistent ex ante pricing of risk. This is particularly true with short historical samples of data or narrow samples of properties to analyze, which is still what we are faced with in real estate. The 1990s and 2000s were favorable periods for apartments and major markets in terms of drawing institutional capital, and the result was a secular repricing of those assets, providing a windfall return to their investors. That does not necessarily mean that apartments or major markets are inherently or persistently viewed as more risky and therefore requiring of an expected return risk premium.

There are, however, two risk factors in the studies of private real estate risk and return whose effects on long-run average returns do make some theoretical sense. These are the market beta and the small property (SML) factor. Our presentation of the classical CAPM explains why beta makes sense as a risk factor for which investors should demand a return premium. In the case of smaller properties, these may be of concern to institutional investors because they are perceived as lacking liquidity, or perhaps because they are more difficult for large investment institutions to manage. Or smaller properties may command a premium due to poorer quality of information about them (a type of "uncertainty premium"). The small property return premium is perhaps the most persistent return premium within the private real estate asset class. It is observed in Exhibit 11-8A as the roughly 150–300 basis-point extra risk premium for "noninstitutional" property.[37]

In summary, while there may be some explanatory power for some models of the cross-sectional variation in long-run asset returns within the private real estate market, in general

---

[37]We will show further such evidence in Chapter 25 (see Exhibit 25-9 in particular, based on the CoStar Commercial Repeat Sales Index).

IS IT RISK, OR IS IT EXPECTED RETURN? A QUESTION OF TERMINOLOGY AND INVESTMENT CULTURE

In the practice of macro-level real estate tactical investment analysis, the terminology can often be a bit confusing. In part, this confusion reflects real estate's unique investment "culture," as compared to traditional securities market investment practice. In particular, real estate investment analysts will often refer to differences in risk across sectors. For example, they may make statements such as: "The Atlanta apartment market seems particular risky at present due to a current oversupply of new construction." It is important to distinguish risk as used in this context, from the concept of risk viewed from the perspective of mean-variance investment performance, the perspective that prevails in the stock market. The former use of the word *risk*, deriving from a space market analysis (e.g., the apartment market in Atlanta), actually means that the expected rent and occupancy in the relevant space market over the coming months or years is below "normal" in some sense (e.g., below the long-run equilibrium level). If (and it is a big if), property asset market prices in the subject sector have not responded to reflect this below-normal expectation in rent levels or rent growth (and assuming the expectation is valid given all the currently available information), then expected returns in the asset market sector will also be below normal.

But this does not necessarily imply anything about the risk in the future investment performance of the subject asset market sector, if we define risk from a mean-variance perspective, the way it is usually conceived in the capital market. From this latter perspective, risk refers to periodic return volatility (or derivatives of this volatility, such as beta, the risk that matters from an asset pricing perspective in terms of the investment market's required ex ante return risk premium). For example, Atlanta apartment buildings may have a relatively safe return in the sense that it may be almost a sure bet that their returns will be below normal (or normal, if apartment property prices already reflect the bad news about future rental growth). From the perspective of capital

market and investments terminology, Atlanta apartments may or may not be overpriced, but this is a question largely of their expected return, not of their risk (volatility or beta).*

In a sense, you can think of risk as defined in the former (space market) usage as being more akin to the capital market concept of default risk as it applies in the corporate bond or mortgage market. Risk in this context refers to an expected gap (in an ex ante probabilistic sense) between the normal cash flow (akin to the contractual cash flow in a bond or mortgage) and the realized cash flow ex post. If the asset price does not reflect this probabilistic expectation (as in the par value of the bond or the contractual principal of the mortgage), then the probabilistic expected rate of return on the investment is less than its normal rate (e.g., the stated yield or contractual yield in the case of the bond or mortgage). Thus, application of the space-market-based concept of risk in a real estate tactical investment context suggests that such investment is viewed largely from an underwriting perspective like that which typifies the primary (new issuance) market for bonds or mortgages. This underwriting culture contrasts with the more trading-oriented perspective that prevails in the stock market and the secondary market for bonds. This is another example of how real estate investments (in particular, direct investment in the private property market) fall into a unique category different from traditional mainstream securities investments, often blending characteristics of both stock and bond investments at both the primary and secondary market levels.

---

*Of course, the volatility or uncertainty surrounding the future values of Atlanta apartments could conceivably be above normal (meaning, above its typical or historical level). But it is difficult to quantify property market sector volatility precisely and reliably over time. It is unlikely that the property market holds a very precise or stable idea about the volatility of Atlanta apartments in this regard, at least within the private (direct) property asset market.

results are weak or ambiguous, with the exception of the apparent premium for smaller (or "noninstitutional") properties.[38]

22.5 Chapter Summary

This chapter is built on the foundation of portfolio theory to introduce you to equilibrium asset pricing models, a key tool used in both strategic and tactical investment decision making at the macro-level, and even at the policy implementation level of investment management performance evaluation. We attempted not only to review, at an introductory level,

---

[38]An interesting innovative perspective is taken in a recent study by Professor Liang Peng at the University of Colorado. His study examines the property-level round-trip investment IRRs of thousands of NCREIF properties at the disaggregate level, instead of periodic returns of subindices or portfolios at the aggregate level. Peng's findings suggest strong relationships between some economic and financial factors and property-level returns. However, it is still not clear that such results reflect persistent ex ante expectations or only ex post results reflecting the direct or indirect impact of the economic and financial variables. (See Peng, 2011.)

the use of such models in the stock market (which includes REIT applications), but also to go into more depth regarding applications of macro-level asset pricing theory to privately traded real estate assets in the property market. Asset pricing theory faces some of its most intellectually exciting challenges and potential rewards in its application to privately held property. In this regard, we pointed out the importance of distinguishing two levels of application. The broad, mixed-asset level deals with pricing *across* asset classes or types of investment products and arenas. At this level, an elegant single-index CAPM-type model probably works pretty well. The more specific sector level deals with pricing *within* the private property market. At this level, the difference between institutional quality and non-institutional properties looms large, but beyond that, the evidence for a rational model explaining the cross-sectional differences in long-run average returns based on equilibrium asset pricing is weak and ambiguous (though research continues, and with ever more and better historical return databases).

KEY TERMS

strategic investment decisions	market portfolio	specific (idiosyncratic) risk
tactical investment decisions	beta	segmented markets
capital asset pricing model (CAPM)	security market line (SML)	risk factors
market price of risk	systematic (nondiversifiable) risk	institutional quality real estate

STUDY QUESTIONS

22.1. What are equilibrium asset pricing models? Describe three practical uses for such models.

22.2. Which was developed first, the MPT or the CAPM? Why did the development occur in that order?

22.3. Why is beta referred to as a normalized measure of risk? In this normalization process, what (by definition) has a beta equal to unity?

22.4. In a nutshell, what is the main point of the CAPM? What is an important practical investment strategy implication of this point?

22.5. Describe two different levels, or foci, at which we might hope to apply the CAPM to real estate.

22.6. The CAPM was originally (and is still primarily only) applied within the stock market. Nevertheless, describe the two types of corrections or customizations to this narrow stock market application that allow the classical single-factor CAPM to be applied most elegantly to real estate at the broad-brush (mixed-asset) level. (Hint: The failure to consider these two points frustrated early attempts to apply the CAPM to real estate in the 1980s.)

22.7. Describe some capital market imperfections that render the CAPM a less than complete model of reality, especially for application to real estate.

22.8. How well does the single-factor CAPM seem to work within the institutional quality commercial property asset class? Discuss some possible reasons for your answer.

*22.9. Consider a simple multifactor asset pricing model with only two factors, the market portfolio and unexpected inflation. What would you expect to be the *sign of* the price of risk of each of these factors (+ or −)? (Hint: Other things being equal, would you expect investors to prefer an asset that is positively correlated with unexpected inflation?)

22.10. If the risk-free interest rate is 5%, the market price of risk is 6%, and the beta is 0.5, then, according to the classical single-factor CAPM, what is the equilibrium expected total return for investment in the asset in question?

*22.11. Fill in the first row of the following table (the expected returns) based on the single-factor CAPM, assuming that the market portfolio has an expected return of 10% and consists of equal one-third shares of stocks, bonds, and real estate, and assuming that the risk-free interest rate is 5%.

CAPM-Based Risk and Return Expectations

	Stocks	Bonds	Real Estate
Expected Return ($E[r]$)			
Volatility	20.00%	10.00%	8.00%
Correlation with:			
Stocks	100.00%	60.00%	30.00%
Bonds		100.00%	−10.00%
Real Estate			100.00%

CHAPTER

23

REAL ESTATE INVESTMENT TRUSTS (REITs)

CHAPTER OUTLINE

23.1 Introduction to REITs
    23.1.1 Tax Status and Regulatory Constraints
    23.1.2 A Brief History of REITs in the United States
23.2 REIT Analysis and Valuation
    23.2.1 Introduction to REIT Earnings Measures
    23.2.2 Valuing REITs as a Stream of Cash Flows: the Gordon Growth Model
    23.2.3 Valuing REITs as Collections of Assets: Parallel Asset Markets and NAV-Based Valuation
    23.2.4 REIT Public/Private Arbitrage
23.3 Some Considerations of REIT Management Strategy
23.4 Chapter Summary: Some REIT Investor Considerations

On the Accompanying CD:
Appendix 23 Agency Costs and Conflicts of Interest in REITs

LEARNING OBJECTIVES

After reading this chapter, you should understand:

⊃ The basic process of macro-level valuation at the investment entity level as exemplified in the valuation of public REITs by the stock market.

⊃ The basic regulatory constraints faced by REITs and some of the unique accounting terminology and conventions used in the analysis of REIT stocks.

⊃ The difference between growth and income stocks and the nature of REITs in this regard.

⊃ Some of the major considerations and objectives in REIT management strategy.

Earlier chapters introduced you to the "securitization revolution" of the 1990s that led to the growth and development of the public REIT and CMBS markets and a strengthening of the link between private real estate asset markets (Main Street) and wider capital markets (Wall Street). While Chapter 20 focused on CMBS, the debt side of the public real estate investment quadrant, we turn our attention in this chapter to the equity side. Publicly traded equity REITs are companies that own, and in most cases actively manage, portfolios of properties.[1] A typical large REIT provides vertically integrated commercial real estate goods and services to customers who are tenants or, indirectly, other users of the built space, such as shoppers using a mall. The vertical articulation in a single

---

[1]As noted in Chapter 7, not all REITs focus on property investment. Mortgage REITs invest in mortgages, either through direct lending or by purchasing mortgages and/or mortgage backed-securities. In addition, not all REITs are publicly-traded. Non-publicly-traded REITs may be "incubators" that hope to go public, or they may be a convenient way to organize what is essentially a private equity real estate fund, or they may be part of what is essentially a separate branch of the real estate investment industry that focuses largely on more passive property acquisitions aimed at individual investors primarily for retirement accounts. The present chapter focuses only on the publicly-traded equity REITs, which is the dominant component of the REIT industry by market capitalization and trading activity. The present chapter will focus on REITs in the United States (we leave the international focus to Chapter 24).

firm may span from raw land acquisition and development, through portfolio management (also known as **asset management**), to operational-level property management.

Shares of the major REITs are publicly traded in the stock exchange. But REITs are *real estate* firms, **pure plays** in the sense that their assets and activities are largely restricted to real estate because of their claim to REIT tax-exempt status, which allows them to avoid corporate level income tax. Consequently, it is appropriate to view REITs as macro-level real estate investment entities.

With this in mind, the purpose of this chapter is to introduce you to the modern REIT industry in more depth than we have already covered it (in Chapter 7), and largely from a macro- rather than micro-level perspective (as the latter was already covered in Chapter 12). Our particular concern at this level is with the process and nature of REIT valuation in the stock market. In addition to valuation, we also want to touch in this chapter on some practical and strategic issues regarding the REIT industry from both REIT management and REIT investor perspectives.

23.1 Introduction to REITs

What exactly are REITs, why do they exist, and how and why have they come to be such an important part of the real estate investment universe? REITs are unique creatures. In this section we introduce you to some of the peculiar features and terminology associated with the structure and analysis of REIT stocks. We also provide a brief history of the development of the REIT market.

The REIT investment vehicle was created by Congress in 1960 through legislation called the Real Estate Investment Trust Act, which authorized a real estate ownership structure with tax treatment similar to that of mutual funds: a pass-through entity that distributes most of its earnings and capital gains. The idea was to do for commercial real estate investment what mutual funds had done for stocks; to provide small individual investors ("retail investors") a means to invest in a diversified portfolio of many individual assets without requiring a huge fortune to do so. REITs thus offer investors a *liquid* way to invest in a *diversified* portfolio of commercial property. At the same time, they provide a way for commercial property to obtain equity capital financing via the public stock market.

Until 1986 REITs were prohibited from being "self-administered." That is, REITs had to hire a separate investment management entity to manage the REITs' property holdings. This presumably maintained the parallelism between REITs and stock mutual funds, but it greatly hampered the ability of REITs to maximize their efficiency and effectiveness as property investment vehicles. With the removal of this restriction in the 1986 tax reform, the REIT industry gradually discovered a completely new way of operating, which ushered in the so-called "Modern REIT Era" in the 1990s. Today, REITs are major players in all major sectors of the institutional commercial property market. Exhibit 23-1 estimates the share by value of REIT ownership of the stock of properties over $5 million in value as of 2011. You can see that the REIT share is very substantial, particularly in large retail and apartment properties.[2] Altogether, REITs as of 2011 owned close to $800 billion worth of commercial real estate in the United States.

The hallmark of the "modern REIT" is that it is a vertically integrated operating company, providing commercial real estate investment goods and services throughout the "food chain." While not all publicly traded REITs are in fact vertically integrated (or even self-administered), Exhibit 23-2 depicts the general idea and the modern paradigm that does in fact describe many of the largest equity REITs.

The production and delivery of commercial property investment "goods and services" can begin with raw land acquisition and "land banking" (holding of land for future develop-

---

[2]REITs are particularly dominant in certain major niches, perhaps more so than is reflected in the estimates in Exhibit 23-1, such as major upscale regional shopping malls and global logistics warehouses. Beyond the traditional four "core" sectors shown in the Exhibit, REITs are also prominent in the hotel/lodging sector and the healthcare properties sector.

EXHIBIT 23-1 Estimated
REIT % Ownership of Major
($5M+) CRE Properties by
Value, 2011

Source: Authors' estimates
based on data from NAREIT and
Real Capital Analytics.

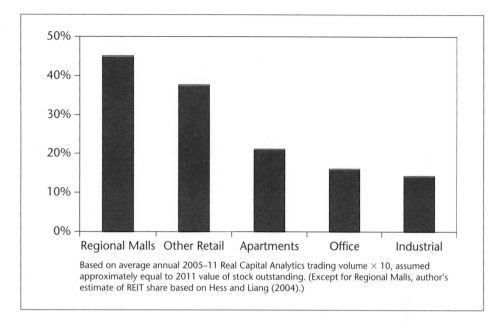

Based on average annual 2005–11 Real Capital Analytics trading volume × 10, assumed
approximately equal to 2011 value of stock outstanding. (Except for Regional Malls, author's
estimate of REIT share based on Hess and Liang (2004).)

EXHIBIT 23-2 Vertical
Integration in REITs
© OnCourse Learning

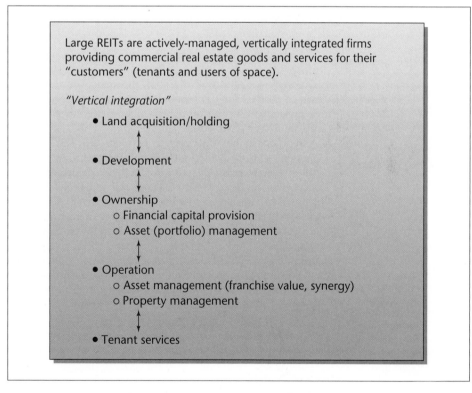

Large REITs are actively-managed, vertically integrated firms
providing commercial real estate goods and services for their
"customers" (tenants and users of space).

"Vertical integration"

- Land acquisition/holding

- Development

- Ownership
  - Financial capital provision
  - Asset (portfolio) management

- Operation
  - Asset management (franchise value, synergy)
  - Property management

- Tenant services

ment). It continues then with the development of structures on the land.[3] Then, the main
component of the entire process, which absorbs most of the time and capital opportunity
cost, is the holding of stabilized operational property assets as investments. Operational

---

[3]However, only a few of the largest REITs have major in-house development capability and engage regularly in building development.

management, including property management, is another major service and can be a major profit center. REITs can offer so-called "downstream" services like tenant services (such as provision of certain utilities and "concierge" type services). This type of vertical integration makes the modern REIT more like a classical "operating company" like other typical corporate denizens of the stock market jungle. However, as noted above, REITs do face some restrictions and still retain some of their original nature as relatively passive investment funds or vehicles, more so in the case of some REITs than in others.

23.1.1 Tax Status and Regulatory Constraints

Perhaps the most notable feature of REITs as compared to most other types of stocks is that REITs are exempt from corporate income tax.[4] The rationale for this exemption is that REITs are viewed as investment vehicles, similar to mutual funds. Exemption from corporate-level taxation enables REIT shareholders to avoid the double taxation of corporate income that characterizes most stocks. In effect, REITs have tax advantages similar (though not identical) to pass-through entities such as mutual funds and partnerships, while retaining the limited liability afforded by the corporate ownership form. Of course, when the IRS giveth, it usually also taketh away. REITs' favorable tax treatment entails a number of regulatory constraints, designed essentially to maintain REITs as a somewhat passive investment vehicle specialized in real estate, not too far removed from the original "mutual fund for real estate" idea, and also to ensure that REIT investment is accessible to small individual investors, which was the original intent of the 1960 REIT enabling legislation. In order to qualify as a REIT, a company must pass, on an ongoing basis, *all* of the following "tests:"[5]

1. **Ownership Test:** A REIT cannot be a closely held corporation, in the sense that no five or fewer individuals (and certain trusts) may own more than 50 percent of the REIT's stock, and there must be at least 100 different shareholders. This is known as the **five-or-fewer rule**. With the **look-through provision** enacted in 1993, pension funds are considered for the purpose of this rule to represent as many owners as there are members of the pension plan. Thus, in effect, institutional investors are not limited by the five-or-fewer rule.

2. **Asset Test:** Seventy-five percent or more of a REIT's total assets must be real estate, mortgages, cash, or federal government securities, and 75 percent or more of the REIT's yearly gross income must be derived directly or indirectly from real property (including mortgages, partnerships, and other REITs). Since 2001, REITs have been allowed to form and own a **taxable REIT subsidiary** (TRS) that allows them to engage in activities and/or service to tenants that were previously not permitted by the IRS under REIT rules. However, no more than 20 percent of its assets can consist of stock of a TRS.

3. **Income Test:** REITs must derive their income (at least 75 percent) from primarily passive sources like rents and mortgage interest, as distinct from short-term trading or sale of property assets. They cannot use their tax status to shield non-real-estate income from corporate taxation. A REIT is subject to a tax of 100 percent on net income from "prohibited transactions," such as the sale or other disposition of property held primarily for sale in the ordinary course of its trade or business. However, if the REIT sells property it has held for at least four years and the aggregate adjusted basis of the property sold does

---

[4]This is commonly stated but not technically true. Dividends paid by REITs are deductible for tax purposes, and as you will learn shortly, REITs must pay out much of their earnings in the form of dividends to shareholders. For most REITs, this implies a corporate tax bill near zero much of the time. On the other hand (and concomitantly), REIT shareholders are not able to take advantage of the lower 15% tax rate on dividends that was applied to most stocks in the 2003 tax law (which may expire or be altered by the time you read this). REIT dividends are generally taxable at ordinary income rates (with some exceptions).

[5]The specific rules governing REITs are changed from time to time by the IRS and/or Congress. We suggest the website of the National Association of REITs (NAREIT) as a good source for updated information.

not exceed 10 percent of the aggregate basis of all assets of the REIT as of the beginning of the year, then no prohibited transaction is deemed to have occurred.[6]

4. **Distribution Test:** At least 90 percent of a REIT's annual taxable net income must be distributed to shareholders as dividends each year.

Obviously, one of the results of these restrictions is that REITs are less able than other firms to retain earnings for investment purposes, as 90 percent of their annual earnings must be paid out as dividends. This means that REITs must go outside the firm to the capital market more frequently than would otherwise be the case to obtain either debt or equity capital in order to make new investments. However, this constraint may not always be quite as binding as you might think, and in fact, many REITs distribute more than the minimum 90 percent of taxable net income in dividends. How can this be? The main reason is that in determining net income, as computed under generally accepted accounting principles (GAAP), REITs are able to depreciate their property holdings and treat depreciation as an expense. Depreciation expenses are a particularly large portion of REIT expenses because REITs are very capital-intensive firms, compared to most other types of stocks. As we pointed out in Chapter 14, depreciation expenses are not like most other types of expenses in that they are not a cash outflow, but represent a purely accrual item.

23.1.2 A Brief History of REITs in the United States

Even though the REIT vehicle has been in existence since 1960, REITs played only a limited role in real estate investment during their first three decades of existence. Starting in 1992, however, the equity REIT market experienced tremendous growth, increasing from a market capitalization of less than $9 billion to nearly $128 billion by 1997. Exhibit 23-3 shows the explosive growth over the 1992–1997 period, in terms of both the number of publicly traded REITs and overall equity market capitalization. It also highlights several important events and developments in the history of U.S. REITs.

Much of the 1990s burst in REIT market capitalization derived from the 1993–1994 **initial public offering (IPO) "boom"** that witnessed a huge upsurge in the number of publicly-traded REITs shown in the solid line in Exhibit 23-3 (relating to the right-hand axis). Over 100 REITs were launched as public companies by 1997. Many of these were not new firms or funds, but had been large and successful real estate investment entities that found themselves unable to access necessary capital through the traditional private market sources after the commercial real estate crash of the early 1990s. Out of necessity and opportunity the real estate investment world discovered the REIT as a vehicle to raise funds on Wall Street required to refinance maturing mortgages and to take advantage of buying opportunities in the depressed property market of the early/mid-1990s. Following the overbuilding of the late 1980s, many developers were sitting on highly leveraged properties encumbered by short-term construction financing and no permanent refinancing to take out the construction lender. Hence, many private firms needed to recapitalize their balance sheets and could not refinance mortgage loans coming due with new mortgage debt because the private debt tap turned off. To survive, these firms either had to find private equity infusions (joint venture partners on specific projects or at the entity level) or go public and raise equity to restructure their balance sheets.[7]

The Kimco IPO in November 1991 is widely credited as the beginning of the modern REIT era, as it was the first of the new breed of large, well-established private real estate companies to *choose* to go public with the REIT status, and at about $130 million, the largest IPO up to that time. However, the $330 million Taubman IPO a year later was an even more

---

[6]This requirement forces REITs to have a longer-term focus when making property investment decisions and implies an average holding period of 10 years with a minimum hold of at least four years. There is some evidence that REITs tend to manage properties for income rather than for price appreciation at the property level, as compared to some other types of investors.

[7]There was also significant pull from Wall Street. With low interest rates and bond yields together with bargain basement prices (high cap rates) well below replacement value for high-quality property, investment bankers saw an opportunity to *arbitrage* private and public real estate markets.

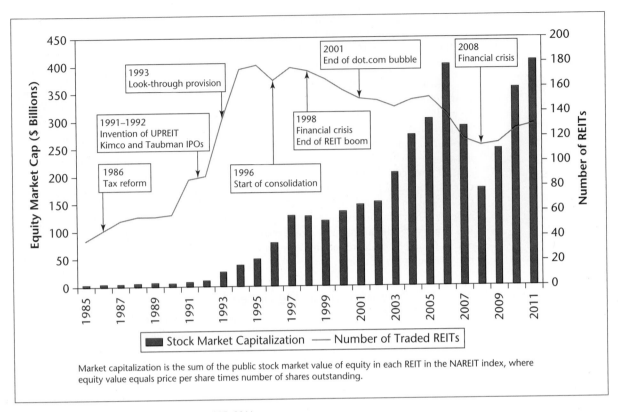

EXHIBIT 23-3 Size of U.S. Equity REIT Sector, 1985–2011

Source: Based on data from the National Association of Real Estate Investment Trusts (NAREIT).

important catalyst because, in addition to its size, it introduced a new structure called the **Umbrella Partnership REIT** (or UPREIT, pronounced up-REIT) that significantly reduced the "cost" of going public for private real estate firms by allowing them to contribute properties to the REIT in a tax efficient manner. As discussed in Chapter 7, the UPREIT structure allows for the contribution of assets in exchange for partnership interests in the REIT without triggering capital gains tax on the properties transferred to the limited partnership. In an UPREIT, the REIT itself does not own any properties but instead owns a controlling interesting in a limited partnership that owns the real estate. At the time of the IPO, the owners of the private real estate company going public as an UPREIT receive **operating partnership (OP) units** in exchange for contributing their property assets to the operating partnership while public shareholders receive common stock. OP units are essentially the same as common stock and, in fact, are usually convertible into common stock on a one-for-one basis. However, OP units are not listed on stock exchanges and hence are not highly marketable. When OP unit holders sell their OP units, it is a taxable event.[8]

The choice by so many private real estate companies to go public with REIT status during this period permanently changed the real estate market. A number of these REITs were of the size (market cap) necessary to attract significant institutional investment. Historically, REIT shares were primarily held by individual investors, given that REIT market capitalizations were too small for large investors to be able to make meaningful investments that would retain their liquidity. The growth in institutional ownership helped to fuel a boom in REIT

---

[8]The UPREIT structure introduces a potential conflict of interest between REIT common shareholders and management that owns UPREIT units as it relates to the sales of properties contributed to the REIT and the differing tax impacts on shareholders and OP unit holders. We discuss this in Appendix 23, which appears on the accompanying CD.

IPOs and then secondary security offerings (SEOs) in 1996 and 1997. For a time, REITs were perceived as "growth" stocks, and during this period of new growth, REIT share prices increased sharply with REITs as a whole being priced at roughly a 30 percent premium to net asset value (NAV) in both 1996 and 1997.

The REIT boom came to a crashing end early in 1998, with share prices and premiums to NAV falling fast and far, a situation that would persist for the next two years. The NAREIT equity price index lost 22 percent in 1998 and by the end of 1999 REITs were priced at about an 18 percent discount to underlying property NAV. The end of the 1990s REIT growth episode and also the length of the downturn were due in part to concerns with REIT pricing in relation to private real estate market fundamentals, emerging concerns about REITs issuing equity simply because it was cheap and then using it to overpay for properties, but also to the emerging "dot-com" stock phenomenon. The collapse in REIT prices coincides with the start of the NASDAQ dot-com "bubble." It was widely thought that the "whoosh" sound heard in the REIT sector was the sound of money being pulled out of REITs and put into dot-com stocks; one sector (REITs) had run its course and it was time for momentum traders (return chasers) to move on to the next "hot" sector. This caused much confusion and concern among REIT managements and investors as the rapid and sustained shock to REIT share prices took place with little change in underlying real property fundamentals. Similar to what we saw with the Russia bond default effect on the CMBS market in 1998, REIT investors learned that REITs are part of the broader capital markets and hence REIT values can at times be affected by factors that appeared to be not directly related to property markets.

Following the turbulent times associated with a new beginning in the 1990s, the REIT sector stabilized and gained credibility. By the 2000s REITs had become an established investment option both for real estate investors to gain long-term exposure to real estate and for stock investors seeking high dividend yields and diversification or inflation protection.[9] Market dynamics have changed dramatically. In the early 1990s, private firms went public because they had to. Today it is a choice. In deciding whether or not to be a REIT, a firm must weigh the tax and access to capital advantages against the costs and constraints from the restrictions on operating and financial structure as well as dividend payout requirements. In addition, REIT management must be prepared to live in the public market fish bowl to some extent, their decisions and actions on display for all to see through required financial disclosure and scrutiny from market analysts.

After the bursting of the dot-com bubble in 2001, REITs regained the favor of stock market investors, and REITs shared amply in the multi-asset-class investment boom of the mid-2000s. Unfortunately, REITs also participated in the excess borrowing that overleveraged the entire financial world at that time. REITs did not lever as highly as many private real estate investors and some private equity funds, because the stock market has always put some brakes on REITs' ability to borrow too much.[10] And while there was a debt-fueled inflation in commercial property prices, the 2000s bubble did not see the amount of rampant overbuilding and resultant *physical* oversupply in commercial real estate that occurred in the housing market and that had occurred in commercial real estate in the previous cycle in the 1980s. Nevertheless, when the bubble burst, REIT share prices took their most drastic pummeling in history, with the NAREIT Equity REIT Price Index falling from a peak of 650 in January 2007 to 480 on the eve of the Lehman collapse in September 2008, into a breathtaking death-defying spiral down to 180 at the beginning of March 2009 (a peak-to-trough fall of 75 percent).

But at that point, with a dividend yield pushed up to over 10 percent by the price crash, REITs found themselves positioned very strongly for a recovery. This was in part because of the relative lack of excess noted in the previous paragraph, and in part because investors were looking for a way to participate in the purchase of distressed properties at distressed prices. Many REITs swallowed the tough medicine of cutting dividends and issuing new shares at

---

[9]The success of the modern U.S. REIT structure has led to a global expansion of REIT or REIT-like formats in a number of countries around the world, a topic we address in more detail in Chapter 24.

[10]This has been so since the REIT crisis of the early 1970s, which we described in Chapter 7.

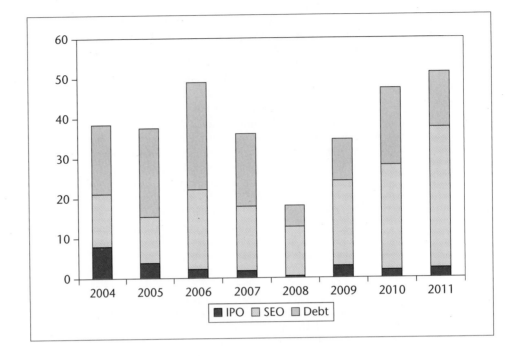

EXHIBIT 23-4 External Capital Raised by U.S. REITs ($billions), 2004–2011

Source: Based on data from National Association of Real Estate Investment Trusts (NAREIT).

their new rock-bottom values, appearing to "dilute" pre-existing shareholders, but using the liquidity of the stock market to raise sufficient cash to perform the refinancing and de-leveraging that they had to do, and then enabling them to participate in buying real estate at the then very-depressed prices prevailing in the commercial real estate market.[11] The private property market was still suffering a liquidity crisis as banks and CMBS sources of capital remained much more constrained than the stock market for several years after the financial crisis. The NAREIT Equity Price Index rebounded from its 180 nadir in March 2009 to 350 by the end of 2009, a jump of 94 percent, and then continued into the upper 400s by 2011, more than doubling from its trough. Exhibit 23-4 shows how REITs were able to raise external capital even during the worst financial crisis in almost a century, thanks to the liquidity and pricing efficiency of the stock market.[12] Note that at the bottom, the stock market was almost the only source of capital available, and REITs raised almost $13 billion in the stock market in 2008 and another $24 billion in 2009. They used this cash to "de-lever" and buy properties at low prices, and emerged from the financial crisis arguably in better shape than almost any other sector of the real estate investment industry. By 2011 REITs were raising over $50 billion per year in external capital, the vast majority of it as equity, and REITs were major buyers in the commercial property price recovery of 2010–2011.

23.2 REIT Analysis and Valuation[13]

As with many other investment questions, perhaps the most fundamental and important issue in analyzing REITs is valuation: How much is a given REIT worth? The answer to this question is obviously important to potential investors in the REIT, as they need to gain

---

[11]To assist REITs in retaining liquidity, the IRS temporarily relaxed the 90% dividend payout requirement to allow REITs to satisfy it by the issuance of stock dividends instead of cash dividends.

[12]Share prices fall far enough and fast enough to maintain a liquid market in the shares even in the face of a collapse in demand. This doesn't happen in the private property market, which tends to freeze up when demand collapses.

[13]The valuation concepts and calculations introduced in this section are illustrated and integrated within a simple yet comprehensive model, "ABC REIT," contained in an Excel file on the CD that accompanies this text.

some comfort regarding whether the stock is priced right. But the question is also important for REIT managers in addressing all sorts of questions about the strategy and operations of the REIT, because they generally want to maximize, or at least avoid losses to, their firm's share price. Not least of these management applications is the acquisition of real property in the private property market: How will a given property acquisition at a given price affect the value of the REIT's stock? Because of the importance of the fundamental REIT valuation question, it will be our major focus in this chapter, although we will turn to some other practical issues of REIT management and other REIT investor considerations at the end in sections 23.3 and 23.4.

REITs are unique among companies in the stock market in that there are two fundamentally different ways to think about the value of the company. As with most stocks, one can view a REIT essentially as a stream of future cash flows generated by the profitable operation of the company. But one can also think of the firm as a collection of real estate assets that are themselves directly valued in the private property market. We noted in Chapter 12 that real estate is unique in that its physical capital (property assets) is traded directly or indirectly in two separate, "parallel" asset markets, the private property market and the stock market for REIT equity shares.

Both the stock market and the private property market are long-established and well-functioning arenas for trading capital assets. As we noted way back in Chapter 1, capital assets are, essentially, long-lived streams of cash flows. Both the stock market and the private property market function as effective information aggregators and equilibrium seekers, although they operate very differently and cater to different investor clienteles. They both bring important information about the value of the real assets they trade. Of course, in the case of REIT equity shares, ultimately it is the stock market that determines their market value, albeit a valuation that changes daily.

Viewed from 30,000 feet (or maybe 60,000), it's probably correct to say that shares of REITs listed on public stock exchanges are valued essentially the same way other stocks are valued. The U.S. stock market is one of the most efficient branches of the capital market in the world, and so it would be surprising indeed to find REITs segmented off in their own corner of a market that is otherwise highly integrated. Within an integrated market, the "Law of One Price" must hold: what is essentially the same thing cannot trade at different prices at the same time. And the stock market generally values stocks by viewing companies as streams of future cash flows. Thus, we will begin by taking this perspective on REITs, and then later turn to the collection-of-assets perspective.

23.2.1 Introduction to REIT Earnings Measures

To analyze REITs as streams of cash flows, we need to begin by giving you some background about how earnings and cash flows are measured and reported in the REIT world. While REIT stocks are valued in much the same way as traditional publicly traded operating companies, REIT **GAAP net income** (or earnings), however, is widely viewed as not being directly comparable to the earnings reported for most other types of publicly traded operating companies. Depreciation expenses under GAAP hide considerable amounts of REIT cash flow from being reflected in taxable income. Furthermore, as we noted in Chapter 14, in the case of real property, depreciation is often not matched by an actual loss in nominal value of the property over time, as inflation may match or exceed the rate of real depreciation in the property. As a result, the REIT industry has adopted a special measure of earnings, known as **FFO (funds from operations)**, as a supplement to the traditional GAAP net income metric. Alas, FFO does not have a definition that is both very precise and also very widely applied in common across all REITs, so it can involve some "apples and oranges." Nevertheless, to gain a basic understanding of REIT earnings and cash flow metrics and how they relate to traditional private property income metrics, let's walk through Exhibit 23-5.

Suppose we start out with a set of commercial property assets that can produce a potential gross revenue of $180 million per year if they were fully leased. As you recall from Chapter 11, this is typically referred to in the property world as PGI (potential gross income). Conceptually, PGI exists whether the properties are held in a REIT or not. Let's see how this

EXHIBIT 23-5
Widely Used Direct Property
vs. REIT Income Measures
© OnCourse Learning

Direct Property		REIT	
PGI	180	PGI	180
Vacancy	−9	Vacancy	−9
Operating Expenses	−71	Operating Expenses	−71
NOI	100	NOI (property level)	100
		General and Administrative Expenses	−3
		EBITDA	97
Interest Expense	−40	Interest Expense	−40
		FFO	57
Depreciation Expense	−20	Depreciation Expense	−20
GAAP Net Income	40	GAAP Net Income (Dividends ≥ 0.9 × Net Income = 33.3)	37
Add back Depreciation	+20	Add back Depreciation	+20
CapEx	−15	CapEx	−15
EBTCF	45*	AFFO (FAD) (Available for plowback up to: 8.7)	42*
		Div/FFO as low as 33.3 ÷ 57 = 58%, Div/FAD = 33.3 ÷ 42 = 79%	

*Direct property EBTCF is not directly available to a passive investor, whereas REIT AFFO is.

set of properties' income might typically be measured and reported in the private (or "direct") property market world and in the REIT world, assuming the (same) properties were held in a REIT.

First we subtract the effect of vacancy and operating expenses to arrive at the property Net Operating Income (NOI). Supposing typical values as in the Exhibit, this gets us down to a $100 million annual operating income bottom line for our portfolio of properties. Most private owners and funds would directly examine and report this property-level bottom line metric, and indeed many REITs also do report their property-level NOI.

Next, in the case of the REIT we subtract firm-level overhead or what is called "general and administrative" expenses. Assuming "G&A" of $3 million, this brings us to the REIT's **EBITDA (earnings before interest, taxes, depreciation, and amortization)** of $97 million. There is not an equivalent deduction or bottom line for direct property income measurement. Of course, in practical reality an investment portfolio of properties generating $100 million in NOI would no doubt require some administrative and management functions above the property level, so this is where we begin to look at "apples vs. oranges" in the typical private direct property income measures as compared to REIT measures. But as a rough correspondence, considering that G&A is usually rather small, EBITDA in REITs is roughly comparable to NOI in the property world, although in the latter case without considering any upper or entity level of expenses in the NOI metric.

Next we take out interest expenses owed on any debt used to finance the properties. At the direct property level we dealt with in Chapter 14 any such debt would have to be property-level mortgages. But in the REIT world the relevant debt could be either mortgages or firm-level ("entity-level") debt such as unsecured bonds or bank loans. Keeping the comparison as fair as possible, we will assume that the interest expense would be the same whether the properties are held in the private property market or in a REIT, so we subtract the same (example) $40 million from each side in Exhibit 23-5. This subtraction does not produce any particularly widely noted metric in the direct private property world, but it gets us to perhaps the most famous and widely quoted measure of REIT earnings, the aforementioned "FFO," Funds From Operations, which we see is $57 million in our example.

Now let us suppose that the set of properties underlying the exhibit can charge $20 million of annual depreciation expense.[14] Subtracting this, we arrive at the major "official" net income bottom line, which is the so-called "GAAP net income." This is the major measure of profit or earnings for most corporations, and is essentially the basis for corporate income taxation. In our example it equals $37 million for the REIT and $40 million for the set of private properties computed directly at the property level.

The REIT must pay out at least 90 percent of this GAAP net income as cash dividends to its stockholders. Thus, the REIT must pay dividends of at least 0.9*37 = $33.3 million. This means that the REIT "retained earnings" in the traditional measure can be no more than $3.7 million from this set of properties which generated $100 million NOI. But this is not the whole story. So far, we have been constructing accrual-accounting-based earnings measures. Now we will adjust these measures to get to actual cash flow, which is more important in practice.[15]

First, we add back the $20 million depreciation expense, since this is not actually a cash outflow. On the other hand, we must now subtract out the capital improvement expenditures made on our set of properties, as these are a cash outflow. As described in Chapter 11, such expenditures are a routine and necessary part of property operations, and typically amount to 10 percent to 20 percent of the NOI over the long run. In REITs as in privately held properties, such routine capital expenditures (aka "capex") are generally financed internally from the cash flow generated by the property itself. Thus, we subtract out an illustrative $15 million from both sides of Exhibit 23-5. And this brings us down to the essential cash flow bottom line on both sides, what we referred to as **EBTCF** (**equity-before-tax cash flow**) at the property level in Chapter 14, and what is often called **AFFO** (**adjusted funds from operations**) in the REIT world.

AFFO is similar to, and sometimes the same thing as, another measure referred to as **FAD** or **CAD** (**funds, or cash, available for distribution**). This refers to the fact that this level of operating bottom line is in principle free cash flow that is available for the REIT to distribute out to its shareholders if the REIT management chooses to do so, and without jeopardizing the long-run health of the REIT's existing properties as we have already subtracted out the (presumably adequate) capital improvement expenditures. The major difference between AFFO and FAD or CAD is that the latter may also subtract nonrecurring or extraordinary capital expenditures, such as for major development projects.

Thus, EBTCF and AFFO are roughly comparable bottom line cash flow measures between the direct property investment and the REIT industries. In our illustrative example in Exhibit 23-5 the property-level EBTCF is $45 million and the corresponding REIT AFFO is $42 million. However, as indicated by the asterisk (*) in the Exhibit, we must not forget that the REIT side is already net of the entity-level overhead and administrative costs of managing the portfolio of properties, whereas we have nowhere taken out such "supra-property-level" costs on the private property side. And note that REIT FFO has no exact analog in the direct property metrics, even though FFO is the most widely cited REIT earnings measure and people often loosely or carelessly try to equate it to the most widely cited earnings metric in the private property world which is NOI. (In fact, the REITs' EBITDA is more comparable to the private property world's NOI.) Furthermore, in common parlance, when people speak of "FFO" or "earnings" for REITs, it's not always clear exactly what they mean (or *should*

---

[14]See Chapter 14 for details regarding property depreciation. As a simplified example and with currently prevailing rules, suppose all the properties are nonresidential commercial buildings (39-year depreciable life) purchased for an historical cost of $975 million of which 20% was land value (hence, depreciable cost basis of 0.80*975 = $780 million, which dividing by 39 gives $20 million/year depreciation). Yet these properties might be worth, say, $1,250 million (8% cap rate applied to $100 million NOI), and if their market value is appreciating at 1.6% per year (which could be quite plausible if inflation is around 3%), then none of the $20 million depreciation expense is actually tracking any loss in value (in nominal terms).

[15]Of course the dividends paid out to the stockholders are certainly a cash flow, and typically a very important cash flow to most REIT investors, as REITs are generally known as "income stocks."

mean), and they may in fact be referring to something closer to what we have defined in Exhibit 23-5 as AFFO.

There are other differences that we should mention even at this broad-brush level. For example, at the level of generality of Exhibit 23-5 FFO appears very clearly and precisely defined. But the devil is in the details, and in fact there is considerable variation in the real world. Unlike GAAP net income (or just "net income" for short), FFO (not to mention AFFO) is not officially and precisely defined. For example, in general, "extraordinary items" of net income, such as income from the sale of properties, are not counted in FFO (in either revenue or expenses). But some REITs that engage more routinely in some sales of their assets (within the constraints of the REIT taxation rules) do include such extraordinary income in their reported FFO.

Some important differences between REIT earnings metrics and traditional property-level metrics result simply from REITs' requirement to apply GAAP accounting, which is accrual-based, whereas tradition in the private property market has always been more cash flow focused. A notable such consideration affects what the property world calls the "Effective Gross Income" (EGI), the gross revenue generated by the property. In the private property world this is measured as the cash flow from the current leases in place. But in the GAAP accrual accounting world long-term leases must be "straight-lined," that is, their rents are reported at their average level across all years in the lease contract. For example, a three-year lease with contracted rents of $100, $105, and $110 in the three consecutive years would be reported under GAAP rules at $105 each year. As leases often contain "step-ups," to increase their rents in later years, this tends to result in GAAP net income over-stating the cash flow in early years and understating it in later years, for any given lease (though this may average out across many leases signed at different times for different terms). As usually constructed, REIT EBITDA and FFO will reflect the GAAP-based straight-lining, while property-level NOI and EBTCF will not. However, most constructions of REIT AFFO will adjust to remove the rent straight-lining effect, making AFFO more comparable to EBTCF.

Property-level operating expenses are generally entirely cash outflows in the private market world. But many REITs are in the property management business, at least for their own properties, and some REITs view property management as a profit center. Some of the property management expenses at the property level are profits at the entity level of the REIT. In effect, this reduces the G&A outflow on a net basis.

Returning to Exhibit 23-5, note that an owner of the properties in the private market would in principle be subject to income taxes on the $40 million of GAAP net income, which would presumably be received by private taxable owners through some sort of pass-through entity such as a partnership or fund. The REIT avoids corporate-level income tax on its $37 million Net Income, but its private shareholders must pay income taxes (to the extent the shareholders are taxable) on any dividends they receive from the REIT, which, as we noted, must be at least $33.3 million. Nothing prevents the REIT from paying out *more* than $33.3 million in dividends. As noted, the REIT in Exhibit 23-5 has $42 million available net cash flow that could be paid out without dipping into reserves or selling assets. To the extent that the REIT pays out in dividends more than its $37 million taxable income, in general the excess would be considered "return of capital," and would not be subject to current income taxation at the level of the shareholder recipients of the dividends.[16]

Any portion of the REIT's cash flow earnings that it does not pay out as dividends are effectively its "retained earnings" on a cash flow basis (or more exactly its "retained cash flow"). For example, if the REIT pays out just the minimum required $33.3 million in dividends, then it will have retained $8.7 million for reinvestment in the firm, presumably largely to buy or substantially improve and redevelop its current property holdings (as we've already subtracted out $15 million in routine capital improvement expenditures). In that case, while the REIT will have satisfied its tax obligation to pay out 90 percent of its taxable earnings,

---

[16]There may be a tax subsequently due when/if the shareholder sells her REIT shares, as return of capital reduces the cost basis of the stock investment.

it will have paid out only 33.3/42 = 79% of its free cash flow (AFFO), and only 33.3/57 = 58% of its FFO (a commonly cited ratio).

In summary, understanding REIT cash flow and making "apples-to-apples" comparisons to property-level or private-market-based cash flow measures is a nontrivial exercise at the very detailed level.[17] But at the broad brush level the picture presented here is accurate and sufficient for a basic and useful understanding.

23.2.2 Valuing REITs as a Stream of Cash Flows: The Gordon Growth Model

Let us now turn to the valuation of a REIT as a stream of future cash flows. As noted, this is the traditional way that the stock market values most corporations. It is particularly congruent with the "modern REIT" model described at the outset of this chapter as a vertically integrated operating firm.

Viewed as a stream of future cash flows, the value of a REIT's equity derives fundamentally from an infinite-horizon DCF valuation similar to that introduced in Chapter 10 at the micro-level of individual property valuation. Now, however, the net cash flows that matter are the dividends paid out by the REIT to its stockholders, instead of just the property-level net cash flow generated by the property assets (PBTCF in Chapter 11). Of course, the REIT's net cash flow for its stockholders must derive ultimately from its property holdings. Letting E represent the current (time zero) value of the firm's equity (equal to the price per share times the number of shares outstanding), we have

$$E_0 = \frac{DIV_1}{(1+r)} + \frac{DIV_2}{(1+r)^2} + \frac{DIV_3}{(1+r)^3} + \cdots = \sum_{t=1}^{\infty} \frac{DIV_t}{(1+r)^t} \qquad (1)$$

where DIV_t refers to the annual dividends expected to be distributed by the REIT in year t and r refers to the stock market's required long-run total return expectation for investments in the REIT's shares.[18] The "Σ" symbol means summation of the discounted dividends.

While formula (1) is the fundamental stock valuation model, a famous shortcut or simplification of (1), known as the **Gordon growth model (GGM)**, is more widely used.[19] It follows directly from formula (1) and the constant-growth perpetuity formula introduced in Chapter 8.[20] The GGM version of the generalized dividend discount model is obtained by assuming that dividends are expected to grow at a constant rate, g, each year into the indefinite future. Under this assumption, the long valuation formula in (1) collapses into a much simpler formulation of the value of a firm's equity, given by

$$E = \frac{DIV_1}{r-g} \qquad (2a)$$

Formula (2a) is obviously a shortcut compared to formula (1) because the analyst does not have to forecast each future year's dividend explicitly. Instead, in the Gordon model,

---

[17]Please consult a professional tax accountant before making any decisions based on the description here.

[18]The discount rate, r, is the REIT's average equity cost of capital, expressed in the form of a single (blended) long-run multiperiod required expected return (like a going-in IRR, but at the level of the firm's equity). In previous chapters, we often labeled this long-run required return expectation $E[r_E]$ to emphasize that it is an *ex ante* expectation of the return to levered equity. Similarly, the DIV_t amounts are expectations. Here we suppress the equity subscript and the $E[.]$ part of the label for simplicity of illustration only. Note that the numerators and denominators on the right-hand side of the valuation equation are measured at the before-tax level from the perspective of the REIT investors. This is convenient, as E refers to the firm's equity market value in the stock market, so DIV_t and r can be related directly to empirically observable public information on the REIT share price and dividends. However, recall from Chapter 12 that market value is determined more fundamentally as the investment value to the marginal investors. In the case of REITs, these marginal investors will generally be taxed individuals. Consistent with Chapter 14, the more fundamental equity valuation equation would use after-tax dividends and the equity-after-tax opportunity cost of capital for the marginal shareholders of the REIT, though this level is not directly observable empirically.

[19]Although the GGM was not originally invented by Gordon, its modern usage is most often attributed to Gordon and Shapiro (1956).

[20]See formula (10) in section 8.2.5 of Chapter 8. If dividends are expected to grow at a constant rate indefinitely, then estimates of first-year dividends (DIV_1) and the growth rate are all that one needs to forecast all future dividends.

the analyst only has to estimate the market's expected long-term average growth rate in the firm's future dividends, g. Note that $(r - g)$ is essentially a "cap rate" applied to firm-level dividends and the shortcut formula in equation (2a) parallels the cap rate approach to private property valuation, $V = NOI/(cap\ rate)$, that real estate investors use as a shortcut to the more fundamentally sound general discounted cash flow (DCF) model as described in Chapter 10.

REIT valuation as a stream of cash flows, therefore, typically revolves around estimates of three variables: DIV_1 and g have to do with the firm's future cash flows (i.e., AFFO) and dividend distributions, while r has to do with the firm's equity risk as perceived by the stock market, and the stock market's preferences for such risk. As the GGM assumes a constant growth rate in dividends over the long run, it is only an approximation of reality. In order to make the model work as well as possible, the variables employed in it should reflect long-run average stabilized and sustainable levels for each variable, the initial annual dividend, the growth rate in those dividends, and the market's expected return on investments in the firm's stock. Temporary aberrations or transient effects in any of these variables can distort the empirical application of the GGM to any given firm, suggesting at times it may not be advisable to rely solely on the simplified constant growth and constant discount rate model, but augment it with a more nuanced DCF model or perhaps the REIT as a collection of assets (NAV) approach that we discuss later.

Let us now briefly consider each of the three variables in the Gordon growth model, DIV_1, g, and r, with particular attention to the cash flow growth rate, g, as this is what most sensitively reflects the valuation view of REITs as streams of future cash flows.

The initial dividends paid out by the REIT, DIV_1, is on its face very easy to empirically observe. However, remember that the GGM must reflect sustainable values. Sustainable dividends must be taken from the net equity cash flow earned by the REIT from its property holdings and sales (i.e., REIT level AFFO plus net sale proceeds, or "FAD"). Thus, stock market analysts and investors must study the nature of the firm's current property holdings and operations, as well as its debt obligations, as these will largely determine the firm's ability to pay dividends in the short run, at least in terms of the stabilized and sustainable rate for such cash payouts.[21] The cash dividend paid out of REIT earnings is also a function of the REIT's dividend policy as reflected in the proportion of net earnings it chooses to pay to shareholders.

We can expand the numerator of the GGM in equation (2a), the expected first-year dividend, by breaking it up into the product of the firm's first-year earnings times one minus the **"plowback ratio"** (p), the proportion of earnings retained by the REIT for reinvestment.[22] That is, $DIV_1 = (1 - p)AFFO_1$, where $(1 - p)$ is the **dividend payout ratio**, and the GGM equation (2a) can be written as

$$E = \frac{DIV_1}{r - g} = \frac{(1 - p)AFFO_1}{r - g} \qquad (2b)$$

With this in mind, consider the second variable in the right-hand-side of the GGM equation, the long-run expected growth rate in the REIT's dividends, g. Fundamentally, g can only reflect one or more of the following three sources of growth: (i) *growth from assets in place* (existing property cash flow growth as levered); (ii) *growth from investment of retained earnings* (i.e., cash flow from investments made with earnings plowed back into the REIT, possibly combined with additional debt to reflect the REIT's capital structure policy); and (iii) *future growth opportunities* (reflecting positive-NPV investments, again, possibly as levered).

---

[21]For example, a firm can temporarily pay out more cash than it earns from operations by selling its assets. But this is clearly not a long-run sustainable source of dividends.

[22]For example, in our previous illustration in Exhibit 23-5, if the REIT paid out exactly 90% of its GAAP net income as dividends, \$33.3 million, then its plowback ratio would be: $p = (42 - 33.3)/42 = 21\%$, where \$42 million is its earnings measured as AFFO as in Exhibit 23-5.

For now, let's ignore the third possibility (positive NPV investments). The first growth component, from **assets in place**, also called **same-store growth**, is growth in what we labeled in Chapter 14 equity-before-tax cash flow (EBTCF) of the static portfolio of properties consisting of the stabilized operating properties the REIT already owns, as levered by existing debt service obligations.[23] This, in turn, reflects the growth in the firm's underlying property (static portfolio) net operating cash flow (PBTCF), as levered by the firm's existing debt.[24]

For example, suppose a REIT holds $1 billion worth of assets producing $50 million property-level net cash flow (PBTCF) per year growing at 2 percent per year.[25] Now suppose the REIT's capital structure is 50 percent debt, such that it consists of $500 million of equity and $500 million of debt which we'll assume is interest-only at a 5 percent interest rate. Then the as-levered same-store REIT returns are (applying the WACC formula (5) from Chapter 13):

- Total return: $r_E = r_D + (r_P - r_D)\text{LR} = 5\% + (7\% - 5\%)2 = 9\%$,
  where LR = Leverage Ratio = $1/(1 - \text{LTV})$;
- Growth: $g_E = g_D + (g_P - g_D)\text{LR} = 0\% + (2\% - 0\%)2 = 4\%$;
- Same-store cash flow yield rate is: $y_E = r_E - g_E = 9\% - 4\% = 5\%$.

The REIT's same-store growth rate is 4 percent (instead of the 2 percent rate of its property assets), and the REIT's AFFO earnings are $25 million.

The second growth source relates to the growth in AFFO attributable to EBTCF from new acquisitions or developments financed with retained earnings (as levered), that is, expansion of the "scale" of the REIT (AFFO plowed back into the REIT) without issuance of new equity. In general, we would expect such expansion to consist of properties similar in risk/return profile to the REIT's existing asset base, acquired at market value in the private market, or development projects requiring the purchase of land at full market value, in other words, zero NPV deals and projects. Annual expected dividend growth, *g*, for the REIT in formula (2b) then derives from the previously described growth in same-store property cash flows plus the plowback-based expansion holding capital structure constant, as the REIT reinvests *p* percent of AFFO each year.

For example, to continue our previous illustration, suppose the REIT pays out $20 million in dividends and retains $5 million in equity cash flow (plowback ratio of 20 percent). This will reduce the REIT's dividend yield from 5 percent to 4 percent (=20/500). However, the plowback will enable the REIT's sustainable growth rate, *g*, to be larger. Suppose the REIT combines the $5 million equity retained cash with $5 million in new debt (to keep the 50/50 debt/equity ratio). Also, over the course of the ensuing year the REIT's same-store property assets have presumably (in steady state long-run average expectation) grown by 2 percent from $1 billion to $1.02 billion in value, allowing an additional $20 million in new debt (again, to keep the D/E ratio at 50/50)

Thus, the REIT invests $25 million of new debt ($5 million plus $20 million as noted) plus the $5 million retained earnings to acquire $30 million worth of new property assets (or expansion of existing assets), to give it now (at the end of the year) $1050 in property assets (the $1020 that the previous year's assets grew to, plus the $30 million new assets). As the debt is now $525 million, so the equity is now $525 million (retaining the capital structure). This is a 5 percent growth rate in the equity (from $500 to $525 million). No new shares have been issued, so the growth in value per share is 5 percent, or 100 basis points more than the 4 percent achieved by the same-store assets as levered, this increment due fundamentally to the 20 percent plowback (holding capital structure constant). As noted, the plowback reduces the REIT's dividend yield from 5 percent to 4 percent (by 20 percent), exactly offsetting the growth in share price, leaving the REIT's total return the same as

---

[23]See Exhibit 14-2 and the discussion in section 14.2.3 in Chapter 14. This is based even more fundamentally on the property-level operating cash flows described in depth in section 11.1 of Chapter 11.

[24]Recall from Chapter 13 that leverage can shift the equity return relatively away from income and towards capital growth (see Exhibit 13-6 in section 13.5).

[25]This would therefore reflect a property-level required return of 7%, since $1000 = $50/(0.07 − 0.02). The property-level same-store 2% growth rate might reflect 1%/year real depreciation if inflation is 3%, for example. Ignore REIT-level G&A expenses in this simple numerical example.

without the plowback, at 9 percent ($r = r_E = 9\%$, which is greater than the underlying properties' 7 percent return, reflecting the REIT's leverage).

We derived the basic GGM model [formulas (2a) and (2b)] in terms of dividends. But the GGM can also be applied directly to REIT earnings. In so doing we have to be careful to use the relevant growth rate in the denominator, the growth rate in same-store earnings (like the 4 percent rate in the above example) rather than the growth rate in dividends which includes the effect of the plowback (the 5 percent rate in the above example). What this means is that we can write the value of equity as a function of current earnings directly with no explicit consideration of the plowback ratio. Specifically

$$E = \frac{DIV_1}{r - g} = \frac{(1 - p)AFFO_1}{r - g} = \frac{AFFO_1}{r - g_E} \tag{2c}$$

with g defined as the long-run growth rate in dividends as above (continuing to assume no NPV > 0 growth opportunities) and noting that this includes the effect of growth due to reinvestment of earnings permitted by the "plowback" of earnings, and g_E defined as the expected growth rate on REIT earnings (i.e., AFFO) from pre-existing or in-place assets only (as levered). Notice that the value of the REITs shares is independent of the plowback ratio the way we have set this up.[26] In this world, shareholders are indifferent between a passive REIT that owns a static portfolio of properties and pays out all property EBTCF as dividends, and an otherwise similar REIT that retains some part of AFFO above the 90 percent of Net Income that must be paid out and expands through acquisitions of properties similar to the ones it currently owns.

In some respects, it is more realistic to apply the GGM model to AFFO rather than to dividends. Most publicly traded companies that pay dividends do not maintain a fixed dividend payout ratio as we have assumed here but instead follow a stable dividend policy, maintaining a roughly constant dollar value of dividend payout that may be increased from time to time to a new higher level but only once the firm feels that it can permanently maintain the higher dividend. Over time, the cash dividends paid have a stair-like pattern for such firms, assuming significant earnings growth over time.[27] Dividend policy may change, but by itself and within reason, that will not change the value of the firm. Therefore, focusing the GGM on earnings and same-store growth can be more accurate and also can provide a sort of "reality check," as ultimately the REIT's value can derive only from the current assets in place plus positive NPV growth opportunities. (And this point, of course, is the basis for the valuation of the REIT as a collection of assets, which we will turn to soon.)

To summarize up to here using our previous simple numerical example, the REIT's dividend growth rate, g, was built up starting from the inherent growth in nominal value of the REIT's same-store assets (which we assumed as 2 percent) by the use of leverage (which bolstered the growth in same-store earnings to the 4 percent rate that we labeled g_E). And the REIT's dividend growth rate was further augmented to 5 percent by the plowback of retained earnings holding capital structure constant. So far, none of this implied any nonzero NPV investment or any expected returns differing from the market's equilibrium return expectations in the private property market (7 percent unlevered, 9 percent levered 50/50). Furthermore, the REIT's earnings/price ratio (inverse of its "P/E," which in our nomenclature is E/AFFO) is $25/500 = 5$ percent (P/E = 20). In this case the earnings yield of 5 percent is

---

[26]For equation (2c) to hold, it must be that $(1 - p)(r - g_E) = (r - g)$, which solving for g yields $g = g_E + p(r - g_E)$. Intuitively, g, which includes the plowback reinvestment effect, is comprised of two parts: growth from existing assets and growth from reinvestment, with the latter given by the levered income yield (y_E) on property equity, $(r - g_E) = y_E$, times the plowback rate: $g = g_E + py_E$.

[27]Publicly traded firms generally do not want to cut dividends, as this tends to be viewed by stock investors as a very negative signal about the firms' earning prospects. Consistent with this notion, Bradley, Capozza, and Seguin (1998) provide evidence that REITs with relatively higher volatility earnings choose a lower dividend payout ratio to reduce the possibility of having to cut their dividend. Chan, Erickson, and Wang (2003, ch. 8) review the existing literature on REIT dividend policy.

the same as the REIT's property-level cash yield of 50/1000 (PBTCF/property value), because the cash yield on the interest-only debt is also 5 percent.[28]

The REIT can also grow in scale (market capitalization) by issuing new shares (secondary public offering, "SEO"). Issuing new shares will increase the "float" (the number of shares outstanding), but does not in itself change the price per share assuming the REIT can only invest at NPV=0. The REIT can also expand in scale by increasing its D/E ratio and issuing more debt. But increasing the D/E ratio will increase the risk in the REIT's equity (holding the riskiness of the assets the same), and still will not increase the value of the REIT's shares if the capital is all invested at NPV=0. Thus, tapping external capital in itself simply to grow the REIT's scale will by itself not increase the REIT's price/earnings ratio.[29]

This brings us to the third component that can affect the stock market's perception of the firm's ability to grow dividends in the long run. This is the ability of the REIT's management to obtain and effectively implement **growth opportunities** per se, in the classical sense of corporate finance, namely, to make *positive NPV* investments. Typical sources of NPV > 0 growth opportunities for REITs include (if any):

- Developable land *already owned*;
- Entrepreneurial abilities (in development or possibly in other activities);
- Firm-level opportunities (such as economies of scale, franchise value, economies of scope);
- Differential micro-level asset pricing between the private property market and the stock market (often referred to as cross-market "arbitrage," as described in section 12.3 of Chapter 12, to be discussed further in section 23.2.4 below).

If we assume that the market now expects management of our previously rather passive REIT to be able to consistently create value by these types of positive-NPV opportunities, then the value of the REIT's shares will exceed that given by the GGM formulas (2b, 2c), by the sum of the expected NPVs from the firm's positive-NPV growth opportunities. In this case,

$$\begin{aligned} E^* &= \frac{(1-p)AFFO_1}{r-g} + NPV(\text{growth opportunities}) \\ &= \frac{AFFO_1}{r-g_E} + NPV(\text{growth opportunities}) \end{aligned} \tag{3}$$

where $E^* > E$, where E (without the asterisk) is our previous valuation ignoring positive-NPV growth opportunities. We can rewrite equation (3) in the GGM form by directly incorporating the expected positive NPV growth opportunities into the presumed dividend growth rate,

$$E^* = \frac{DIV_1}{r-g^*} = \frac{(1-p)AFFO_1}{r-g^*} \tag{2d}$$

where g^* reflects dividend growth from all three components we have discussed: same-store growth in EBTCF, growth in EBTCF from new (NPV = 0) acquisitions financed with retained earnings, plus growth from positive NPV investments. Exhibit 23-6 summarizes the GGM under the different cash flow growth scenarios we have considered.

Much of the fundamental volatility in a REIT's share price probably derives from fluctuations in the market's assessment of these three components of g^*, the long-run growth

---

[28]Recall the leverage ratio version of the WACC: $y_E = y_D + (y_P - y_D)LR$, where $LR = 1/(1-LTV)$. See Chapter 13, section 13.4, formula (5).

[29]A possible exception to this "efficient market" (Miller-Modigliani, aka "MM") result could occur if augmenting the REIT's scale somehow in itself adds value. This possibility will be discussed in section 23.3. Other nuances on the essential efficient-markets MM paradigm described here could result from direct effects of capital structure or dividend policy, such as signaling effects, or if the issuance of new debt creates too much leverage, adding to the potential cost of financial distress or jeopardizing the REIT's management flexibility. See Chapter 15 for a general treatment of capital structure.

Assumptions About Growth Environment	Comments
Case 1: No Expansion [no plowback ($p = 0$), $DIV_1 = AFFO_1$] $E = \dfrac{DIV_1}{r - g_E} = \dfrac{AFFO_1}{r - g_E}$	REIT as a passive, pass-through entity that owns a static portfolio of properties. DIV growth, g_E, is growth in EBTCF from existing assets in place; growth in same-store levered property income.
Case 2: Internally Financed Expansion but No Growth Opportunities $E = \dfrac{DIV_1}{r - g} = \dfrac{(1 - p)AFFO_1}{r - g} = \dfrac{AFFO_1}{r - g_E}$ $0 < p < 1$ $g = g_E + p(r - g_E) = g_E + py_E$	REIT grows by reinvesting $p\%$ of AFFO each year; DIV is less than AFFO. REIT buys properties identical to the ones it currently owns, at market value (i.e., NPV = 0), using retained AFFO and debt, keeping a constant debt/equity ratio ⇒ REIT equity value is unchanged from case 1. DIV growth, g, exceeds same store EBTCF (and AFFO) growth, g_E, but the REIT's price/earnings (E/AFFO) ratio is same as in Case 1.
Case 3: Internally Financed Expansion and Growth Opportunities $E^* = E + NPV(\text{growth opportunities})$ $E^* = \dfrac{(1 - p)AFFO_1}{r - g} + NPV(\text{growth opportunities})$ $\quad = \dfrac{AFFO_1}{r - g_E} + NPV(\text{growth opportunities})$ $E^* = \dfrac{DIV_1}{r - g^*} = \dfrac{(1 - p)AFFO_1}{r - g^*}$	Here REIT is perceived to have the ability to find and execute NPV > 0 deals or projects, possibly at times due to differential pricing in public versus private real estate markets. g^* incorporates future increases in AFFO due to such positive NPV growth opportunities into the growth rate in the GGM; it "merges" the impact of growth opportunities into g_E, thus $g^* > g$, and the Case 3 REIT's price/earnings (E*/AFFO) ratio is greater than that of Cases 1 or 2.

EXHIBIT 23-6 The Dividend (Gordon) Growth Model of REIT Share Prices: A Summary

© OnCourse Learning

expectations for the REIT. Holding the other two variables in the GGM formula constant, even relatively small variations in the market's perception of the REIT's long-run growth rate can have a large impact on REIT value. For example, if g^* increases from 2 percent to 3 percent while the REIT's cost of capital remains at 10 percent, the REIT price as a multiple of its current annual dividend will increase from 12.5 to 14.3, a jump of over 11 percent in share value.[30] A similar fall in share price would occur with a 100-basis-point reduction in long-run growth expectations holding all else the same.

Finally, let us turn to the third of the three variables on the right-hand side of the GGM valuation model of REIT cash flows, the discount rate, r. This variable represents the market's required expected long-run total return, the REIT's **average equity cost of capital**. Like the growth rate, the discount rate also is very sensitively affected by the market's perception of REIT management's long-run abilities. As always, $r = r_f + RP$, so the market's required total return expectation equals the current risk-free interest rate (which is exogenous to the REIT) plus the market's required risk premium for the given REIT. Thus, the market's perception of the amount and nature of risk in the firm's future dividends and share value is crucial in determining r. Fundamentally, the risk in the firm consists of some combination of the risk in the firm's existing assets as levered plus the risk in the firm's management and non-asset-based operations (such as taxable REIT subsidiary activities), as well as (or including) risk in any future positive-NPV growth opportunities the REIT might face. In effect, much of the firm's fundamental equity risk may be attributable to the market's perception of the risk in the firm's management ability (including ability to manage leverage). As noted in Chapter 22, asset value risk also derives from risk in the future discount rate the market will employ. In principle, equilibrium asset pricing models such as the CAPM and other approaches discussed in Chapter 22 can be used to help estimate the market's required

---

[30]The firm value goes from $E = DIV_1/(0.10 - 0.02) = DIV_1/(0.08) = 12.5\ DIV_1$ to $E = DIV_1/(0.10 - 0.03) = DIV_1/(0.07) = 14.3\ DIV_1$.

expected risk premium, *RP*, as this is applicable to a given firm or, more realistically, to a class of similar types of firms.[31]

To summarize this discussion of the cash flow-based valuation of REITs, it should be clear that this is a very challenging exercise. A typical REIT is far more complex and dynamic than an individual property, and so forecasting and evaluating it as a future cash flow stream is much more difficult. Yet REITs are relatively simple and transparent types of companies compared to most corporations that trade in the stock market. REITs at least are limited in the type of business they can do, and even in their dividend policies and ability to trade assets. And the type of business REITs can do is a relatively simple and easy to understand type of business compared to many other industries in the modern stock market. Real estate is not "rocket science." Stock market analysts have traditionally valued most if not all stocks using the GGM and cash flow-based valuation, including many corporations that are much more complicated, dynamic, and unconstrained than REITs. Unlike the CMBS we discussed in Chapter 20, where structured finance presented very new and substantial challenges to the pre-existing analysis community, REITs do not present anything particularly different or challenging at the fundamental level for the traditional stock market analyst world. Cash flows are cash flows. Furthermore, REITs can also be valued using a very different approach, to which we now turn.

23.2.3 Valuing REITs as Collections of Assets: Parallel Asset Markets and NAV-Based Valuation

Analysts and investors do not need to value REITs only from the perspective that they are streams of future cash flows. Uniquely because REITs' physical capital (real estate) trades directly in a well-functioning asset market (the private property market), we can "triangulate" onto an estimate of a REIT's value by valuing it as the collection (or portfolio) of property assets that it holds.[32]

In essence, this approach to valuing a REIT is very straightforward. The main task is to estimate the value of all the properties currently held by the REIT, as these properties would currently be valued in the private property market.[33] You then try to adjust for non-asset-based value the REIT might have, as from taxable REIT subsidiary (TRS) operations such as third-party property management services. (In most REITs, this is usually a minor consideration in the overall firm value.) Then you subtract the value of the REIT's current liabilities.[34] This gives you the **net asset value** (**NAV**) of the REIT. Dividing by the number of shares outstanding (the REIT's "float," or number of shares traded), gives the REIT's NAV per share.

The main task in the above-described procedure is the estimation of the values of the REIT's property assets. However, most REITs hold many properties. It usually isn't possible or practical to individually appraise or estimate the value of each property separately. A type of "mass appraisal" or shortcut estimate of value must be performed. This may involve

---

[31]REITs tend to provide higher returns than predicted by the traditional, single factor CAPM, as they seem to have a "value" stock component to their returns. However, evidence is mixed on how well the Fama-French (1992) three-factor model works for REITs, that augments the market factor with "size" and "book to market (or value)" factors. See, for example, Peterson and Hsieh (1997), and Plazzi, Torous and Valkhanov (2010).

[32]Triangulation is the process whereby surveyors use sightings from two separate points to pinpoint the location of a third point. Knowing the length of a baseline and the two angles of the sightings from ends of the baseline fixes the location being sighted. We're saying that valuing a REIT from the two separate perspectives of cash flow and assets is akin to such a process.

[33]Sometimes analysts try to adjust for property holding considerations. For example, suppose private market valuations of apartment properties currently includes a premium reflecting the possibility of profitable conversion from rental to condominium units. But you know the REIT in question is a long-term holder of apartments as rental units. Then you might try to adjust the value estimate to exclude the condo-conversion premium currently in the private market valuation, to the extent this can be estimated.

[34]You may need to consider the value of the claims of operating partnership unit holders (see our discussion of "UPREITs" in Chapter 7) and preferred stockholders, as well as traditional debt, to arrive at the net claims of the common shareholders.

segregating the REIT's EBITDA (or better yet, its property-level NOI) by market segment (such as the type and location of the properties), and then applying an estimate of typically prevailing cap rates in the private market. In other words, one does a sort of mass-level "direct capitalization" estimate of value as that process was described in Chapter 10. (See section 10.3.)

In effect, one is performing a valuation of future expected cash flow streams, only at the property level and as evaluated by the private property market rather than at the REIT level as evaluated by the stock market. The process is inevitably only an approximation or estimate. Under GAAP accounting rules, REITs in the United States are not required to mark their assets to market (and most don't).[35] Thus, REITs carry their assets on their books at their historical cost (less accumulated depreciation). There may be a tendency to be influenced by the REIT's share price, or by the latest "buzz" and excitement in the private market. No two estimates of a given REIT's NAV made by different analysts are ever exactly the same. Some firms, such as Green Street, are very focused on NAV estimation and devote considerable resources and expertise to the process, and subsequently sell their NAV estimates.

The REIT's NAV/share can be directly compared to the REIT's current stock price per share. Typically this is done by the ratio of share price divided by NAV, or "P/NAV." Any difference of P/NAV away from 1.0 must then be considered. Is it a legitimate and "correct" difference reflecting genuine aspects of the REIT's value not included in the NAV computation? For example, does a P/NAV > 1.0 reflect the REIT's management's ability to add value? This implies positive-NPV opportunities. What are those opportunities, and are they really valuable enough to justify the premium of P/NAV > 1.0? If not, then the REIT may be overvalued in the stock market. On the downside, does a P/NAV < 1.0 justifiably reflect poor management's destruction of value? If not, then the REIT may be undervalued in the stock market. (And if the P/NAV < 1.0 is justified, then what can be done to improve the REIT management or improve its situation that is destroying value? Should it sell assets?)

23.2.4 REIT Public/Private Arbitrage

REIT valuation as a collection of assets is an important exercise at the specific level of analyzing individual REITs. But it also can be aggregated to an industry-wide level, where it may hold additional interesting implications. In particular, industry aggregate or average P/NAV ratios may suggest pricing "disagreements" between the public stock market and the private property market. Such differences, if they are real and substantial and persistent, can hold implications for public/private "arbitrage" in one direction or another.

Real estate's circumstance of trading in two separate "parallel" markets was discussed extensively in Chapter 12 from a micro-level perspective. (See section 12.3.) The key point to reiterate here is that the stock market valuation of property (indirectly, in REITs) and the private property market valuation of property (directly) are not always consistent. The stock market sometimes values properties more highly than the property market does, not just for a few specific REITs or a few specific properties, but generally and widely. At other times the reverse is true. In the long run, the two markets tend to agree. *The ability of capital to flow from one market to the other ensures that such agreement will tend to occur on average over the long run.* But in the short run, often, in historical experience for periods lasting up to several years, the two markets may disagree about value. This disagreement can occur in either direction, but in general, when it occurs, the REIT market tends to be ahead of the private property market in time. In other words, after a period typically ranging from one to three

---

[35]This is in contrast with most other countries, where international accounting standards rely more on the principle of "fair value" than historical cost. Under fair value accounting, which the United States is gradually moving towards, REITs may engage more in their own (or their accountants') estimates of the market values of their properties.

years in historical experience, the property market often follows in the direction in which the REIT market previously led. (But not always.[36])

While there may be extended periods of time in which REIT values and property market values are more or less in agreement, when the stock and property markets disagree about property value, REITs face either positive or negative NPV opportunities from buying properties at market value in the property market. Another way of putting this is to say that there have been prolonged periods in which REITs could implement positive NPV investment strategies either by buying or by selling in the private property market. When the stock market values property more highly than the private property market does, REITs can grow merely by buying properties, and this can turn most REITs temporarily into growth stocks.

Growth stocks are stocks that tend to produce a relatively larger share of their total return from capital growth (through share price appreciation) rather than through income (dividends). In general and on a sustainable basis this requires that such stocks be able to do positive-NPV investments or actions. Therefore, growth stocks tend to have higher price/earnings multiples than **income stocks**. Income stocks are similar to and often the same things as **value stocks**. Normally, most REITs tend to be value stocks or income stocks rather than growth stocks.

When the property market values properties more highly than the stock market does, REITs can in principle earn positive NPV profits for their shareholders by selling properties into the property market. In such periods, REITs need to become "shrinking stocks," for the benefit of their stockholders, although they need not necessarily get out of the real estate *operating* business. REITs may go private via "leveraged buyouts" (LBOs) in which their stockholders are bought out by the use of money borrowed by or on behalf of the REIT, and then the REIT is sold into the private market either in whole or piecemeal, for value in excess of the money borrowed to pay off the REIT's public shareholders. Alternatively, REITs may set up private investment funds and effectively sell some of their properties entirely or partially into the private fund (at private market values), with the REIT still running the fund and managing the properties. Thus, REIT **"public/private arbitrage"** can be performed in both directions, and this can be an important source of positive NPV, at least for some REITs some of the time. However, this type of "arbitrage" is not without risk, so it is not true or traditional "arbitrage" as this term was traditionally defined.

As a result of the shifting relative valuations of property by the stock market and the private property market, REIT investors have to cope with the fact that many REITs can change their stripes, so to speak, from being growth stocks with high price/earnings multiples, to being income stocks with low price/earnings multiples, to occasionally being shrinking stocks with very low price/earnings multiples. Predicting these turning points in REIT valuation is difficult to do very precisely, which is a source of risk in REIT investment and a source of frustration among some REIT investors. However, the private property market is relatively predictable, and this helps to make possible the profitable redeployment of capital between the two types of markets, for some investors.

Exhibit 23-7 displays the average REIT share price premium to NAV reported by Green Street Advisors. It clearly highlights the differential public versus private market pricing for real estate, and it indicates that the premium follows a mean reverting process. That is, there is persistence in either the premium or discount over periods of a few years and then reversal from one to the other.

---

[36]Furthermore, while the stock market (for REITs shares) generally seems to have more effective or efficient price discovery than the private property market in the aggregate and from a longitudinal (across time) perspective, the opposite may be the case at the disaggregate level of individual REITs from a cross-sectional (as of a given point in time) perspective. Gentry, Jones and Mayer (2004) applied Green Street P/NAV ratios to theoretically construct a cash-neutral investment portfolio of REITs, buying REITs whose P/NAV was less than 1.0 using funds from shorting REITs whose P/NAV was greater than 1.0, cashing out and reinvesting monthly. This trading rule appeared to be abnormally profitable even after accounting for likely transactions costs. This suggested that the private property market contained information not yet reflected in individual REIT prices, as if the stock market was excessively "tarring all REITs with the same brush," not sufficiently discriminating among individual REIT values, allowing for a mean reversion or correction within an approximately monthly time horizon.

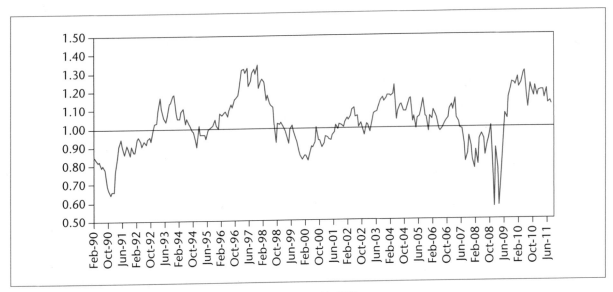

EXHIBIT 23-7 Green Street Average REIT Share Price/NAV Ratio History, 1990–2011

Source: Green Street Advisors, Inc., used with permission.

23.3 Some Considerations of REIT Management Strategy

Back in Part II of this book, where we were describing the urban economic principles that underlie real estate phenomena, we noted the traditional real estate cliché that only three things matter in real estate: location, location, and location. In the 1990s, at the outset of the development of the modern REIT industry characterized by internally managed, vertically integrated corporations, REIT promoters and analysts were fond of paraphrasing that traditional cliché with a new one, claiming that three things mattered in the successful REIT: *management, management, and management.* Like most clichés, what makes this one amusing is that it contains an important grain of truth. In this section, we aim to note briefly several REIT strategic management considerations or goals that are often important.

REITs in the "Land of Growth"   Although it need not be so, the stock market tends to be "the land of growth," that is, the stock market tends to like growth and to reward firms that it perceives as able to grow in share price over the long run. As described in section 23.2, the stock market rewards growth firms with higher price/earnings multiples in their share prices. While the reason or rationale is still a bit of a puzzle, the way the stock market has behaved during much of its history, growth stocks have had higher price/earnings multiples not just because a larger fraction of their expected total return is in the capital appreciation component, but because these stocks actually tend to provide a lower expected total return. This may be more than just the capitalization into present value of future positive-NPV opportunities. In other words, growth stocks really appear to often be more "expensive" than value or income stocks. In part this is just a reflection (or perhaps a cause) of the Fama-French stock pricing model that we described in Chapter 22, where we saw that stocks with high book/market value ratios require an extra "risk premium" in their expected returns. As growth stocks tend to have relatively low book/market ratios, this is just the flip side of the preference for growth stocks.[37]

What does this mean for REITs? Unfortunately, it means they are somewhat out of their element. Real estate is a "cash cow," not a "growth rocket." Whether growth is defined by

[37]Another reflection may be the Fama-French premium for size, as larger capitalization stocks tend to provide lower average total returns in the long run. More on this later when we discuss scale, below.

positive-NPV investments or by simple scale expansion, REITs are at a bit of a disadvantage compared to many other sectors of the stock market.[38] The stock market's relative lack of preference for income or value stocks may be good news for investors in such stocks as it tends to provide them with higher returns. But it is bad news for managers of such stocks because it increases their cost of capital.[39] Keep this challenge in mind as you read about the various strategies described below for how REIT managers try to maximize the share prices of their firms.

Financial Strategy   Financial strategy is a classical component of overall firm-level business strategy. This is particularly true in the case of a capital-intensive industry such as real estate. While the overview of capital structure presented in Chapter 15 is relevant to REITs, we will point out here some considerations that are particularly noticeable in the financial behavior of REITs. The first point to note is that REITs' 90 percent earnings distribution requirement may tend to put some REITs under some added financial stress. The distribution requirement means that, in order to grow, REITs must go to external sources of capital more frequently.[40]

This situation is probably made more acute by the stock market's preference for growth noted above. It is therefore natural for REITs to want to try to grow, and this requires infusions of external capital into the firm. Such capital comes generally in the form of either debt or equity.[41] Equity generally comes with less risk (to the preexisting shareholders) and fewer strings attached than does debt (although it may risk diluting the existing directors' control of the firm in the long run, or diluting existing shareholders' value if the REIT's stock is currently priced low). In addition, REITs do not have the need for corporate income tax shields that most profitable corporations have, which causes those corporations to prefer debt over equity.[42] For these reasons, we might expect that REITs would tend to prefer equity over debt financing.

Yet this natural preference for equity is mitigated to some extent by the growth motivation. We noted in Chapter 13 that financial leverage can often be employed to convert income-oriented, low-growth underlying assets such as stabilized income properties into higher-growth (lower-yield) equity investments. If a REIT can borrow at interest rates lower than its properties' total returns, then positive leverage will exist in the REIT's equity.[43] Indeed, if the REIT can borrow at debt constants (including amortization as well as interest) lower than its properties' current income yields, then it will be able to shift its equity total return relatively toward the capital gain component without sacrificing current yield.[44] These financial leverage considerations may give debt financing considerable appeal to

---

[38]Recall our discussion in Chapter 12 about the difficulty of achieving positive-NPV investments. The private property market is not perfect nor perhaps as informationally efficient as the stock market. But it is still a well-functioning market, and property assets are generally simple and transparent, relatively easy to price fairly. And REITs' dividend payout requirement makes it more difficult to expand scale without recourse to external capital.

[39]It also sets up a temptation. If a REIT can somehow convince the stock market that it is less of a value or income stock, and more of a growth stock, then a one-time "pop" in price/earnings multiple will presumably result, to the benefit of the pre-existing stockholders.

[40]Wu (2005) provides evidence that the payout restriction has a larger effect on smaller REITs making them more likely to be financially constrained. He also documents the increasing importance of bank lines of credit to REIT financing.

[41]Preferred stock is a middle ground that has some popularity among REITs.

[42]Recall our discussion of double taxation in Chapter 14. This also has implications for "signaling" or "pecking-order" theories of preference for debt over equity. REITs may be less subject to such signaling effect on their stock price than taxable corporations. REITs also may be more transparent and subject to less information asymmetry, due to the relatively simple and obvious physical nature of their assets and the fact that they trade in a well-functioning market.

[43]Note that such an increase in the REIT's equity total return expectation does not necessarily (or generally) imply an increase in the REIT's overall firm-level cost of capital, which is measured by its weighted average cost of capital (WACC), including the cost of the debt capital. See section 13.3 in Chapter 13 and section 15.3 in Chapter 15.

[44]See sections 13.4 and 13.5 in Chapter 13.

REITs, even though REITs lack the tax-driven appetite most corporations have for debt financing.[45]

But let's continue on in this point/counterpoint vein. If REITs have a desire for financial leverage, this desire tends to be kept in check by the stock market's squeamishness about REIT debt. The stock market is famously "once bitten, twice shy." REITs have gotten into trouble in the past as a result of being too highly leveraged, most famously in the "REIT debacle" of the early 1970s, and more recently again in the financial crisis of 2008. Excessive leverage played a prominent role in the widespread commercial property financial problems at the end of the 1980s and again in the 2000s. As a result of these memories, perhaps, the stock market has the reputation for severely penalizing REITs that find themselves with large amounts of debt relative to the stock market's valuation of their equity. For the most part, therefore, REITs try to retain debt amounts no greater than about 50 percent of their total asset value. This is less debt than is typically employed by taxable privately held real estate firms but more than most other publicly traded firms.

This relatively conservative debt position, combined with the pressure for growth, makes it easy for REITs to be tempted by a strategy of using low-interest debt to maximize the degree of positive leverage. This typically implies a temptation to borrow using short-term and floating or adjustable rate debt. Of course, there is no free lunch. This type of debt magnifies the REIT's equity risk and can result in an asset/liability maturity gap or maturity "mismatch" problem.[46] Since this is an obvious danger, the type of problem that caused the REIT debacle of the early 1970s, REIT analysts in the stock market tend to be on the lookout for it, and responsible REIT managers are pretty good at resisting the temptation. In short, REIT financial strategy is often a balancing act, a tension between opposing objectives and constraints.[47]

Specialization: Investment Focus and Firm Value A prominent characteristic of REIT management strategy during the 1990s, one that distinguished the new REITs of that decade from the older ones, was the tendency of REITs to specialize or focus on one type of property, or sometimes two closely related types, such as industrial and office properties.[48] Earlier REITs had often been diversified by property type. The idea was that the REIT's investors would want a diversified portfolio of properties. This may have made some sense when REITs were viewed as passive investment vehicles, but in fact, REIT investors can diversify on their own by buying different types of REIT stocks, and the more sophisticated institutional investors of the 1990s preferred to make these types of diversification decisions themselves. Furthermore, once REITs became more actively managed entities, it became clear that management expertise could usually be more effective when it was specialized by property type. Also, perhaps more important, the stock market can more easily understand and analyze a REIT that is specialized into one of a few somewhat standard space market segments.[49] Led by health care REITs in the late 1980s, REITs in the 1990s tended to specialize

---

[45]REITs may still face an indirect tax-based incentive to borrow, because of their 90% dividend payout requirement. Debt shields REIT taxable income, and therefore reduces the amount of dividends that must be paid out to shareholders, and REIT shareholders dividend income is subject to taxation at the personal level. In addition, there are other, non-tax-related arguments both for and against debt financing, as discussed in Chapter 15.

[46]See Chapter 19, section 19.1.4.

[47]Empirical evidence on REIT capital preferences during the 1990s is provided in Ghosh, Nag, and Sirmans (1997). Their study documents a slight tendency to favor equity over debt financing, particularly during periods of favorable stock market valuation of REITs. But in general the academic literature suggests REIT capital structure is heterogeneous and not well explained theoretically, with the lack of strong tax or signaling motivations giving REITs more freedom to choose alternative structures. (See Boudry et al. (2010) and Ertugrul and Giambona (2011) for some recent evidence and discussion.)

[48]Industrial and office properties have similar leasing characteristics and often involve the same firms, or same types of firms, as tenants. Some properties are even hybrids or mixtures of office and warehouse uses.

[49]Capozza and Seguin (1999) provide evidence that the primary value of specialization is not added value in the firm's operating profitability but rather in the stock market valuation of the firm. See Ro and Ziobrowski (2011) for some recent evidence countering the notion of specialization value, and Boer et al. (2005) for an international perspective suggesting that geographical focus can also add value (in contrast to Gyourko and Nelling (1996) and Ambrose et al. (2000)).

in fields such as apartments, shopping malls, smaller retail centers, hotels, and office and industrial properties (or the combination of these two). This trend seems permanent as it has continued throughout the early 2000s. Smaller, more unique niches have also been developed, such as self-storage, manufactured housing, golf courses, and more recently others (such as cell phone tower properties).

Vertical Integration   **Vertical integration** refers to the concept of a single firm controlling several linked stages in the production process, for example, from iron ore to steel to cars in the classical example of the Ford Motor Company early in the twentieth century. The old REITs before the 1990s were confined largely to one phase of the process of the production of commercial property goods and services, namely, the role of capital provision (investment) and ownership of existing income-producing properties, which sometimes included some aspects of the role of portfolio or asset management. Vertical integration involves going "upstream" in the production process to the construction and development of new buildings, and even the acquisition of land sites for future construction. It also involves going "downstream" in the production and delivery process to include property management, leasing, and other related services. A key advantage of vertical integration is that it gives a REIT flexibility to survive, and even profit from, the changes in the relative valuations between the stock and property markets, as described in section 23.2.4. For example, vertical integration allows REITs to profit by selling properties when their NAV exceeds their stock market valuations, while retaining operating scale and geographical scope by continuing to control the operational management of the properties they sell. Most modern REITs exhibit at least some degree of vertical integration, and this has become a hallmark of modern REIT management strategy.

Economies of Scale: Is Bigger Better?   The concept of **scale economies** refers to the phenomenon in which the average cost of production declines with an increasing rate of production, or somewhat more generally benefits to large-scale production. Most capital-intensive industries in the United States exhibit scale economies, at least to a point. Several leaders of the REIT industry in the 1990s argued forcefully that REITs are subject to this same phenomenon, that larger REITs would experience lower average costs than smaller REITs.[50] Supporters of the bigger is better hypothesis suggest that scale economies exist in REIT-level expenses and also in the cost of capital. The implication is that the big REITs will tend to get bigger (presumably by some combination of buying or merging with other REITs, buying properties in the private property market, and/or building new properties themselves), until the scale economies are exhausted. This suggests that the industry will tend to consolidate, as happened in the twentieth century, for example, in such industries as automobile and aircraft manufacturing.[51] If this is true, then REITs can "grow by growing," in a sense. In other words, REITs may face positive NPV opportunities from routine expansion (i.e., even when there is no positive NPV from the investment at the *micro-level*) simply because the increased scale will allow their average total costs to decline. This has obviously important strategic implications, not only for individual REITs but also for investors interested in the industry as a whole. It also provides an argument for raising external capital.

But is it true? Do REITs really face economies of scale, and if they do, are the scale economies very significant, and at what size of firm do they play out and get essentially exhausted? These questions have yet to be answered definitively, although some serious academic research has been focused on this question in recent years. Early empirical studies found evidence of scale economies in REIT administrative and management expenses,

---

[50]Average cost refers to cost per unit of output. In the case of REITs, average cost might be measured as the total cost (including not only the operating costs but also the required return on capital) per year, per square foot of space offered to tenants (or perhaps per dollar of rental revenue). If economies of scale exist in REITs, then REIT expenses should increase but at a decreasing rate as REIT size increases.

[51]Peter Linneman (1997) presented these arguments eloquently.

although the cost advantages appeared to be relatively minor and largely exhausted at fairly small scales.[52] Other studies find little evidence in support of scale economies in REIT expenses, but evidence of substantial scale economies in capital cost, probably driven largely by the increased liquidity of larger-capitalization stocks, and the need of large institutional investors to place capital into more liquid stocks. In other words, controlling for risk, REIT firm-level average capital cost (as measured by the firm-level WACC) appeared to decline significantly with firm size. Furthermore, this cost advantage seemed not to be exhausted even within the largest quartile of REITs (measured by market capitalization).[53]

In an important recent study, Ambrose, Highfield, and Linneman (2005) provide the most extensive investigation of economies of scale in REITs to date. By using a long sample period that extends from 1990 to 2001, the authors are able to overcome an important limitation of many previous studies, most of which employed data from the mid-1990s growth period, making it difficult to separate size-related benefits from REIT market-related effects. They report strong evidence of economies of scale particularly with respect to REIT overhead (G&A) expenses; increasing REIT size lowers average expenses and increases profit margins. Consistent with previous work, they also find that larger REITs have higher liquidity and lower costs of capital.

Perhaps the most compelling evidence in support of the "bigger is better" hypothesis comes from the now long-standing tendency toward consolidation in the REIT industry, now through a couple REIT cycles. REITs on average have become much larger in terms of market capitalization. Looking back at Exhibit 23-3, the industry has been consolidating since its initial 1990s IPO boom. From 1995 to 2011 the average publicly traded REIT grew from a market capitalization of $280 million to $3.1 billion. Even after adjusting for inflation this is almost an eight-fold increase in size. Many REITs have moved out of the small cap realm and are considered mid- and even large-capitalization stocks, with a number among the S&P 500 Index that classically represents large-cap stocks.

Branding Another strategy that some major REITs began to pursue seriously in the 1990s was to add value by building **brand name recognition** and reputation among their ultimate customers, the users of their spaces. This strategy has worked successfully for some firms in other branches of the service sector, such as retail and restaurant chains. Among the most notable attempts to build brand image was that of Simon, a shopping mall REIT. The Simon brand was displayed prominently in all of its malls and promoted through both hard-copy media and the Web. The idea was that if Simon malls were consistent enough in quality and service, then perhaps consumers would attach some value to the brand and choose Simon malls over other more convenient malls when traveling. Moreover, brand recognition may work synergistically with geographical scope to build franchise value. For example, a tenant in a Post Property apartment decides to move to another city and needs to break her lease. Rather than charging the tenant a deposit penalty, the property manager allows the tenant to break the lease provided she moves into another Post Property in her new city. High-quality service and consistent amenities may help such a REIT keep tenants longer and experience lower-than-average vacancy rates in its overall portfolio of properties. So while the strategy of building franchise value remains somewhat unproven in the REIT industry, there is some logic to support the idea of trying to build franchise value when combined with economies of scale and geographic scope.

Power in the Space Market The last major REIT management strategy consideration we will note here is the idea of a REIT using its size and access to capital to corner the market by concentrating its space ownership within a few geographically confined space markets.

---

[52]See Bers and Springer (1997, 1998) and Capozza and Seguin (1998). More recently Ambrose et al. (2005).

[53]Economies of scale in capital cost represent a different scale economy than the classical concept exhibited in manufacturing industries, based largely on financial capital costs rather than on production technology in the underlying physical capital. If such financial-based economies are really important, one wonders whether the financial services and investment industries will be able to come up with methods and vehicles to pool REIT shares or otherwise enable smaller REITs to tap into some of the liquidity-oriented capital cost reductions enjoyed by larger REITs. For example, in a response to the Linneman thesis of scale economies, Vogel (1997) advanced the notion that firms need not own real estate in order to reap scale economy benefits of property management.

Rental markets are often sufficiently segmented so as to enable such concentrated ownership to impart some **market power** (i.e., ability to influence rents) to the dominant space owner, at least in the short run. Yet they are not so segmented as to make such a strategy run afoul of antitrust laws (presumably). Nevertheless, while some REITs did develop semidominant ownership positions in a few markets during the 1990s, it is not clear that this strategy was driven so much by a pursuit of market power as simply by geographical specialization and concentration of local expertise. In fact, it is rare to find geographically constrained space markets that are so unique that they cannot face substantial competition from substitute locations, at least over the medium-term horizon in which new construction can occur. Nevertheless, large REITs do have some ability to pursue a market power strategy, and such a strategy probably does offer some potential profit in many cases. With the increasing consolidation in the industry, rental market power may be becoming more of a reality in some locations and property type sectors.

23.4 Chapter Summary: Some REIT Investor Considerations

This chapter provided an introduction to a fascinating and evolving group of firms that cut across, and link, the stock market and the private property market. REITs are unique whether your perspective is that of a stock market investor or a private property market investor. While unique investments are challenging to understand and deal with, they can provide unique opportunities. In this chapter, we sought to present only the most fundamental and abiding concepts and principles relevant to understanding REIT valuation and REIT investment. Although we also presented some of the nuts and bolts of REIT analysis and terminology, our presentation of strategic considerations was largely from the perspective of REIT managers. In closing this chapter, therefore, we will mention briefly a couple of strategic and tactical concerns and issues from the perspective of REIT investors.

1. Choosing between public and private real estate investment. An important threshold question all real estate investors face is how to place their real estate investment capital: in the public equity market via REITs, or in the private property market (directly or indirectly) via private market vehicles.[54] While there are a variety of considerations in addressing this choice, the major trade-offs were touched on in Chapter 7, and you can now understand them in more depth based on our presentation of portfolio theory in Chapter 21. REITs provide more liquidity than private market investment for the average investor, but they also provide less diversification within a wealth portfolio that is dominated by stocks and bonds, at least over short to medium investment horizons. This is because on a contemporaneous basis REIT returns tend to be more highly positively correlated with stock and bond returns than are private property market returns. The efficiency of the stock market can tend to give REIT investors more protection against making foolish mistakes, and therefore may require less intensive or less sophisticated and specialized due diligence and investment management, assuming investors use common sense and basic investment prudence. Thus, REITs are probably the preferred route for small, nonspecialized investors who want some real estate in their portfolio. Larger, more sophisticated investors will typically have the ability, and gain some benefit, from using both REIT and private market investment vehicles simultaneously in various mixes depending on their objectives and on where they perceive the market to be in terms of the real estate asset market cycle.

It should be noted that, even for large investors, a REIT-based portfolio may be less expensive in terms of management costs than a direct private market portfolio. For example, even large pension funds typically pay asset management fees in the range of 50 to 100 basis points (0.5 percent to 1.0 percent) per year of the value of the assets under management, for relatively simple "core" portfolios of stabilized properties. A passive portfolio of REIT stocks can normally be run for lower costs than that.

---

[54]A third possibility may develop in the near future, in the form of real estate price index based derivatives. One possibility is to base such derivatives on REITs' share prices corrected for leverage and targeted for specific property market segments. (See Chapter 26 for further discussion.)

2. REIT versus general stock returns. Most REIT investors, whether large or small, combine their REIT investments with relatively large holdings in the other sectors of the stock market. It is therefore of particular interest how REITs tend to perform relative to the stock market, including how this performance may tend to differ between "up" and "down" stock markets. While past behavior in this regard is not necessarily a foolproof guide to future behavior, some pretty strong empirical evidence has been compiled regarding REIT behavior relative to the stock market. Much of this evidence seems to present a fairly consistent picture between the "old REITs" of the pre-1992 world and the "new REITs" of the 1990s. In general, REITs are low-beta stocks, but they are certainly not zero-beta assets. Defining beta with respect to the stock market as a whole (S&P 500), REIT betas remained consistently near 0.50 up until about 1996, when they started to fall, just as the modern REIT era really kicked into gear. REIT betas have declined somewhat since the mid-1990s, averaging about 0.30 over the 1996–2005 period prior to the financial crisis, with the decrease due primarily to a significantly lower correlation between REIT and large-cap (S&P 500) returns, as shown in Exhibit 23-8. REITs have consistently shown higher correlations (and betas) with respect to small stocks than with respect to large stocks, and higher betas in declining stock markets than in advancing stock markets.[55] The large increase in REIT corre-

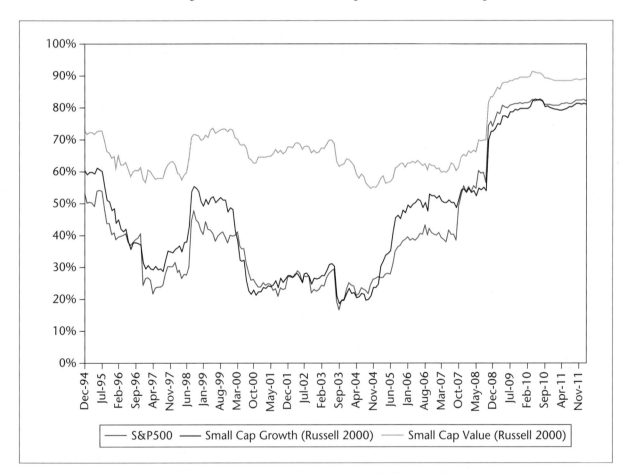

EXHIBIT 23-8 Correlation of Equity REIT Returns with Common Stock Returns (60-month rolling average).
© OnCourse Learning

---

[55]These results are developed and clearly presented in a very readable article by Michael Goldstein and Edward Nelling (1999). More recent evidence using more sophisticated analysis methods is presented in Case, Yawei and Yildirim (2012). Note that REIT volatility has tended to be near that of large-cap stocks, which mathematically implies a beta with respect to large-cap stocks approximately equal to the correlation coefficient.

lations with stocks in the later years of Exhibit 23-8 reflects the particularly high correlations during the financial crisis of 2008-2009. That financial crisis was characterized by abnormally high covariance among all asset classes. For most of the modern REIT era correlation between REITs and the bulk of the stock market has been in the 30 percent to 50 percent range, and this is likely where it will return.

KEY TERMS

asset management
pure plays
look-through provision
five-or-fewer rule
taxable REIT subsidiary (TRS)
initial public offering
    (IPO) boom
Umbrella Partnership REIT
operating partnership
    (OP) units
GAAP net income
funds from operations (FFO)

earnings before interest, taxes,
    depreciation, and amortization
    (EBITDA)
equity-before-tax cash flow (EBTCF)
adjusted funds from operations (AFFO)
funds, or cash, available for
    distribution (FAD or CAD)
Gordon growth model (GGM)
plowback ratio
dividend payout ratio
assets in place
same-store growth

growth opportunities
average equity cost of capital
net asset value (NAV)
growth stocks
income stocks
value stocks
public/private arbitrage
vertical integration
economies of scale
brand name recognition
market power (in the space
    market)

STUDY QUESTIONS

Conceptual Questions

23.1. What is the original purpose for which Congress enacted the REIT enabling legislation in 1960?

23.2. Why are REITs exempt from corporate income taxes?

23.3. What are the restrictions on REIT annual gross revenue sources and taxable income distributions necessary for a REIT to maintain its exemption from corporate income tax?

23.4. What are the two fundamental ways to think about the value of a REIT?

23.5. Define both "funds from operations (FFO)" and "adjusted FFO (AFFO)," carefully detailing differences between the two. Explain why these income measures are often used instead of GAAP net income to quantify the income-producing ability of a real estate investment trust.

23.6. Explain the Gordon growth model (GGM) of stock market equity valuation. What are the major mathematical simplifying assumptions in this model?

23.7. What is the NAV of a REIT, and how is it estimated?

23.8. What is meant by REIT "public/private arbitrage"? How can REITs in principle create positive NPV for pre-existing shareholders when the share price to NAV premium is positive (P/NAV > 1, private market values properties less than the stock market does)? How can REITs in principle create positive NPV for pre-existing shareholders when the share price to NAV premium is negative (P/NAV < 1, private market values properties more than the stock market does)?

23.9. Describe three of the six major REIT management strategy considerations or objectives (other than financing strategy) that were prominent in the REIT industry during the 1990s, as suggested in section 23.3 of this chapter.

23.10. Outline the advantages and disadvantages of investment in public REITs compared to direct real estate investment from investors' perspective, as you see them.

Quantitative Problems

23.11. Middlepoint Industrial Property Trust reports the following financial information, on a per-share basis:

GAAP Net Income [Earnings per Share (EPS)] = $4.00
Depreciation and Amortization (GAAP) = $3.00
Dividend Paid = $4.75
Debt = $50, with an average interest rate = 7%
Estimated share price premium to net asset value = 10%, based on an estimated private property market cap rate of 8% (weighted average firm level cap rate).

  a. Determine the minimum dividend the firm must pay to shareholders to be a REIT.
  b. Explain how the REIT can pay a dividend in excess of earnings per share. Calculate funds from operation (FFO) as part of your answer.
  c. Determine the aggregate NOI on Middlepoint's properties.
  d. Determine the current public market price of a share of Middlepoint stock.

23.12. Colonial Apartment REIT reports the following financial information on a per-share basis:

GAAP Net Income [Earnings per Share (EPS)] = $4.00
GAAP Depreciation and Amortization = $3.00
Reserves for property capital expenditures = $0.80
Dividend paid = $4.50
Debt = $50, with an average interest rate on debt = 7%
AFFO yield of 6.9% based on current share price
Estimated weighted average firm-level private property market cap rate of 8%

  a. Determine Colonial's EBITDA.
  b. Determine the current (public) price of a share of Colonial REIT common stock.
  c. Determine the current share price premium (or discount) to NAV for the REIT.

23.13. Blackstone Properties, a national office REIT, reported GAAP net income of $78,806,000 in 2005. It also reported the following income statement items:

Real estate depreciation: $147,746,000
Preferred stock dividends: $24,468,000
Allocations to OP unit holders: $26,983,000
Net gains from sale of real estate assets: $2,058,000 Net loss from extraordinary items: $13,786,000

  a. What was Blackstone's funds from operations (FFO) for 2005?
  b. Given that Blackstone reported a 2005 net straight-line rental adjustment loss of $14,619,000 and capital expenditures of $27,500,000, what was Blackstone's adjusted funds from operation (AFFO)?
  c. What was Blackstone's 2005 AFFO/GAAP net income ratio?
  d. Given that the REIT paid out $143,826,000 in common stock dividends in 2005, what was its dividend/FFO ratio?
  e. What was Blackstone's plowback ratio based on its AFFO (and deducting distributions to preferred shareholders and OP unit holders as well as common dividends)?
  f. By what percentage did Blackstone exceed the 90% minimum earnings payout requirement (based on GAAP net income)?

23.14. On January 31, 2005, National Growth Properties, a major shopping mall REIT, was trading at a share price of $28.50, at which price its then-current (year-2005) annual dividend of $2.04/share provided a yield of 7.2%. At that time, several analysts who followed National Growth closely were predicting future growth in earnings at a rate of nearly 10% per year for the subsequent five years, although same-store rental growth during the preceding year had been only 5.3%.

a. If the analysts' earnings growth rate expectations accurately reflected the stock market's long-run average growth expectations for National Growth's dividends as of January 31, 2005, then, based on the GGM, what was the stock market's implied long-run average required expected rate of total return for investment in National Growth equity?

b. If the market's long-run growth expectations were better reflected by the previous year's same-store rental growth rate, what was the market's required total expected return?

c. With the 5.3% growth expectation assumption of question (b), what is the market's implied required *ex ante* risk premium for National Growth equity, given that T-bills were yielding about 5.5% at that time?

d. If the required total return expectation you calculated in question (b) was indeed the market's required return for National Growth, but the most accurate long-term dividend growth rate expectation for National Growth was actually halfway between the 5.3% same-store rental growth rate and the analysts' 10% earnings growth rate prediction, then what was the extent of the market's "underpricing" of National Growth stock on January 31, 2005?

23.15. The Donald Grump Corporation, a publicly traded REIT, has expected total return to equity of 13%, average interest rate on its debt of 7.5%, and a debt/total asset value ratio of 40%.

a. What is Grump's equity average cost of capital?

b. What is Grump's firm-level overall average cost of capital? [Hint: Use the WACC formula (1) from section 13.3 of Chapter 13.]

23.16. Bob & Sue Realty (BSR) is a publicly traded REIT that has no debt and a current dividend yield of 8%, with a current share price/earnings multiple of 12.5. The current consensus expectation among stock analysts who follow BSR is that BSR can provide a long-term average growth rate in its dividends per share of 5% per year.

a. What is BSR's plowback ratio (i.e., what proportion of its earnings does it retain and not pay as dividends)?

b. Assuming the stock market agrees with these analysts expectations, what is BSR's firm-level average cost of capital? [Hint: As BSR has no debt, you can use the GGM directly to answer this question.]

23.17. The Rentleg Distribution Center is a warehouse complex near the Cincinnati Airport in Northern Kentucky, in a market where such buildings currently sell at 10% cap rates (net cash flow/property value), with 1.0% expected long-run average annual growth (in both value and cash flow). This property has initial net cash flow of $2,500,000 per year. Both the Grump REIT and BSR (from Questions 23.21 and 23.22) are considering bidding to buy the Rentleg Center.

a. Ignoring possible differential valuation between the stock and property markets, what is the (marginal) opportunity cost of capital for acquisition of the Rentleg Center by either REIT (i.e., what is the *discount rate* relevant for a DCF valuation of the Rentleg Center on the part of either one of the two REITs)?

b. What is the maximum price Grump can offer for the Rentleg Center without its share price being diluted?

    c. What is the maximum price BSR can offer for the Rentleg Center without its share price being diluted?

    d. If BSR is able to purchase the Rentleg Center for $24,000,000, what will be the change in the (aggregate) value of BSR's equity as a result of this transaction (assuming the stock market had not already factored such an expected purchase into its valuation of BSR's shares)?

INTERNATIONAL REAL ESTATE INVESTMENTS: MARKETS, STRATEGIES, AND IMPLEMENTATION

LEARNING OBJECTIVES

After reading this chapter, you should understand:

⊃ The rationale of international real estate investment

⊃ The major obstacles and disadvantages to investing in real estate in foreign markets

⊃ The nature of international institutional investment portfolios and capital flows and the practical considerations shaping them

⊃ The nature of the institutions enabling a successful international real estate strategy

⊃ Risk management strategies associated with successful international real estate investment

Real estate investment was traditionally a very local business, but real estate capital markets are gradually getting more international, as global capital market integration progresses. Cross-border capital flows have increased in all asset markets. Real estate markets have been relatively slow to follow suit, but now seem beyond the tipping point, where more international investment leads to new investment products and supporting institutions that in their turn facilitate yet more international capital flows. The development feeds on itself.

The preceding chapters have looked at real estate markets on a regional or national level, with the last three chapters looking at real estate portfolio theory, capital market theory and the development of the U.S. REIT market. The next logical step is to look at real estate markets from a higher level and broaden the universe from which investment portfolios can be constructed: the global universe. This chapter will begin by looking at the global universe and at international capital flows, and will discuss the institutions aiding the internationalization of the global property markets. After that, we will consider the key arguments for international real estate investment: return opportunities abroad, diversification, and the export of portfolio management and development skills. We will also examine the obstacles and problems associated with international property investment, such as additional costs and risks. The key issue here is the informational disadvantage international property investors are at relative to the local players.

Finally, we will synthesize these issues to come up with viable portfolio strategies for international property investors, based on a combination of direct property investment and the use of the global property share market. One of the key arguments is that different types of investors have different optimal international investment strategies. Especially important in that regard is the question whether one is an intermediate investor, whose shareholders can diversify themselves, or an end-investor, who does not have diversifying shareholders. The chapter ends with suggestions for implementing these strategies, including country allocation, indexing, and currency risk management.

24.1 There's a Big World Out There

Much is happening around the world in terms of the emergence of a global real estate market, and this can be measured by looking at invested capital and capital flows, as well as the size of the market and market segments. This parallels the growth of international corporations with real estate needs around the globe. Besides that, the institutions of globalization are emerging in real estate. In any sector, there is a chicken-and-egg situation where international capital flows are aided by transparency-enhancing market institutions, but in order for these institutions to emerge and be sustained, the capital flows have to emerge. Beyond a certain threshold, the two feed on each other, and the emergence of institutions of international transparency is both a sign of and a catalyst for advancing globalization.

24.1.1 The Global Real Estate Capital Market: Size and Flows

In general, investors favor their own markets above asset markets far away. This so-called home bias has been documented for stock and bond markets, and real estate markets are no different in that respect. The mantra "location, location, location" suggests that real estate markets could be even more local than other asset markets: both supply and demand are driven by local factors. American real estate investors in particular have been reluctant to expand internationally. Of all foreign direct investments made from the United States in the decades through 1995, the average real estate investment has been a mere 0.3 percent.[1]

But internationalization is underway, and the global market has become bigger and more transparent. Exhibit 24-1 depicts size and composition of the institutional real estate markets of Europe and the Asia-Pacific region between 2007 and 2010, divided along the lines of the capital market matrix, as discussed in Chapter 1. In Europe, the market was valued at $3.2 trillion in 2010. The crisis apparently did not hurt market growth in the Asia-Pacific region, and its size has now surpassed that of Europe, reaching a value of $3.5 trillion in 2010. Although the Asia-Pacific market is now the largest in the world, this market value is still very small compared to its likely future value. One should consider that the population of the Asia-Pacific region, including the populous countries of India, Indonesia, and China, is more than ten times that of the United States. When these markets are fully developed, they will require a comparable per capita quantity of real estate as the mature, developed parts of the globe. With such a large population, the combined current value is relatively very low, and a fully developed market could be expected to far surpass the U.S. market in value. In other words, it is likely that the Asia-Pacific real estate markets will need many billions of additional capital over the next decades.

---

[1]Lapier (1998) provides very interesting statistics regarding inward and outward private real estate investments in relation to total foreign direct investments for a number of countries starting in the 1960s and extending through 1995. On the whole, international private real estate investments do not seem to go up as a share of total investments.

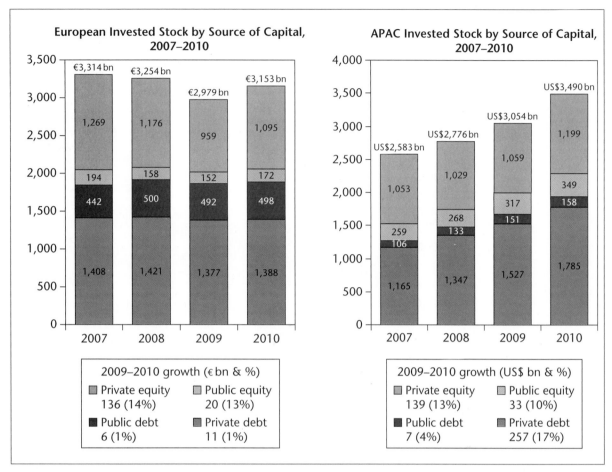

EXHIBIT 24-1 The Composition of Foreign Institutional Property Markets
Source: DTZ Research (2011).

Another important take-away from Exhibit 24-1 is that, both in Europe and in the Asia-Pacific region, the real estate market is still predominantly a private market in both the debt and the equity segments. Regarding securitization, Europe seems a bit more developed in the debt markets, and Asia-Pacific in the equity markets.

It can also be seen that international capital markets are integrating, especially within Europe. Cross-border real estate capital flows among European countries are expanding, and they tend to grow faster than domestic investments. However, many investors stay local, which is illustrated by the behavior of listed property companies. In the global universe of property companies, as measured by Global Property Research (GPR), only around 10 percent are international, in the sense of having any serious holdings in real estate outside their own country. This percentage is rather stable, illustrating that the real estate companies have largely remained local.

In short, this evidence, although incomplete, suggests international capital market integration along regional not global lines. This notion is in line with existing empirical research, which also implies that real estate markets are integrating on a regional basis.[2]

---

[2]See Eichholtz, Huisman, Koedijk and Schuin (1998), who provide evidence that property markets are increasingly driven by continental not global market factors. Gerlach, Wilson and Zurbruegg (2006) show that the Asian crisis of the late 1990s resulted in stronger integration among Asian property markets. More recent, evidence for regional integration are Gallo and Zhang (2010) and Zhou (2011).

EXHIBIT 24-2 The Global
Property Share Market (US$
billion), 1983–2011
Source: GPR.

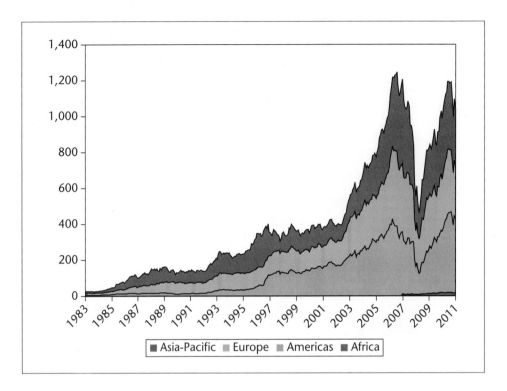

24.1.2 The Institutions of Globalization

International capital market integration requires institutional help, both through the emergence of investment products catering to international investors, and through reliable information sources that make markets more transparent. To start with the former, the development of the public real estate markets, both on the equity and on the debt side, makes it much easier for property investors to allocate significant amounts of capital outside of their home market. Exhibit 24-2 illustrates that the global property share market has been growing in the last three decades. Starting at approximately $25 billion in 1983, the total capitalization of the global property share market had reached $1.2 trillion by 2011, just over 35 percent of which was in North America, with Europe and Asia-Pacific splitting most of the rest. Africa accounts for 1.5 percent of the total market capitalization. The market development has not followed a smooth trend, but instead has been growing in fits and starts, showing strong growth in boom periods, stability in other times and a virtual implosion in 2008, when the global market lost more than half of its value. Interestingly, this was a global phenomenon, as was the equally spectacular recovery that followed.

The overall growth of the global property share market is helped by the proliferation of tax pass-through structures all over the world. The success of the U.S. **REIT** market has prompted regulators in many countries to introduce similar—but differently named—structures. The REIT structure is making rapid progress in many countries. Exhibit 24-3 provides a global overview of tax pass-through property vehicles: property investment entities that do not pay tax at the corporate level, like United States REITs. As the table shows, the REIT structure has been adopted in 22 countries since 2000, among which are important property markets like the United Kingdom, France, Germany, Hong Kong, and Japan.[3] This is an important development for the internationalization of property markets. Without tax transparency, property companies are handicapped relative to direct property investments.

---

[3]The European Public Real Estate Association (www.epra.com) provides and updates an excellent overview of listed tax-exempt property vehicles all over the world.

Country	Structure	Inception	Debt Ceiling	Minimum Payout
Americas				
Brazil	FII	1993	N/A	95% of net income
Canada	MFT	1994	no restrictions	100% of net income
Chile	FII	1989	limit set by internal rules of fund	30% of annual profits
Costa Rica	REIF	1997	50% of real estate / 10% of other assets	no
Mexico	FIBRAS	2004	thin capitalization rules	95% of taxable income
Puerto Rico	REIT	1972	no restrictions	90% of net income
USA	REIT	1960	no restrictions	90% of net income
Africa				
South Africa	PUT	2003	30% of assets	capital gains must be reinvested
	PLS	2009	limited by internal rules of fund	no
Europe				
Belgium	SICAFI	1995	65% of assets	80% of net profit
Bulgaria	SPIC	2004	short terms loans < 20 % of assets	90% of net income
Finland	Finish REIT	2009	80% of assets	90% of net income
France	SIIC	2003	thin capitalization rules	85% of tax exempt profits; 50% of capital gains
Germany	G-REIT	2007	55% of assets	90% of net income; deferral of 50% of capital gains
Greece	REIC	1999	50% of assets	35% of net profits
Israel	REIT	2006	60% of real estate / 20% of other assets	90% of profits
Italy	SIIQ	2003	limited by internal rules of fund	85% of real estate income
Lithuania	Reit	2008	75% of assets	no
Luxembourg	SIF	2007	no restrictions	no
Netherlands	FBI	1969	60% of real estate / 20% of securities	100% of net income
Spain	SOCIMI	2009	70% of assets	50% of capital gains; 90% of rental income
Turkey	REIC	1995	short-term credit < three times NAV	minimum 20% as first dividend ratio
UK	UK-REIT	2007	interest cover test	90% of net income
Asia/Pacific				
Australia	LPT	1971	no restrictions	100% of net income
Dubai	REIT	2006	70% of assets	80% of net income
Hong Kong	HK-REIT	2003	45% of assets	90% of net income
India	REMF	2008	20% of assets	90% of income; 90% of capital gains
Japan	J-REIT	2000	no restrictions	90% + profits from sales
Malaysia	Unit Trust	2005	50% of assets	90% of total income
New Zealand	Unit Trust	1960	possible thin capitalization rules	no
	PIE	2007	possible thin capitalization rules	no
Pakistan	REIT	2008	30% of assets	90% of income
Philippines	REIT	2009	35% of assets	90% of income
Singapore	S-REIT	1999	35% of assets	90% of net income
South Korea	REIC	2001	66% of assets	90% of net income
Taiwan	REIT	2003	35% of assets	pursuant to the REIT contract
Thailand	PFPO	1992	borrowing prohibited	90% of net income; 90% of capital gains

EXHIBIT 24-3 Tax Pass-Through Property Structures and Characteristics

Source: EPRA (2012).

The spreading of tax pass-through property vehicles reverses this disadvantage, allowing international property investors to use the full benefits of the listed property markets, which, due to their relatively efficient pricing, seem particularly fit for acquiring international property exposure.

The global market can also be viewed from a debt point of view. Globally, the market for Commercial Mortgage-Backed Securities (CMBS), which are useful vehicles for real estate debt investors to step into foreign debt markets, had been growing until the 2008–2009 crisis, but has been more or less closed down since then. That crisis has also demonstrated the disadvantages of property market globalization: securitized debt markets have been an important transmission channel of the crisis from one country's banks and investors to the next. Here, international investment turned out to increase risk, rather than reduce it through diversification.

Emerging globalization seems to go hand in hand with a trend for global property markets to become more public. This, in turn, facilitates more internationalization. It is far easier for an investor in Amsterdam or London, for example, to invest in a securitized market in the United States by buying shares of a listed property company on the exchange than to travel there physically, open an office, and set up business as a direct investor. So while the emergence and growth of the securitized market has not by itself made the market international, it has been a conduit and enabling factor for internationalization. On the other hand, the crisis of 2008–2009 has shown that this internationalization also has important drawbacks. The crisis in the U.S. real estate market has become a global banking crisis mainly through the mortgage-backed securities market and its offspring.

Besides the increasing publicness of real estate markets, other new institutions are becoming important for international investors wishing to make direct investments in private real estate. In a private market, the relevant knowledge the real estate investor needs to be successful and perform well remains largely local in nature. In the past, this knowledge was not shared as there were no associations, agencies, or advisors willing to share it, but these are now being created.

This results in the establishment of standards in information quality, governance, and professionalism, both via professional organizations and for-profit firms. National and international research consultants, data providers, and property brokers increasingly supply local data and can help the investor to build up local knowledge. These data include performance benchmarks, up-to-date market information on rents, vacancies, and yields, and information regarding rent contracts. And the quality as well as availability of these data are constantly improving. However, this holds true mainly for the mature markets, as in North America, Europe, Japan and Australia. It is not yet the case for important emerging property markets like those of China, India, Turkey, and Brazil.

Increasing transparency is demonstrated by Jones Lang LaSalle's transparency indicator, a global real estate indicator that measures and ranks countries in order of transparency. Until the crisis of 2008–2009, this indicator was showing ever-increasing transparency, and since its inception in 1999, no country had decreased its transparency. That, however, has changed since the crisis. Especially some of the more transparent countries have shown a decrease, which is mainly due to a lack of transparency in the real estate debt markets. But among the countries that were not very transparent before, Turkey and China have made important steps forward. At the bottom of the list, countries like Ukraine, Egypt, Indonesia, and India have stayed the same and are still opaque. So while transparency is increasing in general, this does not hold for some large and potentially interesting markets. Transparency clearly remains a problem in these markets.[4]

To sum up these developments, we can say that the long-term trend is for real estate markets to become more international, aided by institutions like a growing public market, performance indices and reliable and accessible market information. This leads to the question why these developments are taking place, and what investors should do about them.

---

[4]Lieser and Groh provide a comprehensive analysis of 66 real estate markets, ranking them on their attractiveness for institutional real estate investments.

INSTITUTIONS OF INTERNATIONAL TRANSPARENCY

The internationalization of real estate capital flows has lead to the emergence of supporting institutions. These institutions, some of which are industry associations, while others are for-profit companies, create common international standards and definitions, compare best practices and provide market information. These efforts result in increasing transparency, which facilitates yet more growth in international real estate capital flows. The list below gives information regarding some of the most useful of these institutions.

The Asian Pacific Real Estate Association (APREA) represents the real estate sector in the region. Besides that representative function, it is a network for institutional real estate parties in Asia, and it aims to provide best practice standards. It is also a repository for research on the region, available to members.

CoStar is a data provider for commercial real estate markets, and provides detailed information at the building level, covering prices, rents, quality, and tenants. Its data still cover mostly the United States, but the company is expanding its coverage to the rest of the world.

The European Public Real Estate Association (EPRA) aims to promote, develop and represent the European public real estate sector. EPRA fosters these goals by establishing standards for listed property companies, and by providing information to potential investors. It is the European equivalent of America's National Association of Real Estate Investments Trusts (NAREIT), and besides its European property share indices, it produces a global index in cooperation with NAREIT all together with FTSE.

The European Association for Investors in Nonlisted Real Estate Vehicles (INREV) aims to improve transparency and accessibility of market information and to increase the liquidity of the nonlisted real estate vehicle market in Europe. The organization provides information about this market, tries to foster its professionalism and establishes best practice standards. It is the European equivalent to America's National Association of Real Estate Investment Managers (NAREIM).

Investment Property Databank (IPD) provides investment performance indices for direct property markets. The company has an ever-growing range of indices covering 23 countries (2011). It maintains indices for the standard institutional investment categories, but also covers, depending on the country, the social housing sector, land, and forestry. Representativeness depends to a strong degree on the country.

Global Property Research (GPR) provides performance indices for all listed property share markets in the world. The indices and GPR's database go back to 1984. GPR closely tracks the global universe of listed property companies.

Jones Lang LaSalle provides research rapports on property markets all over the world, and collects market information for over 80 countries to construct their Global Real Estate Transparency Index. Index numbers are based on legal factors, regulatory burden, availability of market information, financial disclosure and governance rules, and availability of investment performance indices.

Real Capital Analytics (RCA) provides information on commercial property transactions all over the world. That involves prices and other transaction details, and also property details and information on the tenants, the buyers, and the sellers. Data coverage is country-dependent. The company also does research based on these data.

Does it mean they should rush to go international and if so, how should they do this and what kind of strategy should they employ? In the next section, we consider the rationale for and obstacles to going international.

24.2 Going International: Rationales and Obstacles

There are strong arguments in favor of international real estate investment. First, there may be good investment opportunities offering better returns outside the home country, especially if the home country has a well-developed, mature property market with little or no growth. Another rationale is that international investment provides diversification benefits, because markets do not move in a synchronized way. The third reason could be to export superior portfolio management or development expertise, especially in emerging markets, where such expertise is likely to be in demand.

However, there are also obstacles and risks attached to going international. International investment entails various costs that are difficult to recoup, and the foreign investor is likely to be at an informational disadvantage relative to his local competitors. Secondly, going international leads to additional risks, like currency risk and political risk, and since international investments are likely to be less liquid than local property investments, these risks could be harder to manage abroad than at home. Lastly, the international investor may be hampered by discriminating regulation, like property ownership restrictions or adverse taxation. The remainder of this section discusses these rationales and obstacles in depth.

24.2.1 Return Opportunities

Prospects of better return opportunities than in the home country come in two varieties. First, return opportunities can be structural, relating to economic development, relative capital scarcity, and demographics. Secondly, return opportunities abroad may be of a cyclical nature. The investor's home market may be at the top of the property cycle, with a big boost to returns beckoning from switching to another market at the bottom of the cycle.

Let's start with the **structural return opportunities**. In economically mature markets, economic growth will be relatively low, and so will growth in property demand. But in emerging markets, rapid economic growth will spur growth in property demand. Similarly, there are mature and immature demographic markets, but these two factors are not the same. Eastern Europe is economically an emerging region but demographically mature. China is an economically booming emerging market, but about to phase out in demographics, with its population peak expected in 2026 because of its one-child per family policy. In India and Malaysia, on the other hand, there is no peak in population in sight.

Regarding the first type of structural return opportunity abroad, economic development is obviously not evenly spread across the globe and the differences are partly of a structural nature. As economic growth in mature markets in the United States, "old" Europe and Japan is weak, so is growth in property demand. Average GDP growth in the euro area has been less than 0.5 percent since 1995, and is forecast to be bad because of the euro-induced austerity measures in a large part of the continent. United States' growth has averaged 2.4 percent since 1995. By contrast, emerging markets in Asia, "new" Europe and the Americas have much higher economic growth. China's economic growth has averaged 10 percent in the past two decades with no slowdown in sight, with India at nearly 8 percent since 2000. Central Europe has shown average growth surpassing 3 percent since 1999, comparable with Brazil. With the exception of Central Europe, these regions have mostly not been very strongly affected by the crises, and continue catching up with the mature economies. They are likely to sustain their impressive growth, even though the growth path will probably not be very smooth.

Economic growth goes hand in hand with property demand. A characteristic of emerging economies is rapid urbanization. China, for example, is creating cities in the millions at a startling pace, housing the rural migrants partaking in the economic boom. Meanwhile, those already living in the cities are becoming richer and consume more space in the form of better housing. This is likely to continue.

Developing societies also need industrial and office properties to accommodate the workers. Cities attract migration from the countryside because there are jobs to be had, initially in manufacturing and distribution, and this requires industrial space such as warehouses and factories. Subsequently, service industries begin to grow rapidly, requiring office space. And finally, as societies gradually become more prosperous, populations adapt similar spending patterns to the West, creating demand for facilities like shopping centers and leisure projects.

These property needs translate into large **structural capital needs**, as housing people at work or home in high-growth urban areas absorbs huge amounts of capital. By contrast, many of the mature economies have mature capital markets, with large institutional investors and a structural oversupply of capital. This is nothing new: in the eighteenth century, the Dutch had a small economy with a big capital market, so their capital went abroad and financed the American economy. Capital markets shift capital from places where it is in surplus to places where it is needed. This probably explains why Dutch and British property investors traditionally have been relatively international: they have had large capital markets relative to their own real estate markets.

Turning to **demographics**, the other major structural factor that could influence returns, it is equally obvious that the demographic tide varies widely across countries. Populations in some countries keep on growing, while in others, they are leveling off or already shrinking. Real estate markets provide the space that people need—working space, living space and recreational space, and these needs are to a large extent driven by population size and composition, i.e. by demographics. To get an idea of future property demand, we need to know how many people there will be as a whole and in different age categories.

As well, different property types are exposed to different aspects of demographic change. Demand for office space depends on the number of people of working age, as these will populate the offices. Demand for retail space depends partly on the total population (because everyone needs clothes and food), and on the population composition as some age groups consume more than others. Purchasing power is a key issue: there are far fewer shops per 1,000 inhabitants in Eastern than in Western Europe, but if purchasing power rises to Western European levels, shopping space will also reach these levels. Housing demand largely depends on household formation, which is driven by population size, but also by average household size: even if the population shrinks, but the average household size also shrinks, the number of households could remain stable or even grow.

However, the exact relationship between demographics and property demand remains unclear. Early research from the late 1980s predicted a fall in American house prices due to the end of the baby boom.[5] The market has proved these predictions wrong by producing the biggest housing boom in recorded history. In effect, what happened is that supply reacted adequately to the new demand situation. More importantly, the end of the baby boom in the United States is a rather nondramatic event compared to demographic developments in other countries, since it implies not a shrinking population but merely a slowing down of population growth: the United Nations does not predict an end to U.S. population growth before 2060. But in some important markets outside the United States, the population is indeed shrinking, and for real estate markets, with their inelastic supply, there is a fundamental difference between slow growth and a shrinking population.[6]

Office market models show that the driver for demand is employment. Over time, employment fluctuates with the economic cycle, but the underlying trend is still determined by the number of people of working age. Job creation matters for office demand only as long as there are people to take the jobs. Exhibit 24-4 shows index numbers of the labor population—the number of people aged 25–64—in Asia, North America, Europe, and the world as a whole starting at 100 in 1960. Asia shows the fastest growth, but will top out at about 2045. North America has had strong growth and keeps on growing through 2060, albeit at a lower pace. In Europe, the situation is totally different, with the labor population already topping out and projected to fall right back to the 1960 level by 2060, though there will be a structural difference as virtually all women will work in 2060 compared with hardly any in 1960. This also means there is some potential for growth in the active labor force left in countries where few women currently participate in the workforce.

Among the mature markets, in the immigration-based group of economies such as Australia and the United States, there is no steady state in sight even in 2060. The labor population growth will continue, albeit at a slower pace. But in mature economies elsewhere, Germany and Japan are already past their peaks; Italy and the Netherlands have reached their peaks and Singapore and Spain are close to it. So besides the immigration-based countries, there are two categories of mature markets: the "not-so-bad" group, like France, Sweden, the United Kingdom, and Singapore, where labor population is projected to be stable or just slightly falling, and the shrinking labor force group, including countries like Germany, Italy, Japan and South Korea, which will all see their labor population go down more than 25 percent until 2060.

---

[5]In 1989, Mankiw and Weil predicted that house prices would fall at the end of the baby boom, but subsequent research and market developments demonstrated that they were wrong.

[6]Glaeser and Gyourko (2005) have theoretically shown that decreasing population may lead to strong declines in property prices.

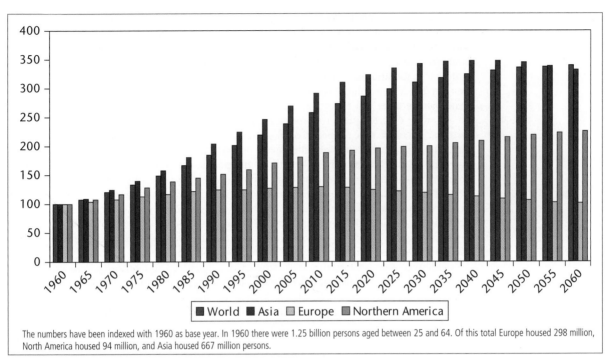

The numbers have been indexed with 1960 as base year. In 1960 there were 1.25 billion persons aged between 25 and 64. Of this total Europe housed 298 million, North America housed 94 million, and Asia housed 667 million persons.

EXHIBIT 24-4 International Labor Force Statistics and Projections (age group 25–64)

Source: United Nations World Population Prospects Database.

One solution could be to shift the property allocation to emerging markets. Here, we can see that non-European markets like Brazil, Chile, and India, plus tenuously European Turkey, look much more promising regarding demographics. But in Eastern Europe, growth is topping out as in the Czech Republic or already falling as in Hungary. These projections may be less reliable in countries that have gone through so much change, as fertility could increase, for example, but the picture looks quite negative apart from Turkey. Central and East European countries may be economically emerging markets, but are demographically mature.

The next question is whether the working population even needs offices. Here the answer has traditionally been yes, because employment growth in the United States, Japan, and Europe in the past decades has only occurred in services. This looks set to continue, but future service employment may require less office space than in the past. The organization of work in services is likely to change fundamentally due to the revolution in communication technology. People will probably work more at home or in the so called "third place," meaning anywhere they happen to be or want to be.[7] This is another reason for less office demand, and it is a global phenomenon.

The data do appear to suggest a gloomy future for European office markets, but there may be some offsetting forces. First, a permanently tight labor market may induce more immigration, later retirement, and stricter social benefits policies. However, in view of the political strength required for such reforms, this will take time, and these developments are much less easy to predict than the demographic growth the markets have been used to. Another key factor will be emigration within countries, with attractive, growing regions and cities pulling in labor from stagnant areas. In real estate, competition between cities will grow with the increasing differences between fast-growth and stagnant cities. This will imply more uncertainty regarding the demand for real estate, in therefore more investment risk.

---

[7]See Malone (2004) for a vision of the business organization of the future, and the role of place in it.

Where the office market used to be driven by a constantly humming demographic engine, with regular and predictable annual growth, it must now rely on unpredictable political and social developments. Even if all possible mitigating factors do emerge, global office demand will grow more slowly due to less labor and the increasing use of alternative locations for work. Either new supply will have to slow down, or prices will fall, and developers as well as investors will feel this.

Macro-demand for retail space, on the other hand, is driven by the number of people and their purchasing power. The number of people and their age composition will determine the quantity of demand: people over 40 are the bigger consumers, and younger people consume less, and consequently need less retail space.[8] The type and location of retail space required and the success of retail formats are also partly driven by the composition of the population. Meanwhile, total purchasing power will determine quantity and quality. Net new space will only be needed if these variables grow, otherwise only replacement space will be required. Nonetheless, expected growth in wealth could maintain the attractiveness of retail real estate in the next decades.

Exhibit 24-5 shows strong variety in historic and expected population developments. Until 2060, the U.S. population is expected to grow approximately 36 percent, while a shrinking population is expected in some European countries—especially those in Central Europe—and in Japan and South Korea. In general, the numbers look better than those for the labor population, with strong expected population growth especially in emerging and immigration-based economies.

Moreover, purchasing power, the second quantitative driver of the demand for retail space is likely to continue growing. Simple extrapolation of GDP real growth since 1970 suggests that by 2030, even the relatively slow growers in Western Europe and North America will be substantially better off than in 2012, suggesting plenty of scope for growth in retail property. In the rest of the world, the potential for real GDP growth is larger, which will translate into more demand for retail space. And as consumers become more affluent, they will demand a western-style shopping experience, rather than the more informal retail arrangements that are currently prevailing in many emerging economies.

But other than in the past, these developments will not translate automatically into consumer spending in physical shops. The global communications revolution breaks down the traditional relation between growth in population and affluence and the demand for retail space. Currently, the money spent on Internet shopping is still a small percentage of overall retail trades. Even in the United States, it is still just around 5 percent. But while high growth rates in Internet retail continue, sales growth in physical shops is sluggish. For example, consumer spending in the crisis of 2008–2009 shrunk in many countries, even as sales in Internet retail kept growing. And this is not a phenomenon that is exclusive to mature economies: China is expected to surpass the United States as the largest e-commerce market in the world by 2015. So even countries where brick and mortar retail is not yet affected very much by this development will surely feel its effects in years to come. Retail property developers and investors will have to rethink the role of their product in societies that spend much of their money on the Web.

The final question is how demographic changes will affect the housing market. This market is driven by income trends, interest rates, and planning rules in the short term, but ultimately by household formation, as every household needs at least one home. Household formation is a function of population size and average household size. Households are generally still getting smaller, partly offsetting the expected decreases in population in many countries. For example, in Europe the number of households is expected to fall from 2015 onwards, but this decline is not nearly as big as the drop in the labor population and will for some time be more of a leveling off.

For countries in which the population is expected to keep on increasing, the decreasing average family size is a driver of even higher growth for housing. Especially in emerging economies, the potential for increased housing demand due to reduced family sizes is big,

---

[8]This is according to Green and Hendershott (2007), who rigorously analyze the relationship between the population age composition and consumption.

	Total Population	Cumulative Growth		Peak in
	2010	1960–2010	2010–2060	
A. Mature Economies				
Australia	22,268	116%	47%	—
Canada	34,017	90%	33%	—
France	62,787	37%	18%	—
Germany	82,302	13%	−12%	2005
Italy	60,551	22%	−5%	2018
Japan	126,536	37%	−18%	2009
Netherlands	16,613	45%	2%	2036
Singapore	5,086	211%	18%	2042
South Korea	48,184	92%	−46%	2041
Spain	46,077	52%	8%	2049
United Kingdom	62,036	18%	19%	—
United States	310,384	67%	36%	—
B. Emerging Economies				
Americas				
Brazil	194,946	168%	11%	2042
Chile	17,114	124%	15%	2046
Mexico	113,423	195%	26%	2050
Asia-Pacific				
China	1,341,335	104%	−10%	2026
India	1,224,614	173%	40%	—
Indonesia	239,871	161%	21%	2050
Malaysia	28,401	248%	60%	—
Europe				
Czech Republic	10,493	10%	1%	2027
Hungary	9,984	0%	−9%	1980
Poland	38,277	32%	−12%	1996
Russia	142,958	19%	−16%	1993
Turkey	72,752	158%	25%	2051
C. World	6,895,889	127%	39%	—

EXHIBIT 24-5 Population (× 1000 persons) in International Perspective, 1960–2060

Source: United Nations World Population Prospects Database.

since economic development is very closely connected with lower fertility rates and smaller families. So even if population growth slows down due to that same lowering of the fertility rate, the growth in the number of households is set to continue for decades, ensuring ongoing demand growth for housing. For example, the average household size in Turkey according to the latest census is 4.5 persons, and it has dropped in each census since 1975. If Turkey's household size falls to the European average in the long run, this alone would lead to a doubling in the demand for housing units.

The other side of the demographic coin is that societies age, and this also seems to have an important impact on the demand for housing. Recent research suggests a strong and positive relation between human capital and the qualitative demand for housing, and it also suggests that this relation is stronger for older families.[9] Since younger generations are better educated than their elders in almost every country, our societies will increase their human capital as time progresses. This, together with the average age of the population, will create demand for higher-quality housing, which implies the need for a continuous adaptation of the housing stock.

Summing up demographic developments, we can say that property markets in many countries are turning into replacement markets; good quality will drive out bad quality, and competition among cities and regions will increase. At the same time, fundamental uncertainty in these property markets will grow as population growth comes to a halt. Market effects will first be felt in the development and construction markets. Because different property types are exposed to different aspects of the demographic tide, demographic changes will first affect office markets and only later, retail and housing markets. Europe and some countries in Asia are very mature demographically, while many emerging countries and countries with a tradition of immigration will follow these trends much later. Thus, investors from demographically mature markets should make strategic allocations abroad, especially to demographically immature markets. This echoes the argument for economically mature markets, but as we have seen, stages of economic and demographic maturity may be in parallel or in opposition, and investors also need to be aware of this.

What does this imply for a property investor? That depends on the home market. For European investors, these numbers provide a clear rationale for investing internationally, and that also holds for investors from Japan and South Korea. For American investors, where the demographics at home look much better, it means they have to be very careful where to invest to achieve a better return/risk profile. They should be aware that there is no strict one-to-one relationship between economically emerging markets and demographically emerging markets. The same holds for investors from other countries in which the demographic situation looks favorable.

In short, for one group of investors, demographics provides a rationale for going international; for another group, it is something they have to be wary of.

The structural return opportunities abroad require a long-run perspective on foreign markets, but **cyclical return opportunities** are a matter of timing the cycle and thus more short-run and opportunistic. The existence of cycles is well documented, and at any given point in time, and for any property type, there will probably be markets around the world at every phase in the cycle. Looking at international cycle snapshots supports this notion.

This may provide market timers with investment opportunities. For example, an opportunistic office investor who feels that the home office market is at the top of the cycle can sell assets and go into foreign office markets close to the bottom of their cycle. Such a strategy of opportunistic international cycle surfing sounds attractive, but to put these cyclical movements into practical investment policies, they need to be predictable. There is some evidence that this is indeed the case, and that the persistence in real estate return series allows profitable tactical allocation policies, even after adjusting for transaction costs.[10] Nevertheless, this has not been tested internationally. Most of the available data is backward-looking, providing a snapshot of situations at various points of time. This may be suggestive of the future direction, but does not really make the market predictable. In that respect, the fact that these cycle snapshots are sometimes called property "clocks" is misleading, since the essence of a clock is its perfect predictability.

---

[9] See Eichholtz and Lindenthal (2012).

[10] Key and Marcato (2005) looked at British private real estate return series and showed that active momentum strategies based on time series information generated from these series are profitable, even allowing for the additional transaction costs associated with these approaches. They do assume instantaneous transactions, which may not be very realistic for private real estate markets.

The international dimension makes matters even more difficult. Opportunistic international property funds investing in, for example, Central and Eastern Europe and in Asian markets like India, have been popular with investors for a while, but generally have not seemed to be very successful in terms of performance. Predicting property markets is hard, and this illustrates that it is even more difficult to make good predictions for someone who is located far away. There is the option of paying a local expert to provide knowledge about the market, but it is questionable whether local players with genuine knowledge will pass it on, rather than keeping it to use for their own benefit. After all, foreign investors are easy to exploit. Advisors may share knowledge for a fee, but how can the foreign investor be sure of the quality of the knowledge?

24.2.2 International Diversification

In considering cyclical rationales for going abroad, we have concluded that markets are not very predictable, and even if they are, acting on the predictions is very difficult, especially for foreign investors. But we do know that markets act in nonsynchronous ways, and this can still be used for diversification. Intuition and straight economic reasoning support this, as diversification is the creation of exposure to different aspects of the economy in such a way that if one part goes down, the other parts still provide protection. Creating exposure to different parts of the property market and different economies provides diversification because business cycles are not synchronous but move out of phase. Countries also have different economic bases, with for example the Netherlands almost entirely a service economy, South Korea a very strong industrial economy, Canada a mining and agriculture economy, and the United States a big mixed economy. Exposure to different economies also provides diversification via exposure to different economic bases and thus reduces risk. Besides that, supply is partly driven by local circumstances such as capital availability and the interest rate, and these vary from country to country as well.

The effect of diversification can be measured by looking at **correlations**. If the fundamentals driving property returns—like GDP growth, inflation, and interest rates—show low international correlations, this is likely to translate into weakly correlated property markets, and therefore strong diversification potential. To take a look at that, we have calculated correlations for these fundamentals across a number of important economies and property markets, based on annual data going back to the mid-1980s. The resulting international correlation matrices are depicted in Exhibit 24-6. These numbers look promising for international diversification potential, as the correlations are generally low. For example, the correlations between the Euro-area's GDP growth and that of the other economies are negative or close to zero, with the exception of the United States and Japan. Correlations with and among emerging economies tend to be lower than those between mature ones, and that also holds for interest rates and inflation. In short, the fundamentals suggest strong diversification potential, and that is clearly visible in the timing of property cycles across the continents. These show phase variability: there are markets to be found in any phase of the cycle whenever a snapshot is taken, and this holds for all property sectors.

Additionally, rental cash flows and their volatility are driven by local market institutions such as rental contracts. In the Netherlands, for example, rental contracts are linked to inflation, partially protecting an office landlord from inflation risk, whereas in other countries, that's not so. But there, retail rental contracts may be linked to turnover, directly linking the investor to consumer confidence and consumer spending. As such practices differ across countries, this creates diversification. The international differences in rental contracts provide diversification benefits through different cash flow streams and risk exposures, as Exhibit 24-7 shows.

Similarly, zoning rules vary, with strong investor protection from strict zoning rules seen in some countries and regions, but paired with less growth, and less zoning protection but more growth in other countries like Poland or China or the United States. Diversification across these can also create a more stable and more predictable return.

Panel A: Correlation Matrix Real GDP % Change

	Argentina	Australia	Brazil	India	Turkey	Indonesia	China	Eurozone	Japan
Australia	−0.28								
Brazil	0.33	0.23							
India	0.13	0.24	0.09						
Turkey	0.29	−0.01	0.22	0.10					
Indonesia	0.05	−0.34	0.18	−0.06	0.19				
China	0.55	0.23	0.45	0.22	0.14	0.11			
Eurozone	0.09	0.20	0.07	−0.11	0.27	0.01	−0.10		
Japan	0.05	0.12	0.10	−0.07	0.41	0.43	−0.04	0.74	
United States	0.02	0.62	0.17	0.02	0.32	−0.20	0.10	0.70	0.53

Panel B: Correlation Matrix CPI Annual % Change

	Argentina	Australia	Brazil	India	Turkey	Indonesia	China	Eurozone	Japan
Australia	0.43								
Brazil	0.56	0.12							
India	−0.10	−0.10	0.07						
Turkey	0.08	−0.07	0.32	0.18					
Indonesia	−0.08	−0.29	−0.12	0.11	0.17				
China	−0.02	0.15	0.55	0.01	0.41	−0.21			
Eurozone	0.72	0.11	0.79	0.28	0.60	−0.02	0.28		
Japan	0.52	0.23	0.41	0.21	0.35	−0.01	0.19	0.67	
United States	0.56	0.51	0.36	−0.11	0.16	−0.20	0.21	0.51	0.66

Panel C: Correlation Matrix Short Term Interest Rate

	Argentina	Australia	Brazil	India	Turkey	Indonesia	China	Eurozone	Japan
Australia	0.38								
Brazil	0.14	0.35							
India	0.46	0.29	0.18						
Turkey	−0.12	0.03	0.03	−0.10					
Indonesia	0.09	0.27	0.20	0.42	−0.05				
China	0.38	0.60	0.63	0.44	0.07	0.28			
Eurozone	0.62	0.51	0.14	0.58	−0.34	0.29	0.36		
Japan	0.38	0.20	−0.12	0.46	−0.24	0.09	0.25	0.55	
United States	0.25	0.69	0.35	−0.01	0.00	0.02	0.49	0.33	0.02

EXHIBIT 24-6 International Correlations of Selected Market Fundamentals across Economies

Source: Authors' calculations based on Thompson Datastream.

There are also theoretical underpinnings to the idea of international diversification. Chapter 21 discussed modern portfolio theory and the concept of the efficient frontier, showing how diversification can enable an investor to reach for a higher expected return with a given level of risk, or a lower risk with a given expected return. The efficient frontier shown

Country	Lease Length	Right to Renew	Rent Reviews		Indexation Basis	
			Period	Basis	Period	Basis
Asia-Pacific						
Australia	Indef. / 3–10 years	Varies	Varies	Varies	Annual	COL
China	2–3 years	Yes	Expiry	Market	N/A	N/A
Hong Kong	2–6 years	No	2–3 years	Market	N/A	N/A
India	3–9 years	Yes	3 years	Market	N/A	N/A
Japan	2–5 years	Varies	6 months prior to lease expiration	Varies	N/A	N/A
Korea	1–2 years	Yes	1–3 years	Market	N/A	N/A
Singapore	2–3 years	Yes	2–3 years	Market	N/A	N/A
Americas						
Argentina	3/5/7/10 years	Not guarantee	2–3 years	CPI	Annual	CPI
Brazil	3 years	Negotiable	End of term	Market	Annual	CPI
Canada	1/3/5 years	Negotiable	End of term	Market	Annual	CPI or specific amount
Mexico	3–10 years	Negotiable	Annual	CPI	Annual	CPI
United States	3–5 years	Negotiable	N/A	Market	Annual	CPI or specific amount
Europe						
France	3/6/9 years	Yes	Expiry	Market	3 times per year or annual	Construction cost
Germany	5–10 years	No	varies	CPI	Annual	CPI
Netherlands	5–10 years	Yes	5–10 years	Market	Annual	COL
Poland	3–7 years; 10 years max	Yes	N/A	N/A	Annual	CPI
Russia	3–5 years	No	6 months–1 year	Varies	N/A	Varies
Spain	1–25 years	Yes	Negotiable	Market	Annual	COL (ipc)
Turkey	1–5 years	No	N/A	N/A	Annual	CPI
United Kingdom	Up to 25 years	Yes	5 years	Market (upwards only)	N/A	N/A

EXHIBIT 24-7 Rental Contract Types in Property Markets across the Globe

in that chapter represented the best possible portfolios in the home market. The question is how the position and shape of the efficient frontier would be affected by going international. Exhibit 24-8 provides a graph of the national and global efficient frontiers. When we look at the global market, we find that the global efficient frontier dominates the national frontier, providing less risk and higher returns. A bigger universe to choose from means greater diversity, so the correlations are lower and the risk is reduced, hence the lower risk of the minimum variance portfolio. As well, it will be possible for a U.S. investor to find a market with higher expected return—and higher associated risk—than would be possible in the American market alone, hence the higher expected returns at the right side of the frontier. Essentially, picking from a larger investment universe provides more diversity, more potential on the upside and more protection on the downside. As a result,

EXHIBIT 24-8 Domestic versus Global Efficient Frontier

© OnCourse Learning

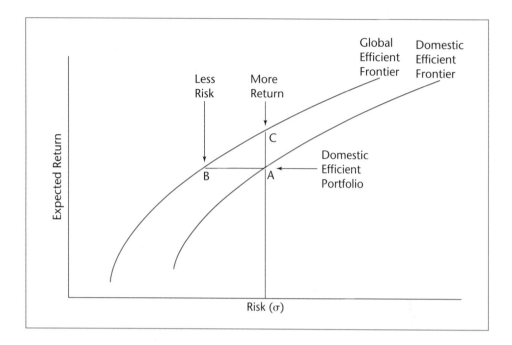

the investor holding domestic portfolio A can reduce his risk by going to international portfolio B or improve his expected return by going to international portfolio C. He can also aim for a combination of these two goals by choosing a portfolio between points B and C on the efficient frontier.

Chapter 22 showed that the risk of an investment can be split in two parts: market risk and specific risk. The more assets and diversification, the lower the risk. If the universe selected from is limited to the local market, the total risk can be reduced only to some extent. But if the market is widened to the global universe, this provides more diversity and more diversification potential. So in a typical situation, the global market risk will be lower than the domestic market risk. A downward shift of market risk can be achieved through an increased universe of assets, as illustrated in Exhibit 24-9. This is not true at any point in time for any market, but holds generally, for a long-run investor. This means it is possible to diversify away a greater part of the total risk and run less risk for a given return. On these grounds, one could argue that all investors should be international.

Looking at Exhibit 24-9, one would be tempted to conclude that the main conclusion from the one-country CAPM could be easily extrapolated to a global setting and that all investors should hold the same **global market portfolio**. However, this is not necessarily the case. The decisive question here is whether capital markets are internationally integrated or segmented. If assets are priced in integrated markets, expected returns will be in accordance to the global systematic risk as depicted in the lower horizontal line in Exhibit 24-9. If, on the other hand, assets are priced in segmented markets, their returns will be in line with the systematic risk of their domestic market. Since this is generally higher, the expected return will be higher as well. This implies that an investor who is able to avoid the cause of this market segmentation will enjoy special benefits from international diversification.

So, the question is whether international asset markets are integrated or segmented. For stocks, the evidence points into the direction of increasing integration, and for the publicly listed real estate market, the same has been documented.[11] But it is not likely that private real estate markets are as integrated as their public counterparts. Direct legal barriers to foreign real estate ownership, and more indirect informational barriers putting international

---

[11]Bardhan, Edelstein and Tsang (2008) show that increasing international openness of the real estate markets leads to lower excess returns relative to the risk-free rate, even though this openness may also increase rents and asset prices.

EXHIBIT 24-9 Domestic and Global Market Risk

© OnCourse Learning

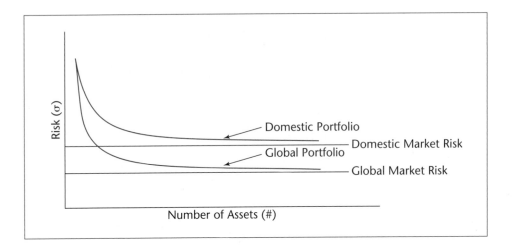

investors at a disadvantage still exist, allowing sustained international price discrepancies. But as noted in the previous sections, markets are slowly becoming more transparent, and foreign ownership restrictions are gradually weakening, so price discrepancies will probably diminish over time.

From a theoretical asset pricing perspective, the difference between a country and the world is that a country has only one currency, while the world has many. The difference between the International Asset Pricing Model (IAPM) and the traditional single-country CAPM discussed in Chapter 22 therefore has to do with currency effects. The IAPM starts with the assumption that investors care about risk and return expressed *in their own currency.* This seems reasonable. Besides that, two more conditions are required: purchasing power parity holds and investors all have the same consumption basket, so inflation is measured the same way in all countries. All assumptions of the single-country CAPM are also applicable to the IAPM. If these assumptions are valid, the outcome of the IAPM as a prescription of what investors should optimally do is very much in line with that of the single-country CAPM: investors should hold a portfolio consisting of risk-free bonds denominated in their own currency and the world market portfolio, optimally hedged against foreign currency risk. In other words, the separation theorem also holds for the IAPM. However, the empirical problems associated with the single-country CAPM are also relevant for the IAPM, and probably even more so. Holding the global market portfolio is even more difficult than it is to hold the home-country market portfolio, especially when it involves private markets—as is still predominantly the case for real estate. As with the single-country CAPM, beta does not explain international return differences very well, and especially financial distress seems not to be captured well by the standard IAPM.[12] But that is no reason to discard the model altogether. Global beta may not be the whole story when it comes to explaining asset returns on an international level, but it is a big part of the story, just like the beta of the single-country CAPM. Additional risk factors probably should be incorporated into the model.

The empirical evidence in the literature regarding international diversification is mostly supportive. The diversification argument critically depends on international correlations, on the question of how synchronized different markets behave. Thus, if correlations are high, the diversification argument is weak, but if they are low, it is strong. Generally, researchers find that international correlations are low: the correlations between real estate markets may be even lower than those between stock and bond markets. This would suggest a clear argument for international investment in real estate, stronger even than for international investment in stocks and bonds. This holds especially when looking at the global universe of property investment opportunities. Within Europe, on the other hand, correlations are quite

---

[12]Ling and Naranjo (2002) show that a global market beta is a significant driver of expected returns on listed property companies and Bond, Karolyi and Sanders (2003) extend this property share research in a multifactor framework.

high, nearly as high as across the regions within the United States. But across Europe, North America and the Far East, correlations are low.[13] The evidence is not all supportive of international real estate diversification, though. Some authors find a dominant global factor driving real estate markets—both public and private—suggesting the international diversification effect is not so great. Others find increasing international integration between real estate markets.[14] However, looking at the body of empirical evidence regarding this matter, it is probably safe to say that international diversification in real estate portfolios is a good idea.

Reviewing the case for international diversification, it is clear that the diversification effect depends on the correlations between international real estate markets. So the question is how stable these correlations are. Unfortunately, they are not stable at all; they tend to move around, even over short horizons. That would probably be acceptable if the correlations merely fluctuated up and down, but if they move in a structural way against the investor, this is a problem. If the correlation would start low and then move in the direction of one, the whole diversification effect would disappear.

At first sight, one might expect globalization and capital market integration to mean that correlations are high and the diversification effect is low. However, pure globalization is not actually what's happening; instead, there is a trend towards regionalization. Continental factors are important and actually increasing in importance. Within the regional blocs, correlations are going up but between regions, they are not. The most defined regional blocs are North America and Europe, while within Asia, the same effect can be seen but it is weaker: correlations are going up in a far weaker way than in Europe and the Americas.

The second question is whether the low correlation is there when it is needed. Diversification is essentially a form of risk management. So when some markets are going down very rapidly, an investor wants to be protected by the others. But in practice, correlations tend to go up in times of crisis, which is when you most need them to be low. Ample evidence shows this effect for stocks and bonds, but in real estate, the correlation increases in times of crisis appear to be somewhat less pronounced. So the diversification effect in real estate is weaker in times of crisis, but still favorable compared to other asset classes. Finally, all of this depends on the investment horizon. If it is long enough, the investor can simply wait out the higher correlations in a crisis, making sure to have a sound international real estate position, with exposure to strong economies and demographics.

24.2.3 Managerial Considerations

The third possible rationale for going international consists of managerial considerations, like exporting management expertise and servicing global customers. To start with the former, it seems obvious that the know-how in real estate investment management built up by investment managers in the mature property markets has a value, and could be exported to emerging markets in Asia and Central and Eastern Europe, for example. With their skills at managing real estate portfolios and developing projects, one would think they could carry out projects that a local player might not be able to do with the same degree of success. Unfortunately, an advantage in know-how in the financial markets is inclined to evaporate rapidly, especially in view of international labor markets and the international market for higher education. Those working for a U.S. investor can also work for a local player and come up with the same projects. Without natural monopolies, advantages in know-how quickly disappear as knowledge is dispersed.

Another question is, how valuable is know-how in general in property investment? Publicly listed property investment companies are sometimes priced at a premium to net asset value—the value of the assets minus the debt and thus the tangible assets in the company.

---

[13]Such supporting evidence has been put forward among others by Eichholtz (1996), Conover, Friday and Sirmans (2002), Hoesli, Lekander and Witkiewicz (2003), De Wit (2010), Liow (2010), and Kroencke and Schindler (2012). The evidence shows that international correlations are relatively low, and especially so across continents and economic blocs. This results in significant benefits from international investment.

[14]Examples are Goetzman and Wachter (2001) and Ling and Naranjo (2002). Good literature reviews can be found in Sirmans and Worzala (2003a and 2003b). Recent evidence for increasing integration can be found in Yunus (2009).

But more often they are priced at a discount, suggesting that the market does not perceive management as a value creator. This does not say much for the value of know-how, and if it does not have much value, there is not much to export and the whole argument collapses. It would seem evident that there is know-how that is important in property development, but even that management premium is doubtful, as recent research suggests that only the land contracts in development have value, and not the management. It would appear that management in real estate companies in general is more or less without value.

The other managerial argument for becoming an international property investor is to follow one's customers. As corporations become more global, so too do the companies that service them. Property investors are part of the business services community. If corporations centralize their global purchasing of services, as they have generally done with accountancy and banking, for example, then it makes sense for the service providers to have the same global footprint as their clients.

To judge the strength of this argument for international property investment, two issues need consideration. The first is how international the property users really are, and the second is how central the corporate real estate decisions are made within these organizations. Concerning the first issue, it is likely that the sector in which the company operates plays a role. For example, the distribution and logistics industry is a global business. That means it makes sense that property companies providing space to that sector are global as well. The American firm ProLogis is a prime example of this strategy, and seems to be doing well.

Retailing is not that international: hardly any of the great American retail chains has successfully set foot in Asia or Europe, and vice versa. However, retail seems to have become more international in the last decade. True global retail formulas are still rare, but European chains, traditionally confined to their own country, are branching out to other European countries. As result, the property companies servicing them, like Rodamco and Corio, are becoming pan-European as well.

The last two main institutional property types, offices and multifamily housing, are even less international than the retail sector. For offices, this may have something to do with a seeming lack of global space occupancy decisions among office users. For housing, demand is simply not international, and likely to remain so. In short, the power of the "follow your customers" argument depends on the property type, but is generally not very strong.

24.2.4 Obstacles to International Property Investment

Having reviewed the advantages and attractions of international real estate investments, we should now consider the disadvantages and obstacles involved. Here, we shall look particularly closely at the costs of investing abroad, including transaction costs and a key element, information costs, where the remote investor is at a major disadvantage. Liquidity is even more of a problem for the international than for the local investor, and this is also true of political risks. Political risks are in any case higher for real estate than for virtually any other asset, as real estate and land is often considered part of the national heritage and therefore emotionally and politically sensitive. Foreign investors are more vulnerable, with their weak political clout. Other obstacles can include unfair laws and even corruption, while in general, the low liquidity of directly held real estate assets makes all these obstacles and risks harder to escape and manage.

One obvious cost disadvantage, particularly for the U.S. investor, relates to property **transaction costs** abroad. In the United States, property transfer tax, for example, scarcely exists, but in many other countries, it is quite high, particularly in countries like Spain (7 percent), Australia (5.5 percent), Korea (4.6 percent), France (5.1 percent) and Brazil (up to 4 percent). Exhibit 24-10 provides information regarding transaction costs for selected international property markets. Besides transfer taxes, investors are faced with agents' fees and legal fees. Agents' fees are also high, while legal fees vary widely. This means the transaction costs of going international in real estate are both high and variable. Total costs for selling a property in countries like France, Brazil, and Spain, for example, will add up to about 10 percent. So investing abroad will either require a fantastic timing strategy or a long-term commitment, in order to recoup these extra costs (or else an indirect approach, such as using public markets or derivatives).

Country	Transfer Tax	Agent's Fees	Legal Fees
Asia-Pacific			
Australia	5.50%	2.50%	0.5–1%
China	1.50%	1.0–2.0% (1–2 Months)	Varies
Hong Kong	0.01–3.75%	1.0%*	Varies
India	6–8%	2%	Varies
Japan	0%	2–3%†	Varies
Korea	Varies (Seller) / 4.6% (Buyer)	1–2%	Varies
Singapore	3% minus $5400‡	1–2%†	Varies
Americas			
Argentina	2.50%	5%§	By Agreement
Brazil	Up to 5%	5–7%	5%
Canada	Varies by Province	1.5–4%	By Agreement
Mexico	2%	5%	By Agreement
United States	Varies by State	1–6%	By Agreement
Europe			
France	5.09%	1–4%	0.9–1.5%
Germany	3.5–4.5%	1–6%	1.50%
Netherlands	6%	1.25–2%	0.25–0.5%
Poland	2%	1–4%	By Agreement
Russia	Nominal	1–3%	By Agreement
Spain	7 or 16% VAT	2–5%	By Agreement
Turkey	1%	1–3%	By Agreement
United Kingdom	4% over £500,000	1%	0.50%

*Both buyer and seller pay (B/S)
†Paid by seller/buyer (PBS/B)
†Paid by buyer (PBB)
§Buyer and seller split the fee equally (50/50)

EXHIBIT 24-10 Transaction Costs in Selected Private Real Estate Markets

Source: NAIdirect.com.

However, the major issue here is **information costs**. These are extremely important in private real estate markets. There is overwhelming academic evidence showing that the public stock markets are mostly efficient in an information sense, implying that the available and relevant information is reflected in asset prices. Having access to information then becomes meaningless, because the information is already incorporated in the prices, and it is not possible to outperform on that basis. This may sound disappointing, but the flip side of the argument is that it not possible to underperform either, at least not due to a lack of information. In such markets, where all assets are fairly priced, it is safe for even completely uninformed investors to make big bets. They only have to make sure they are properly diversified. This, of course, is great news especially for international investors, since they are likely to be the underinformed parties in any market.

Private real estate markets, on the other hand, do not fit this ideal model, and are not efficient at incorporating new information in asset prices. Chapter 12 already discussed the investment implications of this inefficiency, including the danger of doing a bad deal: paying too much, or receiving too little, and doing that in a consistent way. So in the private real estate markets, having access to information probably is a key driver of performance. It is possible to beat the market consistently, and also to be beaten by it consistently, depending on information or the lack of it. It is important to note here that being informed does not accord with the Hamlet principle of "to be or not to be." Rather, it is a matter of degree. Players in domestic real estate markets probably have different degrees of market information, but it is likely that foreign investors are generally badly informed relative to most local investors. Logically, if there are both local and international investors in the market, the local investors will be the insiders, already holding the vital information, while the international investors are more likely to be outsiders without this information. If this is so, it should be reflected in performance.

There is relatively little research providing firm evidence, but the two existing studies do indeed show that this inefficiency issue is an important driver of performance in international real estate markets.[15] Both studies compared the performance of listed property companies holding an international portfolio of private real estate with the performance of property companies investing only in their domestic market. In order to separate the performance effect of information from allocation effects, they looked at the country allocation of each international real estate company for every year, and then constructed a mimicking portfolio of domestic real estate companies with the same country allocation. This was done for every year and every international property company, after which a return index was calculated for each mimicking portfolio. They then aggregated these mimicking indices for the individual companies into one overall index, constructed of local real estate companies with precisely the same portfolio composition as the internationals, to compare the performance of the overall mimicking index with the performance of the index for the internationals, thus eliminating the allocation effect and isolating the information effect. Overall, these two studies cover the period from the mid-1980s to 2007.

What emerges is that international property companies underperform their mimicking index of domestic investors. The difference in return is substantial, at 2.7 percent a year, and this is more or less consistent over time, applying even for subperiods. Only during the last few years does this outperformance of the local investors decrease, which may be related to the increasing international transparency of property markets we have been discussing before.

This strongly suggests that information costs are indeed important performance drivers for international real estate investors. However, it should be noted that this reflected the average underperformance of the universe of international property companies. Within that universe, there were also companies that outperformed their benchmark. The results therefore suggest that information costs make it very difficult to perform well in foreign markets, but that it is not impossible.

The information costs can come in two varieties, both leading to underperformance. The first is that investors do not have the necessary information and therefore make mistakes. They buy lemons; they pay too much when they buy and get too little when they sell. Alternatively, they could try to solve the problem by buying information, for example from local brokers, or by establishing local offices and employing local people. However, that would simply translate the cost of the information disadvantage into the payment of fees and salaries, likewise eroding the return. In any event, these information costs imply that diversification, dubbed as the only free lunch in financial markets, is no longer free.

Along with problems of costs and liquidity, there are specific risks attached to international real estate investment. These can be grouped as political, economic and currency risks. **Political risk** looms larger in real estate than in any other asset class, with the possible exception of art, especially for foreign investors. This is because real estate and land are often considered part of the national heritage. Strong national emotions are then involved. For example, in the late 1980s, when Japanese investors were buying up companies in the United States, the Japanese acquisition of the Rockefeller Center caused more furor than any other transaction at the time. These emotions can provide political support for continuous impediments to foreign real estate ownership. Switzerland is an example of a market nearly inaccessible for foreign real estate investors, and there can be similar ownership problems in Central and Eastern Europe. In China, ownership of land and buildings is still a serious

---

[15]See Eichholtz, Koedijk and Schweitzer (2001), and Eichholtz, Gugler and Kok (2011).

problem, heavily disfavoring foreign investors. Although there may be ways around these types of problems, they are sure to be expensive. There may also be impediments to repatriation of profits from foreign direct investments including direct real estate, wiping out any incentive to invest. Although these issues are gradually becoming less important, especially within trading blocs, this process will take a long time.

In the case of the possible problem of double taxation, this is disappearing more rapidly as more and more tax treaties are concluded and these generally aim to eliminate double taxation.

Besides political risk at a national level, real estate markets are also vulnerable to local politics. In all real estate markets, local government in particular will be extensively involved in matters such as zoning and tenant protection. This will be a far-reaching and structural involvement; local government is not going to go away. Foreign real estate investors are far more vulnerable because of their weak political clout, especially without local partners. They do not represent any voters or contribute funds to election campaigns, nor are they big employers, missing even the political clout other foreign direct investors often have.

Here the information issue resurfaces. One of the big drivers of real estate performance is land use, and the remote investor is not aware of what is cooking politically, either at the level of central government, or at City Hall. The home market investors, on the other hand, will have a much better chance of knowing what is currently being discussed in the corridors of power and what may happen to rules and regulations in the period to come. Land could be changed from industrial to commercial use or from pasture to housing, providing highly profitable opportunities to some, and possible risks to others. To avail of these, the investor needs to be a household name at City Hall, but this is all but impossible for the remote investor, who may not even speak the local language. Besides that, there may also be specific unfair laws against foreign ownership, or laws may be changed against foreign ownership without proper notice to the foreign investor.

Economic risk is partly diversified away by foreign investment, but foreign economies may in themselves be more volatile than the domestic market, especially if the domestic market is mature and the targeted markets emerging. In that case, the higher returns expected in these markets will be accompanied by higher risks, and the investor will move further to the right side of the efficient frontier.

Investors will also be exposed to a **currency risk** if they go abroad, and this could be far bigger than the property risk: volatility in the Eurozone and American property markets, for example, has been lower than the volatility of the euro-dollar exchange rate. In the long run, this is likely to change, due to the general tendency for countries to merge into blocs. The European trade bloc has gone all the way by merging its currencies into the Euro. Although the 2011–2012 travails of the Euro countries do not exactly provide a shining example of how to run a common currency, it is still likely that other regions will also move to link their currencies together. This does not mean that currency risk between blocs will go down, but that it will go down within those blocs, provided these currency links are properly managed.

To end this section, we need to deal with **liquidity**. Always a problem in property markets, but getting more important in far-away markets because the investor will be last in line with the local broker, and will be less successful at monitoring his performance. Especially when pursuing an active trading strategy, this may be problematic. It will be difficult to get into a distant market in times of a boom, as the local people will have seen all the good deals and the international investor is likely to be left with the ones that everyone else has smelled at and walked away from. For example, selling offices in New York when the market is at the top of the cycle to move to London where it is at the bottom may take some time, especially if other investors have similar expectations about the New York market. By this time, London may have moved into a boom with the investor winding up buying near the top of the market instead of the bottom. It will be equally difficult to get out of the market when it turns. The low liquidity of real estate makes the political and economic risks harder to escape. And even if a foreign investor sees economic hardship for the host country on the horizon, he may not be able to liquidate his holdings in time to avoid it.

Some of these risks and obstacles are diminishing in importance through increasing transparency, while others are inherent to international real estate investment. In that case, the international investor either must develop a strategy dealing with these issues, or retreat to the domestic market. The next section will introduce you to some such international investment strategies.

24.3 Developing and Implementing International Real Estate Strategies

Given all the obstacles and risks involved in international investment, how can an investor achieve a satisfactory performance? A successful strategy for international real estate will take advantage of the benefits, while avoiding as far as possible the obstacles and risks: this is effectively the definition of strategy. The way to do this is to determine the key obstacles and risks that are more cumbersome for international than for domestic players, and draw up a strategy to deal with them. They will include information costs, monitoring costs, currency risks, and political risks plus the extra problem of liquidity. The first important resource that can overcome many of these problems is the global property share market. REITs and other listed property companies are mostly local specialists, focusing on their own country. The first question to answer is, to what extent do they overcome the obstacles and risks we have described and what role can investing in REITs play in an international strategy. We can then draw up our strategy, including the question of allocation, and introduce the "home market" concept.

24.3.1 Public Real Estate Investment

To establish how the global REIT market can help the international real estate investor, we will review the obstacles to international investment we have described, and see how REITs measure up. On the costs side, transactions costs for real estate shares (and for shares in general) are low and getting lower. And since the property share market is more or less efficient, information costs are low or nonexistent. Anybody could make a well-informed property share deal in, say, Hong Kong by simply buying shares on the local stock exchange. But if they wanted to buy a private property in Hong Kong, this would be a totally different matter. Listed property companies enable uninformed investors to make well-informed foreign property bets. To make that situation even better, property companies are generally improving their reporting quality, partly forced in that direction by industry associations, but also by accounting rules.

As well, monitoring a foreign real estate portfolio is easy, as investors can free-ride on the local co-shareholders and public information; there will be no need to rush over to Hong Kong to look at your property. Finally, impediments to foreign ownership scarcely arise in the REIT market, as they are simply shares.

Turning to liquidity, this is far better than for direct real estate holdings and comparable to shares in companies of similar size.[16] Besides that, there is a nonlinear relationship between size and liquidity, and since listed property companies are generally growing in market capitalization, their liquidity will go up even more. Discrimination against the foreigner in entering or exiting the market is not likely for listed real estate.

While the economic risk of public property investments is as large as for direct investment, greater liquidity means that investors are better able to defend themselves by withdrawing from the market. The same goes for political risk, with the extra advantage that the manager of the local property company will have the contacts and political clout that the remote direct property investor lacks. Finally, problems relating to regulation will largely disappear, as foreign ownership constraints and barriers to repatriation of foreign-earned returns are usually small or nonexistent for stocks.

In short, the obstacles to international property investment discussed in the preceding section are either not relevant or less important for listed property companies, so they look like an ideal investment channel for global property investors. Indeed, Dutch institutional property investors, who have a long—and sometimes painful—international experience, have exchanged their international direct portfolios almost fully for portfolios consisting of the shares of locally operating property companies in the decades preceding 2012. This has

---

[16]See Brounen, Eichholtz and Ling (2009).

THE DO'S AND DON'TS OF CURRENCY RISK MANAGEMENT

A property investor who crosses the border is faced with currency risk, no matter whether his holdings or public or private. The dollar value of foreign property holdings may go down independently of real estate market movements in the host country, just because the local currency weakened against the dollar. International property investors have to deal with this risk. Over time, different techniques and policies have been suggested to accomplish this.

In the 1970s, when the global regime of fixed currencies was abolished, economists and econometricians aimed to predict currency movements. These predictions could then supposedly be used by corporations and investors as a basis for a currency policy. The idea was to hedge only when the foreign currencies were predicted to fall. However, abundant research since then has shown that currencies mostly follow a random walk, and that currency movements are hard, if not impossible, to predict.

In these circumstances, property investors who decide to run the currency risk if they expect exchange rates to move in their favor do not service their clients well, since they take on speculative positions in a market they probably do not know much about. Besides that, these currency bets take valuable management time, which could better be spent making property decisions. If currency movements are indeed unpredictable, then international property investors will have to hedge not at all or always, and should not make this decision dependent on expectations regarding currency movements.[1]

There are good arguments for not hedging at all. First, there are costs involved in hedging, as in any insurance product. The costs equal the forward premium, which varies across currencies and in time. Using options for currency hedging is even more expensive, since they cover the investor on the downside, while maintaining his exposure to the upside. Second, the international efficient frontier is not very strongly affected by the question of whether returns are calculated in the home currency (representing the unhedged situation) or in local currency (representing the hedged situation), especially in the long run. Lastly, in a broad international portfolio, covering many countries and currencies, the currency risk is partly diversified away.

On the other hand, the arguments for always hedging are also rather convincing, especially for real estate. First, currency risk does increase investment risk, especially for portfolios consisting of few countries, and even more so if the countries involved are emerging markets, which often have very volatile exchange rates. Second, institutional property investors are usually looking for a relatively modest risk-return profile, while currency returns can fluctuate rather strongly. For example, the volatility of the euro/dollar exchange rate has historically been much higher than the volatility of the property markets on either side of the Atlantic, so the targeted risk-return profile may well be thrown on its head because of the currency movements. Third, the development of deep and liquid currency derivatives markets in the last two decades has enabled investors to hedge rather cheaply and quickly.

An inexpensive and easy way to hedge a lot of currency risk is to acquire "natural" hedges though local leverage. For example, a property investor with a 40 percent overall leverage ratio could do all his borrowing at home, but from a currency hedging point of view, it would be far more clever to borrow locally and apply that same leverage ratio to each individual country in the portfolio. That way, the remaining currency exposure would only be as big as the equity position.

To hedge this equity currency exposure, an often-used technique is currency overlay, in which the portfolio is regarded in full and the currency diversification effects are included in the analysis. The investor then decides what percentage of the remaining exposure—after leverage and diversification—he wants to hedge. In effect, an overall risk-return trade-off is made for the currency exposure.

From a cost-benefit point of view, it is wise to concentrate one's hedging on the liquid currencies where possible. For example, the liquidity in the U.S. dollar/Swedish krona market is higher than in the Euro / Swedish krona market, translating in much lower bid-ask spreads. So for a Swedish investor who wants to hedge the currency risk on his euro-area real estate portfolio, it is cheaper to buy dollars for kronor, and subsequently buy euros for these dollars, than to buy euros directly. Likewise, a euro-area investor who wants to buy properties in New Zealand is also better off by going through the U.S. dollar than to buy New Zealand dollars directly. However, these bid-ask spreads change all the time, so the optimal route needs to be determined at the moment the hedge takes place.[2]

---

[1] In that respect, currency hedging is akin to fire insurance. Since it is impossible to predict if and when your house will burn down, you do not take out insurance on the basis of your expectations regarding this. People rarely regret having paid their insurance premium when their house failed to go down in flames.

[2] The three leading textbooks on international finance and investments are Sercu (2009), Solnik and McLeavey (2008), and Levi (2009). All three provide much more detailed advice about currency hedging. Sercu is the more analytical of the three. Solnik and McLeavy focus mostly on investments, and Levi is more concerned with international finance.

happened across the board, including some of the biggest investors like the APG, the pension fund for Dutch civil servants, but also smaller pension funds and life insurance companies. They have largely followed two investment approaches in the global listed market, using a more-or-less passive index tracking approach, or alternatively taking strategic stakes in selected property companies.

The proliferation of listed property companies has also spurred the development of the market for (international) mutual funds investing in their shares. These funds mainly cater to private investors and smaller institutions, and mostly invest in locally operating property companies, thus offering the benefit of one-stop shopping for investors who want to build up exposure to the global property share market.

24.3.2 Determining Country Allocation

For an investor who has decided that the global property share market is indeed the best way to build up international property exposure, a practical question is how to determine optimal portfolio weights. A number of ways have been put forward to accomplish that. The first way is to use modern portfolio theory to find optimally diversified international portfolios, the second is to track international index weights, and the third is to use weights based on GDP.

Using modern portfolio theory, a Markowitz framework or optimizer can be used to establish optimally diversified portfolios in the standard risk/return tradeoff. However, the theoretical basis for using that approach within the real estate portfolio is weak, and this approach also encounters a number of practical problems, like data availability. Studies using this approach have mostly been based on historical time series, and the resulting optimal portfolios were usually very period-specific, making them not very useful in practice. They also tend to deliver what are called corner solutions, which are often very time-dependent. For example, the model's optimal allocation for high risk/high return investors is usually to allocate 100 percent to the asset or country that happened to have the highest return and risk during the sample period. This is hardly a solution for international diversification.

The logical alternative is to track the composition of the global market using the market weight of the global index. In international equity investment, tracking indexes like the global MSCI Index is a widely accepted and frequently used approach. For property companies, such indices are available also: GPR, FTSE EPRA/NAREIT, and S&P Citigroup are leading examples.[17] But basing the portfolio weights on the index weights is liable to the coincidence that market weights are high in countries that happen to have a well-developed property share market. In Europe, for example, the United Kingdom pulls more than its weight in listed property shares, while Germany is underrepresented and in the Asia-Pacific region, the same is true for Australia, which has a dominant property share market, and a relatively small economy. Tracking a global index without making any adjustments for this will probably create unwanted specific risk.

The wisest solution, then, could be to use a combination of market index weights with GDP weights. Investors commonly possess an intuitive map of what the global market should look like, which is partly based on what the capital market looks like, but probably also partly based on what economies look like, for which GDP weighting can be used. Indices have been created in line with this idea, allowing international investors to measure their performance when choosing their international allocation this way.

24.3.3 The "Home Market" Concept

We have seen that all the obstacles to international real estate investment are much reduced or disappear in the case of investing in property companies. However, well-versed real estate investors with experience may have an information advantage in their home market, which could enable them to outperform in direct real estate.

Besides that, there is some concern regarding the diversification effect of listed property shares in the broader mixed-asset portfolio. The early empirical evidence concerning the performance of listed property companies showed that the correlations between property shares and common stock tended to be high, while those between property share returns and direct real estate returns were found to be low. In other words, property shares seemed to behave

---

[17]Serrano and Hoesli (2009) provide a very useful analysis of the available global property share indices.

more like stocks than like property, making them less attractive as a portfolio diversifier. Even though more recent empirical research results indicates that the correlations between property shares and common stock have decreased and seem to stabilize at lower levels, there exists no clear theoretical argument why this should be the case, so it may be just a temporary statistical fluke.[18] This is another argument to keep at least part of the real estate portfolio invested in private property.

Given that direct property markets are inefficient, investors should concentrate their *direct property investments* on market(s) in which they have an information advantage: their **home market**. This does not necessarily need to be defined in a regional way. It could also be that they have expertise, information and valuable networks in a certain property type. So the home market for an investor could be logistics properties in Northern Europe, regional malls in the United States, or multitenant offices in South East Asia. It could also be defined in an even narrower sense, for example offices in Brussels, or conference centers in Singapore. However defined, the key criterion must always be the potential for consistent outperformance, driven by consistently better access to private information than the competition.

Deciding which markets can be considered true home markets in that sense is a difficult process, in which honesty is required, and ego needs to remain in check. After all, we all like to regard ourselves as potential outperformers. However, there is a simple line of thinking to help this process. The consistent outperformance you strive for will have to be accomplished at the expense of the consistent underperformers: the poor underinformed investors. So a home market can be defined as a market in which you can point out the consistent underperformers. If you cannot, you are not an insider, and you had better not become a direct investor in that market. In that respect, real estate investment is just like playing poker: at any poker table, there is a dummy, and if you cannot point him out, you know who it must be.

An important counterargument against this idea of concentrating the investments on the home market is of course diversification. The fact that information costs exist does not nullify the usefulness of spreading your risk internationally. It only means that there is a trade-off between the advantages of international diversification and the information costs this entails. The question, then, is what position an investor should choose on this trade-off.

The answer to that question depends on the nature of the investor. Let's first consider the intermediary investor, like a listed or unlisted property company. For such an investor, diversification does not add value, since the shareholders on whose behalf he is making investments can most likely diversify their holdings. That implies that the most sound investment strategy for an intermediary investor is full concentration on the home market, thereby enabling outperformance of the competition. Most REITs in the United States seem to do that, as they specialize in property types, and hardly invest abroad.

Nonetheless, where the diversification argument may not hold true for a property company, it will still be important for end-investors like pension funds, private investors or family trusts. These end-investors do not have shareholders who can diversify their exposure to them, so they have to diversify themselves. For such investors, it may still pay to determine a home market, or home markets, for the reasons given above. If they do, they should try to manage information costs with a true local presence in the home market(s), and build critical local mass to get access to the best deals and to the information flow required to outperform. This means an effective strategy in private real estate markets rules out covering too many markets. Unlike the intermediary investors, they should not stop there, though. The diversification requirement makes it wise to build up an international portfolio of listed and locally operating property companies to build up exposure outside the home markets. Alternatively, the end-investors may decide that diversification is more important than the potential for outperformance, and hold all real estate exposure through listed property companies. In that respect, it is useful to look at the experiences of the Dutch institutional property investors again. There, the larger institutions have indeed

---

[18]See Brounen and Eichholtz (2003), Newell (2003), and Hoesli and Oikarinen (2012) for international empirical analyses and more discussion.

held on to some of the private property portfolios in their home markets, mostly by putting them in nonlisted property vehicles. PGGM, the pension fund for the health care sector, for example, which has a long experience in the Dutch housing market, has only maintained private investments in that market. All other private real estate exposure has either been sold, or exchanged for stakes in listed property companies. The smaller institutions have mostly sold all of their private real estate holdings, and invest in listed property companies and unlisted property funds instead.

It is now time to broaden the view a bit, and look at other asset markets beside the real estate markets. The analysis in this section and the previous ones was fully focused on diversification issues within the real estate portfolio. But in Chapter 21, we argued that portfolio considerations should not be limited to real estate holdings alone, and should instead be taking the overall wealth portfolio of the investor into account. Following the same line of reasoning provides slightly different investment advice than the previous paragraph, since it is not clear whether a private real estate portfolio in the home market should be complemented with listed property shares or plain common stocks and bonds to reach on optimum on the trade-off between outperformance and diversification. To find the optimal portfolio besides the private real estate exposure in the home market(s), therefore, one has to take all public investment possibilities into account.

24.4 Chapter Summary

This chapter provided you with an introduction into the global real estate capital market. Our goal was to introduce you to the rationale for international investment in real estate, but also to the obstacles for doing that. We then gave some suggestions for international real estate investment strategies that make sense given the nature of real estate assets and markets.

The reasons for investing in real estate outside one's own country are threefold. First, there may be return opportunities abroad (structural or opportunistic) that are unattainable at home. Second, since global real estate markets move in nonsynchronous ways, there are diversification effects related to international investment. The third rationale for going international may be to export know-how in developing and/or managing real estate assets. However, going international can be cumbersome, due to low international liquidity, additional transaction and information costs, and new risks, like currency risk, political risk and economic risk.

These issues suggest that international real estate investment is a trade-off aimed at maximizing its potential gains, while managing the disadvantages as much as possible. Different types of investors will do that in different ways. End-investors, like private investors and pension funds, should aim for diversification, acquiring direct property exposure in a few markets they know well, and using listed and unlisted property companies besides stocks and bonds in other markets. Intermediate investors like property companies, for whom diversification does not add value, should focus on and aim for outperformance in their home market.

KEY TERMS

real estate investment trust (REIT)	international correlations	political risk
structural return opportunities	global market portfolio	economic risk
structural capital needs	transaction costs	currency risk
demographics	information costs	liquidity
cyclical return opportunities	informational inefficiencies	home market
international diversification	risks	

STUDY QUESTIONS

24.1. Why do real estate investors invest internationally?

24.2. How should an international property investor determine his country allocation?

24.3. In what respect is international property investment fundamentally different from international investment in listed stocks?

24.4. How can the global property share market help an international property investor?

24.5. Currency risk is an added risk factor in an international property portfolio. How should an investor deal with this risk?

24.6. Discuss the reluctance of institutional investors to invest internationally in real estate, considering risk exposure and the nature of informational (in)efficiency in the real estate asset market.

CHAPTER

25

DATA CHALLENGES IN MEASURING REAL ESTATE PERIODIC RETURNS

CHAPTER OUTLINE

LEARNING OBJECTIVES

After reading this chapter, you should understand:

⊃ The major types of errors that tend to be present in empirical real estate periodic return data.

⊃ The characteristic signs of such errors and the effects such errors have on analysis relevant to macro-level investment decision making.

⊃ The different ways in which it is conceptually possible to define real estate values and returns, the temporal relationship among these different definitions, and the relevance of different definitions for various types of practical decision problems.

⊃ The new price and return indexing innovations for tracking commercial property, including "repeat-sales" indices based directly on investors' actual experiences in the private property market.

I n Chapter 9, we introduced and defined the concept of periodic returns, or time series of holding period returns (HPRs). At frequent and crucial points throughout this book, we have used such returns, for real estate and other asset classes, in a variety of ways. For example, in Chapter 7, we compared the investment performance of the various asset classes, considering both risk and return, and to make such comparisons we used HPR series. In Chapter 11, real estate periodic returns were important in our analysis of real estate cost of capital. They were also important in our discussion of leverage in Chapter 13, and our discussion of the investment performance of commercial mortgages and their role in the overall investment portfolio in Chapter 19. In Chapters 21 and 22, periodic returns were the raw material for computing or estimating the expected returns, volatilities, and correlations that are necessary to apply modern portfolio theory and develop measures of risk and models of risk valuation and equilibrium asset pricing. Moreover, we will see in Chapter 26 that HPRs are fundamental to measuring and analyzing investment manager performance. In short, particularly (but not uniquely) at the macro-level, modern investment theory and practice absolutely *depend* on the basic data raw material represented by time-series of periodic returns.

The existence, reliability, and meaningfulness of such returns data are taken for granted in the securities industry. For stocks and bonds, the history of such data goes back to the early decades of the twentieth century. The nature of public exchange trading of securities makes it easy to observe and measure periodic returns reliably and precisely, even at frequencies as high as daily for many securities. The existence of such vast quantities of high-quality data is a gold mine for the science of financial economics, the likes of which is the envy of all branches of social science.

In the 1970s, real estate investment industry leaders realized that in order for the investment establishment to perceive private real estate with a degree of credibility and legitimacy approaching that of stocks and bonds, it was necessary to compute, compile, and disseminate series of real estate periodic returns. So, beginning in the 1970s, commercial property periodic returns have been reported and used in the investment industry. The "flagship" **NCREIF Property Index (NPI)** dates from the beginning of 1978, reporting quarterly total returns as well as income and appreciation components ever since, a history that now stretches over a third of a century.

At first, the real estate returns series were viewed skeptically by both academics and industry traditionalists, and their use was not widespread. Over time, they have gradually become better constructed, more useful, better understood, and more widely accepted and used. The 2000s have seen a flowering in the sources and types of commercial property returns data in the United States, as well as an extension of at least basic appraisal-based data in a number of other countries. As a result, in the United States as of 2012 the three major types or sources of commercial property returns time series data, at least for the capital returns or asset price changes that are most important, are (1) appraisal-based, (2) transactions-based, and (3) stock market-based. Each of these types of data has different strengths and weaknesses, and some can be applied in some situations but not in others. Thus, knowledge of all three of these data sources is an important part of the modern educated real estate investor's toolkit, and in this chapter we will introduce you to all three.

But first, it is important to recognize some of the unique issues with private real estate returns data, such as lag bias and statistical noise (and the trade-off between those two). Thus, the chapter will begin with the basics of commercial property returns measurement, including some consideration of valuation at both the disaggregate (individual property) level and the aggregate (collections of properties) level.

25.1 The Basics: Macro-Level Property Valuation

Although this chapter is about indices or time-series data on the periodic returns to populations or portfolios of many properties in the direct (private) real estate asset market, the fundamental data from which most such returns series are created are disaggregate, micro-level value indications of individual properties as of specific points in time. These individual valuations are aggregated or "averaged" to define a central tendency in the asset price change or return across the portfolio or population of properties or investors tracked by a given index. Therefore, before we consider aggregate returns, we must begin this chapter at a more fundamental level by building on concepts introduced first in Chapter 12, considering the valuation, or observation of value, of individual properties.

25.1.1 Transaction Noise and Appraisal Error

In Chapter 12, we noted that observable empirical real estate values are "noisy"—that is, imprecise indications of "true value." The primary empirical indication of value in the direct property market is, of course, the *transaction prices* of properties that actually sell within the

EXHIBIT 25-1 Buyer
and Seller Populations,
Reservation Price Frequency
Distributions
© OnCourse Learning

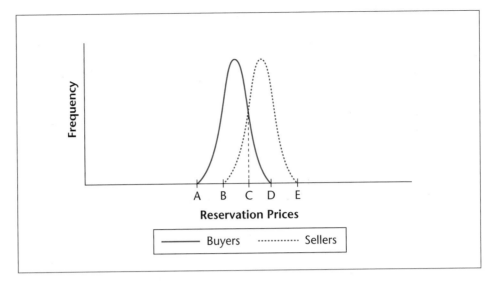

subject market or population of properties. But another important type of empirical value indication for properties is *appraised values* (or *appraisals*), estimates of specific properties' market values as of specified points in time made by professional real estate appraisers. But appraisals are only *estimates* of value, based themselves more fundamentally on transaction price indications.[1]

The key point made in Chapter 12 is that both of these types of empirical value indications contain "error" relative to the "true" *market value* of the properties, at least if we view this process in a statistical sense for developing aggregate indices of market returns. We now need to add nuance to this point, by noting that the **error** falls fundamentally into two major categories: purely *random error* (also known as *noise*) and *temporal lag bias*. Furthermore, in trying to design an optimal value estimation technique, there tends to be a natural trade-off between these two types of error. It is hard to reduce random error without increasing the lag bias, and it is hard to reduce the lag bias without increasing the random error.

To understand these fundamental points, recall the difference between market value and transaction price described in Chapter 12. Exhibit 25-1 reproduces the key picture from Chapter 12's Appendix 12A, showing overlapping reservation price distributions of potential buyers and sellers for some type or within some population of properties as of a given point in time.[2] The exhibit indicates that transactions in this market may occur in the overlap region where some buyers will have reservation prices at least as high as the reservation prices of some sellers, at prices ranging between values B and D. These prices will tend to be distributed around a value labeled C, which we described as the conceptual market value of the property type or the population of properties (e.g., adjusted for quality). Appendix 12A described how this value represents the classical economic concept of equilibrium value, or market-clearing price. We can think of the value C as representing the "true" value as of a

---

[1]The role of appraisal and the relationship between appraisals and transaction prices varies in specific circumstances, and also differs culturally from one country to another. The United States may represent a somewhat extreme case of market independence from appraisals: transaction prices tend to reflect the market directly, while appraisals do so indirectly by filtering transaction price evidence. In other countries where the appraisal profession is strong (such as the United Kingdom), there may be more influence of appraisals on the transaction prices, with a dual direction of causality in which the professional appraisers ("valuers") play a more independent role in helping to determine market values. This could result in there being less systematic difference between appraised values and transaction prices. (For some evidence of this, see Devaney and Diaz, 2011.) In some other countries, neither the appraisal profession nor the markets may be as well developed, and property exchanges may occur more rarely, with exchange prices governed by traditional formulaic value determinations. The primary professional organization governing the appraisal industry as it relates to most commercial and investment property in the United States is The Appraisal Institute. In the United Kingdom and some other countries, the Royal Institution of Chartered Surveyors (RICS) is the major governing body.

[2]Recall from Appendix 12A that the term "reservation price" refers to the private value at and above (below) which the potential seller (buyer) will stop searching or negotiating and agree to the transaction.

EXHIBIT 25-2 Theoretical Cross-Sectional Dispersion in Observable Value Indications

© OnCourse Learning

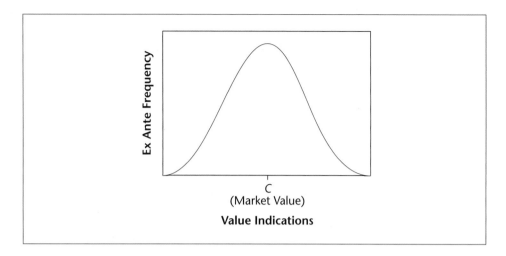

given point in time, with C being unobservable empirically. All we can observe are valuations drawn from the probability distribution around C in Exhibit 25-2.

If the empirical observations are actual transaction prices, the direct and fundamental indications of market value, then the difference between any given price observation and the unobservable true market value is referred to as *transaction price noise*, or *transaction price error*. By definition, this error will be unbiased (equally likely of being on the high side or on the low side), as long as we hold time constant, that is, assuming all the transaction price observations occur at the same time.

Property appraisals are also dispersed cross-sectionally around true market values as of any given point in time. If any two appraisers independently value the same property at the same time, they will almost certainly not make the same estimate of market value. At least one of them must be "wrong," in the sense that their valuation differs from the true market value of the subject property. In fact, both appraisers are probably "wrong" in this sense. The difference between a given empirical appraised value and the (unobservable true) market value is called *appraisal error*, although there is no implication that the appraiser has exhibited any incompetence, negligence, or impropriety.

Although appraised values are dispersed around the underlying true values, unlike transaction prices the appraised-value dispersion is not necessarily centered on the true value. In other words, appraised values may be biased as of any given time. Such bias may result from very rational and proper professional practice on the part of the appraiser, given the nature of the empirical information available in the real estate market. The major bias that is likely to exist that is of concern to us in the present context is that appraised values tend to lag in time behind true contemporaneous market values. This is referred to as temporal lag bias.[3]

25.1.2 A Simple Example of Temporal Lag Bias

Suppose you are thinking of selling a property you own, and you hire an appraiser to help you decide what price to sell it for. The appraiser offers you the following choice. She can give you a value estimate based on appraisal "Method A," in which the value estimate has a

---

[3]Normative and behavioral models consistent with the temporal-lag-bias hypothesis of appraisal have been put forth in the academic literature [e.g., Quan and Quigley (1991), Chinloy, Cho, and Megbolugbe (1997), Geltner and Ling (2006)]. Early quantitative treatments of appraisal lag (or "smoothing") include Brown (1985), and Blundell and Ward (1987). For articles describing empirical or clinical evidence of temporal lag bias, see for example, Chinloy et al. (1997), Diaz and Wolverton (1998), Hamilton and Clayton (1999), and Fisher and Geltner (2000). A survey of the literature is contained in Geltner, MacGregor, and Schwann (2003). It should also be noted that other types of appraisal bias besides temporal lag bias can be of concern in different contexts. For example, appraisers may be biased to provide a valuation that pleases their client, such as, a valuation high enough to help secure a loan that a borrower wants and/or a lender wants to provide. (Another typical context is to provide a valuation low enough to secure a reduction in property tax obligation.) Such agency bias is not the focus of the present chapter.

75 percent chance of being within 10 percent of the true market value of the property. But Method A contains some **temporal lag bias**, in that the expected (or most likely) value of the Method A appraisal is actually the true market value of the property six months ago. Thus, if true market values were, say, 3 percent lower six months ago, then Method A has a 3 percent bias on the low side. Alternatively, the appraiser can base her appraisal on "Method C," which will be unbiased in terms of being completely up to date (i.e., the appraisal is equally likely to be above or below the current true market value).[4] However, the Method C value estimate has only a 50 percent chance of being within 10 percent of the true market value of your property. An additional consideration is that the more precise but temporally biased Method A will provide you with more solid historical evidence explicitly document-ing the estimated value of your particular property. It will do this by providing you with more comparisons of your property with specific comparable sales transactions (known as "comps" in the appraisal field) that in the appraiser's judgment are particularly comparable to your property. The appraiser says she will charge you the same price for either method. Which would you prefer?

The most typical answer is Method A, in part because its greater precision (75 percent instead of 50 percent chance of being within 10 percent of the true value) will probably be more useful to your decision problem relating to the *single* individual property that is the subject of the appraisal, and in part because the greater specific documentation that method provides regarding your particular property can help you to persuade others of the value of the property. Because you control your own decision about the price at which you will actu-ally agree to sell your property, you may be less worried about the bias in Method A. You probably have some sense of the direction of the temporal bias and maybe even a vague sense of its magnitude, just from your familiarity with how the market has been changing over the past six months. And, of course, you will anyway try to sell the property for as high a price as you can, no matter what the appraiser says. In other words, the actual trans-action price you end up with will reflect the current market more than the appraiser's estimate.[5]

25.1.3 The Trade-Off between Noise and Lag

But now let's put ourselves in the shoes of the appraiser. Why did she have to offer you the choice between Method A and Method C. Why couldn't the most precise appraisal also be the least biased (most up-to-date)?

The answer to this question lies in the fundamental relationship between statistics, time, and the generation of empirical data. Recall from Appendix 12A that we can make more accurate inferences about property market value the more transaction price observations we have on which to base our estimate. Indeed, we said this reflects a fundamental law of statis-tical inference known as the **Square Root of n Rule**. The accuracy of our estimate will tend to be inversely proportional to the square root of the number of transaction-price indications of value that we can observe. If the appraiser can use six comps instead of just two, she can make an estimate of value that has $1/\sqrt{3}$ (or about 58 percent) as much error (because $6/2 = 3$). But comps are generated only when transactions actually occur, and transactions occur *through time*. In order to use six comps, the appraiser will have to reach three times as far back in time (on average).

---

[4]We're labeling it "Method C" instead of "Method B," because it is focused on the value "C" in the Exhibits, the unobservable but "true" market value.

[5]Conceptually, this is true *by definition*. We define the "market value" as of a given point in time as the mean of the distribution of potential transaction prices that could occur at that point in time. This does not imply that the trans-action prices (and hence the market value) will not also be subject to some extent to the same type of partial adjust-ment or sluggish incorporation of new information that causes the appraiser to lag the market (perhaps rationally). We already noted in section 12.2 of Chapter 12 (and raised the point again in Chapters 21 and 22) that real estate market values can have inertia and some degree of predictability due to lack of perfect informational efficiency in the market. The difference in this regard between the market values and the appraisals is one of degree, and as noted pre-viously, this degree may vary in different situations and culturally across different countries.

The tradition of professional appraisal is to appraise individual properties, using sales comps that are individually examined and considered for their relevance and appropriateness to the subject property. For appraisal of large-scale commercial and investment properties, which tend to be much more heterogeneous than houses, and to sell much less frequently, this tradition effectively limits the comps sample typically to only a few properties sold in the local market area. The selected comps are supposed to be very similar to the subject and whose differences from the subject are scrutinized and carefully considered. This approach considers unique, idiosyncratic features of the subject property, eliminating the most important potential source of purely random error. But the trade-off is that such comps are scarce in time, and the appraiser must therefore reach back relatively far in time.

Furthermore, appraisers tend to be conservative in adjusting for changes in market conditions, and rightly so. Such adjustments are subjective, and appraisers need to document their value estimations objectively.[6] In fact, statistical and cognitive theory both agree that it is rational to adjust one's prior opinions only partially in the face of new evidence that is less than definitive.[7] If the appraiser truly ignored all past value indications and considered only transactions that have occurred, say, within the past month, no matter how far removed or different from the subject property these transactions were, and no matter how few such transactions were (e.g., maybe there is only one, or none!), then she would probably be considered negligent by the standards of the appraisal profession. And indeed, such an appraisal would likely not be very accurate for the specific subject property being appraised.

25.1.4 The Difference between Aggregate and Disaggregate Valuation

Now let us return to our example of the appraiser who offers you the choice between the "Method A" and "Method C" appraisal. Suppose the purpose of the appraisal is no longer to help you decide on the price of a single specific property, but rather to help you obtain an *up-to-date* estimate of the *aggregate* value of a large portfolio of properties whose value is being tracked by an index, by combining this appraisal with similar appraisals done at the same time of all the other properties in the portfolio. Now which method would you choose?

In this case, if you answered Method C, the one that is *less accurate* (for the individual property appraisal), you would be correct! This is because the purely random error in Method C will be largely diversified away at the portfolio or index level, due to the rather powerful effect of the Square Root of n Rule in a large portfolio, where n is indeed a very large number. For example, if the portfolio contains 100 properties that are each being independently appraised each period, then the aggregate portfolio valuation relevant for index construction (made as the sum or arithmetic average across all of the individual property valuations) will contain only one-tenth $(1/\sqrt{100})$ the purely random error of the typical individual appraisals. By contrast, the temporal lag bias in Method A is systematic and will not diversify out of the portfolio valuation. The portfolio valuation will contain as much lag bias as the average individual property appraisal.

25.1.5 Summarizing Macro-Level Valuation Error

The preceding discussion of property valuation error can be summarized graphically in Exhibit 25-3. In the chart, the two axes represent the two types of error, arranged so that the farther out along the axes (away from the origin), the less the error (and the better the valuation). The horizontal axis represents greater precision in the value estimate, that is, less purely random error. Points farther to the right on the axis have less noise. For example, this dimension might be measured by the inverse of the standard deviation of the value estimates' purely random error component as a percent of the true property value. At least in principle, there is a point on this axis that represents perfection, the elimination of all random error,

---

[6]This may be becoming less of a problem with the advent of more and better transactions-based price indices for commercial property. (See discussion later in this chapter.)

[7]See Quan and Quigley (1989) and Diaz and Wolverton (1998).

EXHIBIT 25-3
Noise-versus-Lag Trade-Off
Frontiers with Disaggregate
and Aggregate Valuation
Methodologies
© OnCourse Learning

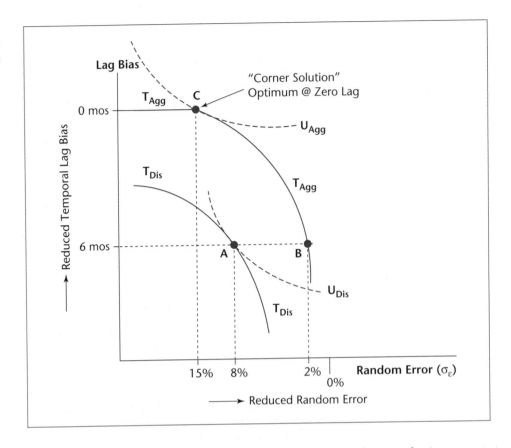

indicated by the short vertical slash and the *0 percent* value label. The vertical axis represents greater "currentness," or less temporal lag bias, the farther up you go along the axis. Again, there is a point of theoretical perfection, where there is zero lag bias in the value estimations, indicated by the *0 months* point on the vertical axis.

The dashed convex curves are *isoquants*, or indifference curves of constant utility, from the perspective of the users of the value estimation information. As users of property value estimates dislike both random-error and lag bias, indifference curves that are farther up and to the right (farther "northeast" in the chart) represent higher levels of utility, like contour lines on a map of a mountain whose peak is in the northeast corner of the chart. The isoquants are convex (bending outward and upward so as not to intersect the axes), because of declining marginal utility for either sort of accuracy.[8] Once a relatively high level of precision is obtained (low noise, toward the left side of the horizontal axis), it is more useful to reduce any significant lag bias in the value estimate than to add another increment to the already high precision of the value estimate. Similarly, once the index is quite up to date (low lag bias, high up on the vertical axis), it is more useful to reduce any significant noise in the value estimate than to reduce the lag bias by another increment.

The exact shape and slope of the utility isoquants will depend on the user and the use of the property-value estimation. For example, most users of individual (disaggregate) property appraisals place a premium on precision and don't care much about lag bias (such as the individual property appraisal to help advise a potential seller that we described earlier). This would be reflected by a utility function with relatively steep isoquants, tilted in a more clockwise or vertical direction like the U_{Dis} curve in the exhibit. On the other hand, many uses of aggregate appraisal (such as to construct an index tracking a population of properties) may

---

[8]The mean squared error (MSE) criterion of statistics [e.g., in Quan and Quigley (1989)] is an example of a property value estimation utility function, and it conforms to the convex isoquants shown in the exhibit.

care more about avoiding lag bias. This would be reflected in a more shallow-sloped or horizontal isoquant like the U_{Agg} curve in the Exhibit.

The thick solid concave curves in Exhibit 25-3 represent the noise-versus-lag trade-off frontier, as provided essentially by the Square Root of n Rule. Points above and to the right of the tradeoff frontier are not feasible and cannot be obtained. There are two different value estimation frontiers shown in the exhibit, representing two different property value estimation circumstances. The curve closer to the origin and farther to the left, labeled T_{Dis}, is the noise-versus-lag trade-off frontier that is relevant for traditional disaggregate, individual property appraisal, in which only a few comps are available to the appraiser to estimate the value of a single, specific property.

The kinked frontier farther up and to the right labeled T_{Agg}, including the straight horizontal section along the zero lag boundary and the steeper curve approaching the zero noise boundary, is the frontier that is relevant for macro-level index construction. Because there are many individual properties in the population or market covered by the macro-level index, the Square Root of n Rule pushes the trade-off frontier far out to the right, near the zero noise boundary Even with no lag bias at all (only current transaction price information used in the value estimation), the size of the aggregate population of properties tracked by the index can potentially give it a relatively low level of noise. As it is impossible to have less than zero temporal lag bias, the aggregate trade-off frontier is kinked at the zero-lag boundary.

There is an important implication of the shapes and locations of the disaggregate and aggregate value estimation trade-off frontiers. The optimal balance between lag bias and random error is always found at the point where the trade-off frontier is tangent to (that is, parallel to and just touching) one of the utility isoquants. This will be the feasible point that achieves the highest possible utility for the value estimation method. The optimal disaggregate-value-estimation method will likely involve some considerable degree of temporal lag bias, in order to get the random error down to an acceptable level. This is indicated by point A, the point at which the T_{Dis} frontier is just tangent to the U_{Dis} level of valuation utility. This appraisal method produces some amount of purely random error, and some amount of lag bias. For example, consistent with our previous illustration (and probably not atypical of commercial property appraisal in the United States) optimal (Method A) type disaggregate appraisal might have six months worth of average lag bias and 8 percent of purely random error (as indicated in the exhibit). Now, if a macro-level return index is produced simply by taking the sum or arithmetic average of such appraisals that are optimal at the disaggregate level, the result for the index will be a point like B, with less noise (due to the larger sample size inherent in the aggregation process) but the same amount of lag bias. But B is clearly not the optimal point for the aggregate index, at least from the perspective of the aggregate-focused users who have utility function U_{Agg}. The optimal noise-versus-lag trade-off at the disaggregate level is not the same as the optimal noise-versus-lag trade-off at the aggregate level.

The optimal aggregate value estimation methodology will tend to occur at or near the "corner solution" with zero or very little lag bias, at a point like C, which contains more noise than B (15 percent instead of 2 percent, might be typical with current commercial property indices in the United States), but virtually zero lag bias. This reflects the difference in your choice of the appraisal methods discussed in sections 25.1.2 and 25.1.4, where in the latter case you preferred the less precise appraisal Method C because it had less lag bias. In practice, an optimal aggregate valuation method such as point C in Exhibit 25-3 will usually be represented by some sort of regression-based transactions price index of the type that have only recently become available in the United States as described in section 25.4.2 later in this chapter.

25.2 From Value Levels to Returns: The General Nature of Performance Measurement Errors

Now that you understand the nature of the two types of errors that characterize property valuations, let's consider how these errors affect the main subject of this chapter, indices or time series of property-level periodic returns in the private real estate market.

To build your intuition in this matter, we will first consider the pure effect of **random noise**, then the pure effect of temporal lag bias, and finally the effect of the two types of errors combined.

25.2.1 The Pure Effect of Random Noise

Consider a static portfolio, that is, a fixed set of properties. Now let's make an unrealistic assumption in order to illustrate a basic point. Suppose all of the properties in the portfolio always sold at the same time each period, say, at the end of each calendar year. The properties are all the same, and the transactions are all synchronous. How will the empirically observable transaction-price-based annual appreciation returns to this portfolio differ from the unobservable appreciation returns to the same portfolio based on the true market value of the portfolio? What does this effect of random noise look like?

The answer to this question is depicted visually in Exhibit 25-4. Panel 25-4A shows an example of the effect of noise on returns, based on a simulation of hypothetical data. Time is on the horizontal axis, with the periodic returns indicated on the vertical axis. The solid line in the chart is the true return realization over time. The dotted line is the empirically observable return realization.[9]

Notice that the empirical return is more volatile. It is also spikier or more saw-toothed in appearance, with large returns tending to be followed by opposite-signed returns. This is typical of excess volatility that reflects overshooting or random errors in the observed value levels that are subsequently corrected in later observations. This is seen more directly in Exhibit 25-4B, which shows the same simulated history, only in the value levels rather than the returns. For example, the empirical valuation in one period might happen to have a positive error, while the valuation in the next period would be just as likely to have a negative error. The result would be a large apparent negative return, due purely to the difference in errors, when the true return was near zero. In general, note that random noise causes the observed value level series to sort of "dance" or "vibrate" around the unobservable true value level series.

What is the effect of this type of return noise on the returns time-series statistics that are of most interest to investors? Well, it does not change the expected value of the periodic return because the expected value of the random valuation error is zero at both the beginning and end of each return reporting period. Hence, the expected value of the difference in errors across each period is zero, and it is this difference that figures in the periodic returns. However, random valuation error does change the volatility, that is, the standard deviation of the periodic returns across time. In particular, it increases the volatility, adding spurious "extra" volatility to the returns over time. Noise also affects the autocorrelation in the returns time series, that is, the way the periodic returns are correlated with each other across time.

In particular, noise reduces any positive first-order autocorrelation (that is, correlation between consecutive returns) that might exist in the true returns, and may make uncorrelated true returns appear to have negative autocorrelation.[10] Noise does not affect the theoretical covariance between the index returns and any exogenous series because, by definition, a purely random variable has no covariance with any other series. Therefore noise does not affect the theoretical beta (or systematic risk) as we defined it in Chapter 22.[11] Finally, combining these **volatility** and **covariance effects**, noise reduces the apparent cross-correlation

---

[9]In the simulation, the true returns were generated randomly from a process that was normally distributed with 5% volatility per period, and the random value level observation error was generated from a process that was normally distributed with a cross-sectional standard deviation of 10%.

[10]The autocorrelation "signature" of pure random noise is negative 50% in the first-order autocorrelation of the returns (first differences of the value levels), and zero for higher-order autocorrelation.

[11]However, noise does make it more difficult to precisely estimate the true beta using empirical returns data. In other words, it does not affect the expected value of the beta coefficient estimate in a regression, but it does increase the standard error in that estimate.

EXHIBIT 25-4A The Pure
Effect of Noise in Periodic
Returns
© OnCourse Learning

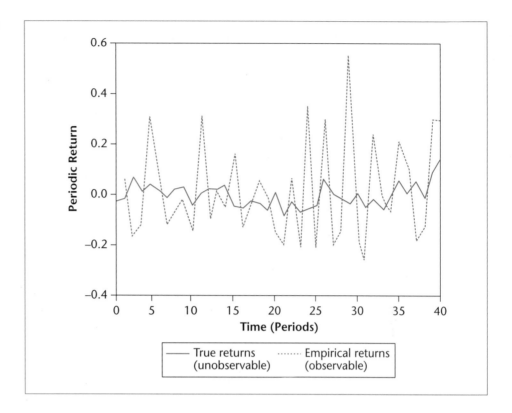

EXHIBIT 25-4B The Pure
Effect of Noise in Periodic
Value Levels
© OnCourse Learning

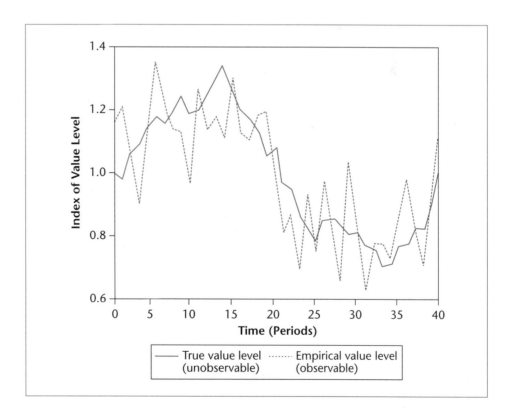

between the noisy series and any other series.[12] Thus, noise can make it appear as if two real estate market segments are less correlated than they actually are.

Unlike true volatility, noise does not accumulate over time in the price value levels. Thus, the longer the interval of time over which returns are measured, the lower the effect of noise will be on any of the return statistics.

25.2.2 The Pure Effect of Temporal Lag

Now let's look at the impact on periodic returns of the other type of error common in real estate valuations, temporal lag bias, the type of error that does not tend to diversify out at the macro-level. To illustrate the pure effect of this type of error, we will consider another unrealistic hypothetical situation. Again we have a static portfolio, but now we will assume that there are an infinite number of properties in the portfolio so that the effect of random noise completely washes away. However, the portfolio valuation each year is based on appraisals rather than transaction prices, and while the appraisals all occur at the end of the calendar year, they display a temporal lag bias in which the appraised value for each property as of the end of year t consists of a one-half weight on the true value as of that time, plus a one-half weight on the true value as of the end of the previous year. The result is that the empirically observed value of the portfolio as of the end of year t, labeled V_t^*, is given by the following formula where C_t is the (unobservable) true market value (and we will assume all values are in logs, so that returns are simple arithmetic differences across time):[13]

$$V_t^* = \left(\frac{1}{2}\right)C_t + \left(\frac{1}{2}\right)C_{t-1} \tag{1}$$

The empirically observable return in the index, labeled r_t^*, is thus

$$
\begin{aligned}
r_t^* = V_t^* - V_{t-1}^* &= \left[\left(\frac{1}{2}\right)C_t + \left(\frac{1}{2}\right)C_{t-1}\right] - \left[\left(\frac{1}{2}\right)C_{t-1} + \left(\frac{1}{2}\right)C_{t-2}\right] \\
&= \left[\left(\frac{1}{2}\right)C_t - \left(\frac{1}{2}\right)C_{t-1}\right] + \left[\left(\frac{1}{2}\right)C_{t-1} - \left(\frac{1}{2}\right)C_{t-2}\right] \\
&= \left(\frac{1}{2}\right)(C_t - C_{t-1}) + \left(\frac{1}{2}\right)(C_{t-1} - C_{t-2}) \\
&= \left(\frac{1}{2}\right)r_t + \left(\frac{1}{2}\right)r_{t-1}
\end{aligned}
\tag{2}
$$

Thus, the empirically observable return consists of one-half weight on the true current return, plus one-half weight on the previous period's true return. The empirical return is called a **moving average** of the true returns across time.

The effect of return lagging like this is pretty obvious, and it is depicted visually in Exhibits 25-5A and 25-5B, which may be compared to their counterparts in Exhibits 25-4A and 25-4B.[14] The empirical returns in Exhibit 25-5A appear "smoothed" and lagged in time behind the unobservable true returns. The same is true of the value levels depicted in Exhibit 25-5B. Note in particular that the observable value level series tends to be shifted to the right in the graph, with turning points tending to occur later in time, as compared to the unobservable true value level series, and the amplitude of any cycle or rise and fall is slightly diminished.

In terms of the effect of temporal lag bias on the periodic returns time-series statistics of interest to investors, first consider the average return across time. Temporal lagging does not

---

[12]The cross-correlation coefficient between two series equals the covariance divided by the product of the volatilities of the two series.

[13]Just to reiterate, there are no random noise terms in equation (1) only because we have "assumed them away," by the device of our hypothetical assumption of an infinite property population in the portfolio. This unrealistic assumption is made to illustrate the pure effect of temporal lag.

[14]All of these exhibits were generated from the same simulated hypothetical historical sample of true returns.

EXHIBIT 25-5A The Pure
Effect of Temporal Lag in
Periodic Returns

© OnCourse Learning

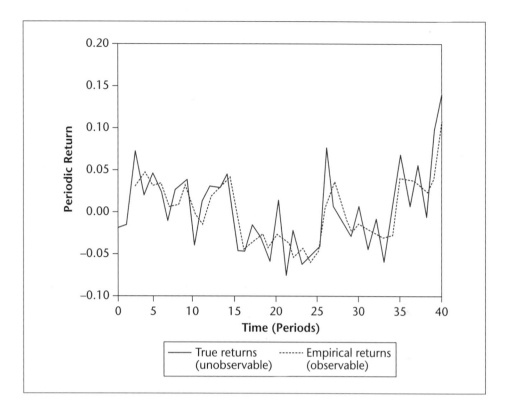

EXHIBIT 25-5B The Pure
Effect of Temporal Lag in
Periodic Value Levels

© OnCourse Learning

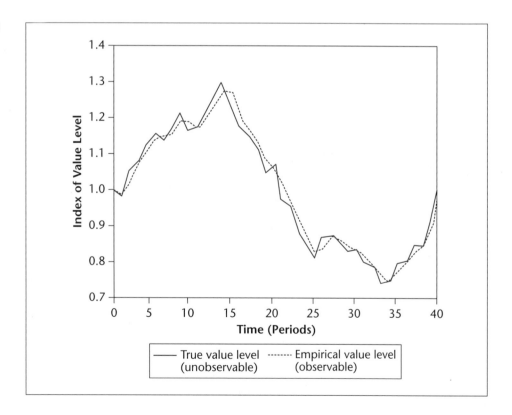

change the long-run (or "unconditional") expected value of the periodic return. However, in any finite sample of time, temporally lagged returns will be "conditionally" biased. That is, the direction of the bias depends on the direction in which the true returns have been trending, if any. For example, if true returns have been increasing over the relevant history, then temporally lagged returns will be biased low, with the average empirical return tending to be lower than the average true return during the history.

Turning to the second moment statistics, the pure effect of lagging in the form of a moving average of the true returns is to reduce the apparent volatility (total risk) of the observable real estate returns. The more important second moment effect of lagging, however, is that it reduces the apparent beta (systematic risk) of the real estate returns measured with respect to any nonlagged series, including a nonlagged risk benchmark such as stock market returns.[15] For this reason, the effect of temporal lagging on periodic returns series is often referred to as **smoothing**, or **appraisal smoothing**, as such lagging in appraisal-based indices is often attributed at least in part to the macro-level valuation impact of the micro-level appraiser behavior described in section 25.1.

What about the cross-correlation and beta of a lagged real estate series with respect to another similarly lagged series? These effects are complicated considering that the underlying true returns are likely to be autocorrelated and contain lagged cross-correlation terms. It is likely, however, that the pure effect of temporal lag bias will in most cases cause only very slight bias, if any, in the cross-correlation and beta statistics between two similarly lagged real estate series. Thus, for example, the beta of a component of the NPI with respect to the total NPI will probably not be seriously biased, as both series have similar lags.

Regarding cross-temporal statistics, the pure effect of temporal lag bias in the returns series is usually to impart apparent positive autocorrelation into the empirical returns series, more so than is present in the unobservable true returns. This tends to exaggerate the effect, noted in the appendix to Chapter 21, that long-interval (lower-frequency) periodic returns become relatively more volatile, compared to nonlagged series, than short-interval (high-frequency) returns.[16] This causes the apparent long-interval betas of lagged series with respect to nonlagged series to be greater than short-interval betas, and this effect tends to be magnified in the apparent beta of a moving average lagged series. Not surprisingly, moving average lagged returns are more predictable in advance than true underlying returns.

25.2.3 Putting the Two Effects Together

In the real world, most practical empirical real estate periodic returns series will contain at least a little bit of both of the "pure" types of errors described in the two preceding sections. The fundamental trade-off between these two sources of error noted in section 25.1 makes it impossible to completely avoid both error sources simultaneously.

---

[15]More precisely, the apparent beta is biased toward zero, as beta can have either a positive or a negative sign in theory. Actually, however, it is only the *contemporaneous* beta that is reduced with respect to a nonlagged risk benchmark such as the stock market (or the REIT market, for example). It is possible to correct such bias by adding the contemporaneous and lagged betas. This can be seen as follows using our two-period moving average lag, defining x_t as a nonlagged (i.e., unpredictable) series, and remembering that $BETA[r_t^*, x_t]$ is defined as $COV[r_t^*, x_t]/VAR[x_t]$

$$COV[r_t^*, x_t] = COV[(1/2)r_t + (1/2)r_{t-1}, x_t] = (1/2)COV[r_t, x_t] + (1/2)COV[r_{t-1}, x_t]$$
$$= (1/2)COV[r_t, x_t]$$

because x_t is not predictable (as in the case of stock market returns, for example). Therefore, $COV[r_{t-1}, x_t] = 0$. Similarly, $COV[r_t^*, x_t-1]$ would also equal $(1/2) COV[r_t, x_t]$, based on the second term in the right-hand-side expansion (while the first term drops out as the unlagged true return component r_t is unpredictable, so the first term on the right-hand-side expansion drops out). Thus, adding the two covariances, you get the complete true covariance (or beta). Of course, these are all theoretical (or "long-history") relationships relating to bias (or the central tendency) in the real estate statistics. Actual results in any finite empirical sample can differ. If the true real estate returns are predictable by the exogenous variable, then the sum of the contemporaneous and lagged betas might overcorrect the smoothing bias. [See Geltner (1991) and Study Question 25-14 at the end of this chapter.]

[16]Both the variance and the covariance with nonlagged series are more than proportional to the length of the return periods in the case of positively autocorrelated periodic returns. For example, annual returns have more than four times the covariance and variance (more than twice the volatility) of quarterly returns, and this effect is magnified the greater is the positive autocorrelation.

The noise component, η_t, will be more important in smaller portfolios and may well dominate in individual property returns.[17] Because of the Square Root of n Rule, noise will be less important in returns to large portfolios or indices. Even though statistical regression is a very efficient tool for handling large amounts of data, noise will still be present in regression-based price indices. Referred to in statistical terms as estimation error, random noise may often be the more important of the two error components in regression-based indices derived from transaction prices, at least provided that the regression is specified and estimated so as to avoid most temporal lag bias.

In contrast, the temporal lag effect will typically dominate in large portfolios or indices that are based on appraised values. Temporal lag effects can also be important in regression-based indices if the transaction observations span across time and care is not taken to control properly for temporal aggregation in the regression specification and estimation process.

It is important to note that the two types of error effects will tend to mask each other in the empirical returns. In reality, it is not possible to separate out the pure effects as we have done in the preceding two sections. For example, the volatility-magnifying effect of return noise will tend to offset, to some degree at least, the volatility-dampening effect of the moving average temporal lag. Similarly, the negative autocorrelation component imparted by the random noise will tend to offset the positive autocorrelation effect of the temporal lag.[18] This type of masking can make it difficult to correct the effect of error on the volatility of the empirical return series. On the other hand, systematic risk (or beta) is more amenable to correction because noise does not affect the theoretical beta, while we know that temporal bias dampens the observable beta toward zero, the more so the greater the lag.

Exhibit 25-6 presents a visual example of the mixed-errors situation, based on the same underlying simulated true returns as those in the previous exhibits. The true returns and market value levels are indicated by the thin solid line. The dotted line reflects the effect of random noise only. In the real world we might observe the dotted line in Exhibit 25-6B as the average transaction price in each period among the properties in the subject population that happened to transact during that period.[19] The dotted line in the returns chart in Exhibit 25-6A is simply the percentage difference in these average prices each period, identical to the returns shown in Exhibit 25-4A.

Now suppose that all the properties in the subject population are appraised at the end of each period, based on appraisers' observations of the transaction prices in the current and past periods (or, equivalently, based on appraisers' partially updating each year their previous year's appraisal based on the new transaction information). In particular, suppose that appraisers apply the following first-order autoregressive (simple exponential smoothing) valuation equation:

$$V_t^* = \omega \overline{V}_t + (1 - \omega) V_{t-1}^* \tag{3}$$

In particular, suppose that the partial adjustment factor, ω, is 0.2.

Under this assumed appraiser behavior, the thick line in Exhibit 25-6 traces out the appraisal-based index appreciation returns and value levels for our simulated population of properties. Note that the appraisal-based returns and values include both random noise and temporal lag effects, and that to some extent these effects mask each other.

Unlike random noise, the lag of the empirically observable appraised values behind the market values does not tend to get washed out, and it is clearly evidenced in Exhibit 25-6B by

---

[17]Periodic returns series of individual property returns are rarely used as such. In the first place, individual properties are typically rather small assets that have relatively little economic or statistical significance by themselves. Furthermore, in addition to the noise and lag effects described earlier, observable individual property value levels are flat (zero appreciation) between appraisals or transaction observations. This gives individual property returns a very spiky appearance and their value level series a very artificial-looking step-like or sticky appearance. For these reasons (among others), the major return measure used at the individual property level is the multiperiod IRR, rather than periodic HPRs. (See Chapters 9 and 26 for additional discussion relevant to this point.)

[18]This is in the first-order statistic only.

[19]This would certainly be a finite, and probably even rather small, sample. Therefore, it could not eliminate the noise as we assumed in the preceding section when we assumed an infinite population.

EXHIBIT 25-6A Periodic Appreciation Returns Based on Market Values, Transaction Prices, and Appraised Values (simulated data)

© OnCourse Learning

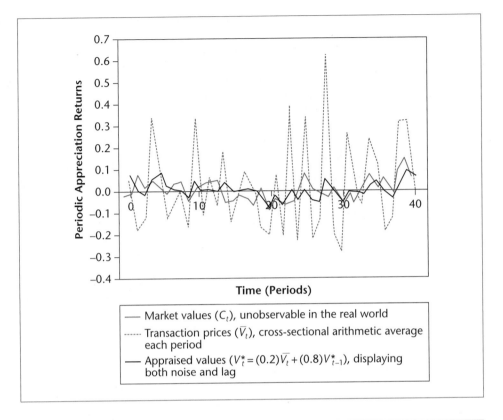

EXHIBIT 25-6B Market Values, Transaction Prices, and Appraised Values (simulated data)

© OnCourse Learning

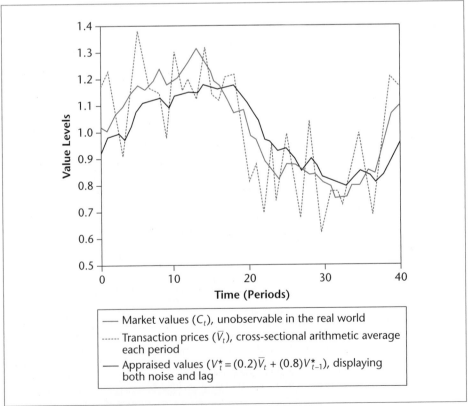

the horizontal gap between the thick and thin lines in the chart. On average, this gap is about four periods long in our example simulation and can be seen most prominently in the lagged turning points in the market value cycle. Of course, this lag would not be directly observable in the real world because the true market returns and values would be unobservable. The same lag also exists between the appraisal-based index and the average transaction prices, which would be empirically observable. However, the noisiness of the transaction price series obfuscates the picture, making it difficult to see clearly the lag in the appraised values relative to the transaction prices.

25.2.4 What about the Total Return?

The preceding three sections introduced you to the major types of measurement errors that are unique to private real estate regarding empirical periodic returns series. The discussion and examples so far considered only the appreciation component of the total HPR. However, most of the volatility in periodic returns series derives from the appreciation return component, so the points made previously about appreciation returns generally carry through to the total returns as well.[20] Furthermore, it is often much easier or more straightforward to accurately observe the income returns (at least for properties in an investment database such as NCREIF or IPD, or for REITs). So the primary challenge in tracking private property market returns is the difficulty of measuring the asset price or capital return component.

25.3 What Is Truth? Lags and the Time Line of Price Discovery in Real Estate

The previous section made clear that one of the major types of errors in private real estate periodic returns data is temporal lag bias. This type of error can be particularly prominent and important in macro-level appraisal-based returns, such as those tracked for large portfolios and benchmark indices such as the NPI. With this in mind, we need now to step back and consider a broader and deeper question.

What do we mean by the "true return"? After all, it is impossible to define *error* without defining a specific conception of the correct value. As a result, it is impossible to appreciate the nature and magnitude of the temporal lag bias problem in real estate without such a definition.

Up to now, we have been defining true returns as those based on market value as this term has been previously defined in this book regarding the private real estate asset market, namely, the *expected* (or ex ante) sale price in the current relevant market for the subject asset. But the problem of temporal lag bias often arises in contexts that are different from or broader than what is implied by this definition of value. For example, consider the following practical decision problems, all of which involve, directly or indirectly, the use of appraisal-based periodic returns data for private real estate:

1. A private market real estate investment manager using a timing-based tactical investment policy wants to know if the institutional office property market "turned around" last quarter, or was it the previous quarter, or two quarters ago, or has it not yet turned?

2. A private market real estate investment manager wants to hedge some of its real estate market risk exposure by taking a short position in a real estate index swap derivative.[21]

---

[20]Remember that the denominator in the formula for the periodic income return component is the beginning period asset valuation. Thus, income return components can be affected directly by valuation errors, particularly in appraisal-based indices. For example, assuming contemporaneous income is accurately observed, the income return component will be biased low when the asset valuation is biased high, and vice versa. These effects will generally be minor, however, at least relatively speaking.

[21]See section 26.3 in the next chapter for a description of real estate index swaps.

3. A consultant considering portfolio allocation strategies wants to know the long-run beta (or long-run relative volatility and correlation coefficient) between real estate and the stock market.

4. An advisor to a wealthy individual trying to decide between private direct investment and REIT shares for the real estate component of her wealth portfolio wants to know the beta of private real estate compared to that of REITs, in both up and down stock markets.

5. An acquisition officer involved in a protracted negotiation for a major property wants to know how far property market values have fallen, in general, during the past calendar quarter.

6. A manager of a large portfolio whose annual incentive fee is pegged to the NPI is wondering why his recently appraised portfolio didn't beat the NPI last year even though he believes his appraisers are competent and he's sure he did better than most of his competitors last year.

7. An appraiser wants to know the approximate ex post time-weighted mean total return risk premium of institutional quality real estate over T-bills during the past quarter century, to help her estimate the appropriate cost of capital to use in a DCF valuation.

8. A pension fund wants to obtain risk and return exposure identical to the NPI by taking a long position in an index swap contract based on the NPI.

For the managers in problems 1 and 2, a definition of market value based on contemporaneous empirically observable transaction prices in the private market, such as would be tracked by a transactions-based index, will be best. The consultant in problem 3 might find something closer to a REIT market-based definition of value more relevant for defining or measuring the temporal lag that is (or should be) of most concern in her problem of measuring long-run beta, at least from the perspective of investors who want to use the public market as their real estate investment vehicle. The advisor and the acquisition officer in problems 4 and 5 might prefer a constant-liquidity definition of private market value, rather than one based only on consummated transaction price evidence. The relevant value for the manager in problem 6 might simply be a fully contemporaneous appraisal-based valuation of his benchmark. Finally, for the appraiser and fund manager in problems 7 and 8, an appraisal-based index that is not completely contemporaneous, like the NCREIF index would be quite adequate (or indeed for the fund manager in problem 8, the NPI specifically is the stated preference).

If you do not have a clear conception of what is the relevant value for the type of problem you are trying to address, then you can get very confused in your attempts to analyze the problem. Yet this question of "truth" (or, what is the relevant conception of value) is so basic and underlying in nature that analysts and decision makers often do not even explicitly consider it. The result is practical decision situations in which the analysts are confused without even knowing they are confused, a potentially dangerous situation! To avoid this situation yourself, we think it is helpful to consider a time line of price discovery as it relates to different types of empirical and conceptual real estate periodic returns series.

25.3.1 Multistep Real Estate Time Line of Information Incorporation into Observable Value

To build your intuition regarding different relevant "true values" in real estate, consider the following simple situation. Suppose that for a long time no new information has arrived relevant to the value of real estate assets. Prices of REIT shares, as well as prices of privately traded property, not to mention appraised values, are all stable and steady. The time is now $t-1$, and all real estate price indices are at a level we can set at 100.

Now into this very dull world a piece of news, that is, *new* information, arrives suddenly, unpredicted (of course, or it wouldn't be news). The information arrives precisely at time t, and it is relevant to the value of all real estate assets. In fact, for illustrative purposes suppose that this information is relevant to all real estate assets in the same direction and same magnitude (although this will not become fully apparent empirically for some time). In particular, as a result of this new information the value of all real estate assets has just decreased by 10 percent. Then, immediately after the arrival of this one piece of news, the world becomes very boring again and no new information relevant to real estate values arrives anymore for a long time.

OK, it's a strange and very unrealistic situation we have just depicted, but it serves to illustrate the time line we want you to become familiar with. Let's think about how different types of real estate price or value indices might respond to the news that arrived at time t. In particular, we will identify and define five different such indices, at a conceptual level: (1) An index based on REIT share prices, (2) a constant-liquidity private market value index, (3) a contemporaneous transaction-price-based private market value index, (4) a contemporaneous appraised value index, and (5) an appraisal-based index with staggered appraisals or some "stale" appraisals such as the NPI. We will consider each of these in turn, as we walk through the index response pattern illustrated in Exhibit 25-7.

Index 1: REIT Share Price Based Index   This index is based on the market prices of publicly traded REIT shares traded in the stock exchange. Most directly, this would include REIT indices such as the NAREIT Index in the United States. It could also include property-level indices (of REIT property assets de-levered from the REITs' financial structure) targeted at specific property sectors, such as the FTSE NAREIT PureProperty™ Index Series launched in 2012. The stock market in which REITs trade is the densest, most liquid market relevant to the trading of real estate equity assets, and so it has the most informationally efficient price discovery. The REIT-based index moves first and fastest. It reflects prices that are always liquid, in the sense that investors can always sell at the prevailing price. However, Index 1 may be subject to some excess volatility, based perhaps on "herd behavior" or overshooting by investors in the REIT shares in the stock market. This is indicated illustratively in Exhibit 25-7 as we depict the REIT index overshooting the mark at index level 90, falling to a level slightly below that, before it corrects itself.[22] Line 1 in Exhibit 25-7 traces the path of the REIT index over time from just prior to the arrival of the news to past the time when all indices have fully reflected the news. In practice, REIT indices show relatively little autocorrelation or inertia, although there may be some minor positive autocorrelation in very short-run returns, followed by a tendency for slight negative autocorrelation at longer frequencies (presumably reflecting correction in the excess volatility noted previously).[23]

Index 2: Constant-Liquidity Private Market Value Index   This is an index of market values in the private property market. However, this index simultaneously reflects both trading volume as well as transaction prices. Volume is as important an indicator as consummated prices for tracking a whole-asset search market like real estate. The constant-liquidity index is meant to represent the asset values that would equilibrate the market with a constant amount of liquidity through time. When bad news arrives, news that suggests market values should fall, real estate market participants become cautious. Potential buyers reduce their reservation prices while property owners on the supply side either don't reduce their reservation prices as much or may even increase them (reflecting uncertainty about the market conditions), causing the two sides of the market to pull away from each other, reducing

---

[22]The existence of this type of excess volatility in the stock market is somewhat controversial, although some tendency in this regard seems to be fairly widely accepted now among financial economists, and there are several theories to explain it (e.g., irrational investor behavior models, noise trader models, and so forth). Excess volatility of this nature has much in common with the random noise described in section 25.1.1 regarding private real estate indices, as far as some of the statistical effects are concerned. However, stock market excess volatility is different in its basic nature and source from the type of noise we considered previously, as it does not generally imply the existence of any measurement error in the market values or returns that are quantified in the index. Furthermore, private property market values in some circumstances bring relevant information to the REIT market, as indicated by the widespread use of NAV data in analyzing REIT stock values. Such information can help correct the overshooting that REIT share prices are prone to in the stock market. See, for example, Gentry, Jones and Mayer (2005).

[23]See Liu and Mei (1994), Graff and Young (1997), and Stevenson (2002). Please note that Index 1 in the exhibit ignores any effect of leverage in the REITs.

EXHIBIT 25-7
News-Response Time Line
for Various Stylized Real
Estate Indices
© OnCourse Learning

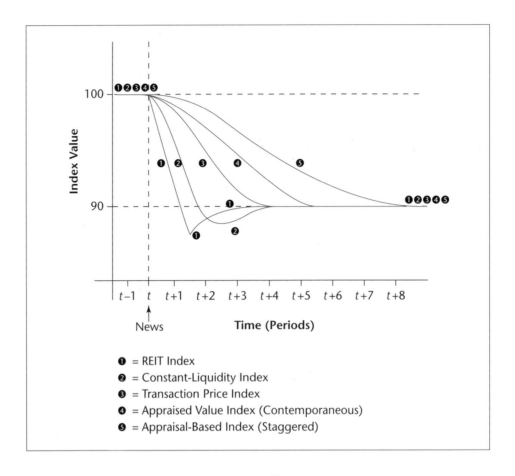

❶ = REIT Index
❷ = Constant-Liquidity Index
❸ = Transaction Price Index
❹ = Appraised Value Index (Contemporaneous)
❺ = Appraisal-Based Index (Staggered)

liquidity and transaction volume in the market.[24] In contrast, when the market turns up, buyers tend to move farther or faster than sellers, bringing reservation prices closer together (with more overlap – recall Exhibit 25-1), increasing liquidity and transaction volume in the market. Thus, liquidity (as reflected by trading volume turnover) in the private market is "pro-cyclical," varying positively with the market cycle. In order to maintain constant liquidity, in other words, to maintain a constant expected transaction turnover ratio, seller reservation prices would have to track those of buyers. An index tracking the buyer (demand) side movements in the property market would therefore tend to reflect greater volatility or faster response to news than an index based on consummated transaction prices. The typical price path of such a constant-liquidity private market index is indicated by line 2 in Exhibit 25-7, in response to our hypothetical single-news event. Note that it lags behind the stock market-based Index 1, and like Index 1 might tend to over-shoot slightly the ultimate value change.

Index 3: Contemporaneous Transaction-Price-Based Index of Private Market Values This is an index reflecting the central tendency (or average) of the sales prices of the actually consummated transactions within each period of time. This type of index can be estimated directly using empirically observable transaction prices. The two major methods to compute such indices are the hedonic and the repeat-sales regression-based methods. The latter is more widely used, as repeat-sales indices reflect the actual round-trip price experiences

---

[24]Recall that reservation prices are the prices at which potential participants in the market will stop searching or negotiating and commit to a deal. This same type of uncertainty happens in the REIT market, but it gets resolved much more quickly there due to the much denser market, with active multiple buyers and sellers publicly trading homogeneous shares with very low transaction costs and the ability to engage in short-selling. Increased uncertainty may be associated with increased volatility in the REIT market.

of investors in the market. Examples of this type of index in the United States include the Moody's/RCA Commercial Property Price Indices (CPPI) and the CoStar Commercial Repeat-Sales Indices (CCRSI). Of course, any empirically based transaction price index would in practice tend to exhibit some estimation error or transaction price noise of the type described in section 25.2.1, though in its stylized representation in Exhibit 25-7 we are ignoring any noise.[25] Since Index 3 represents prices that can reflect widely varying liquidity (transaction volume) over time in the private real estate market, it must be kept in mind that the returns reported in this index do not reflect a constant ease of selling or a fully complete picture of the state of the market in the absence of corresponding trading volume information. Liquidity variation is one reason we would expect consummated transaction prices in the private property market to move slightly behind or smoother than the constant-liquidity values tracked by Index 2. Thus, at least at the conceptual level (in the absence of noise), transaction price indices like Index 3 should be a bit less volatile and slightly more lagged in time as compared to the two previously defined indices, as suggested by line 3 in the Exhibit. But in an important sense Index 3 is the most fundamental indication of property value. The prices it reflects represent the prevailing equilibrium in the property market, the actual prices paid and received by investors on both sides of the market (supply and demand).

Index 4: Contemporaneous Appraised Value Index   This is an index based on micro-level appraised values, that is, the cross-sectional aggregation of individual property appraisals, but with all of the properties being appraised each period as of the current point in time. Thus, conceptually, the only difference between this index and the transaction-price-based index is the temporal lag present in optimal micro-level appraisal, as described in section 25.1 (as in the difference between points B and C in Exhibit 25-3).[26] This index will thus be a bit smoothed and lagged in time behind the transaction price index, as appraisers wait to compile evidence from transaction prices before they finalize their own opinions of how the news that arrived at time t changed the value of real estate. But ultimately an appraisal-based index will settle to the same illustrative "true" value of 90 like the previously described indices, just a little later. The contemporaneous appraisal-based index is indicated in Exhibit 25-7 by line 4.

Index 5: Appraisal-Based Index with Staggered Appraisals   This index is based on the same type of valuation observations as those in the previous index, only in this index not all properties are reappraised in each period that the index is reported, or as of the same point in time within each period. This results in the valuations reflected by the index being partially "stale" (or out of date) and/or spread out over time (which tends to smooth and lag the aggregate value in the index). This makes Index 5 a lagged moving average of the contemporaneous appraisal-based index, as depicted in line 5 in Exhibit 25-7.

Let us now summarize the time line we have just described, as illustrated in Exhibit 25-7. The effect of the news arriving at time t is incorporated at varying rates into the real estate prices or values defined and measured in the five different ways described by these five conceptual indices. The index value levels traced through time from the left-hand edge of Exhibit 25-7 at the old value level of 100 are splayed out and arrive at the new ultimate value level of 90 spread across time. The REIT index, constant-liquidity index, and contemporaneous transaction price index arrive at the new valuation first.[27] They are followed by the

---

[25]In reality, transaction-price-based indices are also potentially susceptible to temporal lag bias. See Geltner (1993a) for additional discussion. However, in the present context, we are defining our conceptual transaction-based index to be contemporaneous, that is, completely free of temporal lag bias, and also free of noise (reflecting the theoretical ex ante mean transaction price each period, not any finite-sample empirical average).

[26]Again, in empirical reality, both this index and the previous could contain random noise, though often there seems to be much less noise in appraisal-based indices than in transactions based indices, as suggested by the example error percentage numbers on the horizontal axis of Exhibit 25-3. As noted, noise is not depicted in Exhibit 25-7. Also, recall our note in section 25.1 that in some countries the appraisal (aka "valuation") process may bear a closer or more "causal" relationship to contemporaneous transaction prices than is apparent in the United States, resulting in less difference between appraisal and transaction based indices such as lines 3 and 4 in Exhibit 25-7.

[27]Probably in that order, that is, the REIT index first, then the constant-liquidity index, then the transaction index.

contemporaneous appraised values. Then the appraisal-based index with the staggered (stale) appraisals pulls up the rear, arriving last at the 90 mark.

Obviously, the temporal lag bias in real estate values depends on which of these five indices one is using, and which one is taken as the truth against which the bias is defined and measured. Each of the five indices represents a different way of measuring real estate value, and therefore, in a sense, a different *definition* of value. If we are using a staggered appraisal-based index such as Index 5 (e.g., an index similar to the NCREIF Property Index – NPI), then the bias is relatively small if the relevant true value is defined by a contemporaneous appraisal-based index such as Index 4. But the temporal lag is much longer, and the smoothing is much greater, when measured or compared against a REIT-based index such as Index 1 or a constant-liquidity transactions-based index such as Index 2.

What do these different conceptual indices of real estate value movements look like in empirical reality? This answer will depend on specific data and estimation methodologies employed to construct the indices, and will no doubt differ across countries reflecting different market and appraisal practices and cultures. Exhibit 25-8 shows the historical price levels for four regularly published indices as of 2012 representing the institutional investment commercial property market in the United States during the 2000–2011 period of history (which of course included a great bull market followed by a major financial crisis and then a recovery).

Exhibit 25-8 shows only four of the five conceptual indices defined in Exhibit 25-7, omitting Index 4 (the contemporaneous appraisal-based index).[28] The representative for Index 1, the stock market-based index, is the FTSE NAREIT PureProperty Index. Being based on REIT share prices, this index publishes daily updates. It is published in both equity and property level versions, with the latter being de-levered so as to track the stock market's valuations of the REITs' property assets directly. As of 2012 REITs owned over $700 billion of commercial property in the United States and the PureProperty Indices represented over 20,000 individual REIT-held properties. The other three indices depicted in Exhibit 25-8 are all based on the NCREIF property database, which as of 2012 contained over 7,000 properties worth over $300 billion, well representing pension fund and other nonprofit institutions' investments in commercial property. The constant-liquidity index in Exhibit 25-8 (corresponding to Index 2 in Exhibit 25-7) has been estimated by combining information from a hedonic model of property prices with a binary choice model of market liquidity (property sale probability).[29] The NTBI transactions-based index reflects the contemporaneous transaction prices of the properties sold from the NCREIF Index each quarter.[30] Finally, the NCREIF Property Index (NPI) is based on the official valuations reported to NCREIF each quarter by the data-contributing investment manager members of NCREIF. The NPI is the oldest (going back to 1977) and most traditional index of U.S. institutional investment property performance (as described previously in Chapters 7 and 9). In recent years NCREIF members have begun reappraising their properties more frequently, and with less seasonal bunching in the fourth quarter, which has enabled the NPI to be more up-to-date than in previous decades.

---

[28]There is not a good representative of Index 4 in the United States. Perhaps the best such index would be the classical annual calendar-year IPD Index of property values in the United Kingdom (where in addition, as noted previously, the appraisals do not differ so much from transaction prices as in the United States).

[29]In essence, the two models—the price model and the sales model—provide "two equations," each of which includes as a fundamental variable two "unknowns," namely, the reservation prices on the demand side of the market and the reservation prices on the supply side of the market. The two equations can be solved for these two unknowns. The resulting index tracing the movements of the reservation prices on the demand side of the market is the constant-liquidity index shown in Exhibit 25-8. (See Fisher, Geltner, and Pollakowski, 2007.)

[30]The NTBI was first developed in 2006 at the MIT Center for Real Estate with NCREIF cooperation. The index was initially based on a hedonic type regression model using the recent appraised values of the sold properties as the major explanatory variable for the transaction prices, with time-dummy variables to capture differences each quarter between the transaction prices and the appraisals (to correct for the lagging and smoothing bias). As of 2011 the TBI was taken over by NCREIF and the methodology was slightly changed, so that the NTBI is now a SPAR (sales price / appraisal ratio) based index in which the average ratio of sales price to recent appraised value across the transactions in each period is multiplied by the appraisal-based index value each period to derive the implied transaction price levels.

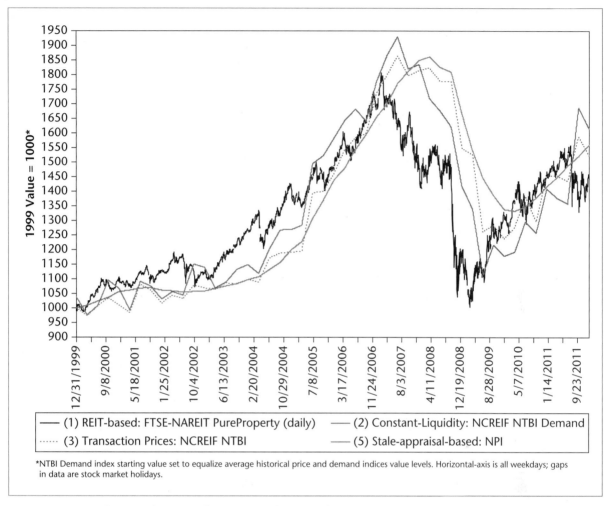

EXHIBIT 25-8 Four Definitions and Measures of U.S. Commercial Property Values, 2000–2011
Source: Author's compilations from FTSE, NCREIF and the MIT Center for Real Estate.

The indices in Exhibit 25-8 are real world indices based on empirical data, and so include some noise and a much more complex behavior than the stylized pure-type indices depicted in Exhibit 25-7 in a simple world where only one piece of information arrived. But the general patterns and relationships depicted in Exhibit 25-7 nevertheless reveal themselves in Exhibit 25-8. All four indices trace a similar history at the broad brush level, including the major boom, bust, and recovery. The stock market-based Index 1 moves first, and crashed a bit farther, only to experience a greater or faster recovery. It also seems to show greater short-run or transient volatility, although part of this may simply be that it is updated so much more frequently (daily instead of quarterly for the other three indices). In fact, measured on quarterly-frequency returns, the FTSE-NAREIT PureProperty Index quarterly volatility during the 2000–2011 period was about the same as that of the NTBI (Index 3).

The solid blue line representing the constant-liquidity Index 2 moved ahead, and more exaggeratedly, compared to the direct transaction price Index 3 (dotted blue line). This difference reflects (and/or causes) the extreme liquidity cycle that occurred in the private property market during the period shown. When the financial crisis struck in 2008 and early 2009, potential investors on the demand side of the market drastically dropped their reservation prices (the NTBI demand index lost 42 percent of its peak value from the end of the second quarter of 2007 through the second quarter of 2009). But property owners held back and did not reduce their reservation prices nearly so much or so fast.[31] The result was a drastic drop in trading volume. Transactions among NCREIF properties declined by more than 60 percent, from over 10 percent of all properties in 2007 to only 4 percent in 2009.

Measured on a calendar quarter basis, the magnitude of the property price crash from each index's respective peak to trough (whose dates can be seen visually in the Exhibit) varied from 41 percent in the PureProperty Index, to 42 percent in the NTBI Demand Index, to 34 percent in the NTBI Price Index, to 28 percent in the appraisal-based NPI. Through the end of 2011 the subsequent recoveries were (as a percent of the trough value), respectively: 36 percent, 45 percent, 26 percent, and 17 percent.

25.4 Innovations in Commercial Property Returns Indices

In this section we will first summarize the major recent developments in indexing commercial investment property prices and returns in the United States. Then we will discuss in more depth a particularly important innovation, that of repeat-sales indices of transaction prices.

25.4.1 Overview of Types of Indices

From the previous sections in this chapter you can see that there are potentially three major different types or sources of data for constructing indices to track commercial property prices and investment returns over time:

- Independent professional appraisals of individual properties;
- Direct transaction price evidence from the property market;
- Stock market-based evidence from REIT share prices.

Indices based on each of these three types of data have different characteristics, strengths, and weaknesses.

Appraisal-based indices have been the only sort of index available until recently in the United States, and still in most other countries. They can be very useful, as they are typically based on a well-defined population of properties whose values and income are reported into the index database using standardized professionally agreed criteria. So, appraisal-based indices tend to be very well documented. They can support detailed performance attribution as well as drill-down into submarkets, and their databases generally allow measurement of total investment return (including net cash flow), not just price change or capital return.[32]

On the other hand, appraisal-based indices may suffer from the smoothing and lagging bias noted earlier in this chapter, and they are relatively subjective or "self-reported" by the property owners or managers, a consideration that can sometimes be an issue. Furthermore, in the United States the appraisal-based NCREIF and IPD indices represent a rather narrow

---

[31]There is also a supply-side reservation price index corresponding to the demand-side index. (Both are updated on an occasional basis by the MIT Center for Real Estate with cooperation from NCREIF, and are available on the MIT/CRE website at http://web.mit.edu/cre.) Over the same period of time (from 2Q2007 through 2Q2009) the supply side index (which had been below the demand index in levels) dropped only 20% (though it ultimately dropped 33% from a later peak to a later trough, between 3Q2008 and 4Q2009).

[32]Performance attribution was introduced at the micro-level in Chapter 10, and will be discussed at the macro-level in Chapter 26. Also, we noted earlier in the present chapter that, while the income component of the total return is quite important, it is not the main challenge or major focus of commercial property investment performance indexing. The main focus here is on tracking asset price changes over time.

and specialized population of properties (though an important one): those owned by pension funds and other investment institutions that must "mark to market" their property values on a frequent basis.[33] The broader population of commercial investment properties is not regularly appraised and cannot be tracked by an appraisal-based index.

There are at least three million commercial properties in the United States, worth in the aggregate over $9 trillion (as of 2010).[34] Several hundreds of thousands of the larger properties, worth about half the total value, make up what may be considered the "professional investment" population of properties. These are characterized by being owned or financed by large investment institutions such as major banks, insurance companies, pension funds, private equity funds, REITs, CMBS, and foreign investors, and are traded relatively frequently. Within this population, the NPI only covers some 7,000 properties worth barely $300 billion, a small fraction of the total.[35]

REITs own $700 billion or more worth of properties (as of 2012) not included in the NCREIF Index. Since REITs are effectively "pure plays" (essentially owning nothing but commercial property investment assets), they can provide another important source of information about commercial property values indirectly via their share prices in the stock market. As noted in the previous section, FTSE launched the first stock market-based index of property values in 2012, and it may be that this type of index will become important in the coming decade.[36] But we described in Chapter 23 how the stock market and the private property market do not always "agree" on the value of commercial property. For the present, the vast bulk of commercial properties in the United States can only be tracked by direct, transaction price evidence from the private property market.

Transaction price evidence is arguably the most fundamental type of evidence about property value, as noted in our previous discussion of Index 3 in Exhibit 25-7. Appraisers depend heavily on observations of transaction prices in order to make their valuation judgments. As property assets actually trade in the private property market, it is their transaction prices in that market that most fundamentally underpin and reflect the actual experiences of real estate investors. With this in mind, let us now focus on the major innovation in commercial property indices of the past decade: the advent of repeat-sales-transaction-based indices of commercial property price performance.

25.4.2 Repeat-Sales Indices of Commercial Property Price Performance

Until recently there were insufficient databases of commercial property transaction prices in the United States to compile a price index based on them. But by the turn of the present century CoStar, Real Capital Analytics, and a few other companies had developed large,

---

[33] As U.S. GAAP accounting standards, which generally use historical cost, evolve more towards international standards that rely more on fair value, it may be that broader populations of properties in the United States will begin to be frequently and regularly appraised. This may allow an expansion of the population of properties that could be tracked by appraisal-based indices.

[34] See Florance et al. (2010).

[35] Although this chapter is focused primarily on the U.S. market, we should note that the situation described here may differ substantially in other countries. We have already noted that in the United Kingdom, for example, the appraisal-based IPD Index there covers a much larger fraction of all U.K. commercial investment properties, and in a market and institutional environment where the appraisals differ from transaction prices less than in the United States. (See Devaney and Diaz, 2011.)

[36] See Section 26.3.3 in the next chapter for more discussion of the PureProperty Index. Also, please note that the FTSE-NAREIT PureProperty Index should not be confused with the Green Street Advisors Commercial Property Price Index (GSA-CPPI). We described in Chapter 23 how Green Street is a leading company regularly estimating the values of REIT property assets as an input to produce their proprietary Price/NAV ratio estimates for the REITs. In 2009 Green Street began publishing the GSA-CPPI as an index tracking REIT property asset values, based on Green Street's NAV estimation process. The GSA-CPPI aims to track values in the private property market, not stock market based valuations, and therefore is not an example of what we are defining here as a stock market based index. (A stock market based index would be based on the numerator in the P/NAV ratio, whereas the GSA-CPPI is based on the denominator.) The GSA-CPPI also differs from the formal repeat-sales regression-based indices we will describe in the next section based directly and purely on transaction price evidence in the private market.

sophisticated, and constantly updated databases of commercial transactions. This combined with advances in econometric and computational technology for producing price indices in private whole-asset markets to enable the production and regular publication of statistically rigorous indices of commercial property prices.

Given a good database of asset prices, it is easy to tabulate average or median price per square foot each period. Such indices have long been produced for the housing market in the United States. But commercial property is much more heterogeneous than housing, and there will generally be a serious "apples-versus-oranges" problem if you take a simple comparison of average price in one period, compare it to the average price in the preceding period, and try to infer from that comparison a price change or capital return as experienced by investors. For example, in the market downturn in 2008–2009 some average price indices at first showed an increase. But that was only reflecting a "flight to quality," as nervous investors shifted their activity toward buying nothing but the highest quality, most prime properties. Even in the housing market, the leading price indices now used in most sophisticated analyses are based on statistically rigorous procedures that formally control for the apples-to-oranges problem of different houses trading in different periods. The most widely used such procedure is the **repeat-sales price index**.

A repeat-sales (RS) price index (RSPI) is based only on properties that have sold at least twice, and the index is based directly and purely on the percentage *change* in price (or log price difference) between the "buy" and the subsequent "sell" in each paired-sale observation. The index is thus based entirely on the actual round-trip investment price change experiences of the investors in the market. This is arguably the most relevant measure of interest to investors.[37] The model regresses the percentage price changes onto a sequence of time-dummy variables representing the historical periods in the index. In a common specification, for each paired-sale observation the time-dummies are set to equal zero for any time periods before the first sale (the "buy") or after the second sale (the "sell"), and in between (during the holding of the investment) they are set equal to one. Thus, given many repeat-sale pairs spanning all the historical time periods in numerous different combinations of holding spans, the regression model is able to parse out how much of the percentage price changes realized in the investors' round-trip experiences are attributable to each historical time period.

Let's take a very simple numerical example. Suppose there are two investors and two periods of time. Suppose the first investor bought his property for $100 at the beginning of the first period, and sold it for $115.50 at the end of the second time period. Suppose the second investor bought his property at the beginning of the second time period for $200 and sold it at the end of that period for $210. Then the time-dummy variable for the first time period would have a value of one for the first investor's experience and a value of zero for the second investor's experience, since the second investor was not in the market during that period. The time-dummy variable for the second time period would have a value of one for both investors since they were both in the market, holding their investments, during the second time period. The regression model data table looks like this:

---

[37]There may be other foci of interest. For example, instead of focusing on investors' experiences, one could focus on the average price trend in the market. Though closely related to investors' experiences, the market average price trend is not exactly the same thing as the average investor's price change experience. Investors buy and sell at specific times at least partly of their own choosing, and they must always sell the same property that they have previously bought. In contrast, the market exists continuously, and its stock of buildings is generally being always updated and rejuvenated with new buildings, such that the same buildings do not characterize the market across time. For example, the average age of the building stock in the market does not increase year for year like the age of any given building. Other types of price models and indices may be more appropriate than repeat-sales for measuring the market price trend, at least in principle, such as hedonic price modeling. (See numerous references on hedonic indexing and the comparison of hedonic and repeat-sales modeling, in the Chapter 25 section of the bibliography at the end of Chapter 26. In particular you might want to look at the articles by: Case, Pollakowski, and Wachter; Case and Quigley; Case and Shiller; Clapp and Giacotto; Englund, Quigley and Redfearn; Hansen; and Wallace and Meese.)

Left Hand Side	Right Hand Side	
	Time Period 1 (dummy):	Time Period 2 (dummy):
115.5 / 100 = 1.155	1	1
220 / 200 = 1.05	0	1

The regression model would then estimate the time-dummy coefficients for the two periods so as to minimize the difference between the model's predicted price-change experiences for the investors and their actual price-change experiences. For this simple example it is clear that the solution is for the first time-period to be given a return of 10 percent and the second period a return of 5 percent. This will cause the first investor's predicted price change experience to exactly equal his actual experience ($115.50 = $100 * (1.10) * (1.05)).[38] The second investor's predicted price change experience will also exactly equal his actual experience ($220 = $200 * (1.05)).[39]

Though this is a very simple example in which we can intuitively see the solution, this is the essence of how the repeat-sales regression-based price index attributes to each historical period the actual realized round-trip price change experiences of the investors in the market. In this sense, the repeat-sales index is very analogous to a stock market price index. It is very relevant to real estate investors, and generally is easily understood by them (which is important). Another practical advantage of the repeat-sales price index is that the model is parsimonious, which means that it requires relatively little information about the transactions, just their prices and dates. The other major rigorous approach to real estate price index construction controlling for differences between the properties that transact from one period to the next, known as "hedonic modeling," requires a lot more information about the properties that are being bought and sold each period. Getting such information, and figuring out the best way to model the property values using the hedonic information, can be problematical in practice, especially for commercial properties. So, the repeat-sales price indices tend to be more "robust" to the data challenges in the real world. They can be used to track investors' price change experiences in any property market that has sufficient repeat-sales data.

With this in mind, let's look at the recent price-change histories evidenced in the first two regularly published repeat-sales indices of commercial property prices in the United States. The first such index was the Moody's/REAL Commercial Property Price Index (CPPI), developed in 2006 at the MIT Center for Real Estate based on transaction price data from Real Capital Analytics (RCA). This index has an inception date as of the end of 2000 and tracks properties generally over $2,500,000 in value, a threshold which roughly distinguishes the previously described "professional investment" segment of the commercial property market from the smaller properties that typically do not trade as frequently and are often occupied and used by their owners. In 2011 the original Moody's/REAL CPPI was discontinued, and replaced in 2012 by a second-generation version labeled the Moody's/RCA CPPI.

In 2010 CoStar Group launched the second major repeat-sales index in the United States, named the CoStar Commercial Repeat-Sales Index (CCRSI). CoStar's transaction database is much larger and includes the smaller commercial properties in an index that goes back through 1998. The CoStar index is interesting in that it is broken out between the smaller properties, which CoStar labels "general," and the larger properties (roughly comparable to the RCA $2.5 million threshold, though CoStar uses a physical criteria) which CoStar

---

[38]The first investor's predicted price change reflects both periods' time-dummy coefficients, since both of those time-dummies have a value of one for that investor. Note that the actual computations are done in logs, so that the returns estimated on the right-hand-side are additive rather than multiplicative.

[39]The second investor's predicted experience by the model only involves the second time period's coefficient (the 5% estimated return) because that investor was only holding his investment during that time period, as he bought at the beginning of that period and sold at the end of it.

labels "investment." This distinction also roughly corresponds to the distinction between the larger "institutional" properties and the smaller "noninstitutional" properties that we have previously noted in Chapters 11 and 22. Exhibit 25-9 shows the differential same-property price experiences of these two major segments in the U.S. commercial property market since 1999. Note that the two segments have behaved quite differently. The smaller ("general," or "noninstitutional") properties exhibited greater price appreciation up to the market peak, and then fell less precipitously during the financial crisis of 2008–2009, but then did not recover as rapidly in the aftermath. This probably at least partly reflects the different types of financing available to investors in the larger ("investment" or "institutional") properties. In particular, investors in the larger properties were able to tap major nonbank sources of financing, such as from private equity funds, pension funds, REITs, and foreign investors.

The different price dynamics between institutional and noninstitutional properties revealed in Exhibit 25-9 suggests the importance of identifying asset market segments in price indexing commercial property in the United States. Even though as we noted back in Chapter 1 asset markets are far more integrated across geography and building type than space markets, the new transaction-based price indices launched in the past decade and covering much broader populations of properties than the NCREIF Index have revealed that segmentation can still be important in the asset market among the broader population of commercial properties, even within the institutional segment of the market.

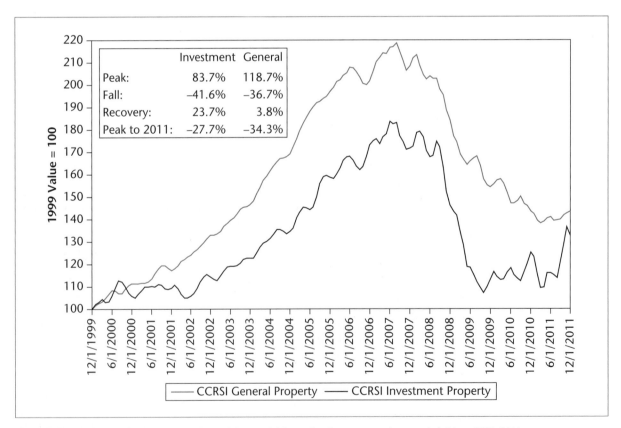

EXHIBIT 25-9 CoStar CCRSI, Investment vs. General Commercial Properties: Same-property (repeat-sales) Prices, 2000–2011

Source: CoStar Group Inc. Index values as of June 2012.

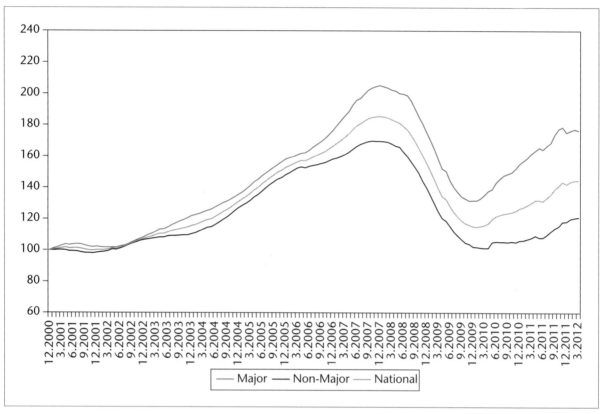

EXHIBIT 25-10 Moody's/RCA CPPI, Major and Non-Major Markets Composite Indices
Source: Real Capital Analytics. Index histories as of June 2012.

This is revealed strikingly in the Moody's/RCA CPPI indices shown in Exhibits 25-10 and 25-11.

Exhibit 25-10 shows the CPPI composite indices for same-property price changes among "Major-Markets" and "Non-Major Markets," and the National Composite Index that is a value-weighted combination of those two segments. The Major-Markets in the indices depicted in the Exhibit were defined as Boston, New York, Washington DC, Chicago, San Francisco, and Los Angeles. The Non-Major Markets consisted of everything else. Keeping in mind that these indices represent only the price-change relevant to the investors' capital returns, not the total investment returns, it is nevertheless striking how different the behavior can be, and this is all within the larger-property ($2.5 million plus) segment roughly corresponding to the "Investment" index in Exhibit 25-9. Exhibit 25-11 shows a finer-grained breakout, tracking five separate sectors (apartments, industrial, retail, CBD-Office, and Suburban-Office) separately for the Major Markets and Non-Major Markets. Both panels of Exhibit 25-11 have the same scale on the vertical and horizontal axes, so they can be directly compared visually. The dispersion in price dynamics is obvious.

In summary, the new repeat-sales price indices developed in the twenty-first century for U.S. commercial property investors have opened a new window on a much broader population of potential investment assets than was previously available through the traditional appraisal-based indices. The field of property price and return indexing is still rapidly developing, and the next decade may see further important innovations.

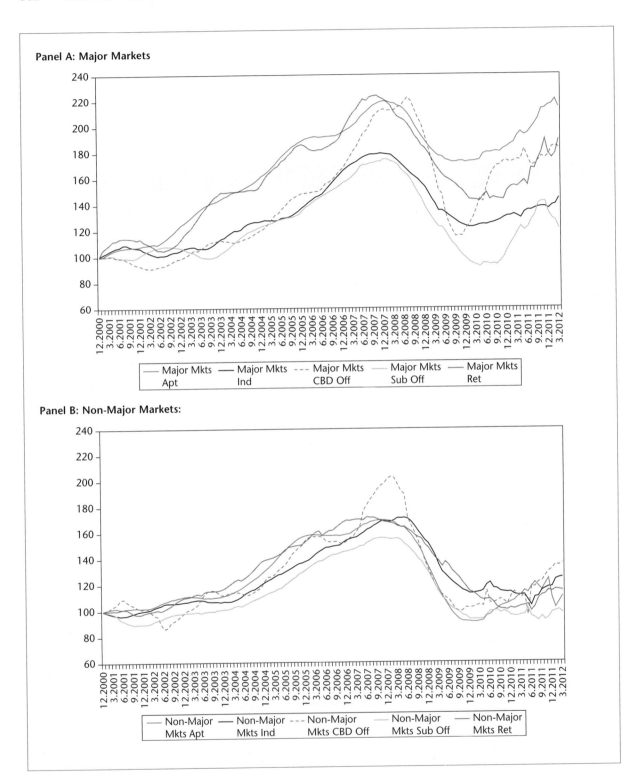

EXHIBIT 25-11 Moody's/RCA CPPI Building-Block Indices

Source: Real Capital Analytics, Inc. (Index histories as of June 2012.)

25.5 Chapter Summary

In this chapter, we have provided an in-depth discussion of the nature of private market real estate periodic price change and investment returns data—the raw material on which virtually all quantitative macro-level real estate investment analysis is based. In Chapter 26, we will address some subjects that practitioners in the real world of macro-level real estate investment deal with on a daily basis. You will see again how the data issues described in this chapter are relevant.

KEY TERMS

NCREIF Property Index (NPI)
error
random noise
Square Root of *n* Rule
temporal lag
volatility effects (of return errors)
covariance effects
moving average
smoothing (or appraisal smoothing)

beta effects
cross-correlation effects
autocorrelation effects
price discovery
Index 1 (REIT-based returns)
Index 2 (constant-liquidity private market returns)

Index 3 (observable contemporaneous transaction price returns)
Index 4 (contemporaneous appraisal-based returns)
Index 5 (staggered appraisal-based index returns)
noise-versus-lag trade-off
repeat-sales price index

STUDY QUESTIONS

Conceptual Questions

25.1. What are the two most common or prominent types of "error" in major indices of private real estate price appreciation?

25.2. Considering appraisal valuations of individual properties, explain the meaning of random error (or noise) component of appraisal "error."

25.3. In the same context as above, what is meant by the temporal lag bias component of appraisal error? What is the typical cause or source of such bias? What is the implication of temporal lag bias for the distribution of appraised values around the underlying true value?

25.4. How can it be rational for an appraiser to only partially adjust her opinion of value of a property in response to the arrival of new information?

25.5. What is the noise-versus-lag trade-off in individual property appraisal? How is this related to the Square Root of *n* Rule? Which of these two types of error is relatively more important at the micro-level of individual property value estimation? What about at the macro-level of static portfolio value estimation as the aggregation of the appraised values of individual properties in the portfolio?

25.6. Describe and contrast the pure effect of random noise and the pure effect of temporal lagging in terms of how an empirical periodic price index would differ from the unobservable underlying true returns. When is the noise effect relatively more important? When is the temporal lag effect typically more important?

25.7. Think back to Chapter 21 where we examined the role of real estate in mixed asset portfolios. Based on your answer to the previous question, what are the dangers of without correction using an appraisal-based real estate return series to examine optimal asset class allocations when real estate is included in the mix?

25.8. In what way can random noise and temporal lag bias mask each other in typical real world price indices? When is such masking likely to be most important?

25.9. Section 25.3.1 presents five different conceptual definitions of commercial property value levels (or periodic appreciation returns).

   a. Describe each of the five value indices starting first with Index 5, which is a staggered appraisal-based index like the NCREIF property index (NPI), and then moving up to Index 1, which is stock market based index such as the FTSE-NAREIT PureProperty Index. As part of your answer, explain the advantage and disadvantage of each index relative to the previous one you just described. What do you gain and what do you lose?

   b. Describe the dynamic behavior of each value definition in response to the arrival of news relevant to the value of real estate assets. (See Exhibit 25-7.)

   c. Which of the indices do you think is the most relevant for each of the eight practical decision problems posed at the beginning of section 25.3? Explain your choice in each case.

25.10. Explain why the dynamic adjustment of a transaction-based (variable liquidity) real estate price index is more sluggish than a constant liquidity version of the index. How is this related to the fact that prices and trading volume are jointly determined in the private real estate asset market? Based on your answers, explain why constant liquidity prices were higher than transaction-prices in the mid-2000s boom years, but lower during the downturn in 2008–09, as seen in Exhibit 25-8.

25.11. What are the three major types of price or investment performance indices publicly available for tracking private commercial property in the U.S. as of the early 2010s?

25.12. What is the essential nature of a repeat-sales price index? That is, in what way does it essentially reflect the experience of investors in the private property market?

Quantitative Problems

25.13. Three nearly identical properties are all sold as of the same date, for prices of $2,650,000, $2,450,000, and $2,400,000.

   a. What is your best estimate of the market values of each of two other properties that are virtually identical to the first three, as of that same date?

   b. If one of those additional properties actually did sell for a price of $2,550,000, what is your estimate of the market value of the fifth property as of that same date?

   c. What is the market value of the fourth property?

   d. What is your best estimate of the error or noise (defined as the difference between the transaction price and the market value) in the observed transaction prices of all four properties?

25.14. In Problem 25.12, how much did the accuracy of your estimate of market value improve as a result of the addition of the fourth empirical valuation observation (i.e., what is your estimation error with the fourth transaction, and what is it with only the first three)?

25.15. Suppose you regress a time-series of appraisal-based index periodic returns onto both contemporaneous and lagged securities market returns that do not suffer from lagging or measurement errors. That is, you perform the following regression, where $r_{M,t}$ is the accurate market return in period t and r_t^* is the appraisal-based real estate return in period t:

$$r_t^* = a + \beta_0 r_{M,t} + \beta_1 r_{M,t-1} + \beta_2 r_{M,t-2} + \beta_3 r_{M,t-3} + \varepsilon_t$$

The resulting contemporaneous and lagged beta values are

$$\hat{\beta}_0 = 0.05$$
$$\hat{\beta}_1 = 0.15$$
$$\hat{\beta}_2 = 0.10$$
$$\hat{\beta}_3 = 0.00$$

What is your best estimate of the true long-run beta between real estate and the securities market index?

25.16. Suppose you have reason to believe that appraisal behavior is well characterized by the following autoregression model relating quarterly appraised values to average transaction prices:

$$V_t^* = 0.30\overline{V}_t + 0.70V_{t-1}^*$$

where the V values are in log levels. Now suppose that a quarterly appraisal-based index (based on fully contemporaneous appraisals, that is, without stale appraisals) indicates an appreciation return of 1% in the current quarter (t), and 1.5% in the previous quarter ($t-1$). Assuming that the appraisal-based index has been cleansed of random noise, what is the implied current period contemporaneous transaction-price-based appreciation return (like Index 3) suggested by a reverse engineering of the appraisal behavior?

REAL ESTATE INVESTMENT MANAGEMENT AND DERIVATIVES

LEARNING OBJECTIVES

After reading this chapter, you should understand:

⊃ What is meant by investment performance attribution at both the macro property level and the portfolio level.

⊃ How to quantify segment allocation versus asset selection effects in a portfolio's differential performance relative to an appropriate benchmark.

⊃ What are the major institutional real estate investment management "styles" and how these may be accounted for in quantitative investment performance evaluation.

⊃ The new concept of real estate equity index derivatives and how such products might be used in real estate investment management.

Recall that at the outset of Part VII we highlighted three major types of macro-level real estate investment decisions: strategic policy, tactical policy, and policy implementation. In this last chapter of Part VII we turn our primary attention to this last question: how to implement real estate investment policy, or more broadly, how to manage real estate investments. This subject is obviously important for those who will be doing the management directly themselves, but it is also important for those whose money will be managed by others with more specialized expertise in real estate management. Decision makers at both levels should be familiar with the principles and tools we will introduce in this chapter. The chapter will begin with macro-level investment performance attribution and manager evaluation. Then we will go into more depth to examine some nuts and bolts of the investment management business with a consideration of benchmarking and real estate investment styles. (More depth and detail is available in the two chapter appendices available on the book's CD.) We will finish the chapter by introducing real estate price index derivatives and the idea of synthetic investment in real estate, an interesting new tool for real estate investment management that may become important in the twenty-first century.

26.1 Macro-Level Investment Performance Attribution

In the field of sophisticated, institutional real estate investment management there is growing potential to apply quantitative analytical tools to help understand and improve investment performance. A fundamental metric that can be useful in this regard is investment **performance attribution**. The idea is to break down into components the ex post total return achieved by a given portfolio or manager in order to learn something about the nature and source of the total return performance. Such dissection can then be combined with **benchmarking**, the comparison of the subject manager's or portfolio's performance results with the average results of some suitably defined index or peer group of similar properties or managers, to gain further insight.[1] Performance attribution is useful for two broad purposes: diagnosis and evaluation. The former purpose is primarily of interest to managers, to help them understand the sources and causes of their realized performance. The use of performance attribution in manager evaluation is of interest both to managers and investor clients, as it can help investors to judge and compare the performance results of competing managers.

26.1.1 The Importance of Property-Level Investment Management

Two salient features of investment in the private real estate market as distinguished from most investment in publicly-traded securities (including REITs) are that: (1) The investor cannot simply passively invest in an index[2] but rather must buy (and hold and ultimately sell) specific individual property assets; and (2) the investor is responsible for the operational management of those assets.

With this in mind, look at Exhibit 26-1. The thick blue line in the exhibit depicts the Moody's/RCA Commercial Property Price Index (CPPI) from its inception at the end of 2000 with a value of 100 through June 2012 when this index tracking same-property prices had a value of approximately 140.[3] The thin gray lines show the price performance of the 10 last-sold properties in that index. Each property is pegged to the index value at the date when it was purchased, and then its value relative to the index is "grown" at a constant rate per month so as to reveal its cumulative price change differential relative to the index by the time of its sale in June 2012. The point is to show graphically how individual property investment performance can differ dramatically from that of the average or aggregate market as a whole which is represented by the index. For example, one of those 10 properties ended up

---

[1]Quantitative performance attribution in real estate investment was pioneered to a considerable degree by the British company, Investment Property Databank (IPD), starting in the 1980s. As late as the 2010s such formal analysis was still more prevalent in the United Kingdom than in the United States, though it is becoming more of a standard state of the art practice among many global real estate investment management firms and funds, and both IPD and NCREIF collect and disseminate data relevant for performance attribution and benchmarking in the United States.

[2]A possible exception will be discussed in the last section of this chapter regarding real estate price index derivatives and "synthetic" investment in real estate.

[3]In between, as you can see, the index peaked around 180 in 2007 and then fell to barely 110 in 2009. See section 25.4.2 in the preceding chapter for a description of repeat-sales indices, the type of price index the CPPI is. (Note that the exact values in the CPPI change as new data is incorporated into the compilation of the average investors' round-trip realized price-change experiences, as described in Chapter 25.)

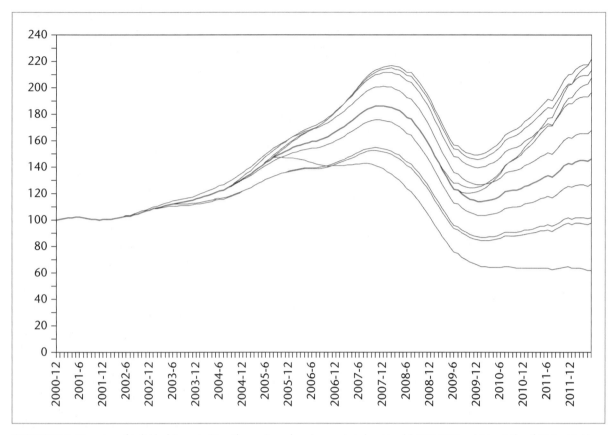

EXHIBIT 26-1 Dispersion of Individual Property Price Change Around an Aggregate Index: Moody's/RCA CPPI and Price Paths of 10 Last-Sold Property Investments as of June 2012

Pegged to starting value on index at time of prior sale (buy), then tracked at constant rate per month to ultimate sale price deviation from index at disposition in June 2012.

Source: Data from Real Capital Analytics Inc. (Used by permission)

more than 50 percent below the aggregate index value, while another couple of properties ended up close to 50 percent above the index. As an investment manager responsible for buying, operating, and selling specific individual properties, how can you try to make sure your properties are among the "winners," or at least not among the worst "losers"? The answer to this question can be significant in determining how successful you are as a real estate investor in the private property market, even apart from what happens with the market as a whole and the average investor.

26.1.2 Macro Property-Level Performance Attribution and the Four Fundamental Responsibilities

In Appendix 10A at the end of Chapter 10, we described *micro-level* performance attribution, an approach to "parsing" (or breaking down into its components) the IRR at the level of the individual property investment so as to provide some insight regarding the sources of the overall multiperiod return on the investment. At what might be termed the **macro property level**, performance attribution can also apply the same IRR parsing as was described in Appendix 10A, only aggregated across an entire portfolio of properties. The objective is to attribute the property-level since-acquisition IRRs of the investments to: (1) the initial cash yield, labeled "IY," (2) the cash flow change during the holding

EXHIBIT 26-2 The Four
Fundamental Property-
Level Investment
Management
Responsibilities Related
to the Three Property-
Level Performance
Attributes

© OnCourse Learning

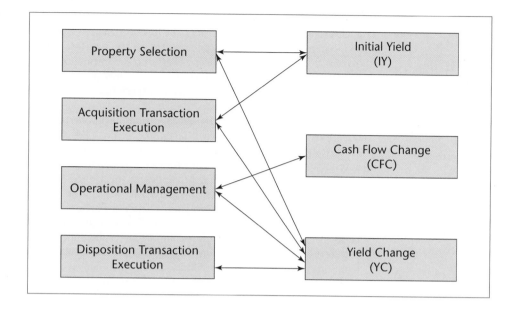

period, labeled "CFC," and (3) the effect of the change in the cash yield between the acquisition and the disposition (or current appraisal if the property is still being held), labeled "YC."[4]

Macro property-level performance attribution is most useful to the investment manager for diagnostic purposes, to help the manager understand the property-level sources of his performance results (e.g., not counting the effect of leverage or capital structure[5]), particularly if the manager's results are compared with an appropriate benchmark of other similar properties owned by competing investment managers in the subject manager's peer universe.

The basic idea in property-level since-acquisition IRR performance attribution is to relate the investment performance to the *four fundamental responsibilities* of property-level investment management:

1. **Property selection:** Picking "good" properties (e.g., bargains as found).
2. **Acquisition transaction execution:** Skillful negotiation and due diligence.
3. **Operational management during the holding period:** Including property-level marketing and positioning, leasing, tenant servicing, expense management, profitable capital expenditure management, and so on.
4. **Disposition transaction execution:** Successful timing, effective search for the right buyer, skillful and efficient sales management, and negotiation.

Property-level since-acquisition IRR attribution can help an investment manager understand their strengths and weaknesses at the property-level because the four fundamental responsibilities relate differentially to the three IRR attributes, as suggested in Exhibit 26-2. Thus, how well the manager scores quantitatively in the three attributes reveals something

---

[4]See Appendix 10A in Chapter 10 for further details and a numerical example. There are also other ways of defining and measuring property-level performance attribution, most notably that promulgated by Investment Property Databank (IPD). The key feature of the system defined in the Appendix 10A is that it is based on the multi-period IRR since the acquisition of each property, including the effect of the acquisition price. This sharpens the focus of the measure onto the round-trip investment performance at the property level, including all four major property-level investment management functions of property selection, acquisition, management during the holding period, and disposition (if the property has been sold).

[5]Performance attribution can in principle be applied to the levered equity performance, or the effect of leverage can be isolated first and treated separately, by comparing the levered equity performance versus the property-level performance without leverage. (See Chapters 13 and 14 for analytical tools relating to the effect of leverage.)

about relative strengths and weaknesses, or at least raises questions which suggest avenues for analysis and perhaps improvement. The links depicted in Exhibit 26-2 are of course not exact or mechanistic. Other factors can intervene to affect performance, such as market movements beyond the control of the manager. Performance attribution is an art, not a science. Nevertheless, careful application of property-level performance attribution analysis may be able to provide insight. It can also help to set an expectation of accountability within the investment management organization.

As is typical with all performance attribution, property-level performance attribution is often most effective when applied in conjunction with benchmarking. The idea is to compare the investment performance of a subject property or portfolio or manager with that of an appropriate cohort of similar properties over the same period of time. For core (stabilized, institutional quality) investment properties in the United States, the NCREIF index can be used to synthesize a benchmark, by converting the appropriate subindex of the NPI into an equivalent multiyear IRR performance. (This information is available on the NCREIF Web site.) Once a benchmark is selected, the difference between the subject property or portfolio performance and the benchmark is computed over the same historical time span, both overall and for each of the three performance attributes. The result will be a comparison that might look something like the bars in Exhibit 26-3, which depicts an example real world application of the since-acquisition IRR attribution benchmarking procedure.

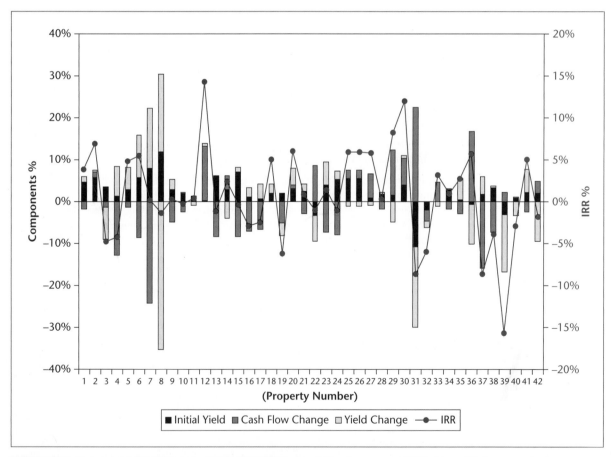

EXHIBIT 26-3 Property-Level IRR Attributes in 42 Round-Trip Investments: Subject Property vs. NCREIF Cohort, IRR Component by Property
Source: Modified from Feng (2010).

The exhibit shows the lifetime performances (from acquisition through disposition) of 42 randomly-numbered institutional real estate investment properties. Each property's overall IRR, as well as its three performance attributes of IY, CFC, and YC, are measured *relative to* a NCREIF benchmark. Only the difference between the property and the benchmark is shown in the exhibit (overall IRR on the right-hand vertical axis, each attribute as indicated by the bars referenced to the left-hand axis). The NCREIF benchmarks are customized to each property. The benchmark is the IRR of a NCREIF subindex representing the same geographic region and property type as the subject property and measured over the same historical holding period as the property. The 42 investments spanned the period from 1981 to 2008 with an average holding period of 10.3 years and average property sale price of $51 million.[6]

The first thing to notice in Exhibit 26-3 is the wide dispersion in the properties' overall IRR results around their benchmarks. This is seen in the blue dots, whose values on the right-hand axis show how the properties' lifetime IRRs differed from their NCREIF benchmarks over the same historical period. The dots are widely dispersed both above and below the horizontal axis, which represents performance just equal to the benchmark. Twenty-four of the investments beat their benchmarks while 18 fell short, with an average IRR difference of just 0.69 percent above the benchmark, implying for the average hold a cumulative outperformance of $1.0069^{10.3} - 1 = 7.3\%$. But the standard deviation of the differential performance across the 42 properties was 5.64 percent, which for the average hold would imply a one-standard deviation cumulative dispersion between +76 percent down to −45 percent.[7]

The performance attribution represented by the bars in the exhibit allow us to gain some insight about the determinants of this range of performance. The initial yield performance is relatively stable and favorable across the 42 investments.[8] Most of the "action" in these properties' performance relative to their benchmarks lies in the other two attributes, CFC and YC, attributes that depend substantially on management of the property investments *subsequent* to the initial selection and acquisition of the properties. Close inspection reveals that it is especially the CFC attribute which, more than any other, determines whether a property beats its benchmark or falls short in terms of the overall IRR performance that is the main investment bottom line. Among the 42 properties 57 percent beat their benchmarks, but among properties with positive CFC components (relative to the benchmark CFC) 69 percent beat their overall IRR benchmarks. All of the sample's top nine performers relative to the benchmark (in terms of IRR) had positive CFC components relative to the benchmark, while seven of the nine worst performers had negative CFC components relative to the benchmark.

These results may reflect property-level investment management strengths and weaknesses of the managers of the sample properties. Relating the performance in the three attributes to the four investment management responsibilities listed in Exhibit 26-2, we can form some hypotheses. The relatively strong and reliable IY performance suggests that these managers were generally able to acquire properties more effectively than the NCREIF peer universe. Exhibit 26-2 suggests that this may have reflected some combination of good property selection and effective acquisition execution. For example, the managers may have been able to effectively utilize deep cash pockets perhaps focused on a few target markets where they could be major players, so as to attract the best brokers to bring them privileged access to the best deals. On the other hand, once acquired, the properties in general seem to have

---

[6]The properties in Exhibit 26-3 represented all regions of the U.S. and the four core usage types of apartment, industrial, office, and retail. The holding periods ranged from 2.9 to 24.5 years, and gross IRRs (per annum, before subtracting benchmark IRRs) ranged from 29.1% (with a 5-year hold) to −1.7% (with a 4-year hold). All the properties were held as core real estate investments by a group of relatively conservative tax-exempt institutions with similar overall investment objectives and policies. Exhibit 26-3 is based on Feng (2010) and is also summarized in Feng and Geltner (2011).

[7]$1.0564^{10.3} - 1 = 1.76$. $(1 - 0.0564)^{10.3} - 1 = 0.55 = 1 - 0.45$. As suggested in Exhibit 26-1, this magnitude of range in individual property lifetime investment performance dispersion seems to be typical among U.S. institutional commercial properties. Similar rates of cumulative performance dispersion appear in the residuals of the repeat-sales regressions underlying indices such as the Moody's/RCA CPPI described in the preceding chapter.

[8]Compared to the overall IRR average relative to benchmark of 0.69% with standard deviation 5.64%, the IY component had average 2.25% with standard deviation 3.54% across the 42 properties.

been not as effectively managed as their benchmarks, particularly regarding on-going cash flow during the holding period. The managers could perhaps improve their overall investment performance by figuring out how they are falling short of their peers in the management of property-level revenues, expenses, or capital improvement expenditures.

This example shows the power and potential of quantitative property-level investment analysis including performance attribution and benchmarking. However, all such formal quantitative exercises must be taken with a grain of salt and applied in an "investigative" spirit. They often bring insights by the questions they raise rather than by providing any definitive answers. They get property and asset managers thinking about how they did and what they did in specific cases, and what impact their actions had in the overall performance. These types of results should never be used mechanistically, without broader and more qualitative analysis, and they should generally be used more for constructive *diagnostic* (i.e., "learning") purposes than for *evaluative* purposes (in our opinion).

In applying performance attribution at any level, we should also remember that return parsing is an inexact science that is sensitive to the length of time over which the return is measured. It is also important to carefully consider the meaning of property-level performance attribution measures. For example, if the yield or income component of the multi-period return does not correspond to the yield at the time when the property was acquired, then it is not clear what implication this component of the return can logically hold regarding the investment manager's performance, even in comparison with a benchmark. Similar questions about meaning may be raised about other components of property-level performance attribution.

26.1.3 Portfolio-Level Performance Attribution

We now move from property-level to portfolio-level attribution. At the **portfolio level**, the key components of investment performance attribution are traditionally defined as **allocation** and **selection**. These are the two major "jobs" that an active portfolio manager may potentially perform. Such a manager may decide how to allocate the total investment capital across a range of exhaustive and mutually exclusive **segments**, that is, classes or types of assets within her purview, and/or she may select which particular individual assets to buy (and sell) within each segment. It is in the selection component that portfolio-level attribution can link down to property-level attribution. We saw in the previous section how asset selection is one of the four fundamental property-level investment responsibilities. But asset selection can also be viewed within the broader or higher-level context of portfolio management.

The terms "allocation" and "selection," like the basic idea of performance attribution at the portfolio level, have their origins in the stock-market-based branch of the investment industry. We need to see how this tool translates into application to investment in the private real estate market. Let's begin with a consideration of the two basic attributes: allocation and selection.

As noted, allocation refers to the chosen segment weights in the portfolio. As an attribute of investment manager performance, allocation is a very similar concept in real estate and in the stock market. In the stock market, segments may refer to industry groupings or sectors in the stock market, or to attributes of the stock, such as market capitalization or current yield. In the private real estate asset market, segments are typically based on the space market to some extent and are usually defined by building usage type and the geographical location of properties. For example, an allocation decision would be to invest 60 percent in warehouses and only 40 percent in office buildings.[9] The basic idea is the same as in the stock market. Segment allocation is a broader-level, more "macro" decision than selection.

Selection, on the other hand, refers to the more micro-level decision of which particular individual assets are picked by the manager to include in the portfolio. In the stock market, investment managers have more freedom of action in asset selection than in the private property market. Within a given segment, an equities manager can invest any amount in any

---

[9]Or to invest 60% east of the Mississippi and only 40% west of the Mississippi. Or to invest 36% in warehouses east of the Mississippi, 24% each in offices east and warehouses west, and 16% in offices west of the Mississippi. You get the idea. (Actually, as we noted in Part II, metropolitan areas usually make more sense as geographical units, rather than broad, multistate regions.)

individual asset (that is, any individual firm's stock). In real estate, an investment manager can decide which individual properties to buy or sell. However, in real estate only assets that are for sale can be bought; so, the manager cannot choose from among the entire potential universe of individual assets. Transaction costs are high in the property market, which usually means long holding periods must be planned for. Finally, as was the subject of the previous section on property-level performance attribution, with private real estate investment the property owner is responsible for the operational management of the assets he selects. Indeed, as we have seen, a large part of the total investment performance may be attributable to operational management.

For all of these reasons (but especially the last), the asset selection function in private real estate is more complicated than it is in stock market investment management. At the portfolio level, it is really not possible to distinguish the component of overall performance due to asset selection per se (as understood in the stock market) from the performance component due to operational management of the assets (though this is where the property-level performance attribution discussed in the previous section can come into play). Nevertheless, there is still some interest and potential usefulness in quantitatively attributing performance at the portfolio level to allocation and selection.

To see how this is done, let's consider a simplified example. Suppose Bob and Sue were each hired at the same time to place $100 million worth of capital into private real estate investments in the industrial and office property segments (and then to manage those investments). Their clients gave them discretion over how much to allocate to each of the two segments. Bob immediately went out and bought $90 million worth of industrial buildings and $10 million worth of offices. Sue did just the opposite, buying $10 million of industrial and $90 million of offices. A few years later, these two intrepid investment managers got to talking at a cocktail reception at a meeting of the Pension Real Estate Association (PREA). Realizing the amazing coincidence of both being hired at the same time for the same type of investment management job, and noting that they had both placed rather strong, and opposite, segment bets, they decided to compare their performances.

The table in Exhibit 26-4 shows the returns both managers earned for their clients, both in total and broken down by segment. Much to his chagrin, Bob had to admit that Sue had beaten him. Over the three years, her annual average return was 9.7 percent, versus Bob's 9.2 percent, a differential of 50 basis points. However, a more careful examination of the returns each manager earned by segment reveals differing sources for their relative performances. Bob clearly beat Sue in property selection performance because *within* each segment Bob's properties earned higher returns than Sue's. His industrial properties returned 9 percent to her 7 percent, while his office properties returned 11 percent to her 10 percent. But Sue beat Bob in allocation performance. Her decision to allocate a greater share of her capital to office than industrial properties turned out to have been advantageous because of the generally better performance of office properties as compared to industrial properties. In this case, Sue's superior segment bet dominated over Bob's superior selection performance to give Sue the overall advantage.

The idea in portfolio-level performance attribution is to break down the total return differential between two managers' performances (or, more often between a manager and a relevant

Weights	Bob	Sue
Industrial	90%	10%
Office	10%	90%
Returns	**Bob**	**Sue**
Total portfolio	9.20%	9.70%
Industrial properties	9.00%	7.00%
Office properties	11.00%	10.00%

EXHIBIT 26-4 Returns Realized for Clients by Bob and Sue

© OnCourse Learning

benchmark) into two components, one based on allocation and the other on selection. However, the overall performance differential is a nonlinear function of the pure allocation and pure selection performance differentials, so there is no unambiguous way to attribute the total differential completely and exactly to these two sources. Nevertheless, some reasonable quantification can be attempted. To see how, let's carry on with our Sue-versus-Bob comparison.

Consider allocation performance first. Suppose we want to quantify how much of Sue's overall 50-basis-point differential over Bob is attributable to her allocation difference with respect to Bob. One way to do this would be to multiply Sue's return performance within each segment by the difference between her allocation and Bob's allocation, and add these products across all the segments. This is demonstrated, in formula (1a):

$$
\begin{aligned}
A_S - A_B &= r_{SI}(w_{SI} - w_{BI}) + r_{SO}(w_{SO} - w_{BO}) \\
&= 7\%(0.1 - 0.9) + 10\%(0.9 - 0.1) \\
&= -5.6\% + 8\% = +2.4\%
\end{aligned}
\tag{1a}
$$

The implication is that Sue outperformed Bob by 240 basis points on the basis of her superior allocation.

The fact that Sue's overall performance differential was less than this, only 50 basis points, reflects the fact that she lost ground relative to Bob in the other attribute of performance, namely, selection. In fact, the simplistic implication is that she lost 190 basis points compared to Bob as a result of her relatively inferior selection: $+2.4\% - 1.9\% = +0.5\%$.

Now suppose we apply the same reasoning to quantify Sue's selection performance differential directly. That is, we multiply the difference between her return and Bob's return within each segment by Sue's allocation weights and sum these products across the segments, as here:

$$
\begin{aligned}
S_S - S_B &= w_{SI}(r_{SI} - r_{BI}) + w_{SO}(r_{SO} - r_{BO}) \\
&= 0.1(7\% - 9\%) + 0.9(10\% - 11\%) \\
&= -0.2\% - 0.9\% = -1.1\%
\end{aligned}
\tag{1b}
$$

By this way of figuring, Sue's inferior selection performance cost her only 110 basis points relative to Bob, instead of the 190-basis-point loss we previously computed as a result of formula (1a). If selection's effect in the differential is only 110 basis points, then allocation's contribution is not 240 basis points, but only 160 basis points, as $1.60\% - 1.1\% = +0.5\%$.

We used a consistent approach across both (1a) and (1b), basing our computation in both cases on Sue's results in the *other* attribute.[10] The only difference in arriving at our two conflicting answers for the performance attribution is the order in which we did the computations. If we compute the allocation effect first, we get an implied attribution of $+2.4$ percent to allocation and -1.9 percent to selection. If we compute the selection effect first, we get an implied attribution of $+1.6$ percent to allocation and -1.1 percent to selection. Which is the real answer?

Well, how about neither. When we use either of these two approaches, we are contaminating the "pure" allocation or selection effects by arbitrarily including the effect of interaction between the two effects with one or the other. For example, in computing Sue's -110-basis-point selection differential in formula (1b), we used Sue's allocation weights. Suppose we had used Bob's allocation weights instead. Then we would have gotten the -190-basis-point effect we computed from (1a):

$$
\begin{aligned}
S_S - S_B &= w_{BI}(r_{SI} - r_{BI}) + w_{BO}(r_{SO} - r_{BO}) \\
&= 0.9(7\% - 9\%) + 0.1(10\% - 11\%) \\
&= -1.8\% - 0.1\% = -1.9\%
\end{aligned}
$$

But why should either Sue's or Bob's allocation weights be "correct" for quantifying Sue's selection effect? Sue's weights are faulty because their use combines the effect of her allocation decision with that of her property selection performance, destroying the "purity" of the

---

[10]That is to say, to quantify the effect of Sue's allocation, we used Sue's selection performance, and to quantify the effect of Sue's selection, we used Sue's allocation.

measurement of her selection performance. Bob's allocation weights are similarly faulty in this context because there is no logical reason to use Bob's allocation weights to quantify Sue's selection performance. What are we to do?

26.1.4 Use of a Benchmark in Performance Attribution

The only way out of our dilemma is to try to identify a reasonable **benchmark**, that is, a reference point that makes sense as a basis on which to quantify a manager's performance. We will discuss the question of an appropriate definition of benchmarks for private real estate performance in the next section. For now, let's suppose that Bob is a good benchmark for quantifying Sue's performance. This might be the case, for example, if Bob's allocation weights across segments and his return performance within each segment were typical of the investment managers in Sue's peer group of investment managers with similar specialties, foci, and objectives to Sue's. Or it might be the case if Bob's segment weights and in-segment returns were broadly representative of the entire market of all the industrial and office properties in the country. In any case, let's assume that Bob's performance is a good benchmark for Sue's performance.

In this case, it makes sense to quantify the pure effect of Sue's allocation performance by computing the effect of the difference between her and her benchmark's segment weights measured *conditional on the benchmark's in-segment return performance*. Similarly, it makes sense to quantify the pure effect of Sue's selection performance by computing the effect of the difference between her and her benchmark returns within each segment, *conditional on the benchmark's segment allocation weights*. Using Bob's results as the benchmark, this perspective reveals that Sue's pure allocation performance effect is +160 basis points, and her pure selection performance effect is −190 basis points:

$$A_S - A_B = r_{BI}(w_{SI} - w_{BI}) + r_{BO}(w_{SO} - w_{BO})$$
$$= 9\%(0.1 - 0.9) + 11\%(0.9 - 0.1) \tag{2a}$$
$$= -7.2\% + 8.8\% = +1.6\%$$

$$S_S - S_B = w_{BI}(r_{SI} - r_{BI}) + w_{BO}(r_{SO} - r_{BO})$$
$$= 0.9(7\% - 9\%) + 0.1(10\% - 11\%) \tag{2b}$$
$$= -1.8\% - 0.1\% = -1.9\%$$

Alas, these two pure effects do not add up to the total performance differential between Sue and her benchmark: $+1.6\% - 1.9\% = -0.3\% \neq +0.5\% = 9.7\% - 9.2\%$. This is a consequence of the nonlinearity of the total return performance differential as a function of the allocation and selection effects.[11] As a result, the total differential between Sue's performance and her benchmark consists not only of the two "pure" effects of allocation and selection, but also of an **interaction effect** that combines these two. In fact, at a fundamental conceptual level, we cannot really account for the interaction effect in a way that is not arbitrary in terms of attributing this effect either to allocation or selection. The most logically sound approach is to leave the interaction effect separate, as a third attribute of the overall performance differential.[12] In our present example, the interaction effect in the differential of Sue's return over her benchmark is +80 basis points, as $+1.6\% - 1.9\% + 0.8\% = +0.5\%$.

---

[11]
$$r_S - r_B = (w_{SI}r_{SI} + w_{SO}r_{SO}) - (w_{BI}r_{BI} + w_{BO}r_{BO})$$
$$= (w_{SI} - w_{BI})r_{BI} + (w_{SO} - w_{BO})r_{BO} = \text{Pure allocation}$$
$$+ w_{BI}(r_{SI} - r_{BI}) + w_{BO}(r_{SO} - r_{BO}) = \text{Pure selection}$$
$$+ [(w_{BI}r_{BO} + w_{BO}r_{BO}) + (w_{SI}r_{SI} + w_{SO}r_{SO})$$
$$- (w_{BI}r_{SI} + w_{BO}r_{SO} + w_{SI}r_{BI} + w_{SO}r_{BO})] = \text{Interaction effects}$$

[12]The interaction effect is sometimes referred to as the cross-product, as that is what it is from a mathematical perspective. Some analysts suggest that the interaction effect itself is indicative of a specific ability on the part of the manager, namely, the manager's success in specialization that leads the manager to overweight segments within which the manager has relatively superior selection skills (even though such segments might not be strategically superior from an overall allocation perspective). But perhaps this is trying to read too much from the "entrails." When all is said and done, the interaction effect is just that, the combined (multiplicative) effect of both allocation and selection.

Attribute	Conditional on Manager Selection	Conditional on Manager Allocation	Unconditional
Allocation	2.40%	1.60%	1.60%
Selection	−1.90%	−1.10%	−1.90%
Interaction			0.80%
Total differential	0.50%	0.50%	0.50%

EXHIBIT 26-5 Sue's Performance Attribution Relative to Her Benchmark

© OnCourse Learning

The performance attributions that result from all three of the approaches we have described are summarized in Exhibit 26-5 for the numerical example we have been working with here. The first two columns in the table depict the approach based on formulas (1a) and (1b), respectively, in which results are conditional on the order in which the effects are computed. The third column depicts the approach represented by formula (2), which is independent of order of computation and provides a logical quantification of the "pure" functional effects, with the interaction effect quantified separately.[13]

26.1.5 The Case for Using Manager Allocation Weights in the Benchmark

Let's return for a moment to the approach represented by formula (1b) in which the manager's allocation weights are applied to the differential between the manager's and benchmark's selection performance in order to quantify the manager's selection performance with respect to the benchmark. In fact, this approach has been employed widely in practice to quantify the manager's selection performance.

The intuitive appeal of this approach is that it can eliminate that pesky interaction effect, and it seems only fair to give credit to managers for their own allocation weights when quantifying the effect of their differential return performances within segments. But keep in mind that in so doing, one is mixing the effects of two performance functions, allocation and selection. By the same reasoning, it would be only fair to apply the formula (1a) approach to quantifying the allocation effect (using managers' own within-segment returns to quantify the impact of their segment weight differences versus the benchmark). Of course, formulas (1a) and (1b) do not add up to the total return differential: 2.4% − 1.1% = 1.3% ≠ 0.5%.

In some circumstances, however, the argument for the use of formula (1b) to quantify the selection effect makes sense. Suppose the manager does not have control over her own allocation (e.g., the client did not give the manager discretion over the segment weights). In such circumstances, it makes sense to "customize" the manager's benchmark by recasting the benchmark segment weights to equal the manager's segment weights. In other words, the manager's benchmark should be computed with the benchmark in-segment returns but

---

[13]It should be noted that the portfolio-level attribution measures described here are essentially single-period measures. In applying such attribution analysis to multiperiod spans of time, a certain amount of arbitrariness or obfuscation tends to occur because in reality segment weights will tend to change gradually over time, both in the manager's and the benchmark portfolio. In practice, alternative approaches to quantifying the attribution measures over multiperiod spans of time include (1) using the initial, terminal, or average (across the overall time span) allocation weights applied to the time-weighted average multiperiod returns within each segment; and (2) computing the single-period attribution measures within each period, and then taking the arithmetic average of the attribution measures across the overall time span. The former approach is somewhat arbitrary and inaccurate in the segment weightings. The latter approach relates to the arithmetic mean time-weighted return, not the geometric mean that is typically used for the overall multiperiod return measure in performance evaluation. However, the latter approach has a better statistical justification, as it does not violate the single-period nature of the attribution measures, but simply views each periodic return as an equally representative sample of time for indicating the manager's performance attribution. The arithmetic time-weighted mean also has the advantage of being completely decomposable into the sum of the arithmetic time-weighted average income return component plus the arithmetic time-weighted average appreciation return component.

the manager's segment weights. In this case, a direct comparison of the manager's return with such a customized benchmark return will be equivalent to formula (1b), and the entire overall performance return differential between the manager and the benchmark will consist purely of the selection effect (the pure allocation and interaction effects will be zero, by construction).

26.2 Investment Performance Evaluation and Benchmarking

Our discussion of manager benchmarks in the previous section is a good steppingstone to our next topic, **performance evaluation**. Performance evaluation is one of the most basic and important tasks in the investment industry. In the context of investment management, performance evaluation refers to the need to arrive at some sort of judgment about how well a given manager has performed, either in absolute or in relative terms. While performance evaluation broadly involves considerations that cannot be well quantified, some aspects of the job can be quantified, and it is to quantitative evaluation that we turn our attention now.[14]

26.2.1 The Basic Idea

A typical performance evaluation of an investment manager or an investment fund is presented in Exhibit 26-6, which depicts the evaluation of two managers, A and B. After a period of time, typically three to five years, the average return achieved over that period is computed for each manager.[15] The returns achieved over that same period of time are also computed for each other manager in a **peer universe** of all the competing managers (or funds) who also specialize in the same type of investments. In Exhibit 26-6, the manager's performance is indicated by the cross. The vertical line indicates the 5th and 95th percentile range of the manager's peer universe. The box indicates the middle two quartiles, and the horizontal line inside the box indicates the median manager's performance within the peer universe. The triangle indicates the return recorded by a passive index that is broadly representative of the type of assets the manager specializes in. (A **passive index** is one whose allocations across assets remain relatively constant.)

In the example shown in Exhibit 26-6, manager A did quite well, performing in the upper quartile of her peer universe and substantially beating the relevant passive index. She will likely be rehired and may have earned an incentive fee. It doesn't look so good for manager B. The investor likely will fire manager B or reduce his allocation in the future, probably

---

[14]Please see the two electronic appendices to this chapter for more depth and detail. They are available on the student CD that comes with the book.

[15]Normally, the time-weighted average return is used (in particular, the geometric average) because at the portfolio or fund level (as distinct from the property-level), the investment manager does not usually have much control over the timing of capital flow. As noted in Chapter 9, time-weighted average returns are neutral with respect to capital flow timing, while dollar-weighted returns reflect the effect of such timing. If the manager does substantially control the timing of capital flow, then the IRR might be a more appropriate measure of the manager's performance. However, the benchmark is meant to be neutral with regard to performance actions. In the case of capital flow timing, such neutrality is represented by the time-weighted average return. The geometric mean is typically used rather than the arithmetic mean because performance evaluation is a backward look at history (rather than a forecasting exercise in which the statistical properties of the arithmetic mean would be useful), and because the geometric mean is not sensitive to the volatility in the periodic returns. (The arithmetic mean is greater the more volatile the returns.) It should also be noted that at the portfolio or fund level being addressed here (as distinct from the property-level considered in section 26.1.1), the periodic HPRs are normally computed as value-weighted (cross-sectional average) returns within each period. That is, within each period, the return to each property is not weighted equally but by the relative value of the property within the portfolio. This type of value-weighting is necessary to enable the HPR each period to reflect the actual return to the portfolio within that period. The focus here (and in the portfolio-level attribution analysis described in Sections 26.1.2–4) is on portfolio-level returns, rather than viewing each property as a sample of the manager's performance.

EXHIBIT 26-6 Graphical Depiction of Typical Investment Manager Performance Evaluation

© OnCourse Learning

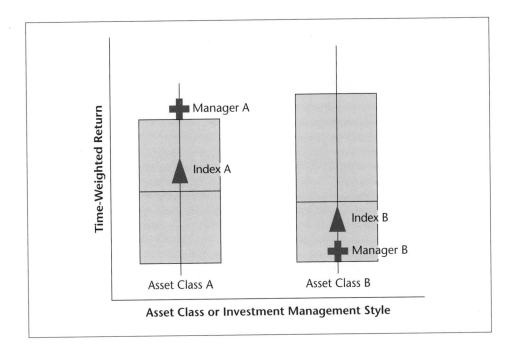

hiring one of his competitors instead. (Note that manager A probably is not a competitor to manager B, as they are in two different asset classes or management styles.[16])

26.2.2 Benchmarks and Investment Styles in the Private Real Estate Asset Class

In Exhibit 26-6, the manager's performance is compared both with respect to the median of her peer universe and with respect to a passive index broadly representative of her asset class. For example, in the public equity investment business, if the manager specializes in large-capitalization stocks, then the peer universe would consist of all the major mutual funds with a similar specialty. The most widely used passive index to benchmark large-stock performance is the Standard & Poor's Composite 500 Index (the S&P 500).

In the example shown in Exhibit 26-6, manager A has beaten both the benchmark index and her average competitor. Manager B has been beaten by both of these reference points. More generally, however, there is potential ambiguity in this process. A manager might, for example, beat the average competitor but fall short of the relevant passive index, or vice versa.

So, which type of reference point is better as a benchmark for judging manager performance? Should it be some central tendency of the manager's peer universe (say, the mean or median), or should it be a passive index? In the securities investment industry, both types of benchmarks are used. But in private real estate a truly passive index is not possible. Fundamentally, this is because of a characteristic of the property market which has been prominent in much of our previous discussion, namely, private real estate investment managers have to be responsible for the operational management of the properties they own on behalf of their clients. Furthermore, as we have noted, private real estate investment necessarily involves long holding periods because transaction costs are high, leading to our previously highlighted fact that much of the overall investment performance is attributable to how well properties

---

[16]The placement of manager A's and manager B's performance evaluations together in Exhibit 26-5 is done merely for illustrative purposes. It is not meant to imply that there should be a head-to-head competition between these two managers. Such direct comparisons would normally only take place between managers within the same asset class or segment (or "style") of investments, to avoid an apples-to-oranges comparison.

are managed while they are held. This is **active management**, of necessity.[17] Passive indices make sense as benchmarks if they represent a plausible alternative that the investor could actually invest in, as through an index fund. But, at least unless or until index derivatives of the type to be described in section 26.3 are available, there can be no such thing as a passive index or an index fund in private real estate.

Instead of passive indices such as the S&P 500, the only type of periodic return indices available to serve as benchmarks in the private real estate asset class are peer group indices. These are indices, like the NCREIF and IPD indices, that essentially reflect the performance of all (or most) of the private real estate investment managers in the country or in the relevant branch of the investment industry. As such, peer group indices correspond conceptually to the central tendency of a given manager's relevant peer group. They make sense as benchmarks because in some sense they represent the average of the "alternatives" that the investor could have achieved if she hadn't picked the particular investment manager that she hired.

The traditional and most widely cited NCREIF and IPD indices are property-level indices, which track the performance of the underlying physical assets. Property-level indices were our focus in Chapter 25. Such indices can be useful as benchmarks for property-level performance analysis and evaluation, as described in section 26.1. However, passive investors who make their real estate investments through investment managers actually experience not the underlying property performance directly, but that performance as managed and realized and passed on to the investor by funds or investment vehicles set up by the investment managers. It is the performance of such funds that investors need to benchmark when evaluating the performance of their hired managers. Both NCREIF and IPD now produce so-called **fund-level indices** for the U.S. institutional real estate investment industry. These are indices that attempt to track the performance actually realized by investors in funds that invest in properties, rather than the performance achieved directly by the underlying properties.

Exhibit 26-7 presents the cumulative total returns (income plus capital appreciation) from 2000 through early 2012 as tracked by the NCREIF Property Index (NPI) and by two institutional investor fund-level indices published by NCREIF in cooperation with the Townsend Group (an institutional investment consultancy).[18] The two fund-level indices represent two different **investment styles**, labeled "core" and "value-added." An "investment style" in this context refers to the types of assets that the investment manager invests in, as well as certain key aspects of the management policies, especially the amount of financial leverage that may be used by the manager. The concept of investment style is a bit fuzzy, as is the exact definition of any given style, but it is important. We will have more to say about styles shortly, but for now let's consider the two fund-level indices in Exhibit 26-7.

The black line in Exhibit 26-7 tracks the performance of investment funds self-described as having a **core** style of investment. This means that they focus on relatively safe fully stabilized (largely leased-up) properties, using relatively little leverage in the investments. Core investment funds have relatively low target returns, but they are also supposed to have little risk. In terms of physical assets, classical institutional quality office, apartment, retail and

---

[17]The term *active management* in the investment management industry has traditionally been defined from a public securities market perspective. In that context, of course, active management does not imply operational management of the investment assets, as this is not possible for investment managers in the securities industry. But in a broader sense, active management refers to the attempt to beat the market, or to outperform the average or typical portfolio of assets, by whatever means are at the disposal of the manager. In the case of securities investment managers, this is limited to the use of investment research and the employment of active trading strategies or target allocations. Private real estate investment managers may employ these types of activities, broadly defined, although in a more sluggish asset market, dealing with assets that are primarily income generators rather than growth plays, and in an environment of high transaction costs. But in addition to these traditional active management tools, private real estate investors can, indeed must, use their control over property-level operational management of the assets to try to improve their investment performance.

[18]As of 2012 fund-level indices for the U.S. were also being introduced jointly by PREA and IPD. Also, NCREIF was planning to launch a global fund-level index in cooperation with ANREV and INREVE (Asian and European Associations for Investors in Non-listed Real Estate).

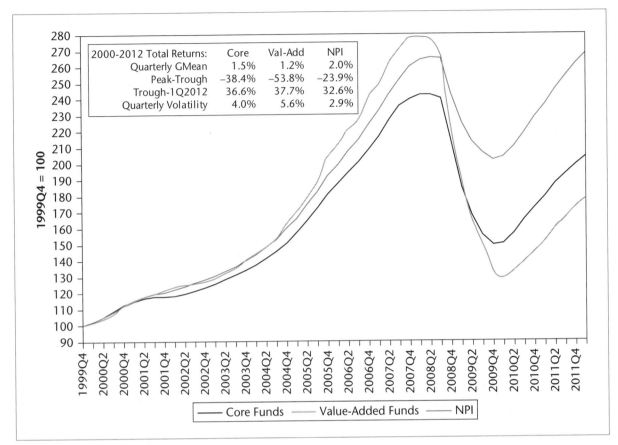

2000-2012 Total Returns:	Core	Val-Add	NPI
Quarterly GMean	1.5%	1.2%	2.0%
Peak-Trough	–38.4%	–53.8%	–23.9%
Trough-1Q2012	36.6%	37.7%	32.6%
Quarterly Volatility	4.0%	5.6%	2.9%

— Core Funds — Value-Added Funds — NPI

EXHIBIT 26-7 NCREIF/Townsend Fund Indices vs. NCREIF Property Index: Cumulative Total Returns, 2000–2012

Based on value-weighted all-funds indices, net of fees. NPI is property level gross of fees.

© OnCourse Learning

industrial properties of the type that largely make up the NPI would be typical investments of a core style fund. Traditionally core investment funds employed little or no financial leverage, but by the 2000s they were often using modest amounts of debt, up to 20 percent to 30 percent loan-to-value ratios (LTVs).

The gray line in the exhibit tracks the performance of **value-added** funds. This investment style is a bit more aggressive than the core style. Value-added funds may invest in assets that are not fully stabilized (still need some leasing) or in need of some turnaround management. Or they may be smaller or less "prime" properties or locations. Perhaps most significantly, the value-added style traditionally allows considerably more financial leverage than the core style, with typical LTVs in the neighborhood of 50 percent or slightly more. This is still conservative by the standards of many real estate investors, but as you recall from Chapters 13 and 18, the impact of leverage on investment risk is nonlinear in the LTV ratio.[19] (A third investment style, "opportunistic," will be introduced shortly, but is not tracked by the same type of NCREIF/Townsend indices as the two styles shown in Exhibit 26-7.)

Since core funds invest in largely the same types of properties as compose the NPI and with little leverage, the performance of the core funds index in Exhibit 26-7 can be compared

---

[19]Look back at Exhibit 18-5. Or recall from Chapter 13 that the effect of leverage on risk is approximately characterized by the leverage ratio: LR = 1/(1 − LTV). Thus a 50% LTV equity investment has twice the risk of the underlying properties. And indeed we see that the Value Added Index has about twice the quarterly volatility of the underlying property index (NPI).

to (and is largely based on) the property-level performance represented by the blue line tracing the NPI. We see that during 2000–2012 the core funds on average provided less total return to their investors than the underlying properties in the NPI. The obvious reason for this is that the fund-level index is net of the funds' investment management fees that they charge their investors, whereas the NPI, being a property-level index, does not reflect such charges. Core funds typically charge close to 100 basis points per year to cover the expenses and necessary profit of the investment management. Another major reason why the core fund index performed below the underlying properties during 2000–2012 was the way the funds on average managed their financial leverage, as we will discuss shortly.

These differences between the core fund index and the NPI are seen in Exhibit 26-7 to be further magnified in the value-added fund index. Value-added funds are more management intensive than core funds and therefore may charge higher asset management fees (a component of which may be performance based). And the greater financial leverage in the value-added funds did not work to their advantage during the 2000–2012 period.

How can financial leverage cause fund performance to fall below that of the underlying physical assets the fund is investing in, when the leverage may have appeared to be "positive" at the time when the loans were taken out?[20] Let's take a simple example. Suppose in the up part of the asset price cycle property values rise from 100 to 150. Suppose by the end of that period an investment fund has a 33 percent LTV ratio, say, $100 in equity and $50 in debt. Now suppose property values fall by one-third, down to 100. The fund still owes $50 and so has lost half its equity value and it now has a 50 percent LTV ratio. At that point the fund probably faces considerable pressure to de-lever, as it is not clear what the future will be in the property market. Somehow the fund raises $17 in new equity, which it uses to pay its debt down to $33 to return it to a 33 percent LTV. Then suppose the property market partially recovers, to a value of 125, leaving the fund with $92 in equity and $33 in debt (to total up to the $125 asset value).

Now for simplicity assume each of the asset price moves occurred in one period and let's compute the simple holding period returns (HPRs), the types of returns tracked by periodic return indices such as those in Exhibit 26-7. In the first period (the crash), the property assets had a −33 percent return (from 150 to 100). The fund had a −50 percent return (from 100 to 50), with its loss compared to the property market exaggerated by its 33 percent LTV at the peak. At this point new equity investors come into the fund (bringing $17 to pay down the debt), diluting the preexisting investors. Such a recapitalization is not reflected in a periodic return index like those in the exhibit. In period two (the recovery) properties gain 25 percent (from 100 to 125). The fund gains 37 percent (from 67 to 92). Across the two periods the property-level HPRs are therefore −33 percent and +25 percent for a time-weighted arithmetic average return (TWR) of −4 percent. The fund-level HPRs are −50 percent and +37 percent for a TWR of −6.5 percent, 250 basis points lower than the underlying properties.

This simplified story is the essence of how poor timing (in retrospect) in the management of leverage during the boom and bust cycle of the 2000s led to widespread fund performance below that of the underlying property assets. This happened not only in private real estate investment management but in many REITs as well (and not just in real estate but in many industries in the 2000s).

Let us return now to the real estate institutional investment management styles, and note that there is a third major style, referred to as "**opportunistic**." This is the most aggressive of the three styles. Opportunistic investment managers and funds aim for high returns (15 percent to 20 percent were typical targets in the 2010s) which can only be achieved by taking on considerable risk. Opportunistic funds may invest in a broad range of asset types, including land, development projects, foreign properties (possibly in emerging markets), distressed debt, or properties or operating entities in need of considerable turnaround. As with the value-added investment style, if opportunistic investing is to actually add value, that is, to "beat the market" in the sense of generating positive-NPV investments (and thereby achieve

---

[20]Recall from Chapter 13 that "positive leverage" refers to the circumstance where the interest rate on the loan is less than the return on the property, implying that the leverage should increase the equity return on average. (See section 13.4.)

IS IT A SAMPLE OR IS IT A POPULATION: THE STATISTICAL NATURE OF BENCHMARK INDICES

Benchmark property-level real estate investment performance indices such as the NCREIF index are often spoken of in common parlance as being a **sample** of a larger underlying population of all the commercial properties of a certain class or type. Indeed, much basic research conducted using such indices effectively treats property indices this way, as they are taken, for example, to represent the performance of an entire asset class (which is generally somewhat vaguely defined). However, it is important to realize that, in the context of performance evaluation of investment managers, benchmark indices such as the NCREIF index are not playing the role of statistical samples of some larger underlying population of properties. Rather, such indices in this context are themselves meant to define an entire **population**, namely, the population of all properties held by the relevant peer group of managers.

In the field of statistical inference, there is a large conceptual difference between a population and a sample of a population.

One implication of this difference is that, if the index is viewed as a sample of a larger population, then, at least ideally, it should not be a value-weighted index, that is, an index constructed as the cross-sectional average of the individual property returns each period weighted by the relative magnitude of the property value within the overall population. Instead, the ideal index from a statistical sampling perspective would be equally weighted across properties within each period. However, the NCREIF index is, quite intentionally, a value-weighted index. This suggests that the designers of that index intended that it be viewed as a population rather than as a sample.*

---

*NCREIF allows members to easily download custom indices that can be constructed by equal-weighting the property-level returns in the database. The transaction based version of the NCREIF Index described in Chapter 25, the NTBI, is published in both value-weighted and equal-weighted versions.

high returns without commensurate risk), it generally must do so through the managers' capabilities with physical assets. (Recall what we said in Chapter 12 about how to earn positive NPV.) However, again as with value-added investing, there is a temptation to reach for high returns simply by taking on more financial leverage and moving out along the Security Market Line (SML) in that way, achieving greater return expectations relatively easily with no real added value but with commensurately greater risk exposure. Opportunistic funds typically employ high amounts of financial leverage, often 50 percent to 70 percent LTVs in spite of more risky underlying assets. This temptation will tend to be greater during boom periods when debt capital is plentiful and interest rates are low.

Opportunistic funds generally cannot be benchmarked using the same type of investment return performance metric as the other real estate investment styles. The indices for core and value-added funds in Exhibit 26-7 are based on period-by-period holding period returns (HPRs) and focused on time-weighted returns (TWRs) to summarize their average performance over time. As described in Chapter 9, such returns do not reflect the timing of when investment capital is placed, or the effect of having different amounts of capital invested at different points in time. TWRs are appropriate for benchmarking investment managers who do not have discretion over equity capital flow into or out of the investments. This is true for all core funds and for many value-added funds, but not for most opportunistic funds. The latter function more like venture capital or private equity funds that set up a capital commitment from the investor and then "call" money into the investments when that is deemed necessary. The preferred return metric to summarize performance over time in such circumstances is a money-weighted average return, most typically measured by the internal rate of return, the IRR (as also defined in Chapter 9).[21]

Exhibit 26-8 is based on an example IRR-based performance report from the NCREIF/Townsend Fund Indices. When benchmarking using IRRs it is very important to control for the "**vintage**," the year or period of time when the peer universe of comparable funds were initiated. It is not fair to compare the IRRs of funds that started at substantially different points in history. The report shows the median and interquartile range of the funds' reported

---

[21]Recall that there is a similar argument for using the IRR metric for the type of property-level performance attribution we described in section 26.1.2. IRR-based metrics may also be appropriate for some value-added funds, depending on how they are structured and report to their investors.

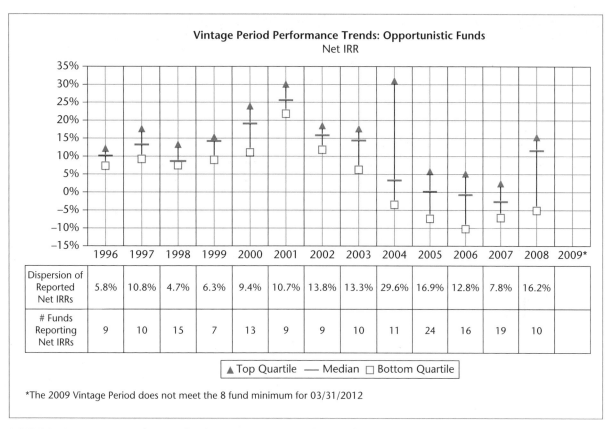

	1996	1997	1998	1999	2000	2001	2002	2003	2004	2005	2006	2007	2008	2009*
Dispersion of Reported Net IRRs	5.8%	10.8%	4.7%	6.3%	9.4%	10.7%	13.8%	13.3%	29.6%	16.9%	12.8%	7.8%	16.2%	
# Funds Reporting Net IRRs	9	10	15	7	13	9	9	10	11	24	16	19	10	

▲ Top Quartile — Median □ Bottom Quartile

*The 2009 Vintage Period does not meet the 8 fund minimum for 03/31/2012

EXHIBIT 26-8 NCREIF/Townsend Report of Real Estate Opportunistic Funds IRR Performance by Vintage Year (as of March 31, 2012)

Source: NCREIF and The Townsend Group, "Real Estate Fund Indices and Vintage Period Performance Report, 1ˢᵗ Quarter 2012f," NCREIF, Chicago, 2012.

net IRRs as of the current reporting date (March 2012 in the exhibit example). Note that the funds are grouped into 13 vintage year cohorts, one for each year from 1996 through 2008, corresponding to the years when the funds were launched. The "vintage year" is defined as the year when the fund first made its capital calls to its investors and began acquiring real estate assets. The report also shows the number of funds in each vintage and the cross-sectional standard deviation among their IRRs as of the current reporting date (labeled "dispersion" in the report). The net IRRs are net of advisory fees, incentives, and promotes (performance based fees as described in Chapter 15, section 15.3), and are based on actual net cash flows to and from investors plus "reversion" values based on current estimated market values of the net assets remaining in the funds (typically evaluated by appraisals).

In Exhibit 26-8 note that as of early 2012 most of the opportunistic funds originated between 1996 and 2008 had not achieved the 20 percent returns that were often stated as the target. Only the 2001 cohort of nine funds was clearly successful in that regard. Indeed, in only three of the 13 cohorts the median fund exceeded a 15 percent IRR, the 2000–2002 vintages launched just before the big boom. The worst performing cohorts were those originated during the peak of the asset price cycle, not surprisingly, during 2005–2007. The 2007 cohort of 19 funds had a median IRR below zero. The 11 funds in the 2004 cohort had a low median performance below 5 percent, but a very high top quartile above 30 percent.

Exhibit 26-9 summarizes the three major styles of institutional real estate investment management. As noted, the boundaries and distinctions between them are fuzzy. The most traditional and well-defined style is core, but it is also rather narrow. Especially with the yield compression of the twenty-first century (the general secular decline in real interest

EXHIBIT 26-9 Schematic
Diagram of Institutional
Real Estate Investment
Management Styles
© OnCourse Learning

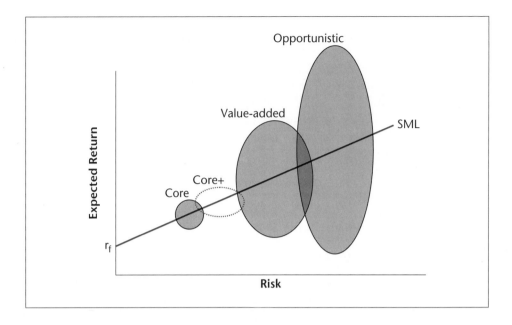

rates and expected returns), there has been a tendency to subtly expand the core style to try to achieve a bit higher returns (and thereby perhaps filling a sort of perceived gap between the value-added and traditional core styles). This has come to be known as "core-plus" (or "core+"), as indicated in the exhibit. Considering just the three major labels, a PREA survey of investors in 2011 found allocations by value among U.S. pension funds of 49 percent to core, 19 percent to value-added, and 32 percent to opportunistic. This contrasted with an earlier 2004 survey (on a similar but not identical set of investors) that found 71 percent core, 17 percent value-added, and 12 percent opportunistic.[22] The trend during the early twenty-first century has clearly been away from the traditional core style and toward the more risky and less transparent styles. This parallels a similar trend more broadly in the investment industry away from traditional publicly traded stocks and bonds and towards more opaque "alternative investments" such as private equity and hedge funds.

26.3 Real Estate Derivatives

This brings us to a rather different subject. Real estate derivatives of the type we will describe in this section could potentially be an important tool of real estate investment management. Indeed, they could conceivably revolutionize the entire industry. To see how, read on!

A **derivative** is a claim whose value depends *completely* on the value of another claim or asset. The most famous type of derivative assets in finance are probably stock options, and you will get an introduction to "real options" (those based on real estate assets) in the next chapter. But here we want to introduce you to a different type of derivative product, one that is new on the real estate investment scene. These are tradable contracts written on real estate investment performance indexes. Trading in this type of derivative developed in the mid-2000s decade primarily in the United Kingdom based on the IPD Index for that country. Trading also started a little later and more fitfully in the United States based on the NPI. Both products were victims of the financial crisis of 2008–2009, and currently new-issue real estate property index derivatives are not being actively marketed or traded. However, this type of investment product is potentially of sufficient importance that we feel we should introduce you to the concept in this chapter, as we hope you will see.

---

[22]PREA Investor Report, August 2012.

In this section we will first introduce the concept of an index swap contract, how it can be useful for investors and the real estate industry, and how it should be priced. Then we will put the role of derivatives in a broader perspective. Finally we will say a few words about how a market for such products might get started, including the type of index that might be involved.

26.3.1 How Index Swaps Can Be Used and Priced

Exhibit 26-10 presents a simple example of an index swap contract. Most fundamentally, such a contract would be written on a specified real estate investment performance index, ideally a total return index that includes both income and capital appreciation. (We will have more to say in section 26.3.3 about the type of index that may work best.) In the example, the swap contract is to be settled quarterly, which means that the underlying index must be updated and reported at least that frequently. The example is a one-year contract on a $100 "notional" amount at a fixed price of 560 basis points (bp). This means that the contract is written and "traded" at "time 0" (the present), with a maturity one year from now, thus envisioning four quarterly "settlements" (potential payments) between now and then. The two parties on the opposite sides of the swap trade are the index "buyer" (the "long" position) and the index "seller" (the "short" position). No cash changes hands up front at time 0, but it will be as though the buyer will receive the quarterly return of the index on $100 worth of index assets, and the seller will receive the fixed return on the same amount of assets based on the 560-bp price. At the end of each of the next four calendar quarters, the index buyer must pay the index seller $560/4 = 140$ basis points times $100, or $1.40. But at the same time the index seller must pay in cash to the index buyer each quarter whatever turns out to be that quarter's index return times $100. If the index return is negative, then the result is additional cash to be paid from the index buyer to the index seller (on top of the $1.40 fixed payment).

Let's walk through the example in the exhibit. Suppose it turns out that in the first quarter after the contract goes into effect the index happened to be flat, a zero percent return. Then the buyer pays the seller $1.40, and that is all for that quarter. Now suppose the second quarter finishes with the index down that quarter by 1 percent (for example, income of $+1$ percent more than offset by a -2 percent drop in capital value). Then the index buyer owes the seller $2.40 that quarter, consisting of the $1.40 fixed payment plus the -1 percent total

EXHIBIT 26-10 Example Index Swap Contract

© OnCourse Learning

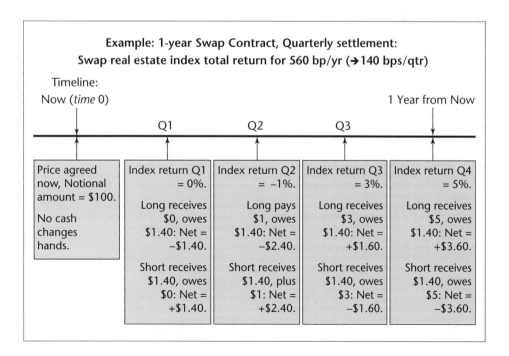

Example: 1-year Swap Contract, Quarterly settlement:
Swap real estate index total return for 560 bp/yr (→140 bps/qtr)

Timeline:
Now (*time* 0)   1 Year from Now

| | Q1 | Q2 | Q3 | |

| Price agreed now, Notional amount = $100.

No cash changes hands. | Index return Q1 = 0%.

Long receives $0, owes $1.40: Net = –$1.40.

Short receives $1.40, owes $0: Net = +$1.40. | Index return Q2 = –1%.

Long pays $1, owes $1.40: Net = –$2.40.

Short receives $1.40, plus $1: Net = +$2.40. | Index return Q3 = 3%.

Long receives $3, owes $1.40: Net = +$1.60.

Short receives $1.40, owes $3: Net = –$1.60. | Index return Q4 = 5%.

Long receives $5, owes $1.40: Net = +$3.60.

Short receives $1.40, owes $5: Net = –$3.60. |

return times the $100 notional amount of the contract. Next, suppose the index produces a +3 percent return in the third quarter. Then the net payment that quarter is $1.60 from the seller to the buyer, consisting of the $3.00 index return (3 percent times the $100 notional value) minus the ever-constant $1.40 fixed payment (sometimes referred to as the "fixed leg"). Finally, suppose the fourth quarter sees a +5 percent return on the index. Then the fourth and final payment on the one-year swap contract would be a net of $3.60 from the seller to the buyer (0.05 × $100 − (0.0560/4) × $100 = $3.60).[23]

Now consider how this swap contract allows the index buyer to effectively construct a synthetic investment in the real estate total return index. Perhaps the buyer is a foreign sovereign wealth fund (SWF) wanting to make a broadly diversified investment in the U.S. institutional real estate market. They are not trying to "beat the market." They just want broad exposure to the market for purposes of meeting a portfolio allocation target to the asset class, perhaps based on a strategic analysis such as we described in Chapter 21, or based on a tactical analysis such as we described in Chapter 22.

The SWF wants to invest $100 cash into the U.S. market. Suppose that the index underlying the swap contract is indeed a broadly diversified index tracking the U.S. institutional property market (effectively the "asset class"), quantifying the average total returns yielded by real estate assets in the U.S. market each quarter (income plus capital return). Then the SWF can take $100 of their own cash and invest it in riskless U.S. government securities with a maturity of one year, which we will presume are selling at a yield of 560 basis points. (It may sound like a coincidence that the Treasury yield equals the swap price, but we will explain shortly.) The SWF then uses the proceeds from the riskless bond investment to cover their fixed payment obligations under the swap contract, leaving their net cash flow from the combined position to provide exactly what the total return would be each quarter on the real estate index. Thus, their cash outlay is $100, and their net returns each quarter exactly equal those of the real estate index total return on a $100 investment. The SWF faces exactly the risk and return of the U.S. real estate index. This type of operation is referred to as a covered long position in the swap, because the investor is investing in a risk-free instrument an amount of their own cash equal to the swap contract notional amount (and for an equal maturity). In this example the covered long position in the equity index swap has allowed the SWF to make an investment effectively in diversified U.S. real estate without having to hire a specialized U.S. real estate investment manager or incur the search and transactions (and learning) costs of actually buying real assets.

Next let's consider how this same index swap contract allows the index seller to hedge, or lay off unwanted risk exposure to the U.S. institutional real estate market. Perhaps the seller is a U.S. pension fund that has $100 too much exposure to the U.S. real estate market. They have invested in a broadly diversified cross-section of U.S. property assets similar to those tracked by the index underlying the swap contract. But their portfolio allocation policy is now calling for $100 less allocation to real estate. (Again, this might reflect strategic or tactical investment considerations such as those described in Chapters 21 or 22; or it might simply result from a "denominator effect," in which relatively high returns to real estate have unbalanced the fund's allocation weights pushing their real estate weight above its target range.)

Because the pension fund already has $100 invested in the type of assets tracked by the index underlying the swap contract, they have a naturally covered short position in the swap. The returns they receive each quarter from $100 worth of their real estate holdings will likely very nearly match the obligations they will face as the short position in the $100 notional swap contract, which is to pay the index returns on $100 worth of investment. Thus, the 560 bp fixed payment (140 bp/qtr) that the pension fund will receive from the swap becomes essentially like a riskless return for them.

---

[23]In this simple example we have ignored the "middle man," the intermediary or bid/ask spread, which would be necessary in the real world to cover transactions costs and the operation of the swap market. For example, the intermediary might "ask" a price of 600 bps from the swap buyer and "bid" a price of 520 bps to pay the swap seller. The resulting 80 bps spread (20 bps/qtr) would be kept by the intermediary. In successful, highly liquid swap markets, bid/ask spreads are usually much narrower than this, but in less liquid over-the-counter markets spreads can be wide, and this can make such trading very profitable for investment banks that deal in the over-the-counter market (which typically trades more customized, "boutique" type derivatives).

If 560 bp is the current yield on riskless government securities (of one year maturity), then this would make the 560 bp fixed payment price of the swap contract "fair" from the seller's perspective. In effect, the swap has allowed the pension fund to substitute a riskless return of 560 bp on a $100 investment (as if in Treasury bonds) for the risky return on their $100 worth of diversified real estate investments, without actually having to sell any of their real estate assets! They thereby avoid sales transactions cost and effort. And they are also able to keep their particular property holdings, which they might particularly like (since they did select them). The pension fund can now use this effectively riskless $100 investment in their portfolio to collateralize the borrowing of cash which they could place into other types or classes of risky investments, effectively substituting another targeted risky investment for the original excess exposure to real estate, if that is their strategic or tactical investment objective for their portfolio.[24]

Now you can see how the "fair" price for the swap contract is the current yield on riskless securities of the same maturity as the swap contract, the 560 basis points in our example. This price provides the seller with a fair return because their covered short position in the swap is essentially riskless (in terms of nondiversifiable systematic risk), and they are essentially receiving a riskless return equal to what they could get by investing in riskless government securities. And the index buyer is also receiving a fair return (in expectation ex ante) because they are exposed to the amount of risk in the real estate index and will be receiving the return provided by the real estate underlying that index. Assuming that the index risk and return accurately reflects the risk and return in the underlying properties, and that the underlying properties are fairly priced so as to provide an expected return risk premium commensurate with their risk (i.e., they lie on the equilibrium Security Market Line (SML) that we have discussed earlier and presented formally in Chapter 22), then the 560 bp price will also be fair from the index buyer's perspective.[25]

---

[24]The operation described here can involve what is called "portable alpha." If the pension fund believes their particular property holdings will beat the market (earn positive "alpha," returns above the Security Market Line), then they are still retaining any such alpha, as they are not actually selling the properties. They are only laying off the "beta" (real estate market) risk exposure. In effect, they move this real estate-based alpha to some other part of their portfolio. However, in this example we are obviously ignoring some complicating aspects of reality. The hedge of the pension fund's real estate investment (beta) will no doubt not be perfect; the returns on their real estate will not exactly mimic the index returns. This will expose the pension fund's hedge to "basis risk." And there will be transaction costs in each leg of the operation (such as the bid/ask spread referred to earlier). And the swap settlements must be paid currently in cash while the capital component of the actual real estate total returns are generally unrealized returns only "on paper" until the properties are actually sold. For these reasons, in the real world the pension fund might demand a fixed payment on the swap somewhat higher than the riskfree interest rate on Government securities (which we assumed was 560 basis points). But on the other hand the SWF on the opposite side of the swap might be willing to pay some extra premium above the riskfree rate to buy the index, in order to avoid all the transactions and management costs associated with actual direct real estate investment (the transactions costs of property purchase, and recall our discussion in section 26.2.2 about fund management fees, and in section 26.1.2 about all the "responsibilities" of direct property investment), not to mention the danger of making bad investments or hiring an unsatisfactory investment manager in a foreign market that is unfamiliar to the SWF. And the pension fund might be willing to absorb a little extra cost, and some basis risk (which is probably purely random and hence very diversifiable), in order to, in effect, purchase "investment risk insurance" for their over-exposure to U.S. real estate.

[25]The assumptions here about the index's accurate reflection of the underlying traded assets, and about the equilibrium pricing of those assets, will not necessarily hold, particularly for traditional types of private market based real estate indices such as appraisal-based or transactions based indices of the types discussed in detail in Chapter 25. This does not make private real estate market price index trading impossible. The "imperfections" in such indices can in principle be reflected and compensated for in the swap pricing. (The "fair" price of the swap might not equal the riskfree interest rate, the 560 basis points in our example.) However, having to deal with such index imperfections does pose an additional hurdle in the way of getting a synthetic real estate investment market started. The swap traders need to become experts in the subtleties and quirks of the index being traded. The general rule for the fair pricing of the swap contract is that the fixed payment rate should equal the expected return on the underlying index over the contract maturity period (which may for example reflect a lag in the index relative to the market) *minus* the expected risk premium that is appropriate for the amount of risk in the traded index (which may differ from the amount of risk in the underlying physical assets tracked by the index). This general rule applies not only to total return indices but to price-change-only (capital appreciation) indices, which can serve as bases for derivatives since almost all of the volatility or risk in asset total returns is in the capital return component. Note that this rule is consistent with our riskfree interest rate price for the swap described in our example. Note also that, contrary to many peoples' initial intuitions, the fair price for the index swap does *not* generally equal the expected return on the index (unless the index is riskless).

26.3.2 The Broader Potential Role of Index Derivatives

Hopefully it is fairly clear how real estate index derivatives such as the swap contract we have just described can help to satisfy the needs of specific investors in specific circumstances, such as our example SWF and pension fund. What is potentially exciting, however, is the general benefits such derivative trading could have for the entire real estate investment industry, if such trading ever develops. The result could be improved liquidity and efficiency in the market. For example, for the first time, the complaint that "you can't short real estate" would no longer be true. Investment managers who can beat the real estate index can earn positive profits even when the overall real estate market is declining, simply by taking the short position in the swap. And investors would not have to hire real estate management expertise, or incur property purchase and sale search and transactions costs, in order to obtain real estate returns in their portfolios.

A big picture perspective on how derivatives could conceivably revolutionize the real estate investment industry is depicted in Exhibit 26-11. The top panel depicts the traditional (and still existing) system. In an important sense, physical and financial capital are "joined at the hip," with results that are suboptimal for both sides. Real estate investment requires ownership and control and management of the underlying physical assets, real property. This is not optimal for the owners of financial capital who want the risk and return characteristics of real estate in their portfolio but don't have the specialized expertise to optimally produce or manage the physical capital. On the other hand there are real estate specialists—"bricks and mortar folks"—who could probably better optimize the physical capital but are buffeted and constrained by real estate's capital intensity, that is, its need for vast quantities of financial capital that must be structured and served to tailor the specific needs of the financial investment industry that then tethers the physical capital to the cyclical ups and downs of the capital markets. How many real estate entrepreneurs have beaten the market in the physical real estate game only to be brought down by the financial capital cycle? How many financial entrepreneurs have been thwarted by high transactions costs, lack of liquidity, and inability to sell short real estate?

The bottom panel of Exhibit 26-11 depicts a potential future structure mediated by derivatives such as the index swaps described in the previous section. The financial and physical sides of the real estate industry could be "disarticulated" (or perhaps we should say, "rearticulated" in a more flexible way, as the two sides would of course still be vitally linked). On the finance side, synthetic investment would allow financial engineering, the development of more varied and creative and efficient real estate based financial investment products. This would allow financial capital to flow into and out of the real estate sector in a manner better tailored to financial needs while buffering the physical capital from extreme swings and particular preferences of investors. For example, capital would flow to and from real estate synthetically by flowing directly in the first instance to and from bonds (as we saw in the swap example in the previous section). Physical real estate entrepreneurs could hedge exposure to the market as a whole and make low-risk, reliable profits from their "**alpha**," excess returns above the Security Market Line, based on their ability to add real value in the physical product. Financial engineering and entrepreneurship, and physical (space market) engineering and entrepreneurship would be linked in a more flexible and buffered manner than in the existing structure. The result could be both greater efficiency and profitability, and better real estate as a physical product.

Of course, there will surely be no utopia. As has been discovered in other branches of the investment industry, derivative trading has its pitfalls.[26] In any case, the

---

[26]An ever present danger with derivatives is that they can make it *very* easy to take on very large amounts of leverage, and in ways that are not always so immediately obvious that they actually do involve large leverage. The types of covered positions we described in section 26.3.1 are the low-risk way of using derivatives. Indeed, the covered short position actually reduced the investor's risk (this is the classical "risk management" purpose of commodities futures exchanges, for example, that motivated the original establishment of commodities exchanges such as the Chicago Board of trade, established in 1848). But in general derivatives trades need not be fully covered, or even covered at all (so-called "naked" positions), in which little or no cash or underlying physical capital is put up or held to offset the risk in the derivative contract *per se*. A derivatives market may be likened unto a Ferrari. It is possible to drive a Ferrari very slowly and conservatively and safely.

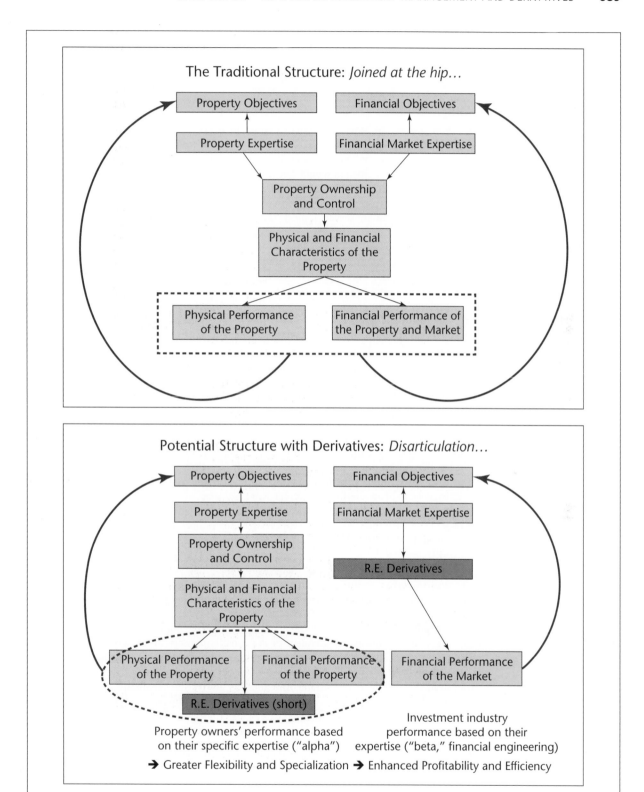

EXHIBIT 26-11 Potential Role of Index Derivatives within the Real Estate Investment System to Facilitate Greater Flexibility and Specialization via Synthetic Investment and Risk Management Hedging

© OnCourse Learning

experience so far has suggested that it will be very difficult to get real estate index derivative trading off the ground. One key barrier is the subject we now turn to in our last section on this topic.

26.3.3 Solving the Index Problem

The largest real estate-based derivatives market to develop to date was not in the type of equity index swaps described here but rather was the market for credit default swaps (CDS) based on mortgage-backed securities. That industry turned out to be a disaster in its initial form, as it helped to cause the great financial crisis of 2008. As we have noted, at that time equity index swaps were just starting, primarily in the United Kingdom, so they had nothing to do with that particular crisis. The financial crisis exposed crucial flaws and weaknesses in several aspects of the derivatives industry and trading system. Responses since the crisis are still being developed, both within the industry and governments. Clearly some fundamental issues must be addressed, including the excessive reliance on over-the-counter (OTC) trading of unique "boutique"-type derivatives that are excessively opaque, illiquid, and expensive, with excessive exposure to counter-party risk.[27] In principle, equity index-based derivatives could help to address such issues, offering relatively simple and homogeneous ("plain vanilla") products that provide the market risk and return of the private property asset class. But a threshold challenge that was not clearly resolved, at least in the United States, before the financial crisis nipped the nascent industry in the bud, was the problem of what index, or indeed what *type* of index, can or should real estate index derivatives be based on?

In Chapter 25 we suggested that there are essentially three major types of rigorously-based price and investment performance indices for tracking the institutional commercial property market in the United States. These include: (1) appraisal-based indices like the traditional NCREIF and IPD property indices; (2) transaction price-based indices like the new repeat-sales indices published by Moody's, Real Capital Analytics, and CoStar; and (3) stock market-based indices like the new FTSE-NAREIT PureProperty Indices. When the index derivatives industry was first trying to develop in the mid-2000s decade, the transactions-based indices were just being born, and the stock market-based indices did not yet exist (except in the form of direct REIT indices, which are arguably a bit different from stock market-based indices of property-level performance, as suggested in our discussion of REITs in Chapter 23). Thus, appraisal-based indices were the only available possibility; indeed, in the United States the only possibility at the time was the NCREIF Property Index (NPI).

There is no question that both appraisal-based and transaction-based indices offer unique and important contributions to the real estate investment information marketplace. But there are serious problems with both types of indices as a base for index derivatives of the type described here, at least in the United States

The appraisal-based indices represent relatively narrow and specialized types of properties, as they require regular and frequent professional appraisals, an expensive process that is not presently generally required of most properties by U.S. accounting standards. The NPI represents only a little over $300 billion worth of property out of over $4 trillion worth of actively traded investment real estate. And there is always the possibility or the perception that appraisal-based indices could be subject to manipulation or bias, as the appraisal process

---

[27]Counter-party risk is the possibility that one of the parties to the contract will default on their obligations under the contract, for example, if either the SWF or the pension failed to come up with their payment in the swap contract we described in 26.3.1. This problem is generally more serious with over-the-counter (OTC) trading of customized contracts, than with centralized exchange-based (or clearinghouse-based) trading of (more "plain vanilla") contracts, as exchanges and clearinghouses are set up to pool counter-party risk and build buffers and protections against it (such as membership or trading fees, as well as standardized margin and collateral or bonding requirements). Exchanges or clearinghouses and the use of more homogeneous contracts can also greatly improve the transparency and information quality in the industry, which can substantially improve efficiency and reduce uncertainty, thereby increasing liquidity in the market.

is inherently somewhat subjective, and the appraisal-based indices generally rely on self-reported valuations by the property owners and investment managers. Furthermore, we described in Chapter 25 the tendency of appraisal-based indices to exhibit smoothing and lagging bias, possibly in ways that are not constant over time. This can make the fair pricing of derivatives based on the indices difficult.[28]

Transaction price based indices also tend to suffer from challenges as bases for derivatives trading. These indices tend to be noisy, which adds to the basis risk that is particularly problematical for traders or users on the short side of the derivatives contracts. Transaction price-based indices also tend to be subject to "backward revisions" (alterations in their historical returns) as more transaction price data becomes available over time and brings new historical perspective on the markets. And transaction-based indices generally have difficulty representing total returns instead of just price-change or capital returns.

Both the appraisal-based and transaction-based indices are not themselves directly "investable." That is, it is not possible for an investor to literally put cash into the physical assets tracked by these indices and reap in cash the returns tracked by the indices. This makes it more difficult to price and trade derivatives products based on such indices, because it is impossible to execute arbitrage or quasi-arbitrage trades or positions replicating the derivative contracts.

None of the above challenges are necessarily fatal to the use of either appraisal-based or transaction-based indices for derivatives trading. And possibly some sort of combination or "cocktail" of various indices would make the best basis for derivatives, as each type of index has different strengths and weaknesses. But there is a third type of index which has more recently been honed that may provide some particular benefits as a potential to underlie equity index derivatives trading for the real estate asset class. This is the advent of **stock market-based property return indices (SMPRIs)**. These are indices designed to track property-level returns based on stock market share price movements of "pure-play"-type stocks that specialize in commercial property investment, such as REITs in the United States. The idea is to de-lever the REIT share prices and use their movements to track how the stock market's valuation of the underlying properties held by the REITs is changing over time. Although SMPRIs are designed fundamentally simply to provide information about the property market, they can in principle also serve as the basis for derivative contracts. The first such index was launched in the United States in 2012 by FTSE in a joint venture with NAREIT, known as the FTSE-NAREIT PureProperty Index. Exhibit 26-12 gives in idea how such indices can work.

In each panel of the exhibit the FTSE-NAREIT PureProperty cumulative total return index is compared over the 2000–2012 period with the corresponding NCREIF transactions-based index, the NTBI, for the same geographic region. The PureProperty Indices are updated daily, while the NTBI is updated only quarterly (with straight line segments drawn retroactively between the end-of-quarter values in the exhibit). The PureProperty indices appear more volatile than the private market based NTBI, but this is somewhat of an illusion, as over the same frequency the two indices have very similar volatility. (The quarterly-frequency index "sweeps under the rug" intra-quartile price movements.) More frequent updating of an index is useful and valuable for derivative trading on the index.[29] Most importantly (as also discussed in section 25.3.1 and Exhibit 25-8 of the previous chapter), the SMPRI trends are very similar to the corresponding private market trends, and the cycles and turning points are also very similar only with the SMPRI index leading the private market indices in time.

All of this suggests that the SMRPI could be a good basis on which to trade institutional commercial real estate returns. The leading nature of the SMPRI is beneficial for derivatives

---

[28]The fair price of the derivative has to include the effect of the lag. It also must reflect the fact that the risk in the index may not exactly reflect the risk in the underlying properties whose long-run returns govern the index long-run returns.

[29]For one thing, this generally means that trading can occur with smaller levels of required margin, as individual price movements tend to be smaller. Frequent news also aids transparency and promotes liquidity.

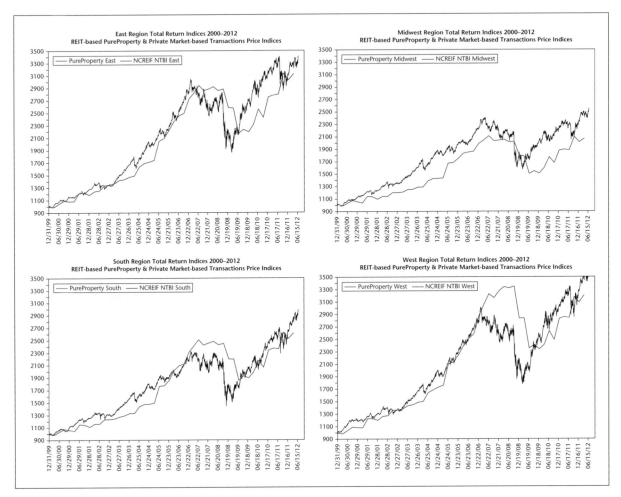

EXHIBIT 26-12 Cumulative Total Returns of FTSE NAREIT PureProperty Indices Compared to NCREIF NTBI for Four Regional Target Segments, 2000–2012

This exhibit shows this relationship for four major geographic regional indices, comparing the cumulative total return of the PureProperty Index with that of the corresponding transaction based NTBI.

Source: FTSE and NCREIF data.

trading as a liquid derivatives market would be predictive, with its prices reflecting any current information relevant to predict future movements in the traded index. Furthermore, the process whereby the SMPRI is constructed is entirely objective and replicable, not subject to manipulation. And the SMPRI indices can be directly investable, as combinations of bonds and long and short positions in liquid, tradable REIT stocks.[30] In summary, either by themselves or perhaps as part of a "cocktail" of different types of indices, SMPRI-type indices may hold considerable potential to overcome the index problem that was a major barrier holding back the development of a real estate equity index swap market in the United States in the decade of the 2000s.

---

[30]The SMPRI returns are actually constructed as the returns to explicit long/short portfolios of REIT stocks. (See Horrigan *et al*, 2009.) The rebalancing and management costs associated with actually operating a mutual fund or exchange traded fund mimicking the SMPRI should not be excessive.

26.4 Chapter Summary

With this chapter, we conclude Part VII, our coverage of the macro-level of real estate investment. This chapter focused in particular on some of the basic principles, tools, and procedures used in the investment management industry, with particular reference to their use in the private property asset class. We described in some detail the techniques of investment performance attribution at both the macro property-level and the portfolio level. We pointed out the importance of formal, quantitative investment performance evaluation in real estate. We also described the nature and role of such evaluation, including some subtleties and unique features that distinguish the private real estate equity asset class in this regard. Finally, we introduced a new real estate investment product concept, property equity index derivatives based on indexes of property-level investment performance, an innovation that could in principle greatly improve the functioning and efficiency of real estate investment at the macro-level.

KEY TERMS

performance attribution
benchmarking
macro property level
    (performance attribution)
property selection
acquisition transaction execution
operational management during
    the holding period
disposition transaction execution
portfolio level
    (performance attribution)
allocation

selection
segments (in the asset market)
benchmark
interaction effect
performance evaluation
peer universe
passive index
active management
fund-level indices
investment styles
core
value-added

opportunistic
vintage
sample
population
derivative
synthetic investment
covered long
hedge
covered short
alpha
stock market based property return
    indices (SMPRIs)

STUDY QUESTIONS

26.1. What are the three major performance attributes, and the four property level investment management responsibilities as identified in Section 26.1.2?

26.2. What is the argument for basing property-level performance attribution on the since-acquisition IRR instead of time weighted returns (TWR)?

26.3. What are the two major performance attributes typically identified at the portfolio management level?

26.4. What is meant by the term *interaction effect* in portfolio-level performance attribution? What issues arise when analysts lump the interaction effect in with either allocation or selection?

26.5. Piet and Yongheng are two apartment property investment managers hired one year ago by two different investors. In both cases the managers were free to use their own judgment regarding geographical allocation between properties in the East versus West of the country. Piet allocated his capital equally between the two regions, while Yongheng placed three-quarters of his capital in the Western region. After one year their respective total returns were as depicted in the following table. As you can see, Piet beat Yongheng by 100 basis points in his total portfolio performance for the year.

Yongheng's and Piet's Returns Realized for Clients		
Weights	**Yongheng**	**Piet**
East	25%	50%
West	75%	50%
Returns	**Yongheng**	**Piet**
Total portfolio	9.50%	10.50%
East	8.00%	9.00%
West	10.00%	12.00%

a. How would you attribute this 100-basis-point differential between allocation and selection performance only (no other component) and you wanted to condition your attribution on computing the allocation performance component first using Piet's return performance (as in Formula (1a) in Section 26.1.3)?

b. How would you attribute this 100-basis-point differential between allocation and selection performance only (no other component) and you wanted to condition your attribution on computing the selection performance component first using Piet's allocation weights (as in Formula (1b) in Section 26.1.3)?

c. How would you attribute this 100-basis-point differential among three components: pure allocation performance, pure selection performance, and a combined interaction effect, if you wanted to compute an *unconditional* performance attribution that was independent of the order of computation and based on Yongheng's results as a type of benchmark or standard?

26.6. In Question 26.5, suppose that Piet did not have discretion to choose his allocation weights between the East and West regions, but was specifically requested by his client to place capital equally between the two regions (as he did). Suppose further that the within-region performance achieved by Yongheng represents an appropriate benchmark for property-level performance within each region. Then what is an appropriate benchmark for evaluating Piet's performance, and what is Piet's performance differential with respect to that benchmark?

26.7. What is the difference between a peer universe and a passive index, as a benchmark for evaluating investment manager performance? Why are the arguments against peer universe benchmarks less persuasive in the private real estate market than in the stock market?

26.8. In what sense (or in what role or uses) is the NCREIF index best viewed as a population (in the statistical sense)? In what sense (or in what role or uses) is the NCREIF index best viewed as a sample?

26.9. What the two major reasons why the NCREIF-Townsend Core Fund Index exhibited greater risk (volatility and down cycle magnitude) and less total return than the underlying NPI property-level index during the 2000–2012 period even though the core funds mostly hold the same properties as those tracked by the NPI?

26.10. Why or how did value added and opportunistic funds perform worse than core funds during 2000–2012 even though such funds are supposed to provide higher returns over the long run than core, because they take on greater risk?

26.11. Why is it often not appropriate to track the performance or to benchmark opportunistic funds using periodic returns time series and time-weighted average holding period returns (TWRs)?

26.12. What is meant by a real estate index swap, and why is it referred to as a "futures" contract?

26.13. Describe two reasons why each party (the long position and the short position) might be willing to pay at least part of a "bid-ask spread" in a real estate index swap contract.

26.14. Suppose the risk-free interest rate is 3% and the equilibrium expected total return risk premium on property investments is 3.5% (hence, equilibrium expected total return on real estate investment is 6.5%). What will be the equilibrium (bid-ask spread mid-point) price (fixed-leg rate) for a real estate index total return swap: (a) If the underlying index is in equilibrium (no lag effect)? and (b) If the expected average annual total return on the index during the period of the contract is 12% (possibly reflecting a lag in the index or the underlying market), but assume that the index exhibits the same risk as the property market such that 3.5% is the appropriate risk premium? (c) Same as (b) only now assume that the lagging and smoothing in the index gives it less risk than the underlying properties whose returns it measures (correctly over the long run) such that the appropriate risk premium for the index is only 2.5% (instead of the 3.5% for direct property investment); and finally (d) Suppose the conditions in (c) except that the index underlying the swap contract now is not a total return index but rather only tracks capital returns or price growth such that its expected return over the contract period is now only 5% (instead of 12%, i.e., there is expected to be 7% income return during the period).

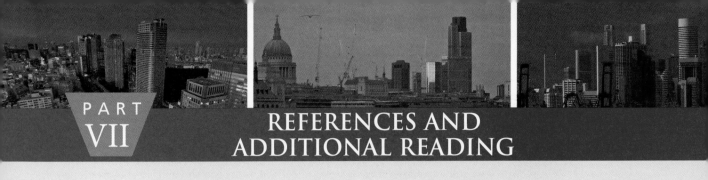

References are grouped by chapter topic. However, some references are relevant to more than one topic area (and may be cited in more than one chapter) but are listed here only once in this bibliography.

Chapters 21 and 22: Portfolio and Asset Pricing Theory

Arrow, K. 1950. A difficulty in the concept of social welfare, *Journal of Political Economy* 58: 328.

Bajtelsmit, V., and E. Worzala. 1995. Real estate allocation in pension fund portfolios. *The Journal of Real Estate Portfolio Management* 1(1): 25–38.

Black, F. Beta and return. *Journal of Portfolio Management* 20: 8–18.

Black, F., M. Jensen, and M. Scholes. 1972. The capital asset pricing model: Some empirical tests, in M. Jensen (ed.), *Studies in the Theory of Capital Markets*, New York: Praeger.

Bond, S. A., S. Hwang, P. Mitchell, and S. E. Satchell. 2007. Will private equity and hedge funds replace real estate in mixed-asset portfolios? *Journal of Portfolio Management*, Special Real Estate Issue.

Bond, S., and S. Slezak. 2011. The Optimal Portfolio Weight for Real Estate with Liquidity Costs, Estimation Error and Uncertainty Aversion, Working Paper, University of Cincinnati School of Business Administration.

Breeden, D. 1979. An intertemporal asset pricing model with stochastic consumption and investment opportunities. *Journal of Financial Economics* 7: 265–296.

Chan, K., P. Hendershott, and A. Sanders. 1990. Risk and return on real estate: Evidence from equity REITs. *AREUEA Journal* 18(1): 431–452.

Chen, P., and Y. Liang. 2000. Optimal diversification: Is it really worthwhile? *Journal of Real Estate Portfolio Management* 6: 7–16.

Chun, G. H., J. Sa-Aadu, and J. Shilling. 2004. The Role of real estate in an institutional investor's portfolio, revisited. *Journal of Real Estate Finance & Economics* 29(3): 295–320.

Ciochetti, B., and J. Shilling. 1999. Pension plan real estate investment in an asset/liability framework. Working Paper, University of North Carolina.

Ciochetti, B., J. Sa-Aadu, and J. Shilling. 1999. Determinants of real estate asset allocations in private and public pension plans. *Journal of Real Estate Finance & Economics* 19(3): 193–210.

Clayton, J., D. C. Ling, and A. Naranjo. 2009. Commercial real estate valuation: Fundamentals versus investor sentiment. *Journal of Real Estate Finance and Economics* 38(1): 5–37.

Coleman, M., and A. Mansour. 2005. Real estate in the real world: Dealing with non-normality and risk in an asset allocation model, *Journal of Real Estate Portfolio Management* 11(1): 37–53.

Craft, T. M. 2001. The role of private and public real estate in pension plan portfolio allocation choices, *Journal of Real Estate Portfolio Management* 7(1): 17–23.

Craft, T. M. 2005. Impact of pension plan liabilities on pension plan investment, *Journal of Portfolio Management*, Special Real Estate Issue: 23–31.

Craft, T. M. 2005. How funding ratios affect pension plan portfolio allocations. *Journal of Real Estate Portfolio Management* 11(1): 29–35.

Dhar, Ravi, and William N. Goetzmann. 2005. *Institutional Perspectives on Real Estate Investing: The Role of Risk and Uncertainty*. Pension Real Estate Society Research Paper.

Eichholtz, P. 1996. Does international diversification work better for real estate than for stocks and bonds? *Financial Analysts Journal* 52(1): 56–62.

Fama, E., and K. French. 1992. The cross-section of expected stock returns. *Journal of Finance* 47(2): 427–465.

Fama, E., and J. MacBeth. 1973. Risk, return, and equilibrium: Empirical tests. *Journal of Political Economy* 81: 607–636.

Fama, E., and W. Schwert. 1977. Human capital and capital market equilibrium. *Journal of Financial Economics* 4(1): 95–125.

Fama, E. F., and K. R. French. 2004. The capital asset pricing model: Theory and evidence. *Journal of Economic Perspectives* 18: 25–46.

Firstenberg, P., S. Ross, and R. Zisler. 1988. Real estate: The whole story. *Journal of Portfolio Management*. 14(3): 22–34.

Garlappi, L., R. Uppal, and T. Wang. 2007. Portfolio selection with parameter and model uncertainty: A multiprior approach. *Review of Financial Studies* 20: 41–81.

Gatzlaff, D. 1995. Pension fund investment: Further analysis of fund allocations to real estate. Working Paper, Real Estate Research Institute (RERI).

Geltner, D. 1989. Estimating real estate's systematic risk from aggregate level appraisal-based returns. *AREUEA Journal* 17(4): 463–481.

Geltner, D., and J. Mei. 1995. The present value model with time varying discount rates: Implications for commercial property valuation and investment decisions. *Journal of Real Estate Finance and Economics* 11: 119–135.

Geltner, D., N. Miller, and J. Snavely. 1995. We need a fourth asset class: HEITs. *Real Estate Finance* 12(2): 71–81.

Geltner, D., J. Rodriguez, and D. O'Connor. 1995. The similar genetics of public and private real estate and the optimal long-horizon portfolio mix. *Real Estate Finance* 12(3): 13–25.

Giliberto, S. M. 1992. The allocation of real estate to future mixed-asset institutional portfolios. *Journal of Real Estate Research* 7(4): 423–432.

Giliberto, S. M., and A. Mengden. 1996. REITs and real estate: Two markets reexamined. *Real Estate Finance* 13(1): 56–60.

Graff, R., and M. Young. 1996. Real estate return correlations: Real-world limitations on relationships inferred from NCREIF data. *Journal of Real Estate Finance & Economics* 13(2): 121–142.

Hartzell, D., J. Heckman, and M. Miles. 1986. Diversification categories in investment real estate. *AREUEA Journal* 14(2): 230–254.

Hoesli, M., J. Lekander, and W. Witkiewicz. 2004. International evidence on real estate as a portfolio diversifier. *Journal of Real Estate Research* 26: 161–206.

Ibbotson, R., J. Diermier, and L. Siegel. 1984. The demand for capital market returns: A new equilibrium theory. *Financial Analysis Journal* 40(1).

Ibbotson, R., and L. Siegel. 1984. Real estate returns: A comparison with other investments. *AREUEA Journal* 12(3): 219–242.

Jones, R. H. 2012. Risk and return in institutional commercial real estate: A fresh look with new data. Masters Thesis, MIT Center for Real Estate.

Kallberg, J., C. Liu, and D. Greig. 1996. The role of real estate in the portfolio allocation process. *Real Estate Economics* 24(3): 359–377.

Karolyi, G. A., and A. Sanders. 1998. The variation of economic risk premiums in real estate returns. *Journal of Real Estate Economics & Finance* 17(3): 245–262.

Lee, S. L. 2005. How often does direct real estate increase the risk-adjusted performance of the U.S. mixed asset portfolio? Working Paper, University of Reading Business School, UK. Retrieved from http://www.reading.ac.uk/REP/fulltxt/1005.pdf.

Lee, S. L., and S. Stevenson. 2005. The case for REITs in the mixed-asset portfolio in the short and long run." *Journal of Real Estate Portfolio Management* 11(1): 55–80.

Lee, S. L., and S. Stevenson. 2005. The consistency of private and traded real estate within mixed asset portfolios. University of Reading (UK) Working Paper presented at the 2005 American Real Estate Society annual meeting.

Liang, Y., F. C. N. Myer, and J. Webb. 1996. The bootstrap efficient frontier for mixed-asset portfolios. *Real Estate Economics* 24(2): 247–256.

Ling, D., and A. Naranjo. 1997. Economic risk factors and commercial real estate returns. *Journal of Real Estate Finance & Economics* 14(3): 283–307.

Ling, D., and A. Naranjo. 1998. The fundamental determinants of commercial real estate returns. *Real Estate Finance* 14(4): 13–24.

Ling, D., and A. Naranjo. 1999. The integration of commercial real estate markets and stock markets. *Real Estate Economics* 27(3): 483–516.

Lintner, J. 1965. The valuation of risk assets and the selection of risky investments in stock portfolios and capital budgets. *Review of Economics and Statistics* 47: 13–37.

Liu, C., T. Grissom, and D. Hartzell. 1990. The impact of market imperfections on real estate returns and optimal investment portfolios. *AREUEA Journal* 18(4): 453–478.

Liu, C., D. Hartzell, T. Grissom, and W. Grieg. 1990. The composition of the market portfolio and real estate investment performance. *AREUEA Journal* 18(1): 49–75.

Liu, C., D. Hartzell, and T. Grissom. 1992. The role of co-skewness in the pricing of real estate. *Journal of Real Estate Finance & Economics* 5(3): 299–319.

Liu, C., D. Hartzell, and M. Hoesli. 1997. International evidence on real estate securities as an inflation hedge. *Real Estate Economics* 25(2): 193–221.

MacKinnon, G. 2011. Private real estate allocations in multi-asset investment portfolios. Chapter 1 in *Real Estate Mathematics,* D. Lynn and T. Wang, eds. London: Private Equity International (PEI).

MacKinnon, G., and A. A. Zaman. 2009. Real estate for the long term: The effect of return predictability on long-horizon allocations. *Real Estate Economics* 37(1): 117–153.

Markowitz, H. 1952. Portfolio Selection. *Journal of Finance* 7: 77–91.

Mei, J., and A. Lee. 1994. Is there a real estate factor premium. *Journal of Real Estate Finance & Economics* 9(2): 113–126.

Miles, M., and T. McCue. 1984. Diversification in the real estate portfolio. *Journal of Real Estate Research* 7: 17–28.

Myer, F., and J. Webb. 1993. Return properties of equity REITs, common stocks, and commercial real estate: A comparison. *Journal of Real Estate Research* 8(1): 87–106.

Pai, A., and D. Geltner. 2007. Stocks are from Mars, real estate is from Venus: The cross-section of long-run investment performance. *Journal of Portfolio Management*, Special Real Estate Issue.

Peng, L. 2011. Risk and returns of commercial real estate: A property level analysis. Leeds School of Business, Working Paper, University of Colorado.

Plazzi, A., W. Torous, R. Valkanov. 2010. Expected returns and expected growth in rents of commercial real estate. *Review of Financial Studies* 23(9): 3469–3519.

Price, S. M., and N. Li. 2005. Multiple asset class investing: Equilibrium asset pricing evaluation of real estate risk and return across four quadrants. MSRED Thesis, MIT Center for Real Estate.

Rehring, C. 2011. Real estate in a mixed asset portfolio: The role of investment horizon. *Real Estate Economics* 40(1): 65–95.

Ross, S. 1976. The arbitrage theory of capital asset pricing. *Journal of Economic Theory* 13: 341–360.

Ross, S., and R. Zisler. 1991. Risk and return in real estate. *Journal of Real Estate Finance & Economics* 4(2): 175–190.

Rubens, J. H., D. A. Louton, and E. J. Yobaccio. 1998. Measuring the significance of diversification gains. *Journal of Real Estate Research* 16: 73–86.

Sharpe, W. 1964. Capital asset prices: A theory of market equilibrium under conditions of risk. *Journal of Finance* 19: 425–442.

Shiller, R. 1981. Do stock prices move too much to be justified by subsequent changes in dividends? *American Economic Review* 71(3): 421–436.

Sirmans, C. F., and E. Worzala. 2003. international direct real estate investment: A review of the literature. *Urban Studies* 40(5&6): 1081–1114.

Titman, S., and A. Warga. 1986. Risk and performance of real estate investment trusts: A multiple index approach. *Real Estate Economics* 14: 414–431.

Webb, J., and J. Rueben. 1987. How much in real estate: A surprising answer. *Journal of Portfolio Management* 13: 10–14.

Williams, J. 1999. Agency, ownership, and returns on real assets. Working Paper, Real Estate Research Institute (RERI).

Young, M., and R. Graff. 1995. Real estate is not normal— A fresh look at real estate return distributions. *Journal of Real Estate Finance and Economics* 10(3): 225–259.

Ziobrowski, B. A. 1995. Exchange rate risk and internationally diversified portfolios. *Journal of International Money & Finance* 14(1): 65–81.

Chapter 23: Real Estate Investment Trusts (REITs)

Ambrose, B., S. Erlich, W. Hughes, and S. Wachter. 2000. REIT economies of scale: Fact or fiction? *Journal of Real Estate Finance and Economics* 20: 211–224.

Ambrose, B., M. Highfield, and P. Linneman. 2005. Real estate and economies of scale: The case of REITs. *Real Estate Economics* 33: 323–350.

Ambrose, B., D. Lee, and J. Peek. 2005. Comovement after joining and index: Spillovers of nonfundamental effects. Working Paper, University of Kentucky.

Ambrose, B., and A. Pennington-Cross. 2000. Economies of scale in multi-product firms: The case of REITs. Working Paper, Real Estate Research Institute (RERI).

Barkham, R., and D. Geltner. 1995. Price discovery in American and British property markets. *Real Estate Economics (formerly AREUEA Journal)* 23(1): 21–44.

Bers, M., and T. Springer. 1997. Economies of scale for real estate investment trusts. *Journal of Real Estate Research* 14: 275–290.

Bers, M., and T. Springer. 1998. Sources of scale economies for REITs. *Real Estate Finance* 14(4): 47–56.

Block, R. 2006. *Investing in REITs: Real Estate Investment Trusts, 3rd ed.* Bloomberg.

Boer, D., D. Brounen, and H. Op't Veld. 2005. Corporate focus and stock performance: Evidence from listed property markets. *Journal of Real Estate Finance & Economics* 31(3): 263–281.

Boudry, W., J. Kallberg, and C. Liu. 2010. An analysis of REIT security issuance decisions. *Real Estate Economics* 38(1): 91–120.

Bradley, M., D. Capozza, and P. Seguin. 1998. Dividend policy and cash flow uncertainty. *Real Estate Economics* 26: 555–580.

Capozza, D. 2005. New rules for real estate investors. Keynote presentation, American Real Estate and Urban Economics Association (AREUEA) annual meetings, Boston, Massachusetts.

Capozza, D., and P. Seguin. 1998. Managerial style and firm value. *Real Estate Economics* 26(1): 131–150.

Capozza, D., and P. Seguin. 1999. Focus, transparency and value: The REIT evidence. *Real Estate Economics* 27(4): 587–620.

Case, B., M. Guidolin, and Y. Yildirim. 2012. Markov switching dynamics in REIT returns: Univariate and multivariate evidence on forecasting performance. Working Paper, Whitman School of Management, Syracuse University.

Case, B., Y. Yawei and Y. Yildirim. 2012. Dynamic correlations among asset classes: REIT and stock returns. *Journal of Real Estate Finance & Economics* 44(3): 298–318.

Chan, S. H., J. Erickson, and K. Wang. 2003. *Real Estate Investment Trusts: Structure, Performance and Investment Opportunities.* New York: Oxford University Press.

Cherkes, M., J. Sagi, and R. Stanton. 2005. Liquidity and closed-end funds. Working Paper, Columbia University.

Cheng, P., L. Yingchung, and L. Zhenguo. 2008. A model of time-on-market and real estate price under sequential search with recall. *Real Estate Economics* 36(4): 813–843.

Clayton, J., and G. MacKinnon. 2003. The relative importance of stock, bond and real estate factors in explaining REIT returns. *Journal of Real Estate Finance and Economics* 27(1): 39–60.

Conner, P., and R. Falzon. 2004. Rational differences between public and private real estate. Research Report, Prudential Real Estate Investors.

Corgel, J., and S. Gibson. 2005. Unlisted REITs, fixed share prices and wealth transfer between investors, Working Paper, Cornell University.

Ertugrul, M. and E. Giambona. 2011. Property segment and REIT capital structure. *Journal of Real Estate Finance & Economics* 43: 505–526.

Fama, E. F., and K. R. French. 1992. The cross-section of expected stock returns. *Journal of Finance* 47: 427–465

Garrigan, R., and J. Parsons (eds.). 1997. *Real Estate Investment Trusts: Structure, Analysis, and Strategy.* New York: McGraw-Hill.

Gentry, W., C. Jones, and C. Mayer. 2004. Do stock prices really reflect fundamental values? The case of REITs. Working Paper, Columbia University Graduate School of Business.

Ghosh, C., R. Nag, and C. F. Sirmans. 1997. Financing choice by equity REITs in the 1990s. *Real Estate Finance* 14(3): 41–50.

Giliberto, S. M., and A. Mengden. 1996. REITs and real estate: Two markets reexamined. *Real Estate Finance* 13(1): 56–60.

Goldstein, M., and E. Nelling. 1999. REIT return behavior in advancing and declining stock markets. *Real Estate Finance* 15(4): 68–77.

Gordon, J., and E. Shapiro. 1956. Capital equipment analysis: The required rate of profit. *Management Science* 3: 102–110.

Grullon, G., and A. Wang. 2001. Closed-end fund discounts with informed ownership differential. *Journal of Financial Intermediation* 10: 171–205.

Gyourko, J., and D. Keim. 1992. What does the stock market tell us about real estate returns? *Real Estate Economics* 20(3): 457–486.

Gyourko. J., and E. Nelling. 1996. Systematic risk and diversification in the equity reit market. *Real Estate Economics* 24(4): 493–515.

Hoesli, M., E. Oikarinen, and C. Serrano. 2011. The long-run dynamics between direct and securitized real estate. *Journal of Real Estate Research* 33(1): 73–103.

Kaiser, R. 1999. The 1990s REIT Boom: Post-mortem of a Wall Street delusion. Paper presented to the American Real Estate Society, Tampa, Florida.

Lee, S., and S. Stevenson. 2005. The case for REITs in the mixed-asset portfolio in the short and long run. *Journal of Real Estate Portfolio Management* 11(1): 55–80.

Ling, D., and A. Naranjo. 1999. The integration of commercial real estate markets and stock markets. *Real Estate Economics* 27(3): 483–516.

Ling, D., and M. Ryngaert. 1997. Valuation uncertainty, institutional involvement, and the underpricing of IPOs: The case of REITs. *Journal of Financial Economics* 43(3): 433–456.

Linneman, P. 1997. Forces changing the real estate industry forever. *Wharton Real Estate Review.*

Naranjo, A., and M. Ryngaert. 1998. The predictability of equity REIT returns. Working Paper, Real Estate Research Institute (RERI).

Ott, S., T. Riddiough, and H. Yi. 2005. Finance, investment and investment performance: Evidence from the REIT sector. *Real Estate Economics* 33(1): 203–235.

Pagliari, J. L., K. A. Scherer, and R. T. Monopoli. 2005. Public versus private real estate equities: A more refined, long-term comparison. *Real Estate Economics* 33: 147–187.

Peterson, J., and C. Hsieh. 1997. Do common risk factors in the returns on stocks and bonds explain returns on REITs? *Real Estate Economics* 25: 321–345.

Plazzi, A, W. Torous, and R. Valkhanov. 2010. Expected returns and expected growth of rents in commercial real estate. *Review of Financial Studies* 23(9): 3469–3519.

Plazzi, A, W. Torous, and R. Valkhanov. 2008. The Cross-sectional dispersion of commercial real estate returns and rent growth. *Real Estate Economics* 36(3): 403–439.

Riddiough, T., M. Moriarty, and P. Yeatman. 2005. Privately versus publicly held asset performance. *Real Estate Economics* 33: 121–146.

Ro, S., and A. Ziobrowski. 2011. Does focus really matter? Specialized versus diversified REITs. *Journal of Real Estate Finance & Economics* 42(1): 68–83.

Sagalyn, L. 1996. Conflicts of interest in the structure of REITs. *Real Estate Finance* 13(2): 34–51.

Sakwa, S., W. Acheson, B. Legg, and C. Schmidt. *REITs: Nuts and Bolts – Primer #1,* Merrill Lynch Equity Research, January 18, 2005.

Shiller, R. 1998. Human behavior and the efficiency of the financial system. Working Paper #6375, National Bureau of Economic Research.

Taylor, L. 1998. Financial analysis of REIT securities. R. Garrigan and J. Parsons (eds.), *Real Estate Investment Trusts.* New York: McGraw-Hill.

Taylor, L., T. Goebel, D. Maloney, and J. Perry. 2002. *REITs for Rookies: Answers to Many FAQs About REITs.* Deutsche Banc Alex. Brown. U.S. Real Estate Equity Research, January 4, 2002.

Vogel, J. 1997. Why the conventional wisdom about REITs is wrong. *Real Estate Finance* 14(2): 7–12.

Wu, F., and A. Yavas. 2004. Do UPREITs suffer tax-timing conflict of interest? Working Paper, Real Estate Research Institute (RERI).

Wu, Z. 2005. Firm investment, financial constraint and banking relationship: Evidence from real estate investment trusts. Department of Real Estate and Urban Economics Working Paper, University of Wisconsin.

Yang, S. 2001. Is bigger better? Reexamining the scale economies of REITs. *Journal of Real Estate Portfolio Management* 7: 67–68.

Yavas, A., and Y. Yildirim. 2011. Price discovery in real estate markets: A dynamic analysis. *Journal of Real Estate Finance and Economics* 42(1): 1–29.

Chapter 24: International Real Estate Investments: Markets, Strategies and Implementation

Bardhan, A., R. Edelstein, and D. Tsang. 2008. Global financial integration and real estate security returns. *Real Estate Economics,* 36(2): 285–311.

Bond, S., A. Karolyi, and A. Sanders. 2003. International real estate returns: a multifactor, multi-country approach. *Real Estate Economics,* 31(3): 481–500.

Brounen, D., and P. Eichholtz. 2003. Property, common stock, and property shares. *The Journal of Portfolio Management,* 129–137.

Brounen, D., P. Eichholtz, and D. Ling. 2009. The liquidity of property shares: An international comparison. *Real Estate Economics,* 37(3): 413–445.

Conover, C., H. Friday, and G. Sirmans. 2002. Diversification benefits from foreign real estate investments. *Journal of Real Estate Portfolio Management,* January/April, 17–25.

DTZ Research. 2011. *Money into Property.*

Eichholtz, P. 1996. Does international diversification work better for real estate than for stocks and bonds? *Financial Analysts Journal,* 56–62.

Eichholtz, P., N. Gugler, and N. Kok. 2011. Property market transparency and the costs of international investment. *Journal of Real Estate Finance and Economics,* 43(1): 152–173.

Eichholtz, P., R. Huisman, K. Koedijk, and L. Schuin. 1998. Continental factors in international real estate returns. *Real Estate Economics,* 26: 493–509.

Eichholtz, P., K. Koedijk, and M. Schweitzer. 2001. Testing international real estate investment strategies. *Journal of International Money and Finance.*

Eichholtz, P. and T. Lindenthal. 2012. Demographics, human capital, and the demand for housing. Working Paper, Maastricht University.

Gallo, J. and Y. Zhang. 2010. Global property market diversification. *Journal of Real Estate Finance and Economics,* 41(4): 458–485.

Gerlach, R., P. Wilson, and R. Zurbruegg. 2006. Structural breaks and diversification: The impact of the 1997 Asian financial crisis on the integration of Asia-Pacific real estate markets. *Journal of International Money and Finance,* 25(6): 974–991.

Goetzmann, W. and S. Wachter. 2001. The global real estate crash: Evidence from an international database, in S. Brown and C. Liu, *A Global Perspective on Real Estate Cycles,* Kluwer Academic Publishers, 5–23.

Glaeser, E. and J. Gyourko. 2005. Urban decline and durable housing. *Journal of Political Economy* 113(2): 345–375.

Green, R. and P. Hendershott. 2007. The impact of age on retail sales. *Journal of Shopping Center Research,* 14 (1): 1–16.

Hoesli, M., J. Lekander and W. Witkiewicz. 2004. International evidence on real estate as a portfolio diversifier. *Journal of Real Estate Research,* 26(2): 161–206.

Hoesli, M. and E. Oikarinen. 2012. Are REITs real estate? Evidence from international sector level data. *Journal of International Money and Finance,* 31(7): 1823–1850.

Marcato, G. and T. Key. 2005. Direct investment in real estate. *Journal of Portfolio Management,* 31(5): 55–69.

Kroencke, T., and F. Schindler. 2012. International diversification with securitized real estate and the veiling glare from currency risk. *Journal of International Money and Finance,* 31(7): 1851–1866.

Lapier, T. 1998. Cross border direct investments. Chapter 2 of *Competition, Growth Strategies and the Globalization of Services; Real Estate Advisory Services in Japan, Europe and the United States,* London: Routledge.

Levi, M. 2009. *International Finance,* 5th ed., London: Routledge.

Lieser, K., and A. Groh. 2011. The attractiveness of 66 countries for institutional real estate investments. *Journal of Real Estate Portfolio Management,* 191–212.

Ling, D., and A. Naranjo. 2002. Commercial real estate performance: A cross country analysis. *Journal of Real Estate Finance and Economics,* 24(1–2): 119–142.

Liow, K. H. 2010. Integration between securitized real estate and stock markets: A global perspective. *Journal of Real Estate Portfolio Management,* 249–266.

Malone, T. 2004. *The Future of Work: How the New Order of Business Will Shape Your Organization, Your Management Style and Your Life.* Harvard Business School Press.

Mankiw, G. and D. Weil. 1989. The baby boom, the baby bust and the housing market. *Regional Science and Urban Economics*, 19(2): 235–258.

Newell, G. 2003. Diversification benefits of European and global property stocks, EPRA Research Report.

Sercu, P. 2009. *International Finance, Theory into Practice.* Princeton University Press.

Serrano, C., and M. Hoesli. 2009. Global securitized real estate benchmarks and performance. *Journal of Real Estate Portfolio Management*, 15(1): 1–20.

Sirmans, C. F., and E. Worzala. 2003a. International direct investment in real estate: A review of the literature. *Urban Studies*, 40(5–6): 1081–1114.

Sirmans, C. F., and E. Worzala. 2003b. Investing in international real estate stocks: A review of the literature. *Urban Studies*, 40(5–6): 1115–1149.

Solnik, B., and C. McLeavey. 2008. *Global Investments*, 6th ed. Upper Saddle River, New Jersey: Prentice Hall.

Wit, I. 2010. International diversification strategies for direct real estate. *Journal of Real Estate Finance and Investments*, 41(4): 433–457.

Yunus, N. 2012. Increasing convergence between U.S. and international securitized property markets: Evidence based on cointegration tests. *Real Estate Economics*, 37(3): 383–411.

Zhou, J. 2011. Downside risk spillover among global real estate securities markets. *Journal of Real Estate Portfolio Management*, 255–270.

Chapter 25: Data Challenges in Measuring Real Estate Periodic Returns

Bailey, M., R. Muth, and H. Nourse. 1963. A regression method for real estate price index construction. *Journal of the American Statistical Association* 58: 933–942.

Basu, S., and T. G. Thibodeau. 1998. Analysis of spatial autocorrelation in house prices. *Journal of Real Estate Finance and Economics* 17(1): 61–85.

Blundell, G., and C. Ward. 1987. Property portfolio allocation: A multi-factor model. *Land Development Studies* 4: 145–156.

Bokhari, S., and D. Geltner. 2012. Estimating real estate price movements for high frequency tradable indexes in a scarce data environment. *Journal of Real Estate Finance and Economics* 45(2).

Bond, S. A., and S. S. Hwang. 2007. Smoothing, nonsynchronous appraisal and cross-sectional aggregation in real estate price indices. *Real Estate Economics* 35(3): 349–382.

Brown, G. 1985. The Information content of property valuations. *Journal of Valuation* 3: 350–357.

Brown, G., and G. Matysiak. 2000. *Real Estate Investment: A Capital Market Approach.* London: Pearson Education.

Bryan, T., and P. Colwell. 1982. Housing price indices. In C. F. Sirmans (ed.), *Research in Real Estate*, vol. 2. Greenwich, CT: JAI Press.

Case, B., O. H. Pollakowski, and S. M. Wachter. 1991. On choosing among house price index methodologies. *Real Estate Economics* 19(3): 286–307.

Case, B., and J. Quigley. 1991. Dynamics of real-estate prices. *Review of Economics and Statistics* 73(1): 50–58.

Case, K., and R. Shiller. 1987. Prices of single family homes since 1970: New indexes for four cities. *New England Economic Review*, Sept.: 45–56.

Case, K., and R. Shiller. 1990. Forecasting prices and excess returns in the housing market. *AREUEA Journal* 18(3): 253–273.

Court, A. 1939. Hedonic price indices with automotive examples. *The Dynamics of Automobile Demand.* General Motors Corporation.

Childs, P., S. Ott, and T. Riddiough. 2000. Noise, real estate markets, and options on real assets. Working Paper, MIT Centre for Real Estate.

Chinloy, P., M. Cho, and I. Megbolugbe. 1997. Appraisals, transaction incentives, and smoothing. *Journal of Real Estate Finance & Economics* 14(1/2): 89–112, January/March.

Clapp, J., and C. Giacotto. 1992. Estimating price indices for residential property: A comparison of repeat sales and assessed value methods. *Journal of the American Statistical Association* 87: 300–306.

Clapp, J., and C. Giacotto. 1998. Price indices based on the hedonic repeat-sales method: Application to the housing market. *Journal of Real Estate Finance & Economics* 16(1): 5–26.

Crosson, S., C. Dannis, and T. Thibodeau. 1996. Cutting-edge, cost-effective valuation for accurate portfolio level appraisal. *Real Estate Finance* 12(4): 20–28.

Devaney, S., and R. M. Diaz. 2011. Transaction-based indices for the U.K. commercial real estate market: An exploration using IPD transaction data. *Journal of Property Research* 28:4: 269–289.

Diaz, J. 1997. An investigation into the impact of previous expert value estimates on appraisal judgment. *Journal of Real Estate Research* 13(1): 49–58.

Diaz, J., and M. Wolverton. 1998. A longitudinal examination of the appraisal smoothing hypothesis. *Real Estate Economics* 26(2): 349–358.

Downs, D., and B. Slade. 1999. Characteristics of a full-disclosure transaction-based index of commercial real estate. *Journal of Real Estate Portfolio Management* 5(1): 94–104.

Englund P., J. M. Quigley, and C. L. Redfearn. 1999. The choice of methodology for computing housing price indexes: comparisons of temporal aggregation and sample definition. *Journal of Real Estate Finance and Economics* 19(2): 91–112.

Fisher, J., D. Gatzlaff, D. Geltner, and D. Haurin. 2000. Controlling for the impact of variable liquidity in commercial real estate price indices. *Real Estate Economics* 31(2): 269–303.

Fisher, J., and D. Geltner. 2000. De-Lagging the NCREIF Index: Transaction prices and reverse-engineering. *Real Estate Finance* 17(1): 7–22.

Fisher, J., D. Geltner, and H. Pollakowski. 2007. A quarterly transactions-based index (TBI) of institutional real estate investment performance and movements in supply and demand. *Journal of Real Estate Finance & Economics* 34(1).

Fisher, J., D. Geltner, and R. B. Webb. 1994. Value indices of commercial real estate: A comparison of index construction methods. *Journal of Real Estate Finance & Economics* 9(2): 137–164.

Fisher, J., M. Miles, and R. B. Webb. 1999. How reliable are commercial appraisals: Another look. *Real Estate Finance* 16(3).

Florance, A., N. Miller, J. Spivey, and R. Peng. 2010. Slicing, dicing, and scoping the size of the U.S. real estate market. *Journal of Real Estate Portfolio Management* 16(2): 111–128.

Gatzlaff, D., and D. Geltner. 1998. A transaction-based index of commercial property and its comparison to the NCREIF index. *Real Estate Finance* 15(1): 7–22.

Gatzlaff, D., and D. Haurin. 1996. Sample selection bias and repeat-sales index estimates. *Journal of Real Estate Finance and Economics* 14: 33–50.

Geltner, D. 1989. Estimating real estate's systematic risk from aggregate level appraisal-based returns. *AREUEA Journal* 17(4): 463–481.

Geltner, D. 1991. Smoothing in appraisal-based returns. *Journal of Real Estate Finance & Economics* 4(3): 327–345.

Geltner, D. 1993a. Temporal aggregation in real estate return indices. *AREUEA Journal* 21(2): 141–166.

Geltner, D. 1993b. Estimating market values from appraised values without assuming an efficient market. *Journal of Real Estate Research* 8(3): 325–346.

Geltner, D. 1999. Using the NCREIF index to shed light on what really happened to asset market values in 1998: An unsmoother's view of the statistics. *Real Estate Finance* 16(1): 69–80.

Geltner, D., and D. Ling. 2006. Considerations in the design and construction of investment real estate research indices. *Journal of Real Estate Research* 28(4): 411–444.

Geltner, D., and W. Goetzmann. 2000. Two decades of commercial property returns: A repeated-measures regression-based version of the NCREIF index. *Journal of Real Estate Finance & Economics* 21(1): 5–21.

Giacotto, C., and J. Clapp. 1992. Appraisal-based real estate returns under alternative market regimes. *AREUEA Journal* 20(1): 1–24.

Giliberto, S. M. 1990. Equity real estate investment trusts and real estate returns. *Journal of Real Estate Research* 5(2): 259–264.

Goetzmann, W. 1992. The accuracy of real estate indices: Repeat sale estimators. *Journal of Real Estate Finance & Economics* 5(1): 5–54.

Goetzmann, W. 1993. The single family home in the investment portfolio. *Journal of Real Estate Finance & Economics* 6(3): 201–222.

Graff, R., and M. Young. 1996. Real estate return correlations: Real-world limitations on relationships inferred from NCREIF data. *Journal of Real Estate Finance & Economics* 13(2): 121–142.

Griliches, Z. and I. Adelman. 1961. On an index of quality change. *Journal of the American Statistical Association* 56: 295, 535–548.

Hamilton, S., and J. Clayton. 1999. Smoothing in commercial property valuations: Evidence from the trenches. *Real Estate Finance* 16(3).

Hansen J. 2009. Australian house prices: A comparison of hedonic and repeat-sales measures. *Economic Record* 85(269): 132–145.

Hoerl, A., and R. Kennard. 1969. Ridge regression: Biased estimation for non-orthogonal problems. *Technometrics* 12(1): 55–67.

Hoesli, M., E. Oikarinen, and C. Serrano. 2011. The long-run dynamics between direct and securitized real estate. *Journal of Real Estate Research* 33(1): 73–103.

Kain J. F., and J. M. Quigley. 1970. Measuring the value of housing quality. *Journal of the American Statistical Association* 65: 532–548.

Lai, T., and K. Wang. 1998. Appraisal smoothing: The other side of the story. *Real Estate Economics* 26(3): 511–536.

Lin, Z. G., and K. D. Vandell. 2007. Illiquidity and pricing biases in the real estate market. *Real Estate Economics* 35(3): 291–330.

Ling, D., A. Naranjo, and M. Nimalendran. 1999. Estimating returns on commercial real estate: A new methodology using latent variable regression. Working Paper, Real Estate Research Institute (RERI).

McMillen, D., and J. Dombrow. 2000. Estimating price indexes in metropolitan submarkets: A flexible Fourier repeat sales approach. Working Paper, University of Chicago.

Mei, J. P., and C. H. Liu. 1994. The predictability of real estate returns and market timing. *Journal of Real Estate Finance and Economics* 8(2): 115–135.

Pace, R. K., R. Barry, J. M. Clapp, and M. Rodriquez. 1998. Spatiotemporal autoregressive Models of neighborhood effects. *Journal of Real Estate Finance and Economics* 17(1): 15–33.

Pindyck, R., and D. Rubinfeld. 1991. *Economic Models and Economic Forecasts.* New York: McGraw-Hill, Chapter 3.

Quan, D., and J. Quigley. 1989. Inferring an investment return series for real estate from observations on sales. *AREUEA Journal* 17(2): 218–230.

Quan, D., and J. Quigley. 1991. Price formation and the appraisal function in real estate markets. *Journal of Real Estate Finance & Economics* 4(2): 127–146.

Quigley, J. M. 1995. A simple hybrid model for estimating real estate price indexes. *Journal of Housing Economics* 4(1): 1–12.

Rosen, S. 1974. Hedonic prices and implicit markets: Product differentiation in pure competition. *Journal of Political Economy* 82(1): 34–55.

Shiller, R. 1991. Arithmetic repeat sales price estimators. *Journal of Housing Economics* 1(1): 110–126.

Stevenson, S. 2002. Momentum effects and mean reversion in real estate securities. *Journal of Real Estate Research* 23(1): 47–64.

Wallace, N. E., and R. A. Meese. 1997. The construction of residential housing price indices: a comparison of repeat-sales, hedonic-regression, and hybrid approaches. *Journal of Real Estate Finance and Economics* 14(1): 51–73.

Williams, J. 2000. Pricing real assets under rational expectations. Working Paper.

Chapter 26: Real Estate Investment Management

Andonov, A., P. Eichholtz, and N. Kok. 2012. Value Added from Money Managers in Private Markets? An Examination of Pension Fund Investments in Real Estate. Working Paper, Maastricht University.

Brodie, Z., A. Kane, and A. Marcus. 1999. *Investments*, 4th ed. Boston: Irwin, McGraw-Hill, Chapter 24.

Buttimer, R., J. Kau, and V. C. Slawson. 1997. A model for pricing securities dependent upon a real estate index. *Journal of Housing Economics* 6(1): 16–30.

Canizo, L., and R. LaFever. 2005. Revisiting performance persistence in real estate funds. Master's Thesis, MIT Center for Real Estate.

Feng, T. 2010. Property-level performance attribution: Demonstrating a practical tool for real estate invest-

ment management diagnostics. Master's Thesis, MIT Center for Real Estate.

Feng, T., and D. Geltner. 2011. Property-level performance attribution: investment management diagnostics and the investment importance of property management. *Journal of Portfolio Management* 37(5): 110–124.

Fisher, J., and D. Geltner. 2002. Property-level benchmarking of real estate development investments using the NCREIF property index. *Real Estate Finance* 19(1).

Geltner, D. 2003. IRR-based property level performance attribution. *Journal of Portfolio Management,* Special Issue: 138–151.

Geltner, D. 2000. Benchmarking manager performance within the private real estate investment industry. *Real Estate Finance* 17(1): 23–34.

Geltner, D., and J. Fisher. 2007. Pricing and index considerations in commercial real estate derivatives. *Journal of Portfolio Management,* Special Real Estate Issue.

Geltner, D. and D. Ling. 2007. Indices for investment benchmarking and return performance analysis in private real estate. *International Real Estate Review* 10(1).

Geltner, D., and D. Ling. 2001. Ideal research and benchmark indexes in private real estate: Some conclusions from the RERI/PREA technical report. *Real Estate Finance* 17(4): 17–28.

Greig, W. 1997. Standardizing information on privately held real estate investments. *Real Estate Finance* 13(4): 59–62.

Hahn, C., D. Geltner, and N. Lietz. 2005. Real estate opportunity funds: Past fund performance as an indicator of subsequent fund performance. *Journal of Portfolio Management,* 31(5): 143–153.

Hamilton, S., and R. Heinkel. 1995. Sources of value-added in Canadian real estate investment management. *Real Estate Finance* 12(2): 57–70.

Horrigan, H., B. Case, D. Geltner, and H. Pollakowski. 2009. REIT-based property return indices: A new way to track and trade commercial real estate. *Journal of Portfolio Management* 35(5): 80–91.

Lieblich, F. 1995. The real estate portfolio management process. In J. Pagliari (ed.), *The Handbook of Real Estate Portfolio Management,* Irwin, Chicago.

Lim, J. Y., and Y. Zhang. 2006. A study on real estate derivatives. Unpublished MS Thesis, Massachusetts Institute of Technology, Department of Urban Studies and Planning.

Lynn, D., and T. Wang (eds.). 2011. *Real Estate Mathematics,* PEI, London.

Mahoney, J., S. Malpezzi, and J. Shilling. 2000. Implications of income property stock data for real estate investment portfolio location. *Real Estate Finance* 16(4).

Mei, J. 1996. Assessing the "Santa Claus" approach to asset allocation. *Real Estate Finance* 13(2): 65–70.

Myer, F. C. N., and J. Webb. 1993. The effect of benchmark choice on risk-adjusted performance measures for commingled real estate funds. *Journal of Real Estate Research* 8(2): 189–203.

Myer, F. C. N., J. Webb, and L. T. He. 1997. Issues in measuring performance of commingled real estate funds. *Journal of Real Estate Research* 3(2): 79–86.

Property Council of Australia. 1998. *Australian Investment Performance Measurement & Presentation Standards*, Property Council of Australia, Sydney.

Rehring, C. & B. Steiningner. 2011. An empirical evaluation of normative commercial real estate swap pricing. *Journal of Portfolio Management*, Special Real Estate Issue: 154.

REAL ESTATE DEVELOPMENT AND OTHER SELECTED TOPICS

The preceding seven parts and 26 chapters have taken you on quite a tour. You have seen the micro-level of real estate transactions and deals, and the macro-level of portfolio strategy, tactics, and investment management. You have seen the urban economic foundation of real estate investment in the space market, as well as the financial economics perspective on both equity and debt investment. But there are still a few particular topics that we have not covered in depth or as a particular focus in any of the previous parts. This last part is therefore a bit of a grab bag, a mixture of topics that we think are important, but that are distinct enough to have been left out of the flow of the previous parts. If there is a common theme in Part VIII, it is to bring you back to the link between the asset and space markets we first described in Parts I and II of this book, but now with a more specific micro-level focus on some topics that are particularly important in commercial property investment.

In particular, Part VIII will focus major attention on the financial analysis of real estate development, beginning with the closely related but more fundamental topic of land valuation, including the real options model. This will occupy Chapters 27 through 29. A second major topic is that of leases and leasing strategy, which will be covered in Chapter 30.

REAL OPTIONS AND LAND VALUE

CHAPTER OUTLINE

LEARNING OBJECTIVES

After reading this chapter, you should understand:

⊃ The call option and how this concept can be used to understand the value of land.

⊃ The binomial model of option valuation, and how and why it works.

⊃ The Samuelson-McKean formula and how it can be used to shed light on land value, development timing, and the opportunity cost of capital for investment in land speculation.

⊃ Some of the insights option valuation theory provides for understanding real estate development behavior, including how over-development can be rational in some circumstances.

Real Options and Land Value

Land value is probably the most fundamental topic in all of real estate. We saw in our discussion of the real estate system in Part I the pivotal role land value plays as the key link between the asset and space markets in the real estate development process. In addition, we saw the crucial role of land value in urban economic analysis and in the shape and dynamics of real world urban development. Indeed, land is the fundamental defining characteristic of real estate, and the nature of land valuation helps to define the investment characteristics of most major real estate assets. In this chapter we will introduce you to a very useful (and Nobel Prize-winning) tool that was developed during the last few decades for the purpose of helping to understand, analyze, and evaluate land and the real estate development process. This tool is **option valuation theory (OVT)**, and especially the branch of that theory known as **real options**.

27.1 The Call Option Model of Land Value

In finance, an **option** is defined as follows:

An option is the right **without obligation** *to obtain something of value upon the payment or giving up of something else of value.*

The person having such a right is referred to as the owner or holder of the option. The asset obtained by the **exercise** of the option is often referred to as the **underlying asset**, while that which is given up is referred to as the **exercise price** of the option. The option holder has the right to decide whether or not to exercise the option. If the option can be exercised at any time (prior to an expiration date, or maturity, if the option has such), then the option is said to be an **American option**. If the option can only be exercised on its expiration date (not before), then the option is said to be a **European option**. In any case, option exercise is irreversible because, in the act of exercising the option, the option itself is thereby given up, that is, an option can only be exercised once.

OVT consists of a body of theory and methodology for quantitatively evaluating options. Included as an integral part of such valuation is the problem of specifying the conditions when it is optimal to exercise the option, if it is an American option. The classical types of options in financial economics for which OVT was first developed are the stock options and warrants that are traded in several public exchanges and widely issued to corporate executives as an incentive component of their compensation. For example, the classical common stock **call option** gives the holder the right, without obligation, to purchase at a stated price per share a specified number of shares of the common stock of a specified company on or before a certain date.

The term "*real options*" refers to the study of options whose underlying assets (that is, either what is obtained or what is given up on the exercise of the option) are real assets (i.e., physical capital) as opposed to purely financial assets. For example, a building or a factory is a real asset, whereas shares of common stock or a release from a mortgage debt obligation are financial assets. The default option in mortgage debt that we noted in Chapter 16 (the mortgagor's put option) is an example of a real option because the borrower is giving up real property. But a deeper and more fundamental level of application of real option theory to real estate is to apply the option model to the land itself, the asset that is characteristic of all real estate. When we do this, we go to the very heart of the real estate system because OVT can now shed light directly on the relation between land value and the timing and nature of the development of buildings on the land.

This application of real options theory to real estate is what may be termed the **call option model of land value**. In this model, land is viewed as obtaining its value through the option it gives its owner to develop a structure on the land. The land owner can obtain a valuable rent-paying asset upon the payment of the construction cost necessary to build the structure. More broadly, the landowner's option includes also the option to demolish and/or redevelop any existing structures on the land. However, unless the existing building is quite old or small, or the development of the city and neighborhood has rendered the existing structure inappropriate for the best use of the location, the cost of demolishing the existing building (in particular, the *opportunity cost* of the forgone revenues that building could earn) will normally be so great as to minimize the redevelopment option value. Thus, the exercise of the option is essentially irreversible; the option is given up through its exercise. The option model of land value is therefore seen to be most applicable either to vacant (or nearly vacant) land, or else to land in transition zones where the highest and best urban use of the land is changing.[1] In any case, it is important to keep in mind that the real option that is viewed as giving land its value is, essentially, the *land development option*.

The reason the call option model of land value can have such a fundamental and central place in furthering our understanding of real estate is that it relates directly to some crucial links in the big picture of the real estate system as we defined this system way back in Chapter 2. Land is the characteristic component that distinguishes real estate from other types of capital assets.

---

[1]Recall our discussion of neighborhood and property life cycles in sections 5.3 and 5.4 of Chapter 5.

The call option model allows us to better understand and quantify land value. Real option theory sheds light on the important link between land value and real estate development. If you recall from Chapter 2 our depiction of the big picture of the real estate system in Exhibits 2-2 and 2-3, you will remember the crucial role that the development industry plays in providing the long-run link between the real estate asset market and the real estate space usage market. From Chapters 4 and 5 you will also recall the crucial role that the land market plays in determining urban spatial form. Finally, recall from Appendix 10C that it is difficult to apply the traditional risk-adjusted discount rate approach to DCF analysis to evaluate development projects because it is difficult to know what is the appropriate opportunity cost of capital to use as the discount rate. All of these issues can be addressed in a rigorous and quantitative way, and can be integrated as never before, using real option theory and the call option model of land value.

27.2 Simple Numerical Example of OVT Applied to Land Valuation and the Development Timing Decision

To gain a more concrete understanding of OVT in its fundamental application to real estate, let's walk through a very simple example of how the development option affects land value and the development timing decision. Consider a vacant land parcel and its potential development as summarized in Exhibit 27-1. Suppose a building worth $100 million today can be developed on the land at a construction cost of $88.24 million, for an immediate profit of $11.76 million.[2] Now suppose that the development option does not expire today, but rather will exist another year. Further suppose that it is reasonable to expect that, if we wait until next year, there is a 70 percent chance that the market will improve and a similar building, newly completed next year, would in that case be worth $113.21 million. On the other hand, there is a 30 percent chance that the market will decline, which would result in a value of only $78.62 million for the new building next year.[3] In either case, construction costs will have increased by 2 percent, to $90 million next year.

Now we can see how the flexibility allowed by the lack of obligatory exercise of the development option enables the landowner to take advantage of the future possibilities. The

---

[2]For now, we will ignore the time that it takes to build, that is, we will assume construction is instantaneous, such that by paying $88.24 million of construction cost today we could immediately have a completed fully operating building worth $100 million. Note that the present value of this building today includes the present value of the net rental income the building would be expected to provide next year (as well as all subsequent years). It does not, however, include the value of any rent received during the current (just past) year. (In other words., we are working with "ex-dividend" asset values). In practice, since the building we could develop on the land does not yet exist, we can only observe the $100 million current value of such a building by observing the current value of similar buildings that do exist, and by extrapolating their rents, occupancy, operating expenses, and capitalization rates to our subject development (perhaps with suitable modification based on our understanding of the relevant real estate market). In effect, we are assuming the existence and observable value of a "twin asset" to the one we would build. This type of "twin asset" assumption actually underlies all DCF analysis, as the OCC used in the discount rate is obtained by observing required returns for "similar investments" (i.e., effectively, "twin assets").

[3]These numbers may seem a bit curious. In fact, they represent a plausible scenario consistent with the value of a newly completed building being worth $100 million today. Note that the expected value of a newly completed building next year is $102.83 million [0.7($113.21) + 0.3($78.62)]. This implies an expected annual growth rate of 2.83% in the value of a new building, roughly consistent with typical inflation expectations in the early 2000s. Suppose a new building completed today would generate net rental income next year equal to 6% of its ex-dividend value at that time. Then the building would generate net rent of 6% × $102.83 = $6.17 million next year. Thus, an investor buying the newly completed building today would obtain a total expected value next year of $102.83 + $6.17 = $109 million. A newly completed building value today of $100 million would then be equivalent in our scenario to assuming that 9% is an appropriate opportunity cost of capital (OCC, or risk-adjusted discount rate for DCF valuation) for investment in completed buildings, and that 6% is a plausible payout rate (or 6.17% a plausible forward-looking "cap rate") for such buildings. Such rates were indeed typical of the office building investment market in the United States in the early 2000s. The assumed range in future value for the building is consistent with an annual building value volatility of approximately 20%, as we will see in section 27.4. An annual volatility assumption of 20% for an individual building is perhaps a bit on the high side, but certainly not out of the range of realistic plausibility. (See section 9.2.5 in Chapter 9, and note that the relevant volatility is that of a single building, not that of a diversified portfolio of many buildings or of a property market index.)

(values in $ millions)	Today	Next Year	
Probability	100%*	30%	70%
Value of developed property	$100.00**	$78.62	$113.21
Construction cost (excludes land cost)	$88.24	$90.00	$90.00
NPV of exercise	$11.76	−$11.38	$23.21
Future values		0	$23.21
(actions)		(Don't build)	(Build)
Expected value of built property	$100.00**	$102.83	
(Probability × Outcome)	(1.0 × 100)	(0.3 × $78.62 + 0.7 × $113.21)	
Expected value of option	$11.76	$16.25	
(Probability × Outcome)	(1.0 × 11.76)	(0.3 × $0 + 0.7 × $23.21)	
PV(today) of alternatives @ 20% discount rate	$11.76	$13.54 = $16.25/1.20	
Land Value Today = MAX(11.76, 13.54) = $13.54			
Option Premium = $13.54 − $11.76 = $1.78			

*Today's values are known for certain (100% probability) because they can be directly empirically observed.
**Today's value of $100 million is for a building already completed today and includes the present value of the building's expected net rental income next year. Assuming a built property OCC of 9%, the present value today of a forward claim on a building to be completed next year would be: $E[V_1]/(1 + OCC) = $102.83/1.09 = $94.34 million.
EXHIBIT 27-1 Numerical Example of Option Premium Value Due to Future Uncertainty in Built Property Value

© OnCourse Learning

landowner can simply choose not to develop if the downside $78.62 million value outcome occurs next year. (The NPV of development at that point would be $78.62 − $90.00 = −11.38 < 0, while the NPV of doing nothing would be zero.) Yet the possibility of developing under the upside $113.21 million contingency would provide a net profit of $23.21 million at that time (the upside building value minus the $90 million construction cost). This gives an expected value for the development option next year equal to $16.25 million, even though there is only a 70 percent chance that the favorable scenario will occur [$16.25 = (0.7)($113.21 − $90.00) + (0.3)($0)]. Thus, the option enables the landowner to avoid much of the negative consequences of the downside outcome of future market volatility, while still retaining the ability to profit from the upside.

Now consider the expected NPV of the development project as of the time of development under the two mutually exclusive alternatives of building today or waiting and building in one year. The NPV in the first case is the $11.76 million that we noted earlier. The NPV in the second case would be the $16.25 million we just calculated.

But this second NPV is as of a time one year in the future. Furthermore, it is an *expected* NPV, based on our expectations as of today about the situation one year in the future. As there is uncertainty about what the future will bring, this future NPV is risky, whereas the NPV of immediate development today is known for certain. To compare the two alternatives, we therefore need to account for the time and risk differences between the two NPVs. This is traditionally done by applying a risk-adjusted discount rate to the second NPV in order to discount it back to a present certainty-equivalent value comparable to the first NPV. The appropriate discount rate to use is the opportunity cost of capital (OCC, or the investment market's expected total return) of the speculative land investment. As such land investment is generally considered to be quite risky, investors would probably require a rather high expected return, say, 20 percent per annum. This would give us a present value of $13.54 million for the second NPV, calculated as $16,250,000/1.20.

Thus, on a present certainty-equivalent basis, the NPV of the first alternative (to build today) is $11.76 million, while the NPV of the second alternative (to wait and possibly build one year from today) is $13.54 million. As these two values are now directly comparable,

NEW INSIGHT INTO THE NPV RULE

One of the first points that is often highlighted from real options theory is its implications regarding the basic NPV rule we introduced in Chapter 10. It is often said in the corporate capital budgeting literature that option theory shows that the classical NPV rule of investment is too simple. Option theory suggests that it will usually not make sense to invest in a project that has a small positive net present value (NPV) as this is quantified in the typical corporate capital budgeting application. Instead, it will usually make more sense in the corporate context to wait until the NPV is substantially positive before investing.

However, a careful reading of the NPV investment rule suggests that option theory does not really negate or modify the old rule as we have stated it in this text. We simply have to be careful about how we apply the rule. Recall from Chapter 10 that the NPV rule is to invest so as to *maximize* your NPV. We don't just invest in any and all positive NPV projects when there are mutually exclusive alternatives. Instead, we pick the alternative that has the maximum NPV. The irreversibility of construction projects means that to invest today excludes the possibility of investing later (e.g., in the same or another construction project on the same land). Building today versus building next year are

mutually exclusive alternatives on a given site. Maximizing the NPV would require selecting the construction timing that has the highest NPV, discounted to today. Applied this way, the NPV rule should still hold.

Another way of seeing this point that is more relevant for real estate applications is to include the current value of the option premium as part of the cost one is incurring by exercising the development option. Whenever one considers the costs and benefits of an investment, one must be careful to include *all* costs and benefits. For an irreversible project, the costs include the option premium that is given up by undertaking the project. The value of this option premium may often be hard to see and to quantify in the case of industrial corporate capital projects, in which highly unique and proprietary types of equipment or physical assets are to be built. But in the case of the typical real estate development project, the option premium should be more readily observable (albeit still not perfectly so) in the current market value of the land. In a well-functioning land market, the development option premium should normally be included in the current market value of the land. This land value is always an *opportunity cost* of the development project (even if the developer already owns the land).

and mutually exclusive, the value-maximizing decision is clearly to wait and develop next year. As the landowner has the right to make this decision, this implies that the land value today must be $13.54 million, not the $11.76 million current exercise value.[4] The difference, $1.78 million, is what is called the **"option premium,"** which clearly derives from the flexibility provided by land ownership to the owner to develop the land at whatever time she chooses, reflecting the land's option value.

Note that if the land is worth $13.54 million, then the NPV of the best current development project, *including the opportunity cost of the land*, is negative (equal to negative $1.78 million, which is the $100 million current newly built property value less the $88.24 million construction cost, minus also the $13.54 million land value). Thus, based on the NPV criterion presented in Chapter 10 including the opportunity cost of the land, development would not currently be optimal, and the highest and best use (HBU) of the land would at this point be to hold the land vacant. Notice that this result is due completely to the option premium of $1.78 million in the land value. Our analysis shows the source of the value of the land and reveals how much of this is due to the option premium. This is, essentially, an example of the **irreversibility premium** described in section 5.2 of Chapter 5.

*27.3 A Rigorous Model of Option Value

The previous illustration demonstrated how future uncertainty about the market for built property interacts with the irreversibility of the construction process (hence, the mutual exclusivity of building today versus building later) to give land value an option premium

---

[4]In a competitive land market, the price of the land would presumably be bid up to $13.54, as any landowner would have the right to postpone development one year.

and make it optimal (value-maximizing) in some cases to delay development (i.e., to engage in "land speculation," that is, holding land for investment purposes for subsequent development). But our example analysis in the preceding section was incomplete and lacking in rigor in at least one major respect that OVT will allow us to address. In particular, we needed to know the OCC of the option to wait in order to evaluate the NPV of that alternative and compare it to the alternative of building today. We *assumed* that this OCC was 20 percent (thereby reducing the expected value of waiting until next year, $16.25 million, to a present value today of $13.54 million). But this assumption was entirely ad hoc. We had no rigorous basis to know if it was correct, no way to know what the true opportunity cost of capital of the option actually was. In this section, we will show how OVT solves this problem, and in the process we shall discover that in fact our assumption of 20 percent was wrong, and hence our evaluation of the land in the preceding section was wrong![5] We will present the OVT solution in two ways, first using an arbitrage argument, and then using the certainty-equivalence valuation procedure that we introduced in Appendix 10C. It turns out that these two approaches are equivalent (and we will explain why).

27.3.1 The Arbitrage Perspective on the Option Value

Let's play like economists for a few minutes and make some admittedly pretty unrealistic assumptions. (It's not that we don't respect the real world; our simplifications are only meant to allow us to see the *essence* of the truth about the phenomenon we are studying.) In particular, we are going to assume the existence of something economists call "complete markets." In fact, we will assume markets that are not only complete but "frictionless" to boot. This means that investors can buy or sell (including short sales[6]) without any trading costs, any fraction or quantity of three types of assets that are traded in three markets:

- Land
- Built properties
- Bonds

The land market trades undeveloped but developable land; the built property market trades completed, fully operational income-producing buildings (together with the land they occupy), and the bond market trades debt instruments (that is, contractual future cash flow obligations that we will assume are riskless).

Suppose further that we can observe the opportunity cost of capital (investors' typical expected total returns) in both the built property market and the bond market. Let's say that the OCC for riskless bonds is 3 percent per year, and the OCC for built properties like the office building that could be built on our land in the example in the previous section is 9 percent per year.

Now let us consider again the option valuation problem we previously considered in section 27.2. In our economist's dream world we could purchase today a 67 percent interest in a future building a year from now just like the building that could be built on our land for $90 million at that time, a building that will be worth either

---

[5]Shame on us. But we don't want to upset you by introducing too many new concepts at once.

[6]In a "short sale," the investor sells an asset *before* he buys it! (Obviously, this is the reverse of the normal, or "long," procedure.) In order to accomplish a short sale, you have to borrow the asset you are selling. This means, of course, that you will have to buy it (or an identical asset) later in order to return it to its rightful owner (in order to "close out your short position"). In a short sale, you receive cash first when you sell the asset, and pay cash later when you close out the short position by buying the asset you previously sold. It's easy to see how short sales can be arranged in the stock market (where shares of a given company are all identical). In real estate, short sales are impossible in reality, but we are going to assume for analytical purposes in this section that they are possible.

$113.21 million or $78.62 million then.[7] Such a purchase would have a price today of $63.29 million, calculated as follows:[8]

$$\$63.29 = (0.67)PV[V_1] = (0.67)\frac{E[V_1]}{1 + OCC} = (0.67)\frac{(0.7)\$113.21 + (0.3)\$78.62}{1 + 9\%}$$
$$= (0.67)\frac{\$102.83}{1.09} = (0.67)\$94.34$$

We could also finance such a purchase in part by borrowing $51.21 million today at the 3 percent riskless interest rate (given that we will certainly pay the money back next year, with interest). Thus, our net investment today would be $63.29 − $51.21 = $12.09 million.

In effect, we would have invested in a portfolio that will mature in one year, consisting of two positions: a "long" position which is a 67 percent share investment in the future completed building, plus a "short" (or negative) investment in a bond that will be worth for certain $52.74 million next year (as $51.21 × 1.03 = $52.74). Exhibit 27-2 depicts the situation we face. If the *up* scenario unfolds (the market for built property improves, which you recall has a probability of 70 percent), then our portfolio will be worth $23.21 million, equal to the $75.95 million value of our 67 percent share of the completed building (which will be worth $113.21 million in that scenario) minus the $52.74 million that we will have to pay back on the loan. If the *down* scenario unfolds (the built property market falls, a scenario that has a 30 percent probability), then our portfolio will be worth exactly nothing, as our 67 percent share in the building will be worth exactly the same as the balance due on our loan ($52.74 = 0.67 × $78.62).

Now compare the future possible values of our portfolio with the optimal net outcome of the development option as described in section 27.2. Comparing Exhibits 27-1 and 27-2, it is obvious that our portfolio will be worth exactly the same amount as the optimal net outcome of the development option, no matter which future scenario happens next year. For this reason, our portfolio is what is called a **"replicating portfolio"** (or a "hedge portfolio"). It replicates the option value in all possible future outcomes.

If our replicating portfolio will have exactly the same value as the option next year no matter what, then it must have exactly the same value as the option today. We have already seen that this value is $12.09 million (that is, we could acquire our portfolio today for $12.09 million net cash outflow). Thus, the option to wait and develop the property next year must be worth $12.09 million, not the $13.54 million that we previously calculated in section 27.2. This option value must be the value of the land, as it is worth more than the $11.76 million immediate development value.

If the land were worth any value different than the $12.09 million we have just determined, then an **"arbitrage"** opportunity would exist in our economist's dream world. That is, investors could earn excess profit risklessly. In effect, you could create a "money machine," as follows.

Suppose, for example, that the price of the land were indeed $13.54 million. The recipe for the money machine would then be to sell the land short and purchase the replicating portfolio. We would take in $13.54 million today from selling the land, and pay $12.09 million to acquire the replicating portfolio (as we previously described). We would thus net $1.45 million today. But what will happen next year?

Next year we will have to buy back the land in order to close out our short position in the land, to pay back to whoever had loaned us the land today a value equivalent to the value of the land next year. If the *up* scenario happens, this will require us to redeem this person a

---

[7]Recall our assumption (for now) that construction is instantaneous.

[8]If you are wondering how we came up with the 0.67 share and the $51.21 million amount to borrow, look ahead to footnote 9. Also, note that numbers in the numerical examples in this chapter (as elsewhere in this book) may appear to not compute exactly. This is due to round-off in the printed text. For example, in this case, the more precise numbers are that we would purchase 67.09% of the underlying asset worth $94.3396 million today: (0.6709)*$94.3396 = $63.29. The exact numbers and methodology for all of the numerical examples in this chapter can be seen in the Chapter 27 Excel file provided on the CD accompanying this book. There, you can also see more precisely how the numbers in this example are derived, and you can change the numbers to match your own assumptions.

EXHIBIT 27-2 Binomial Outcome Possibilities for the One-Period Development Option Arbitrage or "Hedge Portfolio" (values in millions)

© OnCourse Learning

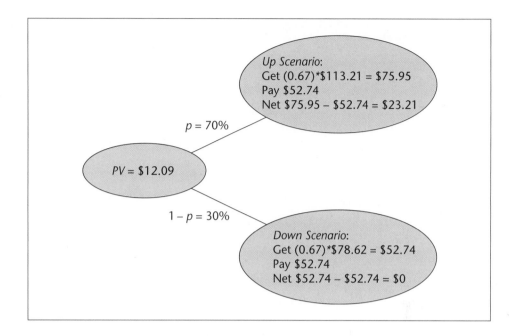

value of $23.21 million, because that would be what the land would be worth next year in the *up* scenario. (Recall that the option expires next year, so it will definitely make sense to develop the office building at that time in the *up* scenario, which will produce an asset worth $113.21 million for a construction cost of $90 million.) Of course, this is exactly the same value as what our replicating portfolio will be worth in that scenario, so we would simply cash in our portfolio and use the proceeds to pay the original landowner and thereby close out our short position with no net cash flow. Suppose instead the *down* scenario occurs. In that case, the land will be worth zero, so we can close out our short position without having to pay the original landowner anything, which is fortunate because our portfolio also will be worth nothing in that scenario. In any case, we will face zero net cash flow next year, for certain, no matter which possible scenario unfolds. Thus, the $1.45 million we could make today is "pure gravy," a safe profit without future liability.

It should be obvious that this same type of procedure could be employed to make an arbitrage profit if the current price of the land were *any* value greater than the $12.09 million value of the replicating portfolio. Similarly, just the opposite strategy would allow us to make riskless profit if the current land price were any value less than the $12.09 million. In that case, we would buy the land today, sell short the replicating portfolio, pocket the difference, and face zero net cash flow next year for certain. Exhibit 27-3 summarizes the arbitrage-based valuation that we have just described, to evaluate the option to wait and develop the land next year.[9] Assuming that in the real world opportunities to make easy riskless profits like

---

[9]A nagging question remains: how did we figure out what the replicating portfolio would consist of? The answer is easy in the binomial world (only two possible outcomes next period) we are working with here. We have two unknown quantities to define the replicating portfolio: the amount of the future completed building to purchase (label this quantity "N"), and the amount to borrow (label this quantity "B"). We need the replicating portfolio to duplicate the development option outcome in each of next period's possible future outcomes. This establishes two equations that are linear in the two unknowns and which will therefore provide a unique solution for our two unknown quantities. Letting P represent the replicating portfolio, V represent the newly built value, C represent the development option net value, and B represent the riskless bond position, we have:

$$\begin{cases} P_1^{up} = NV_1^{up} - (1 + r_f)B = C_1^{up} \\ P_1^{down} = NV_1^{down} - (1 + r_f)B = C_1^{down} \end{cases} \Rightarrow \begin{cases} N = (C_1^{up} - C_1^{down})/(V_1^{up} - V_1^{down}) \\ B = (NV_1^{down} - C_1^{down})/(1 + r_f) \end{cases}$$

In our example:

$N = (23.21 - 0)/(113.21 - 78.62) = 0.67$; $B = [0.67(78.62) - 0]/1.03 = 51.21$. (And we hope to convince you in section 27.4 that this binomial world is not as silly as it first may seem.)

	Today	Next Year	
Development Option Value $C = Max[0, V\text{-}K]$	$PV[C_1] = x$ "x" = unknown value, $x = P_0$, otherwise arbitrage.	$C_1^{up} = 113.21 - 90 = \$23.21$	$C_1^{down} = 0$ (Don't build)
Built Property Value	$PV[V_1] = E[V_1]/(1 + OCC)$ $= [(0.7)\$113.21 + (0.3)\$78.62]/1.09$ $= \$102.83/1.09 = \$94.34$	$V_1^{up} = \$113.21$	$V_1^{down} = \$78.62$
Bond Value	$B_0 = \$51.21$	$B_1 = (1 + r_f)B_0$ $B_1 = (1.03)\$51.21 = \$52.74$	$B_1 = (1 + r_f)B_0$ $B_1 = (1.03)\$51.21 = \$52.74$
Replicating Portfolio: $P = (N)V - B$	$P_0 = (N)\ PV[V_1] - B_0$ $= (0.67)\$94.34 - \$51.21$ $= \$63.29 - \$51.21 = \$12.09$	$P_1^{up} = (0.67)\$113.21 - \$52.74$ $= \$75.95 - \$52.74$ $= \$23.21$	$P_1^{down} = (0.67)\$78.62 - \$52.74$ $= \$52.74 - \$52.74$ $= \$0$

EXHIBIT 27-3 Summary of Arbitrage-Based Valuation of the Development Option

© OnCourse Learning

this would be competed away in the marketplace, the arbitrage based valuation of $12.09 million must therefore be the market value of the option.

27.3.2 The Certainty-Equivalence DCF Perspective on the Option Value

Alright, you say, but that economist's dream world is pretty remote from the reality of real estate markets. We don't really have short sales or frictionless asset markets for land and built properties. We could not actually implement the arbitrages described in the preceding section. While that is true, the option valuation result that we obtained is surprisingly robust. For example, we can get exactly the same result by applying the **certainty-equivalence** approach to DCF valuation that we introduced in Appendix 10C. Certainty-equivalence discounting is simply an alternative way to do DCF present value computation of risky future values or cash flows, equivalent to (but more flexible than) the traditional risk adjusted discount rate (RADR) method that we introduced in Chapter 10. In Appendix 10C we derive and discuss a general certainty-equivalence formula for option valuation in a binomial world, as follows:[10]

$$PV[C_1] = \frac{E_0[C_1] - (C_1^{up}\$ - C_1^{down}\$)\dfrac{E_0[r_V] - r_f}{V_1^{up}\% - V_1^{down}\%}}{1 + r_f} \tag{1}$$

Plugging the relevant values from the previous example into this formula, we obtain:[11]

$$PV[C_1] = \frac{16.25 - (23.21 - 0)\dfrac{9\% - 3\%}{(113.21 - 78.62)/94.34}}{1.03}$$

$$= \frac{\$16.25 - \$23.21\left(\dfrac{6\%}{120\% - 83.33\%}\right)}{1.03} = \frac{\$16.25 - \$23.21(0.1636)}{1.03} = \frac{\$12.45}{1.03} = \$12.09$$

Now recall that we did not employ an arbitrage argument to derive the certainty-equivalence valuation formula in Appendix 10C. We simply assumed that, in equilibrium,

---

[10]See the derivation and discussion of formula (C7) on page 4 of the Appendix 10C, which is equivalent to formula (1) here.

[11]In Appendix 10C, you see that:

$$V_1^{up}\% - V_1^{down}\% = (V_1^{up}\$ - V_1^{down}\$)/PV[V_1].$$

assets in the investment market must trade at prices that reflect the same "price of risk" for all assets. This implies that the investment expected return risk premium per unit of investment risk must be the same for the option and for the underlying asset from which it derives its value. Here, we are simply applying that principle as a cross-market equilibrium condition across the markets for built property and for land. The realism of this condition across those two markets is particularly strong, because the land value is *derivative*, based solely on the value of the office building that can be built on it.[12] We are also employing an assumption that the relative amount of investment risk in an underlying asset and an option that depends upon that asset can be measured by the ratio of the percentage spreads in the underlying asset's and the option's investment returns between the *up* and *down* possible outcomes. This is also a relatively benign assumption for derivatives and their underlying assets, as derivatives must be perfectly correlated with their underlying assets (i.e., when office buildings are worth more, the land on which office buildings are built will be worth more).[13]

27.3.3 Why the Option Valuation Model Works

To clarify what is fundamentally going on in this option valuation approach, let's compute the development option's expected return risk premium. Since the expected value of the option next year is $16.25 million (equal to 0.7 times $23.21 million), and the option's present value today is $12.09 million, the expected return to an investment in the option today is:

$$\frac{\$16,250,000 - \$12,090,000}{\$12,090,000} = \frac{\$4,160,000}{\$12,090,000} = 34.42\%$$

This is therefore the current opportunity cost of capital (OCC) of the development option. (Note that this is quite a bit different than the 20 percent ad hoc assumption that we erroneously made in section 27.2 when we misestimated the option value to be $13.54 million.[14]) As the risk-free interest rate is 3 percent, this implies that the risk premium in the option investment is 31.42 percent. The risk premium in an investment in completed, fully operational office buildings like the one that can be built on our land is 6 percent, computed as the already-noted OCC of 9 percent for such investments minus the 3 percent risk-free rate. Thus, an investment in the development option (i.e., the land speculation) presents approximately 31.42%/6.00% = 5.24 times the expected return risk premium of an investment in a stabilized office building.

---

[12]Recall the residual theory of land value presented in Chapter 4.

[13]To relate this to the CAPM representation of investment risk pricing that we discussed in Chapter 22, recall that the CAPM measure of relative risk, "*beta*," is defined as follows:

$$\beta_V = COV[r_V, r_{Mkt}]/VAR[r_{Mkt}] = CORR[r_V, r_{Mkt}]STD[r_V]/STD[r_{Mkt}].$$

Thus, the ratio of risk between any two assets C and V is just the ratio of the assets' correlations with the market times the ratio of the assets' volatilities. In the case where C is a derivative of V, the two assets are perfectly correlated with each other, which gives them the same correlation coefficient with the market portfolio: $CORR[r_C, r_{Mkt}] = CORR[r_V, r_{Mkt}]$. Thus, relative risk (the ratio of the betas) simply equals the ratio of the two assets' volatilities. In the binomial world, this ratio of volatilities exactly equals the ratio of assets' outcome percentage spreads, thus:

$$\beta_C/\beta_V = (C_1^{up}\% - C_1^{down}\%)/(V_1^{up}\% - V_1^{down}\%).$$

As $C_1^{up}\% - C_1^{down}\%$ equals $(C_1^{up}\$ - C_1^{down}\$)/C_0\$$, the certainty-equivalence formula (1) is seen to be completely consistent with the CAPM presented in Chapter 22. (Note, however, that for purposes of pricing a *derivative* asset *relative to* its underlying asset, formula (1) does not depend on the CAPM, as is demonstrated by the arbitrage argument in section 27.3.1). [See Cox and Rubinstein (1985), and Arnold and Crack (2003), for a more in-depth explanation.]

[14]Note also that we can only determine the option's true OCC *after* we have computed its present value. Thus, we cannot use the classical risk-adjusted discount rate approach to DCF valuation to determine the option value in the first instance. (See Appendix 10C on the CD that accompanies this textbook.)

How does this compare to the ratio of the risk presented by the two investments, as measured by the spreads in their possible investment return outcomes? The spread in the return outcome possibilities for an investment in the future stabilized office building is 36.67 percent, from the \$94.34 million value today to either \$113.21 million or \$78.62 million next year.[15] The spread in the return outcome possibilities for the option is:

$$\frac{MAX[0,\$113.21 - \$90.00] - MAX[0,\$78.62 - \$90.00]}{\$12,090,000} = \frac{\$23,210,000 - \$0}{\$12,090,000} = 192\%$$

Thus, the investment return risk ratio is: 192%/36.67% = 5.24, exactly the same as the ratio of the investment expected return risk premia across the two types of investment assets.

In other words, our option valuation of \$12.09 million is based on the principle that an investment in a stabilized office building and an investment in a development option that gives the right without obligation to build an office building next year both must present the same expected return risk premium *per unit of risk*. (They both present an expected return risk premium of 0.164 percent per 1 percent of investment return outcome spread: 6%/36.67% = 31.42%/192% = 0.164.) That is, the OCC is such as to provide equal risk-adjusted returns across different types of investments (developable land, and built property). This is the key to equilibrium across the markets for built property and land. Otherwise, investors would tend to sell one type of investment (either land or completed buildings) and buy the other. This type of buying and selling would bid up the asset prices in the target market and drive down the prices in the market being sold off, and would go on until the expected return risk premia per unit of risk were equalized across the two types of markets. In a society with well-functioning land and property markets, the competitive drive toward this type of equilibrium across the markets is strong. This is fundamentally what makes the land valuation model described here surprisingly realistic and robust. What we are doing is pictured graphically in Exhibit 27-4.

This points out the sense in which the option valuation model may be viewed as a *normative* tool, not just as a *positive* (empirical) predictor of what the market price of the land will probably actually be. In other words, the model tells us what the "value" of the land is, what its price *should be*, in order to provide a *fair* expected return to investors (relative to the return expectation provided by investment in built property).[16] Actual prices that differ from what the model says present super-normal (or subnormal) investment return expectations either for the land or for the buildings. This is fundamentally why we get the same land valuation result with the arbitrage analysis in section 27.3.1 as we do with the certainty-equivalence valuation in section 27.3.2. Arbitrage opportunities, by definition, present "super-normal" profits.

Finally, note that in both the arbitrage analysis and the certainty-equivalence valuation, wewere able to arrive at a solution only because we were working in a one period binomial world in which investments can have only two possible outcomes. In the next section, we will see how this simple model can be much more realistic and useful than you might at first expect.

---

[15]This can be computed as: (\$113.21 − \$94.34)/\$94.34 − (\$78.62 − \$94.34)/\$94.34 = 20% − (−16.67%) = 36.67%. Alternatively, suppose an investor today pays the full \$100 million for an already existing office building, rather than only \$94.34 million for a forward claim on the building next year. Then the investor would receive next year not only the ex-dividend value of the office building, but also the net rental income it yields. As 100/94.34 = 1.06, the implication is that the net rental payout ("dividend") is expected to be 6% of the ex-dividend value of the asset. Thus, in the "up" scenario the investor will obtain not only the asset worth \$113.21 million, but also 0.06*\$113.21 = \$6.79 million of income, for a total payoff of \$120 million. In the "down" scenario the investor will receive a total payoff of 1.06*\$ 78.62 = \$83.33 million. These payoffs, compared to the initial investment of \$100 million, provide the same percentage spread that we previously computed: 120% − 83.33% = 36.67%.

[16]Assuming one's notion of "fairness" is that investments should provide the same ex ante return risk premium per unit of risk in the investment.

EXHIBIT 27-4 The Option Model Equates the Expected Return Risk Premium *per Unit of Risk* Across the Markets for Built Property and Developable Land

© OnCourse Learning

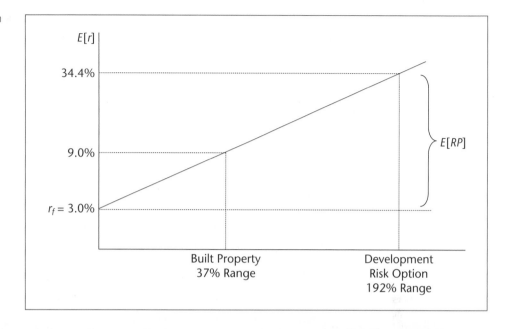

THE THREE MEANINGS OF OPTIONS THEORY

Students often ask how a theory that has been developed originally in the context of perfectly efficient, frictionless markets can be relevant in the less "ideal" world of real estate. To gain perspective on this question, it is useful to think of three different types of market contexts, or "levels," in which option theory applications may occur in the real world. Each of these three different levels corresponds to a different implication about the meaning and use of option theory.

Level 1: Highly efficient markets of commodity-like assets (e.g., public stock and bond markets). In this case, the arbitrage derivation of option theory (such as section 27.3.1) applies directly and in reality. If prices deviate from the option model prediction (assuming the model is good), you can construct a hedge that will allow you to earn supernormal profits risklessly: a true "arbitrage" in the technical sense. This situation does not perfectly exist anywhere, but it comes close to existing in some aspects of the bond market. This is the part of "Wall Street" where "rocket scientists" are in great demand.

Level 2: Well-functioning markets but with some frictions and uniqueness of assets (e.g., most real estate markets in the United States). In this case, the section 27.3.2 derivation of the option model is more relevant, based simply on an argument of "equilibrium" within and across the markets for the relevant types of assets (land, built property, bonds). Equilibrium is a less stringent assumption than exercisable arbitrage. It simply assumes that markets will tend to equilibrate investors' expected return risk premia *per unit of risk*, within and across the markets that people can trade in. In such a world, if prices deviate from what a (good) option model predicts, you may not be able to make riskless profits, but you can make investment

decisions based on the model (buying and selling appropriately as the model suggests) so that you face super-normal expected returns (ex ante). In well-functioning markets, prices are always tending toward equilibrium, but that doesn't mean that they will necessarily ever exactly equal the equilibrium. At this level, the option model still has what in the philosophy of science is referred to as a "positive" (or predictive) basis.

Level 3: No functioning market (e.g., some unique real estate situations in the United States, and many situations in some other countries where the market mechanism is less widely or aggressively employed than in the United States). In this case, the option model loses its "positive" basis. But economics is generally regarded as a "normative" science as well as a "positive" one. That is, it gives guidance on what "ought" to be, in some sense, not just on what "is" (in an empirical sense). Because the option model gives prices (or at this level: "values" rather than prices, as there is no market) that equate the return risk premium per unit of risk (ex ante), those values may be viewed as "normative," or "fair," in that sense. That is, if you want the values you are working with to provide or reflect return expectations that are "fair" in the above sense, then you should use the values predicted by the option model. This could be particularly useful when entering negotiations with other parties about how to allocate or apportion certain costs and benefits of a project or transaction that must occur in the absence of a market. It could also be useful in conducting analyses of trade-offs, or "cost/benefit analysis" from a welfare or social perspective (only bearing in mind that social benefits and costs may differ from those based purely on market prices).

27.4 The Binomial Model of Option Value

The one-period binomial world in which the development option examples of sections 27.2 and 27.3 were presented is obviously a tremendous simplification of reality. In the real world, time is continuous, and asset values can assume many more than just two possible outcomes. But the binomial model is more than just a pedagogical simplification device. It is a building block that can be used to construct a much more general and realistic option valuation and analysis tool. In this context, it is useful to think of an individual binomial scenario (that is, a move in asset value either up or down over one period of time) as like a financial economic "molecule." In chemistry, a molecule is the smallest, simplest particle of a chemical that still retains all of the essential characteristics of that chemical. In the case of financial economics, the essential characteristics are money (or value) across *time* and *risk*. The binomial element contains one unit (period) of time, and the deviation between the "up" and "down" outcomes represents the amount of risk in the particular asset being modeled.

The dynamics of the evolution of the value of built property through time, upon which the land value and the optimal development policy depend, can be modeled as a series of these molecules. Within each period, for each possible future "state of the world" (up or down), we can apply the tools presented in the preceding section. By stitching the individual binomial outcomes together sequentially, we can span as long a time frame as we like, and by making each individual binomial period as short as we want, we can get the model to realistically approach continuous time and continuous pricing.

In section 27A.1 of Appendix 27 on the CD accompanying this book, we present the binomial model of option value in detail, showing how to build realistic binomial value "trees" for the underlying asset and how to evaluate the option by working recursively backwards in time within the value tree. We also provide on the CD an Excel example file that reveals in detail how the model works and that can serve as a template for building your own binomial option valuation models. Here in the text, we will content ourselves with giving you a brief idea how the binomial model works.[17]

First, recall our one-period world in which the underlying asset (a newly completed office building) is worth $100 million today and next year either $113.21 million (70 percent probability) or $78.62 million (30 percent probability). By reducing the period length to a month and stringing together 12 sequential monthly periods, we can produce the binomial value tree for the underlying asset indicated in Exhibit 27-5. As you move from left to right in the table, across the columns, you move into the future, one month at a time. Each column represents the next month in the future. Each value node in the table indicates a possible future value of the underlying asset for the development option, the value of the new office building that could be built on the land. Of course, in reality as the future actually unfolds, only one (true) value for the building will exist at any point in time. But the tree in Exhibit 27-5 models future possibilities as they may be envisioned from the present.

Note that the tree is constructed so that from any possible future value in any given month (each "node" in the tree), it is only possible to move to two possible future values in the next month. (You can only jump to values that are touching the right-hand corners of a given box.) Thus, the tree consists of a series of future single-period binary outcome possibilities, each one of which is conceptually just like the example one-period binomial world we considered in the previous section. We can apply the option valuation approach described in section 27.3 to any of these one-period binomial outcome possibilities, and we can quantify the option values by starting at the right-hand column, the expiration of the option, where its future values are given as the maximum of either zero or the net profit from the development project (just as in the example in section 27.3). We can then work backwards in time, from right to left across the columns, to arrive at the present value of the option.

---

[17]An understanding of the CD material is not necessary to follow subsequent sections of the printed main text.

Month:

Office Building Value Tree:

0	1	2	3	4	5	6	7	8	9	10	11	12
												$184.73
											$175.52	$165.11
										$166.77	$156.88	$147.58
									$158.45	$149.06	$140.22	$131.91
								$150.55	$141.63	$133.23	$125.33	$117.90
							$143.05	$134.57	$126.59	$119.08	$112.02	$105.38
						$135.91	$127.86	$120.28	$113.15	$106.44	$100.13	$94.19
					$129.14	$121.48	$114.28	$107.50	$101.13	$95.13	$89.49	$84.19
				$122.70	$115.43	$108.58	$102.14	$96.09	$90.39	$85.03	$79.99	$75.25
			$116.58	$109.67	$103.17	$97.05	$91.30	$85.89	$80.79	$76.00	$71.50	$67.26
		$110.77	$104.20	$98.02	$92.21	$86.75	$81.60	$76.77	$72.21	$67.93	$63.91	$60.12
	$105.25	$99.01	$93.14	$87.62	$82.42	$77.53	$72.94	$68.61	$64.55	$60.72	$57.12	$53.73
$100.00	$94.07	$88.49	$83.25	$78.31	$73.67	$69.30	$65.19	$61.33	$57.69	$54.27	$51.05	$48.03

EXHIBIT 27-5 One-Year Monthly Binomial Value Tree
© OnCourse Learning

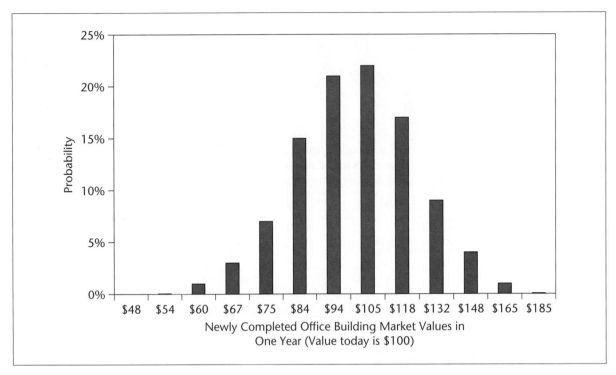

EXHIBIT 27-6 One-Year Value Probabilities for Office Building
© OnCourse Learning

By configuring the *up* and *down* outcomes and the probability of each outcome in a certain manner (as described in section 27A.1), we can ensure that the intermediate outcomes "recombine" as indicated in the table (the move *up* from one future scenario to the next column to the right results in the same value as the move *down* from the scenario immediately above it in the same column).[18] This greatly simplifies the computations that must be performed.

We can also configure the model so that the result at the end of the year is a realistically plausible value probability distribution, such as the value distribution for our office building indicated in Exhibit 27-6.[19] The probability distribution indicated in Exhibit 27-6 is much more realistic than the binary possibilities of only $113.21 million or $78.62 million that we were working with for illustrative purposes in section 27.3. In this way, the binomial option model can be made to well represent the real world. But for more details of exactly how to do this, and an Excel template you may use to apply the model yourself, you will have to go to this book's accompanying CD.

*27.5 A Perpetual Model in Continuous Time

The binomial model described in the preceding sections is the simplest and most intuitive option model relevant to land valuation and optimal development timing. It is useful not only for pedagogical purposes, but we shall see in Chapter 29 how it can be used to analyze

---

[18]For example, the $100 million building today will be worth $99.01 million two months from now either by the market moving up and then down, or by the market moving down and then up, over the intervening two months.

[19]The probability distribution in Exhibit 27-6 has a mean of about $103 million and a standard deviation of about ±$20 million, consistent with an annual new-building value growth rate expectation of 3%, and annual individual building volatility of about 20%. (A diversified portfolio of properties would have a lower volatility.) The model can be configured so that the binomial tree corresponds to whatever mean growth rate and annual volatility we want to input (see section 27A.1 on the accompanying CD).

and evaluate important real estate development project questions, such as project staging, abandonment flexibility, and development privileges that do not last forever. However, the binomial model has an important weakness for purposes of basic land valuation (as a "freehold") and the analysis of simple as-of-right development projects that can be undertaken at any time by the landowner. In particular, the binomial model can only be used to evaluate finite-lived options. Yet, fee simple land ownership rights are perpetual, and the right (without obligation) to build an as-of-right development project on a land parcel never expires. While perpetual development rights can be approximated in the binomial approach by modeling a very long expiration time for the option, it is possible to develop exact models of **perpetual options** in continuous time (i.e., without the artificial discretization of time that exists in the binomial model). It will be worth our while to examine here the simplest and most elegant such model, for the insight it can give regarding the nature of land value, development timing, and the characteristics of investment risk and return in land speculation.

27.5.1 The Classical Samuelson-McKean Formula

Our favorite continuous time option valuation formula relevant for basic land valuation is also one of the first option formulas to be developed in the economics literature. This formula, developed by the Nobel Prize-winning economist Paul Samuelson and his mathematician partner Henry McKean, was first published in 1965 as a formula for pricing "perpetual American warrants" (that is, a perpetual call option that can be exercised at any time on a dividend-paying underlying asset). This **Samuelson-McKean formula** turned out to be very similar to real option models subsequently developed for capital budgeting decisions by Robert McDonald and Daniel Seigel, and for urban land valuation by Joseph Williams, Dennis Capozza, and others.[20]

Although it should be treated as a simplification of the complete land valuation and optimal development problem, the Samuelson-McKean formula is based very straightforwardly on the same type of economic arbitrage and equilibrium analysis as was described in section 27.3.[21] Thus, if you understood section 27.3, then you already understand the economic basis of the Samuelson-McKean formula. Furthermore, unlike much continuous time or perpetual option methodology, the Samuelson-McKean formula can be understood easily without specialized mathematical knowledge, and can be applied easily with no more sophisticated tools than a spreadsheet.[22] In spite of this simplicity, it is a conceptually consistent land valuation and optimal development model, allowing for continuous time and an infinite time horizon.[23]

The Samuelson-McKean formula requires as inputs three parameter values, which describe the underlying real estate and construction markets: the built property current cash yield rate, the volatility in the built property value, and a parameter we shall call the "construction cost yield." This last is the difference between the opportunity cost of capital

---

[20]Some of the urban economic applications extended (and thereby also complicated) the basic model in order to consider optimal density, as well as optimal timing, of the real estate development. (See in particular the articles by Williams and Capozza in the bibliography at the end of this part of the book.)

[21]In continuous time, the replicating portfolio we described in section 27.3.1 is described by partial derivatives, and the arbitrage-avoiding equilibrium condition becomes a differential equation. Solution of this equation with appropriate boundary conditions gives the Samuelson-McKean formula.

[22]The Samuelson-McKean formula is presented in an Excel workbook on the CD accompanying this book.

[23]In some sense, the Samuelson-McKean formula is for real estate what the Black-Scholes formula is for corporate finance, a simplistic but useful tool. The Black-Scholes formula can also be relevant in some real estate situations, and we present it in the Excel workbook provided in the accompanying CD that also contains the Samuelson-McKean formula. The Black-Scholes formula models the value of a European option with a finite expiration time. It would thus be appropriate to value development rights that limit the developer to the right (without obligation) to develop only at a specified single future point in time, a situation that is not very common. However, the European option is useful in other real estate contexts. For example, some lease renewal options may be viewed as giving the tenant a European option on a potential subsequent phase of the leasehold. The lease can be renewed only at its expiration. The lease renewal option is a call option on an underlying asset whose value is the present value of the projected future market rents on the space during the potential renewal phase of the leasehold.

of construction cost cash flows and the expected growth rate in construction costs. Label the construction yield y_K, and let $y_K = r_f - g_K$, where r_f is the risk-free interest rate (which can be proxied by the yield to Treasury bills) and g_K is the expected growth rate in construction costs (which might typically be near the general inflation rate).[24] Let y_V be the built property's current cash yield rate (i.e., the net operating rent as a fraction of the property value, in effect, the cap rate of the property), which can typically be observed in the relevant asset market.[25] Let σ_V be the volatility in the built property market value, measured by the standard deviation of individual property total returns across time. The relevant volatility here is that of properties that are already developed and in operation, not vacant land parcels, and it is the volatility of an *individual* property as distinct from that of a diversified portfolio of properties.[26] Typical values for this volatility measure would be between 10 percent and 25 percent per year, for commercial properties in the United States (see discussion of volatility in section 9.2.5 of Chapter 9).

Given values for these three parameters, we can define the **option elasticity** measure, η, by the following formula:

$$\eta = \{y_V - y_k + \sigma_V^2/2 + [(y_k - y_V - \sigma_V^2/2)^2 + 2y_k\sigma_V^2]^{1/2}\}/\sigma_V^2 \qquad (2a)$$

For example, if $y_K = 1\%$, $y_V = 6\%$, and $\sigma_V = 20\%$, then $\eta = 3.64$. The measure η is referred to as the option elasticity, because when the option is alive (not yet exercised, e.g., the land not yet developed), η gives the percentage change in value of the option (e.g., the raw land) associated with a 1 percent change in the value of the underlying asset (e.g., built property).

Apart from the option elasticity, the other values that enter into the value of a given land parcel are the built value and construction cost of the best project that could be built on the site. Define V_0 to be the presently observable value of newly developed property of the type that would be optimal on the site. Label as K_0 the current construction and development cost (including developer fees for service but excluding land cost and developer general overhead or sunk costs). Then, under the assumptions of the Samuelson-McKean formula, the vacant land value, here labeled C0, is given by:[27]

$$C_0 = (V^* - K_0)\left(\frac{V_0}{V^*}\right)^\eta \qquad (2b)$$

In this formula, V^* is the **hurdle value** (sometimes referred to as the **critical value**) of the developed property below which the land should be held undeveloped for the time being and above which it is optimal to develop the land immediately. In other words, V^* is the current value of the completed project that signals that immediate development of the land is

---

[24]As described here, the Samuelson-McKean formula assumes riskless construction costs that grow deterministically at a constant rate through time. We describe how to relax the riskless construction cost assumption in section 27A.2, located on the CD accompanying this book. Note however that modeling construction costs as "riskless" in this context is often a good approximation of reality. For example, construction costs can often be fixed in advance contractually, and even if not, if the only uncertainty in construction costs has to do with engineering unknowns, then it is reasonable to model the OCC of construction costs as having a zero risk premium (as the uncertainty would be uncorrelated with financial factors, and hence diversifiable). Note also that as construction costs are a negative component in the NPV of the development project, and a lower discount rate will result in a higher present value for such costs, modeling construction costs as "riskless" in this sense actually *magnifies* the negative impact of construction costs in evaluating the development project. This is seen in the Samuelson-McKean formula, as a lower construction yield results in a lower development option value.

[25]The cap rate in this usage should be defined net of a reserve for capital expenditures, so as to reflect a long-run "stabilized" yield rate for the built property.

[26]Thus, this volatility includes idiosyncratic risk components that would diversify out of a large portfolio.

[27]As before, we are here ignoring considerations of time to build, the time required for the construction project to be completed. In effect, we are assuming instantaneous construction. Thus, all three values in formula (2b) are valued as of the same point in time. Section 27A.2 on the CD accompanying this book describes how to account for time to build in the Samuelson-McKean formula.

now optimal. This hurdle value is a simple function of the current development cost and the option elasticity defined earlier:

$$V^* = K_0\eta/(\eta - 1) \tag{2c}$$

Thus, $\eta/(\eta - 1)$ is the **hurdle benefit/cost ratio**, V^*/K_0, that is, the ratio of built property value divided by construction cost exclusive of land cost, which triggers immediate optimal development. Note that this hurdle ratio is purely a function of the option elasticity, which in turn is a function of the three parameters characterizing the relevant asset markets: the built property current cash yield, the volatility of the built-property asset value, and the construction yield rate. Thus, in the Samuelson-McKean formula, the hurdle benefit/cost ratio is independent of the scale of the project(i.e., the size of the land parcel).[28]

27.5.2 General Implications of the Model for Development Timing and Land Speculation Investment Risk and Return Expectations

While the Samuelson-McKean formula may seem a bit daunting at first, it should be clear that anyone with basic spreadsheet skills could easily copy this formula into the cells of a spreadsheet and thereby harness the power of a very sophisticated economic theory to obtain some useful insights not only about the value of a given land parcel but also about the optimal timing of its development.[29] In particular, we see that the Samuelson-McKean formula not only gives the value of the land, but also characterizes the construction benefit/ cost ratio (exclusive of land cost) that is necessary for immediate development to be optimal [formula (2c)]. This in itself is useful and interesting information.

Similarly, the option elasticity measure η, as given in (2a), is not only useful as a stepping-stone to derive the development hurdle ratio and land value, but also contains useful information in its own right. This elasticity is the percentage change in vacant land value associated with a 1 percent change in the values of built properties in the underlying real estate market. In principle, the risk premium in the expected return required by investors holding speculative land should be proportional to this elasticity, according to the following formula:

$$RP_C = \eta RP_V \tag{3}$$

where RP_C is the expected return risk premium (i.e., return over and above the risk-free interest rate) in the vacant land holding, and RP_V is the risk premium for built properties in the underlying real estate asset market.[30] For example, if as in our previous numerical example the risk premium for unlevered investment in built property is 600 basis points (the 9 percent OCC minus the 3 percent risk-free interest rate), and the option elasticity in

---

[28]In 27A.2.1 it is shown how V^*/K_0 is influenced by the time it takes to build the project.

[29]The major technical assumptions used in the derivation of the Samuelson-McKean formula are the following: (1) underlying asset values (in this case built property values) are clearly observable and follow a random walk (with a constant drift rate) in continuous time; (2) instantaneous returns to underlying assets are normally distributed; and (3) the parameters in the model (volatility and yields) are known and constant. Obviously, these assumptions are violated in the real world, not only in the case of real estate but also in other applications of real options theory. Some, but not all, of the unrealistic assumptions can be relaxed with more sophisticated models. [For example, Childs, Ott, and Riddiough (2003) have explored the effect of the inability to observe perfectly the value of the underlying asset.] Nevertheless, the Samuelson-McKean formula seems to work pretty well in the sense that it gives results that are plausible and seem to agree broadly with typical empirical reality. In any case, it is certainly useful for obtaining basic general insights.

[30]The fundamental reason for this result is that options are, formally, derivative assets based on their underlying assets. Thus, the return to the land is in principle perfectly correlated with the return to the built property market, only with a volatility equal to η times the built property volatility. Thus, regardless of the "risk benchmark" on which the capital market bases its pricing of the risk in the built property (i.e., regardless of the basis for the built property's expected return risk premium, such as beta for example, as discussed in Chapter 22), the land will have η times that much risk. This is, in essence, the same point that we made in section 27.3.3 where we described fundamentally how the binomial option valuation model worked, namely, that the option and its underlying asset must provide the same expected return risk premium *per unit of risk*.

the vacant land value is $\eta = 3.64$, then the risk premium in the vacant land expected return would be 21.83% (3.64 × 6%). If the risk-free interest rate were 3 percent, then the total expected return requirement for investors would be 9 percent for built property and 24.83 percent for vacant land.[31]

The relationship between the option elasticity and the investment risk and return expectations for land as compared to built property is particularly useful because the perpetual option model is a *constant elasticity* model. That is, the elasticity does not change as a function of the underlying asset value or of time (per se, holding all else constant). Furthermore, as we see in formula (2a), the option elasticity is not a function of the current "benefit /cost ratio," V_0/K_0. (This is in contrast to the case with finite-lived options.)

The relationship among built property volatility and current cash yield, land value, and the hurdle benefit/cost ratio, as implied by the Samuelson-McKean formula, are displayed graphically in Exhibits 27-7 and 27-8. In these exhibits, the horizontal axis measures the current observable value of the underlying asset, V_0, for example, $100 million in the case of our previous numerical example of the office building in sections 27.2 and 27.3. The straight diagonal line represents the NPV (exclusive of land cost) of immediate development of the land (i.e., the exercise value of the development option).[32] The curved dashed line is the land value based on the Samuelson-McKean formula, as a function of the current built property value. The point at which these two lines meet is the point at which immediate

EXHIBIT 27-7

Samuelson-McKean Model Land Value as a Function of Current Built Property Value

© OnCourse Learning

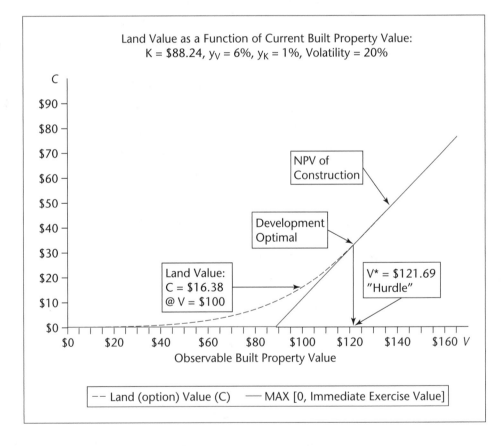

Land Value as a Function of Current Built Property Value:
$K = \$88.24$, $y_V = 6\%$, $y_K = 1\%$, Volatility = 20%

NPV of Construction

Development Optimal

Land Value: C = $16.38 @ V = $100

V* = $121.69 "Hurdle"

Observable Built Property Value

-- Land (option) Value (C)   —— MAX [0, Immediate Exercise Value]

---

[31]Recall that in our discussion of the opportunity cost of capital for real estate in Chapter 11 we suggested that typical return requirements for vacant land were in the range of 10% to 30% per annum, as of the early 2000s.

[32]Negative values of the immediate development NPV exclusive of land value are not shown, but can be inferred as the straight, diagonal line extension below the horizontal axis. Built property values less than construction cost naturally result in negative NPV of immediate development even without considering the opportunity cost of the land. On the other hand, the land itself would never be worth less than zero, as the landowner is not obligated to exercise his option.

EXHIBIT 27-8

Samuelson-McKean Model
Land Value as a Function of
Current Built Property
Value: Two Different
Volatility Assumptions

© OnCourse Learning

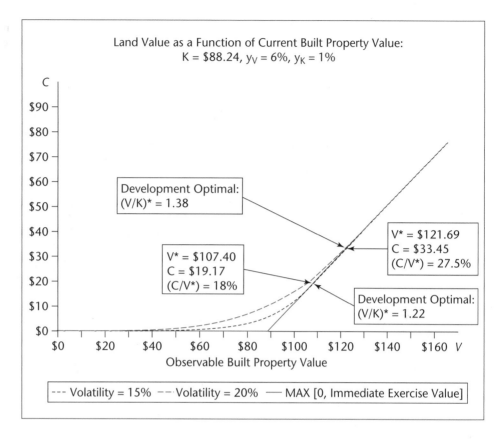

development is optimal, when the built property would have value V^*. This is the first point (i.e., lowest value of V_0) at which the development project would have a nonnegative NPV when the opportunity cost of the land (including its option premium value) is included in the NPV calculus.

Exhibit 27-7 is based on assumptions more or less consistent with the office building example we have been considering previously in this chapter, with current construction cost of $88.24 million (which would be $90 million in a year with a 2 percent inflation rate), completed property cash yield rate of 6 percent, construction yield rate of 1 percent (consistent with a 3 percent OCC and 2 percent growth rate), and completed building volatility of 20 percent. With the current built property value at $100 million, we get an implied land value of $16.38 million.[33] This is considerably greater than the $12.09 million we obtained as the option value in section 27.3. This is because in section 27.3 we assumed that the option to develop expired in only one year. Obviously, if the landowner's right (without obligation) to develop the property lasted for only one year, it would not be worth nearly as much as the perpetual option modeled by the Samuelson-McKean formula.

The Samuelson-McKean valuation of $16.38 million includes $4.62 million of option premium value in excess of the $100 − $88.24 = $11.76 million valuation under the immediate development assumption. This implies that immediate development of the office building would have a negative NPV of $4.62 million, including consideration of the opportunity cost

---

[33]We have already computed the elasticity in formula (2a) to be 3.64. Applying this elasticity value in formula (2c) we obtain a hurdle value of

$V^* = \$88.24[3.64/(3.64 − 1)] = \$121.69$ million.

Applying this hurdle value in formula (2b) we obtain a land value of

$C = (\$121.69 − \$88.24)(\$100/\$121.69)^{3.64} = \$16.38$ million

when the current value of the built property is $100 million ($V_0$).

of the land. (This is found as the $100 million benefit value of the completed built property, minus the $88.24 million construction cost, minus the $16.38 million value of the land.)

In this example, the hurdle value of the built property at and above which it is optimal to develop the land immediately is $121.69 million, equal to the hurdle benefit/cost ratio of 1.3792 times the $88.24 million construction cost.[34] Not unless and until we could sell the completed developed property for at least $121.69 million should we develop the land. Notice that the Samuelson-McKean land value, given by the upward-sloping convex curved line in Exhibit 27-7, exceeds the construction NPV until the point where on the horizontal axis V_0 equals the hurdle value of $121.69 million, in which situation the land (option) would be worth $33.45 million, exactly equal to the construction NPV: $121.69 − $88.24.

For built property values in excess of the V^* threshold, if the land has still not been developed, then there is no more option premium and the value of the land simply equals the NPV of immediate development exclusive of land cost. However, under the assumptions of the Samuelson-McKean model, allowing the potential built property value to rise above V^* without developing the property is suboptimal, and the land should be developed immediately.

Exhibit 27-8 shows how land value and the hurdle built property value V^* both increase with the volatility in built property values. This reveals how greater risk in the underlying real estate market results in greater land value (other things being equal), but more tendency to delay development, as projects must pass a higher benefit/cost hurdle to make immediate development optimal.[35] This is what underlies the urban form result noted in Chapter 5 that cities with more volatile economic bases will tend to have smaller, denser spatial configurations. (See section 5.2 in Chapter 5.)

In fact, a similar effect (greater land value but higher development hurdle) results from a *decrease* in the built property yield rate, y_V, or from an *increase* in the construction yield rate y_K. Note that the option value with the lower volatility in Exhibit 27-8 is reduced for all values of the built property, and the hurdle value at which development is optimal is also reduced. A reduction in relevant volatility from 20 percent to 15 percent reduces the hurdle benefit/cost ratio from 1.38 to 1.22, and reduces the land value fraction of total property value at the moment of optimal development from 27.5 percent to 18 percent of the current built property value.

27.6 Using Option Theory to Understand Overbuilding

Academic researchers have explored the implications of real options theory for several intriguing problems in urban and real estate economics. One of the most important of these is the tendency we noted first back in Chapter 2 of real estate space markets to become overbuilt from time to time. In this context, **overbuilding** may be defined as the production of more space than there is usage demand for at the time the construction is completed. In our presentation of the DiPasquale-Wheaton four-quadrant diagram in Chapter 2, we showed how myopic behavior on the part of investors and developers could explain such overbuilding.[36] But the real options models offer a more rational explanation, that is, an explanation that is consistent with rational expectations and forward-looking land-value-maximizing behavior on the part of developers and investors.

Early research on this phenomenon was done by Grenadier (1995a, 1995b), who noticed that overbuilding seems to be more severe in space markets characterized by large buildings and widespread use of long-term leases, such as CBD office markets. The Grenadier model suggests that overbuilding in such markets may be a rational response to the **leasing option** held by the developer/owner of the building being constructed, that is, the landlord's right without obligation to commit space to a long-term lease at a time of his choosing. As with

---

[34]$1.3792 = 3.64/(3.64 − 1)$.

[35]Of course, increasing built property risk could also reduce the value of built properties, and this effect would reduce the value of the land.

[36]See also section 6.2 in Chapter 6 for a more detailed development of the dynamics of myopic behavior, with implications for cyclicality and overbuilding.

all options, the leasing option presents its holder with flexibility, which can be used to the benefit of the option holder. The magnitude of this potential option benefit may be greater the longer the time to build because longer construction time allows a greater range of extreme outcomes in the space market demand. In effect, the lease option is given a longer maturity the longer the time to build.[37] If demand turns out to be above expectations, the landlord/developer can benefit by locking in high-rent, long-term leases. If the space market turns out to be worse than expected, the landlord does not have to sign long-term leases. The developer can wait for the market to turn around (at least, if he is not too highly levered so that he can maintain control of the project). The asymmetry in this effect of "good" and "bad" leasing outcomes for the landlord can, in some cases, make it worthwhile to commence construction even when there is a substantial chance that usage demand may not be sufficient to fill the building at the time the project is completed.

Additional insight about overbuilding is obtained by considering the fact that it is not possible to observe with perfect accuracy the current value of the underlying asset (the building to be built on the land). While uncertainty in the future value of the underlying asset is an inherent characteristic of all options, in the case of financial options one can usually observe rather precisely the current market value of the underlying asset. For reasons we described in Chapters 12 and 25, real estate is a bit different in this regard. Due to the "thinness" of the property market and uniqueness of each of the whole assets that are traded, asset values can only be observed *approximately*, or with random noise. This can affect the timing of the option exercise and may have implications for the overbuilding phenomenon.

Childs, Ott, and Riddiough (2002) show that when the underlying asset value can only be observed with noise, the option is valued and optimally exercised based on the value of the *best estimate* of what the current true value of the underlying asset is. However, when the current value of the underlying asset is not perfectly observable, there may be heterogeneous information about the true value of the underlying asset (the built property, if it existed today). In particular, different landowner/developers may have different amounts or quality of information and expertise concerning such value. Recent research has shown how such current value uncertainty and information asymmetry can lead to rational herd behavior or follow-the-leader type **cascades** in which periods of very little development are followed by periods of frenzied development.[38]

This relates to an important difference between real and financial options. Typically, the exercise of real options will produce unique, whole assets that will add to the supply side of the market for the use of such assets. In other words, the exercise of real options converts financial into physical capital and thereby impacts on supply and demand in a real market. This is not generally the case for financial options, whose *net supply* is normally zero (as for every option bought, someone else on the opposite side of the deal is either selling or writing the option) and whose exercise does not change the amount of underlying assets (publicly floated shares of common stock). No new shares of the underlying asset corporation are created or issued, and no additional capital flows to the corporation, as a result of option issuance or exercise.

In contrast, suppose in a certain office market there is usage demand for an additional one million square feet of office space. If one landowner/developer decides to build a million-square-foot office building on her land, then her decision to exercise her option causes a flow of financial capital that results in the construction of one million square feet of physical capital (in the form of the office building) in that office market. That one option exercise decision by that one landowner/developer has, in this example, all by itself exhausted the demand for new office space in the relevant market. This, in turn, severely negatively affects the option value of other land parcels that might have served as the sites for new office buildings. This "lumpiness" of real estate supply adds a gaming dimension to the

---

[37]This is not to ignore the negative present value impact of longer construction as the possibility of receiving rents is precluded until the building is completed, but the point is that this cost may be partially offset by the option value. This possibility will be greater in space markets where longer term leases are the norm (see Chapter 30).

[38]See Grenadier (1996). Noise may also cause the first or lead developer to wait longer than she otherwise would. See Childs, Ott, and Riddiough (2002).

development timing decision, in which developers strive to beat each other to the punch, possibly resulting in overbuilding or redundant construction.[39]

The effect of finite demand for new real estate assets, in combination with competition on the supply side (in the form of competing land sights and competing developers), adds a dramatic intensity to the real options model of real estate development. Imagine that as a landowner your development option is perhaps not perpetual after all, but may in fact expire at some point in time. In particular, your development option will expire when the other landowner/developers in the area exercise their development options sufficiently to exhaust the usage demand for new built space in the area. The exact expiration date on your option is therefore unknown and uncertain, as it depends on these other developers' decisions (as well as on the magnitude of usage demand for built space in the area, a quantity that may also be difficult to estimate exactly).

Now it is a basic (and rather intuitive) principle of option theory that the shorter is the time until expiration of an option, the smaller is the option premium value, and the lower are the requirements for immediate exercise of the option to be optimal (that is, profit-maximizing, or rational). In the extreme, it is never optimal to allow an in-the-money option to expire unexercised. Therefore, in the presence of competing developers and a finite usage market demand, there will be strong pressure on you to build immediately as soon as it appears that the market value the newly developed property would have is greater than your construction cost exclusive of your land value (that is, treating your land cost as "sunk"). In effect, the competition pressures you to ignore any option premium in your land value. Your fellow landowner/developers are in the same position as you are. Everyone is under pressure to develop as soon as their development option is in the money. If they all act accordingly (in effect, each one trying to beat the other to fulfill the finite usage demand), they will tend in the aggregate to build too much space too soon. Thus, overbuilding will tend to occur in the space market.

It is important to note that this type of overbuilding occurs even though each individual is acting rationally in his or her own best interest given the available information. Option theory thus allows us to see how real estate's famous overbuilding and boom and bust cycles may result from rational individual behavior, rather than "crazy developers" with "edifice complexes" abetted by bankers pushing easy credit, or from myopic or backward-looking expectations about the future.

The above example should allow you to glimpse an extreme possibility for the implication that competition among developers (and land sites) could have for the real options model of land value and optimal development timing. Research by Steve Grenadier (RFS 2002) suggests that in a highly competitive environment where many competing developers could build many competing developments on similar, substitutable land sites, most of the value of waiting to invest may be eroded away by the competitive pressures. This would lead to individual firm investment at very near zero net present value. In the context of the option model of land value, this would mean that the option premium would be competed away to zero, and land value would simply equal the "residual" difference between the current value of the built property and its construction cost (as we described in Chapter 4). Development would be optimal as soon as the expected construction profit exceeds this land value. In effect, the land value could be conceptualized in essence as only the value that is implied by the location premium of the traditional (deterministic) monocentric city model, which, as you recall, is essentially zero at the fringe of development (or equal to the nonurban opportunity value there).[40]

On the other hand, it is important to note that real estate sites and developments always contain some degree of uniqueness, which makes competition less than perfect.[41] If competition drove away all value of waiting to invest in real estate, we would probably observe much less land speculation and much lower land values than is actually the case

---

[39]See Grenadier (1996), Williams (1993), and Childs, Ott, and Riddiough (2002).

[40]More generally, there would be no option premium in land value, not only at the urbanizing fringe, but anywhere in locations of dynamic evolution of the highest and best use (HBU) as described in Chapter 5.

[41]The relevant theoretical context may be closer to that described by Novy-Marx (2007) than that described by Grenadier (2002).

in locations of dynamically changing highest and best use (HBU). In fact, the option model of land value gives results that seem to be fairly consistent with casual empirical observation, for example, land costs typically between 10 percent and 50 percent of total development cost at the time of development, and we saw values between 18 percent and 27.5 percent in our numerical example in Exhibit 27-8 of section 27.5 (which was based on typical real world numerical values of the relevant parameters). Furthermore, circumstances which effectively give a developer some degree of monopoly power over major land sites, at least temporarily, are not uncommon, especially where local or regional governments are involved in the land use planning and development process (which may often be where optimal land use is changing and development is most dynamic).[42] Recent academic empirical research in North America generally confirms the real option model of land value, though it also suggests that the option premium may be dampened in highly competitive circumstances.[43]

27.7 Chapter Summary

This chapter introduced you to the concept of real options, and to the call option model of land value and optimal development. We also presented a simple option valuation model, the binomial model, and explained the fundamentals of how and why this model works. Finally, we introduced a simple and elegant perpetual horizon, continuous time formula, the Samuelson-McKean formula, which is useful for analyzing and gaining insight regarding land value, development timing, and the opportunity cost of capital for speculative land investments. The perspective and tools presented here are useful for dealing with one of the most fundamental and important issues in all of real estate, whether viewed from an urban economics/space market perspective or a financial economics/asset market perspective. Land valuation and development lies at the nexus of these perspectives, at a central point in the real estate system we described way back in Chapter 2. The next chapter will step back to introduce the financial analysis of real estate development projects, before we extend our treatment of the economics of land development (including real options analysis) in Chapter 29.

KEY TERMS

option valuation theory (OVT)	call option model of land value	option elasticity
real options	certainty-equivalence value	hurdle value (critical value)
option	irreversibility premium	hurdle benefit/cost ratio
exercise of options	option premium	overbuilding
underlying asset	replicating portfolio (or hedge	leasing option
exercise price	portfolio)	cascades (of development)
American option	arbitrage	development timing
European option	perpetual options	
call option	Samuelson-McKean formula	

STUDY QUESTIONS

Conceptual Questions

27.1. Define what is meant in financial economics by the concept of a call option.

27.2. What is a *real* option? How do real options differ from financial option contracts?

---

[42]For example, in China and many other countries (including the United States), government-owned or government-controlled land may be made available to a selected developer for a period of time in order to implement a specified type of development.

[43]See for example: Bulan, Mayer & Somerville (2009); Cunningham (2006); Grovenstein, Kau & Munneke (2011); and Schwarts & Torous (2007). A much earlier study of empirical support is attributed to Quigg (1993).

27.3. Describe the call option model of land value. What is the underlying asset in this model? What is the exercise price? What is the typical maturity of the land development option?

27.4. What do people mean when they say that option theory is an exception to the NPV rule? Do you agree that this is truly a valid exception to the NPV rule? Illustrate your answer with a simple real-estate-related example.

27.5. Explain how the option model of land valuation derives from the principle of equal expected risk premiums per unit of risk across different investment assets. What are the specific asset markets that must be in equilibrium? (Hint: See section 27.3.3.)

27.6. What is meant by the *normative* basis of option value theory, how it can be meaningful even when its prescription may not be implemented or enforced by well functioning markets for the relevant assets.

27.7. Describe two explanations, based on real option theory, for why or how overbuilding can be due to completely *rational* (i.e., profit-maximizing) behavior on the part of developers (landowners).

Quantitative Problems

27.8. **(Option Basics)** Suppose you purchase a call option on a share of ABC Inc. common stock(i.e., go long in an option contract). This option gives you the right, but not the obligation, to buy a share of ABC's stock for $45, which is the exercise price. Assume this is a European option, meaning it can only be exercised at the expiration date, 90 days from today. The option contract costs you $2.50, and ABC Inc. shares are currently trading at $40. (Note: Technically, an option contract is a contract for 100 shares, not a single share, but the economics we are concerned with are unchanged.)

    a. Determine the current *intrinsic value* of the option defined as the payoff if the option were exercised today, where payoff is defined as the current share price less the exercise price. Explain why you would pay more than the current intrinsic value for this call option.

    b. Determine what both the option payoff and your profit will be at the expiration of the contract as a function of the share price at that time (determine these quantities for share prices ranging from $30 to $60 at $5 price increments). (Hint: Profit incorporates the cost of the option contract.)

    c. Graph your payoff function from part (b) with share price at expiration on the horizontal axis and payoff on the vertical axis.

27.9. On a certain parcel of land, you could build a project worth $2 million today, for a construction cost of $1.8 million. If you wait and do not build the project until next year, the project would most likely then be worth $2.2 million, and the construction cost would be $1.9 million. If investors require a 25% expected return for holding land, what is the value of the land today? Should you build the project today or wait until next year?

27.10. In the preceding question, suppose there is a 50% chance that the project next year will be worth $2.6 million and a 50% chance that it will be worth only $1.8 million, with the construction cost still $1.9 million in both cases. The project today would certainly be worth $2 million and cost $1.8 million, as before.

    a. Under these circumstances (and still assuming a 25% required return on land), how much is the land worth today? (Hint: Follow the approach illustrated in Exhibit 27-1.)

    b. Explain why the land is worth more in this problem than in the previous problem. Also explain why it is better not to build the project today even though there is a 50% chance the project will be unprofitable next year.

*27.11. **(No Arbitrage/Replicating Portfolio Approach to Option Valuation)** Continue with the situation in the preceding question. Assume, however, that we do not (yet) know the required return on land but we do know that the required return on built property is 8.5% and the risk-free rate of return (or opportunity cost of default-free bonds) is 4%.

a. Determine the current value of the land using the no arbitrage/replicating portfolio method of section 27.3.1. Specifically, value the land as a call option by valuing a portfolio of built property and bonds that provides the exact same payoffs in the two states Year 1 as the project payoffs you determined in the preceding question. (Hint: This question is similar to the example in section 27.3.1. You should carefully work through that example to replicate key calculations. You need to determine N and B, the number of units of built property and the dollar value of bonds in the replicating portfolio, respectively, using the equations in footnote 9 of the chapter.)

b. Use the certainty equivalence method of Section 27.3.2 to arrive at the same valuation.

c. Determine the implied opportunity cost or required return on the land. How does your answer compare to the 25% assumed in Question 27.10?

*27.12. **(Samuelson-McKean)** Suppose the risk-free (i.e., government bond) interest rate is 4%, the current cash yield payout rate on newly built property is 6.5%, and the annual volatility of individual property total returns is 25% for built properties that are leased up and operational. Use the Samuelson-McKean formula to answer the following questions concerning a vacant but developable land parcel.

a. If built property has a 4.5% risk premium in its expected total return (8.5% total return), what is the risk premium and expected total return for the land parcel? [Hint: Use the elasticity formula (2a) and the risk premium formula (3), and note that with constant riskless construction costs the construction yield rate y_k equals the riskfree rate.]

b. What is the value of the land parcel if a building currently worth $2,200,000 new could be built on the land for a construction cost of $1,900,000?

c. What is the hurdle benefit/cost ratio above which the land should be developed immediately?

d. What value of newly built property does this suggest is required before the land should be developed?

e. Under these conditions, should the land be developed immediately or is it better to wait?

f. What do you suppose is the main reason why the land value as computed here based on the Samuelson-McKean Formula is so much greater than what you computed in Question 27.11 for a parcel with similar characteristics?

*27.13. **(Samuelson-McKean)** Suppose the risk-free (i.e., government bond) interest rate is 6%, the current cash yield payout rate on newly built property is 9%, and the annual volatility of individual property total returns is 20% for built properties that are leased up and operational. Use the Samuelson-McKean formula to answer the following questions concerning a vacant but developable land parcel.

a. If built property has a 5% risk premium in its expected total return (11% total return), what is the risk premium and expected total return for the land parcel? [Hint: Use the elasticity formula (2a) and the risk premium formula (3), and note that with constant riskless construction costs the construction yield rate y_k equals the riskfree rate.]

b. What is the value of the land parcel if a building currently worth $1,000,000 new could be built on the land for a construction cost of $800,000?

c. What is the hurdle benefit/cost ratio above which the land should be developed immediately?

d. What value of newly built property does this suggest is required before the land should be developed?

e. Under these conditions, should the land be developed immediately or is it better to wait?

INVESTMENT ANALYSIS OF REAL ESTATE DEVELOPMENT PROJECTS: OVERVIEW & BACKGROUND

LEARNING OBJECTIVES

After reading this chapter, you should understand:

➲ The typical real estate development project decision process, at a broad-brush level, and the trend towards greener and more sustainable buildings.

➲ The role of financial analysis in development project decision making and the mortgage-based simplified techniques that are widely employed in this role in current practice, including their strengths and weaknesses.

➲ The basics of construction loan mechanics.

W e cannot overemphasize the importance of real estate development. The construction and major rehabilitation of commercial buildings not only is often a make-or-break activity for individual real estate entrepreneurs and firms, but it also has tremendous social and public consequences in the shaping of the future urban environment. Investment analysis is a crucial component of the process of real estate development decision making. Projects that pass the financial screen get funding and get built. Projects that don't pass remain pipe dreams.

The last chapter began our in-depth study of real estate development from an investment perspective, for we saw in our study there of land value that the ultimate end of the land speculation phase is development. In this chapter and the next, we will pick up where that chapter left off, by focusing on the development phase itself. In the present chapter, we will present an overview of the development process and then take an in-depth look at how development project financial feasibility is typically quantified in the real world. Our practical examination of development in this chapter will also include a brief introduction to the mechanics of construction loans.[1] Throughout this chapter and the next, our perspective will be primarily that of the private-sector real estate developer.

It is important to note at the outset of this chapter that the current practice of real estate development project investment analysis relies heavily on *ad hoc* rules of thumb that have intuitive appeal and considerable practical value. These rules of thumb and practical

---

[1]The distinction between construction loans and permanent loans, and the basic method of operation of the construction loan industry, was described in section 16.1 of Chapter 16.

procedures will be the main focus of this chapter. We will see their usefulness, but we will also see here how their *ad hoc* nature causes current practice to fall short in some respects, and this in turn will lead us to the more rigorous framework to be presented in Chapter 29.

28.1 Overview of the Development Decision-Making Process

From an economic perspective, development projects are crucial points in space and time where financial capital becomes fixed as physical capital. More broadly, they are where ideas become reality. In the preface of this book, we pointed out that real estate is a multidisciplinary field. In no aspect of real estate is this more apparent and important than in the development process. In fact, development decision making can be represented as a process that moves iteratively from one disciplinary perspective to another.

Such a model of development was perhaps first articulated by James Graaskamp, a famous real estate professor and the director of the Real Estate Center at the University of Wisconsin from 1964 until his death in 1988. Graaskamp suggested that development decision making in the private sector could typically be described by one of two situations: a *site looking for a use, or a use looking for a site*. In the former case, the site is already under the control of the developer, and the analyst undertakes what is, in effect, a highest and best use (HBU) study. It is not uncommon for developers or land speculators to "inventory" land, that is, to buy and hold land when it is cheaper and not yet ready for development. This results in the **site-looking-for-a-use** type decision making, the type local public sector authorities are often involved in.

On the other hand, in the case of a use looking for a site, the decision maker already knows the type of development it wishes to pursue. The question is where to best pursue such a project: what will be the cost and the level of usage demand and competition at any given location? In a large development firm, the early stages of most development studies are of this **use-looking-for-a-site** type, with the developer having a particular expertise in a certain type of product, such as biotech space, office-warehouse space, senior-oriented housing, and so on. The use-looking-for-a-site activity may characterize "build-to-suit" projects, and tends to be a crucial part of the business of retail firms, many of which work with real estate development firms specializing in retail development.

The process of development analysis, design, and decision making is highly iterative.[2] This is depicted in Exhibit 28-1, which is based on Graaskamp's teaching. Exhibit 28-1 is

EXHIBIT 28-1 Iterative, Multidisciplinary Process of Real Estate Development Decision Making (the Graaskamp Model)

© OnCourse Learning

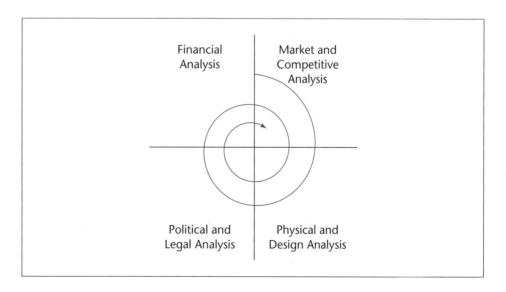

more applicable to the site-looking-for-a-use type of decision making, which will be the major focus of Chapters 28 and 29. A given development concept will cycle through analysis from at least four different disciplinary perspectives: urban economics (the real estate space market), architectural/engineering disciplines (physical analysis), legal/political analysis, and financial economics (the capital market and real estate asset market), not necessarily in that order (or indeed in any fixed order). Expertise is needed in all of these disciplines and perspectives (and sometimes others as well), and just as important, entrepreneurial creativity is needed to integrate and pull together the various perspectives, to synthesize analysis from various fields into a feasible project. With each iteration, the project design and the decision become more synthesized, more detailed, and closer to fruition. This is indicated in the figure by the arrow spiraling toward the center, the point of synthesis and action.[3] While all of the four disciplines and perspectives portrayed in Exhibit 28-1 are important, our focus in this chapter and the next is on the top left quadrant of the picture, the financial analysis of the project from an investment perspective.

From this perspective, Exhibits 28-2 and 28-3 provide an introductory overview of the development project investment process, including the major sources of capital. In these exhibits, the horizontal axis represents time, progressing from left to right. The solid line referenced to the vertical axis on the left-hand side represents the cumulative total amount

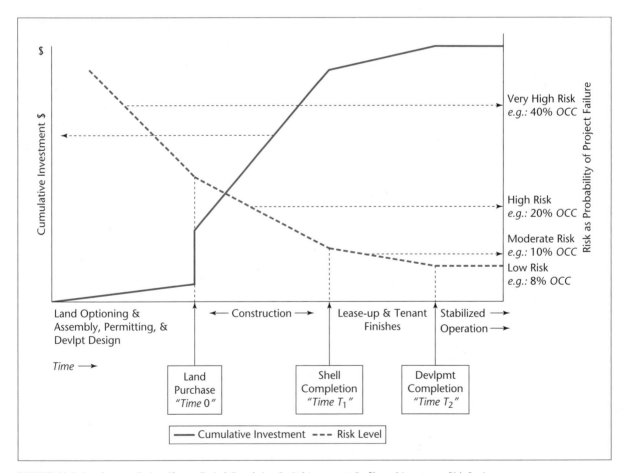

EXHIBIT 28-2 Development Project Phases: Typical Cumulative Capital Investment Profile and Investment Risk Regimes
© OnCourse Learning

---

[3]Hopefully, the diagram in Exhibit 28-1 does not imply a process spiraling out of control!

of financial capital that has been expended on the project up to each point in time on the horizontal axis. In Exhibit 28-2, the dashed line referenced to the right-hand axis represents the degree of risk faced by investors at each point in time, viewed as the probability of financial or economic "failure" of the project. Notice that the risk declines over time as the project progresses and overcomes challenges, and as it comes closer to fruition and more is learned about key factors that determine the project's outcome, such as the nature of the rental market for the project. Notice also that risk declines as more capital is invested (or put alternatively, that more capital can be attracted into the project as its risk declines).

The time line on the horizontal axis in the exhibits can be divided into phases. The first phase, at the left of the horizontal axis, may be viewed as a *preliminary* phase. This is the most creative and entrepreneurial time in the evolution of the project. In most projects, this phase will be led by an entrepreneurial development firm (at least in the United States).[4] In the case of many large, complex projects, this entrepreneurial role will be played by a governmental entity or a partnership among local government, one or more private developers, and perhaps a non–real-estate firm or institution. (Such public/private partnerships are especially likely in large urban areas.[5]) Even in fairly small-scale and routine development projects, this first phase of development often involves the optioning and assembly of separate land parcels,[6] the obtaining of necessary permits (sometimes including variances or other special provisions or infrastructure requirements), and the design of the development project. These tasks will typically proceed in parallel and iteratively with the assembly and permitting process and will include (implicitly if not explicitly) a "highest and best use analysis" of the site. It is in this preliminary phase that the iterative design process described in Exhibit 28-1 is most relevant.

This preliminary phase may take anywhere from a few months to more than a decade! Value creation, if any, occurs because of skills getting through the entitlement process, adept market analysis and targeting, tenant relationships and marketing, and a host of other skills. Furthermore, this phase does not always succeed. The development project may ultimately not be approved or may not prove economically, financially, or administratively feasible. In that case, much if not all of the entrepreneurial developer's time and expenses incurred in the preliminary phase may well have been wasted. This is why this is the riskiest phase in the development process, as indicated by the height of the dashed line in Exhibit 28-2. Referencing the right-hand vertical axis, we see that such high risk carries with it a commensurately high opportunity cost of capital (OCC) in the form of a high expected return for any financial capital invested.

It should be noted, however, that the amount of financial capital actually invested during the preliminary phase is normally relatively small. Most of the resources spent on project development during this phase are better characterized as the normal operational expenses

---

[4]In recent decades a growing number of these development firms are organized as publicly traded REITs or REOCs. Nevertheless, private development firms, both large and small, still dominate the entrepreneurial development field in the United States, and in the early 2000s the growth of the private equity sector in the capital market facilitated continued private ownership. However, it is not uncommon for private, local firms with specialized expertise and local knowledge and connections to partner with larger national firms or funds (public or private) who bring access to the capital markets and national or international connections and expertise.

[5]For example, a university, hospital, or research institution may partner with real estate developers in conjunction with city planners. In recent years, major developments in the infotech and biotech fields have been catalyzed and located adjacent to preexisting university and medical facilities. In other cases, the establishment or expansion of a major industrial or service firm, or the development or redevelopment of a sports facility or transportation terminal, has been the generator and nucleus of complex adjacent development projects.

[6]The "optioning" of land here refers to the widespread practice of developers to offer preexisting landowners a conditional price for the land, contingent on the outcome of the assembly and permitting process. In this way, the developer does not have to actually purchase the land unless and until the entire necessary package of parcels and approvals is obtained. Normally, the land purchase option has a specific finite lifetime, and often the developer pays a nonrefundable fee for such option rights. In any case, the contingent price agreed to in the option is generally designed to enable the developer to obtain a sufficient profit from the land acquisition, if the project succeeds. In return, of course, the developer takes on the expense and risk of site assembly and approval, which is not guaranteed to succeed. In principle, land optioning can be analyzed and evaluated using the real option valuation methodology presented in the previous chapter.

and time, during which overhead of a development firm accrues, rather than as investments of financial capital.[7] Many of these expenses may be recouped in *fees* charged by the developer, during or at the end of the entrepreneurial phase. Profit (including return on any invested financial capital) will hopefully be obtained via the increase in land value that may be created during this phase. To the extent that financial capital has been invested in land acquisition during the preliminary phase, this may be viewed as "land speculation" investment rather than as real estate "development project" investment, and such land speculation investment may be recovered at the end of the preliminary phase if the land is sold to a separate development venture entity. As discussed in Chapter 27, land speculation investment is indeed highly risky, and may be modeled by the use of real options theory. Here in Chapter 28 (and in Chapter 29), our main focus picks up at the end of any such land speculation phase.[8]

At the end of the preliminary phase depicted on the horizontal axis of Exhibit 28-2 (if not before), the necessary land will be purchased or otherwise acquired, to give the developer the right to proceed with construction.[9] Regardless of when and how the land has actually been acquired, from the perspective of the evaluation of the development project as an investment, the economic *"opportunity cost"* of the value of the land is incurred at the time of the start of construction. We label this point *"Time 0"* in Exhibit 28-2. At this point, the land is irreversibly committed to the construction project, and it ceases to be a "land speculation" with real options characteristics. It is important to recognize, however, that the economic opportunity cost of the land at Time *0* may differ from the historical monetary cost of land acquisition. The opportunity cost is the economic value of the land, what it could be sold for at Time *0*, after it has been assembled and permitted and a project design developed. Much of this value of the land may have been created by the entrepreneurial developer during the first phase of the overall development process depicted in the graph. Thus, the actual price paid for the land, which is what is represented by the solid line in Exhibit 28-2, may be quite different from its economic opportunity cost (hopefully, from the developer's perspective, much less).

The development investment *per se* actually begins with the incurring of the land opportunity cost at the beginning of the construction phase. It is during the construction phase that the bulk of the financial expenditures are usually required, for the purpose of paying for the construction of the building(s) on the site.[10] This phase is still quite risky, though less so than the preliminary phase. Development investments are risky for two reasons. First, if the project

---

[7]Recall that the land may not be actually acquired during this phase, but rather may only be "optioned" (as described above), or it may already be owned by the developer (perhaps purchased previously as a land speculation investment, or otherwise acquired for various reasons, or inherited).

[8]For an interesting new perspective on how to model the real estate development (RED) process, see Bulloch & Sullivan (2009, 2010). They conducted an analysis of the normative operations of a typical development firm and modeled the process as a matrix of information flows and tasks, using an analytical tool called the "Design Structure Matrix" (DSM). Bulloch & Sullivan found that the normative RED process involved 91 discretely identifiable tasks involving information generation or usage (an information exchange). The 91 micro-level tasks grouped into the four Graaskamp-identified disciplines (or professions) plus a fifth discipline representing the integration or overall management of the process. The micro-level tasks also fell into six sequential stages or phases: Idea inception, Feasibility analysis, Pre-construction, Construction, Stabilization, and Asset management (or sale). The first three of these six stages contained 63 of the 91 tasks. Thus some two-thirds of the firm's effort in some sense occurred before a shovel turned the earth, in the case of the subject development firm (which should be distinguished from an investment firm or a vertically integrated real estate firm). The end of each stage in the RED process was a type of "gate" through which the candidate project must pass, gaining approval of upper management and in some cases external financing sources. Out of the $91^2 = 8,281$ potential information interfaces in the entire process, the normative RED process actually involved 1.148 binary information exchanges Compared to typical manufacturing innovation processes (the traditional focus of DSM analysis) this is a large number of interfaces, suggesting the complexity of the RED process. 70% of the information interfaces were across two different Graaskamp disciplines (such as between an engineer and a lawyer, or between a construction manager and a banker), indicating the highly interdisciplinary nature of the real estate development process.

[9]This would normally include the exercise of any land purchase options, as described above. (To the extent that some or all of the preexisting landowners are not being paid off at this time, they should be viewed as development partners.)

[10]In some high-value locations, land costs may approach or even exceed construction costs in total magnitude.

is "speculative" (referred to as building "on spec"), then it is not known for certain what occupancy will be achieved within what period of time and at what rental rate. This is fundamental rental market risk, as described in the first two Parts of this text, and in the context of the development project it can be said that spec development is exposed to "**lease-up risk**."

The second reason development investments are risky is that they inherently contain "operational leverage." Even if there is no financial leverage (that is, if the project is financed entirely with equity), and even if there is no lease-up risk (that is, if the project is entirely preleased), development projects still have operational leverage in the sense of having high fixed or committed costs relative to potentially variable revenues. This will be discussed in depth in Chapter 29, but the essence of the matter is that the development investor incurs the land opportunity cost at *Time 0* and commits to paying the construction costs at the end of the construction phase, no matter what the value of the project turns out to be at the time of completion, which we label "*Time T*" in the exhibits.

For example, suppose the opportunity cost of the land at *Time 0* is $20 million, and the construction costs during the development phase are $70 million, with the expectation *as of Time 0* being that the value of the project *upon completion at Time T* will be $100 million. Thus, $20 million is invested at *Time 0* in the expectation of $30 million being returned at *Time T* (the expected difference between project value minus construction cost: $100–$70 million). But the $70 million construction cost must be paid no matter what. If the project turns out to be worth $90 million instead of $100 million (only a 10 percent decline in value), the expected profit is cut by 33 percent (from $30 million to $20 million), and the return on the $20 million *Time 0* investment is reduced to zero. Because of this type of operational leverage, the construction phase of development investments requires a rather high expected return, reflecting an OCC often in the neighborhood of 20 percent per annum (going-in IRR for the development phase only).

The next phase on the horizontal axis in Exhibit 28-2 is described as "Lease-up & Tenant Finishes." This is the phase after the major construction of the "shell" has been completed, during which the space is leased and occupied by its users. For many types of commercial development where long-term leases are involved, this involves some finishing construction work that customizes the space(s) in the building for the tenant(s) who will be occupying the space. While some of these expenditures may be paid for by the tenants, it is not uncommon for much or all of these expenditures to be paid by the developer. Nevertheless, this phase usually involves less capital and less risk than the main construction phase of the development project.[11] As a result, investment in the lease-up phase involves a lower OCC, for example, perhaps around a 10 percent required rate of return (as suggested in the exhibit).

The construction and lease-up phases together represent the "development project" *per se*, the subject of the investment analysis in this chapter. These development phases may take anywhere from a few months to several years. In larger projects (with multiple buildings), the development may often be divided into separate stages, in which there remains flexibility about when (or even whether) to commence the later stages of the development. In such cases, the development project retains real options characteristics, as these were defined in Chapter 27. As will be discussed in Chapter 29, real options based models must be employed for rigorous investment analysis of such multistage projects.

At the end of the development project, the result is an asset in "stabilized operation." The project is completely or nearly leased up, and operating at its long-run steady-state level of profitability (at least relative to the condition of its rental market). This point is labeled *Time T_2* in Exhibit 28-2 (or just *Time T* for short, and to collapse lease-up and construction into a single "development" phase). At *Time T*, the development phase investment is complete, and what exists going forward is an investment in a stabilized operating asset. Usually,

---

[11]With nonspeculative (preleased) development, the lease-up phase may be effectively nonexistent, with the tenant finishes phase absorbed in the main construction phase. At the other extreme, in speculative development of building types that involve major tenant-specific construction, such as biotech space and some types of retail space, the Lease-up & Tenant Finishes phase may involve substantial capital requirement and risk. (For this reason, developers usually try to avoid speculative development of such space.)

there is a recapitalization at this point, because different types of investors typically are in the market for stabilized (low risk) investments. If the construction was financed by a "construction loan" (as it usually is), this loan will be retired (or "taken out"), either by an equity infusion or (more commonly in the case of taxable investors) by taking out a "permanent" commercial mortgage on the property.

The equity investment in the project may or may not be recapitalized at this time by means of a sale of the asset. But whether or not the original equity investors sell the stabilized asset, the risk and return nature of their investment has changed. It now has the nature of the real estate acquisition investments that were the subject of Parts IV and V of this book, and the investment from *Time T* going forward should be analyzed and evaluated as such. It is important in the modern investment world not to "mix apples and oranges." Investment characteristics and performance should be compared among like-kind investments. Therefore, a rigorous framework for the analysis of development investments should take the *Time T* moment of development completion as the ending horizon of the analysis.

Exhibit 28-3 maps the typical sources and types of financial capital onto the previous development project cumulative investment chart. As depicted to the right of the right-hand vertical axis in the chart, there are typically three major types of financial capital provided over the course of the overall development project (including the Preliminary Phase). (Follow the "Order of Investment" arrow in Exhibit 28-3 leading up the capital sources list on the right.) The first to come in is the entrepreneurial developer's seed equity investment, which is invested primarily during the Preliminary Phase and is normally very small in absolute dollar magnitude compared to the other, later sources of capital. The next investment capital to come in is usually external equity, financing the purchase of the land. This external equity requirement is typically much greater than the previous seed equity requirement, and it may come from one or more of a variety of sources (as well as the entrepreneurial developer itself), including opportunity funds, financial institutions (such as pension funds, life insurance companies, or endowment funds), foreign investors, wealthy individuals, private equity vehicles,[12] or in some cases REITs as joint venture partners with the original developer.[13] It is not uncommon for this "external equity" component to include more than one type or class of investor and investment, often in a more or less complex partnership structure, such as was described in Chapter 15 (see section 15.3). It is also not uncommon for some of the capital in this component to come technically in the form of debt, but subordinated debt, such as "mezzanine debt." Finally, the last capital to come in is typically the bulk of the total capital requirement, in the form of a "construction loan," typically from a commercial bank or syndication of such banks (for larger projects). The order of investor payback seniority is typically the reverse of the order of investment but corresponding to the magnitude of capital invested and in inverse order of the amount of investment risk (riskier investments tend to get paid back last).

The original entrepreneurial developer's seed equity investment is represented in the OAFZ region of Exhibit 28-3. This capital comes in first (during the preliminary phase) and typically takes the highest risk, highest residual return position in the overall capital structure of the project. This is appropriate, as the entrepreneurial developer's capital was invested (if at all) during the highest-risk ("preliminary") phase as we described previously in our discussion of Exhibit 28-2.[14] Apart from fee income that may partially or entirely reimburse the developer for operating and overhead expenses, the entrepreneurial developer's return on capital invested will usually be subordinated to that of later and larger capital providers. However, the entrepreneurial developer will retain a disproportionate share of any excess

---

[12]This would include, among others, private REITs and tenant-in-common (TIC) vehicles designed to funnel small individual investor capital into real estate investments.

[13]Of course, in some cases, the REIT will be one and the same as the original entrepreneurial developer. Recall from Chapter 23 that many REITs are "vertically integrated," including everything from land speculation to development to long-term property operation and investment in their range of activities and profit centers.

[14]Alternatively, the entrepreneurial developer may have elected to take all or a portion of her entrepreneurial (Preliminary Phase) investment profits in the form of land sale profit at *Time 0*, by selling the land into the development partnership that would normally be created at that time to include the new, external equity investor partners.

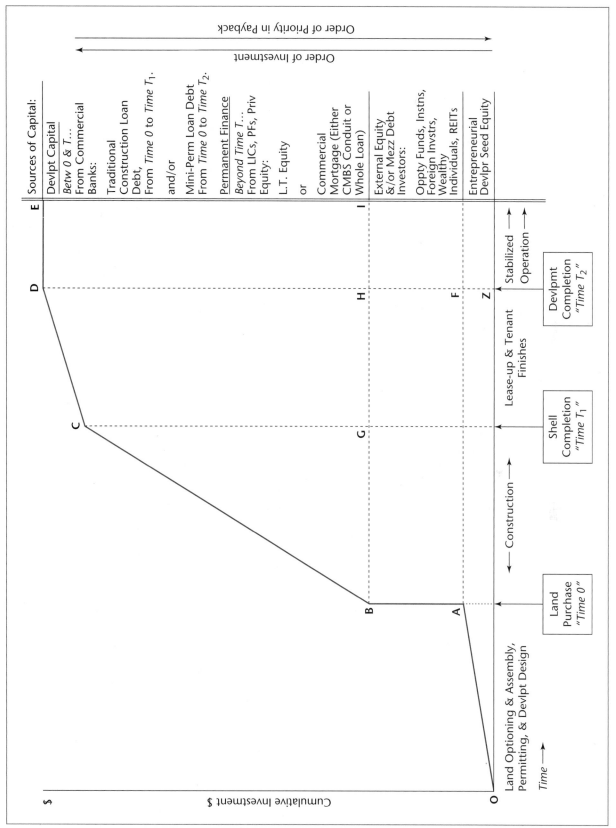

EXHIBIT 28-3 Development Project Typical Sources of Investment Capital

© OnCourse Learning

The figure contains the following labels:

Sources of Capital:

Devlpt Capital
Betw 0 & T...
From Commercial
Banks:

Traditional
Construction Loan
Debt,
From *Time 0 to Time T₁.*

and/or

Mini-Perm Loan Debt
From *Time 0 to Time T₂.*

Permanent Finance
Beyond Time T...
From LICs, PFs, Priv
Equity:

L.T. Equity

or

Commercial
Mortgage (Either
CMBS Conduit or
Whole Loan)

External Equity
&/or Mezz Debt
Investors:

Oppty Funds, Instns,
Foreign Invstrs,
Wealthy
Individuals, REITs

Entrepreneurial
Devlpr Seed Equity

Order of Priority in Payback

Order of Investment

Cumulative Investment $

$

Time

Land Optioning & Assembly,
Permitting, & Devlpt Design

Construction

Lease-up & Tenant
Finishes

Stabilized Operation

Land
Purchase
"Time 0"

Shell
Completion
"Time T₁"

Devlpmt
Completion
"Time T₂"

return available after subsequent senior capital providers have been paid their preferred returns. Given the entrepreneurial developer's normally small investment (in absolute dollar terms), the result can be very large percentage returns, when the project is successful. (For example, it would not be uncommon for an entrepreneurial investor to have an expected return in the neighborhood of the 40 percent OCC suggested in Exhibit 28-2 for capital invested during the Preliminary Phase.) This structure provides the entrepreneurial investor with the maximum incentive to see the project through to successful completion. As the success of the project normally depends most heavily on this developer's expertise, ability, and effort, this is an appropriate, and important, incentive structure.

The external equity investors' investment is represented in the ABIF region of Exhibit 28-3. As noted, this capital normally pays largely for the land purchase, which may or may not include some profit to the entrepreneurial developer. This purchase happens at *Time 0* and kicks off the development project *per se*. This equity investment is normally necessary to secure debt financing in the form of a construction loan. Construction loans normally require first liens on the property, and they require some preexisting equity investment to provide a degree of default (credit loss) protection to the lender.

The external equity investment (possibly including some subordinated debt vehicles such as "mezz debt") is a high risk investment that is looking for high returns if the project is successful. However, such investors will typically accept a less-than-proportional payment of residual returns (after principal payback, relative to the entrepreneurial developer) in return for seniority over the entrepreneurial developer in earning "preferred returns," which are typically intermediate in value.

For example, a typical arrangement might be as follows. Upon completion of the project, the construction lender is paid first, providing perhaps a 6 percent return to the construction loan (assuming no default). Remaining available value in the project then accrues to the external equity and entrepreneurial developer *pari passu* (proportional to their investments) until their investment principal is returned, or, depending on the arrangement, perhaps up until a prespecified preferred return is earned by both partners. In some cases the external equity investors might be paid on a preferred basis until they have earned a prespecified hurdle. Preferred returns might be on the order of 10 percent or so, depending on how risky the project appeared to be at the time of the partnership agreement, and how much external capital was needed by the entrepreneurial developer (and also depending on the seniority structure in the arrangement and on how the remaining residual is to be split). Finally, any remaining value in the project after preferred returns are paid is split in a nonproportional way, with the entrepreneurial developer receiving more than her *pro rata* share (earning a "promote"), but still providing the external equity investors with some considerable additional upside potential. (Exactly how much more varies from case to case.) Including this expected residual component, the external equity might be looking for expected returns in the neighborhood of 20 percent (as suggested by the OCC in Exhibit 28-2 based on the time when the external equity capital came in), but possibly with an asymmetric rightward skew in the return probability if the preferred return has seniority.[15] As noted in Chapter 15, there are infinite specific variations on this general framework of capital structure for the equity portion of the development project's financing.

As noted, the bulk of the actual development capital will typically come in the form of a first-lien construction loan. A classical construction loan will cover the BCG triangle in Exhibit 28-3, covering only (but often *all* of the) construction costs to the physical completion of the project. If the project has a lease-up phase and requires working capital[16] during

---

[15]If the external equity is given seniority in the claim on the preferred return, then there will be ex ante a return probability "spike" at the preferred return rate (for example, 10%), with very small probabilities of earning substantially *more* than the ex ante expectation (for example, 20%). The result is a rightward-skewed return probability distribution. (Though there is also some possibility of earning *less than* the preferred return, including in the worst case a total loss of the equity investment.) However, be careful about taking the 20% target noted here too literally. Development investment returns can be defined in different ways. See for example, Carey (2006), and Altshuler & Schneiderman (2011). (Also see our discussion in Chapter 29.)

[16]Working capital refers to operating cash flow deficits that occur when the building is incurring operating expenses (probably including marketing and leasing expenses) not yet fully offset by rental income revenue.

THE TREND TOWARDS GREENER DEVELOPMENT

The term **sustainable development** refers to real estate development projects with physical characteristics that promote environmental and social improvement. The term "green" is also used to describe sustainable development, though sustainability is not restricted just to environmental considerations; it includes factors such as historical preservation and social and community enhancement. In the twenty-first century green development is especially focused on energy efficiency and the closely related concern about the "carbon footprint" of the construction and operation of the project (considering the entire life cycle, including potential effects of ultimate demolition).

Development has become increasingly green, which is typically defined as either reaching Energy Star label certification or LEED (Leadership in Energy and Environmental Design) certification, or both, or in some cases other measurement standards as we first discussed in Chapter 5 (see boxed feature on page 97). Of course, a fundamental question is whether the costs to develop or retrofit buildings with more sustainable features that save energy or reduce carbon impact are worthwhile? In fact, the new reality is that for investors and developers who are thinking about the long run (if they are at all considering the obsolescence factor in the structures they are building) there is little choice today but to build to a higher standard. This is true for all property usage types. However, the office sector has been the leader in terms of market penetration, with over 15 percent of the U.S. stock now "green" by some measure. But the market standards for all property types are constantly being redefined, and many tenants insist upon such higher standards, such as federal General Services Administration (GSA).[1]

The cost of becoming LEED-certified or Energy Star-labeled is generally minimal to hit the lowest levels of LEED certification (up to "silver") when an experienced contractor and design team is involved. By 2012 many vendors were available in most major markets, providing a variety of improved products and systems ranging from roofs to rainwater capture to urinals to windows to photovoltaic cells and more. However, mastering the learning curve takes time, and not everybody in all markets is convinced that raising the sustainability of a building requires only modest additional investment. Further, the alignment of incentives between landlords and tenants has been an impediment to some less proven technologies that claim to save energy or water, since the landlord requires higher rents to pay for such improvements while the tenants want to see operational costs savings or greater employee productivity before they will pay higher rents. Yet both of these now seem clearly demonstrated. A number of studies have investigated the economics of greening up a portfolio.[2]

In a highly influential study, Eichholtz, Kok, and Quigley documented large and positive effects on market rents and selling prices following environmental certification of office buildings. Furthermore, this capitalization of greenness into rents and values applies to both new construction and retrofits, as shown by Kok, Miller, and Morris in a 2012 study. Rental premiums vary by local market but tend to run 5 percent or so above similar buildings that are not Energy Star or LEED. Premiums for selling prices per square foot are as high as 16 percent. Other studies (Fuerst and McAllister, 2011; Miller, Spivey and Florance, 2008) confirm these findings. Moreover, these results appear robust over the course of the 2008–2009 financial crisis. Other studies mention evidence suggesting positive economic benefits from faster absorption, higher occupancy rates, lower operating expenses, higher residual values as well as greater occupant productivity.[3] What all this means is that no developer of office property will want to develop a building that does not meet a higher benchmark for energy efficiency than the typical building now standing.

Tenants want three features more than any others: natural light, temperature control, and good ventilation. This applies to all property types, but especially office and retail. Whether new development or retrofits, we find the following are common upgrades:

- Reduced plug loads by monitoring occupancy and automatically turning things off when not in use.
- Lighting with LEDs and fluorescents and occupancy sensors that turn off or adjust lighting to the natural light available
- Windows that open; ventilation which is more occupant controllable
- Cooling with chilled beams, under-floor vents, natural air, and screening out the sun's heat by design
- Heating passively with the sun by design and more efficient fuels such as natural gas fuel cells or solar concentrators
- Wind turbines, PV solar cells, reduced water flow features, natural landscaping, and using captured rain water and gray water (water from the building sinks) for irrigation.
- Better insulation and vented wall designs with better glass glazing that reflects heat
- More use of local and recycled materials as well as renewable wood stocks
- No use of toxic chemicals in carpets or glues or wood products

While office property has witnessed the greatest green penetration, we are now observing rapid ramp up for all property types, forcing developers to learn about new technologies and designs, as well as new materials and new benchmarks by which to monitor property performance. Commissioning a building, such as by Energy Star or LEED certification, is the process by which developers improve the operation of the heating, cooling, lighting, and ventilation, so that the building is comfortable and safe as well as efficient. This is becoming standard practice as well.

(continued)

ADDITIONAL RESOURCES

The Journal of Sustainable Real Estate
U.S. Green Building Council
Global Real Estate Sustainability Benchmark (GRESB)
Energy Star Portfolio Manager Information for Commercial
Properties at the EPA
Additional sustainability references appear at the end
of this chapter.

[1]See www.GRESB.com for a group of investors and commercial real estate firms committed to greater market transparency and reporting.
[2]Some of these are mentioned on the reference pages at the end of Part II.
[3]See Pivo, 2010, Fuerst and McAllister, 2009, Miller and Pogue, 2009, Miller, Florance and Spivey, 2008, Miller, Pogue, Saville and Tu, 2010 as examples from the references below.

that period subsequent to construction completion but prior to stabilization, a "bridge loan" may be necessary to cover the GCDH region. Alternatively, a so-called "mini-perm" construction loan may be arranged at the outset, which covers construction costs plus working capital through to stabilization of the property (region BCDH in the exhibit).

Upon stabilization (full or nearly full steady-state occupancy), the construction loan will be paid off using so-called "permanent financing." This can be obtained in the form of either long-term equity and/or a long-term commercial mortgage. The mortgage may come either from a conduit CMBS lender, or from a whole loan portfolio lender (as was described in Part VI of this book). Such long-term investment in stabilized assets, whether equity or debt, normally comes from relatively conservative institutional sources, such as pension funds, life insurance companies, as well as endowment funds, foreign investors, and wealthy private individuals. On an unlevered (property-level) basis, the stabilized asset investor might be looking for an 8 percent return (as suggested by the OCC in Exhibit 28-2), or even less for institutional quality property.[17]

With this overview of the overall real estate development process in mind, we will now focus in the remainder of this chapter on the investment analysis and evaluation of the central step in this process, the construction phase described here, including the commitment of the land to the development project. The commitment of the land and the construction includes the vast bulk of the total capital expenditure on the development project. In focusing on this phase of the process, however, we will keep in mind both the preliminary phase and the subsequent lease-up phase, and we will relate some of our discussion to these phases as well.

28.2 Basic Information: Enumerating Project Costs and Benefits

In the iterative process depicted in Exhibit 28-1, one of the information products that needs to be refined progressively is a realistic budget for the project. In fact, two types of budget are important in development projects, each focusing on a different time period or phase of the project. The first is called the **construction and absorption budget**. It covers the period from the beginning of construction until the building is fully leased and operational. It relates to the investment *cost* side of the NPV equation and includes the cost of land acquisition (or opportunity cost of land development), site preparation, hard and soft construction and design costs, and lease-up costs including the need for working capital until the building breaks even. The second type of budget is known as the **operating budget**. It covers the period beyond the end of the absorption or lease-up of the new structure. The projected operating budget underlies the *benefit* side of the NPV equation, namely, the value of the newly completed built property. This value, as we know from Part IV of this book, is based on the projected net cash flows the completed building is expected to generate.

---

[17]Required return expectations in real estate have been declining in recent years, as they have in other major investment asset classes. Arguably, by 2005, such returns were less than 8% in the United States, especially for institutional grade property. See our previous discussions in Chapters 7, 11, and 22, regarding the OCC for real estate investments.

In analyzing development projects, the operating budget and the resulting estimate of completed project value are often focused on a single so-called **stabilized** year, with valuation based on direct capitalization of that year's NOI rather than on a multiyear DCF analysis. Such a budget is referred to as a *stabilized annual operating budget,* as it applies to a point at which the building's cash flow has become more or less stable, reflecting the building's long-run ongoing operating characteristics.[18] As such, the operating budget is typically characterized by items you became familiar with in Chapter 11:

Potential gross income (PGI)

− Vacancy allowance

= Effective gross income (EGI)

− Operating expenses (and capital reserve)

= Net operating income (NOI)

The development of the operating budget is derived from analysis of the relevant space market, the upper-right quadrant in Exhibit 28-1, based fundamentally on the principles of urban economics and the methods of market analysis.[19]

The other side of the NPV equation, the cost side dealt with in the construction and absorption budget, is a very different animal. It arises from the lower-right-hand quadrant in Exhibit 28-1, based fundamentally on the engineering and architectural disciplines. The major component of the construction and absorption budget typically concerns the construction phase. Costs associated with this phase are traditionally divided into two major categories: **hard costs** and **soft costs**. The former includes the direct cost of the physical components of the construction project: building materials and labor. Soft costs typically include just about everything else in the construction phase, such as design, legal, and financing costs. (The latter includes the interest on the construction loan.) Land acquisition or opportunity cost is sometimes classified as a soft cost, although it is more commonly treated as a hard cost, or as a separate item altogether. Typical hard and soft cost items are shown here:

Hard Costs	Soft Costs
• Land cost	• Loan fees
• Site preparation costs (e.g., excavation, utilities installation)	• Construction interest
	• Legal fees
• Shell costs of existing structure in rehab projects	• Soil testing
• Permits	• Environmental studies
• Contractor fees	• Land planner fees
• Construction management and overhead costs	• Architectural fees
• Materials	• Engineering fees
• Labor	• Marketing costs including advertisements
• Equipment rental	• Leasing or sales commissions
• Tenant finish	
• Developer fees	

---

[18]Recall from our discussion of direct capitalization versus multiyear DCF valuation in Chapter 10 that the latter is most valuable when there is a need to account for existing ("vintage") long-term leases in the property, leases that may have been signed prior to the current conditions in the rental market, or when there is a lease expiration pattern that is not typical for the type of property in question. Of course, development projects usually do not have vintage leases, and it normally does not make sense to expect that they will have atypical lease expiration patterns. Thus, it is usually a reasonable shortcut in analyzing development projects to use the simpler direct-capitalization evaluation procedure for the (projected) completed building, rather than a full-blown multiyear DCF procedure.

[19]A detailed exposition of this quadrant is beyond the scope of this book, although a basic introduction to space market analysis was provided in Chapter 6.

In addition to the construction phase, many development projects will also require the developer to budget for an **absorption** or **lease-up phase**, as indicated by the last items in the previous list. An absorption budget will be necessary when the project is being built at least partially "**on spec**" (short for "on speculation"); in other words, at least some of the space in the project is not preleased at the time the development decision is being made. The developer must line up in advance the financial resources necessary to carry the project through to the break-even point. In addition to working capital necessary to operate a less-than-full building, the absorption phase budget often requires particular expenditures for marketing the new building. The absorption phase may include major expenditures on leasing commissions and tenant improvements or **build-outs**.[20]

From a property-level cash flow perspective, the absorption phase may be considered to be over when the new building begins to break even on a current cash flow basis. However, from a financial perspective, the absorption phase continues until the building is stabilized (as this term was defined earlier, that is, until the building is at or near its expected long-term occupancy level). Not until the stabilization point is reached does the investment risk in the asset fall to that of a fully operational ongoing property, and only then is the permanent lender typically willing to provide a traditional long-term commercial mortgage.

28.3 Construction Budget Mechanics

A key feature of development projects is the fact that construction takes place over a period of time, typically several months to over a year depending on the scale and complexity of the project. Both in theory and in practice, the effect of the temporal spread of construction costs is often dealt with through the device of a **construction loan**, which enables the developer to avoid most cash outflows until the project is completed, at which time the construction loan must be paid back including interest that has accrued on the funds drawn down during the construction project. We will review the basic mechanics of construction loans in this section.[21]

When a construction loan is initially signed, it normally provides for a specified maximum amount of cash for the developer, in the form of **future advances**, based on the projected construction budget and schedule. Funds are **drawn down** out of this commitment as they are needed to pay for construction put in place. The lender verifies the physical construction before disbursing each **draw**. In the classical construction loan, the developer/borrower typically pays no cash back to the bank until the project is completed.[22] At that point, the developer may take out a **permanent loan** secured by the built property and use the proceeds from this loan to pay back the construction lender. Of course, this is not the only way to pay off the construction loan, as the developer may invest his own equity at that point, or may obtain long-term equity partners, or may sell the property.

During the construction period, the developer will draw down the construction loan based on a schedule agreed to at the outset. For smaller projects, invoices and receipts from sub-contractors along with affidavits that all prior work has been completed and paid for will usually suffice for the lender, along with some site inspections, to be sure that the work and materials specified in the budget have actually been used. For large projects, cash might be drawn down from the loan commitment based on a completion schedule of construction phases, such as site preparation, foundation work, framing, and so on, with each component

---

[20]Build-outs (or tenant finish) are tenant improvements on unfinished space, for example, to finish and customize space for a specific long-term tenant.

[21]See section 16.1 in Chapter 16 for an overview of the commercial mortgage industry and the role of construction loans in that industry.

[22]In recent years, and especially for large loans, it is not uncommon for interest-only payments to be required on the current balance on an ongoing basis, even during the construction process.

resulting in the draw for a certain percentage of the total loan. Even though the construction budget normally includes contingency amounts for unexpected costs, lenders often hold back a reserve in the range of 10 percent of the total construction budget. This reserve will only be paid out when the project is completed, as evidenced by a **certification of occupancy** from the local building inspection authority.

At the time the construction loan is being negotiated, the lender will often require an engineering review of the proposed construction budget. At that time, the construction lender will also typically consider the projected lease-up phase and review the projected stabilized operating budget of the completed building from the perspective of permanent loan underwriting criteria, as described in Chapter 18. The construction lender needs to feel confident that the completed project will support a permanent loan sufficient to pay off the construction loan.[23] A permanent loan that is used to pay off a construction loan is often referred to as a **take-out loan**. Indeed, the classical method of construction lending is for the institution making the construction loan to require that the developer obtain a commitment in advance by a permanent lender, sufficient to cover the projected construction loan balance due. The permanent lender considers the projected loan/value (LTV) ratio and debt service coverage ratio (DCR) forecasted for the completed project before committing to the permanent loan.[24] The permanent loan commitment is often contingent on the building achieving a certain occupancy or rent level by a certain time.[25]

In order to develop the construction budget and estimate the amount of cash the developer will have to come up with at the time of project completion (or the amount he must borrow in the take-out loan), a key calculation needs to be performed of the **accrued interest** that will be due when the construction loan is paid off. For example, for a construction loan with an 8 percent interest rate (per annum, monthly compounding), the accrual of interest in the loan balance is illustrated in the following table for the first three months of a construction project, in which a total of $2.75 million of direct construction cost has been expended and financed by the loan. Note that the loan balance exceeds this direct cost amount ($2,780,100 is greater than $2,750,000). This is the effect of the time value of money (including a risk premium for the construction lender), as unpaid accrued interest is added to the balance and compounded forward across time.[26]

Month	New Draw	Current Interest	New Loan Balance
1	$ 500,000	$ 3,333.33	$ 503,333.33
2	$ 750,000	$ 8,355.55	$1,261,688.88
3	$1,500,000	$18,411.26	$2,780,100.14
4	and so on		

In the example in the table, the interest at the end of the first month is computed as $3,333.33 = $500,000(0.08/12). This accrued interest then becomes part of the loan balance on which further interest will accrue. The interest computation in the second month is thus $8,355.55 = ($503,333.33 + $750,000)(0.08/12). The balance at the end of the second

---

[23]Note that, as the permanent loan will typically not be made for more than a 75% LTV ratio, this implies that the construction costs must generally be less than the total value of the completed project. The difference represents the developer's equity in the project, which often equates more or less to the cost of the land.

[24]See Chapter 18, section 18.2.1, for an explanation of these and other commercial mortgage underwriting criteria.

[25]Sometimes the lease-up phase is covered in the construction loan (a "mini-perm" loan), and sometimes it is covered in a separate "bridge loan."

[26]In the example in the table, it is assumed that the draws are made at the *beginning* of each month, and the loan balance refers to the balance at the *end* of the month. This is the most common approach for budgeting, although end-of-month draws or beginning-of-month balances are sometimes used. For budgeting purposes, it does not matter which assumption is made, as long as the requisite interest is accrued as soon as funds are disbursed from the bank. (This is an application of the "four rules" of loan payment and balance computation described in section 17.1.1 of Chapter 17.)

month is computed as $1,261,688.88 = $503,333.33 + $750,000 + $8,355.55. This type of accrual and compounding of interest continues until the construction project is complete. The total balance due on the loan then includes both the direct construction costs and the **financing cost**, or cost of construction capital, namely, the interest on the funds borrowed for construction. In the typical construction budget, this interest cost is listed as a separate item.

28.4 Simple Financial Feasibility Analysis in Current Practice

With the preceding information as background, let's turn to the typical current practice of financial analysis of development projects, focusing on the financial feasibility of the project. This is best done by considering some concrete examples. For this purpose we can call on Bob (you may have guessed), who is a typical real estate developer on Main Street. Bob owns several strategically located, commercially zoned vacant land parcels in Midwest City, and he specializes in building small to medium-size office and retail buildings. Some of his projects can be characterized as a site looking for a use, while others are better described as a use looking for a site. His overall project design and decision-making process can be well described by the iterative approach depicted in Exhibit 28-1. To deal with the financial analysis aspect of this process (the upper-left-hand quadrant in Exhibit 28-1), Bob employs a simple, easy-to-understand methodology. We will call this methodology **simple financial feasibility analysis (SFFA)**, and we will describe it in this section.

28.4.1 Simple Feasibility Analysis Explained

The basic idea in SFFA is, well, *simple*. It is assumed that the developer will "borrow to the hilt," that is, he will take out the maximum permanent loan the completed project will support. (After all, this is what Bob usually does.) With this assumption, Bob does not need to know (or to assume) anything about the capital market except what he can easily observe in the commercial mortgage market. Through his contacts among local mortgage brokers and bankers, Bob can easily keep track of current mortgage interest rates and underwriting criteria such as the maximum allowable LTV ratio and DCR requirements. Combined with the borrow-to-the-hilt assumption, this information is sufficient to ascertain either what sort of rental market is required given a land and construction cost, or what sort of land and/or construction cost can be afforded given a rental market for a completed structure. In other words, Bob can apply SFFA to address the financial feasibility of both the site-looking-for-a-use and the use-looking-for-a-site types of projects.

Take the site looking for a use first. The procedure Bob uses in this case to analyze financial feasibility often starts with a presumed land and construction cost and ends with the required minimum rent per square foot of built structure that will be necessary to make the project financially feasible.[27] The specific steps in this procedure are shown in Exhibit 28-4.

A good example of this procedure in action was a rehab opportunity Bob considered recently. A certain class B office building in a fantastic location had been recently vacated by a major owner/occupant. The building was 30,000 gross SF with 27,200 SF of leaseable area. Bob knew that rents for class C + or B– space in that location were running around $10/SF per year with most operating expenses passed through to the tenants.[28]

---

[27]When the developer already controls the site, he typically has a fairly firm idea of how much the land is worth. The land value, combined with legal/political and architectural/engineering considerations, typically then provides a general implication for the usage type and the scale or magnitude of project that probably makes sense. This, in turn, suggests the rough magnitude of construction cost that would make sense. (In principle, the hurdle benefit/cost ratio described in section 27.5 of Chapter 27 is relevant in this regard, suggesting the magnitude of construction that would make immediate development optimal.) In the iterative analysis, design, and decision-making process characteristic of development projects, this cost information then begs to be checked against what the demand in the space market will support.

[28]Note the iterative nature, or circularity, of the development analysis procedure. Even though this is a site looking for a use, Bob already has a rough idea of the use, at least in terms of the typical market rents.

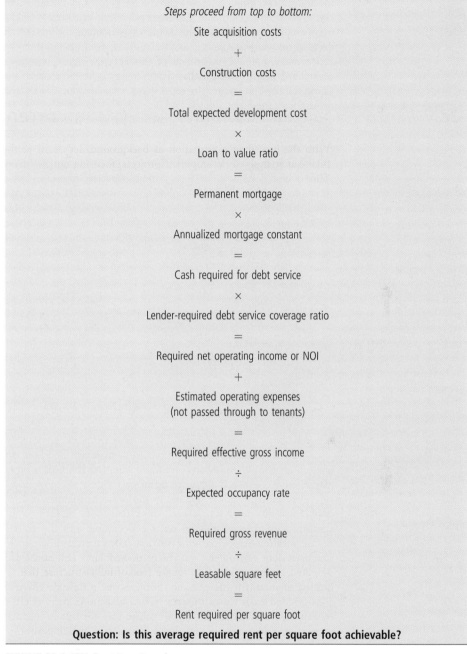

Steps proceed from top to bottom:

Site acquisition costs

+

Construction costs

=

Total expected development cost

×

Loan to value ratio

=

Permanent mortgage

×

Annualized mortgage constant

=

Cash required for debt service

×

Lender-required debt service coverage ratio

=

Required net operating income or NOI

+

Estimated operating expenses
(not passed through to tenants)

=

Required effective gross income

÷

Expected occupancy rate

=

Required gross revenue

÷

Leasable square feet

=

Rent required per square foot

Question: Is this average required rent per square foot achievable?

EXHIBIT 28-4 SFFA Front-Door Procedure

© OnCourse Learning

Bob was pretty sure he could buy the building for $660,000 and fix it up for about $400,000 in hard costs and $180,000 in soft costs including funds for a new marketing program, financing during rehab, and operating costs during the lease-up period, which he estimated would take only a few months. A local lender indicated that they would provide an 80 percent LTV mortgage with a 120 percent DCR if Bob personally signed on the note for 20 percent of the loan balance. The interest rate was 11.5 percent on a fixed rate 20-year amortization monthly payment mortgage. Bob's market research indicated that less than 5 percent vacancy was typical for well-located newly rehabbed projects. Given the superior location of this building, Bob figured a 95 percent stabilized occupancy rate was, if anything, conservative. Bob estimated stabilized operating expenses at $113,000 per year based on prior occupant figures. Even though some of this might be passed through to the tenants, Bob decided to assume initially that the landlord would bear all of these expenses, in order to be conservative, and because much of this expense figure was based on an old (but efficient) centralized heating system that made energy costs difficult to prorate to individual tenants. The question Bob wanted to get a quick take on was, "What are the required rents for this project and, therefore, does it look feasible?"

Applying the procedure in Exhibit 28-4, here is how Bob answered his question:

Site and shell costs:	$ 660,000
+ Rehab costs:	580,000
= Total costs (assumed equal to value):	$1,240,000
× Lender-required LTV	80 percent
= Permanent mortgage amount:	$ 992,000
× Annualized mortgage constant:[29]	0.127972
= Cash required for debt service:	$ 126,948
× Lender-required DCR:	1.20
= Required NOI:	$ 152,338
+ Estimated operating expenses (landlord):	113,000
= Required EGI:	$ 265,338
÷ Projected occupancy (1-vac):	0.95
= Required PGI:	$ 279,303
÷ Rentable area:	27,200 SF
= Required rent/SF:	$ 10.27/SF

Financial feasibility appears to require a gross rent of a little over $10/SF. As Bob's assumptions in applying the previous procedure were (he believed) a bit on the conservative side, and market rents did indeed appear to be around $10/SF, the project looked feasible to Bob.[30]

The SFFA procedure applied in the previous manner is sometimes referred to as **front-door feasibility analysis**. A **back-door feasibility analysis** would go in the reverse order: starting from expected market rents and ending with the amount that can be afforded for site acquisition. Back-door analyses are more typical of use-looking-for-a-site type projects. The back-door version of the SFFA is presented in Exhibit 28-4.

An example application of the back-door version of SFFA was another recent project Bob considered. In this case, the project was a new development, an office building with 35,000 SF of **gross leaseable area (GLA)** and an 85 percent **efficiency ratio**, implying a **net rentable area (NRA)** of 29,750 SF.[31] The idea for this project came from a former business partner of Bob's who was interested in leasing a major portion of such a building, and who

---

[29]From Chapters 8 and 17, we have the monthly mortgage constant:

$$(0.115/12)/[1-1/(1+0.115/12)^{240}] = 0.010664.$$

This figure times 12 is the annual constant: $0.010664 \times 12 = 0.127972$.

[30]Note that to apply this procedure Bob had to assume that the value of the completed project as it would be judged or appraised by the lender would be at least equal to his total projected construction cost of $1.24 million. His familiarity with the local-property-asset market suggested that typical cap rates for similar buildings once fully rented seemed to be around 10.5%. Applying this to the projected NOI of $152,338 implied a projected property value of $1.451 million, well over the $1.24 million construction cost, so Bob felt he was safe in this regard.

[31]Gross leaseable area (GLA) is the total interior space in the structure, including common areas such as lobbies and corridors. Net rentable area (NRA) is the space tenants directly pay for in their leases. Rents are typically quoted in the space market per NRA square foot.

believed that Bob was quite capable of delivering on such a development project in an efficient and effective manner.

Bob believed that, given the proposed design and tenant finishings, the achievable rent in this building would be about $12/SF in any of several suburban neighborhoods where office buildings of this type were in demand in Midwest City. Preliminary design work indicated that the hard and soft costs, excluding site acquisition, would be about $2.14 million. Vacancy rates in the types of space markets relevant for this building were running 8 percent on average. Based on past experience, Bob estimated that operating expenses not passed through to tenants would be $63,000 per year. For this project the permanent lender wanted a DCR of 120 percent and an LTV of no more than 75 percent of finished value, with 9.0 percent interest and 20-year amortization. Bob found a potential site for the project that looked quite promising. The owner of the site wanted $500,000. Bob needed to decide whether it was worth it. He answered this question according to the steps in Exhibit 28-5, as follows:

Potential gross revenue (29,750 × $12):	$ 357,000
− Vacancy at 8%:	$ 28,560
= Effective gross income:	$ 328,440
− Operating expenses not passed on:	$ 63,000
= Net operating income:	$ 265,440
÷ 1.20 (required debt coverage):	$ 221,200
÷ 12 (monthly debt service):	$ 18,433
⇒ Supportable mortgage amount:	$2,048,735
÷ 0.75 LTV (= minimum required value):	$2,731,647
− Construction cost:	$2,140,000
= Supportable site acquisition cost:	$ 591,647

As $591,647 is greater than the $500,000 price the seller was asking for the site, Bob concluded that this project was financially feasible.[32]

28.4.2 Problems with the Simple Approach

The SFFA procedures described here are widely used by developers in real world practice. They have the advantage of being simple and easy to understand without much financial economic expertise. In particular, they do not require any knowledge or assumptions about the capital market or property asset market beyond what can be observed easily in the commercial mortgage market. They are sound enough to have some practical utility as a "back of envelope" tool for preliminary analysis. But it is important to recognize that the SFFA procedures *do not provide a complete or correct financial economic evaluation of a development project.*

As we have noted before, the decision to undertake a real estate development project is a capital budgeting decision, in effect, a capital allocation decision at the micro-level, fundamentally like any other micro-level investment decision in the private real estate asset market. The NPV decision rule that we introduced in Part IV of this book tells whether such

---

[32]Note the sensitivity of this result to the loan interest rate. If the rate were 50 basis points higher, at 9.5%, the affordable loan would be only $1,977,511, resulting in maximum outlays at the 75% LTV of $2,636,682, and implied maximum feasible site acquisition costs of $496,682, less than the $500,000 price. Also note the assumptions that are imbedded in the back-door procedure. The 75% LTV ratio is applied to the estimated supportable loan to derive the minimum required finished building value from the lender's perspective. Yet the building might in fact be worth either more or less than this amount, depending on the prevailing cap rates in the property asset market. If the building would in fact be worth more than this amount, then Bob could actually afford to pay more than $591,647 for the site. If it would be worth less than the affordable loan divided by 0.75, then Bob could not afford to pay as much as $591,647. As you can see, it can often be instructive to apply sensitivity analysis to the SFFA procedure, in a manner similar to what we described in Chapter 11 regarding property valuation, and Chapter 15 regarding deal structuring.

Steps proceed from top to bottom:

Total leasable square feet
(based on the building efficiency ratio times the gross area)

×

Expected average rent per square foot

=

Projected potential gross income (PGI)

−

Vacancy allowance

=

Expected effective gross income

−

Projected operating expenses

=

Expected net operating income

÷

Debt service coverage ratio

÷

Annualized mortgage constant

÷

Maximum loan to value ratio

=

Maximum supportable total project costs
Question: Can it be built for this including all costs?

−

Expected construction costs (other than site)

=

Maximum supportable site acquisition cost
Question: Can the site be acquired for this or less?

EXHIBIT 28-5 SFFA Back-Door Procedure

© OnCourse Learning

decisions are in the interest of those investing their capital. To the extent that the developer is not just a fee-for-service provider, but is in fact a real estate investor as well (which is usually the case), the developer shares this capital budgeting perspective, and should consider **financial feasibility** from a broader and deeper perspective, that of **financial *economic* desirability**. The developer/investor is generally a landowner, either prior to the development or as a result of the development project. As such, the developer/investor wants to know whether it is *optimal* to proceed with the project, in the sense of the question: *Does undertaking the proposed development project now maximize the wealth of the landowner/developer?*

From this perspective, it is easy to see why the developer usually is (or should be) governed by the NPV investment decision rule. Recall from Chapter 10 that this rule requires that undertaking the project must not involve a negative NPV investment, and must maximize the ex ante NPV over all mutually exclusive feasible alternatives. The basis of the NPV rule in the wealth-maximization principle implies that *if the NPV rule is being violated, then money is being left on the table,* that is, the developer is reducing her net worth (or shareholder value) as a result of the project development decision, *compared to what she could have done instead.*

The SFFA procedures fail to account for the NPV rule because they do not quantify the value of the finished project, what we referred to in Chapter 27 as the underlying asset (V). Therefore, the SFFA procedures cannot possibly compute the NPV of the project, either explicitly or implicitly. As a corollary, they fail to provide or even allow for an estimation of the expected return (the going-in IRR) for the development phase of the project. In essence, they look only at how big a loan can be obtained and ignore the evaluation of the equity investment in the development. As a result of these shortcomings, the SFFA procedures make it difficult to relate development financial feasibility analysis and investment decision making to fundamental economic principles and to the mainstream of investment decision making in the broader capital market. To put it a bit simplistically, Wall Street wants to know the expected return to the development project equity so this can be compared to the relevant opportunity cost of capital (OCC).[33]

Even for the purpose of estimating financial feasibility, the SFFA procedures are needlessly restrictive and complex as a result of their implicit assumption that the completed project will be financed to the maximum possible extent with debt. This may be a plausible enough assumption for small individual developers on Main Street, but it is hardly realistic for larger-scale developers, especially those who tap the public equity markets for capital.

Because the SFFA procedures do not provide a complete or correct investment evaluation criterion, when developers use nothing but such procedures, they are placing the entire burden of making correct capital allocation decisions onto the *external* capital providers, typically the construction and permanent lenders. Yet these providers of debt capital have no equity directly at risk, and they face little upside potential from a successful project. Traditional lenders are in the business of investing in loans, and loans are much more homogeneous than real estate development equity, making the lending business more efficiently competitive and driving loan NPVs toward zero. It is a fundamental fact that debt investors do not face the same incentives that providers of equity capital do for making optimal capital allocation decisions about the physical assets.[34]

There is thus a broader social reason, for the sake of the efficiency of capital allocation in the economy, why it is important especially for larger-scale, more sophisticated developers to use financial analysis methods that are more sound from a financial economic and broad capital market perspective. We therefore turn in the next chapter to a discussion of how to apply fundamental economic principles in a more complete model to real estate development investment evaluation and decision making, including the NPV rule. While the primary focus of our presentation in Chapter 29 will be on the land commitment and construction phase of the overall development process outlined here in section 28.1, the basic NPV tool is applicable to the other phases as well.

---

[33]Note that, based on the project NPV estimation, the relevant frame of reference for making the investment decision can vary fundamentally depending on whether the decision maker (investor) is site-oriented or project-oriented. Recall in section 28.1 we pointed out that development projects tend to be either a site looking for a use or a use looking for a site, If it is the former (perspective of the owner of the site), then the relevant mutually exclusive alternatives over which the NPV should be maximized are the alternative uses for the given site. If the decision maker is a development firm (in combination with other passive investors) specializing in producing a certain type of development project, then the relevant mutually exclusive alternatives are other projects which the firm might otherwise undertake on alternate sites using a limited supply of available financial capital. But in either case, the fundamental metric of decision analysis and comparison is the NPV of the alternative projects. And clearly, any given project will have to pass both NPV tests in order to proceed, in principle. (In other words, a landowner will either have to be, or have to find, a willing developer.)

[34]In recent years, external equity capital has begun to play a larger role in the development phase, from sources such as opportunity funds and private equity partnerships. This could improve the economic quality of real estate development investment decision making, assuming that these sources of external equity capital apply economically sound and sophisticated investment analysis and decision principles, as typified in modern corporate finance, and as will be described in Chapter 29.

28.5 Chapter Summary

This chapter built on the theoretical treatment of land value and development timing presented in Chapter 27 to present an overview of the development decision-making process and the basic methodologies and procedures used in current development project feasibility analysis and construction budgeting. While useful at a practical level, these methods fall short of a rigorously grounded framework for development project investment analysis. This will be our subject in the next chapter.

KEY TERMS

site-looking-for-a-use
use-looking-for-a-site
lease-up risk
development project phases
construction and absorption budget
operating budget
stabilized (year or cash flows)
hard costs
soft costs
sustainable development
absorption or lease-up phase

on spec (speculative development)
tenant build-outs
construction loan
future advances
draw-down (of loan commitment)
draw
permanent loan
certification of occupancy
take-out loan
accrued interest

financing costs (construction loan interest)
simple financial feasibility analysis (SFFA)
front-door feasibility analysis
back-door feasibility analysis
gross leaseable area (GLA)
efficiency ratio
net rentable area (NRA)
financial feasibility
financial economic desirability

STUDY QUESTIONS

Conceptual Questions

28.1. Describe the four disciplines or professional perspectives that are involved in the design, analysis, and decision-making process of the typical real estate development project in the private sector.

28.2. What are the four phases of development projects? Give a rough indication of the typical relative amount of risk for financial capital invested in each phase by indicating typical expected returns (opportunity cost of capital) at each phase.

28.3. What are the major sources of financial capital for each of the development project phases noted above?

28.4. Describe the two types of budget that are necessary in the real estate development decision-making process.

28.5. Differentiate between hard and soft development costs.

28.6. How does a *construction* loan differ from a *permanent* mortgage loan? What is a *mini-perm* loan?

28.7. Describe the *front-door approach* to simple financial feasibility analysis? How does this differ from the *back-door approach*?

28.8. We argue in this chapter that SFFA analyses serve as useful preliminary financial analysis tools but should not be relied upon as the ultimate or complete model of the economic desirability or profitability of a proposed development project. What are the major problems or limitations of the simple financial feasibility analysis (SFFA) techniques in this regard?

Quantitative Problems

28.9. You wish to build an office/warehouse project, also known as R&D space or flex space. Market rents seem to be around $15/SF/year with a 5 percent vacancy rate in the local area. All expenses are passed through to tenants except property taxes, insurance, and management, which you estimate at $5/SF/year. Mortgage rates are 11 percent for a 20-year loan with a five-year balloon. Construction costs for your planned 20,000-gross-leaseable-square-foot project are estimated at $1,030,075 in total. All 20,000 SF are rentable. The debt service coverage ratio required is 120 percent, and the maximum LTV ratio is 75 percent.

    a. Use the SFFA *back-door* procedure to determine what you could pay for the land.

    b. Now assume total construction and site acquisition costs (i.e., total development costs) are $1.3 million. Use the *front-door* SFFA procedure to determine what the required rents would be per square foot. Recalculate the required rent assuming a vacancy rate of 15 percent.

28.10. The following table shows the projected draws to pay the construction costs of a project that is expected to take four months to complete. The draws are projected to occur at the beginning of each month. What is the projected balance due on a construction loan at the end of the fourth month if the interest rate is 10 percent per annum with monthly compounding?

Month	Draw
1	$1,000,000
2	$2,000,000
3	$1,500,000
4	$2,500,000

ADDITIONAL SUSTAINABILITY REFERENCES

Eichholtz, P., N. Kok, and J. Quigley. 2011. Doing well by doing good? Green office building. *American Economic Review*, 100(5): 2492–2509.

Fuerst, F., and P. McAllister. 2009. An investigation of the effect of eco-labeling on office occupancy rates. *Journal of Sustainable Real Estate*, 1(1): 49–64.

Kats, G. 2009. *Greening Our Built World: Costs, Benefits, and Strategies*. Washington, D.C.: Island Press.

Kok, N., N. Miller, and P. Morriss. 2012. The economics of green retrofits. *Journal of Sustainable Real Estate* 4.

Langdon, D. 2007. *Costs of Green Revisited*, July 2007, from http://www.davislangdon.com/USA/

May, P. J., and C. Koski. 2007. State environmental policies: Analyzing green building mandates. *Review of Policy Research* 24(1): 49–65.

Miller, E., and L. Buys. 2008. Retrofitting commercial office buildings for sustainability: Tenants' perspectives. *Journal of Property Investment and Finance* 26(6): 552–61.

Miller, N., J. Spivey, and A. Florance. 2008. Does green pay off? *Journal of Real Estate Portfolio Management* 14(4): 385–99.

Pivo, G. 2010. Owner-tenant engagement in sustainable property investing. *Journal of Sustainable Real Estate* 2(1): 183–99.

Pivo, G., and Jeff Fisher. 2011. The walkability premium in commercial real estate investments. *Real Estate Economics*, forthcoming 39(2): 185–219.

Simons, R. A., E. Choi, and D. M. Simons. 2009. The effect of state and city green policies on the market penetration of green commercial buildings. *Journal of Sustainable Real Estate* 1(1): 139–66.

Wiley, J. A., J. D. Benefield, and K. H. Johnson. 2010. Green design and the market for commercial office space. *Journal of Real Estate Finance and Economics* 41(2): 228–43.

CHAPTER

29

INVESTMENT ANALYSIS OF REAL ESTATE DEVELOPMENT PROJECTS, PART 2: ECONOMIC ANALYSIS

CHAPTER OUTLINE

LEARNING OBJECTIVES

After reading this chapter, you should understand:

⊃ The more rigorously correct NPV-based approach to financial evaluation of development projects.

⊃ The relationship of operational leverage to development project risk and return.

⊃ How to estimate the opportunity cost of capital or reasonable expected return for real estate development project investments.

⊃ The role of option valuation theory in analysis and evaluation of multiphase development projects.

The previous chapter introduced you to some of the major tools commonly used to examine the financial feasibility of real estate development projects. We also suggested, however, that those tools fall short in some important respects. Financial "feasibility" is not exactly the same thing as "desirability." And the tools used in current practice tend to be *ad hoc*, not grounded solidly in a rigorous economic framework, generally not fully considering the basic economic principles of market equilibrium and opportunity cost. This not only makes the *ad hoc* procedures subject to possible error or incompleteness, but it makes it difficult for real estate development investment analysis to communicate and relate in a coherent way to the mainstream investments and corporate finance world which is the source of ever more of the capital used to finance development (including not just debt but in recent years much equity capital). Finally, without a rigorous economic framework, the analyst and the decision maker lack the kind of deep understanding that can facilitate greater creativity and innovation in project conceptualization and deal formation.

It is the job of this chapter to remedy this deficiency. In earlier chapters we have already noted that the investment analysis of real estate development projects is essentially an exercise in capital budgeting, a term borrowed from corporate finance literature. Capital budgeting is the field from which the NPV rule arose. It is a micro-level investment decision arena whose basic concepts and principles were treated in Part IV of this book, particularly in Chapters 10 and 12. On top of that, Chapter 27 presented some important fundamental economic principles that relate particularly to real estate development project evaluation and decision making. What remains for us to do in the present chapter is to extend our treatment of this topic to a more practical level. In particular, we will examine how to apply the NPV investment decision procedure to the typical commercial property development project. We will do this in a framework that is consistent with the real options model we introduced in Chapter 27.

29.1 The Basic Idea

As we have said, the essential framework for applying sound financial economic theory to the investment evaluation of development projects is the correct application of the NPV rule. The basic NPV rule was presented and discussed in Chapter 10. In Chapter 14, we extended the basic rule to encompass the use of debt financing, making use of the value additivity principle and the APV rule as a useful shortcut that can avoid unnecessary muddying of the waters when nonsubsidized (market-rate) debt is employed. The principles and procedures introduced in those two chapters are completely applicable to the financial evaluation of development projects. In addition, our discussions of leverage in Chapter 13 and of the real option model of land value and optimal development timing in Chapter 27 are particularly relevant to development investment evaluation. In this section, we will get a bit more specific about this application. In particular, development projects are typically characterized by three somewhat unique features as compared to investments in existing, fully operational properties:

1. **Time-to-build**: In development projects the investment cash outflow is spread out in time, instead of occurring all at once up front. This gives development investments inherent "operational leverage," even if no financial leverage is employed.
2. **Construction loans**: Use of debt financing is almost universal in the construction phase of the typical development project, and this debt typically covers all of the construction cost.
3. **Phased risk regimes**: Because of the operational leverage noted above, development investment typically involves very different levels of investment risk between the construction (or development) phase, the absorption (or lease-up) phase, and the long-term (stabilized or permanent) phase when the completed project is fully operational. The result, as described at a broad-brush level in the first section of Chapter 28, is a very different economic opportunity cost of capital (OCC), and typically different sources of financial capital, for the different phases.

The correct application of the NPV rule to development projects requires a consideration of these three unique features.

29.1.1 Applying NPV to Development Projects

To begin this consideration, recall that in Chapter 10 we defined the NPV of the investment from the buyer's perspective as being equal to the difference between the value of the property being obtained and the cost of obtaining it, which we labeled as

$$NPV = V - P \qquad (1)$$

In the application to investment in existing properties, V is the value of the operating property being obtained, and P is the price of obtaining the property.

In order for the NPV rule to make sense, both the benefit and the cost must be measured in present, certainty-equivalent dollars, that is, in dollars adjusted for risk as of the time the investment decision is being made. Otherwise, we would be comparing apples to oranges. Labeling the present (decision time) as time *0*, we can clarify the NPV evaluation by subscripting the benefit and cost measures to indicate the point when they are measured, as follows:

$$NPV_0 = V_0 - P_0 \tag{1a}$$

In the case of investments in fully operational (stabilized) properties, it is relatively easy to estimate both the benefit and cost as of time *0* and thereby to quantify equation (1a) directly. In the case of development projects, the quantification of (1a) is a bit more complicated, because neither the benefit nor all of the cost is incurred up front at time *0*.

To see this point, let's consider a simple example. Hereandnow Place is a newly completed office property consisting of two buildings with a joint parking lot. Its expected property-before-tax cash flow (PBTCF) is $75,000 per month ($900,000/year, paid monthly), in perpetuity. The property investment market's required expected total return for assets like Hereandnow Place is 9 percent. In other words, the opportunity cost of capital—OCC—for investment in Hereandnow Place is 9 percent per year. We will assume that all rates of return are quoted as nominal annual rates with monthly compounding. Therefore, the 9 percent OCC equates to 9%/12 = 0.75% per month simple return. Thus, Hereandnow Place is worth $10 million today:

$$\$10,000,000 = \frac{\$75,000}{1.0075} + \frac{\$75,000}{1.0075^2} + \cdots = \frac{\$75,000}{0.0075}$$

Because markets are competitive, it is likely that Hereandnow Place would sell for $10 million and an investment in Hereandnow Place would therefore be made at zero NPV (at least from a market value perspective). Thus, the NPV of such an investment would be easily quantified as:

$$NPV_0 = V_0 - P_0 = \$10,000,000 - \$10,000,000 = 0 \tag{1b}$$

At the $10 million price, Hereandnow Place provides the investor with an expected return (going-in IRR) of 0.75 percent per month, or 9 percent per year (ENAR), or $1.0075^{12} - 1 = 9.38\%$ effective annual rate (EAR). Assuming that the risk-free interest rate in the capital market is 3 percent (ENAR, or 3.04 percent EAR), this implies a market risk premium in such investment in stabilized property equal to 6 percent (nominal, or 6.34% = 9.38% − 3.04% EAR).

Now across the street from Hereandnow Place is a vacant and developable land parcel identical to the site on which Hereandnow Place is built. The market for such office properties at this location is still strong, and it is clear that to build an essentially identical development to Hereandnow Place on this new site would indeed be the highest and best use of the site, and that it would make sense to commit irreversibly to such a development right away. Indeed, to eliminate lease-up risk as a source of difference between the development versus stabilized asset we will assume that the new development is already preleased (that is, a forward leasing commitment has been signed) with rental terms identical to those in Hereandnow Place. The new development, to be called FutureSpace Center, would involve construction costs that are contractually fixed and would have to be paid at four points in time, quarterly payments of $1.5 million each at the end of 3, 6, 9, and 12 months from the time when the development decision would be made ("time *0*," which we assume is now). The result would be that the first of the twin buildings would be completed and ready for occupancy six months from time *0*, and the second building would be completed and ready for occupancy 12 months from time *0*. Each FutureSpace Center building, which would be effectively just like the Hereandnow buildings, is expected to produce net cash flow of

$37,500 per month ($450,000/year) each from its time of completion, in perpetuity, based on the already committed leasing arrangements.

The essential development-investment-valuation question in this context is: *What is the price that can be paid today for the FutureSpace land site such that the development investment will be zero NPV?* This is the value of the land, the price the FutureSpace land site would presumably sell for in a competitive market. This question may be equivalently framed as: *What is the NPV of the development project investment apart from the land cost?* The answer to the question phrased in this way tells us not only what is the maximum price that can be paid for the land to produce a nonnegative NPV, but it also enables us to quantify what would be the NPV of the development investment given any specified land price.

To answer this question, we need to quantify V_0 and P_0 for the FutureSpace development project, the certainty-equivalent values of the benefits and costs of the project as of time 0, the present time. The benefits are, of course, the two new office buildings that will be built, and the costs, apart from the land, are the construction costs required to build the two buildings. We will label those construction costs as K. All we have to do is forecast the magnitudes and timings of these benefits and costs and then discount those projected values back to the present, using OCC discount rates appropriate to each type of projected cash flow.

Consider first the benefits, the to-be-completed office buildings similar to Hereandnow Place. The first FutureSpace building (named "FutureSpace One") will be completed in six months. At that time, it will represent an asset projected to be worth $5 million. This is because FutureSpace One will have the same OCC as Hereandnow Place (9 percent per annum nominal, or 0.75 percent per month simple), because FutureSpace One will be essentially the same type of asset as Hereandnow Place and, therefore, will present investors with the same amount of investment risk. Thus, upon its completion, FutureSpace One is expected to be worth:

$$\$5,000,000 = \frac{\$37,500}{1.0075} + \frac{\$37,500}{1.0075^2} + \cdots = \frac{\$37,500}{0.0075}$$

Similarly, the second new building, FutureSpace Two, is expected to be worth $5 million upon its completion in 12 months. Thus, we can compute V_0, the present value of the benefits of the development project, as $9.352 million, as follows:[1]

$$V_0 = \$9,352,000 = \frac{\$5,000,000}{1.0075^6} + \frac{\$5,000,000}{1.0075^{12}}$$

Note that we are simply projecting the values and timing of completion of the assets being produced in the development project and discounting those values back to present at the OCC rate appropriate to investments in such assets. It is as if we were actually planning to sell each building as soon as it is completed. In fact, we could do that, though we need not feel precommitted to doing so. We would get the same answer if we projected receiving the net rents from the first building for the six months from months 7 through 12, at which time we would have two assets worth $10 million together:

$$V_0 = \$9,352,000 = \sum_{t=7}^{12} \frac{\$37,500}{1.0075^t} + \frac{\$10,000,000}{1.0075^{12}}$$

Expressed this way, the equation seems to suggest that we are planning to sell the entire FutureSpace Center project upon its completion in 12 months. In fact, however, this is not necessarily implied by the equation. Whether we sell or keep FutureSpace Center, in month 12

---

[1]Note that what we are referring to as the gross "benefits" of the development project here equates to what we called in Chapter 27 the "underlying asset" of the land development *option*.

the development project is expected to produce an asset worth $10 million at that time (as well as having produced six months worth of net rents by then). We can decide later what to do with the asset.

The key point here at time *0* is that month 12 is the end of the development (or construction) phase of the investment. From that time onward, any continued investment on our part (or any new investment by a purchaser) would be a standard investment in a stabilized operating property as described in equation (1b) and like what we are familiar with analyzing in Chapters 10 and 11. Here we are interested in analyzing development project investments, so it makes sense to cut off the analysis horizon after month 12. As described previously, this is important from an investment-analysis perspective because the development phase investment has very different risk and return characteristics than the stabilized operating phase investment. Different types of investors will typically be interested in these two different phases, and "apples-to-apples" comparisons of risks and returns require that we not mixed investments of very different risk-and-return characteristics into a single, undifferentiated analysis frame.

Note that the present value of the gross benefits, V_0, is less for the development project FutureSpace Center than for the stabilized property Hereandnow Place across the street ($9.352 million versus $10 million), even though the buildings are identical. This is because part of Hereandnow Place's value is the present value of 12 months worth of $75,000/ month net cash flow from months 1 through 12. During the 12-month development phase, the FutureSpace Center project will only generate half that rate of monthly cash flow and for only the last six of the 12 months starting from time *0*. Obviously, this is because the FutureSpace buildings need to be built, whereas the Hereandnow buildings are already complete.

Now let's consider the cost side of the NPV equation. The FutureSpace Center project will require $6,000,000 of construction costs projected as four equal payments of $1.5 million at the end of months 3, 6, 9, and 12. The OCC relevant for discounting these cost outflows is not the same as the 9 percent rate we used to discount the project benefits. Remember from Chapter 10 that discount rate (OCC) must reflect the amount of risk in the asset values or cash flows being discounted, *as the capital market evaluates that risk.* We shall argue that the appropriate OCC for discounting the construction cost cash flows is, at least as a useful approximation, the risk-free interest rate of 3 percent per annum nominal (with monthly compounding, or 3%/12 = 0.25% per month simple).

This may require a little explanation. It probably seems odd to think of construction costs as being "riskless," when everyone knows that construction cost risk is a big concern of every developer. But keep in mind that when we say that a riskless opportunity cost of capital is the appropriate discount rate to translate projected construction costs across time, we are not using the concept of "risk" in the same way as a developer uses the word "risk" to describe a characteristic of the total construction bill he will ultimately face. The developer means that construction costs could turn out to be greater than first projected and because of such a threat to his profits the careful consideration of construction costs looms large in his thinking. This translates into the (wise) developer giving construction costs a "wide berth" in calculating expected development profits. That is, in effect, the developer builds in contingencies and gives construction costs a relatively large value (as a negative item) in the expected profit calculation. But this is exactly the result that is accomplished when we discount projected construction costs to time *0* using a low discount rate such as the risk-free OCC. The risk-free interest rate is low and hence results in a higher present-value magnitude of the negative item of construction costs when applied to the future projected construction expenditures. Furthermore, a risk-free (or nearly risk-free) OCC for construction costs makes sense from a financial economic viewpoint.

This can be seen from several perspectives. First, consider what could cause unexpected deviations in the raw, direct construction costs, the fundamental source of the developer's construction cost cash outflows. Essentially, these costs would deviate from prior expectations only as a result of engineering factors that change or that had not been accurately estimated to begin with. Such engineering issues will not tend to be correlated with financial or capital market factors, and therefore will lack "systematic risk" as defined in Chapter 22.[2] (In other words, the construction costs themselves will tend to present a zero "beta," in the terminology of the CAPM.) This type of risk can be diversified away and hence is not priced in the capital markets and, therefore, does not command a risk premium in the OCC. Second, in many cases, the developer will obtain a fixed-price or semi-fixed-price contract from the construction firm or general contractor. This will tend to reduce further the deviation in construction cost faced by the developer.

Finally, consider this question from the perspective of a construction lender. As noted, most construction costs in most developments are, in fact, financed by construction loans, typically issued by banks. These loans often carry fairly substantial interest rates in terms of spreads over short-term risk-free floating-rate bonds. But the construction loan interest rate is not the same thing as the lender's expected return on the loan, and it is the latter that reflects the OCC of the loan investment. As we discussed in Chapters 18 and 19, default risk and the resulting expected credit losses cause actual expected returns on loans to be lower than the contractual interest rates on the loans. Construction loan expected returns essentially equal their contractual interest rates minus their expected yield degradation due to credit loss risk. Construction loans are too short term to carry much interest rate risk,[3] but their short-term nature means that yield degradation from credit losses in the event of loan default can be very substantial.[4] Consequently, there is little need for much risk premium in construction loan expected returns, even as there is need for their contractual interest rates to carry substantial spreads over default-free short-term bond yields. When we strip away expected yield degradation, typical construction loan expected returns are probably not much greater than risk-free interest rates.

Although the construction lender's perspective is interesting, it is nevertheless important to note that the OCC of the construction loan is not the same as the OCC of the construction costs themselves. It is the latter that is relevant to the developer in evaluating the construction project. Recall from Chapter 14 that the market-value-based NPV of an equity investment is not affected by borrowing to finance the investment at market interest rates (unsubsidized loans), because the loan transaction itself is zero-NPV. In the case of construction lending, which is typically a rather competitive business, there is no reason to assume that the loan transaction itself, that is, the issuance of a market-rate construction loan, would in general be a nonzero NPV event. (Otherwise, competition in the construction lending industry and/or in the development industry would bid away supernormal profits and drive NPVs toward zero.) If construction lending per se is a zero-NPV event, then the present value as of time *0* of the construction loan's expected cash inflows (payments of interest and principle) must equal the present value as of time *0* of the construction cost cash outflows (that is, the construction draws the bank will pay), and this present value reflects the OCC appropriate to

[2]See Simonton (2004), and Wheaton and Simonton (2007). Their study examined over 60,000 actual contractor tender offers on office and apartment construction projects in six major and diverse metro areas spanning 1967–2004, and used "hedonic" regression to control for project scale and features. They found essentially no correlation between construction costs and the trading volume or price in the real estate market. They also found a secular trend of a slight decline in the real cost of construction over the historical period. In general, construction in the United States is apparently supplied with sufficient price elasticity such that perturbations in market demand do not much affect the price of construction materials, labor, and services. Similar results were found by Gyourko and Saiz (2006) using a different type and source of data.

[3]Actually, most construction loans are floating rate, and so have no interest rate risk from the bank's perspective. However, the floating rate loans are often "swapped" in the derivatives market for fixed-rate, such that the developer (borrower) actually experiences a fixed interest rate. In any case, interest rate risk is minimal in construction loans. But interest rate risk is quite different from default risk, as described in Chapters 18 and 19.

[4]Recall our illustration of loan yield degradation in section 18.1.1 of Chapter 18. In our example 10% loan there, a 30%-loss default in the third year of the loan caused an 1,112 basis-point yield degradation while a similar default in the second year caused a 1,711 bp degradation.

the construction cost outflows themselves which, we have argued, is near the risk-free interest rate.

With this in mind, we can now easily quantify the time *0* value of the cost component of our NPV equation:[5]

$$K_0 = \$5,889,000 = \frac{\$1,500,000}{1.0025^3} + \frac{\$1,500,000}{1.0025^6} + \frac{\$1,500,000}{1.0025^9} + \frac{\$1,500,000}{1.0025^{12}}$$

Thus, the NPV of the development project investment as of time *0*, apart from land cost, is:

$$V_0 - K_0 = \$9,352,000 - \$5,889,000 = \$3,463,000 \tag{2}$$

This value of $3.463 million should be interpreted as the net economic value of the particular development program represented by the FutureSpace Center project as we have specified that project. If the price of the FutureSpace Center land site is $3.463 million, then the total economic cost of the investment in the development project, P_0, will be $9.352 million, and the investment will have a zero NPV as of today, the time when the development investment decision must be made. If the price of the land is any value *x*, then the NPV_0 will be $3,463,000 − *x*. If this is nonnegative, then it makes *economic*

---

[5]To see how this might relate to a construction loan, suppose that the lender expects a 5% probability of default when the loan comes due at the end of construction in 12 months, and suppose that in the event of default the loss severity would be 25% (that is, 25% of the outstanding loan balance would not be recoverable through the foreclosure process). Then in an environment where the riskfree interest rate and the OCC of construction costs is 3%, the construction loan would have to charge a contractual interest rate of at least 6.335% in order to cause the loan issuance to be zero NPV, as follows.

Assuming interest accrues from the time each construction draw is made, the OLB due at the end of 12 months would be:

$$\$1,500,000(1 + 0.06335/12)^9 + \$1,500,000(1 + 0.06335/12)^6 + \$1,500,000(1 + 0.06335/12)^3 + \$1,500,000 = \$6,145,000$$

The bank's expected cash flow in month 12 from this credit, given the default probability and conditional loss severity, would be:

$$(0.95)\$6,145,000 + (0.05)(1 - 0.25)\$6,145,000 = \$6,068,000$$

The bank's expected future value of its construction cost liabilities evaluated as of month 12, based on the 3% risk-free OCC of the construction cost outflows themselves, would be:

$$\$1,500,000(1 + 0.03/12)^9 + \$1,500,000(1 + 0.03/12)^6 + \$1,500,000(1 + 0.03/12)^3 + \$1,500,000 = \$6,068,000$$

Thus, the projected NPV at month 12 would be: $6,068,000 − $6,068,000 = 0, which would also imply a zero NPV at the time of loan issuance at time *0*, provided the default-based credit losses are uncorrelated with capital market returns (such that the expected month 12 inflow to the bank can be discounted to time *0* at the same 3% risk-free rate as the construction outflows).

If credit loss incidence in the loan is positively correlated with capital market variables, then the OCC appropriate for discounting the bank's expected cash inflow of $6.068 million at month 12 would be greater than the 3% rate applicable to the construction costs (because of the bank's inability to diversify away all of the default risk). This would result in a lower present value for the inflow to the bank, and hence a negative time *0* NPV for the lender. This might be overcome by an up-front loan origination fee in addition to the interest charge in the loan. Alternatively, a contractual interest rate higher than 6.335% could be charged on the loan in order to equate the time *0* values of the expected inflows and outflows on the loan. It is important to note, however, that such credit losses on the loan are not deadweight losses to the construction project as a whole, but rather "internal" transfer payments from the debt investors to the equity investors in the project, as the borrowers exercise their "put option" right to default with limited liability (assuming lack of lender recourse). That is, the loss experienced by the bank is an increment of loss that is not experienced by the developer (assuming limited liability).

In any case, competition in the construction lending market must result in an ex ante zero NPV for the loan transaction as of time *0* (when the loan decision is made). This implies a time *0* present value of the loan's expected cash inflows (payments from the developer to the lender) equal to the present value of the loan's expected outflows (payments from the bank to the construction contractor), the latter of which equals: $6,068,000/(1 + 0.03/12)^{12} = \$5,889,000$, based on the construction cost OCC of 3%. Thus, we arrive at the same time *0* present value of the construction costs faced by the developer, whether or not a loan is actually used to finance the construction.

A BRIEF DIGRESSION: HIGHEST AND BEST USE ANALYSIS ...

Although our primary focus in this section is on investment in the land commitment and construction phase of development projects, it may be worthwhile to step back for a brief digression to consider applicability of this analysis framework to the preliminary phase. Recall that we specified at the outset of our description of the FutureSpace Center example that this project is the highest and best use (HBU) of the site. Referring back to the multistage overall development process outlined in section 28.1 of the previous chapter, the determination that FutureSpace is indeed the HBU for this site would have been made during the preliminary phase, just prior to what we are calling *time 0*. During the preliminary phase, explicit HBU analysis should be based on the same metric as we quantified in equation (2), the net economic value of the project (exclusive of land cost), what we labeled "NPV_0" in that context. The project design that maximizes this NPV_0 exclusive of land cost is the HBU for the site.

Normally, the value of the land, what we have labeled "x" above, would reflect that HBU. (Thus implying zero NPV for the HBU, negative NPV for any other use, including the land cost. If the land value is greater than the HBU then the site is not yet "ripe" for development; we are still in the land speculation real option phase.) However, it is possible for an entrepreneurial

developer to envision, design, and bring to site-feasibility (e.g., by land assembly and permitting) a project that is more valuable [i.e., that has a higher equation (2) NPV_0 exclusive of land cost] than anyone else could do. Through such a process, the developer adds value during the preliminary phase of the overall development process. This added value is ultimately reflected in the *investment* value of the land (as assembled and permitted) for the particular developer, though it may not be entirely reflected in the *market*-value-based opportunity cost of the land, x, if no other developer could execute the project.[1] In any case, the fundamental NPV decision rule of maximizing the NPV over all mutually exclusive alternatives governs the HBU analysis in the preliminary phase of the overall development process, with NPV defined as we have done here, exclusive of land cost.[2]

---

[1]In the terminology introduced in section 12.1.2 of Chapter 12, the subject developer is the "most-motivated" developer, while the "second-most-motivated" developer is the one who determines market value of the site.
[2]And recall, as noted above (and addressed in depth in Chapter 27), that one mutually exclusive alternative is to wait to hold open the option to develop the land later.

---

sense to undertake the development investment, given that it is the highest and best use of the site.[6]

When a project makes economic sense, then it should be possible to find some combination of participants and to structure the financing and control of the deal in a manner that makes the project feasible and provides fair returns to all parties ex ante. When a project does not make economic sense, it will not be possible to put together such a package to make the project feasible without at least one party (one contributor) not achieving a fair expected return going into the deal.

29.1.2 Operational Leverage and Estimation of the OCC for Development Investments

We have previously noted that a salient feature of development project investments is that, because of the operational leverage inherent in the project, the risk and return characteristics of such investments are very different from those of stabilized operating properties. In particular, development phase investments are more risky and, therefore, must provide higher expected returns going in than investments in stabilized properties. Understanding this difference is very important, because (as we have repeatedly noted in this book) the supply side of the capital market (those who have money to invest) is divided into different types of investors who are looking for different levels of ex ante risk and return in their investments. In this section, we will show you how to quantify rigorously the difference between development

---

[6]Recall from Chapter 27 that consideration of option value could make it optimal to wait before investing in the development project. Such "option premium" value and optimal waiting should normally be reflected in the market value of the land. Hence, in this case, it would be reflected in a value of x greater than $3.463 million. However, recall that at the outset of our discussion of this example we posited that it was indeed optimal to commit irreversibly to immediate development of the FutureSpace Center project. To relate this to the discussion in Chapter 27, the current underlying asset value of $9.352 million (signaled by an observable comparable completed asset current value of $10 million as seen in the value of Hereandnow Place) apparently equals at least the "hurdle value" that makes immediate development optimal, as described in section 27.5.1 of Chapter 27.

phase investment risk and stabilized operating phase investment risk, based on fundamental economic principles.

The extra risk in development investments is easily seen in our previous FutureSpace Center project illustration. We already ascertained that $3.463 million is the zero-NPV fair market value of the up-front investment in the FutureSpace Center development project (the opportunity value of the land). We can, therefore, easily compute what is the fair market expected return on the development phase investment in FutureSpace Center. The going-in expected return on this development investment is seen to be 16.59 percent per annum EAR (1.29%/month simple, or 15.44% ENAR with monthly compounding), by computing the IRR of the development phase cash flows as follows:[7]

$$\$3,463,000 = \frac{-\$1,500,000}{(1 + IRR/mo)^3} + \frac{\$3,500,000}{(1 + IRR/mo)^6} + \frac{-\$1,500,000}{(1 + IRR/mo)^9} + \frac{\$3,500,000}{(1 + IRR/mo)^{12}} \quad \text{(3a)}$$

$$\Rightarrow IRR = 1.287\%/mo, \Rightarrow (1.01287)^{12} - 1 = 16.59\%/yr$$

Now compare this to the expected return on an investment in the otherwise identical stabilized property across the street at Hereandnow Place. Recall that the zero-NPV (fair market value) expected return on an investment in Hereandnow Place is 9 percent (or 9.38 percent EAR). Considering the 3.04 percent risk-free interest rate, the expected return risk premia for the two investments are (in EAR terms):

$$9.38\% - 3.04\% = 6.34\%, \text{ for Hereandnow;}$$
$$16.59\% - 3.04\% = 13.55\%, \text{ for FutureSpace.}$$

Thus, the development project investment has a risk premium that is 13.55/6.34 = 2.14 times that of the stabilized property. Given that both of these are fair market return risk premia and, therefore, must provide the same expected return risk premium *per unit of risk*, the implication is that the development investment has 2.14 times the risk of the stabilized property investment (as the capital market perceives and evaluates risk).

This difference reflects the **operational leverage** in the development project. It exists even in development projects that are entirely preleased, such that there is no lease-up or rental market risk. Essentially, operational leverage occurs whenever an investment involves future cost outlays that are not perfectly correlated with the values of the future gross benefits to be obtained from the investment. In other words (using our previous NPV terminology), operational leverage arises whenever P does not occur entirely at time 0 and is not perfectly and positively correlated with the subsequent realization of V. In general, the greater the relative magnitude of the construction costs, K, compared to V, and the earlier the realization of asset value, V, occurs in time relative to the incurring of K, the greater will be the amount of operational leverage in the development project. For example, other things equal, a developer can increase operational leverage by selling off completed assets sooner. Investments in stabilized properties have no operational leverage, because the investment cost occurs entirely at time 0 the same time as asset value is realized.[8]

To make this point more concrete, let's suppose that in our FutureSpace and Hereandnow examples the ex post asset values turn out to be 10 percent less than had been expected

---

[7]Here we are assuming sale (or valuation realization) of each building upon completion. Thus, the net cash flow in months 6 and 12 is $5,000,000 − $1,500,000 = $3,500,000. Other approaches to realization of the project benefits will yield different IRRs. A "canonical" approach to quantifying consistently development project investment returns will be discussed later in this section.

[8]Obviously, the investor can add *financial leverage* by the use of debt financing of the investment, as described in Chapter 13. But here, to illustrate fundamental principles, we are considering investment without use of debt financing. Also, some properties may have a type of operational leverage in their stabilized phase if the landlord is responsible for paying operating expenses that are relatively fixed, while the rental income is variable and not correlated with those expenses. One example is a property subject to ground lease rental payments (as described in Chapter 14). However, to the extent this type of stabilized phase operational leverage exists, it should be completely reflected in the stabilized phase OCC (e.g., the 9.38% in our previous example) and, therefore, fully accounted for in the value of the stabilized asset, V.

at time *0*. Instead of achieving its expected IRR of 9.38 percent, the investment in Hereand-now would actually achieve a lower return, namely −1.04 percent, computed as:

$$\$10,000,000 = \sum_{t=1}^{12} \frac{\$75,000}{(1 + IRR/mo)^t} + \frac{\$9,000,000}{(1 + IRR/mo)^{12}}$$

$$\Rightarrow IRR = -0.087\%/mo, \Rightarrow (0.99913)^{12} - 1 = -1.04\%/yr$$

Thus, the ex post investment result for the year would fall short of the ex ante expectation by 9.38% − (−1.04%) = 10.42%. But the investment in FutureSpace Center would suffer much more on a percentage basis, experiencing an actual return of −13.42 percent in the ex post IRR calculation based on valuations of the two buildings at $4.5 million instead of $5 million at the times of completion in months 6 and 12:

$$\$3,463,000 = \frac{-\$1,500,000}{(1 + IRR/mo)^3} + \frac{\$3,000,000}{(1 + IRR/mo)^6} + \frac{-\$1,500,000}{(1 + IRR/mo)^9} + \frac{\$3,000,000}{(1 + IRR/mo)^{12}}$$

$$\Rightarrow IRR = -1.19\%/mo, \Rightarrow (0.9881)^{12} - 1 = -13.42\%/yr$$

Compared to FutureSpace's ex ante expected return of 16.59 percent, this is a 30.01 percent return shortfall, some 2.9 times the 10.42 percent return shortfall of the investment in the stabilized property. In other words, the particular type of risk event described here is "levered" almost three times in the development investment return compared to the stabilized property investment return.[9]

This kind of effect is essentially the same type of impact on risk and return as was described in our discussion of leverage in Chapter 13. The effect described in Chapter 13, however, was due to *financial leverage* (use of debt financing of the investment), whereas here no debt financing is being employed (hence, no financial leverage).

With this in mind, let us return to our question of how to compute the OCC of development phase investments. It should now be clear that the development phase OCC is greater than that in an otherwise similar stabilized property, because the investment risk is greater due to the operational leverage. But how much greater? If we know the OCC for the stabilized property being built, how can we compute the OCC for an investment in the development phase?

Before we answer this question, let's step back a minute and put it in perspective. Why do we feel a need even to ask this question? In investment analysis we generally want to know the OCC of an investment in order to use the OCC as the discount rate for purposes of computing the NPV of the investment. But as our FutureSpace project illustration shows, we do not need to know the development phase OCC itself in order to compute the NPV of the development phase investment. We can compute the development NPV by separately discounting the gross benefit (*V*) and cost (*K*) cash flow (and/or asset value) streams, using OCC rates appropriate to each as described in section 29.1.1. In this context, the development phase OCC emerges as an *output* from the NPV computation rather than as an *input* to it. For example, we determined that the OCC of the FutureSpace Center development project was 16.59 percent.

Yet this 16.59 percent output was seen to be an interesting number. We used it to quantify the amount of investment risk in the FutureSpace project relative to that in an otherwise similar stabilized property investment, based on the principle that the expected return risk premium must be the same *per unit of risk* across these different types of investments. This principle applies not just from a normative perspective, but fundamentally in a positive (empirical) sense, because investors can trade across and between the markets for these different types of investments. That is, they can buy and sell development investments and investments in stabilized properties. If the two types of investments do not present the same going-in expected return risk premia per unit of risk (the same **price of risk**), then investors

---

[9]This ratio is greater than the 2.14 ratio in the ex ante risk premia computed earlier, because here we are making a bit of an "apples-vs.-oranges" comparison. We are hypothesizing that the Hereandnow investment does not take the "hit" until 12 months from now in its asset value at that time, while the FutureSpace investment takes half of the hit (in the FutureSpace One building value) upon its completion in only six months and the other half in 12 months. The earlier registration of the loss causes a larger impact on the return.

will tend to sell the type of investment that presents the lower risk premium per unit of risk and buy the type of investment that presents the higher risk premium per unit of risk. Over time, this will drive market prices of the different types of investments to levels that will present investors with the same risk premium per unit of risk.[10]

If we agree that development phase investment OCCs are interesting numbers and that we know how to derive them as *outputs* from the NPV analysis as described above, we still face a practical consideration that can be awkward for some analytical purposes. In particular, the specific numerical value of the development phase OCC depends on the particular cash flow and value realization timing assumptions employed in the IRR computation. For example, the 16.59 percent OCC we derived for the FutureSpace project was based on the cash flow timing assumptions of equation (3a). These included the assumptions that:

- Each building's complete value would be fully realized (including the present value of any subsequent net rents) when, and only when, each building was completed (in months 6 and 12), and
- The construction costs would be paid during the project as they were incurred (months 3, 6, 9, and 12).

We could have made alternative assumptions. For example, suppose we replaced the first assumption above with an assumption that asset values would be realized only at the end of the complete two-building development phase at month 12 (for both buildings). Then our going-in IRR calculation would be as follows:

$$
\$3,463,000 = \frac{-\$1,500,000}{(1 + IRR/mo)^3} + \frac{\$1,500,000}{(1 + IRR/mo)^6} + \sum_{t=7}^{8} \frac{-\$37,500}{(1 + IRR/mo)^t}
$$

$$
+ \frac{-\$1,462,500}{(1 + IRR/mo)^9} + \sum_{t=10}^{11} \frac{\$37,500}{(1 + IRR/mo)^t} + \frac{\$8,537,500}{(1 + IRR/mo)^{12}} \quad (3b)
$$

$$
\Rightarrow IRR = 1.07\%/mo, \Rightarrow (1.0107)^{12} - 1 = 13.58\%/yr
$$

The resulting IRR of 13.58 percent is quite different from our previous calculation of 16.59 percent, yet it is clearly a valid representation of the expected return on the development investment. Which IRR represents the "true OCC" of the development phase investment?

In fact, they can both be true. As long as they represent a feasible and plausible strategy for the actual cash flow realizations of the development phase investment, any number of valid OCC rates can be generated for a typical development phase investment. Comparisons among these rates can provide some insight as to how to manage and finance the project so as to achieve a target risk/return profile. For example, as we have just seen, planning to sell each building upon its completion will add to both the expected return and the risk in the FutureSpace project, as indicated by the difference between the 16.59 percent versus 13.58 percent IRRs computed in equations (3a) and (3b).[11]

---

[10]Recall that this fundamental cross-market equilibrium argument was also used in our development of the certainty-equivalent DCF valuation formula in Chapter 10, Appendix 10C, and in our development of a rigorous option model of land valuation in section 27.3 of Chapter 27.

[11]Remember, you can't get something for nothing in economics! Equilibrium across markets drives market values toward levels that eliminate supernormal profits (or more specifically in this context, that eliminate supernormal expected return risk premia). Recall how the $3.463 million present value of the FutureSpace site was derived back in equation (2). Equilibrium across the markets for investment in stabilized property, in contractually fixed cash flows (bonds), and in developable land leads to the $3.463 million valuation of the site. No scope for supernormal profits is provided for in this valuation. Thus, the higher 16.59% expected return in equation (3a) merely reflects a commensurately greater degree of risk involved, from an ex ante perspective, in planning to sell the assets upon the completion of each one, relative to the plan implicit in equation (3b) of holding the assets through month 12. Of course, if the the sale timing decision can be made ex post based upon subsequent realization of values, such possibilities can indeed be advantageous in terms of ex post realized IRR. Such considerations can be important in determining partnership "waterfall" partitioning of profits as described in Chapter 15 (see Section 15.3), for example, to surpass an IRR hurdle. At a more fundamental level, if the project involves substantial phasing possibilities and timing flexibility then it can be better and more rigorously analyzed using option theory as discussed in section 29.4 to follow.

Nevertheless, it can be useful to have a more standardized formula for defining the OCC of development project investments. This can provide a common framework and, in some contexts, facilitate comparisons across projects. Fortunately, an approach to standardizing the measurement of development project OCC naturally suggests itself in the very widespread use of construction loans to finance the construction cost component of development project investment. As noted in Chapter 28, the classical construction loan results in all of the construction cost cash outflow being paid by the developer (the loan borrower) at one point in time, namely, upon completion of construction (when the construction loan is due). This dovetails nicely with the intuitively appealing conceptualization of the net benefits of the development being realized as of a single future point in time, namely, the time of completion of construction of the entire project.

Thus, a sort of "canonical" development cash flow pattern can be proposed, in which all cash flow occurs at two, and only two, points in time: (i) "time *0*" (the present) when the irreversible commitment to the development project must be made and the cost of the land is effectively incurred;[12] and (ii) "time *T*" when the construction is essentially completed and the developer obtains the net difference between the gross value of the built property as of time *T* minus the construction costs compounded up to time *T*.[13] This canonical assumption of land investment at time *0* and net construction profits realized all at time *T* is not particularly helpful for complex, multistage projects or for projects that involve production and sale of many separate assets over a long period of time (such as most single-family housing developments). However, it provides an intuitively appealing picture of many development projects.

The **canonical formula** for the OCC of development investments can be expressed by the following condition of equilibrium across the markets for developable land, built property, and contractually fixed cash flows or debt assets (see Exhibit 29-1):

$$\frac{V_T - K_T}{(1 + E[r_C])^T} = \frac{V_T}{(1 + E[r_V])^T} - \frac{K_T}{(1 + E[r_D])^T} \tag{4}$$

where:

V_T = Gross value of the completed building(s) as of time T.
K_T = Total construction costs compounded to time T.
$E[r_V]$ = OCC of the completed building(s).
$E[r_D]$ = OCC of the construction costs.
$E[r_C]$ = OCC of the development phase investment.
T = The time required for construction.

In most cases, all of these variables can be observed or estimated with relatively high confidence, except for the OCC of the development phase investment, $E[r_C]$. Solving (4) for $E[r_C]$ we obtain:

$$E[r_C] = \left[\frac{(V_T - K_T)(1 + E[r_V])^T (1 + E[r_D])^T}{(1 + E[r_D])^T V_T - (1 + E[r_V])^T K_T} \right]^{(1/T)} - 1 \tag{4a}$$

Another way of writing this is to define $NPV_0 = V_0 - K_0$ as the result of equation (4), the net economic value of the project exclusive of land cost, which can be computed from either the right-hand or the left-hand side of equation (4). Computing it from the right-hand side, we can then solve for the development OCC as:

$$1 + E[r_C] = \left(\frac{V_T - K_T}{V_0 - K_0} \right)^{1/T} \tag{4b}$$

In equation (4), the left-hand side represents the investment in developable land, which produces the net difference between the built property value and its construction cost at

---

[12]Remember that the economic opportunity cost of the land at time *0* is its market value as of that time (what it could be sold for as a developable land parcel), not necessarily equal to its historical acquisition cost.

[13]The time between time *0* and time *T*, the duration of construction, is what we labeled in section 27A.1.3 (in the CD Appendix to Chapter 27) as the "time-to-build" (*ttb*).

EXHIBIT 29-1
The "Canonical" Formula
© OnCourse Learning

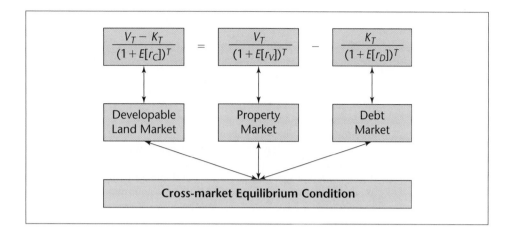

time T. The right-hand side of equation (4) represents essentially a way to duplicate this development investment by investing in a combination of the following: a long position in built property of the type being developed and a short position (borrowing) in an asset that pays contractually fixed cash flows (debt) in the amount of the construction costs of the project. The equation must hold in order for investments across these three types of asset markets (land, built property, and debt) to provide investors with competitive risk-adjusted return expectations (that is, equal expected-return-risk premia per unit of risk across the three types of investments).

Equation (4) represents exactly the same argument and model as in section 27.3 of Chapter 27, where we presented the real option model of land value and optimal development timing. The only difference is that here we are assuming that the timing is ripe to begin the development project, so that the development investment OCC is based on a definite commitment to proceed with the project.[14]

To see how equation (4) works in practice, let us apply it to our previous illustrative example of the FutureSpace Center development investment. For this project, it would be logical to define time T as the end of month 12, the time when the second building is projected to be completed. We would grow the FutureSpace One building completed value or cash flow forward in time to month 12 at the OCC rate appropriate to built property (9 percent). We would then combine that with the projected $5 million value of the FutureSpace Two building as of month 12 to arrive at the total value of V_T, as follows:

$$V_T = \$5,000,000(1.0075)^6 + \$5,000,000$$
$$= \sum_{t=7}^{12}\$37,500(1.0075)^{12-t} + \$10,000,000 = \$10,229,000$$

Similarly, with the construction costs we would grow the four projected payments forward to month 12 at their OCC rate of 3 percent to obtain K_T:

$$K_T = \$1,500,000(1.0025)^9 + \$1,500,000(1.0025)^6$$
$$+ \$1,500,000(1.0025)^3 + \$1,500,000 = \$6,068,000$$

---

[14]It can be verified that equation (4) will provide the same OCC for the development (land) expected return as what is implied by the binomial option model presented in Chapter 27 (with period length equal to T) for any state of the world in which it is optimal to develop the property in both of the two subsequent binomial outcomes: in other words, whenever there is a definitive commitment to develop the project. If, contrary to our assumption in this example, it were optimal to wait and not begin immediate development of the FutureSpace site, then equation (4) would imply a value of $E[r_C]$ greater than the true OCC of the land (development option) investment, causing the time 0 valuation implied by equation (4) (the valuation of the formula on either its left-hand side or right-hand side) to be less than the actual land value including the value of the option to wait. This, in turn, would result in a negative NPV calculation for the immediate development project when the opportunity cost of the land is netted out. (See the boxed feature in section 27.2 entitled: *"New Insight into the NPV Rule."*)

Thus, the projected net development profit as of month 12 is:

$$V_T - K_T = \$10,229,000 - \$6,068,000 = \$4,161,000$$

Substituting in equation (4) and solving for $E[r_C]$ as a simple monthly rate gives:

$$\frac{\$10,229,000 - \$6,068,000}{(1 + E[r_C])^{12}} = \frac{\$10,229,000}{(1.0075)^{12}} - \frac{\$6,068,000}{1.0025^{12}}$$

$$\Rightarrow$$

$$E[r_C] = \left[\frac{(\$4,161,000(1.0075)^{12}(1.0025)^{12}}{(1.0025)^{12}\$10,229,000 - (1.0075)^{12}\$6,068,000} \right]^{(1/12)} - 1 = 1.542\%/mo$$

$$\Rightarrow (1.01542)^{12} - 1 = 20.16\%/yr$$

Thus, the "canonical" OCC of the FutureSpace development investment is 20.16 percent (EAR), which compares to 9.38 percent for the corresponding built property investment in Hereandnow Place and 3.04 percent for risk-free investment. This suggests that the development project has approximately 2.70 [= (20.16% − 3.04%)/(9.38% − 3.04%)] times the investment risk as the built property based on the canonical cash flow timing.

Considering that the difference in risk between the development and built property investments results essentially from leverage, it will not be surprising that the canonical OCC of the development investment can be equivalently derived using the WACC formula we introduced in our discussion of leverage in Chapter 13. If we reproduce the WACC formula of section 13.4 in its leverage-ratio form and with the variable labels we are using here, the WACC formula for the development OCC is:

$$E[r_C] = E[r_D] + LR(E[r_V] - E[r_D]) \tag{5}$$

Defining *LR* as the leverage ratio, $V/(V − K)$, based on the time *0* valuations of the asset to be built and the land value:

$$LR = \frac{V_0}{V_0 - K_0} = \frac{\$9,352,000}{\$9,352,000 - \$5,889,000} = 2.70$$

we have the development (land) OCC given as:

$$E[r_C] = 3.04\% + 2.70(9.38\% - 3.04\%) = 20.16\%.17^{[15]}$$

Note that in whatever manner the canonical OCC is determined, it will, of course, yield the same NPV of the development project (land value) as we derived originally back in equation (2):

$$\frac{\$4,161,000}{1.2016} = \frac{\$10,229,000}{1.0938} - \frac{\$6,068,000}{1.0304} = \$9,352,000 - \$5,889,000 = \$3,463,000$$

Prior knowledge of this NPV is not necessary to ascertain the canonical OCC of the development project, as $E[r_C]$ is determined solely by the variables on the right-hand side of equation (4) [or equivalently of (5)].

Exhibit 29-2 portrays graphically what we have just discovered about the relative risk and return for investments in Hereandnow and FutureSpace, using the familiar equilibrium risk/return diagram with the Security Market Line (SML) that you have seen so often in this book. Note that the exact outcome percentage ranges on the horizontal axis in the exhibit are just illustrative (see Section 29.2 below for their derivation). The point is that the ratio of the

---

[15]Recall that the WACC formula is only an approximation for fractional or multiperiod returns; it works exactly only for simple returns, that is, a simple single period ratio, with all cash flows at the beginning and end of the period. While the canonical formula does move all expected cash flows to those two points in time (using appropriate OCC rates), the application of the simple WACC formula to the resulting canonical OCC of the development project will only be exactly consistent with a per annum IRR metric in the special case where the project lasts exactly one year (as is true in our FutureSpace illustration).

EXHIBIT 29-2
FutureSpace and
Hereandnow Risk and
Return Based on the
Canonical Formula
© OnCourse Learning

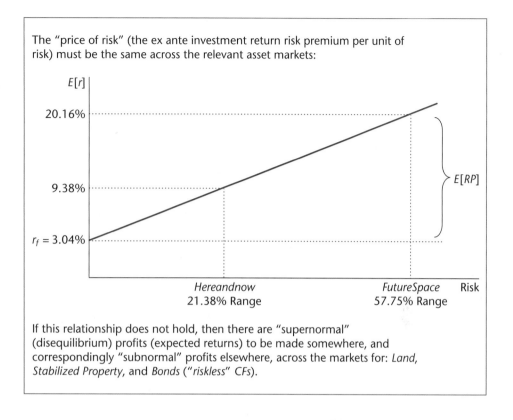

amount of risk between the development project and the stabilized asset, as indicated on the horizontal axis, is the 2.70 ratio that we have just computed, the same ratio as between the two expected return risk premia.

29.1.3 The Development Risk Ratio and Implications for Characteristic Development Regions

The canonical formula for the OCC of a development project, which is most useful in projects that produce a single asset in a single phase, yields an interesting by-product: the **development risk ratio**, which is the ratio of the amount of investment risk in the development project to the amount investment risk in an unlevered investment in an otherwise identical stabilized property. As noted above and illustrated in Exhibit 29-2, the development risk ratio in our FutureSpace project example is 2.70, determined as the ratio of the risk premium in the development project canonical OCC (20.16% − 3.04%) divided by the risk premium in the asset being produced by the development project (9.38% − 3.04%). As we have seen, this ratio is a measure of the amount of operational leverage in the development project.

We can use the development risk ratio to analyze the characteristic economics of the development project in a little more depth by combining the implications of the canonical OCC analysis with the real options model of land value introduced in Chapter 27. After all, the development project is the (presumably optimal) exercise of such a real option. As will be shown in the next section, the development project OCC equals the real option (land speculation) OCC at the moment when it is optimal to develop the land (that is, exercise the real option). Now recall from Chapter 27 that the ratio of the real option OCC risk premium to the underlying asset OCC risk premium is given by the option elasticity (which we labeled η, "eta," in section 27.5). Under the assumptions of the Samuelson-McKean formula this elasticity is a simple function of, among other things, the volatility and the payout ratio or yield rate (similar to the cap rate) of the underlying asset (the property to be built). In particular, greater volatility and/or lower payout (lower cap rate) in the real estate market implies lower option elasticity. Furthermore, the development project's land value fraction—that is, the fraction of land value in the total value of the to-be-built asset at the time of optimal development—is simply the inverse of the option elasticity.[16] Thus, greater volatility and/or lower cap rates imply greater land value fraction.

Greater volatility and/or lower cap rates are thus associated with higher land values and less propensity to build. In effect, the developer must hold back and wait for a greater "irreversibility premium," as this term was defined in Chapter 5. (See section 5.2.) This means that the city with greater volatility and lower cap rates in its real estate market will tend to be a denser city with higher rents, other things being equal. Higher land value fractions also tend to be associated with lower real depreciation rates in built property assets, as land value does not generally depreciate, only structure value. This would imply higher nominal appreciation rates in areas with greater volatility and/or lower cap rates. And indeed, lower cap rates would be directly associated with higher asset value appreciation rates holding constant the risk (and therefore the expected total return) in the built assets.

Greater volatility and/or lower cap rates will also be associated with less operational leverage and therefore less additional risk in the development project investment (other things being equal, and as compared to the risk in unlevered investment in the stabilized property). This simply reflects the lower development risk ratio (or equivalently, the lower option elasticity), which is just the flip side of the coin of the higher land value fraction (since the land value fraction is the inverse of the option elasticity). This means less operational leverage, that is, more of the value of the completed project is in the value of the land, relative to the cost of construction, in high land cost locations. However, this does not mean that the absolute physical amount of construction per acre (capital intensity) will be less, as high land value generally implies high density HBUs. The resulting implication for construction project duration may counteract to some extent the tendency for high land value to be associated with low development risk ratios, as long construction duration tends to increase operational leverage.

In some cases the development risk ratio can be used to help flag a particularly risky or aggressive development project, or in the other extreme, one that is not making full use of the value of the site. For example, suppose you are in a high volatility or low cap rate type of real estate market, that is, the type of market where the option elasticity and therefore the development risk ratio should normally be relatively low (corresponding to a high land value ratio). Yet the development project you are planning seems to pencil out at an (honestly) estimated very high risk ratio based on the canonical formula. This suggests that the construction project may not be adding enough value to the site, particularly if it is not a very long-duration capital-intensive project. The high risk ratio in the planned project in such circumstances likely reflects projected stabilized property value not sufficiently in excess of the projected construction cost, resulting in a present-value profitability, $V_0 - K_0$, that is too low. (Perhaps it is the wrong type or scale of building for the site.) While this might be seen by a direct NPV analysis comparing $V_0 - K_0$ with the land value, it might be difficult to accurately estimate the land value. Alternatively, suppose you are in a low-volatility or high cap rate real estate market (the type that normally supports projects with high risk ratios), but your project presents a low risk ratio. Then the structure you are building may be too small or "cheap" for the site. A relatively high $V_0 - K_0$ measure of present-value profitability (which could cause a low risk ratio) might actually be indicating

---

[16]Rearranging formula (2c) of section 27.5.1, we have:

$$V^* = K_0\eta/(\eta - 1), \implies (V^* - K_0)/V^* = 1/\eta$$

where as in Chapter 27, V^* is the current value of the completed project (at the moment of optimal development), K_0 is the present value of the construction costs, and η is the option elasticity.

that your project is relying too much on the (already low) land value and not enough on value added by the structure.[17]

*29.2 Advanced Topic: The Relationship of Development Valuation to the Real Option Model of Land Value

As noted, the development project valuation and relative risk analysis described here is completely consistent with the real option model of land value described in Chapter 27, only we are here assuming that the point has arrived where it is optimal to make an irreversible commitment to construct the entire development project. In this context, the canonical formula demonstrates the equivalence of the approach described here and the real options valuation model of Chapter 27.

To see this, consider again our FutureSpace Center example. Suppose that risk in the market for stabilized office property can be thought of as making the expected development asset value upon completion, what we have quantified as: $V_T = \$10,229,000$, a random variable that has the following possible outcomes at time T:

$$V_T = \$11,229,000; \text{ or}$$
$$V_T = \$9,229,000.$$

with ex ante probability of 50 percent for each outcome. Then applying the certainty-equivalence form of the DCF present value model that we first introduced in Chapter 10 Appendix 10C (on the CD) and which formed the basis of the binomial option value model we described in Chapter 27, we have the following present value computation for the Future-Space project as of time 0:[18]

$$PV[C_1] = \frac{E_0[C_1] - (C_1^{up}\$ - C_1^{down}\$)\dfrac{E_0[r_V] - r_f}{V_1^{up}\% - V_1^{down}\%}}{1 + r_f}$$

$$PV[C_1] = \frac{\Big((0.5)(11.229 - 6.068) + (0.5)(9.229 - 6.068)\Big) - \Big((11.229 - 6.068) - (9.229 - 6.068)\Big)\dfrac{9.38\% - 3.04\%}{(11.229 - 9.229)/9.352}}{1.0304}$$

$$= \frac{\$4.161 - \$2.000\left(\dfrac{6.34\%}{120.07\% - 98.69\%}\right)}{1.0304} = \frac{\$4.161 - \$2.000(0.2964)}{1.0304} = \frac{\$3.568}{1.0304} = \$3.463$$

Thus, the certainty-equivalence and binomial option models yield the same $3.463 million valuation of the project, and therefore the same implied OCC of 20.16 percent, as we derived previously:

$$1 + E[r_C] = \frac{E[C_T]}{PV[C_T]} = \frac{\$4.161}{\$3.463} = 1.2016$$

Note that in percentage terms the investment outcome spread (which may be viewed as a measure of risk) is:

$$(\$5,161,000 - \$3,161,000)/\$3,463,000 = \$2,000,000/\$3,463,000 = 57.75\%$$

---

[17]Again, an accurate assessment of land value would presumably cause the NPV of a low risk ratio project in a low land value region (where risk ratios should be higher) to appear negative (net of land cost), as the small scale or cheap nature of the project (causing the K_0 value to be small) would cause the $V_0 - K_0$ value to be lower than the land value. But the land value may be difficult to accurately estimate independent of the proposed project's economics (the $V_0 - K_0$ value itself). So the risk ratio may be a telling indicator. However, please note that this type of use of the development risk ratio metric is only suggestive. It may flag situations that deserve further looking into, but does not necessarily imply a suboptimal development plan or timing. Ultimately the NPV Decision Rule (applied net of true land opportunity cost) should be the guiding principle.

[18]Recall that $V_T^{up}\% - V_T^{down}\% = (V_T^{up}\$ - V_T^{down}\$)/PV[V_T]$, and that $PV[V_T]$ is $\$10,229,000/1.0938 = \$9,352,000$.

in the FutureSpace development project, whereas for this project's "underlying asset" (the assets to be built) the percentage investment outcome spread is only:

$$(\$11,229,000 - \$9,229,000)/\$9,352,000 = \$2,000,000/\$9,352,000 = 21.39\%$$

The ratio of these outcome spreads (risk): 57.75/21.39 = 2.70, is exactly the same as the ratio of the ex ante risk premia between the development project and its underlying asset: (20.16% − 3.04%)/(9.38% − 3.04%) = 17.12%/6.34% = 2.70. This demonstrates our previous point that the project valuation model presented here is based on the assumption that the "price of risk" (the ex ante investment return risk premium per unit of risk) must be the same across the relevant asset markets, in this case, the market for development projects (land) and the market for the stabilized assets those projects produce.

29.3 Broadening the Perspective

The preceding sections have presented you with a rigorous framework for analyzing and evaluating basic real estate development projects from an investment perspective. Now it is time to step back and take a breath. In this section, we want to broaden your understanding, from two different perspectives. First, we want to go back and look at how developers typically think about the investment evaluation question. Then, we want to broaden our frame to consider phases before and after the construction phase itself.

29.3.1 How Developers Think about All This

By now, if we have done our job right, you should be thinking that the development investment analysis model we have presented in this section makes sense at a fundamental level. Indeed, though you may not want to admit it (and we would hate to think we've done it to you), you may actually be "thinking like an economist." After all, our investment analysis model is nothing if not based squarely in fundamental economic principles, including opportunity cost and market equilibrium.

But slap yourself, or take a walk in the fresh air, and surely you'll come back down to earth and ask that question we love from students:

> *Do developers and lenders really use this NPV-based method to evaluate development investment projects? And if they don't, then how could it possibly be relevant to the real world?*

We owe you a straight answer.

We must admit that the methodology described in this section is not widely used *explicitly* in current practice. But, we argue, it must be used *implicitly* among the more successful developers and investors. Furthermore, because of its grounding in market-based principles of opportunity cost and equilibrium, we would argue that actual *results* in the real world must tend to conform to the implications of our model, at least in places where markets for land and property and capital function reasonably well. In general, even in other places, our model can be argued to provide a rigorous *normative* framework to guide investment decision making.[19]

Why do we think most successful developers use the NPV framework implicitly if not explicitly? Perhaps we are making an "heroic" assumption. You don't have to be a genius to see that some pretty bad real estate development decisions get made in the real world. (Of course, hindsight helps, but some projects had to have been turkeys even when the decisions were made.) Nevertheless, we suspect that most real estate development decisions are in fact at least approximately consistent with the correct application of the NPV rule (ex ante), even though the developers and lenders may not be explicitly or consciously thinking of their decision process along the lines of the NPV rule. Why do we say this?

---

[19]See the boxed feature at the end of section 27.3 of Chapter 27.

Astute developers do not make crucial decisions just on the basis of whether a project looks feasible according to incomplete procedures such as the mortgage-based SFFA described in Chapter 28. The other, broader part of their decision reasoning is often, however, intuitive and qualitative rather than explicit and quantitative. Developers usually face a capital or resource constraint in practice, or believe they do. That is, they can only do so many projects at once. This means they cannot do all the projects that appear to be financially feasible (and that they might think they would like to do, if they could). As a result, developers are forced, in effect, to rank-order projects and consider feasible combinations of projects. It seems likely that a big part of what makes developers successful is their ability to do this rank-ordering rationally, that is, to choose among mutually exclusive alternatives to pursue those that look best on the basis of the magnitude of the perceived profit or surplus.[20]

In other words, virtually by definition, successful developers are those who maximize their wealth. And that is what the correct application of the NPV procedure does: by definition and construction, the NPV decision rule maximizes wealth. Thus, successful developers are doing the same thing that the NPV decision rule does. So, implicitly if not explicitly, they must be applying the NPV rule. Another way of saying this is to say that application of the NPV rule ensures that developers cover their cost of capital. Less successful developers may not be applying the NPV rule, but they tend to fall by the wayside over time, as any firm that does not cover its cost of capital eventually shrinks or dies.

What we would like to suggest is that even successful developers may find it useful to make more explicit and quantitative that which they have been doing all along implicitly, and less successful developers may be able to improve their performance significantly by the use of the NPV rule. Furthermore, as the mainstream investment world of Wall Street and sophisticated corporate finance grows more relevant to real estate with the rise of the REIT and CMBS markets and the growth of professional, institutional investor interest in real estate and the private equity investment industry, sophisticated methods consistent with global standard corporate capital budgeting practice will come to be more widespread and more necessary in the real estate industry.[21]

But if developers do not apply the NPV analysis procedure described in this section, then what do they do? Admittedly, in some cases, developers may not perform any overall project evaluation at all, satisfying themselves with the type of simple financial feasibility analysis described in Chapter 28. But as noted, that is not really a complete evaluation, and many developers do in fact attempt to perform some sort of evaluation. Not surprisingly, developers and their investors typically do this by applying somewhat simplistic, but quantitative, rules of thumb to evaluate development projects. The three most common such approaches are: profit margin ratios, enhanced cap rates on cost, and blended long-run IRRs. We'll discuss each of these in turn, and relate them specifically back to our FutureSpace example project.

Developers often judge the investment appeal of a development project by its **profit margin ratio**. This is simply the expected gross value of the completed project divided by the total costs of producing the project. Present value discounting is usually ignored, and land may or may not be included in the costs in the denominator, and if land is included it may be included at historical acquisition cost rather than current opportunity cost. By this criterion, developers often shoot for something like a 20 percent margin when land is included. That is, they want the expected completed project value to exceed the all-in costs

---

[20]This is the "use looking for a site" framework of development decision making described in Chapter 28. Yet our main analytical focus in the present chapter has been more from the "site looking for a use" perspective. But as described as far back as Chapter 4, these two perspectives interact in a well-functioning land market, such that optimization occurs in effect simultaneously from both perspectives, thereby maximizing land value. (See section 4.1.2.)

[21]Also, it must be recognized, even proper decision making does not guarantee that all decisions will prove to be optimal ex post. No one has a true "crystal ball." Unforeseeable events can intervene, mistakes can be made in project execution, and assumptions upon which the decision was based, however valid at the time, can prove later to have been incorrect with the arrival of new information. (Alas, this can happen in any field of life.)

by 20 percent. The intuitive appeal of this measure is obvious, as it seems to present a very direct measure of the "profit" of the development project.[22]

Suppose we applied this measure to our FutureSpace project. It would imply that the land value is something like $2.333 million:

$$1 + Margin = \frac{V_T}{K + C} = \frac{\$10,000,000}{\$6,000,000 + C} = 1.20$$

$$\Rightarrow$$

$$Land\ Value = C = \frac{V_T}{1 + Margin} - K = \frac{\$10,000,000}{1.20} - \$6,000,000 = \$2,333,000$$

This is more than a million dollars less than the $3.463 million we previously determined was the true land value or value of the development project (before subtracting land cost) based on true opportunity cost and market equilibrium value.

But in fact, in the real world, a developer applying the margin ratio criterion might not end up so far off from our more sophisticated calculation. Perhaps the developer would decide that 20 percent is an excessive margin to require for such a quick and easy development project, one that produces a fully operational $5 million building in six months, and another six months after that, completely preleased. Or perhaps the developer would apply the margin ratio to historical land acquisition cost, which might well have been much less than the current opportunity cost of the land.[23] What we know is that if investors in the land, built property, and bond markets are to earn expected returns that provide ex ante risk premia proportional to their risk (the condition necessary for equilibrium across these investment markets), then developers applying the margin ratio criterion to evaluating the FutureSpace Project will have to end up figuring the margin ratio in some manner that produces a time *0* project value of $3.463 million (given our OCC assumptions of 9 percent and 3 percent for the built property and the construction costs).[24] The market may allow idiosyncratic deviation from this value (and recall that "idiosyncratic" deviation means deviation on *either side*), but systematic results will tend to be consistent with equilibrium valuation.

The second rule of thumb developers often apply is the **enhanced cap rate on cost**. As you recall from Chapter 10, a common method of estimating property value is the "direct capitalization" method, in which property NOI (stabilized) is divided by the market "cap rate," defined as the prevailing current earnings yield based on the NOI observed in transactions in the relevant asset market. For example, in the case of our FutureSpace project, the relevant cap rate is 9 percent, as the property market value of the project is estimated to be $10 million (based on the indication of the market provided by the observable stabilized "comp," Hereandnow Place), which equals the annual NOI of $900,000 divided by 9 percent.

---

[22]Sometimes the profit margin criterion is expressed in a slightly modified form as an "equity multiple" requirement, which is simply the ratio of the expected value of the project benefit (less construction cost or loan OLB) divided by the land and other equity investment value. While no formal present value discounting is implied in the equity multiple measure, the criterion often requires a higher multiple for longer projects.

[23]Recall that prior to development the land is a speculative investment that must provide an expected return (ex ante) commensurate with the risk suggested by the real options model presented in Chapter 27. Such an expected return (option OCC) was seen in Chapter 27 to be typically quite high. And land speculation return can normally be provided only by appreciation in the land value, as the raw land produces no positive income. (Indeed, raw land typically produces a negative income, due to property taxes and other expenses, unless the land has agricultural value.) To give a rough idea, for example, suppose that the options-based OCC is 20% per annum. Then, ignoring land holding expenses, the simple fact of providing this equilibrium speculation return would imply a purchase price of $2.333 million at a time 2.17 years prior to *time 0*: $2.333 × $(1.20)^{2.17}$ = $3.463. If we add a 2% per annum premium to cover land holding expenses, the implied land purchase date at the $2.333 million price is just two years ago, as: 1.99 = ln[$3.463/$2.333]/ln[1.22]. We might also note that in the numerical example in section 27.5 we computed an option elasticity value of 3.64, quite a bit higher than the 2.70 value in our FutureSpace example in the present chapter. The 3.64 value was based on volatility of 20% and property yield of 6%, whereas FutureSpace has a yield of 9.38% and presumably much higher volatility (perhaps considering uncertainty in both property value and construction costs). (For further explanation, see on the book's CD the "Sam-McK Formula" tab in the Excel appendix file for this chapter, as well as section 27A.2.1 and Formula (A.7) in the Appendix 27 to Chapter 27.)

[24]In our example, this would be a profit margin of 5.7%, as $10,000,000/($6,000,000 + $3,463,000) = 1.057.

Because of the extra risk in a development project, investors would require a higher cap rate than 9 percent. A typical rule of thumb might require an extra 100 basis points, or in this case a 10 percent cap rate. However, this cap rate is applied to total development cost, again, typically without particular care to discounting. Thus, if the developer of FutureSpace expects the completed assets to have a market value of $10 million, with a stabilized NOI of $900,000, then the project would appear desirable if it presented total development costs no more than: $900,000/10% = $9,000,000. Given construction costs of $6 million, this would imply land value (or net project value at time *0*) of $3 million.

While not too far off from our estimate of $3.463 million, the problem with this approach is that there is no rigorous basis for the developer's rule-of-thumb requirement of exactly 100 basis points in the cap rate enhancement. Hopefully, you can see that, unlike our estimate of $3.463 million, a value estimate of $3 million for the FutureSpace project will not be consistent with true opportunity cost and investment market equilibrium.[25]

The third major rule of thumb developers use to gauge development projects is the **blended long-run IRR**. In this approach, the project's stabilized operating cash flows are projected well beyond the completion of the development phase, typically including a 10-year horizon beyond stabilization. Thus, we have an overall project cash flow projection over a horizon equal to 10 years plus the length of the construction phase ($10 + T$ years in our previous nomenclature). A single IRR is then computed over this entire period. The result is, of course, a "blended" IRR that mixes the return earned by the development investment during the development phase with the return earned by the stabilized investment during the operational phase. The latter dominates, both because the capital is fully invested by the time of the operational phase (recall from Chapter 9 that the IRR is a *"dollar weighted"* rate of return) and because the 10-year operational phase projection is typically a much longer period of time than the construction phase. However, the degree to which the stabilized return dominates varies from project to project.

More to the point, from an investment analysis perspective it does not make sense to mix and blend these two investment phases and expected investment returns. They have very different risk characteristics, and so have very different OCC rates.

Furthermore, in the modern investment market, typically different types of investors and/or different types of investment vehicles with different types of investment objectives and different risk/ return targets provide the source of financial capital for the two different phases. Because of this, the blending of the two investment phases muddies the waters. The developer calculates the long-run blended IRR and then stares at that number, and, if he is honest with himself, really does not know what to make of it. What is the appropriate OCC to which he should compare the IRR he has just calculated? On what *rigorous* basis would one determine the *hurdle* IRR by which to evaluate the project?

In practice, of course, rules of thumb and conventional wisdom take hold in the marketplace. It would not be unusual for developers to require, say, an extra 100 basis points in the long-run blended IRR as compared to a typical otherwise similar stabilized property's going-in IRR (without leverage, or more than that for the equity investment component assuming projection of permanent debt financing). Thus, for example, in our FutureSpace project, where the market's going-in IRR for stabilized investment is 9 percent (as observed in the nearby Hereandnow Place market value), the developer might require a 10 percent going-in IRR on the FutureSpace development project including a projected 10-year hold after completion. In the case of FutureSpace, this would

---

[25]Of course, one can always "back out" the implied enhanced cap rate on cost rule of thumb value that would be consistent with a rigorous NPV analysis of a projected development, *after* the rigorous analysis has been completed. For any given specified projected asset market cap rate, rent, construction cost and construction duration, and based on an NPV analysis reflecting actual economic OCC as described in section 29.1, you can derive the implied enhanced cap rate on cost (and hence, the implied development project premium in that cap rate compared to the asset market cap rate). For an illustrative example reflecting the FutureSpace project, see the Chapter 29 Excel file on the book's CD (tab labeled "EnhancedCapRateOnCost"). But bear in mind that in general the cap rate on value for stabilized properties is the fundamental parameter reflecting equilibrium value in the asset marketplace, while the corresponding enhanced cap rate on cost is a derived value reflecting the amount of profit necessary for development in that asset market.

imply a net project (land residual) value of \$3.017 million.[26] This approach is therefore seen to be a rather roundabout way of getting to essentially the same point as the enhanced cap rate on cost approach discussed above. This approach, however, not only lacks rigor, but also is no easier to implement (in terms of number of calculations that must be done) than the rigorous opportunity cost and equilibrium-based procedure described in section 29.1.1.

*29.3.2 "Soup to Nuts:" Including Lease-up and Land Assembly: *"Unblending"* the Blended IRR

Although our primary focus in this chapter is on the major capital investment phase of development, involving the irreversible commitment of the land to the construction phase, it is of interest now to step back to the question of how the framework and analysis presented in this chapter relates to the overall development process described in the first section of Chapter 28. There we suggested that there are several stages in most development projects, with different risk and return regimes across the stages. The basic NPV approach presented here can be applied to any one of the phases of the overall development process, not just to the construction phase considered here, and in fact it should be applied separately to each of the phases. Here is how.

We have repeatedly noted that the project valuation implied by the methodology developed in section 29.1.1 is based on the concept of equilibrium across the relevant asset markets. Assuming that these markets function reasonably well, then the prices of development projects (or equivalently, the price of land ripe for development) that we observe in the world should tend to conform to the normative value implied by the methodology of section 29.1.1. To the extent that this is true, no matter which rules of thumb developers apply in the real world, the successful bidders must end up applying those rules such that they end up with the value implied by the section 29.1.1 methodology. For example, in the case of the FutureSpace Project that has a value of \$3.463 million, we noted that if the developer applied a profit margin criterion of 5.7 percent, he would arrive at the \$3.463 million valuation. Similarly, an enhanced cap rate on cost of 9.51 percent (that is, 51 basis points of enhancement instead of 100), or a blended long-run IRR of 9.74 percent (that is, 74 bps of premium over the stabilized 9 percent rate), would provide the \$3.463 million valuation.

Therefore, assuming that markets are functioning reasonably well, we can use typical developer rules of thumb for typical project cash flow profiles to "back out" the market's true OCC rates for each phase of the overall development process as described in section 28.1 in Chapter 28.

To illustrate this procedure, we can consider a recent application to midsized developers of mixed-income rental housing in the Boston metropolitan area.[27] Cash flows for all phases of the development and stabilized operation were estimated for typical mixed-income rental housing projects in the Boston area, from the preliminary phase through the stabilized operating phase. Developers were then asked what sort of long-run going-IRR premium over stabilized property IRRs they would require to enter the project at either the permitting, the construction, or the lease-up phase. In other words, developers were asked to quantify their decision making based on a common rule of thumb they were comfortable with, namely what we previously termed the blended long-run IRR approach.

By working backwards (starting out with the implied stabilized asset value), computing the value of the development asset at the beginning and end of each phase of the development process based on the cash flows within each and all subsequent phases and on the

---

[26]Calculated assuming the four quarterly construction draws of \$1.5 million each with the first building being completed and generating net cash flow of \$37,500/month starting in month 7 and the second building another \$37,500/month starting in month 13, with an assumed sale of both buildings at a 9% cap rate in month 132. (See the Chapter 29 CD Excel file on the book's student CD, the last tab on the right.)

[27]See W. T. McGrath, "Financial Economics and 40B: A Framework to Mediate the Fight Over Money," CRE Working Paper/ CRE Working Paper, 2005.

EXHIBIT 29-3 An Example of Risk and Return Regimes for Phases of the Development Process (taken from a study of affordable housing development in Massachusetts)

© OnCourse Learning

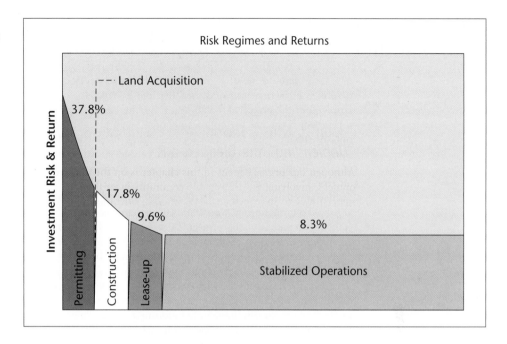

long-run IRRs stated by the developers, the IRR implied specifically *within* each phase was determined.[28] The result is presented in Exhibit 29-3. The study found that for developments producing properties that had stabilized investment required return expectations of 8.3 percent (going-in IRR based on a 10-year hold), the lease-up phase investment alone would require approximately a 9.6 percent going-in IRR,[29] the construction phase investment alone would require a 17.8 percent going-in IRR,[30] and the preliminary phase investment (land assembly and permitting) would require a 37.8 percent going-in IRR.[31]

---

[28]For example, if this procedure were applied to our illustrative FutureSpace Project, developers would presumably state a required long-run IRR rate of 9% for the stabilized investment phase and 9.72% for the development investment phase (noting that this preleased project has no lease-up phase). The stated required 9% stabilized investment rate would then be applied to determine the completed project value of $5 million for each building, and the stated required 9.72% development project rate would be applied to determine the $3.463 million value of the construction phase investment. These two values in combination with the construction phase cash flows would then allow us to "back out" the implied development phase IRR that is required by the developers, which we saw to be 20.16%, using the canonical cash flow assumption. (See the Chapter 29 Excel file on the book's student CD, the last tab on the right.)

[29]Thus, an additional risk premium of approximately 130 basis points for lease-up risk, compared to the stabilized asset. An alternative approach to estimating the lease-up phase OCC is to use the "inter-lease discount rate" described in Appendix 10A of Chapter 10, which can be estimated from more readily observed market variables in the manner described in that appendix. However, it should be noted that lease-up risk may be perceived as more than just the type of space market risk reflected in the inter-lease discount rate risk premium, as the typical inter-lease discount rate implied in a stabilized property is based on an existing operating property whose current and past rental performance is known, unlike the case for a new speculative development. In general, new assets with lease-up risk (but no construction phase leverage) command expected returns (OCC or discount rate) in the range of 50 to 200 basis points above otherwise equivalent fully stabilized property returns.

[30]Based on the "canonical" cash flow timing assumption and a one-year construction phase.

[31]As we noted in section 29.1, relatively little financial capital is typically invested during the preliminary phase (labeled "Permitting" in Exhibit 29-3). Much of the "investment" in this phase is the application of the human resource of the developer's "entrepreneurial labor," which may appear as part of the routine operating expenses of the development firm (some or all of which may be recouped in a "Developer's Fee"). To the extent that there is investment of financial capital, much of this might be in the form of land speculation (discussed in general from an investment perspective in Chapter 27). However, there may be additional value added by the developer in the preliminary phase, as assembly, permitting, and project design add value to the site. In the case of the Boston mixed-income housing development study, the investment outlays in the preliminary phase consisted primarily of nonrefundable land optioning payments, plus direct expenses of project permitting and design. These preliminary phase investments totaled only about 3% of the land acquisition and construction cost investments of the subsequent phase.

29.4 Evaluating Multiphase Developments: Real Options Theory and a Simplification

We took care to note at the outset that the development project valuation procedure described up to now assumes that the time is "ripe" for irreversible commitment to the construction of the project. Prior to that time, the landowner is in the position of a land speculator, in which she has the option to choose when to build. In Chapter 27, we showed how real options theory could be useful for evaluating developable land and characterizing the conditions when, indeed, irreversible commitment to construction is optimal. However, in the case of large, multibuilding development projects, it often does not make sense to commit fully to an irrevocable completion schedule for the entire project all at once, at a single " time *0*." Rather, it often makes sense to divide the project into phases or stages. The first phase is irreversibly committed to at time *0*, but there remains flexibility to delay or cancel altogether the subsequent phases of the project. In such situations, optionality remains in the project, and the project-evaluation methodology described in section 29.1.1 is no longer appropriate. Rigorous evaluation of multiphase projects requires use of real options theory, even when the time is ripe for irreversible commitment to the first phase.

Broadly speaking, the phases of a multibuilding project may be characterized as either **parallel** or **sequential**. If the phases are independent of one another, such that it is possible to construct them simultaneously (and one phase can be built whether or not the other phase is built), then the phases are parallel in nature.[32] In this case, each phase may be viewed as an independent simple-call option on the underlying assets (the buildings) that would be produced in each phase. Each of these options is like the simple land-development options described in Chapter 27. It may well be that the time is not yet ripe for all of the phases to begin at once. This would be indicated by the current valuations of the underlying assets of some phases still falling below their "hurdle values," as we defined this term in Chapter 27.[33] Valuation of the overall project is simply the sum of the values of all of the simple options characterizing the phases.

In other cases, the phases have a natural temporal order of construction, based on physical or economic dependence. For example, one phase cannot be started until a preceding phase is completed or at least already started. In this case, the phases are sequential, and the correct application of real option theory would model the overall project as a series of **compound options**. The term "compound option" refers to an option on an option. The construction of each phase not only obtains the underlying asset associated with that phase, but also obtains the option to construct the next subsequent phase.[34] Compound options can be evaluated using the same type of binomial model as was presented in Chapter 27. The analyst works backwards in time, modeling the option on the final phase first as a simple option, then evaluating each previous phase in reverse order until you come to the time *0* value (and optimal exercise policy) for the first phase, which thereby includes the valuation of the options on all the subsequent phases within it. Appendix 29 on the CD accompanying this book presents a simple numerical example (and spreadsheet template) for such a multistage project evaluation.[35]

---

[32]If the phases not only *can be* but *must be* constructed simultaneously (they are mutually dependent), then they are not really separate phases and should be treated as a single phase.

[33]This could be due to temporary oversupply of the existing stock of space of the type to be built in a given phase, resulting in a temporary depression in the current underlying asset valuation, as realistic longer-than-normal absorption would depress the time *0* valuation of the to-be-built asset. In the context of classical option models, such a situation would also be reflected in a below-normal cash yield rate, y_V in the terminology of Chapter 27 (holding all else constant, including the OCC of the built asset, implying a higher-than-normal growth rate for the underlying asset, as $g_V = r_V - y_V$). This would raise the hurdle benefit/cost ratio in the development option, even as the current depression in underlying asset value lowers the current actual benefit/cost ratio of immediate development.

[34]Sequential phasing can also be used to match product delivery to the space market's capacity to absorb new product. In the option model, this can be simulated by treating subsequent phases as "European" options for a certain time span, that is, making them impossible to exercise until a specified time has elapsed from the exercise of the preceding phase.

[35]See the "Roth Harbor" example in the Excel workbook.

Here in the printed text, we will content ourselves with presenting an *ad hoc* simplified approach to multistage project evaluation that does not require use of option theory. While this approach is not as rigorous or accurate as the option model, it provides an easy extension of the methodology presented earlier in this chapter.

Recall first that the approach to project valuation we have presented in this chapter can be summarized by equation (4), reproduced below:

$$\frac{V_T - K_T}{(1 + E[r_C])^T} = \frac{V_T}{(1 + E[r_V])^T} - \frac{K_T}{(1 + E[r_D])^T} \tag{6}$$

In essence, the basic project valuation methodology presented in section 29.1.1 quantified the right-hand side of this equation, by separately bringing back to time *0* the gross value of the to-be-built project and its construction cost and then performing the subtraction as of time *0* to obtain the $V_0 - K_0$ residual value exclusive of land cost. This was done because it is easier to estimate the values of the parameters on the right-hand side of the formula than to posit directly knowledge of the OCC of the development project itself, the $E[r_C]$ value on the left-hand side of (6). However, we noted in section 29.1.2 that once we have quantified $V_0 - K_0$ using the right-hand side of (6), we can easily solve the equation to "back out" the value of $E[r_C]$. In our FutureSpace example, the value of this OCC of the development investment was seen to be 20.16 percent (based on the "canonical" cash flow timing assumption):

$$1 + E[r_C] = \left(\frac{V_T - K_T}{V_0 - K_0}\right)^{1/T} = \frac{\$10.229 - \$6.068}{\$3.463} = 1.2016$$

Our *ad hoc* suggestion for evaluating multiphase development projects without using option modeling is to apply this approach to each phase, based on the projected most likely time when each phase will begin construction. For each phase, begin by quantifying the right-hand side of equation(6) for that phase only as if time *0* were the time when that phase is planned to begin construction (that is, *T* is the time-to-build for that phase alone). Then solve equation (6) for the $E[r_C]$ value that characterizes that phase. Finally, use this OCC of the phase to bring the *net* value of each phase (its "$V_0 - K_0$" value per equation (6)) back to the overall project's beginning point in time, the present (the real overall "time 0").

For example, suppose that our FutureSpace Center project is double the size we were previously considering, consisting of two identical phases, each of which includes twin buildings and a shared parking lot just like Hereandnow Place across the street. The project we have previously examined is now only the first phase of the overall two-phase project (which has four buildings altogether). Suppose that the first phase will begin construction right away, but the second phase is not slated to begin construction until two years from now. The value of the overall project (gross of land cost) would therefore be approximated as:[36]

$$V_0 - K_0 = V_0 - K_0 \, [\text{Phase I}] + \frac{V_0 - K_0 \, [\text{Phase II}]}{(1 + OCC_{II})^{\text{time to II}}}$$

$$= \$3,463,000 + \frac{\$3,463,000}{(1.2016)^2}$$

$$= \frac{\$10,229,000 - \$6,068,000}{(1.2016)^1} + \frac{\$10,229,000 - \$6,068,000}{(1.2016)^3}$$

$$= \$3,463,000 + \$2,398,000 = \$5,861,000$$

Notice that the value of the second phase within the overall time *0* present value of the project is considerably less than that of the (physically identical) first phase. This is due simply to the

---

[36]Note that it is mathematically equivalent to apply the discounting using the canonical OCC either of two ways: (i) in two steps, first computing the $V_0 - K_0$ value for each phase as of that phase's projected beginning point in time and then discounting that $V_0 - K_0$ value back to present for each phase; or (ii) in one step for each phase by discounting each phase's net $V_T - K_T$ value as of its completion directly all the way back to the present. Both of these approaches are shown in the calculations here. (Recall that the FutureSpace assets have no expected value or rental growth, but in the real world there would often be some expected growth that should be built into the expected future values.)

fact that the second phase is farther out in time and the OCC relevant for discounting such development projects is relatively high (in this case 20.16 percent per year), due to the inherent risk in such projects (fundamentally due to the operational leverage previously described).

While this general result makes sense, it is important to remember that the valuation obtained by this method ignores the value of flexibility in the option to build the second phase later (or, perhaps, earlier, if commencement of the second phase is not dependent on prior actions that will require two years). The valuation obtained through this simplified procedure may be either higher or lower than that implied by the more complete real options perspective. It will tend to be higher if the projected starting dates of the subsequent construction phases are unrealistically early. The simplified valuation will tend to be lower than the more correct option-based valuation if the projected starting dates of construction are excessively late, as this simplified procedure does not explicitly account for the value of timing flexibility for the construction starts.

29.5 Chapter Summary

This chapter is built on the theoretical treatment of land value and development timing presented in Chapter 27 to present an overview of the development decision-making process and a rigorous yet practical methodology for the investment analysis and evaluation of development projects. The main point of this chapter was to present and advocate the use of an NPV-based financial evaluation procedure for real estate development projects. The recommended procedure is based soundly in fundamental economic principles of opportunity cost and market equilibrium, and is consistent with modern corporate capital budgeting and securities investment theory, as well as with the valuation methodology presented in Parts IV and V of this book.

KEY TERMS

financial desirability	canonical formula of development	blended long-run IRR
time-to-build	project OCC	IRR "unblending"
phased risk regimes	real options model of land value	parallel development phases
operational leverage	developmental risk ratio	sequential development phases
price of risk	profit margin ratio	compound option
	enhanced cap rate on cost	

STUDY QUESTIONS

Conceptual Questions

29.1. Describe the three features that characterize real estate development projects and distinguish them from investments in fully operational (aka "stabilized") properties.

29.2. What is *operational leverage* in the context of a real estate development project? Explain why this characteristic causes investment in a development project to be riskier than investment in an otherwise similar stabilized property.

29.3. Explain why the opportunity cost of capital (OCC) of construction costs is usually not much greater than the riskfree interest rate.

29.4. Explain why a lender's expected return on a construction loan is lower than the stated construction loan interest rate and generally not much higher than the risk-free rate.

29.5. What two points in time are useful to define for the purpose of applying the NPV investment rule to development projects and for quantifying the development phase OCC?

29.6. Explain the economic intuition underlying the "canonical" formula for the development phase opportunity cost of capital (OCC), $E[r_C]$, in equation (4).

29.7. Under what condition is equation (4) consistent with the real option model of land value and optimal development timing of section 27.3?

29.8. In general what is the relationship between the highest and best use of a vacant site, the NPV of development exclusive of land cost, and the land value, assuming the site is ripe for development?

29.9. Describe the "enhanced cap rate on cost" technique developers often employ to examine the financial viability of development projects? How can this approach be consistent with the economically rigorous evaluation methodology developed in this chapter?

Quantitative Problems

29.10. **(NPV-Based Front Door & Back Door)** This problem revisits the proposed 20,000 SF office/warehouse flex space development first introduced in Problem 28.9 and gets you to apply an NPV-based back-door financial evaluation related to the approach recommended in this chapter. Market rents are about $15/SF and the local area has a 5% vacancy rate. All operating expenses are passed through to tenants except property taxes, insurance, and management, which you estimate at $5/SF per year. Construction costs are estimated at $1,030,075 as of project completion in one year (assume that construction is riskless). Lease-up is assumed to be instantaneous and the projected cap rate on the completed stabilized property NOI is 10%. The opportunity cost of capital for stabilized property is 11% and the riskfree rate is 6%.

    a. Use an NPV-based back-door approach to estimate the maximum land acquisition costs that can be supported by this project, assuming there are no other up-front development costs or fees other than land acquisition. [Hint: Determine the time *0* value of the developer's NPV exclusive of land cost as in the right-hand side of equation (4).]

    b. How does your answer in part (a) compare with the answer to Problem 28.9 part (a)? Which one is the better indicator of the true economic value of the site, and why? What information that is used in the Chapter 28 SFFA approach is not used in the NPV-based version, and vice versa?

    *c. Now apply an NPV-based front-door investment evaluation of the development and derive the required rent assuming the up-front land acquisition cost (inclusive of any other up-front development fees) is $700,000, and that this figure represents the developer's time *0* equity investment. [Steps: Grow the time *0* investment using the development phase OCC from the left-hand side of equation (4) to determine the minimum required value of the developer's equity as of the time of completion. Combine this with the construction cost as of completion to obtain the required projected stabilized asset value as of time of completion. Apply the cap rate to the result to obtain minimum required NOI, and then proceed as you did with the SFFA version.]

29.11. A developer is evaluating the economic profitability of a large-scale shopping center that will take an estimated 2 years to complete. Total (nonland) construction costs compounded forward to the time of completion are estimated to be $95 million and the estimated value of the completed stabilized property is $128 million. If the OCC of the construction costs is 5% and the OCC (going-in unlevered IRR) of the completed stabilized property is 8.5%, then according to the equilibrium relationship in equation (4), what is the appropriate opportunity cost of the development phase investment? (Assume annual compounding.)

29.12. Consider the development of a 100% preleased office building. Total development costs are estimated to be $55 million. The current (time *0*) opportunity cost, or market value, of the land is $15 million and construction cost draws are projected to be $40 million in total occurring as follows: $10 million at time *0*, $20 million one year later at the end of Year 1, and a final $10 million cost at the time of project completion at the end of Year 2. The value of the completed stabilized property at the end of Year 2 (*VT*) is projected to be $65 million. T-bills are currently yielding 5.5%. The opportunity cost of capital (OCC) for construction costs contains a 50-basis-point risk premium over T-bills and is at 6%. Stabilized built property commands an investment risk premium of 300 basis points over T-bills in its going-in IRR. With this information in mind, answer the following questions related to this development project. [Note, it is recommended that you answer this in an Excel worksheet so you can go back and examine the impact of changes in key variables (e.g. OCCs and property value at completion).]

a. Use the OCC of the construction costs to calculate the present value of the expected construction costs as of time 0, K_0, and use the OCC of stabilized built property to determine the present value of the $65 million estimated value upon completion, V_0.

b. Use your calculations from part (a) to compute the time 0 NPV of the development project ignoring any up-front (time 0) costs other than the land [and the initial construction cost draw, of course, which is already accounted for in your calculation in part (a)].

c. Suppose there is $1 million of additional up-front fees and costs, besides the land. Based on your answer in part (b), what is the implied maximum price the developer could pay for the land such that this development project would still be desirable at the present time?

d. Use your answer from part (c) along with the development cash flows (construction costs & stabilized value) to calculate the OCC of the development phase cash flows. [Hint: Find the IRR or discount rate that sets the NPV of development cash flows, including up-front land and other costs, to zero.]

e. Assuming that $15 million is the true current market value of the land (and that other up-front development fees would be no more than the $1 million), and assuming that the $40 million cost and $65 million value projections are realistic, what does your analysis in part (c) tell you about the relative ability of this developer to use this land parcel as compared to other developers?

f. If the subject developer is the first-best developer of this site, then is it possible that immediate initiation of the $40 million construction project might not be optimal for this developer? Explain.

*29.13. **(NPV of Development with a Lease-Up Phase)** Consider a speculative development project with the following characteristics: The current (time 0) market value of the land is $2 million and there are $200,000 in up-front design fees and developer costs attributable to time 0. Construction is expected to take three years, and the construction contractor is to be paid in three equal annual payments estimated to be $1.5 million at the ends of Years 1 through 3. While the exact amounts may vary ex post due to change orders, these costs are largely fixed by the pre-existing physical design of the structure. A construction loan will be obtained at a projected interest rate of 7.5% plus a $20,000 up-front origination fee (assume the construction loan is riskless so that $E[r_D] = r_D$). The construction loan will cover all of the projected $4.5 million direct construction cost, and the loan will be due in its entirety at the end of Year 3. The opportunity cost of equity capital invested in the development phase is estimated to be 20% per annum. The construction phase is expected to be followed by two years of absorption, with two annual net cash flows during this phase, at the end of Years 4 and 5. The expected net cash flow during Year 4 is −$100,000, as the building is expected still to be largely empty and to be incurring substantial tenant build-out and leasing expenses during that year. The expected cash flow in Year 5 is +$400,000, reflecting more rental revenue and fewer leasing expenses as the building fills up that year. This lease-up phase is less risky than the development phase, but more risky than the stabilized operating phase. The OCC for the absorption phase is estimated at 300 basis points higher than that for the fully operational property (details on this below). The lease-up phase is followed by the long-term fully operational phase of the completed project, starting from Year 6 and extending indefinitely into the future. Net property cash flows from this phase are expected to start out at $800,000 per year and grow annually each year thereafter at a rate of 1% per year. From the perspective of the beginning of Year 6 when the building has first become stabilized, these expected future cash flows have the risk of an unlevered investment in a fully-operational property. This is an amount of risk that warrants a 9% discount rate (going-in IRR from that time forward). *Determine the time zero NPV of the proposed development.* [Hint: Work backwards in time, starting with the stabilized property value after lease-up is completed, V_5. Use this value along with the expected cash absorption/lease-up year cash flows to calculate the estimated property value at the end of construction period, V_3. Be sure to use the appropriate phase-specific OCCs.]

LEASES AND LEASING STRATEGY

LEARNING OBJECTIVES

After reading this chapter, you should understand:

➲ The major characteristics and descriptive terminology used in commercial property leases in the United States.

➲ What is meant by "effective rent," "annuitized lease value," and how to calculate these values.

➲ The major factors determining lease value to the landlord that are left out of the effective rent or annuitized lease value calculation.

➲ Some major leasing strategy issues and trade-offs facing landlords and tenants.

The operating cash flow on which the value of commercial properties is based derives fundamentally from the space market that we explored back in Part II of this book. But more directly, this operating cash flow is mediated by leases, at least on the revenue side. In residential properties, leases are short term, typically yearly or month-to-month. In lodging properties, there are generally no leases at all. But in most other types of commercial property, long-term leases of various types are the norm. In all cases, the nature of leases, and the major considerations in leasing strategy, are key elements in the operational management of commercial properties and important determinants of the investment performance and value of such assets. Without attempting to be fully comprehensive in treating commercial property leases (a topic that would go well beyond the financial economics perspective from which this book is primarily written), we believe that it is nevertheless appropriate in this last chapter to introduce some of the basic terminology, analytical tools, and strategic considerations that are important from an economic perspective regarding commercial property leases and leasing.[1]

As a threshold consideration, let us ask a question that may at first seem too obvious: why does leasing exist? Why don't most users of commercial space build and own the space they use directly themselves? If you go back awhile, say before World War II, you will find that in fact owner-occupancy was much more common in commercial types of property than it is today, and it still is so in many other countries outside the United States. Leasing of commercial real estate has exploded in since the middle of the twentieth century in the United States. Why?

At the end of Chapter 14 we briefly touched on a major answer to this question: income taxes (and we explored that question in more depth in the Appendix 14C). The particular situations of tenants and landlords in the context of specific provisions of the corporate and personal income tax codes can cause leasing to create a tax arbitrage, to save taxes overall on a net basis across the property investors and the tenants (e.g., if the landlord is tax-exempt and the tenant is subject to double-taxation then the deduction of rent expenses from taxable income can more than offset the loss of depreciation tax shields).

But there are other important reasons why leasing exists besides taxes. A good overview and discussion is provided in Benjamin et al. (1998). There it is suggested that a major reason for leasing has to do with specialization of skills and expertise and economies of scale. The operation and management of built space has become a specialized industry in its own right in the United States and other mature economies. Landlords specializing in this business can do a better job of it than one-off owner-occupiers who are not primarily focused on the operation and management of built space per se. And there can be economies of scale in applying this special expertise. There may also be free rider or agency problems that can be solved by leasing. For example, if a single landlord owns all the spaces in which all the shops in a retail center operate, then centralized control can be exercised to optimize the functioning of the center as a whole. Common functions with positive externalities, such as provision of security, become the responsibility of the landlord who can assess the costs optimally from all of the space users via their rent. Location spillovers and synergies can be optimally managed. Other reasons for leasing can arise from heterogeneity or asymmetry in knowledge about the real estate market, in access to credit, or in preference for avoidance or exposure to specific real estate related risks.

For a variety of reasons, therefore, leasing has become the dominant way in which most commercial space is occupied and paid for by the space users in the United States, at least for the larger and more valuable properties that characterize the professional and institutional real estate investment industry. With this in mind, let's explore some of the basic and typical terminology and characteristics of leases.

---

[1]The reader may also want to review the Chapter 6 Appendix on the book's CD, which goes into more depth in particular regarding office rental demand, but also includes some terminology and metrics which are relevant to leases in general.

30.1 Commercial Property Lease Terminology and Typology

A **lease** involves a contract between a holder of property rights and a consumer or user of at least some of those rights, covering a specified period of time. The property owner or land-lord is referred to as the **lessor**.[2] The tenant is referred to as the **lessee**. Normally, the lease gives possession and usage rights but not development or redevelopment rights. An exception to this may occur in the case of very long-term leases of land, often referred to as **ground leases**. The price of the lease is normally called **rent** and is typically paid periodically, although up-front payments may also be included. In addition to possessory rights, the lease normally specifies other rights and duties on the part of the tenant as well as the landlord, and statutory or common law may dictate certain requirements, especially for residential properties. For example, the landlord may be required to provide a certain type of parking or signage. Lease law is an extensive branch of the law, and commercial lease contracts are usually very complex legal documents.[3]

30.1.1 Basic Lease Typology: The Responsibility for Expenses

Commercial property leases vary in how the operating expenses of the building are treated. Some leases require the landlord to pay these expenses, some leases require the tenant to pay them, and others provide for various forms of sharing of the operating expenses. By shifting some or all of the operating expense burden to the tenant, the landlord gains the obvious advan-tage of some protection against inflation in operating costs. The reduction in inflation risk to the landlord is offset by an increase in this risk to the tenant. Broadly, the different ways of handling operating expenses are represented in three types of leases: gross, net, and hybrid leases.

Gross Lease   In a gross lease, the landlord pays the operating expenses. This is also called a *full service lease* because the landlord provides such services as electricity, heat, water, clean-ing, maintenance, security, and so on, at no expense to the tenant. Generally, telecommunica-tions services are not included even in a full service lease.

Net Lease   In a net lease, the tenant is responsible for paying the operating expenses of the building. In a pure net lease (sometimes referred to as **triple net** or **NNN**), all or almost all of the operating expenses of the building are charged to the tenant, including even expenses that are fixed, that is, not sensitive to the level of occupancy in the building, such as property taxes and insurance costs. However, even with a pure net lease, the landlord may cover some expenses, such as the property manager's fees and costs specifically associated with leasing activities. In multitenant buildings, net leases usually provide for all of the building's expenses (even those associated with running the common areas, such as elevators, security, and lighting of lobbies) to be charged to individual tenants on a pro rata basis, determined by the fraction of the total rentable floor area occupied by each tenant. Typically, an estimate of building operating expenses is derived for the current year based on the past year's actual expense record, and monthly expense reimbursements will be paid by the tenants based on this estimate. Periodically (typically at the end of the year), the accounts are squared on the basis of the operating expenses actually incurred as evidenced in an auditable record. The total payments from the tenants to the land-lord thus consist of two components: the net rent payment and the expense reimbursement.

Hybrid Lease   A hybrid lease involves some aspects of both gross and net leases. In other words, the tenant and landlord share the payment of building operating expenses. This may be done in various ways. One common approach is for certain specific expenses to be desig-nated as the tenants' responsibility while other expenses are the landlord's responsibility. For example, the landlord might pay the fixed costs of property taxes and insurance, as well as

---

[2]The lessor is not necessarily the underlying property owner. He may be a leasehold owner, for example, the master tenant subleasing space to a subtenant.

[3]Lease law is beyond the scope of this text. For a treatment of this subject, the reader is referred to the voluminous literature on real estate law and lease law. A very readable introductory example is Jennings (1995).

utilities and services that cannot be metered separately for each tenant, such as water, building security, and common area costs, while the tenants are responsible for other utility and maintenance costs that can be attributed to each tenant.

A different approach to sharing expenses is known as **expense stops**, in which the tenant agrees to pay all operating expenses above a specified annual level known as the "stop." In effect, the expenses for the landlord stop growing at the specified stop level. This technique for sharing expenses is obviously designed to protect the landlord against inflation in operating expenses, as well as to provide the tenant with an incentive to keep operating costs down, while still providing the tenant with something pretty close to a full service lease. The expense stop is usually set at or near the level of operating expenses at the time the lease is signed, thereby guaranteeing the landlord against any effective increase in operating expenses she will have to pay during the life of the lease.

In multitenant buildings, the expense stops are typically negotiated separately for each lease, resulting in each lease possibly having a different stop amount. The expense stop provision causes tenants to be responsible for making expense reimbursement payments to the landlord based on their individual expense stop levels and a pro rata assignment of expense responsibility determined by the fraction of the building's rentable space each tenant occupies. For example, suppose a 100,000 SF building has two tenants, tenant A occupying 60,000 SF and tenant B 40,000 SF. Suppose the total operating expenses of the building are $500,000, (i.e., $5.00/SF) and that tenant A has an expense stop of $4.00/SF while tenant B has an expense stop of $4.50/SF. Then, in addition to their rent, tenant A would owe the landlord $60,000 ([$5.00 − $4.00] × 60,000 SF) and tenant B, $20,000 ([$4.50 − $4.00] × 40,000 SF) in expense reimbursements.

30.1.2 Types of Rent Changes in Leases

One of the most important characteristics of long-term commercial property leases that is of interest to investors is the way the rent is specified to change over time during the term of the lease contract. Rent changes serve several purposes. The most basic purpose is to reflect changes in the relevant space market that cause the equilibrium rent to change for new leases being signed in that market. Another purpose in the case of gross leases is to help protect the landlord from inflation in the operating expenses of running the building. A third purpose, which is important in retail leases, is to allow the landlord to share in the tenant's operating profits, as these profits are typically attributable in part to the store location and/or to the landlord's management of the shopping center of which it is a part. The five most common types of rent change provisions in long-term leases in the United States are described here.

Flat Rent   The simplest type of lease rental agreement provides for a fixed, constant rent level throughout the term of the lease; in other words, no rent change. Virtually all short-term leases have flat rent, and flat rent is not uncommon in longer-term leases as well, particularly during times of low general inflation.

Graduated Rent   The simplest type of lease that provides for a changing rent is called a graduated lease. Such a lease includes specified **step-ups** (or steps) in the rent. In this structure, both the timing and the amount of the rent changes are specified up front in the lease contract. For example, a 10-year graduated lease might start at $15/SF with a provision that at the end of every two years (i.e., after Years 2, 4, 6, and 8), the rent will increase by $1 per SF.

Revaluated Rent   A revaluation lease also specifies in the lease contract the *times* when the rental payments may change, but it does not specify in advance the exact dollar *amounts* of the rent changes. Instead, the lease specifies that the property (or the particular rental space and rental market) will be appraised by a professional real estate appraiser, and the rent will be adjusted accordingly. Sometimes, such revaluations call for upward-only adjustments in rent, while other leases allow the adjustment to be in either direction. In the latter case, this becomes a mechanism to keep the rent current with the changes in the local rental market. For example, a 20-year revaluation lease might specify that after every fifth year the property will be appraised by a certified appraiser and the rent set at one-tenth the property value, per year. Or the lease might call for an analysis of rents on new leases signed on comparable spaces in the local rental market and require the subject rent to be adjusted to the estimated fair market rental rate. Revaluation leases are particularly appropriate for very long-term leases and are traditionally common in the United Kingdom and some other European countries.

Indexed Rent Indexed leases call for the rent to be adjusted according to some publicly observable and regularly reported index, such as the consumer price index (CPI) or the producer price index (PPI). A typical indexed lease might require rents to be adjusted annually at some percentage of the CPI. For example, a 50 percent CPI adjustment would require the rent to be increased by 2.5 percent if inflation had been 5 percent (i.e., if the CPI had increased by 5 percent) during the preceding year. "Full" (i.e., 100 percent) CPI adjusted leases are not uncommon, but often the adjustment is less than full (50 percent being a typical level) because it may be perceived that building operating expenses typically do not grow as fast as inflation, or that the market rents that the building could charge would not grow as fast as inflation.

As a numerical example of how CPI-adjusted rent works, consider a lease that calls for an annual 75 percent CPI adjustment in the rent on the lease anniversary every July, based on the change in the CPI between the previous May and the May prior to that. Suppose the CPI in May of the prior year was 240 and the CPI in May of the current year was 250. Then there was $(250/240) - 1 = 4.17$ percent inflation. Seventy-five percent of 4.17 percent is 3.13 percent. So if the rent had been $12/SF per year (paid as $1/SF each month), then the new rent as of July would rise to $12.38/SF per year ($1.0313/SF paid each month), based on $1.0313 \times 12 = 12.38.

Percentage Rent Percentage leases also involve changes in rent over time. In this case, however, the motivation and nature of the change is rather different from the foregoing examples, and the application of percentage rent is limited to retail property space. In a percentage lease, the rent is a specified percentage of the sales revenue or net income earned by the tenant in the rented space. Often, the rent will include both a fixed component referred to as the **base rent** (which may or may not have any of the previously described change provisions) plus a percentage component. Sometimes the percentage component only applies to revenue or profits above a specified threshold amount. Percentage rents are especially common in class A multitenant retail space, such as shopping malls (and especially for the "in-line" stores rather than the anchor tenants). For example, the rent for a boutique space in a shopping mall might be defined as $10/SF per year plus 5 percent of the gross sales receipts of the store during the preceding year, prorated monthly. Obviously, such a lease would require a provision in the contract enabling the mall owner to audit the books of the shop.

30.2 Lease Characteristics Affecting Value or Rent

A number of characteristics go into the determination of the rent that the parties agree to in a lease, and also into the value the lease then has to the landlord once it is signed. Later in this chapter, we will discuss leasing strategy considerations more broadly from both the landlord and tenant perspectives. At this point, however, it may be useful by way of background to call your attention to several characteristics of the space, the tenant, and the lease itself that help to determine either the rent or the lease value (or both).

The Space The most basic and obvious determinant of the value of the space and, therefore, of the rent the landlord can charge is the nature of the product the tenant is getting in return for the rent, namely, the space itself. Obviously, location is an important characteristic of the space. As noted in the early parts of this book, location is important at several levels, ranging from the metropolitan area to the neighborhood to the specific site and even the location of the space within a multitenant building. For example, higher floors may command higher rents if views are valued or prestige is associated with high locations in the building. Rent and rentability are also strongly influenced by the physical and architectural qualities of the building and of the specific space being leased. In addition, the size, shape, and configuration of the space is also often of great importance in determining its usefulness to the tenant, and therefore the rent that can be charged. Two spaces in nearly identical locations may command very different rents because they are of different sizes or shapes. In general, rent per square foot (SF) tends to be minimized for space sizes near the most typical or widely demanded space size in the relevant space market, for which multitenant buildings are designed and therefore supply is greatest. Particularly large spaces may charge a premium, though occupancy of an entire floor can bring certain efficiencies or benefits to both the landlord and the tenant which can affect the rent.[4] At the other extreme, particularly small spaces can have unique and widely varying rental rates. (See the feature "How Rent Is Related to the Size of the Space Being Rented" on the next page.)

Tenant   Who the lessee is can also be important to the landlord. Some tenants are inevitably more desirable than others due to credit quality, prestige, or synergy with other tenants. The orchestration of positive externalities among tenants is a key part of the job of shopping mall managers, for example, as certain combinations and spatial positioning of types of shops will lead to greater sales volumes for all.[5] Tenants that rent large blocks of space early in the development of a new building provide a particular benefit for the landlord/developer. High-profile, prestige tenants whose names may appear on the outside of the structure also bring a particular benefit to the landlord. Two tenants in nearly identical spaces may not pay the same rent for reasons such as these.

Date and Term of the Lease   The length of time covered by the lease (the **lease term**), as well as the time the lease is signed and when it expires, can have value implications for the landlord. Other things being equal, landlords would typically prefer longer-term leases or leases that do not expire when a large number of other leases in the same building are scheduled to expire.

Rent   Obviously, the level of the rent, and the provisions for rent changes during the term of the lease, are fundamental and direct determinants of the value of the lease to the landlord. Indeed, this characteristic of lease value is so basic that we only mention it here to make the point that rent is not the *only* determinant of lease value. Other characteristics and considerations in this list interact with the rent in the overall determination of lease value for the landlord. Of course, rent by itself only affects the *gross* value of the lease, which is only one part of the NPV of the lease transaction decision, which must also consider the *opportunity cost* to the landlord (what the landlord gives up by entering into the lease agreement).

Concessions   Landlords often provide tenants with various forms of concessions, such as rent abatements and tenant improvement allowances, moving expense allowances, and so forth.[6] In general, concessions reduce the net cash flow the landlord receives from the lease, particularly at the outset or during the early stages of the lease. Landlords provide concessions to tenants as "sweeteners" to get them to sign leases that they otherwise would not agree to, with provisions that are beneficial to the landlord, or at a time when the rental market is unfavorable for the landlord.

Lease Covenants   The value of a lease to a landlord can be influenced by the specific covenants or provisions that are in the lease contract. In general, such provisions may limit or expand the landlord's and the tenant's rights and duties in ways that affect value. For example, tenants have the right to **sublet** (or assign the use of) their space unless this right is explicitly negated or limited in the lease contract. The ability to sublet the space gives the tenant flexibility and potential value. On the other hand, the landlord may want to control the type of tenant that moves in, or to share in any increase in rent.

---

[4]For example, there may then be no need for a common area on the floor.

[5]See, for example, Brueckner (1993).

[6]While some level of tenant improvement may be considered to be normally provided by the landlord (especially in a new or reconstructed building where the space has not been completely finished out), the provision of extra large tenant allowances for either tenant improvements or moving may be viewed as a concession.

Lease Options Leases often provide explicit options to either the tenant or the landlord. Some such options can importantly influence value. As noted in Chapter 27, in general an option refers to a right without obligation to obtain some benefit, perhaps requiring the payment of some additional sum to exercise the option. Options provide valuable flexibility to the option holder, but they may restrict the rights of the opposite party (the option grantor, either the landlord or tenant), thereby reducing value to that party (*ceteris paribus*). The most common lease options that benefit tenants include the following:

- **Renewal option:** Entitles tenant to renew the space at the end of the lease, either at a specified rent, or at prevailing market rents. If it is the latter, this option is similar to a right of first refusal.
- **Cancellation option:** May be written either for the landlord or tenant, entitling the option holder to cancel the lease prior to the end of the lease term (with specified notice).
- **Expansion option:** This may be in the form of a **right of first refusal** to the tenant for space adjacent to the leased space, or it may be a true lease option specifying a rent at which the tenant has the right but not obligation to take specified space during some specified window of time.

HOW RENT IS RELATED TO THE SIZE OF THE SPACE BEING RENTED

The chart shows how rent for office space typically varies by size. (The chart refers to a hypothetical but typical market.) In any given market the rents tend to be lowest at the most typical office space floor-plate size. This is the most substitutable and perfectly competitive space in the market. As tenants require larger and larger spaces there are usually fewer choices in the market. Such space is also more likely provided to an established firm and is often custom-built pre-leased or first generation space customized for the tenant. As such the cost of tenant improvements tends to be higher. For all these reasons the rents tend to be higher. (Exceptions can be found for anchor tenants or for leases used by the developer to launch or define the identity of the entire building.) As the tenant requires less than the average space we find more rental price dispersion. Some tenants are willing to fill in odd sized or small residual pieces within a building, while others are insistent on being in particular locations. Thus we observe the flexible small tenants are able to find relatively cheap space while the particular tenants must pay premiums. This expands the high–low range typically observed for small spaces.

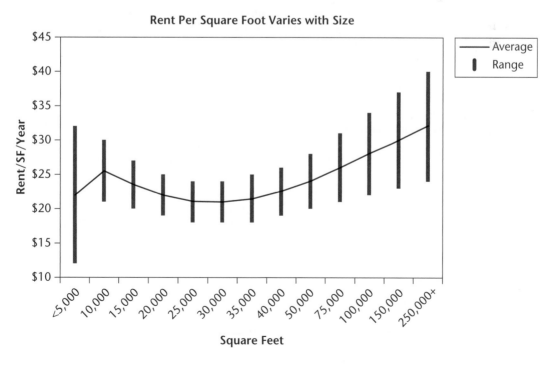

Rent Per Square Foot Varies with Size

30.3 Annuitized Lease Value and Effective Rent

The term **effective rent** is used quite commonly in commercial real estate, but it is often not clearly defined, and people may mean different things when they use the term. Most broadly, effective rent is simply a per annum or per period rental rate that reflects not just the initial stated rent but other aspects of the long-term lease that affect the lease's present value. For example, there may be some free rent given by the landlord to the tenant up front as an incentive to move in. Not uncommonly there may be step-ups in the rent at future points in time within the lease term (as described in section 30.1.2). The concept of effective rent somehow collapses and reflects all (or some) such considerations into a single per period rent number.

The simplest way to do this is to just add up all the rental payments provided for under the lease contract (reflecting step-ups or possibly estimates of conditional step-ups), net of or minus any special concessions or incentives provided by the landlord, and then divide by the total number of rental periods in the lease contract. In this simplest approach there is no attempt to discount for time or risk as in a more rigorous present value analysis. This simple definition of effective rent is often how the term is applied in common practice, especially in the leasing brokerage industry. However, there is also substantial (and growing) use of more sophisticated measures of effective rent that do attempt to account for time and present value. We will focus on such a more sophisticated or rigorous measure, but to make it clear that we are doing so, we shall use the more explicit term **annuitized lease value** (ALV), instead of "effective rent." (But keep in mind that in common parlance what we will now refer to as ALV may often be called "effective rent" in practice.[7])

The ALV of a lease is a level annuity that has the same present value as that of the expected cash flows of the lease. In current practice, the discounting is often done in an ad hoc manner by applying a constant discount rate for all leases and all tenants (10 percent is probably the most widely used rate). However, ALV can be defined more rigorously based on the economic present value of the lease, which of course requires using the economic OCC as the discount rate to compute the annuity. Our focus here will be on the more rigorous, economics-based perspective.

ALV can be computed from either the landlord's or tenant's perspective. When dealing with long-term leases, the rigorous economics-based ALV construct can aid in the comparison across alternative lease structures and lease terms, although one must be careful in making such comparisons. The effective rent typically does not satisfactorily quantify all of the relevant issues to either side. Nonfinancial considerations not captured in the ALV metric may dominate a lease decision, such as exclusive floor access, external signage requirements, exclusive parking access or services, or the nature of co-tenants.

ALV is computed in two steps. First, you calculate the present value of the expected cash flow under the lease. We will label this value LPV:

$$LPV = CF_1 + \frac{CF_2}{1+k} + \frac{CF_3}{(1+k)^2} + \cdots + \frac{CF_T}{(1+k)^{(T-1)}} \tag{1a}$$

where T is the lease term, CF_t is the net cash flow to the landlord in year t, and k is the discount rate.[8] To compute effective rent from the tenant's perspective, the CF_t amounts should represent the tenant's gross cash outflows due to all space occupancy costs, including

---

[7]The CCIM Institute teaches the calculation of effective rent in a manner consistent with what we are calling ALV here. By 2012, CoStar and some other rental market information vendors were also calculating effective rents in the ALV manner.

[8]Here we are depicting annual cash flows for simplicity of illustration, but a more precise calculation would use monthly cash flows for monthly rent, although the ALV is then often quoted in nominal annual terms as 12 times the monthly rent. Also, note that in leases (unlike mortgages and most other financial calculations) payments are usually *in advance* (that is, at the beginnings of the periods, rather than *in arrears*). Thus, the first cash flow is usually at time *0* and therefore undiscounted (already in present value). However, with concessions, this first cash flow may be zero or even negative, for example, if the landlord must pay the tenant's moving costs.

ARE RENEWAL OPTIONS "AT MARKET RENT" WORTHLESS?

Lease renewal options are often written giving the tenant the right to renew at the market rent prevailing at the time of lease expiration. There might be a provision for this market rent to be determined by an appraiser if the tenant and landlord cannot agree as to what the market rent is at that time. In a highly efficient ("information rich") rental market (i.e., one in which there is a lot of easily available information about the rents and other terms in the leases being signed, and in which there is a lot of leasing activity employing relatively homogeneous leases on relatively homogeneous spaces), this option is effectively no more than a right of first refusal. Such rights have value to the tenant, because they enable the tenant to be assured that he can avoid the cost of moving if he doesn't want to move. Otherwise, there will exist what economists call a "holdup problem" to the writing of the lease contract. The landlord could potentially "hold up" the tenant at the end of the lease term, and the tenant would have to factor in the expected cost of this holdup in the rent they would agree to in the first place.

While the "at market" renewal option thus facilitates the lease agreement from the tenant's perspective, it may have some slight cost to the landlord because it removes the potential negotiating leverage the landlord could otherwise use to try to obtain a slightly above-market rental rate from the tenant (on the basis that the tenant would save moving expenses).[1]

In a thin ("information poor") market like many real estate rental markets, the option to renew at market value has an additional value to the tenant (and cost to the landlord). In such a market, it is never obvious exactly what the market rent is for a given space at a given time (hence the possible need for an appraiser to arrive at a value estimation). In such circumstances, the landlord might be able to find a particularly eager tenant who was willing to pay, in effect, more than the going market rent (and more even than the existing tenant, who would face moving costs if he did not renew). While the chance of this happening might be small, nothing prevents the landlord from trying, unless the tenant has a renewal option.[2]

Thus, in real estate a renewal option may have some value to the tenant (and cost to the landlord) even if the option is only for renewal at prevailing market rates and assuming the contract gives the tenant some power over the estimation of what that market rate is (e.g., by giving the tenant a say in the selection of the rent appraiser). Presumably, in equilibrium (in the space market) this value-and-cost is equated in the rent and other terms agreed to by both parties in the lease.

To quantify the value of such a renewal option, one could use a decision tree framework similar to that described in Appendix 30A on the CD accompanying this book. From the landlord's perspective, the upside (opportunity cost) branch of the tree would be based on the difference between the expected market rent and the potential upside that the landlord might be able to get from an eager tenant willing to pay more than market rent (net of the landlord's expected search costs) or from the existing tenant who would avoid moving costs by renewing. From the tenant's perspective, the upside branch would be based on the minimum of either the landlord's differential (noted earlier) or the expected moving costs the tenant would face if required to move to another equivalent space at the market rent. In both cases, the downside branch would have a zero value, as options present rights, not obligations (see Chapter 27). The values would be discounted and multiplied by probabilities, as in the example in Appendix 30A, with the upside probability reflecting the ex ante likelihood that the landlord could get the above-market lease from either a new tenant or the existing tenant.

---

[1]Note, however, that the tenant has a counter-threat in a thin or down leasing market: If the tenant leaves, the landlord will typically have to incur some search and transaction costs to find a new tenant, even without charging more than the "market rent."

[2]Note that optimal search behavior on the part of the landlord does not imply that the ex ante expectation is that the landlord *will* find an above-market tenant, but it may imply some *possibility* of the landlord finding such a tenant.

---

payment of whatever building operating expenses are not covered by the landlord (e.g., in a net lease). In the second step of the ALV calculation, you determine the annualized value (or equivalent level annuity payment) of the LTV:[9]

$$Effective\ rent = \frac{(LPV)k}{(1+k)[1-1/(1+k)^T]} \tag{1b}$$

where k is the same discount rate as previously, and T is again the term of the lease.[10]

---

[9]See equation (8a), in section 8.2.3 in Chapter 8.

[10]Note that in real world practice the annuity in arrears formula is often used, technically incorrectly, although usually it makes little difference.

LEASE TERMS AND THE PROBABILITY OF LEASE RENEWAL BASED ON A MARKET SURVEY

In 2010 one of the book's authors had the chance to partici-pate in several focus group meetings with commercial brokers specializing in tenant representation. The following synopsis is a result of those discussions along with input from principals at CoStar Group. Insight into lease renewal probability is useful because of its significant financial implications for owners of real estate and how it can inform strategic decisions as to lease terms from either the landlord or tenant perspective. For example, from a landlord's perspective it is generally advanta-geous to select tenants with more stability and less rent price sensitivity.

Lease cycles matter. Lumpy surges in supply, fairly pre-dictable trends in absorption and vacancy rates (significant serial correlation), and the tendency to use similar lease terms within a market make it possible to determine if we are in a relatively soft or strong rental market from the landlord's perspective. In a soft market tenants are more able and more likely to bargain for longer lease terms. If the market is soft but expectations are for strong increases in rents in a few years, landlords are more likely to want to use short-term leases.

Tenant size matters. Larger tenants that fill a large portion of a building are riskier in the sense that they have more impact on the proforma if they leave. At the same time it is much harder for tenants to find large contiguous spaces except in the very largest of cities, so renters of large spaces tend to be much more stable tenants, often renewing when leases expire. (See Asser, 2004, for evidence that tenants above 20,000 square feet renewed 82 per-cent of the time compared to 57 percent for those under 20,000 square feet and 52 percent for those under 5,000 square feet.)

Industry type matters. Certain industry types tend to be more stable and renew with greater probability. For example, government offices seldom move, and law firms and architecture firms tend to renew at high rates. Insurance firms and research firms tend to be more sensitive to rent price, and tend to move more frequently because they use more generic space.

Green matters. Certain tenants have committed to greater sustainability and will move unless space is Energy Star or LEED certified. This includes the US GSA, the California GSA and many publicly-traded corporations such as Procter and Gamble, Herman Miller, and others.

30.3.1 Discount Rate in the ALV

In the computation of ALV, it is common practice for the discount rate (k) to be approxi-mated rather casually for the typical tenant, using some conventional rule of thumb. For example, 10 percent per year (or 0.833 percent per month) has been widely used. When such blanket rule-of-thumb discounting is used, with the same rate applied to all leases and all tenants and without regard to the current yields and term structure of interest rates in the bond market, the ALV (or in this case probably referred to as "effective rent") calculation is in theory little more than a type of shorthand way of quoting rents to account for conces-sions and landlord capital expenditures (such as tenant improvement expenditures, TIs).[11] ALV used in this way does not measure very precisely the impact of the lease on the market value of the lessor's property rights. While ALV defined in this simplified way does have some practical usefulness, it is not rigorous from a financial economics perspective, and in the present section we will suggest a more correct and sophisticated approach that is still intuitive and easy to apply.

Suppose we are interested in defining the ALV so that it reflects the market value that the lease would have, say, in a lease-obligation-backed security (LOBS) traded in the bond mar-ket.[12] Then the discount rate used in the ALV calculation should reflect the credit rating of the tenant as well as the current yield curve in the bond market. In other words, k should equate to the rate at which the tenant could borrow money in an unsecured loan with duration equal to the duration of the lease cash flows.[13] After all, the lease cash flows are contractual cash flows backed by the credit of the tenant, similar to loan cash flows pledged to a lender

---

[11]As noted, it is not uncommon in practice for discounting to be ignored altogether in the effective rent calculation (effectively assuming $k = 0$).

[12]LOBS, which is similar to a mortgage backed security, is discussed briefly in section 10.2 in Chapter 10. In actual practice not all leases are effectively "bondable," and even those that are sometimes, are evaluated with a small "illi-quidity premium" in their OCC. Therefore, it might be appropriate to add a small extra premium to the debt OCC of the tenant in estimating the OCC applicable to the lease.

[13]Duration was defined in Chapter 19, section 19.1.1.

when the tenant borrows money.[14] In fact, the tenant's borrowing rate is a good rate to use to compute the ALV from the tenant's perspective, at least for a typical fixed-rent lease.[15]

The computation of ALV from the landlord's perspective may be viewed a little differently. The landlord is typically interested in using the ALV to measure the impact of the lease on the market value of his property. For this purpose, it makes more sense to define the ALV based on the present value attributable to the space that is being leased over the time period covered by the lease. This present value consists of two components. The first is the value of the lease itself, for example, as it would be valued as a component in a LOBS traded in the bond market, as we just described. To evaluate this component of the landlord's value, the tenant's borrowing rate on an unsecured loan would indeed be the correct discount rate, as we described earlier. But another component to the landlord's value is usually associated with the leased space itself. How does that affect the calculation?

If there is a positive probability that the tenant will default on her lease, then discounting the lease cash flows at the tenant's unsecured borrowing rate will reflect the effect of this default probability on the present value of the lease. In other words, the lease present value will be reduced by the probability that some components of the contractual lease cash flow might never be paid by the tenant.[16] These unpaid rents would indeed be losses to the bondholders of a LOBS backed by the lease.[17] But the landlord probably would not face that much loss in cash flow from the leased space in the event of tenant default during the lease term. In a long-term lease, it is likely that the landlord would be able to evict the defaulted tenant and rent the space to a new tenant before the end of the original lease term. For this reason, a lower discount rate, better approximated by the rate at which the tenant could borrow on a *secured* loan, would typically be a more appropriate discount rate to use to compute the effective rent from the landlord's perspective.[18]

30.3.2 ALV Numerical Examples

To illustrate the calculation and usage of the ALV as defined, we will examine two hypothetical leases in this section, from both the landlord's and the tenant's perspectives. Both leases are net, that is, the tenant pays the operating expenses.

Lease A is characterized as follows:

- Term: Five years
- Rent: $20/SF, net
- Concessions: One year free rent, up front
- Tenant still pays operating expenses during rent holiday

---

[14]If the lease includes revaluation, indexing (such as CPI adjustments), or percentage of sales components, then the lease cash flows will not be exactly like those of fixed interest rate bonds, as they will have some contractual volatility. Such differences could affect the appropriate discount rate in either direction. For example, a CPI-adjusted lease results in the lease being a partial hedge against inflation risk (better than bonds), and therefore should probably be discounted at a lower OCC than the tenant's borrowing rate.

[15]Note that the default risk is based on the probability that the tenant will become insolvent or declare bankruptcy. Thus, for example, if the U.S. government is the tenant, then the yield on the appropriate duration Treasury bond would be the correct discount rate for computing the ALV.

[16]Recall from Chapters 18 and 19 that the loan interest rate reflects the stated yield, which includes an ex ante yield degradation component so that the contractual cash flows (without provision for expected losses due to default) will discount at the stated yield rate to the present value of the loan. See, for example, section 19.2.1 in Chapter 19.

[17]Actual LOBS often have default protection provided or paid for by the landlord. For this reason, the yield on LOBS may not be reflective of the appropriate unsecured tenant borrowing rate to use in computing the ALV on a specific lease.

[18]Note that, in principle, the state variable that governs the tenant's lease default event likely has more to do with the net income or value of the tenant's firm than with not the market rent or value in the real estate space or asset market in which the building is situated. In the absence of an explicit cancellation option written into the lease, only limited liability and bankruptcy law enables the tenant to have a put option on their leased space, that is, the ability to avoid payment of remaining rents under the lease. More sophisticated approaches to lease valuation based on real options valuation theory (as introduced in Chapter 27) can often allow a more rigorous valuation of leases, particularly complex leases involving options of various types written into the lease. For example, Steve Grenadier (1995b) developed a procedure that also incorporates the dynamics of the space rental market into the lease valuation procedure.

Assuming a discount rate of 7 percent, lease A's ALV is seen to be \$15.44/SF, computed as follows:[19]

$$LPV = \$0 + \frac{\$20}{1.07} + \frac{\$20}{(1.07)^2} + \frac{20}{(1.07)^3} + \frac{\$20}{(1.07)^4} = \$67.74$$

$$\textit{Effective rent } (A) = \$67.74(0.07)/\{1.07[1 - 1/(1.07)^5]\} = \$15.44/SF$$

Lease B is characterized as follows:

- Term: Six years
- Rent: \$24/SF, net
- Concessions: Two years free rent, up front
- Tenant still pays operating expenses during rent holiday

Again assuming a discount rate of 7 percent, lease B's ALV is seen to be \$14.90/SF, as computed here:

$$LPV = \$0 + \frac{\$0}{1.07} + \frac{\$24}{(1.07)^2} + \frac{\$24}{(1.07)^3} + \frac{\$24}{(1.07)^4} + \frac{\$24}{(1.07)^5} = \$75.97$$

$$\textit{Effective rent } (B) = \$75.97(0.07)/\{1.07[1 - 1/(1.07)^6]\} = \$14.90/SF$$

Other things being equal, the landlord would prefer lease A because \$15.44 > \$14.90.

Now consider these same two leases from the perspective of the tenant. As these are net leases, the tenant must add the expected operating expenses he will have to pay in order to compute the total ALV from his perspective.[20] This is necessary so that comparisons between alternative leases with different expense provisions can be made on an apples-to-apples basis. Supposing that operating expenses are initially \$10/SF and are expected to grow at a rate of 2 percent per year, we have the following ALV calculations from the tenant's perspective. Note that we will use a modestly higher discount rate of 8 percent instead of 7 percent to reflect the lack of residual value in the event of default as described at the end of section 30.3.1.

Lease A (tenant's perspective):

$$LPV = \$10.00 + \frac{\$30.20}{1.08} + \frac{\$30.40}{(1.08)^2} + \frac{\$30.61}{(1.08)^3} + \frac{\$30.82}{(1.08)^4} = \$110.99$$

$$\textit{Tenant ALV } (A) = \$110.99(0.08)/\{1.08[1 - 1/(1.08)^5]\} = \$25.74/SF$$

Lease B (tenant's perspective):

$$LPV = \$10.00 + \frac{\$10.20}{1.08} + \frac{\$34.40}{(1.08)^2} + \frac{\$34.61}{(1.08)^3} + \frac{\$34.82}{(1.08)^4} + \frac{\$35.04}{(1.08)^5} = \$125.86$$

$$\textit{Tenant effective rent } (B) = \$125.86(0.08)/\{1.08[1 - 1/(1.08)^6]\} = \$25.21/SF$$

Thus, not surprisingly, the tenant has the opposite preferences to the landlord. *Other things being equal*, the tenant prefers lease B over lease A, because \$25.21 < \$25.74.[21]

---

[19]Note that the effect of the concession of one year free rent causes the first year's cash flow to the landlord to be zero. In the present example, we have ignored leasing costs borne by the landlord, such as tenant improvement expenditures (TIs). In reality, such costs often cause the first year of the lease to have net negative cash flow for the landlord. In any case, it is important to include the effect of landlord leasing costs such as TIs in the computation of the ALV from the landlord's perspective, for purposes of comparing the value of alternative lease proposals.

[20]Landlord capital expenditures offered to the tenant as part of the lease package (TIs) need not generally be explicitly incorporated in the tenant's ALV calculation. However, in comparing alternative lease proposals, the tenant needs to consider possible differences between the TIs being offered in the different proposals as they may lead to better quality of space in one location or the other. Obviously, common sense must apply in evaluating an overall lease proposal package. It may make sense for a tenant to pay a higher ALV if in return he receives a TI allowance or build-out from the landlord that makes the space sufficiently more attractive.

[21]To facilitate comparisons between alternative lease offers, ALVs should normally be based on net cash flows, that is, *net* rents from the landlord's perspective and *gross* rents from the tenant's perspective.

In reality, where the two parties end up would depend on relative success in negotiation (in part reflecting the current supply-and-demand balance in the space market). That final position would also reflect other considerations important to either party beyond what is included in the ALV calculations described here.

The leases we have examined here are very simple, involving no renewal or cancellation options. Appendix 30A on the CD accompanying this book presents a simple way of approximately adjusting the ALV calculation to incorporate a renewal option.

30.3.3 Summarizing ALV and Effective Rent

Although ALV, when properly calculated based on a risk-adjusted discount rate, gives an important indication of the value of a given lease, neither the tenant nor the landlord should necessarily prefer the lease alternative with the best (i.e., lowest or highest, respectively) ALV. The reason is that important strategic considerations are left out of the ALV calculation. This statement applies doubly for less rigorously defined effective rent not based on the economic present value of the lease. In the remainder of this chapter, we turn our attention to these broader leasing strategy considerations.

30.4 Broader Leasing Strategy Considerations: Term Length and the Space Market Term Structure of Rent

Among the most important leasing strategy considerations not present in the ALV or effective rent calculation is the length of the lease term. We will consider this issue in this section from both the landlord and tenant perspectives, including a consideration of implications for the resulting equilibrium or normative **term structure of rents**, that is, the way rents should vary in the space market at a given time as a function of the lease term. A good way to approach this question is to consider what is left out of the ALV construct we described in the previous section. In other words, why would a landlord sometimes prefer a lease alternative with a lower ALV or a tenant prefer an alternative with a higher ALV?

30.4.1 Interlease Risk

First, consider the pure effect of lease-term length, independent of changes in the relevant rental market. As noted in the previous section, the tenant's borrowing rate reflects the risk *within* each lease once it is signed, that is, the risk that needs to be considered in the **intralease discount rate**. This is the only risk relevant to determining the present value of the lease once it is signed, and hence the only risk that is incorporated in the ALV measure (via the ALV discount rate, k). But the intralease discount rate does not well reflect the risk *between* leases across time, the risk relevant for what we previously called the **interlease discount rate**.[22] The interlease discount rate is the rate applied to discount expected future cash flows from leases not yet signed, discounting across time periods between the successive lease signing dates. The interlease discount rate is usually considered to be higher than the intralease discount rate because the expected cash flows are not contractually fixed between leases: it is not known for certain at what rent level a future lease will be signed. Thus, the expected cash flows beyond an existing lease would be more risky than those within an existing lease.

To the extent this is so, there is an important implication from the fact that interlease risk is not reflected in the ALV calculation: *longer-term leases reduce risk in a way that is not reflected in the ALV calculation*. Longer-term leases reduce the uncertainty in the landlord's future cash flow expectations by contractually fixing more future years' worth of cash flow from the building. This makes the landlord's property rights more like a bond and less like property equity, in terms of investment performance. Other things being equal, this

---

[22]Differential intra- and inter-lease discounting was introduced in Chapter 8 (section 8.2.7) and Chapter 10 (section 10.2.1).

would typically be perceived as making the landlord prefer longer-term leases at the same ALV, or be willing to accept lower ALV for longer-term leases, relative to a projection of what the future short-term (or **spot**) rents will be. Appendix 30B on the CD accompanying this text presents a numerical example and quantitative discussion of this issue.

While the above reasoning and analysis are both intuitively appealing and correct in principle, there are several considerations that mitigate against interlease risk causing a downward-sloping term structure of rents. First, as will be discussed in section 30.4.3, interlease risk considerations only lead to a *relative* downward slope in the rent structure, relative to future spot rental market expectations. Second, as can be seen in Appendix 30B, the magnitude of the downward rent-term structure slope is relatively shallow. Even when we assume a 400 basis-point differential between interlease and intralease OCC (as in the appendix), the result is a 10-year lease annual rent that is only some 15 percent less than that of a corresponding one-year lease rent, assuming a flat rental market.[23]

Third, we are ignoring here two aspects of the bond market that could be important, both of which were discussed in Chapter 19. First is the typical yield curve in the bond market, which we noted in Chapter 19 is upward-sloping due, fundamentally, to interest rate risk. Although even 10-year leases do not have terribly long duration (less than five years), the yield curve could in principle dampen or even negate the interlease risk effect, as the *intralease* OCC for longer-term leases would come from a longer-term (typical intermediate duration) part of the yield curve, while the intralease OCC for short-term leases would come from the short end of the yield curve. This will reduce the interlease-intralease OCC differential the longer the lease term.

The more counter-intuitive point raised in Chapter 19 is that there is some evidence that at least some parts of the bond market view bonds as being very nearly as risky, or perhaps even as risky, as at least some types of real property investment. (Recall our discussion in section 19.2.2 about whether there is "positive leverage" in real estate debt.) The implication could be that the OCC differential between interlease and intralease expected returns is considerably less than the 400bp assumption in Appendix 30B on the CD accompanying this book.

All of these considerations leave somewhat up in the air the question of the impact of interlease risk on the normative lease-term structure of rents. Empirical evidence is still too scarce to shed much light on the question. In part, this is because of other confounding influences on leases, to which we turn in the following sections.

30.4.2 Releasing Costs

Another consideration that is important in leasing strategy, but that is left out of the ALV or effective rent calculation of section 30.3, is **releasing costs**. Typically, both the landlord and the tenant face costs associated with releasing. Many of these costs are not included in the effective rent calculation. For example, landlords face expected vacancy and search costs to find a new tenant whenever a lease expires without being renewed. Tenants face moving costs, including disruption of operations.

Because releasing presents potential deadweight costs to both sides in the lease agreement, releasing considerations generally affect both sides of the lease negotiation, landlord and tenant, in the same direction as far as preferred lease term is concerned. In particular, releasing costs make it advantageous for both sides to prefer longer-term leases, *ceteris paribus*. In this respect, releasing costs are different from the interlease risk we considered in the previous section.

In contrast, interlease risk causes landlords to prefer longer-term leases, while tenants prefer shorter-term leases, *ceteris paribus*. Thus, interlease risk has a clear implication for a

---

[23]Recent theoretical work by Clapham and Gunnelin (2003) also suggests that interest rate risk interacting with rental market risk can in certain circumstances cause the term structure of rents to differ from the simple slight downward slope suggested in the deterministic equilibrium model described above. In other circumstances, the downward slope could be reinforced by these considerations. If we assume that investors view rental markets as being more risky than lease-contractual cash flows (interlease OCC > intralease OCC), the Clapham-Gunnelin model is consistent with the downward-sloping term structure suggested here and in Appendix 30B.

downward-sloping term structure of rents as an equilibrium result in the space market (as shown in Appendix 30B on the CD), while releasing costs do not carry a general implication in principle for the term structure of rents in equilibrium.[24]

Instead, the consideration of releasing costs suggests a general bias toward longer-term leases at whatever term structure of rents prevails in the market, so as to minimize releasing costs over the long run. However, this bias can be mitigated to some degree by the use of contractual devices to reduce the **holdup problem**, at least on one side. (A *holdup problem* is when one party to an agreement can potentially extract unfair advantage of the other party in the future as a result of the situation established in the agreement.) For example, an option to renew "at market" (equivalent to a "right of first refusal"), reduces the ability of the landlord to "hold up" the tenant by threatening to force the tenant to pay moving costs, without the landlord giving up the chance to earn market rents.

In some circumstances, holdup costs are potentially particularly severe and cannot be effectively mitigated by contractual provisions. This is most notably the case when the tenant requires a highly customized space that requires substantial unique investment that cannot be recuperated, and where the space is vital to the tenant's operations. Such unique space in effect does not trade in a space market: because it is so customized for a particular user, there is no other potential demand for it or supply of it, hence no space market. This makes renewal options "at market rent" difficult to enforce. In such cases, the holdup problem from the tenant's perspective tends to lead to very long-term leases or even to "corporate real estate" in which the user-occupant of the space decides to purchase the property outright in fee simple ownership.[25]

30.4.3 Expectations about the Future Rental Market

Expectations regarding the future trend in spot rents in the relevant space market make the opportunity cost of the lease a function of the lease term, and this is not included in the ALV formula we previously presented. For example, if spot rents are expected to rise, then longer-term leases must have higher ALVs than they otherwise would. This is required for both landlords and tenants to be indifferent between long- and short-term leases. With rising spot rent expectations, the expected opportunity cost (to the landlord) or opportunity value (to the tenant) of forgoing a strategy of rolling over short-term leases is greater for longer-term leases within the horizon of rising projected spot rents. If, on the other hand, spot rents are expected to fall, then the opposite is the case, and longer-term leases should have lower ALVs relative to shorter-term leases than would be the case otherwise. To the extent that such expectations reflect both sides of the rental market, they will be reflected in the equilibrium lease term structure of rents. (This is very analogous to the "expectations hypothesis" of the bond market yield curve discussed in section 19.1.3 of Chapter 19.) This expectation effect overlays the generally slightly downward-sloping equilibrium term structure of rents with constant spot-rent expectations due to the interlease risk effect noted in section 30.4.1.[26]

---

[24]Some authors have asserted that considerations of "transactions costs" associated with the leasing transaction would lead to a downward-sloping lease term structure of rent, as landlords would prefer longer-term leases to reduce the impact of transactions costs. [See, e.g., Miceli and Sirmans (1999), and Englund et al. (2004)]. However, this suggestion may be ignoring the tenant's side of the market (or of the lease negotiation), in which the tenant also faces releasing costs. With a deadweight transaction cost burden on both sides of the market, the equilibrium rent implication is ambiguous.

[25]See Fisher (2004). Also see Appendix 14 on the accompanying CD on corporate real estate.

[26]Note that, at least from the landlord's perspective, the spot-rent expectations that matter are those relevant to a given (aging) building, not the average rent in the space market across all buildings currently in that market at each point in time. The age of the average building in the market may not increase with chronological time, as the building stock in the submarket may be renewed. But the opportunity cost of long-term leasing to the landlord is based on what the landlord could rent the space in the given building for in short-term leases rolled over at the prevailing short-term market rent. This is also the relevant opportunity value for the tenant, holding the level of service constant at that provided by the same building over time. It is also important to account for the lease-term length in comparing rental rates across time. As suggested in section 30.4.1, comparisons of long- and short-term lease rental rates at any point in time will be "apples-versus-oranges." See also Englund et al. (2004).

If landlord and tenant expectations differ regarding the future trend in spot rents in the market, such differences might be either complementary or conflicting in terms of reaching a negotiated lease agreement. For example, if the tenant believes rents will rise and the landlord believes rents will fall, then expectations are **complementary** in the sense that it will be easier for the two sides to come to an agreement. If the landlord believes rents will rise and the tenant believes rents will fall, then expectations are **conflicting** in the sense that it will be more difficult for the two sides to agree to a rent level. In the event of conflicting expectations, if one side or the other (or both) can convince the other to change his or her space market rent expectations, at least partially, in the direction of the other's, then agreement will be facilitated. If space market expectations are conflicting and not reconcilable, then agreement will be facilitated by reducing the lease-term length, thereby reducing the impact of future changes in market rents on the opportunity cost of the lease.

In effect, shorter lease-term length provides both the landlord and the tenant more flexibility to take advantage of favorable developments in the rental market. Thus, to the extent that there is uncertainty about future market rents such that landlords and tenants can have significantly conflicting expectations, this can lead both landlords and tenants in the same general direction, namely, toward preferring shorter-term leases. In this respect, space market expectations do not carry an overall general implication for the equilibrium term structure of rents. However, rental market uncertainty alone, without conflicting expectations, does not necessarily lead to a preference for shorter-lease terms, but it does lead to increased incentive to provide explicit options in the lease, for both sides (see section 30.4.4).

A final question regarding the effect of future rent expectations on the lease-term structure of rents is how "rational" are the market's future rent expectations, at least as evidenced in the actual empirical lease rental provisions that prevail in the market. By **rational expectations**, we mean that on average, across many leases and over the long run, the rents agreed to in the leases are unbiased predictors of the actual corresponding future market rents (for similar leases, including similar duration). In other words, are the rental market's apparent expectations about future rents, as implied by long-term lease-rental provisions, born out in reality, on average, by actual future rents? There is little solid empirical evidence that helps to answer this question, and what there is appears to be mixed. Gunnelin and Soderberg (2003), for example, find evidence that office rents in long-term leases in central Stockholm successfully predicted the downturn in that market in the early 1990s. But a more recent and broader study of Swedish markets rejects the hypothesis that the implied "forward rents" in the long-term leases are unbiased predictors of the future rental markets. However, some of this "bias" may be "rational" if it appropriately reflects the downward-sloping term structure described in section 30.4.1.

30.4.4 Uncertainty and the Value of Flexibility and Options in Leases

Certain characteristics of leases and leasing strategy can affect the future decision flexibility of either the tenant or the landlord, or both. Flexibility is valuable because it gives options to decision makers and yet does not reflect the effective rent calculation per se. We have just noted how shorter lease terms increase a certain type of flexibility for landlords and tenants, namely, the flexibility to take advantage of favorable movements in market rents. Shorter leases can also allow other types of flexibility. Other features of leases, such as explicit options and subleasing provisions, can also be useful in this regard.

Tenant Expectations about Future Space Requirements   Expectations regarding the tenant's future space requirements influence the ideal lease-term length from the tenant's perspective. For example, if the tenant knows she will need the space for exactly three years, then a three-year lease term would normally be best. If the tenant expects her business to grow steadily in size, then she may prefer shorter-term leases in expectation of a future need to expand. Lease options on adjacent space or other space in the same building can sometimes also help with such expectations. The ability to sublease space also provides flexibility to the tenant. If the tenant needs to abandon the leased space due to a need to downsize or to move to larger space elsewhere, subleasing can reduce the financial cost to the tenant.

In general, the more uncertainty surrounding the tenant's future space needs, the greater the value to the tenant of retaining flexibility in her space commitments and, therefore, the greater the option value to the tenant either in signing shorter-term leases or using options and subleasing rights to provide flexibility.

Landlord's Redevelopment Option On the landlord side, a lease encumbers the property owner's normal right to demolish or redevelop the leased building structure. A shorter-term lease reduces the length of time for which this right is relinquished, thereby preserving more flexibility for the landlord in this regard. Once again, the option value lies not in the lease, but in the lack of lease, temporally speaking. In the case of very long leases, such as ground leases or the leaseholds that prevail in many European and some Asian countries, the impairment of the redevelopment option can be considerable as the lease term approaches. In such cases, explicit redevelopment options written into the lease can add value to the property.[27]

30.4.5 Staggered Lease Expirations and Releasing Risk

The considerations described above regarding optimal lease term consider each lease separately from the other leases in a building (or portfolio of buildings owned by the landlord). From the landlord's perspective, it may not be desirable to have all (or most) leases expiring at (or near) the same future point in time. If a bunch of leases expire around the same time, the building will be heavily exposed to the vicissitudes of the rental market at a single point in time. The risk or volatility in the building's future cash flow can be reduced by staggering lease expiration dates more uniformly across time. Depending on what the future lease expiration pattern looks like in a given building, this may cause the landlord to prefer either a longer or shorter lease-term length in a given deal than would otherwise be the case.

30.4.6 Summary: Rent Term Structure and Optimal Lease-Term Length

In section 30.4, we raised five considerations of leasing strategy that are not included in the effective rent or ALV calculation: interlease rental market risk, releasing costs, rental market expectations, flexibility considerations, and lease expiration timing considerations for the landlord. The first consideration, interlease rental market risk, implies that, other things being equal (such as the rent), landlords prefer longer-term leases and tenants prefer shorter-term leases. In equilibrium, this likely results in longer-term leases tending to have lower rents than they otherwise would (relative to expectations about future spot rent levels), but given that, it implies that lessors and lessees will be *neutral with respect to lease-term length*. The second consideration, releasing cost, implies that longer-term leases will be preferred by both lessors and lessees, and therefore carries no general implication for the equilibrium term structure of rents. The third consideration, flexibility, implies that shorter-term leases will be preferred by at least one party, probably by both parties in the lease, though potentially mitigated by explicit options (cancellation or renewal) and subleasing rights in the lease. Again, given this implication, flexibility carries no general implication for the equilibrium term structure of rents. However, there are circumstances where flexibility considerations could lead to either a rising or falling (or "humped") term structure in equilibrium (comparable in principle to the "liquidity preference" or "preferred habitat" theory for why bond yields tend to be upward-sloping on average, that is, in this case, differing relative preferences of landlords and tenants). Finally, the fourth consideration, lease expiration timing, will have implications that could go either way regarding lease-term length depending on the specifics of the situation, and therefore holds no general implication for the term structure of rents.

The overall result of all of these strategic leasing considerations can therefore be reduced to the following general principles:

1. The equilibrium term structure of rents may tend to be characterized by a slight downward slope over the lease term (i.e., lower rents in longer-term leases), relative to the general trend in spot market rents (i.e., if rent expectations are sufficiently rising, then

---

[27]See Dale-Johnson (2001).

the term structure of rents will be upward-sloping), though this general result could be mitigated or even reversed by systematic asymmetrical valuations between tenants and landlords regarding the releasing costs and flexibility considerations noted in (2) below.

2. Optimal lease-term length is largely a trade-off between releasing costs and the value of flexibility.

3. Based largely on (2), specific space submarkets or market sectors (property usage types) will typically have characteristic lease-term lengths that largely prevail within each market.

As a result of point (3), here are some stereotypical characteristic lease terms that prevailed in various types of commercial property space markets during the latter part of the twentieth century.[28]

Hotel:	1 day–1 week
Apartment:	1 year
Small retail:	2–5 years
Office:	3–10 years
Anchor retail:	5–15 years
Industrial:	5–20 years
Unique corporate space:	20 + years or user-occupant ownership

In general, releasing costs are lowest in hotels, second lowest in apartments, and highest in anchor retail and industrial leases. The need for (and value placed on) flexibility of lease termination is greatest in hotels and apartments and lowest in anchor retail and industrial space. Small retail and typical office space fall midway between, in both the releasing cost and the value of flexibility dimensions. Very unique space subjects users to potentially large holdup costs that can't be effectively mitigated by options, and so require very long-term leases or outright ownership by the user.

30.5 Other Leasing and Rent Issues

In addition to the optimal term length and term structure of rent considerations described in the preceding section, several other issues that are not internalized within the effective rent or ALV calculation are important in an overall consideration of leasing strategy and leasing behavior. We will briefly note a few of the most important in this section, including microspatial trade-offs and synergies, the use of percentage rents, the use of concessions, and the question of optimal search behavior on the part of landlords for tenants.

30.5.1 Microspatial Trade-Offs and Synergies

Microspatial considerations refer to issues regarding the design and management of space *within* a single property or project. This includes issues and decisions such as externalities, synergies, and trade-offs across tenants and across leasable spaces, some of the most interesting and important considerations in commercial property management. In many cases, the value of a commercial property can be greatly affected by the use of clever mixing and matching of different types of tenants and different types of spaces. These types of considerations are often particularly important in retail, office, and mixed-use properties. Because they are not reflected in the effective rent or ALV calculation, they explain why a landlord might rationally offer a lease with a lower ALV to one tenant, or why a tenant might knowingly choose a lease alternative with a higher ALV. Some examples of microspatial considerations include the following:

---

[28]These characteristic lease terms were fairly widespread and fairly stable over time. Additional factors are also involved in determining the characteristic lease terms, in addition to the releasing cost/flexibility trade-off described here. For example, see Grenadier (1995b and 1995c).

Optimal Space Size   As noted in the earlier text box (see end of section 30.2), there is often an archetypical size of space for any given space usage submarket. Developers will tend to target the supply in speculative or multitenant buildings for this size, and this makes competition on the supply side greater for the most typical space size. The result is that rents are often lowest for such typical size and configuration of space. Smaller spaces (i.e., greater numbers of tenants for the same total building rentable area) involve higher management costs (per SF) for the landlord, and often less efficient use of the building's gross space potentially available (lower **efficiency ratio** in the building, that is, the ratio of rentable space to total space, due to the need for more common areas). Also, it is typically difficult to find tenants for particularly small or irregularly shaped spaces. Furthermore, there is some evidence that larger spaces have higher lease renewal frequency.[29] This reduces the effective lifetime cost for the landlord, enabling larger spaces to rent for less. Space size and configuration issues such as these are particularly important in the design phase of building development or redevelopment, but may also be important whenever long-term leases of large spaces expire, presenting possibilities for subdivision or consolidation and reconfiguration of leasable spaces.

Particular considerations apply in shopping centers or other multitenant properties where there are interaction effects among the tenants. In such cases, "externalities" must be considered to optimally configure and allocate the space among tenants. Some tenants will cause an increase in the profits of other tenants (positive externalities). A landlord may rationally allocate more space to such tenants. See Brueckner (1993) and Benjamin et al. (1998).

Tenant Mix Synergies   Certain types of tenants generate positive externalities by enabling other nearby tenants to earn higher profits. The opposite may also be the case, as incompatible adjacent tenants generate negative externalities.[30] An extreme and important example of positive externalities is what is known as **anchor tenants**. Most prominent in retail development, the anchor in a shopping center draws customers who then shop at smaller tenants' stores. Anchor tenants in office buildings may add prestige to buildings, perhaps by having the building named after them. The landlord is normally able to capture a large portion of such positive externalities in the rents charged to the nonanchor tenants. Therefore, from the landlord's perspective (as well as that of the anchor tenant), it makes sense for the landlord to share such externality benefits with the anchor tenant, and to use such sharing to help lock the anchor tenant into a long-term commitment to the property. This is one reason anchor tenant leases are often for very long terms and at effective rents that are favorable to the tenant. In some cases, the anchor tenant may obtain an equity or equity-like position in the property. In retail properties, the landlord may also, in effect, have an equity-like position in the anchor tenant, as the rent may include a percentage component (this reflects the fact that landlord and anchor tenant are often, in effect, equity partners in the retail development). The art of tenant mixing extends not only to matching the right sort of anchors with the right sort of nonanchor tenants, but also includes optimal mixing, matching, and location of the nonanchor stores. Use of short lease terms and/or renewal and cancellation options on both sides is common in many retail centers to enable the tenant mix to be constantly optimized in the dynamic retail market where flexibility is particularly important.

30.5.2 Why Percentage Rents? (Consideration of Optimal Rent Structure)

Percentage rents, in which the tenant pays to the landlord a proportion of the revenues earned in the rented space, are common in class A retail property, especially among small tenants in multitenant properties such as malls and shopping centers. Usually the lease calls for a fixed "base rent" component, plus an "overage" that equals a percent of revenue over a threshold. Benjamin et al. (1990) show that there is usually a trade-off between these two: larger base rents are associated with smaller percentage rents and higher sales thresholds. This arrangement often makes sense for several reasons.

---

[29]See Asser (2004).

[30]The concept of externalities was defined in Chapter 3, section 3.3.1.

EXHIBIT 30-1 How Percentage Rent Reduces Operating Leverage

© OnCourse Learning

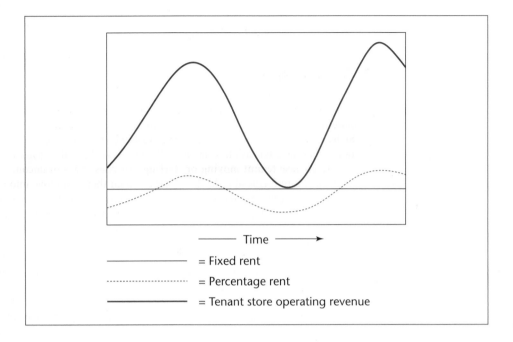

Incentive Compatibility Percentage rents give the landlord a direct incentive to help maximize store revenues. Landlords have some influence over store revenues because landlords control the tenant mix in the shopping center, and some mixes provide more synergy and positive externalities than others. Without sufficient incentive, landlords might not optimize the tenant mix. Wheaton (2000) argues that this must be the major explanation for percentage rents in retail leases, because other explanations would also apply to nonretail leases, and yet we only observe percentage rents in retail leases.[31]

Risk Reduction Many retail tenants are small businesses, and rent is typically a larger portion of the total operating expenses of small retail businesses than it is of other types of firms. This makes such firms more sensitive to the leveraging of their business operating risk caused by fixed rents. If rent is proportional to revenue, then this leveraging effect is reduced. This is depicted in Exhibit 30-1, which shows, in a stylized way, the difference in the net income volatility of the tenant's store with fixed versus percentage rent. The difference between the heavy solid gross operating margin line and the rent line (either fixed or percentage, the latter indicated by the dashed line) is the tenant's net revenue stream over time. Notice that with percentage rents the landlord is, to a degree, like an equity partner of the tenant, sharing in the tenant's operating risk and growth.

In fact, the use of fixed and percentage rent components can be varied so as to produce different effects depending on the nature of the tenant. By increasing the fixed base rent component and decreasing the variable percentage component, the resulting increased operating leverage places the retail tenant under more pressure and more incentive to maximize revenue.[32] The landlord may want to place some tenants under such pressure and incentive, if the tenants are financially strong enough to handle the risk, and if by increasing their revenues the tenants will increase total shopper flow-through in the center, thereby bringing positive

---

[31]However, there could be an enforcement problem with some other types of tenants. It is relatively easy to define and observe the revenues that are generated in a specific store (although Internet sales begin to muddy these waters). It is more difficult to observe the share of a multinational law firm's revenue attributable to a particular space.

[32]Brueckner (1993) argues that optimal percentages decline the greater the positive externality the tenant brings to the shopping center (i.e., the more the tenant attracts shoppers who will also spend money at other stores in the center). Wheaton (2000) finds that the stores with the highest base rents and lowest percentage rents tend to bring in the most revenue.

externalities to the other stores. This argument will tend to apply more to anchor tenants and tenants that are large national chains.

30.5.3 Why Concessions?

Why are quoted rents "stickier" than effective rents? Why do landlords often seem to prefer to give out free rent and generous TI and moving expense allowances up front instead of taking a lower regular rent? For example, in our numerical example in section 30.3.2, why does the $20/SF lease A not simply charge the tenant $15.44/SF every year for five years starting immediately, rather than take no cash flow at all for the first year? Several reasons are worth pointing out.

1. To ease tenant moving or start-up expenses. It is not uncommon for a new tenant to be under more financial or cash flow strain when they first move into a new space. They may be just starting up, or expanding, or incurring large moving expenses. Thus, up-front concessions often help to ease this burden, in effect, matching better the timing of rental expenses with revenue generation by the tenant. This argument particularly applies to concessions such as TIs and moving allowances.

2. Strategic timing of cash flow receipts. There may be some strategy in the timing of cash flow receipts. Higher future cash flows may make it easier to sell the building at a higher price or to refinance the loan on the building, if these events are more likely to occur in the future than in the near term. This might make sense if the landlord has more liquidity at present than she expects to have in the future. It might also make sense if the property asset market is not fully rational, susceptible to NOI illusions in which property buyers or lenders are ignorant of the typical use of concessions on the part of property owners and sellers. This does not sound very likely, but even if there is only a small chance of getting away with such an illusion, why throw away that chance?

3. The value of private information in a thin market. The **quoted rent** (a.k.a. **asking rent**, e.g., the $20/SF in lease A) is what gets reported to the public and to the other tenants. The concessions are usually much more a private matter between the lessor and lessee. Thus, concessions are a way of concealing from other existing or prospective tenants (and from competing landlords, or perhaps even potential investors) exactly how low a rent the tenant is paying and how soft is the demand for the building. In a thin market with imperfect information, keeping such information private may have some value in some circumstances.

30.5.4 Optimal Asking Rent and Optimal Vacancy

What is the optimal vacancy rate for an existing building? Why isn't the optimal rate zero? Of course, vacancy is not an objective or goal as such, so it may seem silly to think of an optimal vacancy rate. Nevertheless, if space is never vacant in a multitenant building, that is probably a sign that the landlord is not maximizing the long-run profit the building can earn. Simply put, if, on average, 10 percent higher rents could be charged if the landlord absorbed 5 percent average vacancy (by taking enough time to search for more eager or appropriate tenants when leases expire), then the result would be 5 percent higher profits for the building. The optimal vacancy rate results from value-maximizing management of the building. It will vary from building to building and can never be pinned down precisely, but we can say something about it by focusing the analysis on a question of more direct relevance to the landlord: what is the **optimal asking rent** as the landlord searches for tenants to fill vacant space?

Recall that in real estate we typically have **noisy price information**. This is typically true in the space market as much as it is in the asset market, and it lies at the root of the concept of **rational vacancy**, the idea that there is an optimal vacancy rate greater than zero for every building. The uniqueness of tenants and buildings and locations underlies the reason it makes sense for there to be some vacancy. Uniqueness of space and tenants makes the rental market **thin**, that is, there are not constantly a lot of very similar potential tenants doing deals for a lot of very similar spaces. Market thinness causes a lack of good information about the nature of the rental market, including the question of what effective rent would clear the market for any given building at any given time. In the absence of perfect information about the price at which a given space can rent, it makes sense to spend some time searching, probing the market. If you want to get a more concrete feeling for this point and see how the concept of optimal asking rent can be analyzed, check out Appendix 30C on the CD. There we present a simple quantitative model of optimal tenant search policy from the landlord's perspective.

30.6 Chapter Summary

Commercial property leases and leasing strategy are among the most fundamental, important, and complex topics in real estate investment and property management. Understanding long-term leases and leasing strategy is also central to many types of professional real estate careers. This chapter only skimmed the surface, presenting an introduction and overview of the leasing topic. Nevertheless, we covered much of the basic terminology and basic analytical tools relevant to current professional practice for finance and investment-oriented users.

KEY TERMS

lease	percentage rent	holdup problem
lessor	base rent	complementary expectations
lessee	lease term	conflicting expectations
ground lease	concessions	microspacial considerations
rent	lease covenants	rational expectations
gross (full service) lease	sublet	efficiency ratio
net lease	lease options	tenant mix synergies
triple net (NNN) lease	right of first refusal	anchor tenants
hybrid lease	effective rent	quoted (asking) rent
expense stops	annuitized lease value (ALV)	optimal asking rent
flat rent	term structure of rents	noisy price information
graduated rent	intralease discount rate	rational vacancy
step-ups	interlease discount rate	thin markets
revaluated rent	spot (or short-term) rents	
indexed rent	releasing costs	

STUDY QUESTIONS

Conceptual Questions

30.1. Describe the differences between gross leases, aka "full service" leases, and triple net leases? Which would the landlord and tenant generally prefer?

30.2. Describe the major ways in which commercial leases specify rental changes over time during the lease term?

30.3. Under what conditions are rent concessions typically offered?

30.4. Why do landlords usually offer rent concessions, such as free rent up front, rather than just reducing the rent?

30.5. Why do we often see higher rents for large tenants even when there is significant vacancy in the market?

30.6. What is the economic rationale for the existence of percentage rents that are common in retail leases?

30.7. Annuitized lease values, ALV, or effective rents that adjust for the uneven cash flows of the lease contract. All else equal the landlord wants the highest possible ALV while the tenant wants the lowest. When might the landlord choose a lease with a lower ALV?

30.8. Discuss why there is often a common prevailing lease term (i.e. 3 or 5 years) in a given rental market.

30.9. Why might a tenant or landlord prefer shorter-term leases, *ceteris paribus?*

30.10. What factors would tend to make tenants or landlords prefer longer-term leases, *ceteris paribus?*

30.11. According to your text the probability of tenant's renewing a lease is systematically related to their size and the kind of business they undertake. Can you provide some examples of tenants that are more likely to be sticky, that is stay in the space longer and wish to renew, independent of the lease term?

Quantitative Problems

30.12. Calculate the ALV of the following leases from the landlord's perspective, assuming the tenant faces a 10% borrowing rate:

   a. 5-year net lease, $15/SF, 1 year free rent up front

   b. 5-year net lease, starting at $10/SF, with step-ups of $1 each year

   c. 5-year net lease, starting at $10/SF, CPI adjustments every year equal to 50% of the change in the CPI. CPI change (inflation) is expected to be 5% per year.

   d. 5-year gross lease, $20/SF, expenses expected to be $8/SF initially, growing at 3% per year

   e. 5-year gross lease, $20/SF, expense stop at $8/SF, expenses expected to grow at 3% per year

   f. 6-year net lease, $15/SF, tenant improvements paid by landlord at beginning in the amount of $20/SF

*30.13. **(Valuing a Lease Renewal Option)** Use the methodology described in Appendix 30A for this chapter contained on the text CD to quantify the impact on the ALV of the lease in Problem 30.12(a), if the lease also includes a renewal option for the tenant, giving the tenant the right (but not obligation) to renew the lease after five years at $16/SF. Assume that the present subjective probability regarding the market ALVs for new five-year leases, five years from now, is that there is a 50 percent chance that the market rent will be $18/SF, and a 50 percent chance that it will be $14/SF. Discount existing lease cash flows at 10% for the purpose of determining ALV or existing lease present value, and future option values at 20% per year for the purpose of determining risk-adjusted present value.

*30.14. **(Lease Term Indifference Rent)** Use the procedure described in Appendix 30B of this chapter contained on the CD to answer this question. You are representing a landlord in a lease negotiation with a prospective new tenant who would occupy a vacant space in a newly completed building. You have proposed a 10-year lease at an ALV of $18/SF. The tenant is interested, but has indicated he might prefer a shorter-term lease. You believe the rental market is currently "in balance" and will remain so over the foreseeable future (i.e., future spot rents will remain about the same as they are today). Assuming a tenant borrowing rate of 8% and an interlease discount rate of 12%, what ALV on a five-year lease would be equally desirable for your client as the $18/SF rent you proposed on the 10-year lease?

*30.15. **(Modeling Optimal Landlord Search)** Use the procedure described in Appendix 30C of this chapter contained on the CD to answer this question. You are a leasing agent working for a landlord who has some vacant space to fill. You believe you can find potential tenants at an average rate of two per month. Typical leases in this market are for five years, with net ALV around $15/SF per year (annual payments in advance, with 8% tenant borrowing rate and 12% landlord required return between leases). Based on your knowledge of the rental market, you feel that the typical potential tenant you would find for this space would have a normal probability distribution of acceptable rent ranging around the $15/SF figure with a standard deviation of ±$3/SF. What is the optimal asking rent so as to maximize the landlord's present value of her building, and what can you tell her about how long to expect until you get a tenant?

Altshuler, D., and R. Schneiderman. 2011. Overpayment of manager incentive fees—When preferred returns and IRR hurdles differ. *Journal of Real Estate Portfolio Management* 17(2): 182–189.

Arnold, T., and T. Crack. 2003. Option pricing in the real world: A generalized binomial model with applications to real options. Department of Finance, University of Richmond, Working Paper, April 15, 2003.

Asser, R. 2004. The determinants of office tenant renewal. MSRED Thesis, MIT Center for Real Estate.

Benjamin, J., G. Boyle, and C. Sirmans. 1990. Retail leasing: The determinants of shopping center rents. *Real Estate Economics* 18: 302–312.

Benjamin, J., C. de la Torre, and J. Musumeci. 1998. Rationales for real estate leasing versus owning. *Journal of Real Estate Research* 15(3): 223–237.

Black, F., and M. Scholes. 1973. The pricing of options and corporate liabilities. *Journal of Political Economy* 81: 637–659.

Brueckner, J. K. 1993. Inter-store externalities and space allocation in shopping-centers. *Journal of Real Estate Finance and Economics* 7(1): 5–16.

Bulan, L., C. Mayer, and C. T. Somerville. 2009. Irreversible investment, real options, and competition: Evidence from real estate development. *Journal of Urban Economics* 65(3): 237–251.

Bulloch, B., and J. Sullivan. 2010. Information—The Key to the real estate development process. *Cornell Real Estate Review* 8: 78–87.

Bulloch, B., and Sullivan, J. 2009. Application of the design structure matrix (DSM) to the real estate development process. *MS Thesis, MIT Center for Real Estate.* Massachusetts Institute of Technology, Cambridge, MA.

Capozza, D., and R. Helsley. 1989. The fundamentals of land prices and urban growth. *Journal of Urban Economics* 26: 295–306.

Capozza, D., and Y. Li. 1994. The intensity and timing of investment: The case of land. *American Economic Review* 84(1): 889–904.

Carey, S. A. 2006. Real estate JV promote calculations: Recycling profits. *Real Estate Finance Journal.*

Childs, P., S. Ott, and T. Riddiough. 1996a. The value of recourse and cross-default clauses in commercial mortgage contracting. *Journal of Banking and Finance* 20: 511–536.

———. 1996b. The pricing of multi-class commercial mortgage-backed securities. *Journal of Financial and Quantitative Analysis* 31(4): 581–603.

———. 2002. Optimal valuation of noisy real assets. *Real Estate Economics* 30(3): 385–443.

Clapham, E., and A. Gunnelin. 2003. Rental expectations and the term structure of lease rates, *Real Estate Economics* 31(4): 647–670.

Cox, J., and M. Rubinstein. 1985. *Options Markets,* Prentice-Hall.

Cunningham, C. R. 2006. House price uncertainty, timing of development, and vacant land prices: Evidence for real options in Seattle. *Journal of Urban Economics* 59(1): 1–31.

Dale-Johnson, D. 2001. Long-term ground leases, the redevelopment option and contract incentives. *Real Estate Economics* 29(3): 451–484.

Dixit, A., and R. Pindyck. 1994. *Investment Under Uncertainty.* Princeton: Princeton University Press.

Dunn, K., and C. Spatt. 1985. An analysis of mortgage contracting: Prepayment penalties and the due-on-sale clause. *Journal of Finance* 40: 293–308.

Englund, P., A. Gunnelin, M. Hoesli, and B. Soderberg. 2004. Implicit forward rents as predictors of future rents. *Real Estate Economics* 32(2): 183–215.

Epperson, J., J. Kau, D. Keenan, and W. Muller. 1985. Pricing default risk in mortgages. *AREUEA Journal* (subsequently *Real Estate Economics*) 13(3).

Fischer, S. 1978. Call option pricing when exercise price is uncertain, and valuation of index bonds. *Journal of Finance* 33(1): 169–176.

Fisher, L. M. 2004. The wealth effects of sale and lease-backs: New evidence. *Real Estate Economics* 32(4): 619–643.

Geltner, D. 1989. On the use of the financial option price model to value and explain vacant urban land. *AREUEA Journal* 17(2): 142–159.

Geltner, D., T. Riddiough, and S. Stojanovic. 1996. Insights on the effect of land use choice: The perpetual option on the best of two underlying assets. *Journal of Urban Economics* 39(1): 20–50.

Graff, R., and M. Young. 1996. Real estate return correlations: Real-world limitations on relationships inferred from NCREIF data. *Journal of Real Estate Finance and Economics* 13(2): 121–142.

Grenadier, S. 1995a. The persistence of real estate cycles. *Journal of Real Estate Finance and Economics* 10: 95–119.

———. 1995b. Valuing lease contracts, a real options approach. *Journal of Financial Economics* 38(3): 297–331.

———. 1995c. Flexibility and tenant mix in real estate projects. *Journal of Urban Economics* 38(3): 357–378.

———. 1996. The strategic exercise of options: Development cascades and overbuilding in real estate markets. *Journal of Finance* 51(5): 1653–1679.

———. 1999. Information revelation through option exercise. *Review of Financial Studies* 12(1): 95–129.

———. 2002. Option exercise games: An application to the equilibrium investment strategies of firms. *Review of Financial Studies* 15(3): 691–721.

———. 2005. An equilibrium analysis of real estate leases. *Journal of Business* 78(4): 1173–1213.

Grovenstein, R., J. Kau, and H. Munneke. 2011. Development value: A real options approach using empirical data. *Journal of Real Estate Finance and Economics* 43(3): 321–335.

Gunnelin, A., and B. Soderberg. 2003. Term structures in the office rental markets in Stockholm. *Journal of Real Estate Finance and Economics* 26(2 and 3).

Gyourko, J., and A. Saiz. 2006. Construction costs and the supply of housing structure. *Journal of Regional Science* 46(4): 661–680.

Jennings, M. 1995. *Real Estate Law*, 4th ed. Cincinnati: South-Western.

Kau, J., D. Keenan, W. Muller, and J. Epperson. 1990. Pricing commercial mortgages and their mortgage-backed securities. *Journal of Real Estate Finance and Economics* 3(4): 333–356.

Margrabe, W. 1978. Value of an option to exchange one asset for another. *Journal of Finance* 33(1): 177–186.

McConnell, J., and J. Schallheim. 1983. Valuation of asset leasing contracts. *Journal of Financial Economics* 12(2): 237–261.

McDonald, R., and D. Siegel. 1986. The value of waiting to invest. *Quarterly Journal of Economics* 101: 707–728.

Merton, R. C. 1973. The theory of rational option pricing. *Bell Journal of Economics and Management Science* 4: 141–183.

Miceli, T., and C. Sirmans. 1999. Tenant turnover, rental contracts, and self-selection. *Journal of Housing Economics* 8(4): 301–311.

Miller, M., and C. Upton. 1976. Leasing, buying, and the cost of capital services. *Journal of Finance* 31(3): 761–786.

Mooradian, R. M., and S. X. Yang. 2002. Commercial real estate leasing, asymmetric information, and monopolistic competition. *Real Estate Economics* 30(2): 293–315.

Myers, S. D. 1977. Determinants of corporate borrowing. *Journal of Financial Economics* 5(2): 147–175.

Novy-Marx, R. 2007. An equilibrium model of investment under uncertainty. *Review of Financial Studies* 20(5): 1461–1502.

Quigg, L. 1993. Empirical testing of real option-pricing models. *Journal of Finance* 48: 621–639.

Riddiough, T., and H. Thompson. 1993. Commercial mortgage pricing with unobservable borrower default costs. *Real Estate Economics* (formerly *AREUEA Journal*) 21(3): 265–292.

Saiz, A. 2010. The geographic determinants of housing supply. *Quarterly Journal of Economics*, 125(3): 1253–1296.

Samuelson, P. 1965. Rational theory of warrant pricing. *Industrial Management Review* 6: 41–50.

Schallheim, J., and J. McConnell. 1985. A model for the determination of "fair" premiums on lease cancellation insurance policies. *Journal of Finance* 40: 1439–1457.

Schwartz, E., and W. Torous. 2007. Commercial office space: Testing the implications of real options models with competitive interactions. *Real Estate Economics* 35(1): 1–20.

Simonton, W. 2004. Creating construction cost indices and examining their cyclic behavior. *MIT Center for Real Estate*, MS Thesis.

Titman, S. 1985. Urban land prices under uncertainty. *American Economic Review* 75(3): 505–514.

Titman, S., and W. Torous. 1989. Valuing commercial mortgages: An empirical investigation of the contingent claims approach to pricing risky debt. *Journal of Finance* 44: 345–373.

Trigeorgis, L. 2002. *Real Options: Managerial Flexibility and Strategy in Resource Allocation.* Cambridge: MIT Press.

Wheaton, W. C. 2000. Percentage rent in retail leasing: The alignment of landlord-tenant interests. *Real Estate Economics* 28(2): 185–204.

Wheaton, W., and W. Simonton. 2007. The secular and cyclic behavior of "true" construction costs. *Journal of Real Estate Research* 29(1): 1–25.

Williams, J. 1991. Real estate development as an option. *Journal of Real Estate Finance & Economics* 4(2): 191–209.

Williams, J. 1993. Equilibrium and options on real assets. *Review of Financial Studies* 6: 825–850.

Additional Sustainability References

Eicholtz, P., N. Kok, and J. Quigley. 2011. Doing well by doing good? Green office building. *American Economic Review*, 100(5).

Fuerst, F., and P. McAllister. 2009. An investigation of the effect of eco-labeling on office occupancy rates. *Journal of Sustainable Real Estate* 1(1): 49–64.

Kats, G. 2009. *Greening our built world: Costs, benefits, and strategies,* Island Press.

Kok, N., N. Miller, and P. Morris. 2012. The economics of green retrofits. *Journal of Sustainable Real Estate* 4.

Langdon, D. 2007. Costs of green revisited, from http://www.davislangdon.com/USA/

May, Peter J., and Chris Koski. 2007. State environmental policies: Analyzing green building mandates. *Review of Policy Research* 24(1): 49–65.

Miller, E., and L. Buys. 2008. Retrofitting commercial office buildings for sustainability: Tenants' perspectives. *Journal of Property Investment and Finance* 26(6): 552–561.

Miller, N., J. Spivey, and A. Florance. 2008. Does green pay off? *Journal of Real Estate Portfolio Management* 14: 385–401.

Pivo, G. 2010. Owner-tenant engagement in sustainable property investing. *Journal of Sustainable Real Estate* 2(1): 183–199.

Pivo, G., and J. Fisher. 2012. The walkability premium in commercial real estate investments. *Real Estate Economics* 39(2): 185–219.

Simons, R. A., E. Choi, and D. M. Simons. The effect of state and city green policies on the market penetration of green commercial buildings. *Journal of Sustainable Real Estate* 1(1): 139–166.

Wiley, J. A., J. D. Benefield, and K. H. Johnson. 2010. Green design and the market for commercial office space. *Journal of Real Estate Finance and Economics* 41(2): 228–243.

INDEX

e = exhibit, n = footnote

A

absorption
  phase, 744
  of space, 33, 103
acceleration clause, 389–390
accrual-based income and tax shelter, 314
accrued interest, 745
accumulated depreciation, 310
accumulated depreciation recapture, 316
acquisition transaction execution, 668
active management, 678
actual returns, 187n
adjustable rate mortgage (ARM), 385, 410–413, 480
adjusted present value (APV)
  marginal investor, application of to, 330–334
  value additivity and, 324–325
adverse selection, 505
AFFO (adjusted funds from operations), 583
after-tax equity valuation, capital budgeting and
  APV applied to marginal investor, 330–334
  DCF and, 320–322
  debt financing, 326–330
  intramarginal investment value, evaluate, 323–324
  marginal investors, shortcuts, 322–323
  value additivity, APV decision rule and, 324–325
after-tax proforma, numerical example of
  about, 311–312
  cash flow components, total return calculations, 317–320
  equity cash flow calculations, 312–314
  example, 313e
  operating cash flow, 314–316
  reversion cash flow, 316
agency cost, 346
agglomeration economies, 46
  land use boundaries and, 87–88
agglomeration shadows, 50
aggregate valuation, 639
agricultural rent, 68
allocation (performance attribution), 671–674
Alonso, William, 67n
alpha excess returns, 687

Alt-A loans, 382n
ALV (annuitized lease value), 790–795
AMB Property Corporation, 601
Ambrose, B., 596n, 598
American Council of Life Insurers (ACLI), 435
American option (call option), 707
amortization of principal (AMORT), 299, 404
Amsterdam, Herengracht location, 92
anchor tenants, 789, 801
annual percentage rate (APR), 415
annual returns, historical statistics on, 141e
annuitized lease value (ALV)
  discount rate in, 792–793
  effective rent, 790–792, 795
  numerical examples, 793–795
annuity
  constant-growth in arrears (present value), 164–165
  convert to future values, 168
  defined, 162
  level in advance (present value), 164
  level in arrears (present value), 163–164
  single-lump sum, 169–170
appraisal-based index with staggered appraisals, 653–656
appraisal-based LTV covenants, 503n
appraisal error, transaction noise and, 635–637
Appraisal Institute, The, 636n
appraisals, 563, 636
appraisal smoothing, 646
appreciation return, period-by-period, 181
APV. See adjusted present value
arbitrage, 270, 592–594
arbitrage perspective, on option value, 711–714
ARCap REIT, 506
area chart, 534
arithmetic average, 190–191
arithmetic mean, 676n
ARM. See adjustable rate mortgage
Arrow, Kenneth, 522n
Ashcraft, A., 484n
Asian financial crisis, 29
Asian Pacific Real Estate Association (APREA), 611
asking rents, 104, 803

asset backed security (ABS), 208
asset class, real estate as
  about, 135–136
  historical investment performance, 138–143
  major investment asset classes, 136–138
  performance of, 140e
asset class choice, expanding, REITs and, 533–536
asset management, 574
asset market
  capital markets, 11–14
  defined, 11
  effect of demand growth in, 34e
  marginal/intramarginal investors and, 263–264
  predictability, 267–269
  pricing correction, 148
  real estate system, 27e
  return expectations and, 203–204
  segmented, 19–21
  valuation concepts and, 276–280
asset price
  calculating, 17–18
  theory, 553–554
asset risk, threshold point and, 554–556
assets in place, 587
asset test, REITs, 576
asset transaction market equilibrium, 263–264
asset-valuation risk, 554–556
asset values, 105n
assignable space, 231n
Atlanta MSA office submarkets, 109e
Atlanta space market data consolidated, 111e
atmosphere, sustainability and, 97
autocorrelation, 548–549
autoregressive integrated moving average (ARIMA), 111
average annual total return, 142e
average current yield, 136–138
average equity cost of capital, 590
average growth, 136–138
average total return on investment, 136–138

B

back-door
  equity return requirement, 753
  feasibility analysis, 748, 750e, 781